The Rise of
American Jewish
Literature

AN ANTHOLOGY OF SELECTIONS
FROM THE MAJOR NOVELS

EDITED BY

Charles Angoff AND Meyer Levin

Simon and Schuster · New York

FIRST PRINTING

SBN 671-20369-X
LIBRARY OF CONGRESS CATALOG CARD NUMBER: 74-101863
DESIGNED BY EVE METZ
MANUFACTURED IN THE UNITED STATES OF AMERICA

ACKNOWLEDGMENTS

For arrangements made with various authors, their representatives, and publishing houses where copyrighted material was permitted to be reprinted, and for the courtesy extended by them, the following acknowledgments are gratefully made. All possible care has been taken to trace the ownership of every selection included and to make full acknowledgment for its use. If any errors have accidentally occurred, they will be corrected in subsequent editions, provided notification is sent to the publisher.

The Rise of David Levinsky by Abraham Cahan. Copyright 1917, 1945 by Abraham Cahan. Reprinted by permission of Harper & Row, Publishers.

Journey to the Dawn by Charles Angoff. Copyright 1951 by Charles Angoff. Reprinted by permission of Thomas Yoseloff Publications.

Call It Sleep by Henry Roth. Copyright © 1960 by Henry Roth. Reprinted by permission of Cooper Square Publishers, Inc.

The Island Within by Ludwig Lewisohn. Copyright 1928 by Harper and Brothers, copyright © renewed 1956 by Ludwig Lewisohn. Reprinted with the permission of Farrar, Straus & Giroux, Inc.

I Can Get It for You Wholesale by Jerome Weidman. Copyright © 1937, 1965 by Jerome Weidman. Published by The Modern Library and reprinted by permission of Brandt & Brandt.

What Makes Sammy Run? by Budd Schulberg. Copyright © 1941, 1969 by Budd Schulberg. Reprinted by permission of Random House, Inc.

Summer in Williamsburg by Daniel Fuchs. From *Three Novels*. Copyright 1934, 1936, 1937 by Daniel Fuchs, copyright © 1961 by Basic Books, Inc. Reprinted by permission of Basic Books, Inc.

The Old Bunch by Meyer Levin. Copyright © 1958 by Meyer Levin. Reprinted by permission of Simon and Schuster, Inc.

The Naked and the Dead by Norman Mailer. Copyright 1948 by Norman Mailer. Published by Holt, Rinehart and Winston and reprinted by permission of the author and his agents, Scott Meredith Literary Agency, Inc.

The Young Lions by Irwin Shaw. Copyright 1948 by Irwin Shaw. Reprinted by permission of Random House, Inc.

Asphalt and Desire by Frederic Morton. Copyright 1952 by Frederic Morton. Published by Harcourt, Brace & World and reprinted by permission of Harold Matson Co., Inc.

Marjorie Morningstar by Herman Wouk. Copyright © 1955 by Herman Wouk. Reprinted by permission of Doubleday & Company, Inc.

Eli, the Fanatic by Philip Roth. From *Goodbye, Columbus*. Copyright © 1959 by Philip Roth. Published by Random House, Inc., and reprinted by permission of Robert Lantz-Candida Donadio Literary Agency, Inc.

The Assistant by Bernard Malamud. Copyright © 1957 by Bernard Malamud. Reprinted by permission of Farrar, Straus & Giroux, Inc.

The Last Angry Man by Gerald Green. Copyright © 1956 by Gerald Green. Reprinted by permission of Charles Scribner's Sons.

Remember Me to God by Myron S. Kaufmann. Copyright © 1957 by Myron S. Kaufmann. Reprinted by permission of J. B. Lippincott Company.

The Pawnbroker by Edward Lewis Wallant. Copyright © 1961 by Edward Lewis Wallant. Reprinted by permission of Harcourt, Brace & World, Inc.

Fathers by Herbert Gold. Copyright © 1962, 1964, 1965, 1966 by Herbert Gold. Reprinted by permission of Random House, Inc.

Stern by Bruce Jay Friedman. Copyright © 1966 by Bruce Jay Friedman. Reprinted by permission of Simon and Schuster, Inc.

To an Early Grave by Wallace Markfield. Copyright © 1964 by Wallace Markfield. Reprinted by permission of Simon and Schuster, Inc.

Herzog by Saul Bellow. Copyright © 1961, 1963, 1964 by Saul Bellow. Reprinted by permission of The Viking Press, Inc.

The Chosen by Chaim Potok. Copyright © 1967 by Chaim Potok. Reprinted by permission of Simon and Schuster, Inc.

Contents

Introduction

We now have an American Jewish literature. The last fifty years have seen the creation of an important body of work, a good deal of it of high critical as well as of popular acclaim. There are those who believe that this literature is, like regional writing or ethnic writing, simply part of the American total. Others believe this work links up with the Jewish literary tradition, particularly of Eastern Europe. Unquestionably it is extensive, rapidly proliferating, and worth considering as an entity.

Several excellent anthologies of short stories have appeared, and of memoirs, poetry, and letters, from the pioneering work of the late Leo Schwarz to the multitudinous collections of Harold U. Ribalow, but we feel that the development of this literature is best traced in the novel. Of the major novels of American Jewish life, some are difficult to obtain, even in libraries, and many are out of print. We have selected twenty-two works, presenting excerpts that are extensive enough to give the reader the flavor of each book. With a few of the shorter novels, when the narrative is strong, we have tried to show the story lines.

Our aim has been to assemble not only samples of literary development but a portrait of American Jewish life in development, a social history through the novel. Naturally, not all of our selections are of equal literary value; we have taken into consideration the public effect of some of the works which do not rank with the highest for artistic merit. Fortunately, literary excellence and representative quality often do go together. We agree about basic values, but it is necessary to say that the views initialed by one of us do not necessarily reflect the views of the other.

In 1954, American Jews celebrated the three-hundredth anniversary of the landing in Manhattan of a score of Spanish Jews from Brazil who were refugees from the still continuing Inquisition; with this little group the American Jewish community as such had its beginning. There was already, at that time, a scattering of Jews in America, but even with the arrival of a cohesive group it would take some two centuries for the community to develop enough to indicate it might one day have a character of its own.

There were, of course, individual Jews of consequence during this early period—Haym Salomon and Joseph Touro at once come to mind—but they were influential as individuals rather than as representatives of a sizable, organized Jewish community. There were Jews in New York and in Boston, in Philadelphia, in Charleston, South Carolina, and in Oglethorpe, Georgia, and there were handfuls in the Far West, but getting together a minyan among them presented a serious problem. It was natural that some Jews married non-Jews, became assimilated, or merely "passed." Formal conversion seems to have been a rarity, but religious integration, as we now call it, was a commonplace. That's how some of the ancestors of "Our Crowd" left the fold. The Jews have always had their John Jacob Astors and their August Belmonts, but Judaism in America did not die out, though even as late as the Civil War, when there were about 300,000 Jews in a total population of thirty million, Jewish life did appear feeble indeed. There are fragmentary portraits of that life in diaries, letters, and documents, with occasional flashes of poetry, up to the time of Emma Lazarus, but there is nothing that may be called a literature.

The fairly substantial immigration of German Jews after the 1848 upheaval in their homeland, though it produced substantive institutions and a definite identity, did relatively little toward developing a creative Jewish community. But toward the end of the century a momentous migration took place that was to affect the history of both American Jewry and world Jewry: the migration of the Litvaks and the Galitzianer to the New World. It went on for nearly three decades, tapering off with the restrictive U.S. Immigration Act of 1920, which went into effect two years later. The significance was not merely that about two million Jews had immigrated here from Eastern Europe; the numbers, of course, were important, but more important was the fact that the center of world Jewish culture had shifted from one continent to another.

Civilization never dies, it only changes its address. In the first two decades of the present century the centers of Jewish civilization moved to America. Vilna moved to New York, Grodno to Philadelphia, and Minsk to Boston. The great Yiddish writers of the time sensed what was happening long before the historians became conscious of it; good writers are always ahead of mere chroniclers, their antennae are more finely attuned. That is why Sholem Aleichem came to New York and why Peretz Hirshbein did the same, along with Sholem Asch and scores of others, including Avram Reisin, Abraham Koralinik, Reuben Brainin, and Joseph Opatashu.

A highly charged Jewish culture quickly proliferated. Indeed, so rich was it that we still do not fully appreciate its variety, its color, its depth, and its stature. The little that has been written about it is in the main mere bookkeeping. Historians, like accountants, can tally the number of talmud torahs that existed at a given time, how many Yiddish newspapers, how many theaters; but they are not likely to convey what went on inside the talmud torahs, the struggle to preserve the old wisdom while adapting to a new environment, and what influence this had on the Jewish population, and how the newspapers served as agencies of Americanization, and how the theaters answered a profound need for their own cultural expression on the part of the immigrants who found the *goldene medineh* not quite so golden, yet recognized it as better than the land of Fonya Ganif. This divided feeling about America began to be expressed in the fiction of Abraham Cahan, editor of the *Jewish Daily Forward*, and of Anzia Yezierska, in her short stories of the longings of immigrant women working in the garment trades.

There were two score superb newspapers and magazines, in both Yiddish and Hebrew. At one time a dozen theaters were in full operation on the East Side, with road companies in Boston, Philadelphia, and Chicago. There was a Jewish labor movement (probably the trailblazer for the entire American labor movement for two decades), and this workers' movement had its own educational facilities. The Labor Temple on Second Avenue antedated the Ninety-second Street Y by nearly half a century as a cultural haven. There was a Jewish music, with magnificent choral groups, there was a Jewish choreography. There was a Jewish social life. There was a Jewish Bohemia.

It was all wonderful—but after a while a curse began to spread throughout the American Jerusalem. The sons and daughters of this first generation in America began to sneer at the culture brought over from Eastern Europe, and, indeed, at all things Jewish. They thought the Jewish tradition was parochial, narrow, uncivilized, and unfit for their serious consideration, let alone dedication. In the classic form of second-generation alienation, they avidly sought total American immersion and feared that even a vestigial connection with Jewish life was an impediment.

The first great novel of American Jewish life, Abraham Cahan's *The Rise of David Levinsky*, the story of a truly lost immigrant generation failing to find a bridge between the Eastern European and American ways of life, might have proven the seed for a self-interpretive literature, but it fell on arid ground. True, there were sentimental portraits of East Side Jews, such as the popular novels of Fannie Hurst, but for a decade there was a literary hiatus. Then out of the ghetto ground that had nurtured Cahan's novel there sprang up a virtual forest of novels of rejection and self-hatred, proliferating in the thirties.

The sons of the ghetto had reached writing age. Encountering neighborhood kike-killers as children, and collegiate anti-Semitism as they grew, many young Jews reacted with inner resentment against the Jewish handicap, and writers among them began to produce "realistic" portraits that, in a closed ghetto world, might have been accepted as self-critical, ironic, and satirical, but that in an open English-reading world had the unhappy effect of confirming from Jewish sources the most strident anti-Semitic summations of "Jewish character." Thus, Ben Hecht's *A Jew in Love* was about a name-changed Jewish publisher who put all of his energy into seducing young women, usually Gentile. This best seller was followed by Jerome Weidman's *I Can Get It for You Wholesale* and Budd Schulberg's *What Makes Sammy Run?*, two skillfully written novels about Jewish business cheats—in the garment and film industries—both doubtless written, with corrective zeal, as satiric exposures, yet raising complex questions of Jewish self-hatred. A host of lesser works pictured Jews as gangsters and exploiters, to the point where the Jewish community began to ask, "Isn't there anything decent to write about?"

Several contributing factors in the period must be noted. These authors, our own generation, were beginning to write during the worst years of the depression. To all the usual difficulties attendant on breaking into print was added the special difficulty that most of us encountered, of a resistance in the publishing world to the use of Jewish background or specific problems of Jewish life as material for fiction. The magazines were cold to such material, and book publishers avoided it with the same avidity with which they were to pursue it three decades later. It was felt that non-Jewish readers would not care to identify with Jewish fictional characters and that even Jewish readers preferred to identify with "real Americans" in fiction. As a result, some talented writers who had begun quite naturally by writing about people and backgrounds with which they were familiar soon abandoned Jewish material or falsified it. They gave Jewish characters in their imaginative vision new, characterless names like Dick Benson or Jane Meredith, and homey Dr. Shapiro could always be endowed with a country twang and changed into Dr. Carruthers. Some who tried to write honestly about the Jewish life they knew, and who even attained critical acclaim, grew bitter over the lack of reader response and over publishing pressure to abandon such material. Still others, like Henry Roth, apparently were so affected as to stop writing altogether.

A second factor affecting young authors in the depression was the rise of radicalism. The writer, with his gift of empathy, is in any case most likely to turn to the left; one has only to recall how great a number of modern revolutionary leaders have been writers not only of polemics but of fiction and poetry. Jews, in general, are usually present far out of proportion to their numbers amongst the proponents of social change, and Jewish writers have a long tradition in this regard. Where other early cultures celebrate their heroes, where their bards produce Odysseys and Eddas, anonymous early Jewish novelists chronicle the moral faults as well as the military victories of a David, and prophets invent the literary form of the parable as an instrument for social criticism. Thus, young Jewish writers in the depression were prominent among the Communists, the Trotskyites, and every splinter radical group, and were often ready to accept formal guidance, even control, in the use of their talents for the creation of "proletarian literature."

Many, having totally alienated themselves from their immediate cultural forebears, were unaware that the Yiddish literary world had been torn asunder by the political dilemma which confronted them now: the problem of subjugating one's Jewish self in favor of "the movement" or "the revolution." Some, of course, saw no need for such a sacrifice, no real conflict involved. But doctrinaire radicals demanded this stance.

At the very outset of the organized Marxist movement in Russia, Jewish intellectuals, drawn to the movement, had become enemies of another equally idealistic set of Jewish intellectuals, drawn to Zionism. Even when Zionists were also Socialists, the "pure revolutionaries" despised them for drawing off energy to a separate cause. The great stream of Eastern European Jewish culture ran on past this argument; though many talented personalities were diverted into the revolution, some of them later to find themselves still identified—and destroyed—as Jews. When American intellectuals in the depression became active leftists, the Jews among them went through the same soul-searching process, and many turned away from a particularist Jewish culture and became hostile to direct forms of identification from religion to Zionism.

Yet through all this, emotional identity was alive. Mike Gold, the popular columnist of *The Daily Worker*, wrote his sketches, *Jews Without Money*, in the direct tradition of folk characterization, including a repulsive pawnbroker landlord, to be sure, but weaving a stark, vivid portrait of Lower East Side life. And a distinguished critic of American literature, the scholar and novelist Ludwig Lewisohn, demonstratively re-adopted the orthodox Jewish tradition just at the moment when things looked bad for Judaism in the United States. As the older immigrants were passing on, it had appeared inevitable that their descendants, rapidly losing interest in religion and showing no interest whatever in Zionism, would totally assimilate.

But then a countercurrent set in. Many Jewish intellectuals had turned their heads in interest when the prestigious Louis D. Brandeis, the first Jew to become an associate justice of the United States Supreme Court, who had been said to be toying with the idea of joining the Unitarian Church, turned actively to Zionism. Then Professor Lewisohn, who also had seemed to be preparing to convert to Christianity, made a complete return to Judaism and wrote his rousing novel *The Island Within* to explain the persistence of identity.

If on no other level, neither the religious nor the national, then the Jewish claim continued to assert itself in a social, historic and cultural consciousness. This became evident in both "negative" and "positive" Jewish novels of the thirties.

As the depression slowly waned, and as Nazism unleashed its full-scale campaign of degradation and destruction on German Jewry, a third generation of American Jewry was entering the colleges, and reacting in the typical pattern of the search for roots. Entering the war, the new generation turned the Jewish literary mood from self-hatred to self-justification. Jewish writers like Irwin Shaw portrayed the young Jew who had only a minimal contact with Judaism, but who reacted to anti-Semitic tauntings with self-assertion, usually by fighting or displaying heroism until he was fully accepted as a man. Or killed in the process.

This became a common theme for war novels, moving the Jewish novel from the particularist to the general scene. And after the war a generation that had encountered the death camps and that then had witnessed the surging birth of Israel, experienced a new stage in American Jewish consciousness, again soon reflected in the novel. This might be called a period of self-examination, ranging from such social novels as Herman Wouk's *Marjorie Morningstar* and Myron Kaufmann's *Remember Me to God* to Bruce Jay Friedman's surrealistic *Stern*.

With the Jewish fate through both destruction in Europe and revival in Israel constantly before the world public as a Jobian mystery and a Mosaic miracle, there seemed suddenly to be no limit to the amount of material about this people that the public, Jewish and non-Jewish, was ready to absorb. Novels, plays, even films on Jewish themes were in demand, and amidst the plethora of Jewish jokes and stereotype nostalgia sketches there appeared a number of books of high literary worth. For at last there was an audience, a Jewish audience as alive to itself—almost—as had been the Yiddish-reading audience in Europe. It seemed to be awakening from a long sleep, and aptly enough there was at last an audience for *Call It Sleep*, republished after thirty years to become a literary phenomenon.

For several years in succession, Jewish authors won the National Book Award with works about Jews. Jewish novels headed the best-seller lists. How remarkable a change from the time when Jewish material was poison in the publishing world! Yet one aspect of this decade in the American Jewish novel was strange. Though the holocaust and the birth of Israel were the conditioning psychological experiences of our era, the most successful novelists seemed to avoid touching on these enormous events, or even showing them as part of the consciousness of American Jewry. For a basic question remained: When is a Jew who writes about Jews a Jewish writer? Among the most distinguished of these novelists were several who felt they should not really be classified as "Jewish writers" but simply as American writers who were Jews, using the Jewish scene for their material. They apparently regarded the "Jewish writer" classification as one that would assign them to Jewish rather than American or cosmopolitan culture.

The Jewish audience, augmented by a college-educated generation of readers, and proud of the American success and prominence of a Saul Bellow, a Philip Roth, a Bernard Malamud, was nevertheless at times brought up short by the distance of such writers from the community. An I. B. Singer was definitely a Jewish writer, but then he wrote in Yiddish, and almost entirely about the old country.

What were the new literary heroes writing about? They no longer, thank heaven, dwelt on business sharpies or gangsters. The typical Jewish character in their fiction was a professor, and he was a respectable intellectual, as in *Herzog, A New Life*, and *Letting Go*. But he was totally detached from the Jewish community. The implied statement was that acculturation and eventual assimilation happened to the best people and was rather inevitable. Some of us, however, asked, Was this literary trend a valid interpretation of postwar Jewish psychology, or was it leading Jews to assimilation by—purposively or not —omitting the inner continuation as well as the creative and identifying activities in Jewish life?

Were the intellectuals missing the real story? For this is not a new problem in Jewish cultural history. It is a classic malaise among Jewish intellectuals and has been since the Greeks attempted to impose their culture on the Jerusalem of the Second Temple. No less an artist than Y. L. Peretz knew all about it when he stated his position more than fifty years ago. He was, of course, accused of parochialism and chauvinism and ghettoism. "Don't you want us to be human beings too, not just mere Jews?" the emancipated progressives asked him. He answered, "I am not talking of shutting ourselves up in a spiritual ghetto. We want to get out of the ghetto, but with our own spirit, our own spiritual treasure, and exchange—give and take, not beg. . . . If you have no God you look for idols. From them comes no Torah."

There was even a famous formal debate that went on for three nights and two days amongst fervid young Jewish intellectuals at the turn of the century. The argument was started in Berne by a graduate student in chemistry named Chaim Weizmann, who wanted to organize a student Zionist group among the many Russian Jews in Switzerland. But numbers of them were passionate followers of the teacher of world revolution, Plekhanov, also an emigré. When the Zionists called a meeting, the revolutionists removed the chairs from the hall. Still, the debate took place. One of the undecided attendants was later to be world-famous as A. Ansky, author of *The Dybbuk*. Weizmann, hard-pressed, called down a young Socialist-Zionist writer from Berlin, Martin Buber, and Buber helped him win a hundred and eighty members for the group, a triumph.

This debate has not yet ended. As we have already pointed out, it affected Jewish writers in the thirties; and through the New Left it affects many writers in the sixties. Some of the most prominent authors in the American Jewish literary renaissance have passed on to the New Left a negative attitude about Jewish continuity that is not, we think, a balanced representation of American Jewish life.

We believe the Jewish experience in its totality is somehow ever present in every Jewish psyche. We believe there is hardly a day when a Jew does not have a shuddery feeling that he too was killed in Auschwitz, an elated feeling that he too walked in Jerusalem, a fearful foreboding: will Auschwitz yet come to Jerusalem? This psychic condition is little reflected in our recent literature, an interesting exception being the intellectual set portrayed by Wallace Markfield in *To an Early Grave*. News headlines show us continuously that American Jewry is psychologically and emotionally involved with all Jewish life, and it is not difficult to see that our Israel involvement is somehow related to a profound and helpless guilt over the holocaust. Few of our best-known writers have touched on this guilt. (Roth did so, but ambiguously, in his short story "Eli the Fanatic.") Even fewer have dared to confront the profound connection with Israel.

To "write Jewish" is in fashion, but recently the Jewishness in much of our fiction has been one of bland nostalgia, a sophisticated look at surface ghetto parochialism; or else it is a Jewishness of mystification cum mysticism, in which the ancient wisdom-image of the Jew is invoked through Hasidic themes or the ideas of Buber; or else it is a Jewishness treated satirically—basically an attack on the complacent middle class.

All this, even with a bow to Hasidism, is negative and essentially induces discontinuation. The most tragic example of discontinuation is, of course, in the Soviet Union, where the destruction of Jewish education is leading directly to the forced assimilation of the Jews. Yet in a subtler way assimilation can be stimulated even in a democracy if writers insistently emphasize that the Jew is becoming "naturally and inevitably alienated from Judaism." What is needed, to keep the balance in our continuously growing collective portrait of the American Jewish experience, is a growth of alertness in the readership. What is needed is a readership that encourages the fullest honesty in all its artists, but resists distortion, a readership that will not take success as a guarantee of truthfulness, that abhors not only tendentiousness but ideological manipulation—for this is a form of censorship. But worse is what comes with it, self-censorship in the artist, and in each individual, and in the community. We need a readership that is able to detect unbalancing omissions, and is able to resist the cliquish Mafia or "family."

The question that links all Jews today is the question of continuation. Subterraneously or overtly this question faces every Jew: Continuation or assimilation?

The continuation question is a fascinating test for the reader himself to put to every piece of Jewish literature, including those in this book. It is interesting, too, to weigh the intentions or even the awareness of each author in this regard.

Shall Jews continue, and if so, how? Can a study of Jewish sources, some sort of contact with the Jewish past and even with a local Jewish community, provide the individual with a more balanced, more intelligent personal stance, even perhaps with gratification and a measure of inner peace? To this end we hope the content of this volume will prove helpful.

The American Jewish community, with all its self-doubt, all its awakened self-probing, will provide a variety of living answers to the question of continuity. Our plea is to let them come freely. Our growing literature should honestly reflect what happens in the Jewish being, rather than attempt to direct what happens.

Fortunately there are signs that we are already emerging from the phase of intellectual negation. Alienated Jewish intellectuals have been saying Kaddish for the Jewish people and for Jewish culture for nearly two thousand years. In the first decade of this century, when our literature was in actuality being born, Professor Leo Wiener of Harvard predicted the death of Yiddish in America and with it the virtual end of Jewishness here. Yet a literature that began with *The Rise of David Levinsky* and some fifty years later can show *The Pawnbroker* has much to be proud of, especially when one considers that it offers at least another fifty novels of solid and enduring worth. Among their authors are many whom we regret being unable to include for lack of space—Albert Halper, Louis Zara, Myron Brinig, Waldo Frank, Paul Goodman, Anzia Yezierska, Irving Fineman, Arthur Miller, Mike Gold, Isaac Rosenfeld, Yuri Suhl, Ben Hecht, Samuel Ornitz immediately come to mind.

American Jewry has awakened from its long, Rip Van Winkle sleep. The writers are only beginning to realize what riches are waiting to be distilled into enduring works. So far they have mined only a small part of these riches. The very complexity of the Jewish experience, the puzzle of the relationship between nationalism and internationalism, awaits to be illuminated. A best seller like *The Chosen* might have attracted some readers for its exotic display of Hasidim flourishing in Brooklyn, yet, more deeply, readers were involved with its portrait of serious young Jews, as American as the baseball they play, profoundly concerned with the continuation of Judaism.

The Jewish authors will come. They always come when material calls them. And it is not at all unlikely that the next fifty years will see a flowering of Jewish literature, especially in the novel form, that will rival the Jewish literature that flourished in the now destroyed community of Eastern Europe. It is not at all beyond the realm of possibility that we will have our own local and universal artists, our own American Mendele Mocher Sforim and Y. L. Peretz and Sholem Aleichem.

CHARLES ANGOFF
MEYER LEVIN

The Rise of
American Jewish
Literature

The Rise of David Levinsky
by ABRAHAM CAHAN

The first major American Jewish novel and in some ways still probably the best is about the garment industry and a Jewish Faust who became trapped in it; it is about Americanization, about good and evil, and about the tension between one's Jewish chromosomes, so to speak, and the heady vapors of freedom and democracy; it is also a novel about the various kinds of love and the bitter loneliness behind some of them; in short, it is a novel about the human conditions in terms of immigrant Jews.

When this book appeared in 1917 it was hailed as a masterpiece by no less a critic than William Dean Howells. Cahan presented a portrait of a Jewish Babbitt five years before Sinclair Lewis unveiled his all-American stuffed shirt. But Cahan, great artist that he was, knew that a Jewish Babbitt suffered from a guilt sense of having failed to fulfill his own spiritual promise, rather than from a simple lack of spirit.

The shorter selection here, "I Discover America," is in itself archetypical for the immigrant's arrival experience; the major selection, "Episodes of a Lonely Life," concludes the book and also sets its tone. David has become a "true American," he has surrendered to the bitch goddess Success, and he knows the dreadful price he has paid. His personal story is a warning for an entire community.

Abraham Cahan arrived in the United States from Russia in 1882, "a wild young man of twenty-two," says Oscar Handlin in Adventure in Freedom, "angry with the Old World of injustices, his mind stuffed with radical new ideas." In 1902 Cahan became editor of the Forward. His ideas dominated a whole era. The extent of his impact is thus described by Jack Rich in his pamphlet, 60 Years of the Jewish Daily Forward, "Under Cahan's direction *the Forward made enormous strides. . . . Nothing like it had been seen before in Yiddish journalism: a paper so clear, so simple, so perceptive of the life and interests of its readers." He also wrote a full autobiography, three novels, and numerous short stories in Yiddish and English. Cahan corralled for the Forward such eminent writers as Abraham Reisin, Sholem Asch, I. J. Singer. Though he is gone his imprint remains: Eli Wiesel and I. B. Singer still write for his paper. And much of the American Yiddish-reading world still lives by it.*

C.A.

The first part of The Rise of David Levinsky portrays Levinsky's life as an impoverished yeshiva bocher, a student of the Talmud, in the town of Antomir. He becomes a tutor, fails to seize a love opportunity, then scrapes up enough money to go steerage to America.

TWO WEEKS LATER I was one of a multitude of steerage passengers on a Bremen steamship on my way to New York. Who can depict the feeling of desolation, homesickness, uncertainty, and anxiety with which an emigrant makes his first voyage across the ocean? I proved to be a good sailor, but the sea frightened me. The thumping of the engines was drumming a ghastly accompaniment to the awesome whisper of the waves. I felt in the embrace of a vast, uncanny force. And echoing through it all were the heart-lashing words:

"Are you crazy? You forget your place, young man!"

When Columbus was crossing the Atlantic, on his first great voyage, his men doubted whether they would ever reach land. So does many an America-bound emigrant to this day. Such, at least, was the feeling that was lurking in my heart while the Bremen steamer was carrying me to New York. Day after day passes and all you see about you is an unbroken waste of water, an unrelieved, a hopeless monotony of water. You know that a change will come, but this knowledge is confined to your brain. Your senses are skeptical.

In my devotions, which I performed three times a day, without counting a benediction before every meal and every drink of water, grace after every meal and a prayer before going to sleep, I would mentally plead for the safety of the ship and for a speedy sight of

land. My scanty luggage included a pair of phylacteries and a plump
little prayer-book, with the Book of Psalms at the end. The prayers I
knew by heart, but I now often said psalms, in addition, particularly
when the sea looked angry and the pitching or rolling was unusually
violent. I would read all kinds of psalms, but my favorite among them
was the 104th, generally referred to by our people as "Bless the Lord,
O my soul," its opening words in the original Hebrew. It is a poem
on the power and wisdom of God as manifested in the wonders of
nature, some of its verses dealing with the sea. It is said by the faithful every Saturday afternoon during the fall and winter; so I could
have recited it from memory; but I preferred to read it in my prayer-
book. For it seemed as though the familiar words had changed their
identity and meaning, especially those concerned with the sea. Their
divine inspiration was now something visible and audible. It was not
I who was reading them. It was as though the waves and the clouds,
the whole far-flung scene of restlessness and mystery, were whispering to me:

"Thou who coverest thyself with light as with a garment, who
stretchest out the heavens like a curtain: who layeth the beams of
his chambers in the waters: who maketh the clouds his chariot: who
walketh upon the wings of the wind. . . . So is this great and wide
sea wherein are things creeping innumerable, both small and great
beasts. There go the ships: there is that leviathan whom thou hast
made to play therein. . . ."

The relentless presence of Matilda in my mind worried me im-
measurably, for to think of a woman who is a stranger to you is a
sin, and so there was the danger of the vessel coming to grief on my
account. And, as though to spite me, the closing verse of Psalm 104
reads, "Let the sinners be consumed out of the earth and let the
wicked be no more." I strained every nerve to keep Matilda out of
my thoughts, but without avail.

When the discoverers of America saw land at last they fell on their
knees and a hymn of thanksgiving burst from their souls. The scene,
which is one of the most thrilling in history, repeats itself in the
heart of every immigrant as he comes in sight of the American shores.
I am at a loss to convey the peculiar state of mind that the experience created in me.

When the ship reached Sandy Hook I was literally overcome with
the beauty of the landscape.

The immigrant's arrival in his new home is like a second birth to him. Imagine a new-born babe in possession of a fully developed intellect. Would it ever forget its entry into the world? Neither does the immigrant ever forget his entry into a country which is, to him, a new world in the profoundest sense of the term and in which he expects to pass the rest of his life. I conjure up the gorgeousness of the spectacle as it appeared to me on that clear June morning: the magnificent verdure of Staten Island, the tender blue of sea and sky, the dignified bustle of passing craft—above all, those floating, squatting, multitudinously windowed palaces which I subsequently learned to call ferries. It was all so utterly unlike anything I had ever seen or dreamed of before. It unfolded itself like a divine revelation. I was in a trance or in something closely resembling one.

"This, then, is America!" I exclaimed, mutely. The notion of something enchanted which the name had always evoked in me now seemed fully borne out.

In my ecstasy I could not help thinking of Psalm 104, and, opening my little prayer-book, I glanced over those of its verses that speak of hills and rocks, of grass and trees and birds.

My transport of admiration, however, only added to my sense of helplessness and awe. Here, on shipboard, I was sure of my shelter and food, at least. How was I going to procure my sustenance on those magic shores? I wished the remaining hour could be prolonged indefinitely.

Psalm 104 spoke reassuringly to me. It reminded me of the way God took care of man and beast: "Thou openest thine hand and they are filled with good." But then the very next verse warned me that "Thou hidest thy face, they are troubled: thou takest away their breath, they die." So I was praying God not to hide His face from me, but to open His hand to me; to remember that my mother had been murdered by Gentiles and that I was going to a strange land. When I reached the words, "I will sing unto the Lord as long as I live: I will sing praise to my God while I have my being," I uttered them in a fervent whisper.

My unhappy love never ceased to harrow me. The stern image of Matilda blended with the hostile glamour of America.

One of my fellow-passengers was a young Yiddish-speaking tailor named Gitelson. He was about twenty-four years old, yet his forelock was gray, just his forelock, the rest of his hair being a fine, glossy brown. His own cap had been blown into the sea and the one he had obtained from the steerage steward was too small for him, so that

gray tuft of his was always out like a plume. We had not been ac-
quainted more than a few hours, in fact, for he had been seasick
throughout the voyage and this was the first day he had been up
and about. But then I had seen him on the day of our sailing and
subsequently, many times, as he wretchedly lay in his berth. He was
literally in tatters. He clung to me like a lover, but we spoke very
little. Our hearts were too full for words.

As I thus stood at the railing, prayer-book in hand, he took a look
at the page. The most ignorant "man of the earth" among our people can read holy tongue (Hebrew), though he may not understand
the meaning of the words. This was the case with Gitelson.

"Saying, 'Bless the Lord, O my soul'?" he asked, reverently. "Why
this chapter of all others?"

"Because— Why, just listen." With which I took to translating
the Hebrew text into Yiddish for him.

He listened with devout mien. I was not sure that he understood
it even in his native tongue, but, whether he did or not, his beaming,
wistful look and the deep sigh he emitted indicated that he was in a
state similar to mine.

When I say that my first view of New York Bay struck me as
something not of this earth it is not a mere figure of speech. I vividly
recall the feeling, for example, with which I greeted the first cat I
saw on American soil. It was on the Hoboken pier, while the steerage
passengers were being marched to the ferry. A large, black, well-fed
feline stood in a corner, eying the crowd of new-comers. The sight
of it gave me a thrill of joy. "Look! there is a cat!" I said to Gitelson.
And in my heart I added, "Just like those at home!" For the moment
the little animal made America real to me. At the same time it
seemed unreal itself. I was tempted to feel its fur to ascertain whether
it was actually the kind of creature I took it for.

We were ferried over to Castle Garden. One of the things that
caught my eye as I entered the vast rotunda was an iron staircase
rising diagonally against one of the inner walls. A uniformed man,
with some papers in his hands, ascended it with brisk, resounding step
till he disappeared through a door not many inches from the ceiling.
It may seem odd, but I can never think of my arrival in this country
without hearing the ringing footfalls of this official and beholding the
yellow eyes of the black cat which stared at us at the Hoboken pier.

The harsh manner of the immigration officers was a grievous surprise to me. As contrasted with the officials of my despotic country,

those of a republic had been portrayed in my mind as paragons of refinement and cordiality. My anticipations were rudely belied. "They are not a bit better than Cossacks," I remarked to Gitelson. But they neither looked nor spoke like Cossacks, so their gruff voices were part of the uncanny scheme of things that surrounded me. These unfriendly voices flavored all America with a spirit of icy inhospitality that sent a chill through my very soul.

The stringent immigration laws that were passed some years later had not yet come into existence. We had no difficulty in being admitted to the United States, and when I was I was loath to leave the Garden.

Many of the other immigrants were met by relatives, friends. There were cries of joy, tears, embraces, kisses. All of which intensified my sense of loneliness and dread of the New World. The agencies which two Jewish charity organizations now maintain at the Immigrant Station had not yet been established. Gitelson, who like myself had no friends in New York, never left my side. He was even more timid than I. It seemed as though he were holding on to me for dear life. This had the effect of putting me on my mettle.

"Cheer up, old man!" I said with bravado. "America is not the place to be a ninny in. Come, pull yourself together."

In truth, I addressed these exhortations as much to myself as to him; and so far, at least, as I was concerned, my words had the desired effect.

I led the way out of the big Immigrant Station. As we reached the park outside we were pounced down upon by two evil-looking men, representatives of boarding-houses for immigrants. They pulled us so roughly and their general appearance and manner were so uninviting that we struggled and protested until they let us go—not without some parting curses. Then I led the way across Battery Park and under the Elevated railway to State Street. A train hurtling and panting along overhead produced a bewildering, a daunting effect on me. The active life of the great strange city made me feel like one abandoned in the midst of a jungle. Where were we to go? What were we to do? But the presence of Gitelson continued to act as a spur on me. I mustered courage to approach a policeman, something I should never have been bold enough to do at home. As a matter of fact, I scarcely had an idea what his function was. To me he looked like some uniformed nobleman—an impression that in itself was enough to intimidate me. With his coat of blue cloth, starched linen

collar, and white gloves, he reminded me of anything but the police-
men of my town. I addressed him in Yiddish, making it as near an
approach to German as I knew how, but my efforts were lost on him.
He shook his head. With a witheringly dignified grimace he then
pointed his club in the direction of Broadway and strutted off
majestically.

"He's not better than a Cossack, either," was my verdict.

At this moment a voice hailed us in Yiddish. Facing about, we
beheld a middle-aged man with huge, round, perpendicular nostrils
and a huge, round, deep dimple in his chin that looked like a third
nostril. Prosperity was written all over his smooth-shaven face and
broad-shouldered, stocky figure. He was literally aglow with diamonds
and self-satisfaction. But he was unmistakably one of our people. It
was like coming across a human being in the jungle. Moreover, his
very diamonds somehow told a tale of former want, of a time when
he had landed, an impecunious immigrant like myself; and this made
him a living source of encouragement to me.

"God Himself has sent you to us," I began, acting as the spokesman; but he gave no heed to me. His eyes were eagerly fixed on Gitelson and his tatters.

"You're a tailor, aren't you?" he questioned him.

My steerage companion nodded. "I'm a ladies' tailor, but I have
worked on men's clothing, too," he said.

"A ladies' tailor?" the well-dressed stranger echoed, with ill-con-
cealed delight. "Very well; come along. I have work for you."

That he should have been able to read Gitelson's trade in his face
and figure scarcely surprised me. In my native place it seemed to be
a matter of course that one could tell a tailor by his general appearance and walk. Besides, had I not divined the occupation of my
fellow-passenger the moment I saw him on deck?

As I learned subsequently, the man who accosted us on State Street
was a cloak contractor, and his presence in the neighborhood of
Castle Garden was anything but a matter of chance. He came there
quite often, in fact, his purpose being to angle for cheap labor among
the newly arrived immigrants.

We paused near Bowling Green. The contractor and my fellow-
passenger were absorbed in a conversation full of sartorial techni-
calities which were Greek to me, but which brought a gleam of joy
into Gitelson's eye. My former companion seemed to have become
oblivious of my existence.

As we resumed our walk up Broadway the bejeweled man turned to me.

"And what was your occupation? You have no trade, have you?"

"I read Talmud," I said, confusedly.

"I see, but that's no business in America," he declared. "Any relatives here?"

"No."

"Well, don't worry. You will be all right. If a fellow isn't lazy nor a fool he has no reason to be sorry he came to America. It'll be all right."

"All right" he said in English, and I conjectured what it meant from the context. In the course of the minute or two which he bestowed upon me he uttered it so many times that the phrase engraved itself upon my memory. It was the first bit of English I ever acquired.

The well-dressed, trim-looking crowds of lower Broadway impressed me as a multitude of counts, barons, princes. I was puzzled by their preoccupied faces and hurried step. It seemed to comport ill with their baronial dress and general high-born appearance.

In a vague way all this helped to confirm my conception of America as a unique country, unlike the rest of the world.

When we reached the General Post-Office, at the end of the Third Avenue surface line, our guide bade us stop.

"Walk straight ahead," he said to me, waving his hand toward Park Row. "Just keep walking until you see a lot of Jewish people. It isn't far from here." With which he slipped a silver quarter into my hand and made Gitelson bid me good-by.

The two then boarded a big red horse-car.

I was left with a sickening sense of having been tricked, cast off, and abandoned. I stood watching the receding public vehicle, as though its scarlet hue were my last gleam of hope in the world. When it finally disappeared from view my heart sank within me. I may safely say that the half-hour that followed is one of the worst I experienced in all the thirty-odd years of my life in this country.

The big, round nostrils of the contractor and the gray forelock of my young steerage-fellow haunted my brain as hideous symbols of treachery.

With twenty-nine cents in my pocket (four cents was all that was left of the sum which I had received from Matilda and her mother) I set forth in the direction of East Broadway.

TEN MINUTES' walk brought me to the heart of the Jewish East Side. The streets swarmed with Yiddish-speaking immigrants. The sign-boards were in English and Yiddish, some of them in Russian. The scurry and hustle of the people were not merely overwhelmingly greater, both in volume and intensity, than in my native town. It was of another sort. The swing and step of the pedestrians, the voices and manner of the street peddlers, and a hundred and one other things seemed to testify to far more self-confidence and energy, to larger ambitions and wider scopes, than did the appearance of the crowds in my birthplace.

The great thing was that these people were better dressed than the inhabitants of my town. The poorest-looking man wore a hat (instead of a cap), a stiff collar and a necktie, and the poorest woman wore a hat or a bonnet.

The appearance of a newly arrived immigrant was still a novel spectacle on the East Side. Many of the passers-by paused to look at me with wistful smiles of curiosity.

"There goes a green one!" some of them exclaimed.

The sight of me obviously evoked reminiscences in them of the days when they had been "green ones" like myself. It was a second birth that they were witnessing, an experience which they had once gone through themselves and which was one of the greatest events in their lives.

"Green one" or "greenhorn" is one of the many English words and phrases which my mother-tongue has appropriated in England and America. Thanks to the many millions of letters that pass annually between the Jews of Russia and their relatives in the United States, a number of these words have by now come to be generally known among our people at home as well as here. In the eighties, however, one who had not visited any English-speaking country was utterly un-familiar with them. And so I had never heard of "green one" before. Still, "green," in the sense of color, is Yiddish as well as English, so I understood the phrase at once, and as a contemptuous quizzical appellation for a newly arrived, inexperienced immigrant it stung me cruelly. As I went along I heard it again and again. Some of the passers-by would call me "greenhorn" in a tone of blighting gaiety, but these were an exception. For the most part it was "green one" and in a spirit of sympathetic interest. It hurt me, all the same. Even those glances that offered me a cordial welcome and good wishes had something self-complacent and condescending in them. "Poor fellow! he is a green one," these people seemed to say. "We are not, of course. We are Americanized."

For my first meal in the New World I bought a three-cent wedge of coarse rye bread, off a huge round loaf, on a stand on Essex Street. I was too strict in my religious observances to eat it without first performing ablutions and offering a brief prayer. So I approached a bewigged old woman who stood in the doorway of a small grocery-store to let me wash my hands and eat my meal in her place. She looked old-fashioned enough, yet when she heard my request she said, with a laugh:

"You're a green one, I see."

"Suppose I am," I resented. "Do the yellow ones or black ones all eat without washing? Can't a fellow be a good Jew in America?"

"Yes, of course he can, but—well, wait till you see for yourself."

However, she asked me to come in, gave me some water and an old apron to serve me for a towel, and when I was ready to eat my bread she placed a glass of milk before me, explaining that she was not going to charge me for it.

"In America people are not foolish enough to be content with dry bread," she said, sententiously.

While I ate she questioned me about my antecedents. I remember how she impressed me as a strong, clever woman of few words as long as she catechised me, and how disappointed I was when she began to talk of herself. The astute, knowing mien gradually faded out of her face and I had before me a gushing, boastful old bore.

My intention was to take a long stroll, as much in the hope of coming upon some windfall as for the purpose of taking a look at the great American city. Many of the letters that came from the United States to my birthplace before I sailed had contained a warning not to imagine that America was a "land of gold" and that treasure might be had in the streets of New York for the picking. But these warnings only had the effect of lending vividness to my image of an American street as a thoroughfare strewn with nuggets of the precious metal. Symbolically speaking, this was the idea one had of the "land of Columbus." It was a continuation of the widespread effect produced by stories of Cortes and Pizarro in the sixteenth century, confirmed by the successes of some Russian emigrants of my time.

I asked the grocery-woman to let me leave my bundle with her, and, after considerable hesitation, she allowed me to put it among some empty barrels in her cellar.

I went wandering over the Ghetto. Instead of stumbling upon nuggets of gold, I found signs of poverty. In one place I came across a poor family who—as I learned upon inquiry—had been dispossessed for non-payment of rent. A mother and her two little boys were watching their pile of furniture and other household goods on the sidewalk while the passers-by were dropping coins into a saucer placed on one of the chairs to enable the family to move into new quarters.

What puzzled me was the nature of the furniture. For in my birth-place chairs and a couch like those I now saw on the sidewalk would be a sign of prosperity. But then anything was to be expected of a country where the poorest devil wore a hat and a starched collar.

I walked on.

The exclamation "A green one" or "A greenhorn" continued. If I did not hear it, I saw it in the eyes of the people who passed me.

When it grew dark and I was much in need of rest I had a street peddler direct me to a synagogue. I expected to spend the night there. What could have been more natural?

At the house of God I found a handful of men in prayer. It was a large, spacious room and the smallness of their number gave it an air of desolation. I joined in the devotions with great fervor. My soul was sobbing to Heaven to take care of me in the strange country.

The service over, several of the worshipers took up some Talmud folio or other holy book and proceeded to read them aloud in the familiar singsong. The strange surroundings suddenly began to look like home to me.

One of the readers, an elderly man with a pinched face and forked little beard, paused to look me over.

"A green one?" he asked, genially.

He told me that the synagogue was crowded on Saturdays, while on week-days people in America had no time to say their prayers at home, much less to visit a house of worship.

"It isn't Russia," he said, with a sigh. "Judaism has not much of a chance here."

When he heard that I intended to stay at the synagogue overnight he smiled ruefully.

"One does not sleep in an American synagogue," he said. "It is not

Russia." Then, scanning me once more, he added, with an air of compassionate perplexity: "Where will you sleep, poor child? I wish I could take you to my house, but—well, America is not Russia. There is no pity here, no hospitality. My wife would raise a rumpus if I brought you along. I should never hear the last of it."

With a deep sigh and nodding his head plaintively he returned to his book, swaying back and forth. But he was apparently more interested in the subject he had broached. "When we were at home," he resumed, "she, too, was a different woman. She did not make life a burden to me as she does here. Have you no money at all?"

I showed him the quarter I had received from the cloak contractor.

"Poor fellow! Is that all you have? There are places where you can get a night's lodging for fifteen cents, but what are you going to do afterward? I am simply ashamed of myself."

" 'Hospitality,' " he quoted from the Talmud, " 'is one of the things which the giver enjoys in this world and the fruit of which he relishes in the world to come.' To think that I cannot offer a Talmudic scholar a night's rest! Alas! America has turned me into a mound of ashes."

"You were well off in Russia, weren't you?" I inquired, in astonishment. For, indeed, I had never heard of any but poor people emigrating to America.

"I used to spend my time reading Talmud at the synagogue," was his reply.

Many of his answers seemed to fit, not the question asked, but one which was expected to follow it. You might have thought him anxious to forestall your next query in order to save time and words, had it not been so difficult for him to keep his mouth shut.

"She," he said, referring to his wife, "had a nice little business. She sold feed for horses and she rejoiced in the thought that she was married to a man of learning. True, she has a tongue. That she always had, but over there it was not so bad. She has become a different woman here. Alas! America is a topsy-turvy country."

He went on to show how the New World turned things upside down, transforming an immigrant shoemaker into a man of substance, while a former man of leisure was forced to work in a factory here. In like manner, his wife had changed for the worse, for, lo and behold! instead of supporting him while he read Talmud, as she used to do at home, she persisted in sending him out to peddle. "America is not Russia," she said. "A man must make a living here." But, alas!

it was too late to begin now! He had spent the better part of his life at his holy books and was fit for nothing else now. His wife, however, would take no excuse. He must peddle or be nagged to death. And if he ventured to slip into some synagogue of an afternoon and read a page or two he would be in danger of being caught red-handed, so to say, for, indeed, she often shadowed him to make sure that he did not play truant. Alas! America was not Russia.

A thought crossed my mind that if Reb Sender were here, he, too, might have to go peddling. Poor Reb Sender! The very image of him with a basket on his arm broke my heart. America did seem to be the most cruel place on earth.

"I am telling you all this that you may see why I can't invite you to my house," explained the peddler.

All I did see was that the poor man could not help unburdening his mind to the first listener that presented himself.

He pursued his tale of woe. He went on complaining of his own fate, quite forgetful of mine. Instead of continuing to listen, I fell to gazing around the synagogue more or less furtively. One of the readers attracted my special attention. He was a venerable-looking man with a face which, as I now recall it, reminds me of Thackeray. Only he had a finer head than the English novelist.

At last the henpecked man discovered my inattention and fell silent. A minute later his tongue was at work again.

"You are looking at that man over there, aren't you?" he asked.

"Who is he?"

"When the Lord of the World gives one good luck he gives one good looks as well."

"Why, is he rich?"

"His son-in-law is, but then his daughter cherishes him as she does the apple of her eye, and—well, when the Lord of the World wishes to give a man happiness he gives him good children, don't you know."

He rattled on, betraying his envy of the venerable-looking man in various ways and telling me all he knew about him—that he was a widower named Even, that he had been some years in America, and that his daughter furnished him all the money he needed and a good deal more, so that "he lived like a monarch." Even would not live in his daughter's house, however, because her kitchen was not conducted according to the laws of Moses, and everything else in it was too modern. So he roomed and boarded with pious strangers, visiting her far less frequently than she visited him and never eating at her table.

"He is a very proud man," my informant said. "One must not approach him otherwise than on tiptoe."

I threw a glance at Even. His dignified singsong seemed to confirm my interlocutor's characterization of him.

"Perhaps you will ask me how his son-in-law takes it all?" the voluble Talmudist went on. "Well, his daughter is a beautiful woman and well favored." The implication was that her husband was extremely fond of her and let her use his money freely. "They are awfully rich and they live like veritable Gentiles, which is a common disease among the Jews of America. But then she observes the commandment, 'Honor thy father.' That she does."

Again he tried to read his book and again the temptation to gossip was too much for him. He returned to Even's pride, dwelling with considerable venom upon his love of approbation and vanity. "May the Uppermost not punish me for my evil words, but to see him take his roll of bills out of his pocket and pay his contribution to the synagogue one would think he was some big merchant and not a poor devil sponging on his son-in-law."

A few minutes later he told me admiringly how Even often "loaned" him a half-dollar to enable him to do some reading at the house of God.

"I tell my virago of a wife I have sold fifty cents' worth of goods," he explained to me, sadly.

After a while the man with the Thackeray face closed his book, kissed it, and rose to go. On his way out he unceremoniously paused in front of me, a silver snuff-box in his left hand, and fell to scrutinizing me. He had the appearance of a well-paid rabbi of a large, prosperous town. "He is going to say, 'A green one,' " I prophesied to myself, all but shuddering at the prospect. And, sure enough, he did, but he took his time about it, which made the next minute seem a year to me. He took snuff with tantalizing deliberation. Next he sneezed with great zest and then he resumed sizing me up. The suspense was insupportable. Another second and I might have burst out, "For mercy's sake say 'A green one,' and let us be done with it." But at that moment he uttered it of his own accord:

"A green one, I see. Where from?" And grasping my hand he added in Hebrew, "Peace be to ye."

His first questions about me were obsequiously answered by the man with the forked beard, whereupon my attention was attracted by the fact that he addressed him by his Gentile name—that is, as "Mr. Even," and not by his Hebrew name, as he would have done in our birthplace. Surely America did not seem to be much of a God-fearing country.

When Mr. Even heard of my Talmud studies he questioned me about the tractates I had recently read and even challenged me to explain an apparent discrepancy in a certain passage, for the double purpose of testing my "Talmud brains" and flaunting his own. I acquitted myself creditably, it seemed, and I felt that I was making a good impression personally as well. Anyhow, he invited me to supper in a restaurant.

On our way there I told him of my mother's violent death, vaguely hoping that it would add to his interest in me. It did—even more than I had expected. To my pleasant surprise, he proved to be familiar with the incident. It appeared that because our section lay far outside the region of pogroms, or anti-Jewish riots, the killing of my mother by a Gentile mob had attracted considerable attention. I was thrilled to find myself in the lime-light of world-wide publicity. I almost felt like a hero.

"So you are her son?" he said, pausing to look me over, as though I had suddenly become a new man. "My poor orphan boy!"

He caused me to recount the incident in every detail. In doing so I made it as appallingly vivid as I knew how. He was so absorbed and moved that he repeatedly made me stop in the middle of the sidewalk so as to look me in the face as he listened.

"Oh, but you must be hungry," he suddenly interrupted me. "Come on."

Arrived at the restaurant, he ordered supper for me. Then he withdrew, commending me to the care of the proprietress until he should return.

He had no sooner shut the door behind him than she took to questioning me: Was I a relative of Mr. Even? If not, then why was he taking so much interest in me? She was a vivacious, well-fed young matron with cheeks of a flaming red and with the consciousness of business success all but spurting from her black eyes. From what she, assisted by one of the other customers present, told me about my benefactor I learned that his son-in-law was the owner of the tenement-house in which the restaurant was located, as well as of several other buildings. They also told me of the landlord's wife, of her devotion to her father, and of the latter's piety and dignity. It appeared, however, that in her filial reverence she would draw the line upon his desire not to spare the rod upon her children, which was really the chief reason why he was a stranger at her house.

I had been waiting about two hours and was growing uneasy, when Mr. Even came back, explaining that he had spent the time taking his own supper and finding lodgings for me.

He then took me to store after store, buying me a suit of clothes, a hat, some underclothes, handkerchiefs (the first white handkerchiefs I ever possessed), collars, shoes, and a necktie.

He spent a considerable sum on me. As we passed from block to block he kept saying, "Now you won't look green," or, "That will make you look American." At one point he added, "Not that you are a bad-looking fellow as it is, but then one must be presentable in America." At this he quoted from the Talmud an equivalent to the saying that one must do in Rome as the Romans do.

When all our purchases had been made he took me to a barber shop with bathrooms in the rear.

"Give him a hair-cut and a bath," he said to the proprietor. "Cut off his side-locks while you are at it. One may go without them and yet be a good Jew."

He disappeared again, but when I emerged from the bathroom I found him waiting for me. I stood before him, necktie and collar in hand, not knowing what to do with them, till he showed me how to put them on.

"Don't worry, David," he consoled me. "When I came here I, too, had to learn these things." When he was through with the job he took me in front of a looking-glass. "Quite an American, isn't he?" he said to the barber, beamingly. "And a good-looking fellow, too."

When I took a look at the mirror I was bewildered. I scarcely recognized myself.

I was mentally parading my "modern" make-up before Matilda. A pang of yearning clutched my heart. It was a momentary feeling. For the rest, I was all in a flutter with embarrassment and a novel relish of existence. It was as though the hair-cut and the American clothes had changed my identity. The steamer, Gitelson, and the man who had snatched him up now appeared to be something of the remote past. The day had been so crowded with novel impressions that it seemed an age.

He took me to an apartment in a poor tenement-house and introduced me to a tall, bewhiskered, morose-looking, elderly man and a smiling woman of thirty-five, explaining that he had paid them in advance for a month's board and lodging. When he said, "This is Mr. Levinsky," I felt as though I was being promoted in rank as behooved my new appearance. "Mister" struck me as something like a title of nobility. It thrilled me. But somehow it seemed ridiculous, too. Indeed, it was some time before I could think of myself as a "Mister" without being tempted to laugh.

"And here is some cash for you," he said, handing me a five-dollar bill, and some silver, in addition. "And now you must shift for yourself. That's all I can do for you Nor, indeed, would I do more if I could. A young man like you must learn to stand on his own legs. Understand? If you do well, come to see me. Understand?"

There was an eloquent pause which said that if I did not do well I was not to molest him. Then he added, aloud:

"There is only one thing I want you to promise me. Don't neglect your religion nor your Talmud. Do you promise that, David?"

I did. There was a note of fatherly tenderness in the way this utter stranger called me David. It reminded me of Reb Sender. I wanted to say something to express my gratitude, but I felt a lump in my throat.

He advised me to invest the five dollars in dry-goods and to take up peddling. Then, wishing me good luck, he left.

My landlady, who had listened to Mr. Even's parting words with pious nods and rapturous grins, remarked that one would vainly search the world for another man like him, and proceeded to make my bed on a lounge.

The room was a kitchen. The stove was a puzzle to me. I wondered whether it was really a stove.

"Is this used for heating?" I inquired.

"Yes, for heating and cooking," she explained, with smiling cordiality. And she added, with infinite superiority, "America has no use for those big tile ovens."

When I found myself alone in the room the feeling of desolation and uncertainty which had tormented me all day seized me once again.

I went to bed and began to say my bed-prayer. I did so mechanically. My mind did not attend to the words I was murmuring. Instead, it was saying to God: "Lord of the Universe, you have been good to me so far. I went out of the grocery-store in the hope of coming upon some good piece of luck and my hope was realized.

Be good to me in the future as well. I shall be more pious than ever, I promise you, even if America is a godless country."

I was excruciatingly homesick. My heart went out to my poor dead mother. Then I reflected that it was my story of her death that had led Even to spend so much money on me. It seemed as if she were taking care of me from her grave. It seemed, too, as though she had died so that I might arouse sympathy and make a good start in America. I thought of her and of all Antomir, and my pangs of yearning for her were tinged with pangs of my unrequited love for Matilda.

MY LANDLADY was a robust little woman, compact and mobile as a billiard-ball, continually bustling about, chattering and smiling or laughing. She was a good-natured, silly creature, and her smile, which automatically shut her eyes and opened her mouth from ear to ear, accentuated her kindliness as well as her lack of sense. When she did not talk she would hum or sing at the top of her absurd voice the then popular American song "Climbing Up the Golden Stairs." She told me the very next day that she had been married less than a year, and one of the first things I noticed about her was the pleasure it gave her to refer to her husband or to quote him. Her prattle was so full of, "My husband says, says my husband," that it seemed as though the chief purpose of her jabber was to parade her married state and to hear herself talk of her spouse. The words, "My husband," were music to her ears. They actually meant, "Behold, I am an old maid no longer!"

She was so deeply impressed by the story of my meeting with Mr. Even, whose son-in-law was her landlord, and by the amount he had spent on me that she retailed it among her neighbors, some of whom she invited to the house in order to exhibit me to them.

Her name was Mrs. Dienstog, which is Yiddish for Tuesday. Now Tuesday is a lucky day, so I saw a good omen in her, and thanked God her name was not Monday or Wednesday, which, according to the Talmud, are unlucky.

One of the first things I did was to make up a list of the English words and phrases which our people in this country had adopted as part and parcel of their native tongue. This, I felt, was an essential step toward shedding one's "greenhornhood," an operation every immigrant is anxious to dispose of without delay. The list included, "floor," "ceiling," "window," "dinner," "supper," "hat," "business," "job," "clean," "plenty," "never," "ready," "anyhow," "never mind," "hurry up," "all right," and about a hundred other words and phrases.

I was quick to realize that to be "stylishly" dressed was a good investment, but I realized, too, that to use the Yiddish word for "collar" or "clean" instead of their English correlatives was worse than to wear a dirty collar.

I wrote down the English words in Hebrew characters and from my landlady's dictation, so that "never mind," for example, became "nevermine."

When I came home with a basket containing my first stock of wares, Mrs. Dienstog ran into ecstasies over it. She took to fingering some of my collar-buttons and garters, and when I protested she drew away, pouting.

Still, the next morning, as I was leaving the house with my stock, she wished me good luck ardently; and when I left the house she ran after me, shouting: "Wait, Mr. Levinsky. I'll buy something of you 'for a lucky start.'" She picked out a paper of pins, and as she paid me the price she said, devoutly, "May this little basket become one of the biggest stores in New York."

My plan of campaign was to peddle in the streets for a few weeks —that is, until my "greenness" should wear off—and then to try to sell goods to tenement housewives. I threw myself into the business with enthusiasm, but with rather discouraging results. I earned what I then called a living, but made no headway. As a consequence, my ardor cooled off. It was nothing but a daily grind. My heart was not in it. My landlord, who was a truck-driver, but who dreamed of business, thought that I lacked dash, pluck, tenacity; and the proprietor of the "peddler supply store" in which I bought my goods seemed to be of the same opinion, for he often chaffed me on the smallness of my bill. On one occasion he said:

"If you want to make a decent living you must put all other thoughts out of your mind and think of nothing but your business."

Only my smiling little landlady was always chirping words of encouragement, assuring me that I was not doing worse than the average beginner. This and her cordial, good-natured manner were a source of comfort to me. We became great friends. She taught me some of her broken English; and I let her talk of her husband as long as she wanted. One of her weaknesses was to boast of holding him under her thumb, though in reality she was under his. Ceaselessly gay in his absence, she would become shy and reticent the moment he came home. I never saw him talk to her save to give her some order, which she would execute with feverish haste. Still, in his surly, domineering way he was devoted to her.

I was ever conscious of my modern garb, and as I walked through the streets I would repeatedly throw glances at store windows, trying to catch my reflection in them. Or else I would pass my fingers across my temples to feel the absence of my side-locks. It seemed a pity that Matilda could not see me now.

One of the trifles that have remained embedded in my memory from those days is the image of a big, florid-faced huckster shouting at the top of his husky voice:

"Strawberri-i-ies, strawberri-i-ies, five cents a quart!"

I used to hear and see him every morning through the windows of my lodging; and to this day, whenever I hear the singsong of a strawberry-peddler I scent the odors of New York as they struck me upon my arrival, in 1885, and I experience the feeling of uncertainty, homesickness, and lovesickness that never left my heart at that period.

I often saw Antomir in my dreams.

The immigrants from the various Russian, Galician, or Roumanian towns usually have their respective synagogues in New York, Philadelphia, Boston, or Chicago. So I sought out the house of worship of the Sons of Antomir.

There were scores, perhaps hundreds, of small congregations on the East Side, each of which had the use of a single room, for the service hours on Saturdays and holidays, in a building rented for all sorts of gatherings—weddings, dances, lodge meetings, trade-union meetings, and the like. The Antomir congregation, however, was one of those that could afford a whole house all to themselves. Our synagogue was a small, rickety, frame structure.

It was for a Saturday-morning service that I visited it for the first time. I entered it with throbbing heart. I prayed with great fervor. When the devotions were over I was disappointed to find that the congregation contained not a single worshiper whom I had known or heard of at home. Indeed, many of them did not even belong to Antomir. When I told them about my mother there was a murmur of curiosity and sympathy, but their interest in me soon gave way to their interest in the information I could give each of them concerning the house and street that had once been his home.

Upon the advice of my landlord, the truck-driver, and largely with his help, I soon changed the character of my business. I rented a push-cart and tried to sell remnants of dress-goods, linen, and oilcloth. This turned out somewhat better than basket peddling; but I was one of the common herd in this branch of the business as well.

Often I would load my push-cart with cheap hosiery, collars, brushes, hand-mirrors, note-books, shoe-laces, and the like, sometimes with several of these articles at once, but more often with one at a time. In the latter case I would announce to the passers-by the glad news that I had struck a miraculous bargain at a wholesale bankruptcy sale, for instance, and exhort them not to miss their golden opportunity. I also learned to crumple up new underwear, or even to wet it somewhat, and then shout that I could sell it "so cheap" because it was slightly damaged.

I earned enough to pay my board, but I developed neither vim nor ardor for the occupation. I hankered after intellectual interest and was unceasingly homesick. I was greatly tempted to call on Mr. Even, but deferred the visit until I should make a better showing.

I hated the constant chase and scramble for bargains and I hated to yell and scream in order to create a demand for my wares by the sheer force of my lungs. Many an illiterate dolt easily outshouted me and thus dampened what little interest I had mustered. One fellow in particular was a source of discouragement to me. He was a half-witted, hideous-looking man, with no end of vocal energy and senseless fervor. He was a veritable engine of imbecile vitality. He would make the street ring with deafening shrieks, working his arms and head, sputtering and foaming at the mouth like a madman. And it produced results. His nervous fit would have a peculiar effect on the pedestrians. One could not help pausing and buying something of him. The block where we usually did business was one of the best, but I hated him so violently that I finally moved my push-cart to a less desirable locality.

I came home in despair.

"Oh, it takes a blockhead to make a success of it," I complained to Mrs. Dienstog.

"Why, why," she consoled me, "it is a sin to be grumbling like that. There are lots of peddlers who have been years in America and who would be glad to earn as much as you do. It'll be all right. Don't worry, Mr. Levinsky."

It was less than a fortnight before I changed my place of business once again. The only thing by which these few days became fixed in my memory was the teeth of a young man named Volodsky and the peculiar tale of woe he told me. He was a homely, commonplace-looking man, but his teeth were so beautiful that their glistening whiteness irritated me somewhat. They were his own natural teeth, but I thought them out of place amid his plain features, or amid the features of any other man, for that matter. They seemed to be more suited to the face of a woman. His push-cart was next to mine, but he sold—or tried to sell—hardware, while my cart was laden with other goods; and as he was, moreover, as much of a failure as I was, there was no reason why we should not be friends. So we would spend the day in heart-to-heart talks of our hard luck and homesickness. His chief worry was over the "dower money" which he had borrowed of his sister, at home, to pay for his passage.

"She gave it to me cheerfully," he said, in a brooding, listless way. "She thought I would send it back to her at once. People over there think treasure can really be had for the picking in America. Well, I have been over two years here, and have not been able to send her a cent. Her letters make holes in my heart. She has a good marriage chance, so she says, and unless I send her the money at once it will be off. Her lamentations will drive me into the grave."

I soon had to move from the Dienstogs' to make room for a relative of the truck-driver's who had arrived from England. My second lodgings were an exact copy of my first, a lounge in a kitchen serving me as a bed. To add to the similarity, my new landlady was incessantly singing. Only she had three children and her songs were all in Yiddish. Her ordinary speech teemed with oaths like: "Strike me blind," "May I not be able to move my arms or my legs," "May I spend every cent of it on doctor's bills," "May I not be able to get up from this chair."

A great many of our women will spice their Yiddish with this kind of imprecations, but she was far above the average in this respect.

The curious thing about her was that her name was Mrs. Levinsky, though we were not related in the remotest degree.

Whatever enthusiasm there was in me found vent in religion. I spent many an evening at the Antomir Synagogue, reading Talmud passionately. This would bring my heart in touch with my old home, with dear old Reb Sender, with the grave of my poor mother. It was the only pleasure I had in those days, and it seemed to be the highest I had ever enjoyed. At times I would feel the tears coming to my eyes for the sheer joy of hearing my own singsong, my old Antomir singsong. It was like an echo from the Preacher's Synagogue. My former self was addressing me across the sea in this strange, uninviting, big town where I was compelled to peddle shoe-black or oilcloth and to compete with a yelling idiot. I would picture my mother gazing at me as I stood at my push-cart. I could almost see her slapping her hands in despair.

As for my love, it had settled down to a chronic dull pain that asserted itself on special occasions only.

I was so homesick that my former lodging in New York, to which I had become used, now seemed like home by comparison. I missed the Dienstogs keenly, and I visited them quite often.

I wrote long, passionate letters to Reb Sender, in a conglomeration of the Talmudic jargon, bad Hebrew, and good Yiddish, referring to the Talmud studies I pursued in America and pouring out my forlorn heart to him. His affectionate answers brought me inexpressible happiness.

But many of the other peddlers made fun of my piety and it could not last long. Moreover, I was in contact with life now, and the daily surprises it had in store for me dealt my former ideas of the world blow after blow. I saw the cunning and the meanness of some of my customers, of the tradespeople of whom I bought my wares, and of the peddlers who did business by my side. Nor was I unaware of certain unlovable traits that were unavoidably developing in my own self under these influences. And while human nature was thus growing smaller, the human world as a whole was growing larger, more complex, more heartless, and more interesting. The striking thing was that it was not a world of piety. I spoke to scores of people and I saw tens of thousands. Very few of the women who passed my push-cart wore wigs, and men who did not shave were an exception. Also, I knew that many of the people with whom I came in daily contact openly patronized Gentile restaurants and would not hesitate even to eat pork.

The orthodox Jewish faith, as it is followed in the old Ghetto towns of Russia or Austria, has still to learn the art of trimming its sails to suit new winds. It is exactly the same as it was a thousand years ago. It does not attempt to adopt itself to modern conditions as the Christian Church is continually doing. It is absolutely inflexible. If you are a Jew of the type to which I belonged when I came to New York and you attempt to bend your religion to the spirit of your new surroundings, it breaks. It falls to pieces. The very clothes I wore and the very food I ate had a fatal effect on my religious habits. A whole book could be written on the influence of a starched collar and a necktie on a man who was brought up as I was. It was inevitable that, sooner or later, I should let a barber shave my sprouting beard.

"What do you want those things for?" Mrs. Levinsky once said to me, pointing at my nascent whiskers. "Oh, go take a shave and don't be a fool. It will make you ever so much better-looking. May my luck be as handsome as your face will then be."

"Never!" I retorted, testily, yet blushing.

She gave a sarcastic snort. "They all speak like that at the beginning," she said. "The girls will make you shave if nobody else does."

"What girls?" I asked, with a scowl, but blushing once again.

"What do I know what girls?" she laughed. "That's your own lookout, not mine."

I did not like her. She was provokingly crafty and cold, and she had a mean smile and a dishonest voice that often irritated me. She was ruddy-faced and bursting with health, taller than Mrs. Dienstog, yet too short for her great breadth of shoulder and the enormous bulk of her bust. I thought she looked absurdly dumpy. What I particularly hated in her was her laughter, which sounded for all the world like the gobble of a turkey.

She was constantly importuning me to get her another lodger who would share her kitchen lounge with me.

"Rent is so high, I am losing money on you. May I have a year of darkness if I am not," she would din in my ears.

She was intolerable to me, but I liked her cooking and I hated to be moving again, so I remained several months in her house.

It was not long before her prediction as to the fate of my beard came true. I took a shave. What actually decided me to commit so heinous a sin was a remark dropped by one of the peddlers that my down-covered face made me look like a "green one." It was the most cruel thing he could have told me. I took a look at myself as soon as

I could get near a mirror, and the next day I received my first shave. "What would Reb Sender say?" I thought. When I came home that evening I was extremely ill at ease. Mrs. Levinsky noticed the change at once, but she also noticed my embarrassment, so she said nothing, but she was continually darting furtive glances at me, and when our eyes met she seemed to be on the verge of bursting into one of her turkey laughs. I could have murdered her.

> *The immigrant struggles to earn a living as a street peddler, then as a garment worker, and finally ventures to open his own shop on the proverbial shoestring, with a moonlighting designer as his partner. A profound Americanization problem for pious immigrants was Sabbath work, required by most manufacturers; Levinsky avoids this and thereby gains a loyal labor force ready to work for less. An American businessman teaches him restaurant manners. His business flourishes, but not his personal life. A boarder, Levinsky typically falls in love with his landlady and, thwarted, has to move out. Later, already wealthy, he finds an exciting atmosphere in the intelligentsia surrounding a Socialist writer. He falls in love with the writer's daughter, contributes money to their causes, is even led into real-estate speculation, but in the end finds himself rebuffed by the daughter, who considers him uncultured.*

IT WAS A severe blow. It caused me indescribable suffering.

It would not have been unnatural to attribute my fiasco to my age. Had I been ten years younger, Anna's attitude toward me might have been different. But this point of view I loathed to accept. Instead, I put the blame on Anna's environment. "I was in the 'enemy's country' there," I would muse. "The atmosphere around her was against me."

I hated the socialists with a novel venom.

Finally I pulled myself together. Then it was that I discovered the real condition of my affairs. I had gone into those speculations far deeper than I could afford. There were indications that made me seriously uneasy. Things were even worse than Bender imagined. Ruin stared me in the face. I was panic-stricken.

One day I had the head of a large woolen concern lunch with me in a private dining-room of a well-known hotel. He was dignifiedly steel-gray and he had the appearance of a college professor or suc-

cessful physician rather than of a business man. He liked me. I had
long been one of his most important customers and I had always
sought to build up a good record with him. For example: other
cloak-manufacturers would exact allowances for merchandise that
proved to have some imperfection. I never do so. It is the rule of my
house never to put in a claim for such things. In the majority of cases
the goods can be cut so as to avoid any loss of material, and if it
cannot, I will sustain the small loss rather than incur the mill's dis-
favor. In the long run it pays. And so this cloth merchant was well
disposed toward me. He had done me some favors before. He addressed me as Dave. (There was a note of condescension as well as
of admiration in this "Dave" of his. It implied that I was a shrewd
fellow and an excellent customer, singularly successful and reliable,
but that I was his inferior, all the same—a Jew, a social pariah. At
the bottom of my heart I considered myself his superior, finding
an amusing discrepancy between his professorial face and the crudity
of his intellectual interests; but he was a Gentile, and an American,
and a much wealthier man than I, so I looked up to him.)

To make my appeal as effective as possible I initiated him into
the human side of my troubles. I told him of my unfortunate courtship as well as of the real-estate ventures into which it had led me.

He was interested and moved, and, as he had confidence in me, he
granted my request at once.

"It's all right, Dave," he said, slapping my back, a queer look in
his eye. "You can always count on me. Only throw that girl out of
your mind."

I grasped his hand silently. I wanted to say something, but the
words stuck in my throat.

He helped me out of my difficulties and I devoted myself to the
cloak business with fresh energy. The agonies of my love for Anna
were more persistent than those I had suffered after I moved out of
Dora's house. But, somehow, instead of interfering with my business
activities, these agonies stimulated them. I was like the victim of a
toothache who seeks relief in hard work. I toiled day and night,
entering into the minutest detail of the business and performing
duties that were ordinarily left to some inferior employee.

Business was good. Things went humming. Bender, who now had
an interest in my factory, was happy.

Some time later the same woolen man who had come to my assistance did me another good turn, one that brought me a rich harvest of profits. A certain weave was in great vogue that season, the demand far exceeding the output, and it so happened that the mill of the man with the professorial face was one of the very few that produced that fabric. So he let me have a much larger supply of it than any other cloak-manufacturer in the country was able to obtain. My business then took a great leap, while my overhead expenses remained the same. My net profits exceeded two hundred thousand dollars that year.

One afternoon in the summer of the same year, as I walked along Broadway in the vicinity of Canal Street, my attention was attracted by a shabby, white-haired, feeble-looking old peddler, with a wide, sneering mouth, who seemed disquietingly familiar and in whom I gradually recognized one of my Antomir teachers—one of those who used to punish me for the sins of their other pupils. The past suddenly sprang into life with detailed, colorful vividness. The black pit of poverty in which I had been raised; my misery at school, where I had been treated as an outcast and a scapegoat because my mother could not afford even the few pennies that were charged for my tuition; the joy of my childish existence in spite of that gloom and martyrdom—all this rose from the dead before me.

The poor old peddler I now saw trying to cross Broadway was Shmerl the Pincher, the man with whom my mother had a pinching and hair-pulling duel after she found the marks of his cruelty on my young body. He had been one of the most heartless of my tormentors, yet it was so thrillingly sweet to see him in New York! In my schooldays I would dream of becoming a rich and influential man and wreaking vengeance upon my brutal teachers, more especially upon Shmerl the Pincher and "the Cossack," the man whose little daughter, Sarah-Leah, had been the heroine of my first romance. I now rushed after Shmerl, greatly excited, one of the feelings in my heart being a keen desire to help him.

A tangle of wagons and trolley-cars caused me some delay. I stood gazing at him restively as he picked his weary way. I had known him as a young man, although to my childish eye he had looked old—a strong fellow, probably of twenty-eight, with jet-black side-whiskers and beard, with bright, black eyes and alert movements. At the time I saw him on Broadway he must have been about sixty, but he looked much older.

As I was thus waiting impatiently for the cars to start so that I could cross the street and greet him, a cold, practical voice whispered to me: "Why court trouble? Leave him alone."

My exaltation was gone. The spell was broken.

The block was presently relieved, but I did not stir. Instead of crossing the street and accosting the old man, I stood still, following him with my eyes until he vanished from view. Then I resumed my walk up Broadway. As I trudged along, a feeling of compunction took hold of me. By way of defending myself before my conscience, I tried to think of the unmerited beatings he used to give me. But it was of no avail. The idea of avenging myself on this decrepit, tattered old peddler for what he had done more than thirty years before made me feel small. "Poor devil! I must help him," I said to myself. I was conscious of a desire to go back and to try to overtake him; but I did not. The desire was a meandering, sluggish sort of feeling. The spell was broken irretrievably.

THE FOLLOWING winter chance brought me together with Matilda. On this occasion our meeting was of a pleasanter nature than the one which had taken place at Cooper Institute. It was in a Jewish theater. She and another woman, accompanied by four men, one of whom was Matilda's husband, were occupying a box adjoining one in which were the Chaikins and myself and from which it was separated by a low partition. The performance was given for the benefit of a society in which Mrs. Chaikin was an active member, and it was she who had made me pay for the box and solemnly promise to attend the performance. Not that I maintained a snobbish attitude toward the Jewish stage. I went to see Yiddish plays quite often, in fact, but these were all of the better class (our stage has made considerable headway), whereas the one that had been selected by Mrs. Chaikin's society was of the "historical-opera" variety, a hodge-podge of "tear-wringing" vaudeville and "laughter-compelling" high tragedy. I should have bought ten boxes of Mrs. Chaikin if she had only let me stay away from the performance, but her heart was set upon showing me off to the other members of the organization, and I had to come.

It was on a Monday evening. As I entered the box my eyes met Matilda's and, contrary to my will, I bowed to her. To my surprise, she acknowledged my salutation heartily.

The curtain rose. Men in velvet tunics and plumed hats were saying something, but I was more conscious of Matilda's proximity and of her cordial recognition of my nod than of what was going on on the stage. Presently a young man and a girl entered our box and occupied two of our vacant chairs. Mrs. Chaikin thought they had been invited by me, and when she discovered that they had not there was a suppressed row, she calling upon them to leave the box and they nonchalantly refusing to stir from their seats, pleading that they meant to stay only as long as there was no one else to occupy them. Our box was beginning to attract attention. There were angry out-cries of " 'S-sh!" "Shut up!" Matilda looked at me sympathetically and we exchanged smiles. Finally an usher came into our box and the two intruders were ejected.

When the curtain had dropped on the first act Matilda invited me into her box. When I entered it she introduced me to her hus-band and her other companions as "a fellow-townsman" of hers.

Seen at close range, her husband looked much younger than she, but it did not take me long to discover that he was wrapped up in her. His beard was smaller and more neatly trimmed than it had looked at the Cooper Institute meeting, but it still ill became him. He had an unsophisticated smile, which I thought suggestive of a man playing on a flute and which emphasized the discrepancy be-tween his weak face and his reputation for pluck.

An intermission in a Jewish theater is almost as long as an act. During the first few minutes of our chat Matilda never alluded to Antomir nor to what had happened between us at Cooper Institute. She made merry over the advertisements on the curtain and over the story of the play, explaining that the box had been forced on one of her companions and that they had all come to see what a "historic opera" was like. She commented upon the musicians, who were playing a Jewish melody, and on some of the scenes that were being enacted in the big auditorium. The crowd was buzzing and smiling good-humoredly, with a general air of family-like sociability, some eating apples or candy. The faces of some of the men were much in need of a shave. Most of the women were in shirt-waists. Altogether the audience reminded one of a crowd at a picnic. A boy tottering under the weight of a basket laden with candy and fruit was singing his wares. A pretty young woman stood in the center aisle near the second row of seats, her head thrown back, her eyes fixed on the first balcony, her plump body swaying and swaggering to the music. One man, seated in a box across the theater from us, was trying to speak to somebody in the box above ours. We could not hear what he said, but his mimicry was eloquent enough. Holding out a box of candy, he was facetiously offering to shoot some of its contents into the mouth of the person he was addressing. One woman, in an orchestra seat near our box, was discussing the play with a woman in front of her. She could be heard all over the theater. She was in ecstasies over the prima donna.

"I tell you she can kill a person with her singing," she said, admiringly. "She tugs me by the heart and makes it melt. I never felt so heartbroken in my life. May she live long."

This was the first opportunity I had had to take a good look at Matilda since she had come to New York; for our first meeting had been so brief and so embarrassing to me that I had come away from it without a clear impression of her appearance.

At first I found it difficult to look her in the face. The passionate kisses I had given her twenty-three years before seemed to be staring me out of countenance. She, however, was perfectly unconstrained and smiled and laughed with contagious exuberance. As we chatted I now and again grew absent-minded, indulging in a mental comparison between the woman who was talking to me and the one who had made me embrace her and so cruelly trifled with my passion shortly before she raised the money for my journey to America. The change that the years had wrought in her appearance was striking, and yet it was the same Matilda. Her brown eyes were still sparkingly full of life and her mouth retained the sensuous expression of her youth. This and her abrupt gestures gave her provocative charm.

Nevertheless, she left me calm. It was an indescribable pleasure to be with her, but my love for her was as dead as were the days when I lodged in a synagogue. She never alluded to those days. To listen to her, one would have thought that we had been seeing a great deal of each other all along, and that small talk was the most natural kind of conversation for us to carry on.

All at once, and quite irrelevantly, she said: "I am awfully glad to see you again. I did not treat you properly that time—at the meeting, I mean. Afterward I was very sorry."

"Were you?" I asked, flippantly.

"I wanted to write you, to ask you to come to see me, but—well, you know how it is. Tell me something about yourself. At this minute the twenty-three years seem like twenty-three weeks. But this is no time to talk about it. One wants hours, not a minute or two. I know, of course, that you are a rich man. Are you a happy man? But, no, don't answer now. The curtain will soon rise. Go back to your box, and come in again after the next act. Will you?"

She ordered me about as she had done during my stay at her mother's house, which offended and pleased me at once. During the whole of the second act I looked at the stage without seeing or hearing anything. The time when I fell in love with Matilda sprang into life again. It really seemed as though the twenty-three years were twenty-three weeks. My mother's death, her funeral; Abner's Court; the uniformed old furrier with the side-whiskers, his wife with her crutches; Naphtali with his curly hair and near-sighted eyes; Reb Sender, his wife, the bully of the old synagogue; Matilda's mother, and her old servant—all the human figures and things that filled the eventful last two years of my life at home loomed up with striking vividness before me.

Matilda's affable greeting and her intimate brief talk were a surprise to me. Did I appeal to her as the fellow who had once kissed her? Had she always remembered me with a gleam of romantic interest? Did I stir her merely as she stirred me—as a living fragment of her past? Or was she trying to cultivate me in the professional interests of her husband, who was practising medicine in Harlem?

When the curtain had fallen again Matilda made her husband change seats with me. I was to stay by her side through the rest of the performance. The partition between the two boxes being only waist-high, the two parties were practically joined into one and everybody was satisfied—everybody except Mrs. Chaikin.

"I suppose our company isn't good enough for Mr. Levinsky," she said, aloud.

When the performance was over we all went to Lorber's—the most pretentious restaurant on the East Side. Matilda and I were mostly left to ourselves. We talked of our native town and of her pious mother, who had died a few years before, but we carefully avoided the few weeks which I had spent in her mother's house, when Matilda had encouraged my embraces. In answer to my questions she told me something of her own and her husband's revolutionary exploits. She spoke boastfully and yet reluctantly of these things, as if it were a sacrilege to discuss them with a man who was, after all, a "money-bag."

My impression was that they lived very modestly and that they were more interested in their socialist affairs than in their income.

My theory that she wanted her husband to profit by her acquaintance with me seemed to be exploded. She reminded me of Elsie and her whole-hearted devotion to socialism. We mostly spoke in Yiddish, and our Antomir enunciation was like a bond of kinship between us, and yet I felt that she spoke to me in the patronizing, didactical way which one adopts with a foreigner, as though the world to which she belonged was one whose interests were beyond my comprehension.

She inquired about my early struggles and subsequent successes. I told her of the studies I had pursued before I went into business, of the English classics I had read, and of my acquaintance with Spencer.

"Do you remember what you told me about becoming an educated man?" I said, eagerly. "Your words were always ringing in my ears. It was owing to them that I studied for admission to college. I was crazy to be a college man, but fate ordained otherwise. To this day I regret it."

In dwelling on my successes I felt that I was too effusive and emphatic; but I went on bragging in spite of myself. I tried to correct the impression I was making on her by boasting of the sums I had given to charity, but this made me feel smaller than ever. However, my talk did not seem to arouse any criticism in her mind. She listened to me as she might to the tale of a child.

Referring to my unmarried state, she said, with unfeigned sympathy: "This is really no life. You ought to get married." And she added, gaily, "If you ever marry, you mustn't neglect to invite me to the wedding."

"I certainly won't; you may be sure of that," I said.

"You must come to see me. I'll call you up on the telephone some day and we'll arrange it."

"I shall be very glad, indeed."

I departed in a queer state of mind. Her present identity failed to touch a romantic chord in my heart. She was simply a memory, like Dora. But as a memory she had rekindled some of the old yearning in me. I was still in love with Anna, but at this moment I was in love both with her and with the Matilda of twenty-three years before. But this intense feeling for Matilda as a monument of my past self did not last two days.

The invitation she had promised to telephone never came.

I came across a man whom I used to see at the Tevkins', and one of the things he told me was that Anna had recently married a high-school teacher.

THE REAL ESTATE boom collapsed. The cause of the catastrophe lay in the nature, or rather in the unnaturalness, of the "get-rich-quick" epidemic. Its immediate cause, however, was a series of rent strikes inspired and engineered by the Jewish socialists through their Yiddish daily. One of the many artificialities of the situation had been a progressive inflation of rent values. Houses had been continually changing hands, being bought, not as a permanent investment, but for speculation, whereupon each successive purchaser would raise rents as a means of increasing the market price of his temporary property. And so the socialists had organized a crusade that filled the municipal courts with dispossess cases and turned the boom into a panic.

Hundreds of people who had become rich overnight now became worse than penniless overnight. The Ghetto was full of dethroned "kings for a day only." It seemed as if it all really had been a dream.

One of the men whose quickly made little fortune burst like a bubble was poor Tevkin. I wondered how his children took the socialist rent strikes.

Nor did I escape uninjured when the crisis broke loose. I still had a considerable sum in real estate, all my efforts to extricate it having proved futile. My holdings were rapidly depreciating. In hundreds of cases similar to mine equities were wiped out through the speculators' inability to pay interest on mortgages or even taxes. To be sure, things did not come to such a pass in my case, but then some of the city lots or improved property in which I was interested had been hit so hard as to be no longer worth the mortgages on them.

Volodsky lost almost everything except his courage and speculative spirit.

"Oh, it will come back," he once said to me, speaking of the boom.

When I urged that it had been an unnatural growth he retorted that it was the collapse of the boom which was unnatural. He was scheming some sort of syndicate again.

"It requires no money to make a lot of money," he said. "All it does require is brains and some good luck."

Nevertheless, he coveted some of my money for his new scheme. He did not succeed with me, but he found other "angels." He was now quite in his element in the American atmosphere of breathless enterprise and breakneck speed. When the violence of the crisis had quieted down building operations were resumed on a more natural basis. Men like Volodsky, with hosts of carpenters, bricklayers, plumbers—all Russian or Galician Jews—continued to build up the Bronx, Washington Heights, and several sections of Brooklyn. Vast areas of meadowland and rock were turned by them, as by a magic wand, into densely populated avenues and streets of brick and mortar. Under the spell of their activity cities larger than Odessa sprang up within the confines of Greater New York in the course of three or four years.

Mrs. Chaikin came out of her speculations more than safe. She and her husband, who is still in my employ, own half a dozen tenement-houses. One day, on the first of the month, I met her in the street with a large hand-bag and a dignified mien. She was out collecting rent.

It was the spring of 1910. The twenty-fifth anniversary of my coming to America was drawing near.

The day of an immigrant's arrival in his new home is like a birthday to him. Indeed, it is more apt to claim his attention and to warm his heart than his real birthday. Some of our immigrants do not even know their birthday. But they all know the day when they came to America. It is Landing Day with red capital letters. This, at any rate, is the case with me. The day upon which I was born often passes without my being aware of it. The day when I landed in Hoboken, on the other hand, never arrives without my being fully conscious of the place it occupies in the calendar of my life. Is it because I do not remember myself coming into the world, while I do remember my arrival in America? However that may be, the advent of that day invariably puts me in a sentimental mood which I never experience on the day of my birth.

It was 1910, then, and the twenty-fifth anniversary of my coming was near at hand. Thoughts of the past filled me with mixed joy and sadness. I was overcome with a desire to celebrate the day. But with whom? Usually this is done by "ship brothers," as East-Siders call fellow-immigrants who arrive here on the same boat. It came back to me that I had such a ship brother, and that it was Gitelson. Poor

Gitelson! He was still working at his trade. I had not seen him for years, but I had heard of him from time to time, and I knew that he was employed by a ladies' tailor at custom work somewhere in Brooklyn. (The custom-tailoring shop he had once started for himself had proved a failure.) Also, I knew how to reach a brother-in-law of his. The upshot was that I made an appointment with Gitelson for him to be at my office on the great day at 12 o'clock. I did so without specifying the object of the meeting, but I expected that he would know.

Finally the day arrived. It was a few minutes to 12. I was alone in my private office, all in a fidget, as if the meeting I was expecting were a love-tryst. Reminiscences and reflections were flitting incoherently through my mind. Some of the events of the day which I was about to celebrate loomed up like a ship seen in the distance. My eye swept the expensive furniture of my office. I thought of the way my career had begun. I thought of the Friday evening when I met Gitelson on Grand Street, he an American dandy and I in tatters. The fact that it was upon his advice and with his ten dollars that I had become a cloakmaker stood out as large as life before me. A great feeling of gratitude welled up in me, of gratitude and of pity for my tattered self of those days. Dear, kind Gitelson! Poor fellow! He was still working with his needle. I was seized with a desire to do something for him. I had never paid him those ten dollars. So I was going to do so with "substantial interest" now. "I shall spend a few hundred dollars on him—nay, a few thousand!" I said to myself. "I shall buy him a small business. Let him end his days in comfort. Let him know that his ship brother is like a real brother to him."

It was twenty minutes after 12 and I was still waiting for the telephone to announce him. My suspense became insupportable. "Is he going to disappoint me, the idiot?" I wondered. Presently the telephone trilled. I seized the receiver.

"Mr. Gitelson wishes to see Mr. Levinsky," came the familiar pipe of my switchboard girl. "He says he has an appointment —"

"Let him come in at once," I flashed.

Two minutes later he was in my room. His forelock was still the only bunch of gray hair on his head, but his face was pitifully wizened. He was quite neatly dressed, as trained tailors will be, even when they are poor, and at some distance I might have failed to perceive any change in him. At close range, however, his appearance broke my heart.

"Do you know what sort of a day this is?" I asked, after shaking his hand warmly.

"I should think I did," he answered, sheepishly. "Twenty-five years ago at this time—"

He was at a loss for words.

"Yes, it's twenty-five years, Gitelson," I rejoined. I was going to indulge in reminiscences, to compare memories with him, but changed my mind. I would rather not speak of our Landing Day until we were seated at a dining-table and after we had drunk its toast in champagne.

"Come, let us have lunch together," I said, simply.

I took him to the Waldorf-Astoria, where a table had been reserved for us in a snug corner.

Gitelson was extremely bashful and his embarrassment infected me. He was apparently at a loss to know what to do with the various glasses, knives, forks. It was evident that he had never sat at such a table before. The French waiter, who was silently officious, seemed to be inwardly laughing at both of us. At the bottom of my heart I cow before waiters to this day. Their white shirt-fronts, reticence, and pompous bows make me feel as if they saw through me and ridiculed my ways. They make me feel as if my expensive clothes and ways ill became me.

"Here is good health, Gitelson," I said in plain old Yiddish, as we touched glasses. "Let us drink to the day when we arrived in Castle Garden."

There was something forced, studied, in the way I uttered these words. I was disgusted with my own voice. Gitelson only simpered. He drained his glass, and the champagne, to which he was not accustomed, made him tipsy at once. I tried to talk of our ship, of the cap he had lost, of his timidity when we had found ourselves in Castle Garden, of the policeman whom I asked to direct us. But Gitelson only nodded and grinned and tittered. I realized that I had made a mistake—that I should have taken him to a more modest restaurant. But then the chasm between him and me seemed to be too wide for us to celebrate as ship brothers in any place.

"By the way, Gitelson, I owe you something," I said, producing a ten-dollar bill. "It was with your ten dollars that I learned to be a cloak-operator and entered the cloak trade. Do you remember?" I was going to add something about my desire to help him in some substantial way, but he interrupted me.

"Sure, I do," he said, with inebriate shamefacedness, as he received the money and shoved it into the inside pocket of his vest. "It has brought you good luck, hasn't it? And how about the interest? He, he, he! You've kept it over twenty-three years. The interest must be quite a little. He, he, he!"

"Of course I'll pay you the interest, and more, too. You shall get a check."

"Oh, I was only joking."

"But *I* am not joking. You're going to get a check, all right."

He revolted me.

I made out a check for two hundred dollars; tore it and made out one for five hundred.

He flushed, scanned the figure, giggled, hesitated, and finally folded the check and pushed it into his inner vest pocket, thanking me with drunken ardor.

Some time later I was returning to my office, my heart heavy with self-disgust and sadness. In the evening I went home, to the loneliness of my beautiful hotel lodgings. My heart was still heavy with distaste and sadness.

GUSSIE, the finisher-girl to whom I had once made love with a view to marrying her for her money, worked in the vicinity of my factory and I met her from time to time on the Avenue. We kept up our familiar tone of former days. We would pause, exchange some banter, and go our several ways. She was over fifty now. She looked haggard and dried up and her hair was copiously shot with gray.

One afternoon she told me she had changed her shop, naming her new employer.

"Is it a good place to work in?" I inquired.

"Oh, it's as good or as bad as any other place," she replied, with a gay smile.

"Mine is good," I jested.

"That's what they all say."

"Come to work for me and see for yourself."

"Will I get good wages?"

"Yes."

"How much?"

"Any price you name."

"Look at him," she said, as though addressing a third person. "Look at the new millionaire."

"It might have been all yours. But you did not think I was good enough for you."

"You can keep it all to yourself and welcome."

"Well, will you come to work?"

"You can't do without me, can you? He can't get finisher-girls, the poor fellow. Well, how much will you pay me?"

We agreed upon the price, but on taking leave she said, "I was joking."

"What do you mean? Don't you want to work for me, Gussie?"

She shook her head.

"Why?"

"I don't want you to think I begrudge you your millions. We'll be better friends at a distance. Good-bye."

"You're a funny girl, Gussie. Good-by."

A short time after this conversation I had trouble with the Cloak-makers' Union, of which Gussie was one of the oldest and most loyal members.

The cause of the conflict was an operator named Blitt, a native of Antomir, who had been working in my shop for some months. He was a spare little fellow with a nose so compressed at the nostrils that it looked as though it was inhaling some sharp, pleasant odor. It gave his face a droll appearance, but his eyes, dark and large, were very attractive. I had known him as a small boy in my birthplace, where he belonged to a much better family than I.

When Blitt was invited to join the Levinsky Antomir Society of my employees he refused. It turned out that he was one of the active spirits of the union and also an ardent member of the Socialist party. His foreman had not the courage to discharge him, because of my well-known predilection for natives of Antomir, so he reported him to me as a dangerous fellow.

"He isn't going to blow up the building, is he?" I said, lightly.

"But he may do other mischief. He's one of the leaders of the union."

"Let him lead."

The next time I looked at Blitt I felt uncomfortable. His refusal to join my Antomir organization hurt me, and his activities in the union and at socialist gatherings kindled my rancor. His compressed nose revolted me now. I wanted to get rid of him.

Not that I had remained inflexible in my views regarding the distribution of wealth in the world. Some of the best-known people in the country were openly taking the ground that the poor man was not getting a "square deal." To sympathize with organized labor was no longer "bad form," some society women even doing picket duty for Jewish factory-girls out on strike. Socialism, which used to be declared utterly un-American, had come to be almost a vogue. American colleges were leavened with it, while American magazines were building up stupendous circulations by exposing the corruption of the mighty. Public opinion had, during the past two decades, undergone a striking change in this respect. I had watched that change and I could not but be influenced by it. For all my theorizing about the "survival of the fittest" and the "dying off of the weaklings," I could not help feeling that, in an abstract way, the socialists were not altogether wrong. The case was different, however, when I considered it in connection with the concrete struggle of trade-unionism (which among the Jewish immigrants was practically but another name for socialism) against low wages or high rent. I must confess, too, that the defeat with which I had met at Tevkin's house had greatly intensified my hostility to socialists. As I have remarked in a previous chapter, I ascribed my fiasco to the socialist atmosphere that surrounded Anna. I was embittered.

The socialists were constantly harping on "class struggle," "class antagonism," "class psychology." I would dismiss it all as absurd, but I did hate the trade-unions, particularly those of the East Side. Altogether there was too much socialism among the masses of the Ghetto, I thought.

Blitt now seemed to be the embodiment of this "class antagonism."

"Ah, he won't join my Antomir Society!" I would storm and fume and writhe inwardly. "That's a tacit protest against the whole society as an organization of 'slaves.' It means that the society makes meek, obedient servants of my employees and helps me fleece them. As if they did not earn in my shop more than they would anywhere else! As if they could all get steady work outside my place! And what about the loans and all sorts of other favors they get from me? If they worked for their own fathers they could not be treated better than they are treated here." I felt outraged.

I rebuked myself for making much ado about nothing. Indeed, this was a growing weakness with me. Some trifle unworthy of consideration would get on my nerves and bother me like a grain of sand in the eye. Was I getting old? But, no, I felt in the prime of life, full of vigor, and more active and more alive to the passions than a youth.

Whenever I chanced to be on the floor where Blitt worked I would avoid looking in his direction. His presence irritated me. "How ridiculous," I often thought. "One would imagine he's my conscience and that's why I want to get rid of him." As a consequence, I dared not send him away, and, as a consequence of this, he irritated me more than ever.

Finally, one afternoon, acting on the spur of the moment, I called his foreman to me and told him to discharge him.

A committee of the union called on me. I refused to deal with them. The upshot was a strike—not merely for the return of Blitt to my employment, but also for higher wages and the recognition of the union. The organization was not strong, and only a small number of my men were members of it, but when these went out all the others followed their contagious example, the members of my Antomir Society not excepted.

The police gave me ample protection, and there were thousands of cloak-makers who remained outside the union, so that I soon had all the "hands" I wanted; but the conflict caused me all sorts of other mortifications. For one thing, it gave me no end of hostile publicity. The socialist Yiddish daily, which had an overwhelmingly wide circulation now, printed reports of meetings at which I had been hissed and hooted. I was accused of bribing corrupt politicians who were supposed to help me suppress the strike by means of police clubs. I was charged with bringing disgrace upon the Jewish people.

The thought of Tevkin reading these reports and of Anna hearing of them hurt me cruelly. I could see Moissey reveling in the hisses with which my name was greeted. And Elsie? Did she take part in some of the demonstrations against me? Were she and Anna collecting funds for my striking employees?

The reports in the American papers also were inclined to favor the strikers. Public opinion was against me. What galled me worse than all, perhaps, was the sympathy shown for the strikers by some German-Jewish financiers and philanthropists, men whose acquaintance it was the height of my ambition to cultivate. All of which only served to pour oil into the flames of my hatred for the union.

Bender implored me to settle the strike.

"The union doesn't amount to a row of pins," he urged. "A week or two after we settle, things will get back to their old state."

"Where's your backbone, Bender?" I exploded. "If you had your way, those fellows would run the whole business. You have no sense of dignity. And yet you were born in America."

I was always accompanied by a detective.

One of the strikers was in my pay. Every morning at a fixed hour he would call at a certain hotel, where he reported the doings of the organization to Bender and myself. One of the things I thus learned was that the union was hard up and constantly exacting loans from Gussie and several other members who had savings-bank accounts. One day, however, when the secretary appealed to her for a further loan with which to pay fines for arrested pickets and assist some of the neediest strikers, she flew into a passion. "What do you want of me, murderers that you are?" she cried, bursting into tears. "Haven't I done enough? Have you no hearts?"

A minute or two later she yielded.

"Bleed me, bleed me, cruel people that you are!" she said, pointing at her heart, as she started toward her savings bank.

I was moved. When my spy had departed I paced the floor for some minutes. Then, pausing, I smilingly declare to Bender my determination to ask the union for a committee. He was overjoyed and shook my hand solemnly.

One of my bookkeepers was to communicate with the strike committee in the afternoon. Two hours before the time set for their meeting I saw in one of the afternoon papers an interview with the president of the union. His statements were so unjust to me, I thought, and so bitter, that the fighting blood was again up in my veins.

But the image of Gussie giving her hard-earned money to help the strikers haunted me. The next morning I went to Atlantic City for a few days, letting Bender "do as he pleased." The strike was compromised, the men obtaining a partial concession of their demands and Blitt waiving his claim to his former job.

My business continued to grow. My consumption of raw material reached gigantic dimensions, so much so that at times, when I liked a pattern, I would buy up the entire output and sell some of it to smaller manufacturers at a profit.

Gradually I abandoned the higher grades of goods, developing my whole business along the lines of popular prices. There are two cloak-and-suit houses that make a specialty of costly garments. These enjoy high reputations for taste and are the real arbiters of fashion in this country, one of the two being known in the trade as Little Paris; but the combined volume of business of both these firms is much smaller than mine.

My deals with one mill alone—the largest in the country and the one whose head had come to my rescue when my affairs were on the brink of a precipice—now exceeded a million dollars at a single purchase to be delivered in seven months. The mills often sell me at a figure considerably lower than the general market price. They do so, first, because of the enormous quantities I buy, and, second, because of the "boost" a fabric receives from the very fact of being handled by my house. One day, for instance, I said to the president of a certain mill: "I like this cloth of yours. I feel like making a big thing of it, provided you can let me have an inside figure." We came to terms, and I gave him an advance order for nine thousand pieces. When smaller manufacturers and department-store buyers heard that I had bought an immense quantity of that pattern its success was practically established. As a consequence, the mill was in a position to raise the price of the cloth to others, so that it amply made up for the low figure at which it had sold the goods to me.

Judged by the market price of the raw material, my profit on a garment did not exceed fifty cents. But I paid for the raw material seventy-five cents less than the market price, so that my total profit was one dollar and twenty-five cents. Still, there have been instances when I lost seventy-five thousand dollars in one month because goods fell in price or because a certain style failed to move and I had to sell it below cost to get it out of the way. To be sure, cheaper goods are less likely to be affected by the caprices of style than higher grades, which is one of several reasons why I prefer to produce garments of popular prices.

I do not employ my entire capital in my cloak business, half of it, or more, being invested in "quick assets." Should I need more ready cash than I have, I could procure it at a lower rate than what those assets bring me. I can get half a million dollars, from two banks, without rising from my desk—by merely calling those banks up on the telephone. For this I pay, say, three and a half or four per cent., for I am a desirable customer at the banks; and, as my quick assets bring me an average of five per cent., I make at least one per cent. on the money.

Another way of making my money breed money is by early payments to the mills. Not only can I do without their credit, but I can afford to pay them six months in advance. This gives me an "anticipation" allowance at the rate of six per cent. per annum, while money costs me at the banks three or four per cent. per annum.

All this is good sport.

I own considerable stock in the very mills with which I do business, which has a certain moral effect on their relations with my house. For a similar purpose I am a shareholder in the large mail-order houses that buy cloaks and suits of me. I hold shares of some department stores also, but of late I have grown somewhat shy of this kind of investment, the future of a department store being as uncertain as the future of the neighborhood in which it is located. Mail-order houses, on the other hand, have the whole country before them, and their overwhelming growth during past years was one of the conspicuous phenomena in the business life of the nation. I love to watch their operations spread over the map, and I love to watch the growth of American cities, the shifting of their shopping centers, the consequent vicissitudes, the decline of some houses, the rise of others. American Jews of German origin are playing a foremost part in the retail business of the country, large or small, and our people, Russian and Galician Jews, also are making themselves felt in it, being, in many cases, in partnership with Gentiles or with their own coreligionists of German descent. The king of the great mail-order business, a man with an annual income of many millions, is the son of a Polish Jew. He is one of the two richest Jews in America, having built up his vast fortune in ten or fifteen years. As I have said before, I know hundreds, if not thousands, of merchants, Jews and Gentiles, throughout this country and Canada, so I like to keep track of their careers.

This, too, is good sport.

Of course, it is essential to study the business map in the interests of my own establishment, but I find intellectual excitement in it as well, and, after all, I am essentially an intellectual man, I think.

There are retailers in various sections of the country whom I have helped financially—former buyers, for example, who went into business on their own hook with my assistance. This is good business, for while these merchants must be left free to buy in the open market, they naturally give my house precedence. But here again I must say in fairness to myself that business interest is not the only motive that induces me to do them these favors. Indeed, in some cases I do it without even expecting to get my money back. It gives me moral satisfaction, for which money is no measure of value.

Am I happy?

There are moments when I am overwhelmed by a sense of my success and ease. I become aware that thousands of things which had formerly been forbidden fruit to me are at my command now. I distinctly recall that crushing sense of being debarred from everything, and then I feel as though the whole world were mine. One day I paused in front of an old East Side restaurant that I had often passed in my days of need and despair. The feeling of desolation and envy with which I used to peek in its windows came back to me. It gave me pangs of self-pity for my past and a thrilling sense of my present power. The prices that had once been prohibitive seemed so wretchedly low now. On another occasion I came across a Canal Street merchant of whom I used to buy goods for my push-cart. I said to myself: "There was a time when I used to implore this man for ten dollars' worth of goods, when I regarded him as all-powerful and feared him. Now he would be happy to shake hands with me."

I recalled other people whom I used to fear and before whom I used to humiliate myself because of my poverty. I thought of the time when I had already entered the cloak business, but was struggling and squirming and constantly racking my brains for some way of raising a hundred dollars; when I would cringe with a certain East Side banker and vainly beg him to extend a small note of mine, and come away in a sickening state of despair.

At this moment, as these memories were filing by me, I felt as though now there were nobody in the world who could inspire me with awe or render me a service.

And yet in all such instances I feel a peculiar yearning for the very days when the doors of that restaurant were closed to me and when the Canal Street merchant was a magnate of commerce in my estimation. Somehow, encounters of this kind leave me dejected. The gloomiest past is dearer than the brightest present. In my case there seems to be a special reason for feeling this way. My sense of triumph is coupled with a brooding sense of emptiness and insignificance, of my lack of anything like a great, deep interest.

I am lonely. Amid the pandemonium of my six hundred sewing-machines and the jingle of gold which they pour into my lap I feel the deadly silence of solitude.

I spend at least one evening a week at the Benders'. I am fond of their children and I feel pleasantly at home at their house. I am a frequent caller at the Nodelmans', and enjoy their hospitality even more than that of the Benders. I go to the opera, to the theaters, and to concerts, and never alone. There are merry suppers, and some orgies in which I take part, but when I go home I suffer a gnawing aftermath of loneliness and desolation.

I have a fine summer home, with servants, automobiles, and horses. I share it with the Bender family and we often have visitors from the city, but, no matter how large and gay the crowd may be, the country makes me sad.

I know bachelors who are thoroughly reconciled to their solitude and even enjoy it. I am not.

No, I am not happy.

In the city I occupy a luxurious suite of rooms in a high-class hotel and keep an excellent chauffeur and valet. I give myself every comfort that money can buy. But there is one thing which I crave and which money cannot buy—happiness.

Many a pretty girl is setting her cap at me, but I know that it is only my dollars they want to marry. Nor do I care for any of them, while the woman to whom my heart is calling—Anna—is married to another man.

I dream of marrying some day. I dread to think of dying a lonely man.

Sometimes I have a spell of morbid amativeness and seem to be falling in love with woman after woman. There are periods when I can scarcely pass a woman in the street without scanning her face and figure. When I see the crowds returning from work in the cloak-and-waist district I often pause to watch the groups of girls as they walk apart from the men. Their keeping together, as if they formed a separate world full of its own interests and secrets, makes a peculiar appeal to me.

Once, in Florida, I thought I was falling in love with a rich Jewish girl whose face had a bashful expression of a peculiar type. There are different sorts of bashfulness. This girl had the bashfulness of sin, as I put it to myself. She looked as if her mind harbored illicit thoughts which she was trying to conceal. Her blushes seemed to be full of sex and her eyes full of secrets. She was not a pretty girl at all, but her "guilty look" disturbed me as long as we were stopping in the same place.

But through all these ephemeral infatuations and interests I am in love with Anna.

From time to time I decide to make a "sensible" marriage, and study this woman or that as a possible candidate, but so far nothing has come of it.

There was one woman whom I might have married if she had not been a Gentile—one of the very few who lived in the family hotel in which I had my apartments. At first I set her down for an adventuress seeking the acquaintance of rich Jews for some sinister purpose. But I was mistaken. She was a woman of high character. Moreover, she and her aged mother, with whom she lived, had settled in that hotel long before it came to be patronized by our people. She was a widow of over forty, with a good, intellectual face, well read in the better sense of the term, and no fool. Many of our people in the hotel danced attendance upon her because she was a Gentile woman, but all of them were really fond of her. The great point was that she seemed to have a sincere liking for our people. This and the peculiar way her shoulders would shake when she laughed was, in fact, what first drew me to her. We grew chummy and I spent many an hour in her company.

In my soliloquies I often speculated and theorized on the question of proposing to her. I saw clearly that it would be a mistake. It was not the faith of my fathers that was in the way. It was that medieval prejudice against our people which makes so many marriages between Jew and Gentile a failure. It frightened me.

One evening we sat chatting in the bright lobby of the hotel, discussing human nature, and she telling me something of the good novels she had read. After a brief pause I said:

"I enjoy these talks immensely. I don't think there is another person with whom I so love to talk of human beings."

She bowed with a smile that shone of something more than mere appreciation of the compliment. And then I uttered in the simplest possible accents:

"It's really a pity that there is the chasm of race between us. Otherwise I don't see why we couldn't be happy together."

I was in an adventurous mood and ready, even eager, to marry her. But her answer was a laugh, as if she took it for a joke; and, though I seemed to sense intimacy and encouragement in that laugh, it gave me pause. I felt on the brink of a fatal blunder, and I escaped before it was too late.

"But then," I hastened to add, "real happiness in a case like this is perhaps not the rule, but the exception. That chasm continues to yawn throughout the couple's married life, I suppose."

"That's an interesting point of view," she said, a non-committal smile on her lips.

She tactfully forbore to take up the discussion, and I soon dropped the subject. We remained friends.

It was this woman who got me interested in good, modern fiction. The books she selected for me interested me greatly. Then it was that the remarks I had heard from Moissey Tevkin came to my mind. They were illuminating.

Most of the people at my hotel are German American Jews. I know other Jews of this class. I contribute to their charity institutions. Though an atheist, I belong to one of their synagogues. Nor can I plead the special feeling which had partly accounted for my visits at the synagogue of the Sons of Antomir while I was engaged to Kaplan's daughter. I am a member of that synagogue chiefly because it is a fashionable synagogue. I often convict myself of currying favor with the German Jews. But then German-American Jews curry favor with Portuguese-American Jews, just as we all curry favor with Gentiles and as American Gentiles curry favor with the aristocracy of Europe.

I often long for a heart-to-heart talk with some of the people of my birthplace. I have tried to revive my old friendships with some of them, but they are mostly poor and my prosperity stands between us in many ways.

Sometimes when I am alone in my beautiful apartments, brooding over these things and nursing my loneliness, I say to myself:

"There are cases when success is a tragedy."

There are moments when I regret my whole career, when my very success seems to be a mistake.

I think that I was born for a life of intellectual interest. I was certainly brought up for one. The day when that accident turned my mind from college to business seems to be the most unfortunate day in my life. I think that I should be much happier as a scientist or writer, perhaps. I should then be in my natural elements, and if I were doomed to loneliness I should have comforts to which I am now a stranger. That's the way I feel every time I pass the abandoned old building of the City College.

The business world contains plenty of successful men who have no brains. Why, then, should I ascribe my triumph to special ability? I should probably have made a much better college professor than a cloak-manufacturer, and should probably be a happier man, too.

I know people who have made much more money than I and whom I consider my inferiors in every respect.

Many of our immigrants have distinguished themselves in science, music, or art, and these I envy far more than I do a billionaire. As an example of the successes achieved by Russian Jews in America in the last quarter of a century it is often pointed out that the man who has built the greatest sky-scrapers in the country, including the Woolworth Building, is a Russian Jew who came here a penniless boy. I cannot boast such distinction, but then I have helped build up one of the great industries of the United States, and this also is something to be proud of. But I should readily change places with the Russian Jew, a former Talmud student like myself, who is the greatest physiologist in the New World, or with the Russian Jew who holds the foremost place among American songwriters and whose soulful compositions are sung in almost every English-speaking house in the world. I love music to madness. I yearn for the world of great singers, violinists, pianists. Several of the greatest of them are of my race and country, and I have met them, but all my acquaintance with them has brought me is a sense of being looked down upon as a money-bag striving to play the Mæcenas. I had a similar experience with a sculptor, also one of our immigrants, an East Side boy who had met with sensational success in Paris and London. I had him make my bust. His demeanor toward me was all that could have been desired. We even cracked Yiddish jokes together and he hummed bits of synagogue music over his work, but I never left his studio without feeling cheap and wretched.

When I think of these things, when I am in this sort of mood, I pity myself for a victim of circumstances.

At the height of my business success I feel that if I had my life to live over again I should never think of a business career.

I don't seem to be able to get accustomed to my luxurious life. I am always more or less conscious of my good clothes, of the high quality of my office furniture, of the power I wield over the men in my pay. As I have said in another connection, I still have a lurking fear of restaurant waiters.

I can never forget the days of my misery. I cannot escape from my old self. My past and my present do not comport well. David, the poor lad swinging over a Talmud volume at the Preacher's Synagogue, seems to have more in common with my inner identity than David Levinsky, the well-known cloak-manufacturer.

Journey to the Dawn
by CHARLES ANGOFF

This is the first book in a continuing series, now in its eighth volume, of Jewish-American life, told in terms of a multigeneration and many-faceted family, the Polonskys, who came from Russia at the turn of the century to settle in Boston. Almost every major aspect of Jewish life is dealt with in the saga: Zionism, socialism, atheism (straight and devout), unionism, religious intermarriage, politics (within the Jewish community and in relation to the "outside" American community), anti-Semitism, education (both religious and "worldly"), Hasidism, secularism, assimilation, the Jew in industry, in business large and small.

The early volumes form a family portrait unmatched in American Jewish literature; the continuing narrative then centers on David Polonsky's experiences in liberal journalism and offers a touching and profound study of the sensitive Jewish intellectual in American life.

Journey to the Dawn, published in 1950, takes the Polonskys from a Russian past both horrendous and strangely glorious to a hard and sorrowful striving for a living in a country that turns out to be far from the goldene medinch of legend, but where opportunities continue to beckon. Heavy prices are paid for these opportunities, and one of the heaviest, leaving profound inner pain, is the need to work on the Sabbath. This theme, touched on in The Rise of David Levinsky, forms our major selection. It is preceded by a portrait of a great figure among impoverished Jewish immigrants, the lodge doctor, and is followed by the death of the family matriarch, Alte Bobbe.

Angoff was born in Russia in 1902. From Harvard he entered journalism, becoming Henry Mencken's managing editor on The

American Mercury, and editor when Mencken left. His book on Henry Mencken proved highly controversial. Veering into teaching as he concentrated on writing, Angoff eventually became a professor at Fairleigh Dickinson University.

Charles Angoff is in love with the whole of Judaism, but chiefly Yiddishkeit; he will go out to lecture at the smallest Jewish community, enjoying the contact. A remarkable number of readers have found their way to the Polonsky series; some of the volumes are now past their fifth editions, having proven more lasting and surely more significant than many a hot "Jewish" best seller.

M.L.

Not LONG after his arrival in this country Mottel suggested to Moshe that he join a lodge, preferably a Jewish lodge, not only for the companionship it would offer a newly arrived immigrant but also because of the very solid benefits it would give a young married man with a family. Mottel took him over to a few meetings of his own lodge, where Moshe could see the membership and where he could get an idea of how a lodge conducted itself, for in Russia there were no lodges, at least among the Jews. Moshe finally joined Mottel's lodge. The annual premium was fifteen dollars. The benefits, as has been said, were sizeable and numerous: there was free burial for all members, including the payment for the funeral and for the plot; small sick benefits ($5 a week for ten weeks for total disability and $2 a week for ten weeks for partial disability); also a loan service (loans up to $50 at 4 per cent per year); and perhaps most important of all, the services of a lodge doctor.

Every member had the right to call upon the services of the lodge doctor for himself and for his wife and all his children as many times as he pleased, and without any expense to himself. The doctor received an annual fee from the lodge for his services. If individual members wanted to give him something—in the way of money or a present—they were free to do so, but such payment was not necessary. Most of the members, if they were working, generally gave the doctor a dollar or a bottle of wine or a bag full of cakes, when he called; but when they were not working, they gave him nothing—

except an apologetic promise that as soon as they could they would do the right thing by him.

There was another feature to lodge life that Mottel forgot to mention but which was a chief attraction to all the members, namely, the annual installation of officers, which was the occasion for considerable festivity, including dancing and refreshments and music by a three-piece band consisting of a violin, a cello, and a bass drum. The members brought their wives and children, and altogether it was a great social event.

The doctor of the lodge Mottel and Moshe belonged to, Dr. Kahn, was ideally suited to his task. He had no ambitions for wealth. He sincerely wanted to minister to the ailments of the poor. Indeed, the poorer the patients the more eager was he to help them, for he had a great pity for the trials and miseries and loneliness and helplessness and occasional hopelessness of the vast and silent majority of mankind upon this planet. Part of this sympathy he got at his own home, which was a poverty-stricken home of Russian-Jewish immigrants; but a great deal of it derived from his own being. His very eyes bespoke deep feeling for all who suffered in any way, and so did his speech and his general bearing.

Professionally, he was a very able man. In fact, he was one of the very best general practitioners in Boston at the time, though few of his poor patients knew it. He had been an honor student at both Harvard College and the Harvard Medical School, and after his internship at the Boston City Hospital—a charitable public institution—he was at a loss what to do. He opened a modest office at the foot of Bowdoin Street, which is a dividing line between the West End slums and the lower realms of Beacon Hill. He hoped to get some patients, in this way, from both elements. Soon enough he discovered the inevitable. The folks of lower Beacon Hill were very slow to seek his advice, and the penurious Jews hesitated to come because few of them had the dollar or two to pay for his services. Thus several months passed, and he had to make a decision.

As a shot in the dark he applied to several fraternal organizations and lodges among the Jews, to become their physician, and it so happened that Mottel's lodge at the time was seeking a physician, for their doctor of many years had decided to "specialize," having moved his office to Commonwealth Avenue, in the heart of the Back Bay, to treat only "nervous disorders."

Dr. Kahn was asked to present himself before the officers of the

lodge, and they all liked him immensely. While they knew nothing
about his competence, they did know that graduating from the
Harvard Medical School with honors in itself meant a great deal.
He also spoke a perfect Yiddish, and in a very gentle and kindly
manner. He was also young, and thus had the strength to make the
many trips to the homes of ill members. Finally, he did not seem to
be greedy for money. All the lodge could offer to pay him was $250
a year, and that was entirely satisfactory to him. The officers said
they hoped to raise this to $300 soon, but they could not promise
when that would be, if ever. It all depended on how many new members the lodge got during the next year or two. Dr. Kahn said he left
that to the officers. Thus, at the next general meeting of the lodge,
Dr. Kahn was quickly and unanimously elected the new lodge doctor.

Immediately after his election he made a brief speech to the
members. He told them not to hesitate to call upon him at any time,
at his office or by telephone. Knowing that most of the members had
no telephone in their homes, he gave them the names and addresses
of three drug stores, so situated as to be handy to nearly all the lodge
members, where the members could ask the druggist to telephone
Dr. Kahn for them. He added, "If you feel you can pay the druggist
for the telephone call, do so; if you can't, don't worry. The druggist
will make the call just the same, and let me worry about the expense." Very often, Dr. Kahn paid for the calls out of his own pocket;
it never occurred to the officers of the lodge that the lodge should
defray the expense of the calls.

Dr. Kahn ended his brief speech by saying, "A miracle man I am
not. Medicine has made amazing progress in the past twenty-five
years, but the field of our ignorance is still far greater than that of
our knowledge. But some things we can do, and the sooner you let
me know your complaints the better for you and for me. You'll recover more quickly, and I'll have time for other patients. One more
thing, no matter what complaint you may have, remember what a
very great doctor at the Harvard Medical School told me. He said
that most people are healthier than they think, and that most ailments get better of themselves, with the help of good food, plenty
of rest, and above all, peace of mind. Psychology is still a new science,
but already we know enough to be sure that the influence of the
mind on the body is very great. The same professor used to tell us
medical students that the amount of harm that worry alone causes
to the body is incalculable. So don't worry. See me when you want

to, and may you all be so strong and healthy that you won't need me. The best doctor is the one who is never needed."

Shortly after Moshe joined the lodge he visited Dr. Kahn to have him look at a sore finger that refused to heal. Dr. Kahn looked at it, put a bandage on it, and said to Moshe, "You should eat a little more meat. Your blood is a little thin." He made a quick examination of a drop of blood, and said, "As I thought. A little anemic."

"What is anemic?" asked Moshe.

Dr. Kahn smiled. "I'm sorry. The word jumped out of my mouth. All it means is like I told you at the beginning. The blood is a little thinned out. If you eat a little more meat and liver for a little while, everything will be fine." Then he added, "I'm glad you came, though, because I like to look over new members, especially those who are not long from the old country."

Dr. Kahn examined him and said, "All our Jews should be as healthy as you are."

"So it's good," said Moshe.

"Of course. Now when your family comes to America, be sure to bring them here, just for me to look them over. It's better for a doctor to examine a person when he's healthy and to keep him healthy, than for a doctor to examine him when he's sick."

Dr. Kahn was a perfect general practitioner. He knew that most of his patients from the lodge suffered chiefly from under-nourishment, malnutrition, and lack of fresh air. Newly arrived Russian Jews were inclined to eat too much starch and too much fat, and far too little vegetables and fruits. They got into this habit for purely economic reasons. Bread and potatoes were cheaper than meat, and fruit was both difficult to get and expensive. Vegetables, it is true, were plentiful, but outside of potatoes and cabbage and carrots, Jews somehow put little stock by them. Moshe, in common with many other Jews, considered most green vegetables as fit only for pigs and cows. His special dislike was for lettuce and celery, and the mere sight of people eating parsley made him laugh.

Dr. Kahn tried to make his patients eat more vegetables, but he had great difficulty in doing so. He therefore centered his efforts upon showing his patients how from the health standpoint to make their little money go the farthest. In those days liver, kidneys, sweetbreads, and other such internal meats were very cheap and Dr. Kahn tried to induce the wives of his patients to get plenty of such meats rather than less of the more expensive meats. One woman had some doubts about this procedure. Dr. Kahn reassured her in this way: "These so-called cheap meats must be good and nourishing. A lion, when he kills a sheep, or any animal for that matter, goes first for the liver and the kidneys. Sometimes, as a matter of fact, that's all he eats: he leaves the rest for the vultures. And I tell you that what's good for the lion is good for the human being. You want your children to be as strong as lions, don't you?"

Dr. Kahn also advised the plentiful eating of fish—particularly the inexpensive herring, haddock and cod. He did not deny that the more expensive mackerel and whitefish tasted good, but he insisted that in food value they were no better than the humble herring and his colleagues of the sea. He said to all who doubted him, "You know that most Russian people and Norwegian people and Swedish people and Danish people and Portuguese people and Spaniards, too, live to a very large extent, and some of them almost entirely, on herring, and they're strong and athletic. So if herring is good for them it is good for you." And always Dr. Kahn insisted that his people eat everything in a fish, for the same reasons that he insisted that they eat everything in a cow or sheep.

Long before it became the fashion in the medical world to use the term, and without knowing precisely what he was doing himself, Dr. Kahn practiced psychosomatic medicine, and often with such success that more celebrated physicians in Boston were astounded. Of course, he believed in the occasional efficacy of pills and elixirs, and he prescribed both whenever he thought them necessary, but he also had the wisdom of a shrewd and observing mother or grandmother.

Dr. Kahn, who in time became the doctor for the entire family, for Leah and Alte Bobbe and their children and grandchildren, was called in one day to examine Yetta, one of David's aunts, who had long been complaining of vague aches and pains, loss of appetite, insomnia, general tiredness, and loss of weight. A Socialist, she first went to her Workmen's Circle doctor, then to a "specialist" recommended by him. Both of them prescribed a variety of pills, special diets, and occasional massages, but to no avail. As a last resort, and largely at the recommendation of Moshe, Dr. Kahn was called in. He examined Yetta carefully and found nothing physically wrong.

He prescribed a small amount of placebos—brightly colored "bread pills," as they were then called among lay people—but he also spent considerable time just talking to her about her work (she operated a machine in a dress-making shop), about her habits, and, very delicately, he probed into her love life. He was led to suspect that she had had a quarrel with her sweetheart, that she wouldn't "lower herself" to take the initiative in calling him, and the sweetheart, for reasons of his own, obviously had not called her. Very gently Dr. Kahn said, with a smile, "Sometimes a woman's pride, instead of bringing her joy, brings her sadness for all her life." To Leah, Yetta's mother, Dr. Kahn said, "I find nothing organically wrong with your daughter. All I can say is that maybe she is having a quarrel with her favorite suitor. Once they make up, I believe all her ailments will disappear."

About the same time Dr. Kahn was called in to examine David's younger sister, Aidel, who had been ailing for a long time, and now was confined to her bed virtually all the time. Mottel had insisted that Moshe call in the son of a prominent member of his synagogue; the son was a "professor"—a term applied to any doctor in those days who charged twice the regular fee of $2 for a house visit—and had his offices in one of the most exclusive sections of Boston. The son examined Aidel thoroughly and left a half dozen prescriptions. A week later he examined her again, and left still more prescriptions. He thought it beneath his dignity to explain his findings to Moshe and Nechame. Aidel did not get better, and pretty soon the great doctor politely gave up the case.

Dr. Kahn had been called in at the very beginning of Aidel's illness, and all he prescribed was a month's vacation somewhere near Boston, where Aidel could get plenty of fresh air, good food, and more constant care than Nechame could give her, what with the other children and the cramped quarters. Now that the great specialist revealed himself as not so great after all, Moshe decided to call in Dr. Kahn again. Moshe told him everything about the specialist, exhibiting the various medicines he had left. Dr. Kahn merely looked at them, smiled, and said, "Different doctors have different ways of doing things." Then he said, "I will examine your daughter again, if you want me to, but I doubt that I'll find anything wrong with her." He examined Aidel, found nothing wrong organically, and said, "Really, all I can suggest is what I suggested in the first place. She needs some special attention for a while—and lots of liver and beef juice and kidneys, and good, clean, fresh air. On the way here I was thinking of suggesting you send her to a certain place that I should have suggested, perhaps, in the first place. Did you ever hear of the Floating Hospital?"

Moshe and Nechame turned pale. They were afraid of hospitals, for they had heard that the Boston City Hospital, where most charity patients went, was a filthy place, which was untrue, and that few people left it alive, which was also not true.

"I see," said Dr. Kahn. "That's why I was afraid, I guess, to mention the Floating Hospital in the first place. But there's nothing to be afraid of. It's not a regular hospital. It's a ship—*floating* hospital, floats, goes on the water. It leaves a pier in the North End every morning at ten and comes back at five. There are beds there. Your daughter will have a bed right on the open deck, she will sleep right in the open, and get all the wonderful fresh ocean air. The boat goes out quite a way into the ocean, not very far, really," he added as he noticed a sudden fear pass across the faces of Moshe and Nechame, "just far enough to get away from all the dirt and soot of the city. And the nurses will feed your daughter beef juice to give her good red blood, and blood, you know, feeds the whole body. The nurses will also give her orange juice, milk, bread and butter. And it will all cost you nothing. If you want me to, I'll telephone the doctor in charge, and perhaps you can start tomorrow. Believe me, you will see a difference in your daughter even after a week."

Moshe and Nechame took turns taking Aidel to the Floating Hospital. Nechame took her home at night, except when David did it. In ten days so great an improvement was noticeable in Aidel that Nechame made an extra large portion of *gefilte* fish for Moshe to take to Dr. Kahn. At the end of two months Aidel had gained almost ten pounds, and for the next month her trips were all pleasure. She ran around the deck and helped the nurses minister to the bed-ridden children. When the head doctor discharged her as in sound health, she cried because she wanted to keep on going on those ocean trips.

It is thus easy to understand why Dr. Kahn's reputation was so high among the poor of the West End slums of Boston. He also enjoyed their companionship and visited them socially. During the Jewish holidays, especially at Passover and Rosh Hashonoh, his office would be filled with all sorts of gifts from his patients, particularly homemade wine and holiday delicacies, and he had dozens of invitations to dinner. So as not to hurt the feelings of anybody he accepted no invitations, but he did visit all the families, and thanked them personally for their good wishes and gifts. It became known that he donated most of the gifts to hospitals and orphan asylums and homes for the aged, and that naturally made him all the more admired and respected in the community.

Not very long after David's arrival in this country, Moshe decided to take him to Dr. Kahn for a general examination, in compliance with Dr. Kahn's specific direction. Moshe was going to take his wife and the other children later. Moshe did not tell David where he was taking him, for fear David would be frightened. Moshe merely said one Sunday afternoon, "Nu, my son, perhaps you would like to take a walk with me to visit a friend. In America, people take walks. It's not very far where we're going, a little up one hill, then down another. Bowdoin Street, you know where that is?"

David said he did.

"So it's good," said Moshe. "Already you know almost as much about this city as I do. And soon, I hope, you will know more than I do." He ruffled the hair of his oldest and favorite child. "Yes, children should know more than their parents. And it won't take you long to know more than I do. Young people learn new ways and new places more quickly than old folks like me."

Moshe held David by the hand, as they walked over Mt. Vernon Street, one of the more elegant sections of the city, then down Bowdoin Street, hard by the State House, and lined on both sides with genteel, old, dignified red-brick houses, the front walls of which were already sprouting ivy leaves here and there.

Moshe tried to make conversation with David, as they walked, but since David was so much smaller than his father, he heard very little of what he was saying. He did hear him ask a few times whether he was tired, and each time David mumbled no. After a while Moshe stopped saying anything to his son, which pleased the son enormously, for he was enjoying this walk very much. The *goyishke* part of the city seemed so quiet and so gentle, as compared to the streets of the Jewish slums, and everywhere David seemed to see wraiths of beautifully dressed women and girls, almost as dainty and delicate as Miss Long, floating in the air above and around them . . . and, in his mind's eye, he could also see the same wraiths walking gracefully and turning this way and that way, smiling at this one and merely looking quietly at someone else. David enjoyed this day-dreaming and hardly was conscious of walking beside his father.

Soon both of them came to a red-brick house that was a bit larger than most of the others on Bowdoin Street. They walked up the few steps, leading to the immaculately white door, and Moshe pulled something and immediately a bell was heard to ring inside. David was thrilled by that bell sound; it added a benediction to all the wonderful day-dreams he was having. It seemed like pure magic to him, and he hoped and hoped that his father would keep pulling the lever that rang the bell for the rest of the day. But very soon a tallish, rather stocky man opened the door, and greeted Moshe very cordially in Yiddish, "Ah, Mr. Polonsky! A good day to you. And this is your little boy?"

"Yes, Dr. Kahn. This is the little boy I told you I would bring to you."

Dr. Kahn patted David's head. "Good, good. Well, the trip from Russia didn't hurt him a bit. Come in, please."

David knew immediately that Dr. Kahn was a physician, and while in general he didn't like physicians, he liked Dr. Kahn at once. Moshe admitted to Dr. Kahn that he hadn't told David he was being taken to a doctor. Dr. Kahn smiled and looked kindly at David and said to him, "Nothing to be afraid of, my son. I don't bite people. You're in America now."

"Yes, America," said Moshe.

"I only want to see how you are," said Dr. Kahn to David. "You look good and healthy to me, but I want to do a few things just to make sure. It will take only a few minutes."

By this time David liked the doctor so much that he was sorry he was going to give him only a few minutes, so David took a little extra time in taking his clothes off. Dr. Kahn examined his heart and lungs and nose and throat and eyes, tapped his stomach and back and felt his neck. Then he felt the biceps of his arms, and said, "You'll be a strong man, my son. A prizefighter!"

David didn't know what a prizefighter meant, but since his father and Dr. Kahn laughed he imagined that being a prizefighter was a worthy thing, and he began to laugh a little himself, out of good spirits.

"A strong little man," said Dr. Kahn to Moshe.

David stared at Dr. Kahn, completely fascinated by him, and his eyes searched the office, fascinated—all those clean, shiny instruments, and that wonderful smell that seemed to hang over the office.

"A bright boy," said Dr. Kahn to Moshe. Then he turned to David and said, "See, it didn't hurt at all, and I hope I don't have to see you again."

"I hope so," said Moshe, and turned to David and told him to dress, which David did very slowly and very reluctantly. Dr. Kahn gave David some chocolates, which not only tasted good, but also presented a good excuse for David to take his time getting dressed.

On their way back home, David said to his father, "I want to be a doctor, like Dr. Kahn."

"If you want to, my son," said Moshe. "In this country that could be."

"Will I have to go to many schools?"

"I think so. Being a doctor is a very noble thing, and it would be an honor both to your father and mother, if you should become a doctor. I have heard it said that Jews make very good doctors. I do know that some of the greatest doctors in the past have been Jews. Maimonides was not only a great rabbi, but also a very great physician. But you have time to make up your mind, my son."

"What is that thing he had in his ears, and put on my chest and on my back, father?"

"I think it's to listen to the heart and the lungs. I once asked him that myself. But I'm afraid I don't know very much more about it."

"What do they call it?" asked David.

"That, too, I don't know, my son. You will have to tell me sometime, when you study medicine and become a doctor yourself."

"And why did he feel me, I mean pinch me, it didn't hurt, why did he feel me with his two fingers in my neck?" asked David excitedly.

"That, too, I don't know," said Moshe, very pleased that his son was so intrigued by the profession of medicine. He thought how seldom he had seen his son so lively in Russia and how often he had been excited since he came from Russia. Out of gratitude to the country, he asked, "So you like it here, David?"

"Yes," said David slowly and with great conviction.

They walked back home, slowly. David now had no time for day-dreaming. He had more interesting things to occupy his mind with: the whole world of medicine, all those strange and tantalizing instruments he saw in Dr. Kahn's office, that lovely whiteness all over the office, the neatness, the penetrating cleanliness, and that smell which David could still feel going up and down his nostrils. He didn't know what that smell was. It was a little acrid and a little sweet, a little thin and a little thick. It reminded him just a little bit of Passover wine, yet it was different, both sharper and mellower. For a while he planned to ask his father about that smell, but he refrained, chiefly because, deep down in his soul, he preferred not to know just now; being blissfully ignorant of the nature and cause of the smell made it all the more exciting. He made up his mind, as he walked along, to tell Velvel and Hyman and Moses and Frank about what had happened to him in Dr. Kahn's office. David was immensely pleased with himself that now he really had something thrilling to tell his new friends. Until now he had to keep quiet most of the time, because he had so little to say.

Dr. Kahn occupied David's mind a great deal during the following days and months. Gradually disturbing rumors reached his ears about Dr. Kahn—in the way in which most rumors reached him, namely, by overhearing his parents talk at night, when they thought all their children were sound asleep. He had developed the habit of taking a half hour or even more to go to sleep and listening to his parents talk over the events of the day or any other matters that called for discussion. This habit grew with the years, so that David began to look forward to overhearing his parents at night. Doing this opened up a world apart to him, revealing his parents to him as nothing else could, drawing him nearer to them, intensifying his admiration and love for them, sometimes, also, increasing his puzzlement with the ways of grown-ups, but always filling him with a strange combination of wonderment and mystery mixed with a slight fear of the unknown.

The rumors regarding Dr. Kahn all concerned one thing: apparently he was living in sin with a woman, and, what was worse in the eyes of many Jews, the woman was a Gentile. David was terrified by these rumors, not because of the moral or religious issues involved, for they meant nothing to him, but because the gossip might hurt Dr. Kahn personally and might even drive him from his post as lodge doctor. From the manner in which his parents discussed the matter, David got the very definite impression that there was a possibility of either or both of these things happening. Not long afterward David's fears were intensified: he heard his father tell his mother that there was a motion on the table in the lodge to oust Dr. Kahn.

David's mother was very sorry to hear this. She said, "It may be wrong for me to say so, but I don't think it's right to do that to Dr. Kahn."

David's father was even more vigorous in his sentiments. He said, "Of course it's not right. It's shameful. To do a thing like that to a man who has done so much good to so many people is a disgrace to the community. I don't know if he's really living with a Gentile girl to whom he's not married. It would be better if he were married to a nice Jewish girl. But what I don't see with my own eyes I don't know. And if I saw and knew, it wouldn't be for me to judge. The rabbis have said many times that scandal-mongering is one of the worst sins. Especially against a man who does good. God forgives a lot to those who do good, and what God does, human beings should do." Then he added emphatically, "I will talk for Dr. Kahn at the lodge."

This show of determination on the part of his father made David feel good for a moment, but then he was as depressed as before. David could imagine his father influencing two or three people, gathered around a table, with glasses of tea and cake on it, but he could not imagine him swaying two, three hundred people. Moshe simply was not an orator. But a few days later, with or without Moshe's pleas, Dr. Kahn was given a unanimous vote of appreciation for his work and told that the job was his as long as he wanted.

Dr. Kahn continued to call on members of the lodge and of Moshe's family. David's love for him grew and grew. Always he made sure, when Dr. Kahn's services were needed, that he was present. David liked to watch him walk down the street, listen to him, see him examine someone. Quickly Dr. Kahn became David's notion of the perfect American grown-up.

One evening Moshe said he had to go to see Dr. Kahn about an infection in one of his fingers, and David instantly asked whether he could come along. Moshe agreed. As Dr. Kahn finished attending to Moshe's finger, the doorbell rang, and Dr. Kahn went to open the door. David heard a soft, lovely female voice at the door, then the sound of a kiss. Soon Dr. Kahn brought her in and introduced her to Moshe and David. Instantly David fell in love with her. She seemed so clean, so white, her hair was airy and so full of summer clouds and sunshine, she walked so gracefully and smiled so disarmingly that he couldn't take his eyes off her.

"I hope you're not sick," she said to David.

David melted inside. He wanted to say something, but he couldn't open his mouth.

Moshe helped him out. "No, I am sick. He is strong—like a prize-fighter."

They all laughed, and again David tried to say something, and again he couldn't open his mouth. He just stared at her—glad for being there, glad for Dr. Kahn, glad for his father, glad for America, glad for the medical profession, glad for everybody and everything.

She excused herself and walked off into another room.

Moshe and David soon left. Moshe said to David, "You should answer when a nice woman speaks to you. It's the polite thing to do."

"I know," mumbled David.

"Don't forget it next time," said Moshe, with a feeble attempt to be stern.

"No," said David.

The two walked on in silence for a few blocks. Suddenly David said, "Is that the woman who caused the trouble?"

Moshe stopped and looked at David. He didn't seem to know what to say. After a few moments, Moshe said, "My son, whatever you hear in the house, you must not repeat. I don't know who she is, you don't know, nobody knows."

David said yes, but he knew at once that she *was* the woman, and he took a great joy in the knowledge. He was glad that she was Dr. Kahn's woman, because he couldn't imagine anybody else worthy of him. Whether or not they were married, whether or not she was Gentile didn't interest him. He was just glad for Dr. Kahn, for her, for both of them, and he felt as if he had achieved something. For days and nights afterwards he was in a state of excitement. All he wanted was to see her again, but he didn't know how. He couldn't ask his father to take him to Dr. Kahn's office, because he couldn't think of a good enough reason. So he merely waited for an opportunity to present itself for him to go to Dr. Kahn's office and perchance see that woman again.

The opportunity never presented itself. A few days later, on a Sunday, Dr. Kahn and the woman were killed in an automobile accident. In accordance with orthodox Jewish custom he was buried the following day. More than two hundred people followed the hearse through the winding streets of Boston till it reached the main highway. David tagged along from behind. He was eager to know that the woman also had a proper funeral, but he didn't know whom to ask, he didn't know where she lived, he didn't know her name, and he didn't know whether or not it was proper for him to ask. He walked back by himself to the building where Dr. Kahn's office was, stared at it for a while, and went home.

A few weeks later another doctor moved into Dr. Kahn's former office. He didn't remove Dr. Kahn's sign, but put his directly under it. At first David was distressed by this. Somehow it seemed a sacrilege to Dr. Kahn's memory. Gradually David changed his mind and soon he learned to respect the new doctor's taste. In the next few months he visited Dr. Kahn's building several times, chiefly to make sure that his sign was not removed. It was not. A year, two years later, the sign was still there. More than thirty years later he visited Dr. Kahn's old building and he was delighted to see that his sign was exactly where he had left it. Though it was barely visible now, the sight of it thrilled him and all the warm emotions of his boyhood leaped across the years to mingle with the poignant emotions of his manhood.

.   .   .   .   .

THE DEPRESSION of 1907, like nearly all depressions in our history, took a far longer time in ending for the poor than for the upper middle class and the very rich. In 1909-1910 doing without became so prevalent that despair gripped the slums of Boston, as well as the slums of other metropolitan centers. And this despair wrought havoc with the convictions and philosophies and emotions of all the people concerned, particularly the new arrivals. These last came over so filled with dreams of this being a land of perpetual prosperity that they had great difficulty adjusting themselves to cold reality, and some of them, as they looked upon their wives and children suffering short rations and clad in threadbare clothing, became very bitter. In the end most of these bitter ones reverted to a saner outlook, but others didn't seem to be able to forgive the United States for not living up to their preconceived notions. The percentage of those who remained disillusioned, among the Jews, was very small, as it has always been small in this country. The Jews are a resilient people, and can bounce back probably more quickly than any other people.

The first one to mention the depression in a serious way was Mottel. The new arrivals had read about it in the *Jewish Daily Forward,* and Chashel and the others had got faint inklings of it at their various places of work—Chashel, for example, had been laid off a day or two every now and then—but somehow they didn't quite grasp the meaning of it all. Things in general were still so very much better, at least more pleasant, than they were in Russia.

One Friday evening, at Leah's house, Alte Bobbe suddenly asked,

"What is it with you, Mottel? All evening you were far away. Is something troubling you? The business, or what? You are among friends, your family, people who are beholden to you, and have only the best wishes for you, you know that, and you know it, too, Bassel," she said as she looked intently at both of them.

Mottel merely wiped his face with his handerchief, and it did not escape his mother's eye that his hand trembled a little. But he said nothing. Alte Bobbe looked again at Bassel.

"It's the business, Bobbe," said Bassel. "It could be better."

"A lot better," said Mottel slowly. "Very much better it could be."

"But nothing really terrible, I hope," said Alte Bobbe, with apprehension.

Mottel forced a smile on his face. "Nothing really terrible, nothing really. Only, like I said, it could be a whole lot better. The plain truth is that we have been having a *crizis* in this country. It hit the millionaires months ago. Now, it is hitting the poor people."

Mottel's placing himself in the class of poor people shocked all of them. They had thought he was a very rich man.

"I don't want to be misunderstood," continued Mottel. "Poor I am not yet, thank God, though a millionaire I have never been. Little by little people are being laid off, first for a day a week, then two days a week, and pretty soon for a week, a month, and then for good. And when the man of the family has little money, or God forbid, no money at all, he doesn't send his children to my store to get candy or ice cream or soda or things like that. After all, what I sell is *nasherei* (dried fruits, bonbons). The world can get along without it very well. So, people don't buy, and my expenses go on. You all know that big soda fountain I have? Well, it has to be my luck, that just before you came over to this country I bought it brand new, and it cost me $2,000, that is, with the marble top, and everything."

"Two thousand dollars!" exclaimed Benjamin, reflecting the astonishment of everybody else.

"Yes," sighed Mottel. "My Bassel, long life may she have, told me not to buy it. The old one was good enough, but I didn't listen."

"Nu, that is in the past," said Bassel, in an attempt to ease his feeling of guilt. "Bigger men than you have made bigger mistakes."

"So," continued Mottel, "to make a long story short, I still owe $1,000 on that fountain, and with interest it will come to even more."

"Aye, aye," sighed Alte Bobbe. "That is real trouble."

Mottel was touched by her concern. "Ah, don't worry, mother.

I'm sorry I even mentioned it. *Erev Shabbes,* too. We're not hungry, and, God willing, we won't be hungry. It's a passing thing."

"*Hallevai,*" said Alte Bobbe. "God will find a way out. Perhaps it won't last so long, and maybe it's over already."

"That cannot happen too soon," said Mottel, "but don't worry. I shouldn't have burdened any of you with my troubles."

After Mottel and Bassel left, the family stayed up to discuss his situation. No one could really contribute anything save sympathy, and that of the vaguest sort, for not one of them understood the financial ways of America, not one of them fully appreciated what was going on in the country, though they had read about it in the Jewish papers. They had been so busy getting accustomed to the new land and its people that their perceptions, for the while, were somewhat dulled. They had been living purely on the surface and were reacting almost wholly emotionally. Suddenly they were brought face to face with reality. And the day or two that almost everyone had been asked to take off the past few weeks took on grave meaning. The same thoughts ran through the minds of all—soon they might be laid off a whole week, then a month, then they might be told that they need not come back at all. But not one of them said anything openly, because they didn't want to alarm Leah or Alte Bobbe.

Alte Bobbe herself, however, was not at all unmindful of what her children and grandchildren were thinking. What she had just heard from her favorite son was bitter enough to her, but what she knew was going on in the minds and hearts of the others was also bitter to her. For the moment she was sure that her Mottel would somehow find a way out of his difficulties, and once again would enjoy the respect of the others. Ah, she would impress upon the others that her Mottel was still not just anybody . . . but a big man, the very important officer of a synagogue, wealthy, a full-fledged American, a big Jew in a big city—her Mottel.

"Nu," she said with a faint smile, as she looked at all about her. "The best news it isn't that we've heard. But my Mottel has managed to twist himself out of messes before, and I'm sure he will manage to do so now again. Besides, and Leah will bear me out on this, Mottel is a funny man. Even when he was but a boy he had a habit of exaggerating bad things and not saying a word about good things. That's how he was years and years ago and that's how he is now, is that not so, Leah?"

"It is so, mother," said Leah, who knew that it wasn't so.

"But you, my children," said Alte Bobbe, "are different. You mustn't worry. From worry come all sorts of *tsores*."

"So far, Bobbe, nothing terrible has befallen us, I mean us here," said Chashel. "We have been out a day or two, but that is all."

"*Hallevai*," said Leah softly, and giving the impression that she was more worried than she cared to express.

"With God everything is possible," said Alte Bobbe. "Everything that Mottel was talking about might just be an ill wind, here one minute and gone the next. After all, didn't Mottel say that this *crizis* has been here for a year, maybe more, so how much longer can it last?"

"That's so," said Moshe, who had been silent most of the evening. "No crisis can last forever."

Aryeh, who felt a little guilty for his lack of concern—he knew that no matter how bad times become, Jews will continue to send their children to Hebrew school—said, "That is so, as Moshe says. It could well be that the crisis is already on the way out."

And yet, deep down in the heart of almost everyone, all this talk of bad times seemed unreal and a little unimportant. In Russia there were bad times, too, but somehow everybody managed. Always there was the family cow to supply the necessary milk and cheese, always there were the chickens to supply eggs and meat, and of course almost everybody, however poor, had a bit of a garden that supplied most of the necessary vegetables. Besides, a neighbor in Russia was a real friend at all times. People were constantly bringing things to neighbors who were having hard luck.

Alte Bobbe herself couldn't quite believe that there was a depression on hand. She, too, remembered Russia, and she also imagined that here, too, people came around and helped. But she realized that they didn't really know anybody here outside of their immediate families; that those they knew were sort of friendly for the moment— they didn't come around to visit; and it occurred to her that the families on the floor above and the floor below were relative strangers to them. And a new fear about Mottel and the other children and grandchildren enveloped her.

She decided to go over to Mottel's house and try to get more information out of him about his plight. She wanted to go alone, because she felt she could learn more from Mottel if he had only her for an audience. She knew that if she told Leah she wanted to visit

Mottel alone, Leah would object and have one of the younger children accompany her, which is exactly what Alte Bobbe didn't want. So one afternoon Alte Bobbe said to Leah, "I think I'll walk down to the park to sit down and watch the water and the trees and the grass. After all, there are not too many trees near our house."

"What about the street cars?" asked Leah. "They run so fast."

"I won't try to hold them back," said Alte Bobbe. "They can run all they want. I'll be back soon."

She went in the direction of Mottel's house. She was a bit uncertain, at first, about the way, but much to her surprise she had no difficulty. Instead of going to the house she dropped off at the store. Only Mottel and Bassel were there; the helper was not there.

Both Mottel and Bassel were astonished to see her. "Mother, you came here, alone!" exclaimed Mottel.

"So I came alone," said Alte Bobbe. "Since when do I have to explain to one of my children where I go and how I get there?"

"Yes, but street cars and automobiles . . . ," said Mottel. "I'm surprised, really surprised that Leah let you."

"Who said she let me? I told her I was going to sit down in the park, and even for that she scolded me. So I'm here."

Mottel and Bassel looked at each other. "Nu, mother, come with me to the house. I was going up anyway for a rest, and now I will have something better than a rest, you," said Mottel.

"I'll go with you, Mottel, but first I thought I'll sit here a while," she said. "A fine, clean store you have here."

"It would be nicer if it weren't so clean but full of people and shouting children," said Bassel sadly. "A clean store is an empty store."

"Nu, nu, it's not so bad, really, mother. It's always a little slow this time of the day. After all, it can't be busy all the time, or we'd go crazy. Even a store-keeper needs a little rest," said Mottel, as he busied himself with tasks which obviously were needless. As he talked Alte Bobbe and Bassel were exchanging glances. "And another thing," continued Mottel, "with less business we don't have to stay open so late . . . ah, such hours we keep . . . like prisoners . . . fourteen, eighteen hours a day. Who ever heard of human beings working such hours? Even horses work only a few hours and then are given food and a chance to rest."

"Around this time of day Mottel takes a rest, so I thought . . .," said Bassel, as she looked at Alte Bobbe.

"Of course," said Alte Bobbe. "I might just as well rest in your home, as in the store. A great attraction for business I am not."

"Business, business," said Mottel. "Let's go upstairs, to our house, mother, and be like human beings. If you need me, Bassel, send up one of the children around here, and I'll run down."

"I will," said Bassel. "Have a good rest. You didn't sleep so well last night and the night before, and you are now eating like a little bird, even less. Pretty soon I won't even have to cook for you."

"Nu, nu," said Mottel. "My stomach wasn't so good. That happens to everybody once in a while."

When they got to the house, Mottel began to make a little tea for himself and his mother, but she stopped him. "I can still make tea for my son and myself. You sit down. Or still better, lie down on the couch or the bed, anywhere. I want to talk to you."

Mottel lay down on the couch and began to smile. "This reminds me of when I was a little boy and you used to say the same thing when I did something bad. Ah, those were happy days."

"Tell me, Mottel, did you let your man, your helper, go?"

"Yes."

There was a silence.

"And Bassel is now taking his place?" asked Alte Bobbe, as she handed him his tea.

He took a sip of his tea, wiped his mouth, cleared his throat, and answered slowly, "Bassel is taking his place."

"And who prepares your dinner, and the children's breakfast and lunch and their dinner and who takes care of the house in general?"

"Bassel."

"It's difficult for her."

"Easy it isn't, mother. Before you I don't have to put on any false pride."

"I don't want to live when that day comes," said Alte Bobbe. "Mottel, you once asked me if I wouldn't come to stay with you?"

"Of course. What do you mean?"

"I am coming to live with you."

Mottel sat up straight. "Mother, please don't make me say no to your staying with us. You know I don't want to. But this is different."

At once she realized that she had hurt him, that her staying with him now would reflect upon him in the eyes of the rest of the family, and she was ashamed of herself for not thinking of these things.

He interrupted her thoughts. "Another thing, mother, you and

Leah have been together so long, she depends upon you so much, especially after Shmooel's death, *olav hasholem*, you understand?"

She realized that there was sense in what he was saying, but she also realized that he was trying to save face, and that cut deep into her heart.

"I know, I know," she said. "Leah needs me. I should have thought of her. Don't sit up. Lie down." She pushed him gently and he reclined.

"Ah," he said "I can't get over you coming here all alone, with that traffic."

"Nothing at all," she said, as she began to take off his shoes.

He objected strenuously, but she snapped right back, "Lie still. I can take off your shoes now as easily as when you were a little boy."

Mottel was made happier by the recollection. "You always told me to take off my left shoe first, because it was luckier, and I insisted on taking my right shoe off first. I was so stubborn."

"And I wasn't so smart in insisting."

"I noticed you took off the left first now."

"Habit. After all I have been taking off my left one first for many, many years. Mottel, I'll come here every day, around noon, to help out, make dinner, clean up. It's the least I can do. I'll keep on staying at Leah's, but I'll do this, too."

"Mother, please, it's such a burden . . . at your age . . . please, mother . . ."

"Quiet. At my age it's easier. I have less things to worry about, less petty nonsense to eat at me. I'm strong, thank God. As it is, there are hours during the day when there is nothing to do at Leah's. The girls help out in the morning before they go to work, and they help out at night, when they come back."

"I don't have to tell you I want you here, mother, but coming here every day . . . who will take you over? . . . and so much trouble."

"So I won't come every day, maybe three, four times a week. Since when has it become a terrible thing for a mother to help out her son and his wife? A shame it isn't. I only thank God I can help. I only hope I will have no more trouble with Bassel than I've had with you. A woman is more offended when another woman enters her house, even if it's only a mother-in-law, or maybe I should say, especially then. And a woman should be offended. A woman's home is her home. It's her own. It's her kingdom, as is proper. But it's also proper for people to help one another. Bassel is a good woman, a diamond, as I said the first moment I saw her, so I think I'll be able to have her let me come over and help out a little bit."

She noticed that Mottel was stroking his forehead.

"Headache?" inquired his mother.

"A little one. Nothing serious."

"I'll fix that," said Alte Bobbe. "Just tell me where a small towel is, and where the vinegar is."

"It's nothing, mother. Besides, how should I know where a towel is and the vinegar. It'll go away soon. I know it will."

"Don't be stubborn," she said and went off into the kitchen. "Lie still and wait till I come back."

She returned shortly with a towel soaked in vinegar, which she tied around her son's forehead. "Now lie still, and don't talk. It's getting a little late. I'll go to the store and talk to Bassel. I'll tell her that I left you asleep and that you'll be down soon."

"What will you tell her?" asked Mottel.

"What will I tell her? I will tell her what I told you. That I want to help out." She noticed that he winced, so she said, "No. I will tell her that I think it's right for me to stay with you for a while . . . oh, for a few days or afternoons a week. That, after all, I hadn't seen you for so many years . . . that Leah has the girls to help her anyway . . . oh, how should I know what I'll tell her? Now, be still and close your eyes."

She bent down to kiss him, and he embraced her tightly. She felt he was beginning to cry . . . and soon she herself was crying. She gave him a quick kiss and walked swiftly out of the room.

In a moment he shouted after her, "How will you go home? Not alone?"

"I won't lose my way," she said and closed the door of the apartment behind her.

After she left Mottel cried profusely and was glad that Bassel was not there to see him . . . that no one was there to see him. He had not cried like this since he was a child. He felt as if a load were lifting from his chest and from his head. He had not been alone with his mother, even for this brief time, for years and years . . . and as he thought of the length and waste and suffering and disappointments and loneliness of those years, he cried more and felt both ashamed and happy. And he went off into a deep sleep, more peaceful than he had had for months and months.

Generally at supper time there was considerable talk by the grown-ups. This time not long after Alte Bobbe's visit with Mottel, there was a little less talk than usual. Alte Bobbe was disturbed. So was Leah. "Almost like in a Christian house we are here, so quiet. Is anything wrong?" she asked.

"Wrong?" asked Benjamin. "What's wrong? I don't see anything wrong."

The others mumbled in agreement and the subject was closed, but Leah still was puzzled. In a few moments she asked again. "Isn't the food good?"

They all mumbled that the food was perfectly good. She asked the young ones how they liked the food; they said it was fine.

"Then maybe I'm just imagining things," said Leah. "May I ask how things were at the shop?" she asked, looking at the older children, and especially at Chashel, for Leah had a fear about Chashel, that sooner or later, because of her interest in socialism, she would get into trouble.

No one answered Leah. Then Leah asked Chashel directly, "By you in the shop it is good, too, Chashel?"

Chashel didn't answer quickly. She made believe that she still had to swallow the food she had in her mouth. Then she evaded an answer. "Why should it be different in my shop than in any other shop? Or maybe I should say my shop and Moshe's shop and Yetta's shop . . ."

"Nothing wrong with Moshe?" asked Leah.

"No."

Leah got a little angry. "All I get is 'No' to everything I ask."

"Don't get yourself excited, Leah," said Alte Bobbe. "Maybe the children don't feel like behaving like Russian hooligans once in a while at the table."

When the dishes were washed and wiped, Chashel decided it was time she told them the bad news.

"Mother," she said, "I've been let go."

Leah looked at her. She knew what Chashel meant, but she wanted to make absolutely sure. "Let go?" she asked softly.

"Tonight I was given my pay and told not to come back. It's so slack that they've decided to lay off a large number. They began with those who came last and worked backward, but they have already reached some who've been here for a year and two years and more."

Leah and Alte Bobbe sat down to listen more closely to Chashel. The others did the same, drawn together by the misfortune unfolding in front of them, the full meaning of which cut slowly into their consciousness.

"That's how it is," said Zayde Tzalel. "I have heard in the synagogue that it's not good anywhere. They're letting people go in all shops, factories. I hear these things from the *zaydes* who come to pray. Children, grandchildren out of work . . . not knowing what to do. Like Mottel says, it's a *crizis*."

The younger school children felt that something important was being discussed and asked Leah what it was all about. Leah looked at them, and said, "It's about something important and please go off in the street to play a little while, but only a little while, and then come back to sleep."

"And Moshe?" asked Alte Bobbe, hardly raising her head.

"So far he still has his job. It seems they need pressers more than finishers. Thank God for that."

"Nu, that's something not to worry about . . . for a while at least," said Leah. Then she added, with a little trepidation, "And Yetta . . . ?"

Chashel began to laugh. "No, mother, I'm the only one honored so far."

Leah's face became stern. "Chashel, tell me, did you do anything or say anything, about socialism or this *meshugaas* about unions?"

"No, mother I didn't. I had planned to, though."

Leah snapped at her. "This is no time for *chochmes*."

"You asked me a question, and I answered you. Anyway, I'll look around and maybe I'll find something. Oh, they let my friend Rose Feinstein go, too. And she told me, coming back from the shop, that she thinks they were going to let her brother Ezra go, too. He works in a different shop, another kind of work."

"And you like her so much," said Leah aimlessly. "And her brother . . . I know now . . . you spoke of him once or twice. A terrible thing it will be for their parents."

"Nu, nu," said Alte Bobbe sorrowfully. "Jews can't be without troubles long."

Chashel somehow felt gay, so she said, "Christians also have troubles."

"Chashel," exclaimed her mother. "What foolishness has got into you? This is no time for laughter."

Chashel still felt devilish. "Crying won't do any good, either. Ezra says, laugh and the world laughs with you; cry and the world turns the other way."

"He must be crazy," said Leah. "Of all the times to make jokes!"

"Maybe he's not crazy," said Alte Bobbe, straightening herself up in her chair, as if she had made a great decision.

"A happy thought it is," said Zayde Tzalel. "A *guter Yid* once said that in Heaven the angels are always laughing, except when they are sad, and then they really don't look sad, but only refrain from laughing for a while."

"Ah," suddenly exclaimed Alte Bobbe. "It will all pass away. I told it to Mottel and now I tell it to you. The world is like a wheel, round and around and up and down and down and up. I haven't lived all these years for nothing. When it's really bad, one knows it's going to get better, and when it's good, real good, well, it means it will get worse soon, but not quite so bad as it was before it got good. God is good, and angry, really angry He never is. Sometimes, He whips us as a father whips a child, and no doubt we deserve a whipping. We did something, and don't always know what it is that we did."

The next few days Chashel spent looking for work. She used to get up early, take along a sandwich and an apple, and go from shop to shop. At noon she would go to the Boston Common, eat her lunch, and then go back to the Market—a neighborhood taking in sections of Washington Street, Hollis Street, and Harrison Avenue, where most of the dress manufacturing shops were located. Everywhere she was told the same story: no work, a great many had already been laid off, and still more would be in the near future. Her friend Rose Feinstein had the same experience. Pretty soon Yetta was also told that she need not come back. Benjamin was told to come in only half days. The family table began to feel the diminution in income. Leah had less money with which to buy food, and she would worry every day what to get to furnish her family decent meals.

She bought more and more cereals and dairy products. Above all, she bought more and more black bread and urged the grownups to dunk it in the thick vegetable soups that she made. This was filling food. After a while the family gave up eating chicken on Friday night and Saturday, pretty much of a ritual among Jews. Instead, Leah made dishes of "lights," and later she bought more and more fish. To the surprise and pleasure of the children, both young and old, the American fish turned out to be very tasty and very inexpensive. Street peddlers used to sell fresh mackerel for as little as ten cents a pound, and flounders for as little as eight cents a pound, and halibut and haddock and cod for five cents.

Even so, the money problem was serious, and when Benjamin was laid off completely at his place of work, Leah began to think of other ways of making ends meet. She gave the school children their usual ration of milk every morning, but for the oldsters she did a little "fixing." They all liked to drink cocoa in the morning, some of them drinking two and three cups of it. The cocoa originally was made entirely with milk. Now she decided to thin the milk with water. The grown-ups noticed it at once but said nothing. Then Leah decided to save a bit on the gas bill. Instead of boiling the children's eggs in a separate pot and on a separate fire, she boiled them in the same pot the cocoa was in. Of course, she first washed the eggs. At first she was ashamed to resort to such housekeeping, but after a while she got used to it.

She and Alte Bobbe also saved on gas by not making any more tea for themselves in the afternoon. They did it without discussing it.

One afternoon, at tea time, as Leah was about to put the kettle on the stove, Alte Bobbe said, "Daughter, somehow I don't feel so thirsty today. And it's pretty hot in the house anyway." Leah looked at her mother and said, "Now that you mention it, I don't think I'm so thirsty either." The next day Leah started to make tea again, and again Alte Bobbe said she wasn't so thirsty, and again Leah said she wasn't either. Thereafter the subject of afternoon tea wasn't mentioned again. Instead, each had a glass of water or nothing at all.

Soon Aryeh told the family at large that he hadn't been paid at his Hebrew school for three weeks now. The parents of most of the children were out of work, and many of them couldn't afford the average tuition of twenty-five cents a week. Leah asked him and Chaneh to eat at their home, at least the main evening meal, and after a little coaxing they agreed, only on the condition that they contribute something.

Leah never did tell Aryeh how much his share was, but the next time he got a check from his Hebrew School, he had Chaneh bring over to Leah's house a huge chicken and a dozen eggs. Occasionally, she also brought over a bagful of vegetables or a big black bread. She noticed that Leah was not buying any more rolls, even for the children, so she sometimes brought over a dozen baigels, saying, "I shouldn't do this, but Aryeh simply loves baigels," and left the bai-

gels at Leah's house. Aryeh would have been surprised had he heard
that he loved baigels. Leah understood, Alte Bobbe understood,
Chashel understood, everybody understood, but no one said anything.

Then Zayde Tzalel announced one evening that not only was he
not paid for the preceding week, but that the president of his synagogue told him that his salary would be cut, from $8 a week to $5,
because of the depression. This was a serious blow to the family ex-
chequer. The family had been relying pretty heavily of late on
Zayde's income. No matter how closely they figured, Leah and Alte
Bobbe just didn't see how they could manage. Cutting down further
on the food was out of the question. Certainly not for the school
children. And not for the older ones, either, for they still went out
every morning in search of work, and walking from one shop to another was labor, and the discouragement on top of that was more
exhausting than the walking.

Zayde Tzalel had an idea. "Some of the people in the synagogue
have been talking about it. The bakeries are now selling old bread.
For much less than fresh bread, and also old rolls. I mean two or
three days old. The men take them, or the women do so, and freshen
them up in the stove, and it's very good. Doesn't hurt the bread at all."

Leah and Alte Bobbe looked at each other, and a light came to
their eyes. "Strange we haven't thought of it before ourselves," said
Alte Bobbe. "A cat's head I have. Bread two, three days old is sometimes even better than fresh bread. After all, everybody knows that
fresh bread is bad for the digestion."

"But for the younger children," said Leah, "I think I'll still get
fresh bread, I mean, in the store, like always. For the rest I don't
mind old bread."

"Ah," said Alte Bobbe, "if only the oven here were bigger, like a
real oven should be, we could bake our own bread. But with such a
little oven, it would cost us a fortune in coal and wood to bake just
a few loaves of bread. I see how long it takes to make just a little
cake."

But the saving made by buying old bread for the grown-ups could
not solve the financial problem completely. In a few days the rent
would be due, and Leah and Alte Bobbe, who bore the burden of
running the house, began to get a little panicky. As usual, Alte Bobbe
was the less distressed. "When the time comes for the rent, something will happen."

"What will happen?" asked Leah.

"Don't ask me any foolish questions. Something will happen. Meanwhile, not a word of any of this to any of the children. They have enough troubles of their own."

Alte Bobbe didn't tell Leah, but for the past few weeks she had been contributing money of her own to the running of the house—money that she had been saving up from the allowances that Mottel had been giving her, and that he insisted on giving her even now. As a matter of fact, she had a *knippel* (a small money bag) of her own. Over the years she would put aside a penny now and then toward a rainy day, and use it at her own discretion, generally to help out a member of the family, to buy gifts at Rosh Hoshonoh and Chanukkah, to buy herself a new shawl, and so on. It used to make her giggle like a girl, inside, when the children wanted to know what she used for money to get this or that. Generally she said, "A little bird brings me money every Thursday, in time to do the shopping for *Shabbes*."

A day before rent day Alte Bobbe went herself to the landlord. He greeted her very politely. "Ah, whenever I see you I think of my own mother, who is still in Russia. In her last picture, she really looks just like you. You could be sisters."

"We could be," said Alte Bobbe. "Mr. Blatt, perhaps you know why I'm here."

"I can't say I do. I hope it's not something bad."

"It's not something good, Mr. Blatt. These are bad times. You know that."

"Do I know it? I know it very well. I wish I didn't know it so well. Half my tenants can pay me only a half or a little more of their rent."

"Nu, Mr. Blatt, it's now going to be more than half. We are decent folk. We always pay our bills when we can, and sometimes even when we can't. We have scrimped and scrimped. I can't tell you how much. The children are not working."

"Yes. Some of them I have seen during the day, and I have wondered."

"For a while at least, Mr. Blatt, I hope you will let us pay, not a half, but two-thirds of the rent. God forbid, we may be able to pay only a half in a month or two or three. But now we want to pay more. We will pay it all back as soon as we can. We are good Jewish people, not hooligans."

"I know that," said Mr. Blatt. "Of course. Pay what you can. A drunken Russian policeman I am not. I have feelings, too. In times like these . . . I know."

Very proudly Alte Bobbe got up, smiled, and shook his hand. "Mr. Blatt, you will not regret your kindness. A very good year to you and your family and may you and your wife live to dance at the wedding of every one of your children and their children, too."

"*Hallevai*," said Mr. Blatt. "Everything we do is for the children. Otherwise who would slave and scrimp?"

Soon Zayde Tzalel wasn't paid every third, then, every second week, though his synagogue promised to pay him, eventually, everything owed him. Leah and Alte Bobbe were now harder put than ever before to meet expenses. For long they held out on charging things at the grocer's. They had done so in Russia, but the grocer there was almost like one of the family. Here, the grocer seemed like a stranger, though he was polite and considerate enough. Charging things with him appeared to them almost like borrowing money from someone they had just met. But a day came when they needed milk and bread and they didn't have the money to pay for them. Leah didn't know what to do. Again Alte Bobbe handled the situation. She had noticed many times before, when she had been at the grocer's, that some women would nonchalantly say, "Put it on the books, please," and the grocer didn't say a word. She decided to do the same. She ordered bread and milk, and, looking straight at him, said, "I wonder whether you wouldn't charge it. I haven't the money at the moment."

The grocer said, "Of course. You haven't an account here?"

"No. We have always paid in the past."

"I know. I know," said the grocer pleasantly enough, as he started a new page for the account of Alte Bobbe and Leah.

"You can trust us," said Alte Bobbe.

"Trust you! Hah ha! I wish I were so sure the dirty, putrid Czar of Russia would drop dead," said the grocer. "And the sooner he does that little favor for me the happier I will feel and the happier will all of us Jews feel."

The experiences with the landlord and the grocer were humiliating, even to Alte Bobbe, but they were also exhilarating. They made them and the rest of the family—who found out about them soon enough—feel more at home in America. "A land full of wild animals America is not," said Leah.

"Jews are Jews, after all," said Alte Bobbe. "A Jewish heart has mercy. And the hearts of poor Jews have the greatest amount of mercy. After all, how much richer than us is the grocer . . . and even the landlord?"

"We should have their money," said Benjamin.

"Who knows, who knows," said Alte Bobbe. "Who knows what troubles they have. One must always be satisfied with one's lot. God knows best."

Economic difficulties brought the whole community together more closely. The women began to talk to one another more intimately in the stores, and lent one another eggs, cups of milk, pepper, pieces of cheese, rolls, candles for the Sabbath, and they exchanged recipes that called for inexpensive ingredients. "Ah, last night I made a stew, so thick with vegetables and pieces of bread that my man, God bless him, thought it was made with meat . . . he felt so full . . . and *kreplach* made with cheese is just as good and nourishing as *kreplach* made with liver . . . And a good, thick *tsimes* with pieces of fat is good, too. . . . Once, I put in some mackerel in *kreplach*, and my husband the smart one thought it was chicken. . . The American beans, baked beans they call them, are good and rich, too. A plate of those is a nice meal, with a little tea and lemon, of course. After a fat dish, tea with lemon is refreshing. It slides right down the throat."

People who lived in the same house, who had hardly exchanged sentences before, now got to know each other. The wives saw one another's husbands around during the day, and all knew the reason. The husbands began to visit one another, the wives followed suit, and soon lending and barter went on from floor to floor, and from apartment to apartment. It was in this way, indeed, that Leah learned that it was possible to buy second-hand shoes at almost any shoemaker's, at a price far below that for new shoes. And she also learned that second-hand clothes for both men and women could be bought at the Salvation Army stores for but a few cents—in fact, she learned that she could buy a perfectly nice dress for herself for a dollar.

The new spirit of camaraderie among the slum Jews brought together many *landsleit*. And soon whole groups joined in going to the park and having picnics on the grass . . . and just passing the time of day or night. "From troubles," said Alte Bobbe, "we have become more *menschlich*. And America has become more *haimish*."

And the younger folk got to know each other better. They made the same daily treks in search of work, they ate their lunches about the same time in the Boston Common or the Esplanade, and in the evening they walked home pretty much the same way across the Common and down Beacon Hill into the slums on both sides of Cambridge Street. Thus many romances started which later ended in marriages—or in heartaches.

The older men did not go every day in search of work. They went three or four times a week, and trusted in friends to tell them how the "market" was. Thus the streets of the slums were generally filled with older men walking around, with and without their children. They discussed life in general and exchanged rabbinical stories, but their plight was not wholly absent from their faces or their manner; they sighed frequently, even as they told tales, and they mopped their brows when there was obviously no need for doing so, and they snapped at their children every now and then for no good reasons and to their own regret and the mystification of their children. They also congregated near the synagogues, and they attended services three times a day a good deal of the week. The rabbis were pleased, but their pleasure was mixed with sorrow for the plight of their flocks. They encouraged them spiritually and often told a father where he could possibly get a day's work—as a janitor, as a helper on a beer wagon, as a window washer, and so on. As always in Jewish history, misery brought the Jews together more closely and helped them to bear their troubles more easily. Some complained, but most of them took their situation philosophically.

"A *klog zu Colombus*" one would say. "So this is the *goldene medine!* Pooh!"

But another would say, "Nu, the human race still has a lot of distance to go to solve its economic problems. Ah, so rich and so big and so what-shall-I-say country shouldn't have unemployment problems. Anyway, they don't kill Jews here, and we can say anything we want about the country or the President without having to look around to make sure a Russian policeman or secret service man is not listening in. After all, even in Palestine, when the land was ours and we had our own government and Kings and courts and everything, even there there were troubles."

And a third would say, "Nu, it says in the Bible, on account of what Eve did, not only all women have to suffer but all people, men and women alike. Men sin, and God has to punish them."

Generally the rabbi of the synagogue would give his interpretation. "Worldly things I do not know, but the great rabbis of the Talmud knew more worldly things than any of the so-called experts do now-adays. The rabbis said that basically it is greed that is behind eco-nomic crises. It's the search for economic security that is the cause of so much trouble. I should say the search for more than economic security. The search for economic security for oneself and one's fam-ily is a fine and noble thing. No. The trouble is that men search for more than security, for two homes instead of one, twelve pairs of shoes instead of two good pairs, a dozen big diamonds for their wives and daughters instead of one or two pretty ones, five chickens for Saturday instead of one or two which would be plenty for any or-dinary family. And when one looks and strives for more than se-curity, for all these additional things I have mentioned, one has to deprive others of their just shares. For, as the rabbis have also said, the good Lord provided enough and a little more than enough for everybody in this world, yes, enough for everybody to live in peace and plenty, without having to live a life of slavery. There is enough for the birds and the rabbits and the cows and the fish and all the animals. They are not greedy. Not even a lion will kill a cow, if he has just eaten. He lets the cow alone. But man is different. He hasn't enough. He must take away from his neighbor, from his friend, from his very brother. Human beings are not beasts! If they would only be like beasts in some respects, they would be more civilized. Men are worse than beasts. They are devils. So it's greed, I tell you, that is behind all these economic troubles. Man is his own worst enemy."

Moshe had lately been among those who had been spending con-siderable time at the synagogue in his neighborhood. He had things on his mind. He still had a job at the shop where Chashel and Yetta and Rose and the others had worked. But already he had been put on a three-day week and only last Friday he had been told that be-ginning with the following week he would be put on a two-day week. He knew what that meant. It meant that soon he would be wholly without a job.

He knew something else. He would have to decide once and for all whether he would stick by his resolve not to work on the Sab-bath. Some of those who had been working with him and who had previously kept the Sabbath, had been forced to desecrate the Sab-bath for purely economic reasons.

Since Moshe still had a job, the problem had not yet confronted him, and his colleagues who had given in envied him. In fact, they were so ashamed of what they had done that for several days after they had become, in their own words, worse than *goyim*, they evaded him and when they passed him they turned their faces away. Moshe didn't know what to do—to run after them and comfort them, or to argue with them, or what. To comfort them meant that he somehow forgave them, and this, in turn, meant that he had the power to forgive, which was clearly not true. Arguing with them meant that he was better than they. Who was he to judge others?

Moshe's own problem was complicated by the fact that Nechame was with child again. If he decided to work on *Shabbes*, how could he face his Nechame? How could he face Alte Bobbe and Leah and the others? How could he face his memories—the memories of his upbringing, of his mother and father and boyhood Hebrew school teacher, of the rabbi who married him and Nechame, of his neighbors in his little village? How could he face his children? How could he go into his synagogue now—even now, as these thoughts passed through his mind?

In Russia a Jew who worked on the Sabbath, for no matter what reason, was looked upon as a person unworthy of human society. Even socialists, who were not overly religious, subscribed to this attitude. Moshe did not recall a single Jew in his little village who desecrated the Sabbath, though he knew two or three who personally would not have hesitated to do so, if public opinion was not so strongly against it. Moshe had heard of Jews in outlying villages and, of course, in big cities, who did work on the Sabbath, but nearly all of them were doctors, who had special dispensation from the rabbis. But even doctors were ill at ease when going about their business on the Sabbath.

Moshe had been sure that he himself would never be tempted to break the Sabbath. As a matter of fact, he had told Nechame once, he would no more think of desecrating the Sabbath than he would of shaving his beard. He was a good Jew, and he intended to remain one.

Now he wasn't so sure. And in a few weeks he was not sure at all. He had been laid off completely at his shop. He had saved a little money since his family came here, but it amounted to less than $25, and he knew that frugal as his Nechame was she could not stretch that very far. The first thing he did was go back to his bottle-washing place, where he had his first job. They had been very good to him and he wondered whether they wouldn't take him back, if only for two or three days a week. But he was told that it was bad with them, too, and besides, they already had several men working part time, and they simply didn't have any more work for anybody, but they told him to drop in once in a while on the chance that there might be something.

Since Moshe knew a great deal about horses—he made his living by trading in them on a small scale in Russia—he inquired in various stables whether they needed help of any kind. They didn't. For a while he played with the idea of asking Mottel whether he could use him in any capacity in the store—if only for a couple of days a week. But he decided not to do that. The rumor was that Mottel's business was getting worse by the day, and Moshe was sure that despite his difficulties Mottel would probably hire him for a while, and Moshe didn't want that. He was so determined about this that he told Alte Bobbe not even to mention it to Mottel. Alte Bobbe had been coming rather frequently of late to Moshe's—to help out in the house during Nechame's pregnancy, and to offer such sympathy as she could while Moshe was unemployed. Alte Bobbe promised him that she wouldn't tell.

Moshe then inquired at several synagogues whether they needed *shamosim*, even if only for Saturday. They didn't. He also made an effort to get pupils to teach them Hebrew and to say the proper prayers at *bar mitzvah*, but after a few inquiries he gave up. Finally, he even went to several saloons in the neighborhood, in the hope that they might need a cleaning man, but the saloon-keepers saw that Moshe was not created for saloon work. Moshe then began to think seriously of becoming a customer peddler, about which he had been hearing a great deal.

A large number of immigrant Jews, who had no trade and who refused to work in shops, traveled in the outlying districts of Boston and sold such things as watches, clocks, baby carriages, stockings, underwear, irons, and even sewing machines. The light objects they carried with them. As for the heavier objects, they carried several pictures of them, and they relied mostly on the names of the manufacturers. Most immigrant families, for example, had heard of Singer sewing machines, and all a customer peddler had to do was to say that he handled Singer machines, and generally that was all the prospective customer wanted to hear. Few of the customers had enough money to pay cash, so the peddler carried their accounts on his books and came around at regular intervals to collect.

Moshe pondered the idea of becoming a customer peddler for several days and then gave it up. To be a peddler he had to make an initial investment of a considerable amount of money, which he didn't have. The various stores would not give credit to beginners. Besides, he suspected that he was not a salesman and certainly he was not a traveler. The only advantage he could think of was that he would probably be his own employer and would not have to work on Saturday.

Nechame knew what was going through her Moshe's mind, and many times she wanted to discuss it with him, but the subject was a serious one and she herself was not feeling so well these days, so she let it slide. Moshe also wanted to talk it over with his wife, but he didn't want to trouble her in her condition. Besides, her condition also was worrying him. With none of her previous pregnancies did she have any difficulty whatever, but with this one she seemed to be out of sorts pretty constantly. A doctor at the Lying-In-Hospital had examined her and said there was nothing wrong, but obviously something was wrong.

Moshe wanted to talk over the matter of working on *Shabbes* with Alte Bobbe, but he was ashamed. Asking her whether he should work on the Sabbath, he felt, was like asking her whether he should become a Christian. But Alte Bobbe sensed that Moshe was troubled deeply by something and she determined to find out what it was. One day when she was visiting at Moshe's house, she asked him point blank, "Moshe, what is eating you?"

"What's eating me? Who said something is eating me?"

"Tell me, Moshe. It's better to talk things out. Your hiding things is not good, and it's not good, too, for Nechame. Isn't that so, daughter?"

Nechame hesitated. "Nu, of course, when Moshe worries I worry. I am only sorry that with this pregnancy I am an additional worry to him. I don't know what it is that is wrong. I used to boast that having a child is so easy for me. I shouldn't have boasted, perhaps."

"You shouldn't feel that way, Nechame. These things happen to all women. Sometimes a pregnancy is easy, sometimes it isn't. It happens the way it happens. Moshe, what is it?"

"To tell you the truth, Bobbe and Nechame, terrible thoughts are running through my mind. Thoughts that shouldn't run through the mind of any Jew. Shameful, horrible thoughts." He turned his face to hide the tears that were collecting in his eyes. "Ah, that I should come to this! Even to think of it!"

"To think of what?" asked Nechame.

"What, Moshe?" asked Alte Bobbe.

He kept his face turned away and did not answer.

"Tell us, Moshe," pleaded Nechame.

"Nu," said Moshe, as he turned to face the two women and revealed much agony in his face, "I will soon have to make a very important decision. About *Shabbes.*"

"Oh," said both women who understood what he was referring to.

Then he told them the situation at the shop, that very likely he would be offered an occasional day's work, and that sometimes that day might be Saturday. "And many days' work there are not these days, at the shop or anywhere else."

"Yes, yes," mumbled Alte Bobbe.

"So that's what's been worrying me," said Moshe quietly.

"Moshe," said Alte Bobbe, "nobody doubts that you are a good Jew. The angels know it."

"They do," agreed Nechame. "They do."

"Only a good Jew would worry the way you do now," said Alte Bobbe. "If there is any comfort for you in what I am going to say, I hope you get comfort from it. Other good Jews have been faced with your problem." She hesitated a moment. "And I know that some people very close to me have not observed *Shabbes* for a while, anyway."

Nechame looked at Alte Bobbe, surprised that she knew about Mottel. Then Moshe looked at her, too, wondering how she found out. As far as he knew, he, Moshe, was the only one among the new arrivals, except Nechame, who knew.

Alte Bobbe sensed their surprise. She did not look at them, for what all three in the room knew was not a pretty thing, and for a mother to acknowledge knowing it about her own son was a cruel confession.

Nechame felt she had to say something to comfort Alte Bobbe, but she didn't know what to say. So she merely mumbled, "Ah, America, America!"

"We mustn't talk against America," said Alte Bobbe. "In Russia there was no such problem, of *Shabbes*, but who can say that Russia is a better country? For Jews it's not perfect anywhere. We are the

hunted and the persecuted. Angels not one of us can be, but everything depends upon the attitude with which an un-Jewish act is done,
even one so horrible as desecrating the Sabbath. I know that many,
I should say, nearly all Jews who are forced to desecrate the Sabbath
have stabs in the heart when they work on *Shabbes*. What can be a
greater shame for a Jew? For *Shabbes* is the Jews' most beautiful holiday. On that day God Himself rested. The great rabbis say that even
Yom Kippur is not a greater holiday than *Shabbes*. So, as I say, I cannot believe that any Jew is proud of working on Shabbes, God forbid.
And that shame will be considered on the Day of Reckoning."

"I know, I know," said Moshe helplessly. "But the mere thought
of so monstrous a thing. Believe me, Bobbe, nights I haven't slept,
and days I have gone around like a dazed man."

"Of course," said Alte Bobbe.

"Ah," said Nechame as she looked sadly at her husband.

"I wish I knew what to say, Moshe," said Alte Bobbe. "To tell you
to work on Shabbes I cannot."

"If I don't take a day's work, if it should fall on a Saturday, how
will I pay for food?" asked Moshe. "And other expenses? A man
must think of his family. On the other hand, if I do work, then I'm
a *goy*, and coming home to the family becomes a strange thing."

"Ah, ah," moaned Nechame.

"Of course," said Alte Bobbe.

"What would my father, *olav hasholem*, think if he knew I was
even considering working on the holy Sabbath? And my mother?
And . . . everybody?"

Alte Bobbe looked at Moshe and at Nechame, pity mounting in
her soul for these two people. Tears began to come to her eyes and
she struggled to hold them back. She wondered what she could say to
help Moshe and to calm Nechame. She whispered to herself, "Help
me, God, help Moshe and Nechame. Help us." And she prayed
silently and repeated the greatest prayer of the Jews, "*Shma Yisroel,
Adonai Elohaynoo, Adonai Echod* (Hear, O Israel, the Lord Our
God, the Lord is One)." Then a thought came to her to relieve her
burden, and she fondled the thought and caressed it and smiled at
it and her whole being became warm and the warmth became light
and the light and the warmth made her feel good all over. And then
she did not feel so good, for the intent of the thought was clear to
her, as it no doubt was clear to God. Now she was warm and light-
hearted, now she was cold and heavy-hearted. Then she said to her-

self, as tears seemed to fill her very heart, "Forgive me, God. You understand. Forgive me, God, O my dear God."

Then she turned to Moshe and Nechame and now she felt better. She was sure God would forgive her for what she was about to say to these two good people, who were in such agony of soul. "Moshe, I was thinking. A great rabbi I am not, or even a little rabbi, or even a little rabbi's wife, or even a little rabbi's niece or grand-daughter. No person can do more than try to be a good Jew. If you don't work for any reason, you will have no money to give to Nechame to buy the necessary groceries."

"That is true," said Moshe.

"In that case it is possible, God forbid, that somebody in the family might get sick. After all, we are all human beings. We must eat, even a little, to keep well. That is especially true of children and pregnant women. And if someone is ill, you have to call a doctor, and a doctor may have to come on Shabbes. So the rabbis have held. God forgives a doctor. Nu, suppose you are the doctor, Moshe, would you light a light on Shabbes, and tear things on Shabbes, and ride on a street car on Shabbes to help your ill children, God forbid, and to get them medicines?"

Moshe and Nechame were startled by the thought and by the clear implication of it.

"If I were a doctor," said Moshe slowly, "I would, of course, do anything for my children. On Shabbes, too, for the rabbis permit it."

"Of course, you would," said Alte Bobbe, "because you are a good Jew. Nu, did it ever occur to you that food is a medicine, too?"

"That is so," said Moshe, wondering, for a moment, where she was leading him.

"And he who gives medicine is, in a sense, a doctor," continued Alte Bobbe.

"Yes," said Moshe. "A real doctor."

"I meant a real doctor. And if food is a medicine, then he who gives or provides food also provides medicine, so he is a sort of doctor. Isn't that so, Moshe?"

Moshe looked at Nechame, wondering if she realized what Alte Bobbe was doing. On her part, Nechame was wondering whether Moshe realized what Alte Bobbe was doing.

"I suppose it is so," said Moshe slowly.

Alte Bobbe wiped her face. There was a moment of silence. She looked at the clock and said. "Nu, I must be going to help Leah."

After she left, Nechame and Moshe did not discuss what Alte Bobbe had said. Nechame merely said, "Aye, Moshe, too much worrying is not good for anybody. God will help you in some way. He always helps, Moshe. I wish there were something I could do."

"Of course, God will help," said Moshe.

He looked at the clock and said, "Nu, I think I better go to the synagogue for *minchah*. The other unemployed Jews are expecting me. It could also be that today I will lead the prayer. I will be back soon."

"All right, Moshe," said Nechame sadly. When he closed the door, she put her head in her hands and wept much.

At the synagogue Moshe found the rabbi and a handful of men. They were discussing the depression and wondering how long it would last. One said that his son had told him that the English paper said that there was already a bit of an upswing in various sections of the country, "and President Taft himself is very optimistic." Another said that he had read or heard somewhere that this was really not much of a depression, and that on the whole the Taft administration had brought prosperity to the United States, and what was happening now was very mild, indeed. To this a third man said, "Him, President Taft, it doesn't seem to hurt much. He could go hungry for quite a while, and he would still be a hundred or more pounds overweight. No wonder, he is always smiling." Here Moshe entered the discussion, "He seems to be a kindly man, much more so than Nikolai of Russia, short may his years be."

Still another, who had been quiet, said slowly, "There is a proverb I heard a long, long time ago. It says that God loves the poor, but He helps the rich. Of course, that is an atheistical thing to say, but, God forgive me, there sometimes seems to be some truth in it." All the others smiled at the proverb, but were afraid to say whether it was true or not. After all, they were in a synagogue, and there was no point in looking for trouble.

In the corner of the basement chapel, where all the weekday prayers were held, and where the men were now congregated, sat the rabbi, reading a holy book. The men kept at a respectful distance. Soon he called over the *shames* and asked whether there was already a *minyan*. The *shames* counted everybody, including the rabbi and himself, and said, "No, rabbi, only nine. Pretty soon I'm sure there will be another."

The rabbi smiled and pondered for a moment. Then he said, "Nine rabbis don't make a *minyan*, but ten shoemakers do."

The men heard the rabbi's remark, which pleased them all.

"A very wise man he is," said one of the men. "Really, the Jewish religion shows no *yichoos* (regard for social station). All are equal before God, the rabbi is no better than the shoemaker or the butcher."

"And why shouldn't that be?" asked another man. "After all, it says in the first chapter of Genesis that we are all made in the image of God, we are all God's children, the rich, the poor, the learned, the stupid. There may be, and there is, a difference about the minds of people and their place in society, but there is no difference in souls."

A third man said, "Of course. Ah, that was a very fine proverb the rabbi said. *Geshmak*. Recently a man asked the rabbi about shaving. May a good Jew in America shave his beard for any reason, for business reasons, or for just social reasons, because so many Jews do it? Is shaving, in short, a great sin? he asked the rabbi. The rabbi smiled and said, 'There are sins and sins. Coming a minute late to the synagogue on Shabbes or Yom Kippur even, is different from eating pork. That is clear. And even the eating of pork is not a simple sin. If one eats pork *lehachis* (maliciously), he is clearly committing a greater sin than he who eats pork with a Russian soldier's bayonet behind his back and the threat that if he doesn't eat it, he will kill him and his whole family. And so I could go on. Our God is at least as just as the courts of the *goyim*. He is a merciful God, and takes everything into consideration. Now about shaving, the same principle applies there as in the examples I hav given you. In a foreign country—and all countries, except Palestine, are foreign to us Jews—in a foreign country, a Jew is sometimes forced to do things against his beliefs, and he must do them for his economic welfare, for the sake of his wife and children, and for a thousand other reasons. Shaving may well belong in this category. Remember I don't say it does belong. I say only that it may belong. Now, to answer your question, *Reb Yid*, I can best do that by repeating what my own great teacher, the great Rabbi Yechonon of Pinsk, once said, namely, 'Better a Jew without a beard than a beard without a Jew.' "

All the men agreed that this last proverb was truly profound and well spoken. But to Moshe it had a special significance. It seemed to offer some light out of his dilemma. It made it easier for him to consider working on the Sabbath for his family's sake, for after all, better a Jew without a beard than a beard without a Jew, better half a Jew than no Jew at all, better a Jew who obeys most of the precepts of Judaism than no Jew at all, better a Jew, who despite his own lacks in orthodoxy, yet sees to it that his family, especially his sons, obey the Jewish laws and regulations.

Soon three more men came in, there was now more than a *minyan*, and Moshe volunteered to lead the group in prayer. He was particularly eager to do so now, for he had a great deal on his mind, now happy, now sad, and he wanted to appeal to God somewhat more directly than could a mere member of the congregation. He knew that strictly this made no sense. All Jews praying are equal before God, even the rabbi himself. Still, he felt, as did, indeed, all orthodox Jews, that he who leads in prayer somehow has God's ear more readily. So Moshe fervently led the congregation, and on two or three occasions he even attempted a bit of singing, though little more than recitation was required during *minchah*. After the prayer he felt uplifted, and when others complimented him on his leadership, he was very happy. "You *daavened* with real *geshmak*. You will be a *chazen* yet some day," said several of them.

Moshe instantly thought what a wonderful way this would be out of all his troubles. As a *chazen* he would always be occupied with synagogue work, he would never be troubled with whether or not he should work on the Sabbath, and in general he would be well off. So unblushingly—and rather strangely for so modest a man—he said, "*Foon aiyer moil in Gott's ever* (From your mouth in God's ear)." Then he caught himself and smiled. "Ah! What am I talking about? I'm not a *chazen*. I can pray, thank God, as every good Jew can, but I am no singer."

Moshe kept on making calls in his old shop—and at other shops. Then, one Friday, the foreman at his old shop said to him, "I have a little work for you, but it's for tomorrow, Saturday. As I see it now, it's at least a full day's work, and it may run over into Monday and maybe Tuesday, too. A quick and very important pressing job. Nu, do you want it?"

Moshe blushed and sighed. "Aye, what can I say?" he pleaded.

The foreman said to Moshe, "I can't tell you what to say. You have to tell me."

"Maybe I'll come," said Moshe softly.

The foreman snapped, "No maybe. You must tell me now, yes or no."

"Yes," said Moshe slowly and walked away.

The foreman looked at him as he departed, then wiped his forehead.

The next day, Saturday, Moshe arose very early and prayed at home. Nechame understood what his praying at home meant. So did David. So did the younger children. But no one said anything. While Moshe prayed Nechame prepared his breakfast and also his lunch (a fish sandwich, a cold baked potato, a piece of cake, and an apple). Moshe tried not to look at his wife while he ate his breakfast, and Nechame kept her eyes off him as much as she could. She noticed that it was rather early for work, but she said nothing about it. There was no reason for Moshe getting up so early. He simply could not sleep any longer, and he was eager to pray and to prolong his prayer as much as he could. Some parts of the Saturday morning prayer, indeed, he said twice in the hope that somehow God would listen to him more closely and understand his plight. And as Moshe prayed he made up his mind that some things he would not do, ever: he would not light the stove in the house on Saturday, he would not tear paper out of the shop, he would not allow anybody in the house to desecrate the Sabbath. In short, he would remain as he always had been outside the shop, and only in the shop would he desecrate the Sabbath.

When he left the house he took a new direction to get to his shop. He was ashamed to meet anybody going to the synagogue. And he walked fast, very fast, till he got lost in the activity of Washington Street where everybody was working and no one could point the finger of shame at anybody.

IMPROVING business conditions brought a change in the mode of living of Leah and her family and of Moshe and his family. The first group moved to a five and a half room apartment on Anderson Street, a slightly better street than West Cedar Street, and Moshe and his wife and children moved to a four-room back apartment on Phillips Street, which was also a bit better than Grove Street. Moshe's apartment looked out upon a smallish yard that appealed very much to Nechame, for she could put her younger children out there and keep an eye on them.

Every Sunday one of Leah's boys would bring some ice cream from a neighborhood candy store, and the whole family would have a party—all except Leah, Alte Bobbe, and Zayde Tzalel, who suspected there was some pork product in the ice cream. In Russia they would have forbidden the children to eat any suspect food, but here they didn't have the heart. As Alte Bobbe said, "Too fanatic we cannot be, especially since we are not sure. And the children shouldn't feel as if they are not like other children. All the Jewish children seem to be eating ice cream. Nu, if it is a sin, then we are all sinning. It's a new world we're living in, my daughter, and the new world has new ways."

In Moshe's house they "discovered" soda water. Every Sunday, while the "boom" lasted, that is, Moshe would give David three cents and a big pitcher. David would rush the pitcher to the candy store at the corner of Phillips Street and West Cedar Street, and shout at the man at the counter, "Three cents strawberry soda" or "Three cents chocolate soda." Then he'd rush back home, making sure he didn't spill any of the precious liquid, and the whole family would drink it slowly, savoring its full flavor. The gas would bring tears to Nechame's eyes, so she would generally have only a little, but Moshe and David loved it, gas and all. Moshe and David, indeed, loved it so much that sometimes, as their soda was going down in the glass, they would add a bit of ordinary water, hoping that the water would somehow soak up a few of the remaining gas bubbles.

David heard a great deal from his school friends about the movies, and now that he felt his father could afford it, he asked him to take him to the Olympic, a motion-picture theatre at the foot of Cambridge Street, not far away, where a double feature played from noon till midnight every day, and where the admission fee was five cents for children under twelve and ten cents for adults. Moshe balked for a while, because he didn't see any sense in this motion picture business, and he was ashamed of going to it. But Nechame pleaded with him, and finally the three of them went on a Sunday afternoon— while Alte Bobbe watched the younger children.

The main picture was "Orphans of the Storm," with the Gish sisters starring. The music, of course, was supplied by a piano in the pit. David was in ecstasy. Here was a magnificence the like of which he had never dreamt of. Moving pictures! People running around there on the screen, snow falling, ice moving, everything, just everything. And he took pleasure in the fact that he could make out the meaning of most of the titles, and he was proud that his parents asked him to tell them what the titles said. Nechame also enjoyed the picture and the general excitement of the place. Moshe was embarrassed. It all looked so silly to him, almost atheistic. When they were outside, he raised his voice, which was unusual for him, "Never again," he said. "If other people are crazy, it doesn't mean we should be crazy. And I don't see what good it does for a little boy to see those girls running around that way, with men not far away. Plain *meshuge*, and not very nice. That's what I say."

Nechame tried to pacify him. "It's not so terrible, Moshe. There were other children there, and the whole country can't be crazy. I don't say we should go there all the time. But some time, for David's sake..."

Moshe didn't answer. He was too flabbergasted by the whole experience, and a bit annoyed that Nechame didn't agree with him. Lately, in fact, she rather surprised him in many ways. She had suggested, only recently, that he eat lettuce and tomatoes. This astonished him. "Such food is for horses or cows," he said, "not for a human being." Nechame pointed out that even the *Forward* said that vegetables were good. To this Moshe answered, "Then all I can say is that in America many Jews go crazy." Nechame also suggested one day that Moshe might buy, next time, low shoes, or Oxfords as they were then called, instead of the high shoes he had hitherto worn. He looked at her in astonishment. "But they'll fall off," he protested. "Do you want me to walk in the street in my stocking feet?" Quietly she said that she had noticed that many men on Phillips Street were wearing low shoes, that they were probably more comfortable and healthier for the feet. But he wouldn't listen. She didn't press her point on the matter of low shoes or vegetables or anything else of this nature. She knew it was of little use, for her Moshe had a stubborn streak that lately, especially since he started working Saturdays, had become more prominent. It was years before Moshe risked wearing low shoes or eating tomatoes.

The matter of working on Saturday was a silently troublesome matter in the family. Shortly after Moshe started working on the Sabbath, Chashel and the others did the same. The theory was that once the depression was over they would not work on Saturday any more, but now that conditions were a little better they kept on working on the Sabbath, for some compulsive reason that not one of them really understood. Perhaps the strongest element in that compulsion was that nearly all the other immigrant Jews were doing the same. The younger folk didn't mind, but Moshe and his generation minded a great deal and they never quite got rid of their shame. Alte Bobbe was particularly disturbed by it, but she said nothing.

Nobody really knew how old she was. She herself didn't know either. Whenever any one of her children, grandchildren or great-grandchildren would ask her when her birthday was she would smile and say, "Who knows such things? Only in America people remember birthdays. What difference does it make? I was born when the good Czar Alexander II was a little boy, God have mercy on his soul. Don't ask me any more foolish questions." But on the basis of the information her daughter Leah and her son Mottel had she must have been ninety-five at the very least when she died, and probably more than one hundred.

Her advice was sought by all members of the family and by many friends of the family. She was very disturbed by the fact that Chashel and Yetta were not yet married. She herself was married at the age of fifteen, and while she thought that was perhaps too young, she thought that every girl should have a husband by the time she was eighteen. She used to say, "A woman must have a husband to make up her mind for her, and to give her children." She looked upon childless marriages as a curse. Any family with less than six or seven children was not a real family. She said that in all her life she never knew a woman who was really happy without a flock of her own children around her.

Her ideas about the relationship between a husband and wife were very clear. Whenever a woman complained about her husband she would say, "I don't care what he did or what he said. If there is a quarrel between a wife and husband, it's always the wife's fault. Look into your heart and change your ways." To the men she spoke with equal plainness. To one of them who was a miser she said, "Yes, they'll erect a golden gravestone in your memory." To another who was mean-spirited and selfish she said, "Consider how small you are. When a fine Jew says, 'Good-day' to another, the other replies, 'A good year to you.' A whole year for one day! You don't even say 'Good-day.'"

She got to love this country to the very roots of her soul. "A country that has sidewalks," she said, "is God's country," and she insisted, humorously, that there were sidewalks in Heaven. The village she came from had no sidewalks. A board every few hundred feet served as the sole sidewalk. The roads were dusty or muddy all year round. She was very pleased that Woodrow Wilson was elected President. She said, "He has so much grace and learning. Ah, it's a wonderful country where a professor, a learned man like that, can become the head man. When he makes a mistake, it's only like bad weather. It goes away." Her favorite among public men, however, was Louis D. Brandeis, whom she considered a close neighbor, because he lived in Boston. She said that his face was "like evening on a mountain." She regretted that he didn't have a beard. "A Jew should have a beard, as a mountain should have foliage." But she forgave him.

Not long after Leah moved to Anderson Street Alte Bobbe began to weaken perceptibly. David, who used to walk with her almost every Saturday morning to the synagogue—a journey that meant going down a steep hill and crossing a congested street junction—noticed that she was beginning to hold on to his arm more firmly than before. David also noticed that in synagogue, where she sat in the women's section in the balcony, she dozed off a bit more often than hitherto, and when she returned from synagogue, she rested longer.

Her children pleaded with her to permit Dr. Stone, the family physician, to examine her. She would say, "I think Dr. Stone is a fine man, and I shall see him, but I won't let him examine me. There's nothing wrong with me. I'm only a little tired. When my time comes he won't be able to help. That's in God's hands. Besides, I've lived long enough. All my children are married happily, and that's all a woman really wants in life. So don't bother Dr. Stone. He has more important things to do than to see an old woman."

Dr. Stone knew Alte Bobbe very well. He used to talk with her at length when he visited others in the family. Once in a while she would allow him to put the stethoscope to her heart, but no more. He told the men folk in the family that her heart was none too good, that age was beginning to take its toll. A few times he told her to rest more often, but she would reply, "I'll take a good long rest when I'm dead. You'll die before me with all your medicines. Now tell me how your wife is, and the children. You don't look so good yourself. You should sleep more and have more chicken soup," one of her favorite remedies for many ailments.

The inevitable last day came. One morning she was unable to get up from her bed to wash and go to the parlor, where she used to pray by herself before breakfast. She asked Leah to give her a little tea. She finished the tea and then said, "Call all the children. This is the end.

I'm not afraid. It's God's will. I thank God I am dying in my own house, with all my children around, and in a good country, where Jews are treated like human beings. I'm sorry I'm not leaving anything of value. I make only two requests: remember me every year by burning a lamp on this my last day, and put a picture of the whole family in my coffin." The entire family had had a group picture taken a year before at her suggestion.

Leah protested such talk. Alte Bobbe said, "Do as I tell you."

All the children and grandchildren and some of the great-grandchildren came over as soon as possible, about thirty in all. Dr. Stone was also called. He examined her. She did not object. After the examination he walked out of Alte Bobbe's bedroom, his eyes red. Three, four hours later, Alte Bobbe breathed her last, fully conscious to the end and as peaceful as anybody could have wished. In accordance with orthodox Jewish custom she was picked up from the bed and put down on the floor. Two candles were placed at her head. The entire family then walked by her and asked her to plead for them in the other world. Each said a prayer as they passed by. David said a prayer, which his mother quickly taught him, as he passed by. Alte Bobbe looked the same as he had always known her, calm, kindly, and as beautiful as snow on a hill not far away. He saw the family picture by her feet. He was inexpressibly glad that he was in it.

Call It Sleep

by HENRY ROTH

The history of this book is of special importance. First published
in 1934, it received little attention and was promptly forgotten
by the general public, but it continued to have a small, admiring
audience who didn't let it glide into total oblivion. In a lecture
at a Jewish community center in Queens, New York, in 1958, I,
as usual when discussing American Jewish writing, spoke of Call
It Sleep and added that the author had not been heard from
since and seemed to have vanished. At the end of the lecture a
woman approached and told me she was Roth's sister. She gave
me his address. I wrote at once, and told others, and thus began
one of the strangest revivals in American literary history. Harold
Ribalow, the anthologist and critic, journeyed up to see Roth,
who actually was operating a poultry farm in Maine. He had for
a time worked for a state hospital; his wife taught school.
Ribalow arranged for republication of Call It Sleep in 1960;
again the hard-cover failed, but the paperback edition was given
an unprecedented front-page review in The New York Times
Book Review, and at long last this important work found its
audience and became a best seller.

The novel is about a Jewish boy on New York's Lower East
Side some fifty years ago, as he learns of the sexual conflict between his parents, of moral and spiritual degradation, of an utterly bewildering world that seems to be filled with hate and indifference. The material here reprinted presents David in a
physical and psychological collapse, leading to a brilliantly conceived, poetically rendered apocalyptic scene that brings the
novel's catharsis.

Roth's style has been compared to that of Joyce, and his material to Farrell's in A World I Never Made. But Call It Sleep is

really sui generis, in both style and content, an eruption of the
Jewish soul in the alien, beckoning, fearful and wonderful milieu
of America.

C.A.

Tenderly petted by his lonely young mother, fearful of his vio-
lent, maladjusted father—who has a whip—David Schearl has
slowly made a tenuous friendship with a few goyish neighbor-
hood kids who practice the marvels of kite-flying from a roof and
sidewalk roller-skating, and who even do bad things with little
girls in basements.

WITHOUT TELLING his mother where he was going
he had started out early that morning for Aunt Bertha's candy store.
It had been a long walk, but high hopes had buoyed him up. And
now he saw a few blocks away the gilded mortar and pestle above a
certain drugstore window. That was Kane Street. His breast began
pounding feverishly as he drew near.

What if she didn't have any skates. No! She must have! He turned
the corner, walked east. A few houses and there was the candy store.
He'd look into the window first. Jumping up eagerly on the iron scrolls
of the cellar railing beside the store window, he pressed his nose
against the glass, scrutinized the display. A wild, garish clutter of Indian bonnets, notebooks, pencil boxes, pasteboard females, American
flags, uncut strips of battleships and ball players—but no skates for
his flitting eyes to light upon. Hope wavered. No, they must be inside.
Aunt Bertha would be foolish to keep anything so valuable in the
window.

He peered in through a crevice in the chaos. Seated behind the
counter, one hand poising a dripping roll above a coffee cup, Aunt
Bertha had turned her head toward the rear of the store and was
bawling at someone inside. David could hear her voice coming through
the doorway. He got down from the rail, sidled around the edge of
the window and went in—

"Sluggards! Bedbugs foul!" she shrilled unaware of his entrance.
"Esther! Polly! Will you get up! Or shall I spit my lungs out at you!
Quick, stinking heifers, you hear me! No?"

Aunt Bertha had changed since David had seen her last. Uncorseted, she looked fatter now, frowsier. The last remnant of tidiness in her appearance had vanished. Her heavy breasts, sagging visibly against her blouse, stained by fruit juice and chocolate, flopped slovenly from side to side. Fibres of her raffia-coarse red hair twined her moist throat. But her face was strangely thin and taut as though a weight where her apron bulged were dragging the skin down. "Wait!" she continued. "Wait till your father comes. Hi! He'll rend you with his teeth! Stinking sluts, it's almost nine!" She turned. "Vell?" and recognizing him. "David!" The hectic light in her eyes melted into pleasure. "David! My little bon-bon! You?"

"Yea!"

"Come here!" she spread fat arms like branches. "Let me give you a kiss, my honey-comb! I haven't seen you in—how long? And Mama, why doesn't she come? And how is your father?" Her eyes opened fiercely. "Still mad?" She submerged him in a fat embrace that reeked of perspiration flavored with coffee.

"Mama is all right." He squirmed free. "Papa too."

"What are you doing here? Did you come alone? All this long way?"

"Yes, I—"

"Want some candy? Ha! Ha! I know you, sly one!" She reached into a case. "Hea, I giff you a pineepple vit' emmend. Do I speak English better?"

"Yea." He pocketed them.

"End a liddle suddeh vuddeh?"

"No, I don't want it." He answered in Yiddish. For some reason he found himself preferring his aunt's native speech to English.

"And so early!" She rattled on admiringly. "Not like my two wenches, sluggish turds! And you're younger than they. If only you were mine instead of— Cattle!" She broke off furiously. "Selfish, mouldering hussies! All they know is to snore and guzzle! I'll husk them out of bed now, God help me!" But just as she started heavily for the doorway, a man stepped into the store.

"Hello! Hello!" He called loudly. "What are you scurrying off for? Because I came in?"

"No-o! God forbid!" she exclaimed with mock vehemence. "How fares a Jew?"

"How fares it with all Jews? A bare living. Can you spare me a thousand guilders?"

"Ha! Ha! What a jester! The only green-rinds I ever see are what I peel from cucumbers." And turning to David. "Go in, sweet one! Tell them I'll sacrifice them for the sake of heathens if they don't get up! That's my sister's only one," she explained.

"Comely," admitted the other.

David hesitated, "You want me to go in?"

"Yes! Yes! Perhaps you'll shame the sows into rising."

"Your fledgelings are still in the nest?"

"And what else?" disgustedly. "Lazy as cats. Go right in, my bright."

Reluctantly, David squeezed past her, and casting a last vain glance at the jumbled shelves, pushed the spring door forward and went in. Beyond the narrow passageway, cramped even closer by the stumpy mottled columns of pasteboard boxes carelessly piled, the kitchen opened up with a stale reek of unwashed frying pans. The wooden table in the center was bare except for a half-filled bottle of ketchup with a rakish cap. Pots, one in another, still squatted on the gas-stove. From a corner of the stove-tray under the burners, coffee dripped to a puddle on the floor. The sink was stacked with dishes, and beside it on the washtub a bag-full of rolls lay spilled all over. Splayed newspapers, crumpled garments, shoes, stockings, hung from the chairs or littered the floor. There were three doors, all closed, one on either side and one with a broom against it opening on the yard.

—Gee! Dirty. . . . Which one?

A giggle at his left. He approached cautiously.

"Is she commin'?" A guarded voice inside.

"Sh!"

"Hey," he called out in a non-committal voice, "Yuh momma wants you sh'd ged op!"

"Who're you?" Challengingly from the other side.

"It's me, Davy."

"Davy who?"

"Davy Schearl, 'Tanta Boita's nephew."

"Oh! So open de daw."

He pushed it back—The clinging stench of dried urine. Lit by a small window that gave upon the squalid grey bricks of an airshaft, the room was gloomy. Only after a few seconds had passed did the features of the two heads that pronged the grey, mussed coverlets separate from the murk.

"It's him!" A voice from the pillow.

"So wodda yuh wan'?" He finally distinguished the voice as Esther's.

"I tol' yuh," he repeated. "Yuh momma wants yuh sh'd get op. She tol' me I shul tell yuh." The message delivered, he began to retreat.

"Comm beck!" Imperiously. "Dope! Wodda yuh wan' in duh staw I asked."

"N-nott'n."

"So waddaye comm hea fuh?" Polly demanded suspiciously. "Kendy?"

"No, I didn'. I jost comm to see Tanta Boita."

"Aaa, he's full of hoss-cops—C'mon, Polly!" Esther was the one nearest the wall. "Ged out!" She sat up.

Polly clung to the covers. "Ged oud yuhself foist."

"Yuh bedder! Yuh hoid w'ad mama said."

"So led 'er say." Peevishly.

"I ain' gonna clean de kitchen by myself," Esther stood up on the bed. "You'll ged!"

"Don' cross over me. Id's hard luck."

"I will if yuh don' get out!"

"You jus' try—go over by my feet—"

But even as she spoke, Esther jumped over her.

"Lousy bestia!" Polly screeched. And as her sister jounced with unsure footing on the bed, she clutched at the hem of her nightgown and yanked her back. Esther tumbled heavily against the wall.

"Ow! Rotten louse!" Esther screamed in return. "Yuh hoit my head." And swooping down on the coverlets, flung them back. "Yeee!" she squawled as Polly, taken by surprise lay for an instant with nightgown above naked navel, "Yeee! Free show! Free show!"

"Free show, yuhself!" Furiously, Polly clawed at the other's nightgown. "Yuh stinkin' fraid cat! Shame! Shame! Free show!" Immediately four bare thighs kicked, squirmed and locked, and the two sisters rolled about in bed, slapping each other and shrieking. After a minute of this, the disheveled Esther, with a last vicious slap, at the other, broke loose, leapt from the bed and squealing rushed past David into the kitchen.

"I'll moider you—yuh rotten stinker!" Polly screamed after her. "I'll break yuh head!" she rolled out of bed as well.

"Yea, I double dare you!" Quivering with spite, Esther bent fingers into claws.

"I'll tell mama on you! I'll tell 'er watchuh done!"

"I ain' gonna go down witchoo." Her sister spat. "Just fer dat, you go yuhself."

"So don't. I'll tell him too!"

"I'll kill yuh!"

"Yea! Yuh know w'ot Polly does?" Esther wheeled on him. "She pees in bed every night! Dat's w'at she does! My fodder has to give her a pee-pot twelve a'clock every night—"

"I don't!"

"Yuh do! Dere!"

"Now I'll never take yuh down, yuh lousy fraid-cat. Never! Never!"

"So don't!"

"An' I hope de biggest moider boogey man tears yuh ass out."

"Piss-in-bed!" Esther taunted stubbornly. "Piss in bed!"

"An he'll comm, Booh!" Polly pawed the air, eyes bulging in mimic fright. "Booh! Like de Mask-man in dc serial! Wooh!"

"Aaa, shoddop!" Esther flinched. "Mama'll take me down."

"Yea!" her sister gloated. "Stinkin' fraid-cat! Who'll stay in de staw?"

"You!"

"Yuh should live so!"

"So I'll pee in de sink." Esther threatened.

"Wid de dishes in id! G'wan, I dare yuh! An' yuh know w'ot Mama'll give yuh w'en I tell 'er."

"So I'll waid! Aaa! He'll go down!" she shrilled in sudden triumph. "Mbaa!" her tongue flicked out. "Mbaa! Davy'll go down wit' me!"

"Yea? Waid'll I tell Sophie Seigel an' Yeddie Katz you took a boy down in de toilet and let 'im look. Waid'll I tell!"

"Sticks and stones c'n break my bones, but woids can nevuh hoit me-e!" Esther sang malevolently. "I ain'gonna led 'im look. C'mon, Davy! Waid'll I ged my shoes on."

"Don' go!" Polly turned on him fiercely. "Or I'll give yuh!"

"An' I'll give you!" Esther viciously hooked feet into shoes. "Such a bust, yuh'll go flyin'! C'mon, Davy!"

"Waddayuh wan'?" He looked from one to the other with a stunned, incredulous stare.

"I'll give yuh kendy," Esther wheedled.

"Yuh will not!" Polly interposed.

"Who's askin' you, Piss-in-bed?" She seized David's arm. "C'mon, I'll show you w'ea tuh take me."

"W'ea yuh goin'?" He held back.

"Downstairs inna terlit, dope! Only number one. Srooo!" She sucked in her breath sharply. "Hurry op! I'll give yuh anyt'ing inna store."

"Don'tcha do it!" Polly exhorted him. "She won't give yuh nott'n! I'll give yuh!"

"I will so!" Esther was already dragging him after her.

"Leggo!" He resisted her tug. "I don't want—" But she had said anything! A vision of bright-wheeled skates rose before his eyes. "Awri'." He followed her.

"Shame! Shame!" Polly yapped at their heels. "Ev'ybody knows yuh name. He's goin' in yuh terlit!"

Cringing with embarrassment, he hurried across the threshold to Esther's side.

"Shoddop! Piss-in-bed! Mind yuh own beeswax!" She slammed the door in her sister's face. "Over dis way."

A short flight of wooden steps led down into the muggy yard, and a little to the side of them, another flight of stone dropped into the cellar. At the sight of the nether gloom, his heart began a dull, labored pounding.

"Didntcha know our terlit was inna cella'?" she preceded him down.

"Yea, but I fuhgod." He shrank back a moment at the cellar door.

"Stay close!" she warned.

He followed warily. The corrupt damp of sunless earth. Her loose shoes scuffed before him into dissolving dark. On either side of him glimmered the dull-grey, once-whitewashed cellar bins, smelling of wet coal, rotting wood, varnish, burlap. Only her footsteps guided him now; her body had vanished. The spiny comb of fear serried his cheek and neck and shoulders.

—It's all right! All right! Somebody's with you. But when is she— Ow!

His groping hands ran into her.

"Wait a secon', will yuh?" she whispered irritably.

They had come mid-way.

"Stay hea." A door-knob rattled. He saw a door swing open—A tiny, sickly-grey window, matted with cobwebs, themselves befouled with stringy grime, cast a wan gleam on a filth-streaked flush bowl. In the darkness overhead, the gurgle and suck of a water-box. The dull, flat dank of excrement, stagnant water, decay. "You stay righd hea in de daw!" she said. "An' don' go 'way or I'll moider you—Srooo!" Her sharp breath whistled. She fumbled with the broken seat.

"Can I stay outside?"

"No!" Her cry was almost desperate as she plumped down. "Stay in de daw. You c'n look—" The hiss and splash. "Ooh!" Prolonged, relieved. "You ain' god a sister?"

"No." He straddled the threshold.

"You scared in de cella'?"

"Yea."

"Toin aroun'!"

"Don' wanna!"

"You're crazy. Boys ain't supposed t' be scared."

"You tol' me y'd give anyt'ing?"

"So waddayuh wan'?" In the vault-like silence the water roared as she flushed the bowl.

"Yuh god skates?"

"Skates?" She brushed hastily past him toward the yardlight, "C'mon. We ain't got no skates."

"Yuh ain'? Old ones?"

"We ain' god no kind." They climbed into the new clarity of the yard. "Wadduh t'ink dis is?" her voice grew bolder. "A two-winder kendy staw? An' if I had 'em I wouldn' give yuh. Skates cost moncy."

"So yuh ain' god?" Like a last tug at the clogged pulley of hope. "Even busted ones?"

"Naaa!" Derisively.

Despair sapped the spring of his eager tread. Her smudged ankles flickered past him up the stairs.

"Hey, Polly!" He heard her squeal as she burst into the kitchen, "Hey, Polly—!"

"Giddaddihea, stinker!" The other's voice snapped.

"Yuh know wot he wants?" Esther pointed a mocking finger at him as he entered.

"W'a?"

"Skates! Eee! Hee! Hee! Skates he wants!"

"Skates!" Mirth infected Polly. "Waddaa boob! We ain' god skates."

"An' now I don' have to give 'im nott'n!" Esther exulted. "If he wants wot we ain' got, so—"

"Aha!" Aunt Bertha's red head pried into the doorway. "God be praised! Blessed is His holy name!" She cast her eyes up with exaggerated fervor. "You're both up! And at the same time? Ai, yi, yi! How comes it?"

The other two grimaced sullenly.

"And now the kitchen, the filthy botch you left last night! Coarse rumps! Do I have to do everything? When will I get my shopping done?"

"Aaa! Don' holler!" Esther's tart reply.

"Cholera in your belly!" Aunt Bertha punned promptly. "Hurry up, I say! Coffee's on the stove." She glanced behind her. "Come out, David, honey! Come out of that mire." She pulled her head back hurriedly.

"Aaa, kiss my axle," Polly glowered. "You ain' my modduh!" And snappishly to David. "G'wan, yuh lummox! Gid odda hea!"

Chagrined, routed, he hurried through the corridor, finding a little relief in escaping from the kitchen.

"Skates!" Their jeers followed him. "Dopey Benny!"

He came out into the store. Aunt Bertha, her bulky rear blocking the aisle, her breasts flattened against the counter was stooping over, handing a stick of licorice to a child on the other side.

"Oy!" She groaned, straightening up as she collected the penny. "Oy!" And to David. "Come here, my light. You don't know what a help you've been to me by getting them out of bed. Have you ever laid eyes on such bedraggled, shameless dawdlers? They're too lazy to stick a hand in cold water, they are. And I must sweat and smile." She took him in her arms. "Would you like what I gave that little boy just now—ligvitch? Ha? It's as black as a harness."

"No." He freed himself. "You haven't got any skates, have you Aunt Bertha?"

"Skates? What would I do with skates, child? And in this little dungheap? I can't sell five-cent pistols or even horns with the red, white and blue, so how could I sell skates? Wouldn't you rather have ice-cream? It is very good and cold."

"No."

"A little halvah? Crackers? Come, sit down awhile."

"No, I'm going home."

"But you just came."

"I have to go."

"Ach!" she cried impatiently. "Let me look at you awhile—No? Take this penny then," she reached into her apron. "Buy what I haven't got."

"Thanks, Aunt Bertha."

"Come see me again and you'll have another. Sweet child!" She kissed him. "Greet your mother for me!"

"Yes."

"Keep hale!"

> *An atmosphere of doom hangs over the little family; there seems to be some secret horror from "back home" that haunts David. From his father's accusation about his mother, David develops a fantasy that he is not the son of his parents, and he babbles such a tale to his Hebrew teacher.*

AT THE second landing of the unlit hallway, the harsh stench of disinfectants rasped the grain of his nostrils. Behind that doorway where the voices of children filtered through, Mrs. Glantz's brood had the measles. Upward and beyond it, wearily, wearily. And at the turn of the stairs, the narrow, crusted, wire-embedded window was open. He loitered again, stared down. In the greying yard below, a lean, grey cat leaped at the fence, missed the top and clawed its way up with intent and silent power. And he upward also, wearily.

—Her fault. Hers. Ain't mine. No it ain't. It ain't. Ask anybody. Take a step and ask. Is it mine? Bannistersticks, is it mine? Mine is . . . Mine ain't . . . Mine is . . . Mine ain't. Mine is . . . Mine ain't . . . There! See! Chinky shows! Her fault. She said about him. Didn't she? She told it to Aunt Bertha. Her fault. If she liked a goy, so I liked. There! She made me. How did I know? It's all her fault and I'm going to tell too. Blame it on her. Yours Mama! Yours! Go on! Go on! Next! Next floor! Mama! Mama! Owoo!

And leaving the third landing where the stale reek of cabbage and sour cream filled the uncertain light, a low whimper forced its way through his lips and echoed with an alien treble in the hollow silence. And upward, clammy palms clinging to the bannisters and squealing in thin reluctance as they slid. And again the turn of the stairs and the open window framing a soft clarity with the new height. Across the alley, a face between curtains grimaced, tilted back; crooking fingers plucked the collar off.

—Stop hollerin'! Stop! You, inside, stop! Don't know. They don't know. Who told them? Tell me, who could've? Well, tell me? There! See! Polly didn't tell—Esther wouldn't let her. She ran after her. But maybe she didn't catch. She did! She didn't. She did! But even if—so what? Aunt Bertha wouldn't tell. Aunt Bertha likes me. See? Aunt Bertha wouldn't tell on me for a million, zillion dollars. Don't she hate Papa? Didn't she want me 'stead of them? Didn't she? So she wouldn't tell. Gee, ooh, God! 'Course she wouldn't tell. So what? What am I scared of? (He leaned against the bannister in an ecstasy of hope) Nobody knows! Oooh, God, make nobody know! Go on then! Make believe nothing happened. Gee, nothing-but—but him. Rabbi? Aaa, he forgets. Sure he does! All the time. What's he got to remember for? Go on, gee, God! Go on! But—but where were you? It's way late. Me? Where was I? Got lost, that's what. Way in the other side of Avenue A. Why? Thought it was the other side. That's where I was. Go on! Oooh, God! Wish I broke a leg. Ow! Don't! Yea! Sh!

The pale blue light of the transom obliquely overhead.

—Nobody—in?

He crept to his doorway, stiff ankle-joints cracking like gun-shots. A blur of voices behind the door.

—Sh! Who? Who's there?

Pent breath trembling in his bosom, he leaned nearer, leaned nearer and poised for flight.

Someone laughed.

—Who? She? Mama? Yes! Y*es!*

Again, out of a mumble of voices, again the laugh—strained, nervous, but a laugh. Hope clutched at it.

—She! Laugh is hers! She don't know! Don't know nothing! Wouldn't laugh if she knew. No! No! Don't know! Can go!

His brain flew open as though a light were swung into it—

—Nobody knows! Can go!

Yet his whole being shied in terror when he reached out his hand for the door knob—

The door that clicked open, clicked shut upon their voices. And—

"David! David, child! Where have you been?"

"Mama! Mama!" But not soon enough could he fling himself into her bosom, not deep enough nest his eyes there before he saw in a blur of vision the bearded figure before the table.

"Mama! Mama! Mama!"

Only the sheltering valley between her breasts muffled his scream of fear to her heart. Convulsive, unerring hands flew up to her neck, sought and clasped the one upright pillar of this ruin.

"Hush! Hush! Hush child! Have no fear!" Her body rocked him.

And at his back, his father's voice, morose, sardonic, "Yes, hush him! Comfort him! Comfort him!"

"Poor frightened one!" Her words came to him from her bosom and lips. "His heart is beating like a thief's. Where have you been, life? I'm dead with anxiety! Why didn't you come home?"

"Lost!" he moaned. "I was lost on Avenue A."

"Ach!" She clasped him to her again. "Because you told a strange tale?"

"I was just making believe! I was just making believe!"

"Were you?" Behind him his father's cryptic voice. "Were you indeed!"

He could feel his mother start. The heart beneath his ear begun to pound heavily.

"Hi! Yi! Yi! Yi! Yi!" From another corner of the room, the rabbi's dolorous groan broke up into a train of sighs. "I see I have wrought badly coming here. No?" He paused, but none answered his question. Instead,

"Stop your whining, you!" his father snapped.

"But what was I to do?" The rabbi launched himself again. His voice, so uncommonly unctuous and placating, sounded strange to David's ears despite his misery. "Had he been a dullard, a plaster golem, such as only the King of the Universe with his holy and bounteous hand knows how to bestow on me, would I have believed him? Psh! I would have said—Bah! Ox-brained idiot, away with this drool! And then and there would I have fetched him such a cuff on the jowls, his children's children would have cried aloud! Hear me, friend Schearl, he would have flown from me like a toe-nail from a shear! But no!" His voice heightened, deepened, grew rich with huskiness. "In my cheder he was as a crown in among rubbish, as a seraph among Esau's goyim! How could I help but believe him? A yarn so incredible had to be true. No? His father a goy, an organ-grinder—an organ player in a church! His mother dead! She met him among the corn—"

"What!" Both voices, but with what different tones!

"I said among the corn. You, Mrs. Schearl, his aunt! What! The like will not be heard again till the Messiah is a bride-groom. Speak! No?"

Again that silence and then as though the silence were creaking with its own strain, the ominous grating sound of a stretched cable, his father's grinding teeth. Under his ear, the heavy beat of the heart tripped, fluttered, hammered raggedly. The stricken catch of the quick breath in her throat was like the audible sublimate of his own terror.

"But uh—uh—now it's a jest, no? Uh—ah, what! A jest!" His hurried nails could be heard harrying his beard. "Not-eh-ah-poo! Not a doubt!" Stumbling at first, his speech began to tumble, growing more flustered as it grew heartier. "It's your child now. No! It's your child! Always! What's there to be disturbed about? Ha? A jest! A tale of a— of a hunter and a wild bear! Understand? Something to laugh at! Ha! Ha—hey, scamp, there! You won't gull me again! What these imps can't invent! Ha! Ha! A jest, no?"

"Yes! Yes!" Her alarmed voice.

"Hmph!" Savagely from her husband. "You agree readily! Where did he get this story? Let him speak! Where did he? Was it Bertha, that red cow? Who?"

David moaned, grasped his mother closer.

"Let him alone, Albert!"

"You say so, do you? We'll find out!"

"But uh—you won't hold it against me—uh—I mean that I told you. May God requite me if I came here trying to meddle, to stir up rancor. Yes! May I wither where I sit! Hear me! Not a jot did I care to pry! Let the feet grow where they list, I cared not! Not I! But I thought here am I his rabbi, and I thought it's my duty to tell you —at least that you might know that he knew—and in what way he was made aware."

"It's all right!" She unclasped one arm. "I beg you don't be disturbed."

"Well then, good! Good! Ha! I must go! The Synagogue! It grows late." The creak of his chair and scrape of his feet filled the pause as he rose. "Then you're not angered with me?"

"No! No! Not at all!"

"Good-night then, good-night." Hastily. "May God bestow you an appetite for supper. I shan't trouble you again. If you wish I'll start him on Chumish soon—a rare thing for one who has spent so little time in a cheder. Good-night to you all."

"Good-night!"

"Hi-yi-yi-yi-yi-! Life is a blind cast. A blind caper in the dark. Good-night! Hi-i! Yi! Yi! Evil day!"

The latch ground. The door opened, creaked, closed on his hi-yi-ing footsteps. And of the silence that followed the beating of her heart condensed the anguish into intervals. And then his father's voice, vibrant with contempt—

"The old fool! The blind old nag! But this once he wrought better than he knew!"

He felt his mother's thighs and shoulders stiffen. "What do you mean?" she asked.

"I'll tell you in a moment," he answered ominously. "No, on second thought I won't need to tell you at all. It will tell itself. Answer me this: Where was my father when I married you?"

"Do you need ask me? You know that yourself—he was dead."

"Yes, I know it," was his significant retort. And his voice tightening suspiciously. "You saw my mother?"

"Of course! What's come over you, Albert?"

"Of course!" he repeated in slow contempt. "Why do you smirk at me with that blank, befuddled look? I mean did you see her before I brought her to you myself?"

"What is it you want, Albert?"

"An answer without guile," he snapped. "You know what I'm talking about! I know you too well. Did she come to you alone? In secret? Well? I'm waiting!"

As though her body were compelled to follow the waverings of an immense irresolution, she swayed back and forth, and David with her. And at last quietly: "If you must know—she did."

"Ha!" The table slid suddenly along the floor. "I knew it! Oh, I know her nature! And she told you, didn't she? And she warned you! Of me! Of what I had done?"

"There was nothing said of that—!"

"Nothing? Nothing of what? How can you be so simple?"

"Nothing!" she repeated desperately. "Stop tormenting me, Albert!"

"You wouldn't have said nothing." He pursued her relentlessly. "You would have asked me, what? What I had done? She told you!"

His mother was silent.

"She told you! Is your tongue trapped in silence? Speak!"

"Ach—!" and stopped. Only David heard the wild beating of her heart. "Not now! Not with him here!"

"Now!" he snarled.

"She did." Her voice was wrung from her. "And she told me I ought not to marry you. But what difference—"

"She did! And the rest? The others? Who else!"

"Why are you so eager to hear?"

"Who else?"

"Father and mother. Bertha." Her voice had become labored. "The others know. I never told you because I—"

"They knew!" he interrupted her with bitter triumph. "They knew all the time! Then why did they let you marry me? Why did *you* marry me?"

"Why? Because no one believed her. Who could?"

"Oh!" sarcastically. "Is that it? That was quickly thought of! It was easy to shut your minds. But she swore it was true, didn't she? She must have, hating me afterwards as she did. Didn't she tell you that my father and I had quarreled that morning, that he struck me, and I vowed I would repay him? There was a peasant watching us from afar. Didn't she tell you that? He said I could have prevented it. I could have seized the stick when the bull wrenched it from my father's hand. When he lay on the ground in the pen. But I never lifted a finger! I let him be gored! Didn't she tell you that?"

"Yes! But, Albert, Albert! She was like a woman gone mad! I didn't believe it then and I don't believe it now! Let's stop now, please. Can't we talk about it later?"

"Now that it's all become clear to me you want to stop, is that it?"

"And why is it suddenly so clear?" her tone held a sharp insistence. "What is so clear to you? What are you trying to prove?"

"You ask me?" ominously. "You dare ask me?"

"I do! What do you mean?"

"Oh, the gall of your kind! How long do you think you'll hide it! Will I be lulled and gulled forever? Must I tell you? Must I blurt it out! My sin balances another? Is that enough for you?"

"Albert!" her stunned outcry.

"Don't call to me!" he snarled. "I'll say it again—they had to get rid of you!"

"Albert!"

"Albert!" He spat back at her. "Whose is he? The one you're holding in your arms! Ha? How should he be named?"

"You're mad! Dear God! What's happened to you?"

"Mad, eh? Mad then, but not a cheat! Come! What are you waiting for? Unmask yourself! I've been unmasked to you for years. All these years you said nothing. You pretended to know nothing. Why? You knew why! I would have asked you what I've just asked you now! I would have said why did they let you marry me. There must have been something wrong. I would have known! I would have told you. But now, speak! Speak out with a great voice! Why fear? You know who I am! That red cow betrayed you, didn't she? I'll settle with her too. But don't think there was no stir in this silence. All these years my blood told me! Whispered to me whenever I looked at him, nudged me, told me he wasn't mine! From the very moment I saw him in your arms out of the ship, I guessed. I guessed!"

"And you believe a child's fantasy?" She spoke with a fixed flat voice of one staggered by the incredible. "The babbling? The wandering of a child?"

"No! No!" he bit back with a fierce sarcasm. "Not a bit of it. Not a word. How could I? It's muddled of course. But did you want a commentary. Let him speak again. It might be clearer."

"I've thought you strange, Albert, and even mad but that was pride and that made you pitiful. But now I see you're quite, quite mad! Albert!" She suddenly cried out as if her cry would waken him. "Albert! Do you know what you're saying!"

"A comedienne to the end." He paused, drew in the sharp breath of one marveling—"Hmph! How you sustain it! Not a tremor! Not a sign of betrayal! But answer me this!" His voice thinned to a probe. "Here! Here's a chance to show me my madness. Where is his birth certificate? Ha? Where is it? Why have they never sent it?"

"That? Was it because of that one single thing your blood warned you so much? Why, dear God, they wrote you—my own father did. They had looked for it everywhere and never found it—lost! The confusion of departure! What other reason could there be?"

"Yes! Yes! What else could it be? But we—we know why it stayed lost, don't we? It was better unfound! After all, was I there to see him born? Was I ever there to see you bearing him? No! I was in America —on their money, notice! The ticket they bought me. Why were they so eager to get rid of me? Why such haste, and I not married more than a month?"

"Why? Can't you see for yourself? There were nine in my family. Servants, others, outsiders began to know. They had hoped I would follow you soon. There was no money at home. The store was failing. The sons weren't grown yet. You couldn't send for me—"

"Oh, stop! Stop! I know all that! Who is it they began to know of —you or me?"

"Do you still persist? Of you, of course! Your mother went around telling everyone."

"And they were ashamed, eh? I see! But now I'll tell you my version. Here I am in America sweating for your passport, starving myself. You see? Thousands of miles away. Alone. Never writing to anyone only to you. Now! He's born a month or two too soon to be mine—perhaps more. You wait that time. That month or two, and then, why then exactly on the head of the hour you write me—I have a son! A joy! Fortune! I have a son. Ha! But when you came across, the doctors were too knowing. Fool your husband, they said. You were frightened. Seventeen months were too few for one so grown. Twenty-one then! Twenty-one they might believe, and twenty-one of course I thought he was. There you are! Wasn't that it? I haven't forgotten. My memory's good. An organist, eh? A goy, God help you! Ah! It's clear! But my blood! My blood I say warned me!"

"You're mad! There's no other word!"

"So? But good enough for your kind. That's what they reasoned back home—the old, praying glutton and his wife—Did you know an organist? Well, why don't you answer?"

"I—oh, Albert, let me alone!" She moved David about frantically under her arms. "Let me alone in God's name! You've heaped enough shame on me for nothing. It's more than I can bear. You're distraught! Let's not talk about it anymore! Later! Tomorrow! I've suffered twice for this now."

"Twice! Ha!" He laughed. "You've a gift for blurting things out! Then you knew an organist?"

"You claim I did!" Her voice went suddenly stony.

"Did you? Say it."

"I did then. But that was—"

"You did! You did" His words rang out again. "It fits! It matches! Why look! Look up there! Look! The green corn—taller than a man! It struck your fancy, didn't it? Why, of course it would! The dense corn high above your heads, eh? The summer trysts! But I—I married in November! Ha! Ha!—Sh! Don't speak! Not a word! You'll be ludicrous, you're so confounded!"

"And you believe? And you believe? This that you're saying! Can you believe it?"

"Anhr! Do I believe the sun? Why I've sensed it for years I tell you! I've stubbed my feet against it at every turn and tread. It's been in my way, tangled me! And do you know how? Haven't you ever seen it? Then why do weeks and weeks go by and I'm no man at all? No man as other men are? You know of what I speak! You ought to, having known others! I've been poisoned by a guess! Corruption has haunted me. I've sensed it! I've known it! Do you understand? And it's been true!"

She rose. And David still in her arms, still clasping her neck, dared not breathe nor whimper in his terror, dared not lift his eyes from the shelter of her breast. And his father's voice, nearer now, broke like a rod of stiff, metallic words across his back.

"Hold him tightly! He's yours!"

She answered, a kind of cold deliberate pity in her voice. "And now, now that you know what you think you know, the corruption's drained. Is that how you are? The fog is split. Why didn't you tell me sooner what clouded you? I would have freed you sooner."

"And now like any discovered cheat you'll mock me, eh?"

"I'm not mocking you, Albert. I'm just asking you to tell me exactly what it is you want."

"I want," his teeth ground into his words. "Never to see that brat again."

She sucked in her breath as if making a last attempt. "You're driving me mad, Albert! He's your son. Your son! Oh, God! He's yours. What if I knew another man long before I met you—! It was long ago, I swear to you! Can he, must he be his? He's yours!"

"I'll never believe you! Never! Never!"

"Why then I'll go!"

"Go. I'll caper! I'll dance on the roofs! I'll be rid of it! Be rid of it, I tell you! The nights in the milk wagon! The thoughts! The torment! The stables—hitching the horse. The other men! The torment! I'll be rid of it! His—"

But as though answering his suppressed scream of exaltation, noises in the hallway, wrangling, angry, confused, battered like turbulent waves against the door. He stopped as though struck. About David's legs the clasp of his mother's arms tightened protectingly. Again the cries threatening, reproachful and a stamp and shuffling of feet. A sharp crack at the door. Flung open, it banged against a chair.

"Now let me go! I'm here! I'm going to speak!"

He knew the voice! One wild glance he threw over his shoulder— Aunt Bertha grappling with her husband seemed less strange to him now than that the light of the kitchen had grown so grey. With a whimper of despair, he clutched at his mother's neck, buried his face frenziedly into the crook of her throat. And she, bewildered—

"Nathan! You? Bertha! What is it? You look so frantic!"

"I—I am angry!" Uncle Nathan gasped tormentedly. "I have much—!"

"It's nothing!" Aunt Bertha beat his words down. "My man is a fool! Look at him! He's gone crazy!"

"Let me speak! Will you let me speak!"

"Be strangled first" She flew at him venomously. "He wants—do you know what he wants? Can't you guess? What does a Jew want? Money. He's come to borrow money! And why does he want money? To make a bigger store. Nothing else! He's out of his head! I'll tell you what happened to him. He dreamt last night the police came and stripped off his boots, the way they did his bankrupt grandfather in Vilna. It's gone to his head. He's frightened. His wits are in a foam. Ask him where he is now. He couldn't answer you. I'm sure he couldn't. And how are you, Albert! It's a fair brace of months since I have seen you! You ought to visit us sometimes, see our little store, and vast variety of bon-bons. Cheh! Cheh! Und heva suddeh-waw-deh!"

David's father made no answer.

And lightly as though she expected none. "And why are you holding him in your arms, Genya?"

"Just to—just to feel his weight," his mother replied unsteadily. "And he is heavy!" She bent over to put him down.

"No, Mama!" he whispered, clinging to her. "No, Mama!"

"Only a moment, beloved! I can't hold you in my arms so long. You're too heavy!" She set him on his feet. "There! Once he gets up, he won't come down." And still keeping her trembling hand on his shoulder, she turned to Nathan. "Money? Why—?" She laughed confusedly. "I think the world's gone mad! What makes you come to us of all people? Are you in your right senses, Nathan?"

Fixing his glowering, harassed eyes on David, Nathan opened his mouth to speak—

"Of course!" Aunt Bertha outstripped him. "Of course, you haven't any money." She dug her elbow viciously into her husband's ribs. "That's what I told him. To the very words! Didn't I?"

Almost giddy with terror and guilt, David had dodged behind his mother. At her side stood his father, arms folded across his chest, aloof, nostrils still slowly flaring in the ebb and flow of passion. In the greying light, his face looked like stone, only the nostrils and the crooked vein on his brow alive. Then he uncrossed his arms. His dense, smoldering eyes traveled from face to face, brushed David's who jerked his head away in panic, traveled on and returned, cleaving there. Without turning to look, David knew himself regarded, so palpable was that gaze, so like a pressure. Enveloping him, it seemed to sap him from without. He grew dizzy, reached out numb hands for his mother's dress, hung there faintly. His father shifted his gaze. And as though he had been struggling under water until this moment, David gulped down breath, heard sounds again, voices.

"And you won't sit down?" His mother was asking solicitously, "You're tired, both of you. I can see it. Why, supper for two more would take no longer. Please stay!"

"No! No! Thanks, sister!" Aunt Bertha was positive. "But if he would go hunting for rusty horseshoes before he's had his supper, why he can wait a little longer—I'm as tired as he is. And I warned him!"

"I'm sorry we can't help you, Nathan. You know we would if we had it! Oh! It's all so mixed! I'm confused! Why!" She laughed ruefully. "If it weren't so absurd, Nathan, it would be flattering that you should think we had any money."

Biting his lips, Uncle Nathan stared at the floor, swayed as if he might fall. "I have nothing to say," he answered dully. "She's said it all."

"You see?" There was a note of triumph in Aunt Bertha's voice. "He's ashamed of himself now. But now I like him!" She began nudging him toward the door. "Now he's my man and as good a man as ever ate prunes with his meat. Come, good heart! Mrs. Zimmerman is waiting— My customers will think I'm burying you."

"You've a cunning way!" He answered, shaking her off sullenly. "You've clogged my chimney well! But you wait! You'll laugh in convulsion yet!"

"Come! Come!" She gave him a push toward the door. "Hoist up your nose! That venture you want money for can wait!"

Uncle Nathan wrested his arm away, shook a desperate, baffled finger at his wife. "A curse on you and your money and your whole story! I'll stay! I'll speak!"

Aunt Bertha ignored him, opened the door. "Good night, sister! Forgive him! He's always been a good husband, but to-night— You know how men are! When they're a little unstrung, they revel in it. Come, you!"

Cowering behind his mother, David watched Aunt Bertha drag her stubborn husband toward the door. Their going would be no deliverance—one doom postponed, another waiting. There could be no less terror if they stayed, or if they went. Whatever way the mind turned it faced only fear. This he had escaped. Aunt Bertha had saved him. But his father! His father again! Their going abandoned him to that fury! But—

"Wait!"

For the first time since they had come, his father spoke. And now he uncrossed his arms and stalked suddenly to the door.

"Wait!" He gripped Uncle Nathan's shoulder, towered above him. "Come back!"

"What do you want of my man!" Aunt Bertha snapped in angry surprise. "You let him alone. He's distraught enough without you troubling him. Come, Nathan!" She redoubled her tugging at the other shoulder.

"It's you who should let him alone!" her brother-in-law growled dangerously. "You and your cursed deceit! Come in, Nathan!"

Staring amazed from face to face, Uncle Nathan could muster no more than a bewildered grunt.

"I say let him go!" Aunt Bertha shrieked furiously. "Wild beast, take your paws off!"

"When I'm done!"

"Albert! Albert!" his mother's frightened voice. "What are you doing! Let him alone!"

"No! No! Not till he's spoken!"

For a moment, half in the thickening light of the kitchen, half in the gloom of the corridor, they wrestled for him, Uncle Nathan's pale, alarmed face, bobbing back and forth between them, and all three struggling figures, shadowy, unreal as nightmare. A moment longer, and with one vicious yank, David's father pulled them back into the room, and with such force, the other man pitched forward, his hat flying to the floor. He slammed the door.

"Listen to me, Nathan!" He drummed his stiff hand against the other man's chest. "You came here to say something, now say it. Stifle the she-ass and her guile! Say it! It isn't money!"

"N-nothing! Nothing! So help me, G-God!" Before the thrust of the other's hand, Uncle Nathan fell back against his wife. "Bertha told you everything! May evil befall me if she didn't! A store! I wanted! I saw! That was all! No, Bertha?"

"You fool!" She spat at her husband. "Didn't I warn you not to come here! Didn't I tell you you'd groan and remember? I've a good mind to—What do you want of him?" She wheeled furiously on her brother-in-law. "You let him alone, ungovernable beast! Do you hear? He's come for money and nothing else! How many times do you want to be told? I don't have to endure any more of your rages! Remember that!"

"Hold your tongue!" His father was beginning to quiver. "You treacherous cow! I know you of old. I know what you've already done. Speak, Nathan!" He smashed his fist down on the wash tub. "Don't let her trick you! Speak! Whatever it is! Have no fear of me! Only the truth! I have reasons! It may do me good to hear!"

"What's he saying?" Aunt Bertha's eyes bulged. "What new insanity gripes him!"

"Albert, I beg of you!" his mother had seized her husband's arm. "If you've any quarrel, it's with me. Let the man alone. He's told you all."

"Has he? So you think! Or pretend, maybe! But I know better! I have eyes! I have seen! Will you speak?" Wrath stretched him to his full height. Teeth bared, he advanced, dwarfing the other man who cowered.

"I-I've already s-said everything," his lips trembling, Uncle Nathan reached behind him for the door. "I must leave! Bertha! Come!"

But David's father had rammed his palm against the door.

"You'll wait! You hear me? You'll wait till you answer me one thing! And you'll answer it!"

"W-what do you want?"

"Why, when you opened your mouth to speak—Before that she-ass brayed you out of words and will—Why did you stare at him?" He hammered the air in David's direction. "Why that look? What was it you were trying to say about him?"

"I—I have nothing to say. I didn't look at him. Let me alone in God's will. Genya! Bertha! Don't let him quarrel with me."

"Albert! Albert! Stop torturing the man!"

"A curse on you! You fiend!" Aunt Bertha tried to squeeze in between them. "You madman! Let him alone!"

He flung her viciously aside. "And you, will you tell me what he did? Or do you want my fury to burst—!"

"Oh! Oh! Woe me! Woe me!" Aunt Bertha filled the room with a loud gasping and lament. "Woe me! Did you see what he did? He threw me? And me with a child in my belly. Monster! Mad dog! It's not drawers you've ripped this time. It's a child you've destroyed! On your head my miscarriage. Oh you'll pay for this! May they hang you. May you—"

"Not if you had twins would it trouble me. Your breed is well destroyed. But I will find out what he did. That brat there! I'm waiting!" His voice became strangled. "I tell you I'm at the end of my patience!"

Uncle Nathan began to sag as though about to faint.

"He—uh—uh— oy! oy! He—!"

"Not a word!" Aunt Bertha screamed. "Open that door or I'll shriek for help! Let us out!"

They faced each other in a silence so awful it seemed as if the very room would burst with the tension in it.

Blind with terror, unnoticed by any, David had already reeled toward the stove. (—*It's there! It's there!*) A tortured, anguished voice babbled within him. (—*It's there! She put it there! It's there!*) Groping, tottering hands reached into the dark niche between the stove and the wall—

"Speak!" In the shrunken, shadowy room, his father had become all voice, and his voice struck with the brunt of thunder.

"Bertha!" Uncle Nathan wailed. "Save me! Save me, Bertha! He's going to strike! Bertha! Bertha!"

"Help!" she screamed. "Let go the door! Help! Help! Call! Genya, throw up the window! Help!"

"Albert! Albert! Have mercy!"

"Speak!" Above their screaming, the horrible gritting of his teeth.

"I— I— uh—he— it was he— uh. Oh, Bertha! Noth—"

"Anh!" That insensate snarl. The shadowy arm drew back. "You—!"

"Papa!"

The bent arm hung in air, hung motionless. The writhing face above it turned.

"Papa!" In the swirling, crumbling, darkened mind, that one compulsion rallied the body and the brain like a standard. A dream? No, not a dream. Not a dream nor the memory of a dream. An act, ordained, foreseen, inevitable as this very moment, a channel of expertness, imbued for ages, reiterated for ages, familiar as breath.

He approached. The rest stood spellbound.

"I— It was me, papa—"

"David! Child!" His mother sprang toward him. "What have you got in your hand!"

But before she could reach him, he had lifted the broken whip into his father's curling fingers.

"David!" She seized him, drew him out of danger. "A whip! Near him! What are you doing!"

"This?" The lids dropped over his father's consuming eyes. "Why do you—? Why is this given? You know what happened to this? Is it your fate you're begging for?"

"I— I— Please, papa!"

"You shan't touch him! You hear me, Albert! I won't endure it!" All entreaty, all timidity had vanished, in its stead a fierce resolve. She bowed over David like a ledge of rock. "Whatever he's done or anyone thinks he's done, you shan't touch him!"

"Band against the alien, the stranger!" His father's voice was hollow and perilous, "But let me hear him!"

"Say nothing, child!" Aunt Bertha's warning cry.

But he was already speaking. And the words he spoke were like staggering burdens he bore up a great steep where his own sighs battered him, where he floundered in his own tears.

"I was—I was on—the roof. Papa! I was on the roof! And there was a b-boy. A big one—and—and he had a kite—k-kite, they called it. Kite —goes h-higher than r-roofs—it goes—"

"What are you talking about!" His father ground. "Stop your candle-gutter! Hurry!"

"I'm—I'm—" He gasped for breath.

"God's fool!" Aunt Bertha rasped under her breath. "My man! My man! May earth gape for you this very hour! You see what you've wrought!"

"Me?" Uncle Nathan groaned. "My fault? How did I—"

"So—s-somebody—wanted to take it. The k-kite. And I called. And I said—look out! Look out! So I—I was his friend. Leo. He had skates and then—Ow! Papa! Papa! And we went to Aunt Bertha's. And we got Polly on the other side—in the yard. He got her—And he gave her the skates. And then, ow! Ow! He took her in—in the cellar. And he —he—"

"He what!" The implacable voice was like a goad.

"I don't know! Ow! He p-played—he played—bad!"

"Anh!"

"Don't you come near him!" his mother screamed. "Don't you dare! That's enough, child! Hush! That's enough!"

"H-he did! Not me, Papa! Papa, not me! I didn't! Ow! Papa! Papa!" He clung frenziedly to his mother.

"That's hers! Her spawn! Mark me! Hers!" He seemed to be stifling in a wild insane joy. "Not mine! Not a jot of me! Bertha, cow! Not mine! You, Nathan! Rouse your sheep-wits! Your mate's betrayed my wife! Do you know it? Blabbed her secret! Told him whose he was. An organist somewhere. How I harbored a goy's get! A rake! A rogue's! His and hers! But not mine! I knew it! I knew it all the time! And now I'm driving her out! Her and him, the brat! Let him beat her in time to come. But I'm free! He's no part of me! I'm free!"

"He's mad!" The other two whispered hoarsely and shrank away.

"Hear me!" He was slavering at the mouth. "I nurtured him! Three years I throttled surmise, I was the beast of burden! Good fortune I never met! Happiness never! Joy never! And—and that was right! Why should I meet anything but misfortune! That was right! I was tainted. I was bridled with another's sin. But for that—for all that suffering I have one privilege! Who will deny me? Who? One privilege! To wreak! To quench! Once!"

And before anyone could move, he had lunged forward at David's mother.

"Ow! Papa! Papa! Don't!"

Those steel fingers closed like a crunching trap on David's shoulders —yanked him out of her hands. And the whip! The whip in air! And—

"Ow! Ow! Papa! Ow!"

Bit like a brand across his back. Again! Again! And he fell howling to the floor.

His mother screamed. He felt himself grabbed, pulled to his feet, dragged away. And now his aunt was screaming, Uncle Nathan's hoarse outcry swelling the tumult. In the shadows, figures swayed, grappled—And suddenly his father's voice, exultant, possessed, hypnotic—

"What's that? That! Look! Look at the floor! There! Who disbelieves me now? Look what's lying there! There where he fell! A sign! A sign I tell you! Who doubts? A sign!"

"Unh!" Uncle Nathan grunted as though in sudden pain.

"Woe me!" Aunt Bertha gasped in horror. "It's—! What! No!"

Terror impinging on terror, David squirmed about in his mother's arms—looked down—

There, stretched from the green square to the white square of the checkered linoleum lay the black beads—the gold cross framed in the glimmering, wan glaze. Horror magnified the figure on it. He screamed.

"Papa! Papa! Leo—he gave them! That boy! It fell out! Papa!" His words were lost in the uproar.

"God's own hand! A sign! A witness!" his father was raving, whirling the whip in his flying arms. A proof of my word! The truth! Another's! A goy's! A cross! A sign of filth! Let me strangle him! Let me rid the world of a sin!"

"Put him out! Genya! Put him out! David! David! Him! Hurry! Let him run!" Aunt Bertha and Uncle Nathan were grappling with his father. "Hurry! Out!"

"No! No!" his mother's frenzied cry.

"Hurry! I say! Hurry! Help! We can't hold him!" Uncle Nathan had been shaken off. With knees bent, Aunt Bertha was hanging like a dead weight from his father's whip-hand. "He'll slay him," she shrieked. "He'll trample on him as he let his father be trampled on. Hurry, Genya!"

Screaming, his mother sprang toward the door—threw it open— "Run! Run down! Run! Run!"

She thrust him from her, slammed the door after him. He could hear the thud her body flung against it. With a wild shriek he plunged toward the stairs—

On the whole floor and even on the one below it, doors had been opened. Spears of gas-lamps crisscrossed in the unlit hallway. Gaping, craning faces peered out, listening, exclaiming, reporting to others behind them—

"Hey, boychick! Vus is? A fight! Hey vot's de maddch? Hooz hollerin'? Leibeleh! Dun' go op! You hea' vot I say. Dun go op! Oy! Cull a cop! Tek keh! Quick! Vehzee runnin'? Hey, boychick!"

A reeling smear of words, twitching gestures, fractured lights, features, a flickering gauntlet of tumult and dismay. He never answered, but plunged down. None stopped him. Only a miracle saved him from crashing down the dark steps. And now the voices were above him, and he heard feet trampling on the stairs, and now all noises merged to a flurried humming and now almost unheard—his down-drumming feet had reached the hallway—

Blue light in the door-frame.

Arms up and gasping like a runner to the tape—

The street.

The street. He dared to breathe. And stumbled to the sidewalk and stood there, stood there.

Dusk. Storelight and lamplight condensed—too early for assertion. The casual, canceled stir and snarling of distance. And on the sidewalks, men and women striding with too certain a gait, and in the gutter, children crossing, calling, not yet conceding the dark's dominion. The world dim-featured in mouldering light, floating, faceted and without dimension. For a moment the wild threshing of voices, bodies, the screams, the fury in the pent and shrunken kitchen split their bands in the brain, flew out to the darkened east, the flagging west beyond the elevated, the steep immensity of twilight that dyed the air above the housetops. For a moment, the rare coolness of a July evening dissolved all agony in a wind as light as with the passing of a wand. And suddenly there was space even between the hedges of stone and suddenly there was quiet even in the fret of cities. And there was time, inviolable even to terror, time to watch the smudged and cluttered russet in the west beckon to the night to cover it. A moment, but a moment only, then he whimpered and ran.

—Can't! Ow! Can't! Can't run! Can't! Hurts! Hurts! Ow! Legs! Mama!

He had no more than reached the corner when every racked fibre in his body screamed out in exhaustion. Each time his foot fell was like a plunger through his skull. On buckling legs, he crossed Avenue D, stopped, wobbling with faintness, rubbed his thighs.

—Can't go! Can't! Hurt! Ow! Mama! Mama!

Fearfully, he peered over his shoulder, eyes traveling upward. From the first to the third floor of his house, the lighted kitchens behind bedrooms cast their dull stain on the windows—one dusky brass, one fawn, one murky grey. A column of drab yet reassuring light—except his own on the fourth floor, still sullen, aloof and dark. He caught his breath in a new onslaught of terror. Waves of fear serried his breast and back—

—Ain't not yet! Ow! Fighting yet! Him! What's he doing! Mama! Mama! He's hitting! Ow! Can't run! Some place! Stay here! Find! Watch! Wait till— Wait! Wait! Scared! Hide! Some place . . . Where?

A short distance to his left, the closed dairy store between Ninth and Tenth was unlit. He stumbled toward it. Behind the barricade of milk cans chained to the cellar-railing, he crouched down on the store-step, fixed lifted, imploring eyes to his windows. Dark, still dark. Baleful, unrelenting, they hid yet betrayed the fury and disaster behind them. He moaned, bit his fingers in agony, stared about him with a wild, tortured gaze.

Across the street the bar of green light in the photography shop blazed out. People passed, leisurely, self-absorbed, and as they entered the radius of the light, it fixed them momentarily in caustic, carrion-green. None marked him there, but drifted by with too buoyant and too aimless a gait for his own misery, drifted by with bloated corroded faces, as if heaved in the swell of a weedy glare, as if lolling undersea. Too sick to endure it, he looked away, looked up.

—Dark yet up. Dark . . . First, second, third is light. Mine Dark. Dark mine only. Papa stop. Stop!, Stop, papa. Light it now. Ain't mad no more. Light it, mama. Now! One, two, three, now! One, two, three, now! Now! Aaa! Ain't! Ain't! Ow! Run away, mama! Don't let him! Run away! Here! Here I am! Run! Mama! Mama! Mama!

He whimpered.

A man, paunched, slow-footed, his bulky body rolling on baggy unbending knees drew near. Opposite David, he turned a slow head toward the light, palmed a strange, corrupt-purple splotch on his jowls, pinched his under lip and lumbered on.

—With the whip. The busted one. Here he hit too. Him like from wagon. And I gave it. Won't bust no more. If he—Don't let him! Don't let him! Run in! Bedroom! Hold door. Tight! Don't let go! Aunt Bertha! Uncle! You too! Hold it! Fast! Don't let him hit her! Hold it, Ow! Mama, Stop, Stop, papa! Please! Ow! Look! Is—dark— dark yet. Dark.

Beside him on the ground floor of the same house where he sat concealed, a window squawked, whirred open. And a man's voice in sing-song harangue:

"Aaa, dawn be a wise-guy! Hooz tuckin' f'om vinnin'! A dollar 'n' sexty fife gestern! A thuler 'n' sompt'n' —ova hadee cends—Sonday! An' Monday night in back f'om Hymen's taileh-shop, rummy, *tuh* sevendy. Oy, yuh sh'd die. An' I sez if yuh ken give a good dill, Abe, yuh sheoll dill in jail auraddy! An' if I luz again, a fire sol dich bald urtreffen!" The voice retreated.

—If it lights, so what? What'll I do? He'll ask me. What'll I do? What? What? Papa, nothing. I wanted . . . I wanted. What? The —The—on the floor. Beads. Fell out—pocket. What for you—? Ow! Papa, I don't know What? Why? He'll look. He'll say. Ball. Ball I wanted Ball? He'll say—ball? Yes. Ball. In my head. Ow! I can't tell. Must! In my head seen. Was. In the corner. By milk-stink baby car- riages. White. Wasn't scared. What? What? What? Yes. Wasn't scared. How I seen one once, when—When? Sword in the fire. Tenth Street. Ask the rabbi. Sword. In the crack light and he laughed. When I read that he—Fire. Light. When I read. Always scared till then— and they made me. Goyim by river. And They—So had. So lost. Wanted back, Papa! Papa! Wanted back. And he said yes. Leo. Like inside-outside guts burning. And he said would. Come out of box. Said God on—Wait, Papa! Papa! Don't hit! Don't! Ow! Didn't want a big one, only twentier. Littler even. Only nickel-big. Down under fished—like when—Ow! That's why, Papa! That's why! Didn't—Ow! Ain't! Ain't! Ain't lit yet! What'll I do? Ain't lit yet!

They had gathered across the street before the house beside the barber shop on the corner, boys, nimble, nervous and shrill. And one stood threateningly on the stoop while the rest crouched tensely on the curb—

"Wolf, are yuh ready?"

"I'm geddin' ouda bed!"

"Wolf, are yuh ready?"

"I'm goin' t' de sink!"

"Wolf, are yuh ready?"

"I'm washin' op mine face—"

With precious, mincing gait, two women approached, scanning with dead caressing flutter the dead faces of the men who passed them. Their cheeks in the vitriolic glare of the photography-shop window were flinty yet sagging; green light glazed the velvet powder, scummed the hectic rouge, livid over lurid. One, the nearest, swelling her bosom to the figment strand she lifted from it, sent a glancing beam at David from casual polished, putrescent eyes. They sauntered on trailing a languid wake of flesh and perfume, redolent for all the ten foot gap between them, emphasizing by denying their corruption.

—Milk—stink here too. Where? Cans, because. Milk—stink big cans. What's that—there by—cellar? What? Sword it—No! Don't care! Don't care! Mama! Mama!

"Wolf are yuh ready?"

"I'm putt'n' on my shoes—"

—If she runs, runs away. Don't look for me. Can't see. If she—like she said. Never see her again. Take, me, mamma! Don't run away! Mama! Here I am, Mama! By cans I'm hiding! By store! Dark yet—is dark. Dark always! She went already. Didn't look! Don't want to find me! Never! Never! She went! She went! Ow! Look someplace else Look! Look someplace! Sword by cans! No, ain't. Forgot! He forgot. Store-spoon, milk-spoon. Why! Ow! Mama! Mama! Ain't light! Never! Never!

"Wolf, are yuh ready?"

"I'm pudd'n on my drawz—"

"No fair! Hey, yuh pud on de drawz a'reddy!"

"Awri'! So I'm pudd'n' on my shoit!"

"Wolf, are—"

The clatter of a horse-car drowned them out. And from the window beside him loud and sudden laughter—

"A bluff, ha? Nisht by Mudjkih! Ha! Ha! Ha! Ha! Ven 'Erry says a full-house is a full—"

—If it was—! If it was a sword. So what? You're scared. Ain't not! You're scared! I ain't! I ain't! I ain't! Yes, you know because it ain't. Double dare me? Double dare me? You know it ain't? Could! Even if it ain't a sword, could go in the crack. Where it splashes, hold cup like where you held sword. You're scared. Triple dare me? Somebody'll see. Let 'em! Don't care! Can't get it out. Anyway. Cans too heavy—Can too. Empty. I triple dare you? Wait! Aaaa, knew you was scared. Wait! Three waits! No more! No more! Only three waits. No more! (He was muttering aloud now) "Yuh gonna lighd winder? Winder! Winder! Yuh gonna lighd winder?"

"Wolf, are yuh ready?"

"I'm tieingk op mine shoe-laces!"

—Winder, secon' chance! Yuh gonna lighd winder? I'll go! I'll go! Winder! Mama! Mama! I'll go!

He had risen to his feet. Once more his anguished eyes beseeched the window, and then a fit of horrible rage convulsed him and he writhed and beat the wall beside him. Seconds passed. The fit left him and he tasted the salt blood on his bitten lip and peered with a new, strange feeling of craftiness up and down the greenish street.

Humanity. On feet, on crutches, in carts and cars. The ice-vendor. The waffle-wagon. Human voices, motion, seething, throbbing, bawling, honking horns and whistling. Troubling the far clusters of street lamps, setting storelights guttering with their passing bodies like a wind. He shuddered, looked near at hand. Across the street, the wolf was crouching, ready to spring; the boys that baited him, twitched warily, giggled nervously at each cry. In the photography-shop, the enlarged pictures of age gazed out at him, mummified and horrible. From wall and sidewalk, lamplight and mercury vapor had crowded the gloaming into night; above the streets the hollow cobalt air dissolved heaven's difference with the roof tops. No one was watching him.

In hatred this time, in challenge, his eyes stabbed the window. Dark. He defied it.

Stealthily, he sidled to the nearest milk-can, took hold of the cover and handle. Under his palms, the metal was cold, the heavy can unwieldy, a shifting steely glimmer under his eyes. He leaned against it—

harder. It budged, sounded hollow. Again he braced himself, thrust—
Clank!

Wedged between the shoulder of the can and the cellar grill, the long, grey, milk-dipper clattered to the ground. He stooped to pick it up—

"Tadam, padam, pam! Thew! Thew! He had to get under, get out and get under—" With a jaunty, swaggering stride and nasal hum and toothy whistle, a tall, square-shouldered man drew abreast. "To fix up his little machine!" Between cap and black shirt, frosty green-blue eyes winked down at David, turned away, and passing, left their chill fire lingering in the air. "Pam! Pam! Prra! To fix up his little machine!"

The coast was clear now. Across the street, the children were shrieking with excitement. David picked up the dipper, crept out of the store entrance, and with the scoop of the dipper under his armpit, long, flat handle in his hand, he slunk quickly toward Tenth Street—

"Wolf are yuh ready!" their voices pursued him.

"I'm co-o-o-o-omin'—down—duh—st-o-o-op!"

—Goin'! I'm goin', winder! Winder! Winder! I'm goin'!

Uphill, the faint slope, steep to aching legs, he ran, avoiding the careless glance of the few who noticed. Tenth Street. A street car crossed the Avenue, going west. The river wind blew straight and salt between a flume of houses. He swung sharply into it, entered the river-block, dimlit, vacant. Ahead of him, like a barrier, the one beer-saloon, swinging door clamped in a vise of light, the mottled stained-glass window bulging with a shoddy glow.

—Somebody'll see.

He skulked in the shadows against the rough wall of the iron-works, crept forward. In the ebb of river-wind, the faint bitter flat beer spread round him. Gone in the quick neaping of wind—A man knuckles to mustache, flung back the swing-door—whirred reiteration of bar and mirror, bottles, figures, aprons—David slunk past him into deeper shadow.

And now the old wagon-yard, the lifted thicket of tongues; the empty stables, splintered runways, chalked doors, the broken windows holding still their glass like fangs in the sash, exhaling manure-damp, rank. The last street lamp droning in a cyst of light. The gloomy, massive warehouse, and beyond it, the strewn chaos of the dump heap stretching to the river. He stopped. And where a shadowy cove sank between warehouse wall and dump heap, retreated.

—Yuh dared me . . . Yuh double-dared me . . . Now I gotta.

The tracks lay before him—not in double rows now but in a single yoke. For where he stood was just beyond the work of the switch, and the last glitter on the tines lapsed into rust and rust into cobbles and cobbles merged with the shadowy dock and the river.

—Scared! Scared! Scared! Don't look!

He plucked his gaze away, tossed frenzied eyes about him. To the left, the chipped brick wall of the warehouse shut off the west and humanity, to the right and behind him, the ledge of the dump heap rose; before him land's end and the glitter on the rails.

—Yuh dared me . . . Yuh double-dared me . . . Now I gotta. I gotta make it come out.

The small sputter of words in his brain seemed no longer his own, no longer cramped by skull, but detached from him, the core of his surroundings. And he heard them again as though all space had compelled them and were shattered in the framing, and they boomed in his ears, vast, delayed and alien.

—Double-dared me! Now I gotta! Double-dared me! *Now I gotta make it come out.*

Inside the Royal Warehouse, located on the East River and Tenth Street, Bill Whitney, an old man with a massive body, short-wind and stiff, rheumatic legs, toiled up the stairway to the first floor. In his left hand, he held a lantern, which in his absent-mindedness, he jogged from time to time to hear the gurgle of its fuel. In his right hand, clacking on the bannister at each upward reach of his arm, he held a key—the key he turned the clocks with on every floor of the building—the proof of his watch and wakefulness. As he climbed the swart stairs, stained with every upward step by shallow, rocking lanternlight, he muttered, and this he did not so much to populate the silence with ephemeral, figment selves, but to follow the links of his own, slow thinking, which when he failed to hear, he lost:

"And wut? Haw! Ye looked down—and—sss! By Gawd if there waren't the dirt-rud under ye. And. Ha! Ha! Haw! No wheels. Them pedals were there—now waren't they? Saw 'em as clear—as clear—but the wheels gone—nowhere. By Gawd, thinks I— Now by Gawst, ain't it queer? Old Ruf Gilman a'standin' there, a'standin' and a'gappin'. Jest a'standin' and a'gappin' as plain— And the whiskers he growed afore the winter . . . By the well with the white housing. A'savin' his

terbaccer juice till he had nigh a cupful . . . Whawmmmmm! Went
plumb through the snaw in the winter . . ."

> *Resounded, surged and resounded, like*
> *ever swelling breakers:*
> *—Double! Double! Double dared me!*
> *Where there's light in the crack,*
> *yuh dared me. Now I gotta.*

In the blue, smoky light of Callahan's beer-saloon, Callahan, the
pale fattish bar-keep jammed the dripping beertap closed and leaned
over the bar and snickered. Husky O'Toole—he, the broad-shouldered
one with the sky-blue eyes—dominated those before the bar (among
them, a hunchback on crutches with a surly crimp to his mouth, and
a weazened coal-heaver with a sooty face and bright eye-balls) and
dwarfed them. While he spoke they had listened, grinning avidly.
Now he threw down the last finger of whiskey, nodded to the bartender, thinned his thin lips and looked about.

"Priddy wise mug!" Callahan prompted filling his glass.

"Well." O'Toole puffed out his chest. "He comes up fer air, see?
He's troo. Now, I says, now I'll tell yuh sompt'n about cunt— He's
still stannin' by de fawge, see, wit' his wrench in his han'. An I says,
yuh like udder t'ings, dontcha? Waddayuh mean, he says. Well, I
says, yuh got religion, aintcha? Yea, he says. An' I says, yuh play de
ponies, dontcha? Yea, he says. An' yuh like yer booze, dontcha? Sure,
he says. Well I says, none o' dem fer me! Waddayuh mean, he says.
Well, I says, yuh c'n keep yer religion, I says. Shit on de pope, I says—
I wuz jis' makin' it hot—an' t'hell witcher ponies I says—I bets on a
good one sometimes, but I wuzn' tellin' him—an' w'en it comes t'
booze I says, shove it up yer ass! Cunt for me, ev'ytime I says. See,
ev'ytime!"

They guffawed. "Yer a card!" said the coal heaver. "Yer a good
lad!—"

> *As though he had struck the enormous bell*
> *of the very heart of silence, he*
> *stared round in horror.*

"Gaw blimy, mate!" Jim Haig, oiler on the British tramp Eastern
Greyhound, (now opposite the Cherry Street pier) leaned over the
port rail to spit. "I ain't 'ed any fish 'n' chips since the day I left 'ome.
W'y ain't a critter thought of openin' a 'omely place in New York—
Coney Island fer instance. Loads o' prawfit. Taik a big cod now—"

> *Now! Now I gotta. In the crack,*
> *remember. In the crack be born.*

"Harrh! There's nights I'd take my bible-oath, these stairs uz higher." On the first floor, Bill Whitney stopped gazed out of the window that faced the East River. "Stinkin' heap out there!" And lifting eyes above the stove-in, enameled pots, cracked washtubs, urinals that glimmered in the back snarl, stared at the dark river striped by the gliding lights of a boat, shifted his gaze to the farther shore where scattered, lighted windows in factories, mills were caught like sparks in blocks of soot, and moved his eyes again to the south-east, to the beaded bridge. Over momentary, purple blossoms, down the soft incline, the far train slid like a trickle of gold. Behind and before, sparse auto headlights, belated or heralding dew on the bough of the night. "And George a'gappin' and me a'hollerin' and a'techin the ground with the toe of my boot and no wheels under me. Ha! Ha! Mmm! Wut cain't a man dream of in his sleep . . . A wheel . . . A bike . . ." He turned away seeking the clock. "And I ain't been on one . . . not sence . . . more'n thirty-five . . . forty years. Not since I uz a little shaver . . ."

> Clammy fingers traced the sharp edge of
> the dipper's scoop. Before his eyes
> the glitter on the car tracks whisked . . .
> reversed . . . whisked . . .

"Say, listen O'Toole dere's a couple o' coozies in de back." The bar-keep pointed with the beer knife. "Jist yer speed!"

"Balls!" Terse O'Toole retorted. "Wudjah tink I jist took de bull-durham sack off me pecker fer—nuttin'? I twisted all de pipes I wanna we'en I'm pissin'!"

"No splinters in dese boxes, dough. Honest, O'Toole! Real clean—"

"Let 'im finish, will ye!" the hunchback interrupted sourly. "O'Toole don' have to buy his gash."

"Well, he says, yea. An' I says yea. An' all de time dere wuz Steve an' Kelly unner de goiders belly-achin'—Hey trow us a rivet. An' I sez—"

> —Nobody's commin'

Klang! Klang! Klang! Klang! Klang!

The flat buniony foot of Dan MacIntyre the motorman pounded the bell. Directly in front of the clamorous car and in the tracks, the vendor of halvah, candied-peanuts, leechee nuts, jellied fruits, daw-dled, pushing his pushcart leisurely. Dan MacIntyre was enraged. Wasn't he blocks and blocks behind his leader? Hadn't his conductor been slow as shit on the bell? Wouldn't he get a hell of a bawling out from Jerry, the starter on Avenue A? And here was this lousy dago blocking traffic. He'd like to smack the piss out of him, he would. He pounded the bell instead.

Leisurely, leisurely, the Armenian peddler steered his cart out of the way. But before he cleared the tracks, he lifted up his clenched fist, high and pleasantly. In the tight crotch of his forefingers, a dirty thumb peeped out. A fig for you, O MacIntyre.

"God damn yuh!" He roared as he passed. "God blast yuh!"

> —So go! So go! So go!
> But he stood as still and rigid as
> if frozen to the wall, frozen fingers
> clutching the dipper.

"An' hawnest t'Gawd, Mimi, darlin'." The Family Entrance to Callahan's lay through a wide alley way lit by a red lamp in the rear. Within, under the branching, tendriled chandelier of alum-bronze, alone before a table beside a pink wall with roach-brown moundings, Mary, the crockery-cheeked, humid-eyed swayed and spoke, her voice being maudlin, soused and reedy. Mimi, the crockery-cheeked, crockery-eyed, a smudged blonde with straw-colored hair like a subway seat, slumped and listened. "I was that young an' innercent, an' hawnest t' Gawd, that straight, I brought it t' the cashier, I did. And, Eeee! she screams and ducks under the register, Eeee! Throw it away, yuh boob! But what wuz I t'know—I wuz on'y fifteen w'en I wuz a bus-goil. They left it on a plate—waa, the mugs there is in de woild—an' I thought it wuz one o' them things yuh put on yer finger w'en ye git a cut—"

"A cut, didja say, Mary, dea'?" The crockery cheeks cracked into lines.

"Yea a cut— a cu— Wee! Hee! Hee! Hee! Hee! Mimi, darlin' you're a comical! Wee! Hee! Hee! He! But I wuz that young an' innercent till he come along. Wee! Hee! Hee! Hawnes' t' Gawd I wuz. I could piss troo a beerbottle then—"

> Out of the shadows now, out on the dimlit, vacant
> street, he stepped down from the broken
> curb-stone to the cobbles. For all
> his peering, listening, starting, he
> was blind as a sleep-walker, he was
> deaf. Only the steely glitter on the
> tracks was in his eyes, fixed there like
> a brand, drawing him with cables as
> tough as steel. A few steps more and

he was there, standing between the
tracks, straddling the sunken rail.
He braced his legs to spring, held
his breath. And now the waving point
of the dipper's handle found the long,
dark, grinning lips, scraped, and
like a sword in a scabbard—

"Oy, Schmaihe, goy! Vot luck! Vot luck! You should only croak!"

"Cha! Cha! Cha! Dot's how I play mit cods!"

"Bitt him vit a flush! Ai, yi, yi!"

"I bet he vuz mit a niggerteh last night!"

"He rode a dock t' luzno maw jock—jeck I shidda said. Cha! Cha!"

"He's a poet, dis guy!"

"A putz!"

"Vus dere a hura mczda, Morr's?"

"Sharrop, bummer! Mine Clara is insite!"

Plunged! And he was running! Running!

"Nutt'n'? No, I says, nutt'n'. But every time I sees a pretty cunt come walkin' up de street, I says, wit' a mean shaft an' a sweet pair o' knockers, Jesus, O'Toole, I says, dere's a mare I'd radder lay den lay on. See wot I mean? Git a bed under den a bet on. Git me?"

"Haw! Haw! Haw! Bejeeziz!"

"Ya! Ha! He tella him, you know? He lika de fica stretta!"

They looked down at the lime-streaked, overalled wop condescendingly, and—

"Aw, bulloney," he says, "Yeah, I says. An' booze, I says, my booze is wut I c'n suck out of a nice tit, I says. Lallal'mmm, I says. An' w'en it comes t' prayin', I says, c'n yuh tell me anyt'ing bedder t' pray over den over dat one!" O'Toole hastily topped the laugh with a wave of his hand. "Yer an at'eist, yuh fuck, he hollers. A fuckin' at'eist I says— An' all de time dere wuz Steve and Kelly unner de goiders hollerin', hey trow us a riv—"

Running! But no light overtook him,
no blaze of intolerable flame. Only
in his ears, the hollow click of iron
lingered. Hollow, vain. Almost within
the saloon-light, he slowed down, sobbed
aloud, looked behind him—

"But who'd a thunk it?" Bill Whitney mounted the stairs again. "By Gawd, who'd a thunk it? The weeks I'd held that spike for 'im

. . . Weeks . . . And he druv and never a miss . . . Drunk? Naw, he warn't drunk that mornin'. Sober as a parson. Sober. A'swingin' of the twelve pound like a clock. Mebbe it was me that nudged it, mebbe it war me . . . By Gawd, I knowed it. A feelin' I had seein' that black sledge in the air. Afore it come down, I knowed it. A hull damned country-side it might of slid into. And it had to be me . . . Wut? It wuz to be? That cast around my leg? A pig's tit! It wuz to—"

> *Like a dipped metal flag or a gro-*
> *tesque armored head scrutinizing the*
> *cobbles, the dull-gleaming dipper's*
> *scoop stuck out from between the rail,*
> *leaning sideways.*
> *—Didn't. Didn't go in. Ain't lit. Go back.*
> *He turned—slowly.*
> *—No—body's—look—*

"Bawl? Say, did I bawl? Wot else'd a kid've done w'en her mont'ly don' show up—Say! But I'll get even with you, I said, I'll make a prick out of you too, like you done t' me. You wait! You can't get away with that. G'wan, he said, ye little free-hole, he called me. Wott're ye after? Some dough? Well, I ain't got it. That's all! Now quit hangin' around me or I'll s-smack ye one! He said."

"Where d'ja get it?"

"I borreed it—it wuzn't much. She called herself a m-mid-wife. I went by m-meself. My old-huhu—my old l-lady n-never—O Jesus!" Tears rilled the glaze.

"Say—toin off de tap, Mary, f'Gawd's sake!"

"Aw Sh-hu-hu-shut up! Can't I b-bawl if I—I—uh-hu-uh—G-go peddle yer h-hump, h-he says—"

"But not hea', Mary, f'r the lova Pete. We all gets knocked up sometimes—"

> *—Horry op! Horry op back!*

"They'll betray us!" Into the Tenth Street Crosstown car, slowing down at Avenue A, the voice of the pale, gilt-spectacled, fanatic face rang out above all other sounds: above the oozy and yearning "Open the door to Jesus" of the Salvation Army singing in the park; above the words of the fat woman swaying in the car as she said, "So the doctor said cut out all meat if you don't want gall-stones. So I cut out all meat, but once in a while I fried a little boloney with eggs—how I love it!" Above the muttering of the old grey-bearded Jewish peddler (he rocked his baby carriage on which pretzels lay stacked like quoits

on the upright sticks) "Founder of the universe, why have you teth-
ered me to this machine? Founder of the universe, will I ever earn
more than water for my buckwheat? Founder of the universe!" Above
the even enthusiasm of the kindly faced American woman: "And do
you know, you can go all the way up inside her for twenty-five cents.
For only twenty-five cents, mind you! Every American man, woman
and child ought to go up inside her, it's a thrilling experience. The
Statue of Liberty is—"

> *—He stole up to the dipper warily,*
> *on tip—*

"Shet up, down 'ere, yuh bull-faced harps, I says, wait'll I'm troo!
Cunt, I says, hot er snotty 'zuh same t' me. Dis gets 'em' hot. Dis gets
em hot I sez. One look at me, I says, an yuh c'n put dat rivet in yer
ice-box—t'ings 'll keep! Yuh reams 'em out with dat he says—kinda
snotty like. Shit no, I says I boins 'em out. W'y dontcha trow it t'dem,
he says, dey're yellin' fer a rivet. Aaa, I don' wanna bust de fuckin'
goider I says. Yer pretty good, he says. Good, I says, didja ever see dat
new tawch boinin' troo a goider er a flange er any fuck'n' hunka iron
—de spa'ks wot goes shootin' down—? Didja Well dat's de way 'I
comes. Dey tol' me so. An' all de time dere wuz Steve and Kelly
unner de goiders havin' a shit-hemorrage an' yellin' hey, t'row—"

> *toe, warily, glancing over his*
> *shoulders, on tip-toe, over serried*
> *cobbles, cautious—*

"Wuz t' be. And by Gawd it might hev gone out when I went to
bed a' suckin' of it. By Gawd it hed no call t' be burnin'. . . . Wuz
to be—Meerschaum, genuwine. Thankee I said. Thankee Miz Taylor.
And I stood on the back-stairs with the ice-tongs. Thankee and thank
the Doctor . . . Boston, the year I—Haw, by Gawd. And the hull
damn sheet afire. And Kate ascreamin' beside me . . . Gawd damn
it! It hadn't ought to 'a' done it . . . A'lookin' at me still now . . .
A'stretchin' of her neck in the white room . . . in the hospital—"

> *As though his own tread might shake the*
> *slanting handle loose from its perch*
> *beneath the ground. And now, and—*

"Why not? She asks me. Pullin' loaded dice on Lefty. The rat! He
can't get away with that y'know. I know, Mag, I said. It'd do my heart
good to see a knife in his lousy guts—only I gotta better idee. What?
She asks me. Spill it. Spill it is right, I says t' her. I know a druggist-
felleh, I said, good friend o' mine. O yea, she looks at me kinda funny.

Croak him with a dose o'—No! I said. No poison. Listen Mag. Throw a racket up at your joint, will ye? Give him an invite. He'll come. And then let me fix him a drink. And I winks at her. Dintcha ever hear o' the Spanish Fly—"

over it now, he crouched,
stretched out a hand to

"They'll betray us!" Above all these voices, the speaker's voice rose. "In 1789, in 1848, in 1871, in 1905, he who has anything to save will enslave us anew! Or if not enslave will desert us when the red cock crows! Only the laboring poor, only the masses embittered, bewildered, betrayed, in the day when the red cock crows, can free us!"

lift the dipper free. A sense almost
palpable, as of a leashed and imminent
and awful force

"You're de woist fuckin' liar I ever seen he sez an' ducks over de goiders."

focused on his hand across the hair-
breadth

"Yuh god mor'n a pair o' sem'ns?"

gap between his fingers and the
scoop. He drew

"It's the snug ones who'll preach it wuz to be."

back, straightened. Carefully bal—

"So I dropped it in when he was dancin'—O hee! Hee! Mimi! A healthy dose I—"

anced on his left, advance—

"Yeah. I sez, take your pants off."

ed his right foot—
Crritlkt!
—What?
He stared at the river, sprang away
from the rail and dove into the shad-
ows.

"Didja hear 'im, Mack? De goggle-eyed yid an' his red cock?"

The river? That sound! That sound
had come from there. All his senses
stretched toward the dock, grappled with
the hush and the shadow. Empty . . . ?

"Swell it out well with batter. Mate, it's a bloomin' goldmine! It's a cert! Christ knows how many chaps can be fed off of one bloody cod—"

Yes . . . empty. Only his hollow nos-
trils sifted out the stir in the
quiet; The wandering river-wind seamed
with thin scent of salt

"An' he near went crazy! Mimi I tell ye, we near bust, watchin—"
decay, flecked with clinging coal-tar—
Crrritlkt!

"Can't, he sez, I got a tin-belly."
—It's— Oh— It's—it's! Papa. Nearly
like. It's—nearly like his teeth.
Nothing . . . A barge on a slack hauser or
a gunwale against the dock chirping
because a

"I'll raise it."
boat was passing.
—Papa like nearly.
Or a door tittering to and fro in the wind.

"Heaz a can-opener fer ye I sez."
Nothing. He crept back.

"Hemm. These last durn stairs."
And was there, over the rail. The
splendor shrouded in the earth, the
titan, dormant in his lair, disdain-
ful. And his eyes

"Runnin' hee! hee! hee! Across the lots hee! hee! jerkin' off."
lifted

"An' I picks up a rivet in de tongs an' I sez—"
and there was the last crossing of
Tenth Street, the last cross—

"Heazuh a flowuh fer ye, yeller-belly, shove it up yer ass!"
ing, and beyond, beyond the elevateds,

"How many times'll your red cock crow, Pete, befaw y' gives up?
T'ree?"
as in the pit of the west, the last

"Yee! hee! hee! Mary, joikin'—"
smudge of rose, staining the stem of

"Nawthin' t' do but climb—"
the trembling, jagged

"Show culluh if yuh god beddeh!"
chalice of the night-taut stone with

"An' I t'rows de fuck'n' rivet."

the lees of day. And his toe crooked into
the dipper as into a stirrup. It
grated, stirred, slid, and—

"Dere's a star fer yeh! Watch it! T'ree Kings I god. Dey came on huzzbeck! Yee! Hee Hee! Mary! Nawthin' to do but wait fer day light and go home. To a red cock crowin'. Over a statue of. A jerkin'. Cod. Clang Clang! Oy! Machine! Liberty! Revolt! Redeem!"

Power

Power! Power like a paw, titanic power,
ripped through the earth and slammed
against his body and shackled him
where he stood. Power! Incredible,
barbaric power! A blast, a siren of light
within him, rending, quaking, fusing his
brain and blood to a fountain of flame,
vast rockets in a searing spray! Power!
The hawk of radiance raking him with
talons of fire, battering his skull with
a beak of fire, braying his body with
pinions of intolerable light. And he
writhed without motion in the clutch of
a fatal glory, and his brain swelled
and dilated till it dwarfed the galaxies
in a bubble of refulgence—Recoiled, the
last screaming nerve clawing for survival.
He kicked—once. Terrific rams of dark-
ness collided; out of their shock space
toppled into havoc. A thin scream wobbled
through the spirals of oblivion, fell like
a brand of water, his-s-s-s-s-ed—

"W'at

     "W'ut?

          "Va-at?

               "Gaw blimey!

       "W'atsa da ma'?"

The street paused. Eyes, a myriad of eyes, gay or sunken, rheumy, yellow or clear, slant, blood-shot, hard, boozy or bright swerved from their tasks, their play, from faces, newspapers, dishes, cards, seidels, valves, sewing machines, swerved and converged. While at the foot of Tenth Street, a quaking splendor dissolved the cobbles, the grimy

structures, bleary stables, the dump-heap, river and sky into a single cymbal-clash of light. Between the livid jaws of the rail, the dipper twisted and bounced, consumed in roaring radiance, candescent—
                              "Hey!"
          "Jesus!"
"Give a look! Id's rain—
                    "Shawt soicit, Mack—"
                    "Mary, w'at's goin'—"
                    "Schloimee, a blitz like—"
                    "Hey mate!"
On Avenue D, a long burst of flame spurted from underground, growled as if the veil of earth were splitting. People were hurrying now, children scooting past them, screeching. On Avenue C, the lights of the trolley-car waned and wavered. The motorman cursed, feeling the power drain. In the Royal Warehouse, the blinking watchman tugged at the jammed and stubborn window. The shriveled coal-heaver leaned unsteadily from between the swinging door—blinked, squinted in pain, and—
"Holy Mother O' God! Look! Will yiz!"
"Wot?"
"There's a guy layin' there! Burrhnin'!"
"Naw! Where!"
                    "Gawd damn the winder!"
              "It's on Tent' Street! Look!"
"O'Toole!"
The street was filled with running men, faces carved and ghostly in the fierce light. They shouted hoarsely. The trolley-car crawled forward. Up above a window slammed open.
"Christ, it's a kid!"
"Yea!"
      "Don't touch 'im!"
"Who's got a stick!"
                    "A stick!"
"A stick, fer Jesus sake!"
      "Mike! The shovel! Where's yer fuck'n' shov—"
"Back in Call—"
                    "Oy sis a kind—"
                    "Get Pete's crutch! Hey Pete!"
"Aaa! Who touched yer hump, yuh gimpty fu—"
                    "Do sompt'n! Meester! Meester!"

"Yuh crummy bastard, I saw yuh sneakin'—" The hunchback whirled, swung away on his crutches. "Fuck yiz!"

"Oy! Oy vai! Oy vai! Oy vai!"

"Git a cop!"

"An embillance—go cull-oy!"

"Don't touch 'im!"

"Bambino! Madre mia!"

"Mary. It's jus' a kid!"

"Helftz! Helftz! Helftz Yeedin! Rotivit!"

A throng ever thickening had gathered, confused, paralyzed, babbling. They squinted at the light, at the outstretched figure in the heart of the light, tossed their arms, pointed, clawed at their cheeks, shoved, shouted, moaned—

"Hi! Hi down there! Hi!" A voice bawled down from the height. "Look out below! Look out!"

The crowd shrank back from the warehouse.

W-w-whack!

"It's a—"

"You take it!"

"Grab it!"

"Gimme dat fuck'n' broom!"

"Watch yerself, O'Toole!"

"Oy, a good men! Got should—"

"Oooo! De pore little kid, Mimi!"

"He's gonna do it!"

"Look oud!

"Dunt touch!"

The man in the black shirt, tip-toed guardedly to the rails. His eyes, screwed tight against the awful glare, he squinted over his raised shoulder.

"Shove 'im away!"

"Go easy!"

"Look odda!"

"Atta boy!"

"Oy Gottinyoo!"

The worn, blackened broom straws wedged between the child's shoulder and the cobbles. A twist of the handle. The child rolled over on his face.

"Give 'im anudder shove!"

"At's it! Git 'im away!"

"Quick! Quick!"

Once more the broom straws rammed the outstretched figure. He slid along the cobbles, cleared the tracks. Someone on the other side grabbed his arm, lifted him, carried him to the curb. The crowd swirled about in a dense, tight eddy.

"Oy! Givalt!"

"Gib'm air!"

"Is 'e boined?"

"Bennee stay by me!"

"*Is* 'e boined! Look at his shoe!"

"Oy, de pooh mama! De pooh mama!"

"Who's kid?"

"Don' know, Mack!"

"Huz pushin'?"

"Jesus! Take 'im to a drug-store."

"Naa, woik on 'im right here. I woiked in a power house!"

"Do sompt'n! Do sompt'n!"

The writhing dipper was now almost consumed. Before the flaring light, the weird white-lipped, staring faces of the milling throng wheeled from chalk to soot and soot to chalk again—like masks of flame that charred and were rekindled; and all their frantic, gnarling bodies cut a carting splay of huge, impinging shadow, on dump-heap, warehouse, river and street—

Klang! The trolley drew up.

"Oyeee! Ers toit! Ers to-i-t! Oye-e-e-e!" A woman screamed, gagged, fainted.

"Hey! Ketch 'er!"

"Schleps aveck!"

"Wat d' hell'd she do dat fer—"

"Vawdeh!"

They dragged her away on scuffing heels to one side.

"Shit!" The motorman had jumped down from the car and seized the broom—

"Fan 'er vid de het!"

"Git off me feet, you!"

"At's it! Lean on 'im O'Toole! Push 'im down! At's it! At's it! I woiked in a power house—"

And with the broom straws the motorman flipped the mangled metal from the rail. A quake! As if leviathan leaped for the hook and fell back threshing. And darkness.

Darkness!

They grunted, the masses, stood suddenly mute a moment, for a moment silent, stricken, huddled, crushed by the pounce of ten-fold night. And a voice spoke, strained, shrunken, groping—

"Ey, paizon! She 'sa whita yet—lika you looka da slacka lime alla time! You know?"

Someone shrieked. The fainting woman moaned. The crowd muttered, whispered, seething uneasily in the dark, welcomed the loud newcomers who pierced the dense periphery—

"On side! One side!" Croaking with authority, the stone-grim uniformed one shouldered his way through. "One side!"

"De cops!"

"Dun't step on 'im!"

"Back up youz! Back up! Didja hea' me, Moses? Back up! Beat it! G'wan!" They fell back before the perilous arc of the club. "G'wan before I fan yiz! Back up! Let's see sompt'n' in hea'! Move! Move, I say!" Artificial ire flung the spittle on his lips. "Hey George!" He flung at a burly one. "Give us a hand hea, will yiz!"

"Sure! Git back you! Pete! Git that other side!"

The policeman wheeled round, squatted down beside the black-shirted one. "Don' look boined."

"Jist his shoe."

"How long wuz he on?"

"Christ! I don't know. I came ouda Callahan's an' de foist t'ing I know somebody lams a broom out of a winder, an' I grabs it an' shoves 'im off de fuck'n t'ing—"

"Sh! Must a done it himself— Naa! Dat ain't de way! Lemme have 'im." He pushed the other aside, turned the child over on his face. "Foist aid yuh gits 'em hea." His bulky hands all but encompassed the narrow waist. "Like drownin', see?" He squeezed,

Khir-r-r-f! S-s-s-s-.

"I hoid 'im!"

"Yeah!"

"He's meckin' him t' breed!"

"See? Gits de air in 'im."

Khir-r-r-f! S-s-s-s.

"Looks like he's gone, do. W'ere de hell's dat ambillance?"

"Vee culled id a'reddy, Ufficeh!"

"Arh!"

"Rap 'im on de feet arficer, I woiked in a power—"

Khir-r-r-r-f! S-s-s-s

"Anybody know 'im? Any o' youz know dis kid?"

The inner and the craning semi-circle muttered blankly. The policeman rested his ear against the child's back.

"Looks like he's done fer, butchuh can't tell—"

Khir-r-r-r-f! S-s-s-s.

"He sez he's dead, Mary."

"Dead!"

"Oy! Toit!"

"Gott sei donk, id's nod, mine Elix—"

Khir-r-r-r-f. S-s-s-s.

"Sit im helfin vie a toitin bankis." The squat shirt-sleeved Jew whose
tight belt cut his round belly into the letter B turned to the lime-
streaked wop—squinted, saw that communication had failed. "It'll
help him like cups on a cawps," he translated—and tapped his chest
with an ace of spades.

Khi-r-r-r-f. S-s-s-s.

(*E-e-e-e. E-e-e-e-.*

One ember fanned . . . dulling . . . uncertain)

"Here's the damned thing he threw in, Cap." The motorman shook
off the crowd, held up the thinned and twisted metal.

"Yea! Wot is it?"

"Be damned if I know. Hol! Jesus!"

Khir-r-r-f. S-s-s.

(*E-e-e-e-e.*

*Like the red pupil of the eye of darkness, the ember dilated, spun
like a pinwheel, expanding, expanding, till at the very core, a
white flaw rent the scarlet tissue and spread, engulfed the margin
like a stain—*)

"Five hundred an' fifty volts. What a wallop!"

"He's cooked, yuh t'ink?"

"Yea. Jesus! What clse!"

"Unh!" The policeman was grunting now with his efforts.

Kh-i-r-r-r-f! S-s-s-s.

"Hey, Meester, maybe he fell on id—

De iron—"

"Sure, dot's righd!"

"Id's f'om de compeny de fault!"

"Ass, how could he fall on it, fer the love O Jesus!"

The motorman turned on them savagely.

"He could! Id's easy!"

"Id vuz stink—stick—sticken oud!"

"He'll sue, dun' vorry!"

"Back up, youz!"

Khi-r-r-r-f! S-s-s.

> *(Eee-e-e-e*
> *And in the white, frosty light within*
> *the red iris, a small figure slanted*
> *through a desolate street, crack-paved,*
> *rut-guttered, slanted and passed, and*
> *overhead the taut, wintry wires whined*
> *on their crosses—*
> *E-e-e-e.*
> *They whined, spanning the earth and sky.*
> *—Go-d-d-b! Go-o-o-ob! G-o-o-b! G'bye! . . .)*

"Makin' a case fer a shyster. C'n yuh beat it!"

"Ha-a-ha! Hunh!"

"I'm late. Dere it is." The motorman dropped the gnarled and blackened dipper beside the curb.

"An Irisher chuchim!"

"Ain't it a dirty shame—"

"Noo vud den!"

"Wat's happened, chief?"

"Dere give a look!"

"Let's git troo dere!"

"Unh!"

Kh-i-r-r-r-f! S-s-s-s.

> *(—G'by-e-e. Mis-s-s-l-e. M-s-ter. Hi-i-i-i.*
> *Wo-o-o-d.*
> *And a man in a tugboat, hair under*
> *arm-pits, hung from a pole among the*
> *wires, his white undershirt glittering.*
> *He grinned and whistled and with every*
> *note yellow birds flew to the roof.)*

"T'ink a shot o' sompt'n' 'll do 'im any good?"

"Nuh! Choke 'im if he's alive."

"Yeh! If hiz alife!"

"W'ea's 'e boined?"

"Dey say id's de feet wid de hen's wid eveytingk."

"Unh!"

Khi-r-r-r-f! S-s-s-s.

> (We-e-e-e-
> *The man in the wires stirred. The*
> *Wires twanged brightly. The blithe*
> *and golden cloud of birds filled the*
> *sky.*)

"Unh!"

> (Klang!
> *The milk tray jangled. Leaping he*
> *neared. From roof-top to roof-top,*
> *over streets, over alley ways, over*
> *areas and lots, his father soared with*
> *a feathery ease. He set the trays*
> *down, stooped as if searching, paused—*)

"Unh!"

> (A *hammer! A hammer! He snarled,*
> *brandished it, it snapped like a whip.*
> *The birds vanished. Horror thickened*
> *the air.*)

"Unh!"

> "He's woikin' hard!"
> "Oy! Soll im Gott helfin!"
> "He no waka."

> (Around *him now, the cobbles stretched*
> *away. Stretched away in the swirling*
> *dark like the faces of a multitude aghast*
> *and frozen*)

"Unh!"

> (W-e-e-e-e-p! Weep! Overhead the
> *brandished hammer whirred and whistled.*
> *The doors of a hallway slowly opened.*
> *Buoyed up by the dark, a coffin drifted*
> *out, floated down the stoop, and while*
> *confetti rained upon it, bulged and*
> *billowed—*)

"Unh!"

Khi-r-r-r-rf! S-s-s-s-

> (—Zwank! Zwank! Zwank!
> *The man in the wires writhed and*
> *groaned, his slimy, purple chicken-*

guts slipped through his fingers.
David touched his lips. The soot
came off on his hand. Unclean.
Screaming, he turned to flee, seized
a wagon wheel to climb upon it. There
were no spokes—only cogs like a
clock-wheel. He screamed again, beat
the yellow disk with his fists.)

"Unh!"

Kh-i-r-r-rf! S-s-s-s.

"Didja see it?"

"See it? Way up on twelft'!"

"I could ivin see id in de houz—on de cods."

"Me? I vas stand in basement—fok t'ing mack blind!"

"Five hundred an' fifty volts."

(*As if on hinges, blank, enormous*
mirrors arose, swung slowly upward
face to face. Within the facing
glass, vast panels deployed, lifted a
steady wink of opaque pages until
an endless corridor dwindled into
night.)

"Unh! Looks Jewish t' me."

"Yeah, map o' Jerusalem, all right."

"Poor bastard! Unh!"

"Couldn't see him at foist!"

"Unh!"

Kh-ir-r-rf! S-s-s-s.

(*"You!" Above the whine of the*
whirling hammer, his father's voice
thundered. "You!"
David wept, approached the glass,
peered in. Not himself was there,
not even in the last and least of
the infinite mirrors, but the cheder
wall, the cheder)

"Junheezis!"

Kh-i-r-r-rf! S-s-s-s.

(*Wall sunlit, white-washed. "Chadgodya!"*
moaned the man in the wires. "One

> *kid only one kid." And the wall dwindled*
> *and was a square of pavement with a foot-*
> *print in it—half green, half black,*
> *"I too have trodden there." And*
> *shrank within the mirror, and the*
> *cake of ice melted in the panel be-*
> *yond. "Eternal years," the voice*
> *wailed, "Not even he.")*

"Unh!"

    "Gittin' winded? Want me to try it?"

"Nunh!"

    "Look at 'im sweat!"

      "Vy not? Soch a coat he's god on!"

    "Wot happened, brother?"

    "Cheh! He esks yet!"

    "Back up, you!"

"Unh!"

   Kh-i-r-r-r-f! S-s-s-s.

> *(And faded, revealing a shoe box full*
> *of calendar leaves, "the red day must*
> *come.")*

"Unh! Did he move or sumpt'n?"

 "Couldn't see."

> *(which lapsed into a wooden box with*
> *a sliding cover like the chulk-boxes*
> *in school, whereon a fiery figure*
> *sat astride a fish. "G-e-e-e o-o-o d-e-e-e-!"*
> *The voice spelled out. And shrank and was*
> *a cube of sugar gripped be-)*

"Unh!"

   Kh-i-r-r-r-f! S-s-s-s.

       "Shah! Y'hea id?"

       "W'a?"

      "Yea! It's commin!"

       "Id's commin'!"

       "I sees it!"

  "Meester Politsman de—"

  "Back up, youz!"

A faint jangle seeped through the roar of the crowd.

"Unh!"

(tween the softly glowing tongs. "So
wide we stretch no further—" But when
he sought to peer beyond, suddenly the
mirrors shifted, and—
"Go down!" his father's voice thun-
dered, "Go down!" The mirrors lay
beneath him now; what were the groins
now jutted out in stairs, concentric
ogives, bottomless steps. "Go down!"
Go down!" The inexorable voice beat
like a hand upon his back. He
screamed, de—)

     Jangle! Angle! Angle! Angle!
    "Dere! It's comin'!"
  "Look! Look hod dere!"
 "Orficer!"
Angle! Jang!
"Christ's about time!"

  The crowd split like water before a prow, reformed
in the wake, surged round the ambulance, babbling,
squall—

(scended. Down! Down into darkness,
darkness that tunneled the heart of
darkness, darkness fathomless. Each
step he took, he shrank, grew smaller
with the unseen panels, the graduate
vise descending, passed from stage
to dwindling stage, dwindling. At
each step shed the husks of being,
and himself tapering always downward
in the funnel of the night. And now
a chip—a step-a flake-a step-a shred.
A mote. A pinpoint. And now the seed
  of nothing, and nebulous nothing, and
  nothing. And he was not. . . .)

ing, stabbing the dark with hands. "Ppprrr!" Lips flickered audibly as
the blue-coat rose. With one motion, palm wiped brow, dug under
sweat-stained collar. Softly bald, the bareheaded, white garbed interne
hopped spryly from the ambulance step, black bag swinging in hand,

wedged whitely through the milling crowd. Conch-like the mob surrounded, contracted, trailed him within the circle, umbiliform—

"Lectric shot; Doc!"

"De hospital!"

"Knocked him cold!"

"Shock?"

" 'Zee dead?"

"Yea, foolin' aroun' wid de—"

"Shawt soicited it, Doc!"

"Yea, boined!"

"Vee sin id Docteh!"

"Git back, youz!" The officer crouched, snarled, but never sprang.
"I'll spit right in yer puss!"

"Mmm!" The interne pinched the crease of his trousers, pulled
them up, and kneel—

"Guess yuh better take 'im witchuh, Doc. Couldn't do a goddam
t'ing wit—"

"He's gonna hea' de heart! See?"

(*But—*)

ing beside the beveled curbstone, applied his ear to the narrow breast.

"Shoe's boined. See it, Doc?"

(*the voice still lashed the nothingness
that was, denying it oblivion. "Now find!
Now find! Now find!" And nothingness
whimpered being dislodged from night,
and would have hidden again. But out
of the darkness, one ember*)

"Take it off, will you, let's have a look at it."

(*flowered, one ember in a mirr—*)

"Sure!" Blunt, willing fingers ripped the

(*or, swimming without motion in the
motion of its light.*)

buttons open,

"Hiz gonna look."

(*In a cellar is*)

dragged the shoes off,

(*Coal! In a cellar is*)

tore the stocking down, re—

(*Coal! And it was brighter than the*)

pith of lightning and milder than pearl,)
vealing a white puffy ring about the ankle, at
   (And made the darkness dark because
   the dark had culled its radiance for
   that jewel. Zwank!)
       "Is it boined?"
       "Can't see, c'n you?"
which the interne glanced while he drew
  "Waddayuh say, Doc?"
a squat blue vial from his bag, grimaced, un-
   (Zwank! Zwank! Nothingness beati-
   fied reached out its hands. Not cold
   the ember was. Not scorching. But as
   if all eternity's caress were fused and
   granted in one instant. Silence)
corked it, expertly tilted it before
   (struck that terrible voice upon the
   height, stilled the whirling hammer.
   Horror and the night fell away. Ex-
   alted, he lifted his head and screamed
   to him among the wires—"Whistle,
   mister! Whistle!)
the quiet nostrils. The crowd fell silent, tensely watching.
  "Amonya."
       "Smells strong!"
       "Stinks like in de shool on Yom Kippur."
   (Mister! Whistle! Whistle! Whistle!
   Whistle, Mister! Yellow birds!)
On the dark and broken sidewalk, the limp body gasped, quivered.
The interne lifted him, said sharply to the officer. "Hold his arms!
He'll fight!"
       "Hey look! Hey look!"
       "He's kickin'!"
  (Whistle, mister! WHISTLE!")
"W'at's he sayin'?"
"There! Hold him now!"
  (A spiked star of pain of conscious-
  ness burst within him)
       "Mimi! He's awright! He's awright!"
        "Yeh?"

"Yea!"

"No kiddin'! No kiddin'!"

"Yeh!"

"Yuh!"

"Yeh!"

"Oi, Gott sei dank!"

"THERE you are, sonny! There you are!" The interne's reassuring drawl, reached him through a swirl of broken images. "You're not hurt. There's nothing to be scared about."

"Sure!" the policeman was saying beside him.

David opened his eyes. Behind, between them and around them, like a solid wall, the ever-encroaching bodies, voices, faces at all heights, gestures at all heights, all converging upon him, craning, peering, haranguing, pointing him out, discussing him. A nightmare! Deliverance was in the thought. He shut his eyes trying to remember how to wake.

"How does that foot feel, sonny?" The routine, solicitous voice again inquired. "Not bad, eh?"

He was aware for the first time of the cool air on his naked leg, and below it a vague throbbing at the ankle. And once aware, he couldn't shake off the reality of it. Then it wasn't a dream. Where had he been? What done? The light. No light in the windows upstairs . . . His father. His mother. The quarrel. The whip. Aunt Bertha, Nathan, the rabbi, the cellar, Leo, the beads—all swooped upon him, warred for preeminence in his brain. No. It wasn't a dream. He opened his eyes again, hoping reality would refute conviction. No it wasn't a dream. The same two faces leaned over him, the same hedge of humanity focused eyes on his face.

"Looks like he's still too weak," said the interne.

"Yuh goin' t'take him wid ye?"

"No!" Grimacing emphatically, the interne shut the black bag. "Why, he'll be able to walk in less than five minutes. Just as soon as he gets his breath. Where does he live?"

"I don' know. None o' dese guys know— Say, w'ere d'yuh live? Huh? Yuh wanna go home, dontchuh?"

"N-nint' street." He quavered. "S-sebm fawdynine."

"Nint' Street." The crowd reechoed. "Say ufficeh," a coatless man came forward. "Det's on de cunner Evenyuh D."

"I know! I know!" The policeman waved him back with surly hand. "Say, Doc, will ye give us a lift."

"Sure. Just pick him up."

"Yea, ooops! Dere ye go!" Burly arms went under his knees and back, lifted him easily, carried him through the gaping crowd to the ambulance. His head swam again with the motion. He lay slack on a long leather cot between greenish walls, aware of faces whisking by the open doorway, peering in. The interne seated himself at the back, called to the driver. The bell clanged, and as the wagon jolted forward, the policeman mounted the low step in the rear. Behind the ambulance, rolling on rubber-tired wheels on the cobbles, he could hear the voices calling the way. "Nint' Street! Nint' Street!" The throb in his ankle was growing in depth, in dullness of pain, permeating upward like an aching tide within the marrow. What had he done? What had he done? What would they say when they brought him upstairs. His father, what—? He moaned.

"That doesn't hurt you that much, does it?" asked the interne cheerily. "You'll be running around to-morrow."

"Yer better off den I tawt ye'd be," said the policeman behind him. "Cheezis, Doc, I sure figgered he wuz cooked."

"No. The shock went through the lower part. That's what saved him. I don't see why he was out so long anyway. Weak, I guess."

Behind beating hooves and jangling bell, he felt the ambulance round the corner at Avenue D. The policeman turned to look behind him and then squinted sideways at David's foot.

"His shoes wuz boined in front. An' he's got it up on de ankle."

"Narrowest part."

"I see. Dat'll loin yuh a lesson, kid." He disengaged one hand from the ambulance wall to wave a severe finger at David. "Next time I'll lock yiz up. Wot flaw d'yuh live on?"

"T-top flaw."

"Would have t'be," he growled disgustedly. "Next time I will lock yiz up—making me woik, an' takin' de Doc away from a nice pinocle game. Wot dese goddam kids can't t'ink of. Geez!"

The ambulance had rounded the second corner and came to a stop. Grinning, the interne leaped down. Stooping over and grunting as he stooped, the policeman lifted him in his arms again and bore him quickly through the new throng that came streaming around the corner. On the stoop, several children recognized him and bawled excitedly, "It's Davy! It's Davy!" A woman in the gaslit corridor cradled cheek in palm in terror and backed away. They mounted the stairs, the interne behind them and behind him remnants of the crowd, children of the house, following eagerly at a wary distance, jabbering, calling to him, "Watsa maddeh? Watsa maddeh, Davy?" Door opened on the landings. Familiar heads poked out. Familiar voices shrilled at others across the hallway. "It's him! F'om opstehs. Veh de fighd voz!" As they neared the top the policeman had begun breathing heavily, shedding thick hot breath on David's cheek, grunting, the lines on his scowling, tough, red face deep with exertion.

The top floor. David's eyes flashed to the transom. It was lit. They were in. What would they say? He moaned again in terror.

"Where is it?" the red face before him puffed.

"Over—over dere!" he quavered weakly.

The door. The arm under his knees slid forward. Beefy knuckles rapped, sought the knob. Before an answer came, the door, nudged forward by his own thighs, swung open.

Before him stood his mother, looking tense and startled, her hand resting on his father's shoulders, and below seated, his father, cheek on fist, eyes lifted, sourly glowering, affronted, questioning with taut and whiplike stare. The others were gone. It seemed to David that whole ages passed in the instant they regarded each other frozen in their attitudes. And then just as the policeman began to speak, his mother's hand flew to her breast, she gasped in horror, her face went agonizingly white, contorted, and she screamed. His father threw his chair back, sprang to his feet. His eyes bulged, his jaw dropped, he blanched.

For the briefest moment David felt a shrill, wild surge of triumph whip within him, triumph that his father stood slack-mouthed, finger-clawing, stooped, and then the room suddenly darkened and revolved. He crumpled inertly against the cradling arms.

"David! David!" His mother's screams pierced the reeling blur. "David! David! Beloved! What is it? What's happened?"

"Take it easy, missiz! Take it easy!" He could feel the policeman's elbow thrust out warding her off. "Give us a chanst, will yuh! He ain't hoit! He ain't a bit hoit! Hey Doc!"

The interne had stepped between them and David staring weakly through the sickening murk before his eyes, saw him pushing her resolutely away. "Now! Now! Don't get him excited, lady! It's bad! It's bad for him! You're frightening him! Understand? Nicht ver—Schlect! Verstehen sie?"

"David! My child!" Unhearing, she still moaned, frantically, hysterically, one hand reached out to him, the other clutching her hair. "Your foot! What is it, child! What is it darling?"

"Put him down on the bed!" The interne motioned impatiently to the bedroom. "And listen, Mister, will you ask her to stop screaming. There's nothing to worry about! The child is in no danger! Just weak!"

"Genya!" his father started as if he were jarred. "Genya!" He exclaimed in Yiddish. "Stop it! Stop it! He says nothing's wrong. Stop it!"

From outside the door, the bolder ones in the crowd of neighbors that jammed the hallway had overflowed into the kitchen and were stationing themselves silently or volubly along the walls. Some as they jabbered pointed accusingly at David's father and wagged their heads significantly. And as David was borne into the bedroom, he heard one whisper in Yiddish, "A quarrel! They were quarreling to death!" In the utterly welcome half-darkness of the bedroom he was stretched out on the bed. His mother, still moaning, had followed, and behind her his restraining hand upon her shoulder came the interne. Behind them the upright, squirming bodies, pale, contorted faces of neighbors clogged the doorway. A gust of fury made him clench his hands convulsively. Why didn't they go away? All of them! Why didn't they stop pointing at him?

"I was just this minute going down!" his mother was wringing her hands and weeping, "Just this minute I was going down to find you! What is it darling? Does it hurt you? Tell me—"

"Aw, Missiz!" the policeman flapped his hands in disgust. "He's all right. Be reasonable, will yiz! Just a liddle boined, dat's all. Just a liddle boined. Cantchuh see dere's nutt'n' wrong wid 'im!"

She stared at him uncomprehendingly.

"Schreckts ach nisht! Schreckts ach nisht!" The chorus of women in the doorway translated raggedly. "Sis im goor nisht geshehen! S' goor nisht geferlich!"

"Dat's it, you tell her!" The policeman shouldered his way through the door.

The interne had undressed him, pulled the covers down and tucked him in. The smooth sheets felt cool on his throbbing foot.

"Now!" He straightened, turned decisively to David's mother. "You can't help him by crying, lady. If you want to help him go make him some tea. A lot of it."

"Kein gefahr?" she asked dully, disbelievingly.

"Yes! Yes! That's right!" he answered impatiently. "Kein gefahr! Now make him some tea."

"Teh, Mrs. Schearl," a woman in the doorway came forward. "Geh macht eem teh!"

"Teh?"

"Yes! Teh!" the interne repeated. "Quick! Schnell! Yes?"

She turned numbly. The woman offered to help her. They went out.

"Well, how's the kid?" the interne grinned down at him. "Feel good?"

"Y-yeh."

"That's the boy! You'll be all right in a little while."

He turned to leave. A fattish, bare-armed woman stood at his shoulder. David recognized her. She lived on the same floor.

"Ducktuh!" she whispered hurriedly. "Yuh shoulda seen vod a fighd dere vus heyuh!" She contracted, rocked. "Oy-yoy! Yoy-u-yoy! Him, dat man, his faddeh, he vus hittin' eem! Terrible! A terrhible men! En' dere vus heyuh his cozzins—oder huh cozzins—I don't know! En' dey vus fighdingk. Oy-yoy-yoy! Vid scrimms! Vid holleringk! Pwww-eeyoy! En' den dey chessed de boy all oud f'om de house. En den dey chessed de odder two pipples! En' vee vus listeningk, en' dis man vos crying. Ah'm khrezzy! Ah'm khrezzy! I dun know vod I do! I dun' know vod I said! He ses. Ah'm khrezzy! En' he vus cryingk! Oy!"

"Is that so?" the interne said indifferently.

"Id vus terrhible! Terrhible! En' Ducktuh," she patted his arm. "Maybe you could tell me fah vy my little Elix dun eat? I give him eggks vid milk vid kulleh gedillehs. En de don' vonna eat nottingk. Vod sh'd I do?"

"I don't know." He brushed by her. "You'd better see a doctor."

"Oy bist du a chuchim!" she spat after him in Yiddish. "Does the breath of your mouth cost you something?"

His mother returned. Her hair was disheveled. Tears still stained her cheek though she had stopped crying. "You'll have some tea in a minute, darling." A tremulous gasp of after-weeping shook her. "Does your foot hurt very much?"

"N-no," he lied.

"They told me you were at the car-tracks," she shuddered. "How did you come there? You might have been— Oh! God forbid! What made you go? What made you do it?"

"I don't—I don't know," he answered. And the answer was true.

He couldn't tell now why he had gone, except that something had forced him, something that was clear then and inevitable, but that every passing minute made more inarticulate. "I don't know, mama."

She groaned softly, sat down on the bed. The fat woman with the bare arms touched her shoulders and leaned over her.

"Poor Mrs. Schearl!" she said with grating, provocative pity. "Poor Mrs. Schearl! Why ask him? Don't you know? Our bleeding, faithful mother's heart they think nothing of wringing. Nothing! Woe you! Woe me! Before we see them grown, how many tears we shed! Oy-yoy-yoy! Measureless. So our children bring us suffering. So our men. Alas, our bitter lot! No?" Her see-saw sigh heaved gustily, pitched audibly. She folded her hands on her loose flabby belly and rocked sorrowfully .

His mother made no answer, but gazed fixedly into his eyes.

In the kitchen, he could hear the policeman interrogating his father, and his father answering in a dazed, unsteady voice. That sense of triumph that David had felt on first being brought in, welled up within him again as he listened to him falter and knew him shaken.

"Yes. Yes," he was saying. "My sawn. Mine. Yes. Awld eight. Eight en'—en' vun mawnt'. He vas bawn in—"

"Wait a minute!" The policeman's voice interrupted him. "Say, Doc, befaw yuh go, tell us, did I do it good. You know—dat foist-aid business. Waddayer say? In case dere's a commendation er sompt'n."

"Sure! Fine! Couldn't have done it better myself."

"T'anks, Doc. An' say, gimme de medical repawt, will yuh? Shock? Foolin' aroun' wit' de car-tracks wit—Heh! Heh!—merlicious intent."

"Oh—er—just say, shock . . . caused by . . . short circuiting . . . trolley power—what d'you call it—rail."

"Yea."

"Then—electrical burn . . . on ankle . . . right foot . . . second degree. Got it?"

"Secon' degree, yea."

"Applied artificial respir—"

"Aw Doc, have a heart, will yuh!"

"You want a commendation, don't you?" the interne laughed. "Well anything—first aid. Child revived— I've left a slip for you, Mister. On the table. Carron oil. Smear it around the ankle tonight and tomorrow. The blib ought to be gone in a day or two."

"Yes."

"And if he doesn't feel well tomorrow, take him to the Holy Name

Hospital—it's on the slip. But he'll be all right. Well, Lieutenant, I'll see you again."

"Yea. So long, Doc."

The woman who had gone out with David's mother came in balancing a cup of tea. Silently his mother propped him up on the pillows and began feeding him out of the spoon. The hot, sugared tea quickened his blood. He sighed, feeling vitality return, but only enough to know his body's weariness. There were no more cool places between the sheets for his throbbing foot. The women in the doorway had turned their backs to him and were listening to the policeman who was holding forth in the kitchen.

"An' say," his reassuring voice boomed out. "I woiked over 'im, Mister, an' no foolin'! Yuh hoid wot de Doc sez, didntcha? If it wuzn' fer me, dat kid wouldn' be hea. Yessir! People don't appreciate a cop aroun dis neighborhood. But w'en dere in dutch— Say, I seen 'em boined, Mister! I'm tellin' yuh. I seen a switchman was so boined— say! He musta fell on de rail. An' nobody knew a t'ing about it. Out dere in de car-barns on a hunner'n fifty-fift' an Eight' Avenoo. Must a been on dere fer hours. An' de foist t'ing you know, his bones was troo de elevated—right down t' de ground—black as zat stove, Mister! Y'hadda gadder 'im up in a sheet. Yessir! So he wuz gettin' off easy, dat kid o' yours. But even so if it hadn'ta been fer me— Say, d'yuh wan' all o' dese people in hea?"

"I—I don'—" His father sounded stunned. "I—I—you—"

"Sure. C'mon goils. De kid's gotta get some quiet now. Waddayuh say? All right, gents."

"Vee know dem," voices objected. "Vee liff heyuh."

"Not hea'," indulgently. "Not all o' yiz. C'mon. Come in later— one at a time—"

There was a general shuffling of feet, murmured protests.

"Er fumfit shoin far a bissel geld," sneered the woman with the bare arms as she went out. "Gitzeem a krenk!"

"I god Davy's shoes and stockin', Mister," a boy's voice piped. "He goes to my cheder."

"Atta boy. Just leave 'em hea. C'mon de rest o' yiz. Dat goes fer you too, Solomon."

Feet went through the doorway, voices dwindled. The door was shut.

"Well, I got de place quiet for yuh," said the policeman. "Funny all de trouble dese kids o' ours gives us, huh? You said it. Geeziz I'm a cop an' I can't keep mine in line, bringin' home repawt co'ds dat'd make yer hair toin grey. Well, my beat's aroun' hea' in case yuh wanna see me sometime. Walsh is de name." He loomed up in the doorway. "How're yuh feelin' now, kid? He'll be all right. Sure. He's full o' de devil a'reddy. I'll fan yuh wit' me stick if I catch yuh foolin' aroun' dem tracks again. See? 'Night." He flicked an open palm, turned and went out.

He had finished his tea. The sudden, flushing surge of heat that filled the hollows of his tired body drove stipple of perspiration to his brow and lips. His underwear clung to him cutting at the crotch. The trough of the bedding where he lay had become humidly warm and uncomfortable. He wriggled closer to the cooler edge of the bed where his mother was seated and lay back limply.

"More?" She asked putting the cup down on the window sill.

"No, mama."

"You've had nothing to eat since the morning, beloved. You're hungry, aren't you?"

He shook his head. And to ease the throbbing in his right foot, slid it furtively from under the covers at her back to cool it.

His father stood in the doorway, features dissolved in the dark. Only the glitter in his eyes was sharply visible, fixed on the puffy gray ankle. His mother turned at his tread, spied the swollen foot also. Her sucked breath hissed between pain-puckered lips.

"Poor darling! Poor child!"

His father's hand fell heavily against the door-frame. "He's written down the name of some medicine for us to get," he said abruptly. "To smear on his foot."

"Yes?" She half rose. "I'll go get it."

"Sit there!" His peremptory tone lacked force as though he spoke out of custom, not conviction. "It will be quicker for me to get it. Your neighbors outside won't delay *me* with their tongues." But instead of going he stood where he was. "He said he'd be better in a day or two."

She was silent.

"I said he'd be better in a day or two," he repeated.

"Yes. Of course."

"Well?"

"Nothing."

There was a pause. His father cleared his throat. When he spoke his voice had a peculiar harshness as though he were at the same time provoking and steeling himself against a blow.

"It— it's my fault you'd say. Is that it?"

She shook her head wearily. "What use is there to talk about faults, Albert? None foresaw this. No one alone brought it on. And if it's faults we must talk about it's mine as well. I never told you. I let him listen to me months and months ago. I even drove him downstairs to—to—"

"To protect him—from me?"

"Yes."

His teeth clicked. His chest rose. The expulsion of his breath seemed to rock him slightly. "I'll go get it." He turned heavily out of the doorway.

David listened to his father's dull, unresilient footfall cross the kitchen floor. The door was opened, closed. A vague, remote pity stirred within his breast like a wreathing, reveling smoke, tenuously dispersed within his being, a kind of torpid heart-break he had felt sometimes in winter awakened deep in the night and hearing that dull tread descend the stairs.

"Perhaps you'll be hungry in a little while," his mother said persuasively. "After you've rested a bit and we've put the medicine on your foot. And then some milk and a boiled egg. You'd like that?" Her question was sufficiently shored by statement to require no answer. "And then you'll go to sleep and forget it all." She paused. Her dark, unswerving eyes sought his. "Sleepy, beloved?"

"Yes, mama."

He might as well call it sleep. It was only toward sleep that every wink of the eyelids could strike a spark into the cloudy tinder of the dark, kindle out of shadowy corners of the bedroom such myriad and such vivid jets of images—of the glint on tilted beards, of the uneven shine on roller skates, of the dry light on grey stone stoops, of the tapering glitter of rails, of the oily sheen on the night-smooth rivers, of the glow on thin blonde hair, red faces, of the glow on the outstretched, open palms of legions upon legions of hands hurtling toward him. He might as well call it sleep. It was only toward sleep that ears had power to cull again and reassemble the shrill cry, the hoarse voice, the scream of fear, the bells, the thick-breathing, the roar of crowds and all sounds that lay fermenting in the vats of silence and the past. It was only toward sleep one knew himself still lying on the cobbles, felt the cobbles under him, and over him and scudding ever toward him like a black foam, the perpetual blur of shod and running feet, the broken shoes, new shoes, stubby, pointed, caked, polished, buniony, pavement-beveled, lumpish, under skirts, under trousers, shoes, over one and through one, and feel them all and feel, not pain, not terror, but strangest triumph, strangest acquiescence. One might as well call it sleep. He shut his eyes.

The Island Within

by LUDWIG LEWISOHN

It was Ludwig Lewisohn probably more than any other writer who pioneered in helping to make serious fiction about American Jewish life a subject of widespread discussion. But later in his career, like virtually all pioneers, he suffered neglect and even ridicule for his attempts. The Island Within, published in 1928, was the first major fictional portrayal of the problems resulting from religious intermarriage. It was, incidentally, among the first novels in which the hero is a psychoanalyst, though the writing itself, unlike much of more recent modern fiction, does not lean on the materials of analysis.

It is interesting that Lewisohn, who was born in Germany, does not, as did Abraham Cahan with Yiddish-speaking Jewry, offer a genre portrait, but, rather, presents a personal problem resulting from assimilation. The section here selected deals with the climax of the ill-fated marriage between Arthur Levy and Elizabeth Knight. Dr. Lewisohn seems to say that the marriage was doomed from the beginning because the Jewish chromosomes and the Gentile chromosomes are incompatible.

Twice, early in his adult life, Lewisohn is said to have been close to adopting the Christian religion. But after a crisis similar to that described in this novel, he returned to orthodox Jewish observance.

Ludwig Lewisohn was a scholar and a creative writer with a sometimes unfortunate gift for becoming notorious. His marital affairs were repeatedly accompanied by melodrama, yet from one of his mismarriages came a searingly honest novel, The Case of Mr. Crump (1926), again a pioneer work, in this case because of its frankness about sex relations, that was for many years a suppressed, underground book. In contrast, Lewisohn's studies in world literatures were college texts. After teaching at Ohio

State and Wisconsin universities, he lived some years abroad.
His authoritative volume, Expression in America, appeared in
1937. Lewisohn's last years were spent on the faculty of Brandeis
University.

C.A.

Elizabeth KNIGHT and Arthur Levy had been married for two years. After the birth of John, Elizabeth had taken up her work again. She had not gone back to her old position. Through the influence of Eugene and Joanna Adams, as well as of other friends, she had been given a chance to write feature articles for the Sunday papers as well as for certain spectacular magazines. Browsing in Arthur's library, getting him to translate for her extracts from German books—case histories more especially from the psychoanalytical journals—she had very vividly and agreeably put together a series of articles which she called "The Cure of Souls." She had a pleasant fluidity in her writing and a frank, simple way of stating things. It was around 1921 and the American interest in psychoanalysis was at its height. Everywhere in the country a few individuals among the younger generation were beginning to resist neo-Puritan pressure, if only in the inwardness of their minds. Elizabeth sold her articles to a woman's magazine of national circulation at a price that staggered Arthur. He was doing reasonably well himself now. Patients were not too many and he labored with them conscientiously. But they would not have trusted him had he not charged them as much as other practitioners of very high standing. Nevertheless, Elizabeth's single check for seventy-five hundred dollars took his breath away. She had been very sweet about it. She had pursed her lips, and the little girl in her which at rare intervals made his father call her *shiksele* had come out. "Really, you know, I owe it all to you." Arthur had tenderly deprecated his part in her undertaking.

"What shall we do with all that money?" Elizabeth had asked. "Jiminy, I didn't know there was that much money in the world."

"Invest it for John," Arthur had said.

"Oh, bother. John'll have half of your father's money some day. Let's have a good time."

"It's your money, darling."

Elizabeth had bought herself two new fur coats and a fur coat for Arthur and half a dozen frocks specially designed for her by the studios of Baron de Meyer, and had sent a check for a thousand dollars to her father, and had then borrowed money from Arthur that she might send his mother flowers for her birthday.

"Never mind," she said. "I've got a lovely notion for some more articles. And I'm going to write some stories, too—stories about my childhood and the upstate farmers. So be a nice husband and give me a check." She had written both the articles and the stories. She sold everything she wrote. In her stories she had a blending of precision and naïveté, a childlike earnestness with moments of sudden bubbling humor that had true charm and yet managed to hit the taste of a very large public. Checks poured in. Also invitations poured in. Miss Knight became more and more of a figure in that literary New York which is so tremendously in the public eye, is, in fact, one of the sights of the town and sustains so fragile and precarious a connection with literature, after all. That world took to Elizabeth with a kind of passion. There are very many Jews in it, Jews who never speak of themselves as Jews and try hard not to think of themselves as such. Elizabeth being a Gentile, but being married to a Jew, was bound, aside from her personal charm and talent, to be much-beloved. One invited Miss Knight; one had luncheon at the Algonquin with Miss Knight. One was supremely comfortable with Miss Knight. She could have no subtle reserves, no hidden judgments upon one. She was, in the end, Mrs. Levy; she was the mother of John Levy. She was an out-and-out Gentile, and yet (far was it from these ladies and gentlemen to use such a phrase except in the innermost privacies of thought) "one of our own people." The postman groaned under the morning mail for Miss Knight, whose name was duly, under that of Arthur Levy, M.D., on the door of the apartment; the telephone rang all day and voices asked for Miss Knight. Elizabeth enjoyed herself hugely. Of the precise character of the situation she was wholly unaware. So great was her naïveté in this matter that once, being at an all-Gentile editorial conference and hearing for the first time since her marriage the stereotyped remarks about the business acuteness of Jewish writers and the hospitality of Jewish publishers to radical and immoral books, she not only said with a glowing sense of doing the right thing: "Remember, please, that my husband is a Jew!" She not only did that in all sweetness and purity of motive, but came home and told Arthur about it and assumed her little-girl air and expected to be praised for her loyalty and frankness. And Arthur, violently uncomfortable but unable to analyze his own discomfort at the moment, praised her in the expected sense.

They went to parties almost every night. One couldn't, Elizabeth pleaded, go to So-and-so and slight So-and-so. Moreover, one met a terribly useful crowd. She picked up commissions and he picked up patients. One made no effort, but the thing happened. It was undeniably true. Arthur was asked to treat more and more members of the literary or editorial set. His patients were nearly all Jews. He found that their psychical aches and inhibitions and discomforts were all flights from an obscure reality. They substituted; they interposed the barriers of phobias between themselves and reality; they were in perpetual flight. There was no earth under their feet, no heaven over their heads. There was an apartment and the Algonquin at noon and a party at night and the gnawing of a mystic tooth at the soul. . . . They railed and jeered at the neo-Puritan obsession, at the Fundamentalists. They made common cause with Bertrand Jones in his famous fictional attacks on the nation's brutal and massive attempts to draw its traditional forces together and extrude the people and the influences that seemed to it to threaten its fierce loyalties and ignorances and solidarities. . . . They did this, overlooking, feigning to themselves not to have observed, the fact that Jones, more drunk than usual one day, had told his partner at dinner that *he* belonged, and that she had better go back to the ghetto where *she* belonged. . . . Arthur had a curious feeling about these Jewish intellectuals one day —a curious and prophetic feeling. He could not imagine them growing old. What would they do when they could no longer hurry hither and thither and write witty articles and columns and go to luncheons and meetings and support all good negative causes and protest and huddle together for warmth against one another in the meeting-places of New York? What busy souls they were! And how drained of anything of their own! How essentially poor, poorer than the poorest Gentile who, from fraternizing and protesting and jeering with them, could withdraw to his hearthstone built on his bit of earth and trust in the long historic process of his people. But he had the haunting conviction that with these Jews movement of the nimble mind and body was identical with life. They had no center to which to retire; when they could no longer whir about the periphery they would drop and die. . . . Tentatively he said these things to Elizabeth. She listened with that earnest attentive air she had.

"'Gene Adams said to me one day that the Jews are the worst anti-Semites. What you say, Arthur, almost makes me think he's right. Why, it doesn't seem to me that our Jewish friends are any different from anybody else! Why should you, of all people, judge them so funnily and so harshly?"

He laughed and kissed her hair. "You're a dear," he said. "I suppose I would be hurt and disappointed if you took any other attitude."

He left her. She was busy. He, too, was expecting a patient. That night there was a party at the house of a Jewish playwright, an extremely brilliant and gifted man whose plays were a concentrated bitterness of protest against the hardness and dulness, against the inconceivable (to him inconceivable) life of the American masses. Arthur and Elizabeth did not get to bed till nearly three o'clock in the morning. He had to get up at eight and left her asleep, and saw her pile of mail, and answered the telephone which angrily demanded Miss Knight, and went through the empty rooms to his study.

VERY OFTEN during the two years of his married life he remembered that scene with his father and mother, that last scene before he had brought Elizabeth to visit them. He saw them at the table in the old dining-room which still had in it the furnishings of his childhood. The scene had not impressed him greatly at the time. Later it seemed stamped and graven upon his mind.

It had been upon the following Sunday that Arthur and Elizabeth had gone to his father's house. In the hall Elizabeth had suddenly reminded him of Georgie Fleming. There had been a vague shrinking and distrust in her eyes, and, had she not lifted her fine straight nose in the ghost of a sniff? To have taxed her with that attitude would, of course, have been monstrous. She was utterly unconscious and innocent. Why would she, under the circumstances, not be a little shy? The older generation always has its conservative moral reserves. And Arthur, convinced in some obscure inner region, blamed himself for attributing to that momentary shyness and shrinking of hers any quality that it would not normally and universally—granting the circumstances—have had.

The door had opened. His mother had appeared and at once folded Elizabeth to her bosom. The old amethyst ring with the tiny diamond flower in it had glowed on Elizabeth's shoulder. Elizabeth had tried hard to yield; she had had no conscious impulse against yielding.

Arthur took all that in with his psychical antennæ. But she had simply not been able to soften suddenly and unexpectedly under this thing that was to Mrs. Levy a mere matter of course and had to her the quality, even though beautiful, of an unforeseen emotional attack. She had felt in that embrace more than a gesture of affection and good will. She had felt in it a subtle reaching out after her and possessing of her and drawing her irrevocably in. And against that assumption of her no longer belonging wholly to herself or her kind, but of being, by a gesture that was also a ceremonial, absorbed into a community of fact and feeling and interests the very existence of which she had not suspected—against that her instincts rebelled. She and Arthur had met freely in a free world of more or less detached human beings. One was nice, to be sure, as nice as one could be, to the relations of one's husband. But one wasn't, at least nowadays and in America, sucked into a clan. . . . Arthur and Elizabeth had never discussed this matter. Arthur knew that Elizabeth would have denied, and very honestly and sincerely denied, these various emotional imputations. Honestly, because any formulation in words made the whole thing intolerably gross—the thing which, in itself, was the shadow of a shadow in the twilight of the mind.

The embrace, which had lasted but a moment, had been crucial. Arthur's mother had experienced the subtle rebuff which she had expected. She would have been happy not to have felt it. But she was not, being human and a woman, wholly dissatisfied to have her foregone conclusions proved and to be able to assume the generous, unweariedly giving and slightly tragic maternal rôle which, ever since Arthur's announcement, she had been prepared to assume. She put her arm through that of her strange new daughter and drew her into the living-room. Arthur was suddenly aware of the fact—he hadn't ever noticed it before—that the furnishings were somber and old-fashioned. He also saw that the watchchain across the chest of his father, who stood there with arms outstretched, was too thick and showy. Slowly the outstretched arms dropped. Mr. Levy came up to Elizabeth and kissed her lightly on the forehead. They all sat down.

The moment had weighed upon them. Stones seemed to lie upon their hearts. Arthur's father had said: "Our son tells us det you write." Elizabeth did not, of course, realize the terribleness of this remark. How it showed a blending of hopeless estrangedness with a self-tormented desire to propitiate. A Jewish daughter-in-law—well, if she had written, he would have teased her about it later. First he would have asked her quite other questions. Or, rather, there would have been no need to ask questions. All that would long ago have been eliminated. They would be, they would have been from the beginning, on some bit of common ground. But Arthur, shivering a little at his father's question, knew suddenly why Jews were sometimes psychically unmannerly. On different grounds, emotionally out of touch, aiming wildly, one aims amiss. One is, for all practical purposes, blind and bungles and stumbles and crashes. He remembered the story that had been told him of a colleague introduced into the Gentile milieu of his betrothed and behaving abominably. Poor Dr. Bergmann, afraid of seeming distant and a stranger, had, out of the depth of his Jewish conception of the family, been overintimate. He had asked questions which would in Jewish circles have been taken as a warm and gracious sign of interest on the part of so new a member of the clan, but which here sounded and, in truth, were excessively prying and rude. He had been glad that, upon the whole, his father and mother were not expansive people. He could imagine Elizabeth with the elder Goldmanns. She had, at all events, regarded his father's words as natural and kindly and had turned to him with relief. She had been in those early days quite deprecatory about her writing. She had joked about it, in fact. His father had smiled and something of the heaviness of the moment had been lifted from them all. . . . But during the dinner it had descended upon them again. Arthur saw that his mother was burning to speak, almost to cry out, to assault Elizabeth and break something in her, break down the invisible barrier which she felt. But it was precisely the intangibleness of the barrier that made the situation so hopeless. Elizabeth was friendly and even cordial. No fault could be found with her. But she was cordial as with people of whom she wanted to make friends. He could hear his father, had his father's articulateness in English extended so far: "Frients! De vife of my only son sits dere like a strange lady vanting to make frients wit me! Better she shoult begin by hating me ent I could show her det I hef for her de heart of a fadder!" Oh, it was hopeless! Elizabeth pulled herself together. Elizabeth was charming in a way that seemed to Arthur's mother unbearably casual and detached. As a last resort Mrs. Levy brought out photographs of Arthur taken from year to year all through his childhood and boyhood, and the two women, going toward the window, seemed to have a moment that drew them together. Then, alas, Mrs. Levy offered to part with some of these treasures and Elizabeth said: "They're awfully sweet and I love them. But you'd better not give me any. I lose things so easily."

At last it had been over and Arthur and Elizabeth had been walk-

ing home along West End Avenue. He took off his hat and let a cool
wind of early autumn blow through his thick hair. They had not
spoken. Arthur had wondered vaguely what Elizabeth's thoughts had
been. He felt utterly dispirited. Intellectually he was entirely on Elizabeth's side. No fault could be found with her. She had, in all sincerity, done her best. On the other hand, there tugged and gnawed
at him the profound sense of his parents' grief. He felt this so strongly
that he rebelled against its irrational causes. Why the deuce did one
have to be so sentimental about family matters? Why did one have
at a first meeting of this kind to melt? What function did this immense Jewish sense of family solidarity have in modern life? Of
course Elizabeth couldn't even comprehend what had been expected
of her. . . . And all the while below these thoughts he knew how
happy he would have been, how instinctively and completely happy,
if his wife could have assumed the part of a Jewish daughter and he
could have come out of his father's house on that day with the conviction that the bonds of solidarity and love had been sustained and
strengthened.

IN THE MANY succeeding months the inevitable results of the life that
Arthur and Elizabeth led and of the character of that first meeting
had become more and more emphatic. They had quite literally no
time for any social life that was not part of the life of the circle in
which they moved. Had Elizabeth been strongly drawn to Arthur's
parents, a distinct effort would no doubt have been made. On the
other hand, Arthur felt morally certain that, had Elizabeth's own
father lived in New York, she would have seen very little of him, too,
and that her conscience would not have troubled her at all. Then
how could he, except at very rare intervals, ask her to add another
burden to her already overburdened professional and social life? On
Sunday she was usually quite tried. He, too, valued their Sundays
alone together. They were so rarely alone together, anyhow. Hence he
drifted into the habit of going home alone on occasional afternoons,
on occasional early evenings. But these visits were of no comfort to
him. His father and mother took it for granted that Elizabeth did not
want to come in an actively negative sense which was utterly unjust
to the real state of her feelings. If he reported her words exactly:
"Darling, I know it's shabby of me not to have been to see your people in all these weeks or to have asked them. But you know they'd

disapprove of our friends, just as much as Dad would in another way. And I'm just broken today. Do go and give them my love and tell them I'm not as low as they think!"—if he repeated these words exactly, he was believed. But under those words his parents felt something which was not there. For the casualness of that attitude was inconceivable to them, the security of belonging instinctively into one's world and not wanting to belong, not feeling the need of belonging to one's given group. They understood attraction or repulsion. They did not understand the specific detachments of the children of a soil. . . .

Those had been weeks of great comfort to his mother when Elizabeth had been in the Sloane Maternity Hospital. She had gone there daily with fresh flowers and had been able to be tender and protective a little in her attitude to her daughter and to her grandson. But the two women had not fundamentally drawn closer together even then. And next had come the burning issue of the child's circumcision. Arthur knew that his parents had taken counsel together when his father had called him up and had asked him not whether but when the ceremony would take place. Arthur had put his father off and gone to Elizabeth.

"Father's just called up. I know from his tone that he's scared to death you won't permit the baby to be circumcised."

Elizabeth, still weak, had smiled rather wanly. "All modern doctors recommend it as a matter of health. I needn't tell you that. And John's name is Levy. So I have nothing against it, Arthur. How do you feel about it?"

He had stopped in front of her and reflected. "It's more troublesome to me than it is to you, dear. It opens the whole problem for me. I know you think there isn't any. But I think I'll just be guided by my father's feeling, if you don't mind."

"Not a bit," she answered.

So Arthur was able to invite his parents for a certain date on which a more or less religiously-minded Jewish surgeon of his acquaintance introduced little John into the company of Israel. Arthur was astonished at his own satisfaction. He interpreted it as relief in his parents' relief and as a result of the very rational consideration that a boy named John Levy and uncircumcised might find himself from the start in a puzzling situation. But Elizabeth had one of her flashes of insight.

"I didn't know you were so Jewish in your feelings."

"Do you mind ?" he asked.

She smiled. "I have atavistic attacks myself when I hear Gospel Hymns."

He shook his head. Somehow it was different, different. . . . Life was becoming more confusing for him from day to day. It had never been clear. There had never been in it a fundamental order. Now he often grasped his head. It seemed to spin. Aside from the strange alienation from his parents, from the friends of his youth, aside from the restlessness of his life with Elizabeth, there was another factor which had become more and more acute and to which, both as a man and as a psychologist, he could not but allow great weight. . . . It was a subtle and difficult and delicate matter. . . . One could not cope with it by either words or action. . . . It was there . . . Elizabeth was very busy. She was always tired at night. . . . She was desperately afraid of having another baby. . . . When they had been out to a party Elizabeth almost fell asleep in the taxi home. When they spent an evening at home, she begged to be allowed to go to bed early in a sweet and child-like manner. . . . Once Arthur had said:

"But, darling, we might as well not be married."

She had pouted. "Is *that* what marriage means to you?"

He had smiled. "You are a little Puritan, just the same."

She had grown grave. "Not in my opinions, Arthur. But I don't really think that that side of life means much to me personally." After that she was careful to create occasions once in a while and to give herself to him. But it was a weary and deliberate and joyless process. . . .

He wondered afterward why he had not rebelled long before. But Elizabeth was disarming in her sweetness, her reasonableness, her instinctiveness. She was that sort of a woman. The sort that keeps her name, goes on working, thinks of marriage rather as a pleasant companionship than as a deeper and more tragic union. She was without blame within her ethical universe. Moreover, all modern ideas were on her side. She was entirely in the right. For opposed to her conception of marriage was the old sex-slavery of the Puritans with its cruel subjection of woman, its denial of divorce, its fierce and ugly repressions. No wonder that the women of her race and her tradition had rebelled and were now at times tempted into extremes. No wonder. And Arthur knew that if he protested she would take immediate fright; she would think that he was protesting from the point of view of that old Puritan notion of marriage which had crushed her mother, from the point of view of the dominant Gentile male. And how was he to tell her and, above all, to convince her, that what he had in mind was something different, was a third kind of condition or estate which he felt to exist but which he himself could neither precisely define nor describe? All he knew was this, that, except in imitation of their Gentile sisters and more or less from the lips outward, Jewish women were not dissatisfied with their position and did not protest against the dominance of the male. He knew of none that did not rule unquestioned in her sphere nor of any that was not her husband's most valued councillor in his. He knew no Jewish home in which the children were not brought up in equal obedience and respect for both parents and in which the equality of the parents in function, wisdom, worth, was not silently and fundamentally taken for granted. But that was not all. There was an indefinable element. As women grew older among Jews they were instinctively treated with a touch of unquestioning reverence as though they were the repositories of some special grace or wisdom. And this thing went so far that he had seen grave and learned men listen dutifully and even cheerfully to the inconsequential babble of old ladies, because these old ladies were their mothers. No, he couldn't explain it! he didn't know enough; he had to rely solely on instinct and casual observation. But he knew with the utmost certainty, just the same, that if he felt cheated in his marriage with Elizabeth, it wasn't because he wanted to be like the older generation of Anglo-Saxon men; he wanted to exercise neither the male arrogance combined with chivalry of the upper classes among them, nor the brutalities of the lower. But in any male resistance to her present theory or method Elizabeth immediately scented, with a touch of hot terror or rebellion, either the one attitude or the other.

IT WAS toward the end of their third summer. Elizabeth and the child had been visiting the Adamses, who had a large bungalow in Atlantic Highlands. Arthur had been kept in town by two patients who were afraid of interrupting their treatment. He could perhaps have soothed them and put them off. He didn't because there was no place for him to go. He had suggested to Elizabeth that they should buy a place in the hills or by the seashore. But Elizabeth had a terror of possessions, of material entanglements. She liked to feel free, unbound, unrooted. She felt at home everywhere and so had no need to localize the feeling of home. The problem of the summer was one of several unspoken problems between them. Places where people named Jones and people named Levy could dwell together in amity were rapidly disappearing from the land. Wherever the Levys came the Joneses withdrew. From their refuge to which they withdrew the Levys were sternly excluded. So the Joneses lived alone with their kind, and the Levys with theirs. Arthur had gathered, quite unintentionally, a little library of prospectuses of places of summer sojourn, in each of which it was stated, in forms of varying emphasis, that Hebrew guests were not wanted. . . . He couldn't possibly "see" Elizabeth in the hotel at Far Rockaway where his father and mother were old and happy and comfortable guests. He couldn't "see" her in any place to which they would have access. Had his name been Cone or Freefield—he smiled at the recollection of his sister's old miseries—he and Elizabeth might, as the Negroes put it, have "passed" in the summer. But the name of Levy is an indelible stamp. Just once the year before Elizabeth had said to Joanna Adams:

"I don't care, but I'd like to see them keep me out."

"Not if you register as Elizabeth Knight, of course," Joanna had answered.

Elizabeth, in one of her sudden adventurous moods, had taken the baby and his nurse and had gone to a fashionable hotel in the Adirondacks. The clerk had assured her that there was a suite vacant before she had registered. Afterward the manager had informed Mrs. Levy that a mistake had been made. The suite was bespoken. Would she forgive him for changing her quarters. She had been assigned a small, hot room over the kitchens. She had fled. It was Eugene Adams who had told Arthur of this incident. The two men had looked at each other. Then Adams had said, awkwardly: "It's a passing phase, a postwar reaction." Arthur had changed the subject. He disagreed wholly with Eugene. But he had no arguments. He had dropped in to see Joe Goldmann, a thing he rarely did in these later days, and had told him the story. Joe had chuckled.

"A hell of a passing phase. That passing phase has managed to turn up with the regularity of clockwork for a good bit over two thousand years. It's the contrary that is a passing phase when it occurs."

Arthur had barely listened to Joe's economic interpretation of the causes. "Look here, Joe," he had said, "you're always chasing some Gentile girl, just the same."

Joe's golden-brown eyes had their old quenchless melancholy. "The thorn is in my flesh. But they're not ladies. I'm not marrying one, you observe."

Now the heat of early September rose over the city like a burning tower and Elizabeth had written that she was coming home. She loved Joanna, but she was tired of 'Gene and of other guests who were in the bungalow. It was too bad for the baby, of course. She supposed it was hot in town. But she thought she would come home, just the same. It was, he supposed later, her casualness about the baby that had wounded and angered him. It was also a way she had of never telling him precisely when she was going or coming, as though she feared that exact knowledge on his part would assign to him a quality of authority. She called his solicitude "bossiness." With a smile. But the misunderstanding rankled.

She now came in, as was her wont, unexpectedly, with the child and its nurse on an evening of still, great heat. She kissed him lightly. "Ooh, isn't it just sticky!" He could not bring himself to answer. He went in and looked at his little son. The child was hot and fretting. He came back. Elizabeth had thrown her hat on the floor. She lay back in a chair and fanned herself with a newspaper.

"You can't keep John in town in this weather."

His tone stung her.

"Can't, Arthur? Well, suppose you provide a place for us."

"I've been anxious to build or buy a place. You haven't wanted me to."

"Because you know, yourself, it would be a nuisance."

Her tone was conciliatory now. There was nothing angry or ugly in Elizabeth. Only, it seemed to him, a little ultimate core of hardness that nothing could reach. It was he who burst through the repressions of the long months.

"It wouldn't be a nuisance if you had any time for your duties as a wife and a mother instead of scribbling inutilities. I want both a house in town and a house in the country. I'm sick to the soul of this casual existence and these silly parties and these everlasting engagements. I'm amazed that John has pulled through as well as he has. I love you as much as ever, Elizabeth, but I feel with the utmost seriousness that you are not a wife to me at all."

She drew herself up. Her eyes were very dark. "The old Adam."

He raised his hand in protest.

She nodded. "You're right, Arthur. This is really our first quarrel, isn't it? But of course I've seen how you've held in. You are nice.

There's no doubt about that. And I'm dreadfully sorry. But I can't do what you want me to do."

"Why not?"

"I'm not fit for it and all my instincts rebel against it. If I gave up my work and just kept house for you and took care of John, I should feel unutterably useless and degraded."

He was walking up and down. "Then why did you marry at all?"

"Can't a woman have a love-life without becoming so disgustingly domesticated?"

"Love-life!" He couldn't keep the irony out of his voice. "It's precisely because you have no real love-life that the normal instincts of womanhood don't function in you. I personally have no warmer desire than to become domesticated. I want a home with all the responsibilities that it entails. I want another child—"

She jumped up. "And if I give up my work and my connections and my friends—I know you've never really liked them—and spend myself on taking care of a house or two and children, what will become of us?"

"I don't understand you, Elizabeth."

"Do you expect me to be satisfied with the society of the Goldmanns and the Bergmanns and of some of your—ugh—colleagues and their wives?"

"Jewish colleagues, you meant to say."

"No, I didn't, Arthur. I give you my word. At least it wasn't in any derogatory sense."

He bit his lips. There was no use going on with that question. It opened abysses unexplored, deliberately unexplored by himself. He stopped. He took her hand.

"Are you happy, Elizabeth?"

Tears came into her eyes. She shook her head.

"Then why not try my plan of living?"

"Because it would mean becoming more hopelessly involved." Her voice was hard and yet sorrowful.

"What is lacking between us, Elizabeth?"

She withdrew her hand.

"Nothing." She laughed a pathetic, weary little laugh. "Everything. I don't know." She walked to the window. "You'd better send baby and his nurse to your mother at Far Rockaway. She'll be very good to him. I think I'll run away for a week and see Dad. Do you mind?"

"Of course not, Elizabeth. But what then, what afterward?"

"I don't know. I can't tell. You're always generous, Arthur. Leave it just so. Will you?"

He assented. Next morning he telephoned to his mother, who immediately came into the city to fetch her grandchild. By the time Mrs. Levy arrived Elizabeth was already gone. Mother and son avoided any confidences.

"You look tired, sonny. Why don't you run over to Boston? Hazel and Eli have always wanted you to visit them. And they have a fine house and a beautiful car."

"I believe I will," he said, passing his hand over his forehead. "I need a change."

THE SINZHEIMERS lived on a sunny street in Brookline. It was a new street and all the houses in the street were new and handsome and had magnificent mechanical equipment of all sorts and large concrete garages. The trees were young and small and gave no shade, and the concrete sidewalks had no cracks, and the awnings over the verandahs were striped blue and white or orange and white and looked as though they had been bought yesterday, and the patches of well-sprinkled lawn were emerald-green even in this September weather. Each house in the street was a little different in shape from every other. But it was clear to any observer that this outward variety concealed an inner sameness. But that sameness could not be helped because perfection in a special kind is perfection and cannot be changed without becoming less than itself.

Arthur was amazed at the eager joyfulness of his reception. His brother-in-law called for him in his new Apperson car and bubbled with enthusiasm about the car and business and his house and Arthur's scientific distinction and new phonograph records and the brilliancy of Lenore, his and Hazel's only child. Hazel, he said, looked magnificent and was lovelier than ever, but he wasn't a bit satisfied with her nervous health, and for that reason, in addition to all the others, he was delighted to see Arthur. He wanted to do something definite for Hazel. Money was no object. He had cleaned up fifty thousand dollars the previous year in spite of the fact that he had been "stuck" with a large number of women's high shoes, which had gone out of fashion with a completeness that he had not seen equalled. Under all this brave talk Arthur perceived clearly a want of ease and of inner peace, and this perception grew stronger as Eli launched out into the more or less inevitable bragging about the excellence and the reliability of his bootlegger and the "slickness" with which, if you could pay the price, real Scotch from Canada was made to flood New England. . . .

They drew up before the spick and span house and there Hazel stood on the verandah, lovely, as Eli had said, though a little matronly in her contours. But what was gone from her wholly was the tenseness, the something fine and blade-like, which had characterized her girlhood. She embraced Arthur and tears came to her eyes. She struggled with a sob and Eli looked significantly at his brother-in-law. She drew forward her little girl, a dark, beautiful, glowing, very Jewish-looking child with clear wise eyes. And the child, too, seemed inordinately glad to see her uncle from New York and clung to him with a quiet affection from the first.

Arthur rested and dressed in his airy guest-room with its mahogany furnishings, including a four-poster bed and the charming hooked-rugs on the highly polished floors. The room was a model of all the elegant standardized amenities of modern American life. No last descendant of a Back Bay family could have found a false note either here or in the rest of the house. Arthur became aware of this as, just before dinner, Eli insisted on taking him through all the rooms. Around the walls of Lenore's sweet white room was a Maxfield Parrish frieze; Eli and Hazel had adjoining rooms discreetly and exquisitely furnished and decorated; the bathroom was a marvel; the living-rooms downstairs had spaciousness and dignity; the objects in them were well chosen and not too many. And the entire house had, despite its unemphatic luxury, a touch of austerity and simplicity that blended in with the New England tradition. It was, in brief, a Boston house, and through it, in this mild weather, there went a breath of desolation that blew upon Arthur like a harsh wind from some outer space beyond the habitations of men. . . . The objects of wood and fabric in this house were stiff and recalcitrant to the people who lived here. They had not been broken into any love or even familiarity. No relation had existed and none had been established. The house, so full of life, was an empty house. . . . The Sinzheimers camped here. They had no home; their child had no home. . . .

Dinner began with chilled grapefruit. The silver was Colonial. A neat Irish maid passed softly in and out. Conversation was formal and hesitant. Everything was icily correct and dead. Chicken. French ice-cream. Salted almonds. The food was rather tasteless and rather meager. Both Eli and Hazel had a tendency toward plumpness; so had little Lenore. They all ate this flat American food without pleasure; they seemed impelled by a sense of duty. . . . Once, when the maid was out of the room, Hazel told Arthur that her husband would go every now and then to his mother's house to eat. She couldn't stand those greasy, old-fashioned messes herself. They were so frightfully fattening, anyhow. She had a terrible time preventing Lenore from sneaking over to her grandmother's house and being stuffed with pastry. . . . All the while she looked critically at her dry bit of roast chicken. And so Arthur knew that poor Hazel suffered perpetual hunger for the sake of her American conformity and an American silhouette.

After dinner they gathered in the drawing-room and Eli played a Wagnerian record on the Victrola, and then a great violinist's performance of the "Kol Nidre," and for a few minutes a human warmth came into the room. But when the instrument was silent that warmth faded again, and suddenly—Arthur never remembered how the subject was broached—they were talking about the more and more intense anti-Jewish feeling in Boston. They had no Gentile friends; their neighbors on both sides ignored their existence. When little Lenore went out into the street the mothers of the other little boys and girls on the block immediately called their children in. It was terrible. Arthur asked Eli whether his parents felt the same way. Eli smiled. "Well, no. They live in what is virtually a ghetto and father is president of a congregation and they have a swell time." Suddenly there was something handsome and natural about the man. "They have magnificent Passover celebrations and guests every Friday evening, and Dad still fasts and weeps on the Day of Atonement. They don't give a damn. But"—his voice grew small and cramped—"that's nothing for Hazel and me. I've sometimes thought that it mightn't be a bad thing for Hazel to join the Council of Jewish Women; she might meet some very fine people there. But Hazel has her own ideas on the subject."

Arthur turned to his sister. A pained, dissatisfied, struggling expression was on her face. She was simply inhibited on that subject. Something subtle and terrible of which Arthur was unaware must have happened to her in her childhood or infancy. She had so shattering and crushing and tragic a Jewish inferiority complex that she could not sustain her life psychically at all without nursing a strong sense of superiority to some one, without despising some one. And the only people whom she dared to despise were her own people. Thus, Jewish to the core by every instinct, she lived in misery and loneliness and dread and clung to life and sanity on these tragic terms by despising all that she yearned for, all that she needed. . . . The old story, Arthur thought. A psychic hurt and then flight from reality, flight from that reality through which the hurt had come. A kind of madness. Like all flights from reality. . . . Gently he asked Hazel why she felt as she did.

"I don't like Jews; I want to bring up my child as an American. All that doesn't mean anything to me."

Eli looked sad. "You see how it is, Arthur. I don't know that I blame Hazel. But it doesn't make life very pleasant. I've thought of moving to New York. But I really can't do it. The shoe business is here and it's here to stay."

Once more Hazel asked after Elizabeth. She had done so at once, of course, when she had seen Arthur. He had made a conventional reply. Now he got up and went over to Hazel.

"I'm not at all sure that Elizabeth and I will go on living together."

"Why, Arthur, I'm shocked! I've so wanted to meet her and know her."

Eli looked concerned. "What's wrong?"

"Nothing," Arthur said. He felt a sudden sense of liberation. "Nothing except that she's a Gentile and I am a Jew. We're fond of each other and we understand each other intellectually, but at the emotional basis of life there is—no, no opposition—there's a divergence. You've heard of the parallel lines that can never meet? It isn't very clear to me yet—the whole thing; I haven't probed it. But I feel as though I'd never been married at all. Maybe I'm wrong and it's just because Elizabeth is a very modern woman and I am, by instincts, an old-fashioned man. But I don't think that that explanation suffices. There's something deeper. Elizabeth has, in my special sense which I'm forced to believe a Jewish sense, no heart. Mind you, only in that sense. She's a splendid woman and I hope she finds her true happiness sooner or later."

Eli got up. "How about your boy, Arthur?"

Arthur lowered his head and he felt the corners of his lids burning. "I don't know . . . I don't know."

They gathered about him after that first evening, his sister and his brother and even their child, as though to protect him from the blows of untoward circumstance. Something streamed from them that was deeper than affection. An immemorial solidarity? Creatures always exposed to the storms of earth and having to cling together for protection? He could not tell. He only knew it warmed him—this attitude of his kinspeople—warmed him and cleared his brain. It warmed them, too, in their desolateness. They begged him to stay another day and another. But patients were clamoring in New York and he had a wistful tragic longing for Elizabeth—a longing like the longing one feels for autumn, for leave-takings, for the end of a feast in its midst, for night at high noon, for the ache of loneliness. . . .

ELIZABETH was already at home when he returned. She seemed rested and softened. She clung to him for a moment when they met and he blamed himself for feeling even in that clinging the presage of farewell. The child was still in Far Rockaway and so Arthur and Elizabeth were alone together as they had been during the early days of their union. The memories of those early days were here to haunt them with their pathos in the bright, tense, perishing autumnal days. . . . They had dinners out and Elizabeth told Arthur of the renewed impressions she had received of the countryside and the people of her childhood. She thought she would like to spend a rather quiet winter and try to do a novel, a slightly new kind of novel for a contemporary American of their set. Not a book of implicit and explicit criticism and protest, but a sort of idyll, recounting those simple lives of the Protestant farmers from within, from their own point of view. The center and pivot of the story would be a full-length portrait of a man like her father. She lifted her head in that proud, sweet, girlish way which had never lost its magic for Arthur and said:

"Dad was too dear and pathetic for words. He asked me whether you and I were quite happy. I told him that I was afraid that I wasn't altogether the right kind of a wife for you. Do you know what he answered?" Arthur shook his head. " 'You must try to obey and please your husband in every way—especially in this case.' I was curious and asked: 'Why especially in this case?' 'Because,' Dad said—and you should have seen the utter innocence and conviction in his eyes—'because you might bring him to Christ.' " She played with a spoon in front of her and looked down at the table. "Does that seem very ridiculous to you?"

"Not at all. It was beautifully in character, of course."

She looked up. "Isn't life funny? Father is quite Christ-like. So, in the sense of patience and kindness and not judging, are you. Oh yes, you are! It came all over me—I hadn't seen Dad in three years, you know—how alike you and he are. It's conviction with him and instinct with you. I'm the rebel and the pagan. But I can't help it."

They were silent for a while. He put his hand over hers.

"What are we going to do, Elizabeth?"

"Don't know yet, darling. Do you mind this uncertainty terribly? Of course, it depends a little or, rather, more than a little, on you."

He withdrew his hand. "It's not for me to be impatient or intolerant, Elizabeth. I only know that I seem to be living in a void. And it seems to me more and more as though many Jews are living in a void. Now what they do is to settle down and establish a real home in the quite old-fashioned sense and cling to that and so shut out the sense of emptiness and of not belonging anywhere. I have the same impulse, but it seems that this complete settling down is repugnant to your instincts. You don't need it. You're not living in a void. You belong somewhere and in fact everywhere. Even if you forced yourself to do outwardly as I wish, I doubt whether that would solve the problem. I'm on the edge of perceptions that I dare not admit even to myself. They are so extreme that you would laugh at them. They are so extreme that my father and mother would think that I'd lost my mind; my Jewish colleagues would be quite sure of it. So, you see, I have no more certitude than you have. I have less, in fact, far less. Who am I to be impatient?"

She looked at him earnestly. "I'm a fairly intelligent human being, Arthur. Why don't you tell me what's really in your mind?"

"I will as soon as it is clear and so articulate. Today it isn't. I don't know enough. I'd like to spend a quiet winter, too, and take up some studies that have nothing to do with either medicine or psychiatry. But I want to raise a practical problem that cuts into the root of the matter: How are we going to bring up John?"

She nodded. "Dad raised the same question. But I put him off. He is afraid, of course, that John's soul won't be saved. Well, we're not."

"I am." He saw her utterly astonished look. "You're saved, Elizabeth, because you live in a stream of tradition that is native to you. The stream changes. You don't believe what your father believes. The intellectual processes and assents are different. But the stream is the same. You are an American Protestant. Your divergences from your ancestors are normal divergences within the native tradition of your race and blood and historic experience. But I and many like me have tried to live as though we were American Protestants or, at least, the next best thing to that. And we're not. And the real American Protestants know we're not. And so we live in a void, in a spiritual vacuum. The devil of it is we don't know exactly what we are. Now, to come back to John. I'd be perfectly willing to have him brought up as a partaker in your tradition and have him feel at home in his country and its life as a Protestant American. But I can't help to bring him up that way. And, what's worse, his name *is* Levy and the more of a Protestant American he were in his heart and soul the more disastrous to him would be the things which in a Protestant American civilization are bound to happen to someone named Levy. I don't see all that clearly enough yet. But I see it."

Her eyes were wide. "I think I see what you mean, Arthur. But don't you think you overestimate the prejudice?"

"No, I'm afraid not. Your international literary crowd in New York is no criterion."

A look of fear, instinctive and unavertable, came into Elizabeth's eyes. "You don't mean to say, Arthur, that you would think of having John brought up as a religious Jew?"

He did not answer at once.

"Tell me, Arthur," she repeated. "Is that what you mean?"

"I'm not prepared to go as far as that. I told you that I was only on the edge of perceptions. But your instinctive terror at the very thought is enormously instructive."

She drew herself up. "It's all a nightmare. Can't we all just be human?"

Arthur smiled. "What is it to be human? Nothing abstract. Show me a human being who isn't outwardly and inwardly some *kind* of a human being, dependent, though he were the most austere philosopher, in his human life on others of more or less the same *kind*. There is no place of *kindless* people in the world. And if you established a colony of extra-religious and supra-national philosophers and sages, male and female, their extra-religiousness and supra-nationalism would establish their kind and their inner kinship, and, far from having broken up the families of mankind, we would have added but another family—a magnificent one, I grant you—to those that already exist. In a word, this vague cry, let us be human—it's a favorite cry among Jews—means nothing and gets you nowhere."

Elizabeth smiled. "How brilliant you are, Arthur. You ought to write something about that. It would make a gorgeous article."

They laughed together.

"You know I don't write. And, anyhow, what good would that do John?"

"Poor little John," she teased. "Don't let's be so solemn and intellectual about it all. I have a notion that it will all take care of itself in some natural way. As Dad always says, God is good."

A few days later the elder Levys returned to the city and the child with its nurse came home. The summer had done the little fellow good. He was sturdier and more vivid. He looked more and more like Hazel. His nose was almost as straight as Elizabeth's. But he was, in coloring and expression, a Jewish child. He had never been continuously with his grandparents before. He had taken a tremendous fancy to them. He wanted his grandpa and his grandma. Elizabeth said with a tang of bitterness:

"Of course he's spoiled. Your mother bettied around after him all day long. I can't quite do that." John was on Arthur's lap. Elizabeth looked at them. "I suppose you think that's what I ought to do."

"No, I don't think *you* ought to do it."

"Which is to say that you wish John had a mother who would and could and wanted to."

Arthur put the child down. "It isn't like you, Elizabeth, to try to pick that sort of a female quarrel."

"I suppose not. But don't be so terribly superior. I must say, Arthur, I do think that that is a Jewish characteristic. It's probably an excellent thing for John that the world doesn't rotate about him when he's at home. Run along to nurse, John. No, you must obey mother. Run along. You see, Arthur, he's very nearly unmanageable." Her face was slightly red.

"What's irritated you so, Elizabeth?" Arthur asked quietly.

"I don't know. I'm sorry."

"Is it that John struck you as looking particularly Jewish today?"

She tugged at a little handkerchief which she was holding. "I think you're trying to goad and nag today, Arthur. That isn't like you, either. The best thing for me to do will be to go out. Don't wait dinner for me. I'll be late."

He sat beside the child's crib until late that night. He sent the nurse to bed and watched the sleeping child hour after hour.

He did not think; he did not reason. Neither can it be said that he indulged in vivid emotion. He brooded over the child, over himself. He recalled his own childhood and boyhood and its difficulties and he wondered how this boy of his would adjust himself, by what inner means of adaptation or resistance he would adjust himself, by what inner means of adaptation or resistance he would adjust himself to a hostile and complicated world. . . . He remembered his own clinging to his father's house, later to streets and squares. John did not even have a house to cling to, only an apartment, an office, a passageway. . . . But perhaps he would not need that sense of protection and refuge; perhaps, like his mother, he would be at home in the world. . . . At home in the world . . . at home in the world. . . . How did one achieve that? His father and mother had it upon some terms that Arthur could not quite make clear to himself. His generation had lost it—he and Hazel and Joe; and even Eugene and Joanna only persuaded themselves and feigned to themselves to have it by a specific kind of refuge in a small and unique society. . . . Where would be the spiritual dwelling-place of his boy? . . . He heard the latch click. Elizabeth was coming. He was glad that she had a little trouble with the key. It gave him time to slip unobserved into his own bedroom. . . .

I Can Get It for You Wholesale

by JEROME WEIDMAN

It is doubtful whether Jerome Weidman thought of I Can Get
It for You Wholesale, which appeared in 1937, as a next-genera-
tion Rise of David Levinsky, yet as both novels are about making it in the garment industry, the way their respective heroes
attack the same problem offers a fascinating character contrast.
Both David Levinsky and Harry Bogen get into manufacturing
by luring a top designer away from a leading firm through persuading him into a partnership. But talmudic Levinsky is honest
with his partner, while American-born Bogen not only switches
the firm's money into his personal account, but slickly makes his
partner liable for his own swindles. Levinsky feels sad over his
materialistic life; Bogen gloats.

There is nothing redeeming about Harry Bogen, despite his
love for Mama and her blintzes, and his repressed love for a nice
Jewish girl she finds him. He is not only a total business cheat
but a Jew who chases after a blond stage star, finally resorting to
diamonds to secure her favors.

Exhibiting a remarkable narrative gift, Weidman also showed
an early understanding of the anti-hero. Written in clipped Hem-
ingway manner, this brutal first novel can be defended as a purga-
tive. In the Sinclair Lewis vein of social caricature, it is shockingly recognizable. Its sequel, What's in It for Me?, caused such
extreme community alarm on publication that the author, realizing it could be misunderstood and misused, particularly in the
heyday of Nazism, agreed to abstain from further editions. A
generation later, Wholesale became a musical comedy. Another
Weidman musical, a great hit and a Pulitzer Prize winner, was
the warmhearted Fiorello!, projecting his innate New Yorkish
feeling.

A ghetto product who studied law but turned writer, Weid-man, born in New York in 1913, is a natural storyteller. He has been highly prolific and uneven, but unquestionably his best works, such as Wholesale, have lasting quality. In several best sellers, including a tale of a successful intermarriage called The Enemy Camp, *a ghetto background haunts his characters, but in a later novel,* The Sound of Bow Bells, *the alienated hero cele-brates a bar mitzvah for his son. Such, it might be said, has been the Jewish pattern of Weidman's time.*

M.L.

Playing on the labor sentiment of the thirties, Harry Bogen gets a stooge to call the garment-district delivery boys out on strike. Then Harry hustles around to the manufacturers, offering a de-livery service. The strike is broken but Harry Bogen is in busi-ness. He brings home gifts to Mama.

I PUT MY ARMS around her quickly and kissed her, lifting her off the ground a few inches. In public I could kill guys that did things like that.

"Heshie!" she said sharply, but she put her own arms around me and kissed me back.

"Come on, now, Ma," I said, kissing her again. "Didn't I say I wouldn't be home for the night?"

"Sure you said it," she said. "But just the same you weren't home, were you?"

I laughed and hugged her, lifting her off the ground again.

"Say, you want to watch your figure, there, Ma," I said. "Pretty soon I won't be able to lift you up any more."

"Never mind," she said. "Don't tell me any stories. I weighed myself only yesterday."

"Yeah?" I said. "How much?"

For answer she walked over to the table and began to undo the packages.

"Come on, now," I said. "How much?"

She looked at me and we both began to laugh.

"It's okay, Ma," I said, putting my arm around her. "You put on as much weight as you want. I'll like you just the same."

"I know, Heshie," she said. "But promise me you won't stay away no more. It gets lonesome at night and I start worrying and I don't know what happened."

I snapped my fingers.

"That reminds me," I said. "That's another thing we're getting. A telephone."

"Don't try to mix me up what I'm saying," she said. "At least you could call me up by Mrs. Hirsch, from downstairs. Even three o'clock in the morning she would call me to the telephone. Last night, for a a nickel, you could—"

"What?" I said. "And have Mrs. Hirsch know that I called up my mother?"

"What's the matter? It's something to be ashamed of?"

"Of course not," I said, "but she don't have to know my business."

Letting Mrs. Hirsch know something was like buying fifteen minutes on WEAF.

"But Heshie—"

"Aah, you don't have to worry about me, Ma," I said.

"Sure I don't have to," she said. "But what am I going to do when it comes night—oh, Heshie!" She'd finally gotten the packages open and seen the cakes. "You didn't forget!"

"Me forget?" I said. "How could I forget a thing like that?"

She broke off a corner of the cheese cake and bit into it. "A taste?" she said, holding it out to me.

"Later," I said, going over to the gas range and lifting the cover of a pot. "What, no blintzes?" I said, turning back to her.

"Of course, no blintzes," she said. "If you let me know in advance when you're coming home, I'll make you blintzes. But like this, you don't come home two nights, you don't call me up, you come home five o'clock in the middle of the day, without telling me anything, how should I know to make them?"

"That's a fine how-do-you-do," I said, striking a pose like an actor. "A hard-working son like me, I nearly wear myself out and kill myself starting a delivery business, so my mother should have diamonds and furs, and when it comes to a little thing like blintzes, I can't get them!"

"Stop already with the fancy speeches," she said, laughing. "Somebody would think I was starving you. So you'll have them to-morrow. But tell me, Heshie, how did it go with the business? Everything is all right?"

For answer I pulled out the roll of bills and held it up.

"I think everything is all right," I said. "How does it look to you, Ma?"

"Oy, yoy-yoy, yoy-yoy," she said, shaking her head a little and holding her hand to her face. "I thought you said it was a delivery business? You didn't tell me it was also a bank!"

"I thought you'd know that," I said reprovingly. "Would I go into any business, Ma, if it wasn't at least as good as a bank?"

"Let me *tokke* take a look," she said, reaching for the roll.

"One second, Ma," I said, dodging her skillfully. I peeled off six fives quickly and held them out to her. "This is for you for the house," I said. "You ought to be able to make plenty of blintzes on that. You be a good girl, Mom, and make them like I like them, and you can have that every week. All right?"

"I should say it's all right," she said, looking important. "Business is business." She folded the money and put it into her small purse carefully. Then her face became pleasantly sad. "Ai, Heshie," she said, shaking her head, "you're a good boy."

Well, that was one thing about my mother. I was sure she liked me.

"This is nothing, Ma," I said. "This is only the beginning."

I snapped a rubber band around the rest of the roll and held it out to her.

"Now take a look at the rest of it, Ma," I said.

She took it and squeezed it a little and bounced it in the palm of her hand. Then she handed it back to me.

"That's a lot of money for a young boy like you to carry around, Heshie," she said. "Maybe it would be better if—"

"Don't worry about it, Ma," I said. "Any time you want any, no matter how much or what for, you just ask for it. Okay?"

"I know that, Heshie," she said. "I wasn't thinking about that." Maybe she wasn't. "I was just wondering—" Her face took on a ___ look. She leaned toward me a little as she spoke. "You're ___ in a nice way?" she asked.

___ id. "All I have to do is stand on Forty-Second Street ___ dress out a ___ and people go by and ___ e to touch

___ took its

"Now you're joking with me," she said. "But maybe it's better I shouldn't worry. I'm sure if it's your business, Heshie, it must be nice."

That was *one* way of looking at it.

"For the time being," I said, "it'll do."

"I'm only a little worried," she said. "I mean, now you're making so much, what are you gonna do with—?"

"Come on, and I'll show you," I said, taking her hand. I led her through the kitchen and the foyer to the living room and stopped in the dorway. "First of all," I said, "look at that sofa. How long've we had it?"

Harry decides to refurnish the house and insists that Mama buy herself new clothes.

"Come on," she said, "you're such a good boy, I'll make you some blintzes."

"But what about the stuff you already got on the stove?" I said.

"Don't stick your nose in my pots," she said. "Let me worry about the cooking. You want blintzes, so I'll make you blintzes. The other things we'll save for to-morrow, or we'll throw it out or—"

"What kind of throwing out?" I said, imitating her voice and scowling. "Who do you think you are, Mrs. Rockefeller?"

"Good things you learn quick," she said laughing.

"Not good things, Ma," I said. "Smart things."

"Is the same," she said.

"Maybe," I said.

"So all right," she said. "So we won't throw it out. So we'll save it for to-morrow."

We went into the kitchen arm in arm, laughing. I sat down at the kitchen table, and she began to mix the batter.

I rolled up my shirtsleeves and stretched my legs far under the t and watched her. It felt good to be looking at her. I realized su that this was the first rest, the first real rest, I'd had in wee always that way when she was around. It was like putt on a log after a tough s why I didn't hair. It scared place to r

"Here
mix tha

After a few moments she looked up from the gas range and said, "What are you looking at, Heshie?"

"Nothing, Ma," I said. "I was just thinking, why don't you—why don't you go to the beauty parlor once in a while, like the other women?"

Take it from me, it's no cinch telling your own mother she isn't perfect.

She stopped pounding the potatoes to stare at me.

"What are you all of a sudden, Heshie, a little crazy?"

"What do you mean, crazy?" I said. "All the other women do it."

"If all the other women are going to run up on the roof and jump off, so I'll have to do it, too?"

"That's not the idea, Ma," I said. "It's just that you're still a young woman. Why shouldn't you—?"

"Aah, Heshie, please! Don't talk like a baby," she said, bending over the pot in her lap. But I could see her blush a little and I knew she was pleased. "What are they going to do in the beauty parlor, make a young chicken of sixteen out of me again?"

"No," I said, "but they could make you look as young as you really are, and not older."

"Yeah," she said, trying to sound sarcastic and taste the mixture of mashed potatoes and fried onions at the same time, "they're going to make me look young!"

"Of course they will, Ma," I said. "They touch up your hair a little and they manicure your nails and they fix up your eyebrows—"

She set the pot of potatoes down suddenly and shook with laughter.

"What's so funny about that?" I asked.

"You," she said. She held up her clean, worn hands, with the dishwater scars all over them. "In the first place, the girl in the beauty parlor, she'll take one look at these hands, she'll get the cholera. And secondly, other boys, they come your age, they go into business, they make a little money—they start looking around for a nice quiet girl she should make a good wife. But you, instead you should look around for a wife, you start sending your mother to beauty parlors."

"So what's wrong with that?"

"It's not wrong," she said. "It's crazy, that's all."

"All right," I said, "so it's crazy. But don't forget, there I like some cheese blintzes, too, not only potato ones."

"Aah, you always eat with your eyes, Heshie," she said. "This is enough."

"Never mind," I said, grinning at her. "By me it's not blintzes unless I get both kinds."

She went to the icebox and took out the cheese.

"I'd just like to see if your wife, when you get one, if she'll cook for you two kinds of blintzes also."

"Don't worry," I said. "I'll find that out in advance. No blintzes, no wife."

She looked at me slyly.

"Maybe you got already a girl, you're keeping it a secret?" she said.

I looked at her as though I had been highly insulted.

"Ma!" I said. "Would I keep a secret from you?"

"So all right, then," she said. "If you haven't got a girl, I'll get you one. I got one that's for you just right."

Maybe it wouldn't have so many curves. But it'd be kosher all right. Leave it to Mama.

"Don't do me any favors, Ma," I said. "Just watch out for those blintzes, there."

Unless my nose had suddenly lost its sensitivity, my guess was that the old lady had been giving this matrimonial business a little more than just a passing thought. If I knew what was good for me, I'd get her mind onto other things, quick.

"Did you ever hear of such a thing?" she said, addressing the frying pan as she poured the batter in. "Instead of thinking about a wife, he's worrying about stuffing his stomach."

"That's the way it should be," I said. "Wives are easy to get. But blintzes like these—aah, Ma, that's not so easy to find. You ought to see some of the junk they give you in restaurants."

She picked the hot thin pancake out of the frying pan with a fork, put it on a plate, and rolled it full of mashed potatoes. She worked swiftly and silently at this, the most important part of the process. But I knew she was thinking deeply, because when she set the first plate of hot blintzes before me, she said:

"Maybe you're right, Heshie," she said. "Maybe you got time with a wife. Maybe you got other plans, hah?"

If my biographer ever wanted to find out from which side of the family I got my brains, I guess he wouldn't have much difficulty.

"Sure I got other plans," I said. "I always have other plans, Ma."

"Maybe now you're got a little more money, now you don't work so hard, Heshie, maybe now," she said hopefully, "you'll go to school at night like Papa wanted you should, and you'll become a lawyer?"

My dear Mrs. Bogen, unless you drop your recently acquired critical tone, and pay more strict attention to business, I'm afraid we'll have to drop you from the payroll.

"Aah, Ma, please," I said gently. "Let's not start that all over again."

"Why not, Heshie?" she said, sitting down across the table from me. "You know it's what Papa always wanted you should be. And now, now you got a business, you're making money, you're still young, you could go at night easy. Plenty boys they study at night and they become big lawyers. What's the matter? They're smarter than you? You're just as smart as they are." Smarter yet! "If by Mrs. Heimowitz that dumb Murray of hers, *he* could become a lawyer by studying at night, then you could do it in a one, two, three, Heshie. You know that."

"Sure I know it, Ma," I said. "But what's the sense of me wasting my time? You know what lawyers are making today? You know how many of them are starving? Why, for crying out loud, Ma, I make more in one week in that delivery business of mine, than most lawyers they make in a *year*."

"That's nothing, Heshie," she said. "For a good one, there's always room."

"You must've been listening to Mrs. Heimowitz again," I said, reaching for more blintzes. "That's what they all say. For a good one there's room. They're crazy. For a good one there's *never* enough room. Well, I'm good, Ma, and there's plenty of room all right, but not in the law business. Not for me. I got bigger plans than that."

"All right, Heshie," she said, "so you *don't* make so much money at the start. But look at the respect. Look how nice it is for Mrs. Heimowitz she should walk down the street and everybody should say that's the lawyer's mother. Don't you want people should look after your mother and say that?"

"No," I said. "I want people should look after my mother in the street because she's wearing diamond rings and fur coats and they should say there goes Mrs. Bogen, she's got a good son."

"But Papa, when he was alive, he always wanted—"

"Yeah, I know," I said. "I know what Papa wanted. But that's just what was the trouble with Papa. That's why we lived on the East Side and in the Bronx all our lives on twenty bucks a week. Because Papa couldn't be bothered figuring out what was the best and quickest way to make money. . . ."

Aspiring now to become a manufacturer, Harry tries to persuade Meyer Babushkin, a star designer, to become his partner. He invites Babushkin to meet Mama. Mama tells Harry she has invited a nice girl for supper.

"Aah, Heshie, don't be a baby. What did I spoil for you, what? You want to talk business, so talk business. A girl by the table is going to spoil everything?"

"You bet she's not," I said. "Because as soon as we finish eating, I'm taking my friend into the living room where we can talk and you can do what you want with your Ruthie."

"All right, all right," she said, pushing me back toward the living room. "In the meantime, show at least the little bit good manners I taught you. Don't leave a girl she should sit alone in the front room by herself."

I straightened my tie and went back into the living room. She smiled as I came in. I hated to admit it, but when she smiled in that soft appealing way, she had something. Why does a gift like that have to be given to a girl from the Bronx?

"I'm afraid I'll have to call you by your first name," I said, walking over to the sofa across the room from her. "My mother is a pretty determined woman, and she's put her foot down about it."

I stopped for a moment, surprised. I wanted to say it again, just to make sure I'd heard myself right.

"I learned that already," she said with a little laugh. "She threatened to spank me if I didn't call you Harry."

"Well, I guess that makes it even," I said.

It was too bad there wasn't a stenographer present. That brilliant conversation should really have been recorded for posterity.

"I'll tell you," she said. "My name is Ruthie, of course—but all my —I mean—all my friends, they call me Betty." She blushed a little. "I mean, if it's all the same to—"

"I get it," I said, smiling reassuringly, and marking it up as dumb trick number one. "All right, then, Betty it is."

But it wasn't. Betty didn't fit her. Ruthie was the word for that softness that was the first thing you noticed about her. Not even Ruth. Just Ruthie. . . .

Mother had four chairs arranged around the kitchen table, and she had Ruthie sitting directly across from me, so that while I couldn't do much talking, I could watch her.

As soon as the blintzes were served, I had another mark to chalk up in her favor. She handled a fork like it was something with which to carry food to your mouth, not like it was a thermometer that had just been used on a typhoid case.

"Oh, Mrs. Bogen," she said, leaning toward Mother and smiling, "these are *delicious!*"

Mother beamed.

"You like them, hah?"

"I certainly do," she said, "they're wonderful!"

"All right," Mother said, "so after supper, I'll show you how to make them. It's a handy thing for a girl to know."

Hey, Mom! Enough is enough!

I turned to Babushkin.

"How're they coming, Meyer?" I said.

"Fine," he said, with his mouth full. "Very good."

It was a good thing I had an opinion of my own about those blintzes, because I never would have been tempted to try them on *his* recommendation.

"Have some more," I said, loading up his plate.

When we finished I lit a cigarette and passed the pack toward her.

"Have one?" I said.

"No thanks," she said with a pleasant little shake of the head, "I don't smoke."

I was glad she didn't say it like she was showing off a medal.

"Well, then, now, look," I said, leaning on the table with my elbows. "Mr. Babushkin and I, here, we have a little business to discuss. So if you ladies will sort of excuse us, we'll go into the living room and get it over with. But don't you run away, now," I said, shaking my finger at her and kicking myself at the same time. "We won't be long."

"Don't worry," Mother said, waving us away. "I'm going to teach her how to make blintzes. So go already, go, with your business. All the time business, business, business, business, business, business, business!"

I laughed and got up and Babushkin followed. We went through the foyer to the living room and I pointed to the armchair.

"Take a seat, Meyer," I said, and sat down on the sofa, facing him.

"Well, Meyer," I said, cheerfully, "how are things up at Pulbetkal?"

"Oh, you know. Just about the same."

"Struggling along, eh?"

"You know," he said, shrugging.

"How's my friend Mr. Pulvermacher? I'll bet he don't feel so good this week. He probably only made three million dollars this week instead of the six he usually makes? Hah?"

He smiled a little. The way he did it you'd think it was against the law.

"Well, that's the dress business for you," I said. "If you've got a good combination, you can make money faster than the mint. That Pulvermacher, he must be worth all kinds of dough."

He didn't look very happy and he began to chew on his thumbnail.

"You make up your mind yet on that thing we were talking about the other day?" I said.

He swallowed the piece of thumbnail he had in his mouth and began to talk to the floor.

"I'll tell you, Mr. Bogen," he said slowly, "I been thinking about it, you know, I been thinking about it a lot, but, well, I don't know, it's such a big thing you know, that, well, aah, I don't know—"

"Sure it's a big thing," I said. "But all good things are big." Oh, yeah? "That's not really an objection, is it? Because if that's all that's—"

"No," he said. "It's not that. It's just that, well, you know, you can't be sure what's gonna happen. Like this, now, at least I know I got a good job, and every week, regular, like clockwork, I get—"

I love this.

"Listen, Meyer," I said quietly, putting my hand halfway across the small room so I could touch his arm. "You're no baby and I'm not going to talk to you like you were a baby. I'm not going to give you any of this nothing ventured nothing gained stuff. You and I we're about the same age, maybe you're even a little older—how old are you, Meyer?"

"Twenty-six and a half."

"So it's just like I said. You're even a little older than I am. So there's no sense in my trying to give you advice or anything like that. But one thing you and I know, Meyer. When you go into business, nobody goes around giving you a written guarantee you'll make a million dollars the first month. It's a risk. Everybody takes a risk. Don't forget, Meyer, I have a running business of my *own* that I'm stepping out of. I don't have to tell you that. And how about Mr. Ast? He's the crack salesman there for Toney Frocks, you think he's not thinking twice before he goes in for this thing? You can just about bet he's thinking about it. And so am I, too. We're all thinking about it. But a man's gotta make a break sometimes. You can't go on working for another man all your life. You have to make a break *some* time. You've been on Seventh Avenue longer than I have, Meyer." This was true. "And you know a little more about it than I do." But this wasn't. "But in my business, the way I have to keep circulating around all the time, keeping in contact with all my clients, my accounts, I pretty nearly get into every dress house in the industry. I sort of get the feel of the way things are running a little better than anybody else. Every place I go, what do I hear? All I hear is what a great line Pulbetkal is got this season. Every place it's the same thing. 'Pulbetkal is got a line that's hot.' 'That Pulvermacher is some little smart one, all right.' 'Look at the business he's doing.' 'Look at the line he's got.' All day long, wherever I go, that's all I hear. But nobody is kidding me, Meyer. Why is Pulbetkal's line hot? Why is Pulvermacher, Betschmann & Kalisch, Inc. making so much money? Because Pulvermacher is got a bald head, or because he wears glasses with a black ribbon, or because he smokes twenty-cent cigars, or maybe because he's president of the Associated Dress Manufacturers? All that stuff is the bull. Pulvermacher is cleaning up because in the back, in his factory, he's got the best factory man on Seventh Avenue, a man that also happens to be one of the best designers in the business. He's got Meyer Babushkin."

It's a funny thing about spilling the crap. If you don't watch out the way you sling it, you're liable to get snowed under yourself.

However, Harry keeps pouring it on, until Meyer is in a daze.

"You really think we'll have enough to go into business?" he asked doubtfully.

"Do I *think* we'll have enough?" I said. "Look. Let's see what we've got. First there's you. You said six last time, didn't you?"

He nodded slowly.

"All right, then, we have six. Then there's Ast. I think he said something about thirty-five hundred or four, wasn't it? Well, all right, it doesn't matter. Let's say four. So your six and his four makes ten. After all, we can't expect him to have more. You know how those things are. He's a salesman. They can't save any money. If it isn't clothes it's entertainment and this and that and God alone knows what. They spend twice as much as they make. Every cent they make is on their backs. Every one of them has twenty-seven suits and twenty-seven cents. It's yet a wonder to me, Meyer, that he's got the four. But anyway, that's the way it is. So far we have ten. And me, last time I said seven, didn't I? Well, I'm gonna borrow three or four extra, like I just told you. That'll make ten or eleven from me. So what've we got? We've got twenty thousand dollars or over. Why, for God's sakes, Meyer, you know what we can do with twenty thousand dollars? We can start *three* dress houses not one. I'll bet three-quarters of the dress houses in the neighborhood start with a capital of less than ten. And plenty of them start with five, too. But what's the sense of my telling you things like that? You've been in the dress business too long for me to tell you these things. You know all about these things." I certainly was taking a lot for granted. "Of *course* we've got enough. We've got enough to not only start, but to start off with a *bang*."

Suddenly I heard the front door open and close and then I heard Mother's footsteps walking back through the foyer to the kitchen. And all at once I had it. I knew what it was in that girl's face that had puzzled and attracted me and had kept going around and around in my mind all the time I had been talking. I saw, too, the resemblance between them that I had missed because of the difference in their ages. She had that same way of making you feel rested just by looking at her that Mother had. I could sit there, in the same room with a dope like Babushkin, and think of that girl's face as it had looked across the table from me in the kitchen, and I got that same feeling of having reached a place where I could drop my guard and draw my breath after having gone through something tough.

I didn't like the idea of Mother's footsteps having gone back to the kitchen alone. I wanted to see that girl again and talk to her. But I couldn't until I got rid of Babushkin.

"So don't worry about it, Meyer," I said, talking quickly. "We're as good as in right now."

He waved that worried face of his up and down in front of me a few times. It was the best thing he did.

"So what do you say, Meyer?" I said, getting up and coming toward him. "Are we in this thing together?"

He nodded slowly, but that didn't mean anything to me any more. For all I knew he might have been saying no.

"I think so," he said, and I was surprised that his voice didn't break.

"Just give me a little more time to think it over, give me a chance I should talk it over with my wife, and I'll let you know," he said.

Suddenly I had an idea. Maybe I ought to meet his wife. I wanted to hurry this along a little. If he couldn't make up his mind, she'd make it up for him soon enough. And if he could talk her into marrying him, I could talk her into anything.

"I'll tell you what, Meyer," I began, and stopped. Maybe it would be better if I didn't go around looking for trouble. She might not be as dumb as he was. And anyway, I didn't want to spend any more time with him just then. I wanted to get back into the kitchen.

"What?" he said.

"Nothing," I said, giving him his hat and walking him toward the door. "You think it over and I'll get in touch with you in a couple of days." It was better not to get him nervous by trying to clinch it right then and there. Besides which, it was faster, too. "Okay, Meyer?"

"Yeah," he said, nodding a little. "I guess that'll be best."

"Good night, then," I said.

"Good night," he said.

I closed the door behind him and hurried toward the kitchen.

MOTHER WAS alone in the kitchen, darning socks, when I got there.

"Hello, Mom," I said, "where's your company?"

"What do you mean, where's my company?" she said. "What are you, anxious or afraid? Take a look at the clock."

I did. It was a quarter to eleven.

"Holy smoke," I said, "was I in there that long?"

"Well," she said with a shrug, "you wasn't out here, so you must've been in there, no?"

"What happened to Ruthie?"

"She went home. What do you think happened to her? To sit here and wait for you to get finished with the business in there, a person could have a hemorrhage, God forbid. The girl has to go to work tomorrow. She can't sit around a half a night with an old woman like me while you're inside with those high-class friends of yours."

"What's the matter with my friends?" I said.

"Nothing is the matter with your friends," she said. "Did I say something was the matter with your friends? Only tell me, Heshie," she said, cocking her head to one side, "is that gonna be your new partner, the one you were telling me about?"

"That's *one* of them," I said. "What do you think of him?"

"He's all right, I suppose," she said, biting off the thread from a freshly darned sock. "He's *your* partner, not mine."

"Okay, okay," I said, sitting down at the table with her and grinning, "let's have it. What do you think of him?"

"Of course, it's none of *my* business—" she began.

"I know," I said, "but since when does that stop you?"

She flicked a sock at me and I ducked.

"Well, to me," she said, "if you really want to know—"

"Yeah, I want to know."

"To me," she said, "he looks like a high-class dope."

"Good," I said, slapping the table. "That's all I wanted to hear. Now I'm positive I'm going into business with him."

"What's the matter?" she said. "Can't you find any smart people in this world, you gotta go around picking out such *schlemiels* like that—?"

"I don't need smart people," I said. "I'm smart enough for three. But dopes, the right kind of dopes, they're hard to find."

"Remember only one thing, Heshie," she said. "To be entirely smart is to be half a fool."

"Yeah, I know, Ma," I said. "Papa used to tell me that, too."

"Well Papa was right, Heshie."

"Let's not go into that now, Ma," I said. "Let's stick to my dope of a partner, Meyer Babushkin."

"I don't know why a person with a little smartness in him should even want to *talk* about a dumbbell like that. Let's talk better about smart people. How do you like Ruthie?"

"Not Ruthie, Ma," I said, raising my hand with the thumb and forefinger forming a circle, "*Betty*, Ma. She doesn't want to be called Ruthie. She wants to be called Betty."

"All right, so it's Betty. Betty, Ruthie, what's something the difference? How do you like her, that's the question?"

"How should I know how I like her?" I said with a shrug. "Before I even got a chance to take a good look at her, she ran away home."

"Well, she didn't run away to Europe. You know where she lives. I got the telephone number. Maybe you don't want to call from here," she said slyly. "You want to take a good look at her, you want to see what she looks like, so you take a nickel, you go into the drugstore, you call her up, and then you go over to her house on Fox Street and you take a look at her. Is that so hard to do?"

It wouldn't be hard. It would be crazy.

"It's not hard," I said, "but it takes too much time. I'm too busy. I can't bother with those things."

"What's the matter, the whole world business fell all of a sudden on your head? One night a week to call up a nice girl like that you haven't got?"

I wouldn't even spend a whole night on the *right* kind of girl. So what chance did a *nice* girl have?

"It's not that, Ma," I said. "I'm planning a new business, too, you know. I've got to see my partners. I've got to arrange for capital. You know, Ma, all that—"

"Who says that by calling up Ruthie—?"

"Betty," I interrupted, smiling.

"All right—Betty. Who says that by calling up Ruthie you'll be wasting time?"

Nobody had to say it. I could tell by looking at her.

"I didn't say I'd be wasting time, Ma," I said. "She's a nice girl and all that, and I got nothing against her."

Not yet, anyway.

"You got something against her!" Mother cried, shaking her head from side to side. "She'll gain ten pounds when I tell her that my Heshie said he's got nothing against her! Since when, Heshie, since when you think you're yourself Count Itufski's son? He's got nothing against her!"

I laughed and lit a cigarette.

"All right, all right, Ma," I said, "I didn't mean it that way. I only meant that I can't spare the time now. I have to look after my new business, that's all."

"All right," Mother said. "Now that you're so smart, and you talked so much, so I'll tell you something. It wouldn't hurt you or that new business of yours if you should go out with Ruthie Rivkin. Now what do you think of that?"

"What do you mean?" I asked.

"Nothing," Mother said with exaggerated casualness. "Only Mrs. Rivkin told me that the boy that marries her Ruthie, that boy gets ten thousand dollars to go in business with, that's all."

He ought to get a medal, too.

"Stop kidding me, Ma," I said. "No grocer on Fox Street is giving away ten thousand dollars with a daughter."

"So maybe you know better than the whole world," she said. "But I'm telling you one thing. The boy that marries Ruthie—"

"Betty," I said.

"All right—Betty. The boy who marries Ruthie Rivkin, he gets ten thousand dollars to go in business. Now what do you think of that?"

She'd never forgive me, if I told her.

"What's the matter?" I said. "Is she so hard to get rid of?"

"What do you mean, hard to get rid of? You saw her, didn't you?"

"Well, I sort of did get a quick look at her before she breezed out of here," I admitted.

"Never mind," Mother said, "don't get so smart. If you didn't see her for long enough, it was your own fault, you were so busy with that big lemon of yours, that Babushkin. But you saw her. And you know there's plenty boys they would thank God seven days a week for the rest of their lives if they could only get a nice girl like that even *without* ten thousand dollars. And *with* ten thousand dollars, don't worry, there's plenty boys in the Bronx, so smart like you any day, Heshalle, that they figure it's worth while they should spend a couple nights a week in the parlor there by the Rivkins on Fox Street."

She probably had a younger sister that was a knockout.

"Then how come nobody grabbed her off yet?" I said.

"What's the matter? She looks like a cripple to you, maybe? She's got a glass eye? One leg is by her shorter than the other? She's a good-looking girl, dope. *She's* particular, too, you dope, you!"

"Ma, please," I said, "don't call me a dope."

"Why not?" she said. "Maybe you're something better?"

"Maybe," I said. "But don't call me a dope."

"If you had any sense in that head of yours—that head that you think is the smartest one the Above One ever made—instead of wasting you time on *lemishkes* like Meyer Babushkin, you'd make a try for that ten thousand dollars, and you could go into business the way you want to and you wouldn't need any stupid partners they should get in the way of your feet when you walk."

"I don't need Babushkin for his money only, Ma," I said. "I need him because he's a designer, a factory man. Don't you understand that?"

"Anything *you* understand," she said acidly, "you can be sure *I* understand, too. Don't think the whole world smartness settled all of a sudden in your head, Heshie. What do you think, it's going to hurt that business of yours if you have an extra ten thousand dollars in it?"

"Of course not, Ma. Ten thousand dollars—"

"—Is ten thousand dollars," she finished. "And it isn't every day in the week a young boy your age gets a chance to put his hands on so much money and at the same time get a nice girl like that Ruthie—"

I started to correct her again, but stopped. I liked the idea of Mother's not being able to talk of her in any way but as Ruthie.

"And I'll tell you something else," Mother said, leaning across the table to poke her finger with the thimble on it at me. "She *likes* you."

"Yeah, she likes me," I said. "What did you do, show her a picture of me? She hardly even saw me. How do you know she likes me?"

That was one to stop the presses for. Harry Bogen reaching for a compliment!

"She told me," Mother said.

"Yeah, she told you! When?"

"After supper, when I was teaching her how to make blintzes," she said.

"Oh, boy, Ma," I said, grinning suddenly and shaking my head, "if I told you before, I'll tell you again—would *you* make a marriage broker! Oh, boy!"

"Never mind with that talk," she said. "I'm not a marriage broker. But for my own son, I want he should get a nice girl. Is there anything wrong in that?"

"Not if she's got ten thousand dollars, too," I said, "there isn't."

"So what do you say, Heshie?"

"Well, all right," I said, "give me her phone number. For *you*, Ma, I'll do it."

She grinned at me.

"You should live so, you little tramp, you," she said, the grin turning into a laugh. "For *me* you'll do it!"

> Harry does call Ruthie for a date; she wants to go to a concert at the Lewisohn Stadium, and he is to meet her in front of the nearby Hebrew Orphan Asylum.

During the next hour and a quarter I had a chance to call myself as many different kinds of a horse's ass as I could think of. And I could think of plenty. But after I'd gone through the whole list, it still didn't help. The fact remained that I was going to a concert and, worse than that, that I was actually looking forward to it.

I could think of an answer, of course. I knew how to read and understand English, and I'd seen a movie or two in my day, so I knew what the answer was supposed to be. But I was damned if I'd admit that a thing like that could happen to me.

But being certain of immunity couldn't change the fact that I was pacing around nervously in front of an orphan asylum on Amsterdam Avenue, all but biting my nails, waiting for what my common sense told me was as Jewish-looking a broad as I'd ever seen in my life.

Hell, I said finally, I guess the smartest of us will do more for ten thousand dollars than we're willing to admit.

When I saw her turn the corner into Amsterdam Avenue, I went forward to meet her.

"Hello," I said, taking her arm, "I was beginning to get scared that you wouldn't show up."

"Oh, I don't think you were *scared*," she said.

That's how much *she* knew about it.

"Well, maybe—" I said, staring at her.

She looked frightened and began to examine her dress and purse and hands.

"Is there anything wrong?" she asked.

"No," I said, still staring hard, "nothing's wrong. I'm just trying to discover two things."

"What?"

"Whether you look the same as you did the other night when we had blintzes," I said, "and whether you're as pretty as my mother keeps saying you are."

She blushed suddenly and looked down at her hands with an embarrassed smile and for the first time in my life I knew what it meant to want to kiss a girl. I mean, just to *kiss* her.

"Oh, I think your mother is—I mean, she's too—"

"Maybe she is," I said, still staring. "But I don't think so."

"Well," she said in a slightly higher-pitched tone of voice, "shall we go in?"

"We might as well," I said, putting my arm through hers. It was amazing how warm she was, even through the thickness of a dress and a light summer coat. "I got the best seats in the house."

"You mean the ones at the tables downstairs?" she said, stopping.

"Yeah."

"Oh, you shouldn't have done that. It's—"

"Forget it," I said, patting her arm. "They're only a dollar and a half a piece."

"It isn't that," she said. "But it's so much nicer in the fifty cent seats, high up in the Stadium."

"You mean way up there on those stone seats?"

She nodded.

"It's not as comfortable as the ones downstairs," she said, "but they're not as uncomfortable as they look. And it's really much more —well, sort of private. But it doesn't matter. If you have these already, why—"

"Just a moment," I said. I took the tickets out of my pocket and tore them in half and tossed them in the gutter.

"Oh!" she said, "you shouldn't—"

"Why not?" I said, remembering to kick myself. I don't like that kind of cheap flash. "No sense in sitting out in the open like an actor on a stage with the whole world staring at you. I should've had more sense than to buy those tickets, anyway. Come on, we'll get a couple of those other tickets."

There was quite a crowd going in when I stopped to buy two of the cheaper tickets. It never occurred to me that there were that many people in the world who were willing to spend money to sit on stone steps and listen to music. Well, and I guess it never occurred to me that I'd be one of them, either.

"Let's go over toward this end," she said, leading me toward the left. "We can climb up to the top row there, and it won't be very crowded. Most of the people sit lower down and toward the right."

"You seem to know a lot about this place, don't you?" I said.

"Oh, I come here pretty often," she said.

"Alone?" I asked.

She blushed and I was sorry I'd asked.

"Sometimes," she said awkwardly. "Sometimes with some other girls or some—"

"Hold it a second," I said. "I want to get a couple of these."

I bought two straw mats from a boy that was selling them, and we continued to climb the wide cement steps.

"You don't really need them," she said. "It's just as comfortable sitting on the stone."

"I suppose," I said. But I couldn't imagine her sitting on anything so hard and not hurting herself seriously.

"This ought to be about right," she said finally, and I spread the mats on the cement step and we sat down.

The huge Stadium stretched away below and to the right of us. It was getting dark quickly, but there was still enough light to see the tiers, arranged like the rays from a flashlight, and how crowded they were. Down below, at the focus of the rays, was the orchestra, with the men tuning their instruments. The sky was blue with a few stars beginning to show and a handful of clouds moving across it slowly. I hadn't looked at the sky for a month. Somehow you get out of the habit downtown.

"It's nice, isn't it?" she said.

I nodded and looked around at the people near us. Most of them were couples of about our own age; they were sitting very close to one another and were whispering and holding hands and laughing for all the world as though they were alone up there. And none of them paid any attention to the others. I considered it a good sign. They had sense.

Just as the music started she turned to me suddenly and said, "I've been wanting to ask you, but I forgot in all the excitement about the tickets. What was it you meant when you said to me on the phone before, 'Don't ever say that,' or something like that?"

It was pretty dark, now, and the only lights were down in the center of the Stadium, with the orchestra.

"Oh, I guess I didn't mean anything," I said. "Let's just forget it."

That marked another first in my life. For once I was afraid to say something to a dame.

"But you must have," she said, looking at me. "I could tell by the way you said it, all of a sudden."

"Well, I'll tell you," I said. "I don't know if I can exactly tell you what I mean. And then, again," I added, "maybe you won't like it. So suppose we skip the whole thing and listen to—"

"But, Harry, please," she said. "I'd rather you told me."

It was the first time she'd called me by my given name. And the way she said it made the skin and the little hairs on the side of my jaw stand up and tingle. Well, at least I could say she had better manners than Babushkin.

"Well, it's like this," I said. "Maybe I don't know you long enough to go around telling you these things, but hell, the way I figure, I figure it's important. So don't get sore, or anything like that. Okay?"

"I promise," she said, smiling, and I was sure she meant it.

"All right," I said. "Now don't ask me for explanations or anything like that, because I can't give them to you. All I know is there's something about you, let's say about the way they put your face together when they made it, or the way you sit and walk and even talk—I heard it on the phone to-night—there's something there that's sort of soft and, well, I guess honest is the best word. Anyway, that's the general idea, see? And it reminds me a lot of my mother. And any girl that can do that, I mean remind me of my mother, must be pretty good. You follow me?"

She nodded a little, quickly, without looking at me.

"Now," I continued, "this is where it gets a little thick, but it's the best I can do in the way of an explanation. I mean, if you only let yourself alone, if you only act natural, you can take my word for it you're all right; you can't go wrong. Anything you say or do, any way you sit or walk or I don't know what, if you only do it natural, without adding anything fancy, you don't have to worry; it'll come out right and it'll look and sound right, too. But the minute you try to add some of those touches, you know, the minute you try to do something different than what you would do if you let yourself alone, it sticks out like a sore thumb; it just doesn't ring right. Now take for instance to-night. We were talking there on the phone and everything was okay; then, I don't know exactly where it was, but all of a sudden you said something—yeah, I remember, now—I think you said something about 'Thank you, kind sir,' or something like that. Anyway—now don't get sore—it was, well, it was fake; just like me tearing up that couple of tickets a little while ago was fake. It didn't sound like you and if you wanna really get right down to it, it *wasn't* you talking. So the second you said it, it hit me so wrong that before I even knew what was hap-pening, I forgot all those high-class manners my mother taught me and like a dope I was yelling 'Ouch,' and I was telling you not to talk like that. Naturally, I got no right to tell you what—aah, *hell*," I said suddenly, "what's the sense of talking?"

"That's all right, Harry," she said quietly. "I know what you mean."

It was nice to know that at least *one* of us did.

"Then suppose we forget it," I said, "and listen to the music."

"All right," she said.

We sat quietly for a while, and the music coming up made every-thing seem all right. Then I thought of something, and I said, "There's one more thing."

"Yes?"

"What do you want to have people go around calling you Betty for?" I said. "That's not you. You're Ruthie. You know what I mean?"

She nodded slowly.

"Ruthie," I said, trying it out. "Ruthie. See, that sounds right. Be cause that's you, you know. Ruthie," I said again. "Well, that's set-tled. Your friends, they call you Betty, but me, I'm different."

Boy, I was as casual as a freight car.

I turned back to the orchestra below us. The music came up thin and tinkly and it suddenly occurred to me that I liked it. It was just right for that sort of place.

"I never listened to this stuff before," I said, "but it's pretty good, isn't it?"

She didn't answer.

She sat with her elbows on her knees, supporting her chin in her hands. A man in a white suit stood up under the lights and put a violin under his chin.

"That's Spalding," she said, as he began to play.

I put my arm around her and she leaned against me, resting her head on my shoulder. I leaned my head down and kissed her hair gently. She didn't move.

The music stopped and we left the Stadium with the crowd.

"How about a little bite of something to eat?" I said.

"I'm not hungry," she said, "but if you are—"

"I'm not either," I said. "Shall we walk a while?"

"All right," she said.

We went west, toward the river, and then walked downtown, arm in arm, without talking. In a dark spot, under a tree, we stopped and I tipped her face up toward me with my hand and kissed her on the mouth. It was all right.

She shivered a little and said, "I'm afraid I'll have to be getting home, Harry."

"All right," I said, and hailed a cab.

I sat with my arm around her, holding her hand in mine, and didn't think of anything.

After a while she coughed a little.

"Well," she said, "I guess we'll, well, I guess we'll be getting home soon."

"Yeah," I said.

"Wasn't it nice?" she said.

"Yeah," I said, without thinking. Then I looked at her quickly. "It was all right," I added.

She turned to look at me.

"What's the matter, Harry? Didn't you like it?"

So far, what had there been to like?

"Yeah, sure," I said. "I liked it."

That was just the trouble. What *did* I like about it? It wasn't the music, that was sure. And as far as I'm concerned, a stadium is just a big draft. I guess I liked my mother so much, I got a kick out of taking her girl friends out.

"It was all right," I repeated. Maybe it still would be, at that. "Only I sort of hate to, well, you know, break the whole thing up right now."

A dame was a dame.

She moved closer to me and put her head against my shoulder. I guess it's all in the words you use.

"Harry—" she began.

I put my other arm around her and drew her close. The cab stopped. What a spot! That's what you get when you haven't got a place to go.

"Well, here we are," she said in a quick, relieved voice.

Yeah, home.

We got out and I paid the driver. She stood on the stoop, hesitating.

"Well, good night," she said slowly.

"Good night," I said; then, quickly, "hey, wait a minute!" Where did she get off, making me behave like a gentleman? "What are you doing to-morrow, Ruthie?"

What was I going to do, let her go thinking I went out with her for the sake of her company?

"Nothing," she said. "Why?"

"How would you like to run up to Totem for the day?" What the hell, I had business up there anyway. I'd kill two birds with one stone. "We could leave early—"

"Oh, I couldn't go to-morrow, Harry," she said.

"Why not?"

"It's Saturday. My mother wouldn't let me ride on Saturday."

It was just as well to be warned in advance. Maybe her mother wouldn't let her do other things on Saturday, either.

"Then suppose we make it for Sunday, then?"

"All right," she said, opening the door and stepping into the hall. "I'll tell my mother."

"Okay," I said, smiling. "Tell her not to worry."

She'd be doing that soon enough.

But somehow, as I walked down the street to the subway, I couldn't help thinking that if I had to knock off a dame to prove I didn't like her, there was something wrong.

Harry has stopped seeing Ruthie, and Ma is disturbed.

"What's the matter, Heshie?" she said quietly, looking up at me from the other side of the table. "What are you afraid of?"

She had the word all right.

"Who's afraid?" I said.

"*You* are," she said.

It looked like I was the answer to everything.

"Don't make me laugh," I said. "Afraid!"

But I sat down again.

"Now look, Heshie," she said, leaning forward. "Maybe I'm wrong. I don't think so. I think I'm right, Heshie. I think you like her and I know she likes you and I'm positive she'll make you a wife like you won't find again if you spend the whole rest of your life looking. But anyway, maybe I'm wrong. Let's say for a minute, I'm wrong. Let's say you don't like her. But why, Heshie? Why? Tell me, tell your mother, why? Give me one good reason."

"Aah, Ma," I said, "you can't give reasons about things like that. You either like a person or you don't. That's all."

"Maybe," she said. "But then you're not so positive. But you, you're so positive you don't like her, you must at least have *one* reason. At least *one* reason let me hear!"

"Aah, Ma," I began, squirming a little, and then I blurted, "she's so damn *Jew*ish-looking! You take one look at her, you see right away she's a kike from the Bronx. For crying out loud, what do you want me to do, walk down the street and have everybody giving me the horse laugh because—?"

She flared up so suddenly that for a moment I almost couldn't catch my breath.

"*You* crazy dumbbell without shame!" she cried. "So *that's* what's eating you! You're a Jew yourself, aren't you? Haven't you got a little feeling in you? What are you, ashamed of what you are? What are you going to do, go around hiding from people what you are? Don't think you're so smart, Heshie. The world is smarter," she almost screamed. "They only have to look at you to know. You can try all you want, you stupid dope, you, but it won't help. I'm glad for once that your father is dead. He shouldn't have lived to hear a son of his talk like that, I'm glad." Her voice shifted to a sarcastic note. "So that's why you don't like Ruthie Rivkin! She's too Jewish-looking for you, hah? And maybe *I* look like a *shickseh* to you? Well, let me tell you something, Mr. Dope. That girl is got more fineness in her one little finger than all the rest of those tramps you're all the time running around with. She's got more—"

"I didn't say she didn't have," I yelled.

"Hold your tongue, my fine one," she cried. "Who do you think you're yelling at, those dopes that you got for partners?"

"Keep them out of this," I cried, and was surprised for a second to find myself in a position where I was defending those two klucks. "I only said I didn't—"

"Never mind what you said," she shouted. "I heard what you said. You said enough for one day."

Suddenly she dropped into her seat and was silent. I sat down, too, and tried to reach across the table to take her hand, but she snatched it away. She sat there, staring at her hands.

Finally she said, "Why do you bother coming home altogether, Heshie, if we're going to fight like this?"

"I don't want to fight with you, Ma," I said. "I don't want to stay away from home, Ma."

"If this is what happens when you come home," she said dully, "maybe it would be better—"

"Don't say that, Ma," I said, reaching across for her hand. She let me take it. "I'm sorry if I said anything, Ma. I didn't really mean it."

"That you're sorry, I can believe," she said quietly. "But don't say you didn't mean it, Heshie." She shook her head. "When a person says what you said, it's only because he *does* mean it. It's a terrible thing, Heshie."

"I guess it is, Ma," I said, scowling. "But I can't help feeling the way I do, can I?"

"No," she said. "But me—I don't feel like that."

"But don't ever say you don't want me to come home," I said. "I like to come home here. I *have* to come home, Ma."

"What for? We should fight? You should say things you don't want to say? We should holler at each other like two crazy ones? *That's* what you like to come home for?"

"No," I said. "And that isn't exactly fair, either, Ma. This is the first time we ever even raised our voices to each other, isn't it?"

"That's all those things need," she said slowly. "A beginning."

"That's not true, Ma. Don't feel that way about it. I don't want you to say those things. It means too much to me to come home here for you to say those things."

"When a person begins to think and talk the way you do, Heshie, home doesn't mean anything to him any more," she said.

"Yes, it does, Ma," I said.

"No," she said. "You're a businessman now. You're a big business-man. You don't think any more the way a son should think. You think the way a businessman thinks. What's a home to a business-man?"

"I don't care about what it means to businessmen, Ma," I said. "All I care about is what it means to me. For crying out loud, Ma, this is the only place where I can sit down and take a rest without feeling that somebody is going to jump on me from behind. This is the only place where it isn't dog eat dog. Don't you understand that, Ma? You think I enjoy all this fighting, fighting, fighting all the time, trying to show people you're smarter than they are? All right, maybe I *do* en-joy it. I don't know for sure. Maybe I think I enjoy it because I know it's the only way to *get* any place in this world, it's the only way to make money and buy the things you want and really live like a person, not a dog. But whether I enjoy it or not, that's not the point. The point is you can't stand a thing like that forever. You have to have a place where you can sit down and take a deep breath and know you're with a friend, you're with a person that really cares for you. That's what coming home here at night means to me, Ma. It makes me feel like a human being for a change. I can sit back and stick my legs under the table and eat your blintzes, without thinking about whether somebody is trying to put one over on me or not. Aah, hell, Ma," I said, "don't you see what I mean?"

"Sure I see what you mean," she said, nodding. "You think you're saying something new? Maybe I never said it in the words the same like you use, maybe I never even *thought* of it that way. I suppose maybe I didn't. But *I* know that. You aren't telling me something I never heard. What do you think I want you should go with a nice girl like Ruthie Rivkin? Because she'll be able to wear the diamond rings and the fur coats you'll be able to buy for her? Of course not. Because a wife is to a man what you just said. How long do you think I'll be here for you to come and sit and eat blintzes and talk? I'm not a chicken, Heshie. I'm an old woman already. Never mind," she said when I tried to protest. "What's true is true. I'm getting older, Heshie. What are you gonna do when I'm not here? You've got to have a wife. You've got to have the right kind of a wife. I don't say you *must* marry Ruthie Rivkin. Maybe you know another nice girl, a girl you didn't tell me about yet. If you have, so all right. But that's the only reason I talk all the time about Ruthie Rivkin. Because about *her* I'm sure. A mother can tell those things, Heshie. A young boy, sometimes he can't."

The hell he can't.

"All right, Ma," I said. "Let's forget the whole thing. Let's not fight or argue."

"When are you giving the party in the showroom for the buyers?" she asked. "To-morrow?"

I nodded.

"So why don't you invite Ruthie she should come down to the party, she'll have a nice time, you can—"

"I don't think she can make it, Ma," I said. "You know she works during the day, and this is for the afternoon."

"Don't worry," she said. "For a thing like this she can get off a half a day. You just tell her she should ask her boss, that's all."

"Nah, Ma," I said, "she wouldn't enjoy it. These people are, well, they're tough, Ma. They're hard drinkers and things like that, Ma. A nice girl like Ruthie, she wouldn't enjoy herself at all."

She dropped her eyes from my face and withdrew her hand from mine.

"It's up to you, Heshie," she said quietly.

The grand opening takes place, without Ruthie.

By four o'clock most of them had arrived and had a couple of drinks. So I climbed up onto the platform and rapped for silence. They turned to face me, holding drinks and cigarettes.

"Ladies and gentlemen," I said, flashing my best smile from one end of the room to the other, "may I have your attention?"

The large room became quiet.

"Thank you, ladies and gentlemen, thank you, thank you, thank you. I want you all to know that I really and sincerely appreciate your all showing up like this, and if there's anything I've forgotten, and it's something anybody here thinks will in any way make this a bigger and better party, why, then, folks, let him speak up now and I, as the management, will do my little bit to see that he or she is taken care of properly. What say?"

I looked around the room, smiling, and they smiled back. But nobody spoke.

"All right, then," I said, "let's get on with the christening. The firm," I said, "is Apex Modes. The president"—I pointed to myself— "is Harry Bogen. We are the proud parents, ladies and gentlemen, who present, for your approval, the apple of our eye—our new fall line."

There was a little applause, not much, because most of them were holding glasses or sandwiches, but a little. I ran down the three steps of the platform, stuck my head into the models' room, and said, "Okay, Meyer."

"Okay," he replied, and I stepped back, holding the curtain away from the doorway.

The first girl was a blonde. She stepped through the doorway, climbed the steps of the platform, turned slowly to show the lines of the dress, and moved down the platform. She was followed by a brunette. Then came a redhead and then a platinum. They followed each other like that slowly, a blonde, a brunette, a redhead, a platinum, until the platform was jammed with a long line of them, some twenty strong. They stood like that for a few moments, posing with their hands on their hips or clasped in front of them. Then the whole group turned slowly and came to rest again, like a line of statues.

This time the applause was louder and longer. When I saw some of those boozehounds actually set their glasses down so they could clap their hands, I knew the line was a hit.

"Okay, girls," I said, and they walked off the platform and began to mix with the crowd.

A half dozen buyers, men and women, crowded around me.

"Where did you get the models, Bogen? They're a knockout!"

"Say, that's some bunch of babies. Where'd you get them?"

"Hey, Bogen! I don't see models like that around the other houses. How come?"

"That's easy," I said, laughing. "They're not regular models."

"Who are they?"

"That's the chorus of *Smile Out Loud*," I said.

"You *mean* that?"

"Sure," I said.

"Oh, boy, oh, boy, oh, *boy!* Pick me that little redhead with the you know whats. Gangway, boys, here I go!"

Five minutes after the girls joined the crowd on the floor, the place was in an uproar. People kept slapping my back and spilling their drinks over me, but I didn't mind. The opening was a success. Not only were the dresses pips, but the idea of getting the chorus of a musical comedy to wear them had caught on.

.   .   .   .   .

I turned toward the rest of the room, and stopped with my mouth open. Standing near the platform, talking to two men, was the neatest-looking brunette I'd ever seen. She stood so that I saw her in profile, and for a moment I couldn't catch my breath. She had the kind of tits you could see coming around a corner ten minutes before the rest of her body followed. Ma-*ma!*

I walked over to Teddy and pointed her out to him.

"Who's the dame?"

He looked at me in surprise. "What are you, screwy?" he said.

"Why?"

"You don't know who she is?"

I looked again. She wasn't a buyer, she wasn't one of my models, and she wasn't wearing one of our dresses.

I shook my head.

"That's a hot one all right," he said, screwing up his lips. "You're paying her, and you don't know who she is."

"You mean she's from *Smile Out Loud?*"

"Sure she is."

"Well, how come she isn't modeling one of our dresses, then?"

"Aw, she's not just in the chorus. She does a specialty number. She sings or something."

"Oh, yeah? You know so much about her, how about a knock-down?"

He looked disgusted.

"Aw, Christ! Why don't you keep your mind on your work for a change, Harry? What do you want to bother with those pots for?"

Get an earful of *that!* He was giving me advice!

"Listen," I said, "I'm paying her, ain't I? All right, then. Come on." I took his arm. "By the way, what's her name?"

"Martha Mills," he said.

THERE ARE two kinds of dames. The kind you want to put, but with whom you wouldn't be found dead. And the kind you not only want to put, but with whom you get a kick out of being seen walking down the street. All the others don't count.

This dame was in class two.

For three weeks in a row I took her out every night. We had dinner and talked until it was time for her to go to the theatre. After the show I called for her and we made the rounds. Always, when the time came to take her home, I thought maybe to-night. But always that's as far as I got, her front door.

Harry starts his campaign. He gets himself an apartment.

The elevator stopped at twenty-one without my saying a word. There's some difference between the elevator operators in a loft building and the elevator operators in a classy apartment house like the Montevideo.

I walked to the door at the end of the small hallway and threw the door open. I didn't see a carpenter, but the two painters who were working in the large living room looked up at us and I could hear the plumber in the bathroom.

"There're your chaperons," I said.

She looked at me sideways, smiling a little, and walked in. We paraded through the living room, into the bedroom, out into the living room again, into the kitchen, peeked into the bathroom, came back into the living room and parked ourselves in front of the wide windows that looked out onto the park.

"Well," I said, "what do you think of it?"

"What am I supposed to say, Harry?"

"Oh, there's no script," I said, waving my hand at her. "You can ad lib."

She looked around the large room again, then out the window, and then at me.

"Who's it for, the Salvation Army or something?"

"No," I said, laughing, "it's all for a very close friend of yours. A gent by the name of Harry Bogen. Remember him?"

"I've got a faint recollection," she said, looking around the room once more, then at me, with her tongue in her cheek a little and the kind of a look in her eye that is sometimes referred to as calculating. "What's the big idea?"

"Oh, I don't know. I just got tired of the old dump, that's all. And now, of course," I added, "now that I'm traveling around in such high-class company, you know"—she bowed a little and I bowed back —"why, I figured it was time I moved into a decent place. See what I mean?"

She said she saw.

"Now tell the truth, Martha, what do you think of it?"

"Well," she said, laughing, "all I know so far is that it's one of the nicer apartments at the Montevideo. Which is enough, believe me. But to tell you the truth, Harry"—she waved her hands to take in the room—"it's still kind of empty, isn't it?"

"That," I said, "is where *you* come in."

She looked at me quickly, and I realized suddenly what I'd said. But I didn't bother to correct the impression.

"We're going out this afternoon to buy me some furniture," I said. I patted my breast pocket. "I got the old checkbook with me, and anything you pick out, that's what I buy." Almost anything, anyway. "What do you say?"

"I say okay."

"Great," I said, putting my arm around her and walking her to the door. "Let's eat first."

With her around, it was almost a pleasure to sign checks. She had so much class, that when we walked into a store, the salesmen fell all over themselves for the chance to wait on us. And she had taste, too. None of this fancy crap for her. Personally, I didn't much care what she bought. As long as the furniture included a double bed, I was satisfied. But she was particular. And so long as her being particular didn't mean more money out of my pocket, she could be particular until the salesmen passed out.

After three hours I said, "All right for to-day. We'll get the rest to-morrow. You tired?"

"No," she said; then, "well, maybe a little."

"Come on," I said, "we'll get a hot drink of something and then go for a drive in the park. All right?"

"All right, Harry."

I was a little tired myself, so I drove back to the garage, left the car, and took a cab.

I put my arm around her and held her hand in my lap. After the cab entered the park, I didn't speak for a while. Then, still holding her close, and looking out the window, I said, "What have you got against me, Martha?"

"Nothing," she said, "I've got nothing against you, Harry."

The fact that she wasn't surprised showed she knew what I was talking about.

"Don't you like me?"

"Sure I like you, Harry," she said. Then, as though she were afraid she hadn't made herself clear, she added, "I like you a lot, Harry." Boy, she was smooth.

I figured the time was ripe for a straight shot, right through the middle.

"Why do you turn me down, Martha?" I said, still looking out of the window.

She stiffened a little in the bend of my arm.

"I'm not turning you down, Harry," she said. "I like you a lot and all that, but, well—I'm just not that kind of a girl, Harry."

And I was Little Lord Fauntleroy.

I didn't say anything. I could feel her head turn a little as she tried to get a look at me to see if it had registered. But I continued to look out of the window, without speaking.

"I like you, Harry," she said again, to drive the point home, "but it's just that I don't know you well enough." She began to talk more quickly, as though she'd been struck by a better idea. "That's the trouble with you: you're so sure right away that you're in love, that you want the woman to be the same. But a woman has to take time, Harry, and be really sure. She has too much to lose." What the hell did *she* have to lose? "A woman can't rush into those things."

All right. Call it love. I had my *own* word for it. We'd soon see which of the two was more accurate. I still had a couple of blank checks on me.

I leaned forward and tapped on the glass.

"Driver," I said, "take us to Tiffany's. Thirty-seventh and Fifth." And, to drive *my* point home, I repeated, "Tiffany's."

If IT WAS any other guy I would have said he was a horse's ass and she was taking him over. But I didn't say it for two reasons. Nobody calls me a horse's ass, and nobody takes me over. I knew she thought I was a big sucker. But she wasn't putting anything over on me. I knew what I was doing.

I picked up the receiver and spoke to the girl at the switchboard.

"Send in one of the boys from the back," I said.

Then I wrote two checks. One to Mama for thirty and the other to cash for five hundred. I put the first one in an envelope, addressed it, sealed it, and sat back to wait for the boy.

What if the wrist watch *had* cost four hundred bucks? So what? First of all, half of that was really coming out of Babushkin's pocket, although he didn't know it, which made *that* all right. And secondly, I wasn't even thinking about the price. Some dames are worth ten times that amount. Maybe not to other guys. But what the hell did I care about other guys? I figured like this: when I took, I took hard. And when I gave, I gave hard. If I took more than my share—well, there were some things you had to *give* more for than they were worth. Like Martha Mills. What if she *did* cost a lot? To *me* she was worth it. And until I got what I wanted I'd keep on giving, just as I'd keep on taking.

The boy came in.

"Yes, Mr. Bogen?"

"Take this down to the bank right away and bring back the cash," I said, holding out the check to him. "Get three hundred in twenties and the rest in tens." He took the check and I picked up the envelope. "And drop this down the chute on your way out. Step on it."

"All right, Mr. Bogen."

He went out and I lit a cigarette.

Love? Love my eye! Every one of these guys that goes around looking like he ate something bad and telling you how much he's in love with some tomato is either just shooting you a line of bull, or he's kidding himself. I don't mind when they shovel it at me, but when they throw the shovel at me, too, that's where I draw the line.

I thought of Ruthie Rivkin and I knew that something was cockeyed with my figuring. I got up and walked to the window. But watching the people and the cars passing in the street below didn't help. I knew I was right. I was positive about that. Then how about Ruthie Rivkin? It didn't add up. Where was the mistake?

I threw the cigarette out and lit another one.

"The hell with it," I said. "If I begin to think too much about it, I'll begin to think maybe I'm wrong."

And I knew I wasn't.

I went back to my desk and propped my feet up on the pulled-out top drawer. If it didn't add up, then the hell with arithmetic, that's all. I knew I was right.

Love? I knew what I wanted, and Martha Mills had it. And I was going to get it if it cost me ten times what I'd spent already. And it was going to be good, too. Because I could have gone through the whole chorus of *Smile Out Loud* and half of Broadway besides, for what she was costing me. But I didn't want the chorus of *Smile Out Loud*. I wanted Martha Mills. Do me something.

There was a knock on the door and the kid came in holding the check.

"What's the matter?" I said. "Where's the cash?"

"They wouldn't cash it, Mr. Bogen. The guy at the bank said—"

"They wouldn't *cash* it?"

"That's right, Mr. Bogen. The man said—"

"Why the hell not? Why wouldn't they—?"

"No funds, the man said. He said there wasn't enough in the—"

"Okay. Okay. Gimme the check." I grabbed it out of his hand. "Okay. You can go back to work."

> Harry has been siphoning off the firm's money, spending it fast, and also socking some away for himself. Now he decides to cover himself by passing the money through Babushkin's bank account. He calls in Babushkin and gives him a wild story about saving on taxes.

"I'll tell you," I said. "I've figured out a plan to beat the government. Have you got a personal bank account, Meyer?"

"Yeah, I got in the savings bank a—"

"I don't mean that, Meyer. I mean a regular checking account. You got one of those?"

He shook his head. What I would've liked to have seen was this baby and Coolidge in a gab fest.

"That's fine," I said. "Now here's my plan, Meyer. You open up a personal bank account in your name in the Manufacturers. We're in the National, the firm I mean, so to keep things straight, you open up this personal account in the Manufacturers. Now here's how we work it. The corporation, Apex Modes, Inc., the corporation draws checks to your order. You take those checks, endorse them, and deposit them in your personal account in the Manufacturers. Then you draw checks on your personal account, you draw them to the order of cash, endorse them, get the cash for them in the bank, and you and I, we take that money for ourselves. See what I mean, Meyer? In that way we'll be drawing money out of the business, and nobody'll know how or why or what. If the tax men ever ask us where the money from the corporation checks went, we just tell them we used it to buy goods, to pay labor, or any one of those things, and we say we paid cash for it. See?"

He stared at me without blinking for a few moments, and then started on his favorite indoor sport, picking his nose.

"Do you get what I mean, Meyer?"

He nodded slowly, but that part of his face that wasn't hidden by the hand he was using on his nose still looked worried.

"Let me repeat it again, Meyer," I said. "Here it is, in a nutshell. You open personal account. Corporation draws checks to you. You deposit checks. You draw checks to cash on your personal account. You endorse checks. Get cash. You and I, we split the cash. Government gets a royal screwing. Understand?"

"Yeah, Harry," he said slowly. "I understand all that all right, but how—?"

Wouldn't that jar you? For a week he'll act like a mummy, then when he does open up, the first word out of his mouth is the wrong one. I wasn't answering any questions beginning with the word how.

"That's fine," I said, breaking in on him. "So suppose we get started. I'll have Miss A draw a check to you for a thousand dollars and you can go right down to the Manufacturers and start your personal account."

He continued to stare at me without moving.

"What's the matter, Meyer? Don't you understand how it's gonna work out? You want me to explain it again?"

"I understand all right, Harry," he said. "But what I don't see is how—"

"Listen, Meyer," I said sharply, "you're not trying to pull any of this Teddy Ast stuff on me, are you?"

"Why, no, Harry. What's the matter you're—?"

Boy, did I know my customers! All I had to do was raise my voice to him and he started crapping green.

"Well, gee whiz," I said, raising my voice and slapping my desk. "You'd think I was asking you to go jump off the roof or something. For crying out loud, Meyer, all I'm asking you is to start a personal bank account with firm money, that's all. Is that something to make speeches about? Do I have to write you a whole *megilla* about a little thing like that? I haven't got all day, Meyer. I've got buyers to see and dresses to sell. We can't sit around all day talking. Do you understand what I was talking about, or don't you? If you want me to explain it again, I'll do it. But for God's sakes, don't—"

"All right, Harry, all right. Don't get excited. Couldn't you just wait a day or so? I mean, I'd like to have a chance to—"

I wondered if he even asked his wife which side of the bed to get out on in the morning.

"For crying out loud, Meyer," I said angrily. "Don't you understand plain ordinary English? If I didn't make myself clear, I'll try again. I've got buyers to see. And I've got dresses to sell. I can't sit around all day on my ass waiting for you to make up your mind, Meyer."

Nor could I wait for him to go home and ask his wife about it. She'd probably have sense enough to tell him what to do.

"All right, Harry," he said. "I just didn't—"

"Okay," I said.

I picked up the receiver and spoke into it.

"Send Miss A in here with the checkbook," I said.

Maybe I didn't get boffed when I went out with Ruthie Rivkin, but I certainly got some swell ideas.

When Miss A came in I said, "Did that deposit go down all right?"

"Yes, Mr. Bogen," she said. "I sent one of the boys down with it only five minutes ago."

"All right," I said. "Now draw a check to the order of Mr. Babushkin for a thousand dollars."

"A thousand?"

"Yes, a thousand."

She leaned the book on the desk and wrote the check. Then she tore it out of the book and handed it to me.

"All right," I said to her, "you can go."

When she left, I turned to Meyer.

"Endorse this on the back," I said, "and go right down to the Manufacturers and start an account. Remember, start it in your name, personally, Meyer Babushkin. Get it?"

He nodded and took the check.

"I'll tell you what," I said. "I've got some work here, so I'll be sticking around for about an hour or so. Go right down and when you come back, drop in here for a minute and tell me about it. Okay?"

"Okay," he said, and went out.

Boy, oh, boy, oh, boy, I said to myself, did I have a partner!

As Harry keeps ordering Babushkin to draw out money and hand it over to him so he can pay the bills—while leaving the bills unpaid—the creditors institute bankruptcy proceedings. This gets into the papers. He is about to explain the stories to Mama.

. . . Mother wasn't alone. I could hear voices in the living room. I walked toward them and stood in the doorway.

"Hello, Ma," I said.

She was in the armchair, her hands folded on the apron in her lap. Across the room, on the sofa, sat a young woman with a baby in her arms. She was plump and had dark hair and was neatly dressed. Before anybody spoke I knew who she was. And I was struck at once by her resemblance to Ruthie Rivkin. There was in her face that same softness, that warmth that was so appealing and that Mother called *chein*.

"Hello, Heshie," Mother said, getting up and coming toward me. "We were just talking about you."

She took my hat and put it on the table.

"This is Mrs. Babushkin," she said.

I bowed and smiled.

"Glad to know you, Mrs. Babushkin," I said. "It's really too bad that we should finally have to meet at a time like this."

She didn't smile.

"Sit down, Heshie," Mother said.

I took one of the straight-backed chairs. I crossed my legs and lit a cigarette.

"Where's Meyer?" I asked.

"He's home," she said, staring at me.

What the hell was she looking at? I had a clean shirt on. And I'd shaved, too. Maybe she was fascinated. It began to look like I had a fatal attraction for the warm Jewish type.

"That's the best place for him," I said. "He should be resting up for to-morrow?"

"He's not resting," she said.

What was I supposed to do, act surprised?

"Well, I guess he doesn't need it, really, Mrs. Babushkin," I said. "There's nothing to what's going to happen to-morrow. A little hearing, a few questions, a few answers, and it's all over."

She shifted the baby into a more comfortable position in her arms.

"I didn't tell him I was coming here to-day," she said quietly.

That was a nice way for a married woman with a baby to talk, wasn't it? It was lucky Mother was there to act as chaperon.

"Why, you could—" I began.

"You see, Mr. Bogen," she said, looking me right in the eye, "my husband *trusts* you."

I dropped my eyes to grind out my cigarette.

"Mrs. Babushkin," Mother said, "let me talk."

I looked at her quickly. And I could tell at a glance that I was in for it. She wasn't on my side, either.

"Mrs. Babushkin has been here for more than an hour, Heshie," she said. "She told me the whole story, the things that happened and the bankruptcy and everything."

It must have been a regular field day.

"Well, I can't help that, Ma," I said irritably. "The creditors just cracked down on us, that's all. But there's nothing to worry about. I told Meyer it was nothing. There's gonna be a little hearing to-morrow, the same as the last one, and everything'll come out the same as the other one did. Two weeks from now our business'll be running again. That's how things happen in business. I can't help those things. It's not *my* fault that those crazy credit men—"

"Nobody says it's your fault, Heshie," Mother said.

They didn't have to say it. I could tell from the way they looked.

I lit another cigarette.

"Then what can I do?" I said.

"Mrs. Babushkin told me," she said, "that her husband trusts you, Heshie."

Why not? Didn't I trust him?

"That's right," Mrs. Babushkin said.

I turned to her with a sarcastic grin.

"But *you* don't, Mrs. Babushkin," I said. "Is that the idea?"

"Yes," she said quietly.

"Well, now look here, Mrs. Babushkin—" I began.

"I don't know what happened downtown, Mr. Bogen," she said, breaking in. "My husband used to talk everything over with me be-fore he did it. This thing he didn't talk over with me. I didn't know what happened until a few days ago. A couple of months ago, he came home and told me about a special bank account you had opened together. I didn't understand it very well from his explana-tion." I couldn't blame her for that. "But he said it was to cheat the government out of income tax."

"Oh, I wouldn't say 'cheat,' Mrs. Babushkin," I said.

"That's what it was for, though, wasn't it, Mr. Bogen?"

"Well, yes, I suppose so," I said. "If you want to look at it that—"

"I warned him at that time not to do it," she said. "I told him it wasn't right." Her face pinched up around the mouth. "But he said it was too late. He said you had started already. He said there was nothing to worry about," she said slowly. "He said you would take care of everything."

"And I did, Mrs. Babushkin," I said quickly. "That had nothing to do with the bankruptcy. This thing is just—"

"Maybe it didn't," she said in a low voice. "But it was the only time he didn't listen to my advice, Mr. Bogen."

"I'm sorry you feel that way about it, Mrs. Babushkin, but I assure you that that account had nothing to do with it. That's a separate thing from this bankruptcy entirely. There's nothing—"

"I don't say there is, Mr. Bogen," she said again. "But it was the only time he didn't listen to what I told him."

Go ahead, tell me again!

"I tell you once more, Mrs. Babushkin, that account had absolutely nothing to do with—"

"Never mind, Heshie," Mother said suddenly. "Let me talk."

"Okay," I said, waving my hand. "Go ahead. You're doing most of it anyway."

"When Mrs. Babushkin came to me an hour ago, Heshie," she said, "and she told me what was happening, I asked her what she wanted me to do. She said she wanted me to make you promise that nothing would happen to her husband."

"For crying out loud, Ma," I said. "I told Meyer Babushkin a dozen times if I told him once. Absolutely nothing is going to happen to him. We're both in this thing and it's one hundred per cent. It's all a big misunderstanding. The creditors think that we haven't got enough money to pay our bills, but they're crazy. We've got plenty. What more can I do? You want me to walk around with Meyer Babushkin and hold him by the hand and see that he doesn't get run over or anything like that?"

"When she was here an hour ago," Mother continued calmly, "I told her there was nothing I could do. I didn't know where you were. But now you're here, Heshie. Now you—"

"What difference does it make where I am?" I said. "I can say it just as well in the Bronx as I can say it downtown. Nothing is going to happen to Meyer Babushkin. You satisfied?"

"Is that the truth, Mr. Bogen?" she asked, leaning forward with the baby in her arms.

I looked her right in the eye.

"That's the truth," I said firmly.

"You promise me that, Mr. Bogen?" she said.

I stood up and waved my arms to the ceiling.

"Jesus Christ alive!" I said. "What do you want me to do, put it in an affidavit for you? You want me to run a full-page advertisement in the paper about it? I just *told* you nothing was going to happen to him, didn't I? What do you want me to—?"

"Stop hollering," Mother said, "and sit down."

I sat down.

"Nobody is going around asking you to make out affidavits," she said, "or anything like that. All Mrs. Babushkin means is you should promise her that *you* won't do anything to hurt her husband."

"*I* shouldn't do anything?" I cried. "Why would *I* want to hurt him? What did he ever do to me? He's my partner, isn't he?"

"Then that's all she wants," Mother said. "She just wants you should promise that nothing'll happen to her husband through anything *you* do. Is that right, Mrs. Babushkin?"

"That's right," she said.

They were both looking at me.

"Do you promise, Heshie?" Mother said.

"That's a nice state of affairs," I said sarcastically. "My own mother and my partner's wife, they want me to *promise* that I'm not going to do anything to get my partner in trouble. Boy, that's pretty good, that is!"

"Don't talk so much," Mother said. "Just say one word, yes or no. You promise?"

"Sure I promise," I said. "Of course I promise. What do you think I am, anyway?"

"That's all I was worried about," Mrs. Babushkin said, getting up. "Thank you, Mr. Bogen."

"Don't even mention it," I said.

Harry has bulldozed Babushkin into testifying at the bankruptcy hearing that the money that went into his personal account was used to buy fabrics, but that he can't recall whom he bought from.

"All right, Your Honor," Golig said, "I'll stipulate the evidence taken at the 21-A hearing."

Siegel looked surprised, but said nothing. He waited until the stenographer made a notation on the record, then he turned to Babushkin.

"According to the testimony that has just been stipulated into the record, Mr. Babushkin," he said, "within ten weeks prior to the bankruptcy of your firm, you made withdrawals, in the form of checks drawn to your order, to the extent of thirty-two thousand five hundred dollars. Those checks you deposited in your personal account, and almost immediately after their deposit, you drew checks on your personal account, to the order of cash, endorsed these checks, cashed them at the bank, and took the cash away with you. You have admitted, Mr. Babushkin, that these moneys were not salaries paid to you by the corporation. And you have insisted, Mr. Babushkin, that you have used that money to pay the debts of the corporation, namely, labor and merchandise purchases. Is that right?"

"Yes, sir."

"Is that the only explanation you wish to make, Mr. Babushkin, as to the disposition of that money?"

"Yes, sir."

"You realize, Mr. Babushkin, do you not, that if His Honor grants this turnover motion against you, and you do not turn that money back into the bankrupt estate, that you will be sent to jail?"

Golig jumped up.

"I object to counsel's attempts to intimidate the witness."

"I'm not trying to intim—"

"Counsel will confine his questions to the issues," the Referee said.

Siegel turned back to Babushkin.

"You realize, Mr. Babushkin, do you not, how silly your explanation of the dispos—"

"I object, Your Honor," Golig cried.

"Sustained," the Referee said.

"Do you want us to believe, Mr. Babushkin, that you spent all that money in ten weeks on labor and piece goods, and   "

"I object," Golig cried again.

"Sustained," the Referee said.

"Do you think a normal man, a man like His Honor, for instance, would really believe, Mr. Babushkin, that you forgot every single name in—"

"I object, Your Honor!" Golig shouted, jumping up and pounding on the table. "This is one of the most outrageous attempts at frightening a witness that I have ever seen. Mr. Siegel is well aware of the fast that his questions are unorthodox and beyond the pale of—"

"Mr. Golig is right," the Referee said. "You will refrain from this line of questioning, Mr. Siegel."

"Very well, Your Honor," Siegel said. But as he turned away I could see him smile.

And all I needed was one look at Babushkin to see why. He was so frightened, that his lips were actually quivering. He kept staring at Siegel as though he had never seen him before, and even from where I was sitting I could see the spit beginning to collect in the corners of his mouth. Boy, but that Siegel was slick. I had to take my hat off to him.

He turned slowly to face Babushkin and asked gently, in a voice so low you could hardly hear him, "Is there any other explanation you *now* want to make as to the disposition of those moneys, Mr. Babushkin?"

Meyer's lips moved, but for a few seconds no words came out. He was the most frightened man I had ever seen. Gradually sounds began to come from his moving lips, but the stenographer could not hear him.

"You'll have to speak a little louder, please."

"M-m-mister B-Bogen can exp-p-plain everything. M-m-mister B-Bogen can exp-p-plain everything."

Harry takes the stand, in turn, and is asked to explain.

"I repeat, Mr. Bogen, can you make such explanation to us now?"

What the hell was his hurry? Couldn't he see I was thinking?

"I cannot," I said.

"I could feel the whole room looking at me, but I kept my eyes fixed on Siegel's face.

"Why not, Mr. Bogen?"

"Because I don't know the first thing about it," I said, talking quickly. I didn't know how groggy Babushkin was, and I had to get it all out before he came to. "This whole thing has been as much of a surprise to me as it has been to everybody else. I was just as astounded at Mr. Babushkin's story at the 21-A hearing as you were. I have always been so busy with the selling end of the business, entertaining buyers, making out-of-town trips, and so on, that I didn't realize until now how I was being victimized by an unscrupulous partner." When it comes to slinging the five-dollar words, I'm as good as any lawyer. "I never did understand how a business as prosperous as ours was could be ruined so quickly. But since I have learned, at these hearings, about Babushkin's personal bank accounts, and the money that has gone through it, the failure of our business is no longer a mystery to me."

"Harry! Harry!"

I could see every eye in the room turn toward Babushkin, where he stood screaming. But I didn't look at him. I looked directly at Siegel.

"What are you saying? What are you telling them? Harry! Harry! What are you saying! Harry!"

He started toward me, but Golig and a couple of others grabbed him. He continued to scream and fight with them, trying to get away from them and at me.

"What are you telling them?" he shouted crazily. "Why don't you tell them the truth? Why don't you—?" Somebody clamped a hand over his mouth, but he bit at it and got his head free. "Harry! What are you saying!" he screamed. "Why don't you tell them the truth?" His voice stretched so thin that it cracked, but he didn't stop yelling and fighting with the men that held him. "Harry! Harrr—eeee—ccccc!"

"Get that man out of here," the Referee said, standing up.

Three others joined the ones that were holding him, and between them they dragged him out of the room.

In a few moments the room was quiet again. Slowly I let out the breath I had been unconsciously holding. I patted my forehead gently with my folded handkerchief.

"I'm sorry, Mr. Siegel," I said, "I didn't mean to start anything like this. I mean, I didn't think he'd—"

"That's quite all right, Mr. Bogen," he said. "It's not your fault at all."

He turned to the Referee.

"No more questions, Your Honor," he said. "The trustee rests."

The Referee turned to Golig.

"Any questions?"

Golig shrugged and said, "No questions."

The Referee looked from one to the other.

"Do you gentlemen want time to submit briefs?" he asked.

"I don't intend to submit a brief," Siegel said, shrugging toward Golig.

"Neither do I," Golig said.

The Referee reached for his pen.

"Motion granted," he said.

As soon as I woke up I reached for the house phone and spoke to the doorman.

"Send a boy out to get a *Daily News Record*, will you?"

"A what?"

"A *Daily News Record*. It's a newspaper.

"All right, Mr. Bogen."

"He may not get it right away. Tell him to try a couple of newsstands. Then send it right up, will you?"

"Right, Mr. Bogen."

As I hung up I wondered how much longer I'd be able to afford having these "Yes, Mr. Bogen" heels all around me. Well, I'd find out. I got out my savings-bankbooks, the last statement on my checking account, my check-stub book, a sheet of paper, a pencil, and went to work.

When I finished, I felt a little better. Even after paying Golig his fee, I still had a good bit more than nineteen thousand left, almost twenty. Not bad. Not bad at all. I thought of all the money I'd pissed away in the past year, and for a moment I felt sad. But only for a moment. What the hell, I'd had a good time. And besides, a lot of that was an investment. What was I crying about? I had twenty thousand in the bank. I had an apartment. I had a car. I had a wardrobe. And best of all, I still had my brains. What was there to be sad about? I'd made it once, and I'd make it again. I wasn't worried. For guys like me the world is wide open.

For what I wanted to do right now, I had more than enough. I even had enough to carry me until I got going again. I'd cut down on expenses, that's all. Mama's weekly check would come down for a while, and I'd reduce expenses all along the line. So what was I hollering about? Who was hollering?

There was a buzz at the door.

"Paper, Mr. Bogen."

"Thanks," I said, and paid for it. But I didn't tip him. I was reducing expenses all along the line, wasn't I?

I didn't have to look very hard. It was right on the front page. "Court Upholds Referee In Babushkin Case. Officer Of Defunct Apex Modes, Inc. To Be Sentenced Friday. Federal Judge Francis J. Guernsey, of the Southern District of New York, yesterday confirmed the turnover motion granted by Referee John E. James against Meyer Babushkin, officer of Apex Modes, Inc."

There was a lot more, but I didn't bother to read it. I knew all about it, anyway.

I sat back in my chair, with the paper in my lap, and tried to figure out how I felt. I waited a few moments, half afraid, but the feeling of worry about Babushkin that I was expecting didn't come. It surprised me a little, how he didn't mean anything to me any more.

Then, to make the test harder, I thought of his wife and kid. But there was no reaction. And why should there be? Come to think of it, it was her own fault in the first place. Was it my place to worry if she was so dumb as to get married to a kluck like Babushkin?

I rattled the paper on my knees. I did it a little proudly. I'd worked the thing out all by myself. And it wasn't a bad job. It gave me confidence for the future. Now there would be no more doubts. Now there would be no more scared moments. Because now, with that paper on my lap, I couldn't go back if I wanted to.

Who the hell wanted to?

Instead of feeling worried or scared, I felt happy. I felt so good that I laughed out loud. I had finally arrived.

I got out the phone book and looked up a number. Then I dialed it.

"Hello? My name is Bogen. I don't know if you remember me, but I was in to look at a diamond bracelet a couple of weeks ago—"

"Oh, yes, Mr. Bogen! I remember you quite well."

Who wouldn't?

"Well, have you still got it in stock?"

"We certainly have, Mr. Bogen."

"Well, then, I'll tell you what. I'm coming down for it this morning, or maybe this afternoon. Anyway, some time to-day. You have it ready for me, will you?"

"We certainly will, Mr. Bogen."

I hung up and whistled to myself as I dialed Riverside 9-0437.

"Hello?"

"Is this Miss Mills' apartment?"

"This is Miss Mills talking. Who is this?"

"Why, ah, my name is Bogen. I don't know if you remember me, but—"

"Why, hello, stranger. Where've you been all these years?"

"Oh, I've been rather busy cleaning up some heavy dough in a little unpleasant thing known as a bankruptcy."

"Oh, *Harry!* I'm *so* glad everything turned out all right. I knew it was that crooked partner of yours all the time, Harry. I knew you'd be all right, Harry."

It looked like she still read the papers.

"Thanks," I said. "How are you feeling, Martha?"

"Oh, so-so."

"I see *Smile Out Loud* is still running."

"Yeah."

"By the way, Martha, when did I see you last?"

"Oh, a couple of weeks ago."

"Oh, sure, now I remember. We were looking at something in some sort of a place, weren't we?"

"That's right, Harry, we were—"

"How's your wrist feeling?"

"It's all right. Why?"

"Because if I remember correctly, it was a bracelet we were looking at, wasn't it?"

"That's right, Harry."

"And your wrist feels okay, you say?"

"Uh-huh. Why?"

I love these dames when they try to play dumb.

"You think it's strong enough to hold the weight of that bracelet?"

"Why, *Harry!*"

"Yes, sir, Martha," I said, "I think I'll bring that little trinket up to your place to-night. What do you say?"

"Oh, *Harry*, that'll be *won*derful."

That's just what *I* thought, too.

"I'll tell you, though, Martha, you know what?"

"What, Harry?"

"What with all the trouble I've been having these last few weeks, Martha, I don't feel so strong as I used to."

"Oh, that's too bad, Harry."

Maybe it was. But at least there was room for an honest difference of opinion.

"And carrying a heavy bracelet like that all the way uptown to your place is just about going to knock me out, Martha, with me in the weakened condition I'm in. See what I mean, Martha?"

No answer. But I wasn't worried. I knew she was still on the wire. I could hear her breathing.

"In fact, Martha," I continued, "by the time I get up to your place to-night with all that load, I'll be so tired out, I'll never be able to make the trip home again. Why, I'll bet, Martha, I'll even have to spend the night at *your* place."

What the hell, I figured the time had come for me to talk turkey.

"So what do you say, Martha? Do you think you'll be able to put up a worn-out messenger boy like me?"

"I think so, Harry" she said.

I could tell by her voice that she meant it. But I wanted to make sure.

"Can't you be more positive than that, Martha? I mean, here I am, all worn out, and I'm going to make that trip all the way up there, carrying such a heavy load, and all you can say is you *think* so!"

"All right, Harry," she said, laughing, "I *know* I'll be able to put you up."

"Okay, kid," I said, "I'll be up right after the show, say about eleven."

"At *eleven?*"

"Sure," I said, "I like to start early."

"Okay, dear," she said. "Good-bye."

Look, I was a dear again!

"Good-bye," I said.

Now that it was all over, and I was released from the strain, I felt so nervous and excited that the hand in which I held the receiver was shaking. I tried to steady it, but I couldn't. It rattled against the hook a few times before it dropped into its place. It was all I could do to keep myself from jumping up and down and yelling crazily. I looked into the mirror over the telephone table and grinned at myself.

I knew it was true. I knew it all happened to me. But still it was a little hard to believe.

"Boy," I said out loud to the face in the mirror, "is that Harry Bogen, or am I nuts?"

Two years ago I was just another poor slob from the Bronx. And to-night I'm going to sleep with an actress!

What Makes Sammy Run?

by BUDD SCHULBERG

Virtually a counterpart of Weidman's Harry Bogen, operating in the film industry instead of the garment trade, Schulberg's Sammy Glick was destined to become the symbol for an entire generation of Hollywood producers. And the simultaneous appearance of these two Jewish anti-heroes, both powerfully drawn, made an enormous impact. The duo seemed in themselves to constitute a trend in fiction.

In retrospect, read as an individual work, and without the confluence of Nazism, Schulberg's book stands out for its sharply observed delineation of the film industry; as the son of a noted producer, he was brought up in that milieu. The creator of Sammy is at pains to offer an economics-is-the-cause-of-it-all explanation for his Jewish hero's vulturous doings, yet hedges on the evil character effects of economic determinism by showing us Sammy's idealistic brother Israel, who, under the same conditions, remained in the slum as a social worker.

The author has explained that at the time he was writing Sammy—which appeared in 1941—he was under didactic tutelage by Communists, though he soon revolted. Despite its rigid conception and occasional lapses into stereotyped cleverness, the novel retains the volcanic force of its central character, and the quality of myth.

Schulberg's ghetto flashback, which forms the center of our excerpt, is particularly interesting because it already represents an attitude of research; the Lower East Side is foreign ground for the novel's narrator, himself the son of a Reform rabbi, and himself alienated from Judaism.

Budd Schulberg has not again approached a major Jewish portrait. His best-known work after Sammy was The Disenchanted, a study (again drawn from Hollywood) of an alcoholic author in his decline. Waterfront was about gangsters in unions, and The Harder They Fall about an exploited prizefighter.

Schulberg, born in New York in 1914, has been a writer all his life. Living in Los Angeles, he became active after the Watts riots in helping young Negro writers develop their talents.

M.L.

THE FIRST time I saw him he couldn't have been much more than sixteen years old, a little ferret of a kid, sharp and quick. Sammy Glick. Used to run copy for me. Always ran. Always looked thirsty.

"Good morning, Mr. Manheim," he said to me the first time we met, "I'm the new office boy, but I ain't going to be an office boy long."

"Don't say ain't," I said, "or you'll be an office boy forever."

"Thanks, Mr. Manheim," he said, "that's why I took this job, so I can be around writers and learn all about grammar and how to act right."

Nine out of ten times I wouldn't have even looked up, but there was something about the kid's voice that got me. It must have been charged with a couple of thousand volts.

"So you're a pretty smart little feller," I said.

"Oh, I keep my ears and eyes open," he said.

"You don't do a bad job with your mouth either," I said.

"I wondered if newspapermen always wisecrack the way they do in the movies," he said.

"Get the hell out of here," I answered.

He raced out, too quickly, a little ferret. Smart kid, I thought. Smart little kid. He made me uneasy. That sharp, neat, eager little face. I watched the thin, wiry body dart around the corner in high gear. It made me uncomfortable. I guess I've always been afraid of people who can be agile without grace.

The boss told me Sammy was getting a three-week tryout. But Sammy did more running around that office in those three weeks than Paavo Nurmi did in his whole career. Every time I handed him a page of copy, he ran off with it as if his life depended on it. I can still see Sammy racing between the desks, his tie flying, wild-eyed, desperate.

After the second trip he would come back to me panting, like a frantic puppy retrieving a ball. I never saw a guy work so hard for twelve bucks a week in my life. You had to hand it to him. He might not have been the most lovable little child in the world, but you knew he must have something. I used to stop in the middle of a sentence and watch him go. "Hey, kid, take it easy."

That was like cautioning Niagara to fall more slowly.

"You said rush, Mr. Manheim."

"I didn't ask you to drop dead on us."

"I don't drop dead very easy, Mr. Manheim."

"Like your job, Sammy?"

"It's a damn good job—this year."

"What do you mean—this year?"

"If I still have it next year, it'll stink."

He looked so tense and serious I almost laughed in his face. I liked him. Maybe he was a little too fresh, but he was quite a boy.

"I'll keep my ear to the ground for you, kid. Maybe in a couple of years I'll have a chance to slip you in as a cub reporter."

That was the first time he ever scared me. Here I was going out of my way to be nice to him and he answered me with a look that was almost contemptuous.

"Thanks, Mr. Manheim," he said, "but don't do me any favors. I know this newspaper racket. Couple of years as cub reporter? Twenty bucks. Then another stretch as district man. Thirty-five. And finally you're a great big reporter and get forty-five for the rest of your life. No, thanks."

I just stood there looking at him, staggered. Then . . .

"Hey, boy!" And he's off again, breaking the indoor record for the hundred-yard dash.

Well, I guess he knew what he was doing. The world was a race to Sammy. He was running against time. Sometimes I used to sit at the bar at Bleeck's, stare at the reflection in my highball glass and say, "Al, I don't give a goddam if you never move your ass off this seat again. If you never write another line. I default. If it's a race, you can scratch my name right now. Al Manheim does not choose to run." And then it would start running through my head: What makes Sammy run? *What makes Sammy run?* I would take another drink, and ask one of the bartenders:

"Say, Henry, what makes Sammy run?"

"What the hell are you talking about, Al?"

"I'm talking about Sammy Glick, that's who I'm talking about. What makes Sammy run?"

"You're drunk, Al. Your teeth are swimming."

"Goddam it, don't try to get out of it! That's an important question. Now, Henry, as man to man, What makes Sammy run?"

Henry wiped his sweaty forehead with his sleeve. "Jesus, Al, how the hell should I know?"

"But I've got to know. (I was yelling by this time.) Don't you see, it's the answer to everything."

But Henry didn't seem to see.

"Mr. Manheim, you're nuts," he said sympathetically.

"It's driving me nuts," I said. "I guess it's something for Karl Marx or Einstein or a Big Brain; it's too deep for me."

"For Chri'sake, Al," Henry pleaded, "you better have another drink." I guess I took Henry's advice, because this time I got back to the office with an awful load on. I had to bat out my column on what seemed like six typewriters at the same time. And strangely enough that's how I had my first run in with Sammy Glick.

Next morning a tornado twisted through the office. It began in the office of O'Brien the managing editor and it headed straight for the desk of the drama editor, which was me.

"Why in hell don't you look what you're doing, Manheim?" O'Brien yelled.

The best I could do on the spur of the moment was:

"What's eating you?"

"Nothing's eating me," he screamed. "But I know what's eating you—maggots—in your brain. Maybe you didn't read your column over before you filed it last night?"

As a matter of fact I hadn't even been able to see my column. And at best I was always on the Milquetoast side. So I simply asked meekly, "Why, was something wrong with it?"

"Nothing much," he sneered in that terrible voice managing editors always manage to cultivate. "Just one slight omission. You left all the verbs out of the last paragraph. If it hadn't been for that kid Sammy Glick it would have run the way you wrote it."

"What's Sammy Glick got to do with it?" I demanded, getting sore.

"Everything," said the managing editor. "He read it on his way down to the desk . . ."

"Glick read it?" I shouted.

"Shut up," he said. "He read it on his way to the desk, and when he saw that last paragraph he sat right down and rewrote it himself. And damn well, too."

"That's fine," I said. "He's a great kid. I'll have to thank him."

"I thanked him in the only language he understands," the ´editor said, "with a pair for the Sharkey-Carnera scrap. And in *your name*."

A few minutes later I came face to face with that Good Samaritan Samuel Glick himself.

"Nice work, Sammy," I said.

"Oh, that's all right, old man," he said.

It was the first time he had ever called me anything but Mr. Manheim.

"Listen, wise guy," I said, "if you found something wrong with my stuff, why didn't you come and tell me? You always know where I am."

"Sure I did," he said, "but I didn't think we had time."

"But you just had time to show it to the managing editor first," I said. "Smart boy."

"Gee, Mr. Manheim," he said, "I'm sorry. I just wanted to help you."

"You helped me," I said. "The way Flit helps flies."

While Al is out having a drink before finishing a review, Sammy fills the remaining space with radio notes, using quips borrowed from Somerset Maugham. Behold, he is a radio editor. Soon a nebbish named Julian Blumberg, in the ad department, brings radio editor Sammy Glick a story, asking for his opinion. Sammy sells Girl Steals Boy as his own to Hollywood, paying Blumberg a pittance, and zooms to the Coast. Kit, a Vassar girl in the next writer office, is overwhelmed by Sammy's energy, nerve, and sex. Al Manheim gets to Hollywood also and meets Sammy with Kit. They talk stories. Maugham is still a favorite with Sammy.

"Come on, Kit, stop the clowning, give out with *Rain*."

Sammy was through playing for the evening. She began to tell Maugham's story. She told it well. You could feel the machinery in his mind breaking it down. I kept my eyes on his face. Sharp, well chiseled, full of the animal magnetism that passes for virility, his skin blue-complexioned from his close-shaved heavy beard adding five years to his appearance, he was almost handsome. If it wasn't for that ferret look. In moments like this when he was on the scent of something you could see the little animal in him poking its snout into a rabbit hole.

Just as she was reaching the climax, where the good Sadie starts giving way to the old Sadie again, Sammy suddenly leaned forward and cut in.

"Wait a minute! I got an angle! I've got it!"

There was an old junk dealer in my youth who used to collect all our old newspapers to grind into fresh pulp again. That was the kind of story mind Sammy was developing. Without even warning us he launched into one of the most incredible performances of impromptu story telling I have ever heard—or ever want to.

"All you gotta do to that story is give it the switcheroo. Instead of the minister you got a young dame missionary, see. Dorothy Lamour. Her old man kicked off with tropical fever and she's carrying on the good work. You know, a Nice Girl. Then instead of Sadie Thompson you got a louse racketeer who comes to the Island to hide out. Dorothy Lamour and George Raft in *Monsoon!* Does that sound terrific? So Dotty goes out to save George's soul and he starts feeding her the old oil. Of course, all he's out for is a good lay, but before very long he finds himself watching the sunrise without even thinking of making a pass at her. The soul crap is beginning to get to him, see? He tells her she's the first dame he ever met he didn't think about that way. Now give me a second to dope this out . . ."

I told him I would be much more generous than that, I would gladly give him several decades, but he didn't stop long enough to hear me.

"Oh, yeah how about this—just about the time George is ready to break down and sing in her choir every Sunday morning they get caught in a storm on one of the near-by islands. They have to spend the night in a cave huddled together. Well, you can see what's coming, she can't help herself and lets him slip it to her. When they realize what they've done they both go off their nut. He goes back to his booze, shooting his mouth off about all dames looking alike when you turn them upside down, and Dotty feels she's betrayed her old man, so she goes to the edge of the cliff and throws herself into the ocean. But good old George manages to get there in time and jumps in after her. Then you play a helluva scene in the ocean where you get over the idea that the water purifies 'em. Jesus, can't you see it, George coming up for the third time with Dotty in his arms hollering something like: 'Oh, God, if You get us outa this—I'll work like a bastard for You the rest of my life.' And you're into your final fade with Dorothy and George married and setting up shop together, in the market for new souls to save."

Sammy looked at us the way a hoofer looks at his audience as he finishes his routine.

There was a moment of respectful silence.

"Of course," Sammy explained, falling back on the official Hollywood alibi, "I was just thinking out loud."

"But where," I said, "does the monsoon come in?"

"Jesus," he said, "I'm glad you reminded me. What the hell is a monsoon?"

"A monsoon is a sequel to a typhoon," Kit explained.

"Only bigger," Sammy interpreted. "So the monsoon'll have to be coming up all the time they're in the cave. It'll be a natural for inter-cutting. Symbolical. When she does her swan dive from that cliff she lands right in the middle of it. That will really give the rescue scene a wallop."

"I'm glad you added the monsoon," Kit said. "I couldn't quite see how an ordinary ocean would purify them. But a monsoon makes it convincing."

> Presently Sammy's first picture, Girl Steals Boy, is being pre-viewed. After the show a shabby young man approaches Al. It is the nebbish, Julian Blumberg, begging Al to hear his tale. It is the classic tale of Hollywood woes: how his wife Blanche made him come out to Hollywood to confront Sammy, how they couldn't even get Sammy on the phone, then how Sammy sud-denly summoned him to "try to help on the script," paying him twenty-five dollars a week, and finally telling him that unfortu-nately the studio had turned down all his scenes.

"I guess you must have thought I was a little shell-shocked when you saw me after the preview last night. Well, maybe I was. Because that picture was the biggest shock in my life, Mr. Manheim. How do you think you'd feel going in to a movie cold and suddenly start-ing to realize you're hearing all your own scenes?"

Oh, God, I thought, I'm going to explode. Sammy Glick is a time bomb in my brain and it's going to go off any moment and blow me to bits.

"The whole picture," Julian was saying. "All those scenes I thought I was just doing for practice—actually showing on the screen—all mine—every line, mine—you know what I felt like doing, Mr. Manheim? I felt like jumping up right in the middle and screaming. I wanted to tell everybody there that the only line Glick wrote on *Girl Steals Boy* was the by-line on the cover. I felt like telling all of them that now I know why he had me fly out in such a hurry—because when he got the other writer bounced he knew he couldn't stay on the picture alone—he didn't dare."

"Why didn't you?" I said. "I suppose you'd've been rushed to the psychopathic ward, but it would have been worth it."

"I just got sick to my stomach," Julian said. "I mean actually throwing up, in the men's room. And when I came out Blanche made me talk to Sammy right away. I've seen Blanche mad, but I've never seen her like that before. I thought it might be better to wait and see Sammy in the morning. But she said either I saw him right then and there or she'd go home and move out. You see, Blanche is a funny kid, Mr. Manheim. To look at her you wouldn't think she was anything but a nice, frail little Jewish girl. But . . ."

"So you did have a talk with Sammy last night?" I said.

"I caught him for a moment in the lobby on his way out," Julian said sadly.

> *Al Manheim shames Sammy into getting Blumberg a small studio job. Still haunted by the Glick phenomenon, Al, once more in New York, looks up Sammy's family address in the old copyboy file.*

Half an hour later I was walking into the world of his childhood, a foreign world of clotheslines, firetraps, pushcarts and pinch-faced children that stretched for too many blocks along the East River. I walked down Avenue A, down Allen, down Rivington, wondering at the irony of the fascist charge that the Jews have cornered the wealth of America; for here where there are more Jews than anywhere else in the world, millions of them are crowded into these ghetto streets with the early American names.

The Glicksteins lived between a synagogue and a fish store, in a tenement laced with corroded fire-escapes and sagging washlines. It looked as if one healthy gust of wind would send its tired bricks tumbling down into the narrow street. The hallway gave off a warm, sweet and infinitely unpleasant odor of age, of decay, of too many uncleaned kitchens too close together. I found the name Glickstein on the mailbox, pressed the buzzer for 4C and started up the moldy wooden staircase that groaned protestingly as I climbed to the top floor.

A frail round-shouldered young man with sick skin opened the door as far as the safety-latch would permit. He looked suspiciously at me through the crack.

"Yes?"

Suddenly I was overwhelmed with the ridiculousness of this visit. I had an impulse to turn and hurry off. But it was too late. I had already begun to explain who I was, why I had come. As if I knew, as if I could.

"My name is Manheim," I faltered. ". . . I knew . . . I'm a friend of Sammy Glick's from Hollywood."

"From Sammele!" I heard a woman's voice cry out. "Israel, quick, open up the door!"

As I entered, she rose from her seat at the window. The window was closed, so she could not have been sitting there for the air. After all these years she must have been still curious about what was going on down there in the street. The indoor complexion of her emaciated, wrinkled face was emphasized by the black lace shawl which she wore, peasant-fashion, over her head. My appearance seemed to frighten her, for she hurried over to me, looking up into my face with an anxiety that made me uncomfortable.

"*Oi weh's mir*, my little Sammele! Something has happened to him! Tell me, mister, please. He sent you to tell me, maybe?"

"No, no, Mrs. Glickstein," I said, wondering what had made me walk into this. "There's nothing wrong with Sammy, absolutely nothing, he's getting along fine."

"Please, I'm his momma—so if something's wrong with my Sammele I want I should know."

"Believe me, Mrs. Glickstein," I had to reassure her. "That's not why I came. Sammy couldn't be better."

"*Ach*," she sighed, slowly regaining her composure. "Excuse me, please. When I hear you come from Sammele I get so excited . . ."

"We haven't heard from Sammy in so long that Momma's been worried about him," the sallow-faced Israel explained.

"But Sammele's a good boy," Mrs. Glickstein added hastily. "Every month regular comes his check in the mail. Only he is all the time so busy he never has time for writing."

She looked at me and her face creased into the deeper wrinkles of a smile. "So maybe my son sent you, you should tell me something from him?"

Here I go again, I thought. Sammy's trusted friend bringing the message of devotion from the faithful son. Why do I always have to be defending the bastard?

"He said to be sure and tell you how well he's feeling," I heard myself saying. "He said that even if he hasn't much time to write he wants you to know he is always thinking of you."

In her excitement she had forgotten her customary hospitality.

"This is his brother," she said. "Israel." Israel nodded like an aged Jew in prayer. He was like an old, bent man with a young face. "Izzy, go in the kitchen and make some tea, like a good boy."

I watched Israel as he quietly obeyed his mother's orders. If physical similarity had anything to do with resemblance, he and Sammy would have looked very much alike. But I would never have recognized them as brothers, for Israel's face seemed to reflect despair and bitterness and the gentleness of resignation, and it was strange to see how these qualities had molded his face to one so different from the forward thrust of Sammy's.

The small front room was cluttered with ugly furniture. The warm, sticky smell I had noticed in the hallway downstairs was only the faint essence of the odor that hung over this flat, the smell of rotting woodwork and too much living in one place.

The street below vibrated with the harsh, raw noises of kids yelling at each other in a stoop-ball game, merchants driving their hard bargains, women shouting their gossip from stoop to stoop, radios turned up as loud as possible to drown each other out, automobile horns honk-honking to remind everybody that their marketplace, their playground, their social center, their arena, was still a street.

Mrs. Glickstein, sensitive with the suffering of five thousand years, guessed what I was thinking.

"Sammele wants we should move uptown," she explained, "but it is better here with the synagogue right next door, so I don't have to do no walking, and the Settlement House where Izzy works right around the corner, and everybody on the block I am such good friends with like in the old country."

Israel brought in the tea, in steaming glasses, and some salami and yellow bread. Mrs. Glickstein and Israel poured their tea into saucers and sucked it through the cubes of sugar they held between their teeth.

Then she ceremoniously lifted a picture from the wall. It was a group photograph captioned Lower Grades, P.S. 15. "See if you can tell which one is him?" Mrs. Glickstein challenged me playfully.

I looked across the rows of serious little faces, wondering whether I could pick him out. It was a cinch. My finger went right to him. He was on the left end of the first row, standing a little closer to the camera than anybody else. It looked weird to see that same intense ferret face on this little body in short pants and long black stockings wrinkled over the knees. "That's him," I said.

"And also here," Mrs. Glickstein said mischievously, pointing to the opposite side of the same row. I looked more closely. By God, there he was again, only this time his face was distorted in a big grin. "He ran around behind the bleachers so he could beat the camera," Mrs. Glickstein explained.

I studied this second image. I had seen that same exultant look on his face before. The moment he watched his name flash on the screen for the first time, the night of his dramatic triumph when the flashlights flared around him and Rita Royce. His face told you that this was a triumph too. When the picture was posted on the school bulletin board Sammy's achievement must have monopolized the comment, and the triumphant sneer on that dark little puss revealed that this had already become his goal.

Mrs. Glickstein wanted me to tell her how much Sammy weighed and whether he was any taller and if he were a good boy and had he met any nice Jewish girl. And she went on talking about what a fine baby he had been and what a smart, hard-working boy, distilling the story of his youth with the unconscious censorship of a mother's pride. In English she sounded awkward and ignorant, but when she discovered I understood Yiddish (though I had practically forgotten how to speak it) she became articulate with that mysterious sense of poetry all peasants seem to have.

All the time we talked, Israel sat there hardly saying a word, noisily sipping his tea or chewing on the dry bread. But the twisted way he smiled at his mother's naive account of her little Sammele, an occasional comment he could not resist, gave him away. When Mrs. Glickstein boasted of the regularity with which Sammy's check arrived every week, Israel nodded scornfully, mumbled grimly, "Sure,

sure, he's very thoughtful." I watched him more and more as Mrs. Glickstein talked, wondering how long this hate for Sammy had been fermenting. He was the one to talk, I thought, this was my man.

At sundown we heard a new sound, a singsong chant of many low voices in weird cacophony. The Orthodox Jews were beginning their evening prayers in the synagogue next door. Israel rose to join them. I said I would like to come along. He nodded, flustered and pleased

When I left, Mrs. Glickstein blessed me again, asked me to look after her little boy, and pressed a paper bag into my hand. "*Strudel,*" she said, "still hot. I made it today. Sammele used to say I made the best *strudel* in the whole world."

When she tried to control herself, her eyes only moistened more. "And maybe you will tell him some time he should try to come home and see his momma."

It was like a very little moan for a very deep wound. I went out wondering how many other cruelties of Sammy's she had accepted with the same mild protest.

The synagogue was a bare, shabby place, airless with all the windows shut, where forty or fifty men, mostly aged and bearded, faced east to the Holy Land, humbled themselves before their fierce, demanding God and wailed their songs of endless sorrow. I stood there swaying with them, but only mechanically, for I was raised in the Reformed Temple that these traditional religionists would spit upon, and in recent years I had even strayed from this watered-down Judaism, occcasionally doing lip service on the holy days now but coming to believe that if love for your fellow man is in your heart you need no superstructure to dramatize it for you. And if it isn't, no God and no Church can put it there. So I stood there swaying and wondering. What is a Jew? The anthropologists have proved it is not a race, since the only scientific category is the Semitic, which includes Arabians and Assyrians, some of the most fervent anti-Jews in the world. And if it were merely a religion, all Jews like me would have to be excluded. And if it is only a unit of national culture it is withering away in America, for the customs and traditions that the Glicksteins brought over at the end of the nineteenth century may have been inherited by Israel, droning in his *yarmolka* at my side, but were thrown overboard as excess baggage by anyone in such a hurry as his younger brother.

Afterward we went across to a little bakery, because that was the most convenient place to sit, and ate potato *knishes* and talked.

The poverty of the neighborhood had swallowed Israel. He had worked for the Settlement fifteen years. When he was a child he had developed tuberculosis of the skin, and doctors had been telling him to find a better climate, but something held him here, like an umbilical cord between him and his people, which he would not cut.

"It is hard to explain," he said. "I would always be thinking about them. I would worry about them."

He talked without an accent but with the wailing tone and cadence of the Jewish chants.

"How much can the Settlement do?" I said.

He nodded wearily. "I know. Sometimes I feel like I'm trying to bail out the Hudson with my bare hands." The sing-song of his voice emphasized the futility. "This one has no clothes to go to school. So, when you get the clothes, he can't go to school because the father has no job. So, when you find the job . . ."

He shrugged helplessly. "The same every day, only worse. The Reds say to me, 'What is the use of your Settlement? It is just a patch on the old tire. What we need is to throw the old tire on the dump heap and start with a new one.' I don't know, sometimes I think maybe they are not so crazy. Only more violence? I have seen too much already. And meantime who is going to get the milk for Mrs. Fleischman's baby, or find someone to take care of little Irving whose mother died yesterday . . .?"

He stopped short, swamped with the hopelessness of it.

"Israel," I said, "have you always felt this way about it?"

"I guess I got it from the old man," he said. "If he had lived a long time ago they would have written about him in the Bible. Everybody on the East Side called him Papa Glick. I can remember when I was a kid, Papa was always bringing somebody hungry home for supper, even when we didn't have enough to go round. I remember once he even dragged an Irish bum in off the Bowery for the Passover Feast, and the ceremony made the mick bawl. Whenever anything went wrong, the neighbors always yelled for Papa. They even called him in the middle of the night like a doctor. Poor Papa Glick."

"Where is he now?"

"He's been dead since Sammy was thirteen."

"How did he die, Israel?"

"He was run over. Coming home with his pushcart one night. Poor Papa. It was like he really wanted to get run over."

"Why?" I said. "What was the matter, Israel?"

"What is the use?" he said. "What's past is past. So now that my brother is a big man I would only sound jealous."

"But you really wouldn't want to be Sammy?"

"Me be Sammy!" he said. "May I eat a live pig first."

"How was it with him and your father?" I said. "What kind of a kid was he? You can tell me."

What I was trying to say was that I was on his side and he seemed to understand.

Israel was one of those Jews who cannot look angry. When they want to look angry they only look more melancholy.

"He broke Papa's heart," he said. "He made Papa not want to live any more."

"What happened?" I said. "What did he do?"

"It's a long story," Israel said. . . .

.   .   .   .   .

Max Glickstein was a diamond cutter in the old country, proud of his trade and his religion. After the pogrom that took his first-born, Max brought his wife and other son to America. The child died in mid-ocean. "We must be brave, Momma," Max tried to console her. "Maybe God is trying to tell us that we will carry none of the troubles of the old world into the new. We will have new sons, little Americans. In America we will find a new happiness and peace."

They found Rivington Street. But no diamonds to cut. In time, Max got a job cutting glass at ten dollars a week. "Glass," he complained. "Glass any jackass can cut. But diamonds!"

For years he cut glass every day but Saturday, when he worshiped his God, and Sunday, when the Christians worshiped theirs. And his wife bore him two sons, first Israel and five years later Shmelka. The midwife did not think Shmelka would live. He weighed only five and a half pounds. "Nebbish such a little one," said the midwife. "Were he a little kitten we would drown him already." But survival of the fittest is a more complex process with thinking animals. Even one who thought as simply as Mama Glickstein. She pushed her great breasts into his mouth until he choked, hollered, and began to live.

Because he was puny, Mama spent so much time with him that his growth was precocious. He walked before his first birthday. Talked before his second. When he was three-and-a-half, he changed his own name. One of Israel's friends always teased him with "Whadya say yer name is, Smell ya?" One day Momma called, "Shmelka, come here," and he paid no attention. She called his name again.

"Shmelka isn't my name any more," he said.

"No," Momma said, "then what is it, please?"

"Sammy," he said.

Sammy was the name of an older kid across the hall whose mother was always yelling for him.

The strike came when Sammy was four. The glasscutters wanted twelve-fifty. Papa was a foreman now, making sixteen, but he remembered how it was to live on ten dollars a week. And now it was even worse with the war boom started and prices rising. He walked out with his men.

"Mr. Glickstein, don't be a dope," the owner said. "In another two, three years you will becoming maybe a partner. To cut your own throat, that is not human. And what kind of foolishness is this when I can get plenty immigrants" (the owner having been here twenty years could look down on the aliens) "to take their places?"

Papa Glick's voice was deep and sure as if he were reading from the Bible. "To be a partner in a sweatshop, such honors I can do without."

But the owner was right about one thing. There were too many others. The strike dragged on six months—a year . . . They never saw those jobs again.

Neighbors helped the Glicksteins the way Papa had always helped them. And he picked up a few pennies as the Cantor in schule on Saturday. But he would gladly have served for nothing and often had. There in the synagogue, a dignitary with his impressive shawl, his yarmolka and his great beard, there life was rich and beautiful. The rest were just the necessary motions to keep alive.

And this they barely did. Sammy played in the streets without shoes. For his fifth birthday he was given a pair that Israel had outgrown. But they were still several sizes too large for him, and the way they flapped like a clown's made the other kids laugh. Sometimes when Sammy would run after his tormentors the shoes would fly off, and Sammy would pick them up in a rage and hurl them at his nearest enemy.

Papa Glick finally gave up any hope of resuming his trade again. He was too old. America was a land for young men. Finally he got himself a pushcart like all the others. He sold shirts, neckties and socks, nothing over twenty-five cents. But there were too many push-carts and not enough customers. So Sammy started peddling papers. He was three feet, four inches high. He wanted to play. He couldn't see why Israel shouldn't do it instead. But soon Israel was going to be bar-mitzvah. *After school let out at three o'clock he studied in the* chcdcr *until supper time. Papa was so proud of him. The Melamud had told him Israel had the makings of a real Talmudic scholar. And it was well known that the* Melamud *was a man who never had a good word to say for anyone but God. "God has blessed my son with the heart and brains of a rabbi," Papa boasted.*

Sammy lugged his papers up and down Fourteenth Street yelling about a war in Europe. He used to come home with a hoarse throat and thirty or forty cents in pennies. He would count the money and say, "God dammit, I'm yellin' my brains out for nuttin'."

Papa Glick would look up from his prayer book. "Please, in this house we do not bring such language."

"Look who's talkin'," Sammy said. "Know what Foxy Four Eyes tol' me—he says I wouldn't hafta peddle papers if you wasn't such a dope and quit your job. He says his ol' man tol' him."

"Silence," said Papa Glick.

"He says that strike screwed us up good," said Sammy.

Papa Glick's hand clapped against Sammy's cheek. It left a red imprint on his white skin but he made no sound. By the time he was six he had learned how to be sullen.

"Papa, please," Mrs. Glickstein pleaded. "He's so small, how should he know what he's saying—he hears it on the street."

"That's so he should forget what he hears," said Papa.

Several weeks later Sammy came in with a dollar seventy-eight. Papa, Momma and Israel danced around him.

"Sammy, you sold out all the papers?" said Papa in amazement.

"Yeah," Sammy said. "There's a guy on the opposite corner doin' pretty good 'cause he's yellin' 'U.S. MAY ENTER WAR'. So I asks a cus-tomer if there's anything in the paper about that. So when he says no, I figure I can pull a fast one too. So I starts hollerin' U.S. ENTERS WAR and jeez you shoulda seen the rush!"

"But that was a lie," Papa Glick said. "To sell papers like that is no better than stealing."

"All the guys make up headlines," Sammy said. "Why don't you wise up?"

Sammy worked a year before he entered school.

That first day at P.S. 15, Sheik kept staring at him. He wanted to listen to what Miss Carr was saying, but he couldn't concentrate very well because Sheik's small black eyes kept boring into him. Everybody knew the Sheik. His old lady was Italian and his old man was Irish and the neighbors would always hear them fighting at night over who was the better Catholic. The Sheik was older than anybody else in the class because he had been left back a couple of times. The kids didn't call him the Sheik because he was handsome, but because it was whispered around that he already knew what to do with little girls. There was even a story that he had knocked one up already, but this was probably circulated by Sheik himself who was a notorious boaster and had a habit of appropriating all his big brother's achievements.

The Sheik sat there all through the hour actively hating Sammy. Sammy had taken his seat, the seat he had had for the past two years. He had told Sammy, but Sammy had refused to budge. "OK., yuh dirty kike," Sheik whispered harshly through his teeth. "See yuh after class."

It was lunch hour. Some of the kids were getting up a game of ball. Sammy wanted to play. After school there was cheder. And then papers to sell. Sammy was going to be a ball player when he grew up. He had a good eye and he was fast. But now he had to fight Sheik. Sheik was two years older, half a head taller. Sammy appraised him. He would probably get the bejesus kicked out of him. But he wasn't scared. Just sorry he couldn't get into that ball game. He followed Sheik into a vacant lot across the street, all boarded up and full of old tin cans and whatever anybody had ever felt like throwing there.

As soon as they got inside the Sheik let one go. It cracked against Sammy's nose, and blood spurted. Sammy's nose felt bigger than his whole face and he couldn't see, but he moved in swinging. Sheik caught him on the nose again. Sammy went down with Sheik on top of him, kicking and swinging, spitting into the bloody face under him, his whole body quivering in a frenzy of hate, shrieking until it became a chant, "You killed Christ. You killed Christ . . ."

When Sammy finally stopped fighting back, Sheik left him there and went to eat his lunch. Sammy tried to stay there until he stopped bleeding, but it wouldn't stop, so he had to walk back to the schoolyard that way. Miss Carr ran over and dragged him into the ladies'

room. *While she washed off the blood he stood there terribly white
and terribly silent. No tears. Just his mouth set hard and his eyes
ugly.* "I think your nose is broken," *she said.*

"It don't hurt much," *said Sammy.*

"You'd better come into the office and lie down."

"Jeez, look where I am! The guys better not see me in the girls'
can."

*She didn't know how to treat him. She was new here and she had
never seen kids like this before. If he would only cry she could comfort him like an injured child. But he would not let her.*

"Hey, what the hell's the matter with that guy sayin' I killed
Christ? The dirty bastard."

"You must not talk like that," *said Miss Carr.* "Christ died so that
everyone should forgive each other and live in brotherly love."

"Yeah?" *said Sammy.* "How about Sheik? Don't he believe in
Christ?"

"Well, yes," *said Miss Carr,* "but . . ."

"I gotta sit down," *said Sammy,* "my head's spinnin'."

*Miss Carr tried to put her arms around him, but he drew away. He
was like a little injured animal snarling at the hand that is trying to
help it.*

"You won't have to worry from now on," *she said.* "I'm going to
have a talk with Sheik. And I think I'll ask some of the bigger boys
to look after you."

His voice made her sympathy sound patronizing. "Who ast ya to?
I'm no sissy. I c'n take care-a myself."

*Sheik felt called upon to avenge Christ every day. Sammy accepted
his beatings as part of the school routine. He never tried to avoid
them, to sneak off after school. He just absorbed it with the terrible
calm of a sparring partner. He would come home every night with his
eyes swollen or his lip cut and his mother would hold him in her
arms and cry, Sammele, Sammele, but he never cried with her, only
held himself stiff in her arms, a stranger to her.*

*After a while, there was no satisfaction left in it for Sheik any
more. It had become manual labor, slaughter-house work. Sheik
began to look around for more responsive victims. It even left Sheik
with a strange kind of fear for Sammy. Somewhere along the line
it had become the victim's triumph. Sammy would talk back to Sheik
any time he liked. There was nothing Sheik could do but beat him
up again. All the suffering that Sammy had swallowed instead of*

crying out had formed a hard cold ball of novocaine in the pit of his stomach that deadened all his nerves.

Life moved faster for Sammy. He was learning. The Glicksteins' poverty possessed him, but in a different way from Israel. He was always on the lookout to make a dollar. The way the little Christians put on Jewish hats and mingled with the Jewish boys to get free hand-outs in the synagogue on the holy days gave him an idea. On Saturday he went down to the Missions on the Bowery and let the Christ-spouters convert him. At two-bits a conversion. He came home rich with seventy-five cents jingling in his pockets. His father, struggling to maintain his last shred of authority, the patriarchy of his own home, demanded to know why he was not at cheder. Sammy hated cheder. Three hours a day in a stinking back room with a sour-faced old Reb who taught you a lot of crap about the Hebrew laws. You don't go to jail if you break the Hebrew laws. Only if you got no money and get caught stealing, or don't pay your rent.

"I hadda chance to make a dollar," Sammy said.

"Sammy!" his father bellowed. "Touching money on the Sabbath! God should strike you dead!"

The old man snatched the money and flung it down the stairs.

Sammy glared at his father the way he had at Sheik, the way he was beginning to glare at the world.

"You big dope!" Sammy screamed at him, his voice shrill with rage. "You lazy son-of-a-bitch."

The old man did not respond. His eyes were closed and his lips were moving. He looked as if he had had a stroke. He was praying.

Sammy went down and searched for the money until he found it.

His mother came down and sat on the stairs above him. She could never scold Sammy. She was sorry for Papa but she was sorry for Sammy too. She understood. Here in America life moves too fast for the Jews. There is not time enough to pray and survive. The old laws like not touching money or riding on the Sabbath—it was hard to make them work. Israel might try to live by them but never Sammy. Sammy frightened her. In the old country there may have been Jews who were thieves or tightwads and rich Jews who would not talk to poor ones, but she had never seen one like Sammy. Sammy was not a real Jew any more. He was no different from the little wops and micks who cursed and fought and cheated. Sometimes she could not believe he grew out of her belly. He grew out of the belly of Rivington Street.

When Papa Glick found out how Sammy made his seventy-five cents, he went to Synagogue four times a day instead of twice. He cried for God to save Sammy.

Sammy remained a virgin until he was eleven. But no storks ever nested in his childish fancy. When he was still in his cradle he could hear the creaking of bedsprings and his parents' loud breathing in the same room. Cramped quarters forced sex into the open. When Sammy ran to find a place to hide from the Jew-hunting gangs with rock-filled stockings who roamed the streets on Hallowe'en, he bumped into a couple locked together in the shadow of the tunnel-like corridor, behind the stairs. On sticky summer nights he used to trip over their legs as he raced across the roofs. The first day in the street he learned about the painted women who called out intimate names to men they didn't know. When he was ten he used to turn out the light to watch the lady across the court get undressed. She was fat, and when she let her great flabby breasts ooze out of her brassiere they flopped down like hams as she bent over. Curiosity and then desire began to creep into Sammy's wiry, undeveloped loins.

He even went up to one of the women around the corner and offered her the quarter he had been given to buy groceries, but she just looked down at him, put her hands on her hips and laughed.

"Send your old man around, sonny, you'd fall in."

A couple of days later Sammy was hanging around Foxy's shop when Shirley Stebbins came in. Shirley was several years older than any of them, maybe sixteen or seventeen. She was tall and thin and only needed a little more flesh to have a voluptuous figure. People said her family was having a tough time because she was going to high school when she should be working. She wasn't hard the way the other girls were hard, boisterous and suggestive. Everybody on the block called her Sourpuss because her mouth was always set in a sullen expression of contempt. Foxy Four Eyes had advanced the theory that she was frigid. He said it happened when her father climbed into her bed one night when his wife was in the hospital.

"Foxy, I'm in a jam," she said. "I need ten dollars bad."

"Bad, huh?" he said, managing to give it an off-color inflection as he put his hand on her. "A guy can do · an awful lot with ten dollars."

He winked at the kids as if he had said something witty. A guy called Eddie who was fifteen and knew his way around got it first.

"I'll get in for a buck," he said.

The expression on his face left no doubt about the pun. It had started as a gag, but Foxy egged them on until the nine of them had subscribed six dollars. Foxy's cheeks burned with excitement and his cockeyes looked out at his protégés proudly.

"All right, sister, I'll be a sport," he said. "I'll throw in the other four—just to see ya oblige the boys."

She looked at all of them. They were jumping around her like frantic little gnomes. Sammy hardly reached her shoulder.

"All right," she said in a tired voice. "Let's see the money, you cheap bastards."

In the back room, when it came his turn Sammy was scared. He was sprawled across her, fidgeting foolishly. Foxy Four Eyes could hardly talk, he was laughing so loud. "Hey, fellers, lookit Sammy tryin' to get his first nookey!"

Sammy could feel the blood flushing his head, and her silent contempt, and his panicky impotence.

While he still clung to her ludicrously, she half-rose on her elbows and said, "Somebody pull this flea off me. I'm not going to make this my life's work."

Foxy and Eddie laughingly dragged him off, still struggling for her, like a little puppy pulled from its mother's teats.

Shirley counted the money carefully and left a little more bitter than she came. "Thanks, you cheap bastards," she said.

Sammy ran after her. "Hey, that ain't fair! I oughta get my four bits back."

But that was the initiation fee Sammy had to pay to be inducted into the mysteries of life.

After the war, prices went higher, but there was no change in the pushcart business. The talk at meals was always money now. The Glicksteins were behind in their rent. A newsboy's take was no longer enough to complement the old man's income. The boys had to find regular jobs.

Sammy and Israel both answered a call for messenger boys. There were hundreds of others. For hours they cussed and fought each other for places near the door because their parents had sent them all out with the same fight talk, spoken in English, Yiddish, Italian, and with a brogue—Sammy, Israel, Joe, Pete, Tony, Mike, if you don't get that job today we don't know what we'll do.

Israel was just ahead of Sammy. They had been waiting since six *in the morning for the doors to open at eight. They were chilled outside, nervous inside.*

When the doors opened at last and Israel was finally standing before the checker, he was told:

"Sorry, kid—ain't hirin' no Hebes."

As Israel hesitated there, crying inside, Sammy suddenly threw himself at him and knocked him down.

"What the hell you do that for?" said the checker.

"That dirty kike cut in ahead of me," Sammy screamed.

The checker looked at Sammy curiously. Sammy stood there, small, spiderlike, intense, snarling at Israel.

"Fer Chris-sake, you look like a Jew-boy yerself!"

"Oh, Jesus, everybody's always takin' me for one of them goddam sheenies," Sammy yelled. Then he broke into gibberish Italian. . . .

. . . . . .

Three weeks before Sammy's thirteenth birthday Papa came in too upset to eat.

"Tonight when I come out of schulc *the rabbi wants to talk to me. 'Max, my heart is like lead to tell you this,' he says, 'but your son Samuel cannot be* bar-mitzvah. *He never comes to* cheder. *He does not know his Brochis. The Mclamud says he knows no more about the Torah than a goy.'"*

Bar-mitzvah is the Hebrew ceremony celebrating a boy's reaching the state of manhood at the age of thirteen. He shows off all his knowledge and makes a speech which always begins, "Today I am a man . . ." and everybody gives him presents and congratulates the father and feels very good. It is as vital to the Orthodox Jews as Baptism is to the Christians.

"Oi weh!" Papa cried. "That I should live to see the day when my own flesh and blood is not prepared to become a man."

"Aw, what's that go to do with becomin' a man?" Sammy said. "Just a lotta crap. I been a man since I was eleven."

"Oh, Lord of Israel," Papa said, "how can You ever forgive us this shame? That I, a man who went to synagogue twice every day of his life, should have such a no-good son."

"Yeah," Sammy said. "While you was being such a goddam good Jew, who was hustlin' up the dough to pay the rent?"

"Silence, silence," Papa roared.

"I guess I gotta right to speak in this house," Sammy said. "For Chris'sake I'm bringin' in more money 'n you are."

"Money!" Papa cried. "That's all you think about, money, money . . ."

"Yes, money, money," Sammy mimicked. "You know what you c'n do with your lousy bar-mitzvah. It's money in the pocket—that's what makes you feel like a man."

The day that Sammy was to have been bar-mitzvahed Papa went to the synagogue and prayed for him as if he were dead. He came home with his lapel ripped in mourning. He would have liked to lock himself in all day because he couldn't face the shame of it. But it was a weekday and on weekdays he was just an extension of his pushcart.

People saw him push his cart through the street with his eyes staring dumbly at nothing. The driver who hit him said he sounded his horn several times, but the old man did not seem to hear.

When he was carried upstairs to his bed Israel and Mama sat there crying and watching him die.

Afterward, Israel didn't know what to do, so he went up on the roof to look at the stars. He found Sammy there smoking a butt.

"Is it over?" Sammy said when he saw his brother.

Israel nodded. He had not really broken down yet, but the question did it. He cried, deep and soft, as only Jews can cry because they have had so much practice at it.

Israel was eighteen, but now he was a little boy crying because he had lost his papa. Sammy was thirteen, but he was a veteran; he had learned something that took the place of tears.

When Israel realized that he was the only one crying he became embarrassed and then angry.

"Damn you, why don't you say something?" Israel said. "Why don't you cry?"

"Well, what's there to say?" said Sammy.

"At least, can't you say you're sorry?"

"Sure," Sammy said. "I'm sorry he was a dope."

"I oughta punch you in the nose," Israel said.

"Try it," Sammy said. "I bet I c'n lick you." Sammy sat there dry and tense. "Aw, don't work yourself into a sweat," he said.

"Sammy," Israel pleaded, "what's got into you? Why must you go around with a chip on your shoulder? What do you have to keep your left out all the time for?"

"Whatta you take me for, a sap like you?" Sammy said. "You don't see me getting smacked in the puss."

"But we aren't fighting now," Israel said.

Israel was right about not knowing Sammy. There were no rest periods between rounds for Sammy. The world had put a chip on his shoulder and then it had knocked it off. Sammy was ready to accept the challenge all by himself and this was a fight to the finish. He had fought to be born into the East Side, he had kicked, bit, scratched and gouged first to survive in it and then to subdue it, and now that he was thirteen and a man, having passed another kind of bar-mitz-vah, he was ready to fight his way out again, pushing uptown, running in Israel's cast-off shoes, traveling light, without any baggage, or a single principle to slow him down.

> *Sammy becomes the assistant to Sidney Fineman, a creative early producer who is falling behind the trends. Soon Sammy is saving him by taking over his job. And when the banker Harrington comes West to look over the studio, Sammy throws a party.*

The night of the party Kit and I saw it happen, saw love come to Sammy Glick or something as close to love as Sammy will ever know. Kit and I and little Ruth Mintz.

This is the way it began. The other members of the Wall Street scouting party were punctual, but Harrington didn't show until the buffet dinner was almost over.

He came in with a dame on his arm, an amazing-looking dame, who made an entrance like the star at the end of the first act. The first thing that clicked when I looked at her was the horse shows in the rotogravure section of the Sunday *Times*. Only not the smartly tailored horsewoman in derby and cutaway, but the horse itself. She was a showhorse with a dark red mane, prancing, beautifully groomed, high-spirited, accustomed and proud to be on exhibition.

If Harrington's life were ever screened, he would be played by Lewis Stone, though Stone would have to go easy on the make-up and under-play his scenes to do the role justice.

Sammy spotted them at the door like a master of ceremonies, beckoned Fineman over to do the honors and ran toward them.

"Mr. Glick," Harrington spoke in efficient snaps. "Very glad to meet you, sir. I've been looking forward to this. I'd like you to meet my daughter, Laurette."

Sammy made a nervous little bow and kept on looking at her. She seemed to fascinate him. He went on staring at her with the out-of-this-world look of a monk at the Shrine of the Madonna, or a strip-tease patron.

"I know that girl," Kit said. "Laurette Harrington. She was at Vassar for a little while."

"I think we're on hand for an historic event," I said. "Sammy Glick is falling in love."

"Sammy isn't impetuous enough for that," she said. "He's just falling in love with the idea of being in love with a gal like that."

Kit and I edged our way up to ringside. Ruth Mintz was standing beside Sammy, but she might just as well have been standing in Outer Mongolia.

"Father hates being late," Miss Harrington was saying. "It's all my fault. I came home frightfully late after looking at pictures all day."

"Perfectly all right," Sammy said in his best party voice. "What pictures did you see?"

"Well, one I've really been chasing all over the world," she said. "*Blue Boy.*"

"*Blue Boy?*" Sammy said. "A foreign picture?"

"Not exactly," Laurette said. "It was done in England."

"Oh, Gaumont-British," Sammy said.

"No, by an independent," she said. "Gainsborough."

> *Laurette becomes engaged to Sammy, for reasons of her own. And he has lunch with her father, the banker.*

"Sammy, I'm going East tomorrow. I don't know whether you realize it or not, but we're contemplating some important changes in our organization out here. We feel your record entitles you to a say in this reorganization."

"That's very kind of you," Sammy said. "Of course, it's only fair to tell you how much I've learned from assisting Sidney. He's been like a father to me. Everything I know about producing came from him. In fact, he's taught me everything he knows."

"That's just what I've been wondering. Perhaps he has given you all he has to give. He let too many flops slip into the program this year."

"Only a genius can make pictures on an average of one a week without some turkeys, Mr. Harrington. Sidney is a hard worker. He did the best he could."

"*I appreciate your sentiments. But, to speak frankly, the purpose of my visit was to determine whether his best was good enough.*"

"*The pictures would have made money if the overhead wasn't so terrific. But it isn't entirely his fault if production costs have been too high.*"

"*Then you think production costs are too high?*"

"*You put me in a difficult position, Mr. Harrington, I don't like to speak about my superiors. Especially a man like Fineman, who was such a pioneer in this business. After all, I can remember when I was a kid seeing his nickelodeons.*"

"*Naturally, my boy,*" Harrington said. "*Loyalty is always to be commended. Always. But our first loyalty is to World-Wide, and I wonder if Fineman isn't becoming a little too old.*"

> Soon afterward Fineman dies, perhaps a suicide, and it is Sammy who presents the industry's golden memorial medal to the widow.
>   Then, his wedding.

The wedding was a beautiful production. It was staged in the garden beyond the lawn terrace of the estate in Bel-Air that Sammy had just purchased from a famous silent star who had gone broke after the advent of sound. The wags insisted on calling it Glickfair.

Beyond the garden were the swimming pool and tennis court and just across the private road a freak three-hole golf-course. The house itself was of baronial proportions, an interesting example of the conglomerate style that is just beginning to disappear in Hollywood, a kind of Persian-Spanish-Baroque-Norman, with some of the architect's own ideas thrown in to give it variety.

There were at least a thousand guests milling around—from Norma Shearer to Julian Blumberg, whose first novel had shortened Hollywood's memory of his Guild activities.

People were clustered about the garden like bees, buzzing isn't it lovely, lovely, just too lovely! The flower girls were two little child stars and the bridesmaids who preceded Laurette down the terraced steps all had famous faces.

Laurette's white satin wedding gown made her complexion seem whiter than ever. Her red lips and hair against that milky skin, and the solemnity of the moment as she moved to the funereal rhythm of the wedding march added to the unreality of the spectacle. She was a

ghostly beauty floating through the Hollywood mist. She and Harrington in his striped trousers and top hat were like a satirical artist's study
of the whole grim business of marriage.

Sammy entered the garden from the opposite path, followed by
Sheik, both in gray double-breasted vests and afternoon cutaways.
Sammy was staring straight ahead of him, a smile set hard on his lips
as if it were carved there. . . .

*In the middle of that night Al gets a desperate call from Sammy
and rushes to his mansion to find him alone.*

"After the wedding, a goddam madhouse. Nothing but champagne.
Twenty-five hundred bucks' worth down the drain. People cockeyed
all over the joint. Can't find Laurette. Make a goddam fool of myself
asking everybody if they seen Laurette. Then upstairs in the guest
room. . . Jesus Christ, with that new punk I just signed, Carter
Judd . . ."

He emptied his highball, keeping his face for a long time in his
glass.

"Judd ducked out as I came in. But she just pulled herself together
and waited for me. Just waited for me as if it was nothing at all."

Sammy's face blotched red and white, unable to hide the pain of
his wounded pride. His features became so ugly and distorted I knew
I was going to see him cry. He started to say, "I can't believe . . . I
thought . . ." and the tears came, forming foolishly in the corners
of his fierce little eyes. I wondered why I thought of Surrealism when
I saw him cry and then I remembered the Dali exhibit of rain falling
inside a taxicab. This was no less bizarre, no less grotesque. Sammy's
tears were rain falling inside a taxicab.

After the tears, came, hideously, the tight, strained, hysterical little
sobs he tried so futilely to choke. But he couldn't hold it any longer
and the dam broke and the tears flowed over. He tried to blot his face
with his handkerchief and when the flow could no longer be checked
that way he sat down on the stool with his elbows on the bar and
cried into his nervous little hands.

When he got his voice again he didn't want me to see how he
looked, so he spoke through his fingers latticed against his face. Before his speech had been nervous broken discords. Now his words
came haltingly, absently, one at a time.

"I told her I couldn't understand it. From a lousy casting couch

broad, maybe. But when a high-class girl like her, a lady, an aristo-
crat . . ."

It was no fake. He was devastated. Kit was right. His was no calculating marriage for position. It did not have to be. He had fallen in
love with position, with the name and the power of Harrington, and it
came to him not as something sordid and cold but as love, as deep
respect for Laurette's upbringing and attraction to her personality and
desire for her body.

He paused a long time, the glibness gone. In his mouth was the
thick, sour taste of defeat, and distress was ugly on him. He was sweating with the strain and the shame of it.

"It wasn't so much what I saw. Hell, we were all drunk and kidding
around. It was how she spoke to me, just stood there like a haughty
bitch, saying . . ." His hands began to massage his face slowly again.
"Jesus, I'll never forget what she said. . . ."

*He balanced a desperate moment on the threshold, swaying, his
eyes bulging, terribly sober.*

*She came forward, straight at him, smoothing out her dress, the
lovely cream satin wedding gown that Princess Pignatelli would be
gushing over in her society column next morning.*

*Her voice was vicious and low, drunken and passionate. Ugly and
hoarse to Sammy. "Well?" she said.*

*He waited for her to alibi, plead, weep, swear, apologize. But this was
all she said. He waited for her to wilt beneath his righteous (and horrified, and frightened) stare, but she only stood there, proud and composed, stately and perverse and cruelly self-possessed. These were the
elements he had loved and admired and suddenly he hated them, he
wanted to hide from them.*

*"Don't stand there gasping like a fish out of water," she said.
"What have you got to gasp about? You've got what you want. And
Dad's got what he wants. And little Laurie's going to get what she
wants."*

*"What do you mean?" Sammy said, feeling his words fade off into
the air like a sky-writer's. "What are you talking about?"*

*"Now listen, dear," she said. "We're going to see a lot of each other.
What's the use of trying to fool ourselves? I know why you married
me—for the same reason you do everything else. And don't worry—
I won't let you down. I'll be the best hostess this town ever had. I'll
handle this part of the business, and I'll be careful, I won't let my*

private life interfere with your career. Only you and I just signed a contract—the same goes both ways."

He had wanted the devotion of Rosalie Goldbaum, he had wanted the companionship of Kit, he had wanted the domesticity of Ruth Mintz and the glamour of Rita Royce, and he had thought he was getting the drop on all of them (and something more, something indispensable) in Laurette Harrington.

His chin went forward defensively, he stood there drawing in slack sail, tightening up, and when he answered her his voice was screwed down hard, cold and metallic.

"Sure. But the joint is lousy with snoopy columnists, that's all. You want it to look right, don't you? Now go on back to the party and stay out of the two-shots. Unless they're with me."

Then she smiled at him boldly and she seemed to tower above him as she came forward to take his frenzied little face in her hands and kiss it on the forehead as if they had been married twenty years.

"All right, dear," she said.

> However, Sammy won't have to spend his wedding night alone. Recovering, he orders up a call girl.

"Before you go," he said, "forget everything I told you tonight. I don't know what the hell got into me for a minute. What the hell have I got to kick about? I feel great. I got the world by the balls. Keep in touch with me, sweetheart."

There in the silence I could almost hear the motor in him beginning to pick up speed again.

As I drove off I saw him standing outside on his palatial stone steps, under his giant eucalyptus trees, looking out over his hundred yards of landscaping that terraced down to the wall that surrounded his property. He was a lonely little figure in the shadows of Glickfair, the terrible little conqueror, the poor little guy, staring after my car as it drove out through the main gates, waiting for Sheik to bring the girls and the laughter.

I drove back slowly, heavy with the exhaustion I always felt after being with Sammy too long. I thought of him wandering alone through all his brightly lit rooms. Not only tonight, but all the nights of his life. No matter where he would ever be, at banquets, at gala house parties, in crowded night clubs, in big poker games, at intimate dinners, he would still be wandering alone through all his brightly lit rooms. He would still have to send out frantic S.O.S.'s to Sheik, that virile eunuch: Help! Help! I'm lonely. I'm nervous. I'm friendless. I'm desperate. Bring girls, bring Scotch, bring laughs. Bring a pause in the day's occupation, the quick sponge for the sweaty marathoner, the recreational pause that is brief and vulgar and titillating and quickly forgotten, like a dirty joke.

I thought how, unconsciously, I had been waiting for justice suddenly to rise up and smite him in all its vengeance, secretly hoping to be around when Sammy got what was coming to him; only I had expected something conclusive and fatal and now I realized that what was coming to him was not a sudden pay-off but a process, a disease he had caught in the epidemic that swept over his birthplace like a plague; a cancer that was slowly eating him away, the symptoms developing and intensifying: success, loneliness, fear. Fear of all the bright young men, the newer, fresh Sammy Glicks that would spring up to harass him, to threaten him and finally to overtake him.

.   .   .   .   .

Now Sammy's career meteored through my mind in all its destructive brilliance, his blitzkrieg against his fellow men. My mind skipped from conquest to conquest, like the scrapbook of his exploits I had been keeping ever since that memorable birthday party at the Algonquin. It was a terrifying and wonderful document, the record of where Sammy ran, and if you looked behind the picture and between the lines you might even discover what made him run. And some day I would like to see it published, as a blueprint of a way of life that was paying dividends in America in the first half of the twentieth century.

Summer in Williamsburg

by DANIEL FUCHS

One of the tragedies of American literature is that so many fine authors write book after book, achieve almost no recognition, not even intelligent understanding, and then give up. Yet their books do not always vanish.

Daniel Fuchs wrote three novels dealing with Jewish life in Brooklyn: Summer in Williamsburg, Homage to Blenholt, and Low Company, in the years 1934, 1936, and 1937 respectively. In his preface to the omnibus edition (Three Novels, published by Basic Books in 1961), Mr. Fuchs says: "The books were failures. Nobody seemed to care for them when they came out. . . . The books didn't sell—400 copies, 400, 1,200. The reviews were scanty, immaterial. The books became odious to me."

These novels hold up remarkably well. They are human, and they tell the truth. Mr. Fuchs knows Williamsburg Jewish life as no other major writer has known it, and his ability to portray people and situations is evident on every page. He writes with basic realism but with a touch of fantasy, of fever, that puts him in the company of Nathanael West. Chapters 8 through 11 of Summer in Williamsburg have much of the bewilderment, agony and yearning of what it meant to be a struggling Jew in Brooklyn nearly forty years ago.

Without the flat didactic simplicity of a Mike Gold, or the ferocity of Weidman and Schulberg, Fuchs in modulated tones portrays the same area of society—in Williamsburg instead of on the East Side. His protagonists are mostly youngsters of his own generation; one of them, a would-be writer, responds as much through Weltschmertz as through social bitterness to the revolutionary appeal of the day.

Fuchs, born in 1909 in New York, was one of the writers of

*the thirties who went to Hollywood when the advent of talking
films created a demand for more literate scenarists. Clifford
Odets, Samuel Ornitz, and a host of other talents took the same
road; only a few returned. In later years, Fuchs has written some
incisive short stories that prove his talent is undimmed; his view
remains sharp, and his sense of form has, if anything, developed.*

C.A.

COHEN, waiting for evening and Tessie's wedding, had
been reading a Russian novel in which the characters, fascinatingly
foreign, had been discussing the melancholy in their souls, the huge
lamentation that was life, and the burdens they endured. He marveled at their rich lives and envied them. Here the people lived with
strong emotions. They felt keenly, and they did not restrain themselves when it came to action. What conversation, Cohen gagged to
himself from respect, what talk! And the things they did! Their movements had a beginning and an end, there were so many adventures
life was constantly in meaningful flux. Take Dostoievsky. That was
life, turbulent, profound, meaty, as it should be.

Cohen read Russian novels and he regretted the condition of existence in Williamsburg. People were commonplace, either going to the
movies or returning. Conversation concerned the price of pot-cheese.
And, worst of all, nothing ever happened. Cohen examined his own
life. Nothing had ever happened to him, he had to admit. In spite of
his reading and culture how many cuts was he in the essential richness
of existence above Davey, the kid who ran through the streets with his
gang? The reflection distressed him, but then the thought of Mahler
came to cheer him.

When Cohen entered the shoe store, the old man was sitting before
his iron shoe gigantically engaged in clearing his chest. He nodded to
him and went on with his duties, this time pushing his nose into a
big dirty rag. The stool on which he sat was a chair with its back
knocked off. Around it on the floor was a dusty mess of leather scraps,
paper, and worn ladies' heels, the collection of months. Cohen sat
down near the wall of the store. He liked the smell of the glue the old
man used to paste on the soles. Mahler came out of the rag and asked
Cohen for a cigarette.

"What are you doing out of bed so soon?" Cohen said, giving him one. "You're a sick man."

"To tell the truth, I'd stay in bed another day, but I had to get up or else Yente Maldick would have come again. Another day with her and I would be dead for sure."

"Listen," said Cohen, "isn't it funny? Here I know you so long and I still don't know your first name."

"I'll tell you, young man," Mahler said slowly. "At my naming ceremony a funny thing happened. The guests were all present, the rabbi was saying the words, and the man who was to circumcise me already took out the blade. Just then in rushes a stranger with a yell. 'What are you filthy Jews doing here?' he cries. 'Are you sacrificing an innocent babe so that your filthy God will have something to eat?' And the next thing that happened a bunch of Cossacks swarm into the room and slaughter the people right and left until everyone is lying with his bowels on the floor. So all my life I have to go through torment not only because I am not properly circumcised but also because I have never been given a first name."

Mahler had given the tale with a straight face, solemnly continuing all the time with his work. Nevertheless Cohen was incredulous.

"Is that a true story?" he said.

"Listen, young gentleman," Mahler said, putting the shoe down and rising on his feet, "there doesn't have to be another word said. If you have any doubt, let me prove it right now."

Cohen protested hurriedly. All right, he believed him. The bell on top of the door tinkled and in walked Yente Maldick carrying a tin cup.

"All right," the shoemaker said, returning to his stool. "There's a woman in the store now, but any time you think I have been lying let there not be two words and I'll be happy to show you." He turned to the old woman. "What do you want, missus?" he said, pretending not to recognize her.

"How are you, Mr. Mahler?" she said. "Look, I brought you some hot milk with butter. It will do you good."

"What's the matter with you, woman?" Mahler asked. He looked at Cohen. "What's the matter with this woman? Maybe you know her, mister? Missus, don't you know poor Mahler died last night? He didn't have any bread, so he died."

"It can't happen," Yente said firmly. "America has enough bread for everyone."

"He was eating herring, missus, and a bone got stuck in his throat. 'If I had a piece of bread,' he said, 'I would be able to get rid of the bone. But I have no bread.' So he sat down and waited until he choked to death."

"That's terrible," Yente said. She began crackling her fingers. "What a calamity! What will we do? What will we do?"

"And what's more," Mahler said, "did you hear what happened to poor Yente Maldick? She went to a Turkish bath to get ready for the Holidays. She knew that when she had all her clothes off there would be no way of telling Yente apart from the others, so she tied a piece of red ribbon around her ankle. Everything went well until a terrible thing happened while she was bathing. The red ribbon fell off and Yente Maldick was lost." It was an old trick, but Yente Maldick had never heard of it.

"Oh, woe, oh, woe," said the old woman, uncertain and wondering whether to believe him. "Woe is me."

"Yes," said Mahler, "terrible things are happening all the time because there is no more a God over America. But look, missus, the milk is getting cold. You better go home with it before it gets like ice."

"Yes, yes, my child," she told the old man. "You're right." The wrinkles on her brow multiplied as she considered what Mahler had said, but finally, finding the problem too difficult, she solved it by dismissing it, and, relieved, carried the tin cup out of the door.

Cohen, who had paid no attention while all this was going on, had been thinking. He had hired a tuxedo for Tessie's wedding and it was to be the first time he would be wearing evening clothes, a stiff shirt, and a wing collar. The prospect exhilarated him, made him feel expansive and urbane.

"Listen, Mahler," he said smoothly, "I'm a writer. You did not know that perhaps, but this was because I never mention it."

"Don't be ashamed of it, young gentleman. At your age everyone is a writer. Even me, although I can't tell you what I wrote. Tell me, what have you written?"

"For the present, I am collecting notes, observations on life and general principles of behavior. Just now, however, I intend working on a play. What I want to do, Mahler, is to talk it over with you. A play should reflect life, and certainly you should know life. After all, I realize I am young and there are many things about which I do not know. Now, the plot of this play goes like this. A certain woman spends the night sleeping with three different men."

"All in the same bed?" Mahler asked, aghast.

"No, no. One after the other. There are three scenes. This is the first act."

"But all in one night. Wonderful, wonderful."

"Here is the problem of the play. The second act opens some months later. The woman knows she is going to have a baby, and the problem of the play is to discover which man is the father of the child. Remember, the three men have been carefully portrayed in the first act. They have different temperaments and they are in different conditions of society. You can see how interesting the problem becomes. Can you imagine what a riot the third act will turn into?"

Mahler rose. "Excuse me," he said, "there is something I have to do." He went to the rear of the store.

When he came back, Cohen was on top of him. "Well, what do you think of it? Did you ever hear of a thing like that?"

"I never heard of such a thing," Mahler said.

"Isn't it original? I told the plot to some friends of mine and they all said they never heard of an idea like that either." He was jubilant. Here was Mahler, the man who had lived all over the world, who had lived intensely, even Mahler recognized the uniqueness of his theme.

"What are you calling this thing?" Mahler wanted to know. He sat before the iron shoe and began hammering small nails, taking them one by one from his gums.

"Well, it's a long story," Cohen said, his face very serious. "At first I wanted to call it 'The Whoremonger,' but I thought that would be too raw for prurient New York audiences, so I changed it to 'The Harlot-Master.' I was thinking of calling it that for some time, but then I had an inspiration. I finally decided to call it 'Green Gods in Yellow.'"

"In what?" Mahler shot back, his face wrinkled with surprise.

"You know, yellow. Like in the war, when a man had too much sense to fight, they called him yellow."

"Oh, that's a pity. With a beautiful idea like that you should never burden the play with a title 'Green Gods in Yellow.' Of course you young gentlemen won't listen to an old man, but, if I may say so, I think a better title would be 'Green Gods in Yellow Tights.'"

Cohen thought it over. "Never mind," he said uneasily. "Never mind."

He hated to admit it to himself, in fact he failed to, but often his favorite was a little disappointing. Was he really kidding him? Cohen sat dejected.

"Cheer up," Mahler said. "Don't look so glum. Look, I'll tell you a joke that will make you happy. It's guaranteed. A fat man was running down the street to catch a trolley-car. On his back he was carrying a heavy sack and he was so fat it was hard for him to run. But the trolley was going to leave and he had to run to catch it. So he runs and runs. Just when he comes to the street corner the trolley-car begins to ride away. He stands in the middle of the tracks, looks at the car, and says, disgusted, 'A joke!' "

"What's the point?" Cohen said. "I don't see anything funny."

"Ah, you young American gentlemen," Mahler said sadly. "In spite of all your learning you still know nothing."

Cohen walked out. What kind of a joke was it, where was the point? He went over Mahler's words as well as he could recall them. Where was the point? He was not so much angry with the old man as disappointed. Was Mahler kidding him? Cohen would not admit it, but in spite of himself he was suspicious. He tried to think of the tuxedo. He would be fascinating tonight and already had composed the postures he would assume.

As he passed Yente Maldick's shack he saw her standing outside, still holding the tin cup and reflecting.

"What's the matter?" he asked. He had forgotten all about it.

She looked at him with grief in her eyes. "Tell me, mister," she begged, "please, young gentleman, did Mahler choke on a herring-bone? Did he really die?" Her eyes were wide and tearful. She wanted earnestly to know.

The bums at Halper's Stable, together with Willie Bernstein and his pals, were having a sham fight. On Keap Street there was a great lot, parts of which had already been excavated for the cellars of apartment houses. The men from the stable had divided themselves into two groups which proceeded to do battle against one another. Cohen, on the sidewalk, wiped his spectacles with his handkerchief and watched them ardently. They were grown men, but they fought for fun like kids, and it was a great sight, but so meaningless, so American in its stupidity.

The men slashed long whips to keep the enemy at bay. Others prepared pails, filling them with water from a hose. They sent the pails up and the front line men swished the water in thick waves. No one minded getting wet. They rubbed the water from their eyes and dug into piles of horse-manure. They seized it, rounding the lumps with their hands like snowballs, and flung them, aiming carefully for the faces. Bernstein suddenly grabbed the hose and played it full force into a friend's mouth. They were having a riotous time.

Out of the stable Halper came running down to break up the game. He waved a blank cartridge pistol, fired into the air, and chased the men with his whip. He cursed hotly at them as they scrambled out of reach. Halper was the only one among them who had any sense of responsibility. The fight was over. Halper stormed at the men at the threshold of the stable while they wrung the water out of their clothes. They cleaned off the manure with sticks. A few went inside to wash. The smell and the filth made little difference with the stable bums. The place was quiet again, and dim.

Cohen shook his head and disapproved, but Davey kept hanging around. It was the high spot for boys, an odorous spot where the atmosphere hung rich in adventure, cowboys, and the Wild West. There was always something doing if one waited long enough to watch it break. The stable was owned by an old family of American Jews, cigar smokers, brandy drinkers, and fast livers who in the winter never failed to appear in expensive fur-lined coats. Halper, a stout, solidly built man, ran the place and worried. The trade had fallen off. It was not like the old times when a horse dealer engaged in a fast-moving business. Halper had to squeeze out the work, no longer trading exclusively in work horses but having to handle saddle horses and ponies. His face was fat and florid, and he was always to be seen in a big hat, a cigar working between his teeth and a long whip in his hand. Wherever he went he smelled warmly of the stable. Willie Bernstein, his nephew, was a wild youngster who would never settle down. He had his uncle in a perpetual state of worry over him. Willie had been a successful lightweight prize-fighter until his uncle heard of it and made him quit the game. A memento of those times, he still had a broken nose. . . .

The men who collected at Halper's Stable held great attraction for Davey and the boys of the street. They paid no attention to the stable bums whom Halper took in and fed in return for the work they did about the stable until they wandered off somewhere. These were sorry specimens, lacking color and resembling the garbage scows in flat hues of gray and brown carrying cargoes of nondescript refuse to sea. On the other hand, there was Scotty, a faithful little man who was a mute and could only manage to mumble out things in thin gasps that were unintelligible. He followed Willie Bernstein with devotion. Rusty, a grinning, cheerful Irishman, periodically got drunk every Saturday night, and kind friends made it a point to look for him and toss him into an opened bale of hay. There were others; a short, dark-faced man chiefly interesting because of the scars on his face; another who attracted Davey because the three fingers between his thumb and little finger on his right hand were missing; and a constantly changing group of cowboys, some tremendously robust and big, bulls.

Willie was easily the most popular of the lot. He was a great hero with the boys. Bernstein was whole-spirited, reckless with himself, and carefully considerate of others. Moreover he was the champion of the Jews in a difficult neighborhood. Once an Italian, in the course of some argument, was smacking skinny Yozowitz, the laundry man. Willie rushed out of the stable, yanked the heavier Italian to the gutter, and then neatly cut him up with his fists. . . .

Cohen found the conversation going badly. It was the tuxedo. He held his neck stiffly above the wing collar, the girl was wearing a flowing red dress that swept the floor, and this was a strange sight to behold in the Canal Street subway station. Cohen made a passing remark about the gaping people in an effort to be superior, but even he recognized the failure of the attempt. In addition, there was the complex etiquette of handling a young lady. It was like walking on eggs. Cohen felt constrained all the time, and tight. He never knew exactly when to hop and skip in front of her to hold open doors and let her pass. Often he had to grope awkwardly to express the appropriately smiling sentiments. Cohen regretted his lack of experience with girls.

The lady herself was disgruntled. She was a plump individual, with wide hips and an oily face. Her hair was ornate. It had waves, bangs and dips, all on one head; she had been to the beauty parlor and had spared no expense. She was disgruntled because Cohen had led her to the subway, disregarding the taxi-drivers who had spotted his tuxedo and hailed him repeatedly, to his discomfiture. Her attitude was inconsiderate. Cohen had already gone to the trouble of hiring a tuxedo when a dark business suit would have done just as well. She lived in Bensonhurst. Tessie was getting married in Williamsburg. What could she expect? Besides, and he mentioned it, the subway was faster.

Cohen in his tuxedo tried to overlook the skinny fit of the trouser legs, the way his vest creased out at the sides, and the cut of the collar around his neck and shoulders. He knew his tie made him appear funny. A boy holding his mother's hand stopped flat-footed and nearly tripped in astonishment as he stared directly into the faces of the pair.

Cohen tried to swing easily into stride beside his companion. "Did Tessie mention perhaps that I am a playwright?" he asked, beginning a conversation to kill time until the train came. They couldn't just stand there.

"You write plays?" she said, frozen in her finery. "What did you say your name was?"

He told her.

"Cohen?" she said. "I don't think I ever heard of you."

A train roared in. Cohen felt so discountenanced that he actually said that he wasn't famous as yet. The doors opened and in his embarrassment he entered.

"Not this train," the girl said, standing on the platform. "That's the wrong train. It's an express."

"Come in," Cohen said. "Come in. This train's all right."

"No, get out. You want a Canarsie local. This is an express. Get out." She stood outside, her face screwed with impatience and irritation.

While Cohen stood there thinking, the doors closed. He pushed to open them, but they closed with too much force. He began yelling instructions, but stopped. He didn't know exactly what to tell her and he couldn't think fast enough. She stood magnificent in her cold anger, her eyes glaring terribly to the last.

Cohen was disgusted. The evening was turning out poorly. He had set so much store by it. Here he had a wedding, and for once in his life the opportunity to get dressed up, to wear evening clothes, to stick his handsome head on top of a high wing collar, to have his chest gleaming proudly with whiteness. There were to be potted palms and soft music. Lovely ladies, each looking like a different flower, would sigh at him because he was so unapproachable. He would walk on the tips of his toes, wafting about the palatial halls like the soft music itself. Cohen would seek a secluded corner, slip his hand urbanely into his pocket, pensively light a cigarette. As the train beat the rails Cohen took heart. The evening was just beginning.

At the hall he burst in while the marriage performer was in the middle of his address to Schlausser and Tessie. Cohen's entrance created a disturbance. Everybody had been listening to the speech and welcomed the interruption. The rabbi, a young man combining the smooth traditions of America with those of Judea, smiled kindly and went on. He had a greasy voice and was all smiles, speaking with the

corners of his mouth constantly upturned. He referred to Tessie and
Schlausser as dear bride and groom, at each occasion presenting them
with a flash of gold teeth as he smiled a little more sweetly. A tender
allegory concerning birds and newlyweds was being unfolded. The
marriage performer said, nest, love-making, billing and cooing, and, of
course (a big golden flash), fledglings. He depicted the course of married life, gently warning that there would inevitably be brief storms.
"But where there is such love as I see in your smiling countenances I
know the compromises will be easy to make. The groom will take his
wife into his embrace, kiss away her tears, and the sweet calm that
follows a storm will be doubly welcome because you have cleared away
anger that has been long pent up." Finally he mixed his metaphors a
bit, said something about twin oaks rearing their branches to the great
heavens and growing old entwined, and Schlausser smashed the wine
glass on the floor with his heel. Schlausser had been sagging at the
end. He had shifted weight repeatedly from leg to leg.

The group broke out of its trance. Everybody kissed Tessie, who
tried to get over the veil. Her eyes were a little moist, and she hugged
her mother with passion. People pumped Schlausser's hand. He was
in a hurry and had a difficult time breaking away. He went to the
bathroom. As he came out the marriage performer was there to meet
him. He congratulated the groom, complimented him on his choice,
and said with a wide smile that Schlausser was not to hesitate very
long in calling him again. He performed circumcisions as well as marriage ceremonies. Finally the holy man came to the point, seeing
Schlausser was holding back. He said that in these cases the groom
generally expressed his appreciation in some tangible way to the man
who had bound him to such a lovely wife. Of course, he wouldn't be
expected to know the custom, this being the first time he was getting
married. They laughed, "Hah, hah," but Schlausser was ready for him.
He said just then he hadn't his wallet with him. He'd see him later
in the evening some time.

A five-piece band, mostly brass, began a foxtrot with snap. A few
couples went out on the floor. The man with the cornet stood up and
wagged the horn. Somebody yelled out, "Hotcha," and the dance
was on. The old folks sat stiffly on the chairs which lined the walls
and told stories about the couple when they were young. They all said
time flew, they could remember when.

The girl in the flaming red dress, whom Cohen was to have escorted,
would not favor him with a glance. Nevertheless, he was having a
great time. He had found a group of girls, and in the general excite-

ment at the close of the address he too had unloosened and was talking abundantly. Cohen discovered there was nothing particularly different about girls. He told a few amusing anecdotes about himself. The girls giggled in appreciation. It was easy, it was like talking to Philip. Cohen was carried away with himself. He was feeling brilliant, suave, and self-assured.

Tessie's father became loudly perplexed. He had forgotten the pickled herring. Thereupon Cohen stepped in and offered his services. "Don't bother," he said, stopping the man's protests. "It's no trouble at all. Just give me the key and I'll fetch it. It'll take me a minute." He was off, gallant and dashing. Cohen wondered what kind of an impression he had left with the girls.

He walked to Tessie's home in a few minutes. Now the streets were empty and he walked unmolested. It was late. In the cool breeze, swinging along in his evening clothes, Cohen played with his tie and began to feel like the movies. To have style, to live with grace and elegance, that was the thing. He found the jar of pickled herring and lugged it down to the street with some effort. Cohen stood at the curb and debated with himself. The jug was large, of earthenware, half brown and half white. How would he look dragging that jar through the streets in his tuxedo and wing collar? He calculated the cost of a taxi and his mood won. He lit a cigarette, lifted his arm, and yelled smartly, "Taxi!" He piled in with the herring.

As they came to the wedding hall Cohen opened the door while the cab was still in motion. He bounced out and worked snappily on the brown-and-white jar. His hand slipped, the jar fell to the sidewalk, the pickled fish slipping over Cohen's trousers and sliding onto the ground. Cohen smelled the overpowering stench of herring all over him. He thought of his awkward time with the girl he was taking to the wedding from Bensonhurst, the mishap when they changed trains at Canal Street, and now this. He was just beginning to have a good time, he had been so happy and exultant, that wonderful mood had passed already and it all came back. He almost wept from disappointment and misery. What would he do about the tuxedo? It was stained, ruined, the man who rented them would demand full payment for it. Cohen's heart ached with his unhappiness and he worried about the tuxedo he had rented.

It was late at night. The street cats with bulky faces, crude, like fists, and chewed-up from fights, crept among the garbage cans seeking food. They slinked nervously. Here one jumped up, pawed stonily about, and ripped open a bag of chicken intestines. She gobbled it up, her sharp teeth going all the time while she looked from side to side to ward off possible attacks from other cats. An unhappy group sat crouched in the center of the street, having the light of the lamp-post all to themselves. They cried and whined, and their sounds had a strangely human quality. From time to time there was a long wail, slow and full, unfolding the misery of the world.

In the desolation of the night a baby woke somewhere and began crying. It cried with all its soul, "E-yah, E-yah." It made a deep gasp for breath and sent it all out on the "yah." The cats in the cold went "Ya-ow, ya-ow," and the baby in answer said sharply, "E-yah." Suddenly an alarm clock went off with its harsh clatter. The cats and the baby stopped.

Cohen, condemned to men's laughter, a frustrated human, Cohen the poor simp, walked the lonely streets at night, seeking peace for his soul. He looked at the houses before him. Out of a canvas, it seemed, he saw the tenement buildings erect before him with their yellow and red brick, with an occasional square of light in a window, with the mournful black fire-escapes. He saw the garbage cans forming uneven designs on the sidewalk which was marked up with the colored chalk of kids who had been playing there. In the gutters were newspapers and bags, banana skins, orange peels, and watermelon rinds. Whatever meaning he read in the picture coincided with his own: a biting sadness. He was ugly with his pimples. His hair was thin, and he had to oil it and plaster it over the bald spots. Girls laughed at him, Hayman laughed at him, Mahler laughed at him. He knew now that in speaking of his play he was a liar. He would never write. Cohen verged on a condition of self-pity, and the feeling consumed him with bitter tenderness.

A Mary Sugar Bum competed with the cats for scraps at the garbage can. She was old, rickety, and seemed put together with safety pins. A gray bristling mustache protruded from a face lined with dirt. The seams running from her cheek bones to her mouth were deeply folded. Cohen stopped, observing her. Nothing was strange. She walked past him, her body bent, unseeing, clutching her oilcloth bag filled with choice refuse.

Cohen stood under the lamp light. He suddenly took it into his head to make a speech to the cats, the garbage cans, the mute fire-escapes. It was his last testament. He stated that the world as he knew it was futile, vain, and lying. He had sought industriously for beauty and poetry and had found only ugliness. He had sought something good that would have the power to interest his mind since the world had failed, interest his mind singly, to the exclusion of all else. Therein too he had failed. Life was senseless, it had no dignity. The manifesto was long-winded, turgid in spots, often trite. Cohen spoke and looked up at the stars. He walked off to the Williamsburg Bridge and to his death. He was determined this time.

Cohen saw a tall, very thin man leaning up against the wall of a chicken market. His clothes were black and damp. Cohen was impressed by the color of his face. It was not flesh-like, but ink black, sickly black. Sweat increased it. He wondered whether the wretch was drunk or dying. He had urinated in his trousers and now held his legs apart while a thin thread ran to the gutter. A cop down the street saw him. The policeman wheeled and walked in a long circle to avoid the bother. In a sick gesture of greeting the thin man held up his hand, the fingers spread, and feebly rolled it. He grinned at the cop. The hand fell to his side.

That was life, Cohen said, a man so thin that the legs ran up to his shoulders, leaning against the wall, urinating as he died. Life was Mary Sugar Bums groping among the garbage, hungry cats wailing in the cold, and an alarm clock going off sharply. I am no part of this life, Cohen said, therefore people laugh at me. I have pimples on my face and tears in my eyes. My head is almost bald. Girls ridicule me almost to my face. Everything I say is ludicrous, for mankind is cruel. Not one of my actions goes unheeded and not one is unmocked.

By this time he had reached the deserted bridge. Cohen walked through the lonely lights. Looking from a distance, he saw the lamp bulbs suspended on the cables like a string of pearls. The sky was a million miles up. Cohen walked in the center of the setting, facing the huge towers, the cables coming down to meet him, the lights at the sides shutting out the world. He was alone, and amid these surroundings in spite of his profound emotion he thought he resembled a wood-cut.

Cohen climbed down from the pedestrian walks to the paths for the automobiles. He scaled the railing here. Below was the East River, somber, undulatingly fearsome. The red and green lights of the tugs and barges looked up at him. What are you doing? they blinked, like children in their wonder. What's the matter with you?

Cohen jumped. His legs were outspread, his face covered with his arms. This was a terrible moment. In it Cohen saw reality. He became a speck in the air. His feet churned furiously, he waved his arms like a mechanical toy released. The air rushed up to meet him. Cohen slipped into the water easily. He had struck the river feet first and entered smoothly. Down, down he went. His eyes were opened and he cried with fear at the black desolation of the water. Now he came up, pushing with his arms and kicking. He rose interminably. Finally he bobbed above the water. His eyes were blinded with light.

A tugboat with all its compartments lit rested near him. A man threw a coil of thick twine to him.

"Grab it," he called. "Grab it."

Cohen held on and the men pulled him through the water. He was dazed. The oily smell of the tug, the heat from the boiler, the gleaming brass filled his head.

"Thanks, buddies. Thanks," he said breathless. "It was an accident. I don't know what happened."

"Accident, my old lady, accident," a man said. He had a fat face, and Cohen noticed the way his dirty sailor hat was stretched over his skull. "You were spread out on the railing like Jesus Christ crucified, thinking about your accident."

Cohen meant to sit down, but the deck rushed up to hit him. The bones in his behind hurt. He was exhausted.

Tessie with characteristic consideration and kindness sent Schlausser to visit Cohen at the hospital. This was four days after the wedding, when Schlausser was on his way to his upper New York State tour.

"Why did you want to do a thing like that for?" he asked. He held his grip, ladies' sundries, corsets and brassieres, and the flush of getting married had already worn off. Business was business. "Why?" Schlausser asked a little impatiently. "Why should a man do a thing like this?"

"I don't know," Cohen mumbled. "It was like this. My head was getting bald and I got to thinking. It was just the way it happened. Then the tuxedo got ruined and I didn't know what to do about it. Everything gets mixed up and sometimes a fellow gets crazy."

Schlausser looked at his watch, unable to fathom the enigma that was Cohen. "Well, I guess I got to be running along. Is there anything I can do for you?"

Cohen was still worried about the tuxedo. "What should I do about the suit?" Cohen asked. "I don't know what to do yet. I can't pay him."

"Forget all about it," Schlausser said. "What can the man do to you? He can't kill you, and if he's crazy enough to sue you, let him sue. He can't do anything to you. Is there anything you want?"

Cohen squinted through his weak eyes. His spectacles had been broken and he had not had an opportunity to replace them. However, he forgot about that now and asked Schlausser if he could get him something to read, something interesting, like Lady Chatterley's Lover or Rabelais. It was very dull at the hospital.

"You mean those dirty books?" Schlausser asked, for some reason astonished at the request. "Well, I certainly can't understand some of you fellows, the way you do things. I don't know about the books. I'll write to Tessie when I get to Albany."

Philip Hayman is a neighborhood friend of young Cohen.

PHILIP REACHED Williamsburg late that Friday afternoon. First his mother sat him down to dinner. After the flat smells and lifeless, unspiced Gentile cooking, he looked forward to his mother's warm tasty foods and juicy meats. She set before him chopped liver mixed with onions, cold borscht with cream, and then the brown, soft, roasted duck surrounded by peas, carrots and applesauce. On the table were sweet wine and seltzer. Philip picked up the plate of delicious flesh close to his nose and sniffed it. His mother sat with her hands folded, looking carefully at his face after so long an absence and observing his satisfaction as he ate. Philip examined the roast suspiciously, gingerly brought a morsel to his mouth, and chewed it critically. His eyes suddenly opened wide. His face twisted into grimaces, the muscles worked as if in convulsions, he grabbed his throat and slipped off the chair to the floor. He rolled in pain.

Mrs. Hayman laughed, rocking in her chair helplessly. That was Philip's favorite trick. Whenever children came into the house while he was eating, she always made him go through the performance for their benefit. Philip looked at her from the floor with a bitter expression. "My God," he gasped, "you've poisoned me."

Then he jumped up eagerly, seized the fork, and began eating as though he were administering an antidote.

"Eat with bread, Philip," she said. "Don't eat only the fancy stuff."

"Bread she wants me to eat," he muttered. "Bread. As if I don't know she ground glass into the flour." He sizzled seltzer into the glass of wine.

"How is it, Philip? Do you still like my cooking?"

He rose formally, held the glass and toasted. "To the worst cook in the world. To the lady who doesn't know the difference between a boiled egg and a herring."

Mrs. Hayman brought him a large cut of cold watermelon. "Here, you with your funny business, fill your monkey face with this."

Philip leaned back in his chair and held his stomach. "I'm water-logged. I feel as though all I've got is a belly with arms and legs stuck on."

As he cut the melon into neat geometric shapes, Mrs. Hayman began to talk. How was Harry?

"Don't worry," Philip said. "He's getting fatter and fatter every day. Even though Pop's down on him he's so fat he'll be a great success some day."

"Poppa," Mrs. Hayman said. She had been having trouble with the old man. For the last few years she had been coaxing him to sell his business, and now a man had offered him five thousand dollars for it. She regarded the offer as little short of providential, but the old man refused to sell. He claimed the place wasn't worth the money, wasn't worth anything. "It would be a swindle," he said and that was the end of it.

Philip smiled at the news. It was in character. Philip knew his mother would continue the argument for days until her strength gave out and she dropped it. Knowing his father as he did, he felt that the old man would not fail himself and that he would hold to principle. If his father sold it would be finally rest and a respite. He was old and worn, it would make things easier for him. Philip wanted it for his father, but he admired his refusal to sell because he thought the man would lose by the transaction. His father was thoroughly a man.

"Well," Philip said, "that's Pop. You can't make him over. Tell me, what's happening to Miller?"

"The old man won't die so easily, he fools them. You don't know. It was a whole business, and when you left everybody thought he would be all right soon, and then doctors came and they said he would die any minute. He's paralyzed and has a blood clot and God knows how many other sicknesses, but he keeps on stretching his life along."

"Miller is as bad as that? I thought he'd get over it. It's too bad. I'll have to see him," Philip said. "What else happened while I was away?"

"What should happen? Nothing, and everything. It keeps on going and everything is still the same. Tessie was married. You know that. Look," she said, "I almost forgot. She sent you a letter."

"She did? That was nice. It must be a wedding announcement." He pocketed the letter casually. "And how is my schlemiel, Cohen?"

Mrs. Hayman told him about the bridge. "Go on," Philip said. "I can't believe it. I know he's a nut, but to go ahead and do something like that! Somebody's got to keep an eye on him all the time. It's a miracle he wasn't killed. What else, Mom?"

"What else? I could sit here telling you grandmother's tales all night. A great deal happens all the time and it's nothing. You get excited, and then it passes. It's all over and you forget about it. Things keep on rushing like water boiling in a pot, and when you're all through there's nothing left. I've lived so long there's nothing to expect."

Philip contemplated his mother over his cigarette. "See, Mom," he said, "you're a regular philosopher. Why don't you go up to the college, kick out Overstreet and Cohen, and gives the boys the real lowdown?" He looked at her. She was old and tired but her face had a gentle loveliness. She was sympathetic and human, yet existence was an old story to her, and she remained placid with the world. Philip remembered how she always came to him with her needle. "Thread it for me," she said. "Everything gets old and useless, even my eyes are no good any more."

"Before I forget," Mrs. Hayman said, "Charlie called up two or three times on the telephone. He's home from camp and he said you should call him back when you came home."

"That's nice," Philip said. The news of Charlie Nagleman's return pleased him and helped to round out the pleasantness of his homecoming. At Havers Falls he had always felt an outsider, as though he did not belong to the country, and as his mother gave him the news he felt at home with people he knew. There were many things for him to do. Philip wanted to see the old sage in the long beard, Miller, on his death-bed. He was eager to see Cohen and discover what the latest adventure meant. The letter from Tessie exhilarated him with its warm possibilities. And he always enjoyed the time he spent with Charlie. Meanwhile he waited for his father. The evening grew.

On Friday nights the yellow stars on top of the three candles shed their soft light through the dim room with the gentleness of enchanted fingers. The tablecloth still showed the fresh creases, and on it, in a long oval dish, rested the knotted challee shining from egg yolk Mrs. Hayman's palms had patted on the dough. Philip's family was not very orthodox, but on Friday night a special air of quiet and peace pervaded the rooms, and it was in this atmosphere on those nights that Philip enjoyed lulling his mind into a kind of warm sleepiness.

Earlier, when the dark had first come, over his book he watched, without seeming to watch, his mother light one candle with a match and use this as a taper for the other two. This was, perhaps, a simple thing, but he always observed the ritual, and it affected him. She would soften the heels of the other candles with the flame, press them into the sockets of the candlesticks, and light them one after the other. Then she covered her head with a napkin, placed her fingertips to her eyelids, and moving her lips in a murmur, withdrawn for the moment and apart from the world, she recited the ancient prayer. There was always something strange, a little awesome, in the spectacle.

At eight o'clock Philip's father came home from his shop. He walked with the tired tread of a worker, and the expression on his face was as if glazed, the lips were dry and cracked. But he greeted Mrs. Hayman warmly, to her "Good Sabbath," he answered, "Good year."

"Home already?" he asked as he noticed Philip. He was pleased, and smiled, but there was little ceremony. At the broom closet, where he kept his coat and slippers, he changed shoes. This was one of his customs, performed regularly as he entered the house every night. It was the first thing he did, but it no longer attracted notice. Then Philip had to leave the chair he was sitting in, for it happened to be "Poppa's Chair." When he was home he sat only in this chair and it was given up to him, as a matter of course, whenever he appeared. Now he sat down for his evening meal. He dipped a piece of the white bread into the salty sauce on his fish plate, wetting his throat as he ate. Then slowly, chatting with Philip's mother as she served him, he ate the Friday dinner—the chopped fish, noodle soup, chicken and applesauce.

"That man, Coblenz, he was here again today," he said. "I don't know why he's looking for trouble."

"Well," asked Philip's mother, "are you going to let him buy the business?" She was upon him at once.

"It's ridiculous. He wants to give five thousand dollars. The place

isn't worth it. If I let him have it, it would be a swindle pure and simple." He rustled his newspaper. "Besides," he added, "what would I
do with myself?"

"Sell it," she said. "Don't be silly. See, Philip, it's just like I told
you."

His father read, and his mother, with the marvelous serenity of
older people, cleared the table and washed the dishes. She was finished with the week's work, had bathed, and her long black hair,
washed and combed, hung on her nape in a neat, shining knot. Philip
too was reading, but the pages remained unturned. Philip supposed it
often happened that children had no intimate knowledge of their
parents. His also were distant. That was because he did not understand them; they were strange to him and often even unreal. What
had they been when they were my age? he speculated. Was it possible
that they had been once boy and girl? What had their courtship been
when they were young? And what would happen when the time came
for them to die? It was difficult to imagine that they had been young
once, or indeed that they had ever been other than as he saw them
now. He was, of course, young himself and had no vivid understanding of the remarkable phenomenon of growth, but especially with his
father and mother it was not easily possible for him to think of them
as young, lively, and fresh.

And yet there was an old picture of his mother, taken over thirty
years ago. It was a large picture with a heavy, ornate, old-fashioned
frame, and his mother kept it hidden in the cellar because at a certain
age not only is there no affectation but honest sentiment becomes a
little pretentious. Often Philip gazed at his mother as she was years
ago, deeply impressed and wondering at the young, fine face with the
sad, innocent eyes. He could never picture his mother as a girl, and
here she was, soft, feminine, and really very lovely. At those times too,
Philip thought of earlier days when he himself had been younger and
watched his mother in her bedroom brush her hair or powder her
face. Even then the performance affected him strangely. Once he
examined her box of face powder. The cover was printed in soft,
gray-blue colors, the design was of blossoms and leaves delicately
intermingled, and the French words held a mysterious charm. Pussy-
willow, the box said, and, fascinated, he used to say to himself, pussy-
willow, pussy-willow, hardly knowing what exactly those silky syllables meant. Later, as often happens in such cases, walking, or at a
theater, thinking of other matters, the chance scent of powder would

bring back in a sudden nostalgic wave the memory of his mother in those days and his wondering about her.

On the other hand, even this much could not be said for his father. He had always been, as Philip remembered him, old, and this was something his mother confirmed. Even when she married him, she said, his hair had been white and he had had the appearance of an old man. He was bent now, drier and skinnier, shriveling with age, but except for those changes Philip supposed he was the same. The old pictures sustained this impression. There was one of his father and mother at the tombstone of his older brother. This had been twenty years before, when Philip was born, for while his mother was in bed with him his brother George was pushed off a roof. The picture, rusty-yellow from time, showed his mother still young and slender, but his father with his big mustaches was almost exactly as he was now. He might have been her father.

However, just as Philip remembered his mother's box of face powder and its effect on him, so he could recall his father ten years back. In the summer months he wore a Palm Beach suit, a Panama hat, and he carried a cane, walking with the jaunty step of a young man. And when Philip walked with him, accompanying him along Grand Street where he shopped on Sundays, it was Philip's practice to walk, not along side of him, but some paces to the rear. Mr. Hayman would enter a shop, pick his article and lay the money on the counter, point at Philip with the stick to indicate that he was to be given the package, and walk out, leaving him to follow. In the warm sun Philip would come after him down the street, holding his purchases, waiting until his father felt ready to return home and never thinking of questioning this odd little custom. At that time Philip held great respect for his father because of his dignity, his years, and his noble presence.

While Philip might have had difficulty in visualizing his parents' younger days, they had had them, of course, and it was this realization, as he contemplated them over his book on that Friday evening, that saddened him. For their youth was gone, they were old now, and when something was gone it made no difference whether you had ever had it in the first place or not. It was truly as though it had never been. A memory was unsatisfying solace. His mother, in speaking of herself, would often say with wry humor, "Down hill. We're going down the hill now." They had been young, they would soon come to die, and it would be all finished, a drop of water losing its identity in a sea.

Philip was saddened not only for his parents but for himself. He knew that time was a subtle thief, and even though he was only twenty years old he felt that his own life was running through its rapid course. He had lived a fourth, or even a third, of his life already, and how fast it had gone! Philip remembered how astonished he had been when he was graduated from elementary school. Seven years, measured neatly for him so that he could notice it, had already passed. This was also true of high school, and when he entered college Philip thought: four years, they would be over in no time; and it was true, for already his senior year had come; in a year he would be leaving college.

Time was a sly, deceitful companion; it slipped away in a minute, unsuspected divisions, like a group of boys trying to escape from a classroom, leaving one by one to attract no notice. As he thought of his father it came to him with great force what a pity it was that this sham had been put over on him too. He had worked so hard and honestly, he was old and tired, his life was passing, and it seemed to Philip that in some way his father had been tricked. Further, the calm acceptance, or the resignation, at any rate, the aloof disregard of what seemed to Philip a tragedy, rendered him a noble figure. With the candlelight softly outlining his white head, his father read his newspaper, knowing that tomorrow he would be going to work, that on Sunday he would buy breakfast and spend the day resting, that on Monday he would be going back to his shop again, and that week would follow week and he would leave the house every morning not noticing the street number on the door.

"Max," Mrs. Hayman said to him across the table, "Max, do it for me. I can't understand why you don't sell the place. You ought to stop already and take a rest."

Philip's father looked at her over his newspaper. "I say it would be a swindle, a plain, ordinary swindle, to take money from that man Coblenz. The place isn't worth the money."

"How do you come to say that? The man isn't a baby. He knows what he wants. If he wants to pay five thousand dollars it's not your place to tell him no."

Mr. Hayman exclaimed his impatience in a syllable of a sort, shook his head, and returned to his newspaper.

Philip laughed. "You can't make him over, Mom," he said. "That's the way he is." He rose and fixed his tie.

"You just came home," Mr. Hayman said. "Where are you running?"

"I've got to see some people." The old man had made no fuss over Philip's homecoming, but it was difficult to leave. Philip fingered the letter from Tessie in his pocket. "I'll try to get in early," he said, "but I guess it'll be late."

"Go in good health," his mother said. "Don't listen to him, he's topsy-turvy in his old age. Go, have a good time. You're young."

Among the neighbors is old Mr. Miller, a professional prayer sayer at the cemetery, now himself near death.

In the dinginess of the dark room Mr. Miller lay on his bed, motionless, the blanket over his arms, his beard resting on the quilt, the great face set, the eyes closed, for all the world like a death mask. It was night. The lights from rooms across the yard sent their rays into the dark room. Shadows sat on the chair. Mr. Miller's yellow face lay in a spot of light. He was sleeping, and in his dream also he was sleeping. He had pondered much and long and he was tired, feeling through with thinking and the world.

There was a light slapping sound, rhythmic and regular, annoying him in his sleep in the dream because he did not want to leave his bed and shut out the night air. In his dream or half-dream he was already walking to the window; he eliminated the noise, he was back in the bed again, but of course the slapping continued, he had not moved. Miller dreamed that lately he had been troubled at night. The old superstition was that the bed should not face the door because that was a bad portent, signifying death. Now, Miller understood this, but at night it always appeared that the bed had moved itself of its own accord out of position and that his feet were pointing to the door. Miller had the uncomfortable sensation of being worried, but for vague, undetermined reasons. And the flapping continued. Soon the sound grew stronger, communicating an almost human quality of impatience. The slapping became insistent. It was no cloth disturbed by the wind—it was tapping! Miller opened his eyes.

The faces of these old men were inarticulate, composed of shadows. But there he was, the old man, sitting on the chair, in black shiny clothes, with the strange bulbous shoes. His small body was bent over his stick which he held with both hands, tapping with it on the wooden floor until he had awakened Miller. For years now Miller had been expecting him, although he had never admitted this, even to himself. Recently he had even forgotten about him completely. Seeing him there exposing his self-conceit, Miller had to smile. At this he smiled back, although surely this was an old story with him. The little black man lifted his stick, poking it gently in the air at Miller as if to say in all good nature, come, come, get over with it.

As Miller rose, he left. Miller saw him move ahead, move until he became a black blur, a dot, dissolved into the horizon.

There was time enough. Miller walked with his hands in his pockets, his face set. He knew what to do. As the night progressed the white light from the stars became suffused grayishly by the rising mist. He could hear no sound. The mist thickened until it was a fog. He was alone. The universe was bounded by his fingertips, and now he knew the answers to all the questions.

Miller walked until he reached the top of the hill. Down below him was the town which revealed itself by four or five gauzy lights. It was in every respect a usual town but Miller did not like it, for once he had been standing on this very hilltop looking at the town, and this was during those sun-tinted days of his early youth when he saw it and the people in it as in dreams, water-blue, like reflections in a big soap bubble. This had been illusion, and a long time ago, and all these things appeared now to Miller as he dreamt, but he did not like the town.

Down below, the misty lights of the town blinked. Miller lifted his hands high above his head, pressing the little fingers against the thumbs, and as he pressed the hill-tops moved together, the one upon which he was standing and the one opposite, they closed together, destroying the valley and the town within it. There were no lights, no people, no town. It was all over. Miller smoothed the earth with his foot where the two hill-tops met.

A man does not die, he said. He lives. The whole world dies, he lives.

In the morning Miller woke up smiling. He was almost hearty. For the first time he took notice of his wife and sons. He looked at them regarding his face for the morning inspection of death, and he laughed at their expressions because he read them. They wondered at him.

"Open the windows," he cried. "Pull the curtains over the chair. Let the light come in. Who's going to die today in Golus?"

When Mrs. Hayman came in he greeted her cordially. They had a spirited conversation.

"You're all right, Mr. Miller," she said at the close. "You should be getting out of bed."

"Soon. I will not be in this bed much longer."

In the kitchen, Mrs. Miller complained and said it was all a trick. Miller had never been sick, he was shamming so that they wouldn't nag him about the swindle. He wanted to have an excuse for lying in bed all day and having attention. He had such a terrible disposition, he had used his devil's brains to devise this torment for them. Mrs. Hayman asked her what she was talking about, she shouldn't say those things, it was a sin.

"Tomorrow, sick or not sick, the old sore gets out of bed." She felt as though she had been tricked, and was angry with the old man.

"What is love?" Tessie asked, her eyes big and round with sadness. "Sometimes I think there just isn't anything like it at all. And then again, I think I have been very unfortunate. These things never happen to me. Everyone else has good luck, but nothing ever happens to me."

"What's the matter?" Philip asked. "What's it all about? Here I get home and my mother gives me a letter from a married woman saying: Is everything over? Can't you come and see me? I need you now, perhaps for the first time I really need you. Marrriage should not break old friendships. What's wrong?"

Philip sat on a great chair with a rose design, respectably, at a distance. He was drinking a rye highball and his legs were crossed. While he made his speech he was handling a bronze book-end showing a girl with breasts reaching to the sky for light. It was a particularly apt sentiment. All this new furniture, the baby grand, the etchings on the walls from Liggett's Drug Store, they all looked clean, and it was something to make a good housewife worry wondering how soon these objects would lose their freshness and turn into the junk one saw in longer-established homes.

"Schlausser has done very well by you. What are you complaining about? You're a lady, you serve rye highballs, you lie on a couch reading a book and playing delicately, when nobody is looking, with your nose."

"Are you going to be impossible, Philip?" Tessie asked. "We're not children any longer. We're grown-up people. Please don't become silly and smart, because I need your help so badly. You're my oldest friend, you're my closest friend, Philip, don't make fun of things now."

Philip tried to hide his resentment, but he was having little success. He took out a cigarette and lit it with careful nonchalance.

"Well, what is it? What can I do when Schlausser stands stretched manfully to shield you from harm?"

"Philip, you're angry with me for what I've done to you. You resent him. You still don't understand."

"Don't be foolish," Philip said. "A girl has got to get married. I understand that. She can kid around with boys, but there must be a finish to it, and she has to get married. Only, where does that put me in the picture now?"

"You won't understand, Philip. It's clear you can't miss seeing it, but you're stubborn, you're refusing to let yourself see it. Can't you see that I can't live with him? Can't you see he means nothing to me? I've made a terrible mistake. What have I in common with a man I see three or four times a month? A man who is always on the road peddling lingerie to lady buyers in Rochester and Buffalo? He thinks he's intellectual when he goes to the movies. Books and concerts mean nothing to him. Can't you see how mismated I am? How miserable I am?" Her voice broke.

"Listen, Tessie, are you kidding me? Do you mean to say that you've been married to such a nice fellow like Schlausser for such a short time and you're already beginning to think you're wasting your life on him?"

"Philip," she said, and closed her eyes with pain. She walked to one of the lamps and clicked off the light. The radio dispensed a soft waltz, but she softened it further. She lay down on the couch to be alone with her unhappiness.

She had been reading an English novel of manners in which the heroine spent her time going through mental soliloquies as she decided yes and no over the fates of her husband and her contemplated lover. Eric was solid, dependable, and in his way lovable. He left each morning for the city where he was engrossed in his business. He had many interests, his wife was an accessory to him. Vivian walked through the garden desiring a life of her own. She did not want to be a casual part of her husband, comforting, serving, an incidental receptacle of his affections in stray moments. She thought of Hugh Baden-Thwyte-Baden and wondered. He was madly in love with her. Hugh's profession was love, not business; life with him would have a separate, important part for the woman. Tessie had reached the climax and wondered which way Vivian would turn. Would she remain with the rugged qualities of Eric, or would she courageously break for love and romance? How true to life it was. How easily one might substitute living people for Eric, Vivian, and Baden-Thwyte-Baden. Tessie wondered how it would all turn out, but in stepped Philip and she had had to put the book down. Nevertheless, Tessie had resolved the problem for herself.

"I think I'll be getting along," Philip said. He was still sitting on the big rose, fingering the book-end. Tessie was ridiculous. She was making him ridiculous. It was clear, and Philip saw it. Tessie, who worried about her weight and the styles of next year's clothes, who had studied the amorous postures of movie stars and read the manners of English society, Tessie who once rode on top of a Fifth Avenue bus and saw the signs that would not release her, who would rather have a milk-shake at Sherry's than a full meal at Foltis-Fisher's, Tessie had grown up, married, and was ready for the next of life's experiences. Tessie wanted an affair.

"I think I'll be getting along," Philip said. He understood her.

"Philip," she murmured, "Philip."

"What?"

"Come here."

He looked at the book-end, the lady with the breasts which reached to the modernistic chandelier for light, and he sat down on the couch.

"Philip, if you knew what you mean to me. A moment ago I said I didn't know the meaning of love. That was a lie. I wish it were true. I'm so miserable. I know this is wrong, but I am so alone. Schlausser is gone for a month."

"I know about Schlausser."

"It makes no difference whether he's gone or here," she went on. "It's the same. I always have the feeling of being alone. I'm wretched with unhappiness, Philip. It was a big mistake. You cannot fool yourself in these things, Philip," she said, stroking his face and his head, "Philip."

"I know," he said, "I know." The radio began playing a lively jazz tune. He reached out to turn it off.

Philip woke up late the next day. It was almost twelve. His mother looked into the bedroom and brought him a glass of orange juice.

"I was around to see some friends last night," he said. "I got in late."

Mrs. Hayman sat on the bed watching him drink. "Philip," she said, "what do you think? It's so funny. This morning Mr. Miller looked so well I thought he would get out of bed and be back at his place in the cemetery. He laughed and talked and moved instead of lying in a lump."

"Well," said Philip, "what happened?"

"It was such a surprise to me. I just saw him. He died an hour ago."

"Oh," said Philip. He had meant to see the old man and regretted he had delayed his visit. He really should have seen the old man once again. If he had only known Miller was on the point of death he wouldn't have missed it. That was to have been the final touch to the old man's wryly piercing homilies, the skinny sage with the long beard slowly saying the last smiling pronouncements on his death-bed.

Mrs. Hayman sat on the bed and narrated the details of Mr. Miller's passing.

IT WAS ONE of those dripping days when the clothes feel uncomfortably warm and sticky, the shoes lose all their luster and the scalp is itchy. The pavement in the yard gleamed black and gloom pervaded the tenements. Listlessly the rain fell down in anemic straight lines, moving from the dirty-gray heavens with deliberate slowness until abruptly in the descent it hit the yard with a little smacking noise. It was like the sound a woman makes with her lips when she is busy eating herring.

A boy stood in the yard, calling up to his mother in a flat, expressionless voice. Unmindful of the rain, he stubbornly yawped, "Ma, Ma," at intervals until she was obliged to answer in a fit of irritation from her flat.

"What do you want?" she yelled.

"Stick your head out of the window."

"Well, what do you want?"

"Ma. Throw me down a penny?"

"No!" The window slammed. She had been disturbed under false pretenses.

"Ma!" the boy screamed, overwhelmed with anger. "Ma! Stick your head out of the window! Ma! Every kid on the block gets three cents a day. If I ask you for an extra cent, I don't see what you have to be so stingy about. Ma! Ma! I hate you! I don't see why I've got to have a mother like you for anyhow. I hate you, Momma, you're a dirty Litvack."

Does it always rain at funerals? Philip wondered. Across the yard he could see one of Miller's sons sitting on a box while he waited for

the old women to finish washing the dead man and get him ready for
the coffin. The son had a big face, with both the color and lumpy
texture of Swiss cheese, marked and lined from rashes of pimples he
must have had as a youngster. He sat on an egg-box, in his shirt
sleeves, with the collar detached, the expression of his face showing
that he was waiting, waiting for things to get over. He had been unable to find a black skull cap, and for this solemn occasion he now
wore a boy's orange-and-black-colored bean hat. Miller had died on a
Saturday morning, postponing the funeral until Sunday, and his son
regretted another day of waste, and waited, tired.

Mahler the cobbler came out of the doorway of the cellar and
sadly looked at the interminable rain.

"That finishes your nap," Philip said down to him. "You're nap's
all washed out."

"Maybe it'll stop," Mahler said hopefully. "Sometimes it keeps on
going like this and then the sun comes out and it stops. You can
never tell."

"No, Mahler. I don't like to tell you this, but I was having a conference with God. He says it's going to rain like this forever. It won't
stop for the rest of the summer."

Mahler looked up at him suspiciously. "Listen," he said, "do you
think I've got it again? What's the matter with you?"

"I'm not kidding. It always rains on funerals. According to the
Good Book, if an old man dies on a Saturday and gets buried on a
Sunday and it rains on that day, well, it means we're all finished. It
just keeps on raining."

"Who's getting buried today?" Mahler asked gently, the grim
finger of Death already wagging him into a state of respectable awe.

"The old man, Miller. The one who ripped up the window sills to
fix his shoes."

"Oh," said Mahler. His eyes were opened wide and he nodded to
indicate his comprehension of the sorrowful law of life. After two
minutes of nodding and contemplation, however, he looked up at the
dark sky. There would be no sun for a bit of sleep in Williamsburg
this afternoon.

Philip's mother asked him to go into Miller's flat with her because
there was so much excitement and rush. As they walked in two sons
were in the midst of a heated argument. They talked in restrained
tones because the mute corpse in the bedroom said, quiet, gentlemen,
quiet, but the globular beads of sweat on their foreheads showed how

earnestly they felt. One waited, holding himself silent by almost physical force, until the other got through arguing his side. He explained with great labor and desire to convince, but as soon as he stopped the other began. They changed roles like acrobats waiting for their cues on the trapeze. Mrs. Miller sat at the dining table dressed in her good black garments, ready for the ride to the cemetery. She cried a little and looked out of the window. That was easiest in this time when she didn't know exactly what to do with herself.

Mr. Miller, it had been discovered, had left almost two thousand dollars. One of the sons argued that the money should be given in its entirety to the old lady, who was to live on it until it was all gone. In this way she would be taken care of, and, more, the sons would no longer be required to contribute money for her support. It would be a release for both sides and seemed eminently satisfactory. However, the other son said that the lump sum was an unnecessary temptation. The old lady would be fooled by some trick and swindled just as Miller had been. "Give everybody a piece and it will be safer. No one will have to worry," he said. They argued with increasing violence, their enthusiasm even overpowering the commanding influence from the dark bedroom.

"My God," one of them exclaimed finally. "Argue with him! Try and talk to him. It's like talking to the wall."

The other picked up a seltzer bottle in a spasm of anger. "I got half a mind," he said threateningly, "right here and now."

Mrs. Hayman stepped in for the sake of peace. "Children," she said tearfully, "it isn't at all nice. Is it decent for sons to fight while the father waits to be buried? You can settle this later, the money isn't flying away."

The sons glared at each other and walked sullenly to opposite ends of the room. Off in the yard somewhere a child began practicing on the piano. Laboriously, heavily, came the clipped notes of the Minuet in G. For a while everyone sat in the dingy room saying nothing and listening attentively to the piano. There was nothing else to do while they were waiting. Suddenly a hot quarrel broke out into the yard from the fourth floor of the building opposite. From the voices it was apparent that two couples were involved. The angry murmur of their discourse rested on top of the gentle patter of the smacking noises the rain was making. One man now yelled in a tone that filled the yard, "That's a nasty habit, mister. Don't think you can attract my wife by standing naked in front of the window."

"Please," a woman's voice begged. "Don't shout. Everyone can hear you."

"I don't care who hears," said the other man defiantly. "If your wife didn't have a filthy mind she wouldn't twist her neck until it almost breaks to look at me."

Philip didn't know whether it was disrespectful to show his interest in the proceedings. He looked at the bedroom door where they were laying out the old man, combing his beard and dressing him. Thus went the sage with the long beard, amid dirty arguments, while Mahler regretted the falling rain and a child jerked out Beethoven's minuet into the gloom.

The undertaker strode into the dining room importantly. "All right," he said in a subdued tone which was nevertheless authoritative. "Are you ready here?"

Six men lifted the coffin and squeezed it around the sharp corners of the doors. They moved their legs delicately and watched the big box with their eyes, like a mother bringing a full bowl of soup to the table. The coffin might have been made of thin glass. The staircase running down in squares gave trouble, but in the end they managed to reach the long hall. As they passed, neighbors stuck their heads silently out of their doors to view the strange spectacle. Children leaned over banisters to watch the procession. They were filled frankly with awe. As the pall-bearers carried the box through the hall, an unhappy boy was caught against the wall. He stood back stiffly, as though paralyzed, and as they finally passed him, he could control himself no longer, broke wildly into a spasm of tears and dashed madly up the steps. The sight of death is sometimes terrible, especially when it is covered plainly by greenish new boards. . . .

The ride to the cemetery was long and dull. They had intended to hold a ceremony at the synagogue but it was raining and the undertaker had taken so much time. There would be prayers enough at the cemetery, the holy men said. Philip sat cooped up in the limousine. He had not wanted to go. When his mother had told him his friend Charlie Nagleman was in town he had phoned and arranged to spend all of Sunday with him. He was anxious to see Charlie again, but his mother had begged him to accompany her and he did not know how to refuse her. She asked so little of him. As they drew into the cemetery Philip saw the old men waiting at the gates in the rain for customers. He wondered whether these professional prayer-makers knew that it was their colleague who needed their prayers today.

The yellow earth surrounded the grave in mounds. It was a dismal morning. They grouped around the wet hole, seeking dry spots for their feet. The rabbi stood at the head and went through the form. It was, Philip had to admit, an impressive sight. Nothing stopped these old Jews and their rituals, not even a nasty day. Before the black sky, in that peculiar scene where white gravestones listened respectfully, the holy man was upright, the downpour soaking his clothes until they were heavy and sodden, the water forming in the crown of his hat a little pool that dripped unattended over his nose, his shoes sucking in the mud, the water penetrating until he must have felt cold and wet and miserable, but he went on stolidly uttering eeni-meenie-mini-mo to God who might have been listening but who sent down the fine rain nevertheless.

Mrs. Miller cried. The sons clasped their hands together and looked without positive expression into the grave. The first spadeful of earth hit the wooden box. Philip heard the pebbles as they struck. This was the last of the sage. He tried to deny it to himself, but the sight affected him considerably. This was the end of the sage, he said, but actually he was impressed. Sometimes a boy will find grief contagious and cry himself, and so Philip felt now oppressed, sad, and wondering. He took out a pad and began writing. His mother edged up to him.

"What are you doing, Philip?" she whispered reproachfully.

"Nothing. It was an idea, it came to me when I heard the sound of the earth on the box, and I wanted to write it down so I wouldn't forget."

Mrs. Hayman looked at him chidingly. "Do you bother with that when a man dies?" she said.

The Old Sage was dead and in his grave, but Philip, sitting in Charlie Nagleman's living room, remembered his words. There was one truth, one meaning, and it was money. Twenty was a young age. At twenty a young man might feel rather that purposeful work and love were the important goals, but nevertheless Philip recognized intimately that there was much in what Miller said. The room in which he was sitting was in its way proof. The pictures on the walls, the tasteful furniture, the tall bookshelves that went up to the ceiling, all this made a difference, subtly projecting its influence in a hundred ways, softening the lives of the people who dwelt there. These people lived decorous lives, they rode in Central Park, played tennis and golf, and they attended the various resorts of reputation.

Charlie came into the room. He had been changing his shirt and was now adjusting the suspender buckles.

"I almost sent you the goddamnedest letter while I was at Havers Falls," Philip said. "I still don't know why exactly I held it back."

"What was it all about?"

"All about money and love among the ash-cans of Williamsburg. The terrific importance of a clean shirt and why it is a great thing to have a father who's made a fortune out of vanity cases."

Charlie smiled and went into the bedroom for his jacket. He was tall, blond, and good-looking. Philip had met him one day through college friends and somehow a friendship had developed, although Philip knew it would have to break with time. They were too far apart. Much as Charlie liked him, a difference in settings often proved too great a handicap. Actually, and Philip knew it, the Naglemans weren't very wealthy; there was no great fortune in this home, but it wasn't Williamsburg. The large room, the grand piano, the furniture in neat, handsome summer covers, the cream colored walls, the drapes, the atmosphere of comfortable living, these were simply not to be seen on Ripple Street, and Philip was appreciative, all the more because of the contrast.

For some time Philip had been a little ashamed of his admiration for these things, thinking they were shallow and stupid. Compared to the more serious properties of living they were, he had felt, superficial. But in fact, and he grew bolder in admitting it, the ornaments were often most important. Just as the great disease of pellagra was discovered curable, not by some complicated toxin or treatment, but by the simple addition of fresh meat and milk, or yeast, to the diet, so the texture of existence might be enriched by furniture, books and surroundings. Philip remembered when the gas connections in his tenement house had been taken out of the chandeliers and electric light installed. He saw the white light reflected in the porcelain tops of the washtubs in the kitchen and said, how could there be misery now with all this wonderful clean light? Philip felt that he could see for himself the softening effect that had been caused by the few improvements already instituted in Williamsburg. They were few and rudimentary but their effect was discernible nevertheless. As backyard toilets were succeeded by more adequate plumbing, as hot water was added as a usual service, as tenements were built with greater concern for light and air, it seemed to him that the brutality, the coarseness lessened.

Charlie returned. "Let's go," he said. "It's almost nine."

"I think I'll be going home," Philip said. Charlie was going to a party on Madison Avenue and had asked Philip to accompany him.

"Come along," Charlie said. "You've got nothing else to do."

Philip always felt a little like an intruder when Charlie brought him into these homes. They were not meant for him, he did not belong there, and he tried to dissuade Charlie from taking him there. Tonight, however, his friend insisted. These smart youngsters, in well fitting suits of white linen or in gay chiffons, lived in the restricted residential sections, they went to expensive summer camps and attended the fashionable schools. Philip was not deluded into a state of awe by these facts, but it was true that he could not match their background, that he could not meet them on their own ground. He felt uncomfortable before them, as if he were an imposter. When he had to mention that he attended City College or that he lived in Williamsburg, he always flinched at their considerate acknowledgment.

"Come on," Charlie said. Philip picked up his hat and they went to the door.

It was at this party that Philip met Ruth Kelman. He noticed her immediately and kept his eyes on her. She wore a plaid guimpe with a white organdy blouse, was pretty, and what impressed him particularly was her grace and charm. He kept watching her. Once or twice her eyes met his, and in that embarrassed pause she smiled uncertainly. When she came to him with a bowl of cherries he felt he could talk to her familiarly.

"My name's Hayman," he said. "These people are terrible. I've been watching you ever since I got into this place, but no one tried to do anything about it."

"Well, that's over. Here, eat these cherries."

"I like cherries, only I never know how to handle the pits. I'm sick and tired of swallowing cherry pits just because there are people in the room."

Ruth laughed. Philip, placing the cherry in his mouth, had to smile at her as she laughed.

"What a lovely girl," he said. "In all my life I have never seen such a lovely girl."

Philip asked Charlie Nagleman about her.

"You mean Ruth?" he said. "She's a kid. I didn't know you liked them that young." Charlie told him her name, that her father was a doctor, that he lived on Eighty-eighth Street. "Listen," he said, "I got my own troubles."

That night Philip walked with Ruth to her home. The streets were cool after the hot day and a pleasant breeze blew. At her door he confessed to her that he was quite taken in. "How soon can I see you again?" he asked. He felt exultant with his discovery.

.   .   .   .

Cohen had solved the riddle of the world. Ever since his attempted suicide he had left the hospital and carried himself grim-faced, satisfied, and cool. Neighbors pointed him out in the streets. "That's the one," they said, and shook their heads wisely. "He looks happier because he knows that no matter how terrible life is it's better than to be dead." Cohen disregarded them. He did not even speak to Mahler. Philip was back, he knew, but he took special pains to avoid him. Alone, within himself, Cohen pondered, running his fingers through his oily hair and taking time to look at them carefully for more fallen hairs. He had solved the riddle of the world.

It was a huge fake. He remembered when he was a boy he had always had the feeling that all people were liars. Actually, the entire world existed as far as he could see. That was all. People said the world was large in a concerted effort to give coming generations confidence. Great seas, foreign countries, pictures, ocean liners, were all accessories to the fraud and part of the deception. At this time Cohen's greatest desire was to walk in a straight line and to walk endlessly until he saw what there was of the world. He didn't believe them. Often, even now, he had a momentary feeling that history was manufactured fiction and that the physical properties of the world had been deliberately exaggerated to give people the feeling of dignity.

It was a matter of proportion. To an ant an inch might be a block, a mile, the universe. In ratio to man the earth was big and a lifetime great. But in truth what was known? We could not think of limitless things, Cohen argued, and yet they told us the universe had no bounds. They said the cosmos had no beginning in time, but we could not imagine matter growing from no origin. Nor could we picture the eternality of the universe. Actually, Cohen affirmed, man did not know. He was as ignorant as the ant. At bottom there was complete blank and everything man said, no matter with what authority and self-assurance, was based on a complete want of knowledge.

These were fundamental truths. Cohen pondered long into the night while the big tenements slept, and in passing he wondered whether he would not die of a cerebral hemorrhage, which would have its romantic advantages. Cohen would erase this perpetual laughing, he would show them. In preparation he was working on what was to be a gigantic outline for a book. This was not to be one of the season's output, but revolutionary. It would change the reasoning habits of thousands, dim into silliness the effect of any other man or work. Cohen.

He lay back on his bed to consider the pleasant possibilities. He put his hands over his eyes to keep out the light. They would come to him, Mahler, Philip, and the girl in the sweeping red gown, respectful with awe at his fame. The rotogravure sections would print his casual presence photographed in Paris, Madrid, Budapest. Every morning there would be a fat handful of letters for him. He was the man, Cohen, the world would say, and never take its eyes from him. All the world would drive him to the civilized capitals to do him homage, but Cohen, tormented by a restless soul, would travel interminably alone, scorning women, men, and diversions. With his money he would build fantastic houses in Tibet and gratify every chance whim. And with equal nonchalance he would discard them as soon as they bored him. To have fame, fortune and to be loved, those are what all men desire most, and Cohen, dreaming on his bed, took sharp delight because he would be able to have them by opening his hand but he would be too world-worn to stretch for them. Then they would say how in the old days he had lived in his miserable room, how he had stridden the streets mysteriously at night absorbed in himself and the stupendous projects he was always dreaming of. They would recount his attempted suicide and its miraculous escape. The tugboat that had fished him out would be sought and photographed. Tourists would fill Ripple Street looking for the marks of the master, his poor room, the modest writing table, and the fountain pen he had used.

Cohen rose and stared at the empty white page. His idea was, briefly—he would put it down on paper. His brain was still fogged from his dreams on the bed. To start with, briefly, to get it into words, his idea was—corpuscles. Corpuscles raced through a human body. There were millions of them, like the number of people on the earth, and they formed a perfect society of their own. The man was their universe. Briefly, the idea was, just as corpuscles inhabit the universe of man, racing through him, living long ages of days or of minutes, traveling from organ to organ which they call capes, continents, peninsulas and oceans, so in proportion do we lead our lives, ignorant as the corpuscles and creating a great universe after the same fashion as they, but in proportion. We disregard the society within us but they too have the equivalents of all kinds of phenomena, arts and sciences, experiences and consciousnesses, individuals who sniff through heavy nose colds and anemic youngsters with dull feelings in their bellies and pimples on their faces, all after their own fashion, valid fashions and worthy of tolerance and respect. Cohen squeezed his pen, and in a burst of effort wrote: "We follow our dark paths in the same fashion as corpuscles in a human body. Really, we are all—peoples, houses, land—minute parts of some great body who walks nonchalantly with no concern for our desperate ignorance. We occupy our days senselessly, like water-bugs sliding over the smooth surface of a pond."

That was all. Cohen gripped his pen until his knuckles hurt. He stared at the white sheet of paper. The three lines stood at the top waiting patiently. More, they said, more. Cohen pressed the pen with his fingers and struggled within himself. His intention had been to do a mixed book, fantasy and realism, revealing satirically, creating the life of the corpuscles paralleled by the life of humans. This was to be a piercing, illuminating thing. The three lines at the top silently begged, more, please, more. He re-read them and was distressed by the reference to the water-bugs. He liked that very much, but it was bad. This was a mixed metaphor. You had to cross it out. Cohen threw the pen down in a fit of disgust and walked from the table. He returned, the fit had worn off immediately, and carefully he screwed the cap over the point so that the ink wouldn't dry. He lay down.

Cohen was heartbroken. He knew again that this was going to be a humiliating flop. It was "Green Gods in Yellow" all over again. Cohen felt almost like crying. He rolled over to hide his face in the bed but his spectacles pushed into his eyebrows. He took them off and dropped them on the floor, and this little incident complicated his grief because it made him feel a little ridiculous again. His great idea now sounded flat, the day-dreams were a joke, he knew he would never write.

What had started him off that day was the recollection of that line he had read in a Russian novel, that line everlastingly with him, interminably repeating itself: "I am, as you know, an employe of the post office, but I have always wanted to be a poet." There was something pathetic about it, it might be his own epitaph it applied so accurately to him. Cohen's mood might also have been caused by his persistent dwelling on his appearance, the ridicule he always met, his growing baldness, and the flat, even way of his life in spite of all the dust storms he tried to kick up for himself. He thought of Barbellion whose *Portrait of a Disappointed Man* the librarian had given him in an effort to stabilize the excitable creature she always saw hanging around the bookshelves. Now it seemed to outline with trenchant meaning for Cohen the dreariness of days succeeding one another with petty misfortune, absence of achievement, and in addition his own special heritage of the always-present laughter. Cohen thought again of his trip to the Williamsburg Bridge. That too, meant as a dignified conclusion, escape from misery, was epitome, for he succeeded here only in making himself more ridiculous and more laughable.

.   .   .   .   .

Cohen threaded his way through the moving throngs on Fourteenth Street to his favorite corner. This was where the models in the dress shop above the cigar store walked their coy bodies carrying wraps and dresses. Cohen bought an apple from a push-cart and settled to watch the models as he chewed. His neck grew stiff, but there was a fascination about it. It was like the zoo. Here were humans walking, swaying, pirouetting for the express purpose of having people on the street, like Cohen, look upon them and admire. They kept going around with the frozen expressions on their faces, one foot being placed in front of the other in their elegant strides. From time to time a model slipped through the curtain at the rear, and when she reappeared, lo! she was more radiant than ever. Cohen grew to recognize them in spite of the new coats they wore. He threw the apple core away. His neck ached and he was getting a little dizzy following their movements in the circle.

Across the street on the Square a shirt-sleeved man spoke forcefully from a wooden platform. He waved his arms to emphasize his point while the spittle gathered unheeded at the corners of his mouth. "Well," he shouted, swaying back, "what did Henry Ford do? I'll tell you, my good friends." He had to wait, stopped full in his fury, before he could tell them. A trolley car was taking the curve screechingly. He waited patiently. "I'll tell you what he did," he said, turning on his fury to its former intensity, and he told them.

Cohen stood at the fringe of the crowd. This was always a good show. He admired the passion with which these men spoke, their entire absorption in their work. The man was small, skinny, and sweated. He spoke in the sharp, clipped pronunciations of New England dialect but his accent was also unmistakably Jewish. Occasionally an unfortunate inflection escaped, giving him away disastrously. "Take me," he cried vehemently. "I've been slaving twenty years. I know my trade, fellow workers, not that I want to boast, but I can work hard. What do I get? I am a married man with three small children, and they threw me out like I was the dirt on the floor. I ask you, should we go on with a way where one man gets the fruits of my labor, and of your labor, too, my friends, and we get no accident insurance, no unemployment insurance, no pension?" He paused for breath.

The crowd listened to him with open mouths. The speaker gave a solid story of his own life. He had worked in a dress-shop as a cutter, he had suffered various injustices, and under a more equitable system of government he felt he would have received better treatment. "I come here tonight," he said, the calm tone indicating that he was winding up, "not to bellyache in this hot weather, but with one thought in my mind. If the people understood, if they took an interest in their government, they would all work together for their common good and do something. I come here night after night, I tell you no fancy stories, I give you fact after fact. You stand there and listen to me for half an hour. What are you going to do?"

He climbed down from the platform. A half-dozen younger members of his party walked through the crowd with copies of the *Daily Worker* and kindred literature. They broke into knots. One man with a triangular face calmly smoked cigarettes as he held the center of discussion. He had shaved so carefully that his jaws were greenish and he spoke with the casual wisdom of the ages. Patiently he explained how they did it in Russia.

"Any of you who are interested can come along with me to our room. We can talk there." He moved off. Of the small group about him Cohen alone followed.

"I'd like to hear a little more about this business," he said.

The man with the triangular face inspected Cohen critically. "Come on," he said. "We've got a basement dump, but you're welcome."

On the way down to the basement dump he explained the life to Cohen. He said you had to be altogether serious about it, they didn't want any kidders around. It was a rigorous discipline. "You can't look at it like any other political club. We don't go in for that. We know what we're fighting here. It's everything, we demand sacrifices from you, and you've got to expect it from us."

In the room on Ninth Avenue, a dark basement under the elevated structure, cigarette smoke circled in a blue haze around the single electric bulb. The discussion going on was almost violent. Cohen's friend with the triangular face left him suddenly to shift for himself. He leaned against the wall, taking it in. The young men and women said, "Comrade" and "Party" and uttered their arguments with intestinal sincerity. It was wonderful, Cohen said. How these people gave themselves! That was the answer, to lose oneself in a cause greater than oneself, to become part of some great movement. A man who lived within himself and for himself was rotten and three-quarters dead. Cohen gasped with excitement. This was it.

A heavy girl with a loose face and big lips came up to him wielding a cigarette.

"My name is Shura," she said point-blank and with dreadful solemnity. "Who are you?"

The Old Bunch

by MEYER LEVIN

In many Jewish communities one hears The Old Bunch described as the most loved book of its generation. After thirty years it is still widely read, now by the children of its protagonists, who were themselves the children of Chicago's immigrant West Siders. Recognized not only as a classic of American Jewish literature but as a foremost novel of the Chicago school, The Old Bunch is also now seen as an outstanding period portrait dealing with the twenties-thirties.

The section called "There Is All Kinds of Competition," chosen here, shows the novel's thematic method, using a variety of characters to provide a symphonic effect around a unifying idea.

An activist before the term became common, Levin at times was a decade or two ahead of the fashion in subject matter. Thus, living in Yagur in Palestine in 1927, Meyer Levin wrote the first kibbutz novel, Yehuda. Across from Yagur was Cfar Hasidim, and this led in 1931 to The Golden Mountain, a retelling from the source material of Hasidic legendry, now republished as Classic Hasidic Tales. In his view, today's Jew should understand his ethos in relation to Israel and to European Jewish life. This has not hindered Levin's treatment of such subjects as that of Compulsion, which started the trend in psychiatric documentary crime novels.

Levin's career has included battles over the Jewish question. The first publisher to contract for The Old Bunch required that the Jewish group be changed to a melting-pot collection of Irish, Italians, and Poles, with a few Jews admixed. Another publisher took the book without change, but on Levin's very next novel,

Citizens, pressed for the Jewish strike doctor to be made a non-Jew!

Born in Chicago in 1905, Levin started as a reporter while at the University of Chicago, later was an editor of Esquire. As a war correspondent he centered on the fate of the Jews, described in In Search. In The Fanatic he confronted the question of God and the Six Million. Meyer Levin spends alternate periods in Israel and New York.

C.A.

THERE IS ALL KINDS OF COMPETITION

Competition is the breath of life. Without competition, would Ford ever have perfected the assembly line? Would Columbus ever have discovered America? If a drug store starts on one side of the street, in a month there's a drug store on the other side of the street. Even in a game of casino one wins and one loses. In school, everybody got marks. In life, too, some will get high marks and some will get low marks, only in life the marks will be in dollars and cents.

A real man welcomes competition. It's no fun running unless you're running a race.

Everybody competes every minute of their life. There is competition when you try to get on a streetcar in a crowd, and there is competition when you take a girl to a dance. What would life be, Mort Abramson asks, without competition?

There is all kinds of competition.

Mitch Wilner kept a little whetstone in his locker, and stopped to give his scalpel a few strokes before going to work on his cat. Keep your mind keen, and your tools sharp.

"Hi, Mitch."

"Hi."

Mitch had to wait while Curly Seabury fished his cat out of the barrel . . . and wait some more while Seabury dug out, from under all the other cats, the specimen that belonged to the class beauty. She stood by, her hands dangling like the paws of a sitting-up rabbit. There was a helpless beauty in every class and fellows like Seabury could always be trusted to do their work for them. Seabury might have been a bright guy but she was dragging him down. Beware of women.

Finally, Mitch unwrapped his specimen. He dropped his *Manual*, and set to work.

Seabury opened the window for the class beauty, who stood and drew a deep breath of spring. At the next table Wallace Costa was whistling to himself, "Oh, You Beautiful Baby."

But on the whole, everybody was humping. Already, this quarter, you could feel the process of selection in operation. The classes were still large, but you could begin to tell who would go. It was a beautiful day for a walk, and some of the droops hadn't even bothered to come to class, though the dissection of the semicircular canals of the ear was due for inspection tomorrow.

Within the bone of the skull, back of the ear, lay the three tiny canals, each for a different plane of balance, and in each canal, like a sac in a fountain pen, lay the liquid-filled tube that acted as a level. In humans, the same as in cats. The entire structure that Mitch sought to uncover was no larger than a fingernail. Go slow, now, go easy. He made ghost-thin shavings of the bone.

A howl went up from the table behind him. Mitch drew back his hand, and looked around. Art Schreiber had botched his dissection. "I've been scraping this damn skull all week," he moaned. "Now look!"

"That's all right, a cat has two ears," Weintraub remarked.

Mitch strolled over and saw where Art Schreiber, after making minute shavings for hours, had become impatient and taken one thick cut. Of course that had to be the spot.

"You can still try the vertical," the lab assistant said. "If you keep even one of the tubes intact you'll be doing well for this outfit."

There was a myth that the assistant, in his day, had dissected out all three canals in half an hour.

Mitch bent over his specimen, his nose almost touching the cat. Instead of taking shavings, now, he began to scrape, stopping to blow away the powder after each stroke. He held the head against the light; there was a shadowy spot! Scarcely tickling the bone with his blade, he laid bare the horizontal canal. The tube was perfectly intact. With the needle-point like a sensitive extension of his own fingers, he touched the tube, and felt how it lay freely in its canal.

"Pretty!" he heard the assistant say, behind him. "See if you can get the other two."

Another hour, hunched over the table, and he straightened, only then becoming aware of the stiff cords in the back of his neck, of the crick in his spine. A low whistle went up from Wally Costa. Mitch had made a clean job of the three chambers.

And only then Mitch realized that half the class had grouped around his table, watching him work.

The assistant grinned and said: "If you keep on you'll be nearly as good as I was."

Mitch wrapped up his cat, and put it on top of the pile in the barrel. It wasn't on top when he came to class the next day. He pulled out one cat after another, and finally found his own at the bottom of the heap. When he unwrapped the head, he saw that his perfect work of yesterday had been ruined. The bone was nicked, the canals were mashed.

His hands actually trembled with rage. That anyone could have it in himself to destroy so beautiful a piece of work!

The dirtiness of it, the unfairness!

"Hi, Mitch!"

"Hi, Hank."

"Hi, Mitch!"

"Hi, Art."

But now the chummy feeling was gone. Any one of these fellows might have done it. No, there were a couple he could be sure of, the top men didn't need to do a thing like this. Or, might not they be just the ones . . . ?

The assistant came around. Mitch said, tightly: "I had a pretty fair dissection here, yesterday. . . ."

The assistant looked at the mess. A wry smile came onto his face. Out of a couple of hundred premedics, only about fifty could be admitted into medical school.

There is all kinds of competition; and Runt Plotkin is driving a Yellow cab. It is one of those swell early spring days that come in Chicago, sandwiched between an icy drizzle and a last week of snow. All of a sudden the streets are melted clear and dried. The sun is high, the air is fresh as a schoolgirl complexion, and nobody thinks of riding a hack. Everybody hikes. A fellow farts around the Loop all morning, grinding in low. Suburbanites come out of Northwestern station, stick their noses into the soft wind, kite up their tails, and walk to the office. The taxi stands are crammed with empties, moving up about as fast as the waiting line at the Chicago Theater on a Saturday night.

So Runt cruises.

On Clark Street there's an old fart of a hotel where the Checkers have a concession. Let them have it. The dump is full of farmers and dollar lays. But just as Plotkin is passing the entrance, a guy steps out and hails him. Some guy with a briefcase. There's a line of Checkers, but they've been waiting so long the front guy is snoozing. And this briefcase hails a Yellow. So naturally Runt swerves for the curb.

Do the Checkers wake up! Five horns go off like a pack of barking hounds. The front man steps on it and his jallopy takes one leap, squeezing in on Runt. There is a hit bang; their fenders have clashed, their bumpers are locked.

"All right," says Runt in a murderous low voice. "All right, you f—— Checker bastard. Back the hell out of there and go back to sleep. I got a fare."

The Checker opens his door and leans way out, inspecting the smash. He has a flat baboon face, unshaven. "You bastit! You bastit!" he screams. "That's my own cab! You pay for this!"

Runt rocks his cab, trying to shake the bumpers loose.

"Look out! Stop it, you bastit!"

"Pull your ass out of there!" Runt hollers.

By this time, two Checker drivers have emerged from their cabs. They see the damage is slight. "Go on beat it, you Yellow louse, where the f—— you think you're trying to horn in?"

"Beat it s——! I got a fare."

"Oh, yeah? Scram, you c—— ——, this is a Checker stand."

"That guy called a Yellow, didn't he, you sonsabitches, a guy has a right to call a Yellow any damn place he wants!"

"Who the f—— wants to ride in your robber hacks anyway! Pull outa there before I tear the wheels offa that crap wagon! Listen, you mother-f—— little runt, if you don't——"

"Oh, yeah? You and who else?"

"Come on outa that cab! Come on out and— —"

"This is my pickup, see? All right, ask him. Ask him if he didn't call for a Yellow."

The guy with the briefcase, by this time, is gone.

"You made me lose my fare, you lousy baboon-faced s——eater, you— —"

"Where you tryna horn in, you got standsa your own— —"

"This f—— Yellow cracks up his hack and——"

"Sure, what's it to a f—— Yellow? Listen, bozo, the Checkers are a bunch of respectable family men owning their own cabs. We don't want no trouble. Just pull out and tend to your own stands."

"Pull out, huh? Who the hell is gonna pay for this fender? I wanna know— —"

By this time a cruising Yellow and another have hauled up across the street and the boys have sauntered over. By this time one of the older Checker drivers, a slugger-looking guy, is laying it down hard. "One more peep out of you, you sawed-off little runt, and I'll— —"

"Any day. Any day— —"

Somebody hauls off. Runt staggers clumsily against his radiator. He jumps back, head bobbing, feet prancing. Come on, you sonsabitches. There is a tangle of guys, howling, shoving, barking. "Yellow! Fulla s——!"

Runt ducks his head and squirms into the tangle, punching guys in the guts. Kick them in the nuts. A fist tears at his ear. He gets a sock in the eye.

It doesn't last a minute. A cop comes up from Van Buren, another from Jackson.

Run 'em all in! What the hell they think the streets are for? The Checkers started it. What's the Yellow doing here? Go on, run me in, whatya think we got lawyers for?

One by one, the men go back to their hacks. Runt cuts his wheels sharp, gives her the gas, and nearly tears off the Checker's bumper unhooking the cabs.

The Yellows drive off, and for a while a couple of Checkers follow them, ominously, nosing against them in every traffic jam. Oh, they want a scrap, huh? Runt steers past the big Yellow stand at the I.C. station, and gives the boys the horn. The lousy Checkers. We'll run them off the streets. Trying to give us competition, huh? He touches his blunt finger against his eye. Easy. Easy. It's a shiner all right.

Sol (Chesty) Meisel takes his sheba to the movies. "Florence Reed is playing at the Central, or, say, how about seeing Priscilla Dean in *Conflict*? She's my secret passion."

"Yeah?" says Estelle, with an arch look.

"Yeah, I'm nuts about redheads." And he squeezes her arm. "I read she's got red hair, like you."

After the movie Estelle asks: "Well, how did you like your girl friend?"

"Mmm-mm!" Sol rolls his eyes. "Is she the cat's nuts! Boy, I could go for her!"

"What are you trying to do," Estelle says, "give me some competition?"

Maybe she won't always want to keep Chesty Meisel lapping after her with his tongue hanging out. But a man is the same as a puppy, trotting off to sniff at every passing pair of legs. It isn't only the girls in your own crowd that your boy friend sees, heck, she doesn't have to worry about competition from fatface Celia Moscowitz or bow-legged Aline Freedman or even Ev Goldberg with all her swell clothes, or mama's angel Sylvia Abramson; but Gloria Swanson and Bebe Daniels and Mae Murray and that society girl Mary Baker, they all give men ideas. Being a woman was taking on the whole world, holding the man you wanted against all competition.

"Hey, kid, I'd take you for her any day," Sol said calfishly.

Mort passed up a couple of sure pickups on Sheridan Road. Business before pleasure. Though it certainly was a cinch to pick up the gash in the new Paige. The back seat was as good as a bed.

Maybe on the way home. If he made a deal in Milwaukee.

For he was going out like a knight after the grail. Only, the grail was the kale. First he would tackle the jobbers. And if he couldn't sell the jobbers, Mort had a plan. He would hit straight for the department stores! The old man would squawk if he knew Mort had such an idea, but he wouldn't know unless Mort brought back an order, and an order would make everything jake.

What use are jobbers in the world anyway? Middlemen. They stand in the middle, and collect from both ends. Do they produce anything? No. The manufacturer is necessary, to make the goods. The storekeeper is necessary, to sell the goods. But a jobber just stands in the way and gums things up.

Mort had been thinking about things, recently, refusing to accept what was handed him at face value. He had his ideas on socialism, too. He had an uncle who traveled all over the world, his job having something to do with Jewish charities. And this uncle with his tales of famine, and of the plight of the Jewish middlemen who had no place in the new order of life, had started Mort thinking along various lines.

Once, after an argument with a street-corner communist, Mort even got Karl Marx out of the library—he was slightly surprised to find they had the revolutionary book right there in the public library. Only, it was dull as ditch water. A few pages gave him a headache. This guy Marx took thousands of words to prove what any business man knew to begin with. That a dollar isn't a dollar, but what you can buy for it.

It was as if somebody wrote a long book full of scientific words, the net result of which was to say, if you don't eat, you'll starve.

Mort gave it up after the first few chapters. But one thing he could tell Karl Marx. Laborers weren't the only necessary people. What would become of the goods in the shop if he didn't go out and sell?

For example, take the story in the *Saturday Evening Post*, by Booth Tarkington, that proved exactly the point he wanted to make. In Tarkington's story, there was an owner of a piano factory who suddenly got idealistic and decided to turn his plant over to his workmen. Just before he did this, he happened to turn down a deal for piano-wire because he knew where he could get the stuff cheaper. Soon after the workmen were in charge, the wire salesman happened to call back, saying: "We've lowered our prices." So the workmen gave him a big order. But the joker was that the new price was still much higher than the price which the boss could have bought the wire from another company.

A thing like that just went to show how necessary brains were, to the making of anything.

But what use was the middleman?

The Paige was running smooth as a Rolls. Mort waited until he was through Highland Park, where there was a speed trap. And then he stepped on the gas. Sixty! The segment lines of the concrete road slid under the wheels. He'd be in Milwaukee by two o'clock.

The town looked plenty peppy, even without the beer industry. He eyed the women's hats. Tams, everywhere! No money in tams, too much competition.

Schweitzer was so fat he couldn't turn sidewise in his chair. He wheeled the chair around, and faced Mort. "Well, maybe I did hear of the Glory brand. I can't keep all the little manufacturers in my head." His raggy chewed cigar wiggled up and down on his lips. His small eyes surveyed Mort amusedly. "What's the difference if I heard of you or not? What have you got?"

The old bluffer. Mort knew Schweitzer had picked up plenty of Glory hats from Frumkin, their Chicago jobber. Mort handed him the sample. "There's a nifty little number. I don't have to tell you, Mr. Schweitzer, the cloche model is going to be all the rage this season."

"You don't have to tell me anything," Schweitzer grunted, fingering the hat. "How do you know they will even wear these chamber pots?

You are too young, you don't even know what it's for, but when I was on the road, this was under every bed." He held the hat, brim up. Way down in his guts, disdainful laughter gurgled. "Listen, Mr. Picker, I've been in this business forty-five years, and I can guess as good as the rest of them, and you know how many times I have been stuck?" The cigar pointed. "Every time I tell them what will be the rage next season."

Mort had come in all wound up like an alarm clock, but now he was beginning to slow down and get an idea of his adversary. One of these old geezers that thought they knew everything, and you were the dirt under their feet. All right. Old Schweitzer would sell himself, before Mort got through using psychology on him.

Schweitzer whirled around, pointing out the window. "You see what's going to be the rage? Those flappers are still wearing their tams and that is what you got to sell them."

"The tam is going out," Mort declared. "Why, I've got a sister that's been wearing those things and she's sick of them. The girls all want to wear real hats again."

Back and forth, back and forth; until Mort, battling his adversary every inch of the way, thought he had him to the point of talking prices.

And then Schweitzer pulled a big, kindly, toothy smile, as if to say, Well, boy, I only wanted to see how you would talk, and, turning back to his desk, in dismissal, said: "I'll tell you how it is, son. I get my regular line from Fleischman's in New York. When it comes to bread and butter hats, we got a big factory right here in Milwaukee."

"Why go to New York when you can get the same thing cheaper from us?" Mort cried. "We are not as big as Fleischman's—yet. But we can give you as good a deal, or better. We are looking for an outlet in Milwaukee——"

"What's the matter, you got stuck with this stuff?"

Mort grinned. "Oh, no. We're expanding. We're going outside of Chicago. We——"

But Schweitzer shook his head morosely, in complete dismissal. He was through amusing himself putting a kid salesman through his paces.

Mort felt sore at being pushed around. He took a bitter chance. "I'll tell you frankly, Mr. Schweitzer, we would rather deal with a jobber than with a store direct. But after all we're not a big house and if we can get one department store here as our outlet——"

Schweitzer's heavy, slow-breathing face seemed to swell, reddening, preparing to shoot out a stream of fire.

"Go to the stores, go! Go to the Boston Store, go to Paines's!" His voice cut off, sharp, like a steam whistle. "You think you can get along without the jobber, huh?"

In that moment there seemed a whole world of unknown, threatening disasters which he could hurl against Mort and his Glory hats. Mort sat quaking, wishing he could draw back his last words. Now he had ruined his chances in Milwaukee, probably ruined the whole idea of selling outside of Chicago.

"Go on, do your kike business. Sell direct. What do you need a jobber for? Carry your own warehouse full of stock. Get stuck with your own dead numbers. Pay yourself cash out of your own pocket! What use is a jobber!"

"I—uh—I didn't mean it like that," Mort hedged. "I meant, maybe we were too small for you to bother with."

Schweitzer stopped, mouth open. He looked at Mort for a long while, swinging his cigar from one side of his mouth to the other, rolling it in his lips, wagging it up and down. Finally he snapped: "Nine-fifty, and I'll see if I can handle it for you."

Mort straightened. Ten-fifty was the price; ten dollars a dozen was rock bottom. Schweitzer couldn't be getting this kind of stuff anywhere for less than ten.

"I'll have to make a call."

If the old man answered the phone, it would be all off. It was after four. His mother would have left the factory, to go home and fix supper. Maybe he had better call home. No, then the old man would feel hurt.

But it was Mrs. Abramson that answered the phone. "Mort? I thought maybe you would call, so I waited."

"So that old *Daitcher kopp* wants to chew you down, huh? Well, let him have the fifty cents. Tell him it is for luck, because it is a first sale. But he got to take at least fifty dozen, at this price."

"A new competitor always has to come in a little bit cheaper," Schweitzer stated, as he initialed the order.

The way Rudy saw it, this was a chance he couldn't afford to pass up. He was finishing his premed, and when he entered medical school he would need every dollar he could earn. The Standard Pharmaceutical's drummer tipped him off that K.M. chain needed a night manager in their Madison Street store.

Rudy didn't know how to say good-by.

"Mrs. Kagen, you know I would rather work for you than for anyone else. You know I have passed up chances to make a little more money in other stores, but right now I need the money for school."

The old lady's eyes were watery, and he was beginning to feel weepy himself. It was like saying good-by to a mother. "Go, Rudy, with the best of my wishes," she said. "I wouldn't be the one to stand in your way like my own son! The store will get along, don't worry."

"Maybe I can come in on Sunday afternoons, and if there is any way I can help— —"

"Listen, Rudy," she sighed philosophically. "In this world, everything is to the highest bidder. You are worth more money, and if someone can pay it to you then I can't afford to keep you, ain't that so? That's business. I am a business lady, so I know how it got to be. Come in sometimes, and have a soda," she ended, with quavering laughter, pushing him away from her, with her fingers on his chest. "Go, go!"

"Well! Take care of your lungs and liver!" he chirped. He started to take his white jacket, but instead left it in the closet. "I'll be seeing you. Don't take any wooden nickels."

Mingled with the regret of leaving, Rudy had the rising feeling in his heart of knowing he was wanted in more than one place. He would always be like this in life, leaving only fine memories of himself when he went from each place higher up.

Competition, that is the primary law of life; competition, get it into your heart; even when the two Lous stop into the Y for their daily handball game before supper, competition, kiddo—I'm three up on you. The little birdies are in competition for the worms, the stalks of corn are in competition for sunlight, Fords are in competition with Chevrolets, the Democrats are in competition with the Republicans, men are in competition and nations are in competition. But when you get to the top it is different. Who can compete with Dempsey? All right, who?

"Harry Wills," says Chesty Meisel. "They ought to give him a chance."

"Don't make me laugh!" boos Runt Plotkin. "That shine couldn't last two rounds."

"Carpentier, the Frenchman," says Mort Abramson.

"Yowee!" Runt waves his handkerchief.

"That Dempsey is built like a box car!" even Mitch Wilner says. "I'd like to dissect those muscles!"

No one can beat Jack Dempsey. Who can compete with Charley Erbstein in a divorce case, and who can compete with Clarence Darrow in a criminal court? Has Fritz Kreisler got any competition, or Galli-Curci? Why does Insull offer Mary Garden $250,000 to manage the opera? Why does Babe Ruth get $500 for every home run? Who can compete with America?

Throw away your hammer and get a horn, says Big Bill Thompson, Boost Chicago! Chicago will pass New York, and then who can compete with Chicago? Who can compete with the United States? France was in competition with Germany, and they had a war; England is in competition with Japan, but the U.S.A. is at the top, we have all the dough, we make all the movies, we make all the automobiles, that is what everybody is striving for, in competition, to be like the U.S.A., to be at the top, to be beyond competition, to be the Human Flash of Lightning, the Joie Ray, the Benny Leonard, the Pavlowa, the Dempsey!

The beauty of competition is that it brings out the best of everybody, everybody works their hardest and shows their best quality to win a competition. For instance, if two girls are in competition for a fellow it is decided by their beauty, grace, and goodness. Rose Heller had a crush on Lou Margolis, but there was competition.

Estelle Green mentioned to Celia Moscowitz: "Kid, my brother Lou told me Lou Margolis is trying to get a job in a law office."

So Celia waited for Friday night, when the old man liked to listen, and do things for the family.

Friday night was family night, like in an old-fashioned Jewish home. Celia remembered the real Friday nights when her grandmother had been alive. All her uncles and her aunts and her cousins, complete to the latest baby, would be at the old folks' flat on Fifteenth Street. The table would have been elongated with wobbly extension boards. The old grandfather, Avrum Moscowitz, would sit there in his skull cap, sipping soup from the end of his spoon, with little smackings of his lips, and never getting his beard wet. Like a real old Jew from the Bible.

Now, since the grandmother was dead, Rube Moscowitz, being the eldest son, had to give the Friday night family suppers. To his wife they were a pain in the neck. She was stylish and didn't believe in old-fashioned foolishness.

But Rube would say: "What does it hurt, make the old boy feel good once a week!" The truth was Rube Moscowitz liked to have a lot of people eating at his table.

Besides, old Avrum still owned the business. When his sons demanded that he turn it over to them, he said: "I have not gone crazy yet. I have seen too many old men become beggars at the tables of their sons."

"You have to humor him," Rube said. He gave the old man a few thousand dollars for his Anshe Kneseth synagogue, and ran the business his own way. Once a year the patriarch insisted on seeing the banking accounts, and always squawked.

"Reuben, what is this, are we in the junk business, or in politics business? Why are you paying all this money? Five thousand here, two thousand there, I know, I know what it is, to politicians. Have they got junk to sell?"

"Listen. Why bother your head about it? Look what I paid the car company for that load of scrap. They practically gave it to me!"

"Gave it to you. You paid them four times over, in the elections."

"That's all right, that's all right, that's the way we do business now, just keep out of it, will you, everything will be all right."

But around election time, when even on Friday nights Rube was interrupted every minute by telephone calls, by messengers who would stand at his elbow and wait for an answer, old Avrum would resume his mutterings.

"Politics. Politics. He ain't got time to eat. It's Sabbath eve in a Jewish house!"

And Celia's mother would chime in: "Sure, if it wasn't for politics, we could have moved up on Sheridan Road long ago. But here, I can't even move to the other side of Jackson Boulevard, it would be bad politics!"

"Sheridan Road! Aren't there people enough on the West Side?" Rube would roar.

"You know what kind of people there are here! It's nothing better than a ghetto."

"It ain't politics, it's business," Rube would insist. "If you want people to do business with you, you got to do them a favor once in a while."

"Why can't the street car company do their own dirty work, why do you have to do it for them?" Mrs. Moscowitz would demand.

When Rube was sprawled, stuffed, on the sofa near the grand

piano, Celia could hear her mother having a kind of serious talk with her father.

"Listen, Rube, as far as I am concerned, mix in politics all you want, if you enjoy it. Only I don't like to hear people talk that my husband is a grafter."

"How can you be a politician without grafting a little?" Rube would say, leering, and begin to chuckle from the bottom of his belly.

Naturally, if a man is running the ward, he has to take care of everything in the ward, letting the bootleggers and the widows who run flats and the harmless gamblers contribute to the party funds. If you don't take their money, they'll go elsewhere for protection. You have to play ball, in politics. And the dough mounts up, too.

"Yah," the woman worried, "and look what happened to Len Small, governor or no governor."

"Aw, who told him to buck the *Tribune!*" And Rube's laughter would explode, his cheeks shaking like a fat woman's breasts. "Don't worry, you know I ain't in it from that end! I hand out more than I take in!" he would console her.

How could a woman understand the competition of politics? Republicans and Democrats! One of them gets into that pot of dough-re-me and he's so busy stuffing, cramming, and grabbing he only has time for an occasional back-kick at the other fellow who is on his tail, tearing and shoving to get inside the pot, howling and slinging great gobs of mud and rocks at his head to get him away from the pot. And so finally the pot-eater is shoved aside, and, wow! their positions are reversed. The second fellow hops into the pot, gorging and grabbing, and the first fellow is outside howling, slinging rocks.

Big Bill the Builder is in. Boy, is he in! No wonder he wants to build, and build! Pour the millions! Millions into the drainage canal and millions for a pier, build schools, tear up streets, show them something for their money, and, boy, how the money flows out! See that beautiful bridge, that Michigan Avenue bridge! (And three million smackers' "expert fees" alone, handed to the guys that were supposed to take a look at a few buildings near the bridge to assess their value.) Build Chicago, boys! Show them a bridge, a street for their money!

The Republicans were in, but the Democrats were hot on their tails. The Democrats still had a lot of judges in office, and how those judges could hand out indictments!

Indict Big Bill's grafting governor, boys. Indict Big Bill's grafting school board, boys! Sue Big Bill for those expert fees, smother him with indictments and he won't dare run again. That's giving them competition!

Governors? Mayors? Senators? It's a laugh! Everything goes in competition, boys. Sock them into jail, throw them in the can, they'd do the same to you—if they could—ha ha ha!

The Democrats have got those Republicans by the tail. Rube Moscowitz is a Democrat, and don't you worry, the Republicans can't even compete with him in his own bailiwick. When Big Bill took the town, he didn't take the Democratic Jewish ward.

For, every Passover, Rube Moscowitz would haul a fleet of trucks full of matzoth up Roosevelt Road. Across on Kedzie Avenue, down Sixteenth Street, they went, with Rube handing out the matzoth, personally, to poor Jews. Come and get your matzoths, boys, with noodles and chickens in the baskets.

"A new Moses in America!" his wife would kid him.

But Rube Moscowitz had that ward sewn up tight and it stayed Democratic. A stronghold of Democracy in a Republican town.

Now Big Bill Thompson's gang was on the run: Small, Lundin, and the rest, their tails afire with indictments, and when the Republicans were out and the Democrats were in again, Rube's power would be extended far beyond his ward, he would be a power to be reckoned with, all over the city.

So why shouldn't Insull practically give Rube Moscowitz the scrap iron from the El and street car lines? Insull wanted new franchises from the city council, Insull wanted to extend the El lines into the new Columbus Park neighborhood that was building up fast, into other new fast-building neighborhoods, Chicago was outgrowing the El. Insull wanted that subway question settled; oh, how long, how long would Chicago talk about building a subway? If a subway was going to be built, he wanted control of that, too.

If Big Bill wouldn't play ball, then another mayor would play ball with Insull. Big Bill, talking big about the city owning its own subway! Why should the city try to compete with a business man!

Insull had a fund for the coming mayoralty campaign.

Republicans and Democrats, state your offers. You've got to compete for that little bag of gold.

Rube Moscowitz was passing out some of that Insull money; certain aldermen always needed a little help. Friendly aldermen could vote to extend the El lines, vote new franchises . . . !

The Thompson machine was cracking, sliding in every election.

Why, the graft they had pulled on the school board alone was enough! And the contracts they had handed out for paving: the streets could have been paved with gold!

Sam Insull was going big. Did you see that stock market! A million shares a day, for seven days running! Why shouldn't Insull give Rube Moscowitz a few tips on the market? Good tips, too.

And Rube Moscowitz passed some of the tips on to Alderman Pete Grinnell, his sidekick, his *goyish* pal.

Celia was used to seeing Pete Grinnell in the house; my second home, the alderman called it, and he was always referred to, with big back-slaps by Rube, as "one of the family."

When Avrum Moscowitz had first located the junkyard on Ogden Avenue, this had been an Irish neighborhood. And the Irish alderman could do favors.

Gradually, it changed to a hundred-percent Jewish ward. Pete Grinnell, with his bulldog beefy Irish face, was still alderman. The opposition was always trying to win by running a Jew for alderman of the Jewish ward. But Rube Moscowitz, with the Jewish vote in his pocket, stuck by his Irish alderman.

Committees would come to whisper in his ear while he lay back in his chair in Rosen's barber shop, "Listen, Rube, after all, how long are you going to keep that mick in the council? After all, why shouldn't we have a Jew?"

"Say, he gets us everything we want, doesn't he? Say, that Irishman is a better Jew than a rabbi from Jerusalem."

Pete Grinnell was like all those Gentiles who, even when on intimate terms in a Jewish household, never quite lose the sense of something mysterious about Jewish religion, imagining mystic secret meaning to whatever they witness.

He never failed to look with awe and wonder at the brass *menorah* that was taken from the sideboard, on Fridays, and set on the dining table. "Say, that's a fine candelabrum," he would hint. "Seven branches, huh? That's a holy number, seven."

"It's a family heirloom," Mrs. Moscowitz would reply. She allowed herself to forget that Rube had brought it home from the junkyard, in the early days. "It was brought over by the old grandfather in the steerage." To admit that one's remote ancestors came in the steerage was okay. People could whisper: "Look where they are now!"

For all the years that he had known the family, if Pete stayed to dinner on a Friday evening, or on a Jewish holiday, he would act strained, standing behind his chair until Rube boomed: "Sit down, Pete! Wadaya think this is!"

It was as though the eating itself represented a tribal ceremony to the alderman, and to counteract his diffidence, he would act even more familiar than ever with the family, personally. He would put his arm around Celia and chuckle: "How's my sweetheart? When are we going to elope? Ha ha!"

You could be sure he told all the Gentiles: "Jews? Best people in the world! Why, I know the Moscowitz family like my own! A finer, more wholesome family you never saw!"

What if Rube Moscowitz wouldn't want him in his house, or in the city council? Where could he go, the old ward politician, with his tree-chopping voice, his ever-ready laugh, with the deep lines of long-held smiles on his face? Start in another ward, at his age?

Grinnell would sit there, looking with a kind of boyish awe at old Avrum in his skull cap, waiting for Avrum to begin eating. A special, different food was always brought on different plates, old, thick porcelain, from his dead wife's household, for Avrum. And, long as he had been coming there, Grinnell did not know that this was the *joke* of the Friday night suppers; he thought it some sort of occult Jewish ceremony, the patriarch eating differently from the others, while the fact was that Avrum, suspecting that Mrs. Moscowitz kept only a lax half-kosher in her kitchen, insisted on bringing his own food and dishes for his meal, prepared by his own trusted housekeeper. "With a good heart, I don't want to insult you," he would say, bringing his package each Friday, "but we all know here in America Jewish wives are Yankees," and so, though the Friday night meal was really held for his benefit, he never ate a morsel of it!

"Well, Celia, when am I going to see a grandson-in-law in the business?" old Avrum squeaked, starting his usual Friday night subject. "Before I die, I should like to hold a great-grandchild in my arms." Why was it that as people grew old, all they could think of was propagating the family?

"Celia, sweetheart, you can't refuse an old man a wish like that!" Pete Grinnell kidded. "My, that's wonderful *gefillte fish*, Mrs. Moscowitz!"

"Oh, she's got lots of time," Mrs. Moscowitz said of Celia, and, of the fish: "Yah, the new girl finally learned. That's one terrible thing about trying to get a girl to cook for a Jewish family, you have to learn them everything."

Rube Moscowitz gobbled down two large pieces of fish, and kept eating from the side dishes, chopped liver, radishes, pickles, hurtling the stuff down his throat unchewed, never stopping between the courses. What he loved was pickles. He even ate pickles with his soup.

"Have some pickles, Pete," he yelled down the table. "Try some of those sour tomatoes. That's the real stuff. Kantor's."

In fact, Rube had loaned the delicatessen man ten thousand dollars to start a pickle and sour tomato cannery.

"All I get out of it is free pickles!" he sputtered.

"Say, if he has to supply you with free pickles, what has he got left to sell?" Rube's brother, Moe, snorted.

"Don't eat so fast!" Mrs. Moscowitz cautioned Rube. "Dr. Meyerson told you! You'll get high blood pressure."

This reminded Pincus Moscowitz, another brother, of something: "Hey! Did you see that in the paper where a doctor claimed he didn't have to pay his lawyer for losing a case, so the lawyer sues him, telling the judge, doesn't a doctor get paid even if the patient dies?"

"What would you rather marry, Celia, a doctor or a lawyer?" put in old Avrum.

"Huh?" said Celia.

One of Moe's three little girls, Rosalind, suddenly piped up: "I'd rather marry a lawyer, because doctors have to get up in the middle of the night!"

Pete Grinnell exploded, his laughter shooting morsels of food from his mouth. All the husbands and wives looked at one another, and then began to sputter, burble, and gulp with partly suppressed laughter. Rube Moscowitz swallowed his food and roared.

"Nowadays," said Hannah, Moe's wife, "you can't tell what kind of people your girls go out with. They do anything they want."

"I know all of my girl's friends," said Mrs. Moscowitz, icily. "They are the nicest smartest kids in the neighborhood. Now you take that boy Mitchell Wilner. Wasn't he the—what do you call it, Celia? At graduation?"

"The valedictorian."

"Wilner? . . ." old Avrum repeated. "There is a Wilner in my *shul*. He knows the Talmud backwards!"

Mrs. Moscowitz, watching Celia, tried again. "And who is that other one, Celia, you know, he was so brilliant . . . you know, the debater? . . ."

"What debater? There were lots of debaters," Celia evaded.

"Isn't he studying law or something. . . ?" Mrs. Moscowitz looked full at her, now.

"In the old country, Mistair Grinnell," Avrum put in, with the sing-song that always started his old country reminiscences, "we would make a match already for a girl like Celia. A Talmud student— —"

"This isn't the old country," Celia cried. And then, flushing, but needing to get it over with: "Hey, pop, that reminds me. A couple of the boys in the bunch are looking for jobs in a lawyer's office. Come on, be some use."

"Yeah? Who are they?" Rube said.

"Aha!" Pete Grinnell smacked his lips.

Celia realized how dumb she'd been. Why couldn't she have waited until she got the old man alone!

Still, she had to finish. "Oh, Estelle Green asked me for her brother, and he chums around with Lou Margolis—they've been here, the two Lous."

"Margolis! Oh, that's the one! The debater!" Mrs. Moscowitz piped. "Oh, Rube, you ought to do something for him. He's a brilliant boy!"

"So that's the one!" Pete Grinnell mimed, and giggled. "Well, Celia, I certainly am broken-hearted."

"Oh, I just told Estelle I'd ask," Celia muttered. Was her face red!

"What chance has age before youth?" the alderman went on. "That's too much competition for me. Just invite me to the wedding, Celia."

"Oh, leave her alone, Pete," Mrs. Moscowitz said.

"Say, I know just the place for your friend," Pete Grinnell suggested. "Rube, what about this fellow Preiss? Edelman, Preiss, and LeGrand. They handled the tax business for you, didn't they? A real high-class outfit. I bet they could take in a lad."

"I'll tell you, Celia, if they're friends of yours I'll see what I can do for them," Rube stated in the voice he always used when asked for political favors. "I'll call up Preiss myself, tomorrow. I don't know if I can get in two boys, but maybe one."

"Yah, which one do you want, Celia? Haw haw haw!" sang little Rosalind.

"Wait!"

Aline looked up and down State Street to make sure nobody they knew might be passing before she let Joe get out of the car in front of their father's dump, the Star Hotel.

As Joe came up the dented stairs, he was greeted by the Negro, John, whom all the storekeepers on the block called the Schvartzer Yid.

"Vos macht a Yid?" John delivered in a lip-smacking Yiddish. John was the street joke, claiming he was a member of a Negro tribe of Jews. He had picked up Yiddish and used each word like a mystic password. He also sang Yiddish songs, "Eli, Eli" was his favorite, and this he would sing with the soft melancholy of a sorrowing race, as he emptied the spittoons.

"Is Mike here yet?" Joe asked about the night man.

John put his hand to his cheek, in Yiddish woe. "Oy, oy, shicker is a goy!" he sang.

"Is he too drunk to work?"

"Aw, he'll be okay; you go on, take the old man home, to eat that gefillte fish!" Nigger John licked his teeth. "Mike's just laying in there mourning for all his pals that got shot up."

"Who?"

"You remember Shorty and that One-Eye crazy man? Lots of the regulars hang out here, they all got shot up. That's why there ain't hardly nobody around."

"Yeah? What's all the shootin' for?" Joe quoted.

"Ain't you read all that in the papers? That mine-shootin' down in Herrin, Illinois, that's where all these boys went. That fellow Shorty, he got shot dead, olav hasholem, but he ain't no loss to the world, that ganef."

Joe remembered now reading about some shooting in a mine strike. So that's what the State Street bums did, went down there to work! For an instant he felt a strange, intimate contact with the world of things that happened. These bums who paid their half-dollars to his old man, who shot their streams of yellow tobacco juice into these very spittoons, they were in the papers. Often, watching the bums squatting on the flophouse chairs, he had been struck by the ordinary wonder, where had their lives begun, how would they end? Now it seemed he knew the end, and therefore the total of their lives.

"He have any folks?" he said.

"Yah, Shorty had some folks someplace," John said. "Used to curse 'em all the time."

There seemed no more to ask about Shorty.

"What'd they all want to go down there for and get into trouble?" Joe asked.

"Ten bucks a day, that's what! Man come along from the Quick Employment Agency, he sends them out all the time on those trouble jobs. Wants me to go along to. Not me. I don't want no trouble with strikers."

"What'd they shoot them for?" Joe asked.

The Shvartzer Yid stared at him. "They was down there strike-breakin'," he pointed the obvious.

"You mean they shoot them, for that?"

"Sure, man! You can't fuss with those striking boys! They don't want no competition!"

Joe found his father in the back-stair hole where Mike sat on a cot, fiery-faced, his eyes greenish, his tongue pushing around inside his chewed face.

"What's he been drinking, canned heat?" Joe said. "It's a wonder he don't poison himself."

"Nothing can poison him," said Freedman, as Mike wobbled to his legs, just like some old sick horse that finally, out of sheer loyalty to his master, had decided to get up.

A newspaper strewn on the floor had headlines about the coal miners' strike. The owners stated that if they raised wages they would be unable to meet the competition from Eastern coal fields.

Joe glanced at the name-list of strikebreakers who had been ambushed by the miners. Few had addresses—Joe wondered which name was Shorty's.

Aline was honking impatiently.

"*Gut shabbes!*" the Shvartzer Yid called as his boss got into the new Studebaker.

As they passed along South State Street, there were the familiar bums loitering in front of the beaneries and the *Join the Navy* posters. The bums had always seemed just freaks, drunks, derelicts, outcasts of life. But now Joe felt rotten about them; they were guys that would go anywhere, do anything for ten bucks, and yet you couldn't blame them, they were helpless, they took a job and then got popped at and died with surprised looks on their beery unshaven faces. They were helpless; they had been squeezed out by the competition of life. But who was safe, in this life? He too might end up a State Street bum!

"I hear you lost some customers," Joe said to his father, smirking uneasily.

Nathan Freedman didn't answer his son, about the bums. As they rode along in the Studebaker, Joe felt more and more uncomfortable. His father's silence this time seemed like the silence of a man who knows and feels a great deal, but realizes it is useless to try to make people understand. Let it be that those were just lousy bums, drunks who went out and got shot; their lives were worthless anyway.

Joe rang the Abramson bell and ran up the stairs. He walked plop into a mob of relatives. It wasn't just a Friday night gathering but some sort of special assembly. There was an uncle who had just come from Russia. "He travels all over the world," Sylvia whispered. "It's something to do with Jewish affairs. I think he's here to get a million dollars out of Julius Rosenwald, for Russian Jewry." She slipped away to perform those last-minute rites for which girls keep their callers waiting, and Joe found himself stuck among the relatives. They were having a terrific argument about the Jews. Even Mort was taking part in the discussion. Joe tried to sit there, just looking at them: an ordinary bunch of Jewish relatives, the women bursting their dresses, the men either pouchy or consumptive-looking. But their excitement got hold of him. Maybe because of the queer mood he had been thrown into by the death of Shorty, thinking where people came from and what became of them, maybe because of the personality of this Russian emissary.

Joe had never seen quite such a Jew. His English, while more heavily accented than that of the others, somehow had a distinguished flavor; he made none of the fat-smacking sounds of ghetto Yids; instead of *vot forr* he would say *how?* A European. He was short, stocky, with a solid face that seemed to have achieved its final, inflexible look and form. Parenthetic creases were at the sides of his settled, yet humorous mouth.

They were arguing at a great clip about those old Yids back in the old country. That had always seemed a laughable dead subject to Joe. All life that really mattered had come over here. But now, suddenly, he felt ignorant, and inferior.

Even Mr. Abramson who was usually sprawled out apathetic to the world was sitting erect, tense with argument.

Once Sylvia had told Joe how her father had become so skinny and worn-out looking. As a boy he had smoked himself hollow, deliberately ruined his health in order to be exempt from the Tsar's military service. Then he had escaped from Russia. And similar stories echoed from Joe's own memory, tales heard in childhood of his own relatives' escapes from military service, of wild frightful rides down guard-infested roads, hidden under a load of hay . . . and how some guard jabbed a pitchfork through the hay, but luckily in the wrong spot, or you wouldn't be here, my son. . . .

The older generation was just full of those heroic yarns. Why had the parents so desperately needed to escape from Russia? Just to avoid military service? . . . As this crowd jabbered, astonishing things poured from them. Why, they had been full of ideas, ideals; they had even been socialists, freethinkers; they weren't dead to the world at all! Joe no longer saw them as mere hulks that had had to exist in order to produce Sylvia and himself, as greenhorns who had left that dumb country, Russia, to get to America, the land of gold, and raise smart children, geniuses.

In the intensity of their discussion, they seemed to have brushed aside Mort, himself, all the younger folk to whose importance they usually were so deferential. There appeared a greater concern for something vital, live, back there; and beside that issue, even their smart American sons and daughters were unimportant. They had dropped English, and were arguing in a Yiddish that was no longer a comical language, but the tongue of a self-respecting nation. Mort had to yammer along in a clumsy foreigner's Yiddish.

That fattest of the aunts argued: "Even Emma Goldman said that for the Jews, the Bolsheviki are as bad as the Tsar. Then there were pogroms, and now there are pogroms . . . !"

"Emma Goldman!" Bialystoker, the foreigner, sneered. "She too can talk! They kicked her out!"

"And why did they kick her out? Because she was telling the truth!" the fat aunt insisted.

"They kicked out Emma Goldman?" Mr. Abramson was startled. "But she was a *revolutzionistke!* a socialist, an anarchist!"

The bald-headed emissary laughed.

"And, Bialystoker," the fat aunt shot at him, "maybe there is no famine in Russia either?"

"Food there is not too much, and bread they need, I can tell you," Bialystoker admitted.

"And their Lenin is lying with a bullet through his head, and Trotsky will be next, and then an end to the whole Bolsheviki!" a fat uncle pursued the advantage.

"Like it said in the *Tribune*," Mort put in. "The Russians would trade all their Lenins and Trotskys for a Hoover. Say it with bread."

"Oh, the Tchicago *Tribune*," Bialystoker mocked. Then announced categorically: "Lenin is not dead, and nobody will shoot Trotsky, and the Bolsheviki are not making pogroms. Jews, how can you believe such *dreck*! Only a few Jews who were class enemies, capitalists helping the Whites—naturally they were arrested."

"White, red, a Jew is a Jew!"

"Listen, countrymen. In Russia, we Jews are now like everybody else. The workers will be protected and the capitalists will be destroyed. Why do we have to fool ourselves? The money-world has always been death to us Jews. We have been forced to live in this way and it has been death to us. What does a Jew really want? A chance to work, like other people. Haven't the Bolsheviki given us a whole territory of our own, in Crimea, the richest soil in all Russia? What more can we ask? At last we can go back to the land, work, live, develop our culture, our nation. We will be a nation within the great group of Soviets. How should the Jews be forgotten? Trotsky himself is a Jew."

"Trotsky shmotsky. Such a Jew, the devil himself is! Trotsky's own father disowned him! A *mamser* he must be! His own army makes pogroms!"

"Where do you get such nonsense?" Bialystoker cried indignantly. "From the Tchicago *Tribune*? The truth is, Trotsky gave guns to the Jews. Protect yourself, he said."

"Tea? More tea?" said Mrs. Abramson.

"Yah." Mr. Abramson was cynical. "It will be like in Poland and in Rumania and like with all those other heathen governments, a black year on them. Promises! Come, Jews, settle on the land, build houses! And we send money and the government takes it away from them. As the learned Rabbi of Bialystok said, a guarantee from a *goyish* government, begging your pardon, ladies, is useful to wipe the behind."

"But with the Bolsheviki it is different! . . ."

"Don't make me laugh!" the fat aunt screeched. "The Bolsheviki are different! My aunt had a little grocery in Berdichev, and now she begs for bread!"

"And Chaim Berman's silk factory in Odessa? The man was a millionaire. Now he eats offal! They won't even give him a food card! And what are they doing with the factory? It rots!"

Now a warty, consumptive-looking little man chimed in conclusively: "Aye, children! Why should we try to make a new life in

Russia? We have our own land again, thank God! Let the refugees go to Palestine!"

"Palestine!" Bialystoker exploded. "Don't speak to me of Palestine! When a man is drowning, this is not the time to lie on the grass and dream dreams!"

"What kind of dream! The land is there! Rather than throw money in the ocean to a drowning man let us send him to our homeland, to settle in Palestine!"

"Yes! On the barren mountains! Jews are starving already in your precious Eretz Yisrael!"

"Better than starving in Russia!"

"Ut! there speaks your idealist!"

Pop-eyed, hot-faced, they were all screaming at each other like a bunch of—like a bunch of Jews. Each side accused the other of idealism. Then suddenly the Zionist cried: "Yes, it is an ideal! Why not? We Jews have always been idealists! And see, now, the ideal is coming true!"

"An ideal you call it!" Bialystoker snorted. "To turn back history two thousand years! To sit under your olive tree and have Arab slaves working for you, noble Jew! Good, so the Jews are idealists. And what is it that I am talking about? The great ideal of the human race . . . to build the new order of mankind! That is more important than to build another little colony for England!"

The idealists glared at each other, fuming. And now Joe saw what they were arguing for. The American Jew, the Rosenwald, had his hand in his pocket, and the idealists howled on each side of him—give money! Give for Jews and Zionism! Give for Jews and communism! It was a competition of ideals.

Mort jumped into the argument. "Idealistically communism is fine, but practically it will never work out!" he declared. "There was a swell story by Booth Tarkington in the *Saturday Evening Post* about a guy that gave his factory to his workmen, and when they tried to run it— oh, boy!"

"You will see, there will be pogroms in Palestine, too," Bialystoker was predicting. "Don't forget, the Arabs are there."

"Pogroms! Starvation!" Mr. Abramson cried. And they began worrying about Jewish refugees from Rumania, where should they go? It was this that confused, amused, and yet got hold of Joe. A houseful of relatives on a Friday night, a house on Avers Avenue, Chicago, and, by God, nothing escaped their worry; they worried about the

Polish pogroms, the Lithuanian Jews, the Rumanian exiles, the Gali-
cians . . . they never forgot one, not one.

Sylvia had come back; she was ready, but he wasn't eager to leave.

As they went to the door the whole scene imprinted itself on Joe's
mind, like a scene from a train, a place at once strange and familiar,
to which a man knows he must return.

"Don't stay out late, Sylvie," Mrs. Abramson cautioned.

Like life, Sol thought. He said the words to himself, like life, the
riding, the going around, it was a victrola record going around around,
and the humming buzz of the wheels . . . like life. After the going
around and the going around for half an hour for thirty-five minutes
there was no end there was no time because time was the hands of the
clock going around and you were going around yourself it was all the
same thing, life. Like life, I figured it out for myself. I'm not dumb,
a dumb athlete, Estelle, because here see I am thinking the same time
I am riding. Like life. Around and around in a circle, does the old man
do any better, does anybody do any better, I say everybody does the
same thing, the old man pushing an iron up and back pressing pants.
Around and around in a circle. I hang onto Bobby. Around three
times and then he falls back and I hang onto the Dutchman. And
I pass and someone passes me, and I pass again, and then we go for
a long time the same, nobody passes anybody. Like life. It is a competition. You go for a long time and it is the same if you go to school
or anything else. Come on, Estelle, come down early today. It is the
long drag of the morning but maybe she will come and stand behind
my pullman. Stand behind my pullman, Estelle, and like they say
the earth goes around the sun I'll be going around you. That's a hot
idea, see I am thinking, not so dumb, Estelle. You stand there and
take your hat off, shake out your red hair like the sun blazing, and
you will keep me going around and around keep me going.

The old lady was sore, what kind of a thing is it! A Jewish boy! A
Jewish boy goes to school, to college, is a doctor, a lawyer; but a Jewish boy should do such a crazy thing! But ma, look at Benny Leonard, he is a Jewish athlete and he made a million dollars! Six days
and nights on a bicycle! It is a *meshugass!* Crazy! Not my son, no,
no, I will not let it! He will kill himself! (Boy oh boy did she put up
a squawk! She nearly had Kabibble Cooperstein keeping me off the
track. Keep that crazy mother of yours away from the front office,
Pisano yelled, or Kabibble will scratch you, understan'!) But why is

it crazier? Why is it crazier on a bike than a doctor gets up in the middle of the night, than the old man pushes the pressing iron, than a guy turns the pages of a book, the next page, the next page, like life!

See the blue and white flag on my pullman. What are you, Jewish? Kabibble Cooperstein says when the Wop drags me up the first time. You don't have to ask Kabibble if he's Jewish ha ha it sticks out all over his nose. You tell him, I stutter, says Pisano. . . . Listen, says Kabibble Cooperstein, What's your name? Solly? Well, Solly, don't expect to cop the first race, don't even expect to finish, don't kill yourself the first time. Let me give you a tip, Solly, in every race a couple of teams drop out before the finish. Maybe your team will drop out. Don't worry. It's the first time. I'll keep an eye on you. I just want to see how you can ride. It wouldn't be such a bad idea, if we could pick a couple of nice Jewish kids. . . . Like life. In America. The Wops and the Greeks and the Germans, the dagos and the micks and the sheenies, all go around like when you stir the tea the leaves go around in the cup. Like life. Boy, was I shaking. Me lining up with Reggie MacNamara and Bobby Walthour and Carl Stockholm and those guys. Boy, was I shaking. You don't believe it when they say your knees shake but that's just what they do, like a pair of rattling bones.

That's all right you two kids ride together. Two Chicago kids. You two kids'll get along fine. Hey, Charley? Hey, Solly? Witczik had that green jersey and I had that blue and white jersey, that's the Jewish colors.So then we got red, white, and blue jerseys.

You never think you are a Jew until you sign up and then they say what are you? A Jew, and you see all the other bunks with Italian, German, French, Canuck flags and you go out and say where can I get a Jewish flag and you have to chase all over town but down on Halsted Street there is a place where they got all kinds of religious stuff, *talisses*, and Jewish flags three for a dime. Penny flags. Like life. I ain't riding under no sheeny flag, Charley yells, and it's nearly a scrap. All right, all right, the boy has two ends, you put any flag you want on your end. I put my flag on this end. The American flag, Charley says, that's good enough for me!!

What do you know about the old lady, she gives in, on opening night she drags the old man down, and Aunt Gittel and uncle, the whole damn family. They come and stand behind the box. Estelle is there behind the box. So no use, they have to know each other.

Meet a friend of mine. But the old lady gives her one look, and knows why she's there, standing behind my box. My girl.

So once you do something they brag about you. In the beginning they raise hell and won't let you do it but once you go out and do it they brag. See, that's my boy. That's my Solly.

And the whole bunch. I was the guy. The whole bunch came, Mort Abramson and his sister and Joe Freedman and Foxey and Dave Plotkin and Harry Perlin, and I was the guy. Hey, Solly, who sent the flowers? The girl friend? Don't blush, Solly! . . . And in the third sprint, fresh and new and afraid to step out in front of all those stars, in front of the Iron Man and Goulet, me, a kid, step out in front of them! But, jeez, the fellows and all the girls in the bunch yelling and screaming every time I passed where they were sitting together! So in the third sprint I had to give them something. Solly, keep your head, I said to myself, don't go showing off, you ain't no grandstand rider, but the fifth lap around Bobby dropped back and then just when we passed the field man holding up number six, the Dutchman dropped the lead and I was third in the chain. The sound of the wheels going around like the electric fan in the store, or like a faraway buzz right near, the sound even then the first couple of hours was getting to be something tagging after me and something pulling me on, but the Iron Man was in the lead. The way he looked back with his long face and the mouth hanging open and that hard look in his eyes, come on, you punks, you can't pass the Iron Man.

So you pull out of line wheeling high onto the track around the curve, passing right under the judge's nose on the ninth time around and as the bell begins to ding ding ding you shoot down ahead of the Iron Man pumping pumping pumping running away running away, your teeth on your tongue, head throwing from side to side ding ding ding ding ding bang! made it! and slow down and slow down slower slower last time around and Pisano running toward you while you lean your fingerless glove against the front wheel braking the front wheel and he catches you as you swing off in front of your bunk. Atsaboy! THIRD SPRINT WON BY SOLLY MEISEL OF THE CHICAGO JUNIORS TEAM! You see Estelle standing there right behind the box and as you roll for the bunk flash her the old smile. Not tired at all, but save it, take it easy, stretch.

Is that sonofagun never gonna wake up? Hey, am I supposed to be riding this race myself or have I got a partner? Hey, Lefty, my hour is up pull that guy outa the bunk before I fall off this wheel. That's what the old-timers say, the hour drag in the second morning is worse than the whole race. Well, I got through mine. I'm in.

Jesus Cuurist what a partner. I tear my guts out pumping up a lead to grab off a lap and then I have to hand it over to him and he loses it every time. What does he think this is, a picnic? This is a race, get it, a race, a competition.

You gotta have the right partner. Like life. Cuurist if I had the right partner.

·   ·   ·   ·   ·

Everything Is Perfect

There is all kinds of perfection. Sometimes we speak of a perfect moment, when the surroundings, the company, the things being done, blend into a perfect whole, into something that seems to have a meaning beyond itself, expanding and multiplying until it is the way of life of the whole universe.

Like Harry Perlin said, watching the beautiful new Cadillac that a customer drove into the garage, a new car is perfect until the first scratch, and the first scratch hurts more than a smashed fender later.

To Mort Abramson a girl was something perfect, until she had been had.

A way of doing something may be perfect; all summer Alvin Fox raved about Louis Wolheim's acting in *The Hairy Ape*; that was perfect, he said!

Runt Plotkin told of a stunt pulled by Rube Moscowitz. After wrecking an old sewage plant, the city of Chicago had about fifty thousand dollars' worth of junk for sale. All the junkyards in town were hungry to bid on that stuff. This was one lot Rube Moscowitz wasn't going to get away from them, because there was a law that the city had to advertise for bids on any transaction over five hundred dollars. So how did Rube Moscowitz fix it with the politicians? They divided the fifty thousand dollars' worth of junk into lots worth a few hundred dollars each, and sold it all, lot by lot, to the Moscowitz junkyard! No other dealer had a lookin!

"That was perfect!" said Runt Plotkin.

It was a perfect summer.

Andy Gump running for Congress, that was perfect!

And Henry Ford for President.

Just because you're you, that's why I love you. . . .

Joe Freedman and Sylvia Abramson had perfect hours in the studio Joe had fixed in the basement the Big Ten had used as a clubroom. It was so cool there, and in the late afternoons Sylvia would sit reading poetry while Joe modeled her head. It was modern poetry: Carl Sandburg.

If both the Sox and the Cubs won their pennants, and that's what it looked like to Lou Green, that would be perfect! It hadn't happened since 1909.

Ev Goldberg was going steady with a full-fledged lawyer!

One day the girls felt that their unity was perfect. Their Sunshine Club was having a mah jong party at Celia's to raise their five-dollar monthly pledge for their Belgian war orphan. Skinny Heller hadn't showed up. Then, when it was nearly over, she burst in. And believe it or not, Skinny's hair was bobbed. The girls mobbed her, squealing and exclaiming. "At last! Skinny, how did you ever get up the gumption!"

And it was Lil Klein who noticed that now every one of them had a bob!

It gave them a funny, lumpy, perfect feeling of being together.

Skinny explained how she had finally got the bob. Just for something to do in summer, she had a filing job with S. W. Straus. And the company had two girls' baseball teams, long hairs and short hairs. They had just played a challenge game. The long hairs lost and had to bob their hair! Even though Skinny wasn't on the team, she had been swept along to the shop, and before she knew it— —

"It's marvelous!" Aline exulted. "It's perfect!"

In the study of law you often get cases where a whole chain of whereases fit into each other as perfectly as a set of Chinese boxes and, at other times, there is logical distinction that is beautiful.

Lou Margolis heard such a one, from his boss, Preiss. Lou asked, what is the difference between calling a man a Jew, and calling a man a bugger? It's like the difference between larceny and robbery, or between a civil and a criminal offense. You might insult a man by calling him a Jew, but you might injure him by calling him a bugger. Get it? He liked to tell it, for it was a perfect distinction.

It was a perfect summer. Sometimes Mitch took an hour off for a walk in Jackson Park with Joe, listening to Joe go into ecstasies about his favorite piece of architecture, the crumbling old Fine Arts building. He said it lay like a great bird with spread wings upon the ground. Joe was off the Gothic stuff now, only the classical stuff was perfect; in fact he was leaving the Midway studio and going down to the school of architecture at Urbana. Mitch kind of liked the decay of the crumbling walls, but Joe said it would be a crime if the city failed to rebuild the place.

They went up to Mitch's room. His life was really efficient this summer, in this cubicle of a dorm room, with the mission study table, the goosenecked lamp, the hard narrow bed, and the bare yellow walls. This was the life.

Joe sprawled on Mitch's cot, his head cupped in his interlocked fingers. Mitch was raving about a prof of his, that Russian, Vakhtanov, who had escaped from the Bolsheviki. "He was a big man in Russia," Mitch said. "These dopes here don't even listen to him, but he's got some wonderful theories. For instance, we don't know a damn thing about blood."

"Yah?" Joe didn't raise his head.

"Everybody's looking for germs," Mitch said scornfully.

"Every day they've got serums for t.b. or they've discovered the cancer germ. But let me tell you, they don't even know what happens in the blood, and that's the whole secret of everything. It's in a lot of complicated chemical reactions . . ."

Joe half listened. He liked the earnest excited sound of Mitch, lecturing like a full-fledged medico.

". . . so look, you cluck, I'll put it simply. Maybe even you can understand. You're an architect. So the human body is a city. The veins and the arteries are the streets and alleys, and the bloodstream is the traffic bringing stuff to the cells, taking away waste."

"Ah, Venice!" said Joe.

"All right, Venice. Now in the body you have factories where certain necessary products are made, like the liver and the spleen and the different organs; then you have warehouses where stuff is stored— see, all this stuff travels along the arteries from factory to warehouse to consumer. Suppose your brain tissue needs a little more fat—"

Joe snorted.

"It's like an endless conveyor system, running through the streets, and into the houses, along the hallways, and every cell is a man in a room who pops open his door, grabs what he wants off the conveyor, and shuts the door. Only there isn't any man and there isn't any door. The cell has some way of dragging this stuff out of the bloodstream and pulling it right through the cell wall, yet keeping it inside so it can't get back out through that same wall. To make brains, to make bones, to make fingernails, each cell knows what compounds it needs, and gets them out of the bloodstream, see? How does it work? How come all that perfect organization? Where does the cell get that selectivity? How the heck, with the thousands of varieties of molecules floating along in the bloodstream, how does each individual cell, each particle of tissue, how does it *know* . . . ?"

There was a pause, while the boys shared the same sense of being on the verge of something deep, something incredibly inapprehensible. Like that time last summer, walking together on the beach, under the country stars. . . .

And at the same time Joe was reminded of the feeling the city gave him, this same feeling Mitch was trying to express; sometimes the utterly inapprehensible complication of the city seized upon Joe: the wonder of street after street of houses, of people going in, coming out, carrying packages, of trucks going to stores, dumping goods to be pieced away by people who came to the stores on the street car, El, bus, from Devon Avenue, from Dorchester to Crawford, from Lawndale to Clark Street, who knew just where to buy victrola records, sacks of flour, Chinese lanterns; sometimes it seemed to him that if this maze of people on the way from one place to another and people eating and people pulling levers were suddenly to be stopped, arrested in motion, the whole thing would be seen to be an amazing, perfectly balanced pattern, every movement would be traceable from its source to its destination, and it would be obvious that the whole life of the city was at any one moment a different, but perfectly composed and balanced pattern of motions. Everything would be clear, and yet you wouldn't discover what you were looking for, but you would be choked with wonder at the perfection with which all these interrelated motifs came to balance. And maybe that was what Mitch meant.

Joe circled his arm along the bed, sat up, and for an instant stared straight into Mitchell's earnest brown eyes. They had a feeling of perfect friendship.

"What are these mattresses made of?" Joe said. "Wood?"

> *The depression deeply affects many of the Old Bunch. Sam Eisen becomes an attorney for arrested demonstrators. Harry Perlin starts a little business, building a door-closer for garages— a device he invented—but things are going very badly.*

Pie in the Sky

Sam's office-mates had gone, and he was sitting alone reading *Tobacco Road* when Ella Bodansky arrived. She slumped into the nearest chair, and edged off her slippers. Heaving a loud sigh of relief, she wiggled her toes.

"They've increased our case loads," she mentioned. "Orphan Annie gave me six new ones today. Looks like winter is coming."

Sam shut the book.

"Those damn fools!" she flared. "If we refused to carry any more cases, they'd have to put on more workers. But we've got a lot of nitwits that think they're in a mission or something. Sushal workers," she mimicked. "Hurry up, Sam, I'm starved."

"Well, put your shoes on."

"Where we gonna eat?"

"How about Childs'?"

She made a face. "There's something too damn virginal about Childs'. Let's go to Deutsch's."

In the elevator she regaled him with a story about one of her clients. "Sam, you'll die. You know that family I've been telling you about—we call the old lady Minnie the Moocher? Vespucci, their name is. She's got a couple of boys—and are they a riot! You don't have to tell them anything! They tore down the doors for firewood! So she's been getting eviction notices, and they're actually going to put her out on the street this time. So she keeps screaming: why don't the relief pay her rent? 'Go out and make a fuss, make them take care of you,' I told her. They can't get a cheaper place than the one she's in, they might as well keep her there."

"Where is it?"

"It's an old dump on Thirteenth Street, it's been filling up with Negroes lately. So she's getting chauvinistic and insists on being moved."

"Thirteenth?" Sam said with a premonition. "How far up have the Negroes come?"

"Oh, it's near Wood Street."

"I bet I know the building. A yellow brick, on the north side of the street?"

"Yah. But how—?"

"Nothing. I used to collect rent for a real estate agent around there," Sam said. Such coincidences were meaningless, except to show a fellow how slow his growth had been.

"So you know what Minnie the Moocher does? She hauls something out of her buzzoom, and the look on her face, I thought it might be some of the Lindbergh ransom money, but when she got it unfolded it was a leaflet for a demonstration."

Sam chuckled. "Yah?"

"Al Howard has been organizing the Unemployed Council around there. . . . So Minnie confides in me, real secret-like"—Ella stage-whispered—"'My kid, he bring this home, lady. Is these them Bolsheviks?'"

They laughed together.

"So she was afraid if she got caught at a demonstration she would be taken off relief. I pumped her up a little," Ella confessed. Then remembering a detail, she laughed. "Oh, and, Sam, they had the entire streetcleaning department around the station today. If there is a stick or a pebble left in the whole neighborhood it would take a detective to find it! I never saw that street so clean!"

"Is that a fact?" Sam grinned, but with a touch of melancholy. "Looks like they're preparing a reception."

"Yah. I guess the I.L.D. better scare up some bail money," she said wryly.

"You better tell Minnie the Moocher to bring her own bricks," Sam kidded.

It was a day in the middle of October, and Harry Perlin took a walk. It was a random walk, and yet a number of unadmitted reasons made him go the way he went.

He was thinking: should he sell the car; and it was natural to walk, thinking this out. As if the car were already gone.

What use would it be to sell the old bus, the house was being foreclosed anyway, and a hundred bucks would make no difference.

He walked through Douglas Park, and on down toward the lower West Side, just to see what the old neighborhood was like. Some of those old buildings weren't half bad, even though stove-heated. He could probably get a flat for fifteen, twenty dollars. Good enough for him and the old lady, now that Vic was married to a meal ticket and off their shoulders.

And he was thinking: maybe, instead of moving, they should break up the household altogether, his mother could go and stay with his married sister, and he could put a cot in the shop.

She still had a little pair of diamond earrings that she could sell to pay a little for her keep, and he would pay a little for her, too.

For himself, he could manage to get through the winter. He could build some auto radios and sell them. Maybe it would even grow to a business. Everybody said business would pick up after the election.

And in the spring he could pick up a jallopy, fix it up, and shove off, roaming the country all summer, as he had always wanted to do.

Thirteenth Street didn't look so bad. Though he had heard coons were filtering in.

Harry was going along, thinking over his troubles, when he saw a bunch of cops standing in front of a building. There was a relief station sign on the building. Harry stared at the sign with a funny feeling of covered-up fear.

He could see two cops in the upstairs windows of the building, and even while he watched, another detail of cops sauntered around the corner, with the lazy bored air of cops.

Did they always have police at the relief station, or was something happening? He noticed a few people dribbling around a vacant lot, casting wary glances at the cops, scattering but hanging around.

Harry approached a cop and asked: "What's going on?"

The policeman gave him a funny look, and shrugged. Feeling uncomfortable, Harry moved along.

On the corner, he asked a young fellow in a sweater: "What's up?"

"They're having some kind of demonstration."

"Oh," Harry said. A handbill lay on the sidewalk; standing over it he read:

DEMAND

ADEQUATE RELIEF

STOP ALL EVICTIONS

JOIN THE UNEMPLOYED COUNCIL . . .

So Harry figured he would stick around and see what one of these demonstrations looked like.

There still seemed to be more cops around than anything else. But a few people were collected at the vacant lot, across the street from the relief station. A short, hollow-cheeked fellow without a hat was talking. There used to be more people than that around the soapbox orators on Roosevelt Road.

Harry drifted along, but couldn't quite leave.

An old Dodge was parked around the corner. A fellow and a couple of girls sat inside watching the scene. They looked Jewish, so Harry stood near them.

"Has anybody started to talk yet?" one of the girls asked him. She was wearing a raccoon coat.

"No," Harry said.

"I never saw so many cops," the other girl laughed. "Rusty must be sitting in his office with a machine gun guarding the door."

"Yah, and I bet Orphan Annie has barricaded herself in the ladies' room!" the girl in the raccoon coat joked.

Harry gathered they were social workers.

"What can Rusty do?" the fellow at the wheel said boredly. "He can only hand out what he gets."

"Don't you worry. If he squawks downtown, they'll do something about it. How are they going to know, unless somebody squawks? Remember when they tried that ten percent relief cut? I told all my clients to go out and yell their heads off."

"I wouldn't brag about it, Bodansky," the fellow said. "Somebody is liable to hear you broadcasting."

"Nuts."

"Say, wait a minute, isn't that Captain Wiley?" The girl in the raccoon coat leaned out, squinting. She wore glasses, but Harry thought she had a very sweet face.

"Yah, that looks like him."

A police captain was crossing the street toward the gathering demonstrators.

"I believe he's actually going to talk to them."

"Go on, drive over, Louie, let's see what's going on."

"Uh-uh. This is close enough. Lousy as it is, I value my job."

The girl with glasses smiled at Harry. "See what he says," she suggested.

Harry ambled over. Everything seemed strangely easy, and even dull. The hollow-cheeked leader had come forward to meet the officer.

"Go on, get your meeting started and get it over with. I'm not going to hang around here all day," the captain said with what seemed like good humor. "Get on your soapbox."

"We want to see the district—" the leader began.

"Yah, yah, I know all about it. . . . Hey!" the captain called across the street. "Bring the comrade a chair here, he ain't even brought along his soapbox!"

There was a blurt of laughter along the street. Encouraged, the people shuffled into the vacant lot—women in mangy sweaters, men in coats different from pants, lots of neighborhood kids, some of them on their home-made scooters, a few Negro women and here and there a more neatly dressed person, just curious.

A cop came out of the relief building carrying a wooden folding chair; he placed it in the middle of the vacant lot.

"How's that?" the captain said with mock solicitude.

"Thanks," the leader replied.

"All right. We'll give you twenty minutes. Then scatter." The captain went back to the station. He watched, from the stairs.

The cops were certainly being decent, Harry thought. The people had crowded around the speaker, who stood on the folding chair, yelling the usual stuff. "Comrades, a lot of you here are living on food cards, faced with eviction. We want a committee to go in there and demand . . ."

Harry was just going back to the girls in the car when he noticed some of the cops crossing to listen to the orator.

Then more cops crossed, and fringed the crowd.

Puzzled, and uneasy, Harry stood frozen to the sidewalk.

A cop yelled at the speaker: "Hey! Come down offa there!"

Harry turned to walk away. He was no part of this. He walked square into a cop.

"Where you going, comrade?" the young cop asked with heavy sarcasm.

Before Harry could answer he was shoved; stumbling backward, he lost his balance and sprawled on the pavement, his mouth still open to explain himself.

And before he could get up, he heard feet; the rest of the cops were running at the crowd; Harry scuttled aside on all fours. A heavy shoe scraped his ankle.

Now Harry managed to get to his feet. The whole scene had changed. Cops were already dragging people off the lot; almost on top of him, a huge fat woman in a dirty dark red sweater buttoned awry was squirming in the grip of a cop who held her two arms from behind. She was squalling in Italian. In the same flash, and while he was thinking: why, the cops told them to go ahead, and then jumped them! Harry saw a man wrench a cop's stick from him and swing it wildly. He caught snatches of yells, grunting, and a kid's scream; but the general impression was a scuttling, scared silence.

Harry realized he was in the midst of a riot, the kind of thing that was in the papers about radicals, reds, only these were just people from around the block, and why had it turned into a riot?

Someone running hurtled against him, whirling him around. He saw a few figures escaping into passageways. He saw two cops chasing a Negro, catching him, distinctly heard the clop of stick on skull as the Negro went down. That was within ten feet of the Dodge, which was just moving away.

Harry started to run, to catch the car, to go with them. His sleeve tore half off his coat as he was jerked back. A cop on each side of him, he was rustled across the street. A final push landed him into a small group of people already rounded up. He felt himself all over everybody's feet. "I—I—excuse me—" he blurted, automatically.

Then he saw that they were being guarded by cops with drawn guns.

This was the first moment when a furious emotion of complete outrage flooded Harry. Nobody had to guard him with guns! At the same time he bitterly realized it was useless to try to explain anything.

Across the street, a free-for-all had developed. He saw a woman momentarily detached from the crowd fling something in the face of a cop coming toward her. The cop bent double with his arm covering his eyes.

A knowing, suppressed chortle went through the arrested group. "Pepper."

Now the fight was in clumps, like football pile-ons. As they disentangled, some broken-looking human would be dragged up and half kicked, half carried across the street.

Suddenly a wild, gloating yell arose. And Harry saw that one of those pulled out of a pile was in uniform. His coat in shreds, blood dripping from a claw-nailed tear in his cheek.

"It's the captain!" the word went around with exultation, and fear.

"Hope they tore his eyes out!" someone muttered.

"Yah? We'll get it if he's hurt!"

A paddy wagon had appeared; it must have been waiting. As Harry was booted up the step, he received a fist-clout on the side of his head.

"You don't have to hit people!" he found himself screaming, as he tumbled into the wagon. . . .

.   .   .   .   .

"There's the whole Moscowitz tribe," Mort observed, "right below us in those ten-dollar box seats. I guess Rube is trying to get rid of his money before he has to turn it over to the government."

"What do you mean?" asked Sylvia.

"Rube Moscowitz is getting into some trouble about his income tax. He forgot to mention a few hundred-thousand-dollar items."

"Say! That's a serious thing!"

"Well, who would give him away? He's so popular, he hasn't any enemies," Aline pointed out.

"Yah? What about that Irish alderman he double-crossed? And old man Klein is burned up because of a dirty trick Rube pulled on him; they were partners in some receiverships and Rube sold them to Jaffe's bank, leaving Klein out cold. Rube got about a quarter of a million dollars out of the deal, just before the bank closed."

"That fox!" Mrs. Abramson said admiringly. "Some trick!"

"You mean Lil Klein's father?" Aline asked.

"Kid, whatever became of her?" Sylvia inquired.

"Kid, I heard she's getting married again but I don't know to who!"

"But you don't mean to say that Rube Moscowitz may actually go to jail?" Sylvia asked Mort.

"Oh, he has too much political pull!" Aline interposed.

"I'm not so sure about that. When Cermak got bumped off, the Irish got back into control. They're sick of having the Jews and the Polacks and the dagos running politics, the Cermaks and Zintacks and Moscowitzes, so now that the Irish are in control again, Rube can't expect any favors. He's no good to them anyway since Insull is *kaput*."

"Oh, Lou Margolis will probably find some technicality for Rube to wiggle out of his case." Sylvia was confident.

"It's after nine o'clock," Mr. Abramson complained.

Just then the *shofar* blew.

The quavering and uncertain sound spread thinly over the field, and then like a Jew encouraged by tolerance, it stiffened, and rose between a wail and a brag. Carried strongly now, the full-blown call of the ram's horn grew through a hundred amplifiers, and filled the

Stadium and rolled over the entire World's Fair.

This was the one truly Jewish sound in the world; no other people owned, no other people fitted, the cry of the ram's horn.

Lil Eisen was with her new friend, Irwin, watching the folk dances in the quaint old Belgian village, and she heard the ram's horn's wailing, broadcast over the loudspeaker system, and she laughed.

"Hurray for the Fourth of July!"

And her friend squeezed her hand because she was so cute and clever, and what a smart little business woman!

She made a resolve that she would find a good modern Hebrew Sunday school, for Jackie; later in life, if he wished, he could forget all about Jewishness, but after all maybe there was something to it.

"Why so pensive?" Irwin said.

Alvin and Eunice heard the *shofar*'s call; they were walking along the top wall of the Stadium, for Alvin had had to buy a couple of tickets for the firm. The sound spiraled around them, and Alvin realized that in all her years of being married to a Jew, Eunice had not until now heard the *shofar* sound.

"That's the ram's horn, isn't it?" she asked with the intelligent curiosity of a good-willed stranger.

"Yes, I haven't heard it for years. They blow it on holidays."

"Oh, on Yom Kippur?" she essayed.

"No, on Rosh Hashanah—New Year's. To blow in the new year."

"It's exciting," she said.

Let her have the kid this time; a little half-Jew who would be free of racial sentiment. That was the best thing after all.

The whitish outlines of the pillars were still against the vapory, warm night air. Shrouded figures could be discerned crossing the field, taking their places on the stages.

Then was felt the eager, twittering Jewishness of the crowd, all assembled with their dollars that would take German Jewish refugees to Palestine; in the anticipatory pause there was felt the all-inclusiveness of these months of communal preparations, the hundreds of daughters in all the Junior Hadassah clubs and in all the temple dramatic clubs who had rushed to rehearsals, the swarm of separate little hopes of meeting new boy friends and new girl friends in this activity, the swarm of little plots and cabals, the little loves

and necking parties and even marriages that had grown out of this
activity; the ticket selling; the innumerable phone calls that had been
made, each with its conditions of social politics, shaming people into
more expensive tickets, the whispers and campaigns and comparison,
oh, for such a wonderful cause. . . . And now, the whole Jewish community of Chicago collected in this darkness, waiting, while south-
ward, over the World's Fair lagoon, Fourth of July firecrackers
streaked in parabolas.

Below the stands, it had been a terrific day of last-minute troubles.
A truck, arriving with the huge image of Moloch constructed by Joe
Freedman, crashed right through the pavement of the eight-million-
dollar stadium. It turned out that the concrete floor was only half
as thick as specified. But meanwhile Joe labored among the cheesecloth Miriams and bearded patriarchs, patching up his Moloch. At
last, resting, he looked up into the great circle of filled seats, and
remembered the amphitheater in Mount Scopus, filled with Jews
from Jerusalem, and it was the same crowd. Why, in Chicago there
were about as many Jews as in all of Palestine.

A mellifluous voice intoned: "And it was said: V*ayheey ohr*—and
there was light . . ."

Gradually, a dawn of light came up, revealing a swaying gray mass
creeping, unfolding like primeval waves. This was the birth of humanity, of themselves, a Jewish humanity, way back there in the
deserts of Chaldea somewhere.

"There are over three hundred people on that stage," Mort said.
"Every ten is in the charge of a leader. Ora is in charge of a group,
there."

And suddenly his mind went to the shop. "You know who I think
is the trouble-maker?" he whispered to his mother. "I think Pauline
Stopa is organizing the girls. She's the only one they'd listen to."

"It's not Pauline. I talked to her yesterday," Mrs. Abramson said.

In his mind, Mort listed over the other workers in the shop.

A chorus sang.

"That's real ancient Hebrew music," Celia mentioned. "It was
dug up in Palestine."

"Yah?" Lou cracked. "How was it buried? On phonograph
records?"

Now came a procession of long-braided virgins dragging the colossal idol, Moloch.

"Ora's leading one of those crews of virgins," Mort informed them. "I guess she's been fooling me all these years," he cracked.

There was a girl for you! Tosses off a couple of kids, and her figure snaps back tight and lithe as a girl's, full of pep and dance.

"The trouble is that dope we got down there in Washington," Mrs. Abramson mused. "What is he doing for the Association? Whatever Roosevelt tells him, he says fine. A yes man we don't need to send to Washington."

"They've got a union all set," Mort revealed. "They're just waiting for those codes to come out. They'll strike the same day."

"A President we needed, to give them excuses to strike," Mrs. Abramson complained.

"Ah, it's the same as four years ago, they won't get to first base," Mort said.

A theatrical fire hissed in the huge maw of the Moloch, and the Virgin was sacrificed.

"Give me the old days!" Mort smacked his lips.

It was the scene of the Spanish expulsion of the Jews.

"Look at Spain now," Lou Margolis said. "They never amounted to anything since they expelled the Jews. The same thing will happen to Germany."

"How do I know they're even trying?" Rube complained nervously. "Those Irishmen have got it in for us. They claim they talked to Washington but how do I know they ain't giving me the runaround? Anyway, what can they do? They barely got their own income taxes fixed up. If it wasn't for the cardinal and those Catholic votes they'd be out of luck. Y' think they can ask the cardinal to put it in for a Hebe?"

On the stage, a little Jew smothered under a bearskin was prancing, while Cossacks snapped long whips about his legs.

"You think this is exaggerated?" said Mr. Abramson. "I have seen this myself, in my young days in Russia."

"And right today!" Rudy put in. "I saw a picture of a poor old German Jew harnessed to a garbage wagon, dragging it through the street."

"Thank God, my kids will never know of such things," Aline said. "In America such things don't happen."

"Yah! What about the Ku-Klux Klan?" Sylvia reminded her. "And when a doctor can't get into Rochester just because he's a Jew?"

"Well, I don't see many gentiles on the Israel staff," Aline countered.

"Those *Daitche Yehudim*," sneered Mrs. Abramson. "I am not saying Hitler is right, but if it had to happen to Jews someplace, then they are the ones that deserve it most. So high class! A Russian Jew, to them, was to spit on."

"Don't worry," Sylvia said. "Now they remember they are Jews like anybody else."

"They're even taking Russian Jews into the Prima Club," Mort revealed. "They had such a big mortgage on their new downtown building. I understand Lou Margolis is a member."

"When this is over, let's all go to the Streets of Paris," Alice suggested. "I want to see that fan dancer they arrested last week. What's her name? Sally Rand. Do you think she really comes out naked?"

"It's just a publicity stunt," Sylvia said.

"Ora knows all about it. She was there," Aline insinuated at Mort.

"Maybe it would pay us to send our own man to Washington to see what they are putting in those codes," Mrs. Abramson worried. "Better to spend a little money now than to spend a fortune fighting it afterwards."

"A real *Chassidishe nigun!*" Mr. Abramson repeated, humming with the singer a wordless melody that he remembered from his Talmud days.

> "Dai, dai,
> Da da dee dee dee. . . ."

People, people! It was the thickness of them, the swarming fullness of this vast Stadium, stirring one to a strange sweet kind of racial love. They were stamping through the Palestinian settler's *hora* now, the field was a sworl of circles. Emotion rose out of the Stadium, rolled over the field like an intoxicating vapor, drugging all.

The whole pageant was rushing through Joe's blood, all his life, and the life of the race that made him. He recalled his own journey, seeking and seeking, going backward on the trail that the Jews had traveled, to Poland, to Bialystok, and then he had had to go again, to Palestine. Now, here, it added up.

Jews, shopkeepers and buttonhole makers, and their educated American children; there seemed a goodness in people when they came together in celebration of themselves. Perhaps they were mistakenly united in this common tradition of their past, in wandering, suffering, learning; perhaps it was from this feeling of cultural equality that the poor buttonhole makers got the delusion of living in a world of human equality. But granting error, and pathos, and clumsiness, and cheating sentimentality, and stampeding emotion, this was beauty too. And at a moment like this, a man didn't want to let go of the world. However silly and involved and stupid human motives might become, there was a life-lust that rolled all into one.

A hand pulled him into the whirl. Joe sang out a Palestinian cry, and danced like a real *chalutz*. The faces all around him, all, all were beautiful.

The crowd tore around Alvin. Some were surging downward, to join the dancers on the field. Others were driving, twisting toward exits. He drew back with Eunice, to a place high on the ledge of the Stadium.

Jews, always afire, damn Jewish Fourth of July.

Moments, there, he had been touched. But what did it all prove? Look at them, with their sweat-beaded faces, their belching corned beef breaths, fat, fat, an ugly people. Clutching pop bottles. What did it all prove, except that the Jews had always been a race of intruders? Even that first time in Palestine, they had been the invaders, taking the land away from the Canaanites, the Philistines, the native tribes. And now again, they would take it away from the Arabs.

What would happen when the swarm of German Jews landed in Palestine?

"You'll see," he predicted to Eunice. "They'll send thousands of German Jews over there, and it'll be worse than in 1929. The Arabs will have an excuse."

"But where else can they go?" Eunice said.

Where? They could disappear. As he saw it now, disappearance was the eventual answer. Eventually, why not now, ha ha. Sure, the Soviets might toy with a Jewish colony in Siberia, but in a few generations that too would be Russianized.

"Oh, it's exciting," Eunice said, looking down onto the self-intoxicated crowd.

"Let's get the hell out of here," he said. In the crowdstream, paunches pressed against him, he could hardly keep from striking out, tearing a space for himself, so he could be free, alone.

The Naked and the Dead

by NORMAN MAILER

Often declared by himself, by his partisans, and also by objective critics to be the best contemporary American writer, Norman Mailer is unfailingly arresting, frequently superb. Occasionally he writes chiefly for effect, and as is inevitable he then sometimes sinks to sensationalism. But his powers of observation never leave him, and he has great gifts of observation and pitying empathy. Is he a Jewish writer? Yes and no. He has never written a "wholly Jewish" novel, yet it would be absurd to deny that something vaguely Jewish runs through his apparently totally non-Jewish writing, and there are critics who explain An American Dream in terms of Mailer's Jewishness.

The Naked and the Dead, which still remains Mailer's "big" novel, is, of course, a group story about World War II. In this authentically American portrait, Mailer, the Jewish boy raised in Brooklyn to be a Harvard prodigy, covers our entire multicultural spectrum through the heterogeneous composition of his army platoon, and he is at pains to keep the Jewish G.I.s Roth and Goldstein from erupting out of the general frame. A subtle distinction is made between them; one of them is able to adjust, to assimilate, but the other cannot leap a final abyss and falls to his death. This theme is excerpted here.

Norman Mailer, born in Long Branch, New Jersey, in 1923, has chosen to make part of his creative contribution as an action personality, and much of his work recently has been in the realm of reportage or documentary novelization of events in which he takes part, producing for the reader a fusion of what Mailer is and what he writes. He has explored mind-expanding drugs, made underground films, and exhibited amusing vestiges of Bo-

hemianism, such as the construction of his Brooklyn Heights
eyrie which can be reached—as in the critical Jewish episode in
this novel—only by leaping across a small chasm. (A similar dare
appears in An American Dream.) Happily, Norman Mailer nearly
always lands firmly when he leaps.

C.A.

THE REPLACEMENTS remained on the beach for another
day or two. The evening after Croft had talked to Captain Man-
telli, Roth walked forlornly through the replacement bivouac. The
man with whom he was bunking, a big good-natured farm boy, was
still over at another tent with his friends, and Roth didn't want to
join them. He had gone along the previous night and, as it usually
happened, he had felt left out of things. His bunkmate and his bunkmate's friends were all young, probably just out of high school, and
they laughed a lot at stupid jokes and wrestled with each other and
swore. He never knew what to say to them. Roth felt a familiar wistful urge for somebody he could talk to seriously. He realized again
there wasn't anyone he knew well among the replacements—all the
men with whom he had come overseas had been separated from him
at the last replacement depot. Even then, it wasn't as if they had
anything special about them. They were all stupid, Roth thought.
All they could think about was getting women.

He stared gloomily at the pup tents scattered over the sand. In
a day or two he would be sent up to his new platoon, and the
thought gave him no joy. A rifleman now! It was such a dirty trick.
At least, if they hadn't told him he was going to be a clerk. Roth
shrugged. All the Army wanted you for was cannon fodder. They
even made riflemen out of men like himself, fathers, with poor
health. He was qualified for other things, a college graduate, familiar
with office work. But try and explain it to the Army.

He passed a tent where a soldier was pounding some stakes into
the sand. Roth paused, and then recognized the man. It was Goldstein, one of the soldiers who had been assigned with him to the
reconnaissance platoon. "Hello," Roth said, "you're all occupied,
I see."

Goldstein looked up. He was a man of about twenty-seven with very blond hair and friendly serious blue eyes. He stared intently at Roth as if he were nearsighted, his eyes bulging slightly. Then he smiled with a great deal of warmth, cocking his head forward. Because of this and the staring concentration of his eyes he gave an immediate impression of great sincerity. "I'm just fixing my tent," Goldstein said now. "I was thinking and thinking about it today, and I finally decided what the trouble was. The Army never designed tent pins to be used in sand." He smiled enthusiastically. "So I cut some branches off a bush, and I'm making stakes out of them now. I bet it'll hold up in any kind of a wind." Goldstein's speech was always earnest but a little breathless as if he were afraid of being interrupted. Except for the unexpectedly sad lines which ran from his nose to the corners of his mouth, he would have looked like a boy.

"That's quite an idea," Roth said. He couldn't think of anything to add, and he hesitated for a moment, and then sat down on the sand. Goldstein kept working, humming to himself. "What do you think of our assignment?" he asked.

Roth shrugged. "It's what I expected. No good." Roth was a small man with an oddly hunched back and long arms. Everything about him seemed to droop; he had a long dejected nose and pouches under his eyes; his shoulders slumped forward. His hair was clipped very short and it accentuated his large ears. "No, I don't care for our assignment," he repeated a little pompously. Altogether, Roth looked like a frail mournful ape.

"I think we were pretty lucky," Goldstein said mildly. "After all, it isn't as if we're going to see the worst kind of combat. I hear a headquarters company is pretty good, and there'll be a more intelligent type fellow in it."

Roth picked up a handful of sand and let it drop. "What's the use of kidding myself?" he said. "The way I look at it, every step in the Army turns out to be worse than you expected, and this is going to be the worst of all." His voice was deep and sepulchral; he spoke so slowly that Goldstein became a little impatient for him to finish.

"No, no, you're too pessimistic," Goldstein told him. He picked up a helmet and began to use it as a mallet on one of the stakes. "If you'll excuse me for saying so, that's no way to look at it." He pounded several times wiith the helmet and then whistled sadly. "Very poor steel in these," he said. "Look at the way I dented it just hitting in a stake."

Roth smiled a little contemptuously. Goldstein's animation irritated him. "Aaah, it's all very well to talk," he said, "but you never do get a break in the Army. Look at the ship we came over on. They had us packed in like sardines."

"I suppose they did the best they could," Goldstein suggested.

"The best they could? I don't think so." He paused as if to edit his woes and select the most telling ones. "Did you notice how they treated the officers? They slept in staterooms when we were jammed in the hold like pigs. It's to make them feel superior, a chosen group. That's the same device Hitler uses when he makes the Germans think they're superior." Roth felt as if he were on the edge of something profound.

Goldstein held up his hand. "But that's why *we* can't afford to have such an attitude. We're fighting against that." Then as if his words had rubbed against a bruised part of his mind, he frowned angrily and added, "Aaah, I don't know, they're just a bunch of Anti-Semiten."

"Who, the Germans?"

Goldstein didn't answer right away. ". . . Yes."

"That's one approach to it," Roth said, a little pontifically. "However, I don't think it's as simple as that." He went on talking.

Goldstein did not listen. Gloom had settled over him. He had been cheerful until a moment ago, and now suddenly he was very upset. As Roth talked, Goldstein would shake his head from time to time or make a clucking sound with his tongue. This had no relation to what Roth said. Goldstein was remembering an episode which had occurred that afternoon. Several soldiers had been talking to a truck driver and he had heard their conversation. The truck driver was a big fellow with a round red face, and he had been telling the replacements which companies were good and which were not. As he meshed his gears and started to pull away he had shouted back, "Just hope you all don't get in F Company, that's where they stick the goddam Jewboys." There had been a roar of laughter, and someone had yelled after him, "If they stick me there, I'm resigning plumb out of the Army." And there had been more laughter. Goldstein flushed with anger recalling it. But more, he felt a hopelessness even in his rage, for he knew it would do him no good. He wished he had said something to the boy who had answered the truck driver, but the boy didn't matter. He was only trying to be smart, Goldstein thought. It was the truck driver. Goldstein saw again his brutal red face, and despite himself he felt fear. That *grobe jung*, that peasant, he said to himself. He felt an awful depression: that kind of face was behind all the pogroms against the Jews.

He sat down beside Roth and looked off moodily at the ocean. When Roth finished talking, Goldstein nodded his head. "Why are they like that?" he asked.

"Who?"

"The Anti-Semiten. Why don't they ever learn? Why does God permit it?"

Roth sneered. "God is a luxury I don't give myself."

Goldstein struck the palm of his hand with his fist. "No, I just don't understand it. How can God look down on it and permit it? We're supposed to be the chosen people." He snorted. "Chosen! Chosen for *tsoris!*"

"Personally, I'm an agnostic," Roth said.

For a time Goldstein stared at his hands, and then he smiled sadly. The lines deepened about his mouth, and he had a sarcastic indrawn look on his lips. "When the time comes," he said solemnly, "they won't ask you what kind of Jew you are."

"I think you worry too much about those things," Roth said. Why was it, he asked himself, that so many Jews were filled with all kinds of old wives' tales? His parents at least were modern, but Goldstein was like an old grandfather full of mutterings and curses, certain he would die a violent death. "The Jews worry too much about themselves," Roth said. He rubbed his long sad nose. Goldstein was an odd fellow, he told himself; he was enthusiastic about almost everything to the point of being a moron, and yet just start talking about politics or economics or about anything that was current affairs, and like all Jews he would turn the conversation to the same topic.

"If we don't worry," Goldstein said bitterly, "no one else will."

Roth was irritated. Just because he was a Jew too, they always assumed he felt the same way about things. It made him feel a little frustrated. No doubt some of his bad luck had come because he was one; but that was unfair; it wasn't as if he took an interest, it was just an accident of birth. "Well, let's stop talking about it," he said.

They sat watching the final brilliant striations of the sunset. After a time, Goldstein looked at his watch and squinted at the sun, which was almost entirely below the horizon. "It's two minutes later than last night," he told Roth, "I like to keep tracks of things like that."

"I had a friend once," Roth said, "who used to work at the weather bureau in New York."

"Did he?" Goldstein asked. "You know I always wanted to do work like that, but you need a good education for it. I understand it takes a lot of calculus."

"He did go to college," Roth admitted. He preferred a conversation like this. It was less controversial. "Yes, he went to college," Roth repeated, "but just the same he was more lucky than most of us. I'm a graduate of CCNY but it never did me any good."

"How can you say that?" Goldstein asked. "For years I wanted to be an engineer. Think of what a wonderful thing it is to be able to design anything you want." He sighed a little wistfully and then smiled. "Still I can't complain. I've been pretty lucky."

"You're better off," Roth assured him. "I never found a diploma any help in getting a job." He snorted bitterly. "Do you know I went two years without any job at all. Do you know what that's like?"

"My friend," Goldstein said, "you don't have to tell me. I've always had a job, but some of them are not worth mentioning." He smiled deprecatingly. "What's the use of complaining?" he asked. "Taken all together, we're pretty well off." He held out his hand, palm upward. "We're married and we have kids—you have a child, don't you?"

"Yes," said Roth. He drew out his wallet, and Goldstein peered through the evening light to discern the features of a handsome boy about two years old. "You've got a beautiful baby," he said, "and your wife is very . . . very pleasant looking." She was a plain woman with a pudgy face.

"I think so," Roth said. He looked at the pictures of Goldstein's wife and child, and returned the compliments automatically. Roth was feeling a gentle warmth as he thought of his son. He was remembering the way his son used to awaken him on Sunday mornings. His wife would put the baby in bed with him, and the child would straddle his stomach and pull feebly at the hairs on Roth's chest, cooing with delight. It gave him a pang of joy to think of it, and then, back of it, a realization that he had never enjoyed his child as much when he had lived with him. He had been annoyed and irritable at having his sleep disturbed, and it filled him with wonder that he could have missed so much happiness when he had been so close to it. It seemed to him now that he was very near a fundamental understanding of himself, and he felt a sense of mystery and discovery as if he had found unseen gulfs and bridges in all the familiar drab terrain of his life. "You know," he said, "life is funny."

Goldstein sighed. "Yes," he answered quietly.

Roth had a flush of warmth for Goldstein. There was something very sympathetic about him, he decided. These thoughts he had were the kind of things you could tell only to a man. A woman had to be concerned with her children, and with all the smaller things. "There are lots of things you can't tell a woman," Roth said.

"I don't think so," Goldstein said eagerly. "I like to discuss things with my wife. We have a wonderful companionship. She understands so much." He paused as if to find a way to phrase his next thoughts. "I don't know, when I was a kid of about eighteen, nineteen, I used to have a different idea of women. I wanted them, you know, for sex. I remember I used to go to prostitutes, and I would be disgusted, and then after a week or so I would want to go again." He gazed at the water for a moment, and then smiled wisely. "But being married made me understand a lot about women. It's so different from the way you think of it when you're just a kid. It's . . . I don't know, it isn't so important. Women," he said solemnly, "don't like it the way we do. It doesn't mean as much to them."

Roth was tempted to ask Goldstein some questions about his wife, but he hesitated. He was relieved by what Goldstein had said. The private aches, the self-doubts he had known when he heard soldiers talking about their affairs with women were a little soothed now. "That's true,"he admitted gladly. "Women just aren't interested in it." He felt very close to Goldstein as if they shared a deep knowledge. There was something very nice, very kind, about Goldstein. He would never be cruel to anybody, Roth thought.

But even more, he was certain that Goldstein liked him. "It's very nice, sitting here," Roth said in his deep hollow voice. The tents had a silver color in the moonlight and the beach glistened at the water's edge. Roth was full of many things he found difficult to utter. Goldstein was a kindred soul, a friend. Roth sighed. He supposed a Jew always had to go to a fellow Jew to find understanding.

The thought depressed him. Why should things be that way? He was a college graduate, educated, far above nearly all the men here, and what good did it do him? The only man he could find who was worth talking to sounded a little like an old Jew with a beard.

They sat there without talking for several minutes. The moon had gone behind a cloud, and the beach had become very dark and quiet. A few muted noises of speech and laughter from the other pup tents filtered through the night. Roth realized he would have to return to his tent in a few minutes, and he dreaded the prospect of being awakened for guard. He watched a soldier come walking toward them.

"I guess that's Buddy Wyman," Goldstein said. "He's a nice kid."

"Is he coming to that reconnaissance platoon with us?" Roth asked.

Goldstein nodded. "Yes. When we found out we were both going to the same place we decided to bunk together if they let us."

Roth smiled sourly. He should have known. He moved aside as Wyman crouched to come into the tent, and waited for Goldstein to introduce them. "I think I saw you when they got us all together," Roth said.

"Oh, sure, I remember you," Wyman said pleasantly. He was a tall slim youth with light hair and a bony face. He dropped on one of the blankets and yawned. "Boy, I didn't think I'd be talking that long," he apologized to Goldstein.

"That's all right," Goldstein said: "I got an idea on how to fix the tent, and I think it's going to stay up tonight." Wyman examined it, and noticed the stakes. "Hey, that's swell," he said. "I'm sorry I wasn't here to help you, Joe."

"That's okay," Goldstein said.

Roth felt as if he were no longer wanted. He stood up and stretched his body. "I guess I'll be taking off," he said. He rubbed his hand along his thin forearm.

"Stay around awhile," Goldstein said.

"No, I want to get some sleep before guard." Roth started walking back to his tent. In the darkness, his feet dragged. He was thinking that Goldstein's friendliness did not mean very much. "Just a surface part of his personality. It doesn't go deep."

Roth sighed. As he walked, his feet made soft slushing sounds through the sand.

.   .   .   .   .

Roth dreamt that he was catching butterflies in a lovely green meadow when Minetta wakened him for guard. He grumbled and tried to go back to sleep, but Minetta kept shaking him. "All right, all right, I'm getting up," he whispered angrily. He rolled over, groaned a little, got on his hands and knees, and shook his head. "Three hours' guard tonight," he realized with dread. Morosely he began to put on his shoes.

Minetta was waiting for him in the machine-gun emplacement. "Jesus, it's spooky tonight," he whispered. "I thought I'd be on forever."

"Anything happen?"

Minetta gazed out at the black jungle before them. It was just possible to discern the barbed wire ten yards beyond the machine gun. "I thought I heard some Japs sneaking around," he muttered, "so keep your ears open."

Roth felt a sick fear. "Are you sure?"

"I dunno. The artillery's been going steady for the last half hour. I think there's a battle going on." He listened. "Wait!" A battery fired a few miles away with a hollow clanging sound. "I bet the Japs are attacking. Jesus, recon is gonna get caught right up the middle of it."

"I guess we're lucky," Roth said.

Minetta's voice was very low. "Yeah, I dunno. Being doubled up on guard ain't so good either. Wait, you'll see. Three hours on a night like this is enough to make you flip your lid. How do we know that the Japs won't break through and before your shift is over they'll be attacking right here? We're only ten miles from the front. Maybe they'll have a patrol out here."

"This is serious," Roth said. He remembered the way Goldstein's face had looked when he was making his pack soon after the storm. Goldstein was up there now, seeing combat. Roth had an odd sensation. He might even be killed. Any of them—Red, Gallagher, Sergeant Croft, Wyman, Toglio, or Martinez or Ridges or Wilson; they were all up there now, right in the middle of it. Any one of them could be gone by tomorrow. It was horrible the way a man could be killed. He wanted to tell Minetta some of this.

But Minetta yawned. "Jeez, I'm glad this is over." He started to go and turned back. "You know who you wake up?"

"Sergeant Brown?"

"That's right. He's sleeping on a blanket with Stanley over there." Minetta indicated the direction vaguely.

Roth muttered, "Just five of us on this part of the perimeter. Think of it, five men having to hold down a whole platoon's part of the perimeter."

"That's what I mean," Minetta said. "We ain't getting any break. At least there's a lot of men where the first squad is." He yawned quietly. "Well, I'm going," he said.

Roth felt terribly alone after Minetta left him. He gazed into the jungle, and got into the hole behind the machine gun as silently as he could. Something like this was beyond him, he told himself; he didn't have the nerves for it. This took a younger man, a kid like Minetta or Polack, or one of the veterans.

He was sitting on two cartridge boxes, and the handles cut into his bony rump. He kept shifting his weight, and moving his feet about. The hole was very muddy from the evening storm, and everything about him felt damp. His clothes had been wet for hours, and he had had to spread his blankets on the wet ground. What a way to live! He would have a cold by morning, he was certain. He'd be lucky if it wasn't pneumonia.

Everything was very quiet. The jungle was hushed, ominous, with a commanding silence that stilled his breath. He waited, and abruptly the utter vacuum was broken and he was conscious of all the sounds of the night woods—the crickets and frogs and lizards thrumming in the brush, the soughing of the trees. And then the sounds seemed to vanish, or rather his ear could hear only the silence; for several minutes there was a continual alternation between the sounds and the quiet, as if they were distinct and yet related like a drawing of some cubes which perpetually turned inside-out and back again. Roth began to think; there was some heavy thunder and lightning in the distance, but he did not worry about the threat of rain. For a long time he listened to the artillery, which sounded like a great muffled bell in the heavy moist night air. He shivered and crossed his arms. He was remembering what a training sergeant had said about dirty fighting and how the Japs would sneak up behind a sentry in the jungle and knife the man. "He'd never know at all," the sergeant had said, "except maybe for one little second when it was too late."

Roth felt a gnawing, guttish fear, and turned around to look at the ground behind him. He shuddered, brooding over such a death. What an awful thing to happen. His nerves were taut. As he tried to see the jungle beyond the little clearing past the barbed wire, he had the kind of anxiety and panic a child has when the monster creeps up behind the hero in a horror movie. Something clattered in the brush, and Roth ducked in his hole, and then slowly peeked above it, trying to discern a man or at least some recognizable object in the deep shapes and shadows of the jungle. The noise stopped, and then after ten seconds began again. It was a scratching urgent sound, and Roth sat numbly in the hole, feeling nothing but the beat of his pulse throughout his entire body. His ears had become giant amplifiers and he was detecting a whole gamut of sounds, of sliding and scraping, of twigs cracking, of shrubs being rustled, which he had not noticed before. He bent over the machine gun, and then realized that he didn't know whether Minetta had cocked it completely or left it half-loaded. It meant that he would have to pull back the bolt and release it in order to be certain, and he was terrified of the noise it would make. He took up his rifle, and tried to loose the safety lever quietly, but it clicked into place quite audibly. Roth flinched at the noise, and then gazed into the jungle, trying to locate the particular place from which the sounds were coming. But they seemed to originate everywhere, and he had no idea of their distance and what caused them. He heard something rustle, and he turned his rifle clumsily in that direction, and waited, the sweat breaking out on his back. For an instant he was tempted to shoot, blindly and furiously, but he remembered that that was very dangerous. "Maybe they don't see me either," he thought, but he did not believe it. The reason he did not fire was for fear of what Sergeant Brown would say. "If you fire without seeing anything to aim at, you just give away the position of your hole, and they'll throw a grenade in on you," Brown had told him. Roth trembled. He was beginning to feel resentful; for some time he had been convinced that the Japs were watching him. Why don't you come on? he wondered desperately. By now his nerves were so taut that he would have welcomed an attack.

He pressed his feet into the thick mud of the hole, and, still looking into the jungle, picked some mud off his boots with one hand and began to knead it like a piece of clay. He was unconscious of doing this. His neck had begun to pain him from the tension with which he held himself. It seemed to him that the hole was terribly open and that there was not enough protection. He felt bitter that a man should have to stand guard in an open hole with only a machine gun before him.

There was a frantic scuffling behind the first wall of jungle and Roth ground his jaws together to keep from uttering a sound. The noises were coming closer like men creeping up, moving a few feet and then halting, before approaching another few feet. He fumbled around the tripod of the machine gun to find a grenade, and then held it in his hand wondering where to throw it. The grenade seemed extremely heavy, and he felt so weak that he doubted if he could hurl it more than ten yards. In training he had been told the effective range of a grenade was thirty-five yards, and he was afraid now that he would be killed by his own grenade. He replaced it beneath the machine gun, and just sat there.

His fear had to ebb after a time. For perhaps half an hour he had been waiting for the noises to develop into something, and when nothing occurred, his confidence began to come back. He did not reason that if there were Japs they might spend two hours in advancing fifty yards toward him; because he could not bear the suspense, a part of him assumed that they could not either, and he became convinced there was nothing in the jungle but some animals scurrying about. He lay back in the hole with his shirt against the damp rear wall, and began to relax. His nerves calmed slowly, rousing to a pitch of fear again every time some sudden noise came out of the jungle, but still becoming more and more composed like a receding tide. After an hour had passed he grew sleepy. He thought of nothing, listened only to the profound pendant silence of the wood. A mosquito began to sing about his ears and his neck, and he waited for it to bite him so that he could crush it. It made him think that there might be insects in the hole with him, and his body began to crawl, and for a few moments he was certain an ant was traveling down his back. It recalled to him the roaches that had infested the first apartment he had had when he was married. He remembered how he had reassured his wife. "There's nothing to worry about, Zelda. I can tell you from my studies that the roach is not too vicious a pest." Zelda had got some idea that there must be bedbugs also, and no matter how many times he reassured her, "Zelda, roaches eat bedbugs," she would start up in bed, and grasp him with fear, "Herman, I know there's something biting me."

"But I tell you that's impossible."

"Don't tell me about your roaches," she would whisper angrily in the darkened room. "If roaches take care of bedbugs they have to get into the bed to do it, don't they?"

Roth felt a mingled pleasure and wistfulness in remembering. Their life together had not been all that he had hoped. There were so many fights, and Zelda had a cruel tongue; he recalled how she had taunted him with his education and the fact that he could make no money. It had not been entirely her fault, he thought, but then it had not been his either. No one was to blame. It was just that you didn't get everything you had hoped for when you were a kid. He wiped his hands on his fatigue trousers with a slow thorough motion.

Zelda had been a good wife in some ways. Their quarrels had become as difficult for him to remember as her face. He mused about her now, and in his mind she became another woman, many women. He began to construct a lewd fantasy in his mind.

Roth dreamt he was taking pornographic pictures of a model whom he had dressed as a cowgirl. She was wearing a ten-gallon hat, and a leather fringe about an inch wide across her breasts, and a leather holster and cartridge belt slung at an angle across her hips. He imagined now that he was telling her which way to pose and she was obeying with a tantalizing insouciance. His groin began to ache, and he sat there, brooding, dreaming.

After a time he became sleepy again, and tried to fight against it. Some artillery was firing steadily a mile or two away, the sounds loud, then muffled, then loud again. It gave him a secure feeling. He hardly listened any longer to the jungle. His eyes kept closing, remaining shut for many seconds while he yawned away on the edge of slumber. Several times he was about to fall asleep when a sudden noise in the jungle would rouse him with a start. He looked at the luminous dial of his watch and realized with dismay that he had still an hour of guard. He lay back, closed his eyes with the full intention of opening them in a few seconds, and fell asleep.

It was the last he remembered until he awoke almost two hours later. It had begun to rain once more, and the gentle drizzle had soaked his fatigues and penetrated to the insides of his shoes. He sneezed miserably once, and then realized with dismay how long he had been asleep. "A Jap could have killed me," he said to himself, and the thought sent electric wakening shudders through his body. He got out of the foxhole and stumbled over toward where Brown was sleeping. He would have missed him but he heard Brown whisper, "What the hell are you thrashing around for like a pig in the brush?"

Roth was meek. "I couldn't find you," he whined.

"Hell of a note," Brown said. He stretched once in his blankets, and stood up. "I couldn't sleep," he said. "Too many goddam noises . . . What time is it?"

"After three-thirty."

"You were supposed to wake me at three."

Roth had been afraid of this. "I began to think," Roth said weakly, "and lost track of the time."

"Shit!" Brown said. He finished tying his shoes and walked out to the emplacement without saying anything else.

Roth stood still for a moment, his rifle strap chafing his shoulder, and then began looking for the place where he and Minetta were sleeping for the night. Minetta had pulled the blankets over him, and Roth lay down beside him gingerly, and tried to tug them away. At home he had always insisted on having the sheets tucked in tightly; now with the blankets drawn up over his feet he was miserable. Everything seemed wet. The rain kept falling on his exposed legs and he became very chilled. The blankets were midway between sopping and damp; they had a musty wet odor which reminded him of the smell of feet. He kept turning over, trying to find an accommodating place on the ground, but it seemed as if a root were always sticking into the small of his back. The drizzle teased him when he pulled the blankets off his face. He was sweating and shuddering at the same time, and he was convinced he would be sick. Why didn't I tell Brown he ought to be glad I stood an extra half hour of guard for him? he asked himself abruptly, and felt frustrated and bitter that he had failed to answer him. Wait, I'll tell him in the morning, he assured himself angrily. Of the men in the platoon he decided there was not one of them he really liked. They're all stupid, he said to himself. There wasn't a single one of them who was the least bit friendly to a new man, and he felt a spasm of loneliness. His feet were cold. When he tried to wriggle his toes, the hopelessness of warming them overwhelmed him. He tried to think of his wife and son and it seemed to him there could be no more perfect life than to return to them. His wife had a soft mothering look now in her eyes, and his son was staring at him with delight and respect. He thought of his son growing up, discussing serious things with him, valuing his opinion. The drizzle tickled his ear, and he pulled the end of the blanket over his head again. Minetta's body was warm and he huddled toward it. He thought once again of his infant son, and felt a swell of pride. He thinks I'm someone. Roth said to himself. I'll show them yet. His eyes closed and he loosed a long whispering sigh, immensely wistful in the soft drizzling night.

That fuggin Roth, Brown said to himself, falling asleep on guard and maybe getting us all killed. No man's got a right to do something like that; he lets his buddies down and they ain't a worse thing a man can do.

No, sir, Brown repeated, they ain't a worse thing a man can do. I may be afraid and I may have my nerves shot all to hell, but at least I act like a sergeant and take care of my duties. There's no easy way to get ahead; a man's got to pull his share, take his responsibilities, and then he gets what he earns. I've had my eye on Roth from the beginning. He's no good, he's lazy, he's shiftless, and he don't take an interest in anything. I hate these fathers who bitch because they finally got caught. Hell, what about us who been sweating it out for a couple of years and Lord knows how long to come? We were fightin' when they were screwin' their wives, and maybe screwin' ours too.

Brown shifted his weight angrily on the cartridge boxes and looked out at the jungle, rubbing his hand reflectively over the bridge of his short snubbed nose. Yeah, what about us, he said to himself, sitting out here in a lousy hole in the rain, sweatin' out every goddam noise while those women are on the loose havin' their own sweet time?

I should have known better, marrying a two-timing bitch like that. Even when we were in high school, she was rubbing up against everything that wore pants. Oh, I know a lot more now, I know that it's a mistake to marry a woman 'cause you can't make her any other way, holding out on me for all that time, and even now I don't know if she was cherry. There ain't any such thing as a clean decent woman any more, when a man's sister will go up to him and tell him to mind his own business because she's fooling around and her husband's out of town, it's time for a man to open his eyes. There ain't a one of them a man can trust out of his sight; how many times have I picked up a piece from a married woman with kids, it's disgustin' the way they all act.

Brown took his rifle off his knees and laid it against the machine gun. It's bad enough with all a man's got to worry about out here, with guys like that fuggin Roth who fall asleep on guard, and trying to keep the details straight so no man has to work more than his share, and always wondering if today is the day you get it, so that you'd think a woman would have the decency to keep her legs closed, but, no, there isn't one of them that's worth a snowball in hell. All the time we're out here beating our meat for company, doing it till it's disgusting, but what the hell else is there? I oughta quit 'cause it breaks down your confidence, and I'd be feeling stronger, but how can ya without a goddam woman and nothing to think about? All the men do it. Sure.

And right now what is she doing, she's probably right in bed talking to a guy this very minute and they're figuring out what they're gonna do with the ten thousand insurance on me when I get knocked off. Well, I'm gonna fool them, I'm gonna live through the goddam war and then I'm gonna get rid of her, and then I'm gonna make my mark. There'll be a lot of ways for a man to make some money after the war if he isn't afraid of some hard work and taking on some responsibility, and I'm not afraid. All the men say I'm a good noncom. I may not be as good a scout as Martinez and I may not have ice instead of blood in my veins the way Croft has, but I'm fair, and I take my job seriously. I'm not like Red, always goofing off, or thinkin' of a smart crack instead of working, I really try hard to be a good noncom 'cause if you succeed in the Army there isn't any other place you won't succeed. If you have to do something you might as well do it right, that's what I believe.

Some artillery fired continuously for several minutes, and Brown listened to it tensely. The boys are really getting it now, he told himself, sure as hell, the Japs are attacking and recon's bound to be in the middle of it. We're a hard-luck platoon, there's no doubt about it, I just hope nobody gets hurt tonight. He stared into the darkness. I'm real lucky being left behind, he told himself, I'm sure glad I'm not in Martinez's shoes. It's going to be real rough tonight, and I don't want any part of it. I've had my share of the close ones, running across a field with a machine gun ticking after me or swimming in the water that time the Japs had the AA gun turned on us is enough for any man to have to take. I'm proud I'm a sergeant, but there are times when I wish I was just a buck private and all I had to do was bitch like Roth. I've got to look out for myself because no one else will, and I've sweated this war out long enough not to get hit now.

He fingered one of the jungle ulcers on his mouth. I just hope to hell none of the boys get hurt tonight, he said to himself.

The truck convoy ground sullenly through the mud. It was over an hour since recon had left its bivouac area, but it seemed much longer. There were twenty-five men packed inside the truck and, since there were seats for only twelve, over half the men sat on the floor in a tangle of rifles and packs and arms and legs. In the darkness everyone was sweating and the night seemed incomparably dense; the jungle on either side of the road exuded moisture continually.

No one had anything to say. When the men in the truck listened they could hear the front of the convoy grinding up a grade before them. Occasionally the truck to their rear would creep up close enough for the men to see its blackout lights like two tiny candles in a fog. A mist had settled over the jungle, and in the darkness the men felt disembodied.

Wyman was sitting on his pack, and when he closed his eyes and let the rumble of the truck shake through him he felt as if he were in a subway. The tension and excitement he had felt when Croft had come up and told them to pack their gear because they were moving forward had abated a little by now and Wyman was drifting along on a mood which vacillated between boredom and a passive stream of odd thought and recollections. He was thinking of a time when he had accompanied his mother on a bus trip from New York to Pittsburgh. It was just after his father died, and his mother was going to see her relatives for money. The trip had been fruitless and, coming back on a midnight bus, he and his mother had talked about what they would do and decided that he would have to go to work. He thought of it with a little wonder. At the time it had been the most important night of his life, and now he was going on another trip, a far more eventful one, and he had no idea what would happen. It made him feel very mature for a moment; these were things which had happened just a few years ago, insignificant things now. He was trying to imagine what combat would be like, and he decided it would be impossible to guess. He had always pictured it as something violent, going on for days without halt. And here he had been in the platoon for over a week and nothing had happened; everything had been peaceful and relaxed.

"Do you think we'll see much tonight, Red?" he asked softly.

"Ask the General," Red snorted. He liked Wyman, but he tried to be unfriendly to him because the youth reminded Red of Hennessey. Red had a deep loathing of the night before them. He had been through so much combat, had felt so many kinds of terror, and had seen so many men killed that he no longer had any illusions about the inviolability of his own flesh. He knew he could be killed; it was something he had accepted long ago, and he had grown a shell about that knowledge so that he rarely thought of anything further ahead than the next few minutes. However, there had been lately a disquieting uncomfortable insight which he had never brought to the point of words, and it was bothering him. Until Hennessey had been killed, Red had accepted all the deaths of the men he knew as something large and devastating and meaningless. Men who were killed were merely men no longer around; they became confused with old friends who had gone to the hospital and never come back, or men who had been transferred to another outfit. When he heard of some man he knew who had been killed or wounded badly, he was interested, even a little concerned, but it was the kind of emotion a man might feel if he learned that a friend of his had got married or made or lost some money. It was merely something that happened to somebody he knew, and Red had always let it go at that. But Hennessey's death had opened a secret fear. It was so ironic, so obvious, when he remembered the things Hennessey had said, that he found himself at the edge of a bottomless dread.

Once he could have looked ahead to what he knew would be bad combat with a repugnance for the toil and misery of it, and a dour acceptance of the deaths that would occur. But now the idea of death was fresh and terrifying again.

"You want to know something?" he said to Wyman.

"Yeah?"

"They ain't a thing you can do about it, so shut up."

Wyman was hurt and lapsed into silence. Red felt sorry immediately afterward, and drew out a bar of tropical chocolate, bent out of shape and covered with tobacco grains from the silt of his pockets. "Hey, you want some chocolate?" he asked.

"Yeah, thanks."

They felt the night about them. In the truck there was no sound except for an occasional mutter or curse as they hit a bump. Each vehicle by itself was making all the noises that trucks can make; they creaked and jounced and groaned over the bogholes, and their tires made wet singing sounds. But, taken all together, the line of trucks had a combined, intricate medley of vibrations and tones which sounded like the gentle persistent lapping of surf against the sides of a ship. It was a melancholy sound, and, in the darkness, the men sprawled uncomfortably on the floor, their backs propped against the knees of the man behind them, their rifles pitched at every odd angle or straddled clumsily across their knees. Croft had insisted they wear their helmets, and Red was sweating under the unaccustomed weight. "Might as well wear a goddam sandbag," he said to Wyman.

Encouraged, Wyman asked, "I guess it's gonna be rough, huh?"

Red sighed, but repressed his annoyance. "It won't be too bad, kid. You keep a tight ass-hole, and the rest of you'll take care of itself."

Wyman laughed quietly. He liked Red, and decided he would stay near him. The trucks halted, and the men moved around inside, shifting their positions and groaning as they flexed their cramped limbs. They waited patiently, their heads dropping on their chests, their damp clothing unable to dry in the heavy night air. There was barely a breeze and they felt tired and sleepy.

Goldstein was beginning to fidget. After the trucks had remained motionless for five minutes, he turned to Croft and asked, "Sergeant, is it all right if I get out and take a look at what's holding us up?"

Croft snorted. "You can stay right here, Goldstein. They ain't none of us gonna be getting up and getting lost on purpose."

Goldstein felt himself flush. "I didn't mean anything like that," he said. "I just thought it might be dangerous for us to be sitting here like this when there might be Japs around. How do we know why the trucks stopped?"

Croft yawned and then lashed him in a cold even voice. "I tell you what, you're going to have enough things to worry about. Suppose you just set down and beat your meat if you're gettin' anxious. I'll do all the goddam masterminding." There was a snicker from some of the men in the truck, and Goldstein was hurt. He decided he disliked Croft, and he brooded over all the sarcastic things Croft had said to him since he had been in the platoon.

The trucks started again, and moved jerkily in low gear for a few hundred yards before they stopped. Gallagher swore.

"What's the matter, boy; you in any hurry?" Wilson asked softly.

"We might as well get where we're goin'."

They remained sitting there for a few minutes, and then began to move again. A battery they had passed on the road was firing, and another one a few miles ahead also had gone into action. The shells whispered overhead, perhaps a mile above them, and the men listened dully. A machine gun began to fire far away, and the sound carried to them in separate bursts, deep and empty, like a man beating a carpet. Martinez took off his helmet and kneaded his skull, feeling as though a hammer were pounding him. A Japanese gun answered fire with a high penetrating shriek. A flare went up near the horizon and cast enough light for them to see one another. Their faces looked white and then blue as though they were staring at each other across a dark and smoky room. "We're gettin' close," someone said. After the flare had died, it was possible to see a pale haze against the horizon, and Toglio said, "Something's burning."

"Sounds like a big fight going on," Wyman suggested to Red.

"Naw, they're just feeling each other out," Red told him. "There'll be a helluva lot more noise if something starts tonight." The machine guns sputtered and then became silent. A few mortar shells were landing somewhere with a flat thudding sound, and another machine gun, much farther away, fired again. Then there was silence, and the trucks continued down the black muddy road.

After a few minutes they halted again, and somebody in the rear of the truck tried to light a cigarette. "Put the goddam thing out," Croft snapped.

The soldier was in another platoon and he swore at Croft. "Who the hell are you? I'm tired of just waiting around."

"Put that goddam thing out," Croft said again, and after a pause, the soldier snuffed it. Croft was feeling irritable and nervous. He had no fear but he was impatient and overalert.

Red debated whether to light a cigarette. He and Croft had hardly spoken to each other since their quarrel on the beach, and he was tempted to defy him. Actually he knew he wouldn't, and he tried to decide whether the real reason was that it was a bad idea to show a light or because he was afraid of Croft. Fug it, I'll stand up to that sonofabitch when the time comes. Red told himself, but I'll damn sure be right when I do.

They had begun to move once more. After a few minutes they heard a few low voices on the road, and their truck turned off and wallowed through a muddy lane. It was very narrow and a branch from a tree swept along the top of the truck. "Watch it!" someone shouted, and they all flattened themselves. Red pulled some leaves out of his shirt and pricked his finger on a thorn. He wiped the blood on the back of his pants and began searching for his pack, which he had thrown off when he first got into the truck. His legs were stiff and he tried to flex them.

"Don't dismount till you're told," Croft said.

The trucks came to a halt, and they listened to the few men circling around them in the darkness. Everything was terribly quiet. They sat there, speaking in whispers. An officer rapped on the tail gate and said, "All right, men, dismount and stick together." They began to jump out of the truck, moving slowly and uncertainly. It was a five-foot drop into darkness and they didn't know what the ground was like beneath them. "Drop the tail gate," someone said, and the officer snapped, "All right, men, let's keep it quiet."

When they had all got out, they stood about waiting. The trucks were already backing away for another trip. "Are there any officers here?" the officer asked.

A few of the men snickered. "All right, keep it down," the officer said. "Let's have the platoon noncoms forward."

Croft and a sergeant from the pioneer and demolition platoon stepped up. "Most of my men are in the next truck," the noncom said, and the officer told him to move his men together. Croft talked in a low voice to the officer for a minute and then gathered recon around him. "We got to wait," he said. "Let's stick around that tree." There was just enough light for them to notice it, and they walked over slowly. "Where are we now?" Ridges asked.

"Second Battalion headquarters," Croft said. "What've you been working on the road for all this time if you don't even know where you are?"

"Shoot, Ah just work, Ah don' spend mah time lookin' around," Ridges said. He guffawed nervously, and Croft told him to be quiet. They sat down around the tree and waited silently. A battery fired in a grove about five hundred yards away and it lit up the area for a moment. "What's the artillery doin' up this close?" Wilson asked.

"It's cannon company," someone told him.

Wilson sighed. "All a man does is sit around an' get his tail wet."

"It seems to me," Goldstein said formally, "that they're managing this thing very poorly." His voice was eager as if he were hoping for a discussion.

"You bitching again, Goldstein?" Croft asked.

The anti-Semite, Goldstein thought. "I'm just expressing my opinion," he said.

"Opinion!" Croft spat. "A bunch of goddam women have opinions."

Gallagher laughed quietly and mockingly. "Hey, Goldstein, you want a soapbox?"

"You don't like the Army any more than I do," Goldstein said mildly.

Gallagher paused, then sneered. "Balls," he said. "What's the matter, you want some gefüllte fish?" He stopped, and then as if delighted with what he had said, he added, "That's right, what Goldstein needs is some of that fuggin fish." A machine gun began to fire again; because of the night it sounded very close.

"I don't like the way you express yourself," Goldstein said.

"You know what you can do," Gallagher said. He was partially ashamed, and to drown it he added fiercely, "You can go blow it . . ."

"You can't talk to me that way," Goldstein said. His voice trembled. He was in a turmoil, revolted by the idea of fighting, yet recognizing the deep necessity for it. The goyim, that's all they know, to fight with their fists, he thought.

Red stepped in. He had the discomfort a display of emotion always roused in him. "Let's take it easy," he muttered. "You guys'll be getting plenty of fight in a minute." He snorted. "Fightin' over the Army. As far as I'm concerned, it's been a goddam mess ever since they put Washington on a horse."

Toglio interrupted him. "You've got the wrong attitude, Red. It ain't decent to talk about George Washington that way."

Red slapped his knee. "You're a regular Boy Scout, ain't you, Toglio? You like the flag, huh?"

Toglio thought of a story he had read once, *The Man Without a Country*. Red was like the man in that, he decided. "I think some things aren't fit for kidding," he said severely.

"You want to know something?"

Toglio knew a crack was coming, but against his judgment he asked, "What?"

"The only thing wrong with this Army is it never lost a war."

Toglio was shocked. "You think we ought to lose this one?"

Red found himself carried away. "What have I got against the goddam Japs? You think I care if they keep this fuggin jungle? What's it to me if Cummings gets another star?"

"General Cummings, he's a good man," Martinez said.

"There ain't a good officer in the world," Red stated. "They're just a bunch of aristocrats, they think. General Cummings is no better than I am. His shit don't smell like ice cream either."

Their voices were beginning to carry above a whisper, and Croft said, "Let's keep it down." The conversation was boring him. It was always the men who never got anywhere that did the bitching.

Goldstein was still quivering. His sense of shame was so intense that a few tears welled in his eyes. Red's interruption frustrated him, for Gallagher's words had pitched Goldstein so taut that he needed some issue desperately now. He was certain, however, that he would start weeping with rage if he opened his mouth, and so he remained silent, trying to calm himself.

A soldier came walking toward them. "Are you guys recon?" he asked.

"Yeah," Croft said.

"Okay, you want to follow me?"

They picked up their packs and began walking through the darkness. It was difficult to see the man ahead. After they had gone a few hundred feet, the soldier who was leading them halted and said, "Wait here."

Red swore. "Next time, let's do it by the numbers," he said. Cannon company fired again, and the noise sounded very loud. Wilson dropped his pack and muttered. "Some poor sonsofbitches are gonna catch hell in 'bout half a minute." He sighed and sat down on the wet ground. "You'd think they had somepin better to do than have a whole squad of men walkin' around all night. Ah can't make up m' mind if Ah'm hot or cold." There was a wet heavy mist over the ground, and alternately they shivered in their wet clothing and sweltered in the airless night. Some Japanese artillery was landing about a mile away, and they listened to it quietly.

A platoon of men filed by, their rifles clanking against their helmets and pack buckles. A flare went up a short distance away, and in its light the men looked like black cutouts moving past a spotlight. Their rifles were slung at odd angles, and their packs gave them a humped misshapen appearance. The sound of their walking was confused and intricate; like the truck convoy, it resembled the whisper of surf. Then the flare died, and the column of men passed. When they were some distance away, the only sound that still remained was the soft metallic jingle of their rifles. A skirmish had started at some distance and Jap rifles were firing. Red turned to Wyman and said, "Listen to them. Tick-boom, tick-boom. You can't miss it." A few American rifles answered, their fire sounding more powerful, like a leather belt slapped on a table. Wyman shifted uneasily. "How far away do you figure the Japs are?" he asked Croft.

"Damned if I know. You'll see 'em soon enough, boy."

"Hell he will," Red said. "We're going to be sitting around all night."

Croft spat. "You wouldn't mind that, would you, Valsen?"

"Not me. I'm no hero," Red said.

Some soldiers walked passed in the darkness, and a few trucks pulled into the bivouac. Wyman lay down on the ground. He was a little chagrined that he would spend his first night in combat trying to fall asleep. The water soaked through his shirt, which was already wet, and he sat up again, shivering. The air was very sultry. He wished he could light a cigarette.

They waited another half hour before receiving the order to move. Croft stood up and followed their guide while the rest trailed behind. The guide led them into a patch of brush where a platoon of men was grouped around six antitank guns. They were 37s, small guns about six feet long with very slender barrels. One man could pull one gun without too much difficulty over level hard ground.

"We're going along with antitank up to First Battalion," Croft said. "We got to pull two of them guns."

Croft told them to gather around him. "I don't know how muddy the damn trail is going to be," he began, "but it ain't too hard to guess. We're going to be in the middle of the column, so I'm going to cut us into three groups of three men each, and they'll be one group restin' all the time. I'll take Wilson and Gallagher, and Martinez can take Valsen and Ridges, and Toglio, you got what's left— Goldstein and Wyman. We're scrapin' the barrel," he added dryly.

He went up to talk to an officer for a few seconds. When he came back, he said, "We'll let Toglio's group have the first rest." He got behind one of the guns and gave it a tug. "The sonofabitch is going to be heavy." Wilson and Gallagher started pulling it with him, and the other platoon, which had already divided into a few men on each gun, began to move out. They tugged the guns across the bivouac area, and passed through a gap in the barbed wire where there was a machine gun emplacement. "Have a good time, men," the man at the machine gun said.

"Blow it out," Gallagher answered. The gun was beginning to drag on his arms already.

There were about fifty men in the column, and they moved very slowly down a narrow trail through the jungle. After they had moved a hundred feet, they were no longer able to see the men in front of them. The branches of the trees on either side of the trail joined overhead, and they felt as though they were groping through an endless tunnel. Their feet sank into the deep mud and, after a few yards, their boots were covered with great slabs of muck. The men on the guns would lunge forward for a few feet and then halt, lunge forward and halt. Every ten yards a gun would bog down and the three men assigned to it would have to tug until their strength seeped from their fingers. They would wrestle the gun out of its rut and plunge it forward for fifteen feet before their momentum was lost. Then they would pull it and lift it for another few yards until it sank into a hole once more. The entire column labored and stumbled at a miserable pace along the trail. In the darkness they kept ganging up on each other, the men on one gun sometimes riding it up onto the muzzle of the one ahead, or falling behind so far that the file at last broke into separate wriggling columns like a worm cut into many parts and still living. The men at the rear had the worst of it. The guns and men that preceded them had churned the trail until it was almost a marsh, and there were places where two teams would have to combine on one gun and carry it above the ground until they had passed the worst of the slime.

The trail was only a few feet wide. Huge roots continually tripped the men, and their faces and hands became scratched and bleeding from the branches and thorns. In the complete darkness they had no idea of how the trail might bend, and sometimes on a down slope, when they could let the gun roll a little distance, they would land at the bottom with the field piece completely off the trail. Then they would have to fumble in the brush, covering their eyes with their arms to protect them from the vines, and a painful struggle to bring the gun back on the path would begin.

Some Japanese might easily have been waiting in ambush, but it was impossible to keep silent. The guns squeaked and lumbered, made sucking sounds as their tires sank into the mud, and the men swore helplessly, panted with deep sobbing sounds like wrestlers at the end of a long bout. Voices and commands echoed hollowly, were lost in a chorus of profanity and hoarse sobbing, the straining sweating noises of men in great labor. By the time an hour had passed, nothing existed for them but the slender cannon they had to get down the track. The sweat drenched their clothing and filled their eyes, blinding them. They grappled and blundered and swore, advanced the little guns a few feet at a time with no consciousness any longer of what they were doing.

When one team was relieved by another, they would stagger alongside the guns trying to regain their wind, falling behind sometimes to rest for a little while. Every ten minutes the column would stop to allow the stragglers to catch up. During the halts the men would sprawl in the middle of the trail not caring how the mud covered them. They felt as though they had been running for hours; they could not regain their breath, and their stomachs retched emptily.

Some of the men began to throw away their equipment; one after another the men threw their helmets aside or dropped them on the trail. The air was unbearably hot under the canopy of the jungle, and the darkness gave no relief from the heat of the day; if anything, walking the trail was like fumbling through an endless closet stuffed with velvet garments.

During one of the halts, the officer leading the file worked his way back to find Croft. "Where's Sergeant Croft?" he shouted, his words repeated by the men along the trail until it reached Croft.

"Here, sir." They stumbled toward each other through the mud.

"How're your men?" the officer asked.

"Okay."

They sat down beside the trail. "Mistake trying this," the officer gasped. "Have to get through."

Croft, with his lean ropy body, had borne the labor comparatively well, but his voice was unsteady and he had to talk with short quick spates of words. "How far?" he asked.

"Have to go one mile . . . one mile yet. More than halfway there, I think. Never should have tried it."

"They need the guns bad?"

The officer halted for a moment and tried to speak normally. "I think so . . . there's no tank weapons there . . . up on the line. We stopped a tank attack two hours ago . . . at Third Battalion. Orders came to move some thirty-sevens over to First Battalion. Guess they expect attack there."

"Better get them through," Croft said. He was contemptuous because the officer had to talk to him. The man ought to be able to do his own job.

"Have to, I guess." The officer stood up and leaned for a moment against a tree. "If you get a gun stuck, let me know. Have to cross a stream . . . up ahead. Bad place, I think."

He began to feel his way forward, and Croft turned around and worked his way back to the gun he was pulling. The column was over two hundred yards long by now. They started to move, and the labor continued. Once or twice a flare filtered a wan and delicate bluish light over them, the light almost lost in the dense foliage through which it had to pass. In the brief moment it lasted, they were caught at their guns in classic straining motions that had the form and beauty of a frieze. Their uniforms were twice blackened, by the water and the dark slime of the trail. And for the instant the light shone on them their faces stood out, white and contorted. Even the guns had a slender articulated beauty like an insect reared back on its wire haunches. Then darkness swirled about them again, and they ground the guns forward blindly, a line of ants dragging their burden back to their hole.

They had reached that state of fatigue in which everything was hated. A man would slip in the mud and remain there, breathing hoarsely, having no will to get to his feet. That part of the column would halt, and wait numbly for the soldier to join them. If they had breath, they would swear.

"Fug the sonofabitchin' mud."

"Get up," somebody would cry.

"Fug you. Fug the goddam gun."

"Let me lay here. I'm okay, they ain't a thing wrong with me, I'm okay, let me lay."

"Fug you, *get up!*"

And they would labor forward a few more yards and halt. In the darkness, distance had no meaning, nor did time. The heat had left their bodies; they shivered and trembled in the damp night, and everything about them was sodden and pappy; they stank but no longer with animal smells; their clothing was plastered with the foul muck of the jungle mud, and a chill dank rotting smell somewhere between leaf mold and faeces filled their nostrils. They knew only that they had to keep moving, and if they thought of time it was in so many convulsions of nausea.

Wyman was wondering why he did not collapse. His breath came in long parched shudders, his pack straps galled, his feet were ablaze, and he could not have spoken, for his throat and chest and mouth seemed covered with a woolly felt. He was no longer conscious of the powerful and fetid stench that rose from his clothes. Somewhere deep inside himself was a wonder at the exhaustion his body could endure. He was normally a sluggish youth who worked no more than he was obliged to, and the sensations of labor, the muscle strains, the panting, the taste of fatigue were things he had always tried to avoid. He had had vague dreams about being a hero, assuming this would bring him some immense reward which would ease his life and re-move the problems of supporting his mother and himself. He had a girl and he wanted to dazzle her with his ribbons. But he had always imagined combat as exciting, with no misery and no physical exer-tion. He dreamed of himself charging across a field in the face of many machine guns; but in the dream there was no stitch in his side from running too far while bearing too much weight.

He had never thought he would be chained to an inanimate monster of metal with which he would have to grapple until his arms trembled helplessly and his body was ready to fall; certainly he had never imagined he would stumble down a path in the middle of the night with his shoes sucking and dragging in slime. He pushed at the gun, he lifted it with Goldstein and Toglio when it became mired in a hole, but the motions were automatic by now; he hardly even felt the added pain when they had to pull it out by the wheel hubs. His fingers were no longer able to close, and often he would tug helplessly until his hands slipped away with the gun still mired.

The column was proceeding even more slowly than it had at the start, and sometimes fifteen minutes would elapse before a gun could be moved a hundred yards. Every now and then a man would faint, and would be left by the side of the trail to make his way back alone when he recovered.

At last a message began to carry back along the trail, "Keep going, we're almost there," and for a few minutes it served as a stimulant so that the men labored with some hope again. But when each turning in the trail discovered only another ribbon of mud and darkness, the men began to feel a hopeless dejection. Sometimes for as much as a minute they would not move at all. It became harder and harder to pitch themselves against the guns again. Every time they stopped they felt like quitting.

There was a draw they had to cross a few hundred feet before they reached 1st Battalion, and its banks sloped very steeply down to a little stony brook, then ascended again abruptly to about fifteen feet above the bottom. This was the stream the officer had mentioned. When the men reached it, the column stopped completely, and the stragglers caught up. Each team of soldiers waited for the men and gun in front of them to cross the stream. In the night it was an extremely difficult business at best and took a long time. The men would go sliding down the bank trying to restrain their field piece from turning over at the bottom, and then they would have to lift it over the slippery rocks of the brook before attempting to wrestle it up the other side. The banks were slimy, and there was no foothold; time and again a team would force their gun up almost to the top of the draw only to slip back again futilely.

By the time Wyman and Toglio and Goldstein had to move their gun, a half hour had passed and they were a little rested. Their wind had returned and they kept shouting instructions to each other as they nosed the gun over the edge of the bank. It began to pull away from them, and they had to resist desperately to keep it from crashing to the bottom. The exertion drained most of the strength they had recovered, and after they had carried the piece across the stream, they were as exhausted as they had been at any time during the march.

They stopped for a few moments to gather whatever force was left in them and began the struggle up the bank. Toglio was wheezing like a bull, and his commands had a hoarse urgent sound as if he were wrenching them from deep inside his body. "Okay, PUSH . . . PUSH," he growled, and the three of them strove numbly to roll the gun. It resisted them, moved sluggishly and treacherously, and the strength began to flow out of their trembling legs. "HOLD IT!" Toglio shouted "DON'T LET IT SLIP!" They braced themselves behind the gun, trying to wedge their feet into the wet clay of the bank. "PUSH AGAIN!" he shouted, and they forced it upward a few more feet. Wyman felt a band was stretching dangerously inside his body, and would snap at any moment. They rested again, and then shoved the gun another few yards. Slowly, minute by minute, they came closer to the top. They were perhaps four feet from the crest when Wyman lost the last reserves of his strength. He tried to draw some few shreds of effort from his quivering limbs, but he seemed to collapse all at once, and just lay stupidly behind the gun supporting it with no more than the weight of his sagging body. The gun began to slip, and he pulled away. Toglio and Goldstein were left at each of the hubs. When Wyman let go, they felt as though someone were pushing down against the gun. Goldstein held on until the sliding wheels pulled his fingers loose, one by one, and then he just had time to shout hoarsely, "WATCH IT!" to Toglio, before the gun went crashing down to the bottom. The three men fell after it, rolling in its wake. The gun struck some rocks at the bottom, and one of the wheels was knocked completely awry. They felt for it in the darkness like pups licking the wounds of their mother. Wyman began to blubber with exhaustion.

The accident caused a great deal of confusion. Croft's team was on the gun waiting behind them, and he began to shout, "What's holdin' you up? What's happening down there?"

"We had . . . trouble," Toglio shouted back. "Wait!" He and Goldstein succeeded in turning the gun on its side. "The wheel's shot." Toglio shouted. "We can't move the gun."

Croft swore. "Get her out of the way."

They tried, and couldn't budge it.

"We need help," Goldstein shouted.

Croft swore again, and then he and Wilson slid down the bank. After a while they were able to tumble the gun over enough times to move it down the creek bed. Without saying anything, Croft went back to his gun, and Toglio and the others climbed up the far bank and went staggering down the trail till they reached 1st Battalion's bivouac. The men who had arrived before them were lying on the ground motionless. Toglio stretched out in the mud, and Wyman and Goldstein lay down beside him. None of them spoke for ten minutes. Occasionally, a shell might burst somewhere in the jungle about them and their legs might twitch, but this was the only sign they gave of being conscious. Men were moving about constantly, and the sounds of the fighting were closer, more vicious. Voices kept coming to them out of the darkness. Someone would shout, "Where's the pack train for B Company?" and the answer would be muffled to the men lying on the ground. They hardly cared. Occasionally they would be aware of the sounds of the night; for a few instants they might concentrate on the constant thrumming that emanated from the jungle, but they always relapsed into a stupor, thinking of nothing once more.

Croft and Wilson and Gallagher brought their gun in a short while later, and Croft shouted for Toglio.

"What do you want? I'm here," Toglio said. He hated to move.

Croft came toward him in the darkness and sat down beside him. His breath was coming in long slow gasps like a runner after a race. "I'm going to see the Lieutenant . . . tell him about the gun. How the hell did it happen?"

Toglio propped himself on an elbow. He loathed the explanations that were to come, and he was confused. "I don't know," he said. "I heard Goldstein yell 'Watch out' and then it just seemed to rip out of our hands." Toglio hated to give excuses to Croft.

"Goldstein yelled, huh?" Croft asked. "Where is he?"

"Here I am, Sergeant." Goldstein's voice came out of the darkness beside them.

"Why'd you yell 'Watch out'?"

"I don't know. I felt suddenly as if I couldn't hold it any more. Something pulled it away from me."

"Who was the other man?"

Wyman roused himself. "I guess I was." His voice sounded weak.

"Did you let go?" Croft asked.

Wyman felt a trace of fear as he thought of admitting that to Croft. "No," he said. "No, I don't think so. I heard Goldstein yell, and then the gun started to come down on me. It was rolling back so I got out of the way." Already he was uncertain exactly how it had occurred, and a part of his mind was trying to convince him that he spoke the truth. With it, however, he felt a surprising flush of shame. "I guess it was my fault," he blurted out honestly, but his voice was so tired that it lacked sincerity, and Croft thought he was trying to protect Goldstein.

"Yeah," Croft said. A spasm of rage worked through him, and he turned on Goldstein and said, "Listen, Izzy."

"My name isn't Izzy," Goldstein said angrily.

"I don't give a damn what it is. The next time you pull a goddam trick like that, I'm going to put you in for a court-martial."

"But I don't think I let go," Goldstein protested weakly. By now, he too was no longer sure. The sequence of his sensations when the gun had begun to pull out of his hands was too confused for him to feel righteous. He had thought that Wyman stopped pushing first, but when Wyman declared he was to blame, Goldstein had a moment of panic. Like Croft, he believed Wyman was protecting him. "I don't know," he said. "I don't think I did."

"You don't think," Croft cut him off. "Listen, for as long as you've been in the platoon, Goldstein, you've done nothing but have ideas about how we could do something better. But when it comes down to a little goddam work, you're always dicking off. I've had enough of that bullshit from you."

Once again Goldstein was feeling a helpless anger. A reaction he could not control, his agitation was even greater than his resentment and choked him so that he could not speak. A few tears of frustration welled in his eyes, and he turned away and lay down again. His anger was now directed toward himself and he felt a hopeless shame. Oh, I don't know, I don't know, he said.

Toglio had a mingled relief and pity. He was glad the onus of losing the gun was not his, and yet he was unhappy anyone should be blamed. The bond of common effort that the three men had known while struggling with the weapon was still with him, and he said to himself, poor Goldstein, he's a good guy; he just had hard luck.

Wyman was too exhausted to think clearly. After he declared it was his fault, he was relieved to discover he was not to be blamed after all. He was actually too depleted to think consecutively about anything, or indeed remember anything. By now, he was convinced it was Goldstein who had deserted the gun, and his main reaction was one of comfort. The image still most vivid to him was the agony he had felt in his chest and groin as they had started up the embankment, and he thought, I would have let go two seconds later if he didn't. For this reason, Wyman felt a dulled sense of affection for Goldstein.

Croft stood up. "Well, that's one gun they ain't going to rescue for a little while," he said. "I bet it stays there for the whole campaign." He was enraged enough to strike Goldstein. Without saying anything more, Croft left them and went in search of the officer who had led the column.

The men in the platoon settled down and began to sleep. Occasionally a shell would burst in the jungle nearby, but they hardly cared. The battle had been threatening all evening like a thunderstorm which never breaks, and by now it would have taken a barrage to move them. Besides, they were too weary to dig holes.

> *They get a little sleep, but are awakened to go farther up the trail, where an attack is expected.*

The mortar shells were falling perhaps fifty yards in front of the platoon at his left, and Croft spat quietly. It was too close to be merely harassing fire; someone had heard something in the jungle on the other side of the river or they would never have called for mortars so close to their own position. His hand explored the hole again and discovered a field telephone. Croft picked up the receiver, listened quietly. It was an open line, and probably confined to the platoons of A Company. Two men were talking in voices so low that he strained to hear them.

"Walk it up another fifty and then bring it back."

"You sure they're Japs?"

"I swear I heard them talking."

Croft stared tensely across the river. The moon had come out, and the strands of beach on either side of the stream were shining with a silver glow. The jungle wall on the other side looked impenetrable.

The mortars fired again behind him with a cruel flat sound. He watched the shells land in the jungle, and then creep nearer to the river in successive volleys. A mortar answered from the Japanese side of the river, and about a quarter of a mile to the left Croft could hear several machine guns spattering at each other, the uproar deep and irregular. Croft picked up the phone and whistled into it. "Wilson," he whispered. "*Wilson!*" There was no answer and he debated whether to walk over to Wilson's hole. Silently Croft cursed him for not noticing the phone, and then berated himself for not having discovered it before he briefed the others. He looked out across the river. Fine sergeant I am, he told himself.

His ears were keyed to all the sounds of the night, and from long experience he sifted out the ones that were meaningless. If an animal rustled in its hole, he paid no attention; if some crickets chirped, his ear disregarded them. Now he picked a muffled slithering sound which he knew could be made only by men moving through a thin patch of jungle. He peered across the river, trying to determine where the foliage was least dense. At a point between his gun and Wilson's there was a grove of a few coconut trees sparse enough to allow men to assemble; as he stared into that patch of wood, he was certain he heard a man move. Croft's mouth tightened. His hand felt for the bolt of the machine gun, and he slowly brought it to bear on the coconut grove. The rustling grew louder; it seemed as if men were creeping through the brush on the other side of the river to a point opposite his gun. Croft swallowed once. Tiny charges seemed to pulse through his limbs and his head was as empty and shockingly aware as if it had been plunged into a pail of freezing water. He wet his lips and shifted his position slightly, feeling as though he could hear the flexing of his muscles.

The Jap mortar fired again and he started. The shells were falling by the next platoon, the sound painful and jarring to him. He stared out on the moonlit river until his eyes deceived him; he began to think he could see the heads of men in the dark swirls of the current. Croft gazed down at his knees for an instant and then across the river again. He looked a little to the left or right of where he thought the Japanese might be; from long experience he had learned a man could not look directly at an object and see it in the darkness.

Something seemed to move in the grove, and a new trickle of sweat formed and rolled down his back. He twisted uncomfortably. Croft was unbearably tense, but the sensation was not wholly unpleasant.

He wondered if Wilson had noticed the sounds, and then in answer to his question, there was the loud unmistakable clicking of a machine gun bolt. To Croft's keyed senses, the sound echoed up and down the river, and he was furious that Wilson should have revealed his position. The rustling in the brush became louder and Croft was convinced he could hear voices whispering on the other side of the river. He fumbled for a grenade and placed it at his feet.

Then he heard a sound which pierced his flesh. Someone called from across the river, "Yank, Yank!" Croft sat numb. The voice was thin and high-pitched, hideous in a whisper. "That's a Jap," Croft told himself. He was incapable of moving for that instant.

"Yank!" It was calling to him. "Yank. We you coming-to-get, Yank."

The night lay like a heavy stifling mat over the river. Croft tried to breathe.

"*We you coming-to-get, Yank.*"

Croft felt as if a hand had suddenly clapped against his back, traveled up his spine over his skull to clutch at the hair on his forehead. "Coming to get you, Yank," he heard himself whisper. He had the agonizing frustration of a man in a nightmare who wants to scream and cannot utter a sound. "We you *coming-to-get*, Yank."

He shivered terribly for a moment, and his hands seemed congealed on the machine gun. He could not bear the intense pressure in his head.

"We you coming-to-get, Yank," the voice screamed.

"COME AND GET ME YOU SONSOFBITCHES," Croft roared. He shouted with every fiber of his body as though he plunged at an oaken door.

There was no sound at all for perhaps ten seconds, nothing but the moonlight on the river and the taut rapt buzzing of the crickets. Then the voice spoke again. "Oh, we come, Yank, we come."

Croft pulled back the bolt on his machine gun, and rammed it home. His heart was still beating with frenzy "Recon . . . RECON, UP ON THE LINE," he shouted with all his strength.

A machine gun lashed at him from across the river, and he ducked in his hole. In the darkness, it spat a vindictive white light like an acetylene torch, and its sound was terrifying. Croft was holding himself together by the force of his will. He pressed the trigger of his gun and it leaped and bucked under his hand. The tracers spewed wildly into the jungle on the other side of the river.

But the noise, the vibration of his gun, calmed him. He directed it to where he had seen the Japanese gunfire and loosed a volley. The handle pounded against his fist, and he had to steady it with both hands. The hot metallic smell of the barrel eddied back to him, made what he was doing real again. He ducked in his hole waiting for the reply and winced involuntarily as the bullets whipped past.

BEE-YOWWWW! . . . BEE-YOOWWWW! Some dirt snapped at his face from the ricochets. Croft was not conscious of feeling it. He had the surface numbness a man has in a fight. He flinched at sounds, his mouth tightened and loosened, his eyes stared, but he was oblivious to his body.

Croft fired the gun again, held it for a long vicious burst, and then ducked in his hole. An awful scream singed the night, and for an instant Croft grinned weakly. Got him, he thought. He saw the metal burning through flesh, shattering the bones in its path. "AII-YOHHHH." The scream froze him again, and for an odd disconnected instant he experienced again the whole complex of sounds and smells and sights when a calf was branded. "RECON, UP . . . UP!" he shouted furiously and fired steadily for ten seconds to cover their advance. As he paused he could hear some men crawling behind him, and he whispered, "Recon?"

"Yeah." Gallagher dropped into the hole with him. "Mother of Mary," he muttered. Croft could feel him shaking beside him.

"Stop it!" he gripped his arm tensely. "The other men up?"

"Yeah."

Croft looked across the river again. Everything was silent, and the disconnected abrupt spurts of fire were forgotten like vanished sparks from a grindstone. Now that he was no longer alone, Croft was able to plan. The fact that men were up with him, were scattered in the brush along the bank between their two machine guns, recovered his sense of command. "They're going to attack soon," he whispered hoarsely in Gallagher's ear.

Gallagher trembled again. "Ohh. No way to wake up," he tried to say, but his voice kept lapsing.

"Look," Croft whispered. "Creep along the line and tell them to hold fire until the Japs start to cross the river."

"I can't, I can't," Gallagher whispered.

Croft felt like striking him. "Go!" he whispered.

"I can't."

The Jap machine gun lashed at them from across the river. The bullets went singing into the jungle behind them, ripping at leaves. The tracers looked like red splints of lightning as they flattened into the jungle. A thousand rifles seemed to be firing at them from across the river, and the two men pressed themselves against the bottom of the hole. The sounds cracked against their eardrums. Croft's head ached. Firing the machine gun had partially deafened him. BEE-YOWWWW! A ricochet slapped some more dirt on top of them. Croft felt it pattering on his back this time. He was trying to sense the moment when he would have to raise his head and fire the gun. The firing seemed to slacken, and he lifted his eyes cautiously. BEE-YOWWW, BEE-YOWWWW! He dropped in the hole again. The Japanese machine gun raked through the brush at them.

There was a shrill screaming sound, and the men covered their heads with their arms. BAA-ROWWMM, BAA-ROWWMM, ROWWMM, ROWWMM. The mortars exploded all about them, and something picked Gallagher up, shook him, and then released him. "O God," he cried. A clod of dirt stung his neck. BAA-ROWWMM, BAA-ROWWMM.

"Jesus, I'm hit," someone screamed, "I'm hit. Something hit me." BAA-ROWWMM.

Gallagher rebelled against the force of the explosions. "Stop, I give up," he screamed. "STOP! . . . I give up! I give up!" At that instant he no longer knew what made him cry out.

BAA-ROWWMM, BAA-ROWWMM.

"I'm hit, I'm hit," someone was screaming. The Japanese rifles were firing again. Croft lay on the floor of the hole with his hands against the ground and every muscle poised in its place

BAA-ROWWMM. TEEEEEEEEN! The shrapnel was singing as it scattered through the foliage.

Croft picked up his flare gun. The firing had not abated, but through it he heard someone shouting in Japanese. He pointed the gun in the air.

"Here they come," Croft said.

He fired the flare and shouted, "STOP 'EM!"

A shrill cry came out of the jungle across the river. It was the scream a man might utter if his foot was being crushed. "AAAIIIIII, AAAIIIIIIIII."

The flare burst at the moment the Japanese started their charge. Croft had a split perception of the Japanese machine gun firing from a flank, and then he began to fire automatically, not looking where he fired, but holding his gun low, swinging it from side to side. He could not hear the other guns fire, but he saw their muzzle blasts like exhausts.

He had a startling frozen picture of the Japanese running toward him across the narrow river. "AAAAIIIIIIIIIIIH," he heard again. In the light of the flare the Japanese had the stark frozen quality of men revealed by a shaft of lightning. Croft no longer saw anything clearly; he could not have said at that moment where his hands ended and the machine gun began; he was lost in a vast moil of noise out of which individual screams and shouts etched in his mind for an instant. He could never have counted the Japanese who charged across the river; he knew only that his finger was rigid on the trigger bar. He could not have loosened it. In those few moments he felt no sense of danger. He just kept firing.

The line of men who charged across the river began to fall. In the water they were slowed considerably and the concentrated fire from recon's side raged at them like a wind across an open field. They began to stumble over the bodies ahead of them. Croft saw one soldier reach into the air behind another's body as though trying to clutch something in the sky and Croft fired at him for what seemed many seconds before the arm collapsed.

He looked to his right and saw three men trying to cross the river where it turned and ran parallel to the bluff. He swung the gun about and lashed them with it. One man fell, and the other two paused uncertainly and began to run back toward their own bank of the river. Croft had no time to follow them; some soldiers had reached the beach on his side and were charging the gun. He fired point blank at them, and they collapsed about five yards from his hole.

Croft fired and fired, switching targets with the quick reflexes of an athlete shifting for a ball. As soon as he saw men falling he would attack another group. The line of Japanese broke into little bunches of men who wavered, began to retreat.

The light of the flare went out and Croft was blinded for a moment. There was no sound again in the darkness and he fumbled for another flare, feeling an almost desperate urgency. "Where is it?" he whispered to Gallagher.

"What?"

"Shit." Croft's hand found the flare box, and he loaded the gun again. He was beginning to see in the darkness, and he hesitated. But something moved on the river and he fired the flare. As it burst, a few Japanese soldiers were caught motionless in the water. Croft pivoted his gun on them and fired. One of the soldiers remained standing for an incredible time. There was no expression on his face; he looked vacant and surprised even as the bullets struck him in the chest.

Nothing was moving now on the river. In the light of the flare, the bodies looked as limp and unhuman as bags of grain. One soldier began to float downstream, his face in the water. On the beach near the gun, another Japanese soldier was lying on his back. A wide stain of blood was spreading out from his body, and his stomach, ripped open, gaped like the swollen entrails of a fowl. On an impulse Croft fired a burst into him, and felt a twitch of pleasure as he saw the body quiver.

A wounded man was groaning in Japanese. Every few seconds he would scream, the sound terrifying in the cruel blue light of the flare. Croft picked up a grenade. "That sonofabitch is makin' too much noise," he said. He pulled the pin and lobbed the grenade over to the opposite bank. It dropped like a beanbag on one of the bodies, and Croft pulled Gallagher down with him. The explosion was powerful and yet empty like a blast that collapses windowpanes. After a moment, the echoes ceased.

Croft tensed himself and listened to the sounds from across the river. There was the quiet furtive noise of men retreating into the jungle. "GIVE 'EM A VOLLEY!" he shouted.

All the men in recon began to fire again, and Croft raked the jungle for a minute in short bursts. He could hear Wilson's machine gun pounding steadily. "I guess we gave 'em something," Croft told Gallagher. The flare was going out, and Croft stood up. "Who was hit?" he shouted.

"Toglio."

"Bad?" Croft asked.

"I'm okay," Toglio whispered. "I got a bullet in my elbow."

"Can you wait till morning?"

There was silence for a moment, then Toglio answered weakly, "Yeah, I'll be okay."

Croft got out of his hole. "I'm coming down," he announced. "Hold your fire." He walked along the path until he reached Toglio.

Red and Goldstein were kneeling beside him, and Croft spoke to them in a low voice. "Pass this on," he said. "We're all gonna stay in our holes until mornin'. I don't think they'll be back tonight, but you cain't tell. And no one is gonna fall asleep. They's only about an hour till dawn, so you ain't got nothin' to piss about."

"I wouldn't go to sleep anyway," Goldstein breathed. "What a way to wake up." It was the same thing Gallagher had said.

.   .   .   .   .

. . . Wilson looked around and saw Goldstein sitting alone at the next tent, writing a letter. Abruptly, it seemed shameful to Wilson for them to drink without including anyone else in the squad. For a few seconds he watched Goldstein scribbling busily with a pencil, moving his lips soundlessly as he wrote. Wilson decided that he liked Goldstein but he was vaguely irritated that Goldstein did not drink with them. That Goldstein's a good fella, he said to himself, but he's kind of a stick-in-the-mud. It seemed to Wilson that Goldstein was missing a very fundamental understanding of life.

"Hey, Goldstein," he roared, "come over here."

Goldstein looked up, and smiled diffidently. "Well, thanks, but I'm writing a letter to my wife now." His voice was mild, but it had an expectant fearful quality in it as if he knew he would be abused.

"Aw, forget that ol' letter," Wilson said, "it'll wait."

Goldstein sighed, stood up, and walked over. "What do you want?" he asked.

Wilson laughed. It seemed an absurd question to him. "Ah, hell, have a drink. What do ya think Ah asked ya for?"

Goldstein hesitated. He had heard that the liquor made in the jungle stills was often poisonous. "What kind is it?" he temporized. "Is it real whisky or is it jungle juice?"

Wilson was offended. "Man, it's just good liquor. Y' don' ask questions like that when a man offers ya a drink." Gallagher snorted. "Take the goddam drink or leave it, Izzy," he said.

Goldstein reddened. Out of fear of their contempt he had been about to accept, but now he shook his head. "No, no, thank you," he said. To himself, he thought, What if it should poison me? That would be a fine way, to leave Natalie to get along as best she can. A man with a wife and child can't take chances. He shook his head again, looking at their hard impassive faces. "I really don't want any," he said in his mild breathless voice, and waited with apprehension for their answer.

All of them showed contempt. Croft spat, and looked away. Gallagher looked righteous. "None of *them* drink," he muttered.

Goldstein knew that he should turn around and go back to his letter, but he made a feeble attempt to justify himself. "Oh, I drink," he said. "I like a little sociable drink once in a while, before meals or at a party . . ." He trailed off. A part of his mind had known with a certain bitter understanding that he was in trouble the moment Wilson called him, but that had served only to send random disconnected warnings which he was incapable of obeying.

Wilson looked angry. "Goldstein, you're chicken, that's what you *are*." Out of his superiority and well-being, he felt a condescending annoyance at anyone who was too stupid to appreciate the chance he had given Goldstein.

"Aaah, go write your letter," Red bellowed. He was in an ugly mood, and Goldstein's expression of humiliation and bewilderment offended him. He felt contempt that Goldstein could not hide his feelings; more, he had had a bitter amused knowledge from the moment Wilson had offered Goldstein a drink. He had known exactly what would happen and it gave him an ironic pleasure. Deep inside him he was feeling a trace of sympathy for Goldstein, but he smothered it. "A man ain't worth a damn if he can't even take care of himself," Red muttered.

Goldstein turned around abruptly and walked away. The circle of men who were drinking drew closer, and there was an almost tangible bond between them now. They opened the third canteen.

"It was jus' a mistake," Wilson said, "to try an' be nice to him."

Martinez nodded. "Man pay for liquor, drink it. No free drinks."

Goldstein tried to become absorbed in his letter again. But he found it impossible to write. He kept brooding over what the men had said and what he had answered, and he kept wishing that he had given the replies he was thinking of now. Why do they give me all this aggravation? he wondered, and for a moment felt like weeping. He picked up his letter and read it through again, not quite able to concentrate on the words. After the war he was planning to open a welding shop, and he and his wife had been discussing it in letters ever since he had been overseas. Just before Wilson had called him, Goldstein had not been writing. He had held his pencil in his hand, and he had thought with excitement and joy of what it would be like with a shop of his own, becoming an established man in the community. He had not been daydreaming about the shop; he had the place picked out, and he had figured very nicely how much money he and his wife would save if the war lasted one year or at most two—he was very optimistic about its ending soon—he had even calculated how much they could save if he were to make corporal or sergeant.

It was the only pleasure he had since he had left the States. At night in his tent he would lie awake and plan for his future, or think of his son, or try to imagine where his wife would be at that moment. And sometimes, if he decided that she would be visiting her relatives, he would attempt to create their conversation, and would shake with suppressed glee as he remembered the family jokes.

But now he could not bury himself in those thoughts. As soon as he would try to hear the light cheerful sound of his wife's voice, he would become conscious of the bawdy laughter of the men who were still drinking at his left. Once his eyes filled with tears and he shook his head angrily. Why did they hate him so? he asked himself. He had tried so hard to be a good soldier. He had never fallen out on a hike, he was as strong as any of them, and he worked harder than most of them. He had never fired his gun once when he was on guard, no matter how tempted he had been, but no one ever noticed that. Croft never recognized his worth.

They were just a bunch of Anti-Semiten, he told himself. That was all the goyim knew, to run around with loose women, and get drunk like pigs. Deeply buried was his envy that he had never had many women and did not know the easy loud companionship of drink. He was tired of hoping to make friends with them; they didn't want to get along with him, they hated him. Goldstein smacked his fist against his palm in exasperation. How can You permit the anti-Semites to live, God? he asked. He was not religious, and yet he believed in a God, a personal God with whom he could quarrel, and whom he could certainly upbraid. Why don't You stop things like that? he asked bitterly. It seemed a very simple thing to accomplish, and Goldstein was irritated with the God he believed in, as if he were a parent who was good but a little thoughtless, a little lazy.

Goldstein picked up his letter and began to write again. "I don't know, honey, I get so sick at the whole thing at times I want to quit. It's a terrible thing to say, but I hate the soldiers I have been put with, they're a bunch of *grobe jungen*. Honestly, honey, it's hard to remember all the fine ideals. Sometimes even with the Jews in Europe I don't know why we're fighting. . . ." He reread what he had written, and then crossed it out violently. But he sat there for a minute or two with a cold fear.

He was changing. He realized it suddenly. His confidence was gone, and he wasn't sure of himself. He hated all the men with whom he lived and worked and he could never remember a time in the past when he hadn't liked nearly everyone he knew. . . .

> *The unit has gone through the most brutalizing difficulties. Goldstein is helping a wounded man back to the beach while the others struggle on over a mountain ledge. Roth lags.*

In time he began to irritate the platoon. Croft would not let them sit down and the enforced wait until Roth was able to walk again annoyed them. They began to wait for Roth to fall and the inevitable recurrence of it rasped their senses. Their anger began to shift from Croft to Roth.

The mountain was becoming more treacherous. For ten minutes Croft had been leading them along a rocky ledge up the side of a sheer bluff of stone, and the path in places was only a few feet wide. At their right, never more than a yard or two away, was a drop of several hundred feet, and despite themselves they would pitch at times close to the edge. It roused another fear in them, and Roth's halts made them impatient. They were anxious to get past the ledge.

In the middle of this ascent Roth fell down, started to get up, and then sprawled out again when no one helped him. The rock surface of the ledge was hot but he felt comfortable lying against it. The afternoon rain had just begun and he felt it driving into his flesh, cooling the stone. He wasn't going to get up. Somewhere through his numbness another resentment had taken hold. What was the point of going on?

Someone was tugging at his shoulder, and he flung him off. "I can't go on," he gasped, "I can't go on, I can't." He slapped his fist weakly against the stone.

It was Gallagher trying to lift him. "Get up, you sonofabitch." Gallagher shouted. His body ached with the effort of holding Roth.

"I can't. Go 'way!"

Roth heard himself sobbing. He was dimly aware that most of the platoon had gathered around, were looking at him. But this had no effect; it gave him an odd bitter pleasure to have the others see him, an exaltation compounded of shame and fatigue.

Nothing more could happen after this. Let them see him weeping, let them know for one more time that he was the poorest man in the platoon. It was the only way he could find recognition. After so much anonymity, so much ridicule, this was almost better.

Gallagher was tugging at his shoulder again. "Go 'way, I can't get up," Roth bawled.

Gallagher shook him, feeling a compound of disgust and pity. More than that. He was afraid. Every muscle fiber demanded that he lie down beside Roth. Each time he drew a breath the agony and nausea in his chest made him feel like weeping too. If Roth didn't get up, he also would collapse.

"Get up, Roth!"

"I can't."

Gallagher grasped him under the armpits and tried to lift him. The dead resisting weight was enraging. He dropped Roth and clouted him across the back of his head. "Get up, you Jew bastard!"

The blow, the word itself, stirred him like an electric charge. Roth felt himself getting to his feet, stumbling forward. It was the first time anyone had ever sworn at him that way, and it opened new vistas of failure and defeat. It wasn't bad enough that they judged him for his own faults, his own incapacities; now they included him in all the faults of a religion he didn't believe in, a race which didn't exist. "Hitlerism, race theories," he muttered. He was staggering forward dumbly, trying to absorb the shock. Why did they call him that, why didn't they see it wasn't his fault?

And there was something else working. All the protective devices, the sustaining façades of his life had been eroding slowly in the caustic air of the platoon; his exhaustion had pulled out the props, and Gallagher's blow had toppled the rest of the edifice. He was naked another way now. He rebelled against it, was frustrated that he could not speak to them and explain it away. It's ridiculous, thought Roth in the core of his brain, it's not a race, it's not a nation. If you don't believe in the religion, then why are you one? This was the prop that had collapsed, and even through his exhaustion he understood something Goldstein had always known. His own actions would be expanded from now on. People would not only dislike him, but they would make the ink a little darker on the label.

Well, let them. A saving anger, a magnificent anger came to his aid.

For the first time in his life he was genuinely furious, and the anger excited his body, drove him on for a hundred yards, and then another hundred yards, and still another. His head smarted where Gallagher had struck him, his body tottered, but if they had not been marching he might have flung himself at the men, fought them until he was unconscious. Nothing he could do was right, nothing would please them. He seethed, but with more than self-pity now. He understood. He was the butt because there always had to be a butt. A Jew was a punching bag because they could not do without one.

His body was so small. The rage was pathetic, but its pitifulness was unfair. If he had been stronger, he could have done something. And even so, as he churned along the trail behind the men there was something different in him, something more impressive. For these few minutes he was not afraid of the men. His body wavering, his head lolling on his shoulders, he fought clear of his exhaustion, straggled along oblivious of his body, alone in the new rage of his person.

.   .   .   .   .

The ledge was no more than a foot wide now. The platoon worked along it very slowly, taking a purchase on the weeds and small bushes that grew out of the vertical cracks in the wall. Each step was painful, frightening, but the farther they inched out along the ledge the more terrifying became the idea of turning back. They hoped that at any moment the ledge would widen again, for they could not conceive of returning over a few of the places they had already crossed. This passage was dangerous enough to rouse them temporarily from their fatigue, and they moved alertly, strung out over forty yards. Once or twice they would look down, but it was too frightening. Even in the fog they could see a sheer drop of at least a hundred feet and it roused another kind of faintness. They would become conscious of the walls, which were of a soft gray slimy rock that seemed to breathe like the skin of a seal. It had an odious fleshlike sensation which roused panic, made them want to hasten.

The ledge narrowed to nine inches. Croft kept peering ahead in the mist, trying to determine if it would become wider. This was the first place on the mountain that demanded some skill. Until now it has been essentially a very high hill, but here he wished for a rope or a mountain pick. He continued along it, his arms and legs spread-eagled, hugging the rock, his fingers searching for crevices to latch upon.

He came to a gap in the ledge about four feet wide. There was nothing between, no bushes, no roots to which they could cling. The platform disappeared and then continued on the other side. In the gap there was only the sheer drop of the ridge wall. It would have been a simple jump, merely a long step on level ground, but here it meant leaping sideways, taking off from the left foot and landing with the right, having to gain his balance while he teetered on the ledge.

He slipped off his pack carefully, handed it to Martinez behind him and hesitated for a moment, his right leg dangling over the gap. Then he leaped sideways, wavering for a moment on the other side before steadying himself.

"Jesus, who the fug can cross that?" he heard one of them mutter.

"Just wait there," Croft said, "I'm gonna see if the ledge widens out." He traveled along it for fifty feet, and discovered it was becoming broader again. This gave him a deep sense of relief, for otherwise it would have meant turning back to find another route. And he no longer knew if he could rouse the platoon to go up again.

He leaned over the gap and took his pack from Martinez. The distance was short enough for their hands to touch. Then he took Martinez's pack and moved a few yards farther away. "Okay, men," he called, "let's start coming over. The air's a helluva sight better on this side."

There was a nervous snicker. "Listen, Croft," he heard Red say, "is that fuggin ledge any wider?"

"Yeah, more than a bit." But Croft was annoyed at himself for answering. He should have told Red to shut up.

Roth, at the tail of the column, listened with dread. He would probably miss if he had to jump, and despite himself his body generated some anxiety. His anger was still present, but it had altered into a quieter resolve. He was very tired.

As he watched them pass their packs across and leap over, his fear increased. It was the kind of thing he had never been able to do, and a trace of an old panic he had known in gym classes when he waited for his turn on the high bar rose up to torment him.

Inevitably, his turn was approaching. Minetta, the last man ahead of him, hesitated on the edge and then skipped across, laughing weakly. "Jesus, a fuggin acrobat." Roth cleared his throat. "Make room, I'm coming," he said quietly. He handed over his pack.

Minetta was talking to him as though he were an animal. "Now, just take it easy, boy. There's nothing to it. Just take it easy, and you'll make it okay."

He resented that. "I'm all right," he said.

But when he stepped to the edge and looked over, his legs were dead. The other ledge was very far away. The rock bluffs dropped beneath him gauntly, emptily.

"I'm coming," he mumbled again, but he did not move. As he had been about to jump, he had lost courage.

I'll count three to myself, he thought.

One.

Two.

Three.

But he could not move. The critical second elongated, and then was lost. His body had betrayed him. He wanted to jump and his body knew he could not make it.

Across the ledge he could hear Gallagher. "Get up close, Minetta, and catch that useless bastard." Gallagher crawled toward him through Minetta's feet, and extended his arm, glowered at him. "C'mon, all you got to do is catch my hand. You can fall that far."

They looked weird. Gallagher was crouched at Minetta's feet, his face and arm projecting through Minetta's legs. Roth stared at them, and was filled with contempt. He understood this Gallagher now. A bully, a frightened bully. There was something he could tell them. If he refused to jump, Croft would have to come back. The patrol would be over. And Roth knew himself at this instant, knew suddenly that he could face Croft.

But the platoon wouldn't understand. They would jeer him, take relief from their own weakness in abusing him. His heart was filled with bitterness. "I'm coming," he shouted suddenly. This was the way they wanted it.

He felt his left leg pushing him out, and he lurched forward awkwardly, his exhausted body propelling him too feebly. For an instant he saw Gallagher's face staring in surprise at him, and then he slipped past Gallagher's hand, scrabbled at the rock, and then at nothing.

In his fall Roth heard himself bellow with anger, and was amazed that he could make so great a noise. Through his numbness, through his disbelief, he had a thought before he crashed into the rocks far below. He wanted to live. A little man, tumbling through space.

Early the next morning, Goldstein and Ridges set out again with the litter. The morning was cool and they were traveling at last over level ground, but it made little difference. Within an hour they had plummeted quickly into the same level of stupor as the day before. Once more they toiled forward a few feet, set Wilson down, and then strained forward. All about them were the gentle foothills rolling backward toward the mountain in the north. The country spread out in an endless peaceful vista of pale yellow, like sand dunes mounting into the horizon. Nothing disturbed the silence. They trudged forward, panting and grunting, bent under their burden. The sky had the pale effortless blue of morning, and far toward the south beyond the jungle a string of puffball clouds tugged after one another.

This morning their torpor had taken a new form. Wilson's fever had become worse, and he moaned for water continually, pleading and begging, screaming, abusing them. They could not bear it. It seemed as if hearing were the only sense left to them, and that was partial; they did not notice the humming of the insects or the hoarse sobbing sounds they made when they drew a breath. They could hear only Wilson, and his moans for water grated on them, burred stridently through their resistance.

"Men, y' jus' gotta gimme water." A pinkish spittle had dried at the corners of Wilson's mouth, and his eyes moved uncomfortably, erratically. From time to time he would thrash about on the litter, but without any real strength. He seemed smaller somehow; the flesh over his large frame had settled. For minutes at a time he would blink vacantly at the sky, sniffing delicately at the odors about him. Without realizing it he was smelling himself. Forty hours had elapsed since he was wounded, and in that period he had soiled himself frequently, bled and sweated, had even absorbed the dank moist odors of the damp ground they had slept on the night before. He moved his mouth in a weak elaborate grimace of disgust, "Men, ya stink."

They heard him without much feeling, gasping again for breath. As they had got used to living in the jungle and being wet all the time, as they had forgotten what it was like to live in dry clothing, so they had forgotten now how it felt to draw an effortless breath. They did not think about it; certainly they did not think of when their journey would end. It had become all existence.

That morning Goldstein had roused himself long enough to contrive an aid. Their stiffened fingers had been slowing them most of all. They were unable to hold onto the litter for more than a few seconds before its weight would slowly force their hands open. Goldstein had cut the straps from their pack, tied them together and yoked the line over his shoulders onto the handles of the stretcher. When he could

grasp them no longer with his fingers he would transfer the weight
to the strap, and plow forward until his hands were able to hold them
again. Ridges followed his example soon afterward, and they plodded
onward in their harness, the burden of the litter swaying slowly between them.

"Water, goddammit, y' fuggin . . ."

"No water," Goldstein gasped.

"**Y'** goddam Jewboy." Wilson began to cough again. His legs ached.
The air that played over his face had the flushed heated quality of a
kitchen when the oven has been on too long and the windows are
closed. He hated the litter-bearers; he was like a child being tormented. "Goldstein," he repeated, "always snuffin' around."

A thin weak smile formed on Goldstein's mouth. Wilson had hurt
him, and he envied Wilson suddenly because Wilson had never been
forced to think about what he said or did. "You can't have water,"
Goldstein mumbled, waiting in a rather delicious expectancy for Wilson's abuse to continue. He was like an animal so used to the whip
that he found it a stimulus.

Suddenly Wilson screamed. *"Men y' gotta gimme some water."*

By now Goldstein had forgotten the reason why Wilson mustn't
drink. He only knew that it was forbidden, and was irritated that he
could not remember the explanation. It caused him panic. Wilson's
suffering had affected Goldstein oddly; slowly, keeping pace with his
exhaustion, it had entered his own body. When Wilson screamed,
Goldstein felt a twinge; if the litter lurched abruptly, Goldstein's
stomach plummeted as if he were dropping in an elevator. And every
time Wilson pleaded for water Goldstein was thirsty again. Each time
he opened his canteen he felt a sense of guilt, and he would do without water for hours, rather than provoke Wilson. It seemed that no
matter how delirious Wilson might become he would always notice
when they took out their canteens. Wilson was a burden they could
not leave. Goldstein felt as if he would be carrying him forever; he
could not think of anything else. The limits of his senses were confined to his own body, the litter, and Ridge's back. He did not look
at the yellow hills or wonder how far they had to go. Infrequently,
Goldstein would think of his wife and child with a sense of disbelief.
They were so far away. If he had been told at that moment that they
had died, he would have shrugged. Wilson was more real. Wilson
was the only reality.

"Men, Ah'll give ya anythin'." Wilson's voice had changed, become almost shrill. He would talk in long spates, droning on and on, his voice singsonging almost unrecognizably. "Jus' name it, men, Ah'll give it ya, any ol' thing, y' want some goddam money Ah'll give ya hundid poun' you jus' set me down, gimme drink. Jus' gimme it, men, that's all Ah ask."

They stopped for a longer halt, and Goldstein lunged away and fell forward on his face, lying motionless for several minutes. Ridges stared dully at him, then at Wilson. "What you want, some water?"

"Yeah, gimme that, gimme some water."

Ridges sighed. His short powerful body seemed to have condensed in the last two days. His big slack mouth hung open. His back had shortened and his arms become longer, his head bent over at a smaller angle to his chest. His thin sandy hair drooped sadly over his sloping forehead and his clothing sagged wetly. He looked like a giant phlegmatic egg set on a stout tree stump. "Shoot, Ah don't know why y' can't have water."

"You jus' gimme it, they ain' anythin' Ah won' do for ya."

Ridges scratched the back of his neck. He was not accustomed to make a decision by himself. All his life he had been taking orders from someone or other, and he felt an odd malaise. "Ah ought to ask Goldstein," he mumbled.

"Goldstein's chicken . . ."

"Ah don' know." Ridges giggled. The laughter seemed to come from such a distance. He hardly knew why he laughed. It was probably from embarrassment. He and Goldstein had been too exhausted to talk to each other, but even so he had assumed that Goldstein was the leader, and this despite the fact that he knew the route back. But Ridges had never led anything, and out of habit he assumed that Goldstein was to make all the decisions.

But Goldstein was now lying ten yards away, his face to the ground, almost unconscious. Ridges shook his head. He was too tired to think, he told himself. Still, it seemed absurd not to give a man a drink of water. Little ol' drink ain't gonna hurt nobody, he told himself.

Goldstein knew how to read, however. Ridges balked at the idea of breaking some law out of the vast mysterious world of books and newspapers. Pa use' to say somethin' about givin' a man water when he's sick, Ridges thought. But he couldn't remember. "How you feel, boy?" he asked doubtfully.

"You gotta gimme water. Ah'm burnin'."

Ridges shook his head once more. Wilson had led a life full of sin and now he was in the fires of hell. Ridges felt some awe. If a man ended up a sinner, his punishment was certainly terrible. But the Lord Christ died for pore sinners, Ridges told himself. It was also a sin not to show a man some mercy.

"Ah s'pose y' can have it." Ridges sighed. He took out his canteen quietly and glanced at Goldstein again. He didn't want to be reprimanded by him. "Here, you jus' drink it up."

Wilson drank febrilely, the water splattering out of his mouth to trickle down his chin, wetting the collar of his shirt. "Oh, *man.*" He drank lavishly, eagerly, his throat working with lust. "You're a good sonofabitch," he mumbled. Some water caught in his throat, and he coughed violently, wiping the blood from his chin with a nervous furtive motion. Ridges watched a droplet of it which Wilson had missed. Slowly it spread out over the moist surface of Wilson's cheek, faded through progressive shades of pink.

"Y' think Ah'm gonna make it?" Wilson asked.

"Shore." Ridges felt a shiver. A preacher had once given a sermon about the way a man resisted the fires of hell. "Y' cain't avoid it, you're gonna get caught if you're a sinner," he had said. Ridges was telling a lie now, but nevertheless he repeated it. "Shore you're gonna be awright, Wilson."

"That's what Ah figgered."

Goldstein put his palms against the ground, forced himself upward slowly. He wanted so very much to remain lying on the ground. "I suppose we ought to go," he said wistfully. They harnessed themselves again to the litter and trudged forward.

"You're a good bunch of men, they ain't anybody better'n you two men."

This shamed them. At the moment, still enmeshed in the first pangs of setting out again, they hated him.

"It's all right," Goldstein said.

"Naw, Ah mean it, they ain't any two men like you to be found in the whole fuggin platoon." He was silent, and they settled into the stupefaction of the march. Wilson was delirious for a while, and then sober again. His wound began to ache and he abused them, screaming once more with pain.

Now it bothered Ridges more than Goldstein. He had not thought very much about the agony of the march; it was something he had assumed was natural, perhaps a little more extreme than any work he had ever done, but he had learned when he was very young that work was what a man did with most of his day and it was pointless to wish to do anything else. If it was uncomfortable, if it was painful, there was nothing you could do about it. He had been given the job and he was going to do it. But now for the first time he hated it genuinely. Perhaps there had been too many fatigue-products, perhaps the accumulative labor had dissolved and reshaped the structure of his mind, but in any case he was wretched with this work, and as a corollary he understood suddenly that he had always hated the drudgery of his farm work, the unending monotonous struggle against an arid unyielding soil.

It was too much of a realization; he had to retreat from it. And that was not difficult. He was not accustomed to threshing out a solution with his mind, and now he was too blunted, too completely tired. The thought had come into his head, exploded, and shaken a great many patterns, but the smoke had cleared quickly, and there was nothing now but a vague uncomfortable sense of some wreckage, some change. A few minutes later he was merely uneasy; he knew he had thought something sacrilegious, but what it was he could not guess. He was fastened to his load again.

But this was mixed with something else. He had not forgotten that he had given Wilson the water, and he remembered the way Wilson had said, "Ah'm burnin'." They were carrying a man who was already lost, and that meant something. He was made a little uneasy by the idea that they might be contaminated by him, but that really was not what bothered him. The ways of the Lord are dev'us. It meant something else; they were being taught by example or maybe they were paying for their own sins. Ridges did not work it out for himself, but it gave him a mixture of dread and the variety of exaltation that comes with too much fatigue. We gotta git him back. As with Brown, all the complexities and cross-purposes canceled out into that simple imperative. He lowered his head and bulled on for another few yards.

"Men, you might as well lea' me." A few tears worked out of Wilson's eyes. "They ain't no use y' killin' yourself for me." His fever was torturing him again, and it sent a leaden aching ecstasy through his body. He felt consumed with the desire to express something. "Y' gotta lea' me. Gowan ahead, men." Wilson clenched his fists. He wanted to give them a present, and he was frustrated. They were such good men. "Lea' me." It was plaintive, like a child weeping for something it will never get.

Goldstein listened to him, tempted by the same inevitable suite of rationalizations that Stanley had followed. He wondered how to suggest it to Ridges, and was silent.

Ridges mumbled. "You jus' shut up, Wilson. We ain't leavin' ya."

And therefore Goldstein could not quit. He would not be the first one; he was a little afraid that Ridges then would bundle Wilson on his back and continue. He was bitter and thought of fainting. That he wouldn't do, but he was angry with Brown and Stanley for deserting them. They quit, why don't I quit? he wondered, and knew he wouldn't.

"Jus' set me down an' gowan, men."

"We'll git ya back," Ridges muttered. He too was playing with the idea of deserting Wilson, but he pushed it away in a spasm of disgust. If he left him it would be murder, an awful sin if he left a Christian to die. Ridges thought of the black mark it would be on his soul. Ever since he had been a child he had imagined his soul as a white object the size and shape of a football, lodged somewhere near his stomach. Each time he sinned an ineradicable black spot was inked onto the white soul, its size depending upon the enormity of the sin. At the time a man died, if the white football was more than half black he went to hell. Ridges was certain that the sin of leaving Wilson would cover at least a quarter of his soul.

And Goldstein remembered his grandfather saying, "Yehuda Halevy wrote that Israel is the heart of all nations." He lunged along, carrying the litter through habit, not conscious of the torments of his body. His mind had turned inward; he could not have concentrated more intensely if he had been blind. He just followed Ridges without looking where they went.

"Israel is the heart of all nations." It was the conscience and the raw exposed nerve; all emotion passed through it. But it was more than that; it was the heart that suffered whenever any part of the body was ill.

And Wilson was the heart now. Goldstein did not say this to himself, he did not even think of it, but the idea worked through him beneath the level of speech. He had suffered too much in these past two days; he had traversed all the first nauseas of fatigue, the stupors that followed, the exaltation close to fever. There were as many levels to pain as to pleasure. Once his will had forbidden him to collapse, Goldstein burrowed deeper and deeper through exhaustion and agony, never quite plumbing the pit of it. But he was in a stage now where all the banal proportions were gone. His eyes functioned enough for him to notice automatically where he walked; he heard and smelled isolated little events; he even felt some pain from his racked body; but all this was separate from him, like an object he might hold in his hand. His mind was both blunted and exposed, naked and stupefied.

"The heart of all nations." But for a few hours, after two days and fifteen miles of staggering forward under a tropic sun, after an eternity of wrestling Wilson's body through an empty and alien land, this could be true for him. His senses dammed, his consciousness reeling, Goldstein fumbled through a hall of symbols. Wilson was the object he could not release. Goldstein was bound to him by a fear he did not understand. If he let him go, if he did not bring him back, then something was wrong, he would understand something terrible. The heart. If the heart died . . . but he lost the sequence in the muck of his labors. They were carrying him on and on, and he would not die. His stomach had been ripped apart, he had bled and shit, wallowed through the leaden swells of fever, endured all the tortures of the rough litter, the uneven ground, and still Wilson had not died. They still carried him. There was a meaning here and Goldstein lumbered after it, his mind pumping like the absurd legs of a man chasing a train he has missed.

"Ah like to work, Ah ain't a goddam fug-off," Wilson mumbled. "If you're job, do goddam thing right, that's what Ah say." His breath was gurgling again out of his mouth. "Brown and Stanley. Brown and Stanley, shit!" He giggled feebly. "Little ol' bugger May when she's a kid, always crappin' her pants." He rambled through a cloudy memory of his daughter when she was an infant. "Smartest little devil." When she was two years old she would drop her faeces behind a door or in a closet. "Goddam, step in it, git dirty." He laughed, only it sounded more like a feeble wheeze. For an instant he recalled vividly his mixture of exasperation and merriment when he had discovered her leavings. "Goddam, Alice'd git mad."

She had been angry when he had seen her in the hospital, angry again when they discovered he was sick. "Ah always say a dose ain't gonna hurt a man a goddam bit. What the hell's a lousy little dose? Ah had it five times an' it never came to a goddam thing." He stiffened on the litter and shouted as if arguing with someone. "Jus' get me some pyrdin whatever the hell y' call it." He twisted about, managed almost to prop himself on an elbow. "If goddam wound gits y' opened maybe Ah won' need the op-per-ration, jus' gits rid of all the pus." He retched emptily, watching through dimmed eyes the blood trickling and spattering out of his mouth onto the rubber fabric of the litter. It was so distant and yet it sent a shudder through him. "Whatdeya say, Ridges, does it git rid of it?"

But they hadn't heard him, and he watched the blood fall in droplets from his mouth and then lay back again moodily.

"Ah'm gonna die."

A shudder of fear, of resistance rippled through him. He could taste the blood in his mouth, and he began to tremble. "Goddammit, Ah ain't gonna die, Ah ain't gonna," he wept, choking on his sobs when some mucus clotted his throat. The sounds terrified him; he lay abruptly in the tall weeds, his blood sopping into the sun-warmed earth, the Japanese chattering beside him. "They're gonna git me, they're gonna git me," he shouted suddenly. "Jesus, men, don' lemme die."

Ridges heard him this time, stopped lethargically, set the litter down, and unyoked himself from the pack straps. Like a drunk proceeding slowly and elaborately to unlock a door, Ridges moved over to Wilson's head, and knelt beside him.

"They're gonna git me," Wilson moaned, his face contorted, his unconscious tears slinking out of his eye sockets, racing down his temples to become lost in the matted hair about his ears.

Ridges bent over him, fingering numbly his own scraggly beard. "Wilson," he said hoarsely, a little imperatively.

"Yeah?"

"Wilson, they's still time to turn."

"Wha . . . ?"

Ridges had made up his mind. It might not be too late. Wilson might not yet be damned. "Y' gotta return to the Lord Jesus Christ."

"Uh."

Ridges shook him gently. "They's still time to turn," he said in a solemn mournful voice. Goldstein looked on blankly, vaguely resentful.

"Y' can go to the Kingdom of Heaven." His voice was so deep that it was almost lost. The sounds quivered heavily in Wilson's head like the echo of a bass viol.

"Uh-huh," Wilson mumbled.

"Y' repentin'? Y' askin' forgiveness?"

"Yeah?" Wilson breathed. Who was talking to him, who was bothering him? If he would agree they would let him alone. "Yeah," he mumbled again.

A few tears mounted in Ridges' eyes. He felt exalted. Maw told me 'bout a sinner was caught on the deathbed, he thought. He had never forgotten her story, but he had never imagined that he too would do something so wonderful.

"Git out, y' goddam Japs."

Ridges started. Had Wilson forgotten his conversion already? But Ridges did not dare to admit this. If Wilson repented and then threw it away, his punishment would be doubly awful. No man would ever dare that.

"You jus' 'member what you said," Ridges muttered almost fiercely, *"Jus' watch yourself, man."*

Afraid to listen any longer, he stood up, went to the head of the litter, rearranged the blanket over Wilson's feet, and then worked the strap over his neck and under his armpits. In a moment, after Goldstein was ready, they moved on.

They reached the jungle after an hour's march, and Ridges left Goldstein with the stretcher, and explored to his right until he found the trail the platoon had cut four days earlier. It was only a few hundred yards away. Ridges felt a feeble glow of pleasure that he had been so accurate. Actually he had done it almost instinctively. Permanent bivouacs, roads through the jungle, stretches of beach always confused him; they always looked the same, but in the hills he could travel with a sure and easy sense.

He returned to Goldstein, and they set out again, reaching the trail in a few minutes. The foliage had sprung up again considerably since it had been cut, and the floor of the path was muddy from the rains. They blundered along, slipping frequently, their thickened feet finding no hold in the slick mud. If they had been less tired, they might have noticed the difference; the fact that the sun no longer beat on them would have been noted with pleasure, and conversely the uncertain footing, the sluggish resistance of the bushes and vines and thorns would have angered them. But they hardly detected all that. By now they knew there was no way to carry the stretcher without travail, and the individual circumstances that obstructed them had no force.

Still they progressed even more slowly. The trail had been cut no wider than the breadth of a man's shoulders, and the litter became lodged in several places. Once or twice there was no way at all to carry Wilson through, and Ridges would lift him off, drape him over his shoulder and lumber forward until the trail widened. Goldstein would follow with the stretcher.

At the point where the trail reached the river they took a long break. It came about through no decision on their part; they had halted to rest for a moment, and the minute passed, stretched out to half an hour. Toward the end, Wilson became restless and began to thrash about on the litter. They crawled over to him, attempted to quiet his movements, but he seemed absorbed in something and waved his big arms, cuffing them feverishly.

"Rest a little," Goldstein said.

"They're gonna kill me," Wilson wailed.

"No one's gonna touch ya." Ridges tried to restrain his arms but Wilson wrestled free. Sweat laved his forehead again. "Oh, man," he whimpered. He made an effort to slide off the litter but they forced him back. His legs kept twitching, and every few seconds he would begin to sit up and then groan, fall back again. "Baawoowwwwwm," he mumbled, imitating the sound of a mortar, his arms protecting his head. "Oh, here they come, here they come." He whimpered again. "Sonofabitch what the fug 'm Ah doin' here?"

The memory frightened them all. They sat quiet beside him, averting each other's faces. For the first time since they had re-entered the jungle it seemed malign.

"Quiet down, Wilson," Ridges told him. "You'll be gettin' the Japs on us."

"Ah'm gonna die," Wilson mumbled. He started up, almost reached a sitting position, and then fell back. When he looked at them again his eyes were clear but very weak. After a moment or two he spoke. "Ah'm in bad shape, men." He spat tentatively but the spittle did not quite clear his chin. "Can't even feel the hole in mah belly." His fingers trembled toward the soiled clotted dressing of the wound.

"Fulla pus." He sighed, licked his tongue dryly over his lips. "Ah'm thirsty."

"You can't have any," Goldstein said.

"Yeah, Ah know, cain't have any." Wilson laughed feebly. "You're a goddam woman, Goldstein. If you wasn't so chicken you'd be a pretty good boy."

Goldstein made no answer. He was too weary to get any sense from the words.

"What you want, Wilson?" Ridges asked.

"Water."

"Y' had some."

Wilson coughed and more blood inched out of the crusted sticky corners of his mouth. "Mah ass's givin' blood too," he grunted. "Aaah, git away, you men." He was silent for several minutes, his lips working abstractedly. "Never could figger out if Ah'd go back t' Alice or t'other one." He could feel new processes going on inside himself. His wound seemed to have dropped through his body; he had the sensation he could put his hand in the hole and find nothing. "Oh." He looked blearily at the men. For an instant or two his vision focused, and he saw them clearly. Goldstein's face had drawn back so that his cheek-bones stood out and his nose was beak-like. His irises had become a bright painful blue in the reddened ovals of his eyes, and his blond beard looked red and brown and filthy, was matted over the jungle sores on his chin.

And Ridges looked like an overworked animal. His heavy features hung even more slack than usual, his mouth open, his lower lip drooping. He breathed with a regular panting rhythm.

Wilson wanted to say something to them. They were good men, he thought. They didn't have to carry him this far. "Ah 'preciate what you done, men," he mumbled. But that wasn't it. He had to give them something.

"Listen, men, they's a goddam little still Ah been waitin' to build out in the woods yonder some'eres, on'y damn trouble is we never stay put long enough. But Ah'm gonna git it goin'." A last facsimile of enthusiasm worked in him. He believed himself while he spoke. "Ain't any 'mount of money a man cain't make ifen he gits one set up. Jus' turn it out, an' have all y' want to drink yourself." He was drifting, and he forced himself back. "But Ah git one made soon as we git back, an' Ah'll give you men a canteenful of it each. Jus' a free canteen." There was no expression on their gaunt faces, and he shook his head. It wasn't much to offer for what they'd done. "Men, Ah'll give ya all y' want to drink anytime, don' matter a goddam. You jus' ast me for it an' it'll be yours." He believed all of it; his only regret was that he had not built it already. "Jus' all y' want." His belly dropped again, and then a spasm seized him, and he slid backward into unconsciousness, grunting once with surprise as he felt himself turning over. His tongue protruded, and his breath gave a last rasping sound. He rolled out of the litter.

They pushed him back. Goldstein picked up Wilson's wrist and searched for a pulse, but his fingers felt too weak to support the arm. He dropped it, and then prodded with his forefinger along the flesh of

Wilson's wrist. But his fingertips were too blunted. He could not feel the skin. After a while he just looked at him. "I think he's dead."

"Yeah," Ridges mumbled. He sighed, thought vaguely of praying.

"Why, he was just . . . talking." Goldstein reeled through the shock, balanced for a moment in his mind all the unutterables.

"We might as well be goin'," Ridges mumbled. He stood up heavily, and began to fit the litter straps over his shoulders. Goldstein hesitated, and then followed him. When they were ready, they staggered out onto the flat shallow falls of the river and began moving downstream.

They did not think there was anything odd about moving this way with a dead man. They were too accustomed to picking him up at the end of each halt; the only thing they understood was that they must carry him. Even more, neither of them really believed he was dead. They knew it but they did not believe it. If he had shouted for water they would not have been surprised.

They even talked about what they would do with him. In one of the breaks Ridges said, "When we git him back, we'll give him a Christian burial 'cause he repented."

"Uh-huh." And even so they talked without feeling the words. Goldstein did not want to realize Wilson was dead; he held his mind away from the knowledge rigidly, thinking of nothing, merely sloshing forward through the shallow water upstream, his shoes sliding on the flat smooth rocks. There was something he could not face once he understood.

And Ridges was bewildered too. He was not convinced Wilson had begged for forgiveness; it was all jumbled in his mind; and he fastened on the thought that if he could get Wilson back, get him buried decently, the conversion would take. And more, both of them felt a natural frustration with having carried him this far only to die. They wanted to complete their odyssey with success.

Very slowly now, more slowly than they had moved at any time, they shambled through the water, the litter swaying between them. Overhead the trees and foliage met; as before, the river wound a tunnel through the jungle. Their heads drooped, their legs moved stiffly as if afraid of collapsing if they were hinged at the knee. Now when they rested they would flop in the shallow water, leaving Wilson half submerged while they sprawled beside the litter.

They were almost unconscious. Their feet blundered along the

floor of the stream, crunching on the river pebbles. The water flowing past their heels was chill, but they hardly felt it. In the dim light
of the jungle aisle they stumbled onward, following the current
dumbly. The animals chattered at their approach, the monkeys
screaming and scratching at their haunches, the birds calling to one
another. And then as they would pass the animals would be silent,
and remain quiet for many minutes after they had gone. Ridges and
Goldstein reeled forward like blind men, their bodies expressing a
mute eloquence. Behind them the animals were silent, passing a
warning through the congested channels of the jungle. It might have
been a funeral march.

They descended a waterfall from one flat waist-high rock to another, Ridges dropping down first, and standing in the foam while
Goldstein slid the litter over, and flopped down to join him. They
struggled through the deeper water, which lashed at their thighs,
floating the litter between them. They worked along the riverbanks,
splashed through shallow water again. They stumbled and staggered
and fell many times, Wilson's body almost washing away. They could
not go more than a few feet without halting, and their sobbing fitted
into the murmurs of the jungle, was lost in the washing of the
water.

They were bound to the stretcher and the corpse. Whenever they
fell they would lunge first at Wilson's body, and become conscious
only when they had secured him of the water pouring into their own
mouths. It went deeper than any instinct they had ever had. They
did not think of what they would do with him when they reached
the end, they did not even remember any longer that he was dead.
His burden had been the vital thing. Dead, he was as much alive to
them as he had ever been.

And yet they lost him. They came to the rapids where Hearn had
carried the vine diagonally across the stream. It had washed away in
the four days that had elapsed and the water churned viciously
through the rocks now with no support to guide them. They hardly
realized their danger. They stepped down into the rapids, took three
or four steps, and were upset in the swirling of the water. The litter
ripped out of their enfeebled fingers, dragged them in their harness
after it. They wallowed and tumbled through the rough water, glancing off rocks, choking and swallowing. They made feeble efforts to
free themselves, tried desperately to stand up, but the current was
too violent. Half drowned, they let the water carry them.

The litter split against a rock, and they heard the canvas ripping, but the sound was only an isolated sensation in the panic they felt at swallowing water. They thrashed once more and the litter broke completely in two, the harness ripping free from their shoulders. Gasping, virtually insensible, they washed out of the worst part of the rapids, and stumbled toward the bank.

They were *alone*.

A fact which obtruded slowly through their bewilderment. They could not quite grasp it. One moment they had been carrying Wilson, and now he had disappeared. Their hands were empty.

"He's gone," Ridges mumbled.

They staggered down the river after him, pitching and falling, and reeling on again. At a turn in the stream they could see for several hundred yards, and far in the distance Wilson's body was just disappearing around a bend. "C'mon, we gotta catch him," Ridges said weakly. He took a step and fell forward on his face in the water. He got up very slowly, and then began to walk again.

They came to the other bend and stopped. The stream spread out into a swamp beyond the turn. There was a thin ribbon of water in the middle and bog land on either side. Wilson had washed into it, was lost somewhere in the foliage and swamp. It would take days to find him if he did not sink.

"Oh," Goldstein said, "he's lost."

"Yeah," Ridges mumbled. He took a step forward and stumbled in the water once more. It felt pleasant lapping against his face, and he had no desire to stand up. "Come on," Goldstein said.

Ridges began to weep. He struggled to a sitting position, and cried with his head on his folded arms, the water swirling around his hips and feet. Goldstein stood over him tottering.

"Mother-fuggin sonofabitch," Ridges mumbled. It was the first time he had cursed since childhood, and the words pulled out of his chest one by one, leaving behind a vacuum of anger and bitterness. Wilson would not have his burial, but somehow that was not important now. What counted was that he had carried this burden through such distances of space and time, and it had washed away in the end. All his life he had labored without repayment; his grandfather and his father and he had struggled with bleak crops and unending poverty. What had their work come to? "What profit hath man of all his labour wherein he laboureth under the sun?" The line came back to him. It was a part of the Bible he had always hated.

Ridges felt the beginning of a deep and unending bitterness. It was not fair. The one time they had got a decent crop it had been ruined by a wild rainstorm. God's way. He hated it suddenly. What kind of God could there be who always tricked you in the end?

The practical joker.

He wept out of bitterness and longing and despair; he wept from exhaustion and failure and the shattering naked conviction that nothing mattered.

And Goldstein stood beside him, holding onto Ridges' shoulder to steady himself in the current. From time to time he would move his lips, scratch feebly at his face. "Israel is the heart of all nations."

But the heart could be killed and the body still live. All the suffering of the Jews came to nothing. No sacrifices were paid, no lessons were learned. It was all thrown away, all statistics in the cruel wastes of history. All the ghettos, all the soul cripplings, all the massacres and pogroms, the gas chambers, lime kilns—all of it touched no one, all of it was lost. It was carried and carried and carried, and when it finally grew too heavy it was dropped. That was all there was to it. He was beyond tears, he stood beside Ridges with the stricken sensation of a man who discovers that someone he loves has died. There was nothing in him at the moment, nothing but a vague anger, a deep resentment, and the origins of a vast hopelessness.

"Let's go," he mumbled.

Ridges got up at last, and they wavered slowly through the water, feeling it recede to their ankles, become shallow once more. The stream broadened, rippled over pebbles, became muddy and then sandy. They staggered around a bend and saw the sunlight and the ocean beyond.

A few minutes later they staggered up on the beach. Despite their exhaustion they walked on for a hundred yards. Somehow it was distasteful to stay too near to the river.

As if in mutual accord, they sprawled out on the sand and lay there motionless, their faces on their arms, the sun warming their backs. It was the middle of the afternoon. There was nothing to do but wait here for the platoon to return and the landing craft to fetch them. Their rifles had been lost, their packs, their rations, but they did not think about this. They were too depleted, and later they could find food in the jungle.

They lay like this until evening, too weak to move, absorbing a faint pleasure from resting, feeling the sun upon them. They did not talk. Their resentment had turned toward each other and they felt the dull sour hatred of men who have shared a humiliating failure together. The hours passed and they drowsed, became conscious again, fell asleep once more, woke with the nausea that comes from slumbering in the sunlight.

Goldstein sat up at last, and fumbled for his canteen. Very slowly, as though learning the motions for the first time, he unscrewed the cap and tilted it to his mouth. He had not realized how thirsty he was. The first taste of the water in his mouth was ecstatic. He made himself swallow slowly, setting the canteen down after each gulp. When it was half empty he noticed Ridges watching him. Somehow it was obvious that Ridges had no water left.

Ridges could walk up to the stream, and fill his canteen but Goldstein knew what that meant. He was so weak. The thought of standing up, of walking even a hundred yards, was a torment he could not bear to face. And Ridges must feel the same way.

Goldstein was annoyed. Why hadn't Ridges been more thoughtful, saved his water? He felt stubborn and tilted the canteen to his mouth again. But the drink tasted suddenly brackish. Goldstein was conscious of how warm it had become. He forced himself to take one more drink.

Then, feeling an unutterable sense of shame, he handed it to Ridges.

"Here, you want a drink?"

"Yeah." Ridges drank thirstily. When he had almost emptied the canteen he looked at Goldstein.

"No, finish it."

"We're gonna have to rustle in the jungle for food tomorrow," Ridges said.

"I know."

Ridges smiled weakly. "We'll git along."

The Young Lions
by IRWIN SHAW

If the Jewish G.I. who feels overly driven to show his valor, in order to refute the anti-Semites, eventually became a stereotype in novels of World War II, he was nevertheless a fresh character when Irwin Shaw created him in The Young Lions, and Noah Ackerman remains the most convincing portrait of this type. Indeed, The Young Lions remains among the best novels of the war, regardless of or perhaps because of its centrality on the question of Germans and Jews, used as symbols of the death and life principle. For with classic simplicity Shaw has focused his work on two characters doomed to meet: a Nazi soldier, so purely a killer that one ceases to shudder at his workmanlike satisfaction in destruction, and a Jew, even in war searching for belief in humanity.

We have selected portions that show this relationship, as well as the fated donouement. For Noah Ackerman, it is a further typicality that he is not strongly self-identified as a Jew; he lives in the open world of urban American society, and he finds himself accepted by a nice Gentile girl and by her New England family. Only not accepted by the brutes of his army unit.

Irwin Shaw, born in 1913, gained renown with Bury the Dead, a prize-winning antiwar play of the thirties. His most memorable drama was The Gentle People, an antifascist parable. As a short-story writer he has, like many an author, found himself identified with one talked-of tale, in his case "The Girls in Their Summer Dresses." But he has written in a cosmopolitan range; not particularly concentrated on Jewish material, he has let it come naturally into his work, and produced a number of memorable stories on Nazism, refugees, Israel. Shaw covered the

Eichmann trial, and with Jules Dassin he made a documentary
film about the Six-Day War.

A Hemingwayesque figure, big and powerful, a good drinker,
Irwin Shaw chose G.I. status in the war; attached to the film
section, he saw much of the concentration camps. Shortly after
the war he moved to Switzerland, writing stories, plays, novels,
sometimes a touch on the slick side. The Young Lions remains
his most impressive work.

M.L.

O N THE WESTERN EDGE of America, in the sea-coast town of
Santa Monica, among the flat sprawling streets and the shredding
palms, the old year was coming to an end in soft, gray fog, rolling in off
the oily water, rolling in over the scalloped surf breaking on the wet
beaches, rolling in over the hot-dog stands, closed for the winter, and
the homes of the movie stars, and the muffled coast road that led to
Mexico and Oregon.

The streets of the town were deserted, left to the fog, as though
the new year were a public disaster that all the inhabitants of the
place were avoiding by wisely staying in their homes until the danger
was past. Here and there a light shone wetly, and on some streets the
fog was tinged the garish neon-red which has become the color of
night-time city America. The flickering red tubes advertised restaurants, ice-cream parlors, moving-picture theatres, hotels, drive-ins,
but their real effect in the soundless, sorrowful night was tragic and
foreboding, as though the human race were being given a furtive
glimpse, in the mist, of its last home, cavernous and blood-colored
through gray, shuffling curtains.

The electric sign of the Sea View Hotel, from which at no time,
even on the clearest days, could any body of water be observed,
added its baleful, minor tone to the thin, sifting fog outside Noah's
window. The light filtered into the darkened room and touched the
damp plaster walls and the lithograph of Yosemite Falls above the bed.
Splinters of red fell on Noah's father's sleeping face on the pillow,
on the large, fierce nose, the curving, distended nostrils, the rigid, deep
eyesockets, on the high, imposing brow, the bushy white hair, courtly
moustache and Vandyke beard, like a Kentucky colonel's in the

movies, ludicrous and out of place here, on a dying Jew in the narrow, hired room.

Noah would have liked to read as he sat there, but he didn't want to wake his father by putting on the light. He tried to sleep, sitting in the single, hard-upholstered chair, but his father's heavy breathing, roaring and uneven, kept him awake. The doctor had told Noah that Jacob was dying, as had the woman his father had sent away on Christmas Eve, that widow what was her name . . . Morton— but Noah didn't believe them. His father had had Mrs. Morton send him a telegram in Chicago, telling him to come at once. Noah had sold his overcoat and his typewriter and the old wardrobe trunk, to pay the bus fare. He had rushed out, sitting up all the way, and had arrived in Santa Monica light-headed and exhausted, just in time to be present for the big scene.

Jacob had brushed his hair and combed his beard, and had sat up in bed like Job arguing with God. He had kissed Mrs. Morton who was over fifty years old, and sent her from him, saying in his rolling, actorish voice, "I wish to die in the arms of my son. I wish to die among the Jews. Now we say goodbye."

That was the first time Noah had heard that Mrs. Morton wasn't Jewish. She wept, and the whole scene was like something from the second act of a Yiddish play on Second Avenue in New York. But Jacob had been adamant. Mrs. Morton had gone. Her married daughter had insisted on taking the weeping widow away to the family home in San Francisco. Noah was left alone with his father in the small room with the single bed on the side street a half mile from the winter ocean.

The doctor came for a few moments every morning. Aside from him, Noah didn't see anyone. He didn't know anyone else in the town. His father insisted that he stay at his side day and night, and Noah slept on the floor near the window, on a lumpy mattress that the hotel manager had grudgingly given him.

Noah listened to the heavy, tragic breathing, filling the medicine-smelling air. For a moment he was sure his father was awake and purposely breathing that way, labored and harsh, not because he had to, but because he felt that if a man lay dying, his every breath should announce that fact. Noah stared closely at his father's handsome patriarchal head on the dark pillow next to the dimly glinting array of medicine bottles. Once more Noah couldn't help feeling annoyed at the soaring, bushy, untrimmed eyebrows, the wavy, theatrical, coarse mane of hair, which Noah was sure his father secretly bleached white, the spectacular white beard on the lean, ascetic jaws. Why, Noah thought, irritably, why does he insist on looking like a Hebrew King, on an embassy to California? It would be different if he had lived that way . . . But with all the women he'd gone through in his long, riotous life, all the bankruptcies, all the money borrowed and never returned, all the creditors that stretched from Odessa to Honolulu, it was a sour joke on the world for his father to look like Moses coming down from Sinai with the stone tablets in his hands.

"Make haste," Jacob said, opening his eyes, "make haste, O God, to deliver me. Make haste to help me, O Lord."

That was another habit that had always infuriated Noah. Jacob knew the Bible by heart, both in Hebrew and English, although he was absolutely irreligious, and salted his speech with long, impressive quotations at all times.

"Deliver me, O my God, out of the hand of the wicked, out of the hand of the unrighteous and cruel man." Jacob rolled his head, facing the wall, and closed his eyes once more. Noah got up from his chair and went over to the bed and pulled the blankets up closer around his father's throat. But there was no sign from Jacob that he noticed any of this. Noah stared down at him for a moment, listening to the bitter breathing. Then he turned and went to the window. He opened the window and sniffed at the dank, rolling mist, freighted with the heavy smell of the sea. A car sped dangerously down the street between the straggling palms, and there was the sound of a horn blown in celebration, lost in the mist.

What a place, Noah thought irrelevantly, what a place to celebrate New Year's Eve! He shivered a little in the influx of cold air, but he kept the window open. He had been working in a mail-order house in Chicago as a filing clerk, and, being honest with himself, the excuse to come to California, even if it was to watch his father die, had been a welcome one. The sunny coast, the warm beaches, he had thought, the orchards tossing their leaves in the sun, the pretty girls . . . He grinned sourly as he looked around him. It had rained for a week. And his father was prolonging his death-scene interminably. Noah was down to his last seven dollars and he had found out that creditors had a lien on his father's photographic studio. Even under the best of circumstances, even if everything were sold at high prices, they could only hope to recover thirty cents on the dollar. Noah had gone down to the shabby little studio near the ocean and had peered in through the locked plate-glass door. His father had specialized in very artistic, very terrible retouched portraits of young women. A hundred heavy-lidded local beauties draped in black velvet, with startling high lights and slumbrous eyes had peered back at him through the dusty neglected glass. It was the sort of business his father had had again and again, from one end of the country to another, the sort of business that had driven Noah's mother to an early death, the sort of business that appears and disappears in down-at-the-heel buildings for a season, makes a ragged little flourish for a few months then vanishes, leaving behind it only some inconclusive, tattered books, a smattering of debts, a stock of aging photographs and advertising signs that are finally burned in a back alley when the next tenant arrives.

In his day Jacob had also sold cemetery lots, contraceptive devices, real estate, sacramental wine, advertising space, second-hand furniture, bridal clothing, and had even once, improbably, set himself up in a ship chandler's store in Baltimore, Maryland. And at no one of these professions had he ever made a living. And in all of them, with his deft, rolling tongue, his archaic rhetoric, loaded with Biblical quotations, with his intense, handsome face and vital, broad-handed movements, he had always found women who made up for him the difference in what he secured by his own efforts from the economic battlefield around him and what it took to keep him alive. Noah was his only child, and Noah's life had been wandering and disordered. Often he had been deserted, often left for long periods with vague, distant relatives, or, lonely and persecuted, in shabby military schools.

"They are burning my brother Israel in the furnace of the heathen."

Noah sighed and closed the window. Jacob was lying rigid now, staring up at the ceiling, his eyes wide open. Noah put on the single light which he had shaded with pink paper that was a little singed now in spots and added its small smell to the general sick-room atmosphere when the light was on.

"Is there anything I can do for you, Father?" Noah asked.

"I can see the flames," Jacob said. "I can smell the burning flesh. I can see my brother's bones crumbling in the fire. I deserted him and he is dying tonight among the foreigners."

Noah couldn't help being annoyed with his father. Jacob hadn't seen his brother in thirty-five years, had, in fact, left him in Russia to support their mother and father when Jacob had made his way to America. From everything that Noah had heard, Jacob had despised his brother, and they had parted enemies. But two years before, somehow, a letter from his brother had reached him from Hamburg, where Jacob's brother had gone in 1919. The letter had been desperate and pleading. Noah had to admit that Jacob had done everything he could—had written countless letters to the Immigration Bureau, had gone to Washington and haunted the corridors of the State Department buildings, an improbable, bearded, anachronistic, holy vision, half rabbi, half river-gambler, among the soft-spoken, impervious young men from Princeton and Harvard who shuffled the papers vaguely and disdainfully on their polished desks. But nothing had come of it, and after the single, wild cry for help, there had been the dreadful silence of official Germany, and Jacob had returned to his son and his photographic studio and his plump, widowed Mrs. Morton in Santa Monica and had said no more about it. But tonight, with the red-tinted fog sighing at the window, and the new year standing at the gate, and death, according to the doctor, a matter of hours, the deserted brother, caught in the welter of Europe, cried piercingly through the clouding brain.

"Flesh," Jacob said, his voice still rolling and deep, even on his last pillow, "flesh of my flesh, bone of my bone, you are being punished for the sins of my body and the sins of my soul."

O God, Noah thought, looking down at his father, why must he always speak like a blank-verse shepherd giving dictation to a secretary on a hill in Judea?

"Don't smile." Jacob peered sharply at him, his eyes surprisingly bright and knowing in the dark hollows of his face. "Don't smile, my son, my brother is burning for you."

"I'm not smiling, Father." Noah touched Jacob's forehead soothingly. The skin was hot and sandy and Noah could feel a small, twitching revulsion in his fingertips.

Jacob's face was contorted in oratorical scorn. "You stand there in your cheap American clothes and you think, 'What has he to do with me? He is a stranger to me. I have never seen him and if he dies, in the furnaces in Europe, what of it, people die every minute all over the world.' He is not a stranger to you. He is a Jew and the world is hunting him, and you are a Jew and the world is hunting you."

He closed his eyes in cold exhaustion and Noah thought, if he only talked in simple, honest language, you would be moved, affected. After all, a father dying, obsessed with the thought of a murdered brother five thousand miles away, a single man at his loneliest moment, feeling the ghost insecure and fleeting in his throat, mourning for the fate of his people all over the world, was a touching and tragic thing. And while it was true that to him, Noah, there was no sense of immediacy or personal tragedy in what was happening in Europe, intellectually and rationally he could feel the somber weight of it. But long years of his father's rhetoric, his father's stagy gesturing for effect, had robbed Noah of all ability to be moved by him. All he could think of as he stood there looking at the gray face, listening to the heaving breath, was, Good God, the old man is going to keep it up to the end.

"When I left him," his father said, without opening his eyes, "when I left Odessa in 1903, Israel gave me eighteen rubles and he said to me, 'You're no good. Congratulations. Take my advice. Stick to women. America can't be that different from the rest of the world. Women will be idiots there too. They will support you.' We didn't shake hands, and I left. He should have shaken my hand, no matter what, don't you think, Noah?" Suddenly his father's voice was changed. It was small and without timbre and it did not remind Noah of a stage performance.

"Noah . . ."

"Yes, Father?"

"Don't you think he should have shaken my hand?"

"Yes, Father."

"Noah . . ."

"Yes, Father. . . ."

"Shake my hand, Noah."

After a moment, Noah leaned over and picked up his father's dry, broad hand. The skin was flaked, and the nails, usually exquisitely cared for, pared and polished, were long and jagged and had crescents of dirt under them. They shook hands. Noah could feel the thin, restless, uneven pressure of the fingers.

"All right, all right . . ." Jacob said, suddenly peevish, and pulled his hand away, caught in some inexplicable vision of his own. "All right, enough." He sighed, stared up at the ceiling.

"Noah . . ."

"Yes?"

"Have you a pencil and paper?"

"Yes."

"Write this down . . ."

Noah went over to the table and sat down. He picked up a pencil and took out a sheet of flimsy white paper with an engraving of the Sea View Hotel on it, large, surrounded by sweeping lawns and tall trees, without basis of real life, but convincing and holiday-like on the stationery.

"To Israel Ackerman," Jacob said in a plain, business-like voice, "29 Kloster Strasse, Hamburg, Germany."

"But, Father," Noah began.

"Write it in Hebrew," Jacob said, "if you can't write German. He's not very well educated, but he'll manage to understand."

"Yes, Father." Noah couldn't write Hebrew or German, but he didn't see any sense in telling his father.

"My dear brother . . . Have you got that?"

"Yes, Father."

"I am ashamed of myself for not having written sooner," Jacob began, "but you can well imagine how busy I've been. Soon after coming to America . . . Have you got that, Noah?"

"Yes," Noah said, making aimless little scratches on the paper. "I have it."

"Soon after coming to America . . ." Jacob's voice rolled on, low and full of effort in the damp room, "I went into a large business. I worked hard, although I know you will not believe it, and I was promoted from one important position to another. In eighteen months I became the most valuable member of the firm. I was made a partner and I married the daughter of the owner of the business, a Mr. von Kramer, an old American family. I know you will be glad to know that we have a family of five sons and two daughters who are a joy and pride to their parents in our old age, and we have retired to an exclusive suburb of Los Angeles, a large city on the Pacific Ocean where it is sunny all the time. We have a fourteen-room house and I do not rise till nine-thirty every morning and I go to my club and play golf every afternoon. I know you will be interested in this information at this time . . ."

Noah felt a clot of emotion jammed in his throat. He had the wild notion that if he opened his mouth he would laugh, and that his father would die on peal after peal of his son's laughter.

"Noah," Jacob asked querulously, "are you writing this down?"

"Yes, Father." Somehow Noah managed to say it.

"It is true," Jacob went on in his calm, dictating voice, "that you are the oldest son and you were constantly giving advice. But now, oldest and youngest do not have the same meaning. I have traveled considerably, and I think maybe you can profit from some advice from me. It is important to remember how to behave as a Jew. There are many people in the world, and they are becoming more numerous, who are full of envy. They look at a Jew and say, 'Look at his table manners,' or 'The diamonds on his wife are really paste,' or 'See how much noise he makes in a theatre,' or 'His scales are crooked. You will not get your money's worth in his shop.' The times are getting more difficult and a Jew must behave as though the life of every other Jew in the world depended on every action of his. So he must eat quietly, using his knife and fork delicately. He must not put diamonds on his wife, especially paste ones. His scales must be the most honest in the city. He must walk in a dignified and self-respecting manner. No," Jacob cried, "cross all that out. It will only make him angry."

He took a deep breath and was silent for a long time. He didn't seem to move on his bed and Noah looked uneasily over at him to make sure he was still alive.

"Dear Brother," Jacob said, finally, his voice broken and hoarse, and unrecognizable, "everything I have told you is a lie. I have led a miserable life and I have cheated everyone and I drove my wife to her death and I have only one son and I have no hope for him and I am bankrupt and everything you have told me would happen to me has happened to me. . . ."

His voice stopped. He choked and tried to say something else, and then he died.

Noah touched his father's chest, searching for the beating of his heart. The skin was wrinkled and the bones of his chest were jagged and frail. The stillness under the parched, flaked skin and the naked bone was final.

Noah folded his father's hands on his chest, and closed the piercing, staring eyes, because he had seen people doing that in the movies. Jacob's mouth was open, with a realistic, alive expression, as though he were on the verge of speech, but Noah didn't know what to do about that, so he left it alone. As he looked down at his father's dead face, Noah could not help realizing that he felt relieved. It was over now. The demanding imperious voice was quiet. There would be no more gestures.

Noah walked around the room, flatly taking inventory of the things of value in it. There wasn't much. Two shabby, rather flashy double-breasted suits, a leather-bound edition of the King James Bible, a silver frame with a photograph of Noah, aged seven and on a Shetland pony, a small box with a pair of cufflinks and a tiepin, made of nickel and glass, a tattered red manila envelope with a string tied around it. Noah opened the envelope and took out the papers: twenty shares of stock in a radio-manufacturing corporation that had gone into bankruptcy in 1927.

There was a cardboard box on the bottom of the closet. Noah took it out and opened it. Inside, carefully wrapped in soft flannel, was a large, old-fashioned portrait camera, with a big lens. It was the one thing in the room which looked as though it had been treated with love and consideration, and Noah was grateful that his father had been crafty enough to hide it from his creditors. It might even pay for the funeral. Touching the worn leather and the polished glass of the camera, Noah thought, fleetingly, that it would be good to keep the camera, keep the one well-preserved remnant of his father's life, but he knew it was a luxury he could not afford. He put the camera back in the box, after wrapping it well, and hid the box under a pile of old clothes in the corner of the closet.

He went to the door and looked back. In the mean rays of the single lamp, his father looked forlorn and in pain on the bed. Noah turned the light off and went out.

He walked slowly down the street. The air and the slight exercise felt good after the week in the cramped room, and he breathed deeply, feeling his lungs fill, feeling young and healthy, listening to the soft muffled tap of his heels on the glistening sidewalks. The sea air smelt strange and clean in the deserted night, and he walked in the direction of the beach, the tang of salt getting stronger and stronger as he approached the cliff that loomed over the ocean.

Through the murk came the sound of music, echoing and fading, suddenly growing stronger, with tricks of the wind. Noah walked toward it and as he got to the corner, he saw that the music came from a bar across the street. People were going in and out under a sign that said, "No Extra Charge for the Holiday. Bring the New Year in at O'Day's."

The tune changed on the jukebox inside and a woman's low voice sang, "Night and day you are the one, Only you beneath the moon and under the sun," her voice dominating the empty, damp night with powerful, well-modulated passion.

Noah crossed the street, opened the door and went in. Two sailors and a blonde were at the other end of the bar, looking down at a drunk with his head on the mahogany. The bartender glanced up when Noah came in.

"Have you got a telephone?" Noah asked.

"Back there." The bartender motioned toward the rear of the room. Noah started toward the booth.

"Be polite, boys," the blonde was saying to the sailors as Noah passed. "Rub his neck with ice."

She smiled widely at Noah, her face green with the reflection from the jukebox. Noah nodded to her and stepped into the telephone booth. He took out a card that the doctor had given him. On it was the telephone number of a twenty-four-hour-a-day undertaker.

Noah dialed the number. He held the receiver to his ear, listening to the insistent buzzing in the earpiece, thinking of the phone on the dark, shiny desk, under a single shaded light in the mortuary office, ringing the New Year in. He was about to hang up when he heard a voice at the other end of the wire.

"Hello," the voice said, somehow vague and remote. "Grady Mortuary."

"I would like to inquire," Noah said, "about a funeral. My father just died."

"What is the name of the party?"

"What I wanted to know," said Noah, "is the range of prices. I haven't very much money and . . ."

"I will have to know the name of the party," the voice said, very official.

"Ackerman."

"Waterfield," said the thick voice on the other end. "First name, please . . ." and then, in a whisper, "Gladys, stop it! Gladys!" Then back into the phone, with the hint of a smothered laugh, "First name, please."

"Ackerman," said Noah. "Ackerman."

"Is that the first name?"

"No," said Noah. "That's the last name. The first name is Jacob."

"I wish," said the voice, with alcoholic dignity, "you would talk more clearly."

"What I want to know," said Noah loudly, "is what you charge for cremation."

"Cremation. Yes," the voice said, "we supply that service to those parties who wish it."

"What is the price?" Noah asked.

"How many coaches?"

"What?"

"How many coaches to the services?" the voice asked, saying "shervishes." "How many guests and relatives will there be?"

"One," said Noah. "There will be one guest and relative."

"Night and Day" came to an end with a crash and Noah couldn't hear what the man on the other end of the wire said.

"I want it to be as reasonable as possible," Noah said, desperately. "I don't have much money."

"I shee, I shee," the man at the Mortuary said. "One question, if I may. Does the deceased have any insurance?"

"No," said Noah.

"Then it will have to be cash, you understand. In advance, you understand."

"How much?" Noah shouted.

"Do you wish the remains in a plain cardboard box or in a silver plated urn?"

"A plain cardboard box."

"The cheapest price I can quote you, my dear friend . . ." The voice on the other end suddenly became large and coherent. ". . . is seventy-six dollars and fifty cents."

"That will be an additional five cents for five minutes," the operator's voice broke in.

"All right." Noah put another nickel into the box and the operator said, "Thank you." Noah said, "All right. Seventy-six dollars and fifty cents." Somehow he would get it together. "The day after tomorrow. In the afternoon." That would give him time to go downtown on January second and sell the camera and the other things. "The address is Sea View Hotel. Do you know where it is?"

"Yes," the drunken voice said, "yes, indeedy. The Sea View Hotel. I will send a man around tomorrow and you can sign the contract . . ."

"Okay," Noah said, sweating, preparing to hang up.

"One more thing, my dear man," the voice went on. "One more thing. The last rites."

"What about the last rites?"

"What religion does the deceased profess?"

Jacob had professed no religion, but Noah didn't think he had to tell the man that. "He was a Jew."

"Oh." There was silence for a moment on the wire and then Noah heard the woman's voice say, gayly and drunkenly, "Come on, George, les have another little drink."

"I regret," the man said, "that we are not equipped to perform funeral services on Hebrews."

"What's the difference?" Noah shouted. "He wasn't religious. He doesn't need any ceremonies."

"Impossible," the voice said thickly, but with dignity. "We do not cater to Hebrews. I'm sure you can find many others . . . many others who are equipped to cremate Hebrews."

"But Dr. Fishbourne recommended you," Noah shouted, insanely. He felt as though he couldn't go through all this again with another undertaker, and he felt trapped and baffled. "You're in the undertaking business, aren't you?"

"My condolences to you, my dear man," the voice said, "in your hour of grief, but we cannot see our way clear . . ."

Noah heard a scuffle at the other end of the wire and the woman's voice say, "Let me talk to him, Georgie." Then the woman got on the phone. "Listen," she said loudly, her voice brassy and whiskey-rich, "why don't you quit? We're busy here. You heard what Georgie said. He don't burn Kikes. Happy New Year." And she hung up.

.   .   .   .   .

Noah opened the door with careful deliberation, silently, and stepped into the dark room. The smell was there. He had forgotten the smell. Alcohol, medicine, something sweet and heavy . . . He fumbled for the light. He felt the nerves in his hand twitching and he stumbled against a chair before he found the lamp.

His father lay rigid and frail on the bed, his mouth open as if to speak in the bare light. Noah swayed a little as he looked down at him. Foolish, tricky old man, with the fancy beard and the bleached hair and the leatherbound Bible.

Make haste, make haste, O God, to deliver me . . . What religion does the deceased profess? Noah felt a little dizzy. His mind didn't seem to be able to fix on any one thing, and one thought slid in on top of another, independent and absurd. Full lips. Twenty-five dollars for the sailors and nothing for him. He had never had particular luck with women, certainly nothing like that. Trouble probably made a man attractive, and the woman had sensed it. Of course she had been terribly drunk . . . Ronald Beaverbrook. The way the flowers had waved on her skirt as she rolled toward the ladies' room. If he had stayed he'd probably be snug in bed with her now, under the warm covers, the soft, fat, white flesh, onion, gin, raspberry. He had a piercing, sharp moment of regret that he was standing here in the naked room with the dead old man . . . If the positions had been reversed, he thought, if it was he lying there and the old man up and around, and the old man had got the offer, he was damned sure Jacob would be in that bed now, with the blonde and the Four Roses. What a thing to think of. Noah shook his head. His father, from whose seed he sprang. God, was he going to get to talk like him as he grew older?

Noah made himself look for a whole minute at his father's dead face. He tried to cry. Somehow, deserted this way, at the end of a year, on this winter night, a man, any man, had the right to expect a tear from his only son.

Noah had never really thought very much about his father, once he had got old enough to think about him at all. He had been bitter about him, but that was all. Looking at the pale, lined head, looming from the pillow like a stone statue, noble and proud as Jacob had always known he would look in death, Noah made a conscious effort to think of his father. How far Jacob had come searching for this narrow room on the shore of the Pacific. Out of the grimy streets of Odessa, across Russia and the Baltic Sea, across the ocean, into the sweat and clangor of New York. Noah closed his eyes and thought of Jacob, quick and lithe, as a young man, with that handsome brow and that fierce nose, taking to English with a quick, natural, over blown rhetorical instinct, striding down the crowded streets, his eyes lively and searching, with a ready bold smile for girls and partners and customers and travel . . . Jacob, unafraid, and dishonest, wandering through the South, through Atlanta and Tuscaloosa, quick-fingered, never really interested in money, but cheating for it, and finally letting it slip away, up the continent to Minnesota and Montana, laughing, smoking black cigars, known in saloons and gambling halls, making dirty jokes and quoting Isaiah in the same breath, marrying Noah's mother in Chicago, grave-eyed and responsible for a day, tender and delicate and perhaps even resolved to settle down and be an honorable citizen, with middle age looming over him, and his hair touched at the ends with gray. And Jacob singing to Noah in his rich, affected baritone, in the plush-furnished parlor after dinner, singing, "I was walking through the park one day, In the merry, merry month of May . . ."

Noah shook his head. Somewhere in the back of his mind, echoing and faraway, the voice, singing, young and strong, resounded, "*In the merry, merry month of May,*" and refused to be stilled.

And the inevitable collapse as the years claimed Jacob. The shabby businesses, getting shabbier, the charm fading, the enemies more numerous, the world tighter-lipped and more firmly organized against him, the failure in Chicago, the failure in Seattle, the failure in Baltimore, the final, down-at-the-heels, scrubby failure in Santa Monica . . . "I have led a miserable life and I have cheated everyone and I drove my wife to death and I have only one son and I have no hope for him and I am bankrupt . . ." And the deceived brother, crumbling in the furnace, haunting him across the years and the ocean, with the last, agonized breath. . . .

Noah stared, dry-eyed at his father. Jacob's mouth was open, intolerably alive. Noah jumped up, and crossed the room, wavering, and tried to push his father's mouth shut. The beard was stiff and harsh against Noah's hand, and the teeth made a loud, incongruous clicking sound as the mouth closed. But the lips fell open, ready for speech, when Noah took his hand away. Again and again, more and more vigorously, Noah pushed the mouth shut. The hinges of the jaw made a sharp little sound and the jaw felt loose and unmoored, but each time Noah took his hand away the mouth opened, the teeth gleaming in the yellow light. Noah braced himself against the bed with his knees to give himself more leverage. But his father, who had been contrary and stubborn and intractable with his parents, his teachers, his brother, his wife, his luck, his partners, his women, his son, all his life, could not be changed now.

Noah stepped back. The mouth hung open, pitiful and pale under the swirling white moustaches, under the noble arch of the deceptive dead head on the gray pillow.

Finally, and for the first time, Noah wept.

Back in New York, Noah soon meets Hope, a lovely, determined young lady, who eventually takes him to her New England family for approval. Soon after their marriage Noah is drafted. At a camp in the South he gets the kike treatment. Money he has saved for a gift for Hope is stolen.

THERE WERE some men sleeping in the barracks when Noah got there. Donnelly was snoring drunkenly near the door, but no one paid any attention to him. Noah took down his barracks bag and with maniacal care he went through every article there, the extra shoes, the wool shirts, the clean fatigues, the green wool gloves, the can of shoe-dubbing. But the money wasn't there. Then he got down the other barracks bag, and went through that. The money wasn't there. From time to time he glanced up sharply, to see if any of the men were watching him. But they slept, in the snoring, hateful, unprivate, everlasting way. Good, he thought, if I caught any of them looking at me, I would kill them.

He put the scattered things back into the bags, then took out his box of stationery and wrote a short note. He put the box on his bunk and strode down to the orderly room. On the bulletin board outside the orderly room, along with the notices about brothels in town that were out of bounds and regulations for wearing the proper uniforms at the proper times, and the list of promotions that had come through that week, there was a space reserved for lost-and-found notices. Noah tacked his sheet of paper up on top of a plea by PFC O'Reilly for the return of a six-bladed penknife that had been taken from his foot-locker. There was a light hanging outside the orderly room, and in its frail glare, Noah re-read what he had written.

> *To the Personnel of Company C . . . Ten dollars has been stolen from the barracks bag of Private Noah Ackerman, 2nd Platoon. I am not interested in the return of the money and will press no charges. I wish to take my satisfaction, in person, with my own hands. Will the soldier or soldiers involved please communicate with me immediately.*
>
> > *Signed,*
> > *Private Noah Ackerman*

Noah read what he had written with pleasure. He had a feeling as he turned away, that he had taken the one step that would keep him from going mad.

The next evening, as he was going to the mess hall for supper, Noah stopped at the bulletin board. His notice was still there. And under it neatly typed, was a small sheet of paper. On the sheet of paper, there were two short sentences.

We took it, Jew-Boy. We're waiting for you.
                              Signed,

P. Donnelly	*B. Cowley*
J. Wright	*W. Demuth*
L. Jackson	*E. Riker*
M. Silichner	*R. Henkel*
P. Sanders	*T. Brailsford*

Michael was cleaning his rifle when Noah came up to him.

"May I talk to you for a moment?" Noah said.

Michael looked up at him with annoyance. He was tired and, as usual, he felt incompetent and uncertain with the intricate clever mechanism of the old Springfield.

"What do you want?" Michael asked.

Ackerman hadn't said a word to him since the moment on the hike.

"I can't talk in here," Noah said, glancing around him. It was after supper, and there were thirty or forty men in the barracks, reading, writing letters, fiddling with their equipment, listening to the radio.

"Can't it wait?" Michael asked coldly. "I'm pretty busy just now . . ."

"Please," Noah said. Michael glanced up at him. Ackerman's face was set in withered, trembling lines, and his eyes seemed to be larger and darker than usual. "Please . . ." he repeated. "I've got to talk to you. I'll wait for you outside."

Michael sighed. "O.K.," he said. He put the rifle together, wrestling with the bolt, ashamed of himself, as always, because it was so difficult for him. God, he thought, feeling his greasy hands slip along the oily stubborn surfaces, I can put on a play, discuss the significance of Thomas Mann, and any farm boy can do this with his eyes closed better than I can . . .

He hung the rifle up and went outside, wiping the oil off his hands. Ackerman was standing across the Company street in the darkness, a small, slender form outlined by a distant light. Ackerman waved to him in a conspiratorial gesture, and Michael slowly approached him, thinking, I get all the nuts . . .

"Read this," Noah said as soon as Michael got close to him. He thrust two sheets of paper into Michael's hand.

Michael turned so he could get some light on the papers. He squinted and read first the notice that Noah had put up on the bulletin board, which he had not read before, and the answer, signed by the ten names. Michael shook his head and read both notes over carefully.

"What the hell is this?" he asked irritably.

"I want you to act as my second," Noah said. His voice was dull and heavy, and even so, Michael had to hold himself back from laughing at the melodramatic request.

"Second?" he asked incredulously.

"Yes," said Noah. "I'm going to fight those men. And I don't trust myself to arrange it myself. I'll lose my temper and get into trouble. I want it to be absolutely correct."

Michael blinked. Of all the things you thought might happen to you before you went into the Army, you never imagined anything like this. "You're crazy," he said. "This is just a joke."

"Maybe," said Noah flatly. "Maybe I'm getting tired of jokes."

"What made you pick on me?" Michael asked.

Noah took a deep breath and Michael could hear the air whistling into the boy's nostrils. He looked taut and very handsome in a rough-cut, archaic, tragic way in the blocked light and shadows from the hanging lamp across the street. "You're the only one," Noah said, "I felt I could trust in the whole Company." Suddenly he grabbed the two sheets of paper. "O.K.," he said, "if you don't want to help, the hell with you . . ."

"Wait a minute," Michael said, feeling dully that somehow he must prevent this savage and ludicrous joke from being played out to its limit. "I haven't said I won't help."

"O.K., then," Noah said harshly. "Go in and arrange the schedule."

"What schedule?"

"There are ten of them. What do you want me to do—fight them in one night? I have to space them. Find out who wants to fight me first, who wants to fight me second, and so on. I don't care how they come."

Michael took the sheets of paper silently from Noah's hand and looked at the names on the list. Slowly he began to place the names. "You know," he said, "that these are the ten biggest men in the company."

"I know."

"Not one of them weighs under a hundred and eighty pounds."

"I know."

"How much do you weigh?"

"A hundred and thirty-five."

"They'll kill you."

"I didn't ask you for advice," Noah said evenly. "I asked you to make the arrangements. That's all. Leave the rest to me."

"I don't think the Captain will allow it," Michael said.

"He'll allow it," said Noah. "That son of a bitch will allow it. Don't worry about that."

Michael shrugged. "What do you want me to arrange?" he asked. "I can get gloves and two-minute rounds and a referee and . . ."

"I don't want any round or any referees," Noah said. "When one of the men can't get up any more, the fight will be over."

Michael shrugged again. "What about gloves?"

"No gloves. Bare fists. Anything else?"

"No," said Michael. "That's all."

"Thanks," Noah said. "Let me hear how you make out."

Without saying good-bye, he walked stiffly down the Company street. Michael watched the shadowy, erect back vanishing in the darkness. Then he shook his head once and walked slowly toward the barracks door, looking for the first man, Peter Donnelly, six feet one, weight one hundred and ninety-five, who had fought heavyweight in the Golden Gloves in Miami in 1941 and had not been put out until the semi-final round.

Donnelly knocked Noah down. Noah sprang up and jumped in the air to reach Donnelly's face. Donnelly began to bleed from the nose and he sucked in the blood at the corner of his mouth, with a look of surprise and anger that supplanted the professional expression he had been fighting with until now. He held Noah's back with one hand, ignoring the fierce tattoo of Noah's fist on his face, and pulled him toward him. He swung, a short, chopping vicious blow, and the men watching silently went "Ah." Donnelly swung again as Noah fell and Noah lay at his feet in the grass.

"I think," Michael said, stepping forward, "that that's enough for this . . ."

"Get the hell out of here," Noah said thickly, pushing himself up from the ground with his two hands.

He stood before Donnelly, wavering, blood filling the socket of his right eye. Donnelly moved in and swung, like a man throwing a baseball. There was the noise again, as it hit Noah's mouth, and the men watching went "Ah," again. Noah staggered back and fell against them, where they stood in a tight, hard-eyed circle, watching. Then he slid down and lay still. Michael went over to him and kneeled down. Noah's eyes were closed and he was breathing evenly.

"All right." Michael looked up at Donnelly. "Hurray for you. You won." He turned Noah over on his back and Noah opened his eyes, but there was no light of reason in them as they stared thoughtlessly up at the evening sky.

Quietly the circle of watching men broke up and started to drift away.

"What do you know," Michael heard Donnelly say as Michael put his hand under Noah's armpit and lifted him slowly to his feet. "What do you know, the little bastard gave me a bloody nose."

Michael stood at the latrine window, smoking a cigarette, watching Noah, bent over one of the sinks, washing his face with cold water. Noah was bare to the waist, and there were huge red blotches on his skin. Noah lifted his head. His right eye was closed by now, and the blood had not stopped coming from his mouth. He spat, and two teeth came out, in a gob of red.

Noah didn't look at the teeth, lying in the basin. He dried his face thoughtfully with his towel, the towel staining quickly.

"All right," Michael said, "I think that did it. I think you'd better cancel the rest . . ."

"Who's the next man on the list?"

"Listen to me," Michael said. "They'll kill you finally."

"The next man is Wright," Noah said flatly. "Tell him I'll be ready for him three nights from now." Without waiting for Michael to say anything, Noah wrapped the towel around his bare shoulders and went out the latrine door.

Michael looked after him, shrugged, took another drag on his cigarette, threw the cigarette away and went into the soft evening. He did not go into the barracks because he didn't want to see Ackerman again that evening.

Wright was the biggest man in the company. Noah did not try to avoid him. He stood up, in a severe, orthodox boxing pose, and flashed swiftly in and out among the flailing slow hands, cutting Wright's face, making him grunt when he hit him in the stomach.

Amazing, Michael thought, watching Noah with grudging admiration, he really knows how to box, where did he pick it up?

"In the belly," Rickett called from his post in the inner circle of the ring, "in the belly, you dumb bastard!" A moment later it was all over, because Wright swung sideways, all his weight behind a round, crushing swing. The knotted, hammerlike fist crashed into Noah's side. Noah tumbled across the cleared space to fall on his hands and knees, face down, tongue hanging thickly out of his open mouth, gasping helplessly for air.

The men who were watching looked on silently.

"Well?" said Wright, belligerently, standing over Noah. "Well?"

"Go home," Michael said. "You were wonderful."

Noah began to breathe again, the air struggling through his throat in hoarse, agonized whistles. Wright touched Noah contemptuously with his toe and turned away, saying, "Who's going to buy me a beer?"

The doctor looked at the x-rays and said that two ribs were broken. He taped Noah's chest with bandage and adhesive, and made Noah lie still in the infirmary bed.

"Now," Michael said, standing over Noah in the ward, "now, will you quit?"

"The doctor says it will take three weeks," Noah said, the speech coming painfully through his pale lips. "Arrange the next one for then."

"You're crazy," said Michael. "I won't do it."

"Deliver your goddamn lectures some place else," Noah whispered. "If you won't do it, you can leave now. I'll do it myself."

"What do you think you're doing?" Michael asked. "What do you think you're proving?"

Noah said nothing. He stared blankly and wildly across the ward at the man with a broken leg who had fallen off a truck two days before.

"What are you proving?" Michael shouted.

"Nothing," Noah said. "I enjoy fighting. Anything else?"

"No," said Michael. "Not a thing."

He went out.

"Captain," Michael was saying, "it's about Private Ackerman."

Colclough was sitting very erect, the little roll of fat under his chin lapping over his tight collar, making him look like a man who was slowly being choked.

"Yes," Colclough said, "What about Private Ackerman?"

"Perhaps you have heard about the . . . uh . . . dispute . . . that Private Ackerman is engaged in with ten members of the Company."

Colclough's mouth lifted a little in an amused grin. "I've heard something about it," he said.

"I think Private Ackerman is not responsible for his actions at this time," Michael said. "He is liable to be very seriously injured. Permanently injured. And I think, if you agreed with me, it might be a good idea to try to stop him from fighting any more . . ."

Colclough put his finger in his nose. He picked slowly at some obstacle there, then pulled his finger out and examined the treasure he had withdrawn. "In an army, Whitacre," he said in the even, sober tone which he must have heard from officiating ministers at so many funerals in Joplin, "a certain amount of friction between the men is unavoidable. I believe that the healthiest way of settling that friction is by fair and open fighting. These men, Whitacre, are going to be exposed to much worse than fists later on, much worse. Shot and shell, Whitacre," he said with grave relish. "Shot and shell. It would be unmilitary to forbid them to settle their differences now in this way, unmilitary. It is my policy, also, Whitacre, to allow as much freedom in handling their affairs as possible to the men in my Company, and I would not think of interfering."

"Yes, Sir," said Michael. "Thank you, Sir."

He saluted and went out.

Walking slowly down the Company street, Michael made a sudden decision. He could not remain here like this. He would apply for Officer Candidates' School. When he had first come into the Army, he had resolved to remain an enlisted man. First, he felt that he was a little too old to compete with the twenty-year-old athletes who made up the bulk of the candidate classes. And his brain was too set in its ways to take easily to any further schooling. And, more deeply, he had held back from being put into a position where the lives of other men, so many other men, would depend upon his judgment. He had never felt in himself any talent for military command. War, in all its thousand, tiny, mortal particulars, seemed to him, even after all the months of training, like an impossible, deadly puzzle. It was all right to work at the puzzle as an obscure, single figure, at someone else's command. But to grapple with it on your own initiative . . . to send forty men at it, where every mistake might be compounded into forty graves . . . But now there was nothing else to do. If the Army felt that men like Colclough could be entrusted with two hundred and fifty lives, then no over-nicety of self-assessment, no modesty or fear of responsibility should hold one back. Tomorrow, Michael thought, I'll fill in the form and hand it in to the orderly room. And, he thought grimly, in my Company, there will be no Ackermans sent to the infirmary with broken ribs . . .

Five weeks later Noah was back in the infirmary again. Two more teeth had been knocked out in his mouth, and his nose had been smashed. The dentist was making him a bridge so that he could eat, and the surgeon kept taking crushed pieces of bone out of his nose on every visit.

By this time Michael could hardly speak to Noah. He came to the infirmary and sat on the end of Noah's bed, and they both avoided each other's eyes, and were glad when the orderly came through, crying, "All visitors out."

Noah had worked his way through five of the list by now, and his face was crooked and lumpy, and one ear was permanently disfigured in a flat, creased cauliflower. His right eyebrow was split and a white scar ran diagonally across it, giving the broken eyebrows a wild, interrogating twist. The total effect of his face, the steady, wild eyes, staring out of the dark, broken face, was infinitely disturbing.

After the eighth fight, Noah was in the infirmary again. He had been hit in the throat. The muscles there had been temporarily paralyzed and his larynx had been injured. For two days the doctor was of the opinion that he would never be able to speak again.

"Soldier," the doctor had said, standing over him, a puzzled look on his simple college-boy face, "I don't know what you're up to, but whatever it is I don't think it's worth it. I've got to warn you that it is impossible to lick the United States Army singlehanded . . ." He leaned down and peered troubledly at Noah. "Can you say anything?"

Noah's mouth worked for a long time, without sound. Then a hoarse, croaking small noise came from between the swollen lips. The doctor bent over closer. "What was that?" he asked.

"Go peddle your pills, Doc," Noah said, "and leave me alone."

The doctor flushed. He was a nice boy but he was not accustomed to being talked to that way any more, now that he was a Captain.

He straightened up. "I'm glad to see," he said stiffly, "that you've regained the gift of speech."

He wheeled and stalked out of the ward.

Fein, the other Jew in the Company, came into the ward, too. He stood uneasily next to Noah's bed, twisting his cap in his large hands.

"Listen, Pal," he said, "I didn't want to interfere here, but enough's enough. You're going at this all wrong. You can't start swinging every time you hear somebody say Jew bastard . . ."

"Why not?" Noah grimaced painfully at him.

"Because it ain't practical," Fein said. "That's why. First of all, you ain't big enough. Second of all, even if you was as big as a house and you had a right hand like Joe Louis, it wouldn't do no good. There's a certain number of people in this world that say Jew bastard automatically, and nothing you do or I do or any Jew docs will ever change 'em. And this way, you make the rest of the guys in the outfit think all Jews're crazy. Listen, they're not so bad, most of 'em. They sound a lot worse than they are, because they don't know no better. They started out feeling sorry for you, but now, after all these goddamned fights, they're beginning to think Jews are some kind of wild animal. They're beginning to look at *me* queer now . . ."

"Good," Noah said hoarsely. "Delighted."

"Listen," Fein said patiently, "I'm older than you and I'm a peaceful man. I'll kill Germans if they ask me to, but I want to live in peace with the guys around me in the Army. The best equipment a Jew can have is one deaf ear. When some of these bastards start to shoot their mouths off about the Jews that's the ear you turn that way, the deaf one . . . You let them live and maybe they'll let you live. Listen, the war ain't going to last forever, and then you can pick your company. Right now, the government says you got to live with these miserable Ku Kluxers, O.K., what're you going to do about it? Listen, Son, if all the Jews'd been like you we'd've all been wiped out 2000 years ago . . ."

"Good," Noah said.

"Ah," Fein said disgustedly, "maybe they're right, maybe you are cracked. Listen, I weigh two hundred pounds, I could beat anyone in this Company with one hand tied behind me. But you ain't noticed me fightin', do you? I ain't had a fight since I put on the uniform. I'm a practical man!"

Noah sighed. "The patient is tired, Fein," he said. "He's in no condition to listen to the advice of practical men."

Fein stared at him heavily, groping despairingly with the problem. "The question I ask myself," he said, "is what do you want, what in hell do you want?"

Noah grinned painfully. "I want every Jew," he said, "to be treated as though he weighed two hundred pounds."

"It ain't practical," Fein said. "Ah, the hell with it, you want to fight, go ahead and fight. I'll tell you the truth, I feel I understand these Georgia crackers who didn't wear shoes till the Supply Sergeant put them on their feet better than I understand you." He put on his cap with ponderous decision. "Little guys," he said, "that's a race all by itself. I can't make head or tail of them."

And he went out, showing, in every line of his enormous shoulders and thick neck and bullet head, his complete disapproval of the battered boy in the bed, who by some trick and joke of Fate and registration was somehow linked with him.

It was the last fight and if he stayed down it would be all over. He peered bloodily up from the ground at Brailsford, standing above him in pants and undershirt. Brailsford seemed to flicker against the white ring of faces and the vague wash of the sky. This was the second time Brailsford had knocked him down. But he had closed Brailsford's eye and made him cry out with pain when he hit him in the belly. If he stayed down, if he merely stayed where he was on one knee, shaking his head to clear it, for another five seconds, the whole thing would be over. The ten men would be behind him, the broken bones, the long days in the hospital, the nervous vomiting on the days when the fights were scheduled, the dazed, sick roaring of the blood in his ears when he had to stand up once more and face the onrushing, confident, hating faces and the clubbing fists.

Five seconds more, and it would be proved. He would have done it. Whatever he had set out to demonstrate, and it was dim and anguished now, would have been demonstrated. They would have to realize that he had won the victory over them. Nine defeats and one default would not have been enough. The spirit only won when it made the complete tour of sacrifice and pain. Even these ignorant, brutal men would realize now, as he marched with them, marched first down the Florida roads, and later down the roads swept by gunfire, that he had made a demonstration of will and courage that only the best of them could have been capable of . . .

All he had to do was to remain on one knee.

He stood up.

He put up his hands and waited for Brailsford to come at him. Slowly, Brailsford's face swam into focus. It was white and splotched now with red, and it was very nervous. Noah walked across the patch of grass and hit the white face, hard, and Brailsford went down. Noah stared dully at the sprawled figure at his feet. Brailsford was panting hard, and his hands were pulling at the grass.

"Get up, you yellow bastard," a voice called out from the watching men. Noah blinked. It was the first time anyone but himself had been cursed on this spot.

Brailsford got up. He was fat and out of condition, because he was the Company Clerk and always managed to find excuses to duck out of heavy work. His breath was sobbing in his throat. As Noah moved in on him, there was a look of terror on his face. His hands waved vaguely in front of him.

"No, no . . ." he said pleadingly.

Noah stopped and stared at him. He shook his head and plodded in. Both men swung at the same time, and Noah went down again. Brailsford was a large man and the blow had hit high on Noah's temple. Methodically, sitting with his legs crumpled under him, Noah took a deep breath. He looked up at Brailsford.

The big man was standing above him, his hands held tightly before him. He was breathing heavily, and he was whispering, "Please, please . . ." Sitting there, with his head hammering, Noah grinned, because he knew what Brailsford meant. He was pleading with Noah to stay down.

"Why, you miserable hillbilly son of a bitch," Noah said clearly. "I'm going to knock you out." He stood up and grinned as he saw the flare of anguish in Brailsford's eyes when he swung at him.

Brailsford hung heavily on him, clinching, swinging with a great show of willingness. But the blows were soft and nervous and Noah didn't feel them. Clutched in the big man's fat embrace, smelling the sweat rolling off his skin, Noah knew that he had beaten Brailsford merely by standing up. After this it was merely a matter of time. Brailsford's nerve had run out.

Noah ducked away and lashed out at Brailsford's middle. The blow landed and Noah could feel the softness of the clerk's belly as his fist dug in.

Brailsford dropped his hands to his sides and stood there, weaving a little, a stunned plea for pity in his eyes. Noah chuckled. "Here it comes, Corporal," he said, and drove at the white, bleeding face. Brailsford just stood there. He wouldn't fall and he wouldn't fight and Noah merely stood flat on the balls of his feet, hooking at the collapsing face. "Now," he said, swinging with all his shoulder, all his body behind the driving, cutting blow. "Now. Now." He gained in power. He could feel the electric life pouring down his arms into his fists. All his enemies, all the men who had stolen his money, cursed him on the march, driven his wife away, were standing there, broken in nerve, bleeding before him. Blood sprayed from his knuckles every time he hit Brailsford's staring, agonized face.

"Don't fall, Corporal," Noah said, "don't fall yet, please don't fall," and swung again and again, faster and faster, his fists making a sound like mallets wrapped in wet cloth. And when he saw Brailsford finally begin to sway, he tried to hold him with one hand long enough to hit him twice more, three times, a dozen, and he sobbed when he no longer could hold the rubbery bloody mess up. Brailsford slipped to the ground.

Noah turned to the watching men. He dropped his hands. No one would meet his eyes. "All right," he said loudly. "It's over."

But they didn't say anything. As though at a signal, they turned their backs and started to walk away. Noah stared at the retreating forms, dissolving in the dusk among the barracks walls. Brailsford still lay where he fell. No one had stayed with him to help him.

Michael touched Noah. "Now," Michael said, "let's wait for the German Army."

Noah shook off the friendly hand. "They all walked away," he said. "The bastards just walked away." He looked down at Brailsford. The clerk had come to, although he still lay face down on the grass. He was crying. Slowly and vaguely he moved a hand up to his eyes. Noah went over to him and kneeled beside him.

"Leave your eye alone," he ordered. "You'll rub dirt in it this way." He started to pull Brailsford to his feet and Michael helped him. They had to support the clerk all the way to the barracks and they had to wash his face for him and clean the cuts because Brailsford just stood in front of the mirror with his hands at his side, weeping helplessly.

We have met Christian Diestl as a ski instructor before the war, and again in the conquest of France, when he traps and kills some soldiers of the Resistance holding a roadblock. We meet him on leave in Berlin, making love to his officer's wife. And then in North Africa, where he saves himself in the retreat, with more cool killing. And again in France, in the invasion battle, where he kills, kills. And finally we find him across the Rhine, in the homeland, in the debacle.

IT DIDN'T LOOK BAD, it looked almost like an ordinary Army camp, quite pleasant, in the middle of wide green fields, with the sloping, forested hills behind it. The barracks-like buildings were a little close together, and the doubled, barbed-wire fences, spaced with watch towers, tipped you off, of course—and the smell. Two hundred meters away, the smell suffused the air, like a gas that, by a trick of chemistry, is just about to be transformed into a solid.

Still, Christian didn't stop. He limped hurriedly along the road toward the main gate, through the shining spring morning. He had to get something to eat, and he needed information. Maybe somebody inside the camp was in telephone communication with a functioning headquarters, or had been listening to the radio. . . . Maybe, he thought hopefully, remembering the retreat in France, maybe I can even pick up a bicycle.

.   .   .   .   .

"Open the gate," Christian said. "I want to go in."

"You want to go in?" the guard said incredulously. "What for?"

"I am making a list of summer resorts for the Strength Through Joy Headquarters in Berlin," Christian said, "and this camp has been suggested to me. Open up. I need something to eat, and I want to see if I can borrow a bicycle."

The guard signaled to another guard in the tower, who had been watching Christian carefully. The gate slowly began to swing open.

"You won't find a bicycle," the Volkssturm man said. "The SS took everything with wheels away with them when they went last week."

"I'll see," Christian said. He went through the double gates, deep into the smell, toward the Administration Building, a pleasant-looking Tyrolean-style chalet, with a green lawn and whitewashed stones, and a tall flagpole with the banner fluttering from it in the brisk morning wind. There was a low, hushed, non-human sounding murmur, coming from the barracks. It seemed to come from some new kind of musical instrument, designed to project notes too formless and un-pleasant for an organ to manage. All the windows were boarded up, and there were no human beings to be seen within the compound.

Christian mounted the scrubbed stone steps of the chalet and went inside.

He found the kitchen and got some sausage and ersatz coffee from a gloomy sixty-year-old uniformed cook, who said, encouragingly, "Eat hearty, Boy, who knows when we'll ever eat again."

There were quite a few of the misfits of the Volkssturm huddled uneasily in their second-hand uniforms along the halls of the Admin-istration Building. They held weapons, but did so gingerly, and with clear expressions of distaste. They, too, like the guard at the gate, were waiting. They stared unhappily at Christian as he passed among them, and Christian could sense a whisper of disapproval, disapproval for his youth, for the losing war he had fought . . . The young men, Hit-ler had always boasted, were his great strength, and now these make-shift soldiers, torn at the heel end of a war from their homes, showed, by the slight grimaces on their worn faces, what they thought of the retreating generation which had brought them to this hour.

Christian walked very erect, holding his Schmeisser lightly, his face cold and set, among the aimless men in the halls. He reached the Commandant's office, knocked, and went in. A prisoner in his striped suit was mopping the floor, and a Corporal was sitting at a desk in the outer office. The door to the private office was open, and the man sitting at the desk there motioned for Christian to come in when he heard Christian say, "I wish to speak to the Commandant."

The Commandant was the oldest Lieutenant Christian had ever seen. He looked well over sixty, with a face that seemed to have been put together out of flaky cheese.

"No, I have no bicycles," the Lieutenant said in his cracked voice, in answer to Christian's request. "I have nothing. Not even any food. They left us here with nothing, the SS. Just orders to remain in con-trol. I got through to Berlin yesterday and some idiot on the phone told me to kill everybody here immediately." The Lieutenant laughed sourly. "Eleven thousand men. Very practical. I haven't been able to reach anybody since then." He stared at Christian. "You have come from the front?"

Christian smiled. "Front is not exactly the word I would use."

The Lieutenant sighed, his cheese-like face pale and creased. "In the last war," he said, "it was very different. We retreated in the most orderly manner. My entire Company marched into Munich, still in possession of their weapons. It was much more orderly," he said, the accusation against the new generation of Germans, who did not know how to lose a war in an orderly manner, like their fathers, quite clear in his tone.

"Well, Lieutenant," Christian said, "I see you can't help me. I shall be moving on."

"Tell me," the old Lieutenant said, appealing to Christian to stay just another moment, as though he were lonely here in the pretty, well-cleaned office, with colored drapes on the windows, and the rough cloth sofa, and the bright blue picture of the Alps in winter on the paneled wall, "tell me, do you think the Americans will get here today?"

"I couldn't say, Sir," Christian said. "Haven't you been listening on the radio?"

"The radio." The Lieutenant sighed. "It is very confusing. This morning, from Berlin, there was a rumor the Russians and the Americans were fighting each other along the Elbe. Do you think that is possible?" he asked eagerly. "After all, we all know, eventually, it is inevitable . . ."

The myth, Christian thought, the continuing, suicidal myth. "Of course, Sir," he said clearly, "I would not be at all surprised." He started toward the door, but he stopped when he heard the noise.

It was a flood-like murmur, growing swiftly in volume, swirling in through the open windows, past the pretty drapes. Then the murmur was punctuated, sharply, by shots. Christian ran to the window and looked out. Two men in uniform were running heavily toward the Administration Building. As they ran, Christian saw them throw away their rifles. They were portly men, who looked like advertisements for Munich beer, and running came hard to them. From around the corner of one of the barracks, first one man in prisoner's clothes, then three more, then what looked like hundreds more, ran in a mob, after the two guards. That was where the murmur was coming from. The first prisoner stopped for a moment and picked up one of the discarded rifles. He did not fire it, but carried it, as he chased the guards. He was a tall man with long legs, and he gained with terrible rapidity on the guards. He swung the rifle like a club, and one of the beer advertisements went down. The second guard, seeing that he was too far from the safety of the Administration Building to make it before he was overtaken, merely lay down. He lay down slowly, like an elephant in the circus, first settling on his knees, then, with his hips still high in the air, putting his head down to the ground, trying to burrow it. The prisoner swung the rifle butt again and brained the guard.

"Oh, my God," the Lieutenant whispered at the window.

The crowd was around the two dead men now, enveloping them. The prisoners made very little noise as they trampled over the two dead forms, stamping hard again and again, each prisoner jostling the other, seeing some small spot on the dead bodies to kick.

The Lieutenant pulled away from the window and leaned tremblingly against the wall. "Eleven thousand of them . . ." he said. "In ten minutes they'll all be loose."

There were some shots from near the gate, and three or four of the prisoners went down. Nobody paid much attention to them, and part of the crowd surged, with that dull, flickering non-tonal murmur, in the direction of the gate.

From other barracks other crowds appeared, coming into view swiftly, like herds of bulls in the movies of Spain. Here and there they had caught a guard, and they made a community business of killing the man.

There were screams from the corridor outside. The Lieutenant, fumbling at his pistol, with his dear memories of the orderly defeat of the last war bitter in his brain, went out to rally his men.

Christian moved away from the window, trying to think quickly, cursing himself for being caught like this. After all he'd been through, after so many battles, after facing so many tanks, artillery pieces, so many trained men, to walk of his own free will into something like this . . .

Christian went out into the other office. The trusty was there alone, near the window. "Get in here," Christian said. The trusty looked at him coldly, then walked slowly into the private office. Christian closed the door, eyeing the prisoner. Luckily, he was a good size. "Take off your clothes," Christian said.

Methodically, without saying anything, the prisoner took off his loose striped-cotton jacket and began on his trousers. The noise was getting worse outside, and there was quite a bit of shooting now.

"Hurry!" Christian ordered.

The man had his trousers off by now. He was very thin and he had grayish, sackcloth underwear on. "Come over here," Christian said.

The man walked slowly over and stood in front of Christian. Christian swung his machine pistol. The barrel caught the man above the eyes. He took one step back, then dropped to the floor. There was almost no mark above his eyes. Christian took him by the throat with both hands and dragged him over to a closet door on the other side of the room. Christian opened the closet and pulled the unconscious man into it. There was an officer's overcoat hanging in the closet and two dress tunics and they gave off a slight smell of cologne.

Christian closed the closet and went over to where the prisoner's clothes lay on the floor. He started to unbutton his tunic. But the noise outside seemed to grow louder, and there was confused shouting in the corridor. He decided he didn't have time. Hurriedly, he put the pants on over his own trousers, and wrestled into the coat. He buttoned it up to the neck. He looked into the mirror on the closet door. His uniform didn't show. He looked hastily around for a place to hide the gun, then bent down and threw it under the couch. It would hold there for awhile. He still had his trenchknife in its holster under the striped coat. The coat smelled strongly of chlorine and sweat.

Christian went to the window. New batches of prisoners, the doors of their barracks battered down, were swirling around below. They were still finding guards and killing them, and Christian could hear firing from the other side of the Administration Building, although on this side, no one seemed to be trying to handle the prisoners at all. Some of the prisoners were knocking down a double door on a barn-like structure a hundred meters away. When the door went down, a large number of the prisoners surged through it and came back eating raw potatoes and uncooked flour, which smeared their hands and faces a powdery white. Christian saw one prisoner, a huge man, bent over a guard, whom he held between his knees, choking him. The huge man suddenly dropped the guard, who was still alive, and bulled his way into the warehouse. Christian saw him come out a minute later with his hands full of potatoes.

Christian kicked open the window and, without hesitating, swung out. He held by his fingers for a second, and dropped. He fell to his knees, but got right up. There were hundreds of men all around him, all dressed like him, and the smell and the noise were overpowering.

Christian started toward the gate, turning the corner of the Administration Building. A gaunt man with the socket of one eye showing in empty, scarred tissue was leaning against the wall. He stared very hard at Christian and began to follow him. Christian was certain the man suspected him, and tried to move quickly, without attracting attention. But the crowd of men in front of the Administration Building was very dense now, and the man with one eye hung on, right behind Christian.

The guards in the building had surrendered by now, and were coming out of the front door in pairs. For a moment, the newly released men were strangely quiet, staring at their erstwhile captors. Then a big man with a bald head took out a rusty pocket knife. He said something in Polish and grabbed the nearest guard and began to saw away at his throat. The knife was blunt and it took a long time. The guard who was being slaughtered did not struggle or cry out. It was as though torture and death in this place were so commonplace that even the victims fell into it naturally, no matter who they were. The futility of crying out for mercy had been so well demonstrated here, so long ago, that no man wasted his breath today. The trapped guard, a clerkish man of forty-five, merely slumped close against the man who was murdering him, staring at him, their eyes six inches apart, until the rusty knife finally broke through the vein and he slid down to the lawn.

This was a signal for the execution of the other guards. Due to the lack of weapons, many of them were trampled to death. Christian watched, not daring to show anything on his face, not daring to make a break, because the man with one eye was directly behind him, pressing against his shoulders.

"You . . ." The man with one eye said. Christian could feel his hand clutching at his coat, feeling the cloth of his uniform underneath. "I want to talk to . . ."

Suddenly Christian moved. The ancient Commandant was against the wall near the front door and the men had not reached him yet. The Commandant stood there, his hands making small, placating gestures in front of him. The men around him, starved and bony, were for the moment too exhausted to kill him. Christian lurched through the ring of men and grabbed the Commandant by the throat.

"Oh, God," the man shouted, very loud. It was a surprising sound, because all the rest of the killing had taken place so quietly.

Christian took out his knife. Holding the Commandant pinned against the wall with one hand, he cut his throat. The man made a gurgling, wet sound, then screamed for a moment. Christian wiped his hands against the man's tunic and let him drop. Christian turned to see if the man with one eye was still watching him. But the man with one eye had moved off, satisfied.

Christian sighed and, still carrying his knife in his hand, went through the hall of the Administration Building and up the steps to the Commandant's office. There were bodies on the steps, and liberated prisoners were overturning desks and scattering paper everywhere.

There were three or four men in the Commandant's office. The door to the closet was open. The half-naked man Christian had hit was still lying there as he had fallen. The prisoners were taking turns drinking brandy out of a decanter on the Commandant's desk. When the decanter was empty, one of the men threw it at the bright-blue picture of the Alps in winter on the wall.

Nobody paid any attention to Christian. He bent down and took his machine pistol out from under the couch.

Christian went back into the hall and through the aimlessly milling prisoners to the front door. Many of them had weapons by now, and Christian felt safe in carrying his Schmeisser openly. He walked slowly, always in the middle of groups, because he did not want to be seen by himself, standing out in relief so that some sharp-eyed prisoner would notice that his hair was longer than anyone else's, and that he had considerably more weight on his bones than most of the others.

He reached the gates. The middle-aged guard who had greeted him and let him in was lying sprawled against the barbed wire, an expression that looked like a smile on his dead face. There were many prisoners at the gate, but very few were going out. It was as though they had accomplished as much as was humanly possible for one day. The liberation from the barracks had exhausted their concept of freedom. They merely stood at the open gate, staring out at the rolling green countryside, at the road down which the Americans would soon come and tell them what to do. Or perhaps so much of their most profound emotion was linked with this place that now, in the moment of deliverance, they could not bear to leave it, but must stay and slowly examine the place where they had suffered and where they had had their vengeance.

Christian pushed through the knot of men near the dead Volkssturm soldier. Carrying his weapon, he walked briskly down the road, back toward the advancing Americans. He did not dare go the other way, deeper into Germany, because one of the men at the gate might have noticed it and challenged him.

Christian walked swiftly, limping a little, breathing deeply of the fresh spring air to get the smell of the camp from his nostrils. He was very tired, but he did not slacken his pace. When he was a safe distance away, out of sight of the camp, he turned off the road. He made a wide swing across the fields and circled the camp safely. Coming through the budding woods, with the smell of pine in his nostrils and the small forest flowers pink and purple underfoot, he saw the road, empty and sunfreckled, ahead of him. But he was too tired to go any farther at the moment. He took off the chlorine- and sweat-smelling garments of the trusty, rolled them into a bundle and threw them under a bush. Then he lay down, using a root as a pillow. The new grass, spearing through the forest floor around him, smelled fresh and green. In the boughs above his head two birds sang to each other, making a small blue-and-gold flicker as they darted among the shaking branches in and out of the sunlight. Christian sighed, stretched, and fell asleep.

THE MEN in the trucks fell quiet as they drove up to the open gates. The smell, by itself, would have been enough to make them silent, but there was also the sight of the dead bodies sprawled at the gate and behind the wire, and the slowly moving mass of scarecrows in tattered striped suits who engulfed the trucks and Captain Green's jeep in a monstrous tide.

They did not make much noise. Many of them wept, many of them tried to smile, although the objective appearance of their skull-like faces and their staring, cavernous eyes did not alter very much, either in weeping or smiling. It was as though these creatures were too far sunk in a tragedy which had moved off the plane of human reaction onto an animal level of despair—and the comparatively sophisticated grimaces of welcome, sorrow and happiness were, for the time being, beyond their primitive reach. Michael could tell, staring at the rigid, dying masks, that a man here and there thought he was smiling, but it took an intuitive act of understanding.

They hardly tried to talk. They merely touched things—the metal of the truck bodies, the uniforms of the soldiers, the barrels of the rifles—as though only by the shy investigation of their fingertips could they begin to gain knowledge of this new and dazzling reality.

Green ordered the trucks left where they were, with guards on them, and led the Company slowly through the hive-like cluster of released prisoners, into the camp.

Michael and Noah were right behind Green when he went through the doorway of the first barracks. The door had been torn off and most of the windows had been broken open, but even so, the smell was beyond the tolerance of human nostrils. In the murky air, pierced ineffectually here and there by the dusty beams of spring sunshine, Michael could see the piled, bony forms. The worst thing was that from some of the piles there was movement, a languidly waving arm, the slow lift of a pair of burning eyes in the stinking gloom, the pale twisting of lips on skulls that seemed to have met death many days before. In the depths of the building, a form detached itself from a pile of rags and bones and started a slow advance on hands and knees toward the door. Nearer by, a man stood up and moved, like a mechanical figure, crudely arranged for the process of walking, toward Green. Michael could see that the man believed he was smiling, and he had his hand outstretched in an absurdly commonplace gesture of greeting. The man never reached Green. He sank to the slime-covered floor, his hand still outstretched. When Michael bent over him he saw that the man had died.

The center of the world, something repeated insanely and insistently in Michael's brain, as he kneeled above the man who had died with such ease and silence before their eyes. I am now at the center of the world, the center of the world.

The dead man, lying with outstretched hand, had been six feet tall. He was naked and every bone was clearly marked under the skin. He could not have weighed more than seventy-five pounds, and, because he was so lacking in the usual, broadening cover of flesh, he seemed enormously elongated, supernaturally tall and out of perspective.

There were some shots outside, and Michael and Noah followed Green out of the barracks. Thirty-two of the guards, who had barricaded themselves in a brick building which contained the ovens in which the Germans had burned prisoners, had given themselves up when they saw the Americans, and Crane had tried to shoot them. He had managed to wound two of the guards before Houlihan had torn his rifle away from him. One of the wounded guards was sitting on the ground, weeping, holding his stomach, and blood was coming in little spurts over his hands. He was enormously fat, with beer-rolls on the back of his neck, and he looked like a spoiled pink child sitting on the ground, complaining to his nurse.

Crane was standing with his arms clutched by two of his friends, breathing very hard, his eyes rolling crazily. When Green ordered the guards to be taken into the Administration Building for safekeeping, Crane lashed out with his feet and kicked the fat man he had shot.

The fat man wept loudly. It took four men to carry the fat man into the Administration Building.

There was not much Green could do. But he set up his Headquarters in the Commandant's room of the Administration Building and issued a series of clear, simple orders, as though it was an everyday affair in the American Army for an Infantry Captain to arrive at the chaos of the center of the world and set about putting it to rights. He sent his jeep back to request a medical team and a truckload of ten-in-one rations. He had all the Company's food unloaded and stacked under guard in the Administration Building, with orders to dole it out only to the worst cases of starvation that were found and reported by the squads working through the barracks. He had the German guards segregated at the end of the hall outside his door, where they could not be harmed.

Michael, who, with Noah, was serving as a messenger for Green, heard one of the guards complaining, in good English, to Pfeiffer, who had them under his rifle, that it was terribly unjust, that they had just been on duty in this camp for a week, that they had never done any harm to the prisoners, that the men of the SS battalion who had been there for years and who had been responsible for all the torture and privation in the camp, were going off scot-free, were probably in an American prison stockade at that moment, drinking orange juice. There was considerable justice in the poor Volkssturm guard's complaint, but Pfeiffer merely said, "Shut your trap before I put my boot in it."

The liberated prisoners had a working committee, which they had secretly chosen a week before, to govern the camp. Green called in the leader of the committee, a small, dry man of fifty, with a curious accent and a quite formal way of handling the English language. The man's name was Zoloom, and he had been in the Albanian Foreign Service before the war. He told Green he had been a prisoner for three and a half years. He was completely bald and had pebbly little dark eyes, set in a face that somehow was still rather plump. He had an air of authority and was quite helpful to Green in securing work parties among the healthier prisoners, to carry the dead from the barracks, and collect and classify the sick into dying, critical and out-of-danger categories. Only those people in the critical category, Green ordered, were to be fed out of the small stocks of food that had been collected from the trucks and the almost empty storerooms of the camp. The dying were merely laid side by side along one of the streets, to extinguish themselves in peace, consoled finally by the sight of the sun and the fresh touch of the spring air on their wasted foreheads.

As the first afternoon wore on, and Michael saw the beginning of order that Green, in his ordinary, quiet, almost embarrassed way, had brought about, he felt an enormous respect for the dusty little Captain with the high, girlish voice. Everything in Green's world, Michael suddenly realized, was fixable. There was nothing, not even the endless depravity and bottomless despair which the Germans had left at the swampheart of their dying millennium, which could not be remedied by the honest, mechanic's common sense and energy of a decent workman. Looking at Green giving brisk, sensible orders to the Albanian, to Sergeant Houlihan, to Poles and Russians and Jews and German Communists, Michael knew that Green didn't believe he was doing anything extraordinary, anything that any graduate of the Fort Benning Infantry Officers' Candidate School wouldn't do in his place.

Watching Green at work, as calm and efficient as he would have been sitting in an orderly room in Georgia making out duty rosters, Michael was glad that he had never gone to Officers' School. I could never have done it, Michael thought, I would have put my head in my hands and wept until they took me away. Green did not weep. In fact, as the afternoon wore on, his voice, in which no sympathy had been expressed for anyone all day, became harder and harder, more and more crisp and military and impersonal.

Michael watched Noah carefully, too. But Noah did not change the expression on his face. The expression was one of thoughtful, cool reserve, and Noah clung to it as a man clings to a very expensive piece of clothing which he has bought with his last savings and is too dear to discard, even in the most extreme circumstances. Only once during the afternoon, when, on an errand for the Captain, Michael and Noah had to walk along the line of men who had been declared too far gone to help, and who lay in a long line on the dusty ground, did Noah stop for a moment. Now, Michael thought, watching obliquely, it is going to happen now. Noah stared at the emaciated, bony, ulcerous men, half-naked and dying, beyond the reach of any victory or liberation, and his face trembled, the expensive expression nearly was lost . . . But he gained control of himself. He closed his eyes for a moment, wiped his mouth with the back of his hand, and said, starting again, "Come on. What are we stopping for?"

When they got back to the Commandant's office, an old man was being led in before the Captain. At least he looked old. He was bent over, and his long yellow hands were translucently thin. You couldn't really tell, of course, because almost everyone in the camp looked old, or ageless.

"My name," the old man was saying in slow English, "is Joseph Silverson. I am a Rabbi. I am the only Rabbi in the camp . . ."

"Yes," Captain Green said briskly. He did not look up from a paper on which he was writing a request for medical materials.

"I do not wish to annoy the officer," the Rabbi said. "But I would like to make a request."

"Yes?" Still, Captain Green did not look up. He had taken off his helmet and his field jacket. His gunbelt was hanging over the back of his chair. He looked like a busy clerk in a warehouse, checking invoices.

"Many thousand Jews," the Rabbi said slowly and carefully, "have died in this camp, and several hundred more out there . . ." the Rabbi waved his translucent hand gently toward the window, "will die today, tonight, tomorrow . . ."

"I'm sorry, Rabbi," Captain Green said. "I am doing all I can."

"Of course." The Rabbi nodded hastily. "I know that. There is nothing to be done for them. Nothing for their bodies. I understand. We all understand. Nothing material. Even they understand. They are in the shadow and all efforts must be concentrated on the living. They are not even unhappy. They are dying free and there is a great pleasure in that. I am asking for a luxury." Michael understood that the Rabbi was attempting to smile. He had enormous, sunken, green eyes that flamed steadily in his narrow face, under his high, ridged forehead. "I am asking to be permitted to collect all of us, the living, the ones without hope, out there, in the square there . . ." again the translucent wave of the hand, "and conduct a religious service. A service for the dead who have come to their end in this place."

Michael stared at Noah. Noah was looking coolly and soberly at Captain Green, his face calm, remote.

Captain Green had not looked up. He had stopped writing, but he was sitting with his head bent over wearily, as though he had fallen asleep.

"There has never been a religious service for us in this place," the Rabbi said softly, "and so many thousands have gone . . ."

"Permit me." It was the Albanian diplomat who had been so helpful in carrying out Green's orders. He had moved to the side of the Rabbi, and was standing before the Captain's desk, bent over, speaking rapidly, diplomatically and clearly. "I do not like to intrude, Captain. I understand why the Rabbi has made this request. But this is not the time for it. I am a European, I have been in this place a long time, I understand things perhaps the Captain doesn't understand. I do not like to intrude, as I said, but I think it would be inadvisable to give permission to conduct publicly a Hebrew religious service in this place." The Albanian stopped, waiting for Green to say something. But Green didn't say anything. He sat at the desk, nodding a little, looking as though he were on the verge of waking up from sleep.

"The Captain perhaps does not understand the feeling," the Albanian went on rapidly. "The feeling in Europe. In a camp like this. Whatever the reasons," the Albanian said smoothly, "good or bad, the feeling exists. It is a fact. If you allow this gentleman to hold his services, I do not guarantee the consequences. I feel I must warn you. There will be riots, there will be violence, bloodshed. The other prisoners will not stand for it . . ."

"The other prisoners will not stand for it," Green repeated quietly, without any tone in his voice.

"No, Sir," said the Albanian briskly, "I guarantee the other prisoners will not stand for it."

Michael looked at Noah. The expensive expression was sliding off his face, melting, slowly and violently exposing a grimace of horror and despair.

Green stood up. "I am going to guarantee something myself," he said to the Rabbi. "I am going to guarantee that you will hold your services in one hour in the square down there. I am also going to guarantee that there will be machine guns set up on the roof of this building. And I will further guarantee that anybody who attempts to interfere with your services will be fired on by those machine guns." He turned to the Albanian. "And, finally, I guarantee," he said, "that if you ever try to come into this room again you will be locked up. That is all."

The Albanian backed swiftly out of the room. Michael heard his footsteps disappearing down the corridor.

The Rabbi bowed gravely. "Thank you very much, Sir," he said to Green.

Green put out his hand. The Rabbi shook it and turned and followed the Albanian. Green stood staring at the window.

Green looked at Noah. The old, controlled, rigidly calm expression was melting back into the boy's face.

"Ackerman," Green said crisply. "I don't think we'll need you around here for a couple of hours. Why don't you and Whitacre leave this place for awhile, go out and take a walk? Outside the camp. It'll do you good."

"Thank you, Sir," Noah said. He went out of the room.

"Whitacre," Green was still staring out of the window, and his voice was weary. "Whitacre, take care of him."

"Yes, Sir," said Michael. He went after Noah.

They walked in silence. The sun was low in the sky and there were long paths of purple shadow across the hills to the north. They passed a farmhouse, set back from the road, but there was no movement there. It slept, neat-white and lifeless, in the westering sun. It had been painted recently, and the stone wall in front of it had been whitewashed. The stone wall was turning pale blue in the leveling rays of the sun. Overhead a squadron of fighter planes, high in the clear sky, caught the sun on their aluminum wings as they headed back to their base.

On one side of the road was forest, healthy-looking pine and elm, dark trunks looking almost black against the pale, milky green of the new foliage. The sun flickered in small bright stains among the leaves, falling on the sprouting flowers in the cleared spaces between the trees. The camp was behind them and the air, warmed by the full day's sun, was piney and aromatic. The rubber composition soles of their combat boots made a hushed, unmilitary sound on the narrow asphalt road, between the rain ditches on each side. They walked silently, past another farmhouse. This place too was locked and shuttered, but Michael had the feeling eyes were peering out at him between cracks. He was not afraid. The only people left in Germany seemed to be children, by the million, and old women and maimed soldiers. It was a polite and unwarlike population, who waved impartially to the jeeps and tanks of the Americans and the truck bearing German prisoners back to prison stockades.

Three geese waddled across the dust of the farmyard. Christmas dinner, Michael thought idly, with loganberry jam and oyster stuffing. He remembered the oak paneling and the scenes from Wagner painted on the walls of Luchow's restaurant, on 14th Street, in New York. They walked past the farmhouse. Now, on both sides of them stood the heavy forest, tall trees standing in the loam of old leaves, giving off a clear, thin smell of spring.

Noah hadn't said a word since they had left Green's office, and Michael was surprised when he heard his friend's voice over the shuffle of their boots on the asphalt.

"How do you feel?" Noah asked.

Michael thought for a moment. "Dead," he said. "Dead, wounded and missing."

They walked another twenty yards. "It was pretty bad, wasn't it?" Noah said.

"Pretty bad."

"You knew it was bad," said Noah. "But you never thought it would be like that."

"No," said Michael.

"Human beings . . ." They walked, listening to the sound of their composition soles on the road deep in Germany, in the afternoon in spring, between the aisles of pretty, budding trees. "My uncle," Noah said, "my father's brother, went into one of these places. Did you see the ovens?"

"Yes," said Michael.

"I never saw him, of course. My uncle, I mean," Noah said. His hand was hooked in his rifle strap and he looked like a little boy returning from hunting rabbits. "He had some trouble with my father. In 1905, in Odessa. My father was a fool. But he knew about things like this. He came from Europe. Did I ever tell you about my father?"

"No," said Michael.

"Dead, wounded and missing," Noah said softly. They walked steadily, but not quickly, the soldier's pace, thirty inches, deliberate, ground-covering. "Remember," Noah asked, "back in the replacement depot, what you said: 'Five years after the war is over we're all liable to look back with regret to every bullet that missed us.'"

"Yes," said Michael. "I remember."

"What do you feel now?"

Michael hesitated. "I don't know," he said honestly.

"This afternoon," Noah said, walking in his deliberate, correct pace, "I agreed with you. When that Albanian started talking I agreed with you. Not because I'm a Jew. At least, I don't think that was the reason. As a human being . . . When that Albanian started talking I was ready to go out into the hall and shoot myself through the head."

"I know," Michael said softly. "I felt the same way."

"Then Green said what he had to say." Noah stopped and looked up to the tops of the trees, golden-green in the golden sun. " 'I guarantee . . . I guarantee . . .' " He sighed. "I don't know what you think," Noah said, "but I have a lot of hope for Captain Green."

"So do I," said Michael.

"When the war is over," Noah said and his voice was growing loud, "Green is going to run the world, not that damned Albanian . . ."

"Sure," said Michael.

"The human beings are going to be running the world!" Noah was shouting by now, standing in the middle of the shadowed road, shouting at the sun-tipped branches of the German forest. "The human beings! There's a lot of Captain Greens! He's not extraordinary! There're millions of them!" Noah stood, very erect, his head back, shouting crazily, as though all the things he had coldly pushed down deep within him and fanatically repressed for so many months were now finally bursting forth. "Human beings!" he shouted thickly, as though the two words were a magic incantation against death and sorrow, a subtle and impregnable shield for his son and his wife, a rich payment for the agony of the recent years, a promise and a guarantee for the future . . . "The world is full of them!"

It was then that the shots rang out.

Noah is killed by Christian, and Christian is killed by Michael, who, in finality, carries Noah's body back to the liberated concentration camp.

Asphalt and Desire

by FREDERIC MORTON

Although he became widely known for his popular biography
of the Rothschild family, Frederic Morton's literary power is
essentially novelistic. Born in Vienna in 1924, he came out with
his family in 1939, among the last escapees. At twenty-two, Morton succeeded in winning a Dodd, Mead literary fellowship with
his first novel, The Hound, a study of the upbringing of a son of
Austrian officialdom and of his collapse in the face of Nazism.
Then came The Darkness Below, a New York passion tale about
a refugee doctor working nights in a bakery (Morton had worked
as a baker). It was with Asphalt and Desire (1952), written
while he was a university English teacher, that Frederic Morton
reached his full powers. Dealing this time with an American Jewish family in the Bronx, and revealing a remarkable sense of
dialogue idiom, he produced an exceptionally vivid portrait of a
Hunter College girl trying to free herself from her virginity and
the Bronx. Iris Leavis stands as a fully valid characterization of
the surface-sophisticated maiden with feelings of intellectual
superiority and social inferiority. Her brother, Mister, a character discovered by Frederic Morton over a decade before this
type became familiar on the scene, is the mixed-up, protesting,
brilliantly failing hippie of our time.

We have selected a number of scenes revolving around the
most understanding, if unuttered, relationship in the novel—
that between brother and sister. The family scenes as a whole
are written with an unusual control that achieves candor without cruelty.

A significant aspect of Asphalt and Desire is that Iris makes
her first sexual contact with a young German, who brings her
to the open world of nature. There is no Nazism in Egon, yet

*in this relationship Morton reacts to the symbiosis between Jews
and Germans, a theme more overtly explored in a Berlin setting
in his later novel* The Schatten Affair. *Still more recently he has
published a novel about international show-offs,* The Snow Gods,
in which an unregenerate Nazi composer figures prominently.

*Living in New York but returning often to Europe, Morton, it
is to be expected, is not done with this unresolved theme that
links two areas in his life and the life of the Jews.*

M.L.

LET THEM who can afford the luxury tax, be good. Let
the rest, like me, be smart. We haven't got time for anything else.
We're caught in a non-stop rollercoaster where it's Hold on, hold your
own, scream a little if you want to, and make sure this is fun. Who
knows? Maybe it is.

Once, though, I wanted to settle back a little. It was two o'clock
in the afternoon in late June and the sun came down upon Park
Avenue with an architectural passion. I was young that Tuesday afternoon, I lived in the April of eternity, I was a pretty girl, a flower
fingered but not yet plucked, I was any number of roseate and boring
definitions. And I was about to leave a women's college for the wide
co-ed world.

"Bye, Iris, good luck!" someone called through the open door.

"So long, Muriel, old chap."

I was famous for calling girls chap. I was famous, period. Witty,
sharp and all that rot. At the moment I stood in the editorial room
of the Hunter College *Bulletin*, making, as outgoing editor, my farewell speech to the staff. I said all the right things.

"There's a buck and a half in the till," I said, "for the incoming
administration to buy themselves dice with."

They tittered.

"Last words of wisdom," I said. "Don't let Margot, our talented
business manager, sleep with the printer unless he reduces the column
rates. Promote the newsprint company from Assistant to Associate
Creditor: it will please them. Keep the faculty advisers male."

They tittered. They tittered. A little dutifully, much too regularly—
some as if they considered me a dying emperor whose last hour had

to be humored, others because they calculated I'd soon be a professional reference with whom they better get in on the ground floor—and maybe a few laughed in honor of the times we had had together. Maybe. Anyhow, this was it. Good-bye and get it over with.

But Zoe Ralnik, my successor, stood before me.

"A little token . . . ," she murmured, red bangs atremble with momentousness.

I felt the metal cool on my palm. A silver cigarette case inscribed: *To Iris Leavis from Bully Staff '48.*

The traditional gift, yet for a moment the crispness of the scene was wavering. I wanted to thank the kids, I wanted to tell them what a grand bunch—

"Ah, sweet of you people," I said. "Honor-bright, it'll end up only in the best of hock shops."

They tittered, in their men's shirts and overalls.

I stood up. I smoothed the skirt, slapped the white gloves into my palm. This was going to be done right.

"It was grand fun, chaps, thanks for your cooperation—and much luck. Make it good."

I rose in the full graduate glory of pleated silk skirt and batwing sleeves, shining my adult elegance on their jeans. My heels clacked steady, my silhouette was a tall groomed shadow against the glass doorpane. Smartly, cleanly, definitely, the door closed.

Let them hear you march away against the world.

> *Iris makes a last visit to the weekly school dance; a man—not a collegian—asks her to go hunting with him sometime. Meanwhile a classmate with high-class connections has made a house-party date for her on this very graduation day. It may lead to a magazine job via seduction. Iris has left a note about her departure for her mother, who at last gets her on the phone.*

"DAUGHTER!" Mrs. Levin said. "I called at your office—"

"I know you did," I said with braced iron evenness. "It is no longer mine. How may I help you?"

"You don't know, Iris? Are you playing dumb, mine dear? Maybe you never left a note for me? Maybe—"

"But of course I left a note for you," I said evenly.

"But maybe you think it's nice to leave such a note to your parents who work years to let you study. We give you a college education—"

"So you did. As a result you will find the note correctly spelled."

"Please—no jokes with me. Don't jump away from the topic. You really want to go away tonight—"

"Wonderful! I spell correctly, you read correctly, all is well."

"Only yesterday I told Mrs. Lasaritz, mine daughter is going to get a college medal tomorrow. We were going to close the store. Your father already bought a flower for his buttonhole—"

"Look, just a moment—"

"We had the car washed too. And you—"

"Let's get this straight: Did I go to school to get something out of life, or did I wear out my derrière studying for four years so you can pat yourself on the back on commencement day?"

"You never heard of respect for your parents? A little bit of gratitude?"

"Go ahead, dear Mother, beat the same old horse all over again."

"You think a smart mouth is everything? One day before graduating she must go in the country, lie in the grass—"

"It says nothing whatsoever in my note about lying in the grass and it says very plainly, if you'll read it again, that I knew nothing definite about the trip until Sylvia called me this morning."

A little cunning pause on the part of Mrs. Levin.

"Oh—so? *Sylvia* called you? Good I got it out of you. That fine no-good girl! What trip is she going to lead you on?"

"S-y-l in the note means *Syl*. Don't sound so surprised. And the trip happens to be about a job."

"A job? Is that so? A what one calls it, an agency isn't good enough for you? You never satisfied? What else can I—"

"No, dear Mother. An agency is where I throw my education away. If you want me to be a lap-sitter for the Assistant Editor of the *Garbage Collectors' News*, I'll stick to agencies. If not, kindly rely on my initiative."

"And where does that fine Syl want you to go on graduating day when everybody else gets the diploma—"

"I am going to be interviewed by somebody who owns a magazine and who happens to live upstate."

A second pause of Mrs. Levin's, still more cunning and weighty than the first.

"Somebody is a man?"

"Yes, dear Mother. Give your evil imagination a good workout."

"I could tell! Four years you learn big things in college and you still dumb enough to think a man invites you to his place for a job."

"Yes, Mother. I am going to be sold by a white slaver to the highest bidding sultan. Does that please you?"

"You really going? You really going to throw yourself away like that on your graduating day? Everything is a sarcasm? Don't you think you can get hurt? You got no backside where somebody can give you a kick? But wait—"

Funny, nothing kept me from slamming the hook down. But I've never been able to hang up on her. Maybe that's the only way we can talk to each other. Maybe I need her abuse to tell me I'm not like her, that I won't end up like her. And there's a queer secret pride in her screaming too, that she was elected to have such terrible and extraordinary children. But whatever it is, the mutual need between us, it is secret, unsayable, bitter.

"I apologize deeply," I said, "for trying to be fair to my future."

"Don't talk to me about fair! Look who is talking about fair! I don't want to listen to you, every word hurts me in my heart—"

"Thank you for wishing me God speed on my trip."

"Don't you think I want to wish you? Don't you think I want a daughter I can love? But I got none. I got no son and I got no daughter! I give you up! Both!"

"Do you notice that you always talk about yourself and your feelings?"

"I am through with you, you can hurt me no more—"

"See you Thursday, kind Mother."

"I don't want to see you . . . Your father says Be careful, but I don't say anything. I am finished."

"My thanks to Paw—"

"That's what *he* says. I say Good-bye. It gives me pain to say this, believe me, but I say I don't care. I got enough of—"

"Good-bye, people," I said, almost softly. The ritual had fulfilled itself.

> Iris goes to the three-couple party of rich phony sophisticates, but balks when seduction time approaches. Back home, her virginity unsold, she finds her brother arrived from Cornell, and presently Ma and Pa come home, lugging the food they had bought for her graduation celebration.

FIRST THEY PUT DOWN the bags, the heavy, greasy bags, the tons and tons of food bought at the A&P and stored for them at the butcher's next door. And then they saw light in Mister's room. And they shuffled in and tentatively had a reunion after his three weeks' absence. Paw shaking hands with Mister, and Mister saying "How's ze busineez, Paw?" and Paw wincing and replying "O.K., I guess," and Maw kissing Mister and then the discovery of the open icebox door and Mister claiming he had just touched it, and Maw saying, Really he shouldn't put nutshells in the living room. But it was tentative, for the real contact had not come yet. Then they saw light in my room, and Maw said, "Hello, back so soon?" pulling a face as she took off her hat to indicate she knew everything and it was the worst. But I kept quiet and so did she, for the real thing had not come yet.

Then they took off their good clothes and returned to the kitchen, Paw in his distended underwear and panting jowls, Maw in her old kimono. And silently they began to make tea and to start digging through the immense stained paper bags, digging through grease-soaked wax paper for lox, herring, butter, onion rolls, salami, ice cream, halvah, eating as they dug. They ate while they unwrapped and while they dragged back and forth, boiling water or pottering for the slicing knife, their jaws working, their eyes opening and closing slowly, the roaches in the corners scattering for cover. They settled down finally to just eating, a heap of soiled saucers and crumpled napkins mounting in the middle of the table. They ate in silent furious asceticism. They champed their cheap and heavy delicatessen. They didn't touch the thick steaks in the icebox. That was for us. They didn't use the big comfortable birch table in the living room, they cramped around the small one in the kitchen. They never lived in the living room. They entered it only to show it to guests, or to rearrange the expensive furniture, or to polish off anxiously a little nick in the wood. They only slept, never lingered or relaxed, in their beautiful twelve-piece W. & J. Sloane bedroom. They didn't like to touch their valuable things. They had built them laboriously in the 'twenties, they had lost them in the 'thirties, they had pieced them together again out of the thousands of dingy coins which pinch-faced people bled day after day for laxatives, suppositories or aspirins into the cash registers of successive dingy cracked-tile stores in Williamsburg, in Brownsville, and now in the Bronx. There was too much worry, too much fret in their important possessions. They couldn't enjoy them, nor even touch them without pain. They hated their glossy furniture because it wouldn't give them the satisfaction they had bargained for; they moved the heavy shiny pieces into new patterns but still there was no contentment. So they were reduced to squatting in the kitchen, working over their food and glowering at their treasures with dire possessiveness.

And that's how they felt about us, only that they had built us, nursed us, fondled us, shifted us so much longer than the furniture, and for that reason, by that degree, hated us so much more. We were their star disappointments, handsome and gifted children who had brought nothing but anguish and anger. They needed the misery we visited upon them to tell that they owned us, loved us, for in their lives misery had become the companion emotion of desire. They could not reach us except through extremity. . . . Mister knew it, I knew it, we've both inherited part of it in ourselves. For just as I always feel shut out and Mister is too unendurable to make intimate friends, so they have nobody either. Even relatives visit us only on holidays. And the curse of loneliness is compounded when the four of us are together, it quivers between us like live wire wound round our wrists. We might try to ignore it, suppress it by sheer will, remain apart, normal, polite, but then somebody would break down, Maw usually, and the four of us would rush upon each other, pound each other, try to scrape the plague off one another, be together.

But not yet. They still crouched in the kitchen. Paw sipping his tea, one hand folded over the elephantine belly; sometimes putting the cup down and coaxing the toaster which withheld the slice too long, poking at it ineffectually, humming a very low, insecure sing-song as though trying to ignore some indignity. And Maw just sat there, very tense, holding the painted cup of mineral water, pinkie curved. Maw in her faded incongruous kimono, always draped in some youthful eccentricity, the cast of her face too young for the lines between her eyes. As Mister says, she's a born child, motherhood was the wrong racket for her She arched forward on the table, really like a moppet surprised by middle age, ambushed by disappointment, a badly treated child prepared to grow obnoxious, obstreperous, bad-tempered and bad-grammared in revenge.

And then it started. In stages, as usual.

"How is your college?" she asked.

"Hunkydunkydory, Maw."

"What? What you mean?"

"It means fine, Maw. Wonderful. Ipsi-pipsi."

"You don't mind if I ask? I miss mine children. I am interested to know what they doing."

"That's very nice. We appreciate that very much, Maw."

"Why don't you relax," Paw said to him. "Join with us. Take a chair."

"I'm happy here," Mister said, twisting on the couch.

"And how is your bookwriting?" Maw asked.

"I am bookwriting terrific."

"Yeh? Well, maybe my son is going to be famous yet. Don't think I wouldn't be happy. I would be the happiest person in the world."

And then there is only the slurping of tea, the crack of herring bones, the tortured yielding of the sofa springs. A quiet on which the imminence of something gnaws.

"So you got any plans for summer?"

"This summer I'm gonna take life by the horns, Maw."

"What? What you mean?"

"You're not going to help out in the store?" Paw said.

"All I'm asking is that you get somebody else. O.K.? Fair warning? All right? If you please?"

"Listen here, mine dear young man, you can't take off a few hours a week to give a hand to your parents?"

"Aw, be big about it. Give an unemployed family father the opportunity."

"You think we're not going to pay you or something? I didn't want to say nothing, but if you think we stingy, why did you have to send a telegram for money for a plane? The train isn't good enough any more?"

"I wanted my mothahs flowahs to arrive freshshly," Mister said à la Winston Churchill.

"Oh!"

Maw was flying toward the askew petals on the shelf. "Isn't that beautiful! I smelled something when I came in! Oh, that's lovely of mine son! You know how easy it is to make a mother happy!"

Mister twisted on the couch.

"Look what he brings his poor old mother, look at the beautiful yellow ones!" She was whisking them round the rooms, gesturing them in my face. "I feel like his best girl! Aren't I your best girl! You see the ones with the red spots? Oh!"

"Daaaah," Mister groaned off her attack before it came too near. She pirouetted and skipped to Paw and kissed him and tickled the flowers under his helpless nose. Her perennial frantic adolescence reddened and fevered her like a rash. It was mortifying.

But she herself threw it off.

"Ah, if you sweet enough to bring your mother flowers, don't tell me you not going to be nice and not work a little in the store?"

"You get yourself a more trustworthy person, Maw."

"I don't care about trustworthy. I want my son to be with me a little. That's not asking much."

"I'll be busy this summer, Maw."

"You going to run around again with these World People, these communists?"

"Not communists, Maw. Gangsters."

"Listen, you talking to your mother—"

"That's what you called them last time, gangsters."

"Do you hear me? I want you to talk like you're talking to your mother, not to a street scum."

"Will you leave me alone?"

But he didn't even close the door. For it was here. It had come. The icebox whispered rustily. With laborious embarrassment Paw screwed on the infra-red lamp that's supposed to kill off all the germs; a tiny cockroach was panicky under the cupboard. We were all braced for the ordeal of togetherness. The question of working in the store didn't matter, the words were irrelevant, but the shout was important, the bawl, the howl was paramount for we were reared in it, they had fed it to us with aching throats. It's the only thing we truly know, we must return to it from time to time, to the ancient intimacy of its pain. Loneliness is farthest off when we cry out against each other.

"What did God give you all that brains for? To hurt your mother? You are home half an hour and you have to act up like that?"

"Yeah, you'd all be so much better off without me. A happy harmonious family you'd be, eating prayers for breakfast."

"Go on, destroy everything with your talk."

"Yeah, I destroy everything. I'm a spoiler. I'm evil. I like to make love to young tawny-haired boys who died of diphtheria. And you know my biggest trouble? I *exist!*"

"Go on, destroy. I can take it. You done it before—"

"I've been *existing* for nineteen years steady. Can't stop. It's a vice, you know. Ain't it tough, having an exister for a son—"

"Talk, go on, talk! And you know something? I wouldn't have you work in the store if you gave me a million dollars! I'm very happy you not working in that store. You destroy that too."

"Oh, yes, I'm an exister of the deepest dye, I'm the ten plagues, I'm the black angel, the canker, the nemesis of all nice mothers who do everything for their sons—"

"Since you are that little I remember you had to ruin everything. You can't come home nice? Talk with me, be like a human being? No, you've got to ruin the conversation—"

"Yes, I'm the scorpion, the adder, the scourge of the Levins—"

"For years I've been begging you. I want to talk to you like a son. I've been the best mother in the world to you, but it didn't do any good. You've got all the brains there is but it's no good. I thought maybe after you went to the university it would be different, but you still the same, you've got no manners, nothing—"

"You shouldn't bother with a boy like that," Paw said. "He'll find out himself." He was still screwing the lamp on, trying to participate in the intensity but lagging behind, as usual, sighing at the lamp socket.

"But he *is* bothering me. He's destroying me. Remember what he did with the five dollars in the store?"

"Yes, I remember," Mister said. "Do you hear, I remember, I'm sorry for it, I remember, you don't have to tell me again."

"You think that was funny? Was that so smart? He's got to give five dollars to a stranger which belong to his family—"

"Help! Listen, I'm going to the blood bank to bleed out five dollars. I'm gonna go into the coal mines to make money, I'll sell my suits. I'll go naked for the five bucks. But don't *say* it again!"

"So you got a bad conscience? You don't know for five dollars I've got to stand in the store all day with my bad feet—"

"Shut up! I'm warning you. I'm not kidding either!"

"Pearl, don't bother," Paw said at the socket, trying to be in tune. "We got over the depression. We will get over him too."

"He's an ungrateless no-good. He doesn't care that for five dollars—"

The vase with the flowers in it shattered to the floor.

From the bed I could see them all with ear or eye or blood-pounding intuition. Mister staring at the vase he'd dashed down, then sprawling back onto the couch, turning away with a snarl of springs. Paw mountainous, still humming, like a raw growth in underwear, a non-malignant growth but with a tumor's wastefulness and grossness, still trying to get the lamp into the socket. And the hapless hum made me think of the wedding portrait in the bedroom in which a slim young man in a snappy tuxedo has his hand slung around Maw's waist, hat tilted spontaneous against the dark hair, and the dark lips open in what might also have been a hum but probably was the inhaling of a giddy happiness instead. And I tried to imagine that zippy young buck buried inside the tumor by the lamp socket. And the terrible thing was that I could. Paw's history had never been sobbed and stamped into us like Maw's but you could tell from the significant nods of aunts and the asides of old cousins, and somehow from his own trampled face. He was a man to whom something had happened. He was an unhappy ending in which the beginning, the intermediate stages could still be spotted. Yeah, I'm a great expert on the decline and fall of Paw. First, the Warsaw *Juengel* so brilliant in Talmud Torah school that his family decides to send him to America where he should study himself into something famous. Then the sensitive young dandy doing pharmacy at Fordham, holding deep intellectual discussions in the Jewish Workers' Circle, persuading, with flashing and guileless brows, the daughters of coal merchants to "espouse" Fabian socialism. Then Pearl Schrecker, all of a sudden. The dandy in the album holding tight and overcome hands with the auburn-haired salesclerk he has fallen for. And, later, from the wedding picture, from the curiously lax lips in a still taut face, you can see it has already started to happen to him. She does not love me. She doesn't love me. It's not a simple fact, it's a process which continues that nibbles inside him like a tiny but growing beast. She doesn't love me. Other things about her are worse but beside it they don't matter. For instance, that she is a shrill piece of violence, temperamentally unsuited to him; that she carries with her and spreads around him a strenuous, unrelievable and brightly enameled loneliness. That she wants everything she can't get, that she always poses the young lovely suffering from the low blows of fate. That she takes over his future; claims pharmacy is too slow, too silly for him; drives out his foolish socialist ideas; pushes him into the glamorous, wealthy jewelry line she always wanted to be in, persuades him to invest the liberal allowance he gets from the old country in the house of Berger, Levin & Co. There is a picture of him and his partner arranged in Big Deal attitudes around a desk, with telephones, secretaries, memo pads clustered in proud profusion; a havana is stuck into his smile like a carrot into a snowman. And what is happening to him has become more definite. The slight puffing of the cheeks show it, the groggy grin; the eyes are dilated with inward incredulity. She doesn't love me. By now he knows that there is nothing in the world he can do to make her love.

Nothing in the world to make him stop loving. No compromise is possible, no *modus vivendi*, it's endless, hopeless, inexorable. And perhaps he knows also that her very intensity energizes the predicament she caused in him. His life has an edge it never possessed before. He recognizes that this thing which is happening to him is a potentially tremendous thing; that his is the job of not merely surviving it, but of expressing it, giving it its proper scope . . . But at first he only endures it. He plays husband to the Big Jeweler's Wife; uses the appropriate gesture when, arrived appropriately late and conspicuous in the Second Avenue Theater, he hands Pearl's mink to the wardrobe mistress. Then 1930. The jewelry proposition which was never really Big Deal bites the dust. He finds himself delivering ice, then struggling as a hand-to-mouth druggist in a Brooklyn alley. And abruptly the thing that has happened to him comes into its own; like a toadstool it flashes out in the fat folds of his jowls, the oily cushions of his hands, the drooping, overloaded shoulders, the rims around his now immobilized eyes. His hunger has finally found its balance—in squalor and inertness. He doesn't care about his new indignity, nor the impoverishment and death of his elegant Polish family, the family which had attracted her to him. It doesn't matter that the stress of digging up a living bloats, muddies him, guts his face. It doesn't matter precisely because these things are such a disgrace to her. At last he can balance her insensibility with an insensibility of his own. He lets himself slump into a turgid spider, he lurks behind splintery drug counters for the quarters of subway conductors' wives, he walks around half-clothed and unwashed at home, he doesn't bother to hide his dirty fingernails before his family, his creased buttocks, his sweaty haunches. He grins at himself sheepishly. He still loves her but he has taken comfort in hopelessness. He is striking back. He lets life go to seed. He tries to guide his children no more than his wife does; he listens to his family tear itself to pieces but does not arbitrate or pacify, he merely bulges his underwear, makes a token attempt, recedes again, hums a little insecurely. He feels he is not loved, only tolerated, and he gloats over his own intolerableness, over his outrageous bulk, his mediocrity as a money-earner, over the fallowness of his intelligence, his utter incompetence as a father, his ugliness and insufficiency as a husband. For in these he has found revenge. At last he can cope with what is happening to him. He repays enormity with enormity. Deep down he proudly bears the supreme wrong of not being loved by her whom he still loves so very much.

And now he was a tumor, scratching into the socket the infra-red lamp which was supposed to cure his ever-swollen gums. His eyes did not move. I could see him and Maw, her back turned to him, tensed away from the fragments of the vase that had sprayed to her feet. As though she were the victim of matricide. In stunned shock against the brutality of things as though she hadn't been through the same scene a hundred times before. Always bullying her wrinkles into the fresh stridency of youth. She never could tone down her rejection of Paw to make it less obvious to her own children, or at least to make it less necessary for him to be a tumor. She wouldn't get rid of him either because she needed him to be oppressed. She commanded him to oppress her with his monstrous bulk so that her nagging might have biblical stature, that she might play the Chosen Woman, elevated and tormented at the same time by an ineffable God. Didn't her husband have the best background and the finest prospects? And what had become of him? Hadn't she been the most gorgeous girl in Warsaw and hadn't everybody said she would marry a millionaire if she went to America? And what had become of her? Wasn't I the prettiest girl in New York—especially since I had her hair—and wasn't I throwing my life away by not having married Alvin Zucker two years ago? Wasn't Mister with his scholarship the intellectual light of the universe, and wouldn't he end up on the electric chair with his behavior?

Oh, I knew what would happen next. The vehemence in which she reveled wasn't complete yet. I was still missing for the grand finale.

She kicked the fragments away and ran into my room.

"Did you see what your brother did?"

I didn't move.

"I'm asking you, did you see? Why don't you talk to him? Maybe he still listens to you! Why don't you tell him I'm his mother, he can't hurt me like this!"

"Please leave me out of it."

"Nobody is left out of this, you hear? As long as I live I will fight for him. They operated me twenty hours when he was born—"

"Mother. Please!"

"What? You are such a big smart lady you can't help your mother? It's not enough you didn't go to the graduation—"

"Look, you bothered *him* enough. Have at least enough sense to leave me alone."

"Leave you alone? You wait, mine dear. First I'm going to ask you a few questions. How come you back so early?"

I squeezed my pillow hard but didn't answer.

"If it was so important you couldn't even go to the graduation, how come you back already? Will you tell me that, mine daughter? Maybe everything didn't go so nice with the man Sylvia arranged for you?"

I turned my back to her.

"So he is through with you? He used you? Didn't I warn you a hundred times—"

It was too much. Exactly what she wanted, of course, to have me flare up and participate in her great spectacle, but it was too much. I should have had the strength to say to myself that I was above all this. The shrill yaps, the jerky gestures, the Bronx whine. What right did they have to be my family? I was Iris Leavis, Phi Beta Kappa, who only yesterday had turned down a flossy Anglo-Saxon seduction. I should have been above the accident of birth. I should ignore all this messy howling. I ought to lie on my bed with rigid and bored hauteur, pondering the gauche fate that had dropped an antelope into a pigsty. Or I ought to get up, calm and impervious, wither these screaming Levins with a glance, taxi down to the Astor bar and get high with the first naval officer above ensign rank who walked in.

I should, I should, but I never could. I saw her coming at me, her carmine-nailed fist lifted in childlike ferocity, I saw her raising her hand, gaudy and futile, against fate, raising it ever since she had run out of the Warsaw slums to become Mrs. Rockefeller. I saw her rawness and vulgarity, the incongruity of paint upon a wrinkled though still creamy skin, but I saw the anger that held it all together too, I saw it was the only thing she had which made her carry on, and I saw that it was, despite everything, hypnotic. It was the doomed, painful prideful anger of the prophets exalting themselves with God's wrath. And I saw, for the dozenth time, that it was my anger too. She was vicious, ridiculous, hysterical, but she reached you, she ripped the heat of response right out of you, she purged something urgent and age-old, she made you rise up from the depths, steamed-up, helpless, yet puzzlingly grandiloquent, shouting:

"Get your filth out of my room!"

"Is that what you say to me! You got no heart? Wait till you have a child. You will see how it hurts—"

"For Christ's sakes—"

"Don't you say Christ in this house!"

"Then get out of this room!"

"Twenty years I try to bring you up. I'm not going to let Sylvia spoil mine daughter. I'm going to fight for you."

"And I'm sick of your bathroom solicitude. I'm not going to have my virginity made into a weekly cannon fodder for your neuroses."

"You know what? You worse than your brother. If you had seen what he did—"

"I know what he did. Get out! I'm not interested—"

"Daaah." Mister stormed in. "Go on. Tell her what Foul Mordecai did!"

"Will you please get!" I said to him. "You're only going to work up that monster some more."

"Oh, let us hear what our gentle mother has to say about me. Let us all listen to that caressing voice!"

"Why the hell don't you stay up in Cornell?" I said. "Do you have to make trouble with that idiot every time you come down?"

"An idiot you call your parents? You think I can listen to this year after year? I can take it no more. I am better off dead."

"Go ahead. Go into your act. Rub ashes on your brow. Makes it more convincing."

"For that I gave mine daughter all the education, so she can feel superior to her mother? So that she can call me names—"

"Goddamn you," Mister said, "if you loaned Foul Mordecai your typewriter he could have worked on the novel up at college. He wouldn't have to come down into this madhouse—"

"You should talk respectful to your mother," Paw said from the kitchen, screwing the lamp.

"It's a terrible thing to say for a mother, but right now I feel I would be better off I had never had any children!"

"Will you get all your carcasses out of my room!"

"You forget there is a God up there, mine daughter? He is hearing every word you say. He's taking it down—"

"Yeah, He's taking down too what Foul Mordecai did. Tell Him what he did, Maw. Give Him the latest version."

"Listen! I tell you something, my son. Not a red cent for college allowance for you. You don't help in the store, we don't help you. I'm through with you—"

"Sure. Disown Foul Mordecai. That *exister!* That Kierkegaard! But sometimes even an exister gets fed up—"

"You going away? Maybe it's better. But I love you, I can't live without mine children. I'm a mother, you know that? A President you could have been with your brains, maybe even a bookwriter. But you got no heart. A bum got more heart than you. But not a red cent for you even if you come to me a poor bum—"

"It's good there's an echo," Paw said. "Even children get children. They will find out."

"You're supposed to be parents," I said, completely fed up by the farce, "not third-rate vaudeville hams."

"When your mother is dead you will regret every word you said to her. You will pray to God He should forgive—"

"Will you get out of my room?"

"You know, I almost wish God should teach you. If you get punished you will know why—"

But Paw interrupted us all. He had broken the infra-red lamp.

"I told you not to use that plug for the electric razor!" he shouted at Mister, thumb bleeding, face red, at least momentarily in rhythm with us.

"What do you want me to do, chrissakes!" Mister shouted. "*Persuade* the whiskers to fall off?"

"Don't say Christ in this house!" Maw sobbed.

> *Iris conceives a great idea for breaking into journalism. She will offer a personal-experience expose of sin in hotels. First she must persuade some editor to buy the idea, then she intends to get an innocent swain to register with her in a sin hotel. So she rushes out to secure a list of editors from her brother, who is picketing downtown.*

YOU CAN always pick him out. He was the biggest bump in a snake of pickets before the Biltmore, and from the rumpled height of his big face he looked down upon the well-pressed passers-by with extravagant pity, as though it were hard to conceive that they could be stupid enough to accept the world, that they should be so cowardly as to be normal, so blind as to be prosperous; and he swung his banner saying *Abolish Frontiers, Abolish Tariffs* in a lofty and robust torment. And when he shouted the slogan in chorus with his band of fanatics (all of whom looked smugly like cartoons of Bolshevik bombthrowers in the *Journal-American*), you could hear his derisive bullfrog roar louder than any of the others' and see the exaggerated weaving of his trunk. His manner seemed to satirize his words; it seemed to imply that he was not entirely one of the pickets either, that he saw through them too, and that he associated with them only because they were relatively closest to him in his total defiance of environment. And the slight disorderly glimmer underneath the deadpan gaze of his eyes told his disenchantment as so lonely and absolute and uncompromising as to be secretly skeptical even about itself.

Then he saw me.

"Miss. Bless you. Let me get you a poster."

"I want to ask you for the addresses of those editors," I said. I had to run up and down alongside him.

"Come on. The Tariff Commission is meeting in there. A couple of turns. Act global."

"Look. May I have those references?"

"Ah," he said, "I see. You don't want to be young and foolish."

"No."

"How's Mayfair?" he said. "And perfumed mammon? And Tennis Anybody?"

"All right. You're having a little fun with me."

"No, I just thought you didn't need my connections."

"I changed my mind. I won't be able to get the right job without them. Am I sufficiently on my knees?"

"Shucks, and Mordecai hoped to use them himself."

"Don't worry, you'll never stoop that low."

"ONE WORLD, ONE DESTINY, NO FRONTIER, NO TARIFF," he roared.

"Mister! I am asking you."

"Daaah. The furor of the marketplace," he said.

It took him five minutes to give me the addresses. He had to shout the slogans and sometimes mixed up words of the slogans into the addresses, and fumbled elaborately for his pocketbook to make plain to his fellow pickets that this contact he had through me with the outside world was quite ridiculous, difficult to him; he was at pains not to take me seriously, yet he murmured guiltily about trying to help out, to be fair to his little social butterfly of a sister; he waved his banner and groaned his slogans and labored under his antagonistic scruples, and on top of it all maintained an air of cynicism against his own finely divided sensibility. So that he not only forced me to seesaw beside him, but also, as usual, to admire the great sufferer.

ONE WORLD, ONE DESTINY . . . and me having to run up and down alongside him.

"Thanks!" I said.

"Daaah! Peddle your wares nobly, young woman!" he called after me.

> The sin-hotel expose turns into a wild fiasco when her reliable swain, Alvin Zucker, fails to appear and Mordecai registers in his place, only to flee down the fire escape when rent is demanded.
>   Still tempting seduction, Iris takes up the hunting invitation. It is by motorcycle—and brother Mordecai rides along in the sidecar. At the camp, she is off with her huntsman to the woods.

. . . YOU RIDE behind a man on a motorcycle. You have to clamp your arms round him. You and he vibrate commonly to each jump of the wheels. Every time he dips sideways in taking a bend you must follow along. There is that kind of cooperation. Furthermore, innocent of these consequences, I had been foolish enough to accept his offer in a bathing suit; now he sat between my bare legs, two obscene white knees sticking out on either side into the air, and my middle, left bare by the two-piece, chafing against his belt. As if that weren't enough, there was something not kosher about the atmosphere of that day; it had started out foggy but by two it had not merely cleared up, it insisted on clearing up still more. A moon of cotton candy stuck in the sky and the sun shiny like a toy furnace. The air crackled with a transparency impossible in the city, I could glimpse the veins on each leaf as we brushed by them. The air was so sight-facilitating, it was positively peeping-tommish. I felt pornographic. I had an irresistible hunch that the sight of nude Leavis riding behind a fully clad boy would be carried down by the oomb-sheesh of the forest; down into civilization it was borne, fastening upon everybody's eyes. They were leering at the camp; in the Bronx Maw was tearing at her hair with shame; Maggie laughed and Syl smirked. For a moment it went so far, I thought the boy I was clasping was not Egon but Lionel— Lionel Krieg of Taft who used to give me riding lessons on his bike but never made a pass at me, just stared at me hard and whom I once caught kissing the seat after a lesson; whom I had never been able to look in the eye afterward because I'd felt as compromised as he.

But he wasn't Lionel. It would have been almost better if he had been. His blue shirt had the tang of faint fierce masculine sweat. He had short curly hairlets on the back of his neck which he pushed against my mouth rudely whenever he pulled his body back in changing gears. I felt suddenly that we had better stop, that I'd better get sore quickly. But that was asinine. We swung down from the mountain and the troubled idea floated off into an open valley, was lost in the sweep of galloping down freely, with no clothes between me and the singeing, singing air.

At last we stopped.

"Look at it," he said.

We both did, sitting one behind the other on the bike.

In the hollow of the plateau lay the morning-blue lake, breathing with soft movement like a child aslumber. It twinkled, miles and miles of blueness deep. A thousand little suns lazed light upon the ripples, and the willows with their streaming boughs along the shore fell wide open beyond the brush with a breeze of calm eternal surprise, as if golden, green and blue were colors just invented for them, as if they would stay forever freshly glimpsed, as if you could see them endlessly for the first time, just as they were, willow and water, shadow and reflection, golden, green and blue, in sovereign virginity, and nothing could change the picture, not time and not sickness, neither season nor sunset.

It was beautiful, honest. It made poetry excusable.

"And over there is the water tower," he said.

It was a gray structure, craggy like a serpent's tooth, pushing up from among the trees. From the pump, I discovered, issued the oomb-sheesh. But it sounded different, had slowed and deepened; the interval between systole and diastole had vanished, merged into the total beat; silence had become part of sound, sound of silence, and the whole a part of the rhythm of brightness upon shade, hues upon horizon, quiver upon calm. And I wondered why the same sound should be a fever down below, a fondling up here; I wondered, even though I knew this was nonsense, I wondered why they fretted far from it in the lowland when they could bask in its tranquillity at the source. Why did they bother when there was such a thing?

He leaped, came down with a twig of leaves in his fist.

"Rub out the tire tracks with that," he said. "The road's still muddy from the rain."

He wheeled the bike into the underbrush. I looked at him.

"Hey, rub out the tracks," he laughed. "You want the patrol to get us?"

And when I rubbed I saw the barbed wire stitched into the willows. It was a reservoir. Off limits. The same old story. The barbed wire as the hallmark of beauty, here or on Fifth Avenue. He came out of the brush. The cage dangled from his hand with the dog in it squirming keenly but still soundless as before, a small pent-in wilderness rapier-eyed and golden-fleeced with sun; his eyes mirrored the innocent-invincible blueness of the lake. Only here the wire didn't matter.

"No," he said; he dropped the cage. "You wipe it easy, like this. Otherwise they see somebody monkeyed around."

And I knew I had been tricked into this. He had pulled the tranced colors, the heaving golden peace out of his sleeve, the dark sleeve, but it was fake and forbidden. I ought to just swim and flirt and tan and maybe write the camp essay, but not stay with him, not that way at least and not so long. I ought to get away from this swarthy Zeusling who broke out of the bush with a dog and a gun like two thunderbolts under each arm, and who looked at me. I didn't want to hunt, to walk into the green dazzle of his parlor and be used there for his pagan purpose. I felt like a frightened bobbysoxer. Oh, I was so smart.

"I'm not going to do anything right," I said.

"Aah," he laughed.

"You didn't pick the right type," I said.

He snapped the cage door open, caught the dog's glistening lunge, held it, leashed it, not exactly ignoring what I said but responding to it somehow with the stance of his entire body, half-facing me, saying soundless "Ha?"

"I am not right for this," I said.

He threw the empty cage into the brush. "Sure you are. Attaboy, Schatzi." He ducked, coiled, leaped once more, reached high while holding on to the leash, crashed down with a heavy oak branch in his palm.

"You hit each trunk with it until one jumps out."

"I don't know what you mean," I said, turning the knobby thing.

"There'll be just one. They don't come in couples this time of year."

"You hear? I don't understand!" I said.

"Well, we usually hunt them at night. In the daytime they hole up and you've got to scare them out."

And he was already starting for the woods and I didn't want to be treated like that, I would show him. "Look," I said, "why didn't you get your blonde companion from the camp—"

"All you've got to do is hit it. Let's go."

And by some mistake I was walking forward.

"That's right. I'm right behind you with the Mauser. How do you like that Mauser?"

"Fabulous," I said. "Everything is absolutely fabulous."

"O.K. Here we go. We want to make a meal out of it yet."

Behind me was the dog, straining at leash, advancing toward me. On both sides lay the laconic splendor of the lake. I was really walking forward, into the trees. I was thinking hard this might make an anecdote in the camp essay, it might come in handy, and that birds, quails, whatever it was I was supposed to be flushing, were harmless little animals who didn't jump at you from behind. And we couldn't be hunting anything else and that in any case he with the gun was right behind me. I penetrated deeper. No paths or empty beer cans or carved lovers' hearts or picnic litter. No footprints of culture. It was unlike any forest I had known, just a primeval jungle. I whacked the trees for reassurance but the beeches locked their boughs above my head, the foliage rose round me like a curtain. I waded, a white nude bird, through the twilight of a green cellar. It was quiet. The pump's breath was muffled in leaves. But it was a secretive, crawling quiet. Myriad mysteries had been waiting for my footsteps. They'd been prowling for my arrival for years and now they mobilized, scrabbled to attack me. Tiny flies began an assault, the antennae of beetles, soft wasps and pointed petals. Twigs and leaves lanced me, shot little torpedoes of sap, pricked under my bathing suit. I wanted to scratch, but *he* was following—and looking behind me, I saw he wasn't there. And scratched and wished he were nearer, though I knew he had to keep a distance. I whacked the trees harder but couldn't drive away the green silence that was infiltrating me, which slid between wool and skin, itched in the most awful places. I passed some pink-tipped shrubs, I whacked them, avoided them, but they coiled out, their smooth shoots explored, seeped, sprouted into me, spurted some untamed tang into my blood which swelled, reared, roared into rhythm, a response of my own to the oomb-sheesh gliding through the boughs. Just then I saw the shadow. Shiver of motion across the haze, blot scuttling up along a bole. But I wasn't frightened. The fear of animal boiled into greed, the emerald savagery in me sang out, I shouted, I think, I pursued, thrashed with my switch. I clawed for it with bare arms and legs, surged after it as it sailed from branch to branch, lunged for it—

A root kicked me and I flopped, foaming full length along the leaves.

Two shots spoke out.

A silence dropped. Dragonflies drew discreet exotic circles in the air. Moss throbbed against my arms. Then panting laid the silence open. Hoarse and louder panting, rumoring, rustling, rioting straight

toward me in the brush. I sat up. I awaited it, switch gripped, unafraid. And it rocketed out of the trees—the dog—not to attack but,
as I had somehow foreseen, to jubilate, to display to me the prize of
the feathery shadow clamped between its teeth. It whipped to my
right, it wheeled to my left, it blazed furious brown circles of exaltation round me, its ebony snout plowing the grass, teeth gleaming, tail
flagellating gloriously. It even had found tongue: a deep triumphant
growl demanding again and again that I recognize its victory, admire
the fabled cargo in its mouth.

And I found I could answer. I cried, *"We did it!* We *got him!
Didn't we!"* I ran at the dog and it ran at me. I fell again and it circled me. And all my dusty frustrations died and an ardor rose under
my breast that was strong and incandescent and wise about all that
was made of breath and blood and which bit into the core of life. I lay
there mad and heard myself answer the dog's cries with my own.
Round and round I rolled to follow the delight of its revolutions and
whenever, in headlong ritual, it scurried near me as if to surrender the
prey I reached out with my arms, whenever it ran off again withdraw-
ing the offer, I beckoned it to return again. We almost danced a war
dance together, full of indomitable and crazy exhilaration.

Until Egon appeared, abruptly. He broke through the branches,
rifle slung back. ·

"Man," he said, "he was a fast one."

My limbs snapped together. Leavis, you ass.

I adjusted my suit and sprang up.

I didn't have it in me to watch him pluck it. I wasn't that far gone.
After I had followed him to a little brook I sat down on a stone, my
back turned. But not Schatzi, the dog. Schatzi watched the process
with pitiful longing; it sat right by me, paws prayerfully close together,
tail atwitch with supplication. Sometimes it even slid forward a begging little inch, a bit closer to the quarry. But it was swept right back
again, either by some ingrained ethic of the hunt or perhaps a motion
of Egon's who whistled easy to the cracking of the bones. Queer, I
had suddenly become friends with the dog. When it gave up the forbidden inch it whinnied at me under the assumption that I too shared
its great hankering; it'd add a low yowl to warn me against being as
fresh as it; and would end up by nudging its foxy head against my
side.

Then I had to turn around to watch him too. He squatted on his heels, bobbing as he worked, as though his thighs were springs. The bird was quite large, already peaceful looking in his hands; there was surprisingly little blood. He had just finished stripping the wings. A moment later he started to scrape out a hollow, using the metal sheath of his knife, digging the earth in long fluid motions. One movement gave birth to the next, how naturally he draped action over his body: bike, gun, shot and prey. His hair toppled down again and again I wanted to touch it. It would give me power. I wanted to be a hunter like him. For I'd just realized what I wanted out of the city which was waiting for me down below; what I wanted was not its jewels or its minks but its submission. I wanted to lick the city like that, it had the same kind of challenge for me, I wanted to take it by the horns as he did, and lay it on its back and skin and pluck it, whistling. . . .

. . . Out of his knapsack he hauled a grate, onto the grate he distributed what I could no longer think of as pieces of cadaver, for in his hands they became morsels, pungent, pink-boned, toothsome. As the lower sides roasted with a sizzle, he slipped under the flat of his knife, flipped them over, and at the same time reached with his left into the brook, flung a fist of spray across the grate that flashed into a rainbow, that made the flames squirm and growl, and finally crackled up as savory brown steam while drops of newly formed gravy beaded the grate bars. Not only that but he produced, again out of his knapsack, some dark bread which he cut into thick slices, laid them across the well-done but still roasting pieces so that the rye's gusty sour mixed with the bite of wild meat and the faint bitter of slightly scorched bread crust. And his knife was a fascination. All the world's good flavors clung to its clouded steel; easily he picked out with it the embers in the earthen brazier, exploded them into the brook for fun, grinning, quickly raked in new stalks, green and juicy, to keep the fire slow, all with his knife, wiping the blackness of the blade against the crust of the breast piece. So easy. . . .

It was time to eat, then; not only to eat but to taste, to talk, to lean against the patina of blood-warm rock, to talk, to look out across the lake. To calm Schatzi who had at last been granted his spoils of feathers and bones and who tossed them about in fierce simulation of a second chase; to laugh at him (for he had really become a *him* now, not just an *it*) and to talk, to comb your hand through the swift cool of the brook, to let the wild new flavor play against the tongue; to recapture what was somehow a lost rite which should have been there always. For this was not a gulped-down calorie-charted, steak-coffee-juice refueling, lubricated with liquor and amenities bitterly bartered for tips. This was a feast. There was ritual in this, a rightness and richness, a sharing, a leisurely aesthetic, a sunken memory of a Passover evening I had once spent at my grandmother's. Our talk was in it, and Schatzi's capers, and the wide glitter of the water beveled in maroon and rose now, ripe with afternoon but still steeped in freshness, and the sun much softer against the willows' graceful green, and, slow and deep, deep and slow, the refrain from the old tower. That, the tang of the fire, and the talk. . . .

He talked.

"You like flowers?" he said. "Girls like flowers. That's marigolds over by the willows. Something funny. When I was a kid, the orphan home sent me up for a couple of days. So once we took a hike around and I'd never seen a flower close by. I plucked one and hid it in the pillow at night like you do, you know, with a swiped candy. Next morning I wanted to smell at it but it was all mashed up." The grate hissed with another spray of brook water. "It was just shreds, that pansy," he said. "It looked awful. What a stupid kid."

"Tell me more," I said.

He took out his pipe, knocked it against the rock, stuffed it and lit it. And the embers shifted in the glow, the old water tower confided its refrain. Schatzi came running with the feathers, wanted me to pull at them, pull hard so Schatzi could hold them with proud teeth and show how much they were Schatzi's, how Schatzi possessed them. And suddenly I felt I had set something off again in him; one shoulder rose higher than the other, and it was there, he was fighting it.

"That time I didn't know about flowers," he said.

I pulled at the feathers.

"What didn't you know?" I had to ask it. I was meant to. "Flowers are free," he said. "Anything you can grab is free." And Schatzi held fast and growled Rrrr with ownership while *he* shot a smoke-ring far across the hill.

"This is my hide-out," he said. "They don't come up here from the camp because the hike is too long. The path isn't big enough for cars either. But I can handle the cops. Boy, I'd like to see them try to catch me on my bike. But when I'm up here all alone I feel like I own the whole place. Like a baron." He paused and exhaled. "But that's fooling yourself. A lot of hooey. It don't belong to you. You got to keep watching for those cops." He sent more rings, swift, high, above afternoon and lake, willow and rhythm. It hit whatever he fought but it hit it so smooth, the rose roundelay of the waves was not disturbed or the warmth against me of his elbow.

"I'm going to have the same out in California, in Monterey," he said. "Except it'll really be my place. Flowers all year round. That's the way it is on the Coast. As many as I want and not just looking. I'll have a garden. With petunias, larkspur, asters, phlox, peonies and so on. They got some special semi-tropical varieties. There is a page with pictures in the Knowledge encyclopedia."

"It sounds nice," I said.

"I am going to plant them all," he said.

"Tell me more about your future."

"All of them," he said. "And you know when I'm out there I'll read the Encyclopedia Britannia."

"Britannica," I said. Schatzi, a happy little demon, rolled on the feathers.

"Britannica," he said. "But I'm going to read it. I decided the other day. The Knowledge encyclopedia was just for getting used to the big words. I'm going to read the big one when I get out there."

"By that time you might have a wife and six kids."

"No," he said.

"Why not?" I said.

He was ever so cute even if that happened to be a bobbysoxer word, and there was an ugly fold on his shirt I had to smooth. "Flowers are good for kids," I said.

"I'm going to read the science articles first," he said.

The fold was very obstinate. The lake had lovely ripples.

"It takes a long time, reading up on all that stuff. But that's the only way. You got to get at the idea behind this popular mechanics business, you've got to understand the scientific laws. Then you know you got something. You're not just fooling around."

Abruptly he sat up. "Sometimes I got a feeling I'm just fooling around." His arm left me.

"Let's do something," he said. "You play Catchfinger?" He scratched his head; the hair rose in black petulance. He showed me how: to place my downward palm against his upward palm, the idea being to hit me before I could draw back.

It was a crazy game. There was no reason in the world why we should play it. But he always hit me, it was good to feel the pounce of his anger.

"But I'm going to keep at it. I'm going to read science books," he said. "I'm going to set up a laboratory in Monterey."

And a wind came, very gentle with the gold of the afternoon. He hit me, his hair rose, the hurt was sharp, tiny, like no hurt had ever been before.

"And if you set up a laboratory fertilizing new kinds you can make money even with flowers."

I laughed; a laugh that jumped out of my throat like candy, sweet and sleek, I didn't know something like that was in me.

He stopped. The hurt from his fingers was gone and I wished it back. And there was another fold in his shirt I had to smooth.

"You think reading the Knowledge book is foolish?" he said.

"No," I said, laughing, aching for the vanished ache.

"You told your brother about it?"

"My brother?" I said. "Let's play more."

"Your brother would think it's foolish."

"My brother thinks many things he doesn't mean."

"He doesn't like the bike either. But I'm not going to get a car till I can afford a Jaguar."

"Your bike is lovely."

"Does he go to college—your brother?"

"In his fashion," I said. "Play?"

"I can tell. He doesn't like uneducated people."

I hit his hands. My fingertips cried out for contact, for being hit again. But we were not playing any more.

"So you like my motorbike?"

"I love it," I said. "It's like horseback riding."

"I'm going to keep it in California too."

"Promise to take me for a ride sometime?"

"Out there?"

"Especially out there."

"Sure," he said, and his chest moved, a long deep breath of smoke scattered upon the lake and his arm came back round me, all the way round me, and I knew he had fought it out. And the arm was so good. "Laugh like that again," he said.

"Why?" I said.

"I like it. Laugh like that,"

"If you'll take me to Monterey, I will."

"Sure."

And I knew he was going to kiss me. The hour's ease had burst. He leaned over, his shirt blotted out the sky, the lake drowned in the guileless sea-strong morningblue swiftness of his eyes. I tried to laugh the way he liked it.

"I can't, I can't," I said.

It came, his mouth somewhat smaller than I had imagined, softer than I remembered, his shoulders warm mounds above my breast. The moment before I had been parched for touch, the moment after I was flooded, I was coasting, I couldn't hold him in as I had at Biml's. I had to steady myself, I thought Pleasant, I thought, This is really all right, a way of saying thank you to him for the nice trip, a manner of obliging: I had brought it on myself, I had provoked it, I should be able to control it. But that didn't help. His lips were soft plows, his mouth and arms churned into me, questioning and fathoming, dredging me up. Under his pressure I split into drifting bits, then forced myself together again thinking in panicked irony, What a man, Leavis, will you let him quite? And his drive grew so near, so intimate, I felt what he wanted, he wanted to complete himself in me, he wanted the Britannica in me, the Phi Beta Kappa crowned queen of the college dance, he wanted the sophistication of my flesh just as I wanted the untaught strength of his. And seconds long it was lovely, it was all right, I felt I wouldn't have to feel horrible afterward, for he needed me, it was mutual, his hair was like black silk through my fingers, his mouth like an apple on a summer night.

Then came fear, flickering. His hands reached too far, his legs searched; he was really direct—and no, I wasn't ready. I was withered, dry, I wasn't worthy. I was suddenly drained, far from being jungle-juicy as I had fancied myself during the hunt. No, vanity, my sophistication was phony, my eloquence no good, my yap. I wasn't even a woman who could say yes or no with a smiling depth, I was just a terrified wriggle thrashing out against him, for I couldn't let him go further, let him find out how meager, how scared and rank I was; there was nothing to answer his great surge with; I couldn't fool him the way I had fooled Alvin or the others, he was too strong. I would never be able to know a man after this, this humiliation. I was doomed to lifelong frigidity. I fought him. Fear was a constriction from my lips to my loins.

And since I couldn't cry out, I opened my eyes. Opened them wide, clutching at the adolescent myth that if you looked at a boy while kissing, it didn't count, it wasn't a kiss, the kiss would die. But the kiss wouldn't stop. I only saw the purple light riding the waters and the trellis of shadows tossed on it by the willows, black against purple, beautiful and unmoved by my predicament, and I cursed myself for being a miserable virgin. I saw Schatzi uneasy about this queer thing going on between us, unable to participate in it as a third, circling us with whimpers. I saw it all painfully clear, even him, the taut blue seam of his shirt, his tanned neck with the d.a. haircut, his almost feminine long lashes pressed blind and passioned together, the slanted onslaught of his body. And I tried to detect some treachery, some leering premeditation but there was none, just the wild purity of his wanting. So I had to fight that, and fight it harder because the kiss wouldn't stop but grew inwards deeper and I had nothing left but black resistance. I fought with my eyes wide open, throat dried into dumbness while sunset shimmered lavender and Schatzi teetered on his paws, watching open-jawed, snarling along with us, trying to join, uncomprehending.

Then came the noise. The distant rattle.

> *The noise may mean a game warden. Egon hurries her away. But that night he takes her up on the mountain.*

ONCE I STUMBLED and through an opening saw the bonfire, red and yellow with a little green. He never stumbled. He didn't use the flashlight tinkling from his belt. It was a single movement, pulling me up across pebbles and shrubs, across hundreds and hundreds of yards of matted black and none of us talking, reaching a clearing, sitting me down on it, then the pure tiny fierceness of his stubble, the cool yielding of the grass as I was pressed into it, all one. Not abrupt queasy steps, but a single movement, a need like a wellspring. And I was less ready for it than ever. I tried to persuade myself not to be bourgeois, that I wouldn't be damaged goods; I recalled the many times I had dreamed how I would offer myself when the time came, how I would make my body into a satiny, accessible yet mysterious joy, the body I had saved up so long; how I had thought out all the little gestures, even if I had nothing on any more I would still be clothed in a certain little smile that would make my nakedness unfathomable. And now it was here, and the man not at all as I had fancied and my own state still more shocking. I sweated, my flesh was the jail of some frightened demon, I had to resist mutely while his face burned mutely into mine. He spoke, then, he said unwhispering: "Iris, Iris . . ." but I couldn't even say No, I was tensed crazy, every fiber of me, despite the cool yielding of the grass. I wished I were back with the pale shifty wolves of the Bronx with whom you invest nothing but a night-club evening of glib hostility and cheap banter, whom you can dirty-deal with a shabby good-night kiss because they want to dirty-deal you, who kiss to neck and neck to pet and pet to go the limit and go the limit to entertain the boys next morning. With them you could be tough and lonely, with him you couldn't, and I craved back to the safety of loneliness. But he was upon me with a soft strong darkness-tentacled demand, with a bone-deep lust that desires so overwhelmingly and dizzyingly and sucks you out. I wanted to appeal to him with reason, even with humility, to say, Stop, please, this is to big for me, I am not ready for it yet, I must prepare myself, perhaps I have lived wrong for I am not used to giving myself, oh, let me prepare for it. But I couldn't speak, and so I tried anger, I thought he was a rapist, his stubble would raise a rash on my face since he hadn't even bothered shaving— But that didn't work out either, his lunge was too deep and swift, a tingling tiger in the dark, his lips so strong, even his hands, momentarily buttonbaffled, so honest in their power, so animal-clean. I felt giddy and had to hold on to him, I even thought I would throw up but I was too faint even for that and knew only from afar that it was too late for struggling anyhow, that I was pained and impaled—and here it was at last for the first time. And then, strange, drenched in limpness as I lay there was a wrench down there in unmentionability (for I mustn't use, mustn't even think any other word else I'd feel unbearably cheap), an erupting searing kindling of a thousand nerves, and the oomb-sheesh came down upon me with a mighty rhythm, we rode the bicycle again in the old interpierced togethered speed, the night leaped open under it and we traveled as equals, even though I was merely following, fumbling, my need was as vast as his, we sped, we met, we met and mined each other for unheard-of marvels.

"Don't do that," he said.

For in the end I had shivered into coldness. Into wet and separation. The grass was suddenly so hard.

"Why do you cry?" he said.

"Because I can't find my tissues."

He had them somehow and gave one to me and it quieted me. I couldn't see anything. The leaves cut off the moon. I felt alone and askew.

And then there was the awful question I had to get rid of. It boiled out of me.

"Was it bad?"

"Ha?" he said. He was lying next to me, one hand fisted round the branch of a bush and his arm swinging from it shadowy and curved. And me such a trembly stupid wretch.

"I mean . . . was it messy?" I had to say.

"No," he said. "It doesn't matter."

"Yes, it does and you know it."

I needed another tissue. I tried to order myself. I was sneezing, of all moronic things. I asked him to give me all my Kleenex so I wouldn't have to beg for them one by one, humiliatingly.

"Don't worry, I took precautions," he said.

"Stop it. Do you have to make it sound so sordid?"

"See, there's the Big Dipper. One two three four five six seven stars. But it looks like an outboard motor to me." And he bent a branch down and tickled his neck with it. But it didn't do me any good.

"I know it was sordid and you shouldn't pretend it wasn't."

"You sound cute when you cry. You got a baby voice."

"Stop it. Please, stop it."

He tickled my neck with the branch, but it didn't help me. I was still sneezing.

"I was a virgin," I said, "so I was no good. What the hell do you expect from a virgin?"

"You were just different," he said. "And a girl doesn't have to be good."

"A girl does so have to be good. That's male superiority. And I was no good."

"It was very nice."

"Because of you. Not because of me."

Suddenly I thought he had kissed me. As an answer. I wasn't sure. The touch was so light on my side and I couldn't see. And everything was better. But it had to be still better.

"But why did you—why did you insist?"

"I just did," he said.

"But what did you feel about me? You must tell me."

"I felt—very strong. Since the time I went to the play with you."

"But what feeling did you have? Did you love me? You must tell me."

"I loved you."

And then I sensed his arm had been round my shoulder all the time. And I cried. Not as before, but much deeper, freer against his arm. Because he had said it. I had waited so very long for him to say it. I had to push him into it and he had not said it quite right. But he had said it just the same. That was the important thing. And now I could really cry and it was wonderful. For years I hadn't cried like that, hot and deep and liberating, washing the tautness and the meanness out of me, until I was clean and open. And then I could talk. I could say all the things.

> But Egon is simply interested now in setting off a floater rocket he has made for the fireworks display. He drags her down to the camp and runs to the barn to get the rocket. Iris runs to Mordecai, and they seize Egon's motorcycle.

"COMEDY," Mister said, sudden and solemn, into the nothing, "sees the life of man as a career upon the banana peel, as a pratfall out of the womb. Hmm."

"All right," I said. "Let's get the bike going."

"Tragedy is solitary. Comedy is social and semi-detached. Hmm. Comedy is the housemaids tittering from the window as *homo Mordecai* tumbles on the belly. Tragedy is the lone pang in *homo Mordecai's* heart as he sinks. Hmm."

"I wish I could rant like you."

"At a distance of twenty feet *homo Mordecai* is a witty little clown. At the distance of an inch he is a tragic hero. Hmm."

And then it became too much. I had to let him have it.

"I was deflowered, you know," I said.

He must have dropped something. At least there was a noise like it.

"Miss," he said. "Literally?"

"Literally," I said. "Funny, isn't it?"

"Where is he?" he asked.

"Who cares . . . Think we'll get home before daybreak?"

"Where is he, Miss?" he asked.

"The buses run every two hours from Pompheim, don't they?"

"Probably."

"What's that to us where he is? What are you bothering for?"

"I just asked."

"Probably looking for his bike. Isn't that obvious?"

"Oh. Yes."

Mister had stood up. He was tapping the grass for what he had lost.

"The main thing is I've got the bike. I am not accepting it. I am not just another notch on his gun. Don't you see?"

"No," he said, "I don't see the whole thing."

"I am not taking it. I am not a quiet heartbroken doll. I am vicious about it. Will you get the point! I stole his bike."

"Sure."

"You're a great help, Mister. A great help."

"That tough guy."

"He has a mind. He happens to have a mind. If you had listened to him—"

"Yeah, he was great." He was still tapping for something.

"I am stating the facts. I am looking at it dispassionately, from both sides. I am not taking it and he's not dumb. Do you understand that? And will you stop pestering me about it?"

"No, he is not dumb."

"He only sized you up right. We talked about you, among other things. It's not just the way you think. And your whole shocked attitude is just male superiority. That a girl can't get initiated—that's the double standard. And . . . and you are very bourgeois."

"Haven't got a handkerchief," he said.

"Did I ask you? Did you ever have a handkerchief? Were you ever of any help to anybody?"

"No," he said, "Mordecai was never of any help to anybody."

> They fall into a ditch, get going again, the motorcycle gives out, they hitchhike the wrong way. Finally they wait in a coffee shop for a bus. Mordecai tells her he is leaving college.

"I AM GOING to look for soft places," Mister said. Not very clearly. His mouth was still lying on his fist.

"The bus will be here soon," I said.

"Far away Mordecai will go. All the soft places he will try. In a little book he will write where the softest grass is and the softest upholstery and the softest earth. And the softest spring and maybe even the softest girls."

As a practice run I imagined the camp had never been there and the thing had never happened. It almost worked.

"The most wonderful things are soft things," Mister said, low and dreamy. "With your fingers you first try it. Then you let yourself down on it, first only with your backside but then with everything, you let yourself go and you drink it up. Softness is really the most important thing in the world. It's the only thing that doesn't kid you. If it's soft, it's soft. And it never runs away from you. It's always there. A soft thing is so full of sincerity. It's the only thing you can really know. Mordecai knows."

He sat up. His face coiled into sadness. Into tautness. It was almost as if his lips had interrupted his words.

"Miss, I am going away."

"What?" I said.

"I am leaving college."

"On the level?" I tried imagining that.

"I wrote a letter to the Dean demanding they set up a Department of World Government like their Department of Religion. So they threw me out."

"Just like that?"

"The Dean wrote back a huffy letter. So we organized some pressure. We got out leaflets. They say I cut too many classes too."

He was an idiot. I remembered the intercepted letters. But he had brought it up merely to divert me from my Great Grief. It was undoubtedly true but he was taking pity on me.

"Congratulations," I said.

"We'll hike down to South America in August. We got three different nationalities among us. We'll put up some sort of a show. *One World or Bust.* I am writing some skits. All stupid. And we already got some Spanish leaflets. Some kids are working on the Portuguese."

"My blessings."

"We want to cover all cities over a hundred thousand. You got to do something. You can't just wait for the bombs. You've got to try, you've got to reach for something."

"And I'll be left alone with Maw and Paw."

"You come along too."

"I'll have to listen to the howling day after day. Thanks a lot."

"We'll take you with us, Miss."

I tried imagining that for a change. And I got very mad.

"You moron," I said, "you think it's worth it? You think the world is tremendous, don't you?"

"Yeah, crazy," he said. "Yeah, we're young and foolish and globally conscious." His hands grazed the table, his dirty epic hands. "It's doing something. You see there's got to be a big soft spot somewhere and we'll go find it and there'll be softness enough in it for every last mean son of a bitch. And we'll tell everybody where it is and how they can find it. And they will all lay down on it, on the softness, and there won't be any more atom bombs. That's the theory behind it."

"But it's not worth it," I said. "There's nothing tremendous in the world. I found out just now."

Suddenly his mouth dropped down on his fist again.

"Yeah," he said.

And I tried to make him listen, to say something that would make him grasp my meaning. "Listen," I said, "this is life. Either you kibitz or you lose. There is no pot. Either you laugh or you pay through the nose. I'm telling you, I just found out." But that was a weary wise-guy wisdom and it was no good.

"We're conked out and profound," he said distortedly.

"We're miserable," I said.

"Yeah."

"Well, anyway, I wish you luck."

"Mordecai is going out into the world," he said, "to look for soft places." And he pretended to fall asleep on his own fist. And the green scarf hung sad, fantastic, down from his neck.

I sat there, waiting. Kibitz or lose. The ignition key of the bike was on my lap and I guarded it. Without really knowing why or how come. Mister actually seemed asleep. He had wet his fist. I had to guard him too. A thought jumped up. Nothing can happen to me now because everything already has. I guarded that thought too. And the kibitz-or-lose idea also. Though it wasn't really worth it. The jukebox was playing Frank Sinatra, *Oh, What It Seemed To Be*. The diner swayed in a somnambulistic haze, a portrait of tiled musical inferno. An old man opposite ordered his third slice of greasy apple pie. "You bet," said the waitress. But oh, what it seemed to be. It was like a trip to the stars. To Venus and Mars. "You bet," said the waitress. Suddenly the bus came.

THERE THEY WERE. They squatted on the damp furniture in the wee damp hours of the morning and the rancid yellow of the electric light curdled on the floor while the dawn slopped over it from the window. They were suspended in tired desperation, tensed forward a little by our movement at the door. Paw bloated, shapeless, striped in his pajamas, a sticky tongue of chest-hair peeking out between two buttons, arms spread and weighing on his thighs, striving to sag a little against the stress. And Maw with her dressing gown wrinkled round the chemise, twitching new never-seen-before folds around her mouth, and a vein convulsed around her ankle. I saw instantly how it had been. They had argued all day long about us. What had happened to us.

Whether they should call the police. Whether it was just another trick. Perhaps we merely tried to torment them in a different way. Or maybe, God forbid, we had been kidnaped. Or were sick, or dead. Behind the cluttered drug counter they had gone over all the old ground: How come we were that way. That we had inherited the bad blood from Maw's uncle who had been a wandering actor in Poland. That we had been hopeless to begin with and should have been packed off to a military school, both of us; that Maw had foreseen all this. That we were really exceptionally smart children but spoiled because Paw hadn't bothered to help his wife in educating us. That maybe they should have sent me to Vassar. And then they had ordered their disheveled faces as a customer came in and they sold him a large bottle of milk of magnesia and resumed. That we were really most brilliant and everything had gone right until the depression had ruined it all. What they should do if we were really found dead. That they shouldn't even think such thoughts. Who was responsible for letting Mister go to seed. That Mister must have started this trouble and dragged me down with him. But Iris was the elder, Iris was responsible. But no, that Syl was actually responsible for demoralizing Iris . . . I could see them arguing all afternoon, closing up the store, then adjourning their old passionate pain to the kitchen; debating whether they should call Maw's cousin Morris, the lawyer; hoping that perhaps he would know what to do about missing persons; hoping and debating through the evening with Paw not really participating but just keeping enough exchange going to satisfy Maw; and then their deciding against Morris because the less the relatives knew about our troubles the better, but casting about for another person who could locate us discreetly and not finding any and not coming to any conclusions either, just eating their fried kippers slowly while the kitchen clock crawled past midnight. Until Maw said Enough. She was finished with her children forever. She had suffered enough. She would sell the store and go to Palestine. She didn't care any more. She wanted to go to sleep and forget the family. She would go to bed. And Paw saying they should wait a little more; murmuring it was good to be ready in case a call came. And Maw screaming he was torturing her, he had been torturing her all her life, it was his fault they had such terrible children, he had never given her enough money to bring the children up right, he had bungled the jewelry business away; and Maw going to bed with violence, with Paw following slowly behind, trying to sag. And then in bed the tossings, the mutterings, the asking again and again what time it is, the opening of windows, and the journeys to the bathroom for relief, for aspirins, throat and nose clearings, mouth rinsings and back to bed again. And finally Maw screaming she could stand it no more in bed, she would get up. And her putting on the dressing gown and Paw bumbling behind, balloon in search of inertia amid gusts, and the endless grinding accusations continuing in the kitchen without decision, without action.

And then I saw why they hadn't jumped up at our entrance. And why, sensing him, I was so wide awake.

Egon. By the icebox. In the same red shirt.

He must have come in just before us. His hair still gleamed from the light drizzle outside. He turned. He walked toward me and I toward him and for a moment, for a single moment—

"Where is my bike?" he said.

He is here, I thought. And again: He is here. He is here, he is here, until the surging of surprise split upon the fisted eyes, the anonymous mouth. Puma died many memories away. All in one moment, surprise and disaster.

"Here are the clothes you left," he said.

The clothes. He handed them to me. Really just the clothes. And the bike. His face was solid dedicated practicality. No recessed softness anywhere, no message or hidden recollection. Just the clothes, the bike. And under the wet hair his eyes on me angry, like two smooth sledge hammers. And I had to stop the nonsense. I had to and I would. I said to Mister, loud:

"Give him the address of the garage."

"And the bike key?" he said.

That was too much, entirely too much. I ran into my room, tormented by the hot awkward drum of my own feet, clutched against the closed door, drew a splinter somewhere, cursed but did not cry, and felt the edge of the blasted key against my chest: that there shouldn't be a single glimmer or intimation in his face and voice, no special mask, no put-on coldness, no anger-on-the-rebound, that there was no need for him to use insincerity, that he shouldn't display one excess born of a hurt that could balance my own excess of having stolen his bike. I hated not only his not loving me, but I also loathed his healthy energy and matter-of-factness, hated his not having to hate me; envied it, abominated it, pushed the edge deeper into my skin.

And they came alive out there. The unsure shuffle of Maw's slippers, her voice against the door. "Iris, what's the matter with you?"

and me not answering, wishing she'd die, and Paw mumbling something and Maw again, turned in another direction, "A nice fellow like
you . . . ," and Paw rising heavily, drivenly, pulling the slumped pajamas over his hairiness (for I could see it plainly through the wood,
I could see the impotent maneuvers, the loud gauche complexities of
all us Levins circling around the black rock of calmness that was
Egon), Paw saying, "Just a minute, I want to ask you, are you the one
my children were with since yesterday morning—" And myself screaming suddenly, "Don't ask him! Don't ask him! Kick him out!" And
Maw breaking in with a scream of her own because once we are in the
screaming stage it doesn't matter whether we help or hate each other,
our lungs become the bellows of a cosmic and undiscriminating ache,
Maw crying, "What you mean by saying before mine daughter has
taken something! Mine daughter never stole anything in her life!
Mine daughter is an honor student in her school. She is a beautiful
girl, she will become famous, you hear?"

No, I didn't want to hear. I stuck my thumbs into my ears; round
and round I wandered in the walled-in, too-well-known space where
I had spent too many years, too many hopes, too many different kinds
of striving youth, walls frayed by the silent chafing of too many secret
thoughts, whose clotted wall paint bore the scars of too many captive
dreams; the room into which I had escaped as one escaped from a
courtroom into a jail, from the roarmouthed trials in the kitchen
where my parents had accused me of being one of them, one no-good
spouting worm among no-good spouting worms, from which I had
escaped so often into my room that had turned prison at the locking
of my door, turned indictment into a verdict saying that, yes, I was a
no-good spouting worm to whom the heart's promise of freedom and
grace, Cadillacs along Concourse, bough-dipped night-steeped whisper
on Riverside Drive, silked stroll along Fifth Avenue, laughter in the
evening, to whom all that was lost daily, glimpsed again, and lost once
more in the kicking maze of my own striving.

I paced the rectangle that was myself, I passed the overcurtained
window, the scratched victrola case, the wall prints Alvin had sent me,
the gee-tar, the tacked-up Bully clippings, the self-stitched bed cover
with the Eustace Tilley design, the cupboard with two agency postcards on it, one saying *Steno with Leather Trade Journal* $50, the
other *Ass't Editor Girl Scout Magazine* $45, and one letter from
Alvin, the dresser with the surrealistic perfume flask, the album, the
overcurtained window, the scratched victrola case, the wall prints

Alvin had sent me. . . . Like a spiked wheel the room raked me—but gently now for these were all old stings that had driven deep calloused ruts into memory, deep furrows into longing, they had shaped me, carved me, cut me for so long I had almost forgotten they were knives.

And, stopping, I unthumbed my ears to see if the sounds still hurt. A fly buzzed instantly at the window, Maw swelled into saying, did Mr. Biml realize how much blood a mother put into a daughter, could Mr. Biml blame her for defending her? And Paw, grasping at patriarchal gravity, wanted to know what had really happened since yesterday, he meant he had a right to know, those were his children! Weak, voluble they shifted around him. Maw said she was sure if Mr. Biml was a gentleman— And abruptly he knocked on my door.

It was him. I knew. I knew so well the sweep of his hands, the raps touched me. I stood rigid. Mister shouted from the bathroom, shower on, somebody throw him a towel instead of fooling with that naaaasty man. . . .

I moved again. As though someone had tapped me on the shoulder to say "It doesn't matter." And it was true.

I was through with it.

None of the sounds hurt me, for I was through with them. Through with the room and its penthouse-high hopes, with Maw and Paw— and through with *him* too, for though he had ended the phase, he was part and parcel of it, though he had kicked me out of my old state I was for that reason proof against his power, I could ignore him as only a corpse can cut its executioner, he had made me die and even death is a trifle to the dead. Done, the snarled littered grace-haunted Bronx nights, when I had battled the monsters in the kitchen, the chinchillas in my brain, when Maggie and I had kneaded the future with visions and words, yet never came near it since in our virgin world the future had been too great for touching. From the extremity of thirst I had ogled at the extremity of fulfillment and never dared jump the glittering vast between. But now I had leaped at last—and lost—and gained the loss. I had tried to write the great scoop and lost, I had fallen, after all these cautious years, in great love and come a cropper. And now I hurt like hell but I was wise. I had latched on to the secret of maturity: the domestication of failure. I had acquired the adult courage for compromise. Experience is the name men give to their mistakes and all that rot, but it was true. I was mistaken, I was experienced, and how. But that was all right. Tremendousness was gone. And so, slowly my cramped hand relaxed, revealed the key I would return in a minute because it was useless, there was no longer any reason to keep him knocking. Tremendousness had taken a powder. I would take the Scout job for forty-five bucks. I would move away. I would move away with Maggie, not into a Village duplex but a small midtown room. I would let myself love again, and hope for being loved, and yes, be a she-burgher, catch a man, marry and worry about safe ludicrous things, about nonirritating diaphragms and fur coats and whether my man would not get bald too soon. And for Christ's sakes, Leavis, get the goddamn business over with.

I grabbed the forty-five-dollar postcard, not for any immediate reason but because it hugged the new anti-tremendous resolve closer to me, I held the key. I opened, opened the door.

There he stood, of course, a young boulder, the hair not dry yet, so painful. In a minute nothing would be left of him.

I gave it to him. Eyes severely business. In a way all this was merely growing up.

"Good-bye."

"I don't get you," he said.

"Don't try," I said, and wanted to shout to heaven in thanks that he didn't get me, that he would never understand the convolutions, the contradiction, the writhing ruses of loving too much, for in understanding he would have to pity and to be pitied by him was a thing I would die of endlessly through a thousand years.

"But listen—" he said, and I marveling how purely his hesitation was made of puzzlement, how clean the slant of his black hair, how fresh, uncalculated the inclination of his head, how animal-noble his brows, how free of unreasonableness, the moist ulterior intent of love, his interest for me.

Then he *had* to get out, otherwise the whole crazy thing would start again.

"Good-bye."

"But what'd you do such a crazy thing for?"

"If you don't know . . ."

"I don't. And you should've seen my floater rocket. I set it off from a tree—"

"Will you please leave!"

"I don't see it. Not just about the bike. We could have had such times together. They were dancing till two in the morning, wonderful weather. I had a little surprise for you too. A rocket with your initials—"

"No," I said, "I can't listen, not now!"

"It's easy, making rockets with initials. But this one's special." He pulled at something in his pocket.

"I don't want to see it!"

It would kill me, the unused unexploded gray sight of it.

"I wish you'd watch it. The first one I made myself."

"Some other time. Go!"

"You mean it?"

"Yes. At this moment!"

He went. While even the kitchen was quiet, the shower droned. Gone.

Gone. I would move to midtown, somewhere near the park and not think of him and work for the Girl Scouts of all people. It didn't matter. In a way all this were merely growing up.

Another moment quiet and I saw from the afterrigidity of their sitting that they knew. And knew even better that now was the time to stay away from me. But they wouldn't, couldn't. My pain or Mister's draws them like dogs smelling a bitch, they come trotting heavily, not content till they share the last little drop of agony. They rose, Maw asked, why hadn't Mr. Biml said good night to her and what was going on, she was not going to sleep till she knew. And Paw went to the bathroom and demanded through the door, demanded with compulsive but sagging tyranny that Mister should tell his parents everything, did he hear? Everything!

"Had a picnic," Mister said, coming out. I watched them soberly. In a way all this was merely growing up.

"A picnic?" Paw said, following Mister along. "All day and all night for a picnic? And who do you think is helping in the store?"

"We were celebrating a hotcha occasion," Mister said.

"Apart from everything," Paw said, "don't you know that when a girl like your sister goes away with a man overnight, don't you have some responsibility—"

"We were celebrating Mordecai's declaration of independence," Mister said. "I was kicked out of Cornell."

"Kicked . . . ," Paw mumbled. And I observed them. I had grown up.

Maw, all set for a renewed swoop on me, swiveled round. She cried out that she had felt it. She had felt it ever since Mister had won the scholarship; for three years she had carried it around in her heart, but she had never wanted to say it, she had hoped it wouldn't happen.

Mister, fixing up his bed, said, Yup, just one of those things. Paw said, Look at him, he's proud of it. And Maw swore she would go up to Cornell, she would talk to the university president herself until they had told her the reason why, she would fight for her son. And Paw said maybe it would teach him a lesson; there was still time for him to learn pharmacy. But Maw sobbed: Pharmacy! Never! A brilliant boy like her son should never be trapped in pharmacy the way it had trapped her, she hated pharmacy, it had poisoned her life, she should have never come to this country, everything had gone wrong, there was a curse on her. Paw watched her with his flogged fat eyes, watched her with fatigue and desire, the hair still showed through his pajamas and slowly he sat down on the kitchen chair.

I could go then, because Mister had released me. He had taken them upon himself. While I went, he walked around the kitchen, burly and heavy-footed, his shoulders heaving into an old man's hunch for the weight of our parents' stinging love was upon them and ran down his arms and trailed behind. He moved like a stag born for the hungers of all the world's hounds. And since I had to love somebody that moment, I loved him.

And so I went to bed. I locked the door and drew the shades against the gray. I would sleep until infinity tomorrow. I shook off my clothes and lay down for my first real rest in five days. I thought of all the things that had happened and it was pretty bad. But I consoled myself with the idea that all those things were just another way of growing up. But the consolation was somewhat out of order and I couldn't sleep. I wrapped myself in tiredness and thought of all the things I would do tomorrow, the definite, solid, nice things. How I would take the job and wear a chartreuse beret for the interview and borrow money from Maw to buy a Scotch-plaid stole. I thought how comfortable life had become now that it had shrunk. I thought of that, it was a good, cool thought. Life became smaller, cozier, darker, till it almost disappeared. I dozed off. But suddenly I heard Mister roar out at something. And though I couldn't distinguish the words, I came to; I knew that breath was still fit for shouting, and for him the future still to be bitten into with vast courage, vast cynicism, vast despair, that tremendousness would never leave him and he be forever young —while I, for the first time, had aged. And, sweet horror, Egon suddenly floated back to me as though I had never gotten rid of him, the whole strong simple wondrousness of him, I suddenly remembered he had tiny black hairs on his shoulders, I felt like running out naked as

I was into the streets to catch him, call him back—but then I reminded myself I was too tired. Perhaps tomorrow I'd give him a ring and ask him to explode my initials in Claremont Park for me and—and hell, I didn't want to think. I was too tired. The bed came round me again. Another way of growing up. I relaxed. I thought of definite comfortable things. The Girl Scout job was a little asinine, I could graduate from there to *Seventeen*, maybe *Mademoiselle*. Forty-five bucks, but I could try free-lancing on the side. And one day I would travel with Mister to stay young with him. I would get married to an artist who didn't mind damaged goods or to a foreign correspondent and Mister would travel with us. We would travel all the time some day, though never in New Jersey. Some day I would have enough to support my brother and let him have everything he wanted. And sometime somesoon I would even go to sleep.

Marjorie Morningstar

by HERMAN WOUK

Gentleman's Agreement, by Laura Z. Hobson, was the first American novel on a Jewish theme to reach best-sellerdom, but Marjorie Morningstar really catapulted interest in Jewish material to a lofty high. First published in 1955, it has sold into the millions in both hard-cover and paperback editions, and has been translated into many languages, as well as filmed.

Wouk's portrait of a Passover seder, presented here, perhaps best epitomizes, out of all the typical material in the novel, the author's double view, in which the realistic rendition of certain vulgarities is paralleled by a feeling for certain simple souls and some understanding of those who, like the half-artist Noel Airman, suffer from their pretentions and limitations.

The seder episode shows the partial breakdown of this ancient family rite in American Jewish homes; not a pleasant picture, and surely not a total one, but there is truth in it. The second selection, "The Man She Married," tries to get into the soul of an "emancipated" Jewish girl who has experimented, if lightly, with various aspects of the sophisticated life, but who in the end surrenders to suburban values. The man she marries is rather shadowy, after the portrait we have had of Noel Airman, but what takes place—the actual marriage and the reasoning behind it—is recognizable.

Wouk, who was born in New York in 1915, came to wide notice with earlier novels, particularly The Caine Mutiny, a study of authoritarianism focusing on a trial in which a Jewish lawyer, reacting powerfully to the results of insane authoritarianism in the holocaust, exposes it among the military. A still earlier novel, The City Boy (1948), is a charming pastiche of a Jewish child's activities in a summer camp.

Like Budd Schulberg, who wrote of an F. Scott Fitzgerald figure in The Disenchanted, Wouk novelized a Thomas Wolfe figure in Youngblood Hawk. A desire to identify? Wouk has attracted a wide audience with his book about his faith as a traditional, observing Jew, This Is My God.

C.A.

The Seder

WHEN MRS. MORGENSTERN first suggested inviting Noel and his parents to the family's Passover dinner, the seder, Marjorie thought it was an appalling idea. On reflection, however, she decided that there was some hard good sense in it.

With Noel doing well at Paramount, with their relationship becoming each week more intimate and hopeful, it did seem to her that the time had come for his parents and her own to confront each other. She also thought Noel had better see the Family and glimpse her religious background. At fourteen and fifteen she had hated seders, barmitzvas, and all the rest, and she had taken pleasure in shocking her parents with atheistic talk. In recent years, however, she had found the seder oddly appealing, and she wanted to see how he would react. The complex rituals and symbols of the Passover feast—the matzo, the horseradish, the four cups of wine, the pounded nuts and apples, the hard-boiled eggs in salt water, the great goblet of wine for Elijah— these things, with the old family songs and the annual jokes at the same points in the Hebrew service, had attractive bitter-sweet nostalgia for her. It was fun in a way, too, to see the Family once a year, and find out which of the cousins had married, and see the new babies, and marvel at the rapid growth of the old babies. There was a risk, of course, that Noel and his parents would be dismayed and put off by the seder; but she didn't think it was much of a risk, and anyway she was prepared to take it.

She was rather afraid to bring the subject up with Noel. But to her astonishment he agreed very readily to come. He knew nothing whatever about seders, except that matzo was eaten; but when she described the ceremonies to him he said, "Why, it sounds very colorful and alive. My father will undoubtedly make a bloody ass of himself, as usual, but that might prove amusing, too."

"I should warn you that all the relatives from miles around get to-gether at this thing, and the children, and the grandchildren, and it's a pretty noisy mess."

"Oh." Noel looked thoughtful, then he brightened. "Well, don't you think that may be a good thing? I may well go unnoticed in the crush. Of course, all your relatives will gossip about us, but if you don't mind I don't."

"Honestly, Noel, you're a chameleon. If there was ever anything I dreaded, it was mentioning this thing to you. And here you are, being just as nice as pie about it."

"Darling, you really do me an injustice. I have a heart of gold. My only faults are that I'm totally selfish and immoral. Tell your mother it's okay—my folks and all."

He arrived late. The seder guests were already crowded in the smoky living room, with children darting between their legs and around the furniture, laughing and squealing. Four babies in baskets and portable cribs were howling in Marjorie's bedroom, and their young mothers, wild-haired and with blouses coming out of their skirts, were rushing to and fro through the foyer, brandishing bottles, diapers, pots, and rattles. Noel grinned at Marjorie, cocking his ear to the noise, as he slipped out of his coat. She said, "Well, didn't I warn you?"

"Why, it sounds very exuberant. My father here?"

"Yes, and your mother, and they're both in evening clothes. They go from here to a Democratic banquet."

The doorbell rang, and Marjorie's cousins, Morris and Mildred Sapersteen, came in with their son, Neville. Marjorie was amazed to see how the child had grown. She remembered him as a particularly loud-bawling blond infant, but he was now a large redheaded boy. "Gosh, how old is Neville, anyway?" she said to the father, who was carrying a black suitcase. Neville's mother began taking off his coat, which was no simple thing to do, since he was rearing and tearing to get at the children in the living room, shouting, "Hi, Suzy Capoozy! Hi, Walter Capalter!"

"He's five, just turned five," Morris Sapersteen said. He was Uncle Shmulka's oldest son, a writer of advertising copy, a sad-faced young man not much bigger than his father. He set down the suitcase with a sigh. "Gosh, you'd never believe how heavy those things can be."

"What have you got there?" Marjorie said.

"Airplanes."

"Airplanes?"

"Forty-seven airplanes, Neville won't go anywhere without them."

Neville, disentangling his arms from the sleeves of his coat, was off into the living room like a rocket. Marjorie introduced Noel to the Sapersteens. Morris's wife, Mildred, a thin freckled girl with very large front teeth, and black straight hair cut like an inverted bowl, was a piano teacher of sorts, and sometimes played at family gatherings. She looked very tired.

Morris opened the suitcase. It was really crammed to the top with toy airplanes of every shape, color, and size, all tumbled in a tangle of wheels and wings. "Where can I put this, Margie? Just so he can get at them when he feels the need for them. I don't want it to be in the way——"

Marjorie indicated a corner in the hallway. "It's a nuisance," Mildred Sapersteen said, "but we've tried taking him places without them, and it sets up all kinds of traumas. The planes have become a sort of security symbol for him."

Noel said gravely, "A substitute for the father image, would you say?"

"Well, possibly," Mildred said, "but we think it's a compensatory mechanism for a rather small sex organ. It's well within the normal range, but—— Morris, leave the lid up, he goes into a frenzy if he sees it down——"

"I'm leaving it up, I'm leaving it up," Morris said. "I say it's a surrogate for masturbation, myself, but whatever it is, he won't go anywhere without these damn planes, that's for sure. Whew! There we are." He stood and peered into the clamorous living room. "Well, I see the panic is on. Let's go, Mildred. Where is he, anyway?"

When they were out of sight Noel collapsed against the closet door, shaking with laughter.

"That's right," Marjorie muttered, "laugh at my crazy cousins——"

"Crazy!" Noel gasped. "Honey, nearly every young married couple I know talks that way. I bait them for hours sometimes, and they never tumble. Morris, leave the lid up, or he'll get a trauma——" He choked, his shoulders quivering. "Now you know why I won't get married. . . . Forty-seven airplanes——"

Mrs. Morgenstern, flushed, and with an apron over a fine new purple dress, poked her head into the foyer. "What are you two billing and cooing about in a corner? We're starting the seder. Come in."

The flower-festooned glittering table, extended with all its leaves and eked out with a card table, stretched from the windows to the far wall of the long narrow dining room, under a blaze of bright white electric bulbs. An auxiliary table had been improvised in the living room, visible through the opened French doors, and the children were shepherded out there by Mildred Sapersteen, who volunteered to stay with them, so as to keep an eye on Neville. The children objected raucously to being steered away from the adults' table, and Neville, in the course of his objections, put his foot through a pane in the French doors. But the glass was cleared away, the children pacified with a round of Pepsi-Cola; and against the background of rich lively noise, mingled with the quarrelsome chattering of the children and the muffled but powerful howls of the babies in the bedrooms, the seder began.

The liveliness did not extend to the table of the adults. Here, as the ceremonies proceeded, there gradually fell a strained queer quiet, unlike the atmosphere of other years. The little people of the Family, old gray tailors, candy-store keepers, mechanics, and their wives, were terrorized by the presence of a judge and his lady; and their grown-up sons and daughters, usually a joking and irreverent band of ordinary young Americans, wore awkward company airs. The fact that the Ehrmanns were in evening clothes did not help matters. Tiny Uncle Shmulka, the laundry sorter, jammed in his cheap frayed brown suit against the resplendent judge, kept trying in vain to shrink away, and not contaminate the great man with the rub of poverty. Seth, too, sat clumsy and glum beside Mr. Morgenstern, supporting his father's opening chants over the wine and the matzo with his uncertain baritone voice, and shooting occasional suspicious looks at Noel.

Noel, though his behavior was faultless, seemed to make the Family even more uneasy than his parents did. A chill radiated from him, causing much of the lameness of the singing, the stumbling of the Hebrew responses, and the embarrassed side glances among the relatives. The skullcap perched on his thick blond hair somehow looked as incongruous as it would have on an animal's head. His bearing was sober, his comments courteous; Marjorie could not accuse him of deliberately trying to appear out of place and trapped. Nor was there anything intentionally offensive in the way he kept looking around. But the effect was to make the Family, including Marjorie, feel increasingly like painted Africans performing a voodoo rite. Mrs. Morgenstern didn't improve things by trying to explain the ceremonies to Noel. She would get all tangled up in theology, and dead silence would drop over the table while she painfully bumbled her way through; and Noel all the while would nod brightly, saying that it was really terribly interesting. This happened over and over.

Worst of all, however, was the absence of the Uncle.

Until this year, Marjorie had not realized how central Samson-Aaron had been to the seder. Her father always had sat at the head of the table, as he sat now, conducting the service out of the beautifully illustrated Hagada printed in England. Samson-Aaron had seemed merely the fun-maker, the heckler, of the feast. Now Marjorie saw that he had been nothing less than the soul of it; and he was gone. He had warmed the air. Single-handed, he had dispelled the stiffness of a year's separation, and the frost of all the permanent quarrels, of all the sad unchangeable differences in income. His bubbling jokes, his bellowing of the songs, his pounding of the rhythms with fist and foot, his cavorting, his fabulous eating and drinking, had gradually wakened the spirits of the Family, brought the old ties of blood to life, and welded the scattered estranged group, at least for the evening, into something like the close-knit tribal Family of the old country. Without him, the seder was but a moribund semblance; and it was enacted with less and less heart as the evening went on, under the fixed smiles of Judge and Mrs. Ehrmann, and the cool observant eyes of their son.

If anyone promised to save the seder as an institution, it was Neville Sapersteen. He was giving the occasion what liveliness it had. The children's table was a vortex of noise and motion, all of it churning around Neville. Snatching the other children's Pepsi-Cola, breaking matzos over their heads, drinking off the salt water, throwing plates, forks, pepper, flowers, hard-boiled eggs, Neville was exhibiting enough vivacity for ten children. His mother stayed one step behind him, as it were, catching the plates before they broke, putting back the flowers, wiping up the wine, comforting the other children when Neville drank their Pepsi-Cola, and persuading them not to break matzos over Neville's head, on the grounds that revenge was an unworthy motive. Marjorie's back was to the living room, so that she missed much of the byplay; but at every sudden burst of noise she would look around fearfully, to make sure that nothing jagged or wet was sailing her way.

Matters broke out of control very suddenly in the living room, just as Mr. Morgenstern was putting down the three wrapped matzos after reciting *This bread of affliction*. There was an explosion of laughter and yammering, with Neville's voice rising in infuriated soprano shrieks over the din. His mother yelled, "Morris, Morris, come quick! The airplanes! They're into the airplanes!" While Morris struggled frantically to get out of the seat where he was wedged between two fat aunts, half a dozen children came giggling and shrieking into the dining room, swooping toy airplanes in their hands and making noises like airplane motors—"*Braah! Braah!*" After them charged Neville, his face dark purple, waving his fists and uttering hideous choked sounds. The children dived under the table and under chairs; they flew between the legs of their pursuing parents, in and out of the clutching arms of Mildred and Morris Sapersteen, into the bedrooms and round and round the living room, all the time roaring "Braah! Braah!" Neville did a remarkable simulation of running in fourteen directions at once, whimpering, screeching, and snapping his teeth. The seder stopped dead for ten minutes, while all the parents joined the chase. The airplanes were at last rounded up, and the children herded back to their chairs; it was a difficult business, because they kept snatching new airplanes from the suitcase after being deprived of the ones they had, and galloping around again.

Morris Sapersteen stood at bay in the middle of the living room, clutching the suitcase, while Mildred attempted to quiet Neville, who was lying on his back, kicking the floor with both heels, and yelling. Morris said, "I'll just have to lock the lid, I guess."

"No, no," Neville screamed. "I want the box open!"

His mother said, "There's only one answer. These kids are impossible. You'll have to hold the suitcase open on your lap."

"Gosh, Millie, how will I eat?"

"Look, Morris, it wasn't my idea to come to this thing, it was yours. I warned you." She led Neville off, and Morris stumbled back into his chair, and sat with the suitcase on his lap.

Peace ensued; but not for long.

The next part of the seder was the reciting of the Four Questions. Essentially the seder was a sort of pageant, or religious drama, performed at home. The youngest child who could memorize Hebrew delivered four queries about the table symbols: the horseradish, the matzo, the salt water, and so forth: and the adults in reply chanted the tale of the Exodus from Egypt, explaining the symbols as the story unfolded. Marjorie had scored great triumphs with the Four Questions from her fourth to her eighth year. The Family had all said even then that she was a born little actress.

This year the Questions were admirably performed in a sweet pip-
ing voice, in flawless parroted Hebrew, by Susan Morgenstern, a
chubby six-year-old from the Newark branch of the family. She retired
to the children's table, after curtsying to the applause. The adults
had hardly begun the concerted chant of the response when the most
horrible imaginable scream rang out from the living room, and Neville's mother was heard exclaiming, "Neville, that was cruel! You're
not supposed to be cruel!"

Neville, it developed, had sneaked up in back of Susan Morgenstern and bitten her with all his might on the behind.

Again the seder stopped while the four parents hurriedly unscram-
bled the children; for Susan was rolling with Neville on the floor,
trying to strangle him, and making fair headway.

It happened that there was bad blood anyway between the Newark
branch and the Far Rockaway branch, which was Neville's, and a
nasty argument sprang up when Neville's father tried to say that the
bite had actually been a good thing. He said that Neville had gotten
rid of the hostility naturally created by Susan's spell in the limelight,
and so in reality the bite had drawn the cousins closer. "Holy cow,
Morris!" exclaimed the father of Susan, a heavy good-natured young
butcher named Harry. "If he bit her he bit her. But I'll be god-
damned if I'll let you say it was a good thing, too. Why, for crying
out loud, suppose all the other kids had—what'd you call it?—gotten
rid of their goddamn hostility like him? My girl would have been
chewed to death."

"Harry, please, don't curse at the seder table," said Mrs. Morgenstern, smiling pathetically at the judge and his wife.

"Perfectly normal, nothing to get excited about," the judge said,
craning his neck and watching the flailing Neville in the other room
with some alarm.

"Neville's exceptionally aggressive," his father said. "It's the normal
pattern of the only child, especially the insecure male."

"It's not that at all," his mother shouted angrily. She was squatting,
trying to hold Neville still while she straightened his clothing. "It's
all this primitive magic and symbolism and Hebrew he's being exposed to. It upsets his nerves. He's been brought up rationally, and
he's at a stage where all this poppycock disturbs him deeply!"

Morris Sapersteen, fumbling at the open suitcase on his lap,
glanced around at Mr. and Mrs. Morgenstern. "All right, Millie,
there are other people here besides us, who think a little differently
——"

"Oh, it's all right. He's got to be exposed to all these folkways sooner or later, I guess, but we might have waited a couple of years, that's all."

The Family meantime, with all the excitement, had become a little livelier. There was chatter around the table, instead of stiff gloom. Harry Morgenstern, Susan's brawny father, sneaked himself a couple of drinks of the Palestinian plum brandy to calm his nerves. He immediately became very red in the face, and began to pound the table with his fists. "What the hell, people, is this a seder or a funeral? Come on, put some life into it! The judge here is going to think he's in an old folks' home!" And he started to bawl a song, and several of the Family joined in.

Judge Ehrmann waved at him and laughed. "Don't worry about me. I'm thoroughly enjoying myself, I assure you."

"This is nothing, Your Honor," Harry shouted. "We warm up a little, we'll show you what a seder is all about! Come on, Dora, come on, Leon—sing!"

Mr. Morgenstern said, "That's the spirit, Harry, that's what we need. You sound like the Uncle." He beat time on a glass with a fork, and after a moment broke into the song himself. Everybody sang. Mr. Morgenstern returned to the Hebrew chanting with more zest and heart, and the Family's responses became stronger, too.

Noel turned to Marjorie, his eyes lively. "Well, I begin to get the idea."

"Oh, this is nothing," Marjorie said. Her spirits were rising. "This is a ghost of what it used to be. We used to have Samson-Aaron."

"I can imagine," Noel said. "I'm really beginning to understand him, a little bit—and you too, for that matter."

The seder continued to pick up momentum and gaiety, and soon it was more or less in the old swing. Harry the butcher showed some promise of leadership, bellowing and pounding with energy equal to the Uncle's, if with less charm and flavor. Marjorie felt the familiar old warmth enveloping her. The sweet grape taste of the wine woke childhood recollections. She began to care less what Noel and his parents were thinking, and she joined in the songs with abandon. She noticed that both Noel and his father had taken to reading the English translations in their Hagadas, watching the others to see when pages were turned. Noel looked to her at one point and said, "Do you understand all this Hebrew?"

"Well, fortunately, yes, we've gone over and over it for so many years—otherwise my Hebrew is pretty rusty——"

Noel said, "The English is absolutely atrocious, at least this translation furnished by the matzo company is. But I do get a dim idea of what it's all about. It has terrific charm and pathos, actually—and power, too. I rather envy you."

The ritual had arrived at another song, and as the family burst into it with gusto, Judge Ehrmann glanced up from the book, his high bald brow wrinkled. "Why, I believe I know that one," he said to Uncle Shmulka. He hummed a few bars with the others, and Shmulka nodded with delight. "Well!" the judge said. "I guess that's one that percolated through to the German Jews. My mother used to hum it to me when I was a baby. I remember it distinctly, though I haven't heard it in fifty years." Waving a stiff extended finger high in the air, Judge Ehrmann joined in the song. The effect on the Family was tremendous. When the song ended Harry bawled, "Three cheers for the Judge!" And the Family cheered, and gave him a round of applause. He bowed here and there with pleased dignity, his long face flushed, his gray fringe of hair a little disordered, a pulse throbbing in his neck.

A crash of crockery from the living room now indicated that Neville Sapersteen was emerging from his doldrums. Marjorie looked over her shoulder, and saw Mildred Sapersteen on her hands and knees, picking up the pieces. Mildred caught her look and said angrily, "Well, there's just so much I can do. Susan is impossible. She keeps calling Neville 'Neville the Devil.' No child with any brains would stand for that——"

Harry Morgenstern shouted into the living room, "Susan, you stop that, do you hear? No more calling Neville 'Neville the Devil.' Understand me?"

"Yes, Daddy," piped Susan, and added, "Just one last time, all right, Daddy? Neville the Devil!"

Now that it was officially forbidden, all the children took up the cry and bayed rhythmically, "Ne-ville the De-vil! Ne-ville the De-vil! Ne-ville the De-vil!"

Neville left his chair and catapulted into the dining room, yelling, "Daddy, I want my airplanes! Give me my airplanes!"

Morris jumped up, forgetting that the suitcase was open on his lap; the suitcase slipped, he clutched at it and upset it, and the forty-seven airplanes went clanking and tinkling all over the floor under the table. There was a moment of silence after the crash; even Neville shut up, staring pop-eyed at his father.

"All right," Mildred Sapersteen said in an icy tone. "Nice going, Morris. Now pick them all up."

"No, no," screeched Neville, "I don't want them picked up. Leave them there. I've got to make a parade!" He dived under the table and could be heard crawling, and sliding airplanes along the floor.

"What's he going to make?" Mrs. Morgenstern said nervously to Mildred. "Get him out from under the table, please."

"A parade," Mildred said. "He won't harm anything. He just lines them up three abreast. In perfect formation."

"Mildred dear," said Mrs. Morgenstern, "not under the table, please, with people's feet and everything——"

Morris said, "Aunt Rose, if you want some peace and quiet, believe me this is the best idea. A parade absolutely absorbs him. You won't know he's there. Take my word for it. Just ignore him and——"

At that moment Judge Ehrmann leaped to his feet with an incredibly loud snarl, upsetting his chair, clutching at his leg. "Aaarh! MY GOD!"

"My parade! You kicked my parade!" Neville squealed from under the table.

"Good heavens," the judge choked, "the little monster has really bitten my ankle to the bone!" He pulled up his trouser leg, peering anxiously at his thin bluish shank.

Morris Sapersteen plunged under the table and pulled Neville out, thrashing and howling. "My airplanes! My parade! I want my parade!"

The whole table was in an uproar. The judge said to Morris, "Good Lord, man, forgive me for being blunt, but what that child needs is the whipping of his life. He needs it desperately."

"Morris!" shrilled Mildred, glaring at the judge. "Let's go home."

"Take it easy, Mildred, for God's sake," Morris said.

"We're going home, I say! Pick up the airplanes!"

"I've got *him*, Millie," Morris panted, still struggling with Neville, as with a large live salmon.

Uncle Shmulka said, "Mildred, dolling, don't go home, it's a seder. You didn't eat nothing yet." He held out his arms to Neville. "Come to Grandpa, sveetheart." Neville with astonishing readiness stopped writhing, slid from his father's arms into little Shmulka's lap, and nestled. The judge edged slightly away. "There, Mildred, everything's fine," Shmulka said. "He'll sit vit me and be good. For Grandpa, he's alvays good."

"Oh no, I'm not going to have that again." Mildred's mouth was a black line, her brows were pulled in a scowl. "That lulling is all wrong, and that grandfather-fixation business is really sick, and I'm not having it in my family. *Get* the airplanes, Morris, and let's go." She folded her arms and leaned in the doorway. The children behind her were still.

Morris looked around with a smile, his eyes big and sad. "Sorry folks, I think it's best, maybe." He dropped on his hands and knees, and knocked and shuffled under the table.

Mildred was standing almost directly behind Marjorie. Impulsively getting out of her chair, Marjorie put her arm around Mildred's waist. "Millie, you're right to be upset. But I think you'll be more upset, and Morris certainly will be, if you walk out now. It's only another hour ——" she faltered. Mildred Sapersteen's eyes, curiously flat and shiny as they looked into hers, horrified her.

Mildred said, "Marjorie dear, you're very sweet and pretty, and you've got everything in the world, I know, but I've just got a son, and I've got to do what's best for him."

Harry said to Marjorie, "Give up. She's just a goddamned pill. She's enjoying this."

Mildred whirled, glared at Harry, then looked around at the table. "Well! Thank God we live in a time when you can pick and choose your own culture. Nobody can say I haven't tried to cooperate, but this mumbo-jumbo is impossible, and Neville senses it, and I've always said so. If I have anything to say, we'll wind up joining the Unitarian Church. They have all the answers, anyway." There was a horrid silence. "All right, Morris. Get the baby and let's go."

Uncle Shmulka said in a small tired voice, "He fell asleep." Neville indeed, the storm center of the wrangle, was curled in a ball in his grandfather's lap, eyes closed, breathing peacefully.

The last thing Morris said after fumbling goodbyes, as he carried the slumbering boy out of the room, was, "Papa, she didn't mean that about the church. We're not joining any church."

"I know, Morris, I know you're not. She's a good girl, she's upset. Be vell," said Uncle Shmulka.

As Morris trudged out of sight one of the children called out half-heartedly, "Neville the Devil."

Mrs. Morgenstern said to the Ehrmanns, "I don't know what you must think of us."

Judge Ehrmann smiled, and his voice was deep and soothing. "You should see our family get-togethers, Rose. When blood doesn't flow, it's considered dull. Now I know you've got a big happy family."

He had not used her first name before. Mrs. Morgenstern glowed, and the drawn countenances all around the table relaxed. Harry Morgenstern said, "By God, Judge, you're right. We do have a big happy family. There's one of those in every family, and to hell with her. Come on, Aunt Rose, we're through with the Hagada, aren't we? Where's the eats?"

It was a heavy delicious feast: chopped chicken liver, stuffed fish, fat beet soup, matzo balls, chicken fricassee, potato pancakes, fried chicken and fried steaks. Judge Ehrmann went at the food with startling enthusiasm, saying there was nothing in the world that he loved like Jewish cooking. The relatives, who had been fearing that they would have to eat daintily in the judge's presence, fell to joyously. Soon everybody was very merry except Aunt Dvosha, who sat nib bling at a platter of dry chopped-up carrots, lettuce, tomatoes, raw potatoes, and apples. She had recently given up cooked vegetables, on the grounds that vitamins were destroyed by heat. As she looked around at seventeen people stuffing themselves with vast quantities of fried meat, her face became long and gloomy, and she grumbled to herself, and to whoever would listen to her, about stomach linings, amino acids, protein poisoning, and sudden death.

The judge began glancing at his watch when the dessert came. After finishing his second cup of tea, he deliberately removed his skullcap, folded it on top of his napkin, and cleared his throat. The gesture and the single sound were enough to make all the guests stop eating and drinking, and turn their faces toward him.

"My dear Rose and Arnold, Mrs. Ehrmann and I certainly regret that we have to leave this warm and lovely family circle, and these beautiful ceremonies, and this marvelous food, and go to a dull political dinner, the kind of thing I have to do almost every night in the week, but I can't——"

"It's perfectly all right, Judge," Mrs. Morgenstern said, not quite realizing that this was a preamble rather than conversation.

The judge rolled over her smoothly with a smile, "—but I can't, I say, leave this sumptuous, and may I say sacred, table without a word of appreciation." Noel slumped. His eyes dulled, and his face was so morose that Marjorie was afraid others would notice. But all eyes were on the judge. "Come what may tonight," Judge Ehrmann said, "I've eaten Rose Morgenstern's food. And I'm even more grate-

ful for the spiritual food I've received tonight. Mrs. Ehrmann and I
aren't religious people in any formal sense, I'm afraid, but I trust in
all our actions, we've always showed ourselves good Jews at heart.
You see, we're both descended from the old German families who
have pretty well dropped all that. Sitting here tonight, I asked myself, were my grandfathers really so wise? Twentieth-century psychology has some very complimentary things to say, you know, about the
power of symbol and ceremony over the conduct of men. And I wonder whether it isn't going to turn out that these old-time rabbis knew
best. The marvelous warmth and intimacy of your ceremonies tonight! Even the little family quarrel only made things more lively. It
gave the evening—well, tang. I was going to say bite, but I'd better
not." He paused skillfully for the laugh. "The little Hagada, with
its awkward English and quaint old woodcuts, has been a revelation
to me. I've suddenly realized, all over again, that I'm part of a tradition and culture that go back four thousand years. I've realized that it
was we Jews, after all, with the immortal story of the Exodus from
Egypt, who gave the world the concept of the holiness of freedom
——"

"Oh lawks a mercy me," Noel muttered.

"Shut up," Marjorie whispered angrily.

"But somehow," the judge said, "your seder has done more than
even that for me. Somehow I've almost seen the Exodus come alive
tonight. While you've chanted the Hebrew, which regrettably I don't
understand, I've closed my eyes and seen the great hordes of Israel,
with the majestic gray-bearded giant, Moses, at their head, marching
forth from the granite gates of Rameses into desert sands by the
light of the full moon. . . ." Judge Ehrmann proceeded in this vein
for perhaps ten minutes, drawing a vivid picture of the Exodus and
then the revelation on Sinai. The relatives sat spellbound. Marjorie,
for all of Noel's sarcastic mutterings, was thrilled and amazed. Noel
had described his father as a ridiculous windbag; but actually, though
his language was flowery and his manner magisterial, the judge had
eloquence and humor. Describing the Israelites heaping their ornaments before Aaron for the making of the golden calf, he said, "Earrings, finger rings, ankle rings, nose rings, gold, gold, in a clinking,
tumbling, mounting pile! Just picture it! They stripped themselves
bare! They gave away their last treasures for this folly, this golden
calf, these impoverished Israelites with the light of the Sinai still on
their faces!—and to this day, my friends, a Jew, no matter how poor,
will always dig up ten dollars for a pinochle game." The relatives

roared, and the older men nudged each other and winked. The judge sat quietly, waiting for the laugh to die, his eyes alert, his face serious, the pulse in his neck throbbing, and Marjorie was forcibly struck by his resemblance to his son. Noel, too, never laughed at his own jokes, but sat solemnly, timing his pauses to the laughter of his hearers. The deep-set clever blue eyes were identical in the two men, now that the judge's were roused into vigor. The gap of age, and Noel's smooth handsomeness and mass of blond hair, could not hide the fact that he was, after all, his father's son.

And as Noel sat sunk low in his chair, staring at a wine stain on the tablecloth, and slowly crumbling a hill of matzo crumbs over it while his father talked, Marjorie could see him sitting so at his father's table from perhaps his thirteenth year onward, sullenly enduring eclipse. One thing was obvious: at a table where Judge Ehrmann dominated, there were no other attractions.

When he rose to go, after finishing his talk with, "—and now goodbye, God bless you, and happy Pesakh," everybody at the table stood, crowding toward him, offering their hands, chorusing compliments. He had a handshake and a word for everybody. He remembered which children belonged to which parents, and mentioned them by name in making his farewells, a feat which stunned all with delight. Mr. and Mrs. Morgenstern accompanied the Ehrmanns to the foyer, and several of the guests followed, still exchanging jokes with the judge. Noel's mother, a richly dressed small wraith of a woman, with makeup a little too pink, stopped to kiss Noel on the forehead, and then she kissed Marjorie. "You have a lovely family, Marjorie dear, really lovely. You're a girl to be envied. Good night. I wish we could stay."

Marjorie said, when she was gone, "I think your mother's a darling. And your father's charming, too. Why did you paint him to me as such an idiot?"

He glanced briefly at her with a dip of the head, and a smile that was not pleasant. "Did you believe any of that speech, by some chance?"

"I thought it was moving, I don't care what you say."

"Really? Just remember, dear, he's a politician, and your house is in his district. When will this thing be over? Can I take this off?" He reached for the skullcap.

"Well, the ceremony starts up again now, Noel, and some of the best songs come——"

"How much longer?"

"Oh, not much, not even an hour. I appreciate that you've been very patient——"

"Well, it's been interesting, but frankly I do have the idea now."

She said at once, "Noel, it's perfectly all right if you want to leave now. Everybody will understand."

"I'll settle for some more of that Palestine brandy." He poured a stiff drink—he had been drinking brandy steadily since the dessert —swallowed half of it, and stared at the amber liquid. "Curious taste. Rough, not quite civilized. Primitive, potent, exotic. Well suited to the occasion."

The change in tone was marked when the seder resumed. The glory was departed. The guests were all stuffed with food, and sleepy with wine and brandy, and more interested in talking about the wonderful judge than in following the ceremony. Mr. Morgenstern had to rap for quiet several times.

There soon ensued a lot of glancing toward Noel and Marjorie among the Family, with winks, and nods, and whispers. Marjorie began to be uneasy. The rite that came next was the traditional occasion for teasing sweethearts and engaged couples. Noel, oblivious, was leafing through the Hagada in a bored way, sipping plum brandy. Even Aunt Dvosha became lively and gay, whispering across the two vacant chairs to Uncle Shmulka. The arch faces she made at Marjorie would have frightened an alligator. In the expectant quiet that settled over the table, Uncle Harry said, "Okay, who opens the door this year?"

The relatives giggled, pointing at Marjorie. Noel looked up. "What on earth——?" he said mildly.

"This is it, Noel," Harry said. "The door's got to be opened, you know." There was more laughter.

Noel said, "For whom?"

"Elijah, the prophet Elijah. Don't you know? Elijah comes in now and drinks his cup of wine."

Noel said, "Well, he's no friend of mine, but I'll be glad to open the door." At the howls of mirth that followed, he turned to Marjorie. "Was that funnier than I thought?"

"Margie and Noel open the door," squealed Aunt Dvosha, and collapsed on the table, laughing.

Noel said, "I begin to understand. . . . Well, let's go." He took her hand and stood amid ribald guffaws.

Marjorie, completely scarlet-faced, said, "It means nothing at all, nothing." They went out to jocular shouts. "Just some nonsense about making a wish, but a boy and a girl are supposed to go together."

"Well," Noel said, as she halted in the hallway. "Do we open it now?"

"No. One moment." A chant began in the dining room. "Now. Go ahead, open the door."

With a wry smile, Noel did so. The empty tiled outside hall, and the rows of doors, looked strange. He glanced at her. "Damned if I didn't feel a cool wind on my cheek. The power of suggestion——"

"I've felt that wind every year since I was four," Marjorie said.

"How long does Elijah stay?"

"Just for a minute."

"Am I supposed to kiss you, really?"

"Not at all. Skip it, by all means."

He kissed her lightly. He had drunk a lot of brandy; he smelled of it. In a swift motion he had his coat out of the closet, draped over his arm. "Margie, make my excuses to your folks, will you? I'm going out on the town with the prophet Elijah." She stared at him. He said, "Really, it's best. They're sweet people, and I've had a wonderful time, the judge's oration notwithstanding. It's been a revelation to me, really it has. But I think at this point I'd better run along."

She said faintly, "It's probably an excellent idea. Goodbye."

"I'll call you," he said. He looked at the empty air in the hall. "Elijah, wait for baby!"

The door closed.

.   .   .   .   .

The Man She Married

When Marjorie finally did get married, it happened fast.

Not that she was expecting it, or looking for it, when it came to pass. Quite the contrary, she was in another time of dull despair, worse in a way than what had gone before, because there was no dream of recapturing Noel to brighten the future.

Yet she never regretted refusing Noel. Once that tooth was out, the hole rapidly healed. He sent her a lot of eloquent letters after she returned from Europe. Some she read, some she tore up without reading. She answered none, and after a month or so they stopped coming.

Mike Eden filled her thoughts during her homeward voyage, and for a long time afterward. She nurtured a hope that he would some-how turn up again, and she even took a volunteer job with a Jewish refugee-aid committee; partly influenced by all that Mike had told her, but partly in the selfish hope that she might pick up news of him. Months passed. The hope began to fade, and she kept on with the work for its own sake. Most of what she did was routine typing and mimeographing. Now and then she helped a family find a place to live, or guided girls to jobs. She didn't exactly enjoy the work, but the emptiness at her heart went unnoticed while she was doing it; and at night she slept, untroubled by the sense of exasperated futility that had broken her rest during her years of haunting Broadway and battling with Noel.

Once she bought a drug trade journal and wrote to some of the companies that advertised, inquiring after Mike Eden. He had been careful to withhold from her the name of the firm he worked for. She had no luck, and she gave up the attempt; there were hundreds of such companies. After four or five months—especially after Hitler in-vaded Poland, and the headlines and radio bulletins filled everyone's conversation and thoughts, and the refugee work grew tumultuous —her interest in Mike lost substance. She still daydreamed and wor-ried about him, and wondered whether he was alive or dead. But he began to seem almost like someone she had heard or read about rather than actually known.

One Friday evening early in November, Seth came home from school in the blue and gold uniform of the Naval Reserve Officers' Training Corps. It was the first the family knew of his having joined. As if this were not shock enough for his sister and parents, he an-nounced at the dinner table that he intended to become engaged to Natalie Fain, the Barnard freshman whom he had been dating regu-larly for a year. Seth was a few weeks short of being nineteen. Poland had already been crushed, and the queer lull called "the phony war" had ensued in Europe; there was hope that real fighting might never break out. All the same it chilled Marjorie to see her gangling baby brother in military garb, the pink pimply razor-nicked face ridicu-lously stern under the white cap with gold insignia. If fighting came, this child would have to fight! As for his becoming engaged, they would all have laughed at him, and Mrs. Morgenstern would perhaps have told him to go wipe his nose—if not for the uniform. It blasted grown masculinity at them; it would not be denied.

The Friday-evening dinner at the candlelit table was different from all the hundreds of Sabbath meals that this little family had eaten through the years. The stuffed fish was as tasty as ever, the chicken soup with noodles as boring as ever, the pot roast and potato pudding as fat and satisfying as ever. But time had struck a brazen gong in the Morgenstern home. The father, whose round face had lost many worry lines when Marjorie returned from Europe cured of Noel, kept glancing at his son, and the worry lines came back, with some new ones. Mrs. Morgenstern relieved the mournful silence with brave jokes about seasickness and child marriage; and she addressed Seth all evening as Admiral, but her face was far from merry. As for Marjorie, she was simply stricken dumb. She could hardly eat. A picture haunted her: Aunt Marjorie, her wan face without makeup, her graying hair pulled straight back in a bun, serving as baby sitter while Seth and Natalie in evening clothes went off to the opera; Aunt Marjorie, the querulous fat spinster in steel-rimmed glasses, reading "The Three Pigs" to a couple of pudgy children in yellow pajamas.

Next morning she telephoned Wally Wronken. He seemed extremely pleased to talk to her, and readily made a date to meet the following day at twelve-thirty in the lobby of the St. Moritz Hotel, where Wally now lived, and to have lunch at Rumpelmayer's.

Marjorie came five minutes early for the date, dressed exactly as she had been for her meeting with Noel in Paris. She was aware of this, and slightly bothered by it; but the black and pink outfit was the best she had, and there was no point in looking anything but her best. She sat in a lobby armchair and smoked a cigarette, swinging her ankle; uneasy, almost distraught, more than a little ashamed of herself. The admiring glances of men sitting near her or walking by gave her no satisfaction. She knew by now that she was reasonably good-looking, and that it didn't take much to win stares from men; neatly crossed legs in good stockings were enough.

She was uneasy because Wally had been, if anything, too pleasant, too smooth, too glad to hear from her, too willing to take her to lunch. She greatly feared she had heard condescension in his voice. He had, of course, every right to condescend. He was the success, the young man of twenty-three with a hit on Broadway; not a smash hit, true, nothing that presaged a major literary career, but still a comedy that was in the fourth month of its run. Wally had sent her a pair of matinee tickets; she had seen the play with Seth. There had been several empty seats in the house, and she had not particularly liked the play, but the audience had laughed and applauded solidly. It was a farce about the radio broadcasting business, full of echoes, she thought, of successful farces of the past ten years. Her objections to Wally's writing remained in general what they had been at South Wind. It was commercial, mechanical; he was too eager for success, too ready with cynical imitation. But she had to acknowledge his competence; cheap and slight though Wally's play might be, it was superior to Noel's *Princess Jones*, with its precious and pallid whimsey, which she had, in her lovesick blindness, mistaken for high wit. Wally's reach was at least proportioned to his grasp. Moreover, he had set out to break into Broadway as a writer, and he had done it, while her own dream of being Marjorie Morningstar had blown away like vapor. She had not found it hard to write him a note of warm congratulation. He had answered with warm thanks, and there things had rested between them until she had taken the initiative and telephoned him.

The clock over the hotel desk crept past twelve-thirty. Her uneasiness mounted. She was regretting the impulse that had led her to call him up; she had in fact been regretting it ever since she hung up the receiver, disagreeably suspecting him of condescending to her. What was she doing, really? Was she trying to change things between them at this late date and get him to marry her, now that he was a success? It was nothing so definite or so stupid. She wasn't at all sure how she would feel when she saw him. More than anything else, she wanted to be reassured that she was still attractive, and Wally had always done that for her during the racking years with Noel.

Her conscious intention had been to tell him about Seth, and about her own fears of being an old maid. She wanted to laugh with him over the nightmare picture of herself baby-sitting for Seth's offspring, and so get herself back into good humor. But Marjorie had come a long way in self-knowledge. She couldn't be blind to the fact that she also was vaguely hoping for something more to come of this lunch, if not with Wally, then with somebody else, somebody successful and interesting, somebody whom she might meet by starting to go around with Wally again. It was this not very admirable notion that lay at the root of her uneasiness, and that made her shame and humiliation increase with each passing minute after twelve-thirty.

Those minutes lengthened. She lit another cigarette, promising herself to leave when it was smoked out. Disordered miserable thoughts possessed her. As a drowning man is said to do, she saw years of her life tumble past her mind's eye. She saw herself in other hotel lobbies, in bars, in grills, in cars, in restaurants, in night clubs, with men—George Drobes, Sandy Goldstone, Wally Wronken, Noel Airman, Mike Eden, Morris Shapiro, and dozens of others who had come and gone more casually. It was a strange set of customs, she thought, that drove a girl to conduct the crucial scenes of her life outside her own home; usually in a public place, usually over high-balls, usually when she was a little tight or quite tight. As girls went nowadays, she was probably respectable, even a bit prudish. Yet this had been her story.

It occurred to her too, as the cigarette went from white tube to gray ash, shrinking fast, that whatever subconscious hope she had of winning Wally was not only nonsensical but almost depraved. She had been Noel's mistress. She knew that Wally, Broadway-wise though he was, somehow had convinced himself that this was not so. He had said things to her that left no doubt in her mind what he believed. At the time she had seen no point in undeceiving him, so she had lied by omission, by saying nothing. Evidently he had found it necessary or pleasant to idolize her; she had felt herself under no obligation to disillusion him with uncomfortable confessions.

But how could she possibly marry him, or even take to dating him again, without telling him the truth? How much of a liar was she? And yet, how could she ever tell Wally Wronken that she had been Noel Airman's bed partner, after all? How could she face the moment that would follow the shattering of his picture of her—the one good girl in a world of chippies? The fact that he made free with chippies —it was obvious that he did—had nothing to do with it. He wasn't supposed to be pure; she was. It might not make sense, but that was exactly how things stood.

The butt had been growing warm in her fingers; now the glowing end stung her skin. She crushed the cigarette out and stood, brushing ash from her black skirt. It was eighteen minutes to one. She went to the house phone and called his room. The telephone rang and rang, but there was no answer. Her face became fiery. Obviously he had been polite to her on the phone and then had completely forgotten the date. He was a Broadway playwright, and she was an aging West End Avenue girl from his dead past, trying to clutch at a shred of his glamor. He probably thought of her as little more than an autograph hunter. She put the receiver down, walked out of the hotel, and dazedly got into a cab.

The cab had hardly turned the corner when Wally Wronken,

dressed as for a birthday party, with a gardenia corsage in a box under his arm, came whirling through the revolving door, scanning the lobby anxiously. He walked up and down the lobby, he walked through Rumpelmayer's, he questioned the headwaiter and the bell-boys in the lobby. He went up to his suite and called Marjorie's home, but she wasn't there. He ate a cheerless lunch by himself in his living room overlooking Central Park, where the trees were bright with the colors of autumn.

He telephoned her the next day to apologize, but she wasn't in. He telephoned her several times during the ensuing week. By the time he did get to talk to her it was too late—if it had ever not been too late. She was pleasant, distant, and preoccupied. She had met another man.

It was fifteen years before Marjorie found out what had delayed him.

There was a fitting irony, perhaps, in the fact that it was Marsha Michaelson who brought her together with this man; Marsha, at times her dearest friend, at times her worst enemy; Marsha, who had greased her descent into Noel's bed. She met him at a dinner party in Marsha's New Rochelle home, the evening after her aborted lunch date with Wally. A long time later she found out that Marsha had planned the dinner with the purpose of bringing them together. He was Michaelson's young law partner, the pleasant round-faced man who had cut off the noise of the beserk theremin at the wedding by pulling the plug out of the wall. She dimly recalled that he had almost made a date with her before Noel had spirited her away on that fatal night. Placed side by side at the table, they fell into conversation easily because they had met once before; and by the time the meal ended they were talking with rapid easy intimacy, all but oblivious to the rest of the party. She hoped he would ask to see her again. He did. He wanted to see her the next day. She knew that by the usual rules she should put him off for a week or so; instead she said yes with an eagerness that made her blush a little.

After the second date, she knew she wanted to marry him. The headlong torrent of her feelings scared her, but she couldn't help herself. It wasn't at all a blind urge to get married off at last. Since her return from Europe she had been meeting eligible men and having as many dates as she wanted; but none of them had waked her feelings. With this man, her heart had come to almost instantaneous hot life. There was something undignified, something not quite adult, she felt, about falling for someone new so soon and so hard; after all, the days of George Drobes were over, weren't they? But her own skepticism and disapproval made no difference whatever to her emotions. Nothing seemed to matter but the fact that she was falling in love.

He was far from perfect. He was a bit short, though athletically built, not quite a head taller than herself. His speech was slow, calm, and direct, with just a touch of quiet humor, in sharp contrast to the quick nervous wit and fantastic vocabulary of Noel, and the stinging insight and mordant eloquence of Mike Eden. Marjorie had been almost sure that in the end she would meet and marry another of these wild talkers, since the type seemed to be her weakness, but Milton's measured speech and deliberate thinking seemed to suit her well enough. The fact was, some of his ideas on politics and religion were decidedly old-fashioned—she might have said banal, describing somebody else who seemed less reliable, sound, and sure. He wanted, for instance, to have a traditionally religious home, and was obviously pleased to learn of Marjorie's family background. It was amazing how little all that concerned her, anyway. The one thing she couldn't understand—that she fiercely regretted—was that she had failed to warm to him the first time she had met him at Marsha's wedding.

After her third date she was in agony, because she was sure she had looked badly, and talked stupidly, and cooled his interest. After the fourth date—all four dates were in one week, Monday, Wednesday, Thursday, Saturday—she knew he was falling in love as hard and as fast as she was, and that he was going to propose.

He never did propose. They met early Sunday morning after that crucial Saturday-night date, and were together all day long and all evening, driving in his new gray Buick far out into New Jersey, supposedly to see the fall foliage. They did drive through marvelous vistas of red and yellow flame, but they didn't take much notice. They lunched and had dinner at roadside taverns; they parked for hours in the moonlight. By the time he brought her home, about half-past four in the morning, they were discussing the wedding date, and where they would live, and how they would break the news to their parents. Only when she found herself alone in her bedroom, staring dazed at her face in the mirror—the most familiar face in the world, looking like a stranger's to her, the makeup smeared, the hair in disorder, the eyes heavily shadowed but shining joyously—only then did she begin to realize what an upheaval had taken place in her life.

It didn't seem like an upheaval. Marrying him seemed natural and inevitable, parts of the ordinary sequence of things, like graduating from college at the end of her senior year. Earlier in the week she had fought against this feeling, had tried to summon objections to marrying this stranger, had tried to maintain the modesty and reserve she knew she ought to have. But her old identity had all but melted in his presence. She felt like his wife before the week was out. It was an effort to keep up the pretense that she didn't feel that way. Her relief was overwhelming when, sometime during the drive in New Jersey, he told her that he hoped she wouldn't consider him presumptuous or crazy, but he couldn't help thinking of her as his wife. It was shortly after he made this confession, and she made a similar one, that they parked in a leafy side lane and kissed with enormous gusto and began to speak of their marriage as a thing settled.

They went rapidly past the mutual delight of finding out how much they loved each other, and talked about how many children they would like to have, and what their religious feelings were, and how much money he had to live on; all the time necking as a man and a woman do who have discovered each other, but with the necking secondary, part of the exchange of confidences as it were, rather than an attempt to get pleasure for the moment out of sex. About the ridiculous speed of it all, Marjorie felt that she ought to be ashamed and worried—but she couldn't summon shame or worry from any corner of her spirit. His touch, his kiss, his hands, his voice, were all familiar, sweet, and wonderful. He actually seemed part of her, in a way that Noel Airman, despite his hypnotic fascination, never had. Nor was she too surprised to find that a man so different from Noel could stir and please her. She had learned from the encounter with Mike Eden that there really was more than one man in the world—the piece of knowledge that more than anything else divides women from girls. As long as there were two, there could be three, or ten; it was a question of good luck or God's blessing when she would encounter the one with whom she could be happy.

She fell asleep that morning dreaming confusedly and deliciously of diamond rings and bridal dresses, as the windows turned gray in the dawn.

She woke a couple of hours later to an immediate and wretched problem: when and how should she tell him about Noel?

For she had not yet done so. No consideration in the world could have brought her to tell him, before she was sure he loved her and wanted to marry her. It might have been calculating and not quite honest to let his feelings flame up without telling him. She thought that perhaps it had been dishonest. But she didn't care. Her life was at stake. She knew she would have to tell him now, and the prospect made her sick, but she was ready to do it.

The question was whether it was right for her to reveal the engagement to her parents—right away, in the next ten minutes, at breakfast—instead of waiting until he knew about Noel. Quite possibly he might want to break off with her. Clearly he had assumed she was a virgin; it had never occurred to him to question the fact. Like Wally Wronken, he had fallen into the accursed way of regarding her as a goddess, instead of realizing that she was just another girl stumbling through life as best she could. Supposing now she told her parents, and forty-eight hours later would have to tell them that it was all off? How could she endure it?

Marjorie went and did the natural, perhaps the cowardly, probably the inevitable thing. She told her parents at breakfast. This was what she had agreed with him to do. He was going to tell his parents, and they were coming with him to the Morgenstern home in the afternoon. To stop the rolling event, she would have had to telephone him and tell him to hold off because she had a serious disclosure to make to him first. Quite simply, she hadn't the guts to do it. So she plunged ahead, hoping for the best. In the whirl of her parents' joy— for they knew him, approved of him violently, and had been holding their breaths during the stampeding week when what was happening, became pretty plain—at the center of the whirl, she sat in a quiet shell of black fear.

He came, radiating pride, love, and masculine attraction, the bridegroom in his hour of power. His parents were—parents: a plump short gray woman, a spare tall gray man, both well spoken, well dressed, and at first quite stiff and cold, especially the mother. The Morgensterns, for their part, were cautious, faintly defensive, and at the same time assertively proud of their daughter. Tense and scared though she was, Marjorie was able to find amusement at the way the prospective in-laws, suddenly dumped together in a room, sized up each other with hackles raised. His mother kept remarking, not always relevantly, that he was her only child, that he owned his own new Buick convertible, and that she knew of no young lawyer half as successful as he was. These statements, sometimes coming abruptly out of nowhere, tended to stop the conversation dead. The atmosphere warmed slightly when Mrs. Morgenstern served tea and a marvelous apple strudel she had baked in a hurry that morning. Then it turned out that his father was the president of his Zionist chapter; and since her father was the president of *his* chapter, that helped a lot. The first real thaw came when it developed that the mothers had emigrated from neighboring provinces in Hungary. Shortly thereafter, when it appeared that both fathers admired President Roosevelt, and that both mothers couldn't stand the lady who was president of the Manhattan chapter of Hadassah, the ice was fairly broken. It was observed, and it was considered extremely remarkable, that Marjorie resembled her mother and that the bridegroom resembled *his* mother. His father, after the second piece of strudel, swung over to extreme joviality, and uncovered a gift for making puns and a taste for chain smoking. As the two sets of parents disclosed facts about themselves little by little, for all the world like bridge players playing out their cards, it became clear that at least in background it was a fairly balanced match. True, his father was a native-born American. Mr. Morgenstern's accent sounded loud and pungent that afternoon in Marjorie's ears. On the other hand, Marjorie soon gathered that his father had not been successful in business. He spoke vaguely of stocks and bonds, became respectful when Mr. Morgenstern described the Arnold Importing Company, and made no puns for a while afterward. Mrs. Morgenstern managed to say to Marjorie, when they were together in the kitchen for a moment, that she was sure the son was supporting the parents (as usual, Marjorie was very annoyed at her, and as usual, she turned out in the end to be quite right). She also remarked that she couldn't for the life of her see what right his mother had to be standoffish, inasmuch as West End Avenue wasn't at all the same above Ninety-sixth Street, and they lived on the corner of 103rd. However, Mrs. Morgenstern quickly added—when she saw the dangerous light in Marjorie's eye—that they were lovely people, and she couldn't be happier about the whole thing.

In time Mrs. Morgenstern brought out cherry brandy, and scotch, and the occasion became reasonably lively. The parents began debating whether this meeting constituted the religious occasion in the course of a courtship known as "T'nayim." Marjorie had never heard of T'nayim before. Her parents were emphatic and unanimous in declaring that this get-together certainly amounted to T'nayim. His mother was equally sure it was far too early for T'nayim, and that all kinds of other things had to be done first, though she was most foggy as to what those things might be. His father stayed out of the argument, contenting himself with seven cigarettes in a row and a number of unsuccessful puns on the word T'nayim. In the end Mrs. Morgenstern settled the matter, in her customary way, by going into the kitchen and coming out with a large soup plate from her best china set. She called the couple to the dining-room table, and told them to take hold of the plate and break it on the table. They did so, looking puzzled at each other. The fragments flew all over the floor, and the parents embraced each other, shouting congratulations and weeping a bit. That, evidently, was T'nayim.

The parents were happily planning the wedding, the honeymoon, and the general future of the couple when the bridegroom-to-be announced that he was taking Marjorie out for a drive. This was a tremendous joke to the two fathers, who had by then drunk a lot of scotch between them. The winks, guffaws, and elbow-nudges were still going on when they left. At the last moment, just as Marjorie was preceding him out the door, her future mother-in-law sprang at her, fell on her neck, kissed her, said she loved her, and fell into a paroxysm of wild sobbing, which she declared was due to an excess of happiness. Mrs. Morgenstern firmly peeled her off Marjorie, and the couple left her being quieted by the other three parents.

They drove out to New Jersey again. The tavern where they had dined the night before, he said, had the best food and drinks in the whole world; didn't she agree? She agreed. She said little during the drive. He did all the talking. He drew perceptive amusing sketches of both her parents, and was especially shrewd about her mother. "She's going to give me trouble," he said, "but she's all there." He told her a lot about his own parents. He pressed her to name a date for the wedding, but she turned him off in one way and another. He talked about the places they could go to for a honeymoon trip despite the war: the Canadian Rockies, South America, Hawaii, Mexico. He had an odd notion that Alaska might be fun. He wanted to go as far from home as possible; he wanted to be alone with her, he said, somewhere on the outer rim of the world. All the time he talked she sank deeper into fear and misery, though she kept up a smiling face. It seemed impossible to break into this run of pure bubbling high spirits with the revelation about Noel. Yet she knew that she had to do it tonight.

They drove across the George Washington Bridge in a gorgeous sunset. He became quiet and just drove, now and then reaching over and touching her face with his hand. He was a picture of a supremely happy man.

She had her rebellious moments during that sorrowful ride, behind the smiling face. This was the twentieth century, she told herself. He was an honor graduate of Harvard; he ought to know what life was all about! Obviously at thirty-one he himself wasn't a virgin. Most likely he hadn't been at her age, twenty-four. She hadn't claimed to be one. Inwardly she raged at the injustice of his assuming that she must measure up to the standards of dead Victorian days. Virginity was a trivial physical detail, meaningless between two people truly in love; anybody knew that, all the books said it. Her guilt over having had one affair was childish. Everybody had affairs nowadays, the world had changed. . . .

In all these reasonable thoughts, however, Marjorie could find no trace of relief or hope. The fact was, she had passed herself off as a good Jewish girl. Twentieth century or not, good Jewish girls were supposed to be virgins when they married. That was the corner she was in. That was the dull brute fact she faced. For that matter, good Christian girls were supposed to be virgins too; that was why brides wore white. She couldn't even blame her Jewish origin for the harrowing trap she was in, though she would have liked to.

They came to the tavern. They had one drink, and another. He wasn't talking much, just holding her hand, worshipping her, and once in a while saying something nonsensical and sweet. She had all the opportunity she needed to talk, but she couldn't.

Then, all at once, at the very worst moment, just after the food was set before them, the story somehow broke from her in a stammering rush of words; every word like vomit in her mouth.

That ended the evening. He remained cordial, but he was quenched. She had never seen such a change in a man's face; he went in a few minutes from happiness to sunken melancholy. Neither of them could eat. About her affair with Noel, he said never a word. It was as though she hadn't told him. When the food was taken away, he asked her correctly and pleasantly whether she wanted more coffee, or some brandy, or anything else. Then he drove her home, saying nothing at all on the way. She remembered that drive for years as the worst agony she ever endured. It was like being driven to a hospital, dying of a hemorrhage.

She telephoned him early next morning after a ghastly night. His mother answered, full of concern and excitement. He wasn't at home or at his office. He had gone off, leaving a short note saying he was very tired and was taking a vacation for a week or so in the mountains. But he hadn't said what hotel, or even what town he was going to. What on earth had happened? Had something gone wrong? His mother was not successful in keeping a note of pleasure out of her voice, if she was even aware of it. Marjorie evaded her questions, and hung up.

Three days passed. His mother called every morning and evening, wanting to know if Marjorie had heard from him. This, with the mournful atmosphere in her own home, the unspoken questions and terrible worry in the faces of her parents, became unendurable. Marjorie got up very early one morning, left a similar note for her parents, and went to a hotel in Lakewood, a New Jersey resort a couple of hours from the city. It was the wrong time of the year for Lakewood. The hotel she stayed in was almost empty; the town was deserted. There was nothing to do but read, go to movies, or walk around the lake. Marjorie read magazines, newspapers, books, whatever she could lay her hands on, without the slightest idea of what she was reading. She was at the hotel six days, and the time passed as though she were in delirium. She couldn't remember afterward any details of what she had done in those six days; they were blanked from her mind as by amnesia. She came home with a severe cold and a temperature of a hundred and three. She had not eaten at all, and she had lost twelve pounds. She came home because her mother telephoned her (unlike him, she had disclosed where she was going). "He's back, and he called this morning. Better come home."

"How did he sound?"

"I don't know. Come home." Mrs. Morgenstern didn't seem very cheerful.

Sick as Marjorie was when she arrived home, she brushed off her mother's alarm at the way she looked and her insistence that she go to bed. She telephoned his office. It was four in the afternoon, a raw snowy day, already growing dark. He said abruptly, coldly, that he would like to see her as soon as possible for a little while.

In the same clothes she had worn travelling home, dishevelled and shivering, she went straight downtown and met him, at a dingy bar near his office. Naturally it would be at a bar; it had always been at a bar. He was already at a table, in a gloomy far corner.

There was a long quiet pause after they greeted each other and ordered drinks. Bad as she looked, he looked worse. He had actually aged. His face was white, lined, and wretched. He studied her face during that pause, and she felt as though she were about to be executed. When he finally spoke, what he said was, sadly and gruffly, "I love you." He opened a jeweler's box and put it before her. She stared dumfounded at what she thought must be the largest diamond in the world.

It was a good thing they were in a dark corner, because she had to turn her face down and cry bitterly. She cried a long time, in an excess of the deepest bitterness and shame, before he shyly brushed the tears from her face with his hand.

He never said anything about Noel thereafter; not for the rest of their lives. But she never again saw on his face the pure happiness that had shone there during the drive across the George Washington Bridge in the sunset. He loved her. He took her as she was, with her deformity, despite it. For that was what it amounted to in his eyes and in hers—a deformity: a deformity that could no longer be helped; a permanent crippling, like a crooked arm.

> *My object all sublime*
> *I shall achieve in time . . .*

The song popped into Marjorie's head as her mother was buttoning her into her wedding dress, in an anteroom of the Gold Room of the Pierre Hotel, less than an hour before the ceremony. So great was her nervous tension that, once established, the melody drummed on and on in her brain. She was holding her veil high in the air with both hands, for it interfered with the buttoning, and as she stood so, with both arms high, she had begun to hum, and then to sing, unaware of what she was singing.

> *My object all sublime*
> *I shall achieve in time . . .*

After a few moments she heard herself, and quietly laughed, realizing why she was singing it. She had held her arms up in just this way on the stage at Hunter College, strutting through her first acting triumph as the Mikado. The electric excitement of that forgotten moment had welded the words and the tune in her brain to the act of throwing her arms high. Six years later—the better part of a lifetime, it seemed to Marjorie—the weld was still there. But how everything else had changed!

"What are you laughing at? Am I tickling you?" her mother said.

"An old joke, Mama, nothing. . . . Hurry, for heaven's sake, the photographer should have been here long ago."

"Relax, darling. You'll be married a long, long time."

All through the photographing, all through the frenzied last-minute rehearsals of cues with the caterer's hostess in charge of the sacred formalities, all through the hot hurried last embraces with her ecstatic mother, her beaming father, both looking astonishingly young and well in fine new evening clothes—and with her white-faced grim brother, stiff and unyielding as a post in his first top hat, white tie, and tails—and with her weeping mother-in-law and desperately punning and smoking father-in-law—all that time the song ran on and on in her mind. . . . *My object all sublime, I shall achieve in time* . . . It cut off sharply when the procession began and she heard the organ, far below in the ballroom, playing the wedding march.

For there was an organ, of course. And there were two cantors, a handsome young man and a marvelously impressive gray-bearded man, both in black silk robes, and black mitres with black pompons. There was a choir of five bell-voiced boys in white silk robes, and white hats with white pompons. There was a broad canopy of white lilies, on a platform entirely carpeted and walled with greenery and white roses. There were blazing blue-white arc lights, a movie photographer, and a still photographer. There was a rose-strewn staircase for her to descend; there was a quite meaningless but quite gorgeous archway with gates at the head of the staircase, covered and festooned with pink roses, through which she was to make her entrance. There were banks of gold chairs, five hundred of them, jammed solid with guests, and with spectators who had read the announcement in the *Times* and knew the bridegroom or the bride. After the ceremony there was to be as much champagne as anyone could drink, and as many hot hors d'oeuvres as the greediest guest could stuff into himself. There was to be a ten-course dinner beginning with imported salmon, featuring rare roast beef, and ending in flaming cherries jubilee. There was to be a seven-piece orchestra, more champagne, a midnight supper, and dancing till dawn.

It was the Lowenstein Catering Company's number-one wedding, the best there was, the best money could buy—sixty-five hundred dollars, tips included. Marjorie and her bridegroom had discussed accepting the money, instead, as a wedding present from her father. Mr. Morgenstern, who had accumulated the money and set it aside for the wedding over twenty years, had diffidently made the offer. They had decided instead to have the wedding, rococo excess and all. Their decision filled all four parents with joy. It was obviously what everybody wanted.

Marjorie stood behind the closed rose-covered gate at the head of the stairs, with the perspiring hostess at her elbow, listening to the music as the wedding procession filed in below from the lobby of the ballroom. She couldn't see anything through the heavy sweet-smelling screen of roses, but she knew what was happening. In the number-one Lowenstein wedding—the only one featuring the rose gate—all the others came in first and took their places; then the bride came down the flower-strewn steps in lone splendor, white train dragging, while her father waited for her at the foot of the staircase. Then he was to take her arm, and escort her to the canopy. Marjorie had seen this pageant several times at the weddings of other girls. The day before, at the rehearsal, she had been amused by the amateurish theatricalism of it all. At the same time, she secretly rather liked the idea of making such a grand entrance. Her only worry was that she might trip on her train and sprawl headlong down the stairs. But the hostess had assured her that every bride had had exactly the same fear, and not one had ever tripped.

The music stopped. That meant they were all in place: the four parents, the rabbi, Seth, the best man, and his betrothed, Natalie Fain, the maid of honor. Marjorie could hear the gossiping chatter of the guests. She swallowed hard, clutched her little bouquet of white orchids and lilies of the valley, and glanced at the hostess. The little flushed woman inspected her from head to toe, minutely adjusted her train, pulled Marjorie's hotly clasped hands with the bouquet to the exact center of her midriff, kissed her damply, and nodded at the yawning waiter with the gate rope in his hand. He hauled on the rope. The gates swung open, and Marjorie stood in a white spotlight under the arch of pink roses, revealed to public view.

There was a general gasp and murmur below, then a total hush. The organ began to play *Here Comes the Bride.* Slowly, regally, Marjorie came down the staircase, hesitating on each step, in time to the music.

Perhaps the spotlight shining in her eyes made the tears well up;

perhaps it was the emotions of the moment. She blinked them back as well as she could, glad that she was veiled. She could see dimly the guests below, stretching in orderly ranks forward to the canopy. Their faces were turned up to her. There was one look on all of them: stunned admiration.

Marjorie was an extremely beautiful bride. They always say the bride is beautiful, and the truth is that a girl seldom looks better than she does at this moment of her glory and her vanishing, veiled and in white; but even among brides Marjorie was remarkably lovely. For years afterward Lowenstein's hostess said that the prettiest bride she ever saw was Marjorie Morgenstern.

The Goldstones were there, in one row near the back; and Marsha and Lou Michaelson, and the Zelenkos, and Aunt Dvosha, and Uncle Shmulka, and Geoffrey Quill, and Neville Sapersteen in a dark blue suit, and the banker Connelly, and Morris Shapiro, and Wally Wronken—these familiar faces and dozens of others she recognized, though her eyes scarcely moved. She had taken but two or three steps downward when she also saw, in the very last row of the array of black-clad men and beautifully gowned women, the tall blond man in brown tweed jacket and gray slacks, with an old camel's hair coat slung over one arm, incongruous as he was startling. She had not even known Noel Airman was in the United States; but he had come to see her get married. She could not discern his expression, but there wasn't a doubt in the world that it was Noel.

She didn't waver or change countenance at all; she continued her grave descent. But in an instant, as though green gelatins had been slid one by one in front of every light in the ballroom, she saw the scene differently. She saw a tawdry mockery of sacred things, a bourgeois riot of expense, with a special touch of vulgar Jewish sentimentality. The gate of roses behind her was comical; the flower-massed canopy ahead was grotesque; the loud whirring of the movie camera was a joke, the scrambling still photographer in the empty aisle, twisting his camera at his eye, a low clown. The huge diamond on her right hand capped the vulgarity; she could feel it there; she slid a finger to cover it. Her husband waiting for her under the canopy wasn't a prosperous doctor, but he was a prosperous lawyer; he had the mustache Noel had predicted; with macabre luck Noel had even guessed the initials. And she—she was Shirley, going to a Shirley fate, in a Shirley blaze of silly costly glory.

All this passed through her mind in a flash, between one step downward and the next. Then her eyes shifted to her father's face, rosily happy, looking up at her from the foot of the stairs. The green gelatins slid aside, and she saw her wedding again by the lights that were there in the room. If it was all comical in Noel's eyes, she thought, he might derive from that fact what pleasure he could. She was what she was, Marjorie Morgenstern of West End Avenue, marrying the man she wanted in the way she wanted to be married. It was a beautiful wedding, and she knew she was a pretty bride.

She reached the bottom of the stairs. Her father stepped to her side. Taking his arm, she turned a bit and squarely faced into Noel Airman's expected grin; he was not ten feet from her. But to her surprise Noel wasn't grinning. He looked better than he had in Paris: not so thin, not so pale, and he appeared to have gotten back all his hair. His expression was baffled, almost vacant. His mouth hung slightly open; his eyes seemed wet.

The organ music swelled to its loudest. Marjorie marched down the aisle with solemn gladness to her destiny, and became Mrs. Milton Schwartz.

Eli, the Fanatic

by PHILIP ROTH

The best of Philip Roth is in this remarkable story, published with the novella Goodbye, Columbus in the volume that won the author the National Book Award in 1960. Then twenty-six, he was already renowned as an important American Jewish writer among both avant-garde and conservative critics.

In describing the identity problem of the self-aware young-marrieds in suburbia, Philip Roth displayed his caustic wit and his ear for catch-phrases, in this case the psychoanalytic jargon with which a confused generation pretended self-understanding. (A touch already introduced by Herman Wouk in the Seder scene in Marjorie Morningstar.) But "Eli, the Fanatic" has profound reverberations which are absent in such hard-edged Philip Roth social portraits as Portnoy's Complaint and Goodbye, Columbus itself.

Eli Peck, the young lawyer who sends a suit of his own clothes to a yeshiva Jew so that he will no longer parade around town in outlandish garments, then feels compelled to don those very garments when they are left on his doorstep, and to parade through town in them, when he goes to visit his newly born son Eli's friends call his therapist, and he is carted off. Identification with the Jewish past, Roth would seem to be saying, drives the modern Jew off balance.

Such negative statement of the Jewish condition has at the very least provoked enormous discussion. Roth's own career is illustrative. Goodbye, Columbus, about Jewish middle-class vulgarities, was followed in 1962 by Letting Go, whose Jewish characters were alienated. In 1967 came When She Was Good, a study of a Midwestern non-Jewish environment that was, by some, considered not so good. During this period Roth was a visiting writer and teacher at the University of Chicago, Princeton and other colleges. The sensational success of Portnoy's Complaint marked a return to Jewish material.

While this collection otherwise has used excerpts from novels, the clarity of "Eli, the Fanatic" as regards the American Jewish psyche seemed to make this story the best representation for Philip Roth here. Roth doubtless feels himself an American writer using the material with which life has provided him—unfortunately, or perhaps quite fortunately, Jewish. Like Eli Peck, like Portnoy, he is haunted by that Jewish self.

C.A.

Leo TZUREF stepped out from back of a white column to welcome Eli Peck. Eli jumped back, surprised; then they shook hands and Tzuref gestured him into the sagging old mansion. At the door Eli turned, and down the slope of lawn, past the jungle of hedges, beyond the dark, untrampled horse path, he saw the street lights blink on in Woodenton. The stores along Coach House Road tossed up a burst of yellow—it came to Eli as a secret signal from his townsmen: "Tell this Tzuref where we stand, Eli. This is a modern community, Eli, we have our families, we pay taxes . . ." Eli, burdened by the message, gave Tzuref a dumb, weary stare.

"You must work a full day," Tzuref said, steering the attorney and his briefcase into the chilly hall.

Eli's heels made a racket on the cracked marble floor, and he spoke above it. "It's the commuting that's killing," he said, and entered the dim room Tzuref waved open for him. "Three hours a day . . . I came right from the train." He dwindled down into a harp-backed chair. He expected it would be deeper than it was and consequently jarred himself on the sharp bones of his seat. It woke him, this shiver of the behind, to his business. Tzuref, a bald shaggy-browed man who looked as if he'd once been very fat, sat back of an empty desk, halfway hidden, as though he were settled on the floor. Everything around him was empty. There were no books in the bookshelves, no rugs on the floor, no draperies in the big casement windows. As Eli began to speak Tzuref got up and swung a window back on one noisy hinge. "May and it's like August," he said, and with his back to Eli, he revealed the black circle on the back of his head. The crown of his head was missing! He returned through the dimness— the lamps had no bulbs—and Eli realized all he'd seen was a skullcap. Tzuref struck a match and lit a candle, just as the half-dying shouts of children at play rolled in through the open window. It was as though Tzuref had opened it so Eli could hear them.

"Aah, now," he said. "I received your letter."

Eli poised, waiting for Tzuref to swish open a drawer and remove the letter from his file. Instead the old man leaned forward onto his stomach, worked his hand into his pants pocket, and withdrew what appeared to be a week-old handkerchief. He uncrumpled it; he unfolded it; he ironed it on the desk with the side of his hand. "So," he said.

Eli pointed to the grimy sheet which he'd gone over word-by-word with his partners, Lewis and McDonnell. "I expected an answer," Eli said. "It's a week."

"It was so important, Mr. Peck, I knew you would come."

Some children ran under the open window and their mysterious babble—not mysterious to Tzuref, who smiled—entered the room like a third person. Their noise caught up against Eli's flesh and he was unable to restrain a shudder. He wished he had gone home, showered and eaten dinner, before calling on Tzuref. He was not feeling as professional as usual—the place was too dim, it was too late. But down in Woodenton they would be waiting, his clients and neighbors. He spoke for the Jews of Woodenton, not just himself and his wife.

"You understood?" Eli said.

"It's not hard."

"It's a matter of zoning . . ." and when Tzuref did not answer, but only drummed his fingers on his lips, Eli said, "We didn't make the laws . . ."

"You respect them."

"They protect us . . . the community."

"The law is the law," Tzuref said.

"Exactly!" Eli had the urge to rise and walk about the room.

"And then of course"—Tzuref made a pair of scales in the air with his hands—"The law is not the law. When is the law that is the law not the law?" He jiggled the scales. "And vice versa."

"Simply," Eli said sharply. "You can't have a boarding school in a residential area." He would not allow Tzuref to cloud the issue with issues. "We thought it better to tell you before any action is under-taken."

"But a house in a residential area?"

"Yes. That's what residential means." The DP's English was per-haps not as good as it seemed at first. Tzuref spoke slowly, but till then Eli had mistaken it for craft—or even wisdom. "Residence means home," he added.

"So this is my residence."

"But the children?"

"It is their residence."

"*Seventeen* children?"

"Eighteen," Tzuref said.

"But you *teach* them here."

"The Talmud. That's illegal?"

"That makes it school."

Tzuref hung the scales again, tipping slowly the balance.

"Look, Mr. Tzuref, in America we call such a place a boarding school."

"Where they teach the Talmud?"

"Where they teach period. You are the headmaster, they are the students."

Tzuref placed his scales on the desk. "Mr. Peck," he said, "I don't believe it . . ." but he did not seem to be referring to anything Eli had said.

"Mr. Tzuref, that is the law. I came to ask what you intend to do."

"What I *must* do?"

"I hope they are the same."

"They are." Tzuref brought his stomach into the desk. "We stay." He smiled. "We are tired. The headmaster is tired. The students are tired."

Eli rose and lifted his briefcase. It felt so heavy packed with the grievances, vengeances, and schemes of his clients. There were days when he carried it like a feather—in Tzuref's office it weighed a ton.

"Goodbye, Mr. Tzuref."

"Sholom," Tzuref said.

Eli opened the door to the office and walked carefully down the dark tomb of a corridor to the door. He stepped out on the porch and, leaning against a pillar, looked down across the lawn to the children at play. Their voices whooped and rose and dropped as they chased each other round the old house. The dusk made the children's game look like a tribal dance. Eli straightened up, started off the porch, and suddenly the dance was ended. A long piercing scream trailed after. It was the first time in his life anyone had run at the sight of him. Keeping his eyes on the lights of Woodenton, he headed down the path.

And then, seated on a bench beneath a tree, Eli saw him. At first it seemed only a deep hollow of blackness—then the figure emerged. Eli recognized him from the description. There he was, wearing the hat, that hat which was the very cause of Eli's mission, the source of Woodenton's upset. The town's lights flashed their message once again: "Get the one with the hat. What a nerve, what a nerve . . ."

Eli started towards the man. Perhaps he was less stubborn than Tzuref, more reasonable. After all, it was the law. But when he was close enough to call out, he didn't. He was stopped by the sight of the black coat that fell down below the man's knees, and the hands which held each other in his lap. By the round-topped, wide-brimmed Talmudic hat, pushed onto the back of his head. And by the beard, which hid his neck and was so soft and thin it fluttered away and back again with each heavy breath he took. He was asleep, his side-locks curled loose on his cheeks. His face was no older than Eli's.

Eli hurried towards the lights.

The note on the kitchen table unsettled him. Scribblings on bits of paper had made history this past week. This one, however, was unsigned. "Sweetie," it said, "I went to sleep. I had a sort of Oedipal experience with the baby today. Call Ted Heller."

She had left him a cold soggy dinner in the refrigerator. He hated cold soggy dinners, but would take one gladly in place of Miriam's presence. He was ruffled, and she never helped that, not with her infernal analytic powers. He loved her when life was proceeding smoothly—and that was when she loved him. But sometimes Eli found being a lawyer surrounded him like quicksand—he couldn't get his breath. Too often he wished he were pleading for the other side; though if he were on the other side, then he'd wish he were on the side he was. The trouble was that sometimes the law didn't seem to be the answer, *law* didn't seem to have anything to do with what was aggravating everybody. And that, of course, made him feel foolish and unnecessary . . . Though that was not the situation here— the townsmen had a case. But not *exactly*, and if Miriam were awake to see Eli's upset, she would set about explaining his distress to him, understanding him, forgiving him, so as to get things back to Normal, for Normal was where they loved one another. The difficulty with Miriam's efforts was they only upset him more; not only did they explain little to him about himself or his predicament, but they convinced him of *her* weakness. Neither Eli nor Miriam, it turned out, was terribly strong. Twice before he'd faced this fact, and on both occasions had found solace in what his neighbors forgivingly referred to as "a nervous breakdown."

Eli ate his dinner with his briefcase beside him. Halfway through, he gave in to himself, removed Tzuref's notes, and put them on the table, beside Miriam's. From time to time he flipped through the notes, which had been carried into town by the one in the black hat. The first note, the incendiary:

To whom it may concern:

Please give this gentleman the following: Boys shoes with rubber heels and soles.

> 5 prs size 6c
> 3 prs size 5c
> 3 prs size 5b
> 2 prs size 4a
> 3 prs size 4c
> 1 pr size 7b
> 1 pr size 7c

Total 18 prs. boys shoes. This gentleman has a check already signed. Please fill in correct amount.

> L. Tzuref
> Director, Yeshivah of
> Woodenton, N.Y.
> (5/8/48)

"Eli, a regular greenhorn," Ted Heller had said. "He didn't say a word. Just handed me the note and stood there, like in the Bronx the old guys who used to come around selling Hebrew trinkets."

"A Yeshivah!" Artie Berg had said. "Eli, in Woodenton, a Yeshivah! If I want to live in Brownsville, Eli, I'll live in Brownsville."

"Eli," Harry Shaw speaking now, "the old Puddington place. Old man Puddington'll roll over in his grave. Eli, when I left the city, Eli, I didn't plan the city should come to me."

Note number two:

Dear Grocer:

Please give this gentleman ten pounds of sugar. Charge it to our account, Yeshivah of Woodenton, NY—which we will now open with you and expect a bill each month. The gentleman will be in to see you once or twice a week.

L. Tzuref, Director

(5/10/48)

P.S. Do you carry kosher meat?

"He walked right by my window, the greenie," Ted had said, "and he nodded, Eli. He's my *friend* now."

"Eli," Artie Berg had said, "he handed the damn thing to a *clerk* at Stop N' Shop—and in that hat yet!"

"Eli," Harry Shaw again, "it's not funny. Someday, Eli, it's going to be a hundred little kids with little *yamalkahs* chanting their Hebrew lessons on Coach House Road, and then it's not going to strike you funny."

"Eli, what goes on up there—my kids hear strange sounds."

"Eli, this is a modern community."

"Eli, we pay taxes."

"Eli."

"Eli!"

"*Eli!*"

At first it was only another townsman crying in his ear; but when he turned he saw Miriam, standing in the doorway, behind her belly.

"Eli, sweetheart, how was it?"

"He said no."

"Did you see the other one?" she asked.

"Sleeping, under a tree."

"Did you let him know how people feel?"

"He was sleeping."

"Why didn't you wake him up? Eli, this isn't an everyday thing."

"He was tired!"

"Don't shout, please," Miriam said.

" 'Don't shout. I'm pregnant. The baby is heavy.' " Eli found he was getting angry at nothing she'd said yet; it was what she was going to say.

"He's a very heavy baby the doctor says," Miriam told him.

"Then sit *down* and make my dinner." Now he found himself angry about her not being present at the dinner which he'd just been relieved that she wasn't present at. It was as though he had a raw nerve for a tail, that he kept stepping on. At last Miriam herself stepped on it.

"Eli, you're upset. I understand."

"You *don't* understand."

She left the room. From the stairs she called, "I do, sweetheart."

It was a trap! He would grow angry knowing she would be "understanding." She would in turn grow more understanding seeing his anger. He would in turn grow angrier . . . The phone rang.

"Hello," Eli said.

"Eli, Ted. So?"

"So nothing."

"Who is Tzuref? He's an American guy?"

"No. A DP. German."

"And the kids?"

"DP's too. He teaches them."

"What? What subjects?" Ted asked.

"I don't know."

"And the guy with the hat, you saw the guy with the hat?"

"Yes. He was sleeping."

"Eli, he sleeps with the *hat?*"

"He sleeps with the hat."

"Goddam fanatics," Ted said. "This is the twentieth century, Eli. Now it's the guy with the hat. Pretty soon all the little Yeshivah boys'll be spilling down into town."

"Next thing they'll be after our daughters."

"Michele and Debbie wouldn't look at them."

"Then," Eli mumbled, "you've got nothing to worry about, Teddie," and he hung up.

In a moment the phone rang. "Eli? We got cut off. We've got nothing to worry about? You worked it out?"

"I have to see him again tomorrow. We can work something out."

"That's fine, Eli. I'll call Artie and Harry."

Eli hung up.

"I thought you said *nothing* worked out." It was Miriam.

"I did."

"Then why did you tell Ted *something* worked out?"

"It did."

"Eli, maybe you should get a little more therapy."

"That's enough of that, Miriam."

"You can't function as a lawyer by being neurotic. That's no answer."

"You're ingenious, Miriam."

She turned, frowning, and took her heavy baby to bed.

The phone rang.

"Eli, Artie. Ted called. You worked it out? No trouble?"

"Yes."

"When are they going?"

"Leave it to me, will you, Artie? I'm tired. I'm going to sleep."

In bed Eli kissed his wife's belly and laid his head upon it to think. He laid it lightly, for she was that day entering the second week of her ninth month. Still, when she slept, it was a good place to rest, to rise and fall with her breathing and figure things out. "If that guy would take off that crazy hat. I know it, what eats them. If he'd take off that crazy hat everything would be all right."

"What?" Miriam said.

"I'm talking to the baby."

Miriam pushed herself up in bed. "Eli, please, baby, shouldn't you maybe stop in to see Dr. Eckman, just for a little conversation?"

"I'm fine."

"Oh, sweetie!" she said, and put her head back on the pillow.

"You know what your mother brought to this marriage—a sling chair and a goddam New School enthusiasm for Sigmund Freud."

Miriam feigned sleep, he could tell by the breathing.

"I'm telling the kid the truth, aren't I, Miriam? A sling chair, three months to go on a *New Yorker* subscription, and *An Introduction to Psychoanalysis*. Isn't that right?"

"Eli, must you be aggressive?"

"That's all you worry about, is your insides. You stand in front of the mirror all day and look at yourself being pregnant."

"Pregnant mothers have a relationship with the fetus that fathers can't understand."

"Relationship my ass. What is my liver doing now? What is my small intestine doing now? Is my island of Langerhans on the blink?"

"Don't be jealous of a little fetus, Eli."

"I'm jealous of your island of Langerhans!"

"Eli, I can't argue with you when I know it's not me you're really angry with. Don't you see, sweetie, you're angry with yourself."

"You and Eckman."

"Maybe he could help, Eli."

"Maybe he could help you. You're practically lovers as it is."

"You're being hostile again," Miriam said.

"What do you care—it's only *me* I'm being hostile towards."

"Eli, we're going to have a beautiful baby, and I'm going to have a perfectly simple delivery, and you're going to make a fine father, and there's absolutely no reason to be obsessed with whatever is on your mind. All we have to worry about—" she smiled at him "—is a name."

Eli got out of bed and slid into his slippers. "We'll name the kid Eckman if it's a boy and Eckman if it's a girl."

"Eckman Peck sounds terrible."

"He'll have to live with it," Eli said, and he went down to his study where the latch on his briefcase glinted in the moonlight that came through the window.

He removed the Tzuref notes and read through them all again. It unnerved him to think of all the flashy reasons his wife could come up with for his reading and rereading the notes. "Eli, why are you so *preoccupied* with Tzuref?" "Eli, stop getting *involved*. Why do you think you're getting *involved*, Eli?" Sooner or later, everybody's wife finds their weak spot. His goddam luck he had to be neurotic! Why couldn't he have been born with a short leg.

He removed the cover from his typewriter, hating Miriam for the edge she had. All the time he wrote the letter, he could hear what she would be saying about his not being *able* to let the matter drop. Well, her trouble was that she wasn't *able* to face the matter. But he could hear her answer already: clearly, he was guilty of "a reaction formation." Still, all the fancy phrases didn't fool Eli: all she wanted really was for Eli to send Tzuref and family on their way, so that the community's temper would quiet, and the calm circumstances of their domestic happiness return. All she wanted were order and love in her private world. Was she so wrong? Let the world bat its brains out —in Woodenton there should be peace. He wrote the letter anyway:

Dear Mr. Tzuref:

Our meeting this evening seems to me inconclusive. I don't think there's any reason for us not to be able to come up with some sort of compromise that will satisfy the Jewish community of Woodenton and the Yeshivah and yourself. It seems to me that what most disturbs my neighbors are the visits to town by the gentleman in the black hat, suit, etc. Woodenton is a progressive suburban community whose members, both Jewish and Gentile, are anxious that their families live in comfort and beauty and serenity. This is, after all, the twentieth century, and we do not think it too much to ask that the members of our community dress in a manner appropriate to the time and place.

Woodenton, as you may not know, has long been the home of well-to-do Protestants. It is only since the war that Jews have been able to buy property here, and for Jews and Gentiles to live beside each other in amity. For this adjustment to be made, both Jews and Gentiles alike have had to give up some of their more extreme practices in order not to threaten or offend the other. Certainly such amity is to be desired. Perhaps if such conditions had existed in pre-war Europe, the persecution of the Jewish people, of which you and those 18 children have been victims, could not have been carried out with such success—in fact, might not have been carried out at all.

Therefore, Mr. Tzuref, will you accept the following conditions? If you can, we will see fit not to carry out legal action against the Yeshivah for failure to comply with township Zoning ordinances No. 18 and No. 23. The conditions are simply:

1. The religious, educational, and social activities of the Yeshivah of Woodenton will be confined to the Yeshivah grounds.

2. Yeshivah personnel are welcomed in the streets and stores of Woodenton provided they are attired in clothing usually associated with American life in the 20th century.

If these conditions are met, we see no reason why the Yeshivah of Woodenton cannot live peacefully and satisfactorily with the Jews of Woodenton—as the Jews of Woodenton have come to live with the Gentiles of Woodenton. I would appreciate an immediate reply.

Sincerely,
Eli Peck, Attorney

Two days later Eli received his immediate reply:

Mr. Peck:
The suit the gentleman wears is all he's got.

Sincerely,
Leo Tzuref, Headmaster

Once again, as Eli swung around the dark trees and onto the lawn, the children fled. He reached out with his briefcase as if to stop them, but they were gone so fast all he saw moving was a flock of skullcaps.

"Come, come . . ." a voice called from the porch. Tzuref appeared from behind a pillar. Did he *live* behind those pillars? Was he just watching the children at play? Either way, when Eli appeared, Tzuref was ready, with no forewarning.

"Hello," Eli said.

"Sholom."

"I didn't mean to frighten them."

"They're scared, so they run."

"I didn't do anything."

Tzuref shrugged. The little movement seemed to Eli strong as an accusation. What he didn't get at home, he got here.

Inside the house they took their seats. Though it was lighter than a few evenings before, a bulb or two would have helped. Eli had to hold his briefcase towards the window for the last gleamings. He removed Tzuref's letter from a manila folder. Tzuref removed Eli's letter from his pants pocket. Eli removed the carbon of his own letter from another manila folder. Tzuref removed Eli's first letter from his back pocket. Eli removed the carbon from his briefcase. Tzuref raised his palms. ". . . . It's all I've got . . ."

Those upraised palms, the mocking tone—another accusation. It was a crime to keep carbons! Everybody had an edge on him—Eli could do no right.

"I offered a compromise, Mr. Tzuref. You refused."

"Refused, Mr. Peck? What is, is."

"The man could get a new suit."

"That's all he's got."

"So you told me," Eli said.

"So I told you, so you know."

"It's not an insurmountable obstacle, Mr. Tzuref. We have stores."

"For that too?"

"On Route 12, a Robert Hall—"

"To take away the one thing a man's got?"

"Not take away, *replace*."

"But I tell you he has nothing. *Nothing*. You have that word in English? *Nicht? Gornisht?*"

"Yes, Mr. Tzuref, we have the word."

"A mother and a father?" Tzuref said. "No. A wife? No. A baby? A little ten-month-old baby? No! A village full of friends? A synagogue where you knew the feel of every seat under your pants? Where with your eyes closed you could smell the cloth of the Torah?" Tzuref pushed out of his chair, stirring a breeze that swept Eli's letter to the floor. At the window he leaned out, and looked, beyond Woodenton. When he turned he was shaking a finger at Eli. "And a medical experiment they performed on him yet! That leaves nothing, Mr. Peck. Absolutely nothing!"

"I misunderstood."

"No news reached Woodenton?"

"About the suit, Mr. Tzuref. I thought he couldn't afford another."

"He can't."

They were right where they'd begun. "Mr. Tzuref!" Eli demanded. "*Here?*" He smacked his hand to his billfold.

"Exactly!" Tzuref said, smacking his own breast.

"Then we'll buy him one!" Eli crossed to the window and taking Tzuref by the shoulders, pronounced each word slowly. "We-will-pay-for-it. All right?"

"Pay? What, diamonds!"

Eli raised a hand to his inside pocket, then let it drop. Oh stupid! Tzuref, father to eighteen, had smacked not what lay under his coat, but deeper, under the ribs.

"Oh . . ." Eli said. He moved away along the wall. "The suit is all he's got then."

"You got my letter," Tzuref said.

Eli stayed back in the shadow, and Tzuref turned to his chair. He swished Eli's letter from the floor, and held it up. "You say too much . . . all this reasoning . . . all these conditions . . ."

"What can I do?"

"You have the word 'suffer' in English?"

"We have the word suffer. We have the word law too."

"Stop with the law! You have the word suffer. Then try it. It's a little thing."

"They won't," Eli said.

"But you, Mr. Peck, how about you?"

"I am them, they are me, Mr. Tzuref."

"Aach! You are us, we are you!"

Eli shook and shook his head. In the dark he suddenly felt that Tzuref might put him under a spell. "Mr. Tzuref, a little light?"

Tzuref lit what tallow was left in the holders. Eli was afraid to ask if they couldn't afford electricity. Maybe candles were all they had left.

"Mr. Peck, who made the law, may I ask you that?"

"The people."

"No."

"Yes."

"Before the people."

"No one. Before the people there was no law." Eli didn't care for the conversation, but with only candlelight, he was being lulled into it.

"Wrong," Tzuref said.

"We make the law, Mr. Tzuref. It is our community. These are my neighbors. I am their attorney. They pay me. Without law there is chaos."

"What you call law, I call shame. The heart, Mr. Peck, the heart is law! God!" he announced.

"Look, Mr. Tzuref, I didn't come here to talk metaphysics. People use the law, it's a flexible thing. They protect what they value, their property, their well-being, their happiness—"

"Happiness? They hide their shame. And you, Mr. Peck, you are shameless?"

"We do it," Eli said, wearily, "for our children. This is the twentieth century . . ."

"For the goyim maybe. For me the Fifty-eighth." He pointed at Eli. "That is too old for shame."

Eli felt squashed. Everybody in the world had evil reasons for his actions. Everybody! With reasons so cheap, who buys bulbs. "Enough wisdom, Mr. Tzuref. Please. I'm exhausted."

"Who isn't?" Tzuref said.

He picked Eli's papers from his desk and reached up with them. "What do you intend for us to do?"

"What you must," Eli said. "I made the offer."

"So he must give up his suit?"

"Tzuref, Tzuref, leave me be with that suit! I'm not the only lawyer in the world. I'll drop the case, and you'll get somebody who won't talk compromise. Then you'll have no home, no children, nothing. Only a lousy black suit! Sacrifice what you want. I know what I would do."

To that Tzuref made no answer, but only handed Eli his letters.

"It's not me, Mr. Tzuref, it's them."

"They are you."

"No," Eli intoned, "I am me. They are them. You are you."

"You talk about leaves and branches. I'm dealing with under the dirt."

"Mr. Tzuref, you're driving me crazy with Talmudic wisdom. This is that, that is the other thing. Give me a straight answer."

"Only for straight questions."

"Oh, God!"

Eli returned to his chair and plunged his belongings into his case. "Then, that's all," he said angrily.

Tzuref gave him the shrug.

"Remember, Tzuref, you called this down on yourself."

"*I* did?"

Eli refused to be his victim again. Double-talk proved nothing. "Goodbye," he said.

But as he opened the door leading to the hall, he heard Tzuref. "And your wife, how is she?"

"Fine, just fine." Eli kept going.

"And the baby is due when, any day?"

Eli turned. "That's right."

"Well," Tzuref said, rising. "Good luck."

"You know?"

Tzuref pointed out the window—then, with his hands, he drew upon himself a beard, a hat, a long, long coat. When his fingers formed the hem they touched the floor. "He shops two, three times a week, he gets to know them."

"He *talks* to them?"

"He sees them."

"And he can tell which is my wife?"

"They shop at the same stores. He says she is beautiful. She has a kind face. A woman capable of love . . . though who can be sure."

"*He* talks about *us*, to *you?*" demanded Eli.

"You talk about us, to her?"

"Goodbye, Mr. Tzuref."

Tzuref said, "Sholom. And good luck—I know what it is to have children. Sholom," Tzuref whispered, and with the whisper the candles went out. But the instant before, the flames leaped into Tzuref's eyes, and Eli saw it was not luck Tzuref wished him at all.

Outside the door, Eli waited. Down the lawn the children were holding hands and whirling around in a circle. At first he did not move. But he could not hide in the shadows all night. Slowly he began to slip along the front of the house. Under his hands he felt where bricks were out. He moved in the shadows until he reached the side. And then, clutching his briefcase to his chest, he broke across the darkest spots of the lawn. He aimed for a distant glade of woods, and when he reached it he did not stop, but ran through until he was so dizzied that the trees seemed to be running beside him, fleeing not towards Woodenton but away. His lungs were nearly ripping their seams as he burst into the yellow glow of the Gulf station at the edge of town.

"Eli, I had pains today. Where were you?"

"I went to Tzuref."

"Why didn't you call? I was worried."

He tossed his hat past the sofa and onto the floor. "Where are my winter suits?"

"In the hall closet. Eli, it's May."

"I need a strong suit." He left the room, Miriam behind him.

"Eli, talk to me. Sit down. Have dinner. Eli, what are you doing? You're going to get moth balls all over the carpet."

He peered out from the hall closet. Then he peered in again—there was a zipping noise, and suddenly he swept a greenish tweed suit before his wife's eyes.

"Eli, I love you in that suit. But not now. Have something to eat. I made dinner tonight—I'll warm it."

"You've got a box big enough for this suit?"

"I got a Bonwit's box, the other day. Eli, *why?*"

"Miriam, you see me doing something, let me do it."

"You haven't eaten."

"I'm *doing* something." He started up the stairs to the bedroom.

"Eli, would you please tell me what it is you want, and why?"

He turned and looked down at her. "Suppose this time you give me the reasons *before* I tell you what I'm doing. It'll probably work out the same anyway."

"Eli, I want to help."

"It doesn't concern you."

"But I want to help *you*," Miriam said.

"Just be quiet, then."

"But you're upset," she said, and she followed him up the stairs, heavily, breathing for two.

"Eli, what now?"

"A shirt." He yanked open all the drawers of their new teak dresser. He extracted a shirt.

"Eli, batiste? With a tweed suit?" she inquired.

He was at the closet now, on his knees. "Where are my cordovans?"

"Eli, why are you doing this so compulsively? You look like you *have* to do something."

"Oh, Miriam, you're supersubtle."

"Eli, stop this and talk to me. Stop it or I'll call Dr. Eckman."

Eli was kicking off the shoes he was wearing. "Where's the Bonwit box?"

"Eli, do you want me to have the baby right *here!*"

Eli walked over and sat down on the bed. He was draped not only with his own clothing, but also with the greenish tweed suit, the batiste shirt, and under each arm a shoe. He raised his arms and let the shoes drop onto the bed. Then he undid his necktie with one hand and his teeth and added that to the booty.

"Underwear," he said. "He'll need underwear."

"Who!"

He was slipping out of his socks.

Miriam kneeled down and helped him ease his left foot out of the sock. She sat with it on the floor. "Eli, just lie back. Please."

"Plaza 9-3103."

"What?"

"Eckman's number," he said. "It'll save you the trouble."

"Eli—"

"You've got that goddam tender 'You need help' look in your eyes, Miriam, don't tell me you don't."

"I don't."

"I'm not flipping," Eli said.

"I know, Eli."

"Last time I sat in the bottom of the closet and chewed on my bedroom slippers. That's what I did."

"I know."

"And I'm not doing that. This is not a nervous breakdown, Miriam, let's get that straight."

"Okay," Miriam said. She kissed the foot she held. Then, softly, she asked, "What *are* you doing?"

"Getting clothes for the guy in the hat. Don't tell me why, Miriam. Just let me do it."

"That's all?" she asked.

"That's all."

"You're not leaving?"

"No."

"Sometimes I think it gets too much for you, and you'll just leave."

"What gets too much?"

"I don't *know*, Eli. Something gets too much. Whenever everything's peaceful for a long time, and things are nice and pleasant, and we're expecting to be even happier. Like now. It's as if you don't think we *deserve* to be happy."

"Damn it, Miriam! I'm giving this guy a new suit, is that all right? From now on he comes into Woodenton like everybody else, is that all right with you?"

"And Tzuref moves?"

"I don't even know if he'll take the suit, Miriam! What do you have to bring up moving!"

"Eli, I didn't bring up moving. Everybody did. That's what everybody wants. Why make everybody u*nhappy*. It's even a law, Eli."

"Don't tell me what's the law."

"All right, sweetie. I'll get the box."

"*I'll* get the box. Where is it?"

"In the basement."

When he came up from the basement, he found all the clothes neatly folded and squared away on the sofa: shirt, tie, shoes, socks, underwear, belt, and an old gray flannel suit. His wife sat on the end of the sofa, looking like an anchored balloon.

"Where's the green suit?" he said.

"Eli, it's your loveliest suit. It's my favorite suit. Whenever I think of you, Eli, it's in that suit."

"Get it out."

"Eli, it's a Brooks Brothers suit. You say yourself how much you love it."

"Get it out."

"But the gray flannel's more practical. For shopping."

"Get it out."

"You go overboard, Eli. That's your trouble. You won't do anything in moderation. That's how people destroy themselves."

"I do *everything* in moderation. That's my trouble. The suit's in the closet again?"

She nodded, and began to fill up with tears. "Why does it have to be *your* suit? Who are you even to decide to give a suit? What about the others?" She was crying openly and holding her belly. "Eli, I'm going to have a baby. Do we need all *this?*" and she swept the clothes off the sofa to the floor.

At the closet Eli removed the green suit. "It's a J. Press," he said, looking at the lining.

"I hope to hell he's happy with it!" Miriam said, sobbing.

A half hour later the box was packed. The cord he'd found in the kitchen cabinet couldn't keep the outfit from popping through. The trouble was there was too much: the gray suit *and* the green suit, an oxford shirt as well as the batiste. But let him have two suits! Let him have three, four, if only this damn silliness would stop! And a hat— of course! God, he'd almost forgotten the hat. He took the stairs two at a time and in Miriam's closet yanked a hatbox from the top shelf. Scattering hat and tissue paper to the floor, he returned downstairs, where he packed away the hat he'd worn that day. Then he looked at his wife, who lay outstretched on the floor before the fireplace. For the third time in as many minutes she was saying, "Eli, this is the real thing."

"Where?"

"Right under the baby's head, like somebody's squeezing oranges."

Now that he'd stopped to listen he was stupefied. He said, "But you have two more weeks . . ." Somehow he'd really been expecting it was to go on not just another two weeks, but another nine months. This led him to suspect, suddenly, that his wife was feigning pain so as to get his mind off delivering the suit. And just as suddenly he resented himself for having such a thought. God, what had he become! He'd been an unending bastard towards her since this Tzuref business had come up—just when her pregnancy must have been most burdensome. He'd allowed her no access to him, but still, he he was sure, for good reasons: she might tempt him out of his confusion with her easy answers. He could be tempted all right, it was why he fought so hard. But now a sweep of love came over him at the thought of her contracting womb, and his child. And yet he would not indicate it to her. Under such splendid marital conditions, who knows but she might extract some promise from him about his concern with the school on the hill.

Having packed his second bag of the evening, Eli sped his wife to Woodenton Memorial. There she proceeded not to have her baby, but to lie hour after hour through the night having at first oranges, then bowling balls, then basketballs, squeezed back of her pelvis. Eli sat in the waiting room, under the shattering African glare of a dozen rows of fluorescent bulbs, composing a letter to Tzuref.

Dear Mr. Tzuref:

The clothes in this box are for the gentleman in the hat. In a life of sacrifice what is one more? But in a life of no sacrifices even one is impossible. Do you see what I'm saying, Mr. Tzuref? I am not a Nazi who would drive eighteen children, who are probably frightened at the sight of a firefly, into homelessness. But if you want a home here, you must accept what we have to offer. The world is the world, Mr. Tzuref. As you would say, what is, is. All we say to this man is change your clothes. Enclosed are two suits and two shirts, and everything else he'll need, including a new hat. When he needs new clothes let me know.

We await his appearance in Woodenton, as we await friendly relations with the Yeshivah of Woodenton.

He signed his name and slid the note under a bursting flap and into the box. Then he went to the phone at the end of the room and dialed Ted Heller's number.

"Hello."

"Shirley, it's Eli."

"Eli, we've been calling all night. The lights are on in your place, but nobody answers. We thought it was burglars."

"Miriam's having the baby."

"At home?" Shirley said. "Oh, Eli, what a fun-idea!"

"Shirley, let me speak to Ted."

After the ear-shaking clatter of the phone whacking the floor, Eli heard footsteps, breathing, throat-clearing, then Ted. "A boy or a girl?"

"Nothing yet."

"You've given Shirley the bug, Eli. Now she's going to have *our* next one at home."

"Good."

"That's a terrific way to bring the family together, Eli."

"Look, Ted, I've settled with Tzuref."

"When are they going?"

"They're not exactly going, Teddie. I settled it—you won't even know they're there."

"A guy dressed like 1000 B.C. and I won't know it? What are you thinking about, pal?"

"He's changing his clothes."

"Yeah, to what? Another funeral suit?"

"Tzuref promised me, Ted. Next time he comes to town, he comes dressed like you and me."

"What! Somebody's kidding somebody, Eli."

Eli's voice shot up. "If he says he'll do it, he'll do it!"

"And, Eli," Ted asked, "he said it?"

"He said it." It cost him a sudden headache, this invention.

"And suppose he doesn't change, Eli. Just suppose. I mean that *might* happen, Eli. This might just be some kind of stall or something."

"No," Eli assured him.

The other end was quiet a moment. "Look, Eli," Ted said, finally, "he changes. Okay? All right? But they're still up there, aren't they? *That* doesn't change."

"The point is you won't know it."

Patiently Ted said, "Is this what we asked of you, Eli? When we put our faith and trust in you, is that what we were asking? We weren't concerned that this guy should become a Beau Brummel, Eli, believe me. We just don't think this is the community for them. And, Eli, we isn't me. The Jewish members of the community appointed me, Artie, and Harry to see what could be done. And we appointed you. And what's happened?"

Eli heard himself say, "What happened, happened."

"Eli, you're talking in crossword puzzles."

"My wife's having a baby," Eli explained, defensively.

"I realize that, Eli. But this is a matter of zoning, isn't it? Isn't that what we discovered? You don't abide by the ordinance, you go. I mean I can't raise mountain goats, say, in my backyard—"

"This isn't so simple, Ted. People are involved—"

"People? Eli, we've been through this and through this. We're not just dealing with people—these are religious fanatics is what they are. Dressing like that. What I'd really like to find out is what goes on up there. I'm getting more and more skeptical, Eli, and I'm not afraid to admit it. It smells like a lot of hocus-pocus abracadabra stuff to me. Guys like Harry, you know, they think and they think and they're afraid to admit what they're thinking. I'll tell you. Look, I don't even know about this Sunday school business. Sundays I drive my oldest kid all the way to Scarsdale to learn Bible stories . . . and you know what she comes up with? This Abraham in the Bible was going to kill his own *kid* for a sacrifice. She gets nightmares from it, for God's sake! You call that religion? Today a guy like that they'd lock him up. This is an age of science, Eli. I size people's feet with an X-ray machine, for God's sake. They've disproved all that stuff, Eli, and I refuse to sit by and watch it happening on my own front lawn."

"Nothing's happening on your front lawn, Teddie. You're exaggerating, nobody's sacrificing their kid."

"You're damn right, Eli—I'm not sacrificing mine. You'll see when you have your own what it's like. All the place is, is a hideaway for people who can't face life. It's a matter of *needs*. They have all these superstitions, and why do you think? Because they can't face the world, because they can't take their place in society. That's no environment to bring kids up in, Eli."

"Look, Ted, see it from another angle. We can convert them," Eli said, with half a heart.

"What, make a bunch of Catholics out of them? Look, Eli—pal, there's a good healthy relationship in this town because it's modern Jews and Protestants. That's the point, isn't it, Eli? Let's not kid each other, I'm not Harry. The way things are now are fine—like human beings. There's going to be no pogroms in Woodenton. Right? 'Cause there's no fanatics, no crazy people—" Eli winced, and closed his eyes a second—"just people who respect each other, and leave each other be. Common sense is the ruling thing, Eli. I'm for common sense. Moderation."

"Exactly, exactly, Ted. I agree, but common sense, maybe, says make this guy change his clothes. Then maybe—"

"Common sense says that? Common sense says to me they go and find a nice place somewhere else, Eli. New York is the biggest city in the world, it's only 30 miles away—why don't they go there?"

"Ted, give them a chance. Introduce them to common sense."

"Eli, you're dealing with *fanatics*. Do they display common sense? Talking a dead language, that makes sense? Making a big thing out of suffering, so you're going oy-oy-oy all your life, that's common sense? Look, Eli, we've been through all this. I don't know if you know—but there's talk that *Life* magazine is sending a guy out to the Yeshivah for a story. With pictures."

"Look, Teddie, you're letting your imagination get inflamed. I don't think *Life's* interested."

"But I'm interested, Eli. And we thought you were supposed to be."

"I am," Eli said, "I am. Let him just change the clothes, Ted. Let's see what happens."

"They live in the medieval ages, Eli—it's some superstition, some *rule.*"

"Let's just *see*," Eli pleaded.

"Eli, every day—"

"One more day," Eli said. "If he doesn't change in one more day. . . ."

"What?"

"Then I get an injunction first thing Monday. That's that."

"Look, Eli—it's not up to me. Let me call Harry—"

"You're the spokesman, Teddie. I'm all wrapped up here with Miriam having a baby. Just give me the day—them the day."

"All right, Eli. I want to be fair. But tomorrow, that's all. Tomorrow's the judgment day, Eli, I'm telling you."

"I hear trumpets," Eli said, and hung up. He was shaking inside—Teddie's voice seemed to have separated his bones at the joints. He was still in the phone booth when the nurse came to tell him that Mrs. Peck would positively not be delivered of a child until the morning. He was to go home and get some rest, he looked like *he* was having the baby. The nurse winked and left.

But Eli did not go home. He carried the Bonwit box out into the street with him and put it in the car. The night was soft and starry, and he began to drive the streets of Woodenton. Square cool windows, apricot-colored, were all one could see beyond the long lawns that fronted the homes of the townsmen. The stars polished the permanent baggage carriers atop the station wagons in the driveways. He drove slowly, up, down, around. Only his tires could be heard taking the gentle curves in the road.

What peace. What incredible peace. Have children ever been so safe in their beds? Parents—Eli wondered—so full in their stomachs? Water so warm in its boilers? Never. Never in Rome, never in Greece. Never even did walled cities have it so good! No wonder then they would keep things just as they were. Here, after all, were peace and safety—what civilization had been working toward for centuries. For all his jerkiness, that was all Ted Heller was asking for, peace and safety. It was what his parents had asked for in the Bronx, and his grandparents in Poland, and theirs in Russia or Austria, or wherever else they'd fled to or from. It was what Miriam was asking for. And now they had it—the world was at last a place for families, even Jewish families. After all these centuries, maybe there just had to be this communal toughness—or numbness—to protect such a blessing. Maybe that was the trouble with the Jews all along—too soft. Sure, to live takes guts . . . Eli was thinking as he drove on beyond the train station, and parked his car at the darkened Gulf station. He stepped out, carrying the box.

At the top of the hill one window trembled with light. What *was* Tzuref doing up there in that office? Killing babies—probably not. But studying a language no one understood? Practicing customs with origins long forgotten? Suffering sufferings already suffered once too often? Teddie was right—why keep it up! However, if a man chose to be stubborn, then he couldn't expect to survive. The world is give-and-take. What sense to sit and brood over a suit. Eli would give him one last chance.

He stopped at the top. No one was around. He walked slowly up the lawn, setting each foot into the grass, listening to the shh shhh shhhh his shoes made as they bent the wetness into the sod. He looked around. Here there was nothing. Nothing! An old decaying house— and a suit.

On the porch he slid behind a pillar. He felt someone was watching him. But only the stars gleamed down. And at his feet, off and away, Woodenton glowed up. He set his package on the step of the great front door. Inside the cover of the box he felt to see if his letter was still there. When he touched it, he pushed it deeper into the green suit, which his fingers still remembered from winter. He should have included some light bulbs. Then he slid back by the pillar again, and this time there was something on the lawn. It was the second sight he had of him. He was facing Woodenton and barely moving across the open space towards the trees. His right fist was beating his chest. And then Eli heard a sound rising with each knock on the chest. What a moan! It could raise hair, stop hearts, water eyes. And it did all three to Eli, plus more. Some feeling crept into him for whose deepness he could find no word. It was strange. He listened—it did not hurt to hear this moan. But he wondered if it hurt to make it. And so, with only stars to hear, he tried. And it did hurt. Not the bumblebee of noise that turned at the back of his throat and winged out his nostrils. What hurt buzzed down. It stung and stung inside him, and in turn the moan sharpened. It became a scream, louder, a song, a crazy song that whined through the pillars and blew out to the grass, until the strange hatted creature on the lawn turned and threw his arms wide, and looked in the night like a scarecrow.

Eli ran, and when he reached the car the pain was only a bloody scratch across his neck where a branch had whipped back as he fled the greenie's arms.

The following day his son was born. But not till one in the afternoon, and by then a great deal had happened.

First, at nine-thirty the phone rang. Eli leaped from the sofa— where he'd dropped the night before—and picked it screaming from the cradle. He could practically smell the hospital as he shouted into the phone, "Hello, yes!"

"Eli, it's Ted. Eli, he *did* it. He just walked by the store. I was opening the door, Eli, and I turned around and I swear I thought it was you. But it was him. He still walks like he did, but the clothes, Eli, the clothes."

"Who?"

"The greenie. He has on man's regular clothes. And the suit, it's a beauty."

The suit barreled back into Eli's consciousness, pushing all else aside. "What color suit?"

"Green. He's just strolling in the green suit like it's a holiday. Eli . . . is it a Jewish holiday?"

"Where is he now?"

"He's walking straight up Coach House Road, in this damn tweed job. Eli, it worked. You were right."

"We'll see."

"What next?"

"We'll see."

He took off the underwear in which he'd slept and went into the kitchen where he turned the light under the coffee. When it began to perk he held his head over the pot so it would steam loose the knot back of his eyes. It still hadn't when the phone rang.

"Eli, Ted again. Eli, the guy's walking up and down every street in town. Really, he's on a tour or something. Artie called me, Herb called me. Now Shirley calls that he just walked by our house. Eli, go out on the porch you'll see."

Eli went to the window and peered out. He couldn't see past the bend in the road, and there was no one in sight.

"Eli?" He heard Ted from where he dangled over the telephone table. He dropped the phone into the hook, as a few last words floated up to him—"Eliyousawhim . . . ?" He threw on the pants and shirt he'd worn the night before and walked barefoot on to his front lawn. And sure enough, his apparition appeared around the bend: in a brown hat a little too far down on his head, a green suit too far back on the shoulders, an unbuttoned-down button-down shirt, a tie knotted so as to leave a two-inch tail, trousers that cascaded onto his shoes—he was shorter than that black hat had made him seem. And moving the clothes was that walk that was not a walk, the tiny-stepped shlumpy gait. He came round the bend, and for all his strangeness—it clung to his whiskers, signaled itself in his locomotion—he looked as if he belonged. Eccentric, maybe, but he belonged. He made no moan, nor did he invite Eli with wide-flung arms. But he did stop when he saw him. He stopped and put a hand to his hat. When he felt for its top, his hand went up too high. Then it found the level and fiddled with the brim. The fingers fiddled, fumbled, and when they'd finally made their greeting, they traveled down the fellow's face and in an instant seemed to have touched each one of his features. They dabbed the eyes, ran the length of the nose, swept over the hairy lip, until they found their home in the hair that hid a little of his collar. To Eli the fingers said, *I have a face, I have a face at least.* Then his hand came through the beard and when it stopped at his chest it was like a pointer—and the eyes asked a question as tides of water shifted over them. *The face is all right, I can keep it?* Such a look was in those eyes that Eli was still seeing them when he turned his head away. They were the hearts of his jonquils, that only last week had appeared—they were the leaves on his birch, the bulbs in his coach lamp, the droppings on his lawn: those eyes were the eyes in his head. They were his, he had made them. He turned and went into his house and when he peeked out the side of the window, between shade and molding, the green suit was gone.

The phone.

"Eli, Shirley."

"I saw him, Shirley," and he hung up.

He sat frozen for a long time. The sun moved around the windows. The coffee steam smelled up the house. The phone began to ring, stopped, began again. The mailman came, the cleaner, the bakery man, the gardener, the ice cream man, the League of Women Voters lady. A Negro woman spreading some strange gospel calling for the revision of the Food and Drug Act knocked at the front, rapped the windows, and finally scraped a half-dozen pamphlets under the back door. But Eli only sat, without underwear, in last night's suit. He answered no one.

Given his condition, it was strange that the trip and crash at the back door reached his inner ear. But in an instant he seemed to melt down into the crevices of the chair, then to splash up and out to where the clatter had been. At the door he waited. It was silent, but for a fluttering of damp little leaves on the trees. When he finally opened the door, there was no one there. He'd expected to see green, green, green, big as the doorway, topped by his hat, waiting for him with those eyes. But there was no one out there, except for the Bonwit's box which lay bulging at his feet. No string tied it and the top rode high on the bottom.

The coward! He couldn't do it! He couldn't!

The very glee of that idea pumped fuel to his legs. He tore out across his back lawn, past his new spray of forsythia, to catch a glimpse of the bearded one fleeing naked through yards, over hedges and fences, to the safety of his hermitage. In the distance a pile of pink and white stones—which Harriet Knudson had painted the previous day—tricked him. "Run," he shouted to the rocks, "Run, you . . ." but he caught his error before anyone else did, and though he peered and craned there was no hint anywhere of a man about his own size, with white, white, terribly white skin (how white must be the skin of his body!) in cowardly retreat. He came slowly, curiously, back to the door. And while the trees shimmered in the light wind, he removed the top from the box. The shock at first was the shock of having daylight turned off all at once. Inside the box was an eclipse. But black soon sorted from black, and shortly there was the glassy black of lining, the coarse black of trousers, the dead black of fraying threads, and in the center the mountain of black: the hat. He picked the box from the doorstep and carried it inside. For the first time in his life he *smelled* the color of blackness: a little stale, a little sour, a little old, but nothing that could overwhelm you. Still, he held the package at arm's length and deposited it on the dining room table.

Twenty rooms on a hill and they store their old clothes with me! What am I supposed to do with them? Give them to charity? That's where they came from. He picked up the hat by the edges and looked inside. The crown was smooth as an egg, the brim practically thread-bare. There is nothing else to do with a hat in one's hands but put it on, so Eli dropped the thing on his head. He opened the door to the hall closet and looked at himself in the full-length mirror. The hat gave him bags under the eyes. Or perhaps he had not slept well. He pushed the brim lower till a shadow touched his lips. Now the bags under his eyes had inflated to become his face. Before the mirror he unbuttoned his shirt, unzipped his trousers, and then, shedding his clothes, he studied what he was. What a silly disappoint-ment to see yourself naked in a hat. Especially in that hat. He sighed, but could not rid himself of the great weakness that sud-denly set on his muscles and joints, beneath the terrible weight of the stranger's strange hat.

He returned to the dining room table and emptied the box of its contents: jacket, trousers, and vest (*it* smelled deeper than black-ness). And under it all, sticking between the shoes that looked chopped and bitten, came the first gleam of white. A little fringed serape, a gray piece of semi-underwear, was crumpled at the bottom, its thready border twisted into itself. Eli removed it and let hang free. What is it? For warmth? To wear beneath underwear in the event of a chest cold? He held it to his nose but it did not smell from Vick's or mustard plaster. It was something special, some Jewish thing. Spe-cial food, special language, special prayers, why not special BVD's? So fearful was he that he would be tempted back into wearing his traditional clothes—reasoned Eli—that he had carried and buried in Woodenton everything, including the special underwear. For that was how Eli now understood the box of clothes. The greenie was saying, Here, I give up. I refuse even to be tempted. We surrender. And that was how Eli continued to understand it until he found he'd slipped the white fringy surrender flag over his hat and felt it clinging to his chest. And now, looking at himself in the mirror, he was mo-mentarily uncertain as to who was tempting who into what. Why *did* the greenie leave his clothes? Was it even the greenie? Then who was it? And why? But, Eli, for Christ's sake, in an age of science things don't happen like that. Even the goddam pigs take drugs . . .

Regardless of who was the source of the temptation, what was its end, not to mention its beginning, Eli, some moments later, stood draped in black, with a little white underneath, before the full-length mirror. He had to pull down on the trousers so they would not show the hollow of his ankle. The greenie, didn't he wear socks? Or had he forgotten them? The mystery was solved when Eli mustered enough courage to investigate the trouser pockets. He had expected some damp awful thing to happen to his fingers should he slip them down and out of sight—but when at last he jammed bravely down he came up with a khaki army sock in each hand. As he slipped them over his toes, he invented a genesis: a G.I.'s present in 1945. Plus everything else lost between 1938 and 1945, he had also lost his socks. Not that he had lost the socks, but that he'd had to stoop to accepting these, made Eli almost cry. To calm himself he walked out the back door and stood looking at his lawn.

On the Knudson back lawn, Harriet Knudson was giving her stones a second coat of pink. She looked up just as Eli stepped out. Eli shot back in again and pressed himself against the back door. When he peeked between the curtain all he saw were paint bucket, brush, and rocks scattered on the Knudsons' pink-spattered grass. The phone rang. Who was it—Harriet Knudson? Eli, there's a Jew at your door. *That's me.* Nonsense, Eli, I saw him with my own eyes. *That's me, I saw you too, painting your rocks pink.* Eli, you're having a nervous breakdown again. Jimmy, Eli's having a nervous breakdown again. Eli, this is Jimmy, hear you're having a little breakdown, anything I can do, boy? Eli, this is Ted, Shirley says you need help. Eli, this is Artie, you need help. Eli, Harry, you need help you need help . . . The phone rattled its last and died.

"God helps them who help themselves," intoned Eli, and once again he stepped out the door. This time he walked to the center of his lawn and in full sight of the trees, the grass, the birds, and the sun, revealed that it was he, Eli, in the costume. But nature had nothing to say to him, and so stealthily he made his way to the hedge separating his property from the field beyond and he cut his way through, losing his hat twice in the underbrush. Then, clamping the hat to his head, he began to run, the threaded tassels jumping across his heart. He ran through the weeds and wild flowers, until on the old road that skirted the town he slowed up. He was walking when he approached the Gulf station from the back. He supported himself on a huge tireless truck rim, and among tubes, rusted engines, dozens of topless oil cans, he rested. With a kind of brainless cunning, he readied himself for the last mile of his journey.

"How are you, Pop?" It was the garage attendant, rubbing his greasy hands on his overalls, and hunting among the cans.

Eli's stomach lurched and he pulled the big black coat round his neck.

"Nice day," the attendant said and started around to the front.

"Sholom," Eli whispered and zoomed off towards the hill.

The sun was directly overhead when Eli reached the top. He had come by way of the woods, where it was cooler, but still he was perspiring beneath his new suit. The hat had no sweatband and the cloth clutched his head. The children were playing. The children were always playing, as if it was that alone that Tzuref had to teach them. In their shorts, they revealed such thin legs that beneath one could see the joints swiveling as they ran. Eli waited for them to disappear around a corner before he came into the open. But something would not let him wait—his green suit. It was on the porch, wrapped around the bearded fellow, who was painting the base of a pillar. His arm went up and down, up and down, and the pillar glowed like white fire. The very sight of him popped Eli out of the woods onto the lawn. He did not turn back, though his insides did. He walked up the lawn, but the children played on; tipping the black hat, he mumbled, "Shhh . . . shhh," and they hardly seemed to notice.

At last he smelled paint.

He waited for the man to turn to him. He only painted. Eli felt suddenly that if he could pull the black hat down over his eyes, over his chest and belly and legs, if he could shut out all light, then a moment later he would be home in bed. But the hat wouldn't go past his forehead. He couldn't kid himself—he was there. No one he could think of had forced him to do this.

The greenie's arm flailed up and down on the pillar. Eli breathed loudly, cleared his throat, but the greenie wouldn't make life easier for him. At last, Eli had to say "Hello."

The arm swished up and down; it stopped—two fingers went out after a brush hair stuck to the pillar.

"Good day," Eli said.

The hair came away; the swishing resumed.

"Sholom," Eli whispered and the fellow turned.

The recognition took some time. He looked at what Eli wore. Up close, Eli looked at what he wore. And then Eli had the strange notion that he was two people. Or that he was one person wearing two suits. The greenie looked to be suffering from a similar confusion. They stared long at one another. Eli's heart shivered, and his brain was momentarily in such a mixed-up condition that his hands went out to button down the collar of his shirt that somebody else was wearing. What a mess! The greenie flung his arms over his face.

"What's the matter . . ." Eli said. The fellow had picked up his bucket and brush and was running away. Eli ran after him.

"I wasn't going to hit . . ." Eli called. "Stop . . ." Eli caught up and grabbed his sleeve. Once again, the greenie's hands flew up to his face. This time, in the violence, white paint spattered both of them.

"I only want to . . ." But in that outfit Eli didn't really know what he wanted. "To talk . . ." he said finally. "For you to look at me. Please, just *look* at me . . ."

The hands stayed put, as paint rolled off the brush onto the cuff of Eli's green suit.

"Please . . . please," Eli said, but he did not know what to do. "Say something, speak *English*," he pleaded.

The fellow pulled back against the wall, back, back, as though some arm would finally reach out and yank him to safety. He refused to uncover his face.

"Look," Eli said, pointing to himself. "It's your suit. I'll take care of it."

No answer—only a little shaking under the hands, which led Eli to speak as gently as he knew how.

"We'll . . . we'll moth-proof it. There's a button missing"—Eli pointed—"I'll have it fixed. I'll have a zipper put in . . . Please, please —just look at me . . ." He was talking to himself, and yet how could he stop? Nothing he said made any sense—that alone made his heart swell. Yet somehow babbling on, he might babble something that would make things easier between them. "Look . . ." He reached inside his shirt to pull the frills of underwear into the light. "I'm wearing the special underwear, even . . . Please," he said, *"please, please, please,"* he sang, as as if it were some sacred word. "Oh, please . . ."

Nothing twitched under the tweed suit—and if the eyes watered, or twinkled, or hated, he couldn't tell. It was driving him crazy. He had dressed like a fool, and for what? For this? He reached up and yanked the hands away.

"There!" he said—and in that first instant all he saw of the greenie's face were two white droplets stuck to each cheek.

"Tell me—" Eli clutched his hands down to his sides—"Tell me, what can I do for you, I'll do it . . ."

Stiffly, the greenie stood there, sporting his two white tears.

"Whatever I can do . . . Look, look, what I've done *already*." He grabbed his black hat and shook it in the man's face.

And in exchange, the greenie gave him an answer. He raised one hand to his chest, and then jammed it, finger first, towards the horizon. And with what a pained look! As though the air were full of razors! Eli followed the finger and saw beyond the knuckle, out past the nail, Woodenton.

"What do you want?" Eli said. "I'll bring it!"

Suddenly the greenie made a run for it. But then he stopped, wheeled, and jabbed that finger at the air again. It pointed the same way. Then he was gone.

And then, all alone, Eli had the revelation. He did not question his understanding, the substance or the source. But with a strange, dreamy elation, he started away.

On Coach House Road, they were double-parked. The Mayor's wife pushed a grocery cart full of dog food from Stop N' Shop to her station wagon. The President of the Lions Club, a napkin around his neck, was jamming pennies into the meter in front of the Bit-in-Teeth Restaurant. Ted Heller caught the sun as it glazed off the new Byzantine mosaic entrance to his shoe shop. In pinkened jeans, Mrs. Jimmy Knudson was leaving Halloway's Hardware, a paint bucket in each hand. Roger's Beauty Shoppe had its doors open—women's heads in silver bullets far as the eye could see. Over by the barbershop the pole spun, and Artie Berg's youngest sat on a red horse, having his hair cut; his mother flipped through *Look*, smiling: the greenie had changed his clothes.

And into this street, which seemed paved with chromium, came Eli Peck. It was not enough, he knew, to walk up one side of the street. That was not enough. Instead he walked ten paces up one side, then on an angle, crossed to the other side, where he walked ten

more paces, and crossed back. Horns blew, traffic jerked, as Eli made
his way up Coach House Road. He spun a moan high up in his nose
as he walked. Outside no one could hear him, but he felt it vibrate
the cartilage at the bridge of his nose.

Things slowed around him. The sun stopped rippling on spokes
and hubcaps. It glowed steadily as everyone put on brakes to look
at the man in black. They always paused and gaped, whenever he
entered the town. Then in a minute, or two, or three, a light would
change, a baby squawk, and the flow continue. Now, though lights
changed, no one moved.

"He shaved his beard," Eric the barber said.

"Who?" asked Linda Berg.

"The . . . the guy in the suit. From the place there."

Linda looked out the window.

"It's Uncle Eli," little Kevin Berg said, spitting hair.

"Oh, God," Linda said, "Eli's having a nervous breakdown."

"A nervous breakdown!" Ted Heller said, but not immediately.
Immediately he had said "Hoooly . . ."

Shortly, everybody in Coach House Road was aware that Eli Peck,
the nervous young attorney with the pretty wife, was having a breakdown. Everybody except Eli Peck. He knew what he did was not
insane, though he felt every inch of its strangeness. He felt those
black clothes as if they were the skin of his skin—the give and pull as
they got used to where he bulged and buckled. And he felt eyes,
every eye on Coach House Road. He saw headlights screech to within
an inch of him, and stop. He saw mouths: first the bottom jaw slides
forward, then the tongue hits the teeth, the lips explode, a little
thunder in the throat, and they've said it: Eli Peck Eli Peck Eli Peck
Eli Peck. He began to walk slowly, shifting his weight down and
forward with each syllable: E li Peck E li Peck E li Peck. Heavily
he trod, and as his neighbors uttered each syllable of his name, he
felt each syllable shaking all his bones. He knew who he was down
to his marrow—they were telling him. Eli Peck. He wanted them to
say it a thousand times, a million times, he would walk forever in
that black suit, as adults whispered of his strangeness and children
made "Shame . . . shame" with their fingers.

"It's going to be all right, pal . . ." Ted Heller was motioning to
Eli from his doorway. "C'mon, pal, it's going to be all right . . ."

Eli saw him, past the brim of his hat. Ted did not move from his doorway, but leaned forward and spoke with his hand over his mouth. Behind him, three customers peered through the doorway. "Eli, it's Ted, remember Ted . . ."

Eli crossed the street and found he was heading directly towards Harriet Knudson. He lifted his neck so she could see his whole face.

He saw her forehead melt down to her lashes. "Good morning, Mr. Peck."

"Sholom," Eli said, and crossed the street where he saw the President of the Lions.

"Twice before . . ." he heard someone say, and then he crossed again, mounted the curb, and was before the bakery, where a delivery man charged past with a tray of powdered cakes twirling above him. "Pardon me, Father," he said, and scooted into his truck. But he could not move it. Eli Peck had stopped traffic.

He passed the Rivoli Theater, Beekman Cleaners, Harris' Westinghouse, the Unitarian Church, and soon he was passing only trees. At Ireland Road he turned right and started through Woodenton's winding streets. Baby carriages stopped whizzing and creaked—"Isn't that . . ." Gardeners held their clipping. Children stepped from the sidewalk and tried the curb. And Eli greeted no one, but raised his face to all. He wished passionately that he had white tears to show them . . . And not till he reached his own front lawn, saw his house, his shutters, his new jonquils, did he remember his wife. And the child that must have been born to him. And it was then and there he had the awful moment. He could go inside and put on his clothes and go to his wife in the hospital. It was not irrevocable, even the walk wasn't. In Woodenton memories are long but fury short. Apathy works like forgiveness. Besides, when you've flipped, you've flipped—it's Mother Nature.

What gave Eli the awful moment was that he turned away. He knew exactly what he could do but he chose not to. To go inside would be to go halfway. There was more . . . So he turned and walked towards the hospital and all the time he quaked an eighth of an inch beneath his skin to think that perhaps he'd chosen the crazy way. To think that he'd *chosen* to be crazy! But if you chose to be crazy, then you weren't crazy. It's when you didn't choose. No, he wasn't flipping. He had a child to see.

"Name?"

"Peck."

"Fourth floor." He was given a little blue card.

In the elevator everybody stared. Eli watched his black shoes rise four floors.

"Four."

He tipped his hat, but knew he couldn't take it off.

"Peck," he said. He showed the card.

"Congratulations," the nurse said. ". . . the grandfather?"

"The father. Which room?"

She led him to 412. "A joke on the Mrs?" she said, but he slipped in the door without her.

"Miriam?"

"Yes?"

"Eli."

She rolled her white face towards her husband. "Oh, Eli . . . Oh, Eli."

He raised his arms. "What could I do?"

"You have a son. They called all morning."

"I came to see him."

"Like *that!*" she whispered harshly. "Eli, you can't go around like that."

"I have a son. I want to see him."

"Eli, why are you doing this to me!" Red seeped back into her lips. "*He's* not your fault," she explained. "Oh, Eli, sweetheart, why do you feel guilty about everything. Eli, change your clothes. I forgive you."

"Stop forgiving me. Stop understanding me."

"But I love you."

"That's something else."

"But, sweetie, you *don't* have to dress like that. You didn't do anything. You don't have to feel guilty because . . . because everything's all right. Eli, can't you see that?"

"Miriam, enough reasons. Where's my son?"

"Oh, please, Eli, don't flip now. I need you now. Is that why you're flipping—because I need you?"

"In your selfish way, Miriam, you're very generous. I want my son."

"Don't flip now. I'm afraid, now that he's out." She was beginning to whimper. "I don't know if I love him, now that he's out. When I look in the mirror, Eli, he won't be there . . . Eli, Eli, you look like you're going to your own funeral. Please, can't you leave well enough *alone?* Can't we just have a family?"

"No."

In the corridor he asked the nurse to lead him to his son. The nurse walked on one side of him, Ted Heller on the other.

"Eli, do you want some help? I thought you might want some help."

"No."

Ted whispered something to the nurse; then to Eli he whispered, "Should you be walking around like this?"

"Yes."

In his ear Ted said, "You'll . . . you'll frighten the kid . . ."

"There," the nurse said. She pointed to a bassinet in the second row and looked, puzzled, to Ted. "Do I go in?" Eli said.

"No," the nurse said. "She'll roll him over." She rapped on the enclosure full of babies. "Peck," she mouthed to the nurse on the inside.

Ted tapped Eli's arm. "You're not thinking of doing something you'll be sorry for . . . are you, Eli? Eli—I mean you know you're still Eli, don't you?"

In the enclosure, Eli saw a bassinet had been wheeled before the square window.

"Oh, Christ. . . ." Ted said. "You don't have this Bible stuff on the brain—" And suddenly he said, "You wait, pal." He started down the corridor, his heels tapping rapidly.

Eli felt relieved—he leaned forward. In the basket was what he'd come to see. Well, now that he was here, what did he think he was going to say to it? I'm your father, Eli, the Flipper? I am wearing a black hat, suit, and fancy underwear, all borrowed from a friend? How could he admit to this reddened ball—*his* reddened ball—the worst of all: that Eckman would shortly convince him he wanted to take off the whole business. He couldn't admit it! He wouldn't do it!

Past his hat brim, from the corner of his eye, he saw Ted had stopped in a doorway at the end of the corridor. Two interns stood there smoking, listening to Ted. Eli ignored it.

No, even Eckman wouldn't make him take it off! No! He'd wear it, if he chose to. He'd make the kid wear it! Sure! Cut it down when the time came. A smelly hand-me-down, whether the kid liked it or not!

Only Teddie's heels clacked; the interns wore rubber soles—for they were there, beside him, unexpectedly. Their white suits smelled, but not like Eli's.

"Eli," Ted said, softly, "visiting time's up, pal."

"How are you feeling, Mr. Peck? First child upsets everyone. . . ."

He'd just pay no attention; nevertheless, he began to perspire, thickly, and his hat crown clutched his hair.

"Excuse me—Mr. Peck. . . ." It was a new rich bass voice. "Excuse me, rabbi, but you're wanted . . . in the temple." A hand took his elbow, firmly; then another hand, the other elbow. Where they grabbed, his tendons went taut.

"Okay, rabbi. Okay okay okay okay okay okay. . . ." He listened; it was a very soothing word, that okay. "Okay okay everything's going to be okay." His feet seemed to have left the ground some, as he glided away from the window, the bassinet, the babies. "Okay easy does it everything's all right all right—"

But he rose, suddenly, as though up out of a dream, and flailing his arms, screamed: *"I'm the father!"*

But the window disappeared. In a moment they tore off his jacket —it gave so easily, in one yank. Then a needle slid under his skin. The drug calmed his soul, but did not touch it down where the blackness had reached.

The Assistant

by BERNARD MALAMUD

After The Natural, a mythic novel about a baseball player, published in 1952, Bernard Malamud's work has almost entirely dealt with Jewish material. The allusively moral tone of this work seems a direct continuation of a kind of writing that reaches from Biblical parables through the Midrash and Yiddish literature, particularly in Hasidic tales, down to our time. Thus in The Fixer the hero, in a weird half-real journey on a disintegrating vehicle, seems to be insistently approaching his fate as an exemplary sufferer for a cause he only instinctively understands.

It was The Assistant that made Malamud's reputation and that remains at this writing his chief work dealing with the American Jewish scene. It is not the suburban scene; the musty, dying store where Morris Bober and his wife and daughter got stuck is part of a row of Jewish shops in a played-out Brooklyn neighborhood where only the liquor business remains good. Around a simple holdup, Malamud weaves a poignant drama. The little family is portrayed with a lyric realism that raises the story to the level of poetry. Some critics have found the holdup man's eventual conversion to Judaism a touch out of key; others, on the contrary, found in it the key that opens the realistic tale to a mystical vista. The novel has a finely sustained rhythm and a consistently felt atmosphere; this is beautifully established in the first section, reprinted here.

A writing method, Malamud has said, "must not be didactic but writing must change the reader," and his readers doubtless agree that from subtle undercurrent to direct illumination his work produces such changes. His achievement helped liberate the Jewish writer in America from a sense of professional limitation if he used his own subject matter.

Malamud has led a scholar's life, if not in the yeshiva then in academe. Born in Brooklyn in 1914, educated at City College and Columbia, he taught English in New York City high schools in the forties, and then at Oregon State, Bennington, Harvard, and the University of Chicago. In 1967 he received the National Book Award for his short stories in The Magic Barrel.

M.L.

THE EARLY NOVEMBER street was dark though night had ended, but the wind, to the grocer's surprise, already clawed. It flung his apron into his face as he bent for the two milk cases at the curb. Morris Bober dragged the heavy boxes to the door, panting. A large brown bag of hard rolls stood in the doorway along with the sour-faced, gray-haired Poilisheh huddled there, who wanted one.

"What's the matter so late?"

"Ten after six," said the grocer.

"Is cold," she complained.

Turning the key in the lock he let her in. Usually he lugged in the milk and lit the gas radiators, but the Polish woman was impatient. Morris poured the bag of rolls into a wire basket on the counter and found an unseeded one for her. Slicing it in halves, he wrapped it in white store paper. She tucked the roll into her cord market bag and left three pennies on the counter. He rang up the sale on an old noisy cash register, smoothed and put away the bag the rolls had come in, finished pulling in the milk, and stored the bottles at the bottom of the refrigerator. He lit the gas radiator at the front of the store and went into the back to light the one there.

He boiled up coffee in a blackened enamel pot and sipped it, chewing on a roll, not tasting what he was eating. After he had cleaned up he waited; he waited for Nick Fuso, the upstairs tenant, a young mechanic who worked in a garage in the neighborhood. Nick came in every morning around seven for twenty cents' worth of ham and a loaf of bread.

But the front door opened and a girl of ten entered, her face pinched and eyes excited. His heart held no welcome for her.

"My mother says," she said quickly, "can you trust her till tomorrow for a pound of butter, loaf of rye bread and a small bottle of cider vinegar?"

He knew the mother. "No more trust."

The girl burst into tears.

Morris gave her a quarter-pound of butter, the bread and vinegar. He found a penciled spot on the worn counter, near the cash register, and wrote a sum under "Drunk Woman." The total now came to $2.03, which he never hoped to see. But Ida would nag if she noticed a new figure, so he reduced the amount to $1.61. His peace—the little he lived with—was worth forty-two cents.

He sat in a chair at the round wooden table in the rear of the store and scanned, with raised brows, yesterday's Jewish paper that he had already thoroughly read. From time to time he looked absently through the square windowless window cut through the wall, to see if anybody had by chance come into the store. Sometimes when he looked up from his newspaper, he was startled to see a customer standing silently at the counter.

Now the store looked like a long dark tunnel.

The grocer sighed and waited. Waiting he thought he did poorly. When times were bad time was bad. It died as he waited, stinking in his nose.

A workman came in for a fifteen-cent can of King Oscar Norwegian sardines.

Morris went back to waiting. In twenty-one years the store had changed little. Twice he had painted all over, once added new shelving. The old-fashioned double windows at the front a carpenter had made into a large single one. Ten years ago the sign hanging outside fell to the ground but he had never replaced it. Once, when business hit a long good spell, he had had the wooden icebox ripped out and a new white refrigerated showcase put in. The showcase stood at the front in line with the old counter and he often leaned against it as he stared out of the window. Otherwise the store was the same. Years ago it was more a delicatessen; now, though he still sold a little delicatessen, it was more a poor grocery.

A half-hour passed. When Nick Fuso failed to appear, Morris got up and stationed himself at the front window, behind a large cardboard display sign the beer people had rigged up in an otherwise empty window. After a while the hall door opened, and Nick came out in a thick, hand-knitted green sweater. He trotted around the corner and soon returned carrying a bag of groceries. Morris was now visible at the window. Nick saw the look on his face but didn't look long. He ran into the house, trying to make it seem it was the wind that was chasing him. The door slammed behind him, a loud door.

The grocer gazed into the street. He wished fleetingly that he could once more be out in the open, as when he was a boy—never in the house, but the sound of the blustery wind frightened him. He thought again of selling the store but who would buy? Ida still hoped to sell. Every day she hoped. The thought caused him grimly to smile, although he did not feel like smiling. It was an impossible idea so he tried to put it out of his mind. Still, there were times when he went into the back, poured himself a spout of coffee and pleasantly thought of selling. Yet if he miraculously did, where would he go, where? He had a moment of uneasiness as he pictured himself without a roof over his head. There he stood in all kinds of weather, drenched in rain, and the snow froze on his head. No, not for an age had he lived a whole day in the open. As a boy, always running in the muddy, rutted streets of the village, or across the fields, or bathing with the other boys in the river; but as a man, in America, he rarely saw the sky. In the early days when he drove a horse and wagon, yes, but not since his first store. In a store you were entombed.

The milkman drove up to the door in his truck and hurried in, a bull, for his empties. He lugged out a caseful and returned with two half-pints of light cream. Then Otto Vogel, the meat provisions man, entered, a bushy-mustached German carrying a smoked liverwurst and string of wieners in his oily meat basket. Morris paid cash for the liverwurst; from a German he wanted no favors. Otto left with the wieners. The bread driver, new on the route, exchanged three fresh loaves for three stale and walked out without a word. Leo, the cake man, glanced hastily at the package cake on top of the refrigerator and called, "See you Monday, Morris."

Morris didn't answer.

Leo hesitated. "Bad all over, Morris."

"Here is the worst."

"See you Monday."

A young housewife from close by bought sixty-three cents' worth; another came in for forty-one cents'. He had earned his first cash dollar for the day.

Breitbart, the bulb peddler, laid down his two enormous cartons of light bulbs and diffidently entered the back.

"Go in," Morris urged. He boiled up some tea and served it in a thick glass, with a slice of lemon. The peddler eased himself into a chair, derby hat and coat on, and gulped the hot tea, his Adam's apple bobbing.

"So how goes now?" asked the grocer.

"Slow," shrugged Breitbart.

Morris sighed. "How is your boy?"

Breitbart nodded absently, then picked up the Jewish paper and read. After ten minutes he got up, scratched all over, lifted across his thin shoulders the two large cartons tied together with clothesline and left.

Morris watched him go.

The world suffers. *He* felt every schmerz.

At lunchtime Ida came down. She had cleaned the whole house.

Morris was standing before the faded couch, looking out of the rear window at the back yards. He had been thinking of Ephraim.

His wife saw his wet eyes.

"So stop sometimes, please." Her own grew wet.

He went to the sink, caught cold water in his cupped palms and dipped his face into it.

"The Italyener," he said, drying himself, "bought this morning across the street."

She was irritated. "Give him for twenty-nine dollars five rooms so he should spit in your face."

"A cold water flat," he reminded her.

"You put in gas radiators."

"Who says he spits? This I didn't say."

"You said something to him not nice?"

"Me?"

"Then why he went across the street?"

"Why? Go ask him," he said angrily.

"How much you took in till now?"

"Dirt."

She turned away.

He absent-mindedly scratched a match and lit a cigarette.

"Stop with the smoking," she nagged.

He took a quick drag, clipped the butt with his thumb nail and quickly thrust it under his apron into his pants pocket. The smoke made him cough. He coughed harshly, his face lit like a tomato. Ida held her hands over her ears. Finally he brought up a gob of phlegm and wiped his mouth with his handkerchief, then his eyes.

"Cigarettes," she said bitterly. "Why don't you listen what the doctor tells you?"

"Doctors," he remarked.

Afterward he noticed the dress she was wearing. "What is the picnic?"

Ida said, embarrassed, "I thought to myself maybe will come today the buyer."

She was fifty-one, nine years younger than he, her thick hair still almost all black. But her face was lined, and her legs hurt when she stood too long on them, although she now wore shoes with arch supports. She had waked that morning resenting the grocer for having dragged her, so many years ago, out of a Jewish neighborhood into this. She missed to this day their old friends and landsleit—lost for parnusseh unrealized. That was bad enough, but on top of their isolation, the endless worry about money embittered her. She shared unwillingly the grocer's fate though she did not show it and her dissatisfaction went no farther than nagging—her guilt that she had talked him into a grocery store when he was in the first year of evening high school, preparing, he had said, for pharmacy. He was, through the years, a hard man to move. In the past she could sometimes resist him, but the weight of his endurance was too much for her now.

"A buyer," Morris grunted, "will come next Purim."

"Don't be so smart. Karp telephoned him."

"Karp," he said in disgust. "Where he telephoned—the cheapskate?"

"Here."

"When?"

"Yesterday. You were sleeping."

"What did he told him?"

"For sale a store—yours, cheap."

"What do you mean cheap?"

"The key is worth now nothing. For the stock and the fixtures that they are worth also nothing, maybe three thousand, maybe less."

"I paid four."

"Twenty-one years ago," she said irritably. "So don't sell, go in auction."

"He wants the house too?"

"Karp don't know. Maybe."

"Big mouth. Imagine a man that they held him up four times in the last three years and he still don't take in a telephone. What he says ain't worth a cent. He promised me he wouldn't put in a grocery around the corner, but what did he put?—a grocery. Why does he bring me buyers? Why didn't he keep out the German around the corner?"

She sighed. "He tries to help you now because he feels sorry for you."

"Who needs his sorrow?" Morris said. "Who needs him?"

"So why *you* didn't have the sense to make out of your grocery a wine and liquor store when came out the licenses?"

"Who had cash for stock?"

"So if you don't have, don't talk."

"A business for drunken bums."

"A business is a business. What Julius Karp takes in next door in a day we don't take in in two weeks."

But Ida saw he was annoyed and changed the subject.

"I told you to oil the floor."

"I forgot."

"I asked you special. By now would be dry."

"I will do later."

"Later the customers will walk in the oil and make everything dirty."

"What customers?" he shouted. "Who customers? Who comes in here?"

"Go," she said quietly. "Go upstairs and sleep. I will oil myself."

But he got out the oil can and mop and oiled the floor until the wood shone darkly. No one had come in.

She had prepared his soup. "Helen left this morning without breakfast."

"She wasn't hungry."

"Something worries her."

He said with sarcasm, "What worries her?" Meaning: the store, his health, that most of her meager wages went to keep up payments on the house; that she had wanted a college education but had got instead a job she disliked. Her father's daughter, no wonder she didn't feel like eating.

"If she will only get married," Ida murmured.

"She will get."

"Soon." She was on the verge of tears.

He grunted.

"I don't understand why she don't see Nat Pearl anymore. All summer they went together like lovers."

"A showoff."

"He'll be someday a rich lawyer."

"I don't like him."

"Louis Karp also likes her. I wish she will give him a chance."

"A stupe," Morris said, "like the father."

"Everybody is a stupe but not Morris Bober."

He was staring out at the back yards.

"Eat already and go to sleep," she said impatiently.

He finished the soup and went upstairs. The going up was easier than coming down. In the bedroom, sighing, he drew down the black window shades. He was half asleep, so pleasant was the anticipation. Sleep was his one true refreshment; it excited him to go to sleep. Morris took off his apron, tie and trousers, and laid them on a chair. Sitting at the edge of the sagging wide bed, he unlaced his misshapen shoes and slid under the cold covers in shirt, long underwear and white socks. He nudged his eye into the pillow and waited to grow warm. He crawled toward sleep. But upstairs Tessie Fuso was running the vacuum cleaner, and though the grocer tried to blot the incident out of his mind, he remembered Nick's visit to the German and on the verge of sleep felt bad.

He recalled the bad times he had lived through, but now times were worse than in the past; now they were impossible. His store was always a marginal one, up today, down tomorrow—as the wind blew. Overnight business could go down enough to hurt; yet as a rule it slowly recovered—sometimes it seemed to take forever—went up, not high enough to be really *up*, only not down. When he had first bought the grocery it was all right for the neighborhood; it had got worse as the neighborhood had. Yet even a year ago, staying open seven days a week, sixteen hours a day, he could still eke out a living. What kind of living?—a living; you lived. Now, though he toiled the same hard hours, he was close to bankruptcy, his patience torn. In the past when bad times came he had somehow lived through them, and when good times returned, they more or less returned to him. But now, since the appearance of H. Schmitz across the street ten months ago, all times were bad.

Last year a broken tailor, a poor man with a sick wife, had locked up his shop and gone away, and from the minute of the store's emptiness Morris had felt a gnawing anxiety. He went with hesitation to Karp, who owned the building, and asked him to please keep out another grocery. In this kind of neighborhood one was more than enough. If another squeezed in they would both starve. Karp answered that the neighborhood was better than Morris gave it credit (for schnapps, thought the grocer), but he promised he would look for another tailor or maybe a shoemaker, to rent to. He said so but the grocer didn't believe him. Yet weeks went by and the store stayed empty. Though Ida pooh-poohed his worries, Morris could not overcome his underlying dread. Then one day, as he daily expected, there appeared a sign in the empty store window, announcing the coming of a new fancy delicatessen and grocery.

Morris ran to Karp. "What did you do to me?"

The liquor dealer said with a one-shouldered shrug, "You saw how long stayed empty the store. Who will pay my taxes? But don't worry," he added, "he'll sell more delicatessen but you'll sell more groceries. Wait, you'll see he'll bring you in customers."

Morris groaned; he knew his fate.

Yet as the days went by, the store still sitting empty—emptier, he found himself thinking maybe the new business would never materialize. Maybe the man had changed his mind. It was possible he had seen how poor the neighborhood was and would not attempt to open the new place. Morris wanted to ask Karp if he had guessed right but could not bear to humiliate himself further.

Often after he had locked his grocery at night, he would go secretly around the corner and cross the quiet street. The empty store, dark and deserted, was one door to the left of the corner drugstore; and if no one was looking the grocer would peer through its dusty window, trying to see through shadows whether the emptiness had changed. For two months it stayed the same, and every night he went away reprieved. Then one time—after he saw that Karp was, for once, avoiding him—he spied a web of shelves sprouting from the rear wall, and that shattered the hope he had climbed into.

In a few days the shelves stretched many arms along the other walls, and soon the whole tiered and layered place glowed with new paint. Morris told himself to stay away but he could not help coming nightly to inspect, appraise, then guess the damage, in dollars, to himself. Each night as he looked, in his mind he destroyed what had been built, tried to make of it nothing, but the growth was too quick. Every day the place flowered with new fixtures—streamlined counters, the latest refrigerator, fluorescent lights, a fruit stall, a chromium cash register; then from the wholesalers arrived a mountain of cartons and wooden boxes of all sizes, and one night there appeared in the white light a stranger, a gaunt German with a German pompadour, who spent the silent night hours, a dead cigar stuck in his teeth, packing out symmetrical rows of brightly labeled cans, jars, gleaming bottles. Though Morris hated the new store, in a curious way he loved it too, so that sometimes as he entered his own old-fashioned place of business, he could not stand the sight of it; and now he understood why Nick Fuso had that morning run around the corner and crossed the street—to taste the newness of the place and be waited on by Heinrich Schmitz, an energetic German dressed like a doctor, in a white duck jacket. And that was where many of his other customers had gone, and stayed, so that his own poor living was cut in impossible half.

Morris tried hard to sleep but couldn't and grew restless in bed. After another quarter of an hour he decided to dress and go downstairs, but there drifted into his mind, with ease and no sorrow, the form and image of his boy Ephraim, gone so long from him, and he fell deeply and calmly asleep.

Helen Bober squeezed into a subway seat between two women and was on the last page of a chapter when a man dissolved in front of her and another appeared; she knew without looking that Nat Pearl was standing there. She thought she would go on reading, but couldn't, and shut her book.

"Hello, Helen." Nat touched a gloved hand to a new hat. He was cordial but as usual held back something—his future. He carried a fat law book, so she was glad to be protected with a book of her own. But not enough protected, for her hat and coat felt suddenly shabby, a trick of the mind, because on her they would still do.

"*Don Quixote*"?

She nodded.

He seemed respectful, then said in an undertone, "I haven't seen you a long time. Where've you been keeping yourself?"

She blushed under her clothes.

"Did I offend you in some way or other?"

Both of the women beside her seemed stolidly deaf. One held a rosary in her heavy hand.

"No." The offense was hers against herself.

"So what's the score?" Nat's voice was low, his gray eyes annoyed.

"No score," she murmured.

"How so?"

"You're you, I'm me."

This he considered a minute, then remarked, "I haven't much of a head for oracles."

But she felt she had said enough.

He tried another way. "Betty asks for you."

"Give her my best." She had not meant it but this sounded funny because they all lived on the same block, separated by one house.

Tight-jawed, he opened his book. She returned to hers, hiding her thoughts behind the antics of a madman until memory overthrew him and she found herself ensnared in scenes of summer that she would gladly undo, although she loved the season; but how could you undo what you had done again in the fall, unwillingly willing? Virginity she thought she had parted with without sorrow, yet was surprised by torments of conscience, or was it disappointment at being valued under her expectations? Nat Pearl, handsome, cleft-chinned, gifted, ambitious, had wanted without too much trouble a lay and she, half in love, had obliged and regretted. Not the loving, but that it had taken her so long to realize how little he wanted. Not her, Helen Bober.

Why should he?—magna cum laude, Columbia, now in his second year at law school, she only a high school graduate with a year's evening college credit mostly in lit; he with first-rate prospects, also rich friends he had never bothered to introduce her to; she as poor as her name sounded, with little promise of a better future. She had more than once asked herself if she had meant by her favors to work up a claim on him. Always she denied it. She had wanted, admittedly, sat-isfaction, but more than that—respect for the giver of what she had to give, had hoped desire would become more than just that. She wanted, simply, a future in love. Enjoyment she had somehow had, felt very moving the freedom of fundamental intimacy with a man. Though she wished for more of the same, she wanted it without after-math of conscience, or pride, or sense of waste. So she promised her-self next time it would go the other way; first mutual love, then lov-ing, harder maybe on the nerves, but easier in memory. Thus she had reasoned, until one night in September, when coming up to see his sister Betty, she had found herself alone in the house with Nat and had done again what she had promised herself she wouldn't. After-ward she fought self-hatred. Since then, to this day, without telling him why, she had avoided Nat Pearl.

Two stations before their stop, Helen shut her book, got up in silence and left the train. On the platform, as the train moved away, she caught a glimpse of Nat standing before her empty seat, calmly reading. She walked on, lacking, wanting, not wanting, not happy.

Coming up the subway steps, she went into the park by a side entrance, and despite the sharp wind and her threadbare coat, took the long way home. The leafless trees left her with unearned sadness. She mourned the long age before spring and feared loneliness in winter. Wishing she hadn't come, she left the park, searching the faces of strangers although she couldn't stand their stares. She went quickly along the Parkway, glancing with envy into the lighted depth of private houses that were, for no reason she could give, except experience, not for her. She promised herself she would save every cent possible and register next fall for a full program at NYU, night.

When she reached her block, a row of faded yellow brick houses, two stories squatting on ancient stores, Sam Pearl, stifling a yawn, was reaching into his corner candy store window to put on the lamp. He snapped the string and the dull glow from the fly-specked globe fell upon her. Helen quickened her step. Sam, always sociable, a former cabbie, bulky, wearing bifocals and chewing gum, beamed at her but she pretended not to see. Most of the day he sat hunched over dope sheets spread out on the soda fountain counter, smoking as he chewed gum, making smeary marks with a pencil stub under horses' names. He neglected the store; his wife Goldie was the broad-backed one, yet she did not much complain, because Sam's luck with the nags was exceptional and he had nicely supported Nat in college until the scholarships started rolling in.

Around the corner, through the many-bottled window that blinked in neon "KARP wines and liquors," she glimpsed paunchy Julius Karp, with bushy eyebrows and an ambitious mouth, blowing imaginary dust off a bottle as he slipped a deft fifth of something into a paper bag, while Louis, slightly popeyed son and heir, looking up from clipping to the quick his poor fingernails, smiled amiably upon a sale. The Karps, Pearls and Bobers, representing attached houses and stores, but otherwise detachment, made up the small Jewish segment of this gentile community. They had somehow, her father first, then Karp, later Pearl, drifted together here where no other Jews dwelt, except on the far fringes of the neighborhood. None of them did well and were too poor to move elsewhere until Karp, who with a shoe store that barely made him a living, got the brilliant idea after Prohibition gurgled down the drain and liquor licenses were offered to the public, to borrow cash from a white-bearded rich uncle and put in for one. To everybody's surprise he got the license, though Karp, when asked how, winked a heavy-lidded eye and answered nothing. Within a short time after cheap shoes had become expensive bottles, in spite of the poor neighborhood—or maybe because of it, Helen supposed—he became astonishingly successful and retired his overweight wife from the meager railroad flat above the store to a big house on the Parkway—from which she hardly ever stepped forth —the house complete with two-car garage and Mercury; and at the same time as Karp changed his luck—to hear her father tell it—he became wise without brains.

The grocer, on the other hand, had never altered his fortune, unless degrees of poverty meant alteration, for luck and he were, if not natural enemies, not good friends. He labored long hours, was the soul of honesty—he could not escape his honesty, it was bedrock; to cheat would cause an explosion in him, yet he trusted cheaters— coveted nobody's nothing and always got poorer. The harder he worked—his toil was a form of time devouring time—the less he seemed to have. He was Morris Bober and could be nobody more fortunate. With that name you had no sure sense of property, as if it were in your blood and history not to possess, or if by some miracle to own something, to do so on the verge of loss. At the end you were sixty and had less than at thirty. It was, she thought, surely a talent.

Helen removed her hat as she entered the grocery. "Me," she called, as she had from childhood. It meant that whoever was sitting in the back should sit and not suddenly think he was going to get rich.

Morris awoke, soured by the long afternoon sleep. He dressed, combed his hair with a broken comb and trudged downstairs, a heavy-bodied man with sloping shoulders and bushy gray hair in need of a haircut. He came down with his apron on. Although he felt chilly he poured out a cup of cold coffee, and backed against the radiator, slowly sipped it. Ida sat at the table, reading.

"Why you let me sleep so long?" the grocer complained.

She didn't answer.

"Yesterday or today's paper?"

"Yesterday."

He rinsed the cup and set it on the top of the gas range. In the store he rang up "no sale" and took a nickel out of the drawer. Morris lifted the lid of the cash register, struck a match on the underside of the counter, and holding the flame cupped in his palm, peered at the figure of his earnings. Ida had taken in three dollars. Who could afford a paper?

Nevertheless he went for one, doubting the small pleasure he would get from it. What was so worth reading about the world? Through Karp's window, as he passed, he saw Louis waiting on a customer while four others crowded the counter. Der oilem iz a goilem. Morris took the *Forward* from the newsstand and dropped a nickel into the cigar box. Sam Pearl, working over a green racing sheet, gave him a wave of his hammy hand. They never bothered to talk. What did he know about race horses? What did the other know of the tragic quality of life? Wisdom flew over his hard head.

The grocer returned to the rear of his store and sat on the couch, letting the diminishing light in the yard fall upon the paper. He read nearsightedly, with eyes stretched wide, but his thoughts would not let him read long. He put down the newspaper.

"So where is your buyer?" he asked Ida.

Looking absently into the store she did not reply.

"You should sell long ago the store," she remarked after a minute.

"When the store was good, who wanted to sell? After came bad times, who wanted to buy?"

"Everything we did too late. The store we didn't sell in time. I said, 'Morris, sell now the store.' You said, 'Wait.' What for? The house we bought too late, so we have still a big mortgage that it's hard to pay every month. 'Don't buy,' I said, 'times are bad.' 'Buy,' you said, 'will get better. We will save rent.' "

He answered nothing. If you had failed to do the right thing, talk was useless.

When Helen entered, she asked if the buyer had come. She had forgotten about him but remembered when she saw her mother's dress.

Opening her purse, she took out her pay check and handed it to her father. The grocer, without a word, slipped it under his apron into his pants pocket.

"Not yet," Ida answered, also embarrassed. "Maybe later."

"Nobody goes in the night to buy a store," Morris said. "The time to go is in the day to see how many customers. If this man comes here he will see with one eye the store is dead, then he will run home."

"Did you eat lunch?" Ida asked Helen.

"Yes."

"What did you eat?"

"I don't save menus, Mama."

"Your supper is ready." Ida lit the flame under the pot on the gas range.

"What makes you think he'll come today?" Helen asked her.

"Karp told me yesterday. He knows a refugee that he looks to buy a grocery. He works in the Bronx, so he will be here late."

Morris shook his head.

"He's a young man," Ida went on, "maybe thirty—thirty-two. Karp says he saved a little cash. He can make alterations, buy new goods, fix up modern, advertise a little and make here a nice business."

"Karp should live so long," the grocer said.

"Let's eat." Helen sat at the table.

Ida said she would eat later.

"What about you, Papa?"

"I am not hungry." He picked up his paper.

She ate alone. It would be wonderful to sell out and move but the possibility struck her as remote. If you had lived so long in one place, all but two years of your life, you didn't move out overnight.

Afterward she got up to help with the dishes but Ida wouldn't let her. "Go rest," she said.

Helen took her things and went upstairs.

She hated the drab five-room flat; a gray kitchen she used for breakfast so she could quickly get out to work in the morning. The living room was colorless and cramped; for all its overstuffed furniture of twenty years ago it seemed barren because it was lived in so little, her parents being seven days out of seven in the store; even their rare visitors, when invited upstairs, preferred to remain in the back. Sometimes Helen asked a friend up, but she went to other people's houses if she had a choice. Her bedroom was another impossibility, tiny, dark, despite the two by three foot opening in the wall, through which she could see the living room windows; and at night Morris and Ida had to pass through her room to get to theirs, and from their bedroom back to the bathroom. They had several times talked of giving her the big room, the only comfortable one in the house, but there was no place else that would hold their double bed. The fifth room was a small icebox off the second floor stairs, in which Ida stored a few odds and ends of clothes and furniture. Such was home. Helen had once in anger remarked that the place was awful to live in, and it had made her feel bad that her father had felt so bad.

She heard Morris's slow footsteps on the stairs. He came aimlessly into the living room and tried to relax in a stiff armchair. He sat with sad eyes, saying nothing, which was how he began when he wanted to say something.

When she and her brother were kids, at least on Jewish holidays Morris would close the store and venture forth to Second Avenue to see a Yiddish play, or take the family visiting; but after Ephraim died he rarely went beyond the corner. Thinking about his life always left her with a sense of the waste of her own.

She looks like a little bird, Morris thought. Why should she be lonely? Look how pretty she looks. Whoever saw such blue eyes?

He reached into his pants pocket and took out a five-dollar bill.

"Take," he said, rising and embarrassedly handing her the money. "You will need for shoes."

"You just gave me five dollars downstairs."

"Here is five more."

"Wednesday was the first of the month, Pa."

"I can't take away from you all your pay."

"You're not taking, I'm giving."

She made him put the five away. He did, with renewed shame. "What did I ever give you? Even your college education I took away."

"It was my own decision not to go, yet maybe I will yet. You can never tell."

"How can you go? You are twenty-three years old."

"Aren't you always saying a person's never too old to go to school?"

"My child," he sighed, "for myself I don't care, for you I want the best but what did I give you?"

"I'll give myself," she smiled. "There's hope."

With this he had to be satisfied. He still conceded her a future.

But before he went down, he said gently, "What's the matter you stay home so much lately? You had a fight with Nat?"

"No." Blushing, she answered, "I don't think we see things in the same way."

He hadn't the heart to ask more.

Going down, he met Ida on the stairs and knew she would cover the same ground.

In the evening there was a flurry of business. Morris's mood quickened and he exchanged pleasantries with the customers. Carl Johnsen, the Swedish painter, whom he hadn't seen in weeks, came in with a wet smile and bought two dollars' worth of beer, cold cuts and sliced Swiss cheese. The grocer was at first worried he would ask to charge—he had never paid what he owed on the books before Morris had stopped giving trust—but the painter had the cash. Mrs. Anderson, an old loyal customer, bought for a dollar. A stranger then came in and left eighty-eight cents. After him two more customers appeared. Morris felt a little surge of hope. Maybe things were picking up. But after half-past eight his hands grew heavy with nothing to do. For years he had been the only one for miles around who stayed open at night and had just about made a living from it, but now Schmitz matched him hour for hour. Morris sneaked a little smoke, then began to cough. Ida pounded on the floor upstairs, so he clipped the butt and put it away. He felt restless and stood at the front window, watching the street. He watched a trolley go by. Mr. Lawler, formerly a customer, good for at least a fiver on Friday nights, passed the store. Morris hadn't seen him for months but knew where he was going. Mr. Lawler averted his gaze and hurried along. Morris watched him disappear around the corner. He lit a match and again checked the register—nine and a half dollars, not even expenses.

Julius Karp opened the front door and poked his foolish head in. "Podolsky came?"

"Who Podolsky?"

"The refugee."

Morris said in annoyance, "What refugee?"

With a grunt Karp shut the door behind him. He was short, pompous, a natty dresser in his advanced age. In the past, like Morris, he had toiled long hours in his shoe store, now he stayed all day in silk pajamas until it came time to relieve Louis before supper. Though the little man was insensitive and a blunderer, Morris had got along fairly well with him, but since Karp had rented the tailor shop to another grocer, sometimes they did not speak. Years ago Karp had spent much time in the back of the grocery, complaining of his poverty as if it were a new invention and he its first victim. Since his success with wines and liquors he came in less often, but he still visited Morris more than his welcome entitled him to, usually to run down the grocery and spout unwanted advice. His ticket of admission was his luck, which he gathered wherever he reached, at a loss, Morris thought, to somebody else. Once a drunk had heaved a rock at Karp's window, but it had shattered his. Another time, Sam Pearl gave the liquor dealer a tip on a horse, then forgot to place a bet himself. Karp collected five hundred for his ten-dollar bill. For years the grocer had escaped resenting the man's good luck, but lately he had caught himself wishing on him some small misfortune.

"Podolsky is the one I called up to take a look at your gesheft," Karp answered.

"Who is this refugee, tell me, an enemy yours?"

Karp stared at him unpleasantly.

"Does a man," Morris insisted, "send a friend he should buy such a store that you yourself took away from it the best business?"

"Podolsky ain't you," the liquor dealer replied. "I told him about this place. I said, 'The neighborhood is improving. You can buy cheap and build up this store. It's run down for years, nobody changed anything there for twenty years.'"

"You should live so long how much I changed—" Morris began but he didn't finish, for Karp was at the window, peering nervously into the dark street.

"You saw that gray car that just passed," the liquor dealer said. "This is the third time I saw it in the last twenty minutes." His eyes were restless.

Morris knew what worried him. "Put in a telephone in your store," he advised, "so you will feel better."

Karp watched the street for another minute and worriedly replied, "Not for a liquor store in this neighborhood. If I had a telephone, every drunken bum would call me to make deliveries, and when you go there they don't have a cent."

He opened the door but shut it in afterthought. "Listen, Morris," he said, lowering his voice, "if they come back again, I will lock my front door and put out my lights. Then I will call you from the back window so you can telephone the police."

"This will cost you five cents," Morris said grimly.

"My credit is class A."

Karp left the grocery, disturbed.

God bless Julius Karp, the grocer thought. Without him I would have my life too easy. God made Karp so a poor grocery man will not forget his life is hard. For Karp, he thought it was miraculously not so hard, but what was there to envy? He would allow the liquor dealer his bottles and gelt just not to be him. Life was bad enough.

At nine-thirty a stranger came in for a box of matches. Fifteen minutes later Morris put out the lights in his window. The street was deserted except for an automobile parked in front of the laundry across the car tracks. Morris peered at it sharply but could see nobody in it. He considered locking up and going to bed, then decided to stay open the last few minutes. Sometimes a person came in at a minute to ten. A dime was a dime.

A noise at the side door which led into the hall frightened him. "Ida?"

The door opened slowly. Tessie Fuso came in in her housecoat, a homely Italian girl with a big face.

"Are you closed, Mr. Bober?" she asked embarrassedly.

"Come in," said Morris.

"I'm sorry I came through the back way but I was undressed and didn't want to go out in the street."

"Don't worry."

"Please give me twenty cents' ham for Nick's lunch tomorrow."

He understood. She was making amends for Nick's trip around the corner that morning. He cut her an extra slice of ham.

Tessie bought also a quart of milk, package of paper napkins and loaf of bread. When she had gone he lifted the register lid. Ten dollars. He thought he had long ago touched bottom but now knew there was none.

I slaved my whole life for nothing, he thought.

Then he heard Karp calling him from the rear. The grocer went inside worn out.

Raising the window he called harshly, "What's the matter there?"

"Telephone the police," cried Karp. "The car is parked across the street."

"What car?"

"The holdupniks."

"There is nobody in this car, I saw myself."

"For God's sake, I tell you call the police. I will pay for the telephone."

Morris shut the window. He looked up the number and was about to dial the police when the store door opened and he hurried inside.

Two men were standing at the other side of the counter, with handkerchiefs over their faces. One wore a dirty yellow clotted one, the other's was white. The one with the white one began pulling out the store lights. It took the grocer a half-minute to comprehend that he, not Karp, was their victim.

Morris sat at the table, the dark light of the dusty bulb falling on his head, gazing dully at the few crumpled bills before him, including Helen's check, and the small pile of silver. The gunman with the dirty handkerchief, fleshy, wearing a fuzzy black hat, waved a pistol at the grocer's head. His pimply brow was thick with sweat; from time to time with furtive eyes he glanced into the darkened store. The other, a taller man in an old cap and torn sneakers, to control his trembling leaned against the sink, cleaning his fingernails with a matchstick. A cracked mirror hung behind him on the wall above the sink and every so often he turned to stare into it.

"I know damn well this ain't everything you took in," said the heavy one to Morris, in a hoarse, unnatural voice. "Where've you got the rest hid?"

Morris, sick to his stomach, couldn't speak.

"Tell the goddamn truth." He aimed the gun at the grocer's mouth.

"Times are bad," Morris muttered.

"You're a Jew liar."

The man at the sink fluttered his hand, catching the other's attention. They met in the center of the room, the other with the cap hunched awkwardly over the one in the fuzzy hat, whispering into his ear.

"No," snapped the heavy one sullenly.

His partner bent lower, whispering earnestly through his handkerchief.

"I say he hid it," the heavy one snarled, "and I'm gonna get it if I have to crack his goddam head."

At the table he whacked the grocer across the face.

Morris moaned.

The one at the sink hastily rinsed a cup and filled it with water. He brought it to the grocer, spilling some on his apron as he raised the cup to his lips.

Morris tried to swallow but managed only a dry sip. His frightened eyes sought the man's but he was looking elsewhere.

"Please," murmured the grocer.

"Hurry up," warned the one with the gun.

The tall one straightened up and gulped down the water. He rinsed the cup and placed it on a cupboard shelf.

He then began to hunt among the cups and dishes there and pulled out the pots on the bottom. Next, he went hurriedly through the drawers of an old bureau in the room, and on hands and knees searched under the couch. He ducked into the store, removed the empty cash drawer from the register and thrust his hand into the slot, but came up with nothing.

Returning to the kitchen he took the other by the arm and whispered to him urgently.

The heavy one elbowed him aside.

"We better scram out of here."

"Are you gonna go chicken on me?"

"That's all the dough he has, let's beat it."

"Business is bad," Morris muttered.

"Your Jew ass is bad, you understand?"

"Don't hurt me."

"I will give you your last chance. Where have you got it hid?"

"I am a poor man." He spoke through cracked lips.

The one in the dirty handkerchief raised his gun. The other, staring into the mirror, waved frantically, his black eyes bulging, but Morris saw the blow descend and felt sick of himself, of soured expectations, endless frustration, the years gone up in smoke, he could not begin to count how many. He had hoped for much in America and got little. And because of him Helen and Ida had less. He had defrauded them, he and the bloodsucking store.

He fell without a cry. The end fitted the day. It was his luck, others had better.

During the week that Morris lay in bed with a thickly bandaged head, Ida tended the store fitfully. She went up and down twenty times a day until her bones ached and her head hurt with all her worries. Helen stayed home Saturday, a half-day in her place, and Monday, to help her mother, but she could not risk longer than that, so Ida, who ate in snatches and had worked up a massive nervousness, had to shut the store for a full day, although Morris angrily protested. He needed no attention, he insisted, and urged her to keep open at least half the day or he would lose his remaining few customers; but Ida, short of breath, said she hadn't the strength, her legs hurt. The grocer attempted to get up and pull on his pants but was struck by a violent headache and had to drag himself back to bed.

On the Tuesday the store was closed a man appeared in the neighborhood, a stranger who spent much of his time standing on Sam Pearl's corner with a toothpick in his teeth, intently observing the people who passed by; or he would drift down the long block of stores, some empty, from Pearl's to the bar at the far end of the street. Beyond that was a freight yard, and in the distance, a bulky warehouse. After an occasional slow beer in the tavern, the stranger turned the corner and wandered past the high-fenced coal yard; he would go around the block until he got back to Sam's candy store. Once in a while the man would walk over to Morris's closed grocery, and with both hands shading his brow, stare through the window; sighing, he went back to Sam's. When he had as much as he could take of the corner he walked around the block again, or elsewhere in the neighborhood.

Helen had pasted a paper on the window of the front door, that said her father wasn't well but the store would open on Wednesday. The man spent a good deal of time studying this paper. He was young, dark-bearded, wore an old brown rainstained hat, cracked patent leather shoes and a long black overcoat that looked as if it had been lived in. He was tall and not bad looking, except for a nose that had been broken and badly set, unbalancing his face. His eyes were melancholy. Sometimes he sat at the fountain with Sam Pearl, lost in his thoughts, smoking from a crumpled pack of cigarettes he had bought with pennies. Sam, who was used to all kinds of people, and had in his time seen many strangers appear in the neighborhood and as quickly disappear, showed no special concern for the man, though Goldie, after a full day of his presence complained that too much was too much; he didn't pay rent. Sam did notice that the stranger sometimes seemed to be under stress, sighed much and muttered inaudibly to himself. However, he paid the man scant attention—everybody to their own troubles. Other times the stranger, as if he had somehow squared himself with himself, seemed relaxed, even satisfied with his existence. He read through Sam's magazines, strolled around in the neighborhood and when he returned, lit a fresh cigarette as he opened a paper-bound book from the rack in the store. Sam served him coffee when he asked for it, and the stranger, squinting from the smoke of the butt in his mouth, carefully counted out five pennies to pay. Though nobody had asked him he said his name was Frank Alpine and he had lately come from the West, looking for a better opportunity. Sam advised if he could qualify for a chauffeur's license, to try for work as a hack driver. It wasn't a bad life. The man agreed but stayed around as if he was expecting something else to open up. Sam put him down as a moody gink.

The day Ida reopened the grocery the stranger disappeared but he returned to the candy store the next morning, and seating himself at the fountain, asked for coffee. He looked bleary, unhappy, his beard hard, dark, contrasting with the pallor of his face; his nostrils were inflamed and his voice was husky. He looks half in his grave, Sam thought. God knows what hole he slept in last night.

As Frank Alpine was stirring his coffee, with his free hand he opened a magazine lying on the counter, and his eye was caught by a picture in color of a monk. He lifted the coffee cup to drink but had to put it down, and he stared at the picture for five minutes.

Sam, out of curiosity, went behind him with a broom, to see what he was looking at. The picture was of a thin-faced, dark-bearded monk in a coarse brown garment, standing barefooted on a sunny country road. His skinny, hairy arms were raised to a flock of birds that dipped over his head. In the background was a grove of leafy trees; and in the far distance a church in sunlight.

"He looks like some kind of a priest," Sam said cautiously.

"No, it's St. Francis of Assisi. You can tell from that brown robe he's wearing and all those birds in the air. That's the time he was preaching to them. When I was a kid, an old priest used to come to the orphans' home where I was raised, and every time he came he read us a different story about St. Francis. They are clear in my mind to this day."

"Stories are stories," Sam said.

"Don't ask me why I never forgot them."

Sam took a closer squint at the picture. "Talking to the birds? What was he—crazy? I don't say this out of any harm."

The stranger smiled at the Jew. "He was a great man. The way I look at it, it takes a certain kind of a nerve to preach to birds."

"That makes him great, because he talked to birds?"

"Also for other things. For instance, he gave everything away that he owned, every cent, all his clothes off his back. He enjoyed to be poor. He said poverty was a queen and he loved her like she was a beautiful woman."

Sam shook his head. "It ain't beautiful, kiddo. To be poor is dirty work."

"He took a fresh view of things."

The candy store owner glanced again at St. Francis, then poked his broom into a dirty corner. Frank, as he drank his coffee, continued to study the picture. He said to Sam, "Every time I read about somebody like him I get a feeling inside of me I have to fight to keep from crying. He was born good, which is a talent if you have it."

He spoke with embarrassment, embarrassing Sam.

Frank drained his cup and left.

That night as he was wandering past Morris's store he glanced through the door and saw Helen inside, relieving her mother. She looked up and noticed him staring at her through the plate glass. His appearance startled her; his eyes were haunted, hungry, sad; she got the impression he would come in and ask for a handout and had made up her mind to give him a dime, but instead he disappeared.

On Friday Morris weakly descended the stairs at six A.M., and Ida, nagging, came after him. She had been opening at eight o'clock and had begged him to stay in bed until then, but he had refused, saying he had to give the Poilisheh her roll.

"Why does three cents for a lousy roll mean more to you than another hour sleep?" Ida complained.

"Who can sleep?"

"You need rest, the doctor said."

"Rest I will take in my grave."

She shuddered. Morris said, "For fifteen years she gets here her roll, so let her get."

"All right, but let me open up. I will give her and you go back to bed."

"I stayed in bed too long. Makes me feel weak."

But the woman wasn't there and Morris feared he had lost her to the German. Ida insisted on dragging in the milk boxes, threatening to shout if he made a move for them. She packed the bottles into the refrigerator. After Nick Fuso they waited hours for another customer. Morris sat at the table, reading the paper, occasionally raising his hand gently to feel the bandage around his head. When he shut his eyes he still experienced moments of weakness. By noon he was glad to go upstairs and crawl into bed and he didn't get up until Helen came home.

The next morning he insisted on opening alone. The Poilisheh was there. He did not know her name. She worked somewhere in a laundry and had a little dog called Polaschaya. When she came home at night she took the little Polish dog for a walk around the block. He liked to run loose in the coal yard. She lived in one of the stucco houses nearby. Ida called her die antisemitke, but that part of her didn't bother Morris. She had come with it from the old country, a different kind of anti-Semitism from in America. Sometimes he suspected she needled him a little by asking for a "Jewish roll," and once or twice, with an odd smile, she wanted a "Jewish pickle." Generally she said nothing at all. This morning Morris handed her her roll and she said nothing. She didn't ask him about his bandaged head though her quick beady eyes stared at it, nor why he had not been there for a week; but she put six pennies on the counter instead of three. He figured she had taken a roll from the bag one of the days the store hadn't opened on time. He rang up the six-cent sale.

Morris went outside to pull in the two milk cases. He gripped the boxes but they were like rocks, so he let one go and tugged at the other. A storm cloud formed in his head and blew up to the size of a house. Morris reeled and almost fell into the gutter, but he was caught by Frank Alpine in his long coat, steadied and led back into the store. Frank then hauled in the milk cases and refrigerated the bottles. He quickly swept up behind the counter and went into the back. Morris, recovered, warmly thanked him.

Frank said huskily, his eyes on his scarred and heavy hands, that he was new to the neighborhood but living here now with a married sister. He had lately come from the West and was looking for a better job.

The grocer offered him a cup of coffee, which he at once accepted. As he sat down Frank placed his hat on the floor at his feet, and he drank the coffee with three heaping spoonfuls of sugar, to get warm quick, he said. When Morris offered him a seeded hard roll, he bit into it hungrily. "Jesus, this is good bread." After he had finished he wiped his mouth with his handkerchief, then swept the crumbs off the table with one hand into the other, and though Morris protested, he rinsed the cup and saucer at the sink, dried them and set them on top of the gas range, where the grocer had got them.

"Much obliged for everything." He had picked up his hat but made no move to leave.

"Once in San Francisco I worked in a grocery for a couple of months," he remarked after a minute, "only it was one of those supermarket chain store deals."

"The chain store kills the small man."

"Personally I like a small store myself. I might someday have one."

"A store is a prison. Look for something better."

"At least you're your own boss."

"To be a boss of nothing is nothing."

"Still and all, the idea of it appeals to me. The only thing is I would need experience on what goods to order. I mean about brand names, and et cetera. I guess I ought to look for a job in a store and get more experience."

"Try the A&P," advised the grocer.

"I might."

Morris dropped the subject. The man put on his hat.

"What's the matter," he said, staring at the grocer's bandage, "did you have some kind of accident to your head?"

Morris nodded. He didn't care to talk about it, so the stranger, somehow disappointed, left.

He happened to be in the street very early on Monday when Morris was again struggling with the milk cases. The stranger tipped his hat and said he was off to the city to find a job but he had time to help him pull in the milk. This he did and quickly left. However, the grocer thought he saw him pass by in the other direction about an hour later. That afternoon when he went for his *Forward* he noticed him sitting at the fountain with Sam Pearl. The next morning just after six, Frank was there to help him haul in the milk bottles and he willingly accepted when Morris, who knew a poor man when he saw one, invited him for coffee.

"How is going now the job?" Morris asked as they were eating.

"So-so," said Frank, his glance shifting. He seemed preoccupied, nervous. Every few minutes he would set down his cup and uneasily look around. His lips parted as if to speak, his eyes took on a tormented expression, but then he shut his jaw as if he had decided it was better never to say what he intended. He seemed to need to talk, broke into sweat—his brow gleamed with it—his pupils widening as he struggled. He looked to Morris like someone who had to retch—no matter where; but after a brutal interval his eyes grew dull. He sighed heavily and gulped down the last of his coffee. After, he brought up a belch. This for a moment satisfied him.

Whatever he wants to say, Morris thought, let him say it to somebody else. I am only a grocer. He shifted in his chair, fearing to catch some illness.

Again the tall man leaned forward, drew a breath and once more was at the point of speaking, but now a shudder passed through him, followed by a fit of shivering.

The grocer hastened to the stove and poured out a cup of steaming coffee. Frank swallowed it in two terrible gulps. He soon stopped shaking, but looked defeated, humiliated, like somebody, the grocer felt, who had lost out on something he had wanted badly.

"You caught a cold?" he asked sympathetically.

The stranger nodded, scratched up a match on the sole of his cracked shoe, lit a cigarette and sat there, listless.

"I had a rough life," he muttered, and lapsed into silence.

Neither of them spoke. Then the grocer, to ease the other's mood, casually inquired, "Where in the neighborhood lives your sister? Maybe I know her."

Frank answered in a monotone. "I forget the exact address. Near the park somewheres."

"What is her name?"

"Mrs. Garibaldi."

"What kind name is this?"

"What do you mean?" Frank stared at him.

"I mean the nationality?"

"Italian. I am of Italian extraction. My name is Frank Alpine— Alpino in Italian."

The smell of Frank Alpine's cigarette compelled Morris to light his butt. He thought he could control his cough and tried but couldn't. He coughed till he feared his head would pop off. Frank watched with interest. Ida banged on the floor upstairs, and the grocer ashamedly pinched his cigarette and dropped it into the garbage pail.

"She don't like me to smoke," he explained between coughs. "My lungs ain't so healthy."

"Who don't?"

"My wife. It's a catarrh some kind. My mother had it all her life and lived till eighty-four. But they took a picture of my chest last year and found two dried spots. This frightened my wife."

Frank slowly put out his cigarette. "What I started out to say before about my life," he said heavily, "is that I have had a funny one, only I don't mean funny. I mean I've been through a lot. I've been close to some wonderful things—jobs, for instance, education, women, but close is as far as I go." His hands were tightly clasped between his knees. "Don't ask me why, but sooner or later everything I think is worth having gets away from me in some way or other. I work like a mule for what I want, and just when it looks like I am going to get it I make some kind of a stupid move, and everything that is just about nailed down tight blows up in my face."

"Don't throw away your chance for education," Morris advised. "It's the best thing for a young man."

"I could've been a college graduate by now, but when the time came to start going, I missed out because something else turned up that I took instead. With me one wrong thing leads to another and it ends in a trap. I want the moon so all I get is cheese."

"You are young yet."

"Twenty-five," he said bitterly.

"You look older."

"I feel old—damn old."

Morris shook his head.

"Sometimes I think your life keeps going the way it starts out on you," Frank went on. "The week after I was born my mother was dead and buried. I never saw her face, not even a picture. When I was five years old, one day my old man leaves this furnished room where we were staying, to get a pack of butts. He takes off and that was the last I ever saw of him. They traced him years later but by then he was dead. I was raised in an orphans' home and when I was eight they farmed me out to a tough family. I ran away ten times, also from the next people I lived with. I think about my life a lot. I say to myself, 'What do you expect to happen after all of that?' Of course, every now and again, you understand, I hit some nice good spots in between, but they are few and far, and usually I end up like I started out, with nothing."

The grocer was moved. Poor boy.

"I've often tried to change the way things work out for me but I don't know how, even when I think I do. I have it in my heart to do more than I can remember." He paused, cleared his throat and said, "That makes me sound stupid but it's not as easy as that. What I mean to say is that when I need it most something is missing in me, in me or on account of me. I always have this dream where I want to tell somebody something on the telephone so bad it hurts, but then when I am in the booth, instead of a phone being there, a bunch of bananas is hanging on a hook."

He gazed at the grocer then at the floor. "All my life I wanted to accomplish something worthwhile—a thing people will say took a little doing, but I don't. I am too restless—six months in any one place is too much for me. Also I grab at everything too quick—too impatient. I don't do what I have to—that's what I mean. The result is I move into a place with nothing, and I move out with nothing. You understand me?"

"Yes," said Morris.

Frank fell into silence. After a while he said, "I don't understand myself. I don't really know what I'm saying to you or why I am saying it."

"Rest yourself," said Morris.

"What kind of a life is that for a man my age?"

He waited for the grocer to reply—to tell him how to live his life, but Morris was thinking, I am sixty and he talks like me.

"Take some more coffee," he said.

"No, thanks." Frank lit another cigarette and smoked it to the tip. He seemed eased yet not eased, as though he had accomplished something (What? wondered the grocer) yet had not. His face was relaxed, almost sleepy, but he cracked the knuckles of both hands and silently sighed.

Why don't he go home? the grocer thought. I am a working man.

"I'm going." Frank got up but stayed.

"What happened to your head?" he asked again.

Morris felt the bandage. "This Friday before last I had here a holdup."

"You mean they slugged you?"

The grocer nodded.

"Bastards like that ought to die." Frank spoke vehemently.

Morris stared at him.

Frank brushed his sleeve. "You people are Jews, aren't you?"

"Yes," said the grocer, still watching him.

"I always liked Jews." His eyes were downcast.

Morris did not speak.

"I suppose you have some kids?" Frank asked.

"Me?"

"Excuse me for being curious."

"A girl." Morris sighed. "I had once a wonderful boy but he died from an ear sickness that they had in those days."

"Too bad." Frank blew his nose.

A gentleman, Morris thought with a watery eye.

"Is the girl that one that was here behind the counter a couple of nights last week?"

"Yes," the grocer replied, a little uneasily.

"Well, thanks for all the coffee."

"Let me make you a sandwich. Maybe you'll be hungry later."

"No thanks."

The Jew insisted, but Frank felt he had all he wanted from him at the moment.

Left alone, Morris began to worry about his health. He felt dizzy at times, often headachy. Murderers, he thought. Standing before the cracked and faded mirror at the sink he unwound the bandage from his head. He wanted to leave it off but the scar was still ugly, not nice for the customers, so he tied a fresh bandage around his skull. As he did this he thought of that night with bitterness, recalling the buyer who hadn't come, nor had since then, nor ever would. Since his recovery, Morris had not spoken to Karp. Against words the liquor dealer had other words, but silence silenced him.

Afterward the grocer looked up from his paper and was startled to see somebody out front washing his window with a brush on a stick. He ran out with a roar to drive the intruder away, for there were nervy window cleaners who did the job without asking permission, then held out their palms to collect. But when Morris came out of the store he saw the window washer was Frank Alpine.

"Just to show my thanks and appreciation." Frank explained he had borrowed the pail from Sam Pearl and the brush and squeegee from the butcher next door.

Ida then entered the store by the inside door, and seeing the window being washed, hurried outside.

"You got rich all of a sudden?" she asked Morris, her face inflamed.

"He does me a favor," the grocer replied.

"That's right," said Frank, bearing down on the squeegee.

"Come inside, it's cold." In the store Ida asked, "Who is this goy?"

"A poor boy, an Italyener he looks for a job. He gives me a help in the morning with the cases milk."

"If you sold containers like I told you a thousand times, you wouldn't need help."

"Containers leak. I like bottles."

"Talk to the wind," Ida said.

Frank came in blowing his breath on water-reddened fists. "How's it look now, folks, though you can't really tell till I do the inside."

Ida remarked under her breath, "Pay now for your favor."

"Fine," Morris said to Frank. He went to the register and rang up "no sale."

"No, thanks," Frank said, holding up his hand. "For services already rendered."

Ida reddened.

"Another cup coffee?" Morris asked.

"Thanks. Not as of now."

"Let me make you a sandwich?"

"I just ate."

He walked out, threw the dirty water into the gutter, returned the pail and brush, then came back to the grocery. He went behind the counter and into the rear, pausing to rap on the doorjamb.

"How do you like the clean window?" he asked Ida.

"Clean is clean." She was cool.

"I don't want to intrude here but your husband was nice to me, so I just thought maybe I could ask for one more small favor. I am looking for work and I want to try some kind of a grocery job just for size. Maybe I might like it, who knows? It happens I forgot some of the things about cutting and weighing and such, so I am wondering if you would mind me working around here for a couple-three weeks without wages just so I could learn again? It won't cost you a red cent. I know I am a stranger but I am an honest guy. Whoever keeps an eye on me will find that out in no time. That's fair enough, isn't it?"

Ida said, "Mister, isn't here a school."

"What do you say, pop?" Frank asked Morris.

"Because somebody is a stranger don't mean they ain't honest," answered the grocer. "This subject don't interest me. Interests me what you can learn here. Only one thing"—he pressed his hand to his chest—"a heartache."

"You got nothing to lose on my proposition, has he now, Mrs.?" Frank said. "I understand he don't feel so hot yet, and if I helped him out a week or two it would be good for his health, wouldn't it?"

Ida didn't answer.

But Morris said flatly, "No. It's a small, poor store. Three people would be too much."

Frank flipped an apron off a hook behind the door and before either of them could say a word, removed his hat and dropped the loop over his head. He tied the apron strings around him.

"How's that for fit?"

Ida flushed, and Morris ordered him to take it off and put it back on the hook.

"No bad feelings, I hope," Frank said on his way out.

Helen Bober and Louis Karp walked, no hands touching, in the windy dark on the Coney Island boardwalk.

Louis had, on his way home for supper that evening, stopped her in front of the liquor store, on her way in from work.

"How's about a ride in the Mercury, Helen? I never see you much anymore. Things were better in the bygone days in high school."

Helen smiled. "Honestly, Louis, that's so far away." A sense of mourning at once oppressed her, which she fought to a practiced draw.

"Near or far, it's all the same for me." He was built with broad back and narrow head, and despite prominent eyes was presentable. In high school, before he quit, he had worn his wet hair slicked straight back. One day, after studying a picture of a movie actor in the *Daily News*, he had run a part across his head. This was as much change as she had known in him. If Nat Pearl was ambitious, Louis made a relaxed living letting the fruit of his father's investment fall into his lap.

"Anyway," he said, "why not a ride for old-times' sake?"

She thought a minute, a gloved finger pressed into her cheek; but it was a fake gesture because she was lonely.

"For old-times' sake, where?"

"Name your scenery—continuous performance."

"The Island?"

He raised his coat collar. "Brr, it's a cold, windy night. You wanna freeze?"

Seeing her hesitation, he said, "But I'll die game. When'll I pick you up?"

"Ring my bell after eight and I'll come down."

"Check," Louis said. "Eight bells."

They walked to Seagate, where the boardwalk ended. She gazed with envy through a wire fence at the large lit houses fronting the ocean. The Island was deserted, except here and there an open hamburger joint or pinball machine concession. Gone from the sky was the umbrella of rosy light that glowed over the place in summertime. A few cold stars gleamed down. In the distance a dark Ferris wheel looked like a stopped clock. They stood at the rail of the boardwalk, watching the black, restless sea.

All during their walk she had been thinking about her life, the difference between her aloneness now and the fun when she was young and spending every day of summer in a lively crowd of kids on the beach. But as her high school friends had got married, she had one by one given them up; and as others of them graduated from college, envious, ashamed of how little she was accomplishing, she stopped seeing them too. At first it hurt to drop people but after a time it became a not too difficult habit. Now she saw almost no one, occasionally Betty Pearl, who understood, but not enough to make much difference.

Louis, his face reddened by the wind, sensed her mood.

"What's got in you, Helen?" he said, putting his arm around her.

"I can't really explain it. All night I've been thinking of the swell times we had on this beach when we were kids. And do you remember the parties? I suppose I'm blue that I'm no longer seventeen."

"What's so wrong about twenty-three?"

"It's old, Louis. Our lives change so quickly. You know what youth means?"

"Sure I know. You don't catch me giving away nothing for nothing. I got my youth yet."

"When a person is young he's privileged," Helen said, "with all kinds of possibilities. Wonderful things might happen, and when you get up in the morning you feel they will. That's what youth means, and that's what I've lost. Nowadays I feel that every day is like the day before, and what's worse, like the day after."

"So now you're a grandmother?"

"The world has shrunk for me."

"What do you wanna be—Miss Rheingold?"

"I want a larger and better life. I want the return of my possibilities."

"Such as which ones?"

She clutched the rail, cold through her gloves. "Education," she said, "prospects. Things I've wanted but never had."

"Also a man?"

"Also a man."

His arm tightened around her waist. "Talk is too cold, baby, how's about a kiss?"

She brushed his cold lips, then averted her head. He did not press her.

"Louis," she said, watching a far-off light on the water, "what do you want out of your life?"

He kept his arm around her. "The same thing I got—plus."

"Plus what?"

"Plus more, so my wife and family can have also."

"What if she wanted something different than you do?"

"Whatever she wanted I would gladly give her."

"But what if she wanted to make herself a better person, have bigger ideas, live a more worthwhile life? We die so quickly, so helplessly. Life *has* to have some meaning."

"I ain't gonna stop anybody from being better," Louis said. "That's up to them."

"I suppose," she said.

"Say, baby, let's drop this deep philosophy and go trap a hamburger. My stomach complains."

"Just a little longer. It's been ages since I came here this late in the year."

He pumped his arms. "Jesus, this wind, it flies up my pants. At least gimme another kiss." He unbuttoned his overcoat.

She let him kiss her. He felt her breast. Helen stepped back out of his embrace. "Don't, Louis."

"Why not?" He stood there awkwardly, annoyed.

"It gives me no pleasure."

"I suppose I'm the first guy that ever gave it a nip?"

"Are you collecting statistics?"

"Okay," he said, "I'm sorry. You know I ain't a bad guy, Helen."

"I know you're not, but please don't do what I don't like."

"There was a time you treated me a whole lot better."

"That was the past, we were kids."

It's funny, she remembered, how necking made glorious dreams.

"We were older than that, up till the time Nat Pearl started in college, then you got interested in him. I suppose you got him in mind for the future?"

"If I do, I don't know it."

"But he's the one you want, ain't he? I like to know what that stuck up has got beside a college education? I work for my living."

"No, I don't want him, Louis." But she thought, Suppose Nat said I love you? For magic words a girl might do magic tricks.

"So if that's so, what's wrong with me?"

"Nothing. We're friends."

"Friends I got all I need."

"What do you need, Louis?"

"Cut out the wisecracks, Helen. Would it interest you that I would honestly like to marry you?" He paled at his nerve.

She was surprised, touched.

"Thank you," she murmured.

"Thank you ain't good enough. Give me yes or no."

"No, Louis."

"That what I thought." He gazed blankly at the ocean.

"I never guessed you were at all remotely interested. You go with girls who are so different from me."

"Please, when I go with them you can't see my thoughts."

"No," she admitted.

"I can give you a whole lot better than you got."

"I know you can, but I want a different life from mine now, or yours. I don't want a storekeeper for a husband."

"Wines and liquors ain't exactly pisher groceries."

"I know."

"It ain't because your old man don't like mine?"

"No."

She listened to the wind-driven, sobbing surf. Louis said, "Let's go get the hamburgers."

"Gladly." She took his arm but could tell from the stiff way he walked that he was hurt.

As they drove home on the Parkway, Louis said, "If you can't have everything you want, at least take something. Don't be so goddam proud."

Touché. "What shall I take, Louis?"

He paused. "Take less."

"Less I'll never take."

"People got to compromise."

"I won't with my ideals."

"So what'll you be then, a dried-up prune of an old maid? What's the percentage of that?"

"None."

"So what'll you do?"

"I'll wait. I'll dream. Something will happen."

"Nuts," he said.

He let her off in front of the grocery.

"Thanks for everything."

"You'll make me laugh." Louis drove off.

The store was closed, upstairs dark. She pictured her father asleep

after his long day, dreaming of Ephraim. What am I saving myself
for? she asked herself. What unhappy Bober fate?

It snowed lightly the next day—too early in the year, complained
Ida, and when the snow had melted it snowed again. The grocer remarked, as he was dressing in the dark, that he would shovel after
he had opened the store. He enjoyed shoveling snow. It reminded
him that he had practically lived in it in his boyhood; but Ida for-
bade him to exert himself because he still complained of dizziness.
Later, when he tried to lug the milk cases through the snow, he found
it all but impossible. And there was no Frank Alpine to help him, for
he had disappeared after washing the window.

Ida came down shortly after her husband, in a heavy cloth coat, a
woolen scarf pinned around her head and wearing galoshes. She shov-
eled a path through the snow and together they pulled in the milk.
Only then did Morris notice that a quart bottle was missing from one
of the cases.

"Who took it?" Ida cried.

"How do I know?"

"Did you count yet the rolls?"

"No."

"I told you always to count right away."

"The baker will steal from me? I know him twenty years."

"Count what everybody delivers, I told you a thousand times."

He dumped the rolls out of the basket and counted them. Three
were missing and he had sold only one to the Poilisheh. To appease
Ida he said they were all there.

The next morning another quart of milk and two rolls were gone.
He was worried but didn't tell Ida the truth when she asked him if
anything else was missing. He often hid unpleasant news from her
because she made it worse. He mentioned the missing bottle to the
milkman, who answered, "Morris, I swear I left every bottle in that
case. Am I responsible for this lousy neighborhood?"

He promised to cart the milk cases into the vestibule for a few
days. Maybe whoever was stealing the bottles would be afraid to go
in there. Morris considered asking the milk company for a storage
box. Years ago he had had one at the curb, a large wooden box in
which the milk was padlocked; but he had given it up after developing a hernia lifting the heavy cases out, so he decided against a box.

On the third day, when a quart of milk and two rolls had again been taken, the grocer, much disturbed, considered calling the police. It wasn't the first time he had lost milk and rolls in this neighborhood. That had happened more than once—usually some poor person stealing a breakfast. For this reason Morris preferred not to call the police but to get rid of the thief by himself. To do it, he would usually wake up very early and wait at his bedroom window in the dark. Then when the man—sometimes it was a woman—showed up and was helping himself to the milk, Morris would quickly raise the window and shout down, "Get outa here, you thief you." The thief, startled—sometimes it was a customer who could afford to buy the milk he was stealing—would drop the bottle and run. Usually he never appeared again—a lost customer cut another way—and the next goniff was somebody else.

So this morning Morris arose at four-thirty, a little before the milk was delivered, and sat in the cold in his long underwear, to wait. The street was heavy with darkness as he peered down. Soon the milk truck came, and the milkman, his breath foggy, lugged the two cases of milk into the vestibule. Then the street was silent again, the night dark, the snow white. One or two people trudged by. An hour later, Witzig, the baker, delivered the rolls, but no one else stopped at the door. Just before six Morris dressed hastily and went downstairs. A bottle of milk was gone, and when he counted the rolls, so were two of them.

He still kept the truth from Ida. The next night she awoke and found him at the window in the dark.

"What's the matter?" she asked, sitting up in bed.

"I can't sleep."

"So don't sit in your underwear in the cold. Come back to bed."

He did as she said. Later, the milk and rolls were missing.

In the store he asked the Poilisheh whether she had seen anyone sneak into the vestibule and steal a quart of milk. She stared at him with small eyes, grabbed the sliced roll and slammed the door.

Morris had a theory that the thief lived on the block. Nick Fuso wouldn't do such a thing; if he did Morris would have heard him going down the stairs, then coming up again. The thief was somebody from outside. He sneaked along the street close to the houses, where Morris couldn't see him because of that cornice that hung over the store; then he softly opened the hall door, took the milk, two rolls from the bag, and stole away, hugging the house fronts.

The grocer suspected Mike Papadopolous, the Greek boy who lived on the floor about Karp's store. He had served a reformatory sentence at eighteen. A year later he had in the dead of night climbed down the fire escape overhanging Karp's back yard, boosted himself up on the fence and forced a window into the grocery. There he stole three cartons of cigarettes, and a roll of dimes that Morris had left in the cash register. In the morning, as the grocer was opening the store, Mike's mother, a thin, old-looking woman, returned the cigarettes and dimes to him. She had caught her son coming in with them and had walloped his head with a shoe. She clawed his face, making him confess what he had done. Returning the cigarettes and dimes, she had begged Morris not to have the boy arrested and he had assured her he wouldn't do such a thing.

On this day that he had guessed it might be Mike taking the milk and rolls, shortly after eight A.M., Morris went up the stairs and knocked on Mrs. Papadopolous' door.

"Excuse me that I bother you," he said, and told her what had been happening to his milk and rolls.

"Mike work all nights in restaurants," she said. "No come home till nine o'clock in mornings. Sleep all days." Her eyes smoldered. The grocer left.

Now he was greatly troubled. Should he tell Ida and let her call the police? They were bothering him at least once a week with questions about the holdup but had produced nobody. Still, maybe it would be best to call them, for this stealing had gone on for almost a week. Who could afford it? Yet he waited, and that night as he was leaving the store by the side door, which he always padlocked after shutting the front door from inside, he flicked on the cellar light and as he peered down the stairs, his nightly habit, his heart tightened with foreboding that somebody was down there. Morris unlocked the lock, went back into the store and got a hatchet. Forcing his courage, he slowly descended the wooden steps. The cellar was empty. He searched in the dusty storage bins, poked around all over, but there was no sign of anybody.

In the morning he told Ida what was going on and she, calling him big fool, telephoned the police. A stocky, red-faced detective came, Mr. Minogue, from a nearby precinct, who was in charge of investigating Morris's holdup. He was a soft-spoken, unsmiling man, bald, a widower who had once lived in this neighborhood. He had a son Ward, who had gone to Helen's junior high school, a wild boy, always in trouble for manhandling girls. When he saw one he knew playing in front of her house, or on the stoop, he would come swooping down and chase her into the hall. There, no matter how desperately the girl struggled, or tenderly begged him to stop, Ward forced his hand down her dress and squeezed her breast till she screamed. Then by the time her mother came running down the stairs he had ducked out of the hall, leaving the girl sobbing. The detective, when he heard of these happenings, regularly beat up his son, but it didn't do much good. Then one day, about eight years ago, Ward was canned from his job for stealing from the company. His father beat him sick and bloody with his billy and drove him out of the neighborhood. After that, Ward disappeared and nobody knew where he had gone. People felt sorry for the detective, for he was a strict man and they knew what it meant to him to have such a son.

Mr. Minogue seated himself at the table in the rear and listened to Ida's complaint. He slipped on his glasses and wrote in a little black notebook. The detective said he would have a cop watch the store mornings after the milk was delivered, and if there was any more trouble to let him know.

As he was leaving, he said, "Morris, would you recognize Ward Minogue if you happened to see him again? I hear he's been seen around but whereabouts I don't know."

"I don't know," said Morris. "Maybe yes or maybe no. I didn't see him for years."

"If I ever meet up with him," said the detective, "I might bring him in to you for identification."

"What for?"

"I don't know myself—just for possible identification."

Ida said afterward that if Morris had called the police in the first place, he might have saved himself a few bottles of milk that they could hardly afford to lose.

That night, on an impulse, the grocer closed the store an hour later than usual. He snapped on the cellar light and cautiously descended the stairs, gripping his hatchet. Near the bottom he uttered a cry and the hatchet fell from his hands. A man's drawn and haggard face stared up at him in dismay. It was Frank Alpine, gray and unshaven. He had been asleep with his hat and coat on, sitting on a box against the wall. The light had awakened him.

"What do you want here?" Morris cried out.

"Nothing," Frank said dully. "I have just been sleeping in the cellar. No harm done."

"Did you steal from me my milk and rolls?"

"Yes," he confessed. "On account of I was hungry."

"Why didn't you ask me?"

Frank got up. "Nobody has any responsibility to take care of me but myself. I couldn't find any job. I used up every last cent I had. My coat is too thin for this cold and lousy climate. The snow and the rain get in my shoes so I am always shivering. Also, I had no place to sleep. That's why I came down here."

"Don't you stay any more with your sister?"

"I have no sister. That was a lie I told you. I am alone by myself."

"Why you told me you had a sister?"

"I didn't want you to think I was a bum."

Morris regarded the man silently. "Were you ever in prison sometimes?"

"Never, I swear to Christ."

"How you came to me in my cellar?"

"By accident. One night I was walking around in the snow, so I tried the cellar door and found out you left it unlocked, then I started coming down at night about an hour after you closed the store. In the morning, when they delivered the milk and rolls, I sneaked up through the hall, opened the door and took what I needed for breakfast. That's practically all I ate all day. After you came down and got busy with some customer or a salesman, I left by the hallway with the empty milk bottle under my coat. Later I threw it away in a lot. That's all there is to it. Tonight I took a chance and came in while you were still in the back of the store, because I have a cold and don't feel too good."

"How can you sleep in such a cold and drafty cellar?"

"I slept in worse."

"Are you hungry now?"

"I'm always hungry."

"Come upstairs."

Morris picked up his hatchet, and Frank, blowing his nose in his damp handkerchief, followed him up the stairs.

Morris lit a light in the store and made two fat liverwurst sandwiches with mustard, and in the back heated up a can of bean soup. Frank sat at the table in his coat, his hat lying at his feet. He ate with great hunger, his hand trembling as he brought the spoon to his mouth. The grocer had to look away.

As the man was finishing his meal, with coffee and cup cakes, Ida came down in felt slippers and bathrobe.

"What happened?" she asked in fright, when she saw Frank Alpine.

"He's hungry," Morris said.

She guessed at once. "He stole the milk!"

"He was hungry," explained Morris. "He slept in the cellar."

"I was practically starving," said Frank.

"Why didn't you look for a job?" Ida asked.

"I looked all over."

After, Ida said to Frank, "When you finish, please go someplace else." She turned to her husband. "Morris, tell him to go someplace else. We are poor people."

"This he knows."

"I'll go away," Frank said, "as the lady wishes."

"Tonight is already too late," Morris said. "Who wants he should walk all night in the streets?"

"I don't want him here." She was tense.

"Where you want him to go?"

Frank set his coffee cup on the saucer and listened with interest.

"This ain't my business," Ida answered.

"Don't anybody worry," said Frank. "I'll leave in ten minutes' time. You got a cigarette, Morris?"

The grocer went to the bureau and took out of the drawer a crumpled pack of cigarettes.

"It's stale," he apologized.

"Don't make any difference." Frank lit a stale cigarette, inhaling with pleasure.

"I'll go after a short while," he said to Ida.

"I don't like trouble," she explained.

"I won't make any. I might look like a bum in these clothes, but I am not. All my life I lived with good people."

"Let him stay here tonight on the couch," Morris said to Ida.

"No. Give him better a dollar he should go someplace else."

"The cellar would be fine," Frank remarked.

"It's too damp. Also rats."

"If you let me stay there one more night I promise I will get out the first thing in the morning. You don't have to be afraid to trust me. I am an honest man."

"You can sleep here," Morris said.

"Morris, you crazy," shouted Ida.

"I'll work it off for you," Frank said. "Whatever I cost you I'll pay you back. Anything you want me to do, I'll do it."

"We will see," Morris said.

"No," insisted Ida.

But Morris won out, and they went up, leaving Frank in the back, the gas radiator left lit.

"He will clean out the store," Ida said wrathfully.

"Where is his truck?" Morris asked, smiling. Seriously he said, "He's a poor boy. I feel sorry for him."

They went to bed. Ida slept badly. Sometimes she was racked by awful dreams. Then she awoke and sat up in bed, straining to hear noises in the store—of Frank packing huge bags of groceries to steal, But there was no sound. She dreamed she came down in the morning and all the stock was gone, the shelves as barren as the picked bones of dead birds. She dreamed, too, that the Italyener had sneaked up into the house and was peeking through the keyhole of Helen's door. Only when Morris got up to open the store did Ida fall fitfully asleep.

The grocer trudged down the stairs with a dull pain in his head. His legs felt weak. His sleep had not been refreshing.

The snow was gone from the streets and the milk boxes were again lying on the sidewalk near the curb. None of the bottles were missing. The grocer was about to drag in the milk cases when the Poilisheh came by. She went inside and placed three pennies on the counter. He entered with the brown bag of rolls, cut up one and wrapped it. She took it wordlessly and left.

Morris looked through the window in the wall. Frank was asleep on the couch in his clothes, his coat covering him. His beard was black, his mouth loosely open.

The grocer went out into the street, grabbed both milk boxes and yanked. The shape of a black hat blew up in his head, flared into hissing light, and exploded. He thought he was rising but felt himself fall.

Frank dragged him in and laid him on the couch. He ran upstairs and banged on the door. Helen, holding a housecoat over her night-dress, opened it. She suppressed a cry.

"Tell your mother your father just passed out. I called the ambulance."

She screamed. As he ran down the stairs he could hear Ida moaning. Frank hurried into the back of the store. The Jew lay white and motionless on the couch. Frank gently removed his apron. Draping the loop over his own head, he tied the tapes around him.

"I need the experience," he muttered.

Morris had reopened the wound on his head. The ambulance doctor the same who had treated him after the holdup, said he had got up too soon last time and worn himself out. He again bandaged the grocer's head, saying to Ida, "This time let him lay in bed a good couple of weeks till his strength comes back." "You tell him, doctor," she begged, "he don't listen to me." So the doctor told Morris, and Morris weakly nodded. Ida, in a gray state of collapse, remained with the patient all day. So did Helen, after calling the ladies' underthings concern where she worked. Frank Alpine stayed competently downstairs in the store. At noon Ida remembered him and came down to tell him to leave. Recalling her dreams, she connected him with their new misfortune. She felt that if he had not stayed the night, this might not have happened.

Frank was clean-shaven in the back, having borrowed Morris's safety razor, his thick hair neatly combed, and when she appeared he hopped up to ring open the cash register, showing her a pile of puffy bills.

"Fifteen," he said, "count every one."

She was astonished. "How is so much?"

He explained, "We had a busy morning. A lot of people stopped in to ask about Morris's accident."

Ida had planned to replace him with Helen for the time being, until she herself could take over, but she was now of two minds.

"Maybe you can stay," she faltered, "if you want to, till tomorrow."

"I'll sleep in the cellar, Mrs. You don't have to worry about me. I am as honest as the day."

"Don't sleep in the cellar," she said with a tremble to her voice, "my husband said on the couch. What can anybody steal here? We have nothing."

"How is he now?" Frank asked in a low voice.

She blew her nose.

The next morning Helen went reluctantly to work. Ida came down at ten to see how things were. This time there were only eight dollars in the drawer, but still better than lately. He apologized, "Not so good today, but I wrote down every article I sold so you'll know nothing stuck to my fingers." He produced a list of goods sold, written on wrapping paper. She happened to notice that it began with three cents for a roll. Glancing around, Ida saw he had packed out the few cartons delivered yesterday, swept up, washed the window from the inside and had straightened the cans on the shelves. The place looked a little less dreary.

During the day he also kept himself busy with odd jobs. He cleaned the trap of the kitchen sink, which swallowed water slowly, and in the store fixed a light whose chain wouldn't pull, making useless one lamp. Neither of them mentioned his leaving. Ida, still uneasy, wanted to tell him to go but she couldn't ask Helen to stay home any more, and the prospect of two weeks alone in the store, with her feet and a sick man in the bargain to attend upstairs, was too much for her. Maybe she would let the Italian stay ten days or so. With Morris fairly well recovered there would be no reason to keep him after that. In the meantime he would have three good meals a day and a bed, for being little more than a watchman. What business, after all, did they do here? And while Morris was not around she would change a thing or two she should have done before. So when the milkman stopped by for yesterday's empties, she ordered containers brought from now on. Frank Alpine heartily approved. "Why should we bother with bottles?" he said.

Despite all she had to do upstairs, and her recent good impressions of him, Ida haunted the store, watching his every move. She was worried because, now, not Morris but she was responsible for the man's presence in the store. If something bad happened, it would be her fault. Therefore, though she climbed the stairs often to tend to her husband's needs, she hurried back down, arriving pale and breathless to see what Frank was up to. But anything he happened to be doing was helpful. Her suspicions died slowly, though they never wholly died.

She tried not to be too friendly to him, to make him feel that a distant relationship meant a short one. When they were in the back or for a few minutes together behind the counter she discouraged conversation, took up something to do, or clean, or her paper to read. And in the matter of teaching him the business there was also little to say. Morris had price tags displayed under all items on the shelves, and Ida supplied Frank with a list of prices for meats and salads and for the miscellaneous unmarked things like loose coffee, rice or beans. She taught him how to wrap neatly and efficiently, as Morris had long ago taught her, how to read the scale and to set and handle the electric meat slicer. He caught on quickly; she suspected he knew more than he said he did. He added rapidly and accurately, did not overcut meats or overload the scale on bulk items, as she had urged him not to do, and judged well the length of paper needed to wrap with, and what number bag to pack goods into, conserving the larger bags which cost more money. Since he learned so fast, and since she had seen in him not the least evidence of dishonesty (a hungry man who took milk and rolls, though not above suspicion, was not the same as a thief), Ida forced herself to remain upstairs with more calm, in order to give Morris his medicine, bathe her aching feet and keep up the house, which was always dusty from the coal yard. Yet she felt, whenever she thought of it, always a little troubled at the thought of a stranger's presence below, a goy, after all, and she looked forward to the time when he was gone.

Although his hours were long—six to six, at which time she served him his supper—Frank was content. In the store he was quits with the outside world, safe from cold, hunger and a damp bed. He had cigarettes when he wanted them and was comfortable in clean clothes Morris had sent down, even a pair of pants that fitted him after Ida lengthened and pressed the cuffs. The store was fixed, a cave, motionless. He had all his life been on the move, no matter where he was; here he somehow couldn't be. Here he could stand at the window and watch the world go by, content to be here.

It wasn't a bad life. He woke before dawn. The Polish dame was planted at the door like a statue, distrusting him with beady eyes to open the place in time for her to get to work. Her he didn't like; he would gladly have slept longer. To get up in the middle of the night for three lousy cents was a joke but he did it for the Jew. After packing away the milk containers, turning bottomside up the occasional one that leaked, he swept the store and then the sidewalk. In the back he washed, shaved, had coffee and a sandwich, at first made with meat from a ham or roast pork butt, then after a few days, from the best cut. As he smoked after coffee he thought of everything he could do to improve this dump if it were his. When somebody came into the store he was up with a bound, offering service with a smile. Nick Fuso, on Frank's first day, was surprised to see him there, knowing Morris could not afford a clerk. But Frank said that though the pay was scarce there were other advantages. They spoke about this and that, and when the upstairs tenant learned Frank Alpine was a pai-

san, he told him to come up and meet Tessie. She cordially invited
him for macaroni that same night, and he said he would come if they
let him bring the macs.

Ida, after the first few days, began to go down at her regular hour,
around ten, after she had finished the housework; and she busied herself with writing in a notebook which bills they had got and which
paid. She also wrote out, in a halting hand, a few meager special-
account checks for bills that could not be paid in cash directly to
the drivers, mopped the kitchen floor, emptied the garbage pail into
the metal can on the curb outside and prepared salad if it was needed.
Frank watched her shred cabbage on the meat slicer for cole-slaw,
which she made in careful quantity, because if it turned sour it had
to be dumped into the garbage. Potato salad was a bigger job, and
she cooked up a large pot of new potatoes, which Frank helped her
peel hot in their steaming jackets. Every Friday she prepared fish
cakes and a panful of homemade baked beans, first soaking the little
beans overnight, pouring out the water, then spreading brown sugar
on top before baking. Her expression as she dipped in among the
soggy beans pieces of ham from a butt she had cut up caught his eye,
and he felt for her repugnance for hating to touch the ham, and
some for himself because he had never lived this close to Jews before.
At lunchtime there was a little "rush," which meant that a few dirty-
faced laborers from the coal yard and a couple of store clerks from
on the block wanted sandwiches and containers of hot coffee. But the
"rush," for which they both went behind the counter, petered out
in a matter of minutes and then came the dead hours of the afternoon. Ida said he ought to take some time off, but he answered that
he had nowhere special to go and stayed in the back, reading the
Daily News on the couch, or flipping through some magazines that
he had got out of the public library, which he had discovered during
one of his solitary walks in the neighborhood.

At three, when Ida departed for an hour or so to see if Morris
needed something, and to rest, Frank felt relieved. Alone, he did a
lot of casual eating, sometimes with unexpected pleasure. He sam-
pled nuts, raisins, and small boxes of stale dates or dried figs, which
he liked anyway; he also opened packages of crackers, macaroons,
cupcakes and doughnuts, tearing up their wrappers into small pieces
and flushing them down the toilet. Sometimes in the middle of eating sweets he would get very hungry for something more substantial,
so he made a thick meat and Swiss cheese sandwich on a seeded hard

roll spread with mustard, and swallowed it down with a bottle of ice-cold beer. Satisfied, he stopped roaming in the store.

Now and then there were sudden unlooked-for flurries of customers, mostly women, whom he waited on attentively, talking to them about all kinds of things. The drivers, too, liked his sociability and cheery manner and stayed to chew the fat. Otto Vogel, once when he was weighing a ham, warned him in a low voice, "Don't work for a Yid, kiddo. They will steal your ass while you are sitting on it." Frank, though he said he didn't expect to stay long, felt embarrassed for being there; then, to his surprise, he got another warning, from an apologetic Jew salesman of paper products, Al Marcus, a prosperous, yet very sick and solemn character who wouldn't stop working. "This kind of a store is a death tomb, positive," Al Marcus said. "Run out while you can. Take my word, if you stay six months, you'll stay forever."

"Don't worry about that," answered Frank.

Alone afterward, he stood at the window, thinking thoughts about his past, and wanting a new life. Would he ever get what he wanted? Sometimes he stared out of the back yard window at nothing at all, or at the clothesline above, moving idly in the wind, flying Morris's scarecrow union suits, Ida's hefty bloomers, modestly folded lengthwise, and her housedresses guarding her daughter's flower-like panties and restless brassières.

In the evening, whether he wanted to or not, he was "off." Ida insisted, fair was fair. She fed him a quick supper and allowed him, with apologies because she couldn't afford more, fifty cents spending money. He occasionally passed the time upstairs with the Fusos or went with them to a picture at the local movie house. Sometimes he walked, in spite of the cold, and stopped off at a poolroom he knew, about a mile and a half from the grocery store. When he got back, always before closing, for Ida wouldn't let him keep a key to the store in his pocket, she counted up the day's receipts, put most of the cash into a small paper bag and took it with her, leaving Frank five dollars to open up with in the morning. After she had gone, he turned the key in the front door lock, hooked the side door through which she had left, put out the store lights and sat in his undershirt in the rear, reading tomorrow's pink-sheeted paper that he had picked off Sam Pearl's stand on his way home. Then he undressed and went restlessly to bed in a pair of Morris's bulky, rarely used, flannel pajamas.

The old dame, he thought with disgust, always hurried him out of the joint before her daughter came down for supper.

The girl was in his mind a lot. He couldn't help it, imagined seeing her in the things that were hanging on the line—he had always had a good imagination. He pictured her as she came down the stairs in the morning; also saw himself standing in the hall after she came home, watching her skirts go flying as she ran up the stairs. He rarely saw her around, had never spoken to her but twice, on the day her father had passed out. She had kept her distance—who could blame her, dressed as he was and what he looked like then? He had the feeling as he spoke to her, a few hurried words, that he knew more about her than anybody would give him credit for. He had got this thought the first time he had ever laid eyes on her, that night he saw her through the grocery window. When she had looked at him he was at once aware of something starved about her, a hunger in her eyes he couldn't forget because it made him remember his own, so he knew how wide open she must be. But he wouldn't try to push anything, for he had heard that these Jewish babes could be troublemakers and he was not looking for any of that now—at least no more than usual; besides, he didn't want to spoil anything before it got started. There were some dames you had to wait for—for them to come to you.

His desire grew to get to know her, he supposed because she had never once come into the store in all the time he was there except after he left at night. There was no way to see and talk to her to her face, and this increased his curiosity. He felt they were both lonely but her old lady kept her away from him as if he had a dirty disease; the result was he grew more impatient to find out what she was like, get to be friends with her for whatever it was worth. So, since she was never around, he listened and watched for her. When he heard her walking down the stairs he went to the front window and stood there waiting for her to come out; he tried to look casual, as if he weren't watching, just in case she happened to glance back and see him; but she never did, as if she liked nothing about the place enough to look back on. She had a pretty face and a good figure, small-breasted, neat, as if she had meant herself to look that way. He liked to watch her brisk, awkward walk till she turned the corner. It was a sexy walk, with a wobble in it, a strange movement, as though she might dart sideways although she was walking forward. Her legs were just a bit bowed, and maybe that was the sexy part of it. She stayed in his mind after she had turned the corner; her legs and small breasts and the pink brassières that covered them. He would be reading something or lying on his back on the couch, smoking, and she would appear in his mind, walking to the corner. He did not have to shut his eyes to see her. Turn around, he said out loud, but in his thoughts she wouldn't.

To see her coming toward him he stood at the lit grocery window at night, but often before he could catch sight of her she was on her way upstairs, or already changing her dress in her room, and his chance was over for the day. She came home about a quarter to six, sometimes a little earlier, so he tried to be at the window around then, which wasn't so easy because that was the time for Morris's few supper customers to come in. So he rarely saw her come home from work, though he always heard her on the stairs. One day things were slower than usual in the store, it was dead at five-thirty, and Frank said to himself, Today I will see her. He combed his hair in the toilet so that Ida wouldn't notice, changed into a clean apron, lit a cigarette, and stood at the window, visible in its light. At twenty to six, just after he had practically shoved a woman out of the joint, a dame who had happened to walk in off the trolley, he saw Helen turn Sam Pearl's corner. Her face was prettier than he had remembered and his throat tightened as she walked to within a couple of feet of him, her eyes blue, her hair, which she wore fairly long, brown, and she had an absent-minded way of smoothing it back off the side of her face. He thought she didn't look Jewish, which was all to the good. But her expression was discontented, and her mouth a little drawn. She seemed to be thinking of something she had no hope of ever getting. This moved him, so that when she glanced up and saw his eyes on her, his face plainly showed his emotion. It must have bothered her because she quickly walked, without noticing him further, to the hall and disappeared inside.

The next morning he didn't see her—as if she had sneaked out on him—and at night he was waiting on somebody when she returned from work; regretfully he heard the door slam behind her. Afterward he felt downhearted; every sight lost to a guy who lived with his eyes was lost for all time. He thought up different ways to meet her and exchange a few words. What he had on his mind to say to her about himself was beginning to weigh on him, though he hadn't clearly figured out the words. Once he thought of coming in on her unexpectedly while she was eating her supper, but then he would have Ida to deal with. He also had the idea of opening the door the next time he saw her and calling her into the store; he could say that some guy had telephoned her, and after that talk about something else, but nobody did call her. She was in her way a lone bird, which suited him fine, though why she should be with her looks he couldn't figure out. He got the feeling that she wanted something big out of life, and this scared him. Still, he tried to think of schemes of getting her inside the store, even planning to ask her something like did she know where her old man kept his saw; only she mightn't like that, her mother being around all day to tell him. He had to watch out not to scare her any farther away than the old dame had done.

For a couple of nights after work he stood in a hallway next door to the laundry across the street in the hope that she would come out to do some errand, then he would cross over, tip his hat and ask if he could keep her company to where she was going. But this did not pay off either, because she didn't leave the house. The second night he waited fruitlessly until Ida put out the lights in the grocery window.

One evening toward the end of the second week after Morris's accident, Frank's loneliness burdened him to the point of irritation. He was eating his supper a few minutes after Helen had returned from work, while Ida happened to be upstairs with Morris. He had seen Helen come round the corner and had nodded to her as she approached the house. Caught by surprise, she half-smiled, then entered the hall. It was then the lonely feeling gripped him. While he was eating, he felt he had to get her into the store before her old lady came down and it was time for him to leave. The only excuse he could think of was to call Helen to answer the phone and after he would say that the guy must've hung up. It was a trick but he had to do it. He warned himself not to, because it would be starting out the wrong way with her and he might someday regret it. He tried to think of a better way but time was pressing him and he couldn't.

Frank got up, went over to the bureau, and took the phone off its cradle. He then walked out into the hall, opened the vestibule door, and holding his breath, pressed the Bober bell.

Ida looked over the banister. "What's the matter?"

"Telephone for Helen."

He could see her hesitate, so he returned quickly to the store. He sat down, pretending to be eating, his heart whamming so hard it hurt. All he wanted, he told himself, was to talk to her a minute so the next time would be easier.

Helen eagerly entered the kitchen. On the stairs she had noticed the excitement that flowed through her. My God, it's gotten to be that a phone call is an event.

If it's Nat, she thought, I might give him another chance.

Frank half-rose as she entered, then sat down.

"Thanks," she said to him as she picked up the phone.

"Hello." While she waited he could hear the buzz in the receiver.

"There's nobody there," she said, mystified.

He laid down his fork. "This girl called you," he said gently.

But when he saw the disappointment in her eyes, how bad she felt, he felt bad.

"You must've been cut off."

She gave him a long look. She was wearing a white blouse that showed the firmness of her small breasts. He wet his dry lips, trying to figure out some quick way to square himself, but his mind, usually crowded with all sorts of schemes, had gone blank. He felt very bad, as he had known he would, that he had done what he had. If he had it to do over he wouldn't do it this way.

"Did she leave you her name?" Helen asked.

"No."

"It wasn't Betty Pearl?"

"No."

She absently brushed back her hair. "Did she say anything to you?"

"Only to call you." He paused. "Her voice was nice—like yours. Maybe she didn't get me straight when I said you were upstairs but I would ring your doorbell, and that's why she hung up."

"I don't know why anybody would do that."

Neither did he. He wanted to step clear of his mess but saw no way other than to keep on lying. But lying made their talk useless. When he lied he was somebody else lying to somebody else. It wasn't the two of them as they were. He should have kept that in his mind.

She stood at the bureau, holding the telephone in her hand as if still expecting the buzz to become a voice; so he waited for the same thing, a voice to speak and say he had been telling the truth, that he was a man of fine character. Only that didn't happen either.

He gazed at her with dignity as he considered saying the simple truth, starting from there, come what would, but the thought of confessing what he had done almost panicked him.

"I'm sorry," he said brokenly, but by then she was gone, and he was attempting to fix in his memory what she had looked like so close.

Helen too was troubled. Not only could she not explain why she believed yet did not fully believe him, nor why she had lately become so conscious of his presence among them, though he never strayed from the store, but she was also disturbed by her mother's efforts to keep her away from him. "Eat when he leaves," Ida had said. "I am not used to goyim in my house." This annoyed Helen because of the assumption that she would keel over for somebody just because he happened to be a gentile. It meant, obviously, her mother didn't trust her. If she had been casual about him, Helen doubted she would have paid him any attention to speak of. He was interesting looking, true, but what except a poor grocery clerk? Out of nothing Ida was trying to make something.

Though Ida was still concerned at having the young Italian around the place, she observed with pleased surprise how, practically from the day of his appearance, the store had improved. During the first week there were days when they had taken in from five to seven dollars more than they were averaging daily in the months since summer. And the same held for the second week. The store was of course still a poor store, but with this forty to fifty a week more they might at least limp along until a buyer appeared. She could at first not understand why more people were coming in, why more goods were being sold. True, the same thing had happened before. Without warning, after a long season of dearth, three or four customers, lost faces, straggled in one day, as if they had been let out of their poor rooms with a few pennies in their pockets. And others, who had skimped on food, began to buy more. A storekeeper could tell almost at once when times were getting better. People seemed less worried and irritable, less in competition for the little sunlight in the world. Yet the curious thing was that business, according to most of the drivers, had not very much improved anywhere. One of them said that Schmitz around the corner was having his troubles too; furthermore he wasn't feeling so good. So the sudden pickup of business in the store, Ida thought, would not have happened without Frank Alpine. It took her a while to admit this to herself.

The customers seemed to like him. He talked a lot as he waited on them, sometimes saying things that embarrassed Ida but made the customers, the gentile housewives, laugh. He somehow drew in people she had never before seen in the neighborhood, not only women, men too. Frank tried things that Morris and she could never do, such as attempting to sell people more than they asked for, and usually he succeeded. "What can you do with a quarter of a pound?" he would say. "A quarter is for the birds—not even a mouthful. Better make it a half." So they would make it a half. Or he would say, "Here's a new brand of mustard that we just got in today. It weighs two ounces more than the stuff they sell you in the supermarkets for the same price. Why don't you give it a try? If you don't like it, bring it back and I will gargle it." And they laughed and bought it. This made Ida wonder if Morris and she were really suited to the grocery business. They had never been salesmen.

One of the women customers called Frank a supersalesman, a word that brought a pleased smile to his lips. He was clever and worked hard. Ida's respect for him reluctantly grew; gradually she became more relaxed in his presence. Morris was right in recognizing that he was not a bum but a boy who had gone through bad times. She pitied him for having lived in an orphan asylum. He did his work quickly, never complained, kept himself neat and clean now that he had soap and water around, and answered her politely. The one or two times, just lately, that he had briefly talked to Helen in her presence, he had spoken like a gentleman and didn't try to stretch a word into a mouthful. Ida discussed the situation with Morris and they raised his "spending money" from fifty cents a day to five dollars for the week. Despite her good will to him, this worried Ida, but, after all, he was bringing more money into the store, the place looked spic and span—let him keep five dollars of their poor profit. Bad as things still were, he willingly did so much extra around the store—how could they not pay him a little something? Besides, she thought, he would soon be leaving.

Frank accepted the little raise with an embarrassed smile. "You don't have to pay me anything more, Mrs., I said I would work for nothing to make up for past favors from your husband and also to learn the business. Besides that, you give me my bed and board, so you don't owe me a thing."

"Take," she said, handing him a crumpled five-dollar bill. He let the money lie on the counter till she urged him to put it into his pocket. Frank felt troubled about the raise because he was earning something for his labor that Ida knew nothing of, for business was a little better than she thought. During the day, while she was not around, he sold at least a buck's worth, or a buck and a half, that he made no attempt to ring up on the register. Ida guessed nothing; the list of sold items he had supplied her with in the beginning they had discontinued as impractical. It wasn't hard for him to scrape up here a bit of change, there a bit. At the end of the second week he had ten dollars in his pocket. With this and the five she gave him he bought a shaving kit, a pair of cheap brown suede shoes, a couple of shirts and a tie or two; he figured that if he stayed around two more weeks he would own an inexpensive suit. He had nothing to be ashamed of, he thought—it was practically his own dough he was taking. The grocer and his wife wouldn't miss it because they didn't know they had it, and they wouldn't have it if it wasn't for his hard work. If he weren't working there, they would have less than they had with him taking what he took.

Thus he settled it in his mind only to find himself remorseful. He groaned, scratching the backs of his hands with his thick nails. Sometimes he felt short of breath and sweated profusely. He talked aloud to himself when he was alone, usually when he was shaving or in the toilet, exhorted himself to be honest. Yet he felt a curious pleasure in his misery, as he had at times in the past when he was doing something he knew he oughtn't to, so he kept on dropping quarters into his pants pocket.

One night he felt very bad about all the wrong he was doing and vowed to set himself straight. If I could do one right thing, he thought, maybe that would start me off; then he thought if he could get the gun and get rid of it he would at least feel better. He left the grocery after supper and wandered restlessly in the foggy streets, feeling cramped in the chest from his long days in the store and because his life hadn't changed much since he had come here. As he passed by the cemetery, he tried to keep out of his mind the memory of the holdup but it kept coming back in. He saw himself sitting with Ward Minogue in the parked car, waiting for Karp to come out of the grocery, but when he did his store lights went out and he hid in the back among the bottles. Ward said to drive quick around the block so they would flush the Jew out, and he would slug him on the sidewalk and take his fat wallet away; but when they got back, Karp's car was gone with him in it, and Ward cursed him into an early grave. Frank said Karp had beat it, so they ought to scram, but Ward sat there with heartburn, watching, with his small eyes, the grocery store, the one lit place on the block besides the candy store on the corner.

"No," Frank urged, "it's just a little joint, I got my doubts if they took in thirty bucks today."

"Thirty is thirty," Ward said. "I don't care if it's Karp or Bober, a Jew is a Jew."

"Why not the candy store?"

Ward made a face. "I can't stand penny candy."

"How do you know his name?" asked Frank.

"Who?"

"The Jew grocer."

"I used to go to school with his daughter. She has a nice ass."

"Then if that's so, he will recognize you."

"Not with a rag around my snoot, and I will rough up my voice. He ain't seen me for eight or nine years. I was a skinny kid then."

"Have it your way. I will keep the car running."

"Come in with me," Ward said. "The block is dead. Nobody will expect a stickup in this dump."

But Frank hesitated. "I thought you said Karp was the one you were out after?"

"I will take Karp some other time. Come on."

Frank put on his cap and crossed the car tracks with Ward Minogue. "It's your funeral," he said, but it was really his own.

He remembered thinking as they went into the store, a Jew is a Jew, what difference does it make? Now he thought, I held him up because he was a Jew. What the hell are they to me so that I gave them credit for it?

But he didn't know the answer and walked faster, from time to time glancing through the spiked iron fence at the shrouded gravestones. Once he felt he was being followed and his heart picked up a hard beat. He hurried past the cemetery and turned right on the first street after it, hugging the stoops of the stone houses as he went quickly down the dark street. When he reached the poolroom he felt relieved.

Pop's poolroom was a dreary four-table joint, owned by a glum old Italian with a blue-veined bald head and droopy hands, who sat close to his cash register.

"Seen Ward yet?" Frank said.

Pop pointed to the rear where Ward Minogue, in his fuzzy black hat and a bulky overcoat, was practicing shots alone at a table. Frank watched him place a black ball at a corner pocket and aim a white at it. Ward leaned tensely forward, his face strained, a dead butt hanging from his sick mouth. He shot but missed. He banged his cue on the floor.

Frank had drifted past the players at the other tables. When Ward looked up and saw him, his eyes lit with fear. The fear drained after he recognized who it was. But his pimply face was covered with sweat.

He spat his butt to the floor. "What have you got on your feet, you bastard, gumshoes?"

"I didn't want to spoil your shot."

"Anyway you did."

"I've been looking for you about a week."

"I was on my vacation." Ward smiled in the corner of his mouth.

"On a drunk?"

Ward put his hand to his chest and brought up a belch. "I wish to hell it was. Somebody tipped my old man I was around here, so I hid out for a while. I had a rough time. My heartburn is acting up." He hung up his cue, then wiped his face with a dirty handkerchief.

"Why don't you go to a doctor?" Frank said.

"To hell with them."

"Some medicine might help you."

"What will help me is if my goddam father drops dead."

"I want to talk to you, Ward," Frank said in a low voice.

"So talk."

Frank nodded toward the players at the next table.

"Come out in the yard," Ward said. "I got something I want to say to you."

Frank followed him out the rear door into a small enclosed back yard with a wooden bench against the building. A weak bulb shone down on them from the top of the doorjamb.

Ward sat down on the bench and lit a cigarette. Frank did the same, from his own pack. He puffed but got no pleasure from the butt, so he threw it away.

"Sit down," said Ward.

Frank sat on the bench. Even in the fog he stinks, he thought.

"What do you want me for?" Ward asked, his small eyes restless.

"I want my gun, Ward. Where is it?"

"What for?"

"I want to throw it in the ocean."

Ward snickered. "Cat got your nuts?"

"I don't want some dick coming around and asking me do I own it."

"I thought you said you bought the rod off a fence."

"That's right."

"Then nobody's got a record of it, so what are you scared of?"

"If you lost it," Frank said, "they trace them even without a record."

"I won't lose it," Ward said. After a minute he ground his cigarette into the dirt. "I will give it back to you after we do this job I have on my mind."

Frank looked at him. "What kind of a job?"

"Karp. I want to stick him up."

"Why Karp?—there are bigger liquor stores."

"I hate that Jew son of a bitch and his popeyed Louis. When I was a kid all I had to do was go near banjo eyes and they would complain to my old man and get me beat up."

"They would recognize you if you go in there."

"Bober didn't. I will use a handkerchief and wear some different clothes. Tomorrow I will go out and pick up a car. All you got to do is drive and I will make the heist."

"You better stay away from that block," Frank warned. "Somebody might recognize you."

Ward moodily rubbed his chest. "All right, you sold me. We will go somewheres else."

"Not with me," Frank said.

"Think it over."

"I've had all I want."

Ward showed his disgust. "The minute I saw you I knew you would puke all over."

Frank didn't answer.

"Don't act so innocent," Ward said angrily. "You're hot, the same as me."

"I know," Frank said.

"I slugged him because he was lying where he hid the rest of the dough," Ward argued.

"He didn't hide it. It's a poor, lousy store."

"I guess you know all about that."

"What do you mean?"

"Can the crud. I know you been working there."

Frank drew a breath. "You following me again, Ward?"

Ward smiled. "I followed you one night after you left the pool-room. I found out you were working for a Jew and living on bird crap."

Frank slowly got up. "I felt sorry for him after you slugged him, so I went back to give him a hand while he was in a weak condition. But I won't be staying there long."

"That was real sweet of you. I suppose you gave him back the lousy seven and a half bucks that was your part of the take?"

"I put it back in the cash register. I told the Mrs. the business was getting better."

"I never thought I would meet up with a goddam Salvation Army soldier."

"I did it to quiet my conscience," Frank said.

Ward rose. "That ain't your conscience you are worried about."

"No?"

"It's something else. I hear those Jew girls make nice ripe lays."

Frank went back without his gun.

Helen was with her mother as Ida counted the cash.

Frank stood behind the counter, cleaning his fingernails with his jackknife blade, waiting for them to leave so he could close up.

"I think I'll take a hot shower before I go to bed," Helen said to her mother. "I've felt chilled all night."

"Good night," Ida said to Frank. "I left five dollars change for the morning."

"Good night," said Frank.

They left the rear door and he heard them go up the stairs. Frank closed the store and went into the back. He thumbed through to-morrow's *News*, then got restless

After a while he went into the store and listened at the side door; he unlatched the lock, snapped on the cellar light, closed the cellar door behind him so no light would leak out into the hall, then quietly descended the stairs.

He found the air shaft where an old unused dumb-waiter stood, pushed the dusty box back and gazed up the vertical shaft. It was pitch-dark. Neither the Bobers' bathroom window nor the Fusos' showed any light.

Frank struggled against himself but not for long. Shoving the dumb-waiter back as far as it would go, he squeezed into the shaft and then boosted himself up on top of the box. His heart shook him with its beating.

When his eyes got used to the dark he saw that her bathroom window was only a couple of feet above his head. He felt along the wall as high as he could reach and touched a narrow ledge around the air shaft. He thought he could anchor himself on it and see into the bathroom.

But if you do it, he told himself, you will suffer.

Though his throat hurt and his clothes were drenched in sweat, the excitement of what he might see forced him to go up.

Crossing himself, Frank grabbed both of the dumb-waiter ropes and slowly pulled himself up, praying the pulley at the skylight wouldn't squeak too much.

A light went on over his head.

Holding his breath, he crouched motionless, clinging to the swaying ropes. Then the bathroom window was shut with a bang. For a while he couldn't move, the strength gone out of him. He thought he might lose his grip and fall, and he thought of her opening the bathroom window and seeing him lying at the bottom of the shaft in a broken, filthy heap.

It was a mistake to do it, he thought.

But she might be in the shower before he could get a look at her, so, trembling, he began again to pull himself up. In a few minutes he was straddling the ledge, holding onto the ropes to steady himself yet keep his full weight off the wood.

Leaning forward, though not too far, he could see through the uncurtained crossed sash window into the old-fashioned bathroom. Helen was there looking with sad eyes at herself in the mirror. He thought she would stand there forever, but at last she unzippered her housecoat, stepping out of it.

He felt a throb of pain at her nakedness, an overwhelming desire to love her, at the same time an awareness of loss, of never having had what he wanted most, and other such memories he didn't care to recall.

Her body was young, soft, lovely, the breasts like small birds in flight, her ass like a flower. Yet it was a lonely body in spite of its lovely form, lonelier. Bodies are lonely, he thought, but in bed she wouldn't be. She seemed realer to him now than she had been, revealed without clothes, personal, possible. He felt greedy as he gazed, all eyes at a banquet, hungry so long as he must look. But in looking he was forcing her out of reach, making her into a thing only of his seeing, her eyes reflecting his sins, rotten past, spoiled ideals, his passion poisoned by his shame.

Frank's eyes grew moist and he wiped them with one hand. When he gazed up again she seemed, to his horror, to be staring at him through the window, a mocking smile on her lips, her eyes filled with scorn, pitiless. He thought wildly of jumping, bolting, broken-boned, out of the house; but she turned on the shower and stepped into the tub, drawing the flowered plastic curtain around her.

The window was quickly covered with steam. For this he was relieved, grateful. He let himself down silently. In the cellar, instead of the grinding remorse he had expected to suffer, he felt a moving joy.

The Last Angry Man

by GERALD GREEN

Set in a pocket of the Brooklyn slums, The Last Angry Man is so vividly authentic that even if one has never lived in such a setting, one feels recognition. Green's more recent novel, To Brooklyn with Love, adds tenderness to this brilliant portrait of what may well be the definitive story of the Jewish doctor.

Not really a community man, Dr. Abelman is nevertheless part and parcel of the community; a nonreligious Jew, he never refuses a contribution to the long-beards who regularly invade his sanctum. Every turn of his character, every obstinacy, every curse at the galoots who throw garbage on his stoop, but whom he never refuses to help, seems to come right out of Talmudic parable. Certain works, like The Assistant, become augmented through a sense of moral intention in the use of Jewish material, but, while with a writer like Malamud one feels this intention, Green is effective because one feels this is simply the material of his life. Novelistically he was less successful, for instance, with The League of Noble Christians, an idea story about a quest in Europe for Christians who had saved Jews. That book was researched. The Brooklyn books are lived.

Green was brought up in a Brooklyn area that was turning Negro, and his remarkable portrait of the neighborhood in transition was predictive for what was soon to erupt as a major urban problem. It is Dr. Abelman's effort to save a Negro boy that is threaded through these excerpts.

While Green's Dr. Abelman and Malamud's Bober appear almost antithetic in character, one a protester, the other resigned, both have the same tough ethical core, and both are killed in the same hostile society. The two novels offer a remarkable contrast to the hard-edged slum novels of the thirties; Malamud and

Green restore to the American Jewish character a profound ethical concern, and rachmones.

Gerald Green, born in 1922, and a graduate of Columbia, worked for some years in television, at one time as producer of the Today show, and still turns his hand to "specials," though he is now more free for his writing. Most recently he has published a remarkable study of the artists in the Theresienstadt concentration camp.

M.L.

T HE BULK of the doctor's office work was crammed together on weekends. Sometimes the waiting room would be filled from mid-morning through late afternoon and Jannine would have to set up bridge chairs to accommodate the overflow. If the weather was pleasant, several patients would adorn the doctor's front stoop, taking advantage of the sunlight filtering through the bright foliage of the Lombardy poplar.

He loved the ritual of the office: opening the double doors to the examining room, inviting the next patient in; the case histories, the preliminary interrogation, the probings. With old hands, he liked to discuss family matters, business affairs; they knew he expected it and they told him everything. With new patients, he delighted in learning the new facts, even though, more often than not, they were a dreary repetition of a hundred similar cases.

It had been a tiring day. A GI series on the Traficanti boy had kept him in and out of the darkroom most of the morning. He didn't like the irregularity of the duodenal shadow; it would gnaw at him all through the day. That was the trouble with medicine—nothing was ever isolated. Every case, every patient was a part of you all the time. Angelo Traficanti's duodenum would occupy him continually, infringing on his concern over Mrs. Abarbanel's arthritis, Shirley Feinman's fainting spells, Mr. McMorris' coronary, and Ed Dineen's gall bladder. All of them would force themselves like driven nails into his consciousness, until his mind was a swarm of problems, self-generating and self-propagating, feeding on each other and on him and shutting out his personal worries. He did not think about the new house very much on weekends.

At five in the afternoon there were still several people in the waiting room, sitting quietly in the dull heat, all of them flecked with the irregular spangles of the tree-patterned sunlight.

He had just given Rabbi Piltz his monthly check-up, and the snuffish odor of the old man lingered in the examining room. The patriarch departed, waving his authoritative cane and mumbling his incomprehensible blessing. Standing between the partly opened doors, the doctor chuckled, addressing the three people in the hot anteroom.

"Well, we're all in good luck today. The rabbi blessed us." He did not notice that two of the people were Negroes, nor did it bother him. In the filth and noise of the savage street he saw an enemy in each dark face; in the office they became real people, identifiable, capable of salvation, worthy of a little dignity.

A stout Negro woman, draped in the outlandish dark clothes which denoted Deep South churchgoing and an eschewal of vulgarity, rose hesitantly. Gently, she guided a thin, café-au-lait youth toward the door. He moved lightly, head down, his manner one of contemptuous indifference. At the door, the third patient, a short fat man in a soiled white shirt leaped from his seat. Boldly, he thrust himself between the doctor and the Negroes, crying coarsely:

"It's my next!"

"It's your next?" the doctor asked pleasantly. "You mean it's your *neck,* and it could use a bath. These people were first."

The fat man looked from the doctor to the Negroes. He said nothing, but the curled upper lip and the eyes transmitted the message: *They are black and I am white and therefore it doesn't matter if they were here first.*

"So you don't take me foist?" he asked.

"If you were first, I'd take you first," the doctor said. "You know— the last shall be first. Ever read the Bible, Ballenberg?"

That was the trouble with most of the doctor's little *ripostes:* they pointed morals and they were much too far above the heads of his audience. Ballenberg ignored him.

"You'll take dem foist?" he persisted.

"Of course," said the doctor. With a deft shove he moved the fat man aside and, opening the doors wider, ushered in the Negro woman and the boy.

"You shouldn't touch me like that!" Ballenberg said. "I'll fix you, Abelman! I'll go by Baumgart! He wouldn't take a *schwartzer* foist! To your own people you do this, *hah?*"

He turned, irate and indignant, slum honor sullied by the doctor's insistence on fair play. The Negro woman looked distraught. "Ah'm sorry, doctor," she said in a barely audible voice. "Maybe you shudda seen him first. You gon' lose a patient."

"Who needs him. Who needs his kind?" And he knew, of course, that he needed all of them, the galoots, the boors, the villains. Yet somehow Dr. Baumgart never seemed to have these troubles with patients; you never heard him arguing with them, moralizing, ordering them out of his office. And how that young guy knew how to collect the big fees! They paid through the nose for his X-ray work, they called him in on consultations, and he sucked them dry.

The shades were partly drawn in the consultation room—a mingled essence of summer flowers drifted into the dim room. Through the cracks between shade and window, slivers of late afternoon sun intruded, falling across the comforting face of Harlow Brooks. He sat the youth to one side of the great desk and the woman perched unhappily at the tip of the deformed Morris chair.

"I think I know you," the doctor said. He squinted over his glasses at the woman. "Are you related to the Jeffersons on Patchen Avenue?"

"No, suh," she answered faintly.

"Well, I'm sure I know *you*," the doctor said, looking at the boy. The youth silently lowered his head, an exquisite knob, molded and shaped like a bronze museum piece. The black burrs on top were an afterthought, a Greenwich Village touch on an authentic Ashanti wood carving.

"Ah don' know you," the boy muttered.

"Well, it's a funny thing, I don't remember you in this office before, or seeing you as a patient, but I could swear I've met you."

The youth jerked his head, the kind of movement a dog makes when being annoyed by flies. "You don' know me. Don' nobody know me," he said flatly. Then, inexplicably, he looked up quickly and, with an impertinent grin, said, "Ah deh man of mystery."

The doctor settled back in the swivel chair, crossing his stubby legs. He enjoyed the challenge of the perverse patient, and the youth's mocking tone had not been wasted on him.

"That's very nice. We should get along fine, because, you see, I'm very good at solving mysteries. If you're a mystery, I'll find it out, young fellah. I'm a kind of detective. But you wouldn't know anything about detectives or cops, would you?"

The boy started to rise, the stringy body uncoiling like a snake. "Ah don' wan' stay here. He talk too much," he told his mother. "You make me come here. Ain' nothin' wrong with me."

She raised her voice and leaned forward, speaking in the hard voice of the deaconess, the church pillar. "You sit down dere, Herman, and be polite to deh doctor. You a sick boy."

The doctor turned to his desk, yanked out a fresh file card, and dipped the non-fillable pen in the clotted inkwell.

"You can stay or get the hell out, young man," he said sharply. "Excusing your presence, lady, I don't need him."

"He gon' stay," she said. It seemed to settle the issue for the time being.

The doctor began his interrogation, writing swiftly and illegibly, salting his notes with the shorthand symbols he still remembered from his days as a male stenographer for Mr. Comerford and Hector O'Bannion. He learned quickly that the boy's name was Herman Quincy, age seventeen, that he neither attended school nor worked. He lived with his mother (father deceased) in a fourth-story walkup. He had no past history of serious disease, and from the doctor's cursory study of him appeared to be in good health, if somewhat sullen and ill-mannered.

"So what's bothering him?" the doctor asked Mrs. Quincy.

She shifted her dark bulk, layered with ungainly petticoats and skirts. "He havin' fits," she said.

"Ah, hell, Ah ain' had nothin' but a little faintin'," Herman said, turning his head away again.

The doctor leaned forward. "What kind of fits?" he asked.

"Jes' fits is all," she said uncomfortably. "He done had three already. He had one las' week runnin' 'round with his no-good friends. An' he had two more at home. Ah seen deh last one."

"Have you been to any other doctor?"

"No, suh. He don' like no doctors."

"Has anyone ever mentioned the word 'epilepsy' to you? To you, Herman?"

They both shook their heads, uncomprehending.

"What was this fit, as you call it, like? Did you pass out right away, Herman? Do you remember anything?"

"Ah don' remember nothin'. Ah ain' sick."

"This last fit, the one you saw, Mrs. Quincy, what happened?"

"It skeer me awful, doctor. He come home late at night an' I hear him moanin' and thrashin'. He layin' on deh bed an' his fingers an' arm, dey jerkin' and twitchin'—"

"Left or right arm?"

"Ah don' recall."

"Well, was it both arms and sets of fingers, or one?"

She ruminated, recalling the tan body writhing on the rumpled bedsheets under the glaring bulb. "Ah ain' sure, doctor, but Ah think at first only one arm and deh fingers, and den deh haid and one leg, and den deh whole body, twitchin' and jumpin'."

"What do you remember, Herman?"

"Nothin'. Ah fainted das all."

Dr. Abelman scowled. "You may be pretty sick, young man. You should realize I'm trying to help you."

"Ah don' need no help."

"What else, Mrs. Quincy? How long did this seizure last?"

"Ah ain' sure, seem lak a whole hour, but could'n' been more den five, ten minutes."

"What happened then?"

"He pass out cold a few minutes," she said. "He right, he fainted, but dat come *after* deh fit. Den he wake up and he say his right arm weak, he cain't move it. How long dat last, Herman?"

"Couple minutes. My arm fall asleep das all."

The doctor looked owlishly at him through thick glasses. His eyebrows bristled over the top rims authoritatively, demanding co-operation.

"How is that right arm now, Herman? Think it's strong enough to hand wrestle me on the desk?"

"Dat arm feel fine. Ah cud pitch a double-header." He was looking up, smiling easily, without the contempt he had evinced earlier.

"Okay big shot, put the arm down here and see who goes down first."

He moved aside his blood pressure apparatus and daybook, grasping the thin brown fist. Their elbows rested on the glass top. Herman looked apprehensively at the huge biceps under the short-sleeved shirt and widened his eyes a fraction.

"You pretty strong for a ole man," he said.

"Strong enough to knock some sense into you," the doctor said. "Ready?"

Herman nodded. They clamped hands, and, after a second of resistance, the doctor slammed the tan arm to the desk top.

"How does it feel now, Herman?"

"Feel funny. Mebbe a little weak." He was examining his right wrist and forearm curiously, wondering how he, Josh the Dill, could be afflicted with any kind of weakness.

The doctor invited him into the examining room, asking Mrs. Quincy to remain behind. You did better with them when you had them alone. Relatives got in the way, particularly when there was palpable hostility between family members. Herman stripped down to his shorts in the interior room. The doctor took his height, his weight, his blood pressure; listened routinely to his chest and heart and found nothing out of the ordinary. He seemed a perfectly healthy child of the gutter: limbs, heart, and lungs defiantly strong. Like so many of his companions, the absence of vitamins, pediatricians, and wheat germ had not affected Herman Quincy's physical well-being.

The doctor was examining his ears, nose, and throat, probing with spatula, the patient seated on a converted piano stool below him, when he noticed the pinpricks in the soft flesh of the tan thigh.

"And what are those, mosquito bites?" he asked grimly.

The boy stiffened again, the hostility returning. "Das my business."

"How much do you take?"

"What Ah can git."

"Can you do without it? Or are you hooked for good?"

He lowered the sculptured head, turning away from the doctor's outraged face, a face which said: *No goddam patient of mine has the right to be addicted.*

"Ah take it or leave it. Ah too smart to be hooked."

"You taking it now?"

"Ain' had it fo' a few days."

The doctor wondered idly if the strange convulsions, the loss of consciousness, the weakness in the right arm could be the result of narcotic addiction—or perhaps abstinence from it. He would have to consult the texts; crazy things happened to addicts, one-in-a-thousand symptoms which had to be taken into account before you even leaned toward other diagnoses. He'd have to probe the boy's medical history. They must have taken him to a clinic of some kind at some time, somewhere there was a medical record available. You couldn't leave anything to guesswork; you researched it as deeply as you could.

He flicked off the overhead chandelier and lit his ophthalmoscope. Preceded by the yellow cone of light, he walked toward Herman again.

"Herman, you get headaches, don't you?"

"How you know?"

"I just guessed. What kind of headaches? Morning, when you wake up?"

He was bending over him now, peering through the instrument into the luminous eyeball.

"Yeh. Dey come an' go quick in deh mornin'. Jes' a few minutes, das all."

"Every morning?"

"Three out of fo' mebbe. Sometime dey come quick when I go to deh bathroom, or bend over fast."

The doctor squinted into the eyeball, trying to focus his own tired eye on the optic disc. On the side of the disc nearest the nose, there was a faint blurring of the edge, and the entire disc itself appeared to be somewhat swollen—papilledema, the books called it. And papilledema could mean several things: hypertension, kidney disease, something worse. . . .

That was the challenge of the profession: the more you knew, the more possibilities you opened up. He was starting with papilledema, a swelling or choking of the optic disc; a slight engorgement of the veins, the blurring and dim streaking that might conceivably have been the start of a hemorrhage. Where would it lead him?

Turning on the overhead light again, he sat Herman on the creaking examining table. He had worn out a dozen leather examining pads on its smooth hard surface: the bright green plastic affair resting there now was his daughter's gift. It didn't ring true next to the smoky wooden sides and legs.

"Just lay still, Herman, completely relaxed."

"Ah relax real good. Man, Ah'm loose."

"Loose as a goose, is that what you fellows say?" He chattered on aimlessly, keeping the patient comfortable and at ease, seeking to avoid the slightest tensing or resistance to his probing fingers. The doctor began with Herman's face, poking at the forehead, the delicate musculature of the eyelids, the muscles around the thick African lips, light pink inside the darker red. He found nothing suspect. Gripping the right arm at the elbow, he tried rotating it, seeking some rigidity, some resistance to the passive motion. There wasn't any—the arm moved freely. The hands and fingers offered no stiffness either, nor did the left arm. Next he tested the extensors of the knees and the plantar flexors of the feet; there was neither resistance nor an exaggeration of the normal reflexes. The whole picture of the limbs was negative. Or had he missed something? Again, the worm of doubt gnawed at him. You could miss the slightest hint, the faintest suggestion of a symptom and go completely wrong the rest of the way. To assure himself he repeated all the tests, flexing and probing the bronze face and limbs again.

"Stand up, Herman," he said. "Now go to the end of the room by the door and walk toward me at your normal pace, no faster or slower."

The boy rolled off the table lightly, stood at the locked double doors, his figure sharp as a paper cutout against the bottle-green shades.

"Walk toward me, son," the doctor said.

Herman walked. The doctor looked intently at his arms and legs, studying particularly the right-hand members, seeking some variance from the normal gait, some faint betrayal of what he suspected. The boy moved as lithely and easily as an oiled machine. There was even a faint swagger to his narrow hips and small athletic buttocks. Did he imagine that the right arm was swinging differently? Was the right knee the slightest bit stiffer than the left?

"Now walk away from me, a little slower," he said.

Herman spun about and proceeded again, toward the shaded doors. The doctor took off his glasses and studied the right arm and right leg once more. It was his imagination: you sometimes started to see signs because you wanted them to be there, to tie together the loose ends of a diagnosis. He told himself that the boy's right knee was indeed stiff, that the right arm was not swinging normally. But comparing them again to their opposite members he decided the difference existed in his mind, in his eagerness to confirm his suspicions.

Herman, his tour of the office completed, stood in front of the physician gazing down at him with bored, detached eyes. The doctor leaned back in the swivel chair and pushed his eyeglasses back on to his forehead.

"Herman, I want you to repeat a sentence after me. You listening?"

"Sho."

"Fine. Say this: *Around the rugged rock the ragged rascal ran.*"

"Whuh?"

"Say it just the way I did. Go ahead."

"Ah don' recolleck it. Whuffo yo' wan' me say dat?" He was as suspicious as an alley cat.

"I want to get you a job as President of the United States, Herman, and you have to speak very nicely in that job. Now you understand? Come on, repeat it: *Around the rugged rock the ragged rascal ran.*"

Herman Quincy did not smile at the old man's joke at his expense; but, reluctantly, he repeated the strange sentence, slurring words and syllables together with deliberate contempt.

"Roun' de ruggah rock de raggah rascahran."

"Wise guy, hey, Herman?" the doctor said. Again he was in furious debate with himself: did the tongue-twister come out any more blurred or indistinct than Herman's normally slothful speech? Was there a hint that the faculty of speech had been impaired? He pointed to Herman's clothes.

"Okay, Herman, you've been very co-operative. Get dressed."

Throughout the examination Mrs. Quincy had remained seated precariously on the edge of the Morris chair in the consultation room. She looked as if she were about to topple over: the flopping black hat on the graying steel-wool hair added to the illusion of unbalance.

"Well, Mrs. Quincy," Dr. Abelman began, "there's something wrong with Herman, but I'm not sure what it is. I need your help and his. I want you to keep a record of his headaches and his fits."

She looked at him blankly, uncomprehending.

"Look. Get a piece of paper with lines and write down whenever Herman gets a convulsion. Here, I'll give you some."

He fumbled in the lower desk drawer, in a pile of old rolled-up EKGS, electric bill stubs, and irregular stack of prescriptions, envelopes, and stationery, and found a ruled pad that Myron had brought from the newspaper office.

"Now listen to me, and you too, Herman. I want you to write down on this paper every time you get a headache. The date, and how long it lasted. Also if you became nauseated and had to throw up. I also want a record of the next fit you have. How long it lasted, exactly what happened. You, Mrs. Quincy, you watch him closely and tell your neighbors, if they're around, to watch him too. Now this is very important: call me when he has the next fit. I don't care how late it is, call me. If I'm in Long Beach, I can't come back, because it would be over by then. But if I'm in my office, or if I can be reached nearby, I want to see the next one—"

"Dey ain' gon' be no next one. Ah'm okay."

"Like hell you are. You're sick. I don't know how sick, but I'm going to find out."

He advised them that a series of X-rays would be needed. He himself would do the routine work in his office; if more specialized pictures were needed (and already he suspected they would be), he would take them to a specialist. She protested—they were very poor, wouldn't the clinic be better?

"No. If you're my patients you have to trust me. Don't worry about the cost. I'll see that you can afford it. What do you think, I'm a professor and charge Park Avenue prices?"

He took two dollars from her for the office visit. The two dollars already represented an hour's hard work and hard thinking; stuffing the rumpled bills in his trouser pocket, he knew the sixty minutes would generate an evening's worry, a few afternoons in the medical library, any number of phone conversations with the doctors he trusted.

The waiting room was vacant. He bid them goodbye and, motivated by a curiosity he could not explain, peered from the screened window as they descended the stoop. On the street, the youth pulled a ridiculous checked cap over his eyes and skipped lightly away from his unwieldy mother. The doctor watched him prance away down the cluttered, steaming street, thinking: *The little bastard, the little son-of-a-bitch*. It didn't have to be the same one, the one who rang his bell and called him names. They all looked alike in the dark. Besides, that cop, Kaplan, had told him his name was something else, Jess, or Joss, or something like that. He couldn't keep unimportant information in his mind any longer; there were too many symptoms and lab tests and techniques and diagnoses and prognoses and therapies to remember. Who could remember the name of a *tunkele* galoot? . . .

> *A television producer has been researching the life of Dr. Abelman, having hit upon him through a news item about one of Herman's delinquencies. The program is to be the first in a series on the ordinary good people of America. For this, Abelman recalls the great flu epidemic during World War I.*

Each day the commissioner would see no cause for alarm, assuring the public that the disease was on the wane. Yet the official figures indicated no such thing; daily death tolls during the week of October 21 were running considerably higher than the previous week. And since the newspapers efficiently printed the totals each day, much in the manner of the standings in the baseball leagues, the numerical facts in agate type were continually at variance with the optimistic reports from the authorities.

The commissioner's office then put its collective finger on the source of guilt. Who else but the doctors could be guilty? If the commissioner said the disease was decreasing, it *had to be* decreasing. Obviously, the doctors were letting cases pile up, accumulating influenza victims by the score, by the hundreds, and not reporting them until they had a fat batch of cards. Thus cases which were a week or so old would be reported at a time when the number of diseased was *actually decreasing! They had to be* decreasing; the commissioner's office said so.

To fail to report influenza patients on a daily basis, the authorities warned sternly, "is a misdemeanor punishable by a fine of $250 or imprisonment for six months or both. Beginning tomorrow, we have asked the Police Department to have policemen from each precinct call on all the doctors having offices in that precinct to remind them that each day's new cases must be reported on that day and no other. We know that the number of new cases is decreasing rather than increasing. . . ."

To Sam Abelman, in drugged sleep at the wheel of his Dodge, the warning conveyed no terror. The finger of guilt pointed at him; he was among the busiest of Brooklyn's doctors and among the most delinquent in reporting his cases. Time had become a blur, a cycle of ringing telephones, ascents of tenement steps, prescriptions, admonitions, advice, collections of one-dollar fees, and now, more and more frequently, certification of death.

Twenty-four hours earlier, shortly after four in the morning, the phone and the nightbell called him simultaneously. At the door were two patients—the Shapover kid complaining his mother wasn't feeling good, and Ed Dineen saying his oldest son had caught it, Jesus God, and lookin' like death itself. The phone call was from the Leiberman family, his brother Aaron's inlaws. They suspected two cases. Before he had dressed, there was another call, in the same building where the Leibermans lived, and as he climbed into the Dodge with Dineen and Hymie Shapover, Sarah called from the window that Sol Pomerantz' cousin, on Saratoga Avenue, wanted him also.

He had never experienced anything like it. It was like the clinical descriptions of a malignancy—you excised it once, only to have it crop up in three other places, sudden, virulent, unpredictable. The early morning calls depressed him; the incidence of deaths was running higher this week, and maybe it was his imagination, and maybe it was based on accurate diagnoses, but it seemed to him the people were looking sicker, the bug was getting more vicious.

Back at Haven Place, after the dawn patrol, the phone interrupted his breakfast. It was going to be one of those days, one of the merry-go-rounds of general practice that neither LeFevre, nor Biggs, nor Brooks had warned him about. No, that wasn't quite accurate. Dousing his face with cold water, he recalled Harlow Brooks' advice about the "day-in, day-out practitioner," the doctor who lives for the routine, the house call, the office patient. The backbone of the profession, Brooks had called them. He may have been a backbone, Sam thought grimly, but his own could stand some propping. He had been averaging four hours' sleep per night for the past ten days, when the presumed "peak" was reached. It seemed more like a steady ascent now, even if the Health Commission *flatly denied* there was an increase in Spanish influenza.

He noticed that three new calls were on the same block, two of them in the same building. He suspected that the half-dozen wretched tenements on March Place had become a focus of infection. Crowding, poor ventilation, primitive sanitation all could speed the spread of the disease.

A twelve-year-old with matted blond hair and a steady drip of snot from his Slavic nose greeted him at the door.

"Doctor you? My papa Widzik. Family all sick. Papa, Mama, two sisters. You come-it with me now?"

"You bet, Polski," he said. "You can ride back with me like Pilsudski at the front." Widzik was a drunken house painter who had done some work for him when he had opened the office. He was an immense, lumpish man, given to executing dance steps on the sidewalk and crooning the folk songs of Lodz, whenever sufficiently sodden. But he was also violent and unpredictable; Sol Pomerantz had once told him to shut up and he all but tossed the bantam druggist through his front window.

As they parked in front of the tenement where Widzik lived, a knot of people gathered around the car. The spokesman was a flabby little man with a head of Brillo and the pallor of the garment loft.

"Dr. Abelman," he cried, "everyone's sick in there! The whole house. I swear, there's twenty cases in 1718 alone!"

He got out of the car and they surged about him with pleading, dumb faces. Selfishly, Sam imagined them as they would be when he asked for his fee: stupidity replaced by cupidity; their plea would become furtive whines.

"Doc, come by me first! My old lady is coughin' like a trained seal act!"

"Me next, doc, Apartment 4-H!"

"Stop by 5-B also. Sherogrodsky. You treated my uncle, Abe Blaufein."

He walked toward the stoop, fingers and hands clutching at his coattails, the frightened voices demanding his reassurances. A basin of sickroom slop sailed in a liquid arc from an upper-story window and he shouted angrily, "Slobs! Don't you do that again! I'll run you in if anyone else throws anything out of a window!"

He turned on them furiously. "Someone get a mop and some ammonia and clean up that mess!" he cried. They did not move. All that concerned them was their own little choked world, their own apartment with its sick and dying. Outside the door, blessed by mezuzah or crucifix, the world could go to hell.

"You!" Sam shouted. He grabbed the little man with the Brillo hair. "You're in charge of the clean-up detail. You and three of these other big galoots, grab mops and pails and clean up the gutter, where all the crap is collecting." He pointed to the overloaded ashcans, crammed with bandages, gauze, sickroom offal. "And I want all the junk in those cans burned right now. Make a pile in the street and light it!"

"But, doctor," the spokesman pleaded. "My father! He's sick!"

"And he'll die, if you don't keep this place free from infection. Get the hell to work!"

Community effort was beyond their understanding; they lived their crabbed lives in little shells. But somehow they were shamed into action by his fierce Indian face, the authoritative mustache. An Italian lady, in eternal black mourning, appeared with a mop and a pail. Two small Yeshiva *bokhers*, earlocks and all, sullied their scholarly hands by rolling ashcans to the gutter. Mermelstein, the corner grocer, donated a bottle of ammonia.

Not all of them were won over. A toothless beshawled granny sneered at him in Yiddish, expecting that this *goyishe* young Jew with his short haircut and bow tie, would not understand her.

"Ai, better Lemkau should have come!" she murmured. "He is a gentleman, a *mensch*! He don't insult people!"

"So call Lemkau," Sam snapped. "You look like the kind who needs professors."

Brillo-head peered up from his sanitational duties. "We tried, doc. But he says he can only handle so much work. He won't recommend no young doctors."

He left the mopping, burning, and wailing, and, with the Widzik boy steering him, entered the house painter's apartment on the ground floor. He raced through the kitchen, steamy with cabbage smells, and into a bedroom. Two small girls, flat-faced blond children, lay on one bed; their wretched mother, a scarecrow at thirty, was stretched on the other bed. He took their temperatures, prescribed aspirin, sponged them all with alcohol, and was giving the boy the phone number of the visiting nurse service, when he recalled that the father was supposed to be sick also. He asked about the painter. The woman raised herself on one elbow. "He go crazy, doctor. Run from house, scream-it. All sick, he kill himself. He blame-it me for children be sick."

"Can you pay me for the visit?" Sam asked apologetically.

"No got-it money," she wailed. "Stashu take all money. Buy whiskey, I know it. Beat me up."

"To hell with him," Sam said. "Look, if the big galoot goes out and deserts you, let's at least use the other bedroom. Mrs. Widzik, we'll move you back in, and put the girls on separate beds. Sonny boy, you can sleep on the couch."

He resigned himself to not getting paid; but there was no point in not finishing the job. He picked up the frail woman, told the boy to take the sheets, and began carrying her into the other room. Halfway across the kitchen, the front door slammed open and the man of the house lurched in. Widzik may have been sick with influenza, but there was no doubt that he was very drunk. He had on his motley painter's overalls. In one hairy fist he wielded a ten-inch brush, dripping with thick scarlet paint.

"Goddammit family, all sick-it," he crooned. "Paint-it up whole goddam house! Teach you lousy wife get-it sick!"

"Take it easy, Stash," Dr. Abelman said. "Put down that brush and get into bed. You're sick also. You'll drop dead if you keep acting like a horse's ass."

He carried the ailing woman into the room, hearing the painter's hoarse curses and moans. The galoot was chasing his son with the brush, swearing at him in Polish.

Returning to the kitchen, Sam was amazed at how much paint Widzik had been able to spread in a few seconds. The ceiling, the kitchen table, the dreary cabinets had all been liberally smeared with scarlet.

"You bum," Dr. Abelman said, "you should paint that well when you do my office over. You stink. You can't even hold a brush right."

The boy poked a head out from under the table. His silken hair was matted with scarlet ooze; pale-blue eyes peered from under a red mask. "Papa's paint-crazy again," the boy said, quite calmly. "Whenever he drinks too much, he goes paint-crazy. He paint-it whole milk wagon and horse yellow New Year's Day."

"Well, no drunken son-of-a-bitch is going to paint *me*," the doctor said. "Specially when he owes me a dollar and a half for three patients. Give me the brush, Stash!"

"You screw-it yourself, you doctor you. You lousy. You play wit' wife in bedroom. I see. You take money, no cure-it. You and lousy wife, make-it sick kids."

He was advancing, one lopsided step after another, brandishing the dripping brush in front of him. A little trail of scarlet dots followed him across the floor. The bloated, speckled face exhaled cheap whiskey. Sam set his feet wide apart, his hands held low, arms spread, like a wrestler. He had no doubt he could handle Widzik, drunk or sober. But the thought of all that thick scarlet slop smearing his new black serge disconcerted him. What did the textbooks on clinical medicine say about *this* kind of situation?

Widzik lunged, swinging the brush at him. He partially deflected the painter's wooden arm, but the worst had happened. A great sticky path had been smeared down his suit jacket, down the front of his trousers. Raging, he twisted Widzik's arm back and almost tore off the right hand at the wrist. The painter screamed and dropped the weapon.

Sam slapped him in the face, once, twice, a third time; not terribly hard, but with enough of a sting to assert his authority. The painter fell into a kitchen chair and wept.

"I sorry, goddammit doctor, I sorry sonofabitch. My lousy, lousy." He reached out for Sam, his two lumpish arms, reddened up to the elbows, pleading.

"Keep your hooks off me, you cheap bum," the doctor shouted. "Just give me a dollar and a half and get the hell to bed. You're no more sick than I am. But your kids are and your wife is. If you're any kind of a man and not just a drunken slob, you'll take care of them. This little boy has more sense than you."

Widzik bawled, softly, intensely. "No got-it money, doctor," he blubbered. "No got-it single penny."

"Spent it on cheap booze, hah, Stash?"

"Spend it all, pay later, I good for it. You know-it me, doctor. I love-it you. You good man. Treat me good like gentleman."

It was going to be a great morning at 1718 March Place, he could see. Done out of his first fee; his new suit ruined with red paint that would never come off, and for which he would never be reimbursed; and a wrestling match with a drunken Polack painter to perk him up.

He doused his face and hands with alcohol, removing most of the sticky mess. Leaving the Widziks for the Sherogrodskys, who lived down the hall, he found himself feeling sorry for the painter. He had had every right to turn the galoot in to the police. But what could you do with them? They tortured and badgered you (and ruined your new black suit) and then they looked at you like crippled dogs and licked your hand.

Sherogrodsky was an easy one—an old man in a skullcap, propped up in bed, spry and talkative. The family was Lemkau's and the patient was recovering. He gave him a routine examination, finding the heart and lungs normal, the temperature almost normal. They paid without a complaint—Lemkau's patients were conditioned to deliver the money without any arguments. The professor took no nonsense from them.

Up one flight, he called on a family named Oestreicher, strangers to him. They were a childless middle-aged couple, the woman a glandular case, freakishly obese, with a child's terrified eyes. He heard the coughing halfway down the hall and found her propped on pillows, alternating helpless gasps for breath with the coughing. She was quite sick; the fleshy face was dull with the look of grippe. Her husband trembled at the bedside while the great mound heaved, bringing up pink sputum into a soiled rag. After each spasm she fell back on the pillows, her lips pursed and petulant, in search of air.

Sam studied her closely. She must have weighed in excess of three hundred pounds; the flesh on her upper arms lay in little flaps and folds and the soft torso inflated the gray blanket.

"Does she always sleep lying down?" he asked the husband.

"Usual," he said.

"Did anyone ever tell you she might be more comfortable in a sitting position?"

He gestured indifferently and the woman hawked again. Hot tears trickled from the childish face as she fell back again, gasping.

"Well, we'll try an experiment," Sam said. "Sit her up in a chair near the window and let some air into this lousy place. I don't want her to lie down for anything. She can breathe easier and cough easier from a sitting position."

"I can't move her by myself, doc," he protested. "You sure it's the right thing?"

Sam tore off his paint-stained jacket, spitting on his hands. "Come on, muscles, get over there. You ready, lady? Wait till I put you on a diet, you'll be a regular Theda Bara."

She smiled coyly, hooking a hand around Sam's neck. Mr. Oestreicher, handling her port side, almost pitched to the floor as they raised the dead weight from the mattress. For a moment Sam thought he would have a compound fracture on his hands also; it seemed as if Oestreicher would buckle under his wife's heft and break one of his pipestem legs. But they made it, Sam carrying the payload, to an overstuffed armchair at the window, looking out on a vista of broken fences and weeds.

"Now keep her here," Sam said. "She should sleep here, take nourishment here, until she's stronger. She can't breathe flat on her back because of the weight pressing against her diaphragm."

They looked at him blankly. He dashed off a prescription, trying to ignore the husband's plaintive query. "A person is sick they should go to bed, no? I never heard a doctor made a sick person sit up."

"Well, you heard it now, sonny boy. And if you throw her back on her spine, you'll be calling Karnofsky, not me."

There was a coal stove, the pipe thrust out of a window, and a pile of egg-size coals in the corner of the kitchen. No effort had been made to keep the coal confined. It lay on the kitchen floor just as the man of the house had deposited it.

"What's that for?" Sam asked.

"To heat it up good," the husband said. "The landlord don't send up enough heat. He says he's a patriot. He's saving coal for the war."

Sam frowned. "Doesn't he know the city is ordering landlords to maintain heat during the epidemic? He can be fined if he doesn't get the heat up."

Oestreicher spread his hands helplessly. "It don't bother him."

"Well, it bothers me. I don't want that coal pile in the same house where there's a respiratory infection. Get it out. Keep it in the hallway and bring in just a little bit at a time. Besides, she isn't that cold. She's got plenty of insulation."

Stuffing the fee in his pocket, the scarlet coat over one arm, he left. His first thought was to get hold of the landlord and give him a little hell; but he never had the chance. They were clawing at his lapels, taking the satchel from his hand, guiding him first here, then there. In the next two hours he made six different stops, calling on every floor of 1718 March Place. The corridors echoed with hacking coughs, groans, and sighs, the whimpering of relatives. He chased visitors out of sickrooms, battled recalcitrant children who hid under the bed, put the match to infected rags, and threatened to punch an old witch, a sorceress of some kind, who refused to let him into Speciale's apartment. The old crone, waving some kind of dried weeds in his face and chattering away in a dialect out of the hills of Calabria, tried to keep him from the sickroom where Charlie Speciale was running 104.5 with a pulse so slow you could hardly clock it. She bit him once when he shoved her aside; a cuff in the neck pried the teeth loose and when he showed her his fist she slithered away.

He hurried back to the street. There were a few cases in the adjoining tenement, 1720, and he wanted to clean them up. There was an OB due in East Flatbush and he wanted to look at Eunice again; what with the disease intensifying, he couldn't be too solicitous of his own child's health. As he reached the sidewalk, he heard shrieking following him. It was Brillo-head, the pasty little man who had mopped up the street.

"Doctor, doctor! You missed us! Top floor—Feuerstein!"

The little man flew at him, pausing, even in his distraught condition, to mark the scarlet smears on the doctor's suit.

"My father, doctor! He's groaning, something terrible. How come you missed us?"

"How come?" he asked. "I made nine calls here. How can I keep track of everyone?"

He was being propelled up the five flights again, finding it tougher and tougher to make the ascent. Sam hurried through the kitchen to the rear bedroom; he heard the rattling breathing and understood he was too late. Brillo-head's father, a shriveled Orthodox Jew, was gasping his last. He heard the *râles*, felt for the fading pulse, and found almost nothing, and sat down at the bed. The old, stained mouth opened, emerging from the mass of white hair, and Sam imagined he heard a blurred, "*Shema Isroel* . . ."

Women were weeping around the cluttered bed. Brillo-head was on his knees, sobbing huge convulsive gouts of tears into the old man's concave chest. Sam lowered the eyelids over the gummy orbs. He raised a bedsheet over the face, stuffing his stethoscope back in his pocket.

"You should have come sooner!" a woman screamed at him.

"I asked you, I asked you!" Brillo-head sobbed, looking up from the corpse. "Why didn't you come here first?"

Sam shook his head. "Listen, he was an old man and he was dying. I couldn't have done anything for him. I'm sorry I was late, but, believe me, he was going to die anyway."

"You're all the same, you doctors!" Brillo-head's wife shrieked. She was a lank sloven, a head taller than her husband. "You want the money, but you won't put yourself out! We won't pay you!"

Another woman seconded the move. "Not a cent! Papa died! The poor old man with no one to help him!"

Brillo-head and another member of the household were removing the body from the bed and placing it on the floor, in keeping with tradition. An old woman was draping sheets over the mirrors.

"When did he get sick?" Sam asked.

"When?" Brillo-head asked. "Two days ago, I guess. A cold, that was all. A little coughing and fever."

"Did you call a doctor?"

"No, of course not. Just a little cold—"

"Why, you fools," Dr. Abelman said. "The old man has been sick two days, and he dies of pneumonia and you blame me! What's the matter, too stingy to pay a buck for an examination? This man needed medical attention immediately! Not the day of his death!"

They looked at him with dull hatred. He was the most convenient object for their bitterness; not only had he been closest to the old man when he died, but in their primitive minds his tardiness certified his guilt. Sam would encounter it a thousand times; yet he never would be able to take it. It pained him that the blame-the-doctor attitude was most prevalent among his own people. A stranglehold on life, that was their trouble. Life owed them too much, including the one thing it could not possibly provide—a guarantee against death.

He made out the death certificate, getting the information on the late Avram Feuerstein, born in Galicia, from Brillo-head. The little garment worker sniffed tears, apologized for his rude behavior and that of his wife and sister, and paid him a dollar. Sam shook hands with him warmly; the little guy had volunteered to mop up the street, he wasn't a bad sort of *shnook* after all. Leaving, he heard the women screaming at the little man—the new scapegoat.

"You paid him, Hymie! You paid him his blood money? *Oi*, and he killed Papa!"

The shrieks unnerved him and he had to stop and remember what his next move was. The tenement next door, 1720, that was it. He still had a call from this morning hanging fire there, and it was now midafternoon. The encounter with Widzik had ruined his timetable as well as his suit; he smelled like the rear of a hardware store. Rather than make the climb down five flights and up five again, he climbed up the escape ladder and through the roof trap door. On top of 1718, he breathed deeply, resting for a minute. There was a four-foot jump across the alley between the houses and he vaulted it easily, landing on the tar surface of 1720. He had barely started toward the trap door when he heard a low growl. Alert as he was to the menace of dogs, he never anticipated the violent rush of black fur, the white teeth, the uncurled red gums. The mongrel, lurking behind the chimney, belonged to the janitor—a stern warning to neighborhood kids to stay away. He dodged the brute, swinging the satchel on the flat skull. The mongrel grunted, wheeled on wobbling legs, and came at him again. Sam ran to the roof door. There was no time to unlatch it before the black mutt was on him again. This time he used the calfskin bag as buckler and shield, shoving it into the snarling maw once, then slamming the heavy load of instruments at the stupid skull. He opened the trap door and descended. On the first landing he checked his bag. There was a row of teeth marks on it; inside, the glass on his sphygmomanometer had been shattered. He was sure that no course at Bellevue had covered what he had just been required to do.

It was early evening when he arrived back at Haven Place; office hours were already begun, and a few patients were waiting for him. He had eaten nothing since the morning, but his appetite was gone. Sarah insisted he at least have some tea and a sandwich. He obliged, visiting Eunice first for a bedside game of "masked rider."

He gave Sarah a wad of bills and a fistful of coins—the day's work since four in the morning, more money than he normally earned in a week. It was impossible to tell how many people he had visited, and the day was not over yet. After office hours, he tried to fall asleep. But he had forgotten about the OB that was ready to pop—that cousin of Sol Pomerantz in East Flatbush. The urgent call from the father-to-be roused him from a black stupor shortly after ten o'clock, and he was off again in the rattling Dodge. The mother was narrow-waisted, a little pale thing with a contracted pelvis, and he earned his money squeezing the infant into the world on top of the kitchen table. The family forced a glass of sweet wine on him and it made him dizzy. Leaving, richer by nine dollars for his obstetrical work, he was stopped at the door by a short woman in the apron of the local candy-store owner.

"You're Dr. Abelman?" she asked him.

"Yes," he muttered. "Don't tell me—someone's got Spanish influenza, and it's on the fifth floor, and you didn't call the doctor yesterday because you were sure the patient only had a cold."

"Such a doctor! He make jokes yet. Nobody's sick by me, thanks God, knock on wood."

"What do you want me for, then?" he asked. He could have slithered down the wall and fallen into a dead sleep at the head of the stairs.

"From your wife, a message. Three more calls you got, and she said it's better you should make them now than come home and go out again."

She pressed a slip of paper into his hand with the names and addresses of three new calls on it. He gave her a nickel for her services and walked slowly down the steps. He had changed his clothes on returning home, yet he still smelled from paint.

He was back at Haven Place after one in the morning, so enervated that he fell asleep at the wheel as soon as he parked the car. Consciousness left him as abruptly as if he had been slugged by five Paddy Lynches. Two hours later, Sarah was shaking him. She was standing on the sidewalk in her flannel bathrobe, shining the flashlight in his face.

"Sam! Sam! What happened? You didn't get held up?"

"Whah—who? What am I doing here? What time is it?"

"It's after three in the morning! Are you all right?"

He felt as weak as if he were coming out of deep anesthesia. It took a few seconds for him to get his arms and legs in motion, and he struggled across the seat, lowering himself to the sidewalk. A chill autumn mist swirled about the deserted street and he saw Sarah only dimly. Toward Rower Avenue, he could see a smoky fire at the curb —somebody committing sickroom towels and gauze to the purifying flame. He wondered how much good these rituals did. A tinkling of wagon bells aroused him, and in the distance, moving slowly through the wet fog, he saw a horse drawing a creaky flatbed.

"It's Karnofsky's assistant," Sarah explained. "He gets so many calls now he keeps a wagon on the street twenty-four hours a day, picking up bodies wherever he can."

The makeshift hearse, four cheap pine coffins resting athwart the wooden boards, rolled by them. A Negro driver slapped the reins across the horse's butt and the bells tinkled wearily. Any minute Sam expected him to cry out, *Nice, fresh coffins, today!*

"Come in, Sam," Sarah said, taking him by the arm. "You're not to make a single call until noon. I want you to get some hot food and a night's sleep for a change. How can you keep it up? Let them call someone else."

He didn't hear her; he was watching the ghostly progress of Karnofsky's night prowler. A fat lot of good it would do the families, he thought sourly. Didn't they know the dead were piling up in the cemeteries? In Queens, the borough of the dead, there were already two thousand unburied stiffs! The city was asking for volunteer gravediggers, but there had been few applicants. Relatives were going out to Queens on the streetcar, armed with picks and shovels to intern their dead. It was particularly tough on the Orthodox Jews, whose law prescribed immediate burial. Karnofsky might be there waiting with his empty boxes, but the influenza victims would be forced into a lonely limbo somewhere on the flat plains of Queens County.

Sarah helped him undress upstairs. He was asleep as soon as he fell against the pillow. It seemed he had just closed his eyes when he saw her again, standing at his bedside, calling him softly. Sunlight was leaking through the drawn green shades; the clock on his dresser told him it was a little after nine in the morning. Dimly, he recalled having heard the phone ring a few times during the night, and Sarah politely making excuses.

"Sam, I hate to wake you," she said.

He sat up blinking, feeling uncomfortably unshaven and unwashed, fatigue clinging to him like a coating, something with mass, odor, a feel of its own. A faint pressure in his temples warned him that a migraine might be in progress; his throat was unnaturally parched, and rising from the bed he sensed a curious lightness.

"Sam, I wanted to let you sleep until noon," she said apologetically. "But there are a couple of people to see you, and they insisted they had to see you right away."

"Okay, okay, *ketzeleh*," he said reassuringly. "I'm fine, just a little weak in the knees. Who are they? Regulars? Or some of Lemkau's deserters?"

"They're not patients," she said timidly.

"Detail men?" he asked suspiciously. "Some guy with a new vaccine?"

"Oh, Sam, I warned you about sending those cards in to the commissioner! It's a policeman—a cop! And somebody who says he's the district health officer! They want to talk to you about not sending in the cards. Sam, why couldn't you have done something so simple?"

He grunted in disgust, walking to the bathroom. "Why didn't you do it for me, wise guy?" He wanted someone to share a little of his guilt.

"Who can ever tell where you've been?" she complained. "You haven't made an entry in the daybook for three days! How do I know how many calls you've made—or how many deaths you've seen?"

"Ah phooey," he said.

"That's a very nice answer," she said, "very polite. For all I care, they can cart you off to jail."

He tried a scalding shower to unloosen the knots in his arms and back, shaved and threw some aspirins down his throat and drank two full tumblers of water. Superficially he felt a little better; but he couldn't set aside the uneasy feeling that something deeper than exhaustion was making him lightheaded.

They were waiting for him in the anteroom: Patrolman Pope of the 77th Precinct, and a small neat man in derby hat and chesterfield.

"Dr. Abelman, the name is Saunders, G. M. Saunders, district health officer, working out of 590 Hopkinson Avenue. Nothing personal in this, I want you to know. Doing my job for the grand City of New York."

"Stop crapping me up, buddy," the doctor said. "You want to know why I haven't sent in my daily reports, is that right?"

"Now don't get huffy on me, doctor," the little man said. Gold teeth peeked through a cracked smile. Sam seemed to remember him at the polling place in the public school, handing out blotters just beyond the No *Electioneering* poster.

"You have been a prime offender in this matter," Saunders said. "As health officer, so appointed by the commissioner, I'm authorized to check on all delinquent doctors. It's you fellows who are ruining the city's fine record, not sending in your reports. Why, there's a fellah like you in Harlem who sent in an accumulation of six days' cases—two hundred and seventeen to be exact. Now how does that make the commissioner look?"

"No worse than not closing the schools," Dr. Abelman snapped. "Or quarantining a ship, or having enough nurses and enough hospital beds ready."

Saunders turned to the policeman. "Read the law to the doctor, officer."

Haltingly, Patrolman Pope read from a booklet.

" 'The penalty for neglecting to observe this provision of the sanitary code is fifty dollars for each offense. Furthermore, neglect of physician to carry out the provision of the sanitary code constitutes a misdemeanor which may be punished by one year in prison, five hundred dollars' fine or both.' "

Sarah had come in to the room. "Why, that's horrible!" she cried. "My husband has gotten three hours' sleep a night since this thing started—he's treated hundreds of people! If it weren't for people like him the city would be a graveyard. He admits he didn't fill out the cards. He was just too busy, too exhausted. We'll do it right now, won't we, Sam? Then, please, leave him alone!"

"Busy is right," Saunders said, showing gold fangs again. "You know what the mayor of our great city said about extortionate doctors getting rich—"

"Why, you cheap Tammany Hall bum! You goddam ward-heeling punk!" Dr. Abelman was advancing purposefully.

Saunders skipped gracefully behind the officer. "Don't try it, doctor," he said confidently. "You're in trouble enough as it is. Right, Pope?"

Pope said nothing. He had no kidney for the job, ever since the district leader had called him in the night before and given him the word. The city wasn't looking too good on this epidemic or pandemic or what the hell else you wanted to call it. And this was an election year, a big election. They had to get the city off the hook on Spanish influenza; and they already had the cue—lay it on a few doctors, make 'em sweat for it. Especially those guys not handing in their reports, making the daily statistics look so rotten, especially when everyone *knew* the disease was on its way out. The district leader had leveled a fat finger at Saunders, reminding him why he had gotten the job of health officer. There was a hint to Pope also that he could be helped if he played along.

"Lookin' through these records," the district leader told them, "I seen this guy Abelman, a young draft-dodgin' sawbones. He's been runnin' through whole buildings like Rochelle Salts. And he ain't handed in his cards for four days now. Let's start with him. Get him down to the district office to fill the cards out. We'll make an example of him, get his name in the papers, and let him go. I know these little Jew-boys with the mustaches. He'll see the blue uniform and he'll fold up. Just hold him long enough to get the information, then call the reporters at Brooklyn police headquarters. I took care of *them* already."

Recalling the briefing, Pope shivered a little.

"I'm sorry, doctor," the policeman said, "I got my orders. You're to accompany Mr. Saunders to the district health office and fill out the cards there."

"Why can't I do it right here?" Sam asked. "My wife and I—it will take us five minutes! Go, Sarah, get the book—I can remember most of them."

"Remember! You mean you got no records of your own?" Saunders asked. He was stationed a foot behind the sweating cop now, calling out his taunts.

"I said I could remember them," Sam said. "You think I'm a chump?"

Saunders shook his head and tugged at the cocky derby. "Not good enough. You will accompany us to my office, and we'll review everything you've done the past few days. We intend to make an example of a few of you fellows. Will you come along, doctor, or must Officer Pope assist you?"

"Oh, God!" Sarah cried. "You're arresting him!"

Eunice, in her mother's arms, started to laugh. "P'leeceman, p'leeceman! I am de mack rider! Bing, I shoot you!"

Pope smiled at them weakly. "It ain't the police station, lady, it's just the health office on Hopkinson Avenue. Doc, we'll make it as quick as possible, honest. We'll get you back in less than an hour, right, Mr. Saunders?"

"I am not promising anything," the health officer said. "I don't like the doctor's attitude one bit."

"Why don't you take a flying leap at a rolling doughnut?" the doctor asked. "Okay, I'll go. I'm too tired to argue any longer. *Ketzeleh*, I'll be back soon. If Sherogrodsky or Speciale get impatient, tell 'em I'm on my way."

Riding in the patrol car, he began to feel the dull ache in his temples again. Now his chest was hurting, and the back of his neck, too. His outrage, his fury with the crap artists, prevented him from worrying about his own symptoms. The nerve of the bastards! He's knocking himself out fighting drunken house painters, crazy relatives, old witches, and mad dogs—and they have to come arrest him like a thief, over a few lousy postcards. He'd complain to someone, the district leader maybe. That would show 'em—the district leader was a friend of Ed Dineen's. He'd take care of them.

The emergency health office had been set up in an empty store, the lower half of a peeling yellow frame building. As the police car approached, Sam could see a crowd of thirty or forty persons collected around the door. The office, which was supposed to supply home service and keep records on the progress of Spanish influenza, had only three nurses available. Two of them had been making calls since eight o'clock, when they came on duty. The third was trying with no success to keep order in the surging mob around the shabby store. She was quite obviously a volunteer—a pretty young *shicksa*, probably from one of the old Protestant families on the Heights, and her good intentions, her pleas for reasonableness, were lost on the aggrieved citizenry. All they knew was that the city was supposed to supply medical aid. Where was it?

"You run a pretty good office here," Sam said to Saunders. "You'll be cited for malpractice, you don't organize that place better."

Saunders glared at him as they started elbowing through the mob. Sam had brought his satchel with him, hopeful of resuming his calls as soon as the ordeal with bureaucracy had ended. Following Pope through the mob, he suddenly felt a hand gripping his suit collar.

"Hallo, you doctor!" It was Widzik, his speckled painter's cap towering over the crowd of stunted Jews and Italians. "You doctor, come-it my house, quick dammit! City no good, no got-it nurse! Tell us come here for nurse, no nurse!"

He heard a voice whine. "Dot's a doctor, yet?"

"He's a doctor! A doctor!"

"Doc, my old lady—570 Saratoga—Apartment 3!"

They were grabbing at his arms, his coat; someone snatched the bag from his hand. Widzik had him in a bear hug and was kissing him.

"Oh, you goddam gentleman, doctor! I love-it you! Come-it me first, I carry bag for you!" He located the satchel-snatcher, a fat little Greek, yanking the bag from his hands. "You give-it me doctor's bag! Everybody want-it Dr. Abelman, one goddam gentleman, I tell you, lousy people. You follow me, see my kids and old lady first, then take-it care all of you! Everybody!"

The mob, whom he would have occasion to detest, to fight, to moralize with, to preach to, and to curse for half a century, was rescuing him. Widzik was wrestling him to the curb, pushing him into the front seat of his paint wagon; the others were climbing onto the back, still shrieking at him, extracting promises that he would visit.

"It's me next, doc—Donoso—I'm a friend of Traficanti the barber!"

"Come by me, Dr. Abelman, I'm next door to Widzik, 1720, you were there yesterday!"

Saunders was screaming at Pope, "Stop him! Stop him, officer! Do your duty or you'll be reported! I'm warning you people—Dr. Abelman is guilty of not filing his reports! He has to answer to the great City of New York and our great Democratic party for this!"

Pope was looking the other way, grinning. He'd think of some excuse. What was he supposed to do? Keep the doctor from helping the sick? Saunders ran to the wagon, shaking a fist at Widzik.

"You're impeding justice, you! And you, doctor, you're an educated man, you should know better! I'll take care of *you!*"

"Ah, go fugg-it yourself, you piss, you," Widzik said. He slapped the reins and the horse trotted off, saving Sam Abelman from civic dishonor and plunging him into the diseased tenements for another day's work.

The work kept him from worrying about his own symptoms; if anything it was worse than the day before. In addition to the new calls, he felt impelled to drop by his old cases, charging them nothing for a quick visit. Mrs. Oestreicher, the three-hundred-pounder, was improving. So was Speciale and so were several others. But there had been another death in 1718, again from pneumonia.

Back home in late afternoon, he knew he had contracted influenza. It was inevitable, he felt, the way he had been exposed to it. He put himself to bed, trying to sleep off the awful pressing pains in his eyes, around his head, his ears. He vomited bile; he dozed in fits and starts; his temperature hit one hundred and five and then dropped precipitously when the aspirin took effect. Sarah called Max Vogel, and the quasi-military doctor came in that night from Fort Jay.

"You look like my Uncle Hymie after Yom Kippur," Vogel told him. "Whaddya trying to do, make all the money in Brownsville?"

"Why not?" Sam asked thickly. "Should I leave some for you?"

"Serves ya right. You'll be flat on your back for a month."

> Thrasher, the television producer, has come to continue his research.

"I GUESS the doctor is back," she said. "I can tell the noise that old car makes a block away."

Diane had risen painfully and was standing at the window, shaggy forepaws on the sill, the absurd tail wagging lazily. Thrasher walked to the dog's side, looking through the leaf-shaded screen to the street below. The doctor was making his usual tour of the sagging automobile, kicking at the weary tires. On the sidewalk, he busied himself collecting an accumulation of tin cans and old newspapers (Thrasher suspected that old man Baumgart had left them there) and stuffed them into a burlap trash bag suspended from the cast-iron railing above the brick wall.

He was about to enter the house when a Negro youth, several shades blacker than Herman Quincy and much broader in the shoulders, ran up to the doctor and clutched his arm. Thrasher could not hear their conversation, but the boy appeared singularly agitated. The doctor was listening attentively.

"Someone's just grabbed your husband," Thrasher said. "Probably one of those emergency calls he hates so."

She reached for a fresh sprig of grapes. "Oh, he complains about them all the time," she said softly. "But, really, that's what general practice is. You'd think he'd be used to it by now."

Thrasher rose, somewhat annoyed by her lack of sympathy.

"I think I'd like to accompany the doctor. Do you think he'd object?"

"Not at all, Mr. Thrasher." She rose slowly, her shapeless form somehow compressed into the rude outlines of the overstuffed armchair. "The doctor is very fond of you."

He thanked her for her information, bade her goodbye, and ran down the stairs. The doctor and the Negro lad had just entered the car, and he called out to the old man to wait for him.

The overworked engine was coughing and gasping when Thrasher opened the rear door and sat on the edge of the faded seat. Dr. Abelman waved a greeting; the old car lurched off, narrowly missing a stickball player.

"How long since your friend Herman had the fit?" the doctor asked the Negro boy.

"It jes' happen."

"This minute? You ran over from the market as soon as he fell down?"

"Yeah. Das right. He fow down, twitchin' and movin' his arms. I remembeh he say he call you ef he gits a fit. So Ah run over."

"You oughta get a medal. You're a smart fellah remembering me. I ever see you before? What's your name?"

"Lee Roy Bishop."

"You have an uncle William Bishop? He had cancer of the rectum two years ago and I took care of him?"

"Yeah. Das my fambly."

"A very nice fellow."

Thrasher leaned against the heat-sodden seat, marveling at the old man's double vision: he would shake his fist and curse eloquently at a dozen Lee Roy Bishops as they shrieked beneath his window— yet a single Lee Roy Bishop had to be invested with dignity and a sense of importance.

They had driven only two blocks when the doctor wheeled the Buick against the curb. Before them was a market block, a street of stores and street stalls, lined with double rows of cluttered pushcarts. It was something out of a different era, a vestige of New York City fifty years ago. Thrasher had passed by the market once before; this was his first close view of it, and it confounded him. For one thing, it was virtually impossible to get an automobile through the traffic lanes. Whatever area the pushcarts did not occupy was crammed with delivery trucks, piles of open crates, assorted garbage, and the overflow of shoppers and merchants. The ramshackle carts sold everything imaginable: plump fruits and lush vegetables, costume jewelry, corsets, eyeglasses, smoked fish, kerchiefs, and men's ties. The stores— most of them specializing in food—were in the ground floors of tenement buildings, and, while the proprietors appeared to be uniformly

Jewish, the tenants of the upper stories were Negroes. They leaned from soiled sills and rusted fire escapes, gazing down on the milling swarm of buyers and sellers.

The doctor made his way through the throng with quick, nimble steps. He apparently was accustomed to threading a path through the market block; Thrasher had trouble following Lee Roy's muscular body as it trailed the old man. The late afternoon heat intensified a dozen strange odors, and soon Thrasher felt a little dizzy. A store labeled APPETIZING (Appetizing what? Appetizing who? Thrasher wondered) gave forth a miasma of garlic and fish; from the gutter arose the rich stench of garbage; all about them was the characteristic smell of unwashed Negro bodies.

The doctor made an abrupt left turn into what appeared to be an arcade of some kind. Over the entranceway was a sign in Yiddish and some crude drawings of chickens. Following Lee Roy into a dark, cool court, his nostrils twitched at two new odors. Thrasher was a country boy, and he knew chicken droppings and chicken blood when he smelled them. The arena was a slaughterhouse for fowl. To the rear he could see crates of chickens, piled ceiling-high. About them were lidless steel drums, and in several of these he could see the dripping carcasses of chickens enmeshed in wire frames to permit the blood to trickle downward. In one, the dying fowl was still screaming and thrashing as blood drained from its half-severed neck.

Dr. Abelman's short legs wheeled around a corner of the slaughterhouse. Lee Roy was running at his side, pointing to a cluster of people gathered about the supine form of Herman Quincy. The boy's lean body was splotched with blood, and for a moment Thrasher thought he was bleeding to death. Then he saw one of the steel drums overturned nearby, and he realized that the huge crimson stains were merely the drainage from a murdered bird. The left side of Herman's face—one sightless eye, lips, and jaw—was twitching irregularly. The long fingers of his left hand lay on the blood-smeared chest, and these too jerked with involuntary imprecision.

A bearded elder in sanguinary white apron and an undented black Homburg greeted Dr. Abelman and addressed him in guttural Yiddish. From the comments of the other observers, Thrasher gathered that Herman and Lee Roy had been making nuisances of themselves in the slaughterhouse, had been ordered to leave, and that in the ensuing argument a drum half filled with chicken blood had been upset. Herman had been struck by the drum and had pitched to the floor in convulsion.

"How long has he been twitching like this?" the doctor asked. He was on one knee at the boy's side, feeling the delicate wrist for the pulse, placing a burlap bag underneath the beautiful head.

"At least ten minutes, doc," a young man in a soiled undershirt volunteered. "He just pooped out in front of us. He's a pleptic, ain't he, doc?"

"Yeah, sure, professor. Is that your diagnosis?" The doctor set his spectacles on his nose, wiping the lenses on an atrocious orange and brown tie.

The bearded slaughterer, gesturing with his lethal knife, indicated he wanted the body removed, and Dr. Abelman protested vociferously. Without the remotest knowledge of the alien tongue, Thrasher understood that the doctor had reprimanded and silenced the chicken-killer in one rude sentence.

Suddenly Herman's twitching became more pronounced. The jerking of the left eyebrow and cheek quickened, until the entire left side of the face was shaking. The spastic movements of the fingers spread rapidly to include the entire hand, then the forearm, and then all of the left arm. Now the left foot was affected, the dandified tan suede shoe flopping about the bloodied cement floor and making the ridiculous tasseled laces fly up and down. From the foot, the agitation diffused to the left leg, and in a few seconds all of Herman Quincy's left side was a mass of clonic motion.

"He gon' die?" Lee Roy asked shrilly. "Man, Ah better git his ma. He look lak he gon' die."

"Not yet. Stay here and shut up."

"Do something for him already. We don't want he should drop dead here!" the young man in the undershirt pleaded. "Somebody dies in a kosher slaughterhouse, it's a whole *megillah* to get it kosher again!"

Dr. Abelman peered up from Herman's bouncing limbs. "How'd you like to take a flying leap at a rolling doughnut, buddy? Just hold your water. He'll pull out of this in a few minutes. Go cut up some chickens."

But Herman gave no sign of recovering. Indeed, the convulsive seizure was now affecting his entire body. Whereas a moment ago only his left side had been in motion, now his entire form was indulging in the crazed dance. The brilliant yellow slacks billowed and rippled as his lean legs kicked and jigged; the arms thrashed from side to side, and the hands grazed knuckles and fingers on the harsh floor.

"He's out cold," Thrasher heard the doctor mutter. "Perfect god-dam syndrome."

Around the corner, the wild screeching of another stabbed bird ricocheted off the unpainted walls; the crowd around the prostrate youth now numbered more than twenty. The normal quota of side-walk practitioners were advising the doctor on therapy, and with every proffered bit of treatment, the doctor would respond with a tired snarl.

"If you'll all keep your traps shut," he muttered, looking up at them through misty lenses, "he'll snap out of it. The next wise guy who tells me to put ice on his neck, I'll turn him in for practicing without a license."

Gradually the convulsion diminished in intensity. The thrashing of arms and legs subsided, the jerking of fingers and face became less pronounced. Soon, the bloodstained form was still except for labored breathing. The doctor felt Herman's pulse again, nodded approvingly, then placed his stethoscope on the frail chest. One fearful eye opened and looked appealingly at the old man. Herman sighed deeply as the murky cloud of the convulsion lifted. Both eyes open and alert, he parted purple lips and sought his voice.

"Just lay here and take it easy, buddy," the doctor said. "Who told you to go running around a chicken market? You're studying to be a *shochet*, maybe?"

The bearded butcher did not think the doctor's joke was funny. *He* was a *shochet*, a ritual slaughterer, an honored professional man. To hint that a Negro, a *goy*, even in jest, could aspire for such a lofty vocation was disrespectful. Again he admonished the doctor to re-move his patient, and again the doctor answered him in one snappish phrase. The butcher raised his voice and the doctor raised his. It was an impasse.

Dr. Abelman propped Herman into a sitting position. He squeezed his left arm, raising it above the boy's head and watching it fall to his side like deadwood. He grasped the underside of the young man's knee, taking a handful of bright-yellow cloth in his massive fist, and jerked the leg into a jackknifed position. The leg fell back lifelessly.

"You feel anything in that leg, Herman?" he asked.

"Feel sleepy. Lak it asleep."

"How about your left arm. Try lifting it."

"Ah cain't. It asleep too."

"Try moving your right arm. Lift it up."

Herman did so. The right arm seemed normal. The doctor made him flex his right leg, and that member, too, betrayed no post-convulsive weakness.

"It's only temporary, Herman. It should go away in a few minutes."

"Yeh. Ah awright. Kin ah have a butt?"

"A what?"

"Cigret. Lee Roy, you got a butt?"

Lee Roy offered his friend a cigarette and struck a kitchen match on the slaughterhouse floor. Herman Quincy inhaled deeply, shutting his eyes and luxuriating in the redeeming smoke. Tobacco vapor spurted from his wide nostrils in thick twin streams.

"Okay, Herman, I'm going to stand you up now and let you walk. Try your left arm now. And jiggle your left foot around."

Hesitantly, the youth tried to raise his left arm, and this time he got it to the level of his neck. Likewise, his foot responded. The doctor placed one powerful arm around the narrow waist and lifted the boy to his feet. Herman swayed and ducked his head a few times and appeared ready to topple, but the doctor's arm sustained him. He gave the boy a slight push.

"Take a walk, buddy. Make believe you're chasing a couple of chippies."

There was a mild laugh from the audience; the butcher turned away disdainfully. It was bad enough having a *schwartzer* almost drop dead in your holy slaughterhouse—but to get a *meshugeneh* for a doctor, one who made dirty jokes, that was too much for one hot day. He clucked reproachfully and wandered off to dispatch a few more hens.

Herman was walking now, around the corner and toward the high sunlit doorway that led to the market street. The doctor was a few yards behind him, squinting at the youth's legs, grasping Thrasher's arm as they followed the wobbling figure.

"Boy, look at that," the doctor whispered. "Perfect. Perfect goddam gait. Was I right or wasn't I?"

"I don't follow you," Thrasher said.

"Yeah, but I follow him," the doctor whispered, grinning at what he took to be a magnificent display of wit under trying circumstances. "Look at that kid wobble like that. The *gait*, the *gait*. Just what you'd expect in a neoplasm of the cerebral hemispheres. I suspected it all the time."

Herman continued his painful excursion toward daylight. The doctor trailed him like a pointer on the track of a wounded bird. Now Thrasher noticed that the youth was walking in a peculiar fashion. The left knee and ankle were not flexing freely, and the entire leg appeared stiffly extended. Moreover, there was a tendency on Herman's part to circumduct the entire left limb; the outer anterior margin of his left shoe appeared to scrape the floor. When he reached the open doorway, Herman rested against the wall, shading his eyes from the burning sun.

"You feeling a little better?" the doctor asked.

"Some. Mah leg still sleepin' a little. Ah cain't feel it too good."

"You wait with your buddy. I'll bring the car over and take you home. I want Dr. Karasik to look at you tomorrow. You may have to go into the hospital today."

"Ah ain't goin' no hospital."

"We'll argue later. Go sit on that milk crate over there, in the shade. I'll be right back with the car."

The doctor patted Herman on the shoulder and resumed his hurried steps toward his parked car. Thrasher had trouble catching up with him. Once he almost tripped over a barrel of redolent pickles standing on the oven-hot pavement.

"What was that all about, doctor?" Thrasher asked breathlessly. "Have you made a diagnosis?"

"The same one I made a week ago. All that crap from Karasik about epilepsy. Idiopathic, my foot. That kid's got a tumor of the motor area of the right cerebral hemisphere. I was right all the time." He sounded fatigued and heavy with despair; his diagnostic triumph was affording him no pleasure.

"How can you tell?"

"That was a Hughlings Jackson convulsion. And a Jacksonian convulsion is typical of an intracranial tumor. Neoplasms in the motor area of the brain causing focal convulsions and generalized attacks. I saw one once before. This was the same thing all over. Followed by Todd's paralysis—weakness in the limbs. The whole damn picture was there, perfect, so perfect that even a crap-artist specialist could figure it out. Did you see him walk? Spastic hemiplegic gait! I'll bet you a plugged nickel if I examine him right now I'll get an exaggerated patellar reflex and the Babinski sign will be present. A lousy, stinking abnormal picture all the way around."

They were in the aged car now, the doctor honking furiously and cursing at assorted peddlers and truckmen in his way, the tires crunching on protesting vegetable crates. Thrasher felt that a blow-out was imminent.

"What's next, Dr. Abelman? Surgery?"

He sighed, a long, weary *Hiiiiiii*. The gears jammed in neutral, and he wrestled them angrily for a second before answering.

"I guess so. Karasik will take some more encephalograms, and maybe we'll need ventriculography to localize the vicious son-of-bitching thing."

Thrasher wiped his forehead. "Well—I mean—does anyone live after these operations?"

"Yeah. You can keep some of them going a long time. But that poor little bastard! I think it's eating him up."

Double-parked at the entrance to the chicken market, they saw that the colored youths had vanished. The doctor leaped from the car, rushing inside the blood-smeared courtyard. But Herman Quincy had reverted to Josh the Dill; he and Lee Roy had vaporized.

"You made your mistake mentioning the hospital," Thrasher said solicitously. "He's probably scared stiff."

He cursed Herman, Lee Roy, the butcher, the neighborhood. Then, pounding his fist against the strident horn in an effort to dislodge a van unloading sides of beef, he included the driver in his litany.

"You'd think these lice would let somebody through. The bastards won't let you live."

> *With television cameras set up in the doctor's house, and the live broadcast little more than an hour away, there is an urgent call from the police. They have caught Herman, and Herman begs to see the doctor. Dr. Abelman, with Thrasher at his side, goes to the police station; he even stops to settle a little matter with the desk sergeant.*

"ABOUT a few weeks ago, sergeant, I called you about my tires getting slashed. Some galoots went crazy on my block and destroyed my sign. You remember that?"

"So what? I get lotsa calls like that. Yeh, yeh, I remember."

"When I made that call, sergeant, you called me 'Petey.' You used it in a disrespectful manner, to try to lower me to your level, sergeant. I'm glad to meet you to tell you to your face that you acted like a galoot. You know why? Because I'm a physician. A physician is entitled to some respect. I worked hard to become a doctor. I didn't get it by graft or by influence or by knowing somebody. I worked my ass off to get 'M.D.' after my name and I'm proud of it. I don't care if you wear a uniform and represent the city of New York. You are a galoot if you don't know enough to address a physician with a little respect."

His homily concluded, he turned away, not waiting for a response, not seeing Sergeant Felice make a halfhearted gesture of *cuckoo,* a circular motion of his finger alongside his ear. Why? Thrasher asked himself. Why was the speech necessary? Herman Quincy lay dying upstairs, Alice Taggart had almost been raped, a million-dollar program hung in the balance, and all that had concerned Sam Abelman had been to put a fresh cop in his place.

At the head of the stairs Kaplan shook their hands and took them into a small room off the corridor. It smelled of alcohol and urine. The walls were a stained smoky brown; plaster peeled in great chunks from the ceiling. On a folding cot, covered with a faded army blanket, lay Herman Quincy.

"Mr. Thrasher," Kaplan said, "the young lady is downstairs with a policewoman. She's not hurt, just a little upset. We gave her a little sedative. I'll take you to see her in a minute."

Herman's eyes were half shut, his breathing labored. The bandage around his head, now soiled and unraveling, gave him the look of a Hindu ascetic, a starveling fakir, stretched on a bed of hot coals. Kaplan pulled back the blanket. One of the yellow trouser legs had been cut off to reveal Herman's thigh, wrapped in a bloodstained bandage.

"He tried to run away. Or I should say, walk away," Kaplan explained. "I had to shoot him in the thigh." He sounded sorry about the whole thing.

"It serves the little rat right," Dr. Abelman said. "Well, Herman, you had to know it all. You had to run out of the hospital and get in with those *fekokteh* friends of yours. Don't you know you're very sick? Don't you know I'm trying to cure you? Haven't you enough to worry about without going out and attacking people in broad daylight?"

"Go 'way," Herman muttered. "Evah since Ah seen you Ah been in trouble."

"Oh sure," the doctor said, matter-of-factly. "I've been very mean to you." Suddenly his calm manner changed and he was raging and screaming at the ruined boy. "What the hell is the matter with you?" the doctor yelled. "What the hell is eating you that you have to be a louse, a rat? Who ever did anything to you? Why must you be a dirty little punk instead of a human being? Don't you love anyone? Don't you ever want to do something for somebody? Who said the world owes you anything? Listen to me, Herman! It doesn't owe *anybody* anything! Who ever did anything for me for nothing?"

Herman moaned and covered his eyes. "Ah, sheeet. Stop yellin' at me. Who evah hep me? Dey all agains' me."

"Oh, is that so?" shouted the doctor. "Am I against you? Is Mr. Thrasher here against you? Is this policeman here against you?"

Herman turned his head away. "Ah ain' gon' lissen to you."

"Yeah, you bet. Well, I used to feel sorry for you, but I wonder why I did."

Thrasher fought nausea; he rested his head against the dirty wall and immersed himself in guilt. He could not possibly explain it to Dr. Abelman, or the boy, or to Louis Kaplan, but the guilt seemed to him so obvious that he was almost annoyed with them for not pointing the finger at him and driving him from the room. He was the custodian of the word; and the word determined what people thought and did; and when they turned out like Josh the Dill and the Twentieth Century Gents, where else could guilt lie?

Dr. Abelman appeared to be raising his right arm, almost as if he wanted to smash the tan, contemptuous face beneath him; but it was a gesture of despair, not anger, and Thrasher felt bound to alleviate his torment.

"It's really not all his fault," the agency man said hoarsely. "You know—what he reads and sees and is told—all of us—I'm sure the policeman understands—all of us have some responsibility—"

"You keep out of it!" the doctor said quickly. "What the hell are you talking about? This punk doesn't need your excuses. He likes what he is."

Kaplan shook his head sorrowfully. "Mr. Thrasher's on my side. We're all responsible to some extent."

"Sure! Sure we are!" the physician cried in agreement. "But so is he! That's all I'm saying." Then, wearily, he raised his arms and let them flop to his sides. "What did you call me here for anyway, Kaplan? Can't you see he hates my guts? He hates me even more for trying to help him."

"He asked for you."

The doctor scratched his head. "He sure doesn't act that way. Come on outside. I want to talk to you."

The three men walked into the dark hallway, out of earshot. They could hear the Negro boy's heavy breathing, a rhythmic, moribund noise.

"He has to go right back to New Hill for radiation, maybe surgery. He's sick as hell. Who can say how long he'll live? How he kept going with those two holes in his skull, I don't know," the doctor said.

"He's under arrest, doctor," the policeman said. "He can only go to a city hospital, to the prison ward. It'll have to be Kings County."

"Okay, Kings County. Karasik is on the staff there. See that he gets there right away. I suppose you'll see to it that your slug is taken out of his leg. He's got enough *tsuris*."

"Sure, doctor. It was nice of you to come. He's very ungrateful, I must say."

"You think he's any worse than the rest of my lousy patients?"

They walked back to the little room. "Herman, you're going to another hospital in a little while. Dr. Karasik and I will come to see you later tonight. Now try to be a good boy for a change. I'll call your mother and tell her. Shall I tell her you asked about her?"

"Go 'way," Herman muttered.

"You're a punk, Herman," the doctor said contemptuously.

They started down the stairs again, Kaplan remaining on the upper story, and promising to notify Dr. Karasik as soon as the patient-prisoner was removed to Kings County. He told Thrasher where he could find Miss Taggart, thanked both men again, and returned to the inner room.

At the bottom of the staircase, the doctor shot a parting glance at Sergeant Felice, but that worthy was not eager for a new exchange. He buried his two-inch brow in the blotter.

"Let's get out of here," the doctor said.

They had taken a step or two when they heard Kaplan's voice calling to them from the stairs.

"Oh, Dr. Abelman! Herman would like to talk to you for a minute."

The doctor turned around. "What does the punk want?"

Kaplan smiled weakly. "He says he wants to apologize to you. He's sorry for what he did."

"Oh, he's sorry, is he? That's just dandy. He shoots up a few people, slashes tires, beats up an old man and rapes a little girl and tries the same on Mr. Thrasher's assistant and then he's sorry. Not to mention getting fresh with me. I'm very glad he's sorry."

"I think he really means it," Kaplan pleaded. "As soon as you left he began to cry. He wants you."

"Tell him to go to hell!" the physician shouted. "I've had enough of his crap! And that goes for all of them!"

Thrasher thought he was going to faint. He battled an attack of vertigo, and, steadying himself, grabbed the doctor's arm.

"Time is running out, doctor," the agency man said. "I do think we should get back for a last-minute check. Remember, we've got a program to do yet. I don't want you to get upset. That boy seems to have unnerved you. Really, he isn't worth it."

"I wish you'd come up, doctor, only for a minute, it might help Herman if you did." The young policeman would not be denied.

"All right, all right. Didn't I tell you something once, Woody? The bastards won't let you live. You go see your little girl and I'll accept His Royal Highness's apology, the louse."

He began trudging up the stairway, his muscular, bent figure growing dimmer in the crepuscular light of the station house. Thrasher watched him walking a little stiffly from the arthritis, and then turned, looking for the room where Alice Taggart was being comforted by the policewoman.

The noise that made the executive spin about, a kind of grunt or cough, the noise that a man would make when punched unexpectedly in the groin, had come from the head of the stairs.

At the top step, the doctor was doubled up, leaning against the banister. Kaplan was standing over him solicitously and again Thrasher heard the peculiar grunt. He raced toward the stairs, flying up the steps, putting his hand on the doctor's back, on the sweat-soaked green shirt.

"What's the matter, doctor?" he cried. "What's wrong?"

"I don't know what's happened," Kaplan said breathlessly. "He was walking up toward me, and when he got to the top, right here, he made that funny noise and bent over, with his hands on his chest."

"Ah. Ah. Ah, you son-of-a-bitch," the doctor groaned. "Oh, you louse. You dirty rat. I'm all right. Not a word to Mrs. Abelman, either of you punks. Oh, you bastard."

He straightened up and they were horrified by his face. It was gray and moist; the creases and wrinkles appeared to have been dug deeper and the dark hollows beneath his eyes seemed to have widened and grown blacker.

"Oh. Ah. Like a lousy vise, closing right in," the doctor said. "Let me lean on you a minute, Woody. I'm fine. I'm all right."

The pain had struck him suddenly—a giant vise squeezing his breastbone. No sooner had it commenced compressing his chest than he felt it radiate to his jaw, his neck, his shoulders, his left arm, right down to the wrist. Resting against Thrasher for a moment, he began to massage his chest, rubbing his right palm and fingers against the offended sternum, cursing and grunting, alternatively.

"Ah. Bastard. What a louse. Won't get the best of me. I'm too tough for any lousy coronary."

Thrasher's legs trembled; they were dissolving and for a minute he feared he would tumble down the narrow stairwell. What amazed him was that the doctor could diagnose his case so quickly and still appear unperturbed. The occasional grunt, accompanied by a hunching of his shoulders and a painful grimace, seemed to be involuntary: gestures that only intractable pain could wring from the stubborn old man.

"Little morphine be very good now. That crazy Maxie, will he have the laugh on me."

It seemed the ultimate in irrelevant nonsense that at this critical point in his life he could be distressed about Max Vogel having the laugh on him. He was still rubbing his chest, trying to ease the relentless pressure, grunting and grimacing every few seconds.

"Can I help?" Kaplan asked. "Would you like to lie down and rest? We have a bed. . . ."

"The officer is right," Thrasher added. "You do look a little pale. A rest might help you catch your breath."

"Rest? Don't kid me, sonny. I got a coronary. Nice thing about being a doctor. Don't you know I'm a helluva diagnostician? I figured it out right away—ah—ah—ah, you bastard."

The policeman and the agency man exchanged terrified glances; at the base of the stairs a group of uniformed cops and detectives gathered.

"What do you want us to do, doctor?" Kaplan asked. "Shall I call an ambulance?"

"Nah. To hell with them. It would just scare Sarah and Eunice. Help me to the car. Woody, you can drive. Now, damn it, when we get home, not a word to Sarah or Eunice. I got indigestion. I ate too much. Don't worry them or I'll knock your block off."

They paused momentarily. From the room where Herman Quincy lay dying they heard the boy's voice drift toward them.

"Whuh happen out deah? Deh doctoh okay? Ah wan' 'pologize. Ah ain' mad at you, Doct' Abelman. You done try hep me. Y'all gon' see my ma? Y'all tell her Ah ain' mad at you. . . ."

Dr. Abelman squinted at Kaplan.

"What the hell do you know. He's a human being after all."

"I don't think you ever doubted it, doctor," Thrasher volunteered.

"Ah—ah—bastard," he grunted. Then, raising his head, he looked toward Herman's room. "I guess I should talk to the little rat. C'mon, Woody, give me a hand."

"I think not," the agency man said quickly. "I think we'd better get you home."

"Yes, I agree," Kaplan added. "I'll convey any message you wish to Herman. I'm sure glad he said those few words."

They each took one of the old man's arms, Thrasher finding it hard to believe that the enormous iron biceps could ever be destroyed, and began the slow descent.

"That little louse Herman," he muttered. "Apologies from him yet. Well, he's not my worry any more. I did what I could."

Step by step, they aided him down the stairs, watching him wince every few seconds, watching the color drain from his face, amazed by the vigor with which he kept massaging his chest. They guided him through the cluster of law officers, down the stone steps and into the ancient Buick. Thrasher climbed behind the wheel and Kaplan sat in the rear.

"I forgot my bag," the doctor complained.

"I'll come back for it," Kaplan assured him. "I think we better get you home in a hurry."

A sooty dusk descended on Brownsville, a warm mist that seemed to soften the tired buildings, the trash-filled streets.

Remember Me to God

by MYRON S. KAUFMANN

An immensely gratifying long novel, with unflagging tension around the question of a mixed marriage, Remember Me to God is remarkable not only for its thorough exploration of this key theme, but because of its extraordinarily vivid characterizations. Least involved in the mixed-marriage theme, for example, is Richard Amsterdam's little sister Dorothy, yet the psychological portrait of this unhappy stutterer captures every fluttering image in her troubled, innocent soul.

Equally well achieved is Kaufmann's portrait of the self-deceiving prig, Richard Amsterdam, who attempts to show that a Jew who learns to ape the manners of the Brahmins can be accepted not only into the Hasty Pudding Club at Harvard but eventually into the soft-speaking world of New England bankers and industrialists, the real American rulers.

Adam Amsterdam, a lower-court judge, with his profound desire to do justice in the squabbles that come before him, his pathetic efforts to continue Jewish customs at home, his willingness to consent, for his son's happiness, to the mixed marriage that tears across his own beliefs, is a monumental and yet unidealized portrait of a good Jew.

One of the postwar writers who most clearly shows the mood of self-examination that followed the self-assertion of the war novel, Kaufmann provides, in his hero's dialogues with a rabbi and a Christian minister, here excerpted, a classic recapitulation of the religious-identity debate. And he has made utmost use of his theme in showing patterns of contemporary Jewish life—the temple activities, the visit to the old shul, the family at home, the college contact with the Gentile world.

Kaufmann, who was born in 1921, is, like Angoff, a product of the Boston Jewish community and Harvard. Working as a news-paperman and writing on the side in the old traditional way (the newer tradition is to work as an English instructor) he took eight years to produce his first novel and another eight for his second, Thy Daughter's Nakedness, again concerned with an American Jewish environment. After several years on a news agency in New York, Myron Kaufmann has returned to live in the Boston area.

M.L.

CAN GOD see me now?" she asked timidly, as Bessie sponged her tummy.

"Yes," Bessie told her.

After her bath she would be put to bed, and often lie awake for a long time in the darkness of her little room, thinking about God. God had remarkable powers, of which the most wondrous was His power to see right through the ceiling. He was always spying on Dorothy naked. She found this out gradually, through constant inquiry. Many times, when she had nothing on, in the bathroom or in her bedroom, she had asked her mother, "Can God see me now?" and her mother invariably answered "Yes," or "God watches you all the time." So Dorothy knew He was always peeking.

Her mother was also privileged to see her naked, but that didn't count, and besides her mother was only a lady. But God was male, and privileged to enjoy a free show every time Dorothy got undressed. It was no use to hide modestly in the closet; the roof was glass to Him. He could even see in the dark. Thus God and Dorothy continued in a relationship of boudoir intimacy, from which she had no escape. She knew He also amused Himself by watching other girls, and by watching big ladies, but He was so terribly great and all-powerful that she felt no jealousy.

Dorothy also loved God for another reason. He was Jewish. So Dorothy and God had that in common: they were both Jews.

She pictured Him as graying and distinguished, with a regular hair-cut, and clean-shaven. His suit was always neat, and He wore cuff links, and had a stickpin in His necktie. His face was straightforward and wide-eyed and artless, very like Daddy's, but many times bigger.

He was thoroughly Good. He had floated through the void as a spirit, and created Himself, and then created heaven and earth. He had made Dorothy.

Dorothy was startled one day to learn that the neighborhood kids also believed in Him. She had thought only Jewish people believed in God, while Proddistins and Cathlicks believed in Jesus Christ, who had a swear for a name. She pictured Jesus Christ as a crafty-eyed sinister man in a white robe, with greasy black hair tumbling to his shoulders, and a Fu Manchu mustache. But the subject came up by chance among the children on the sidewalk, and Dorothy found out to her surprise that the other kids believed not only in Jesus Christ but in God too.

This upset her. She had no way of being sure now that God was really Jewish. The Proddistin kids seemed confident that God was a Proddistin. The Cathlicks were equally sure He was a Cathlick. There were several Proddistins and Cathlicks in this discussion, standing about near the telephone pole they used as goal in hide-and-seek, but only one of Dorothy, so she held her peace. But at night she lay awake worrying.

The homey intimacy of her relationship with God seemed in jeopardy. The Proddistins were the main part of the human race, and there was danger that God might be tempted on that account to be a Proddistin.

She still had a belief that He was really Jewish, but it was anxious and uneasy now. She prayed and pleaded with Him for a miracle, to show that He was Jewish. But nothing happened.

After several days she thought up a setting for a miracle. She acquired one of the cardboards which the laundry sent with Daddy's shirts, and took it to a little table in her room, where she marked the cardboard in pencil with the letter *P*, *C*, and *J*.

Then she shut her eyes tight, clutching the pencil in her fist, and punched the cardboard with random violence again and again, until she persuaded herself that she had forgotten the exact location of the three letters and that God was now guiding her hand. She let her fist come to rest, and slowly opened her ayes. The point of the pencil was on the *J*.

Ah! A miracle! He's Jewish!

She remained sitting at the little table, feeling pleased, but in a few moments doubts again began to trouble her. Had it really been a miracle, or had she remembered where the *J* was and made it come out that way herself? She resolved to try the experiment once more, to see if the pencil could also come to rest on the P.

Again she closed her eyes tightly, and the pencil in her fist punched the cardboard vigorously and repeatedly. It came to rest.

With bated breath she opened her eyes. This time God had come out a Proddistin!

Dorothy hunched her shoulders fearfully, in a gesture unconsciously like her father's. She wished she had had the prudence to be content with the first miracle, instead of angering God by demanding a second one.

> Richard has managed to get onto the business staff of the Lampoon, where he almost feels fully accepted, even by a type called Fertile-head.

THE MOST CONSTANT subject of Fertile-head's humor was the mob of unattractive Jewish students who commuted to Harvard every day from run-down neighborhoods at the other end of the Boston subway, some of them unkempt and others worriedly reading. Richard knew that the spectacle of Jewry was comic in a sense, and that Fertile-head was not altogether wrong. But although Fertile-head somehow failed to identify Richard with these subway boys, Richard identified himself with them. As a very small boy he had lived in the same part of the city they came from, and he could still remember it, and his father working there in a butcher shop after quitting the abattoir. He knew that their families differed from his own only partially, by neighborhood and degree, with infinite merging gradations between—unstable gradations that continued vaguely above the Amsterdams for that matter, with overlapping of relatives.

Richard's family, and all the Jewish families he knew, accepted as a matter of course their nearness to immigrant origin, improving upon it with varying effectiveness, and accepting also the refinements of the nicer neighborhoods to which they had moved. A few of the gentile kids he had known in the suburbs would occasionally mock a Jewish stereotype, but on the other hand he had been sufficiently accepted by other gentile neighbors to take their daughters bowling, so that none of these attitudes was really new to him.

Nevertheless, he began now to watch his own manners, his voice, and his clothing more carefully. The finer, newer points he tried to learn by watching Bill Hodge, in order that he might be above reproach. Some of them he wrote down in a notebook, in his little room on the top floor of Eliot House, in order to clarify his thinking and to keep them for review.

> *With most foods or drinks, it is polite to serve your friends before yourself, but wine is an exception. With wine, you pour a little into your own glass first, then fill your friend's glass, and then finish filling your own. This is so your own glass will get the cork dust floating in the bottle.*

> *If you ask a friend to buy you a nickel's worth of pipe cleaners on his way somewhere, most middle-class people would think it is polite to offer to reimburse him when he brings you the pipe cleaners. But it is even more polite not to offer to reimburse him, as that way you compliment him by showing you think he does not need the nickel.*

> *If you belong to an exclusive club, you never mention this club in the presence of a non-member. If you are not a member, you never mention it in the presence of a member. You act as if it did not exist. This is good form. Also, a boy who goes to debutante parties never refers to them in the presence of a boy who is not eligible and vice versa.*

> *The main thing in a true gentleman is integrity of character. He is kind and tactful by instinct, because he has no snobbery. He is on the level with everybody, whether it is the biddy who sweeps his room, or whether he is being introduced to a king. His respect for his fellowman makes him poised in any situation.*

With passing months Richard's knowledge of the *Lampoon* staff sharpened. He learned that Pillbank and Fertile-head had attended obscure private schools near their homes, Pillbank in Maryland and Fertile-head in New Jersey, and he deduced that while both had made the Hasty Pudding neither had been invited to join a final club. He thought of them secretly as petty climbers. Fertile-head always wore his Pudding necktie. The towering Pillbank was stuffily eager to be pals with all the others.

Yet Bill Hodge, who was more patrician than either of them, seemed less aware of rank, and often seemed to prefer Richard's company to theirs.

Meanwhile Richard's notebook began to contain longer entries, composed in a careful scrawl late at night.

Do not let the snobs get you down. You will go farther than they will in the long run. America is getting slowly more democratic all the time.

But the real Yankees that keep the old Puritan values are another matter. The Jews can learn a lot from them. The Yanks live below their means and they don't care if they look cheap. But they know how to enjoy life, and a father and his sons arise before daybreak together to shoot flying geese from a small rowboat in the marshes. A Jew doesn't know enough to take recreation. He just keeps working, working, working, so his wife can show their friends that they have some new kind of a piece of furniture or rug that all the Jewish ladies have just found out about. His idea of relaxation is to take his wife to a restaurant for lobster or Chinese food and bicker with her there instead of at home. Or if he is the easy-going type that doesn't like to bicker, his wife considers him a dope who has nothing to say. I knew one case of a Jewish couple that kept on going out to lobster restaurants together even though they were not speaking to each other, and the children had to carry messages. Sometimes the men start a Masonic lodge to get away from their wives, but all they do there is get sore at each other in arguments over who should be the officers. A Jewish mother thinks she is a better housekeeper, but actually she is too good. She wants a fireplace, but she won't allow a fire in it, because it might get dirty. She keeps yelling at the kids not to play on the lawn. You hesitate to invite a friend for dinner because you know she will make a whole operation out of it, and spend two days cleaning and cooking too much stuff and worrying and making all kinds of complicated jello molds with whip cream. A Yankee mother reads intellectual books, and if the house is a little dusty she still enjoys life. In a fairly nice Jewish home often the only books are some worn out fairy tale books they bought years ago for the children. Yankees give their daughter horseback lessons, but Jewish mothers just yell at their daughter to practice piano. Of course not everybody can afford horseback lessons, but even if a family is poor they should make every effort to at least send their young children to a neighborhood dancing school, even if for only once a month, instead of always putting piano and music lessons first, because dancing develops poise. Millions of Jewish parents don't seem to realize the importance of that. We have a lot to learn from the Yanks.

He showed the notebook to Jeanie Cooper, and she read it through twice, deeply impressed, telling him it had profound insights. This encouraged him, and he began to think of printing it some day privately, as a guide to other Jewish boys like himself and families like his own who wished to improve themselves. Inside the front cover he scratched a title:

HOW TO BECOME A GENTLEMAN
—(HANDBOOK)—
ANONYMOUS

Jeanie suggested that the text include something about Jewish indifference to alcohol. She told him that after meeting him two years ago she had for a time been uncertain whether he was Jewish or not, because although it seemed he must be for the college to assign him to live with Larry Leavitt, yet he did not look it and never spoke of it, and she had not felt certain that he was until he refused some whisky offered by a drunk at a football game. She said a gentile would either take proffered whisky gratefully, or else make a friendly excuse about being "on the wagon"—but a gentile would not casually dismiss good bourbon without any reaction at all, as though it were water.

"Damn good point," Richard nodded, fixing it in his mind.

The notebook grew to nearly twenty pages, and he visualized it as someday reaching a hundred, and being distributed through the temples discreetly. He considered that he might even expand it eventually for the use of Irish and Italians and Armenians and others, because the more he thought about it, the more he felt that all American minorities were longing for just such a specific handbook as this, to assist and guide them in their efforts to become more dignified, and Jeanie agreed with him that in setting out to compose one he had undertaken a noble task. He believed the need for such a book to be so great that he wondered why no one had ever thought to write it before.

Jews should cultivate a taste for good Scotch. They should not drink so much ginger ale and other tonics.

A boy who happens to have a big hook nose should be especially careful not to walk slumped forward.

Jews are right in wanting to move away from Roxbury and Dorchester as soon as they can, but they should spread out more thin over all towns, instead of beginning to settle thickly in Brookline and Newton. There should never so many move into one neighborhood that the gentiles start to move out, because then they defeat their purpose and are back where they started, only in a different location.

They should also learn to play squash, instead of just hand-ball all the time.

A gentleman, if he had a very good position, or if his father had a very good position, he would avoid telling anybody. For instance, if your father happens to be the president of a very famous bank, and somebody asks you what your father's occupation is, you just answer that he works for a bank. You let it sound as if he were only a clerk or a teller or something. In the same way, if your father is a judge, you shouldn't mention this fact, if possible. You just say your father works for the State, or you say he is a lawyer, or you can just say he works in the courthouse, or something like that, just so it sounds small and unimportant.

A gentleman does not put his wallet in his pants pocket. He puts it in his inside jacket pocket.

Girls should not think it is more refined to get taken to expensive places. They should notice that Yankee girls are not fussy if their boy friends do not spend any money on them. A well brought up girl considers it a good time to just take a walk.

Yet he knew that for the time being at least, he would not dare to show this notebook to anyone but Jeanie. He had the feeling that other people might misunderstand it. In observing the manners of the well-born, he felt that maybe he was doing something that looked undemocratic, although he believed very strongly in democracy.

Lying awake, he would consider that some of the habits he had marked down to be acquired and mastered did indeed have merit, although others were plainly arbitrary and imitative. The fact that he was the only boy on the *Lampoon* who was not eligible for the Pudding came often to his mind. He wondered if the fact of his being a pal now of several Pudding members made him somewhat eligible. But he did not think so.

Richard knew also that it was undemocratic to think of such things, and that he shouldn't. The whole trend in the country was toward greater democracy and the obliteration of social distinction, and Richard was glad it was. Most boys, he was sure, whether in the Pudding or not, would have thought it undemocratic to *want* to be in the Pudding or to give it any importance.

It was confusing. In a way it was undemocratic to want to learn the mannerisms of the eligible, and purely social aristocracies were certainly the most stupid of all aristocracies; but the challenge to learn all their mannerisms was that if he could not—even though their mannerisms be intrinsically no better—then his inability might indeed give the well-born some sort of argument in their own minds as to their superiority over him.

He did not want anyone, even a relatively small society of people, to feel in any way a superior order of being to him; even the fact of knowing that people who thought themselves superior were fools was not enough—he did not want the fools to think it was Richard who was a fool. But he was troubled, because he could not explain this to himself without thinking it sounded illiberal and small-minded.

He felt that such matters were nothing, or should be nothing, and that he shouldn't give them a thought. But he was not sure what quite all the *Lampoon* boys really thought of him, just as for that matter he had not been sure what Mrs. Hodge had really thought of him, so that at times he felt an uneasiness with some of these boys, without even being certain who had started the uneasiness, he or they. And then he reasoned that his uneasiness was itself a Jewish neurosis or mannerism that he ought to try to cure.

But on the other hand, he thought one night as he lay in bed, in a way it *was* democratic to want to break into the Pudding, if his motive was to set a precedent, and open the gates to all those types who were now excluded.

He reflected that the finest of these influential Beacon Hill blue bloods, especially the younger generation of them, were boys who wanted to become more democratic and less exclusive. And by mixing with them, Richard was helping the process along.

*Being on the Lampoon has given Richard entree to a dance,
where he has met Wims, the voluptuous if slightly overblown
daughter of a proper if not top Boston family. Their affair has
progressed to the point where her father—a widower—is alarmed.*

"I DIDN'T GET your message till way late," she explained. "I was out all
afternoon looking for a book. And then I had to wait a long time for a
bus."

She looked small in the big chair. She tried sitting up, far back
in it, her feet not touching the floor, and then she put her feet on
the floor, her back slumping. All the time she kept her eyes on her
father. Her face was wary. Under the oil portrait a square clock with
gold curlycues rang a pretty quarter-hour, and the log popped loudly,
sending up a shower of sparks behind an iron screen.

He poured a little whisky into the bottom of his glass.

"Would you like a cocktail?" he asked.

"No thanks," Wimsy said

"You know, Wims," he said, studying his glass, "I've tried to be
both father and mother to you girls. Of course money isn't easy to
make these days, but I still have my health, and I still have hopes,
although naturally, at my age, a man's career is a race against time.
But I carry a lot of insurance. If anything happened to me, Wims,
your mother's family couldn't say you three girls weren't provided
for. You'd go to live with them, naturally, but the insurance money
would be there when you came of age."

"Did you make me rush all the way home just to go over this
again?" Wimsy asked uneasily.

"No. I didn't." He took a sip slowly, looking into his glass, and
then looked at his daughter again. "As I said, Wims, I've tried to
take your mother's place. But maybe sometimes a girl doesn't con-
fide in her father the way she would in a woman."

He arose slowly, putting down the glass, and went around his chair
to open the drawer of a desk. He took a letter or two from it and a
package of photographs.

"I'm glad to see you're having a good time taking pictures with
the Brownie Kath gave you last Christmas," he said, flipping the
photographs deliberately. "Aggie slipped around to the druggist Sunday to pick up your films, but before she got back you'd rushed back
to Cambridge. You've been in a rush to get out of here lately, Wims.
Kath is the same way. She used to be content to sit on the floor and

let me tousle her hair, and now she isn't." He stopped flipping the photographs and held them in a pack. "I used to look forward to having my girls all together on a weekend. Especially now we're coming out of winter, and the brooks are full, and the woods are going to be green again, I thought we could all pile into the Buick the way we used to, just as soon as it's warmer. But I don't know if you'll want to. You come in at the last moment, sometimes not till Saturday night, and you mope around in a fog, and then you duck out back to Cambridge Sunday before dessert's half off the table. I know you can't be having midyear exams at the beginning of March. Do your courses really need so much study, Wims? Or do you think you've fallen in love with some lad over there?"

She reddened but said nothing, her hands spread on the wide arms of the chair.

Talbot went back to his seat, putting the letters into a pocket of his lounging-jacket, and began to look at the snapshots again.

"These are nice pictures you took, Wims, but kind of monotonous. They're all of the same boy, about forty of them. You must have spent an afternoon walking the whole length of Brattle Street and snapping his picture against every tree." He looked up just enough to ascertain that she had reddened deeper. "That fire is putting a nice red glow in your cheeks," he remarked. "Now about this boy in the pictures. He seems like a good-looking chap—clean cut—mm-hm —not bad—looks like he could defend himself with his fists. Doesn't smile much, though, does he. I guess young people still feel it's smart to be melancholy—and to think I thought that went out with cloche-hats and prohibition. Well now, I see you got him almost smiling in one picture. I guess that's why you took so many—trying to see if you could get him with a smile." He held up the smiling picture a moment and then returned them all to a pocket of his jacket. "Is he nice?"

"He's very nice!" she blurted defiantly.

"I see." He spoke a little louder and not so gently. He stretched sideways and from the opposite pocket drew some folded papers. One rattled as he opened it. "I wonder if those pictures have any connection with a letter I got in yesterday's mail. It's on the stationery of a couple of shysters that call themselves 'Hanrahan & Amsterdam' and it's signed by 'Adam Amsterdam'—how a man gets a silly name like that I don't know."

Wimsy turned ashen.

"This Hanrahan, incidentally," Talbot said, "is none other than The Great Francis Xavier Hanrahan, the so-called Honorable. I had somebody find out."

"Who's Francis Xavier Hanrahan?" Wimsy asked sullenly.

"He's one of the biggest bums in the State Senate, that's who he is. One of Curley's crowd. Or one of Tobin's—it doesn't matter— they're all bums. He was on the Governor's Council for a little while, some years back, and now they say the Catholic Archdiocese slips him some business on property transfers—in return for condemnation tip- offs, no doubt. Where Amsterdam fits in I don't know—I guess Han- rahan needed somebody to write the deeds. It sounds like one of these Jew-Irish law-office teams where Paddy sucks around the poli- ticians and Solomon figures the loopholes."

"He's a judge," said Wimsy.

"Wims, he's the most petty kind of judge. He's not even on a reg- ular salary. He's what they call a special justice. They pay him a few dollars when they need him. It's like a substitute on call, for the lowest kind of court. And apparently his only qualification for the job is simply that he happens to be The Great Hanrahan's law part- ner. He's completely undistinguished. Now do you want to hear his letter?"

Wimsy said nothing.

"Do you? Or aren't you interested?"

"Yes," she said in a weak voice.

He adjusted the position of his bifocals. Some of the long hairs on top of his head slanted upward above him like floating strands of cobweb. "He starts, 'My dear Mr. Talbot.' I notice he's got it 'Wal- bot' on the envelope, but he's got it right inside."

> It has come to my attention that you have a certain daughter Wilma, also known as Wimsy, with whom my son Richard are considering themselves engaged to be married.

He paused and glanced at her pale face. "New paragraph," he said.

> With all due respect to the merits of your daughter, my wife and I have talked this over and feel as I am sure you will agree, namely that such a marriage is not in the best interest of all con- cerned. It so happens that my son Richard and your daughter

Wilma *according to my understanding are of two different religious faiths, and I am sure it is your experience as it is mine if you search the record that such marriages of a mixed background are uncomparable and do not work out for the best interest. I am sure you will understand that this is intended as no personal reflection on your daughter but as I am sure you and your—*

Talbot halted and looked up solemnly at the portrait before lowering his eyes again.

—but as I am sure you and your wife are concerned of the welfare of your daughter, you will advise her that a mixed marriage is not good for anybody.

Thanking you I remain very sincerely yours—

He dropped the letter to his lap and blew a sigh of exasperation.

"Now what's this all about, Wims? Who's he talking about? Is that the boy in the pictures? That you wasted half-a-dozen rolls of film on?"

She lowered her face.

"Have you actually told this whelp you're engaged to him?"

"Yes." She spoke onto her bosom, almost inaudibly.

Talbot was silent a moment, with his lips tight. When he spoke his voice was tired. "Wims, do you know what this letter has done to me in the last couple of days? When I read it, it fell out of my hands. And although I've gone to the office I haven't done a lick of work—I'm a nervous wreck over it. Don't you know what the welfare of you girls means to me? You must know, because I see you had better sense than to bring him here for my approval. You didn't dare tell me. I had to learn of it from the boy's father. Now you might like to hear a letter I've prepared in reply."

He unfolded another sheet of paper noisily.

Dear Sir:

I have received your letter and noted the information therein, and will thank you to keep your boy away from my daughter.

Yours truly,

Frederick G. Talbot

He folded it again and returned it to his pocket, his lips tight and angry. He arose and pushed the iron screen aside, dropping Adam's letter into the fire. It lay there, rocking and browning in the heat, and suddenly caught, flaring and shriveling. Wimsy burst into tears.

Talbot gave a grunt of disgust. He uncorked the whisky and downed a bit more. He looked at his daughter, standing with his legs apart. She wiped her eyes with a handkerchief and controlled herself.

"Damn it, Wims. I didn't send you over to Radcliffe to run around with Jews and gypsies."

"He isn't a gypsy."

"They're all related. What in the name of God has gotten into you, Wims? Last year it was all that Catholic stuff. Nunneries, and flopping down on your knees all over the house. And now this. Next year I suppose you'll join the bolsheviks, or run off with a Frenchman. What do you think life is, a game of make believe? Now calm down and pull yourself together. I don't want your eyes all bloodshot at dinner."

He waited until she blew her nose. Behind him the log broke and tumbled with a soft crush of ashes.

"Listen to your father, Wims," he said quietly. "You think it's smart and clever to run around with a Jew. You think it's glamorous, liberal, romantic. Don't you."

She looked at him, her eyes round and wet, without answering.

"I sent you to Radcliffe, to be near Harvard, with the idea of giving you a solid education. But it's all going awry. You've got a head full of the New Freedom. And I have a suspicion these daffy labor courses have got a lot to do with it."

"I only took one labor course. And they aren't daffy."

"You took others along those lines, though, Wims. I wish you'd major in something solid, like literature, or classics, or geology, instead of all this gaseous stuff like 'social theory'—half the men that teach it are humbugs and fakers, and the fashions in those fields change before you can learn the stuff anyway. You don't get your money's worth out of an education with those courses. There's no meat to them. If you'd stick to something like history, or English literature, or German literature, or astronomy, you'd have something substantial that would always be with you. The basic stuff of an education. But with this sociology stuff, along comes a new professor, and a new windbag, and a new theory in a couple of years, and all the theories you learned in college are out of date. Here today and gone tomorrow. It isn't worth it. I told you that before."

"You said I could major in anything I want."

"I didn't say you could major in Jewish boy friends. I've granted you a lot of freedom, Wims. But unless you show me you can exercise some judgment, I'd sooner spend that dormitory money on taxicabs to bring you back here every day after classes. You're only nineteen, Wims. And you've got a lot to learn. You're still a child. Engaged to be married—God!—do you know what marriage means? Do you think I could take this boy into Mr. Bullock's office and say, 'Mr. Bullock, meet my Jewish son-in-law?' I couldn't, could I. You know I couldn't. It would sound pretty poor, wouldn't it."

"The Hodges associate with him," Wimsy protested. She seemed defiant through her tears. "And he knows the Pauls, too. And he belongs to the Hasty Pudding."

Talbot was somewhat taken aback. "Are you sure of that?" he asked. "He's in the Pudding?"

"Yes."

He shook his head. "Well, maybe they're all breaking down over there. Or else he must be an adventurer or a climber of some sort. And as far as the Hodges and the Pauls are concerned, they're more secure than we are. They're rich, they're eminent families, for generations so to speak, and their position is established. They can afford to have a Jew hanging around—we can't. Wims, don't you see it's your happiness I'm thinking of? You three girls are all the world to me. I want you to have the best that life can offer—I want you to feel at home with good books and good music—I want you to understand plants, and growing things, and the creatures of the field and forest—to hear the rustling in the trees, Wims. And I want you to make a good marriage. I put myself in hock for five years to give you a proper coming-out party. And I'll do the same for Kath, and I'll do it for Liss. So help me, as your mother in Heaven is my witness, I'll earn the money somehow. The least gratitude I can show to your mother's memory, is to see to it that her children don't lose position because of the marriage she made. You've no need to throw yourself away on this boy. On your mother's side you're well-born. You know that. You're connected to the Lees and the Cabots. And do you know what it means to be married to a Jew? It means in effect that you become one yourself, and you've no need to. That boy's name and race would close half the best drawing rooms in Boston to you."

She tightened her face, turning it and lowering it to her shoulder, and wept silently.

"Come to me, Wims."

He extended his arms. She ran and embraced him.

"There, now," he said. "Dry your eyes. You're a good girl. As soon as I put my coat and vest on again we're going into dinner, and you don't want your sisters to know you were bawling."

> *Talbot appears with Wims in his car one day when Wims was to meet Richard.*

"Now just a minute, young fellow," said Talbot. "I came here to talk to you. I've always let Wims have everything she wanted, and I suppose this is no time to stop it. But I'd like to tell you something man-to-man, as a friend, for your own good. Wims isn't in love with you. She may think she is, right now, but you're just a passing craze with her. You'll see. You'll find out. I know my daughter a lot better than you do. And she's only playing with you."

"That isn't so," said Wimsy.

"Wims," her father said, "you're just having an emotional jag feeling a lot of this damn social significance. I know you better than you know yourself. That's all it is, Amsterdam. She'll get over you. That much I'm sure of. But I know she's capable of making herself sick in the meantime, and that's why I'm here."

"Why don't you let Wimsy and me decide if we're in love or not?"

"Yes," said Wimsy.

"She gets these enthusiasms, Amsterdam. She'll tire of you."

"I won't tire of him," she said.

"I'll take that chance," said Richard.

"I'm afraid I'm being forced to take it too," Talbot said to Richard with a little sigh. "I'm going to let her start seeing you again, if she wants to, under certain conditions and with certain stipulations. But I'm making no secret of my hope that nothing comes of it. The whole thing's against my better judgment. But for the time being anyway, I want her to take some food and get a little color back into her cheeks. A few more of these faints like this morning and she'll do herself some damage."

It thrilled Richard to learn that Wimsy had been waging such a campaign against her father on his behalf. But he kept his face solemn.

"But there's something I don't understand about you, Amsterdam,"

Talbot continued. "I notice you're wearing a Pudding tie. And I believe Wims saw you at the Paul girl's coming-out party. Now I know such things are enjoyable, and I know they can be flattering—I wasn't born to them. But they do have a purpose, a function, and in your case you seem a little bit afield. In other words, just why a lad of your faith wants to float around in circles like that, unless he wants to become one of us, is more than I can understand. If you wanted to become a Christian I could understand it. But if you mean to cleave to your own people, as I'm told you do, I don't quite see what you were doing on the Pauls' invitation list. I think you realize that I'm just a little curious as to your motives."

"No motive," said Richard.

"Well, I'm not quite clear what you're up to. I'm not satisfied. And I don't intend to see Wims get hurt."

"You're the one that's hurting her."

"Don't be surly, young fellow! You're spoiling a good impression! I'm older than you, and I've come to you, and you might have the courtesy to address me with a civil tongue."

"Yes, you're not being nice to Daddy, Richard," Wimsy said.

"I didn't get the question," said Richard.

"I asked why you don't convert. I like your looks, and you move in some good circles and seem to have a desire to, and I don't understand why you haven't converted. Especially if those are the circles you want and you feel you'd be all right there. Unless it's a question of your parents' feelings, if they're old-style."

"No, they're not old-style. It's a question of my own feelings. I'm not ashamed of what I am."

"Well, I don't see that. I'd think your type would want to convert. That's what confuses me. I wish you'd clarify the picture of what you are by converting. As you stand now you're neither fish nor fowl, and as much as I hope Wims doesn't end up by making a fool of herself over you, as long as there's a chance that she might I'd feel better about it if I knew you were sincere and willing to go the whole hog and become one of us, and not some kind of adventurer. It goes without saying that you'd convert if you married Wims."

"I didn't think she wanted me to convert."

"She told me she wanted you to and you wouldn't."

Richard looked past him to Wimsy, but she put a finger to her lips for silence, unseen by her father.

"This Stringfellow Todd is another of her crushes," Talbot said, "and she's got her heart set on having you baptized by him."

"I thought Todd was in England," said Richard.

"He's back," Wimsy told him. "He was in the commandos, and he got wounded and he's in the hospital."

"Think it over, Amsterdam," said Talbot. "You're not the orthodox type. You're modern and you've been around, and I assume you've got an open mind. At any rate I'm told that the Pauls and the Hodges think you're a square-shooter. Now, I'm a deeply religious person, and I'd think in that case, you being an alert and openminded fellow, you'd look at it from the viewpoint of your own soul. Your people have for centuries been driven by a feeling of unsatisfied longing, because they haven't accepted the Saviour. And it's that feeling of longing that drives them and makes them the way they are—their genius, and always trying to get money, and dabbling in radicalism, and migrating from country to country in search of a peace they can't find. Every one of those traits is an effort to fill that agonizing emptiness of soul, because their souls are looking for something—because your whole race is bothered by that longing. Maybe you don't feel it."

"He does feel it," Wimsy told her father.

"I don't have any longing," Richard said.

"Oh, Richard," Wimsy pleaded. "Daddy's almost won over and you're complicating it."

Richard felt confused.

"Consider it, boy," Talbot said. "I know you're a stiff-necked people, but I can also see you're too educated for those outworn ways. Look into your soul, with your eyes wide open, and ask yourself, why all this climbing? What possesses you to grasp for clubs and honors, and the invitations of the great? Isn't it another form of that restlessness that plagues all your race? What do you think your hungry soul is crying out for? Maybe you have your own idea about it—I know psychoanalysis is the big thing nowadays. But I'm one of the few people I know that's read the whole Bible right straight through. And religion and the Holy Writ have been a big comfort to me. Maybe it's my rustic background. But I've had grief in my time, and I found then it was Christ I turned to. Christ Jesus. I never knew how religious I was until then. I suppose that's why I'd always stayed Congregational. I never became Unitarian. Search your own history, Amsterdam. Wasn't it after the Jews denied the Saviour that your religion went stale, and got bogged down in these petty regulations and all that Talmud business? That's why it dried up then—that's part of your punishment. When you turned your back on the Saviour you shriveled and dried up."

"Wimsy," Richard asked, "can you get out of the car and have lunch with me?"

"No, she can't," said Talbot. "We've got to pick up her sisters at Sunday school and then we're going for a drive in the country." He switched on the ignition. "I'm about done, Amsterdam, but there's one more thing I want to make clear to you. And that is that I don't consider Wims engaged to you. She can see you, but she's not engaged. And now you'd better go in. You'll catch your death of cold."

"He's got an iron constitution," Wimsy said.

Then, signaling to Richard from behind her father, she puckered her lips to be kissed. He went around the automobile and leaned into her window. She put forth her face.

"Not in my presence, please," Talbot said. The engine began chugging.

"Oh, Daddy," she pleaded.

"Well, then be quick about it." He idled the engine and turned his face away, raising his right hand as a blinder.

Richard stuck his head half into the Buick and she kissed him as passionately as she could. The car began to roll. Richard did not withdraw quickly enough and the metal frame struck the side of his head with a blow that made him see stars. It swung him around and sent him reeling.

The automobile drove off, and he saw Wimsy leaning out to blow a kiss with her gloved hand.

.   .   .   .   .

As HE NEARED A CATHOLIC CHURCH the half-hour sounded high above him in the clock tower, and it occurred to him to go into the church and rest. He crossed the street toward it, glancing in both directions, but westward he could hardly see because of the excessive sunshine and the bright puddles. An automobile splashed his trousers with mud as he reached the opposite pavement.

In the darkness of the church he could see at first only the multicolored circle of stained glass, high and far before him. The Sunday

Masses were over, and there seemed to be no one there. Slowly he went down the aisle, his hand touching each pew. Now he saw panels of stained glass to the sides, and the little tiers of candles in red glasses on racks, and finally the entire soft dimness became visible.

He sat near the front, his eyes resting on a great suffering Christ made of white plaster. As he relaxed he saw a middle-aged woman kneel before the rack of little red tumblers. Apparently she said a prayer, but he did not see her lips move. She lit a candle, and it became a point of light, waving in the red glass, beside a row of others. She's praying for a son at war, Richard thought. He watched her cross herself. Then his gaze drifted above the red tumblers to a dust-covered saint who stood in a corner alcove, a shadow within shadows. It was larger than life-size, a bearded figure, and its gentle hand rested in the air, over the head of the woman who had lighted the candle. The sockets of its eyes were misty, and it seemed to have a sadness that was peace, a poverty that was wisdom. Richard looked at it a long time.

Then he looked again at the plaster Christ, writhing and twisting upon the Cross, the ribs naked and the eyes turned in and upward with horror. The notion of men killing God suddenly struck him with a fascinating and terrible newness, as though he were hearing for the first time the phrases of his childhood playmates. It was an idea alien and fearsome, diabolical yet tempting, like striking out and conquering one's elders. If he had thoroughly escaped from his father and chastised him and beaten him, he could then weep for his father and pity him. The love that was awe would then become the love that was remorse, and that was how Judaism became Christianity. He thought this all at once in a flash, and when he tried to capture it to see if it was an idea worth holding, it seemed as if he had already forgotten important parts of it.

The woman passed Richard, and when he saw the lines in her face he knew she believed. He dwelt for a moment on how different this woman's mind was from his own, and yet such people had always lived side by side with him. He looked again at the plaster images. What a lot of bunk it is, he thought.

He remembered the synagogue, and how at one point three men supposed to be hereditary priests but otherwise quite ordinary had emerged from the congregation to wail a special blessing loudly, their faces hidden under their prayer-shawls like bogymen, and how outlandish it had seemed to him. All religions were alike in this respect, he thought—that some people could vulgarize them in ways that seemed offensive to other people, and that either vulgar people or cultivated people could at times find solace in them, provided they were done up according to taste. He thought of Mrs. Hodge reciting the Twenty-third Psalm, and of the minister Toddy entering battle because of his private theology and now apparently hospitalized with a wound.

It occurred to him that his own life would be much simpler if he had chanced to be born a Protestant. The notion of a divine-yet-human Begotten Son to mediate for mankind was as attractive a myth as any, if one were going to have a myth, and he would have enjoyed a Protestant environment.

Suddenly he remembered the insistence of Mr. Talbot that Richard really wanted to convert without knowing it. Just below the hairline of his forehead he felt himself beginning to perspire. It seemed too easy a surrender. But what argued against it? Except habit of thought and stubbornness? Wasn't there an honesty in admitting he would rather have been born something else, and a greatness in shifting to the form of church that he found most congenial?

For the moment it seemed frightening and impossible. But then it seemed very possible, and quite courageous. He wondered why he had not let himself think of this before. It was obvious now that he had indeed borne an unsatisfied longing all his life, exactly as Mr. Talbot had said, and now that he considered accepting the Saviour, that longing in him really did seem on the verge of fulfillment, just as Mr. Talbot had predicted. It was a remarkable thing—the efficacy of the Christian myth. He really felt different, as if a burden to which he had been used all his life had for the first time been lifted from him.

He arose and walked out preoccupied to the sidewalk and headed toward his room, smiting his hands together once. He had much to think through.

He pictured himself attending church with Wimsy and their children, and mentioning to everyone freely that he had been born a Jew but that he had accepted the Gospels because he had an open mind and had found it a better religion. Better for Richard Amsterdam, anyway—others could do as they liked. What's there to be ashamed of in that? America guarantees freedom of conscience, so why not have the courage of your convictions?

He considered that it was natural, normal, and healthy to want to conform, to succeed according to the standards of one's country, to be a Protestant in a Protestant land, to be in the center of the community in which one lived and grew, and to rise as high in it as one could. To be known in Boston as a banker and head of a family and trustee of cultural institutions—to be known in the nation as an industrialist and adviser to politicians—to feel the nation's pulse throb under his hand.

To be fully a part of things did not mean to shut himself up in a minority, to be two people, to split his personality. If he wanted the Yankees to accept him fully into their way of life, he should accept their way of life fully.

What then was the pull of his own relatives that had held him apart from his friends and acquaintances? Just the notion that he would be a traitor to the Jews if he converted, that was all. And would he be a traitor, actually? Would his conversion do any harm or cost anything to any other Jew? Was it anybody's business but his own? Was anybody going to be slaughtered or persecuted because Richard Amsterdam changed his faith? Nonsense.

There is not one rational reason, he said to himself, why I or anyone like me should continue to be a Jew. No matter what men say about spiritual values, deep down they all want a beautiful wife and ten-thousand-a-year. And why should a modern, educated agnostic force himself to adhere to an unpopular minority sect? If a man really likes that crabbed life, or believes in it as some do, let him adhere. But if he doesn't like it, if his energies cry to expand into the mainstream of human activity, and he yet restrains himself, out of supposed conscience or sentiment, if he thinks he must closet himself in a small cult that doesn't really attract him—sacrifice of that kind isn't noble, it's neurotic. Prejudice was going out, and this compulsive need to cling to a religion you don't like should go out with it.

Let a man test his strength in the market place where he lives. And can he ask for a position of leadership while remaining alien?

As Richard saw it, his conversion would be a truer assertion of himself, because he would insist on his Jewish blood all the more. As a Christian by conviction, of Jewish origin, he would publicly champion various causes of the Jews. Everyone would know exactly what he was.

There was a good feeling that he was indeed making his own life, and that he was unbound, like primal man born anew. He felt vigorous. There seemed nothing he could not do.

Wimsy began to see him again, almost daily, and she was delighted with his new thinking. They decided his baptism should wait until Toddy was well. She said she considered herself engaged to marry him, and that Toddy would perform that ceremony too, and that she was sure her father would agree eventually.

Richard sent Bessie a postcard, saying he was seeing Wimsy again and that he was planning to enter the Congregational Church. He warned in the card that his family need not try to contact him until they were ready to accept him as he was, Wimsy and all.

Every day he did a lot of thinking. He believed that his mind and his emotions had been half-crippled before, and had only now been straightened out. . . .

Richard has broken with his family.

ONE DAY DURING THE NOON HOUR, when Richard climbed to his room in Eliot House to deposit some lecture notes there before lunch, he was surprised to notice that the door of his room was ajar, since it had always been closed in his absence. But without troubling over it, he took advantage of its unlatched state to kick it wide open. His shoe made a dirty mark on the white paint, and the wooden mass swung away from him sluggishly.

There, inside the room, was Adam, seated in the Windsor chair. Richard was startled.

"I've been sitting here waiting for you," Adam said. "I told the janitor who I was, and he let me in." He did not rise from the chair.

"What do you want?" Richard said in a tone of hostility.

"I know you're sore at me," Adam began, attempting a smile.

"I'm not sore," said Richard. "I just don't have anything to discuss with you, that's all. We don't seem to speak the same language."

He tossed away his lecture notebook and it passed in front of Adam and landed on the desk with a smack.

"But we can talk, can't we?" said Adam.

"We'd only get into a fight," said Richard. He was standing with his back to the door.

"Well, I know how you feel," Adam said quietly. "Those letters I sent, to your girl friend's father, and the dean. You feel I was interfering in your business."

"I certainly did."

"Well, I admit maybe it wasn't the best way. But believe me,

Richard, I was only trying to do what I thought was the best thing for your own good."

"You seem to have an uncontrollable urge to do everything you can to hurt me, and then explain it as being for my own good."

"No. Please, Richard," said Adam. "That isn't the truth. How shall I say it? Sometimes I make a mistake. It's a difficult thing to be a parent. You'll find out yourself, when you have children."

"Well, you're forgiven, if that's all you want. You could have saved yourself the trouble of coming down here."

"Richard," Adam said, looking down at his fingers. "I'd like to let bygones be bygones and start paying your bills again." He looked contrite.

"I don't want your dough," said Richard. "I'm getting along all right."

"No strings attached," Adam said.

"No thanks," Richard told him. "I just want you to let me alone, that's all. I don't need your help."

Adam sighed uncomfortably, rubbing and pressing his powerful hands. "Well, that's up to you," he said. "But I just want you to know that I'm your father, and I'm always ready if you need anything. If you're ever in any kind of trouble. In the meantime, I'm here to ask you a little favor."

Richard narrowed his eyes suspiciously.

"You don't have to do it for me," said Adam. "Do it for Mother. Tonight is Passover."

"I won't be there."

Adam was silent a moment.

"Well, it's a free country," he said finally. "But everybody will be there, Aunt Fanny and Uncle Eddie with the children, and Grandma —Aunt Lydia and Uncle Harry and everybody, and they don't know about all this yet. They expect to see you, naturally, like always, and your mother is sick already over what to tell them if you aren't there—"

"Tell them the truth, for Christ sake."

"Please, Richard. I'm begging you. Am I asking anything so difficult? Just to sit there."

"I can't. That supper is a religious service and I can't honestly attend it. I wouldn't feel right."

"Don't keep standing in the door like that, as if I was a stranger. Sit down like a human being, so we can talk."

Richard walked toward the studio couch. As he passed Adam his eye fell on Dorothy's little box of fudge on the upper shelf of the roll-top desk, with two pieces and some crumbs remaining. He offered it but Adam waved a refusal. Richard sat on the studio couch.

"So you're really going to be a Christian, then?" Adam asked.

Richard nodded.

"It's a matter of my conscience—being honest with myself," he said. "And I wish you'd either accept it as such, or else just let me alone." He did not feel like discussing it with his father just now. There was a strange quaver in his voice and a shake in his arms, as if it were cold in the room. He was in his tweed jacket, and he was not sure whether the room was really cold, or whether it was a peculiar nervousness in his body, independent of his mind. He wished he could control it, because the quake kept his voice from sounding firm and dignified.

"Well, I guess I've failed," Adam said.

"You haven't failed," said Richard. "It's not the salesman's fault if the product is unsalable."

"Well," said Adam, "even assuming the salesman's no good, or you don't like the product, and you're making up your mind that you've decided to buy something else—Christianity—even assuming that you like the principles of that religion—did it ever occur to you that there might be certain conditions where Christ and all the saints would like it better if you didn't convert? Where you might be showing more of a Christian charity, if you didn't become a Christian? I remember a certain story, Richard, a fable, about John the Baptist. It seems that John the Baptist and Jesus Christ were going around the country with a jug of water together, baptizing people, and telling everybody they met that they'd go to hell if they didn't get baptized. But one Jewish boy wouldn't get baptized, and he said he'd rather go to hell. He said, 'I'd rather go to hell and look after my poor mother and father, because they never got baptized, and if they're in hell, my place is in hell next to them, so I can fan them a little in the heat, and shoo the flies, and try to make my parents a little more comfortable. So no thank you, I'll stay unbaptized like my parents, because I want to go down to hell if my parents are suffering down there, because they need me.' And so what did Jesus and John the Baptist do? They told the Jewish boy he was absolutely right. They told him to stay Jewish and go to hell with his parents, because he already had more of the true Christian spirit the way he was."

"Where did you get that?" said Richard. "That's a dumb thing."

"It's just a fable," said Adam.

"Whose fable? Where does it come from? It certainly isn't Christian, and it doesn't sound Jewish."

Adam tossed his head sheepishly and gave a little smile. "Well, I made it up, actually," he said. "It came to me a little while ago in the car, while I was driving down here."

"I might have known it was yours," said Richard. "It's not worth anything as an argument anyway. I could invent fables too. You can make up fables to prove anything you want."

"Well, it just brings out the idea that religion should be like a cement, that holds a family together. I don't want you to be mad at me, Richard. Whatever I did, I'm asking—you're the only son I have. I don't want you to hate me."

"I don't hate anybody."

"Well, I'll tell you what," said Adam. "Come out and have lunch with me, like a good feller. Let me buy you a good lunch. And we'll talk it over. Man to man." He arose and took up his coat, looking steadily at Richard with a beckoning gesture.

Richard finally consents to lunch.

. . . Adam looked with approval at the mirrors and the yellowed hunting scenes. Then he studied the menu, and they both ordered the liver plate. Despite Richard's aloofness Adam had an air of jolly camaraderie.

"And bring us each a Scotch and soda, nice and cold," he said.

"The Scotch-and-soda first?" the waiter asked.

"No, with the meal," Adam told him.

"You don't drink that with a meal," Richard said when the waiter had gone.

"Listen, just because you never saw me drink a Scotch-and-soda, that doesn't mean I never had any. I like it once in a while. You and I don't eat out together often—let's make it good, the best of everything."

What a dope he is, Richard thought.

"I know you're used to the highest-class type of associations these days," his father continued. "Don't think I have anything against it. I appreciate a refined type of living as much as the next one."

This remark irritated Richard.

"Listen, Dad," he said. "I wish you'd get one thing straight. Get over the idea that being around the Hasty Pudding is what caused me to convert. I'm not that superficial."

"I didn't say it did."

"But you think my head's been turned by a view of gracious living, and you think wrong. Listen, I'm mature enough to know a Jew can drink Scotch-and-soda without converting. You've got a lot of things confused here. Some Jews may even have a hell of a lot more graciousness than Wimsy's father has, as far as manners goes, if you want to know the truth. He's not especially a well-mannered guy. But what moves my conscience is entirely separate. It's a matter of my inner convictions. Plus the fact that I love someone, and the way I feel about my relation to the whole thing. It's what you could call a kind of unsatisfied longing. It's kind of a pull toward the larger community, that tells Jews in their consciences that this fetish of separatism is wrong. I had it even as a little kid. Mr. Talbot calls it a longing for Christ, and I do have such a longing. It isn't just snobbery—it's this larger liberation that Christ brought, where instead of long chains of father begat son begat grandson, you have individual souls. In the Old Testament they worry about the seed of Edom, and the seed of Amalek, or cut off somebody's seed. Keeping track of everybody's sperm, in other words, as if that were the main thing. But in the New Testament, the soul just floats in independent. I'm not expressing it well because I didn't expect to be talking to you about it and I didn't have my thoughts prepared. But this unsatisfied longing is a spiritual thing. I've felt it."

"Your girl talked it into you that you have a longing for Christ?"

"No, she didn't. Her father just happened to mention it. But he didn't talk me into it. I agreed with it."

"And you fell for that old business?" said Adam. "That argument about the Jews having an unsatisfied longing, it's so old it's got whiskers on it. There's even an old joke about it. Do you know the joke about Jesus and the unsatisfied longing?"

"What's this, another one of your fables?"

"No, it's a real joke," Adam began, smiling expectantly. "It's about this feller Cohen, and he had a feeling of longing. So he mentioned it one day to a Catholic priest that happened to come into the store, and the priest told him, 'Come to Jesus.' So he took a trip up to heaven and he found Jesus there, walking in the garden. And Jesus put on a big smile and He said, 'Well if it isn't Cohen! Hello, Cohen!

So tell me, nu? How's by you? How's business?' So Cohen said, 'Everything's hunky-dory, only sometimes I get a feeling of longing.' And so Jesus said, 'Cohen, should I be frank with you? I have a feeling of longing myself.' "

"I don't get it," Richard said contemptuously.

"Wait a minute," said Adam. "So Cohen said, 'How is it, up here in heaven you should still have a feeling of longing?' And Jesus said, 'I'll tell you. In a ritzy place like this, the butler buys the groceries. And ever since they put that shagetz Saint Peter in charge of the gate, I haven't had a decent piece of pickled herring.' " Adam's smile broadened and he waited for Richard to laugh.

"All right, kid around," said Richard. "I think you're in pretty damn poor taste."

The waiter came with their plates of liver and their glasses of Scotch-and-soda. They began to eat, Adam taking one or two sips from his glass. There was no conversation until each had taken several pieces. Then Adam cleared his throat.

"You know, Richard," he said, "a lifetime is a good long time to be married to the wrong girl."

"She isn't the wrong girl," said Richard. "We've slept together a couple of times, in spite of the so-called difference of race, and brother, we had one-hundred-per-cent compatibility, right at the very beginning. If you know what I mean—right at the same instant, practically. Without any previous experience or anything, and some couples take years to achieve that. If you don't think we were made for each other you're crazy."

Adam had begun to blush while Richard was speaking.

"I didn't realize you slept with her," Adam said in a low voice. "I never slept with your mother before we were married."

"Well, you're out of date on a lot of things. Times have changed since then."

"It's a fine thing, when morality is out of date."

"I don't mean in just that way. I mean all your ideas—what you think about intermarriage, for example. And what would you rather, anyway, that I went out and picked up some cheap bum, instead of sleeping with the one I love and keeping it sacred?"

"Well, no," said Adam. "I don't say you shouldn't go out and have some fun once in a while. But I was a clean-living youngster when I was your age, and it wouldn't do you any harm to live clean either. I was pretty pure when I got married, if you want to know the truth.

If you want to talk about it intimately. I went with the fellers to a prostitution house once, down in the South End somewhere, and I was so disgusted I couldn't do anything. That's the truth. I went downstairs and waited for the other fellers, and I let on I did it. I'm telling you the truth, since we're on the subject. And I never went back there. The only time I wasn't a virgin was over in Paris in 1918, there was this sort of a restaurant where they have ladies that come and sit on your lap with nothing on, and all that kind of business, and you can go with them upstairs, that kind of a place. But outside of that in Paris, that was all, and I didn't get married young, either. I was going on thirty years old. But I've never regretted that I lived clean. I still enjoy good health on account of it. I'll admit there was other times when I could have, but I didn't."

"Well, chacun à son goût."

"What?"

"Everyone to his taste."

"By the way, that reminds me, speaking of that, Dorothy asked an interesting question last night. She wanted to know, if you should marry this girl, and you have some little boys and they're Christians, would they be circumcised or not."

"What does she care?"

"Well, they'd be Dorothy's nephews. She was just curious, I suppose."

"Well, I never thought about it. They might be, for health reasons, I guess. I don't know. Tell Dorothy to mind her own business."

They made their way slowly, each through his piece of liver, Adam occasionally washing down a bite of meat with his stale whisky-and-soda. Sometimes he rotated the glass thoughtfully on the tablecloth. The jaunty spirit had gone out of him and he was beginning to look anxious.

"Richard," he said finally, "can't you see that all I'm asking you to do, is be true to yourself?"

"And can't you see that that's all I'm doing?"

"No, I can't see that," said Adam, "because you're repudiating your parents, and to despise your parents is to despise yourself, because you came from your parents. You can't respect yourself unless you respect the people you came from."

"I don't despise you, I just disagree with you. Can't I disagree with you? Dad, if I were to go on trying to be a Jew, I'd be living a lie. I'd be giving myself a split personality and living two lives and tearing myself apart. That's what I've been doing all my life and I'm sick of it."

"You're trying to be something you're not."

"On the contrary, if I kept on pretending to believe in Judaism I'd be trying to be something I'm not."

"Listen, whatever you believe or you don't believe—am I asking you to go around with a tsitsis hanging out? I'm just asking you to know you're a Jew, to say you're a Jew, that's all. Go ahead, marry the girl if you love her so much. If you're in love with her I'm not going to try to talk you out of it. I'm willing to make compromises. I'll accept her. But don't be a Christian. Let her become a Jew for a change."

The waiter was suddenly upon them, bringing their coffee, and taking their plates. They were both embarrassed, wondering if the waiter had overheard. But he gave no sign. They kept silent while the waiter gathered some peas that Adam had dropped on the tablecloth. Then they both followed him with their eyes, until they were sure he was out of earshot.

"She'll convert if she loves you," Adam said in a lower voice.

"Why should I impose that on her?"

"Because it's your religion. Why shouldn't you? If you're not ashamed of it."

"I've already given ten reasons why I'm not deeply religious, any more than any educated man—we're all moralistic agnostics more or less—these different sects all have their own beauty and their own lesson, and I'm changing sects open and aboveboard. I'm not hiding what I was, and I'm not hiding what I want to be. And if you call that being ashamed, that's a matter of your own definition, but I say it's just a case of not wanting a particular thing. I admit I'm a Jew and I admit I don't want to be. I'm honest about it. What's so ashamed about that? Sure, I admit a guy's a jerk if he's ashamed of being a Jew and doesn't do anything about it. Because a man's sect isn't an uneradicable mark. He can change it. And I say there's nothing wrong with being ashamed of something you can change, if you then go ahead and change it. Like they say a guy shouldn't be ashamed to be poor. But if he's ashamed to be poor, and he works hard on account of it and gets rich, what's wrong with that? I say that's to be proud of. More power to him."

"Why should you even want to change?" Adam said with emphasis.

"Because I want my religion to be something of my own choosing, like my vocation, and not something imposed upon me by something else."

"So why not choose the Jewish religion?" said Adam. "What's wrong with it?"

"Nothing's wrong with it, as such. But I'm not afraid to change because I'm not afraid to grow. The human race wouldn't grow if people were afraid to switch religions. And my natural instinct is to grow in this direction. I've got guts enough to accept the soil on which I was born, and its people, unreservedly, because the man whose instinct is to conform to the majority is the guy who's in step with his country, and that's my natural instinct."

"You can be in step without that. There's plenty of famous Jews in this country that never converted—movie stars—"

"Maybe some of them would have, if their fathers-in-law insisted on it. I don't know. I bet most of them just never converted because they never cared that much, one way or the other. But in the kind of New England life I want, church happens to be part of the fabric of it, and I'm big enough to admit it. You wouldn't think much of an immigrant that refused to learn English."

"You can't compare that. We have freedom of religion."

"And that's what I'm exercising," said Richard. "Look, call it by any name you want. Call it snobbery, or social climbing, I don't care. Maybe I have got a certain amount of natural snobbery, just as we all have, but to the extent it makes me look down on anybody or be rude or unfair to anybody, I'm trying to cure it. I've always tried to make myself a decent person. But the whole Yankee way of life is all around me, and I see its inner values, and it's available. Is that such a God-awful crime, for Christ sake? I've seen Bill Hodge's way of life, and I've seen my own, and these things a man has to work out for himself. You don't shoot him for it. Bill Hodge's whole world is cut from one piece of cloth. And mine isn't. Or hasn't been. The Puritan religious tradition, and Harvard, and those banks down on Devonshire Street are all cut from the same piece of cloth, and they've got the whole history and the flavor of the country tied up with it."

"Well, Richard," Adam answered tiredly, "I don't know what to say. It seems to me there's no point in a man looking for a better religion, because any religion he belongs to, he's an example of it, and if he's good, people are going to say it's a good religion. I used to have some of the same feeling as you when I was a kid and I saw all these immigrants that weren't Americanized. But then I thought, why look at them? Why shouldn't I look at me? One little part of the whole Jewish people is me, and it's as good as I make it. I have that in my power, to this extent. Whatever I do, I'm an example of a Jew, so if I'm honest, who can deny that the Jews are good enough to produce an honest man? Look, Richard, why shouldn't a man stick up for his religion, and make it a good one by being a good result of it? The way I feel, I can't change the fact that I was born a Jew, so I might as well be proud of it. Why should I make a bum out of my ancestors? All those generations that went to the trouble to keep on staying Jewish, so I could know I'm descended from Abraham, Isaac and Jacob, and if I were to turn Christian now, it seems to me I'd be making a monkey out of all those generations. If the Jewish religion in our family is going to die out with me, then our ancestors might just as well have saved themselves the trouble. Either they were being damn fools all that time, or else I have to believe it was worth preserving. And why should I admit I'm descended from damn fools? When you get converted, Richard, it means that the Christian bishops that burned our ancestors at the stake are finally winning the argument the way they predicted, and you make yourself a product of people that were so dumb that they went to the stake for nothing."

"So what am I supposed to do?" said Richard. "Devote my life to being a propaganda poster? Suppose I did stay a Jew—do you think all the Jews would get credit for every good deed I did? People don't think in those terms. I have a right to my own life—it's not as if everything I did or thought was a betrayal of somebody. You might as well say I'm betraying all those Jews over in Germany and occupied Europe."

"You are," said Adam.

"I am not!" Richard answered heatedly. "There's nothing practical I can do to help those people, except fight in the United States Army, and that I'm going to do anyway. And I'll bet half the Jews in Germany never wanted to be Jewish anyhow. They'd probably thank me for defending their right not to be Jewish. There's nothing unique in my ideas."

Adam opened his mouth and shut it again. He seemed unable to think of anything more to say. He looked glumly at their empty coffee cups, and at the Scotch-and-soda glasses. Richard had not drunk his. "Let's go," said Richard. "I've got work to do.". . .

They came in sight of the massive stories and innumerable chimneys of Eliot House. Richard walked a little faster and Adam quickened to keep abreast.

"Don't you believe in the brotherhood of man?" Richard said to him.

"No," said Adam. "I mean yes. Yes, I do. But I believe Christians should be good Christians, and Jews should be good Jews. When the Jews start becoming Christians everything gets unraveled."

He looked overwrought and desperate. Half the iron gate was open, and they passed into a tunnel-like arch, under a wing of the building. Richard stopped, and turned to his father.

"Well, it's been nice talking to you," he said. "Thanks for the lunch."

"Wait a minute," Adam said, catching Richard's arm. "Don't go in yet. I told your mother I'd bring you home."

"Don't be ridiculous."

Richard extricated his arm with a sharp pull, and passed through the dark archway into the sunlight of the big enclosed courtyard, with Adam following him.

In the courtyard he went along a little gravel walk, heading toward the particular entry that led to his quarters. He was embarrassed to have his father dogging him at his heels, and he was conscious of several students crossing the new grass in various directions at a distance, and a number of others emerging from the dining hall.

"Please," his father was saying behind him. "Just sit there at dinner for two hours."

"Leave me alone," Richard said, walking quickly without looking around. "Scram, will ya? I'm not going home."

Adam kept following.

Blushing, Richard hurried up a few stone steps of a little patio, crossed it dodging among students, and descended some steps on the other side. He continued quickly toward the green door of his entry. Adam was half a step behind, up across the patio and down again.

"Be a good feller," Adam pleaded. "Give us a nice Passover for a couple of hours, that's all I ask. Be a sport. I promised your mother."

"You had no right to make a promise like that," Richard said over his shoulder. He had the feeling they were becoming a spectacle.

"Why can't you do such a little thing for Mother's sake?"

"I told you," Richard said, hurrying along without looking around. "I wouldn't feel right. I'd be living a lie. I can't take being two people any more."

As he arrived on the stoop and seized the door handle his father grasped his arm again and swung him around. Richard made a violent gesture in an effort to release himself, but Adam had him firmly by the sleeve of his tweed jacket. Richard's back was to the door and his father's great body was between him and the wide courtyard.

"What'll we tell Grandma? And look at your little cousins, how are we going to explain it?"

"Tell them I'm going to be baptized." He kept his voice lowered, and tried to make it look like a normal conversation even though his father was holding him. "I'm a Christian. They've got to know sometime."

"You don't know what you're saying!"

"I resent that. Let go of my arm." He pulled again, but Adam held. None of the boys walking in the courtyard were staring rudely, as far as Richard could see, but he sensed that some of them must be watching from the corners of their eyes.

"You aren't going in that door!" Adam said. "I told your mother I wouldn't come home empty-handed! Now come on! I'm getting mad!"

"Will you let go of my arm or do I have to sock ya?" Richard asked desperately in a low voice, knowing while he heard his own voice that he had lost control, and regretting his words while he said them.

Adam's eyes flashed and he struck Richard a smashing blow with the back of his hand, across the eye and cheek. Richard stumbled backward against the door, numb and surprised. In the same instant that he felt the sting, far beyond his father he saw among the boys walking in the courtyard the slender, ambling figure of Brooks Garrison, watching with what appeared to be mild curiosity. Adam slapped him again in the other direction. "Don't talk to me like that!" he said. "Now come on."

Richard turned in an agony of mortification and lunged into the door, throwing it open with the force of his shoulder, his red face averted and hidden almost in his armpit.

The green door slammed in Adam's face so violently that the brass knocker flew up and down again with a clunk.

"Richard!" Adam shouted, throwing himself against the door and pressing the handle.

He almost stumbled as it swung open, and at the top of the flight of stairs he could see Richard's legs disappearing around a landing. He already felt remorse for having struck him. He ran up after him.

"Richard!" he shouted hoarsely, climbing two steps to the pace and slipping once to his knee. "Wait!"

As he rounded the first landing he saw Richard's legs again going out of sight a flight above.

A bedraggled old woman was scrubbing the stairs immediately in Adam's path but he did not see her until too late and his foot splashed into the bucket. The scrubwoman gave a little cry and rolled back against the railing. Adam looked at her apologetically for only an instant. He wanted to catch up before Richard could lock himself into his room. He tried to shake the bucket from his foot and run farther upstairs, but his ankle was caught between two rollers which had been attached to the bucket for the purpose of wringing mops, and he fell on the steps, spilling dirty water over himself and the scrubwoman and losing his Homburg.

He got up in haste and confusion and reached down to pull the bucket and rollers off like an overshoe. The cold, muddy water drenched through his shoe and sock.

"Easy does it," the scrubwoman told him, her raw hands competing with his to widen the rollers. She was on her knees, working with grunts at Adam's impatient ankle, the gray strands of her hair and the brown cotton front of her shapeless dress hanging down limply. Several times he thought his foot was nearly freed and he moved as if to run again.

"Don't be running and pulling until I get it open," she said.

"I'm his father," he explained frantically, thinking he must appear to her a lunatic.

> At the insistence of his dean, Richard consents to see the family rabbi.

"YOU'RE TOO LATE to talk me out of marrying Wimsy," Richard said to the Reverend Leo Gabriel Budapester. "She's already set the date of the wedding. It's in just about seven weeks. June fourteenth, to be exact."

He was on the sofa at 3 Wood View Terrace, and the reform rabbi sat in the high-backed chair with carved arms, facing him. Budapester was a stocky, fiery-eyed man in his middle forties, with a great back-swept pompadour, as though his face were jutting into a wind. He also had a neat black mustache and a forward-pointed Vandyke, that added to the appearance his face had of moving ahead at high speed. But his most striking characteristic was his fierce and deep little eyes, which at times moved quickly and at times fixed themselves, under heavy eyebrows and an overhanging wide forehead that rose upward into the pompadour.

Between his fingers, on his crossed knees, he held a cigar, and Richard noticed that he wore a conservative, expensive-looking suit of the softest flannel, with vest.

The rabbi had determined that the house in which Richard had grown up would be the best setting for their interview, and Dean Clark had thereupon insisted that Richard go along with this. They had agreed upon an afternoon hour, and the rabbi had cautioned Adam not to happen in upon them.

Richard had arrived at the house first, traveling by bus, and he had taken a nap on the sofa until the rabbi awakened him with the doorbell. He was still a bit sleepy-eyed as he sat facing the rabbi now, and his shoes were untied.

"I didn't know the wedding date had actually been set," the rabbi said.

"She set it last Saturday afternoon, when we were at the baseball game. We're getting married right after commencement, before I go into the Army. Just a quiet little affair. She's telling her father, and she's going through with it regardless, no matter what he says. But he'll go along with it, though, when he sees he has to."

Budapester arose and took the ashtray from the lamp table at the end of the sofa. He was a short man, but his build was not small, and he had the light step of a man in good physical condition. He placed the ashtray on the carpet beside the high-backed chair and sat down again.

"I love that girl," Richard said. "So don't waste your breath."

"Very well then," said the rabbi. "Let's leave her out of our discussion this afternoon, shall we? You say you're going to marry her in seven weeks, and you don't want to talk about it, so we won't."

"That's okay with me," said Richard.

"Suppose we talk instead about this business of your conversion to Christianity," the rabbi said. "Have you considered, Richard, that you don't have to become someone else in order to become good?"

"What do you mean by that?"

"I mean that I suspect that at the bottom of your desire for conversion is a desire to become someone else—a feeling that your own self is the obstacle to worthiness. I'd like to show you, Richard, that you're worthy while being yourself."

"All right," said Richard. "Being myself should mean I can look over all the religions and pick the one I like best, shouldn't it?"

Budapester looked as though he had not expected this retort. "You're misinterpreting me—," he said.

"Why?" said Richard. "You say I should be myself. I pick my politics, don't I? A man doesn't inherit his politics, so why should he inherit his religion? Being myself ought to mean I've got a right to a clean slate. My father hasn't got a right to ask that I be him. I'm not even letting him pay my bills any more—I don't know if he told you that. But the way I look at it, I don't want to inherit my father's house, and I don't want to inherit the mortgages, either. He's got a right to what he built, but I've got a right to build my own."

Budapester puffed slowly at his cigar. He narrowed his eyes for a little while and let them gradually widen again, staring all the time at Richard.

"Perhaps your problem is this," he said, "—that you feel some nameless guilt, or inadequacy, as so many of us do, and because you can't define it you identify it with your parental religion—this mystic thing that has hovered over you from birth. As if by putting away your parental religion you could put away your nameless fears."

"Are you a rabbi or a psychiatrist?"

"These days a clergyman has to be a bit of a psychiatrist too," said Budapester.

"Well, I can assure you I'm as sane as you are," said Richard.

Neither said anything for a moment, while Budapester took another puff and lowered his hand to flick some ashes into the tray. They kept looking at each other.

"If you're such a hot psychiatrist," Richard said, "you can understand that I'm sick and tired of being a split personality all my life, and that's the main reason why I want to convert."

"A split personality? You mean as between being a Jew and being thoroughly American?"

"Between living in a majority culture, and taking advantage of it, and trying at the same time to pretend that I belong to a special little different group. And all the crazy rationalizations that it led me into, and cruelty to people that I committed on account of it."

"Do you drink your morning orange juice as a Jew or as an American?" Budapester asked him.

"What?"

"Do you drink your morning orange juice as a Jew or as an

American?" Budapester repeated. "Or do I? I resent people, whether Jewish or gentile, who imply that insofar as I'm an American I'm one thing, and insofar as I'm a Jew I'm another thing, as if I were two people, or as if I had two aspects. I don't know where one begins and the other ends. I breathe, I eat, I sit on the toilet, and it's one man. It seems to me that my existence, my person, is visible proof to anyone that there's no distinction between 'American' and 'Jew.' If I catch cold I catch cold, don't I? Is it the Jewish me or the American me that catches it? Richard, I was born here, raised here—I know no other land. And I love to see the white birches of New England, and I love to watch the waves pounding on the shore of Cape Ann, and to think of that rough coast as my own. And yet when I walk there on the sand and throw pebbles as far as I can and skip them on the sea, to amuse my youngest son, it's a Jew walking there, a religious Jew, nonetheless a Jew for being an American. Isn't that a hard fact? Is it illogical, really, for a Jew to speak English as his mother tongue? Do you think, Richard, that our Irish neighbors are less American for wearing green on Saint Patrick's Day?"

"To a certain extent."

"Well, don't ever tell one that. He'll punch you in the nose. They're as American as the police force. The United States wouldn't be recognizable without them. I'll give you another example. I had the good fortune a couple of years ago to visit an Indian village, on the Hopi reservation, just when a young Indian had come home on furlough from the United States Army, and the villagers had gotten up what they call a butterfly dance in his honor. For all I know that lad may be dead now on Bataan. But this one time he was home, in his G.I. uniform, and the old men were beating tom-toms and chanting in his honor, and the young girls were got up in ornate wooden headdresses and masks, all hopping around in line, you know. Now here's the point. When these old Indians interrupted their chant to joke in English, by way of joshing this young lad home from the Army, and there was so much laughter, I saw what a wonderful time that U.S. Army soldier was having, being an Indian again that day —and I thought of what a joy such things can be, whether it's a Christmas dinner on Beacon Hill or a butterfly dance in Arizona. So long as it's your own father, mother, sisters, brothers."

The rabbi leaned forward and gestured slightly toward Richard with his cigar, but Richard looked at him skeptically and did not speak.

"And in the same way, Richard, as that boy enjoyed being an Indian, I enjoy being a Jew. It's fun to be a Jew. What would I do on Passover eve if I weren't a Jew? Walk the streets? It's being a Jew that makes the United States of America such a wonderful place to be on Passover eve. And aren't I a better American for being a whole person? I'll tell you this, Richard—" He tapped Richard on the knee. "—You don't grow by getting rid of culture, and you don't create culture by partial amnesia. America is an abstraction and a void, until you bring your share to it and give it substance. And it's by interchange that we grow, not by discarding. I learned a lot from my Yankee schoolfellows, and perhaps they learned something from me, too. I know I learned a lot about manners from the Yankees. And perhaps they lost some of their insularity, perhaps they gained some of the Jewish sense of personal participation in the ancient history of mankind, a sense of the interlocking character of the history of nations. They don't become worse Yankees for learning from the Jews, and I feel myself a better Jew for having picked up a few Yankee traits. The thing is to add to culture, not subtract from it. We all became better—and closer—by the exchange. I feel special kinship for men around the world for one reason or another, for some because they speak English though they're not of my religion, and for others because they're of my religion, though they don't speak my tongue or know my country. The Jewish experience is mine, and New England is my home, and I can no more deny one than the other. Do you call this a contradiction? My very physical existence proves it's not a contradiction. It's natural to me. Do you follow me, Richard?"

"Oh, I follow you, all right," Richard said. "I just can't imagine a grown man talking such rot."

Budapester leaned back in the chair, with an irked expression.

"Richard," he said, "I have a right to all the world-ties history has given me. I'm an American by virtue of being the son of a Jew—a Jew who chose to come here. And is my personality less unified, simply because my total background is too broad to be described in a single word?"

"All right," said Richard, "but you're beclouding the issue. When you bring in this Indian in Arizona—you don't know what that Indian was thinking—"

Budapester tasted his cigar quietly for several long seconds, regarding Richard. The blue cigar-smoke hung about him in whorls and layers. When he began to speak again, his voice was slower and quieter.

"Put it this way then," he said. "It's through the Jews that you're an American. It was your Jewish father who gave you an American home, here on Wood View Terrace, and it was your Jewish mother who taught you the English language. Isn't it through Jews that the American breakfast table has become a part of you? If you cut your tie to the people nearest you, it's going to mean cutting your strongest tie to the United States. Because a man's tie to his country is first of all through his own little corner of that country. You've had one mother, and one childhood home, Richard, and you'll never have another. And as old as you get, no milk will ever taste quite like your own mother's breast. That's why mankind is made of little congregations, and that's why America is made of little communities—sons attached to the faiths of their fathers, as a peasant in France is attached to his own special hill—and it's those little, particular loyalties that are real, and add up to a nation. A man's own land—his own childhood corner of land—and his own people, are his natural avenues to God. His familiar countryside, his people, his relatives—these are his biggest links to humanity. That's why I say that an American Jew who forsakes the American Jews puts himself out of touch with America. He may take a while to realize it, but that's what he does. He must. Because he's estranged from those particular Americans to whose hearts he has the most intimate access—his own flesh-and-blood relatives. These people, his sisters and his aunts, are the most bound to love him. And how can he know America in general without knowing individual Americans in particular, and what Americans can he ever know more intimately than his own family? Your approach to the United States, like your approach to God, is through the people into which you were born. You cut your tie to the people nearest you, and you cut your closest tie to America. That's why, Richard, that's why I say that an American Jew, who's out of touch with American Jews, is like an expatriate. He's like an American living in Paris, out of touch with his country, and therefore out of touch with the world. A few years ago, Richard, before the war broke out in Europe—do you know Waldo Hamburger's eldest daughter?"

"No."

"Well, Waldo Hamburger's eldest daughter was living on the Left Bank in Paris, trying to be a poetess. And of course her father was trying to get her to come home, so I wrote to her. And indeed it was well she did come home—not only because the war came—but because how could she be in touch with life, except through her own country? An American living out his life in Paris—he doesn't become French and he ceases to be American. He's nothing. He's alone. An American expatriate living in Paris or Florence, like an American who looks to Moscow—how can they hope to understand humanity if they can't understand their very own homeland? A man estranged from his own country loses touch with God. As I wrote to the Hamburger girl, shedding your homeland doesn't make a World Citizen. It makes a Man Without a Country, because you can't reach the general except through the specific. Love, and loyalty, and knowledge are nourished at home. Abstractions are meaningless, until your family, your neighbors, the people you know, give them substance."

"Yeah? Well, it's a good thing everybody else doesn't think like you," Richard said. "Because if they did, the Pilgrim Fathers never would have pulled up stakes to leave their country and their church and come over here. And my grandparents never would have left their native villages in Russia, either."

"That's different," the rabbi said. "When a whole folk migrates, or alters its religion, it carries its internal ties along. That's evolution. It's not like an individual wandering off."

"In other words," said Richard, "you want people to drift with the mob all their life. Well, as it happens, there's people that have got guts enough to try to make their own lives. I happen to think the religious group I was born in isn't for me. It's too bad, and I've had unhappiness on that account. But I'm doing something about it. I've got guts enough to go where I think I'll find peace, just like my grandfather and the Pilgrim Fathers had guts. You say, 'Keep in touch with your people'—but Jesus, let's call a spade a spade. You want me to be a sheep and graze with the herd with my eyes shut, that's all. In the same old pasture. I say, if God is any place, or if humanity is any place, it's every place."

"But the search is easier," said the rabbi, "when a man has a home. A searcher needs a base of operations."

"I'll build a home. Just like my father built this one."

"A home isn't built in a generation."

"I'll have children after me, if they care to finish it."

"Your children will need grandparents."

"Well, damn it, there's such a thing as a guy growing up and striking out on his own! My parents won't live forever. What do you want me to do? Cuddle up in my umbilical cord?"

"No, I want you to know who you are."

"Know who I am—these Jewish arguments always get back to that," Richard said. "Do you realize, rabbi, that the people in this country who most know who they are—best know who they are—are these Yankees, these old Unitarian families for instance, down on Marlborough Street, and down around Dover and Dedham? Those are the people that know who they are. They've got their homesteads, and they're the only people that have records of their whole family tree, back for two hundred years. And they know the part their own ancestors played individually, in every period of the growing of this country. A guy in that set knows exactly who he is. And he knows what families are his friends, and what family runs every museum and every bank. I happened to be in the home of a Yankee friend of mine when the news came of Pearl Harbor, and his mother quoted Ralph Waldo Emerson—in other words she was quoting an American poet of her own race, that her own grandparents maybe knew personally. If you want people to know who they are, those old Yankee families are the ones that know who they are. They've got streets named after them. And by contrast, we're just part of the big, jumbled up middle class that drifts around, without knowing from one generation to the next what city they'll be living in, or where their grandparents were born exactly, just guys moving around trying to figure a way to eke a living, and making friends by accident, hit-and-miss. That's the way people live in America. Except for these old established Boston Yanks, that know where they belong. They're stable, and they run things, and generation after generation they're on top of the whole mess."

"Boston has an Irish mayor, Richard. The rest of us are getting there. I grant you, the Anglo-Saxon race that we call Yanks here in New England are a clever and hardworking lot—they came to an empty continent and built a country. But they don't have a monopoly. Have patience, Richard. Meanwhile, imitate their cleverness and their diligence if you like."

"Why not go the whole hog?"

"Because the fact is that you aren't a Yankee. Your ancestors came here two generations ago from eastern Europe. You're an

American and a New Englander, by birth, but you aren't in the particular ethnic group that people in Massachusetts refer to as the Yankees, so make the best of it."

"In other words, you don't want me to know who I am—you want me to know who I'm not. And frankly, I don't think blood's that important. The gates are open."

"I want you to consider a plain fact—that even if you go through the motions of switching your ethnic group, you become only a first-generation Yankee. It's only as a Jew, that you're of antique stock. As a Yankee you're first-generation, like an immigrant. Your well-to-do Yankee friends in the banking business are of antique stock as Yankees, but you're of antique stock only if you stay a Jew."

"Well, that's all right. I consider myself an original anyway. I look forward, not back. You have ancestors—I have descendants. I mean I will have. Me and Wimsy, we'll have."

The rabbi's cigar-ash had lengthened, and he reached down to drop it into the ashtray he had placed on the carpet. Then he took a long draw, crossing his legs again and regarding Richard with contracted eyes. Finally he held the cigar beside his face.

"What was the passage from Ralph Waldo Emerson that you said your friend's mother quoted?" he asked.

"It was the one about duty."

"I can quote Emerson too," the rabbi said. "Did you know that Emerson said that 'every man is an omnibus on which all his ancestors are seated'?"

"No."

"Well, he did. Emerson said that."

Dorothy has come in during the argument. The rabbi brings up the point of Jewish identity through persecution.

"You'll have to do better than that," Richard said. "I've heard that one before, and I don't see why I should feel I'm different from everybody else just because my ancestors got a bigger than average share of kicking around. Maintaining a separate Jewish race is something I can't intellectually justify."

"Richard, it's not a contest to see who got the biggest kicking around. It's a whole separate concept of God, and law."

"Well, I'm not theology-minded, and I'm not going to decide who

I marry on the basis of some concept about God, because if God is one way, we're sitting here in this living room, and if God is the other way, we're still sitting here in this living room, so I don't see what difference it makes. That stuff is artificial. You invent words, and then you think they're real. Sure, if a Jew is being persecuted in Germany, I'm willing to help him, but I don't see why I should take something to heart that's only a theory and try to feel any more alien, or any more in exile, than I actually have to be."

"Richard, didn't I make it clear before, that when I walk the shores of Cape Ann with my small son, I don't feel in exile? In spite of this grand concept of exile from the Promised Land, the fact is that no Jew is in exile until he's exiled from the Jews. And he's not an alien. It's been said that the Jews are aliens everywhere, but the truth is that we're aliens nowhere. That's the truth—look at it. We're a world-folk." He turned from Richard to Dorothy. She had been attentive for only the first moment or so, and then had begun to fidget absently as though troubled with some private matter, but when she saw the rabbi look at her, she made a new effort to appear as though she had been listening. The rabbi turned again to Richard. "Jewish songsters in America, Jewish parliamentarians in France— don't Jews in every land add to that land something characteristic not of themselves, but something characteristic of that land itself? They enter into a country's life like a vitamin. They give each native culture a salt and flavor, adding to France something French, to Austria something Austrian—look, Richard, how bright and lively America and Britain are with their Jews, and how wretched Germany and France have grown now without them. And beyond that, they give each country they live in a touch of the whole human experience. The country that has Jews, belongs to the human race. It knows that it does. It can't help but know it. Would old Vienna have had its full savor, without its very own Jewish shopkeepers and actors? Jews are everywhere a humanizing leaven, and no country is really raw or savage, once the Jews have given it their touch. That's why a great nation needs her Jews. Perhaps it's because they're the most ancient and far-flung of wanderers, so that the country that contains Jewish blood senses itself in closer touch with all the ages and nations of mankind—less constricted in space and time. America, for example, is a product of the wilderness and frontier, a young land, a land without memory, broken from the past. And to America the Jews have brought a living memory of the Pharaohs of Egypt, a living recollection of the dawn of man. And America needs that. That memory is part of mankind's sense of greatness. America needs her Jews."

"Now wait a minute," Richard said. "It seems to me you've contradicted yourself about a dozen times here. What do you think I am, a dummy?" Dorothy looked up with interest at Richard as he challenged the rabbi.

"How have I contradicted myself?" Budapester asked.

"Well, I'm not sure if I got it all, but it's just a little too slick. It seems to me you're straining just a little too hard to be the same and different at the same time. And as far as this stuff goes about giving a country something characteristic of the country itself, the only example that comes to my mind right now is Jacques Offenbach writing the can-can in Paris, but it seems to me guys like that usually don't give a damn about being a Jew anyway—"

"Oh, I didn't mean just things like that," the rabbi said, raising his hands in a spirited shrug. "I meant the totality of Jews in New York, London—"

"Let me finish," Richard said. "Before you start talking again. And a little while ago you were saying, oh, we're just like the Irish wearing green on Saint Patrick's Day, we're just like the Indians in Arizona. And now all of a sudden we're the great yeast that's going to humanize everybody else."

Budapester smiled. He drew a new cigar from his vest and bit the end from it. The old one lay in the ashtray.

He's stalling for time, Richard thought.

"Do you mind if I smoke?" Budapester said to Dorothy.

She did not seem to hear him at first, and then when she realized she had been spoken to she looked up startled.

"No," she said.

Budapester opened a book of matches, and lighted the cigar.

"There's no contradiction," he said, "in the commonplace fact that many nations and many peoples have each put something unique, something invaluable, into the common cultural pool of mankind, and at the same time each of them has borrowed heavily from this common pool, even relied on it mainly. The common culture of mankind is like a mutual fund, and everyone's indebted to everyone else. In America we Jews think in English, and enjoy Shakespeare and the English poets, but John Milton studied Hebrew, and the English Bible is a translation of ours, so you see, there's a balancing

of accounts. The Jews and western Europe have civilized one another
in turn. I grant you, God's covenant with Israel belongs now to all
the world. But it's our special assignment to keep it fresh, to keep
it in high glow and polish, just as it's a special assignment of the
French to maintain Notre Dame and the boulevards, to thrill and
edify the rest of us again someday, because only they can. It's not
fair to the rest of mankind that we should stop pulling our oar now.
Don't you think the Christians still need us? Isn't the New Testament twice as real to a Christian child, when he can see walking in
his neighborhood the people of whom it speaks?"

"Next you'll be telling me it's the duty of a chicken to lay eggs,"
Richard said, "so that the whole human race can have fresh eggs for
breakfast, or something like that."

Budapester ignored this remark. "How Providence assigns roles, we
can't know," he said, "but to contemplate the particular role given to
the Jew is to see this about it—that the Jew is a summary, a distilla-
tion, a caricature of Man himself, because the Jew has borne Man's
greatest aspirations, and given voice to Mankind's most awesome
hopes, and suffered accordingly the most painful of failures. The
aspiration to carry out the moral law, and the daily failure to do so.
Aspiration, failure, and yet a continuing unwilling dialogue with God,
century after century, generation after generation. Our persisting existence is a dialogue with God. Read our history, beginning with the
earliest pages of Scripture, and isn't it all the story of man's divine
possibility, his failure, and his endless efforts to try again? This is also
the story of all humankind. But it's especially the story of the Jew,
because the Jewish people has been assigned the greatest of tasks,
and voiced the greatest of hopes, so that our failure has been propor-
tionately great. And thus we are Man in a nutshell, Man condensed,
that Man may look at the Jew and see himself with greater meaning."

Boy, can he sling it, Richard thought.

"The Jews are Man in the extreme," Budapester said. "Because the
Jews have been at once the most magnificent and the most wretched
of peoples, and this is the essence of Man. To be at once sacred and
ridiculous, and to live always in danger of slaughter, as Jews do, as
men have lived since Cain slew Abel."

"Speak for yourself only," Richard said.

"What?"

"I said speak for yourself only. You can be ridiculous if you want
to, but I'm not."

Budapester nodded and smiled. "I sincerely hope you are not," he said.

Dorothy was listening now, and looking from one to the other in the exchange.

"Look," Richard said, "you've got an unhealthy attitude, going around telling yourself you're holy and tragic and wretched, and Man in the extreme, and different from other people. It isn't normal. And as far as that goes, for crying out loud, you could say any human being is Man in the extreme. You could say the Scotch are Man in the extreme, or the U.S. Army—look at the Eskimos, why aren't the Eskimos Man in the extreme? They live way up there on the northern edge of Canada, where they have such a hard time making a living— cold and starvation all the time, fighting for life—boy, it seems to me that that's Man in the extreme, if anybody is."

Budapester smiled a bit. "Maybe they are—as you say, all men are. But let's explore the ways in which the Jews are—"

"No, let's talk about the Eskimos," Richard said. "They're my candidate for Man in the extreme."

.   .   .   .   .

"Rabbi," Richard said, "I'd like to ask you a question. And I want an honest answer."

"Yes?" Budapester put his lips around the cigar, holding it between his fingers.

"Do you actually believe in God?" Richard asked.

Budapester took his cigar from his lips, and exhaled the wisp of smoke that was in his mouth. His eyes remained fixed on Richard's eyes.

"Yes," he said.

"It seems to me you hesitated."

"Only because the question itself is blasphemous. The Christians spoke of belief, but the Jews spoke of awe and wonder. We know that beyond what we know, beyond the outer reaches of inspiration and awareness, beyond our conviction of law, we're faced at last with what we know not—what we can only call the Name. The Unutterable."

Richard smiled wryly. There was a short snicker through his nose.

"What's the joke?" Budapester asked him severely.

"You don't believe that stuff any more than I do. You just wish you did."

"Are you a mind reader?"

"I don't have to be. It's plain from the way you answer. You're like my father. Pin him down and he just kicks words around. I don't think either of you really believe in God. Except in the same general way that I do, which is that one church is as good as another, and if I can integrate and be happy with Wimsy in the Congregational Church, that's the church for me."

.   .   .   .   .

Budapester lowered the cigar to the ashtray, beside the stub of the other one. He brushed a handkerchief across his nostrils. Then he looked at his watch. "Well, I've got two other calls to make this afternoon," he said. "I'm afraid we didn't get very far. I'd like to continue this another time, so we can discuss the difference of outlook that divides Christianity from Judaism. That's of course the big thing, and we haven't even gotten up to talking about it. Can we make an appointment?"

"Not unless Cod Clark forces me to."

The rabbi arose to go. Richard got up from the sofa. Even in his stocking-feet he stood several inches above the rabbi. Dorothy also stood up.

"It could be at my study," the rabbi said. "Or I could come to your room at college. I needn't drag you all the way out here again."

"Listen," Richard said, "my mind's made up. I came out here because Cod Clark insisted on it, but as far as I'm concerned, sitting around to jaw about it like this is a waste of valuable study time, and I can't afford it. I've got exams to study for."

The rabbi stood there unhappily a moment. "Well, meanwhile can I give you a lift back to Cambridge?" he offered. "You'll have to wait in the car while I make a couple of short calls, but I promise you they won't be long."

"No thanks. I'm really short on time. As soon as I have a glass of milk I'll go down and catch the bus."

"Very well, then, Richard," Budapester said. "And call me up any time you want to."

"I won't want to," said Richard.

Budapester was a little taken aback by this rudeness. He shook hands with Richard, looking from Richard to Dorothy and back, with an uncomfortable expression.

"Pray for me if you like," Richard said, with a touch of sarcasm in his voice.

"I certainly will," Budapester said darkly. "Believe me."

"And me, too," Dorothy said anxiously.

Budapester looked at her, as if to see whether she also spoke with sarcasm, but when he saw her face his features softened, to the beginning of a kindly smile. "Yes, I will, Dorothy," he said. "I will indeed. And what shall I pray for—that your stammering goes away?"

"No," she said, "just—give Him my best regards, and—"

"Yeah, give Him our regards," Richard said, smiling. He snorted a brief chuckle.

"It's really not necessary that you children laugh at me," said Budapester, darkening again.

"I wasn't laughing!" Dorothy said, her voice suddenly tearful and harassed. "I used to say that when I was a little kid! I just meant—ask Him—oh, I don't know."

She turned her face away. Budapester looked at her soberly.

"I'm sorry," he said to her, in a kindly tone. "I'll gladly pray for you, Dorothy. But don't forget that you don't need me. Jews pray directly, without priests or intercessors."

"I know it," she said, biting her lip.

Richard looked at her. Budapester nodded at Richard again, meeting his eyes for only the briefest possible time. Then he turned to leave. Richard saw the rabbi's back go to the door, and then he saw the door shut. What a windbag, he thought.

He turned and looked at Dorothy, who had sat down twisted on the sofa, hiding her face in some private grief that had overcome her. Richard wondered what madness had seized her now.

But then the noise of Budapester's car distracted him, and he went to the window curtains to watch it go away.

It was a handsome Cadillac.

Then Richard goes to Stringfellow Todd for conversion.

. . . He did not know how to begin expressing the vague feelings he had wanted to discuss with the minister. He realized also that Todd was asking him for something quite specific, such as a personal confession of faith, and he had not thought to prepare any.

"Well, I take life seriously," he began, as best he could. "I'm interested in making myself into the best person I possibly can."

The minister nodded his head, as though he approved, and Richard felt encouraged.

"For instance a person can go along like a domestic animal," Richard said, "never creating his own future, and letting accident and circumstance chart his whole course—a mediocre career or a lousy one, what job he has, or what religion he is, or whether he bothers to get the right kind of a congenial wife or not, and things like that. With some people things just happen to them like the rain. There's thousands of people like that."

"The majority," Todd said, nodding.

"Or a man can be 'the master of his fate and the captain of his soul,' and try to take charge and make some kind of a plan out of his life," Richard said. "I believe a guy just gets one crack at life, and he ought to take the bull by the horns."

"Or you mean, as Sallust put it, 'Quisque est faber fortunae suae,' " said Todd. "My Calvinist forebears might not have agreed with you, strictly speaking, but it strikes me as a useful pragmatic attitude for us lowly mortals."

Richard did not understand the Latin or the reference to Calvinism, and he was uncertain what Todd meant. "I mean, if a guy leads a half-baked life during his one stay on earth, it's a criminal waste," he said. "You only get this one chance, and you should try to start living right. I mean improve yourself as soon as you can."

"I certainly agree," said Todd.

Richard felt reassured.

"Well, there isn't any limit to how much a guy can improve himself, if he's got the will power and he keeps at it," he went on. "I admit it's a lot of work, and if a guy hasn't had the qualities of a gentleman bred in him from his earliest childhood, it's a lot harder for him to make himself over when he's older—it comes a lot easier to a guy that comes from a really fine family and started right out in life with the best examples always around him. But I still say a guy that wants to, and keeps on trying to, and practicing and correcting himself, he can make himself over."

"With faith in God he can be transformed," said Todd.

"That's right—transformed," said Richard. "But it's tough. Like for instance, about a year ago I was trying to teach good manners to this kid from New York. But just looking at him and listening to him, all my own bad manners got stirred up, and we both started yelling and hollering at each other—I sunk right down to his level. And I'm the same way with my family. My father starts making a fool of himself in public and pulling my sleeve or something, so I give him some back talk that I know isn't the way I should talk to my father, and make a fool of *myself*, and that's the way it goes. We both have bad manners, and we provoke each other to worse manners. Anytime you're around anybody that's vulgar, and that's got these same ingrained bad habits that you're trying to get rid of, you get provoked and it makes you revert to type. They rake up all that stuff in you."

"Well, are you making any progress?"

"I don't know. But I've found one thing that makes it much easier—good companions. Pick friends that set a good example. I think that's half the battle."

"There's truth in that," the minister nodded. "Do you know Aesop's fable about the rose and the clay?"

"No."

"No matter. Go on."

"Well, like I say. I've got this friend by the name of Hodge—you probably know of the family. And when I'm visiting that family, it comes natural to me to be on my best behavior, because the way they act is so naturally harmonious and sensible toward one another, that you can't help but be influenced by it. It's like a whole atmosphere of character and mutual respect that they live in."

Todd was scratching his nose thoughtfully, listening to Richard but not looking at him. Richard somehow did not feel at ease, and he thought he was expressing himself badly.

"I don't mean just things like that," he said. "I mean you see the whole Puritan tradition, the way the Yankees maintain it, like for example my friend Bill Hodge volunteered for submarine duty. Nobody has to volunteer for submarine duty, and it's pretty dangerous. But he felt he should, because he had the physical qualifications and there was a shortage of submarine officers. And the fact that he has a whole banking empire and a whole position to inherit didn't mean a thing. Or you—I think of you as the archetype of that kind of self-sacrifice—"

"Oh, I don't think I'm an archetype of anything," Todd said.

Richard felt he had been gauche in praising Todd so bluntly as to force him to be modest. He began to blush a little again. "Well," he said, "I've got this other friend by the name of Cadbury, that's got four million dollars in his own right, and anybody not brought up in that strict Beacon Hill tradition would be a playboy with that kind of money. But he isn't. He studies just as hard as some poor guy trying to get into medical school."

Todd looked at him, and Richard stopped.

"Go ahead," Todd said.

"Well, that's the way of life I believe in. Those people live right. They have a sense of values—the atmosphere in their homes is gracious—it's an atmosphere that lets a man develop, without all these drags on him, and I want to move into that. I mean, these old Puritan families here have got really the best way of life, and an awful lot of them are really fully developed people, and I can develop better if I'm in that atmosphere."

Richard stopped again. Todd continued looking at him with no change of expression.

"Where does Christ figure?" said Todd.

It struck Richard that Christ was what he ought to have been talking about. But before he could get his bearings and think of a suitable reply, Todd spoke again, seeming to change the subject.

"I was a little surprised to hear you describe your father as a provocation to vulgarity," said Todd. "I've always had the highest opinion of him."

"Well, of course you just see him at his best, when he's in court. But he's done certain things to me that are pretty hard to forgive. You probably wouldn't believe that he gave me a sock that almost broke my jaw about a month ago. My own father—you can imagine how I felt. I just turned and ran to get out of the situation. I didn't know what to do." Richard's voice was no longer firm. He was sorry to find himself discussing his father. But Todd had challenged him and forced him into a corner, and he had to explain himself.

"He shouldn't have done that," Todd agreed, with a pained frown. "I don't know what his provocation was, but he shouldn't have hit you."

"Well, his provocation was just his own narrow-minded neuroticism, the same kind that he's trying to impose on me. He's driven by a neurotic compulsion to believe in all that Chosen People hokum, and I admit maybe he can't help it—maybe it's the result of generations of persecution—but I'm healthy enough to want to get away from that stuff. I wished I was dead when he socked me that time. The two of us, father and son, like a couple of bums getting ready for a fist fight in a saloon, only it was right out in public. And his only provocation was that I was planning to marry a girl of a different religion. That's all. He's trying to believe in all these old Jewish things—I don't think he believes in God actually, but he thinks he should, and the harder he tries the more he creates conflicts in himself and the worse he acts. I give him the benefit of the doubt. But can you blame me for wanting to liberate myself from that kind of a mind?"

"If he wronged you, he needs your love all the more. Twice as much."

"Well, he doesn't act like he needs it. He made it pretty clear that he hates the girl I'm in love with, without even having met her. Of course if he wants to shut the door in her face, like he did last winter, that's his business—it's his house and it's his door. But then he went and wrote Mr. Talbot a letter, to poison his mind against me. And that was just plain underhanded."

"You should love those that wrong you," Todd said gently, his eyes twinkling at Richard with a hint of a teasing smile.

"It's all right to say that," said Richard. "I told him he was forgiven, as far as that goes. But the fact is that you don't love people for pulling things like that on you."

"You should. That's when they need your love most."

"Well, listen. I may still love him to a certain extent, because I understand him, but when you say I should love him more because he tried to break up my marriage, that isn't human nature."

"No, it's not human nature. It's Christianity." He continued looking at Richard, with an expression that Richard found hard to fathom. A friendly, shadowy smile continued to flicker elusively about the lean, hard cheeks; yet beneath its friendliness there seemed to be hidden a steel-like hostility. "You were talking a minute ago of 'that Chosen People hokum,' " he said. "Of course you know the Israelites received God's word, and were the conveyors of it until the Messiah came. Now, when you said 'Chosen People hokum,' did you mean that you agree with Saint Paul that there's no difference between Jew and gentile, or did you mean that you disbelieve in the prophecies of the Old Testament? I want to know. Because if you disbelieve the prophecies, you must find it difficult to believe in their fulfillment in Christ."

Richard was discomforted by the mixture of friendliness and unfriendliness which he read in the minister's face.

"I believe in Christ," he said uneasily. The chair tottered under him on its uneven legs. "I mean I believe in it as much as Christians do. The average Christian doesn't take it literally, the theological stuff. I believe in the moral part of it. I believe in the ethical teachings of Christ."

He saw Todd regarding him skeptically. It seemed unfair to him that the minister should seize upon a stray phrase he had used inadvertently in another context, and cross-examine him about the literalness of his belief in Jesus.

"I've sat in Christian churches and I've gotten something out of it," he added. "I feel that the whole Jewish idea is sort of like an unfinished story, unless you add the Christian idea on to it. I mean, I sat in a church once, looking at an image of Christ, and I was thinking that all human beings are sort of lonesome, they're all sort of wondering what it's all about, and the Jewish idea of God is so vague and remote, that that's why they have to have Christ to mediate between God and human beings, so you don't feel so cut off." Richard felt that he had a good deal of respect for all that Christ and the Church stood for, and he had a frustrating sense that he was not making Todd realize this. He knew that in times past he had thought it through in better phrases than he could now bring to mind.

"When you came in here a little while ago asking for baptism," Todd said, "I assumed you believed the literal truth of the birth, death, and resurrection of Our Lord, or that you're prepared to believe it. But I'm not sure now that you don't just think it's all—well —just some sort of allegory."

"Well, it is an allegory." He knew the minister would regard this as a wrong answer, and he felt his cheeks redden darkly. But it was what he believed, and it seemed better to chance the truth than to lie about it. He felt that his motives were sincere.

"Are you a freethinker?" said Todd.

"Well, I suppose so, the same way everybody is."

"Then why on earth do you want to be baptized?"

"I told you why. I'm not trying to be a revivalist or anything. I just want to be an ordinary average Christian like anybody else."

"You mean you want to belong to the Congregational Church, without believing."

"Well, I respect it. I believe it, in a way. I bet I believe it as much as nine Congregationalists out of ten do. I bet if you cross-examined the trustees of your own church you'd find that some of them don't take it literally."

"That's true—I admit we have our hypocrites, even in high ecclesiastical places. But surely you're not asking for conversion with ambitions of imitating hypocrites. I assume that when you ask for conversion, it's because you take Christ seriously."

"Well," Richard said contritely, "I'm asking to be baptized, and

I told you truthfully I take it perfectly seriously and loyally, and any time that's convenient for you, or if—"

"Amsterdam, what bothers me here is that you've actually rationalized a conversion to evangelical Christianity, in your own mind, and you've done it all without reference to God. Apparently God never enters your calculations at all, not even in a formal change of religion."

"Well, I can't help it if I can't believe in Bible stories. Lots of people can't."

"Then I wouldn't think of baptizing you. I couldn't recommend you to our standing committee. I'm trying to bring people to Christ, not to Beacon Hill."

739

The Pawnbroker

by EDWARD LEWIS WALLANT

Edward Lewis Wallant, who died in 1962 at the age of thirty-six, was one of the truly great fictional talents in Jewish-American writing. He left four novels, two published posthumously. It is the first pair, The Human Season and The Pawnbroker, that will probably do most to keep his memory green.

His writing deals with humble folk, the heavy-laden and sore beset, plumbers, pawnbrokers, pimps, prostitutes, dessicated social workers, punks, dying refugees, with old men, with emotionally starved women. He viewed them all with rachmones, yet with complete truth, and, while he never moralized, he was constantly appalled by the indignities heaped upon men and women by life's indifference to human dreams.

The excerpt from The Pawnbroker reprinted here concerns Sol Nazerman, former Polish university teacher, who survived the Nazi concentration camps where his wife and children died, and who now makes a living of sorts running a pawnshop in Harlem. He hides his memories and his misery behind a mask of indifference to all values, but his memories won't leave him, and his despair takes various forms of escape: sharing the pathetic couch of an equally despairing refugee woman; or arguing with a social worker who through her own loneliness almost reaches him, but who cannot restore his emotional spark; or in hard business relations with a long array of slum characters, including racketeers and sluts, petty thieves and major swindlers.

Sol has relatives—Selig, Joan, Morton, Bertha, American Jews who try to understand this strange man who embodies the tragic experience of our time. But he finds a touch of solace of a special sort, a companionship, in reading Chekhov's short stories: "He appreciated emotions evoked, but he was not involved emo-

tionally himself because his invulnerability allowed no exceptions. He was stirred only by a reminiscence of sadness; he was like an archaeologist studying the ruins of an interesting civilization. Sometimes he smiled faintly; breezes of life seemed to play over his bland, buried face."

C.A.

T ESSIE RUBIN OPENED the door to Sol and gave him access to a different kind of smell from that of the hallway of the apartment house. The hallway, with its tile floors and broken windows, smelled of garbage and soot; Tessie's apartment gave forth the more personal odors of bad cooking and dust.

"Oh, it's you," she said, opening the door wider. The immediate apprehension on her yellowish face settled down to the chronic yet resigned look of perpetual fear. "That Goberman has been bothering me for money. He curses—imagine—*curses* me for not giving money to the Jewish Appeal. Is that any way to get charity from people, to curse!"

Sol walked past her, down the hall whose walls were so dark and featureless that they seemed like empty space.

"He pockets it himself," he reassured her as she followed him to the living room.

"He's a devil is what he is. Says to me, 'You of all people should contribute to saving Jewish lives.' What does he want from me, blood? Can't he see how I live? Maybe he doesn't know I haven't a single penny in the house. Every week he comes, and when I give him something he looks at it like its *dreck*. 'Is this what you call a contribution?' he says. What does he want from me, I'm asking you." She fell wearily into an armchair which leaned swollenly to one side under its faded cretonne covering, like an old sick elephant under shabby regal garments. She had a large, curved nose, and her face was very thin; there were hollows in her temples, and her eyes, stranded in the leanness of all the features, were exceptionally large and dismal. She threw her arms outward, splayed her legs in exhaustion: their thinness was grotesque, because her torso was heavy and short, with huge breasts. "Why doesn't he look around how I live?

How can he think I'm a Rothschild, a Baruch! Maybe he should know that I made bread soaked in evaporated milk for supper for me and the *alta*."

"I gave you fifty dollars last week. Why bread and milk?" Sol said angrily as he reclined on the sofa, which was as shapeless as the chair she sat on.

"Why, why! I had to have the doctor twice for him, the old man— *house calls*. Ten dollars each time."

"So, thirty dollars in five days. Not a fortune, but you should have more than bread and milk from it."

"Oh, I go crazy, too, you know. So I took in one little movie, so I bought one little house dress I shouldn't walk around with holes showing. It's a crime?" She glared at him savagely, as though to make up for her unaltered position of repose.

Sol waved his hand to dismiss the subject. "I'll leave you a few dollars before I go. Remind me." He turned his head toward the doorway that led to the two bedrooms. "How is he, the old man?"

"Eh, he lives. How can he be?"

Sol nodded and slid lower on the couch, so that he was lying almost horizontal. He exhaled slowly through his teeth and crossed his arms over his eyes. The ugly grotto of the room permeated him with all its stale, musty odors; and yet oddly, as always, his body went limp with relaxation. He heard Tessie sighing quietly across the small room, seemed to see, even through his covering arms, the crowding, unattractive mementoes she had reclaimed or imitated from her past life: a brass samovar, a twin-framed ornate picture of herself and her late husband, Herman Rubin, a brown depressing tapestry which depicted a waterway in Venice, a fluted china plate teeming with iridescent-green tulips, a picture of her father and her mother in the frozen poses of a half-century ago, an oval-framed portrait of a fat-faced child with slightly crossed eyes—her late son, Morris. The sink in the kitchen leaked steadily, not drops, but in a persistent trickle. From above came the sound of many footsteps, the heavy ones of men and women, the dance of the young. The old man groaned in the bedroom, called out a complicated Yiddish-Polish curse, and then subsided into high, womanish moans, which gradually diminished to little respiratory grunts. There was a smell of sour milk and cauliflower and an all-pervading odor of sweat, as though the building were a huge living creature. Gradually, Sol's body lightened, his breathing came more deeply and regularly. He lay there listening to the sound of his body drifting toward sleep, observing the numbing peace of his limbs, until he slept, deeply and peacefully.

When he woke he couldn't remember where he was for a moment. The room was dark except for the thick beam of light cast on the floor from the kitchen. He lay without moving, listening to the clattering of pots and pans, savoring the nerveless ease of his body.

"Vat is to eat? *Ich bin kronk.* I need strength, *kayach,*" the old querulous voice said. "I eat bread and milk and you . . . vat do you hide and eat ven I sleep? Hah, vat—lox and herring, some juicy smoked fish? *Ich bin kronk, dine aine tata.* You would starve me. Ah, it is all up vit me," he whined.

"Shh, you will wake him, let him sleep. He is so tired, that man, he needs to sleep. I took some money from his pocket and bought some nice fresh eggs, some cream cheese. You like cream cheese, Pa," she said.

"I dream about smoked butterfish. Why can't we have smoked butterfish?" the old man complained.

"I'll fry the eggs hard, the way you like them," the woman's voice said. "Just don't talk so loud, please. He gets his best sleep here."

Sol lay without moving. The smell of the frying eggs came to him, the sounds of the other people in the building. All around him life of various sorts, stone hollowed out and filled with the insect life of humans, the whole earth honeycombed with them. In another pocket of stone or brick or wood, Jesus Ortiz, Morton, George Smith, Murillio, billions. Insects ruining the sweet, silent proportions of the earth. Undermining, soiling, hurting. Where was the gigantic foot to crush them all? Where was blessed silence? Footsteps, pots clanking, voices of strangers, of the old man, the woman in the kitchen. He drifted off to explore a last little void of dreamless sleep.

"Sol, Sol, wake up. I have supper. Come, before it gets cold."

He peered up at her gaunt, bleak face. She nodded to tell him he was awake; she had much experience with the violated borders between reality and dreams, knew enough to take the time to reassure a sleeper. "Eggs and rolls, coffee. Yes, yes, it is only Tessie . . . come."

Slowly he unrolled himself, sat up, then stood. She touched his arm, and he followed her. In the kitchen the old man shrugged at him.

"Hello Mendel," he said.

"Sure, sure," the old man said bitterly. "What do they care? Yeh, don't esk qvestion, it's a Jew—gas him, burn him, stick him through vit hot needles."

"Eat Pa, while it's hot," Tessie said, looking at Sol over her father's head.

They sat down together at the porcelain-topped table. Sol reached for a roll, and Tessie poured coffee while the old man muttered the prayer over the food sullenly, his face like an arid relief map of some forgotten valley. He was seventy-five but he looked a hundred. He had many dents in his bald head, his nose was crushed; but he had been of durable stock, so he was still alive.

"Her husband died in Belsen," the old man said suddenly, pointing a crooked accusing finger at his daughter. "And vat they did to her, yes, yes. And she sits there like a *lady. Oy vay, ich bin zayer kronk.*" He began to weep and dab at his eyes.

"I know, Mendel. Stop that now. Let us eat in peace, for Christ's sake," Sol said. Mournfully, he himself began to eat, as though to set an example. Tessie shrugged and ate, too, with her eyes on the food. She had a tattoo similar to Sol's on the dead-white skin on her arm. The sink dripped, the neighbors pounded on the ceiling, shouted occasionally in Spanish or Yiddish. Someone screamed in the streets, and a police siren sounded, going away from all of it. Here, Rubin, here is your lovely widow, your stately father-in-law; I watch over them for you, keep them in a manner befitting their station. Let your bones lie easy in the earth—you are missing nothing, nothing at all.

Finally they were through. Tessie herded the old man into his room and closed the door. She came back into the kitchen and cleared the dishes away. Sol went into the living room and sat down. He closed his eyes and waited. Soon he heard her come into the room and sit beside him. He opened his eyes; the room was still lit only by the light from the kitchen. She looked at him with glittering, dismal eyes.

"So what do we have in this life?" she said.

"We have, we have. We live."

"I feel like screaming all day long. I feel like screaming myself to death," she said.

"But you don't and I don't and the old man doesn't. We live and fight off the animals."

"They're better off, the dead ones."

"I won't argue. I don't want to talk about it. It is ridiculous to talk about it. I don't feel so good the past week or two anyhow. Don't talk about nonsense."

"So I won't talk," she said.

They sat there in silence for about ten minutes, in the pose of two peaceful people seated on a cool veranda watching the country scene.

After a while she said, "Do you want to?"

"All right," he said.

She took off her dress in the dimness. He lay back on the couch. Finally she pushed her heavy, hanging breasts in his face and lay against him. "You're not too tired?"

He shook his head against her warm body, which smelled old. They turned into each other with little moans. And then they made love on the lumpy couch with the sounds of the old man's groaning madness in the other room, and there was very little of passion between them and nothing of real love or tenderness, but, rather, that immensely stronger force of desperation and mutual anguish.

When it was over, they said nothing to each other. After a few minutes, Sol got up and straightened his clothing. Then he took some money from his pocket and wedged it under the samovar. With his hand on the door, he spoke without turning.

"Maybe Monday, Tuesday I will come again," he said.

"What shall I do about that torturer Goberman?" she asked dully, expecting no illusion of grace from him. Her collapsed body lay wraithlike in the darkened room.

"All right, I will come Monday night. Tell Goberman to come then, that you will settle with him then. I will be here, I will deal with him."

She sighed for answer.

He closed the door on her and her father; it was like administering a drug to himself, that closing of the door, an opiate locking off a corridor of his mind. He went out through the tiled hallway, with its smell of garbage and its resemblance to some ancient, abandoned hospital, until he was on the street, which was erratically lit and smoky with the increasing heat.

Then he walked like a man in a dream toward the subway, sagging with tiredness again at the prospect of the distance between him and his bed.

MABEL WHEATLY HUNG on Jesus Ortiz' arm like a bride; he suffered her possessive embrace because it made him feel manly to walk through the crowd that way. The counterfeit exoticism of the dance hall, garish and frenetic, fell over them as they walked. There was a huge babble of voices, the feathery rustling of dresses. The savage farce of light that came from a rotating prism on the ceiling bathed Jesus and the girl in green, in red, in yellow, in blue. The orchestra crashed rhythmically, with a minimum of tune. Dark faces, white teeth, and fluttering clothes made a shifting corridor for them as they shoved their way along one side of the huge room toward an empty table.

Ortiz plunked the two bottles of beer on the table, and they sat. He scanned the teeming hall with cool, faintly bored eyes, liking the picture of them; him sitting like a man who had been around. Mabel half leaning over the table, holding his hand, her eyes fixed on him. Her expression was a naïve attempt at sultriness; it was her stock in trade, but also the only way she knew how to show emotion. She had on a dress of metallic green, cut low to reveal the tops of her full, brown breasts. Her face was softly curved, wide-nostriled, long-eyed; she offered the best of herself to her companion, but he sat in a sullen reverie, casting his eyes around for something he had no hope of finding there.

"You want to dance, hon?" she asked timidly, brushing her fingers against the back of his hand.

"Let's just sit . . . talk a while. I'm tired. That Jew had me working my *cojones* off all afternoon. Let's just talk," he said idly, his eyes everywhere but on her.

"What you want to talk about, honey?" she asked. She clung to him hungrily with her eyes, yearning toward some odd, bright cleanliness she imagined in him. Half consciously she saw a hope of escape in him. Not that she actually thought her prostitution was a bad way to earn a living. Only she became drugged with hopelessness at times, experienced boredom of such an intense degree, as she indulged the queer fears and lusts of her paying customers, that she had even considered suicide, and passed it by only because of some inexplicable curiosity about what the next day would bring. This boy was so cool, so sweet to look at. He seemed to know something, have some marvelous answer in him. "You got somethin' special in mind, sweety? What?"

"Talk?" He turned to her as though she had brought up the suggestion. "Well now, what could you and me have to talk? Business, you want to talk about what kind of business I should go into?" he said sarcastically. "You an expert or something? All right then, tell me. Should I go into the clothing business like my uncle in Detroit? Or tombstones, or baby carriages, or groceries, or . . . a pawnshop?"

"Good money in that pawnshop business," she said, pretending he hadn't been teasing her with the question. "The Jew teachin' you that business, ain't he?"

"Yeah, he teachin'." Suddenly his eyes went hard with the gleam of desire. "Oh, if I had the f—g dough, the loot. . . ."

"You serious about that business kick, ain't you, hon?" she asked, wondering how to connect herself with his desire.

"I'm serious."

She looked at him cautiously for a moment. "Could I maybe go in with you?" she blurted out.

He looked at her with scornful amusement.

"You sayin' how you need the money so bad. Well, what if I chip in with some? How would that be?"

He smiled and ran his fingers up her arm. He was flattered at being offered money by a whore. How many men got offers like that? Wasn't that evidence that he was a man among men?

"It might be; you never know, Mabel. I like you good enough, you a sweet baby to be with. Of course, I figure my plans for me alone, but you never know. You show me the money, and we could see."

"You see. I get me some money together, gonna start squeezin' for it. I don't want to do what I'm doin' forever either, you know. I get some *gifts*, extra, you know. I already got a load of stuff to hock. You see, honey, I gonna surprise you."

"Yeah, you do that, fine, fine," he said, searching the crowded hall. All around were the myriad, elusive colors, the thumping music entwined with the hundreds of voices and the whispering slide of the many dancers on the floor. The colors played over his delicate head like the reflection of all his fleeting ideas, of his strange, desperate daydreams. He was big and had hands of great brawny power, a face that was tough and brutal and inspired fear and awe; and everyone, himself included, knew his name, for it was graven on the wall of some huge and imposing edifice—JESUS ORTIZ.

Tangee and Buck White sat down at the next table. Tangee was with some strange woman, not his wife, a black, fulsome woman with purple lipstick. Buck White watched his wife shyly. She was a light-skinned girl of frail and tinselly beauty who demonstrated by her bored sullen expression that she had been bought by her slow-witted husband but that her price was going up, right before his despairing eyes.

"Hey man," Tangee called over. "How the pawnbrokin' business?"

"Makin' out," Jesus answered blandly.

"Aw listen to him, *makin' out!* That place *coin* money."

Jesus shrugged. "Ain't mine."

"Whyn't you and the gal come over to sit with us," Tangee offered. "Be sociable."

Jesus looked at Mabel, then got up and went over. She followed him, a shy smile on her face. There was some shifting of chairs, little darts of smile.

"Billy an' Thelma, say hello to Jesus Ortiz an' . . . I didn't catch your gal's name. . . ." Tangee leaned over, the diplomatic link between all their dissimilarities.

"Mabel," Jesus said, and endured the giggling salutations, the embarrassing shifting of Buck, to whom amenities were complex and better avoided. Buck's wife, Billy, stared blatantly at Jesus over her conversation with the other two women, and Buck dreamed of the sacks of gold with which he could earn his wife's febrile attention.

"Now I been wonderin' somethin', Ortiz. I don't want you to take it bad. I'm just curious." Tangee looked at Jesus' small, hairless hands, with their delicate, thin fingers, and noted how he balled them up into little fists under his scrutiny. "How come a smart boy like you got to work in that pawnshop? I mean you used to have faster games than that. I happen to know you worked for that pusher, Kopey, one time. Even numbers a couple years ago. How come you go for that nigger job? What could you make—thirty, forty bucks? You just don't figure like a janitor."

"That my business, Tangee."

"Okay, but it don't make no sense to me."

"I got my plans."

"Sure you do; ain't we all?" Tangee toyed with the ash tray, his eyes on the clenched, childish fists. After a decent interval, casually, he asked, "Say, tell me, that there pawnshop a goin' thing?"

"Much cash," Jesus said, staring hard at Tangee's face to force him off the study of his hands.

"Yes man, that what I thought," Tangee said. "That what Robinson say, ain't it, Buck? Just them same words, 'Much cash.' "

"He say like dat den when he . . ." Buck confirmed, stopping before the words got him out of his depth.

Billy White frowned disdainfully at her husband and began running her eyes from Jesus' hair to his mouth to his hands.

"It somethin' to think on, all that cash," Tangee said.

Jesus looked at him with a flat, unreadable expression while the orchestra pounded the beat on walls and floor, pulling at the smoky-sweet air so people's hands and feet followed the rhythm. The woman Thelma tapped her large, black hand and hummed indistinguishably. The turning prisms on the ceiling swung the phosphorescence of color over faces and bottles. There was, in all the hubbub, the clear sound of the three men's careful, speculative breathing.

"He's cute," Billy White said suddenly. They all turned to look at her. "I mean look at how cute he is," she said, gazing at Jesus' mouth. "Got a face like a girl. And look at his hands—pretty, like a girl's. I like fellas with like delicate hands and all."

Jesus felt his throat close, his whole body go rigid with fury and pain. All the hands seemed displayed on the table; Buck's mammoth ones, Tangee's, Thelma's, even Mabel's were slightly larger than his. Tangee smiled slyly. Buck just lifted his hands with mild amusement; he had never considered them before. Suddenly Jesus felt his arms twitch, as though pulled by someone. A glass turned over and fell to the floor without breaking. Mabel gave a little gasp, bent to pick it up, and then stopped, remembering some devious propriety.

"You just like fellas, period, Billy," Tangee said after a little laugh. But his own gaze followed the chiseled line of the Ortiz features, noted the lovely oversized eyes, the shapely lips, now compressed by some odd tension, and the hands bunched up at the very edge of the table. And his scrutiny was for something he could use, something perhaps too devious for him to seize, but *there*, there all the same. "Don't pay her no attention, Ortiz; she just tryin' to embarrass you is all."

Jesus spread his mouth in a rigid smile and stared insolently at Billy. "Why, she like my type. That's no insult."

Buck stared at his new-found hands and began rubbing their knuckles together, his massive face perplexed, fermenting.

Jesus pushed back his chair and stood. "We got to cut out now," he said softly, the pale smile still in place. Mabel stood up with him.

"It somethin' to think about, all that cash," Tangee said.

"Well then, I think about it," Jesus answered. He gave a little wave to all of them. He looked at Tangee a moment longer, took the other man's veiled, suggestive expression, and returned it unopened.

"Maybe we talk some more, another time, Tangee," he said.

"That be fine if we do, *very* fine," Tangee said after them, and he watched Jesus' slender back with a flat yet avid gaze until it disappeared among the thronging men and women in a last reflection of blue and red from the prismatic light.

Mabel preceded him up the stairs to the Ortiz apartment. His mother would be long gone for her night job downtown, where she still worked as a scrubwoman in a big office building. They walked into the three-room apartment, and Mabel turned on the little radio while Jesus went into the kitchen with the bottle of gin he had bought. She hummed the tune as she waited, her eyes wandering absently over a familiar place, familiar in its resemblance to the ten thousands like it all over the city. She knew that Jesus and his mother had lived in a dozen different places in the last ten years, and that each flat was like another as if they had all been the rooms of one gigantic house. Her gaze was uncritical of the paint-swollen walls, which were lumpy because of the many layers of pigment, as though poverty itself dented the rooms beyond any attempts at concealment. In one corner a little lantern flickered on a saccharine Mary, and farther away a gold-colored crucifix picked up the Mother's light. Shapelessness infected the modestly covered bed and the tired stuffed chairs. You sensed that the peculiar odor of poor living was somehow held slightly at bay by the desperate cleanliness of the woman who lived there. There was a picture of Jane Ortiz, Jesus' mother, a dark-skinned woman with pronounced Negroid features who smiled self-consciously, as though shy at the proximity to her husband in the twin frame. The father, long absent from their lives (Mabel had always been afraid to ask Jesus what had happened to him, well aware of his strange, inexplicable sore spots), looked almost white, a thin-nosed, narrow-lipped man with large, sensuous, slightly goiterous eyes like those of an ancient Spanish grandee.

"Here you go, Baby," Jesus said, handing her a glass full of gin with clumsily broken chunks of ice in it. He put the bottle down on the end table and sat beside her on the couch. There was a light in the kitchen, but the only light in the living room came from the little altar in the corner. The radio played a rock-'n'-roll tune, and Mabel hummed to it, occasionally inserting a string of words she remembered. Her head rested comfortably on his shoulder. Jesus sipped at the drink and stared at the dim colors reflected on the window shade from the scattered neons and street lights. Side-stepping his fearful rage, he placed himself on a great, flat plain with no one in sight, no house or tree, no rise of ground. And then he imagined himself approaching a great light in the earth, filled with an immense trembling excitement, not knowing the source of the light, moving toward it and wondering whether it would be fearsome or exalting.

"Penny for you thoughts, hon," she offered timidly, willing to go infinitely higher.

"Nazerman say to me one day, 'You know how old this profession is?' " His voice was soft and amusing, almost as though he talked aloud to himself. "I say no, how old? And he say *thousands of years*. He say one time the Babylon . . . some crazy tribe, they use to take crops and even people for pawn. A man make loans on his family— wife, kid, anything. I mean you see what a solid business that is thousands of years. Hard to think on thousands of years, people back then. . . ." He laid his head back against the couch, his eyes burning at the dimness. His mind reeled at the succession of rooms he had lived in. He remembered, a thousand times multiplied, those few times his name had been doubted, his paternity jeered at. He recalled the hundred times he had experienced the same humiliation he had felt that same night when the woman had called attention to his delicate face, his small, girlish hands. His home, his name, his gender —all a tenuous, unproved thing. The world had no up or down for him; he floated disembodied in a dark void and he was forever clawing at the random things he passed, seeking a handhold, a mystical history. Only the Pawnbroker, with his cryptic eyes, his huge, secret body, seemed to have some sly key, some talisman of *knowing*.

"Only for the money. I learnin' that business, estimatin' figurin'. If I had me a bundle . . ." He turned to her, and she, mistaking his intention, opened her lips to him. "You got any idea what that Tangee hintin' at, back there in the dance hall?" he asked.

"He didn't say much of anything."

"He didn't *say*. But you know what that man is, who he hangs out with."

"He got that friend Robinson. I know him. You smart you don't get mixed up with that man. He's a ex-con, a real bad, bad man." She studied him for a moment and then lowered her eyes. "Yes," she said solemnly, "I do know what he getting at. But honey, you don't *need* to get in with them. I told you I gonna raise some money, and you save some here and there. Pretty soon you get it—safe!" She looked at him again, and her anxiety was not just for his welfare but for the threat to her contribution, her only possible claim on him.

"Sure, sure," he said blandly, excluding her once more with a covering smile. "Don't worry about a thing, sweety."

Then he pushed her back roughly and began fondling her thighs. The recent rage returned to him, and he demanded she forget how small his hands were by crushing her full breasts with them. He delighted in her groans of pain, saw himself as a great rutting male, for the while, in his assumed brutality. She cried out many times, "I love you, I love you, I love you," ecstatic in the glamour of the unpaid-for love-making she endured under her unfathomable lover.

And later, while she sighed wistfully and cast about in her mind for sudden wealth with which to ensnare him, Jesus puffed on a cigarette as he lay, thoughtfully blowing his scrambling dreams at the ceiling in dim clouds of smoke.

MAYBE I HAVE a tumor, Sol thought with bitter amusement. He tried to visualize that peculiar knot of pressure, tried even to localize it. It would seem to be here, just below the breastbone and then . . . up here near his neck . . . no, more toward his back and down. For a moment he thought of death, that old companion of his youth. Ortiz feather-dusted quietly, and he watched him. That sourly anticlimactic joke; it only made him feel cold, not fearful at all.

"Mail this on the corner," he said.

Ortiz took the envelope and studied the address.

Sol sighed mildly. "Just mail it, will you," he said. "Don't waste time. Maybe when you get back I'll tell you a few things, give you a *lesson* in pawnbroking. You are always after me to."

Ortiz smiled and walked swiftly out on his errand. Sol studied his debts while he was waiting. He made a dozen small calculations which proved he didn't make enough money to pay all his bills. Then he just let the pencil meander over the paper in small, amoebic doodles until his assistant returned.

"All right. That thing you just mailed was the list of yesterday's hocks, the things I loaned money on."

The eager acolyte leaned on the counter, his eyes on the Pawnbroker's mouth, all of him narrowed to that mundane information. It occurred to him that great secrets could come from tiny perforations, inadvertently. He must be patient and receptive.

"All the information about an item of jewelry, for example, must be on that list; the amount loaned on it, the complete description.

In describing a watch, you must have the case and movement numbers, the size, any unusual markings, any engraved inscriptions. In jewelry, you use the loupe to . . ."

The store creaked under the grotesque weight of its merchandise, and the air was respectful of the teacher's voice. No customers came in; the street in front of their doorway seemed deserted and even the traffic sounded distant. It seemed to Jesus that all the city found the time suddenly hallowed, and he offered himself to the Pawnbroker's dark, indrawn voice with an unconscious sensation of privilege.

"To find the purity of gold in something, up to fourteen karat, you scratch a tiny mark. I say *tiny* in the ethical sense. Actually, this is an area for dishonest profit, too; the filings from a year's gouging can add up to a pretty penny. Anyhow, you drop nitric acid on the scratch. If there is brass, you will get a bright green, silver will show up a dirty gray, and iron will give you a blackish-brown color. Now if the gold is about fourteen karat, you must use these special gold-tipped needles and a touchstone. The acid we use for this is secret to the trade. . . ."

"*Secret*, huh," Jesus echoed in a languid voice as the Pawnbroker gave him the barest outlines of the mysteries.

And it seemed to him that many things of great significance just lay in the quality of the big Jew's voice, that he might, at any moment, surprise the great complexity of his employer just in the ponderous breath that carried the droning words. Horror and exaltation seemed to reside in the Pawnbroker's mysterious history, oddly eased and enriched in the imminence of revelation, oddly eased and enriched in the things beyond what he could form in thought, beyond what the older man said.

". . . so you must watch out for the professional confidence men, the gyp-artists. They are shrewd and practiced and they have a huge bag of tricks. In jewelry, for instance. Take a good-quality pearl which has been accidentally ruined by acid or sweat. The con man will peel the vital top layer to expose the second layer. This layer *will* have a similar appearance to the unspoiled pearl. For a few months! But then you will realize that you are stuck with a dull, worthless nothing. It is important to examine the apparently beautiful pearl, for only the original top layer is really smooth; the other layers are coarse by close comparison."

Sol's voice rolled on in the stillness, disdainful of this latter-day craft of his, echoing his vast bitterness for the things he had once considered important and which he now hated because in his loss of them he had been left deprived and ugly.

Yet, not knowing this (nor would he have cared if he had), the smooth-skinned youth with the sly, delicate face basked in his exposure to ancient, terrible wonders, things only faintly shaped by his scattered knowledge of the Pawnbroker's peculiar heritage, his strange survival of fantastic horrors. So he looked at the blue numbers on his employer's arm and tried to work back from that cryptic sum to the figures that had made it; and, more and more, he was involved in an odd current of emotions, softened and blinded and bound.

Until, finally, the Pawnbroker pushed at him almost gently and said, "Enough with the lessons. Get to work now, Ortiz."

And then, to make the severance complete, Mrs. Harmon came in with three suits; Jesus took them upstairs to the loft and went reluctantly back to his cross-indexing, which now must include Willy Harmon's two Sunday suits and the invalid younger Harmon's rare festive change. And Jesus Ortiz muttered about nothing, really cursing the elusiveness of the Nazerman spirit.

"Fee time at my Edith's secretary school," Mrs. Harmon said in her chuckling voice. Then she laughed out loud and shook her head in wonder at the precariousness of her life. "Man d'lifeboats again, another bill. Honest and true, it like bailin' out a leaky ol' boat fill with holes. Pawn somethin' to buy somethin' else, then pawn that. Each time it seem like the boat gettin' lower in d'water. Ain't it a *wonder* a body stay afloat long as it do?" She sighed at her ridiculous resignation. "But you do, somehow you do, one way or another. I declare, sometimes I don't know if the good Lord plan it all this way to test or if he jus' so busy he get to you again and again jus' in time to keep you from goin' under for the third time." And then her rich, imperishable laughter struck on all the objects in the place, stealing all their value by implying that nothing had value without human hands to coax life into it.

"Five dollars for the three suits," Sol said, feeling the buried pressure again. It sent a streak of apprehension through him; he recalled the power of a few blades of grass to grow through and split solid stone.

"I jus' ain't up to horse-tradin' today, Mistuh Nazerman. No use threatenin' to take my suits someplace else. Too tired to bother." She held out her hand for the money. As she buried the bills deep in the shabby purse, she muttered, "Jus' keep them ol' pawn tickets, these and the ones from the candlesticks, too. You an' me both know that what you bury might jus' as well stay dead." For a moment she looked at the gray, untouchable face of the Pawnbroker. "Ain't that right, Mistuh Nazerman?"

"I suppose it is," he answered, his face sightless and only coincidentally directed toward her.

Two women came in with wedding rings to pawn, apparently arrived at similar desperations at the same time. An old Orthodox Jew, wearing a long gabardine coat despite the heat, offered a tiny diamond stickpin; he argued feebly in Yiddish for a few minutes and then took the small loan with a little clucking noise. A Puerto Rican youth brought in a Spanish guitar and took the first price offered without a word; only he plucked a two-note farewell to the instrument on its own strings before abandoning it. A jet-black girl with the face of a fourteen-year-old and a pregnant body gave him her engagement "diamond," which was glass. The Pawnbroker sent her out with it in her hand, stunned and lost.

At noon a man with nut-colored skin and white hair came into the store. He walked over to the counter with an amiability that indicated he had nothing he wished to get a loan on.

"I'm Savarese," he said. He had black eyes and puffy, fighter's features. "I'm agonna giva you d'estimate."

"I expected you yesterday," Sol said.

"I wasa busy.' He ran his eyes in mock appraisal over the store and grinned. "Well, after carefula study, I'ma estimate the complete redecoratin' gonna costa you five G's."

"Who do I make the check out to?"

"Acame Contractin' Corporation," Savarese said, picking at his teeth with a toothpick.

"How do you spell it?"

"It'sa A C M E, *Acame!*"

As Sol began to write, Savarese looked furtively around for a moment, then silently took a thick envelope from his breast pocket and dropped it in front of the Pawnbroker. Sol pocketed it without looking up as he continued writing.

Savarese took the check from him with a parting chuckle.

"Give you a gooda job, Mr. Pawnabroker, paint the whole goddama place pink anda yellow."

Sol waved him away with the offhand gesture he would have used to brush a bug off the counter.

He opened the envelope, and the inside was greasy-green with money. Fifty hundred-dollar bills bulged out. As he stared dully at it, the steps behind him creaked. He turned quickly to see his assistant gazing innocently at the money.

"I guess Thursdays are paydays," Jesus said flatly.

"Mind your own business," Sol said. He took the money back to the huge safe and, hiding the combination with his body, locked it in. Later, as was his custom, he would take it to the night depository of the bank down the street.

A well-dressed woman, white with mortification, brought in a diamond watch. He loaned her ninety dollars on it, and she took the money with a little wince before hurrying out with the pawn ticket clutched in her hand.

"Now she not a virgin any more," Jesus said. "She been in to a pawnshop, sell her soul to the devil."

"I can do without your jokes," Sol said, involved with that peculiar kernel inside him. What was the matter with him, worrying invisible aches like his fearful brother-in-law, Selig? "You have time to be funny? Go instead to the cafeteria and get me some coffee."

Jesus raised his eyes in mocking surprise at his employer's unusual self-indulgence. "Next thing you be takin' afternoons off to go to the track."

"You must be patient with me," Sol answered sourly. "I am getting on in years." He flipped a coin to Jesus.

The youth snapped it out of the air with a dart of his hand and then winked at Sol for his own prowess. "Black, no sugar?"

Sol nodded impatiently.

While Jesus was gone, Mabel Wheatly came in.

"This here a expensive locket," she said challengingly. "No sense foolin' around, I *know* it's gold."

It *was* gold, heavy and pure. Obligatorily, he scratched and tested, but he knew all the time by the very feel of it.

"Fifty dollars," he said.

"Gimme the locket."

"Seventy-five," he revised, offering the figure she would get from anyone else.

"That worth a hundred easy," she said, taking up her property with an assaying glance at his face, emboldened by his one retreat.

"Not to me," he said, looking into her face as though it were a hollow well.

She saw finality in his expression. For a moment she rubbed the gold with her thumb, massaging prodigious value into it. Then she nodded and dropped it on the counter before him.

As he wrote up the article and made out the pawn ticket, she talked her relief like a man who, after a hard day's work, takes satisfaction in his pay, in the money he thinks will advance him along the road to a particular aspiration.

"Ah, you know all about *me*, Pawnbroker," she said in an easy, confiding voice. "You know what I'm in. I don't have to tell you how hard *I* work for my money."

"It is peculiar work," he agreed without judgment.

"Oh brother, peculiar is right." She lit a cigarette and looked back with comfortable melancholy at those hardships already behind her. "Like a woman could go right out of her mind if she thinks on it too much."

"Then I suppose you should not think about it," he said with a little serrated edge to his voice.

"I suppose," she said. She watched her exhaled smoke as it was caught suddenly by the fan and torn to pieces. "Got me a hard boss there, too."

"The woman in charge?" he inquired politely as he finished the little bit of paper work.

"Oh no, she all right. No, I mean the big boss, the owner. He one hard man. Not that he do anything I know of. Only the way he look at us girls, talk in a quiet weird voice. Like you just *know* what he threatenin', if you mess around. Big man, too, got lots of irons in the fire, you know."

Sol looked up for a few seconds to stare at the slow-moving cigarette smoke between them. He was teased with an almost imperceptible sense of recognition, of connection. But the smoke caught in the fan's arc and was wafted away, so he found himself looking at the girl's ordinary brown features, and whatever it was ducked down in his consciousness.

That night, before he left, Jesus asked Sol if he wanted him to accompany him to the bank. "I take one of them duelin' pistols and guard you, huh?"

"If you would only do those things I ask you to, I would be satisfied. Never mind volunteering; I do not appreciate it. Just go on home, I will ask you for what I want."

"You gonna smother my initiative," Jesus said with his wild smile.

"Good night already," Sol said, raising his hand and turning his head away in exasperation. When he looked back, Ortiz was gone.

He went to the safe and took the money out. For the first time he found himself apprehensive over that half-block walk. Formerly, he had always had the policeman on the beat escort him the short way. But in recent weeks, since Leventhal had become so annoying, he had gone alone.

Anyhow, it was still quite light on the street. There were many people around and police were never more than a block or so away. He locked up the store and started down the street.

When he was almost to the bank, he noticed the three men on the far corner, recognized the ash-gray suit, Tangee, the great bulk of Buck White. He hurried the last few dozen feet, and his hands shook as he slipped the envelope into the brass, revolving chamber. But when he looked back at the men after the money was safely deposited, they appeared quite innocent, like any three men commenting idly on the passing scene. And he felt a growing rage at himself, as though his greatest enemy had invaded his body to leave him shaken and unknown to himself.

When he got home that night, everyone but Selig was out for the evening. His brother-in-law sat stiffly in the dim-lit living room. His usually ruddy face was sweaty and pale, and he looked pleadingly up at Sol.

"What is wrong, Selig?"

"I think I'm having a heart attack," Selig whispered in terror.

Sol sat down and took his brother-in-law's wrist to feel the pulse. Selig stared at him like a bewildered animal. The pulse was strong and steady, only a little fast.

"Why do you think you are having a heart attack?"

"I had these stabbing pains in my chest before. Then I got faint. No one was here. It seemed terrible that I might die alone. I'm afraid of dying, Sol. I was afraid to move." He spoke softly, without moving his lips, as though careful to avoid even that tiny strain. "I'm not like you, Solly. I haven't been through the things you have. Your life doesn't seem to interest you very much. Not like me, not like me. I must live! I *love* living—eating, talking. . . . Bertha and I still have . . . love . . . you know what I mean. I'm terrified, please Sol. . . ."

"Does it hurt now?"

"Noo-o," Selig said, his expression one of inward inspection. "I don't think so."

"And just how many *stabbing* pains did you have?"

"About three or four," Selig whispered, just turning his eyes.

"And that was all?"

"Yes, except that I got this *faint* feeling after that."

Sol smiled distastefully. "You will not die now, Selig; relax. You are a very healthy man." Surprisingly, there was a note of gentleness in his scorn.

"You think so?" Selig leaned very cautiously into hope. "What was it, then, the pains, the faintness?"

"The pains were nerves. You were perhaps thinking about the possibility of a heart attack for some reason?"

"A teacher in my school, just my age, fifty-four, keeled over today. Never had a sick day, and, boom, he keels over dead!"

"Aha."

"But the faintness?" Selig asked, not letting go of fear too easily, although a craven smile of relief was beginning.

"A natural reaction to fear. The blood leaves your head, you see things as through a smoked glass, sounds get distant and small."

"Yes, yes, that was it exactly." He breathed delightedly the sweet air of life and began looking around him with great pleasure, like a child drinking in the familiarity of his room after a nightmare. "Oh, Solly, thank you. I wouldn't say this in front of anyone else but . . . well, you are a comfort, a strange comfort to me. You're younger than I am . . . but it's funny, this will sound foolish, I feel as protected with you here as I did when I was a kid still living with my father. Protected . . . a strange thing to say, isn't it? Tomorrow I will want to forget all about this. But now . . ."

"First of all, you are a hypochondriac, Selig. But most of all you are a fool." Sol stood up. "Relax now; your crisis is over. You must take care of *yourself*. I have nothing to do with you. I am not your protector, nor am I your father or your doctor or your rabbi. I give you the courtesy of exposing your own foolishness to you, that is all. I am nothing to you, Selig. Now I am going to bed."

"Yes, Sol, thank you Solly," Selig said, still beyond insult.

And that night, Sol Nazerman was ravaged by dreams again. But mercifully, perhaps, they were torn out of recognition, because he kept waking all through the night, waking up with a strange, nameless alarm.

BUCK WHITE SAT in one corner, brooding in the sound of his wife's flirtatious laughter. When he had been younger, his great muscularity had been an impressive focus for women's attention, but now his laborer's body was just a hard, knotty joke. He had nothing else to offer. Words came out of him in careful couples or trios. When he tried to use more than he needed for request or simple answer, they came out in a garbled winding whose beginning and end were lost to him. Once, he had won several hundred dollars in a crap game, and his winnings had adorned him in suits and an installment car; people had seemed to smile respectfully at the dazzle he made. He sat there yearning savagely for that affluence again, his huge Bantu face lowering and hard as he watched his wife, Billy, parade her face and body for Kopey, the numbers man.

Three other men, Cecil Mapp among them, sat in another corner laughing over their beer. Actually, Cecil was drinking lemonade, under the influence of his wife, who sat with the other women in the kitchen. Billy White was the only woman among the men, and her laughter kept them all swollenly conscious of their maleness; except for her husband, who dreamed furiously of barbaric splendor and kneaded his huge hands.

"I'm going to take a little business trip out to L.A. in a couple of weeks," Kopey said with a blasé expression on his sleek, yellow face. He studied the big star sapphire on his pinky. "Pro'bly run out to Malibu Beach while I'm out there. That L.A. really jumpin'."

"I'm just dyin' to get out there," Billy said, courting him with a smile. "Catch a look at the movie stars, you know. I got a idea it's real crazy out there, loads of fun and all."

"Oh they *move* out there, no question," Kopey said with a last, bored look at his ring.

Buck cleared his throat, and they turned toward him, surprised at this manifestation of life. Billy frowned in anticipation of stupidity.

"I almos' went there . . . once," he said, embarking on the treacherous sea of conversation; it suddenly appeared to him that he had need of greater complexity. "It was like I was in there the army but not befo', not when I was gettin' out like, ony this guy don' remember which because he wasn't in like me the army, ony he said if . . ." His eyes cast around for something that would orient him, searched for anything but his wife's face. He felt himself drowning in the sea of words, but he continued to thrash around, making a great show of swimming. "I . . . if *I* want to go like in the place, not he—*I*," he emphasized as though some clarity were just out of his reach. His face beaded with sweat, and the sudden silence of everyone else in the room was like a sound. "See I still in but not he, he never in at all so he could go ahead to L.A. but only he wasn't able, so he got to get I . . . *me* . . ." It was all so simple in his mind, how a 4F had offered him a chance to go to L.A. to deliver a car because he could get the gas rations on his army papers. How did people get those things across to other people? He stared at all their dumb, pitying faces, and his mouth closed over air. Slowly, he lowered his eyes to his ponderous hands and surrendered.

"I almos' go. . . ."

Billy White flashed her seraglio eyes upward in exasperation, and Kopey commiserated with a good-natured shrug. Then the two of them went on with their devious courtship in talk of the grand and glittering L.A. while Buck returned to his gloomy invocation of legendary riches.

In the kitchen, the other women talked around the table over their glasses of fruit juice. Mrs. Cecil Mapp sat in righteous ease as she castigated the small, wistful sinner who was her husband.

"Church, *him?* Don' make me laugh, sister," she said to Jane Ortiz, the mother of Jesus. "That man so far from God he can't pronounce the word. A fritterin' spineless creature of evil ways. Don' matter to him me and his children wear rags an' tatters. 'What the use anyway,' he say. 'We miserable hopeless people anyway.' Imagine a man like that! So he gives up long ago. Now he courts the bottle, completely lost in the ways of intemperance."

"My Jesus have some wild ways, I admit," Jane Ortiz said, plucking at the tablecloth with a musing expression. "But he never lost to God; that much I can say. 'Course we of a different faith than you, Mrs. Mapp; it's a little different all around. But no matter what kind of devilment he get into, he fin' time to get to church now an' again. He took his communion, makes a confession every so often."

"Well sure, that is somethin' to say for him. His heart in the right place at least, no matter what kind of church," Mrs. Mapp said condescendingly, no real friend of Catholics. (Might as well as be weird as those colored who worshiped in a synagogue.) "But of course with us Baptists you can't just leave your sins on no priest, not so easy with us. We got to fight with the Devil all the time."

"Well, Mrs. Mapp, you might not understand how we works in the *Catholic* Church," Jane Ortiz said, quite proud of her affiliation with the un-Negro faith she had married up to. "You see with us . . ."

Downstairs, the Pawnbroker's janitor, John Rider, sat smoking his new chrome-stemmed pipe, distracted from his reading of the Bible by the shrill voices of the women upstairs.

"It is better to dwell in a corner of d'housetop than wid a brawlin' woman in a wide house," he muttered angrily, yet with a proud smugness, as he slammed the window shut.

"My Jesus is ambitious," Jane Ortiz said with proud irrelevance.

"You people jus' don' believe in d'existence of Hell is your trouble. You think you get everything off you back in them confessions."

"It happen Jesus Christ hisself was a Catholic," Jane Ortiz threw in as a clincher.

"It happen he was a Jew," Mrs. Mapp answered.

"Why, Mrs. Mapp, what a awful thing to say!"

Kopey had an expression of delighted anguish on his shiny yellow face as he talked to Billy White.

"And you should see them night clubs out there in L.A. There's nothin' here to compare. . . ."

Billy sighed with yearning while her husband knotted his immense hands, trying to wring treasure from them.

Jesus sat low in his seat in the dark theater. His knees were crammed up against the seat in front of him, and his eyes were narrow and intense on the movie screen, like slits of fire.

The scene was the patio of a great country house. People in handsomely tailored evening clothes strolled through the parklike grounds, and Japanese lanterns were reflected in a large, free-form swimming pool. An orchestra played sleepily from inside the opened French doors. In the foreground now, a white man murmured languidly against the face of a skinny white woman. The land fell away quietly in a swoop of luxurious privacy; everything was immaculate, rich, and fabulous.

Jesus Ortiz felt a vast shapeless desire, but it was too great and beautiful to attain shape. So he thought about money and the power of *business*.

Mabel Wheatly writhed fetchingly on the white sheets of the

whorehouse as she waited for her third customer of the evening to finish undressing. She murmured lustful catch phrases to him, this fat, balding white man with girlish skin and tiny plump hands. The summer air came hot and smoky in through the cautiously opened window and the man's hand trembled.

"I'll tell you what I want you to do," he said in a voice savage with shame. "First lie over . . . like this. And then keep saying, 'Do it to me, Richy, do it to me,' like that," he said, his shaky hand moist on her bare brown skin.

"Is your name Richy, hon?" she asked with a vampish smile.

"No, no, my name is Don. But you just do what I say and don't ask questions. Do what I say." He fell on her then and began a mad pantomime of mock virility.

"Do it to me, Richy, do it to me, Richy, do it to me . . ." she intoned in a dead voice, contorting herself according to that particular recipe of passion. But his eyes were up on the ceiling, staring at a desperate dream.

Tessie Rubin didn't open the door to the angry knocking of Goberman. She called from behind the closed door in a loud half-whisper she hoped would carry to Goberman and not to her father lying in his raging sleep in the back bedroom.

"What do you mean coming this time of night?"

"Does it make a difference to the slaves in Yemen, the Israelites in the ghettos of Algiers and Alexandria what time it is? Their blood is on you. You must give me money for the Jewish Appeal or your name will go down with Hitler in Hell," Goberman cried in the same wild half-whisper from the hall.

"I'll give, I'll give, you madman," she said. "Only I don't have, now. Come Monday night, come then, I'll take care of you then."

"I'll come then, I'll come like the Angel of Death to the Egyptians. God help you if you don't . . ."

"Monday, Monday," she wailed against the door.

"Vat is the pounding? Are they here again?" the old man roared from the bedroom. "*Ich shtab swai huntret yourn!* I haf died too many times already."

"It's nothing, Poppa, *gay shluphin*; it is just the man from the electric company," she called in a soothing voice as she leaned against the door. "It will all be taken care of, Sol will take care of it." She covered her face with her hands and pressed as hard as she could.

Goberman's footsteps clacked hollowly over the tile floor of the hall, receded out to the street, and then were gone from her ears but not from her head, never from her head.

Miles away, the Pawnbroker sat up rigidly in his bed to escape the long-drawn and endless moaning of his dreams.

His SUNDAYS WERE parodies of Sabbaths; hours to be got through without the insulation of work. He swung his feet to the floor of his bedroom and stared at the leafy shape of sunlight over them; it was like morning discovering the marble of a statue. Outside, there were the sounds of the Sunday gardeners and children's voices slamming at the quiet. A lawn mower chugged in the warm air a half-block away, and a few birds twittered weakly, obligated to August. He was in a warm, safe place. Why then did he creak under invisible weights? Why did he feel that phantom growth deep inside?

For a few minutes he studied the motionless curtains tapestried with sunlight. He began to recognize the edge of something soothingly rational.

"A week from Thursday is the twenty-eighth of August," he said aloud. Every year around the anniversary of his family's death he experienced that now vague sense of oppression. It was only natural; in fact in its mildness it was almost unnatural. He did not grieve or mourn them, because he had been cauterized of all abstract things. Reality consisted of the world within one's sight and smell and hearing. He commemorated nothing; it was the secret of his survival. But August was his bad month, the period of his own mistral, a time when he felt healed scars as a veteran might recall his wounds in damp weather. No more than that; August would come and go, and he would continue to exist. Bleakly comforted at having found a name for his ache, he got up and began to dress.

He put on a pair of fawn-colored summer slacks and an olive sport shirt his niece, Joan, had bought him the Christmas before, which made his complexion take on the yellowish translucence of old marble. In the bathroom, he ran the electric razor over the sparse stubble of his beard, his eyes indifferent to the rest of his pallid face. Then he brushed his teeth, which were his own except for two steel ones a little to the side of his mouth. Amazing that he hadn't lost them all. He spread his lips to observe his teeth and continued the expression in a mirthless smile at that odd persistence; the teeth continued to manufacture calcium, as hair and fingernails continued to grow in the grave.

With his unique spectacles on, Sol went downstairs to where the odor of fresh coffee and rolls and smoked fish filled the rooms pleasantly. Bertha was in the kitchen, the rest of the family reading the different sections of the *Times*.

"Good morning, Uncle Sol. You slept late," Joan said brightly. In her yellow bathrobe, her skin tanned to a lovely maple, she was a bright spot in the sunny room. "And so formal. I wish you would let me buy you a dressing gown."

"Good morning, *Solly*," Selig said with conspiratorial heartiness, reminding his brother-in-law of his lingering gratitude with raised eyebrows.

"Good morning," Sol said, walking over to the livingroom window to gaze blankly at the shaded street.

Morton glanced up from his perusal of the advertised bosoms in the theater section. For a moment he looked at his uncle. Oddly, he felt himself loosen in the presence of the big, shapeless figure, felt certain cords of anguish go limp and become bearable in his uncle's stillness.

Bertha's voice broke into the rustling quiet of the room.

"Come eat," she called from the kitchen.

They went in and sat around the sumptuous spread of rolls, bagels, cheeses, sturgeon, smoked whitefish and lox, huge tomatoes and chunks of sweet tub butter; and what was real between them was the mutual hunger, the greed that lit up their faces with an ersatz amiability. Bertha poured coffee into each of their cups. Sol's was an over-sized novelty inscribed "Grandpa," which Joan had bought the year before on the vacation she and her parents had taken at Sol's expense. It was part of the half-conscious campaign she and her mother waged to make Sol a family "character"; that at least could explain his indefinable personality, could ultimately, they hoped, reduce him to something they could work with and control.

For a while, they talked in little side courses about friends and news events and book reviews. Bertha dug with gleeful savagery at the small failure of one of her friends' children. But when Selig and Joan finished eating and sat back with cigarettes and a second cup of coffee, Joan suddenly noticed her brother's skinny hands.

"Your nails are filthy," she said comfortably, exhaling a twin stream of smoke from her nose. The observation was made without malice, for she was a healthy, unfrustrated girl. "You keep them too long."

Selig cast his face into a father's sternness. "I don't want to see you coming to the table like that," he said.

Morton ate more quickly, as though he expected his plate to be taken away before he was through eating.

"You don't answer people when they talk to you?" his mother said.

"Leave me alone," Morton said, continuing to eat.

Bertha stared at him viciously for a minute, searching for ammunition, feeding her bitter disappointment in him. She had a certain capacity for love, but it was not large. Her life in America had been bright and clean and pretty; she had become accustomed to clean prettiness. She had come to America thirty years before and had gotten the educated, "American-looking" Selig to fall in love with her wholesome good looks. The first child had been a beautiful credit to her. And then Morton! She might have been able to shape a pitying affection for her son, but from early childhood he had been as sour and unreceptive to her condescending attention as he was now.

"I found some indecent pictures in your drawer," she said, not adding that she had studied them curiously for almost ten minutes.

"Ah, the solitary vice, very unhealthy," Selig said belching the essence of smoked fish out with the cigarette smoke. "You're at the age where self-discipline is important, Morton."

"Talk about shame," Morton snarled, "haven't you people got any shame? How can you talk to a person like this? All right, you despise me and I despise you. Yes, let's get it out in the open—*despise!* Well, okay, I don't need you. I'll become an artist and get out on my own. Then you can all go to hell, for all I care!"

"That language in front of your mother and your sister!" Selig half stood in threat. And this, his namesake, his hope of immortality. He was too lazy about discipline. Well, from now on he would take a hand. For an instant he visualized a tall, broad-shouldered Morton with tanned, smooth skin and bright friendly eyes and himself, Selig, introducing this beautiful son to his principal, telling the man that his son had been offered any number of football scholarships but that Morton preferred a particular nonathletic college whose pre-med courses were said to be the best. Selig stayed, half standing, his eyes glazed and forgetful of the purpose of his posture. Gradually, he sank back into his chair as the daydream faded.

"Morton," Joan said, "we don't hate you. What an unhealthy attitude that is! You have many antagonisms against yourself and you try to put them on us. We just want to help you. Our criticism is meant to be constructive."

"That's what a family is for," Selig said.

"Well I certainly hate to see him get like this," Joan said. Then, with a glance at her uncle, the payer-of-fees, "Maybe some professional help would be in order. Mort, would you consider talking to Sid's friend Doctor Klebish? Just informally; the brightest people do it nowadays."

Morton didn't answer, just kept stubbornly eating.

"*Get* like this," Bertha cried scornfully, suddenly flooded with bitter recall. "He was always like this. He sucked my milk till there was blood. At three years old he was still crying for the titty."

"*Really*, Mother!" Joan spoke with delicate distaste. "Now, Mort, you know Mother is just angry—not that I blame her. You get her all upset. Honestly, you don't let anyone relax and be friendly with you. You're so violently antisocial, so . . ."

"He used to pee in his pants when he was already eleven years old, just to embarrass me," Bertha persisted, half enjoying the dim nausea she felt in this attack on her son. It seemed that if she continued it long enough and intensely enough, she would vomit all the sick anger she felt for him, that she might be soothed and eased and patient enough to love him as she should.

"Nowadays we have guidance people in the schools," Selig said. "Perhaps if the people at the school . . . I mean this drawing business is not a solution to all your problems, you know, son. Let's say you are pursuing some modest talent, all well and good, but . . ."

"You don't know anything about it!" Morton cried hoarsely, his eyes bulging and wild. "You people with your slimy, warped little brains, talking about *foreign films* and *book reviews*. What do you know? Beauty, do you really understand about beauty? No, just prettiness, nice clean little things, fashionable, crappy little nothings. And you have the nerve to tell me . . ."

"Those pictures in your drawer maybe, that's beauty?" Bertha said.

Morton snarled miserably, like a trapped animal.

Sol just sat drinking his coffee and contemplating the cold, living stone in his vitals, in a hurry for the hour to end, for the day, the week, the month to be gone. He forced himself to anticipate the peace that would follow his strange seasonal discomfort. The voices of his relatives snapped in a closing circle around the ugly weakness of their prey, but he heard them only distantly, like the sound of some far-off hunt. He squinted at the chrome sparkle of the stove, which threw needles of light into his eyes. He might even take a little holiday in October, walk in some New England wood and just breathe without regret or poignance the pleasant cold air so free of unnatural smells. He would take some books along and stay at a quiet inn and walk and eat and read and be quite content within the walls of his senses. He sat in an autumnal reverie, his face slack and idiotic, his body collapsed sideways in the chair.

But suddenly the noise intruded. Morton was standing with his hands up to his ears and screaming one steady tantrum note.

"That's just childish, Morton," his sister said. "You refuse to take criticism like an adult."

"He's a baby, a nasty baby," Bertha shrilled.

"Get a grip on yourself, boy," Selig shouted.

"Shut up, all of you!" Sol said in a thunderous voice. "Leave him alone!"

"Now, Solly, you must let us work out our paternal problems in our own way," Selig said with polite reproof.

"I said be still, be still!" He towered over them with his anger, and they were reminded that he came out of unknown violences. Selig and Joan sat open-mouthed and intimidated.

But Bertha was made of tougher material.

"You are not yet the dictator around here, Solly," she said. "Maybe you think you can throw up to us the little help you have been willing to give us. But we didn't vote you the head of the house. After all, we give something in return. We have made a home for you, given you a family. What money could buy that?"

Morton forgot to scream. He lowered his hands from his ears and watched his uncle.

Sol turned to his sister with a cold, glistening stare.

"You will be still now," he said. "No more talk at all until I am out of this room. Silence, Bertha, silence. When I am gone from here, you may continue your cannibalism; I do not take sides or interfere with your miserable pleasure. But hear what I say. I do *not* need you for a family—that is *your* myth. If you wish to be able to continue, be silent!"

Then he turned and went from the room.

Morton followed, a careful distance behind his uncle. Like his father, he was prone to imaginative reconstructions. He looked at Sol's wide, bulky back and had no need to create a new and perfect father; he was willing, in his dream, to settle for that one somber, harsh man, would have taken his chances on all the darknesses in the Pawnbroker that would be forever beyond his knowing. He felt, without evidence, that there were murkinesses those eyes could penetrate and understand.

But Sol was only soliciting silence. He went into the yard with a book of Chekhov's short stories. Settled on the plastic-webbed chair, he began to read. He soaked in a fictitious climate which isolated him from the warm sunlight and the voices of all the neighbors, dulled by the heavy summer foliage. And slowly he worked away from the minor irritant of the recent scene in the house. He read avidly, and although he projected himself to a certain extent to the late nineteenth-century Russian town, he derived pleasure mainly from the lucid familiarity of something he had loved and enjoyed in another time. He appreciated the emotions evoked, but he was not involved emotionally himself because his invulnerability allowed for no exceptions. He was stirred only to a reminiscence of sadness; he was like an archaeologist studying the historic ruins of an interesting civilization. Sometimes he smiled faintly, at other times his eyes narrowed slightly; breezes of life seemed to play over his bland, buried face.

During the morning the members of the family came out into the yard for various reasons; Bertha to dump the garbage, Selig looking for a pair of pruning shears, Joan just wandering aimlessly. Each of them skirted his reposing figure with cautious silence and stayed for the shortest time; they were intimidated by Sol's motionless face, stony in the yellow-green light, and by his eyes, obscured behind the thick lenses of his glasses.

Only Morton stayed for a long time in another chair, a good distance away from his uncle. He read intermittently from Gardner's *Art Through the Ages*, and every so often swung his eyes furtively from some Byzantine saint or Renaissance madonna to the motionless figure.

After a while, Sol, too, found himself swinging in and out of the balm of his reading, although he did not lift his eyes from the printed pages. His mind drifted with the apparent abandon of an oarless boat, bumping on this strand and that. His customers ranged through his thoughts, and he examined them harshly, as though he might find the thing responsible for his increasing unease. With his eyes on "A Day in the Country," he checked off Jesus Ortiz and Buck White, Tangee and the blue-eyed Negro. He considered craftily the harsh, sonic whine of Murillio's voice, the sleazy delicacy of George Smith's importuning debate. And he wondered if any or all of them might have anything to do with the way he felt. The buzzing conjecture began to make his nerves tingle, and a slight dizziness came over him.

"But it's just the time of the year . . . an old superstition," he said aloud, gesturing, too, as though in answer to an unseen companion.

"What did you say, Uncle Sol?" Morton asked, as alien with his sallow face in that cheery sunlight as his uncle.

"What . . . oh, nothing, nothing. I was reading aloud . . . it meant nothing," he said softly.

Then he went back to Chekhov with his memory strangled in the grip of his will. And the soft summer sounds fell over him with the sunlight, as unfelt as the lightest rain of pollen.

Fathers

by HERBERT GOLD

The produce market as a background for the sensitive Jew's contact with the rough goyish world might in itself serve as a unifying theme for an anthology, including such items as Louis Zara's life saga of an immigrant fruit-and-vegetable peddler, Blessed Is the Man, the Boston market scenes where Angoff's hero David Polonsky labors and learns about society, and Herbert Gold's Fathers, a self-portrait of a schoolboy as a Saturday assistant in his father's greengrocery in Cleveland.

It was an early story about this store, "The Heart of the Artichoke," that, Gold has said, gave him his first sense of mastery over his material. Gold has a way of reworking his material, and the story of how an ordinary Jew deals with a local fascist is woven into this novel of a son's examination of his origins, culminating in the symbolic and powerful episode of the old-country crippler.

More elliptical in his style than Saul Bellow, who in Herzog makes similar use of early family work scenes, Gold is touching though cool. He has polished his episodes and, as has the slightly younger Philip Roth, assumed the attitude of educated judgment, but there is more sympathy than rage in his irony. His Jews are still connected.

An early novel, The Prospect Before Us, about the owner of a third-rate Cleveland hotel who faces a business crisis when a Negro girl reserves a room in his place, is built around an exceptionally complex characterization of a stiff-necked Jew, a smart urban operator who is still, atavistically, ready to ruin himself over a principle.

A frequent contributor to Playboy and other magazines, Gold has written novels about a failed marriage in Love and Like,

about carnival life in The Man Who Was Not with It, *and about*
New York *careerists in* Salt.

Born in Cleveland in 1924, Herbert Gold received his master's
degree at Columbia, spent a year in Paris on a Fulbright, traveled in Europe and Israel; he has taught at Western Reserve,
Wayne State, Cornell, Harvard, and the University of California
at Berkeley and has made San Francisco his literary keep.

M.L.

I N 1935 MY FATHER had two mighty enemies. Against one
of them he struggled all the long fruit-and-vegetable day, hoisting
the crates and loading a top-heavy truck in early morning, at dawn,
in his wet boots, then meeting the customers until evening in a store
built narrow and dark in the alleyway between a bakery and a Peer-
less showroom. Against the other enemy he fought all night, tossing
and groaning in his sleep, fierce with that strange nightmare which
allows an angry man to be pursued without ever retreating.

His daytime foe was one shared by most other Americans—the
Great Depression. The adversary of his nights was that beast clanking and roaring in the streets of fantastic Deutschland. "Hitler!" he
said at breakfast, shaking the sleep from his head. "I'm almost
ashamed to be human. The other strawberries don't like the rotten
strawberry, they blush rotten red if you don't pluck him out—"

"Have another cup of Wheatena for the strength in it," chanted
my mother, grieving with him like a good wife because of the need
for strength on a troubled planet.

"Sorry, no time—look at the clock!" He hadn't meant to complain;
it was the only earth he knew. "The lettuce is in already, and the
Pascal comes with it." And standing up, jacketed, shod in Army-
Navy boots, he drained his coffee, dropped the cup in the sink, and
was off to the market downtown near the Flats of Cleveland. Before
light on a winter morning, he fought the battered reconditioned motor of his truck, cursed, lifted the hood, wiped the wires and plugs.
Mother opened the kitchen window to watch. Then fits and coughs,
then action. Mother watched him go, and waved. *Action*—his pockets filled with knives, hammers, dollars, a deck of cards, and funny
pictures to show his friends in the chill damp of a January morning.

Down the suburban streets, up the suburban highway he rattled; and through the sleeping city where the street lights abruptly died in the dawn; and only rare bedroom lamps and kitchen noises greeted him on his way.

But the West Side Market was a city in full life. Carloads of vegetables steamed with the haggle and babble of selling under corrugated zinc roofs and no roofs at all. Desperate eaters, standing near the great tureens of soup, could not remember whether this was their second or their third breakfast. My father paced the aisles of lettuce and tender peas, the green corridors of spinach, deep into silent back parlors of early fruit off the railway cars. Private, at one with food, he sniffed gratefully, at his ease, homely, taking the pleasures of business on his tongue and in his deep-breathing lungs. He went to the produce market as to worship—putting Hitler and bank holidays behind him in the glory of America's bounty. He squeezed a plum until the wine spurted. He wiped his eyes.

Joe Rini surprised him in his shadowy lair. "What you doing here, Sam?"

"Same as you! Good, eh?"

"But can we sell it? I still got last week's plums left over."

My father shrugged, the sheepskin ruffling against a crate. "They get soggy in the cooler. What else can we do?"

"Nothing—and these look like prime. Here, let me taste."

"Taste, go on. Me, I'd like to buy."

The fruitmen rivaled, of course, for the favor of the farmers, who were of another breed, not washing in those days as a protest against the cost of living. Their best produce many times rotted in the fields, and the farmers often suffered terrible bellyaches from the hopeless eating of an unbought crop. Even striated beefsteak tomatoes, warmed by sun and dusted with salt, can be too many! The farmers suffered from mortgages, skin diseases, unrepaired fences, chronically pregnant wives. Regularly removed from their lonely land to confront a crazy urban cackle, and perhaps returning without the profit of seed and fertilizer, they too passed cards among themselves.

The immigrant Italian and Jewish fruitmen, with their occasional Greek and Negro colleagues, exchanged printed jokes and dirty pictures. They first competed and argued, then huddled for soup and coffee and gossip, sharing each other's hard times in the pleasure and intimacy of these early mornings. They left dawn with regret, jamming their trucks into gritty day.

The farmers' wives, bundled and red and unfragrant as men, dipped up the last coffee and watched without a word. Drops of fat cream whirled round like crazy fishlets in the tin cups. The farmers too had their whispered consultations, but these never ended in a burst of laughter as they got the point. Their little cards were other dreams, dreams of riding and hunting, gothic fantasies of ritual, celebration, and chastisement. The Black Legion haunted the countryside around Cleveland. It made contact with the Klan in Parma and the Bund in Lakewood, and there were histories of drilling in open fields, the youngsters standing guard with broomsticks. Their cards made them members together for sacred order and vengeance. Cousins who rarely came out saw each other on Sunday after church to listen to screaming harangues from the platforms of pickups. During the dark winter of 1935, some farmers discovered that they had the call—or at least as much a one as the man in blue serge sent down from Black Legion headquarters in a warehouse in Jackson, Michigan.

Al Flavin was a farmer with whom my father had dealt for almost ten years. They had never been friends, but my father gave as good a price as anyone and Flavin took good care of his lettuce; they met in commerce. An angry man who had sometimes wrestled at country fairs, a giant with magnificent hairy paws, he began to know glory for the first time since abandoning his boyish victories on sweaty canvas. Men listened to him. He became a Commander or a Knight or a Dragon, whatever the Black Legion name for it was. He could not pay off the loan on his greenhouse, but he could gather the Legionnaires in before-dawn consultations at the edge of town.

It must have made Al feel distant from himself to discuss the meeting, give the mystic handshake, crushing the wrists of men less mighty than he, climb into a truck with a load strapped on, and then drive meekly off to do business with Sam Gold.

"All right, make it eleven crates for ten," my father said.

"Ten crates," Al repeated stubbornly.

"Eleven. Or ten and my last price."

"No. Ten crates. My price."

"Al, listen to me," my father said. "You *know* I can't buy it your way. Joe Rini will undersell me, he'll throw circulars on all the porches, and then where will I be? You got to make sense in business."

"You heard me."

"What's the matter, you don't feel good today, Al? Something hurting?"

"Joe Rini don't buy from me. I bring in first-quality stuff."

"I know, I *know*, that's why I stand here and argue with you. I *want* your stuff, Al. I like it."

My father rocked, smiling. Al Flavin stood behind his barricade of lettuce. Patience, patience—the soul is tried on earth. At last they were agreed, someplace between demand and offer, and then, joining in the traditional aftermath of successful negotiation, the two of them completed their deal by hoisting the produce into my father's truck. Hot and sighing when this was done, the cash changing hands, usually they came to a moment of benevolent treaty, and the plump fruitman would light up with the burly, brooding farmer. Al Flavin was busy behind his squeezed-shut eyes trying to remember who he was, who other people were.

"Okay, Al," my father said, "have a cigar."

Now he remembered. He felt his card and sorted my father out: "*Kike!*"

"Wh-wh-wh," said my father.

Flavin's shoulder caught my father and half spun him around as the man stamped off in the flapping galoshes which he wore almost into summer. My father stammered, "Wh-wh-wh," meaning *What?* and *Why?* First amazed, then stooped and solemn, pouting with thought. It was well past dawn now, but suddenly the nightmare toppled onto his daytime dream, and he was standing in the sad, crooked streets of old Kamenets.

My father stopped dealing with Al Flavin. This did not put an end to it. He heard Flavin's word every market-day morning, first whispered, then called after him, twice a week. The single note grated on his nerves. The market is supposed to be a pleasure. My mother made him promise not to fight. Flavin, huge, profligate with his wrestler's flesh, yearning to brawl, would crush him in his paws. It was policy. Flavin was a Commander. He hoped to convert the waverers by rolling with Sam Gold in the running wash of the market gutters.

"I'd get him with the peen of my hammer first!" my father yelled.

"Sam, Sam, we don't want trouble."

"I'll break his head with the claw!"

Mother petted him, stroked him. "Think of your business. You got a family, Sam, you got to count them."

"I'll kill him, Frieda."

"Shush, you're making noise, the neighbors. You got to count me, too. No trouble, please for your kids' sake."

"No, no, no." His eyes were red with sleepless thinking. There was an angry scratch in the tender eye-flesh. He breathed as if he were struggling for air. "No, you're right, Frieda. But if he touches me one more time—"

That time came, however, on a morning during the dog days of July, when even at early market hours the men panted and sweated under the bloody-eyed sun before it reared up onto the exhausted city. Ice trickled through the crates of lettuce, rustling, and evaporated on cement still hot from the day before. The overfed market rats loped along on seared paws. Flavin sprang from behind a heap of crates, pretending to be in a hurry, and struck my father with his knee at the belly, so that he lost his balance and stumbled like a drunk. He grunted. He tried but could not quite sob out his breath. It was caught, trapped, exterminated someplace within, and he lay sprawled on the soft market refuse while the little world of pain in his belly spun faster than the earth's turning, and only a moment later, when the hurtling agony at the center of his being slowed down to weakness, and the weakness to a sour sickness that drained into his mouth, did he remember again who he was. It's an assault against life that brings this gnawing, liver-eating agony upon a man gasping for his breath with his head against a crate of lettuce. The blood shrieked like eagles in his ears. It's a wish of murder—extermination. It's a terrible pain that makes a man forget he is Sam Gold.

Flavin roared, pushed the laughter forward with all his weight, and stood with his huge arms welcoming. Once taciturn, he had learned the trick of oratory: "Looks drunk, don't he? Ain't he a rummy? Never did run into a rummy kike before, did you ever, boys?"

An offering of laughter. The rest would gather when the rich noise of brawling crashed out. Flavin was in boots, kicking free of a broken crate, ready.

Sam Gold pained badly in the gut. He climbed up dizzily and shook his head clear. He felt for the silver-pronged crating hammer in his back pocket. Flavin crouched, his long jaw twitching with desire. The buttons of his pants were stretched and a tab of his shirt came out of his fly. Flavin could wait another moment to make himself real. The usual hubbub of commercial dispute hid them now; the life of the market swirled unknowing about the two men, food rising in great towers and vaults above them, around them, and only a couple of farmers watched. Joe Rini, terrified, blowing saliva, also watched.

My father had promised my mother.

He loved life and the right and *to win*.

Flavin might kill him.

My father walked away rapidly, hunched, turning red for shame and white for planning, and grabbed Joe Rini by the sleeve and took him with him. "Joe, Joe," he said, "I got to talk to you. I know you got friends. I got to talk to them too."

"What you got to say, Sam?"

"Oh maybe I could kill him, but then again maybe not. Which it wouldn't be so good if he gave me a beating. Those other Cossacks would feel too nice about it. Or worse. A bad example. No good in that. So . . ."

Eagerly Rini talked into the void. "So you know how they drink. They're drunkards. So don't raise your blood pressure." My father's eye made him stop. Rini agreed. My father decided slowly:

"The way things are going on the market now, Joe, it won't be safe for any of us soon."

"What you thinking, Sam?" Rini asked.

He was thinking, but in his own words: precedent, morale, example. This was a political question, to be answered in the impure, compromising way of politics. A passionate answer—Sam Gold's face bloodied, a crowd secretly smiling over Sam Gold's fallen body, an inflamed Al Flavin finding his dream of power fulfilled—this was the worst possibility which my father's furious body had almost given him. The philosophical thing to do was to master that hot inner twitch, and then, only then, to think out how to discourage the Cossack mob.

Job and Noah had patience; yet Job was permitted his anger. Not an educated man, my father knew that the patriarchs had even spoken for passion on earth, properly used. And he knew no other place for justice except here below, on earth, where he hoped to have more children.

He breathed deeply once, twice, again, that's better, and then thanked God for giving him a sense of responsibility. He thanked the Lord of Creation that his healthy, willing, complaining wife had come to mind. Wistfully he thanked the Almighty for prudence— and also for his friend Joe Rini. He said to Joe Rini: "You're going to help me now."

That very night Joe found the three young friends whom he had in mind and brought them to the house. My father wanted to meet them: "Make your acquaintance, I'm sure." How formal we become under embarrassment. For fifty dollars he could buy a beating with any refinements he named. Except nothing vicious, of course—what do you think, they were queers? They were mere administrators.

"No, *no!*" my mother cried. "So then he'll kill you next, and what's the good? We can't afford it."

"We can't afford not to," my father said stonily. "We're going to do what the Frenchies won't do. When he makes his noise, we march into the Rhineland and stop it good. You don't have to listen to that noise. You stop it the best way you can. You stop it. You *stop* it."

"Sam, O Sam, it's dangerous, it's fifty dollars."

"It's the cost of living, Frieda."

Joe Rini's friends, three young chaps with slicked-down hair, nervous hands, and old jokes, were very sociable. They jiggled and dandled and played beanbag with me as if I were a baby, although I felt as serious as any adult. They took time over the business because my father likes business. Also he wanted to be certain. He did not like this business, and that made him slow and cautious. Mother served liver *with*, the rich slabs covered by curly, glistening onions. How can businessmen discuss matters without keeping up their strength? Mugs of strong black coffee, too.

"For fifty dollars, Mr. Gold," said the leader of the group, "we can maybe kill him for you. It's no extra. We'll be working anyway. His truck has got to stop for a light on the edge of town, and there we are."

"No, no," my father said. "Put him in the hospital, that's all."

"Mr. Rini says he used to work in the commission house with you. He says you're buddies from way back. It's no trouble at all."

"No!" my father said. "The man has a wife and kids, just like me. His big boy is too dumb to run a farm by himself—"

"We got smart kids," my mother interrupted, smiling, politely patting with a napkin, pleased by their appetites. "My big boy, he gets such marks from his teacher—"

"Frieda, shush. Go call up somebody on the telephone if you got to talk. Listen."

The businessmen shrugged apologetically, being brought up in a tradition which favors mothers, and turned regretfully back to hear out my father and his scrupling. They were unaccustomed to fine distinctions, but they came of devoted families; they enjoyed a moth-

er's pride. "So don't do that what you said there," my father repeated. "I just want him to learn a little, have time to think a little.
The hospital."

"Okay," the leader of the trio said reluctantly, "you're the boss.
You get a hold of us if you change your mind, will you? To you the
price remains the same."

"The hospital," my father repeated, making them promise.

"Let us worry about the details, Mr. Gold. Fifty goes a long way
these days."

My father arose angrily, sending his cup ringing against a platter.
"*I said the hospital!*"

"The hospital, hospital," they intoned mournfully, and filed out.

The next morning Flavin did not show up at the market. It was so
easy to follow him from the country in a flivver, stop with him at a
red light, get rid of the cigarettes, and pile quickly onto his truck.
So instead of Flavin, a weary, hard-working young thug appeared
and nodded to Dad, saying that they had been careful, just as he
said. But it would have been no extra trouble, in fact, the reverse.

My father was undelighted. By his veiled eyes he signaled regret
at the weight of the world: he was obliged to send Flavin down to
defeat without earning the kiss of victory. Life had provided him—as
it does everyone—with one more little blemish on the ideal of brave
perfection. He found it a necessary business, nothing more, a merely
rational victory, and he foresaw the possibility of being ambushed in
his turn by a man who might not bother to think of his wife and
children. Nevertheless, reason consoled him.

Another man might have done nothing against his enemy, because
he believed vengeance the worst of sins. He might be a good Christian; he might be a coward. Another man would simply have killed
him or hired him killed. That seemed simple, and it might seem easy
to some. Another man might have stayed home and brooded till his
wife shamed him into desperate combat. These were all ways some
men might have replied to the disaster of assault.

Reason consoled my father. Perhaps he had not taken the right
way, but he found his own way.

Still, he did not like it very much and he was unconsoled by reason. Reason did not help when he cut himself off from his father;
reason did not help when Ben cut himself out of life; reason was
only a way of trying to make the incoherent coherent, and it never
did all the job. It washed over grief, but it left grief intact. It shrunk

grief into a tiny matted lump in the belly, but it left the shame and grief where they lay.

"Okay! Which it is what I had to do," he told my mother. "Okay! I don't want to hear about it."

"Sam, what if he does to you? Where will I and the kids be? Where will *you* be if you're dead?"

He grinned. Coming back to his world. "Well, it's a risk," he said, although he had just said he would not speak any more about it. "But in this life you have to take chances and defend yourself like you can." He frowned angrily. "I don't always like how I can, Frieda."

She was frightened by his face. She waited to see if he had something he wanted to tell her.

"And now let me answer your question: If I'm dead, I'm noplace."

He sent Flavin a five-dollar bouquet of flowers, followed the next morning by a two-dollar plant with thick wet leaves and a decorative sprinkle of spangles. Joe Rini approved. A friend who went to see Flavin in the hospital reported that they were the only flowers he received.

The moral which my father drew was one which he wanted to teach England and France in 1935 and after. Still strong and capable, Flavin came quietly to work in his bandages about ten days later. He sold tomatoes to my father, and they haggled like gentlemen over the price. They mistered each other warily. There was further talk of the Black Legion, but not a gesture from Flavin. In a few years even the talk passed.

Sometimes my father thought that he might be beaten up, but it never happened, although once he was robbed. That was not Flavin's work.

Flavin had taken instruction well, administered according to Aristotelian principles, with moderation, by a man whose fundamental passionate mildness led him to a reasonable strictness: the hospital for Flavin, nothing worse. Nightmares go on, but they have answers—albeit risky, rational, incomplete, and not ideally valorous. Poor Flavin, unused to surprises—he was discouraged.

A few days later Shloimi Spitz telephoned to ask: "Sam, why didn't you let me know? I could of done a better job for no charge—included already."

"You get what you pay for," my father said.

"You don't like me. Aw, you don't like me," said the racketeer extortionist. "And we done business together so long already."

"Monkey business. Foo," said my father.

"I could of crippled him good. My pleasure," said Shloimi. "I protect you good, don't I, Sam?"

"Like clockwork regular," my father said.

"You don't like me," said Shloimi. He waited. When there was no answer, he put the telephone down. My father said he had a bad taste in his mouth. All this monkey business cost too much.

"Fifty dollars," said my mother.

"No. A bad, bad taste. A bad, bad time. Frieda. I should have figured out another way."

But my mother was consoled. Dad made another fifty dollars to replace the ones spent in good works in a bad time.

.   .   .   .   .   .

. . . I TASTED DURING one evening the delights of approval, staying up with Mother and Dad while we discussed the day's business, counted the receipts, and discussed the pros and cons of tangle displays against neat pyramids of cans or fruit. I spoke for tangle displays, Mother for order; Dad listened to us both, sipping his tea with little Ahs through his lump of sugar, and reserved decision. He tried to lasso my head as he used to in a ring of cigar smoke. "It's too big," he complained. "Just like mine, a size seven seven-eights. So look who needs a hat! You want a Stetson?"

We had a long late supper, and before going to bed he slipped me three dollar bills in a secret conspiratorial gesture while Mother stacked the dishes.

"I saw! I saw!" she cried out, her eyes peeping bright in the mirror over the sink. We all giggled together.

Dad slapped her rump, yawned, and said, "Nothing like a good day's work, hey?" in his imitation of Guy Mallin.

"Sam, you crazy?" At peace with each other we parted. "And don't forget whose birthday is next month," my mother said. "Yours. You'll be thirteen, kiddel."

She had it right this time. It was a real truce; I knew its joys. But had anything been altered? As aphoristic Aunt Anna might say, "A leopard coat can't change its spots."

A few days afterward I received a letter. The envelope carried my name on the outside, together with the smart-alecky title "Master," all printed in green ink. I studied it, marveling, my first mail since the revolutionary discovery of INCREASE YOUR WILL POWER FOOL YOUR FRIENDS, and for that I had sent away a coupon and a quarter. I sniffed it. I licked the ink and made a smear of what our art teacher called *graded area*. I tasted my name in green, finding it more artistic than black but approximately as lucid. At last I decided to open the letter.

It was an invitation from Mr. B. Franklyn Wilkerson to go on a Nature Walk a week from Saturday. Mr. Wilkerson, who taught General Science to the seventh grade, had worked out a plan to augment his income during the summer vacation by conveying flower names and leaf shapes to suburban scholars. Small, swarthy, with three daughters and thin black hair artfully spaced and glued into place to cover his scalp, Mr. Wilkerson recited Science (general) with his neck petrified for fear a sudden breeze or emotion might betray his baldness. Zealous, he devoted himself to general-science textbooks, turning the pages slowly to avoid drafts. A real scientist would have perforated the pages to keep from disturbing the air. He was but a general scientist, however, combining, as he thought, the virtues of the practical and the theoretical in Elevating the Young, an intellectual sort whose pink resentful mouth and clenched neck made the expression of someone who had just swallowed a banana sideways.

The first walk, a free trial, would take place on a Saturday, and the Saturday before the Fourth, the third-busiest day of the year in the store. I decided not to go.

Tom Moss was going. Lewis Snyder, who had dates alone with girls, was going. I learned that several of them, including Rosalie Fallon and Pattie Donahue, would be botanically present. I decided to go.

We met, everyone carrying lunch but me, at eleven-thirty. Mother didn't know about it, I had run away from the store, taking my cap from under the cash register and, for some last scruple, telling Myrna to tell my father that I had gone. "Where?"—but I disappeared without answering, subtle as a hungry tomcat unable to hide its rut, sneaking around corners with its yellow eyes scheming. Lewis Snyder had a scout canteen filled with near-beer left over after repeal. I suspected him of planning to offer Pattie some.

Pedantic, amorous, shifty-eyed general scientists, we followed Mr. Wilkerson into the Rocky River reservation. He wore a checkered golf cap, its band black with Sta-Neet, and showed how he had taught his wife to wrap his lunch—cellophane insulated the deviled eggs each from each. "Practical. Sanitary germfree. Vitamins spoil in the open air," he advised us.

Tom Moss, my friend the skeptic, whispered to me that he thought it was supposed to be *good* for you to be out in the fresh air, and then went to step on Rosalie Fallon's heels.

We penetrated the woods, already hungry. "Now right here on your left children we find an interesting phenomenon page one hundred and forty-eight in Brenner's figure sixteen that orange growth over there with the black spots now that's a wild spermaphore," Mr. Wilkerson remarked. "Ess. Pee. Ee. Arrh—"

"Looks like a toadstool to me," I said.

"Spermaphore. Silver spoons unreliable poor quality silver these days no workmanship. Damp places. Twenty-four on a picnic without a general scientist. Could have told them. Whole party dead in eight to ten hours. Horrible. Too bad. Ess, pe—"

A voice occurred behind me, whispering, "Hello, there." It was Pattie. "Toadstools are very poisonous"—she leaned sociably. "Do you like, are you fond of mushrooms?"

I soared into paradise at her feet. "My mother cooks spermaphores with meat loaf," I said, "and stuffed peppers."

"Oh"—a gasp of scandal. "She does not! You'll all be dead . . . Does she?"

"Yes," I lied, death-defying—what could be a better beginning between lovers? All lies come true in the world of supple twelve-year-old facts. It was cool here across the city from the store. Birds soon to be falsely named cocked their heads in the trees and lectured us. Someplace customers swarmed amid the imperatives of telephones, and the distance between my father and me widened past even the nine-month doubt separating an instant of giving from the birth of a son. Fatherhood, a metaphysical idea, was being taken from Dad as Mrs. Rawlings slipped her daily bottle of vanilla extract into her muff, no one to distract her, and as Mr. Wilkerson bravely broke the perfidious spermaphore with a five-foot stick, no academician he, a man of general action in science. Rosalie Fallon gave her pressed-lip assent and moral outrage against hypocritical silver spoons while my thoughts fled back from the store to recall prepared speeches of pas-

sion for Miss Donahue, known by Killer Me and Edward G. as Ulalume or The Lost Lenore.

"Oh-h-h," she was saying.

"Look the bug," I replied.

She pretended to be scared; not. I knew. Death and complicity—
love is not a biological gesture in suburban children, O Mr. Wilkerson! I had forgotten my speeches and Ulalume.

Despite this meeting I again felt deserted, lunchless at lunchtime.
Tom Moss pretended not to notice: excuse him his hunger. "Where's
yours?" Pattie asked, her mouth full.

"Don't have any. My mother didn't. Not hungry anyway."

Girls always have enough to give. Suburban girls (economical) always have enough to invest. Sweetly she murmured, "You can have
one of my bacon and tomato-motto sandwiches and a bite of cottage
cheese with the canopy, please do." Smiling, licking her lipstick, her
eyes calculating under the modest, fluttering, venereal lids, she whispered intimately: "And a cookie the one with the candied cherry in
the middle, please do, really."

"Oh!" I protested.

Take, take, my mother would have said.

"Really, I don't mind, please do," said dainty Miss Patricia
Donahue.

I did.

Later, when we bid farewell to sporting, big-toothed, intellectual
(generally scientific) Mr. Wilkerson, and thanked him for a lovely
nice afternoon, and promised to ask our parents to fork over five
smackeroos for a Program of Nature Walks, Pattie Donahue allowed
it to be known that I was walking her home. Under the circumstances even Lewis Snyder had to count it a date with a girl; the evidence whelmed, overwhelmed. I obeyed the protocol. We had a Coke
and then an ice cream stick. That Snyder must have been eating his
heart out, at least aggravated. All right then—I soliloquied with Tom
Moss *qua* Conscience & Scorekeeper—half credit then for a daytime
date.

At this age my father had already seen the wonder-working rabbi.
He was crossing borders at night to find freedom in America. He had
found it for me too.

"Did you get a free one?" I asked.

She read her ice cream stick. "No," she said.

"Neither did I. Don't believe in luck anyway"—and I expounded my philosophy of will power concentrate your way to fame and/or fortune. Just like a wonder-working rabbi from Lakewood, Ohio. I tried to recite "Ulalume" but forgot it.

My mother's arches were hurting in her Enna Jetticks, but she avoided my father so that he would not order her home. Andy was making off to the vegetable cooler with a bagful of macaroons. Basketwood splintered under orders; customers fidgeted untended; my father wiped his forehead with a paper towel from the pine forests of Maine, leaving crumbs of lint, and mourned his losses: Where was his son?

"I never knew you were so smart," said Pattie Donahue.

We had fallen silent, sitting on the front steps of her house in the shadow of a bush where her mother could not see us. Up the street someone was hosing his car, an incontinent sound, in preparation for a Fourth of July trip. The afternoon was over. Pattie Donahue, an economical creature, an Indian giver, took back her gift in a way which expressed her genius. Business acumen. Operating costs and turnover. Appraising me with her turtle-round eyes, shrewd to calculate the value of an investment, she first created a bear market by sighing, Ohh, rustling her dress, and accidentally touching my arm with her transparent turquoise-veined hands. Cologned and dusted with powder, she breathed on me.

"Yes!" I spilled out, naked in summer smells. "Do you like me, Pattie? I like you."

"Sure I like you"—disappointment and a pout that it had been so easy. Even economy becomes sport with such a housekeeper. "Sure I like you but you're too fat."

"Fat?" I repeated stupidly.

Her laughter tinkled in the July calm by the watered bush. "Fat I mean skinny. I mean you're just a *grocery* boy, you. You just grub around a certain store I could name all the Saturdays I ever heard about, except I suppose today—"

She was a sly old creature, that Pattie Donahue. The lips: *grocery boy.* The frozen iris: the same. Her laughter caroled forth, free, enterprising, resolute, the investment paying off in a Saturday afternoon dividend of power. Not all men are men, her laughter told her. This is a profit forever, my face told her.

"Oh but—oh but—oh but," I said.

She put her little hand to her mouth and delicately closed it. Teehee. She looked at me, unblinking. My father, knowing he was a foreigner, could have accepted this in the perspective of history. I had to discover a fact without a past; it leapt out at me like some fierce fish from the glittering shale of Pattie Donahue's economical eyes.

I stood up. "Thank you for the sandwich and the cookie," I said. (The cookie with a preserved cherry on it.)

"Oh, me, no," she said.

"I was hungry."

"Oh, you're welcome really," she said. "Thank you for the Coke. Thank you for the ice cream."

"Goodbye, Pattie."

"It was nice," she said, "truly very nice."

.   .   .   .   .

THERE WAS NO moment of reconciliation between my father and me. We quarreled, we lived together, we remained in touch, we warred again on occasion, we made it up, we looked ahead, we walked carefully with each other, we were part of a family. One day I noticed that the war with my father was over. I don't remember when that day came. It came more than once. There would still be quarrels, but we had agreed upon the lines of power. We each had our territory. We could each allow the other to live. We were allies.

Now we come to some other wars. There were many, the Depression, the struggle of family, and the one that rose above our personal mortalities. This is the war which almost made private life seem irrelevant, and then became very personal, forcing itself into the kitchen, as if to demonstrate that we are each of us required as individuals for the grand disasters of the human fate.

September, 1939. A cottage on Lake Erie at Cedar Point. My brothers and I had struggled deep into the beach, playing touch football, sand in eyebrows, shins aching. "See it here! See it here!" the youngest kept yelling. I made myself captain. We found other kids on the beach. Smell of Lake Erie, fish and wind, and a few filmy June bugs who had lost track of time—we called them Canadian soldiers . . . There was another captain down the beach and we chose up sides. Lake-sodden, sand-sodden, we clashed and the score mounted. I sent my youngest brother back to the cottage because his shoulders were sunburned. "Aw, see it here," he said, begging to touch the ball one more time.

We spent a last night in the cottage. The evening breezes came up;

we washed; sand in the sink, sand everywhere. My father sat on the porch at dusk, reading *The Cleveland Plain Dealer*. He studied and restudied the large black type, square black letters filled with furry ink—serious news. The newspaper said: WAR. My mother kept asking us to finish the fruit, the nice bananas and pears, she didn't want to have to pack it up for the trip back to Cleveland. My father read until he boiled, and then he threw the newspaper to the floor. He picked it up and read some more. Then, regularly, he threw it down, waited, and picked it up. I took a snapshot of him.

My mother was worrying about whether I had packed my fountain pen, whether the fan belt on the car would last until Cleveland, whether we were men enough to do justice to the bag of fruit she had wrapped together so we wouldn't starve on the two-hour drive back home. She wanted to put butter on my brother's shoulders. He yelled that it didn't hurt. She yelled that a little butter wouldn't hurt. He yelled that it made him feel sticky. She yelled: "What's sticky, you don't want to peel."

I pointed out that there was plenty more skin where that came from.

My father asked everyone please be quiet.

A weekend at the cottage. The newspaper with furry letters. My father was flinging the paper down again and again. I took his picture again.

My mother fought her wars closer to home. I was her battleground; her eldest son was the rough turf over which she struggled toward victory. She determined to root out my flaws before they could appear—particularly the flaw of marrying the wrong woman. There were millions and millions of the wrong women, wherever she looked; they covered the earth, like Sherwin-Williams paint.

Starting from about the age of eleven, I was a worry to her in this traditional way. Would I or would I not marry a nice Jewish girl? My mother debated this question with herself, with my aunts, with my father, and with me. She anticipated the shame, she anticipated the disgrace, she anticipated the moment when my bride would turn on me, holding up one of my socks from the hamper, and crying out that age-old subtitle from the dialogue of an international low-budget nightmare: "Dirty Jew!" Or perhaps it might be metaphysical; suddenly my wife would conclude that I had killed the Saviour. Or that I wasn't good enough for her—a family with a house by the lake. My mother had a nonecumenical view of things.

Like an unsharpened blade, I first must have replied clumsily, sawing back and forth, looking for my way in life. "Well, Ma, everybody's human, we heard in Auditorium today. All boys and girls created equal. Where's my skate key?"

"Oh! Oh! Aie! Human yes! But marry her, no!"

"What her? *Who?* But it's love that counts, Ma. Hey, the peanut butter's all gone."

"In your own kind you'll marry. Otherwise what will happen to us? She'll turn on me because I don't have an accent, you just say I do—on your father, he speaks worse. I learned it from him. Do you think they let us into their country clubs? Do you think they invite us to dinner? You're an aggravation, not a son."

"Okay, I won't marry anyone this year. First I got to get out of junior high, okay?"

"There's the new jar of crunchy peanut butter, dummy. I suppose you want me to make the sandwich too."

And thus the matter was settled for ten minutes. But then it began again.

"You're only fourteen years old."

"Fifteen, going on sixteen."

"You're too young to marry a shiksa."

"Who said I wanted to marry anyone? Just because I'm in love with Pattie doesn't mean I can marry her." Sadistically, ominously, oedipally I added: "Yet."

"Oh! oh! aie!" sobbed my mother, struck at her core.

"Fifteen years old," I pursued her angrily. "Why can't I be my own age?"

For a moment I seemed to seize the advantage. But my mother was a Ulysses S. Grant of discussion. Curse the casualties, disregard the losses. She recaptured the terrain, heroic about costs and logic.

"You're a boy!" she cried. "A boy, my own boy. I want you to be a man, a pride to me. Not a baby, a shame—a man!"

"So far," I said dejectedly, "I'm not sure I'm a adolescent."

"Where'd you learn that word? Where? Come on, tell me."

"On the playground. In the toilet. From a kid in tennis shoes."

"Oy, he'll ruin his feet," my mother said. "Flat feet before twenty, and the arch, and the calluses, and that's how the goyim take care. But their feet hurt, they take it out on the Jews. Pogroms. Prejudice. No Jews in insurance companies, no Jews in the banks, not even a teller."

"Mother, I want to go out now. The kids are waiting. I've got the bat."

"You won't go out and play baseball till you promise me. No shiksas. A nice Jewish girl from a good family, plays the piano, not flat-chested, educated."

"Who?" I asked, suddenly interested.

"Promise," she said. "When the time comes, don't worry."

My father participated gloomily, if at all, in these discussions. He could be awakened by my mother's invocations of the sufferings of the Jews. But he looked at me—skinny, knobby, with an oversized Adam's apple and a trombone voice—and was reassured. No one would have me, of whatever race, creed, or color. Also he could not accept these future risks as disasters. Even future disasters were not yet disasters. When the time came, he would think about it.

"Your father doesn't care," my mother said. "I bear the entire burden of worrying."

"Who needs you to worry?" my father asked. "I'll do the work, which we don't need the worry."

"I don't work?" my mother asked. "I raise a son, and he is lost to us?"

"Can I go read my book now? *Lost Horizon* by James Hilton? It's a grown-up book by an Englishman?"

"Lost, lost, lost," my mother said. "What good is it for me to worry and nag and nag and worry if nobody listens?"

My father was behind his paper, *Der Tag*, which came by mail from New York City. I was behind the movie edition of *Lost Horizon*, which had a photograph of Ronald Colman and Jane Wyatt— or was it Margo?—holding hands on a stone bench in the world of the future, where no one grew old, while old Sam Jaffe, the great High Lama, watched in his robes. ("The years will come and go, and you will pass from fleshly enjoyments into austerer but no less satisfying realms," Sam Jaffe told Conway while I itched with spiritual desire. "Hmm. Chang tells me that Mozart is your favorite Western composer.") I fled the unreality of family life into the reality of the realms of the spirit, where all is peace and tranquility, and Chang reminisces about Mozart, whom he knew personally.

My mother always sought the parting shot. "But you will," she said.

"Will what?"

"The right girl," she said.

And I responded malevolently, before sinking into eternal truth. "Yes, Ma. First Pattie, and then I'll divorce her. Then Lucille, and then she'll divorce me. And then Pattie again, because I'll always love her, she has such a nice red bicycle."

Lucille, of course, was put into play only to poison the wells of discourse. I didn't want to give away my secrets. Pattie was the only girl I could ever love. She hated me.

My mother took aim once more. "What did we give you for your birthday, lummox?"

"A typewriter," I said. "I already thanked you."

"Yah," she said dubiously.

"Thank you again," I murmured.

"Yah," she said, frowning, having lost her point in a notion about the ingratitude of eldest sons, the perilousness of filial love, the risks of devotion to the cause of that son, the future doctor, the future lawyer, the future pride and joy, the future marrier of a—Ah! ah! She caught the thought on the wing.

"Well," she said cunningly, hoping I would catch all the implications of this news, "I heard about a girl lives up the street, only a year or two older than you, I forgot her name, you know her, I won't tell you her name, you should leave her alone, Anna says . . ."

"What's your point, Ma?"

"For her fifteenth birthday her ma and pa gave her a case of beer. That's the kind of people you're going to marry?"

.   .   .   .   .

ACQUIRED CHARACTERISTICS ARE not passed on, but children accept them into the hospitality of their souls through the imitations of love and hate. Acquired wounds do not visibly mark the generations which follow after, but the memory of them goads and troubles. Thus history seeks to survive in every birth.

On an Indian summer day of 1938, during the madness of the Munich surrender to Hitler, my father received a last letter from his grandfather in the Ukraine. I was fourteen; we lived in Lakewood, Ohio; the streetcar stopped at the end of the block, near the corner of Clifton Boulevard and Hathaway Avenue. His grandfather had not spoken with his own son after he had permitted the boy to run away to America, but my father's father had been killed during the First World War and now the old, very old man was dying and wrote one final letter to the boy in America.

Not that he knew he was dying. He was one hundred and seven years old, close to God in heaven, addicted to practical jokes on earth. He had one eye. He liked to fish a purse on a string out into the dirt road; he watched out of his one eye until a passer-by noticed and bent to pick it up, and then he jerked the purse away. And he roared through his beard with his one-hundred-and-seven-year-old laughter. Perhaps he meant some comment on the reliability of purses in the changed universe of Russia. More likely this was the farce of an ancient creature who had very little on his mind except memories, and wanted something to happen today, right now, on the patch of street which he could still make out. His one eye was dimming. He complained of this. His handwriting was precise and small, but he complained that it was difficult to write beautifully with only one dimming hundred-and-seven-year-old eye.

My father answered to ask if he would come to America. He received a brief reply, written by a neighbor, saying that his grandfather was now too blind to write. He had a cataract. My father looked up the word: "opacity of lens of eye, due to toxic states, senility, etc." It would be very difficult to leave the Soviet Union anyway.

A few months later the old man died, and then the war broke out, and then all the rest of the Jews of Kamenets-Podolsk were dead, tumbled into mass graves by machine guns. My father thinks his grandfather would have liked to point his beard at the S.S. murderers and see the end for himself. The circle of life is never completed, but the spiral turns round, remembering other turnings.

Aside from the fact that he was very old when he died, and he died, he did not see all that he might have seen of the nineteenth and twentieth centuries because he had but one eye. The other was taken from him a hundred and thirty years ago by a man called The Crippler, who had been employed for this purpose by his parents. These distances are immense, in time, in blood flowing, in the persistence of flesh and soul. Let us try to negotiate the encrustations of years. The path runs steeply down into shadow, up into fear, and we go naked into these realities. His grandfather, whose last letter my father still possesses, was taken to The Crippler in the 1830's. In the woods and villages of the Caucasus, the Crimea, and the Ukraine, where my family lived, 1830 might as well have been the twelfth century. The people still recalled the dominion of the crazy-hatted Turks. They knew the marauding Cossacks as occasional destroyers, not as neighbors. The sunlit woods were a place of menace. The narrow mud streets ran as readily with gore as with commerce. The people spoke Yiddish. The rest were strangers. The Czar and the Russians were utter strangers. And the work of The Crippler was as essential as that of the undertaker. Like the undertaker, he served the living.

The Great Imam, Shamyl, was just then preparing to lead his Moslem mountaineers in their war against the Russians; the holy slaughter would provide a great victory for the Little Father in 1859. There had been other holy wars for faith and land, and other great victories; dominion on earth must continually be reaffirmed. In this land where Prometheus once lay in chains, where Jason once sought the Golden Fleece, strange waters bubbled in underground springs; pastures, oil, and precious metals lay waiting for human use; the earth was enriched by bodies and pieces of bodies—the Tartars, the Ruthenians, Mazepa's bands, the Poles, the Turks, the Russians, the Jews. The Chazar khans now lay mingled with the dust. The Scandinavian house of Rurik had first conquered, then disappeared. Yesterday the Golden Horde of the Mongols rode their fierce little ponies down the Mamison and the Daryal passes, hoofbeats echoing on rock. Now Circassian princes, married to blond northern ladies, conceived children who ruled, or seemed to rule, or tried to rule. Anarchy gave way to chaos, gave way to bitter autocrats. In reality there were two rulers —swift fear and slow fear. Revenge was utter. Then for a time everyone bathed in the golden sunlight and harvested the swaying grains that replaced some of the pastures.

But always there remained this nostalgia for death and destruction. Precarious life could be reaffirmed by murder. *I* live, *you* die. *You* die, and I can risk turning my back on you. *You* are crushed, and I can walk less warily.

Everyone waits for death, whether he knows it or not, but the Jews waited especially for murder. They bargained, sometimes with mutilations—in this place with mutilations—against the universal fate. In his own way The Crippler intended to save some of the sons.

The Crippler was an old man who lived alone in a hut in the woods, separated from all the world by the horror of his vocation. His job was to cut off the hands and the feet of Jewish boys; he deafened with a little stick, he blinded with another; he cut tendons and he created limps, twisted arms, broken bodies. Did he choose his vocation or was he chosen? How does a man become a crippler? I imagine that he had no wife or children of his own. There must have been some awful consecration in his heart, deeper and more terrible than that of a rabbi. He was the surgeon who treated a fatal malady inflicted upon the Jews by those strangers who carried the plague.

In those days, and for long afterwards, the Czar attempted to settle the irritating matter of his Jews by drafting all the able-bodied men among them for a period of twenty years. An officer rode up and said, "You! you! you!"

"Oh sir, he can't because—"

"Who are you?"

"The child's father, please, Your Excellence, he—"

"The recruit will stand on this spot tomorrow morning." The officer's long Cossack body leaned down along the heaving flanks of his horse. He made a mark in the dust with his sword. "Here! here! Understand?"

"No, sir, he's only a child."

The officer sat immense on his horse, noting it all down. "On this spot tomorrow morning!" And in a swirl of dust he was gone. But the Jews stood silent among the turning motes in the air. He would return as he promised. There was no more hope.

When a boy was taken, his parents brought him to the rabbi. The rabbi pronounced the service for the dead over his head. They would never see him again. Most likely they would never hear from him again. Almost at once, in the Czar's army, he would be forced to eat non-kosher food; other soldiers would sit on him and they would hold his nose until he swallowed and choked on cabbage soup floating with lard, on kasha mixed with bits of pork. The desecration ended his brief life as a man. He would no longer know who he was. He was cast out, he was submitted to use, he was a thing. What defined him as a person had been profaned; he profaned God; he had eaten unclean and forbidden things.

Much of a child's discipline in virtue, obedience, awe, and worship was joined to the duties of food: of cleanliness, of care, of prayer over food, of the appointed time for certain dishes and the absolute rejection of others. Milk and meat were never eaten at the same meal or with the same utensils; the blessed white bread, queen of the Sabbath, was taken with joy and wine on Fridays at sundown; pork and shellfish were abominations, cursed, forbidden; certain blessings had to be performed and rules obeyed in the preparation and the cooking. To violate these commandments was an insult flung in the face of God; it was unthinkable, filth, a horror, obscene. A Jew who could eat pork might do anything, or anything might be done to him. He was lost to humankind. His body would wander the earth like a wild pig's body. He would see the knives stuck in the earth near the Jewish huts—this was one way of cleansing them—and he would blush if there was still blood in his veins. But in his veins ran only madness and despair. He wore the Czar's uniform. He ate pork. He was worse than dead: destroyed, a walking shame to God, a man without even the privilege of martyrdom.

And then, at some indeterminate future date, he would finally die in one of the Czar's wars if he happened to survive the cholera, dysentery, and smallpox which periodically swept the Czar's army. Or if he was not first killed by an officer, a noncom, or a non-Jew. Or perhaps, in the despair of that living death, even by a faithless Jew. But all this, of course, came after the end of his life, since on his very first day under the Czar's dominion he was forced to eat non-kosher food as the symbol of his bondage. His body lay in bondage, waiting to be devoured; his soul was fled. Grief alone remained in his heart. The service for the dead provided for all temporal contingencies; it dealt in the ultimate matter.

The Crippler explored a means to postpone the service for the dead for many of these children. The Czar hungered for healthy Jews, he loved to crunch up their bodies and spit them out, but he had no taste for defective ones. The Crippler manufactured defects to thwart the Czar's appetite. When the time of the boy-collectors arrived, the parents took their children to the hut in the woods where the ferocious old man waited with his instruments. They stood in line, weeping, the boys clinging to their mothers in terror, the fathers morose and determined, the mothers wailing in the birch and pine forests of the fertile Ukraine. Few dared to pray as they waited—would this not be sacrilege? They know what they were doing but they did not ask either divine sanction or divine forgiveness. It was a decision on earth. It was polluted, as decisions must be on earth. Oddly enough, when the moment came, the boys marched into the bloody room without tears, and the mothers stopped weeping, and sometimes only at that time did the fathers begin to wail like women. They saw their sons look brave and manly. The sight undid them.

Within this collaboration in a custom, it was necessary, of course, to be reasonable. The State could not brook ridicule—a rabble of Jews all missing the index finger. That would be absurd. An entire village

of invisible fingers pointing toward the sky with invisible reproach—
absurd! The Czar's collectors knew what was being done, but they
hardly minded, so long as the forms were obeyed. These gentlemen
preserved their dignity. If the Jews chose another way, the battle was
won. And if the Jews chose to destroy themselves, why, so much the
better. The Little Father in Moscow, in his great wisdom, would
smile at how the cursed ones insisted on reading their strange books,
babbled their strange prayers, wore their magical long black coats
and sideburns, but then could be led to devour their own young like
beasts. Let them fabricate a race of cripples. Then they would not
have to be fed by the army. They made poor soldiers anyway; few
were converted, few became Russian; and they died miserably later,
sullen, closed in, deaf to the Little Father's holy will for them.

And so they would rather punish themselves by their own hands?
They would rather invent and choose their own grief, like Jews, like
Jews always, like Jews since the time of the Refusal?

Fair enough. Good. Delicious.

The provincial officials winked at the game. Some officers found it
a marvelous joke over vodka after wearying themselves in obscure
struggles over the cold bodies of the sluts of the village. Some pious
ones discovered an obscure justice in the way of the world. The way
of the world must mean something. The world could not run this
way without some intention. *Slave Bogu:* Glory to God.

Still, the papers had to be filled out, the bureaucracy had its regulations. In this complicity between victim and oppressor, it was the
duty of the victim to make his wounds interesting and varied. The
Crippler performed the ceremony, and also made the rules within
a general code. Judgment was delegated to him. It must seem like a
set of accidents. As the boys lined up, he looked them over and told
the parents, without any expectation of contradiction: "This one I'll
take two fingers. This one I'll take the foot. This one I'll deafen."
He looked sternly at my great-grandfather's parents. If the aggregate
of horror did not satisfy the Russian inspectors, they might come
down drunkenly in the night upon the entire village. "Your son," he
said, "I will blind in one eye." And for the first time he faltered. He
added a few words which might serve as apology. "Only in the left
eye."

My great-grandfather's mother was weeping. His father accepted
fate, but with a murderous withdrawal. He could do nothing for his
son; he was unmanned, as Abraham must have been with Isaac. But

then it was God Who demanded the sacrifice. And God asked only assent to the sacrifice; then He relented.

The boy clung to his mother. The Crippler paused because he had to justify himself to no one, and yet he was human too, although a crippler. He had been crippled himself—he walked with a limp. He fixed the child with his fierce gaze and said, as if to give him courage:

"Out of the right eye he will see like a tiger. How many sights can you see with two eyes? No more than with a good right eye. I'll only take the extra one, come here"—and he bent with his beard jutting toward the terrified child while my grandfather's father suddenly wept and prayed.

"Come here, son. Come here. Here."

Blessed art thou the Lord our God the Lord is One.

The boy screamed.

The Crippler did his deed.

When my father wanted to come to America, his grandfather hissed with rage at the boy's father. Godless America! He showed his scarred socket and said, "I see! So he can escape the army? I see anyway. Is he to be more free than I am? Does he have a right?"

His rage, his fear, and his hurt clinging to the reality of the past was given to his own son as a cautious passivity, and then transformed by my father into its reverse, a controlled will to make his own life; and then somehow, in some other way, it was transmitted to me. The Crippler is an instrument of the way things are, and so are the crippled. We are chosen. Also we sometimes manage to choose our sacrifices—eye, toe, ear, hand; we risk our members—heart, soul, memory, will; we risk our brothers and ourselves; we each of us bear the many marks of sacrifice, compromise, and accommodation.

On his last visit to me in San Francisco, when he stood on my little terrace looking after the Japanese freighter heading east through the Golden Gate, my eighty-year-old father was still plotting his victories for the next twenty years. He had taken great pains to stay alive in these times. He had dared the world and his own weaknesses to defeat him, and sometimes he accepted a defeat, because his failures were as necessary to him as his riding free.

For his pains my father did not resolve the quarrel with death. Nor will any of us. But he sought his own way to the common end, carving his will out of the dreadful void, and may I and other fathers do as much.

Stern

by BRUCE JAY FRIEDMAN

Somewhere between the grotesque and the surrealistic, Friedman's Stern touches the ultimate nerve in sensitivity to anti-Semitism. This remarkable psychological novel, so fresh on the theme, has the added literary virtue, rare in a first book, of being perfectly constructed.

The schnook-hero is no ghetto child driven to rapacity by his inner hatred of being Jewish, but a trembly semisophisticated ad writer, now making it out to the suburbs. A primitive insult from a neighbor drives him to a sanatorium, where this ulcerated Jew becomes a Ulysses in a psychodrama of cripples. Only after he returns home and swagger-sneaks up to his neighbor to make a show of a fight and take his beating can Stern live with his condition.

We have attempted to preserve the story line of the novel while concentrating on the amazing episodes at the sanatorium. Aside from stylistic idiosyncracies, the book has a unique effect of satire within allegory. Friedman's parody of self-pity could be an extension of the wry humor of Sholem Aleichem, as indeed could much of the sophisticated black humor that came into vogue with this author and Joseph Heller. More extreme is Friedman's later novel, A Mother's Kisses, the end-all sketch of the Jewish mama that preceded and even exceeded Roth's Portnoy's Complaint.

Bruce Friedman is another New York product, born there in 1930, but he went to the University of Missouri for a degree in journalism. There followed some experience in publicity and ad writing, which probably contributed to the sloganesque effect of his style, particularly effective in dialogue. Thus, in his successful play, Scuba Duba, a satire of our stock-parts society, even the most advanced attitude resounds as a cliché.

*Taken as a segment of the American Jewish experience, Stern
is typical of the pain and bewilderment of the detached Jew,
married to a non-Jew, free of family or community demands, but
still not free of being a Jew. Possibly this suburbanite will, out of
sheer need for classification, join a temple; just as possibly, he or
his son will opt for discontinuation. Friedman has shown him as
he is, in the interim.*

M.L.

Prologue

ONE DAY IN EARLY summer it seemed, miraculously, that
Stern would not have to sell his house and move away. Some small
blossoms had appeared on one of the black and mottled trees of what
Stern called his Cancer Garden, and there was talk of a child in the
neighborhood for his son, a lonely boy who sat each day in the center
of Stern's lawn and sucked on blankets. Stern had found a swift new
shortcut across the estate which cut his walking time down ten minutes to and from the train, and the giant gray dogs which whistled
nightly across a fence and took his wrists in their mouths had grown
bored and preferred to hang back and howl coldly at him from a distance. A saintlike man in brown bowler had come to Stern with a
plan for a new furnace whose efficient ducts would eliminate the
giant froglike oil burner that squatted in Stern's basement, grunting
away his dollars and his hopes. On an impulse, Stern had flung deep-
blue drapes upon the windows of his cold, carpetless bedroom, frustrating the squadron of voyeurs he imagined clung silently outside
from trees to watch him mount his wife. And Stern had begun to
play "Billy One-Foot" again, a game in which he pretended his leg
was a diabolical criminal. "I'll get that old Billy One-Foot this time,"
his son Donald would say, flinging his sucking blanket to the wind
and attacking Stern's heavy leg. And Stern, whose leg for months had
remained immobile, would lift and twirl it about once again, saying,
"Oh no, you don't. No one can ever hope to defeat the powerful
Billy One-Foot."

It was as though a great eraser had swept across Stern's mind, and
he was ready to start fresh again, enjoying finally this strange house
so far from the safety of his city.

After leaving the home-coming train on one of these new nights, Stern, a tall, round-shouldered man with pale, spreading hips, flew happily across the estate, the dogs howling him on, reached his house, and, kissing his fragrant, long-nosed wife deep in her neck, pulled off a panty thread that had been hanging from her shorts. He asked her if anything was new and she said she had taken their son Donald about a mile down the road to see the new boy she'd heard about. When the children ran together, the boy's father had stopped cutting his lawn, pushed her down, and picked up his child, saying, "No playing here for kikes."

"What do you mean he pushed you down?" Stern asked.

"He sort of pushed me. I can't remember. He shoved me and I fell in the gutter."

"Did he actually shove you?" asked Stern.

"I don't know. I don't remember. But he saw me."

"What do you mean he saw you?"

"I was wearing a skirt. I wasn't wearing anything underneath."

"And he saw you?"

"I think he probably did," Stern's wife said.

"How long were you down there?"

"Just a minute. I don't know. I don't want to talk about it any more. What difference does it make?"

"I didn't know you went around not wearing anything. You did that at college, but I thought you stopped doing that."

Stern knew who the man was without asking more about him and was not surprised at what he had said. The first Saturday after they moved in, Stern had driven around the sparsely populated neighborhood, smiling out the window at people and getting a few nods in return. He had then come to this man, who was standing in the middle of the road. The man had taken a long time getting out of the way, and when Stern had smiled at him, he had tilted his head incredulously, put his hands on his hips, and, with his shirt flopping madly in the wind, looked wetly in at Stern.

Stern had held the smile on his own face as he drove by, letting it get smaller and smaller and sitting very stiffly, as though he expected something to hit him on the back of the head. On one other occasion, Stern had driven by to check the man and had seen him standing on his lawn in a T-shirt, arms heavy and molded inside flapping sleeves, his head tilted once again. And then Stern had stopped driving past the man's house and, through everything that happened afterward, had blacked the man out of his mind. Yet he had waited nonetheless for the day his wife would say this to him.

There was half an hour of daylight remaining. Stern's son flew to the top of a living-room bookcase and said, "Get me down from this blazing fire," and Stern climbed after him, throwing imaginary pails of water on the boy, and then swept him down to administer artificial respiration. They saw Popeye together on television, Stern's wife bringing them hamburgers while they watched the set. When he had eaten, Stern said he was going to see the man, and his wife for some reason said, "Be right back."

He did not take the car, wanting the walk so he could perhaps stop breathing hard. On the way over, he kept poking his fingers into his great belly, doing it harder and harder, making blotches in his white skin, to see if he could take body punches without losing his wind. He hit himself as hard as he could that way but decided that no matter how hard you did it to yourself, it wasn't the same as someone else. As he hit himself, a small temple of sweetness formed in his middle; he tried to press it aside, as though he could shove it along down to his legs, where it would be out of the way, but it would not move. The man's house was small and immaculately landscaped, but with a type of shrub Stern felt was much too commercial. It might have been considered beautiful at one time. A child's fire wagon stood outside. Stern walked past the house, near to the curb, and then walked on by it, stopping fifty yards or so away in a small wooded glade and ducking down to do some push-ups. He got up to nine, cheated another two, and when he arose, the sweetness was still there. He saw that he had gotten something on his hand, either manure or heavily fertilized earth. He wiped it on his olive-drab summer suit pants and kept wiping it as he walked back to the man's house again, past it, and on down the road to his own.

His wife was scrubbing some badly laid tile on the floor of the den, pretending the deep crevasses didn't exist. She was a long-nosed woman of twenty-nine with flaring buttocks and great eyes that seemed always on the edge of tears.

"Can you remember whether he actually shoved you down?" he asked her. "Whether there was physical contact?"

"I don't remember. Maybe he didn't."

"Because if there was physical contact, that's one thing. If he just said something, well, a man can say something. I just wish you had something on under there. I didn't know you go around that way. Don't do it any more."

"Did you see him?" his wife asked.

"No," said Stern.

"It doesn't make any difference," she said, continuing on the tile.

.   .   .   .   .   .

He had met his wife at college after being rejected by a young girl with musical voice and tangles of blond hair who acted in Arthur Wing Pinero plays, doing deep, curtsying walk-ons that made Stern weak in his middle. He had scrupulously avoided taking the blond girl to bed, preferring to think of her as "not the kind of girl you do that with" until, disgustedly, she refused to see him, telling him, "Someday you'll understand." A week later, he met his wife, a girl with great eyes and shining black hair and no music in her voice, and, after an anecdote or two to establish his charm, he went with her to a blackened golf course and, with clenched teeth and sourness, drove his fat hand through her summer-smelling petticoats and, as she moaned "God no," kissed her and tried not to think of curtsies. Later that first night, he went into her a little, and they both froze and clung to each other. Stern at that time boarded off campus with a trembling old ex-bass fiddle player who sat each night wearing truss-like old-man belts and gadgets and twanged his instrument in the basement. The old man was not particularly nice to Stern. He feigned munificence by asking Stern to have glasses of milk but actually used him as a sourness tester. At night, while the old man sat in his bands and trusses, Stern would spirit the petticoated girl into his room, undressing her swiftly and then tasting and biting her, going at her with anger and closed eyes to drive away all traces of Victorian curtsies. She was the only daughter of a man who had missed great opportunities as a baseball executive and now lived with silver tongue and failing eyesight in an Oregon apartment. Her mother was Hungarian, had lost three children in infancy, and spent her time crocheting bitterly, dreaming of three dead sons. Lean of funds, they had sent the girl, with heavy trunkloads of petticoats, for a single year of college and then no more. She dated constantly, afternoons and evenings, an endless succession of boys. Stern asked her what she did on these dates and she said she'd kissed most and allowed some to "kiss her on top."

"You're the only one from New York I've known, and you're different," she said to him. "You care for different things. The others just care about being a good dresser."

Psychology interested her, but she mispronounced words, and it bothered Stern, a man who waded without joy through classics, that she had never tried Turgenev. She had total recall of her childhood and, her voice filled with pain, she told Stern tales that failed to move him. "I had twelve birds, and each time I got to love one, my parents would get rid of it. I'd come home and see it not there and look all over and then I'd realize that they'd given it away. They'd just give me enough time to love it, and then it would get out of the cage and make on the floor and my father would say, 'It's a filthy animal,' and give it to a girl friend." She was aware of her longnosed beauty and would say to Stern, "You should have seen me at eight. I tapered off a little up through ten, but at eleven my face would have killed you. I don't even want to *talk* about my face at thirteen. I was really beautiful then, really something." She complained much of her childhood ordeals, telling Stern, "My mother never gave me sandwiches, even though she knew I would have loved them. She'd give me what was inside, and even the bread, but not sandwiches." Most of the time she would listen to Stern, though, sitting with great and shimmering eyes as he told of New York; and when he was finished, she would say, "You really are different. You're not interested in shoes or dancing. You're the most different person I know." Their talks were only bridges, and when it seemed to Stern they had put in enough time at it so that he could feel they legitimately interested one another, he would begin to kiss her and bite her and stroke her and undress her and examine her while she stood or sat calmly, great eyes shining, and let him explore her body. When he touched her a certain way they would fly at each other and she would do a private, nervous, whimpering thing beneath him. They clung to each other all over the campus, and sometimes she came to his room with nothing beneath her summer dress. She would wheel about him, nude and happy, while Stern feigned calmness and watched her with held breath as though it were a scholarly exercise. Then his loins would go weak and he would sail at her and bite her thighs too hard. He did crazy, tangled things to her, thinking he would break her frail body, but when he had finished she would come to him with great eyes wide, scrape his neck with her nails, and ask him to "be a man again." . . .

There were only three other occasions on which Stern and his wife discussed the kike man. One occurred the very next night when Stern, still in his topcoat, caught her wrists around the oven and said, "I just want to see how it happened."

"What do you mean?" she said.

"I want to get a picture in my mind of what it was all about. Get on the floor and show me exactly how you were. How your legs were when you were down there. It's important."

"I won't do that," she said, breaking through to clean the oven.

"I've got to see it," said Stern, grabbing her again. "Just for a second."

"I'm not going to do anything like that. I told you to forget it."

"I'm not fooling around," he said, and, taking her around the waist, he threw her to the kitchen floor, her jumper flying back above her knees.

"You crazy bastard," she said, flicking a strip of skin from his nose in a quick swipe and getting to her feet.

"All right, then—me," said Stern, getting on the floor. "My topcoat's your dress. Tell me when I'm right." He drew the coat slightly above his knees and said, "This way?"

"I'm not doing this," his wife said. "I don't know what you want me to do."

"Were you this way?" he asked. "Just tell me that."

"No," she said.

He drew the coat up higher. "This?"

"Uh-uh," she said.

He flung the overcoat back over his hips, his legs sprawling, and said, "This way?"

"Yes," she said.

Stern said, "Jesus," and ran upstairs to sink in agony upon the bed. But he felt excited, too.

On the weekend, several days later, as Stern unloaded cans of chow mein from the supermarket, his wife said, "He has big arms."

"Who?" Stern asked, knowing full well who she meant.

"The man," she said. "The man who said that thing."

"Oh," Stern said. "What do arms mean?"

The third and final time was when they sat one day beneath a birch tree while their son dug a hole in the dirt to China. The kike man drove by in his car and Stern's wife said, "I hate that man."

"You're silly," Stern said.

The man's house lay at a point equidistant between Stern's and the estate. Since Stern did not want to pass the man's house on foot any more, he took to driving his car back and forth to the estate each day, leaving it at the estate edge each morning and picking it up at night. Once he was in his car at night, he had a choice of either driving directly past the man's house or taking a more roundabout route that avoided the man's house altogether. Each night, as he boarded the train, he would begin a struggle within himself as to which road to take. The roundabout road presented the more attractive view and Stern told himself there was no earthly reason why he should have to pass up the nicer scenery along this road. The houses were much handsomer and made Stern feel he lived in a more expensive neighborhood. Stern would start off along the finer road, but when he had gone fifty yards, he would throw his car into reverse, back up, and go down the road that led past the man's house. It was much shorter this way, of course, and Stern told himself now that distance should be the only consideration, that if he took the roundabout road, he was only doing it to avoid having to look at the man's house and was being a coward, afraid that the man would pull him out of the car and break his stomach. . . .

.   .   .   .   .   .

On clear weekend days during that summer, Stern was able to look straight down the street as far as a mile or so and make out the man playing softball in the road with neighboring boys. On such days, Stern would go back inside his house, his day ruined. And often, inside the house, he would think about his Jewishness.

As a boy, Stern had been taken to holiday services, where he stood in ignorance among bowing, groaning men who wore brilliantly embroidered shawls. Stern would do some bows and occasionally let fly a complicated imitative groan, but when he sounded out he was certain one of the old genuine groaners had spotted him and knew he was issuing a phony. Stern thought it was marvelous that the old men knew exactly when to bow and knew the groans and chants and melodies by heart. He wondered if he would ever get to be one of their number. He went to Hebrew School, but there seemed to be no time at all devoted to the theatrical bows and groans, and even with three years of Hebrew School under his belt Stern still felt a loner among the chanting sufferers at synagogues. After a while he began to think you could never get to be one of the groaners through mere attendance at Hebrew School. You probably had to pick it all up in Europe. At the school, Stern learned to read Hebrew at a mile-a-minute clip. He was the fastest reader in the class, and when called upon he would race across the jagged words as though he were a long-distance track star. The meaning of the words was dealt with in advanced classes, and since Stern never got to them, he remained only a swift reader who might have been performing in Swahili or Urdu. He had two teachers, one a Mr. Lititsky, who concentrated on the technique of wearing yarmulkes and hit kids with books to keep order in the class. He had poor control over the classroom and would go from child to child, slamming an odd one here and there with a textbook and saying, "Now let's get some order here." By the time he had some, the half hour was up and there was time only for a fast demonstration of how to slip on a yarmulke. Outside, some of those slammed with books would say, "If he does that again, I'm going to hit Lititsky in the titskys," always sure to draw howls of laughter.

His other teacher was a black-eyed beauty from the Middle East named Miss Ostrow who told stories of Palestinian oases, referring to Palestine over and over as "the land of milk and honey," while Stern listened, unable to see why a land filled with those commodities should be so desirable. Miss Ostrow was beautiful and wore loosely cut Iraqi blouses, and Stern loved her, although he preferred to think of her as American-born and not to dwell on her earlier days in the Palestinian date groves. She cast him as the wicked Egyptian king, Ahasuerus, in a Purim play and, until the date of the play, called him "my handsome Ahasuerus." One day, after school, she caught Stern in a crowd in front of a drugstore and embarrassed him by standing on tiptoe and waving, "Ahasuerus."

All Hebrew School led up to the Bar Mitzvah and the singing of the Haftarah. Stern, who had a good voice, took to trilling occasional high notes in his practice Haftarah rendition, and the Haftarah coach would say, "No crooning." On the day of his Bar Mitzvah, Stern sang it flawlessly and his mother, afterward, said, "You had some voice. I could have fainted."

"Yes," said the Haftarah coach, "but there was too much crooning."

No great religious traditions were handed down to Stern by his small, round-shouldered father. He was self-conscious on the subject, and a favorite joke of his was to create some outrageous supposition, such as "Do you know why we're not allowed in the Chrysler Building after eleven at night?" When Stern or his mother would answer "Why?" Stern's small dad would say slyly, "Because we're Jews," mouthing the final word with great relish and pronouncing it "chooze." Stern's mother would then double up with laughter and Stern would join in, too. A bad punster whose favorite gag word was "homogenize" ("I homogenize saw you on the street last night"), Stern's small dad had great fun with such phrases as "orange Jews" and "grapefruit Jews." When Stern would say, "I heard that, Dad," his father would say, "Yeah, but I'll bet you never heard prune Jews."

Stern considered Passover the biggest holiday of the year, and on the first night of the celebration Stern and his parents traditionally attended a Seder in the back-room apartment of his Aunt Edda's hardware store, which was closed for the holiday. (After the final prayers, Aunt Edda switched on the lights of the store and each of the Sedergoers put in a large order for hardware items, which Aunt Edda furnished them at cost.) A small, dark-haired woman with tiny feet, Aunt Edda was much revered by the other members of the family, and Stern's mother often referred to her as a "saint" and then added, "Even though she's got more money than God." When Stern walked into Seders, Aunt Edda would run to him on tiny feet, clasp his arm, and say, "I want to tell you something," after which she would stare into his eyes, hold his arm for a long time, and then say, "You're some darling boy." Aside from arranging the Seder, Aunt Edda's main function was to thrust her tiny body into the center of the Seder fights that broke out annually. One of the main antagonists was Stern's Uncle Sweets, who presided over the ceremonies—a wild-haired man with giant lips who was involved in clandestine Chicago rackets and once, bound hand and foot, had to climb out of a lake in southern Illinois to save his life. Stern was proud of him and referred to him as "my bookie uncle." He took Stern and his parents to restaurants, always ordering meat pies and picking up the checks; outside a seafood villa once, a hobo had asked him for a handout and Uicle Sweets had put a penny in his palm and offered it to the man. When the hobo went to get it, Uncle Sweets had doubled up his palm and driven his fist into the man's nose, spreading the nose across the hobo's face with a sloshing sound Stern never forgot and leaving the man in the gutter. Stern's father said, "Hmm," and his mother said, "Oooh, Sweets is some bitch," with an excited look in her eyes.

Uncle Sweets, wrapped sacredly in embroidered shawls, presided over the entire ceremony with thick lips and heavy lids, pounding his chest, quaffing wine, and singing long passages with the sweet full voice and passionate fervor of an old choir boy, as though this was his one night to atone for all the mysterious goings-on in Chicago. Challenging him each year and breaking in with his own set of more militant chants was Stern's Uncle Mackie, squat, powerfully built, burned black from the sun, a Phoenix rancher who flew in each year for Seders and to have mysterious medical things done to his "plumbing." An eccentric man who had once chased Pancho Villa deep into Mexico at General Pershing's side, Uncle Mackie, when asked about his health, would bare his perfect, gleaming teeth, double over his bronzed, military-trim body, and croak, "I feel pretty lousy." Early in the evening, he would take Stern around the waist, pull him close, and whisper confidentially, "I just want to find out something. Do you still make peepee in your pants?" And then he would explode with laughter, until he checked himself, held his side, and said, "I've got to do something about the plumbing." He continued the peepee inquiries long into Stern's teens. When the Seder began, Uncle Sweets would take long difficult passages to himself, which gave him an opportunity to hit high notes galore, but soon Uncle Mackie, warming to the Seder, would break in with great clangor, doing a series of heroic-sounding but clashing chants that seemed to have been developed outdoors in Arizona. Before long, Uncle Sweets would stop and say to him, "What the hell do you know? You shit in your hat in Phoenix." And Uncle Mackie would fly at him, saying, "I'll kick your two-bit ass through the window." At this point, Aunt Edda would seize both their wrists, say, "I want to tell you something," pause for a long time, looking from one to the other, and then say, "You're both darling boys." The Seder would then continue uneasily, much tension in Uncle Sweets' choruses, Uncle Mackie continuing with much vigor but directing his efforts to another side of the room, as though trying to enlist a faction to his banner and start a split Seder. Stern wondered who he wanted to win in a fight, his bookie uncle or the peepee man who'd gone in after Pancho Villa. At the same point in every Seder, Stern's father would arise to do a brief prayer, reading in a barely perceptible whisper and in a strange accent Stern had never heard in Mr. Lititsky's class. He read uncertainly, flashing his teeth as though charm would compensate for a poor performance; others at the Seder would root him on, hollering out key words, while Stern stared at the floor, ashamed of his father's uncertain whispers and wishing he had a militant chanter for a dad. Toward the tail end of the Seder, Stern and his cousin Flip would sneak off to the bedroom, get a dictionary, and look up dirty words, such as "vulva" and "pudendum." They would then open their flies and compare pubic hair growths, Flip's always being further along since he was six months the elder. They would generally emerge in time for Uncle Gunther's entrance. A onetime Hollywood bit player who had done harem scenes in silents, Gunther worked a lathe in a ball bearing factory, drank heavily, and was always striding into speeding cars. Tension generally built throughout Seders as to whether he'd make it this year; when he did show, there would be great relief that he hadn't gotten caught on a fender. Aunt Edda would fix him an abbreviated Seder meal, and when he had finished it, the others would begin to confer gifts upon him in deference to his lowly lathe job. Uncle Gunther would wave them off disdainfully, saying, "What do you think I am," and finally race out the door and into the street, with the others behind, still thrusting forth their gifts, a crumpled twenty-dollar bill from Uncle Sweets, advice on life from Uncle Mackie of the Far West. Stern's small father would always take off an item of clothing, a vest or belt, and holler, "What do I need it for, you fool," at the fleeing Gunther, who would stop after a while, collect the items, and allow himself to be ushered back to the store, defeated; there, Aunt Edda stood waiting for him, holding sets of pots and pans and the uneaten Seder food, wrapped in packages and tied with string. And thus the curtain would come down on another religious holiday.

.   .   .   .   .

. . . When Stern went to college in Oregon, even the trappings fell away. He told the people he met at school, "I don't care much about being a Jew. There's only one thing: each year I like to go and hear the Shofar blown on Rosh Hashanah. It sort of ties the years together for me." And it was true that for a while Stern's last concession to his early Jewish days was to stand outside synagogues each year and listen to the ram's horn. It was as though listening to the ancient sound would somehow keep him just the tiniest bit Jewish, in case it turned out someday that a scorecard really was kept on people. One year he didn't go, however, and then he rarely went again, even though he kept using that "ties the years together" line when he met new girls and needed impressive attitudes. Before Stern met his wife at college and lived with the old man of dangling pelvic supports, he stayed in a boardinghouse of Jewish students, where the air was thick with self-consciousness. One of his two room-mates was a tall graceful redheaded boy with a monotonous voice that sounded as though he were in a telephone booth. His personality was limited, and since he seemed to have only one joke (When someone asked him for a match, he would answer, "Sure, my ass and your face"), he became known as "Gordon One-Gag."

"I've got lots of jokes," he would protest from inside his booth, to which Stern or the other room-mate would say, "Nonsense, One Gag, you've only got one gag."

Stern's other room-mate was a small, flabby ex-Navy man named Footsy who had motherly-looking breasts and a large fund of anal jokes developed on shipboard. There grew up among the three a jargon and patter, all of which hinged on Jewishness. The motherly Navy man might suddenly arise during a study period, hold his stomach, and leave the room. "Where are you going?" the redhead might ask, to which Footsy would answer, "I can't stand the Jewishness in the room," bringing forth howls of amusement. Or Stern might make a remark about the weather, to which the Navy man would say, "How Jewish of you to say that." If Stern were to utter a pronouncement of any kind, one of his room-mates would invariably retort: "Said with characteristic Jewishness." Long imaginary dialogues were carried on between the redhead and the Navy man in which the redhead was a job applicant and Footsy was an employment director, reluctant to hire him. Finally, Footsy, prodded to explain why, would say briskly, "Well, if you must know, it's because of certain minority characteristics we'd rather not go into," and all in the room would break up laughing. The Navy man would often do a storm trooper imitation, in which he got to say, "Line dem opp against the fwall and commence mit the shooting," and a boy down the hall named Wiegel who had sick feet would come in and do another German officer, saying, "Brink in the Jewish child. Child, ve eff had to execute your parents." The redhead would try Mussolini in his last days, but Footsy, the Navy man, would say, "Stick to your one gag." Footsy would lie in bed for hours twisting lyrics of popular songs to get Jews into them: "Beware my foolish heart" became "Beware my Jewish heart," "Fool that I am" turned into "Jew that I am," and

"I'm glad I met you, wonderful you" emerged "I'm glad you're Jewish, you wonderful Jew." Stern chipped in with a full lyric that went (to the tune of "Farmer in the Dell"):

> *The Jews caused the war.*
> *The Jews caused the war.*
> *We hate the Jews*
> *Because they caused the war.*

On occasion, the president of the boardinghouse, a short boy with quivering old-man jowls, would appear in the room and say, "These things aren't funny," after which Footsy would poke Stern in the ribs and whisper, loud enough for all to hear, "He's being *very* Jewish," and the president would stomp off, jowls in a rage.

Although much dating was done by the social club, little attention was paid to the girls of the single Jewish sorority, who wore the traditional campus skirts and sweaters but who seemed somehow an acne-ed, large-shouldered parody of the brisk, blond girls of the gentile sororities. Only sick-footed Wiegel took out what Footsy described as "laughing dark-eyed beauties." When Wiegel announced that he'd booked another for Saturday night, Footsy would say, "But she's a pig," to which Wiegel would answer, "Yes, but you've got to date the pigs to get to the gentile queens."

Before dates, the redhead, all dressed, might stand before Stern and say, "Check my hair."

"Fine," Stern would say.

"Suit?"

"Excellent."

"Check me for Jewishness."

"Reject," Stern would say, and all would become convulsed. Footsy would then bare a womanly breast and say, "Here, One-Gag, practice on this little beauty." After dates, all would compare how they had done, in crisp, codelike sum-ups.

"Knee and conversation," the redhead might say, and Stern would add he'd gotten "elbow and upper thigh." Footsy, who took out homelier girls, would generally have come through with "outside of bra, heavy breathing, and an ear job." Then Stern and the redhead would get into their beds, turn out the lights, and listen to Footsy do a high-pitched imitation of an imaginary date being seduced by any one of the room-mates. "Oh, Gordon, you're very cute, but I can't possibly do any screwing. I'll take off my panties, but you've got to promise there'll be no screwing. You promise?" Footsy's voice was so convincing and the girl so appealing that Stern and Wiegel (who often came in late at night for the imitations, rubbing his sick feet) would beg him to do another, substituting *their* names.

Going along with the Jewish comedy routines, Stern began to call Footsy, his motherly, good-natured room-mate, "Little Jew." In the morning when he woke up, he'd say, "Morning, Little Jew," and after classes he would ask, "How's Little Jew getting along?" It sounded good on Stern's tongue, nice and comfortable. He said it in two syllables, and it came out "Gee-yoo," and when he said it, he would bare his teeth and get a disgusted look on his face, which he felt would add to the irony and comic effect of the routine.

It was fun to say, and he began to call Footsy "Little Gee-yoo" at every possible opportunity, making terrible faces and then poking Footsy in the ribs with a laugh. It made him feel fine to keep saying it. One day the three room-mates were on their way to the ice-cream parlor where gentile girls hung out after class. Each time a group of girls walked by, Footsy would say to the redhead, "Tell them your one gag, One-Gag. That'll have them swarming all over us." And Stern would say to Footsy, "What did the little Gee-yoo think of that group?" At the ice-cream parlor, Stern held the door for Footsy, saying, "You first, Little Gee-yoo," and Footsy turned and said, "No more."

"What do you mean, Little Gee-yoo?"

"Don't call me that any more."

"The Little Gee-yoo doesn't like to be called Little Gee-yoo. Little Gee-yoo. Little Gee-yoo." It felt so good that Stern said it a few more times.

The three were inside the ice cream parlor now, and Footsy said, "If you keep doing that, I have something I'll call you."

"There's nothing, Little Gee-yoo. Nothing at all."

"All right, Nose. What do you think of that? I'll call you Nose. Hello, Nose. Hello, Nose." With tweed-skirted gentile girls listening, he began to scream out the name—"Nose, Nose. Hello, Nose. What do you say, Nose?"—until Stern, thin-faced and large-nosed at the time, flew out of the door and down the street, the cry following him back to the boardinghouse. At night the room-mates did not speak until, finally, Stern said, "OK, I won't call you the name if you don't call me 'Nose.'" to which Footsy nonchalantly said, "All right." To break the tension, the redhead said, "Let me tell you my one gag. Does anyone have a match?" And Footsy said, "Save it." There was a strain between Stern and Footsy from then on. One day Stern inadvertently called him "Little Gee-yoo" again and added, "I'm sorry. It slipped out." Instead of overlooking it graciously, Footsy said, "That's all right, Nose."

"I said I didn't mean it," Stern apologized.

"That's all right," said Footsy. "You're getting one for one."

At the end of the semester, the room-mates decided that they would separate. . . .

Stern would really like to tell the kike man that he is not much of a Jew, that his bank account is lean, he drives an old car, that no synagogue has seen him in ten years.

But Stern said nothing, continuing to drive hunched and tense past the man's house, until one night he saw a line of giant American flags flying thrillingly and patriotically from the man's every window. At that moment a great flower of pain billowed up within Stern's belly, filling him up gently and then settling like a parachute inside his ribs. He nursed it within him for several weeks, and then one evening, warming tea at midnight by the gas-blue light of the ancient kitchen stove, an electric shaft of pain charged through Stern's middle and flung him to the floor, his great behind slapping icily against the kitchen tile. It was as though the kike man's boot had stamped through Stern's mouth, plunging downward, elevator-swift, to lodge finally in his bowels, all the fragile and delicate things within him flung aside.

Stern is X-rayed by his doctor and sent to the specialist Fabiola

. . . He was holding the pictures of Stern's stomach up to the light when Stern entered, fingers dug into his great belly, as though to prevent the parachute within from blossoming out further. "You've got one in there, all right," said Fabiola. "Beauty. You ought to see the crater. That's the price we pay for civilization."

"Got what?" Stern asked.

"An ulcer."

"Oh," said Stern. He was sorry he had let the doctor talk first; it was as though if he had burst in immediately and told Fabiola what kind of a person he was, how nice and gentle, he might have been able to convince him that he was mistaken, that Stern was simply not the kind of fellow to have an ulcer. It was as though the doctor had a valise full of them, was dealing them out to certain kinds of people, and would revoke them if presented with sound reasons for doing so. Political influence might persuade the doctor to take it back, too. Once, when Stern had been unable to get into college, his uncle had reached a Marine colonel named Treadwell, who had phoned the college and smoothed his admission. Stern felt now that if only Treadwell were to call the doctor, Fabiola would call back the ulcer and give it to someone more deserving.

"Look, I don't think I want to have one of them," Stern said, getting a little dizzy, still feeling that it was all a matter of debate and that he wasn't going to get his point across. "I'm thirty-four." When the doctor heard his age, he would see immediately that he had the wrong man and apologize for inconveniencing Stern.

"That's when they start showing up. Look, we don't have to go in there if that's what you're worried about. We get at them other ways."

"What do you mean, go in there?" said Stern. Going in there was different from simply operating. He had a vision of entire armadas of men and equipment trooping into his stomach and staying there a long time. "You mean there was even a chance you might have had to go in?"

"I don't see any reason to move in," said Fabiola. The old doctor opened the door then and, with eyes narrowed, said, "I knew I heard some tootsies in here." He limped in rakishly and took a seat next to Stern. "Excuse me," he said, "I thought you were a tootsie. My office was always full of 'em. The real cheese, too."

"I think I may be pretty sick," Stern said, and the old man rose and said, "Oh, excuse me. I'll be getting along. Well, boys, keep everything hotcha. Any tootsies, you know who to call.

"Hotcha, hotcha," he said, and winked his way out the door.

"Look," Stern said, leaning forward now. "I really don't want to have one." He felt suddenly that it was all a giant mistake, that some-how the doctor had gotten the impression he didn't *mind* having one, that it made no difference to Stern one way or the other. This was his last chance to explain that he really didn't want to have one.

"I don't see what's troubling you," said Fabiola. "You'd think I'd said heart or something."

"Maybe it's the name," Stern said. "I can't even get myself to say it." It sounded to Stern like a mean little animal with a hairy face. *See the coarse-tufted, angry little ulcer, children. You must learn to avoid him because of his vicious temper. He is not nice like our friend the squirrel.* And here Stern had one running around inside him. . . .

"I can see all of this if I'd said heart," Fabiola said, beginning to write. "All right, we'll get right at her. We can do it without moving in."

"Don't write," said Stern, searching for some last-ditch argument that would force Fabiola to reconsider. The writing would make it final. If he could get Fabiola to hold off on that, perhaps a last-minute call from Colonel Treadwell would clear him.

"I wear these tight pants," Stern said. "Really tight. I think the homosexuals are influencing all the clothes we wear, and it's silly, but I wear them anyway. I can hardly breathe, I wear them so tight. Do you think that might have done it?"

"No," said Fabiola, filling up little pieces of paper with furious scribbles. "You've definitely got one in there."

Once, on a scholarship exam, Stern had gotten stuck on the very first question. There were more than four hundred to go, but, instead of hurrying on to the next, he had continued for some reason to wrestle with the first, aware that time was flying. Unable to break through on the answer, he had felt a thickness start up in his throat and then had pitched forward on the floor, later to be revived in the girls' bathroom, all chances of passing the exam up in smoke. The same thickness formed in his throat now and he toppled forward into Fabiola's carpeting, not quite losing consciousness.

"I didn't say heart," Fabiola said, leaning forward. "I could understand if I'd said heart."

Helped to his feet, Stern felt better immediately. It was as though he had finally demonstrated how seriously he was opposed to having an ulcer.

"I think we ought to bed this one down for a while," the doctor said, writing again. "I know an inexpensive place. Can you get free?"

"Oh, Jesus, I've really got one then," said Stern, beginning to cry. "Can't you see that I don't want one? I'm thirty-four." Fabiola stood up and Stern looked at the doctor's softly rising paunch, encased in loose-flowing trousers, and wondered how he was able to keep it free of coarse-tufted, sharp-toothed little ulcers. Fabiola's belly had a stately, relaxed strength about it, and Stern wanted to hug it and tell the doctor about the kike man, how bad it was to drive past his house every night. Then perhaps the doctor would call the man, tell him the awful thing he'd done and that he'd better not do it any more. Or else Fabiola would ride out in a car and somehow, with the stately, dignified strength of his belly bring the man to his knees.

"It's a little place upstate," said Fabiola, leading Stern to the door. "The way you hit the floor I think we ought to bed it down awhile. They'll be ready for you in about three days."

.   .   .   .   .

Stern, who wrote the editorial material on product labels, traveled eight floors upward to his office now, where he was greeted by his secretary, a tall, somber girl with gently rounded but sorrowful buttocks. She had lost both parents beneath a bus, and although she served Stern with loyalty, she placed a dark and downbeat cast upon all events.

"I've got something lousy in me and I've got to go away," Stern said. "Tell Mr. Belavista I want to see him. I've got to get wound up here so I can get out."

"What is it?" she asked. "The worst?"

"No, it's not the worst," Stern said. "But it's lousy and I'd rather not have it in there."

.   .   .   .   .

. . . Stern had once seen Belavista race swiftly toward a train and dive between its doors, prying them open to get aboard. Stern decided that was really the difference, that was what had made him millions. And if people had all their money and possessions taken away and everyone had to begin all over, the men who plunged daringly toward closing train doors would survive and soon have fortunes again.

Belavista was a gentle man, and Stern often told others, "He's like a father to me." Childless and divorced, Belavista lavished all his attentions on two six-year-old Brazilian nieces, listing them both as corporation directors and sending them expensive gifts. A company joke was that for a Christmas present he had once given each of them a division of IBM. Stern pictured a day in which Belavista would put his arm around him and say that his nieces were foolish, that he had always wanted a son, and would Stern consider accepting a third of the label business, leading eventually to complete control? And then Stern, all considerations of wealth aside, would have a father who leaped bravely for closing train doors.

He went in to see Belavista now and yearned for the man to put his arms around him and take him back to his many-roomed house and keep him there, protecting him from the kike man and eventually calling for his wife and boy.

"Something's come up," Stern said. "I've got to go away. They found something inside me and I have to get it taken care of."

"I'm sorry to hear that," the Brazilian said. "What is it?"

"An ulcer," Stern said. "It just showed up in there."

"Does it nag at you around here?" Belavista asked, pointing between his ribs.

"Yes," Stern said. "That's where it gets you."

"Uh-huh," said Belavista. "I know. I've got it all right." He hollered out to his secretary, "Make an appointment for me with Dr. Torro.

"I know," said Belavista. "Gets you around the back, too, a little."

"A little," Stern said. "You feel as though a baby with giant inflated cheeks is in there."

"I know, I know," said the boss. "I've got it. I'm sure I've got the same thing." He shouted to his secretary, "Make sure it's for today," and then said to Stern, "I've got it, all right. I've got the same thing."

Stern felt a tiny bit of resentment now. It was as though he had finally come up with something that Belavista, with all his millions, could not have, and yet here was the man trying to horn in on Stern and get one too, a finer and richer one. Now Belavista rose and said, "All right, here's what I'm going to do for you," and Stern felt such a thrill of excitement that he had to hold on to his boss's desk. There were those who said that Belavista was a selfish and shrewd man, but Stern had always told them, "I don't see it. He comes through. He's always been very nice to me." Stern was certain Belavista had been waiting for a moment of crisis, a special time to make certain announcements about Stern's future. And now Stern, near tears, wanted to hug him in advance and say, "Thank you. Oh, thank you."

"I'm continuing your salary," Belavista said.

"That's wonderful," said Stern. "It will ease my mind." And then he waited for the list to continue.

"For as long as it takes. I don't care if it's three weeks."

"That's really nice," Stern said. He looked with humility at the floor, as though he expected nothing more.

"You've been pretty good around here and I want to play fair with you," said Belavista. "I've thought it over, and that's the way I'm going to handle it. I'd like to chat some more, but I've got an appointment I can't break. So look, take it easy, get your mind off things, and everything around here will be all right."

.   .   .   .   .   .

A tiny, gray-haired nurse looked up at him and said, "What can I do for you, puddin'?" Stern told her who he was.

"Of course, dumplin'," she said, checking her records. "You're the new intestinal. I'll get Lennie out for you. Does it hurt much?"

Stern said he'd had a bad night and asked what the rate was. She said three dollars a day. "That includes your three meals and your evening milk and cookie."

Stern had been ready to pay ten dollars a day and felt ashamed at getting it for so little. She said, "Everyone pays the same rate, crumb bun," and Stern said, "I'll donate a couch later when I get out."

A tall handsome Negro with powerful jaw muscles came out on steel crutches, moving slowly, adjusting clamps and gears as he clattered forward. He was pushing a baggage cart, and he threw his legs out one at a time behind it, as though he were casting them for fish.

"This is Lennie," said the nurse. "You'll like him. He's a sugarplum. Lennie, this is Mr. Stern, your new intestinal."

"Very good," said the Negro. "Bags on the cart, Mr. Stern. Patients to the left of me as we walk."

"I can handle them," said Stern. The Negro's jaw muscles bunched up, and he said, "Patients to my left. Bags on the cart."

Stern, afraid of his great jaw muscles, tossed his bags on the cart, and the Negro began to clatter forward, clamps and gears turning, leg sections rasping and grinding out to the side, one at a time. Stern fell in beside him, hands in his pockets, feigning a very slow walk, as though he, too, took days to get places.

"Are you originally from New York?" Stern asked. "I just came from there and it's funny, but the last guy I saw was a Negro artist friend of mine."

"There'll be no dinner," said the Negro, sweat shimmering on his forehead as he pushed the cart, looking straight ahead. "That's at five. You're late for milk and cookie, too. One lateness is allowed on that, though. Did the nurse furnish you with milk and cookie?"

"No," said Stern.

. . . . .

Stern's room was long and thin and rancid, as though aging merchant marine bosuns with kidney difficulties had spent their lives in it. A small middle-aged man with a caved-in chest and loose pouches under his eyes sat on one of the two beds in the dim light and said, "Hey, what's this?"

"What?" asked Stern.

The man had arranged his hands in a tangled way, as though he were scrubbing them, and was holding them against a lamp so that a clumping, knobby shadow showed against the wall.

"I don't know what that is," Stern said.

"See the dingus? See the wang-wang?"

"What do you mean?" Stern asked.

"You know. It's sexeroo. Screwerino."

Stern looked at the shadows again and, as the man manipulated his fingers, Stern thought he could make out a rough picture of a pair of sexual organs in contact.

"That's pretty good," Stern said.

"Check these," the man said, pulling a medallion out of his T-shirt and beckoning Stern closer. Stern looked at it, a carving of a lion and a deer, which turned into a pair of male and female genitals when tilted at an angle.

"See the dingus? Can you see the wang-wang? You want to hold it and fool around with it awhile?"

Stern actually wanted to get a better look at it, but he said, "No, thanks. I'm just getting in here and I want to take it easy. I'm going to just lie down and not do anything for a while."

"I got that last set from a guy carved them in prison. Listen, do you want me to do another one on the wall? I can do blowing."

"I just want to lie down here," said Stern, "and take it easy the first night. I have some things on my mind."

Stern got down on the bed and thought again about the man down the street. He imagined coming home and finding out that the man had moved away, unable to make his mortgage payments. Or that he had developed a lower-back injury, so that the least motion would cause him agony. Stern saw himself running over with extended hand and showing the man that he would not take advantage of him, that he would not fight him in his weakened condition, that Jews forgive. He wanted opportunities to demonstrate that Jews are magnanimous, that Jews are sweet and hold no grudges. He pictured the man's boy falling down a well, and Stern, with sleeves rolled up, being the first to volunteer to work day and night digging adjacent holes to get him out. Or the man's child being stricken with a rare disease and Stern anonymously sending checks to pay the medical bills but somehow letting the man know it was really Stern. And then he saw himself and the man becoming fast friends from that point on, Stern inviting him in to the city to meet Belavista, showing the man he didn't mind his work clothes. But mostly he wanted the back injury, and clenched his fists and squeezed his eyes hard, as though just by straining he could make it happen. If only there was a way, he thought, that he could pay to make it happen—even a large figure like $8,000, which he would work off at $10 a week.

His room-mate asked, "Do you mind any farting?" And Stern said, "I don't have any views on that."

"I cut loose a few," said the man, "but I wanted to ask, because I know a lot of the younger ones object."

The room was thick with the smell of merchant marine sheets, and Stern sat up, touching his stomach to see whether it had gotten any better since he had come to the home.

"I've got something in here and I wonder how long I'm going to have to take to get it out of here," Stern said.

"I've got the weakness is all that's wrong with me," said the man. "I've had it ever since I left the circuit. I did comedy vignettes. I used to get fifty-two straight weeks in those days, but snappers killed me off and I can't work any more. You see, I never used many snappers, maybe three a night. What I'd do is work around m'crowd, futz them along a little, nurse them, slowly giving them the business, and then, maybe after twenty minutes, I'd come in with m'snapper. I'd use maybe three a night, four tops. Nowadays the new ducks throw them out a mile a minute, no futzing in between, just one after another. Anyone who books you wants you to shoot out a million snappers before he'll even consider you. Well, I just couldn't change my style, and now I've got the weakness."

"I don't know what to say to any of that," Stern said. "I'm just here to get rid of something I've got in here."

"Suck what?" said the man.

"What do you mean?" asked Stern.

"That's one of them. One of my old snappers. I'd ask a Saturday night bunch if they had any special song requests, and when they hollered out a few, I'd take my time, do a little business with m'feet, and then say to them, 'Suck what?' "

The room seemed to have gotten narrower, and Stern was afraid that someone would seal him in with the merchant marine sheets and the old actor.

"I'm just going to go out and get the feel of the place," Stern said, getting up from the bed.

Stern walked outside in the hall and got his first look at the half man. Starting with his neck and going all the way down his body, about half had been cut away. In the shadows, with a handkerchief around his neck and a violin in his hand, he made a beseeching sound at Stern. His voice seemed to come from some place a foot away from him and sounded like a radio turned on a little too loud and tuned in to a small, dying station in New Jersey. Stern walked ahead, his face frozen, as though he did not see the man, and on the way down the steps he heard an off-key violin melody played with sorrow and no skill, muffled by a closed door. Stern wondered whether at some future date, when halves started to be taken out of him, he too would be farmed off to a home to sit unloved in the shadows and play a tortured violin.

Downstairs on the front porch a scattering of people talked beneath a great insect-covered bulb. An old man, gray-haired, draped over a wooden banister like a blanket, winked deeply and called Stern forward. In the weeks to come, Stern was to see him clinging insect-like against poles, draped over rails, propped up against walls, but never really standing. Whenever the people at Griggs moved somewhere as a unit, to meals or to the outdoor stadium, the strongest would always carry Rooney, who weighed very little, and see that he was perched or propped up or laid comfortably against something. His main concern was the amount of money great people had or earned, and his remarks were waspish on this subject. He poked Stern in the ribs and said, "Hey, the President don't make much dough, does he? I mean, he really has to hustle to scrape up cigarette money." He chuckled deeply and, poking Stern again, said, "You know who else is starving to death? Xavier Cugat. I mean, he really don't know where his next cuppa coffee's comin' from." He became convulsed with laughter. "He goes to one of them pay toilets, he's got all holy hell to scare up a dime. Jesus," he said, choking with laughter and poking Stern, "we wouldn't want to be in his shoes, would we? We sure are lucky not to be Cugie." He started to slip off the rail and Stern caught him and propped him up again. "Thanks, kid," said Rooney. "All them guys are starving, you know."

A tall, nervous, erupting teen-age boy was on the porch, pushing back and forth in a wheelchair a Greek youth who Stern learned had had a leg freshly cut off in a street fight. A blond nurse with flowering hips passed by and the Greek boy said, "The last day I'm going to jazz that broad. They're going to let me out, see. That's when I tear-ass up the steps and catch her on the second floor and jazz her good. I going to jazz her so she stays jazzed."

"Where are you tear-assin'?" said the tall boy. He combed his blond hair nervously with one hand as he pushed the wheel chair. "You got one leg gone."

"Shut up, tithead," said the Greek boy, concentrating hard. "I jazz her. Then they come after me and I cut out to Harlem. I cut out so they never find me."

"Where you cuttin'?" asked the tall, nervous boy. "You can't cut nowhere."

"You're a tithead," said the boy in the wheelchair.

Stern approached the pair and the tall, blond boy said, "How are you, fat ass? Jesus," he said to the boy in the wheelchair, "you ever see such a fat ass?"

Stern smiled thinly, as though this were a great joke and not an insult.

"I've put on a litle weight because of something I've got inside me," he said. "It certainly is a lovely night."

The tall boy erupted in violence. "You trying to be smart or something?"

"What do you mean?" said Stern in panic.

"Talking like that. You trying to make fun of us?"

"Of course not," Stern said.

"What did you say lovely for? We're just a bunch of guys. The way I see it, you think maybe you're better than the rest of us."

"It's just a way to say something, is all," said Stern.

The boy was a strange mixture, exploding with rage one minute and lapsing into a mood of great gentleness the next. The latter quality took over now, and he began to pour out his thoughts as though he might never have another chance to talk to someone so smart; he used "lovely" and it wasn't even showing off. It was as though the occasion called for conversation only on the highest level.

"I've got bad blood," he said, the violence gone. "I couldn't get into the Army with it. I work on high wires, you know. I'm the only one who don't use a safety harness. You know, I'll just swing from one wire to another. The guys see me, they flip out. I'm not afraid of anything. You get killed; so what? Then my blood gets lousy and I have to stay in bed three months, six months, I don't care. I just like to have freedom. A bunch of us guys was sitting around at Coney Island eating a plate of kraut and the man comes over and says it's time to close and takes away my plate of kraut. He didn't say it nice or anything. Right away he's stepping on our head. So we really give it to him and run the hell out of there. I hit him with the whole table.

"But you see what I mean?" he said with an overwhelming tenderness, as though Stern were his first link with civilization and he wanted Stern to interpret his position before the world. "A guy has to have freedom. The whole trouble with everything is that there's always somebody stepping on your head when you're eating a bowl of kraut."

"Sounds pretty reasonable," said Stern.

"Are you sure you're not trying to show us up?" the boy said, erupting again and taking Stern by the collar.

"No," Stern said, imagining the boy hitting him with a table.

"You're all right," the boy said, the gentleness returning. "I'll bet the only reason you have a fat ass is because you're sick, right?"

"That's why," said Stern.

"Maybe one night—George, you, and me—we all go downtown to get some beers."

By sliding and slipping from railings to banisters, Rooney had attached himself to a pole close to the trio. "You know who don't have a pot to piss in?" he said. "The guys who run this place. They don't eat good at all, do they?" he said, chuckling deeply and clinging to the pole like a many-legged insect.

The little staff room inside the front door lit up now, and from within, behind a counter, the Negro attendant said, "Line up for bandage and pill. Staff quarters are not to be entered."

The porch people lined up outside the staff room, Rooney sliding and clinging along as the line moved. The old actor had come downstairs and was standing alongside a dark-haired woman with sticklike legs and a thin mustache. Her head was covered with a kerchief and she tittered shyly as the old actor whispered things into her ear. He was very courtly toward her, making deep, gallant bows, and Stern wondered whether he had shown her any medallions. Stern stood at the end of the line next to a paunchy, middle-aged man who introduced himself as Feldner. "You're an intestinal, I hear," the man said. "I had what you had, only now I'm in here worrying about something else. You're a pretty smart boy. I heard you say lovely to those kids. What do you do?"

"I write labels for products," said Stern.

"I worked the casinos all my life," said the man. "All over Europe, lately the Caribbean. But I was always betting on the wrong rejyme. I'd put my money on a rejyme, see, and then I'd be working a table, making my three clams a week, when bingo, a plane flies over, drops a bomb, and we got no more casino. Once again Feldner's got his money on the wrong rejyme. One rejyme in South America give me an ulcer, what you got. But now I'm worrying about something else. How'd you like to write a book about a guy who always bet his money on the wrong rejyme?"

When Stern's turn came, he saw that the Negro, inside the staff room, had taken off his intern's jacket. He had great turbulent shoulder muscles, and Stern wondered what his legs looked like, all fitted up in their contraptions.

"Bullet got me in the high ass region," he said, his back to Stern, preparing Stern's medication. "Pacific. It pinched off a nerve and caused my legs not to move."

Stern welcomed the sudden intimacy and said, "You get around fine. I never saw anyone handle things so smoothly. When I was a kid, I used to go up to the Apollo on Amateur Night in Harlem. You'd see some really fine acts there. That's where Lena started, and Billy Eckstine." He put his foot inside the door and the Negro turned swiftly, jaw muscles pumped up with rage, and said, "There is not to be any entering of the staff room."

Stern said, "All right." He was the last one in line, and when he had swallowed his medicine, the Negro lowered the staff-room light and Stern went upstairs. On the top step the half man was waiting for him, a bandage around his neck. As Stern approached, he flung open his bathrobe in the shadows and said, "Look what they did to me," his voice coming from a static-filled car radio on a rainy night. Stern pushed by him, making himself thin so as not to touch him, closing his eyes so as not to see him, not daring to breathe for fear he would have to smell the neck bandage. He got into his narrow room and shut the door tight and wondered whether the half man would wait outside the door until he was sleeping and then slip into bed beside him, enclosing the two of them in his bathrobe. . . .

.   .   .   .   .

Most of the climactic events at Grove seemed to take place on the porch during "milk and cookie." Another night, the scowling union man, two places ahead of Stern, fell forward and died. The patients made a circle around him, as though he were "it" in a sick game, and Rooney hollered, "Give him mouth-to-mouth." Afraid he would be called upon to do this, Stern said, "I'll get someone," and ran wildly into the field beyond the building, making believe he was going through the proper procedure for handling recent deaths. He came back after a few minutes to look at the union man on the floor. It was the first dead person Stern had seen, and the man did not look sweet and peaceful, as though he were asleep. He looked very bad, as though he had a terrible stomach-ache. No one had done anything yet, and the half man was now standing in the circle, croaking, "See what happens. See." It was as though he was allowed to stand with the others only on occasions such as this, a thing he knew all about. Finally Lennie arrived, stern and poised, and leaned over the man. "This is a death," he said coolly, and Stern thought to himself, "Why did Fabiola send me here? How can I possibly be helped by seeing guys dying and half men? He made a mistake."

Yet, despite the wild urination and the curled-up dead man, Stern's pain diminished gradually. Sometimes, when he sat in the fields on endlessly long afternoons, waiting for the days to pass, he would probe his middle cautiously, as though he expected to find that the ulcer had only been playing dead and would leap out at him suddenly, bigger than ever. But the circle of pain had grown small and Stern thought how wonderful it would be if the kike man was getting smaller too, if when he got back to his house, he could find the man completely gone, his house erased, all traces of him vanished, as though he'd been taken by acid or never existed.

One morning, late in Stern's stay, word spread that two industrial teams were coming to play baseball for the patients at the Home.

There was much excitement, and Stern felt sorry for those shriveled people whose only fun had been at YMCA's and merchant marine recreation parlors. Not one had ever seen *My Fair Lady*, and it was small wonder they looked forward with such delight to a clash between two industrial teams. In early evening, the night of the game, Stern took his place in the dumb march formation and walked to the field, poking his belly and feeling around for the pain flower. It had been replaced by a thin, crawling brocade of tenderness that seemed to lay wet on the front of his body and was a little better than the other. But he wondered whether the ulcer might not roll forth in a great flower once again, at the first trace of friction, and then he would have the two, the flower and the brocade. He was aware that in just a few days he would have to go back to the kike man. What would happen if he merely drove by once, saw the man's great arms taking out garbage cans, and felt the flower instantly fill his stomach, one glimpse wiping out five weeks at the Grove Rest Home? And what if it went on that way, five weeks at Grove, one glimpse at arms, another five weeks at Grove, arms, until one day the flower billowed out too far and burst and everything important ran out of him and there was no more? . . .

One of the teams represented a cash register company and the other a dry cleaning plant, and as they warmed up, the old actor ran out onto the field, stuck a bat between his legs, and hollered to the grandstand, "Hey, get this wang-wang. Ain't she a beaut?" A tall, light-skinned, austere Jamaican Stern thought might have been a healthy-legged brother of Lennie was the umpire, and he thumbed the actor back into the stands, saying, "Infraction," and then folded his arms and jutted his chin to the sky, as though defying thousands.

In the stands, Feldner, in a bathrobe and slippers, shoulders stooped from years of bending over crap tables, said to Stern, "We had softball games when I was working under one of the Venezuela rejymes. You know how long that rejyme lasted? Four days. I really backed some beauties. That's how I got what you got."

Stern felt sorry for Feldner in his bathrobe, a man whose shoulders had grown sad from so many disappointments, and wanted to hug him to make him feel better. Once, Stern's mother, infuriated at having her clothing allowance cut down by his father, had gone on a strike, wearing nothing but old bathrobes in the street. This had embarrassed Stern, who had turned away from her each time she had walked past him and his friends. Now Stern wanted to embrace

Feldner as though to make it up to his mother for turning his back on her saintlike bathrobed street marches.

Stern watched the men on the two teams pepper the ball around the field and then looked at them individually, wondering if there were any on either team he could beat up. They all seemed fair-skinned and agile, and Stern decided there were none, until he spotted one he might have been able to take, a small, bald one playing center field for the cash register team. But then a ball was hit to the small player and he came in for it with powerful legs churning furiously and Stern decided *he* might be too rough, also. He imagined the small, stumplike legs churning toward him in a rage and was sure the little man would be able to pound him to the ground, using endurance and wiriness and leg power.

A black-haired Puerto Rican girl came to sit with the tall, erupting, blond boy. She helped a nurse take care of a group of feebleminded children connected to the Home and Stern had seen her with a pen of them, doing things slow-motion in the sun. From a distance she seemed to resemble Gene Tierney, but up close he saw that she was a battered Puerto Rican caricature of Gene Tierney, Tierney being hauled out of a car wreck in which her face had gone into the wind-shield. She did things slow-motion, in the style of the retarded children she helped supervise. Sitting on the ground in front of the tall, blond, fuselike boy, she said, "You promised we were goin' dancin'."

"Shut your ass," the tall boy said. "Hey, you want to hear one? Two nudists, man and a broad, had to break up. You know why? They were seein' too much of each other."

The Puerto Rican girl giggled and leaned forward in slow motion to tickle the tall boy. Stern saw her as a Gene Tierney doll man-handled by retarded children in temper tantrums, then mended in a toy hospital.

"Your sense of humor is very much of the earth," she said.

The tall boy introduced Stern to the girl. "This is Mr. Stern," he said. "He's a swell guy, even though he's got a fat ass. I'm sorry, Mr. Stern; only kidding. He's really a good guy. Real smart.

"Listen to this one," the boy continued. "I know a guy who was invited out by Rita Hayworth. He was in her house at the time." The tall boy erupted with laughter and the Puerto Rican girl tickled him again in slow motion. Turning to Stern, she said, "He's a natural man. I'd like to feel his energy coursing through my vitals." . . .

.   .   .   .   .

Sitting in the grandstand now, feeling Feldner's warm, bathrobed bulk against him, Stern, despite the tender sheet that lay wet against the front of his body, felt somewhat comfortable and took a deep breath, as though to enjoy to the fullest the last few days before his return to the kike man. He was afraid of the charged and sputtering boy on his left, afraid that in a violent, pimpled, swiftly changing mood he might suddenly smash Stern back through the grandstand benches. Yet, despite the grenadelike boy, Stern still felt good being at a ball game among people he knew, broken as they were. He had cut himself off from people for a long time, it seemed, living as he did in a cold and separate place, and he thought now how nice it would be if all these people were his neighbors, Rooney in a split-level, Feldner next door in a ranch, and the old actor nearby in a converted barn. Even the half man would not be so bad to have around, living out his time in an adjacent colonial until the last half was taken away. All of them would form a buffer zone between Stern and the man down the street. That way, if the kike man ever came to fight him on his lawn, his neighbors would gather on the property and say, "Hands off. He's a nice guy. Touch him and we'll open your head."

Late in the game, a line drive caught the little bald cash register outfielder in the nose and he went down behind second base with a great red bloodflower in the center of his face. There were no substitute ballplayers, and the austere Jamaican umpire, flipping through the rule book, said, "Forfeit," jutting his chin toward the grandstand, as though ready to withstand a hail of abuse.

"I'll run that coon the hell out of here," said the wheel-chaired Greek, waving his fist. "I come to see a ball game."

"That's right," said the tall boy, pimples flaring, beginning to ignite. Suddenly, his face softened. He grabbed Stern's collar and shouted, "We got someone. This guy here will play. Don't mind his fat ass." To Stern, he said, "I didn't mean that. I know you can't help it." He turned to the Puerto Rican girl and said, "Hey, a man brings home a donkey, see. So all day he goes around patting his ass."

The girl smiled, showing salt-white teeth with only the tiniest chip on a front one. She lay back, putting her head on the tall boy's lap and waggling a leg lazily, so that a gleam of Puerto Rican underwear caught the sunlight. "Boredom and you are ever enemies," she said to the tall boy. "Please sneak out and take me dancin'." The others in the stands were cheering for Stern now, and he stood up, afraid the tall boy's pimples might sputter into violence again and also not wanting to hurt anyone's feelings. It was easy to just start trotting out toward the field. He fully expected to turn back with a big smile and say, "I'm not going out there. Not when I'm sick." But he found himself jogging all the way out to center field, unable to get himself to return. Winded, he stood in a crouch, hands on knees, as though capable of fast, dynamic spurts after balls. He hoped the Puerto Rican girl was watching and would see him as being potentially lithe and graceful, equal to the tall boy. Feldner ran out in his bathrobe and slippers and said, "Do you know what will happen to you? With what you got? You play and you're dead in a minute and a half."

Stern motioned him back, saying, "I'm not sure I have what you had. Everyone's got a different kind of thing." But when Feldner turned away, discouraged, Stern was sorry he had been harsh to a man in a bathrobe.

From the stands, Stern heard the Greek boy shout, "You show 'em, fat ass," and Stern hoped the girl would not think of him only as a man with a giant behind. The austere Jamaican umpire checked Stern, looked at his rule book, said, "Legalistic," and turned stoically toward the wind.

The second hitter hit a pop fly to short center field, and Stern, since childhood afraid to turn his back and go after balls hit past him, joyfully ran forward and caught the ball with his fingertips, so thrilled it had been hit in front of him he almost cried. He did a professional skip forward and returned the ball to the infield, wishing at that moment the kike man was there so he could see that Jews did not sit all day in mysterious temples but were regular and played baseball and, despite a tendency to short-windedness, had good throwing arms.

A sick, reedlike cheer came from the torn people in the grandstand after Stern's catch. At the end of the inning, he trotted toward the dugout and heard the Greek boy say, "Nice one, fat ass, baby," but he averted his eyes with DiMaggio-like reserve and sat on the cash register team's bench. Feldner came over in his bathrobe and said, "What did I tell you?"

"What do you mean?" said Stern.

"Look at yourself. You should see your face."

"I look all right," said Stern. "And I'm playing now." Sitting among the lean, neutral-faced cash register team, he was ashamed of Feldner's bathrobed presence and motioned him away. But, as Feldner left, Stern again regretted his curtness and wanted to shout, "Come back. You're more to me than these blond fellows."

Stern got to bat in the inning. Afraid the dry cleaning pitcher had discovered his Jewishness and planned to put a bloodflower between his eyes, too, he swung on the first pitch, hitting it on the ground. Forgetting to run, he stood on the base path and actually squeezed with his bowels, hoping the ball would get past the third baseman. When it filtered through the infield for a hit, Stern hollered "Yoo" and ran to first, sending home the runner in front of him and tying the score. His team won in that inning and the patients gathered round him on the field. "You clobber their ass, baby," said the Greek boy with genuine sincerity, reaching up from the wheelchair to pat Stern's back. The tall boy, with gentleness in his lips, the ticking in him fading, said, "No fooling, you get around good. I mean, for a guy with a can like yours." The Puerto Rican girl, still lying on the bench with gaping skirt, said, "We're all goin' dancin' tonight. Either alfresco or in my place. The group has much charm." . . .

> The following night they sneak out, propelling the Greek boy in
> his wheelchair. They meet the girl in a bar.

"What about the dancin'?" the girl asked, looking over at the jukebox. "Does my love feel a tango within him?"

"Dancing, shit," said the blond boy. He looked over at the proprietor, who was rinsing glasses, and said, "He comes over here again, we get him. You can be nice up to a certain point."

"He thinks he has a fancy place," said the boy in the wheelchair. "I'll cut his balls."

Stern, his stomach pumping, wanted to say, "Wait. No fighting. You have other things, but I have an ulcer, the kind of thing you shouldn't get excited with. What if I get hit in it and get another new one?" When the proprietor came over to the table, the blond boy arranged his fingers like two donkey's ears and stuck them swiftly in the man's eyes. The proprietor said, "I can't see now," holding his eyes, and the Greek boy grabbed his hair and yanked the man's head down on his lap, saying, "I ought to cut your balls." Then he held the man by the hair in a bent-over position and the tall, blond boy began to kick at the man's upper legs, the kicks making sharp, fresh cracking sounds, like new baseballs off a bat.

Stern, who had stood by doing nothing, wanted to say, "Stop, you're going too far. The hair stuff wasn't so bad, but now you can do spinal injury." But a current began snapping through him and he looked for something to do. There was one other person in the bar, a small man with a toothbrush mustache who was eating a heavy soup. Stern ran over and grabbed him from behind, pinning his arms.

"I'm not in this," said the man.

"That's all right," said Stern, ecstatic over being in the fight, his stomach free and easy. How wonderful it would be, he thought, if he could be transported in this very condition to the kike man's front porch, the current snapping through him, the same excited sweat in his arms. He was certain he would be able to fight him and not feel a single blow, and for an instant he thought of jumping in a cab and speeding back to his house, gritting his teeth to preserve the mood. The cab fare would be $150 or so, but it would be worth it. But what if the current then began to fade, the sweat dry up, and he found himself nearing the man's house with a growing fright, worrying about being hit in the ulcer? He saw that he would have to get there instantaneously or it would not work.

After many kicks, the proprietor said, "That's enough," and the blond boy, as though waiting for him to signal with those very words, said, "Let's cut," shoving his wheelchaired friend through the door. Stern said, "I'm letting you go now," to the mustached soup eater and ran out the door after the girl, looking back at the proprietor. He was relieved to see that the man was standing; it seemed to him that only when people were on the floor might there be police involvement. The quartet ran through blackened, neatly shrubbed residential streets, and Stern wondered how running was for the ulcer. Would jogging up and down disengage it and cause it to take residence in another part of him? He was suddenly struck by the incongruity of the quartet—a grenadelike, blond boy with strange vein problems; a wheelchaired Greek; a heavy Jew with ulcer-filled stomach; and a strange, Tierney-like girl who spoke in literary flourishes. And yet they were comrades of a sort and he was glad to be with them, to be doing things with them, to be running and bellowing to the sky at their sides; he was glad their lives were tangled up together. It was so much better than being a lone Jew stranded on a far-off street, your exit blocked by a heavy-armed kike hater in a veteran's jacket.

They slowed down after a while and Stern put his arm around the girl's waist, as though he had been unable to stop and was using her to steady himself. Her neck was wet from the exercise, and the pungent dime-store fragrance of her hair brought him close to a delighted faint.

"Hey, you grabbin' my girl," said the blond boy, and, with a straight face, whipped a blue-veined, grenadelike fist into Stern's ulcer, stopping at the last possible instant and saying "Pow!" instead of landing the blow. Then he threw his head back and howled, saying, "You grab my girl, I got to give you one. Pow, pow, pow!"

"Suivez-moi to my petite habitat," said the girl, going up ahead of the group. "And a young girl shall lead them."

Not sure whether further waist encirclements were permissible, Stern walked beside her, and she said, "I used to work in a hardware store. You meet a princely selection of spooks there, it being near the main drag. One such spook came in one morning and said his friend wanted to spend the evening with me for $140. I asked him where yon friend was. He said he was across the street in a building watching the two of us with a telescope and would come down if I assented. I replied in the negative, of course. I'll entertain a man, to be sure, but not a telescoping type. You do agree there are many spooks in this land of ours." Stern, flattered that she had told him an anecdote, was not sure what to reply and decided he would tell her about his ulcer, testing her reaction.

"I've got something inside me. That's why I'm at the Home. I'm not sure how all this running around will affect me."

"The shits," she said. "I know them. The shits are a chore." She whirled around now and slid her fingers under the shirt of the tall, blond boy. "Does the darling midnight fool feel a cha-cha within him?" she asked. The blond boy took one hand off the wheelchair, tapped the underside of her breast, and said, "Flippety-flippety. Hey, Stern, you see that? Flippety-flippety."

The girl led them to the last house at the edge of a dead-end street; a sign saying "Tina's Beauty Salon" was in the center of the lawn alongside a thin and graceful tree. It had a white luminescent stripe across the bottom of its slender trunk, making it look like a thoroughbred horse's taped ankle.

"My queenly habitat," said the girl, and led them through the front door and down a long corridor with lined-up rows of hair-drying machines. She opened a door at the end of the corridor and guided them now into a small, sparely furnished room with a single bed and one wall papered with Broadway show posters. The lamplight within was warm, making her features seem smoother and heightening the Tierney resemblance; Stern, weakened now by the bulge of her black sweater, the things she had been saying, and the show posters, wondered how it would be getting a divorce, being bled financially, and starting up anew with the Puerto Rican girl in this very room.

The girl flicked on a victrola, putting a finger to her lips, and said, "I'm just a tattered tenant here." She closed her eyes and swayed to the music as though it were a treatment; her body lagged a trifle behind the beat, in the slow-motion style of the feeble-minded children she watched each day. Holding out her arms to the blond boy, she said, "Step inside this delightful sound." The blond boy came over, pinched her skirt, and said, "Check your oil." Then he pointed to the Greek boy, who sat staring out at the stars, rubbing his hands as though washing them in a sink. "Dance with George," said the blond boy. "Hey, George, dance with the broad." The Greek boy, his back to the others, a lawyer deciding a case, said, "I don't like dancing. I came out with you to do some jazzing."

The tall boy suddenly grabbed the Greek's wheelchair and pushed it out the door, saying, "I got an idea." Inside the beauty parlor room, he picked up a cigarette holder, put on a hairnet, and sat beneath a hair dryer. "Hey, look at me," he hollered back to Stern and the girl. "I'm an old broad."

The girl closed the door and said, "Boredom sets in swiftly." Still swaying to the music, she asked Stern, "What is your work?" Thrilled by her sudden interest and loving the way she had asked the question, Stern said, "Product labels. There's some writing to it, only not literary." Dancing with closed eyes and lagging behind the beat, she said, "Someday I, too, shall write a volume. I shall include the sweetness and bile of my life." She stopped dancing now and said, "One of the spooks at the hardware store asked me to do some modeling. Bearded chap. Does figure work mean you work in the altogether, or does one get to keep a doodad on?"

"I don't get into that in my work," said Stern. "I don't like the sound of what you said, though. I have some friends who are legitimate photographers."

She changed the record to a fox-trot now and, taking off her skirt, said, "How would I look adorning magazines?"

Stern stopped breathing, and it suddenly came home to him that they were only a mile or so from the Grove Rest Home and that he was supposed to be undergoing treatment. He was certain that he would be caught, and he tried to imagine what untold horrors would await him if he were brought before the Home committee. At the very least they would throw him out, marking his records so that he would be banned from other rest homes when, at some later date, new illnesses came on. Then he imagined one gentile on the committee smiling thinly and saying, "No, no, let's let him stay," and then seeing to it that he was given a daily allotment of tarnished pills so that his stomach sprouted an entire forest of ulcers.

She put her hand on her hips in a terrible thirties pose and then took off her sweater, saying, "Oh yes, the bosom culture; I'd forgotten." Her breasts poured forward, capped by slanting, evil, Puerto Rican nipples, and Stern had a sudden feeling that his wife, at that very moment, sad-eyed and chattering with need, was hoisting her own sweater above her head in the rear seat of a limousine, that there was a strange sexual balance wheel at work, and that for every indiscretion of Stern's his wife would commit one too, at best only seconds later.

Like a discharged mortar shell, the tall, blond boy, a salivated look of rage on his face, charged into the room now and said, "Oh, you lookin' at my girl's nips, eh?" He shoved Stern against the wall and shot his fist at Stern's neck, stopping once again at the final instant and saying "Fwot" instead of landing the blow. Then he became convulsed with laughter, doubling up on the bed and howling, "I got you again." The boy stood up then and kissed the girl's nipples with loud, smacking sounds and said to the Greek, "Good set, eh?" Stern, feeling somehow that the girl's breasts were going to get hurt, walked over to her and said, "We were discussing something and she was demonstrating it." The tall boy said softly, "Oh, that's all right. I just like to diddle her boobs a little. George and me will take ten outside and kid around with those dryers." Then, with increasing kindness, he said, "You know the way you say things? Like what you just said? You were *discussing* something. That's nice. The way you have of saying all the thoughts in your head."

Stern noticed now for the first time that the boy's T-shirt had holes in it, and he felt very sorry for possibly having taken something away from him. What if his veins acted up and he had to spend six months in a room, unable to swing from trees and make believe he was going to hit Stern in the ulcer?

"We can all stay here and play around," said Stern, but the blond boy walked out, saying, "That's all right, Mr. Stern, sir." To the boy in the wheelchair, Stern said, "You can stick around," but the Greek youth, rubbing his hands, said, "No, I don't feel like it tonight. You know, some nights you're just not in the mood for jazzing." He wheeled himself out of the room, closing the door behind him, and the girl put her arms around Stern's neck and said, "Sweet riddance. Now, my knighted author, will you be with me on the highest of all levels?"

Minutes previous, when she had taken off her clothes, Stern had planned merely to stare at her and fix her in his memory. Perhaps he would tap her behind and feel her breasts in the style of the other boys and then race back across the streets to the Grove Rest Home. It seemed to him that somehow if he did more, the Home would definitely hear of it, his treatment would be disrupted at an early stage, and he would be doomed to walk the streets forever with a permanent ulcer blooming between his ribs. And, of course, if he were to go further, within minutes his own wife, skirt gaping and great eyes confident, would sink back comfortably on the rear cushions of some strange convertible.

He waited for an outraged knock at the door, the clatter of Lennie's machine-shop legs, but nothing came and he fitted his hands over the girl's nylon-covered buttocks, thinking that he had never held a Puerto Rican behind before and that maybe it *was* a little different. She took his ear between her chipped white teeth, as though she were an animal pawing meat, and said, "Wondrous author of mine, explore forbidden avenues with deponent thine."

She guided him to the bed, did a dipping thing to make herself nude, and said, "Honest, do you think I'm sensitive?"

"Yes," said Stern, who loved the things she said.

She pulled him to her and said, "Then thrill my secret fibers." She put a contraceptive on him and said, "Now, honey, don't spoil it. Really, let's do a good one." It bothered Stern that she had the contraceptive on hand, but he liked the way she managed it, and the idea of her having one ready suddenly threw him into a frenzy. After a moment, she whispered, "We are as pages in a book of sonnets. Really give it to me." He said, "All right," and after a few seconds she rose and said, a little irritatedly, "Oh, you thrilled me, all right. You really thrilled me." She got into her clothes, and then the irritation passed, and she perched on the bed beside him and said, "Such loveliness I have never known." Her bare brown Puerto Rican knees excited Stern and he wanted her again. He had loved the things she whispered to him and the sting of her teeth pulling on his flesh like meat. "Tell me of your literary prowess," she said.

The door opened and the blond boy came in and said, "We're tired of sitting around out there."

Stern looked out in the corridor and saw the Greek boy's wheel-chair against the window. He went outside to him and found the boy crying. "My leg is gone," he said. "I ain't got two fucking legs any more." Stern took the boy's head against his waist and rubbed his neck, trying to think of something to tell him. But there was nothing. What could he say? That the leg would grow back again? "Some people have things even worse than legs in their stomachs," he said finally. He wheeled the boy inside the room, where the girl sat perched on the bed. The tall, blond boy picked up an extra-long broomstick handle and said, "Hey, George, let's give her a ride." He quickly slid the broomstick between the girl's legs, and the boy in the wheelchair, getting the idea, dried his eyes, wheeled close, and caught the other end, so that they had her straddling the stick as though she were on a fence. They began to lift her up and down on the broomstick, the two of them howling at the ceiling, while the girl shouted, "Lemme off, you bastards." Stern shouted, "You'll hurt her down there," but she looked so awkward, he stopped loving her immediately. When she cursed at them, Stern looked at her and said, "I can't do anything."

"Hey, Mr. Stern, keep her up there," said the blond boy, and Stern took the Greek boy's end and tossed her up and down a few times, saying, "I'm going to do this a little, too."

They finally let her down, and for an instant, straightening her skirt, she smoothed her hair and pretended nothing had happened. "Let me tell you further of my book," she said to Stern. But, after seeing her on the pole, the thought of her terrible Puerto Rican writing disgusted him and he said, "No literary stuff now."

She bent over then, holding her crotch, and said, "Ooh, you really hurt me down there, you cruddy bastards." Stern felt good that she had addressed all three of them, not excluding him, and it thrilled him to be flying out of her apartment with his new friends, all three howling and smacking each other with laughter at the pole episode. He wanted to be with them, not with her. He needed buddies, not a terrible Puerto Rican girl. He needed close friends to stand around a piano with and sing the Whiffenpoof song, arms around each other, perhaps before shipping out somewhere to war. If his dad got sick, he needed friends to stand in hospital corridors with him and grip his arm. He needed guys to stand back to back with him in bars and take on drunks. These were tattered, broken boys, one in a wheelchair, but they were buddies. They skidded across the lawn, wildly recalling the night's events.

The blond boy: "You see me kick that guy's ass? Pow, pow, pow!"

The Greek: "We almost ran that broomstick up the broad's kazoo, man."

Stern: "Did you see me hold that strong little guy at the bar?"

They split up at the main gate, each stealing back to his room separately. "Tomorrow night, maybe we do some real jazzing," said the boy in the wheelchair as they parted.

Exhilarated as he slipped past Lennie's darkened office, Stern, approaching his room, felt his stomach and was surprised to find the tapestry still prickling raw against it. Perhaps excitement is not good for it, he thought—even good excitement. But it did not really bother him, and it occurred to him for the first time that if necessary, by God, he would live with the damned thing. He opened his door now and saw the half man, bathrobe flown apart, toothache towel around his jaw, sitting on Stern's bed. The sleeping actor's foot stirred momentarily, tapping the edge of the bed in time to some forgotten vaudeville turn. Stern wheeled around in a panic, wanting to flee the room until the half man was out of there and his bed was scrubbed. He went out into the hall, but the half man chased and caught him, gripping Stern's wrist in a death vise. "Question," he radio-croaked in the dark hall.

"What?" asked Stern, his eyes closed so he would not see the half man, not daring to inhale lest he smell his halves.

"You Jewish?" the man asked, croaking so close his mouth worked against Stern's ear.

"Yes," said Stern, shutting his eyes until they hurt.

"Me, too," croaked the man, wheeling Stern around so that he had to face him. "I'm Jewish, too."

It did not thrill Stern to hear this. It was no great revelation, and it failed to touch him, just as the man's terrible violin playing had not moved him either. He said, "OK," and freed his wrist, but as he walked away a crumbling chill seemed to invade him, starting between his shoulder blades and pouring through all of him. He turned and kissed the man and hugged him and put his nose up against the man's toothache towel, and then, perhaps using some of the courage he had amassed that evening, embraced the man's bad side, too.

He had counted on firm handshakes and hearty goodbyes, exchanged phone numbers, pledges to continue friendships, and deep sincere looks in the eye, but on the morning of his departure he found that the people at Grove hung away from him. He was sitting on the porch with them, after leading the dumb march back from breakfast with Rooney in his arms, and he said to Rooney, "I'm all better and I'm going home today."

Rooney, who had been clinging to a pole and making waspish comments about the wealth of horse owners, turned to Stern and said, "You didn't say anything about that."

The old actor overheard Stern and said, "What did you come up for, if you were only staying such a little time? That's really country, boy, really country."

It was as though by getting healthy he had violated a rotted, fading charter of theirs and let them down. He had come into their sick club under false pretenses, enjoying the decayed rituals, and all the while his body wasn't ruined at all. He was secretly healthy, masquerading as a shattered man so that he could milk the benefits of their crumbling society. And now he felt bad about not being torn up as they were.

"I didn't know you weren't that sick," said Feldner in his bathrobe. "I had what you got, and I needed the warm of a stew in me every day for two years."

"I may have to come right back," said Stern, trying to make the man in the bathrobe feel better.

He went over to the charged-up blond boy, who was leaning on the young Greek's wheelchair, and said, "Maybe you can take a run by my place when you get sprung."

But the camaraderie of the wild evening was gone. "You weren't even in here much," said the blond boy and the Greek youth said, "Yeah, what'd you come up here—to fool around?"

Only Lennie was consistent that morning. He had taken Stern's baggage out of the room himself, and when Stern tried to help him, he said, "No infractions on last days. There are patients who rupture before check-out, and legal suits come about. Patients to the right as we take baggage downstairs." At the bottom of the steps, he loaded Stern's valises onto the baggage rack and walked intricately into his office. "Final pill," he said to Stern, getting one ready in a little cup. When the Negro handed him the pill cup, Stern stuck a folded-up five-dollar bill in the pocket of the intern's jacket. His mother had always stuck bills in the pockets of busboys and waiters and, after each insertion, had said, "I never missed that kind of money. You should see the respect I got for it." Lennie took the bill out of his jacket, examined it, and put it back in his pocket. He started to turn around, but then he changed his mind and asked Stern, "Anyone around?" Stern said everyone was out on the porch, and the Negro said, "Come on in here then," beckoning Stern into the forbidden office. "Have a seat," said Lennie, locking them both in. He sat down himself, releasing gears and switches, and then produced a loose-leaf notebook. He thumbed through it, stopped at a page, and said, "The old actor guy. Guy you roomin' with. He go around saying he got the weakness. He ain't coming out of here. They been trying to get him ready for another operation, but he too weak." He flipped the page and said, "Girl check in here two days ago," referring to a young and pretty blond girl who had kept to herself. "She says she restin'. Well, she got something in her from intercoursin' with a man too big for her. Who else you want to know?"

"None of the others right now," said Stern, wanting to leave the room but afraid to offend the Negro.

"That's all right," said Lennie, turning to another page. "Rooney, the guy you carryin'. Bones softening up; nothing they can do on him. He be here for the duration." He flipped again. "Feldner, the Jew fella. He hit Casino. He gettin' out but ain't got no more'n a year." Without referring to the book, he said, "The half guy you see stalkin' around. He surprisin' everybody. He gawn be around when they all through." . . .

"I thought I'd always have it in there, but the parachute is gone," Stern told his wife as they drove home. "It feels as though I have a hot tablecloth around the front of me now, but it's better than the chute."

She sat beside him with one tanned leg folded beneath her, her great eyes glistening, wet with expectancy. She wore a cotton jumper, and when Stern leaned over to kiss her, he saw that her blouse was loose and he could make out the start of her nipples beneath her half bra. It got him nervous, and he said, "Why are you wearing your blouse like that? When you bend over, people can actually see the nipples. That isn't any damned good."

"It isn't?" she said, teasing him. "Oh well, don't worry; it's only when you get real close."

"None of that's funny," said Stern. "I just got out of the god-damned place for my stomach. Do you still go to that dance class?"

"Oh yes," she said, sitting against the door, her eyes huge. "That's what saved me when you were in there. First we dance like crazy and then we congregate at the overnight diner on Olivetti Street. That's the best part. You should hear one of the girls talk. Dirtier than anything you've ever heard. She's a scream. Then José spins me home, since he lives out our way."

"Is there any more of that tongue stuff?" Stern asked.

"Don't be silly," she said. "He kisses everybody. It's what they do." . . .

Later, when they approached the outskirts of Stern's town, they drove past small houses with neatly kept lawns and Stern nodded in a friendly way to the people who stood outside them. He knew they were all gentiles and he wondered what would happen in a pogrom. Which ones, if any, would hide him and his family from the authorities? Probably quite a few, he thought; ones that would surprise him. Probably the people with the most forbidding gentile faces. Ordinarily they'd never have anything to do with Stern, but if it came to a pogrom, with New England crustiness they'd spirit Stern and his family off to attics, saying to one another, "No one's going to tell us what to do with our Jews."

As they drove past the man's house, Stern held his breath and closed his eyes for a second, as though there were a chance it might not be there. He had been away five weeks, and perhaps part of his cure was that the man's house would be swept away or that it would disappear as though it had never been there, much like his vanished ulcer. But the house stood in the same place, and Stern, as he drove by, inclined his head gently toward it, as though he would face whatever horrors lay inside with softness and gentle ways, melting them with his niceness. As he neared his own house, he wondered fleetingly what he, the man down the street, would do in the event of a pogrom. Would he startle Stern by spiriting his despised Jewish neighbors away in his cellar, hating pogroms as even more un-American than Stern?

In his house, Stern sat down in the easy chair of his sparsely furnished living room and said to his wife, "Softly and easily. That's how it's going to have to be. No noise. No upsets."

His son came out with a bandage on his elbow and said, "What's it like to die?"

Stern said, "I'm not doing any dying for a while. But there'll be no rough playing any more. Everything with Daddy is soft and easy. Where did you get the cut? That's the kind of thing I don't want to get involved in, but where did you get it?"

"I found it on me in the morning," said the boy, beginning to suck a blanket.

Stern's wife, who had been boiling eggs for him in the kitchen, hollered in, "There's one last thing you're going to get a kick out of doing. The kind of thing you'll enjoy. I'll tell you about it later."

Stern started to eat the eggs, but they stuck in his throat and he said, "What's the thing? I don't want to get into anything two minutes after I'm back from a rest home."

"I wouldn't tell it to you, except it's the kind of thing you'll enjoy taking care of. Some kids came by on a bike, older than him, and one of them cut his elbow with a mirror and called him 'Matzoh.' I've been furious, but I saved it for you because I know it's the kind of thing you'll want to settle."

"He doesn't live around here, that bad boy," said Stern's son. "He's just visiting someone here. I wish you'd make the boy die."

"Daddies don't make small boys die," said Stern. The brocade that lay across the front of him began to heat up, and he pressed his fist deep into his stomach and held it there, on guard lest another ulcer begin to sprout forth and fill his ribs.

"Nobody seems to have heard what I've been saying," he said to his wife, but then he clasped his son's head and said, "You're right; it is the kind of thing I'd like to take care of." He took the boy to his car, squeezing his hand, and for a second it seemed that the child was really holding *his* hand, leading Stern and protecting him. He drove the car in a wide arc, as far as possible from the kike man's house, and the child said, "You're going too far. The bad boy won't be around here."

"You point him out to me," said Stern, the front of him on fire, crouched over as though to give the flames less area to ruin. They came to a cluster of seven boys who'd gotten off their bikes to rest, and Stern stopped the car, gripping his son's hand for courage. He went among them and said, "Someone said something to my son and cut him. They said a dirty thing to him, and it had better not happen again."

"Don't make them dead," his son said. "They're not the bad boys."

Stern grabbed the collar of one of them, twisted him close, and said, "I can really get sore, and when I do I can really start swinging. That better not happen again."

The boy looked at him evenly, without fear, and Stern released him. He must have been around twelve, and Stern wondered whether he would remember and two years later, at fourteen, with his body shaping into athletic hardness, come after Stern and pummel him to the ground.

Stern got back into the car with his son and, continuing in the arc, he drove slowly through the streets and stopped alongside a small boy with glasses and large feet who was walking next to the curb, carrying books.

"Someone said something lousy to my son and cut him," Stern said from the car. "I don't like the particular kind of thing they said."

"I'm not a little boy," said the book carrier. "I'm seventeen and finishing high school. I'm small and everyone thinks I'm a kid."

"Don't make him dead, Daddy," said Stern's son. Stern felt very sorry for the small high-school student with his big feet, and yet he was thrilled to find someone in the neighborhood who read books and wasn't fierce. He wanted to invite him to his house and give him books, maybe take him to New York to see Broadway plays.

"Come over if you're near my place," said Stern, and drove off.

"I think the bad boy is visiting over there," said Stern's child, pointing in the direction of the house that darkened Stern's every waking moment. Nonetheless, he knitted his eyebrows, bared his teeth, and gunned the motor, as though, by going through the motions of outrage, he would somehow become outraged and the momentum would carry him right up to the man's front door before he had time to change his mind. He raced toward the man's house, and yet, when he reached it, the fraud of his facemaking became apparent to him and he continued on, realizing that he had never intended for a second confronting the man.

In his own home, Stern's wife asked, "Did you find him?" And Stern said, "I don't want to do any finding. Don't you realize I just came home from a Home a few hours ago?"

For one blissful second then, Stern's vision blurred and it seemed that he had gotten it all wrong, that he had not been away at all, and that he was to leave that very evening for a place where everything would be made better for him. But then he caught the edge of a chair, his eyes cleared, and he realized that he really had been away. The thought that he had come back to find his situation unchanged was maddening. It was as though he had been guaranteed that the treatment would heal his neighborhood as well as his ulcer—and that the guarantee had turned out to have secret clauses, rendering it worthless. The man was still there. The hospital had not had him removed. His wife had not somehow arranged to have him eliminated. His father had not gone down the street to thrust his scarred nose up in the man's face. No hand had reached down from the heavens and declared that the man had never existed. He was still right there in his house, not even seriously sick.

Stern went upstairs, and as he sat on the edge of his bed he felt a small spring inside him stretch and finally break, leaving his body in a great tremble. He lay back on the bed, as though mere contact with a bed could cure anything, but he could not quiet himself, and so he dialed Fabiola.

"A brand new thing has happened," Stern told him. "There's a tremble in me and I can't control it. The thing is, I've just come *back* from the damned rest home. Can you just come back from a place like that and have something like this happen?"

"Yes," said Fabiola. "You'd better avoid tension or you're going to wind up back there again. Remember that and call me if you get into more trouble."

Stern got on his knees now, as though in prayer, clutching fistfuls of sheet and trying to squeeze out the tremble. The bedroom windows were darkening with night when his wife appeared, flinging off her shorts, combing her hair, and saying, "I've got to go to rehearsals."

"Look," Stern said, "I'm going to ask you something, and I really have to. I've got a new thing and I have to have you here. I'm not talking about any ulcer but something really new and lousy."

"You mean you want me to give up the dancing? It's the only thing I have out here."

"You don't know what this new deal is," said Stern. As though to demonstrate, he began to take short, gasping breaths. It started as a plea for sympathy, but when he tried to stop he found he couldn't and he began to cry. "Let's get out of here. Oh, let's sell this house. We don't belong here. You'll have to handle all the details. Oh, I'm really in trouble now."

.   .   .   .   .

. . . Sometimes, writhing and wet on the sheets at midnight, he would tell his wife, "I'm touching bottom," but it wasn't really true. He seemed to be holding on to a twig, halfway down a sheer, rain-slick mountain. How nice it would be to let go. But he had only $800, and it would be eaten up quickly if he were put in a sanatorium. He imagined himself in such a place at the end of three days, the $800 gone, in a terrible panic, unable even to lie back and be crazy with the other patients. And so he held on to the twig and he clutched at people, too, pulling at men's lapels and women's skirts on steaming city streets, telling them he was in bad trouble.

When it got so bad it seemed he'd have to smash himself against something to make the trembling stop, he would take some stranger's sleeve in the city and say, "I know this is going to sound crazy, but I'm pretty upset here and wish you would just talk to me a second." It amazed him that no one was perturbed by this. People seemed to welcome the chance to exchange wisdoms at midday with a strangulating young man. And Stern, no matter how banal their words, would attach great and profound significance to them, adopting each piece of advice as a slogan to live by. "I'm going to tell you something that's going to help you, fellow," an elderly gentleman said to him. "I was in trouble once, too, and I decided then and there never to give anyone more'n half a loaf. You remember that and you'll never go wrong again." And Stern said to him, "You know, that's right. I can see where, if you follow that, you'll always come out right." And he went off, determined to stop giving up entire loaves, convinced he had come up with the key to his trembling. A Negro ice-cream salesman told him, "You got to stop lookin' for things," and a retired jewelry executive, seized in a restaurant, advised him against "letting any person get hold of you." In both cases, Stern had said, "You know, you've really got it. I'm going to remember that."

He recalled being in many places and then running, choking, out of them. Once in a darkened, cavernlike restaurant, he ordered six lunchtime courses and thought to himself, "This is the end of it. I'm going to sit here like all the other men and eat, and when I leave this table it's all going to be over." But the service was slow, he lost his breath, and when the juice came, he gulped it down, threw out clumps of dollars, and flew from the pitlike restaurant, clawing for air. Another time, floundering across the hot city pavements, on an impulse he plunged into a physical culture studio and signed up for a six-

year course. "I want to start right this minute," he said, and was
shown to a locker. In shorts, he went into the gym, where the only
person exercising was a great, bearlike man with oil-slick hair and
huge, ballooning arms. He said to Stern, "Come here. Were you in
the Army?"

"I was a flier," said Stern.

"I took a lot of crap from a drill sergeant in the Marines," said the
man. "He'd stand out there, and the bullshit would come out of him
in quart bottles, but do you know the only thing that saved me?"

"What's that?"

"His arms. They weren't even sixteens. I've got eighteens, myself.
He'd stand there, and the shit would flow about how tough he was,
but all you'd have to do is look at his arms and it didn't mean anything. How am I supposed to respect a man who doesn't have arms?"

"You can't," said Stern.

"Well, I'm going to do some arm work," the man said, and began
to curl a great dumbbell into his lap. Stern watched his arms expand
and said, "I can't seem to get started today." He dressed and then ran,
gasping and unshowered, for the daylight.

Once, when the sound of Belavista's slippered footsteps down the
hall sent him spinning into the streets, he ran into a telephone booth
and called Fabiola.

"This thing isn't getting any better," he said. "It's like I swallowed
an anthill. I'm jumping through my ass. You've got to send me to
someone."

"Psychiatry's up in the air," said Fabiola. "There's the cost, too.
Take a grain of pheno when you feel upset this way."

"I don't care about any expense. I don't think you know what's
going on with me. It isn't the ulcer any more. I'd take a dozen of
those compared to this new thing."

"All right, then," said Fabiola. "There's one good man. He's ten
per session, and he *has* helped people."

"I really want to see him, then," said Stern.

The psychiatrist was a rail-thin man who talked with a lisp and
whose office smelled musty and psychiatric. It bothered Stern that he
had only one tiny diploma on the wall.

"Can it hurt me?" Stern asked.

"No," said the man. "Sometimes you dig down and come up with
something very bad, but generally it helps."

"There's probably something lousy like that in me," said Stern.

"How much is this going to cost?"

"Twenty a session."

Stern began to choke and said, "I heard ten. Oh God, I can't pay twenty." He gasped and sobbed and the man seemed to panic along with him.

"Maybe there's something about money," said the lisping psychiatrist. "Some people think it's dirty."

"No, no, it's the amount. Oh God, don't you just want to *help* people?" He got up, gasping, sucking in musty, psychiatric air, and the psychiatrist, gasping and white, too, said, "Maybe you think money has a smell. We could go into that."

"No, no," said Stern, "we're not going into anything. Imagine how you'd feel expecting ten and then hearing twenty." And with that he ran, crouching, through the door, with the panic-stricken psychiatrist hollering after him, "You've got a money neurosis."

.   .   .   .   .

At the tail end of it, with courage forming along the bottom of him like vegetable shoots, it pleased him to make detailed and shocking phone calls to his mother and sister.

"I actually chew on drapes," he told his mother at midnight. "I pull at my skin and I won't have my job for long. I expect to go into an institution and not come out of it."

"I haven't had that in my life?" she said. "I haven't had much worse? I've had the same thing. You can't scare me."

"How would you like to see your son peeled off the fender of a speeding car? It's going to happen, you know."

And to his sister, long-distance, he said, "Oh, it's a breakdown, all right. Dying doesn't scare me in the least. It'll be in about a week or so. They're going to find me in a tub. I'll bet you're amazed that I can discuss it so calmly. Bet it really shakes you up to think it's happening to your own brother, who used to tell all those jokes."

He expected that if it ever did end, it would peter out, with a little less trembling and choking each day, but it surprised him by finishing up abruptly in a quiet unexplainable way after a talk with a Polish woman who had come to clean his house.

Through it all, amazingly, he had never thought once of the kike man. Sliding down the mountain, he had been too busy casting about for things to clutch to think very much about who had pushed him.

If the man had stopped him on the street, Stern, hunched over, fists planted in his waist to quiet the erupting, might have brushed on by and said, "I have no time to fool around."

On the night that it ended, his wife had gone to the movies, and Stern, a crawling, bone-deep shiver coming over him, had flicked off the television set and found the Polish woman on her knees in the broom closet. A small, pinched wrinkle of a woman, she seemed to have been made from a compound of flowered discount dresses, cleaning fluid, and lean Polish winters. She shook her head continually and muttered pieces of thoughts, finishing none of them. Stern talked to her for two hours and found her scattered, wise-sounding incantations soothing.

"You just can't," she said, rolling her head from side to side. "I mean you just don't go around. . . . You got to just . . . sooner or later. . . . I mean if a man don't. . . . This old world going to. . . . When a fully grown man. . . . Rolling up your sleeves is what . . ."

To which Stern said, "Oh God, how I appreciate this. I think I'm going to be able to get hold of myself now. I really do. Sometimes you just get together with a certain person and it really helps. I think I'm going to be all right. And, you know, as long as I live, I'm never going to forget this and the help you've given me. I really think I'm going to be able to stop it tonight."

"Sure," said the woman, rolling her head from side to side. "Of course. I mean you just . . . you got to. . . . There comes a time . . ."

And that night, when Stern's wife came home, he said, "I think I'm out of it." In bed, he relaxed his grip on the headboard, and then, just as swiftly as it had come over him, it more or less disappeared.

.   .   .   .   .

During his troubled, spinning weeks, Stern had often brushed by the child, saying, "No elephants, no whale questions," and gone to hold on to something or to lie somewhere in a sweat. Now, as though to make up for his brusqueness, he held talks with the boy on an almost formal schedule.

"I can remember being inside Mommy," said the child, taking off Stern's shoe. "I knew about the Three Stooges in there. Now I'm taking your foot's temperature. It's quarter past five."

During dinner, the boy said, "Were you ever a magician before you became my father?"

"Right before," said Stern.

"Could you tear a Kleenex into a thousand pieces and then turn it back into a whole Kleenex again?"

"I could do that one."

"Do you learn about the inside of soda at college?"

"I don't know," said Stern. "I don't know that. No soda now. No pirates. I'm just going to sit here." He was eating an apricot dessert then, and he began to breathe so hard he thought something would fly out of his chest. "I've got to go out and get some air," he told his wife.

"Is it all right for daddies to go out in the dark?" asked the boy, and Stern said, "If they're very careful."

Outside, walking on leaves, Stern could not catch his breath and wondered if he should call a cab. He saw himself walking all the way to the man's house only to collapse, wordless and exhausted, on the doorstep, having to be put outside near the garbage for someone to see and take home. He thought it was unfair for him to be depleting his strength in a long, cold walk while the man sat in a tasteless but comfortable armchair, his forearms bulging after a day at the lathe.

When he had gone a few hundred feet, he thought of turning around and telling his wife where he was headed or at least leaving a note on the porch so that someone would know his whereabouts in case he wound up cracked and bleeding, the life seeping out of him, yet completely out of public view. He imagined people saying of him later, "The funny part is they could have saved him if only they'd been able to find him in time." . . .

There was a simple stone walk through some short grass and a step leading up to a brown oaken door. He had expected the house to have some memorable characteristics, symphonic music to play when he actually set foot inside the fence. He knocked on the door and suddenly shook with hope that the wife would answer and say she was sorry but the man was attending a meeting of the Guardian Sons. It was an election meeting to select officers who would be even more pinched and thin-lipped than the old crew. He would say to the woman, "Your husband said something to my wife and I want to say I know about it and he's not getting away with it. You tell him that." Then he would be able to go back home, his mission accomplished. After all, he had tried. It wasn't his fault the man was not in.

The man opened the door and Stern blinked to see him better, startled that although he stood only two feet away, he still could not really make out his face. It was as though he were looking at the man through an old pair of Japanese binoculars he had once bought. They were expensive, but Stern had never quite gotten them adjusted right and always saw things better with his eyes. He could see that the man was shoeless, however; wore blue jeans and a T-shirt; and kept his head cocked a little in the incredulous style Stern remembered so clearly. The beer had taken some effect; he seemed a little heavier than Stern recalled. His arms were about the same, perhaps a little thicker in the foresection than they had seemed to be from the car.

"Are you the man who said kike to my wife?" asked Stern, happy he had only short sentences to get out.

"I think I remember that."

"About a year and a half ago?"

"That's right."

"You shouldn't say that, and we're going to fight."

"All right. Let me get my slippers on."

Stern had not expected any delays, and when the man closed the screen door he thought of how little insurance he had and wondered if he could call out, "Excuse me just a minute," and run back to take out another policy, then return. He wanted so bad to live he would have settled right on the spot for being a bedpan patient all his life. If only there were someone with whom he could enter into such a bargain. The man came back and said, "Come on around back here," walking toward the rear of the house, and Stern did not follow. He remembered that he had not brought along an observer to run for an intern and wondered if he could hail one now, not to stop the fight, but just to stand by and watch it and know that it was going on. He thought that maybe the man's wife was watching through the shades and, if Stern's head were opened, *she* would call for help, waiting first until he was almost through. He wanted to stop what was happening, take the man aside, and say, "Look, the important thing was for me to come down here. Now that I'm here, there doesn't have to be any fight. I didn't think I could make it, but here I am, and why don't I just go back now?" But, instead, he followed the man to the backyard and said, "I don't know how to begin these." The man paused a moment and then hit Stern on the ear, a great freezing kiss covering the entire side of his face. The lobe seemed to slide around a little before settling in one place, and Stern was so thrilled at still being alive he jumped a little off the ground. But then his joy was erased by a warm shudder of sympathy for the man, who had been unable to knock him unconscious with the blow. It was as though all those years at lathes, building arm power, had gone to waste. More because it seemed to be expected of him than because he felt anger, Stern tried to throw a punch in the smoothly coordinated style of a Virgin Islands middleweight he had watched on TV, but it was as though a belt had been dropped over him, constricting his arms, and the blow came out girlish and ineffectual. Lowering his voice several octaves, as if it were he who had delivered the ear kiss, he said, "Don't talk that way to someone's wife and push her," and only after he had said it did he realize he had fallen into an imitation of an old deep-voiced high-school gym teacher who used to say, "Now, boys, eat soup and b'daders if you want your roughage."

"Shit I won't," said the man, and Stern said, "You better not," still blinking to see the man's face. He saw his socks, though, faded blue anklets with little green clocks on them. They were cut low, almost disappearing into his slippers, and reminded Stern of those worn by an exchange student from Latvia at college who had brought along an entire bundle of similar ones. Now Stern felt deeply sorry for the man's powerful feet, which were always to be encased in terrible refugee anklets, and for a second he wanted to embrace them.

His ear began to leak now, and he walked off the man's lawn, not sure at all how he had done. The hot flush of exhilaration that had come with the punch stayed with him awhile, and yet when he had gone halfway back to his house the cold flew into his shirt and rode his back and he began to shake with fear of the man all over again. Inside his house, his wife was sponging the dinner table and said, "What happened to your ear? It's hanging all off."

"I had a fight with that guy from a year and a half ago. The one who said the thing to you. I can't understand it. I was all right for a while, but now I'm afraid of him all over again."

"That's some ear you've got," she said.

"Ears never worried me," he said. "I don't understand why I still have to be afraid of the bastard. Come on upstairs." They walked to the steps and his wife said, "You go first. I don't like to go upstairs in front of people." And Stern went on ahead, annoyed at being denied several seconds of behind glimpses.

Upstairs, in his son's room, he looked at the six or seven children's books on the floor. Pages were torn out of them, and Stern wondered how the child was ever to become brilliant on so ratty-looking a library. Once, in some kind of sheltering, warmth-giving act he really couldn't explain, Stern had bought children's rugs and hung them all over the walls. The boy had said, "Rugs on the wall?" And Stern had answered, "Of course, and we put pictures on the floors, too. We eat breakfast at night and get up in the morning for a bite of supper. This is a crazy house."

Now Stern walked around the room, touching the rugs to make sure they wouldn't fall on his son's face. Then he said, "I feel like doing some hugging," and knelt beside the sleeping boy, inhaling his pajamas and putting his arm over him. His wife was at the door and Stern said, "I want you in here, too." She came over, and it occurred to him that he would like to try something a little theatrical, just kneel there quietly with his arms protectively draped around his wife and child. He tried it and wound up holding them a fraction longer than he'd intended.

To an Early Grave

by WALLACE MARKFIELD

When this novel appeared it was thought to be much too "in" to attract a wide audience. Even more remote seemed the possibility of a film audience for the slender tale of four hypersophisticated American Jewish writers on their Joycean way to a funeral for the mentor of their group, Leslie Braverman. And yet not only the universality but the speciality of Markfield's view found a wide audience. He had taken the American Jewish novel a step further into the open world.

Though this novel appeared to be part of a wave of Jewish humor that required only the use of a Yiddishism for its effect, it was, in fact, a wryly serious study of a life style. Markfield's characters belong to that special world of intellectuals who make a fetish of Westerns, of the comics, who write for the protest magazines, and whose highest status mark is getting into Partisan Review. They are the precocious scholars from the Bronx who fled home to live in the Village, they are the brothers and future lovers of Frederic Morton's Iris Leavis. What comes as a surprise is that Jewishness still permeates their lives.

Whether it is through cookery, in the jars of Mama's pea soup that Weiner hauls back for the boys (now nearing their forties), or whether it is through the resistance of Hadassah lecturer Felix Ottensteen to a ride in critic Holly Levine's Volkswagen, or whether it is through Morroe Reiff's profession of speech writing for United Jewish Appeal fund raisers, the Jewish experience is ever present for these seemingly detached intellectuals.

The form of the novel is evanescent, and we have tried to convey its flavor in some of the choice episodes, such as the expertise contest in naming minor characters in the comics that

*takes place as they ride to the funeral, or Morroe's touching elegy
among the gravestones on how things are on the scene today.*

*Wallace Markfield was born in New York in 1927. He under-
took his first novel comparatively late, having meanwhile written
for Partisan Review, Commentary, and the Hudson Review, and
worked as a Jewish fund-raising writer. He then took the teaching road, to San Francisco State College.*

M.L.

*To U.J.A. speech writer Morroe Reiff, abed with his wife in an
Upper West Side apartment on a Sunday morning comes a call
from Inez Braverman telling him that his good friend Leslie
Braverman has suddenly died. Will he come to her in the Village to go to the funeral?*

Morroe's wife Etta doesn't want him to go.

"**I** SEE SOMETHING. For the first time it dawns on
me. You have no feeling, you have no compassion." He turned his
wedding band slowly clockwise, then counterclockwise. "A friend is
dead. Let's even say, not a friend. An acquaintance, all right? A
figure, a talent, an original. And in a little while there'll be nothing
left. Before the day is finished he'll be closed over, covered up and
that's it." He saw Leslie in a casket, going into the grave, taking the
weight of earth full on his moon face, on his peeping, despairing
eyes, on the snub nose where the glasses bobbed. Silent, silent forever, the one who could talk you deaf and dumb and blind. And,
whoosh! Without clothes! The way the Orthodox send you off.

He said again, "Make me juice."

"A person without compassion is not a juice-squeezer."

There was rumbling in Morroe's stomach and a huge pocket of gas
was expanding through his chest. In a quivering, vindictive voice he
told Etta, "I give in too much to you. You know? On everything.
When it comes to your family, your *meshpuchah*, it's all right if I
run around and put myself out. It's all right, you know, to give your
cousin Maxie my insurance—though I'm losing a good eighty dollars
a year. And *bar mitzvahs* and birthday parties for their brats and
family-circle meetings. People I can't stand. Yes, for you and yours

it's all right, isn't it? So don't you dare tell me I shouldn't go to Leslie's funeral. Because that—that, I assure you, you will not get from me."

"He is such a mourner." Etta's lips began to curl; her eyes shone at him with reproachful irony. "But when my cousin Harris died, that was another story. He was too sensitive. He couldn't take funerals. He didn't believe in the rigmarole."

"Drop it, change the subject." He made a pass at her like a magician.

"The only one who couldn't pay that last little respect. And it was coming to Harris, I assure you, more than to a hundred Leslies." She hunched forward, tendony, pinched in the neck. Tears sprang into her eyes and she whimpered, "Who—whom—have I got? A mother? She wouldn't let anyone touch my little slips or my dresses. She used to boil a special starch for them while my father laughed and said, 'Lena, Lena, *du bist eine eisel.'* "

And rocking and rocking, this small, dark, pretty girl, whose absurdly large breasts he could stroke and pet by the hour, who, for all her graying bangs, read movie magazines and hummed to foolish radio music as she did her kitchen work, blurted out again the story of her afflictions: how there had been department stores in Cologne and a houseful of servants (a pastry cook, the pride of the Hapsburgs); how her father had ignored warnings and portents; how he had packed her off to an older sister in Liverpool; how he and her mother both had one morning been moved to a convent outside of the city ("Take only one toothbrush and a change of underwear"); how, before long, the chimneys of Buchenwald had belched forth their blood and bone.

And though he was swept through and through by a surge of love for her, Morroe said nastily, "Stop, stop the Ingrid Bergman stuff. And don't embroider every time. Because from my understanding there were no department stores. And how did it suddenly get to be servants? One, one broken-down day worker."

In the pain of the moment, she was almost speechless. When she replied, her color was very high and she looked dazed. "You know what you are? I will tell you what you are. You are a *schmuck!*" She heaved herself off the bed and out of the room.

And Morroe let himself fall back, onto the pillows.

And a "Doo-doo doo-doo-doo-doo" bubbled from his lips.

And he stiffened and arched two fingers and walked them, rocked them, danced them down chest, belly and thighs and leaped them daringly across the abyss between his knees.

And into the circuits of his mind he fed GO and DON'T GO, and also profuse memory and complicated doubts.

And when it came out a clear and simple DON'T GO he roused himself, cast a desperate glance at the clock and hurried into pants, shirt, jacket, deciding against shave and shower and, finally, tie.

"I'm going. Honey, I am going," Morroe bawled, lagging near the kitchen door, ready to trade a pleasant goodbye for half, make it a quarter, of an orange. There was only the ferocious running of water and the banging of bottles in the refrigerator. Good, he thought, very good. I'll pick up the paper, I'll grab a bite in the B & J or the Sabra, I'll do some of the crossword puzzle. Nevertheless, while he let himself out, while he twisted both keys in both locks, he was far from pleased; these were not his habits in the morning, and holding to small habits was a weakness with him.

Near the incinerator he saw Toego, 5K, whom he couldn't stomach. "Howdy like our landlord there, Mr. Rieff?" Toego asked, advancing upon him. His mean, greenish eyes watered for a moment, and he turned away, racked by so many tics and spasms he seemed uncertain which to suffer first. In bathing trunks and felt slippers he seemed all gristle and vein and crabbiness.

"I have no opinion," Morroe said distantly. "Since I live here I've seen him twice: when I signed the lease and when he came to inspect our paint job."

"Yes, but you got the form, didn't you?" There was a resonance of horror in Toego's voice. "He wants fifteen per cent. Hardship. My, my, my! Oi-oi-oi! Hardship!"

"Well, we didn't get one."

"Oh, I see you must be among the favored. Burke, now, he got one. And how is it Lang got one? *And* Volkening? *And* Maggrett? *And* Baerst?" Toego winked, or twitched.

"I wouldn't know," Morroe curtly said.

"Of course, and how would you?" Toego paused, cracked a few knuckles. "The things you see you never saw under the old management. God rest him, Mr. Carmichael had a Christmas tree up every year and a lovely little crèche in the lobby. A wonderful man. Old New York type. Straw hats and bow ties and very gruff in his manner of speaking. 'Youse' and 'dems.' Oh, but a gentleman. Honor, integrity. And service—my Lord! He *ran* the building!"

Morroe began a protracted study of his watch, saying, "Look, today everything is sky high. Whoosh! Labor, materials, whatever you touch. And this is an old house. It's falling apart, it can bleed you of every penny." He turned, rang for the elevator. But Toego followed, raising his hand in the gesture of one about to enter a plea. "They're driving us out," he said. "Oh, it's fifteen per cent now, Mr. Rieff, and then one of these days we'll get a notice. 'Clear out! Go! Never mind where, the building is being torn down.' And it's not even that! The city—why, the whole city is impossible. I'm a native New Yorker and I say that. Like the dirt. Every morning my nose is clogged; I wake up choking. Or you walk around a corner and your nails are black. And you're always smelling that garlic frying, and when it's not garlic it's marijuana or—"

Morroe cut in with, "I have a funeral. People are waiting."

"Oh, say, say." On either side Toego's face veins tapped. "Family? . . ."

"A friend."

"I hadn't seen your father around."

"No, knock on wood, he's fine. Oh, not *fine*, but—"

"Good news!" Toego stepped halfway into the elevator with Morroe. "That friend . . . how old?"

"Forty." Morroe fixed a finger on the lobby button. "Maybe a big forty-one."

"Lord, Lord, younger and younger and younger. My father made eighty-four. And I'm not sixty and I had my first stroke." He gave a snicker of high glee.

He stepped out of the elevator, closing the door carefully behind him. But then his voice was floating down, down the shaft after Morroe: "Hardship. My, my! Oi! . . ."

THE FIRST IMPRESSION Morroe gave was one of intense redness. To his family, he was still "*der Royte,*" not so much for his hair, which, at thirty-nine, was brown and heavy as beaver fur, but for his temper —at four or five, he had launched himself against an older sister and dealt her a scratch that needed stitches and injections. His large glasses shrank his eyes and, with his way of squinting—as though for him all things were in gray outline—gave him a bluff uncomprehending look. When he walked, he bent forward slightly, his arms stiff, with the no-nonsense air of one who is wise to the complications of the city, who can find a subway seat and a restaurant table during the worst hours, a taxi in the rain, a wholesale outlet that beats even discount-house prices, one who kept an electric razor in his desk, Pream for his instant coffee, deposit and withdrawal slips to beat bank lines, sent personal mail through office meters, sneaked home envelopes, clips, pencils, staples and carbon paper, saw that his resumé was up to date, his connections solid.

All the same, he was a latecomer to New York. When he was ten his father, a small, harsh pepperpot of a man who could not bear working for others, moved from Cleveland to Norfolk and opened a laundry near the huge naval base, believing that a good living could be made from the sailors. At four in the morning, in all weathers, he would park his truck and take his stand before the huge sheds, jockeying for position with his rivals, between whom not a look or word passed. Then the sailors would come, by the hundreds, lugging their sea bags, and the line of laundrymen would stiffen and surge forward. They could not solicit; the rule was strict and the smallest infraction got you declared off limits for a week.

But they would call attention to themselves in other ways. They would paint lavish nudes on their doors and fenders, they would bang drums and blow whistles and pitch pipes, they would fire cap pistols and set balloons floating out over the harbor.

And each with his own costume.

There was Leo the Lumberman, taking listless swings with his heavy ax.

There was Hershel the Hawaiian, decked out in leis and hula skirt.

There was Moishe the Mexican, in his Sam Browne belt and *huaraches*.

And there was his father, Cowboy Joe, the last to give in, sullen and unconciliating under the weight of his Stetson hat.

Later, when it was impossible to compete with the laundromats, his father decided on New York, where, after taking heavy losses on a commission bakery and a milk route, he found a gold mine in a candy store near Washington Heights. And though Morroe did his share, his father stubbornly refused to give him more than the dollar and a quarter a week which barely covered the cost of milk in the high school cafeteria and the outlay for G.O. fees and books and gym outfits. Then, in his senior year, there was a terrible quarrel: Morroe had brought friends into the store, gone behind the counter and dished up egg creams, frappés, malteds. His father, in full view

of all, fell upon him with fearful curses, letting him know that he
was not in business for love, that, like it or not, his friends must pay.
They raised hands to each other; before the night was over Morroe
walked out for good, moving in with his Uncle Lazar.

If he did not prosper, exactly, during the years that followed, he
nevertheless came through better than some. He registered at City
College, with the idea of studying medicine. But he had no aptitude
and, besides, he could not bear the night students who jealously
guarded their lecture notes and would not give you so much as a
cigarette; inside of a month he dropped his science courses. He
settled, finally, like most, on English literature, taking just enough
education credits to qualify for the public school system. For a while
he tied bundles and stacked remnants in a dress house. Later, he
landed something with the Hollis Protective Agency, going around to
the smaller chain stores and cafeterias to make sure the help didn't
hold out on the cash register or serve double portions to friends. The
job kept him out in the air, he could charge off meals to the agency
and make a little besides by adding fifteen minutes or a half-hour
to his time sheet. When it folded—once too often he had taken pity
on a short-change artist—a friend wangled something for him in the
college library. There he stayed for over three years.

Morroe graduated into a gloom of a time, when all the civil service
lists were closed, when you knew better than to argue with a snotty
receptionist and read great promise into the personnel man's fish-eyed
grin, when the strongest pull and the best of connections left you no
better off than the next fellow, the one who shared your waiting
room bench and made sure you got no inkling of his stale leads.
Finally, his Uncle Lazar had spoken to a rabbi. Who held out little
hope, but nonetheless made a few calls. And referred him to a Brighton Beach yeshivah, which needed someone for English studies; here
Morroe had his mornings free, to say nothing of the Jewish holidays
and Fridays, when he got out before sundown.

It so happened that the yeshivah held a bazaar, and the principal
turned to Morroe, asking his help with a few fund-raising letters.
Though he was at first wary and disdainful, Morroe soon found he
had a knack for the stuff. He talked a printer into making up some
posters, he sent out press releases, and the *Brooklyn Eagle* ran a small
story on the day of the affair.

The principal, though generally petty and stingy with praise, was
pleased, and steered Morroe onto something good: he had heard

about this giver, Zeigler, a man who sat on every board and committee, a powerful *macher* in Jewish communal affairs, who had passed
around word that he needed a speech-writer. There were other applicants, plenty of them, and Zeigler would be no pleasure to work
with—the principal made this clear—but anyway he pressured Morroe
to try, for the fun of it.

Thus, on a morning when he had other interviews set, Morroe
received a call—a summons, really. He was to come to Zeigler's house,
he was to bring along resumé and samples.

It was an insult, not an interview. Morroe was kept waiting a half-
hour, and then, when Zeigler made an appearance, it was in a bathrobe, mountainous, slovenly, without the grace to offer coffee or rolls
from the tray a maid bore after him. For several minutes he ate and
drank, then fell back in his chair and crossed his hands over his belly.

He said, "So write me a speech."

Morroe started to say something, and fumbled in his pockets for
the resumé.

"No, no, forget that stuff. Write me a speech."

"Well, what do you mean, 'a speech'?" Morroe's voice was congested by rage.

"Do I know?" Zeigler shouted. "A speech. With words. It should
move and sway people."

Praying for restraint, Morroe pointed out that he would have to
know something about the subject. "And how long should it be, and
for whom is it meant? Otherwise I'm completely in the dark."

At which Zeigler laughed and laughed and threw up a pair of
meaty hands. "Only one thing I'll tell you. Israel is the subject.
Money is the theme. Giving is the idea."

And he shook a little silver bell for the maid, who came on crepe
soles and led Morroe to the door.

Morroe was all set, later, to write Zeigler an angry note; such
phrases as "impossible conditions," "ordinary decency" and "contempt for people" ran in his mind. Once at the typewriter, though,
he fell into another mood. He was overtaken by an enormous confidence, by the belief that whatever he put his hand to would at this
moment work in his favor. Without conscious thought, without even
knowing whether one sentence followed another, he turned out a
shrill, high-pitched speech. Which he sent off without even reading.

In two days Morroe was hired, making more money than an
assistant principal or a welfare department supervisor. And if Zeigler

took handling and pestered at all hours, he knew, at least, what he wanted; they got along. Profoundly grateful, Morroe did not spare himself, making sure to come up with fresh approaches, digging up pointed jokes and newspaper items which he wove into the speeches. He was certain his luck had turned. Till the following winter, when Zeigler suffered a diabetic coma in Miami Beach, and was warned to give up absolutely all outside activities. But by then Morroe was known in the field, he had made contacts. Shortly before the New Year he was hired by a medium-sized agency which raised funds to train Israeli farmers in the agricultural sciences.

Meanwhile, he had found himself a cold-water flat near the Village, and he began taking adult education courses and attending forums on Marxism and psychoanalysis and creative writing. So he met Leslie. It was at the Everyman School, on a night when, for the first time, Leslie had given high praise to some little thing he had written about Anna Karenina, and how it had been needless for Tolstoy to kill her. Morroe, a bit shyly, went up to him after class; without ceremony, Leslie took him for coffee, reaching him quickly, talking and talking of things that mattered. When the restaurant closed he dragged Morroe to his place, where Inez, despite the hour, rose to make French toast and put out Polish sausage and a very nice eggplant spread. There was no holding back with them; everything that was his Morroe laid bare over the kitchen table: his father, the days of Norfolk, the yeshivah, Zeigler. He went on and on in a rollicking satire, mimicking and burlesquing with a deftness that was new to him and rendered them, at times, helpless with laughter. After he left for the office—Inez had insisted they stay up all night and await the sun—he was lightheaded, in a state akin to exaltation.

During those years Leslie and Inez gave party after party. Big names came, writers of much promise, people who were publishing right and left. And, always, some busted-up character, someone on the verge of divorce, someone who had the look of a potential suicide or an alcoholic. Wandering near one of the bedrooms you could make out the sound of his weeping, or Leslie's voice, soft, tremulous, counseling and cajoling. Later, Morroe and the boys would stay behind, a small, permanent cadre, while Leslie, spreading out on the sofa, gave them the full story. This bothered Morroe; not so much the betrayal of confidences—he loved gossip as well as the next man —but Leslie's studied Talmudic air threw him off and gave warning that it could be dangerous to put yourself under his power.

At one such party he met Etta. She had been brought by a girl friend, an annoying type, with pretensions to all the arts. Etta, on the other hand, was simple, straightforward, moving uneasily amid the talkers and drinkers. Morroe was greatly pleased by the light spicing of her accent, by her high color and drastic pigtail, by the pendant earrings which would have been vulgar on others, by her accidentally-on-purpose posing so that he could look either up or down her dress. Even her slightly crooked teeth, with their greenish roots, pleased him; and he would gladly have shared with her a common tooth-brush. Morroe began to bait and tease her, rather heavy-handedly. This was his way with girls; but Etta took it well, giving as good as she got. They sang German *Lieder* together, while Leslie accompanied on his recorder, leering over them like a satyr. "Look, look, look," cried Inez, "aren't they cute together; don't they make a nice couple?" All night long she bumbled around them, and at one point beckoned Etta aside, talking to her heatedly for a few minutes, finishing up with a noisy kiss and a little push in Morroe's direction. To his inquiries, Etta, somewhat flushed, answered, "She said you were a guy with certain problems, and I should be good to you." He hadn't believed her; for that matter, still didn't.

Four days later Morroe made up an extra set of keys to his apartment. Yet he could not quite believe in his good fortune; and, sure enough, trouble came. There was a convention of Jewish agencies in Chicago. He spent a week there, increasingly disturbed when Etta failed to reply to the long letters he mailed out every night. On his return he rushed over to her place by cab, but her girl friend would not let him in and, when he made an uproar, picked up the phone and actually started calling the police. By the time he was home and unpacked, Etta had shown up. Half-drunk, her face white and straining, she confessed that from the moment he left she had been sleeping with someone: a West Indian who held down a stockroom job in her office while he studied modern dance. It had nothing to do with her feeling for Morroe, she insisted; she had had certain fears about sex, she wanted to prove herself with other men, and she had chosen this one only because he was handy. It was a piece of nonsense, *mishugass*, and the whole thing had only awakened in her hungry longings for Morroe.

Wild with grief, Morroe slapped her. Then he pushed her out the door. Afterward, he fell into a fit of uncontrollable trembling, and in the morning went straight to her office, dragging her out to the fire stairs, begging her forgiveness with all his might. They waited a month, till her birthday, and went by bus to Arlington, where they were married in a quick civil ceremony.

Not long afterward, his Uncle Lazar died. Morroe caught sight of his father in the chapel, but ignored him. Finally, when the grave was closed, a group of relatives forcibly drew them together, and they embraced. The old man took a liking to Etta and, winking at Morroe, invited her to the candy store. "I'll make you a malted," he promised. "Something special." And whenever he visited he brought a bagful of Hershey bars and Charms and sour balls and chocolate-covered halvah; it became a standing joke between them.

.   .   .   .   .

No MATTER where he lived, no matter how much it annoyed visitors, Leslie Braverman would never put a nameplate over his bell. "Why should I?" he would say. "Why should I make it easy for them when they come looking for me?" By matchlight, Morroe hunted and hunted, till finally, losing patience, he pressed one whole row of bells on the top floor. With the first clicking of the lock he sprinted inside, taking the steps two at time. "Who is it?" someone called down. "Hello." He froze against the landing and fought down an impulse to reply, to make some apology. Then, after he heard doors slam, he continued his climb, breathing heavily, feeling an unexpected tickle of nervous excitement. The Village, he decided. No matter how he knocked it to others, the place gripped and held him. This kid now, brushing past him with her armload of groceries. Where else could you see her kind? She glowed, she positively twinkled and shimmered. He could make out the point of a long Italian bread sticking out of the bag and smell the odor of sour pickle and maybe corned beef or ham. On Sunday morning the Village delicatessens were filled with young people, paying unbelievable prices and taking the kidding and the pointed remarks of the clerks who knew the source of these big appetites. And Morroe chuckled to himself, and as he followed her up the flights he wished long life and good years to her breasts, belly and behind, to her Keds, Amazon belt, copper bracelet, beaten silver ring, to all her parts and all accessories.

But when he stood before Leslie's apartment his mood evaporated. The chink in the peephole was still there; if you leaned and listened you could make out a few words amid the hubbub. Many times Morroe had done this, wondering if he would hear his name, perhaps some comment letting him know whether or not he was welcome. And seconds later he would enter, bearing his pack of troubles, dimly aware that he was talking too much, that Leslie and Inez were not to be altogether trusted. Mind you, he wasn't the only one. Far from it. Why, the very walls dripped troubles! You could peel them off with the laths and tiles, they hung from the clothes dryer in the kitchen, they stuffed up the drains, they killed the plants, they brought in roaches! Every bedspring sang of shack up and abortion and breakdown and louse up and bad ball!

He took a handkerchief and mopped his face. All sorts of things churned in his mind, recollections from which he shrank. "So?" he grunted in annoyance at his clammy hands, his parched throat. "What are you afraid of? What? You've learned a few things, you're a match for her. What you were then, you're not now." Resolutely, he knocked.

Pilar, the older girl, let him in. Still on the small side for her eight years. And chubby; it looks like she'll have Leslie's build, Morroe reflected, though I hope not. She smiled, but her expression was guarded, suspicious, and Morroe hastened to say, "I guess you don't remember me, eh?"

"Well, should I?" There was a certain charm in the way she said this—Leslie's charm, Morroe reflected—which softened what might have been snottiness in the mouths of other kids.

"Whoosh, I think so, I honestly do." He started toward the living room. "Where's your mother, honey?"

"She took Sister to Mrs. Falvey. Dolores is too young to go to funerals. You know, I have a story all made up for her. She's going to ask where Leslie is, and guess what I'll say."

"What? What's that?" He drew up a hassock and sat down heavily, his hands joined over his knees. With silent repugnance he looked around the room. Inez had never been of the housekeeping breed, but this—this was something! The couch looked as if it had been gored by bulls. There were burns on the television cabinet, and a fat grease mark near the center of the screen. And wherever you looked, bottles and cups and magazines from the year one.

"I'm going to say . . . I'll say . . . Leslie went to . . . Africa. On a safari. He heard drums. Boombala, boombala, thump, thump, thump. Miles and miles away. The natives didn't want to go there.

'No go, white chief!' They were very, very scared. But Leslie wasn't scared. Guess why he wasn't scared!"

Morroe looked at her high, wrinkled forehead and conniving eyes, seeing Leslie, only Leslie. He said, "I'm waiting, honey."

"Because . . . Because . . ." She uttered a bark of laughter. "Because he was a . . . *braver* man."

Morroe pretended to shudder. Then he drew her close and rubbed his nose against hers. "You are a character, all right," he informed her gravely. "But continue, proceed."

"Oh, there is no more. I had an idea for a witch doctor, but I'm going to put him in my next story." . . .

Inez arrives.

In a cracked voice Inez said, "Hi, baby." She was heavily made up; under the layers of lipstick her smile was hard and professional, like an airline stewardess or a chorus girl.

Morroe extended both his arms as she came forward, and they clasped each other.

"Inez, Inez, what can I tell you, what should I say? We should meet, next time, under better and happier circumstances."

"Yeah, yeah, better and happier." She wheeled swiftly and began to clear off the couch, saying, "Look, look at him! What's the matter, you're no stranger here. You don't have to wait for me before you sit. Did you eat? I bet you ran out without. Dope, come on, I have so much in the refrigerator. I shopped yesterday for the whole week."

"I ate, I ate," he protested. "Honestly." He sat down beside her, trying to keep himself impassive while he took in her getup. Whoosh! Where had she picked it up? Gold earrings, so heavy it was a wonder she could lift her head. And in this weather a black taffeta dress. What his father called a *shiksa* dress. Yes, but she *was* a *shiksa*. Easy to forget. Her ways and mannerisms were Leslie's. And she could speak Yiddish with the best.

"So tell me what's happening," Inez demanded. "You put on some weight I think, but it doesn't hurt. How's the job? You're still doing . . . the fund-raising work?"

"Still in the Jewish business. Still with the speeches and the releases and the letters. Did you hear we moved? But, of course, that you know."

"And how's Irma? Did she finish that thesis finally? Ooh, what a mind on that kid, I'm telling you!" She gave an ecstatic little shiver.

"Hah?" Morroe's lips stiffened, and he said, a trifle bitterly, "What kind of an Irma? I think you have your signals crossed."

With shaky fingers Inez began a drumming of her brows. She shut her eyes tightly for a moment, then opened them to the full. "Etta, Etta, Etta!" she shouted. "I was thinking of—oh, sure, you know her—the one with the bone condition. Every other day she'd be in the hospital with a fracture."

"Sure, a bone condition." There was a ring of exasperation in Morroe's voice, but he pretended to make the connection. "Yes, definitely, I have that one placed. Anyway, never mind. Let me hear about Leslie. You know how it is over the phone. A million questions . . . and especially when you get up from sleep . . . a person is still groggy."

"Wait, you'll hear, you'll hear!" She sprang up from the couch. "Sweetie!" she called into the kitchen. Pilar entered, chewing a slice of dry white bread. "Look, you'll do me a big favor, yeah? You'll go downstairs. You'll go into Dienstfrey. Make sure *he* waits on you, not the wife; she's a terrible bitch. You'll tell him, 'Mr. Dienstfrey, my mother wants two iced coffees and two—better say four—of the prune Danishes.' You'll bring down some of the deposit bottles and the rest he can charge. Okay? You got it, chutzie?"

Pilar gave her a wise little smile. A sign that she was accustomed to stranger errands and dealings.

"Hey, don't bother," Morroe protested. "It's so fierce out, don't send her up and down the stairs." Then he checked himself as he caught Inez gritting her teeth and flaring her nostrils. She had things to say; she wanted the kid out of the house. Dumb and heavy he sat, watching her zip around the room, bending and hauling and shoving, while bottles chimed over her footsteps. Whoosh! Grief had made her radiant, positively radiant. And that energy. She looked capable of tearing down walls, wrecking entire civilizations. Yet by the time she returned to the couch she had altered herself, collapsing on the cushions like an accident case, too far gone to worry over a hiked-up skirt or the abandoned spread of her legs.

Again Morroe said, "Let me hear now about Leslie. Fill me in."

"Okay, all right, sure. You know we were all set for a divorce?"

Working his feet back and forth on the thinned-out carpet, Morroe said, "I knew and I didn't know. I mean, I ran into Harvey Katzman about a year ago, and he dropped all sorts of hints. Of course, who could be definite? The person isn't alive who can get a direct statement out of him."

"Yeah, yeah, yeah, that louse, that cheapskate! I hate his guts!" But she said this without interest or feeling. "Oh, it was building up for years. I think he lived only to punish and needle me. That's how he got his kicks. If I was a fly he . . ." One shoulder quivered, as though from the tearing of a wing.

"Hey, hey, come on, he wasn't *such* a monster," Morroe contended. "And by talking this way you only do yourself harm."

The look she shot him startled Morroe, filled him with a peculiar dread. "Sure, who am I? What do I know? I was only the coffee server. He was the big shot intellectual, the profound personality and I was the coffee server. He was the intimate friend of Kafka and Kierkegaard while I was rattling cups in the kitchen and making dialogue with the other broken-down wives about wee-wee and formulas and vaginal cream and spaying cats and where do you get the best grated parmesan. Yeah, yeah, yeah, grated parmesan."

In affable, even-minded fashion Morroe said, "Honestly, you're not being fair. He was a writer, a creative person. You couldn't think up his stories and he couldn't make your coffee. And those other things. Tolstoy's wife could make almost the same complaints. Except vaginal cream . . . I don't think . . . in those years . . ."

"Ah, go 'way. You're talking to the little gal who slept with him. I couldn't get him to take a bath, you know that? His feet stank. 'Leave me alone,' he'd tell me, 'that's the odor of sanctity.'"

"Oh, now, come on, Inez, come on." Morroe gave way to a short laugh. "What's so terrible? It's far, far from a revelation. Believe me, nobody ever said Leslie was the cleanest person in the world."

Inez turned down her underlip, and flecks of blood appeared in her pupils. There rose to Morroe's mind images of harpies and witches . . . haters and eaters of men. "You want revelations?" she demanded, speaking with enormous pleasure. "Yeah? Well, one Saturday he gets up, he wants a Pepsi. 'Where is the Pepsi?' 'No Pepsi.' 'No Pepsi?' 'No Pepsi.' He sees I'm not going down, so he goes down. A half-hour, three-quarters of an hour. I grab myself a little snooze. I wake up, it's four hours now. I feed the goldfish, I make a few *latkes*, I paint the kitchen chairs, I stuff the hassock Morty Zelenka got me from Tangiers, I *potchke* with my pottery. Cut a long story short, you know when he came back? Ask me when he came back?"

"I'll bite." Morroe showed teeth. "So when did he come back?"

"I forget. Okay, you no-good, miserable bastard, where were you? Oh, he's amazed that I'm sore. After all, we're modern, ain't we? We don't have to account for every little move. He just ran into Tillie Dreyfus—"

"The dancer? The one who was always telling you how she was going to put out a little magazine?"

"She dances like I dance. But it was a big coincidence. In fifteen years neither of them had been to Steeplechase. Whee! Let's take the subway down, let's get hot dogs and custard and let's go on the rides. Oh, he gave her a ride all right. He probably screwed her ass off."

"Ucch!" said Morroe, and "Whoosh! Tillie Dreyfus! You'd think . . . I don't know. Anybody could hop into the sack with her. Take my word for it and without going into detail, I had plenty of opportunities. Plenty!"

"Look, kid, maybe he had standards in literature, but when it came to you-know-what it was just a question of what could fit on a mattress. If Greta Garbo came along—fine! And if Rose Dreckfresser turned up—also good!" She abruptly laughed. "Did you hear how he carried on at Bentley? All those sweet, juicy little things. He came back with a prostate—"

"Bentley?" cried Morroe. "Where did he come to Bentley?"

"Manny, Manny Ribalow is up there. They were looking around for somebody to give a popular culture seminar and he pushed hard for Leslie."

God almighty! thought Morroe.

From each Leslie had taken and gotten!

Wherever there was a foundation.

Wherever there was a grant.

Wherever there was a publisher to hand out advances.

And he, he himself, out one hundred and thirty-seven dollars. Who would go blocks and blocks to save eight cents on a bottle of shampoo.

His heart quickened and a great roaring started in his ears. "Please," he wanted to tell her, "enough already," while she plunged on and on, carrying him along in the swell of her grievances. Mama, Mama, was this a Leslie! He was her enemy, even as Hannibal was enemy to Rome. If he had been better in the sciences he would have extracted the calcium from her bones. Once he had forced her to wear a crucifix in bed. Unto her ninth month with Pilar she had worked for him. Her stomach dropping, her legs swelling like hydrants. He had a habit of helping himself to whatever was in her purse. He grudged her an old razor blade to shave her legs. No library would issue him books, so he took cards out in her name and in the name of her Bessarabian grandmother. He peed in the sinks. He would go to movies in the afternoon. He would demand all kinds of crazy dishes. He sat in the toilet for three hours at a time. He held on to no jobs. He farted away golden opportunities. He met no deadlines. He could be your best friend and, overnight, disappear like Job's boils.

There was no end to it. There were no words for so many sins and abominations. The human mind could not order or contain them.

To shut her up, he said, "Let me ask you this. What was he doing in Brooklyn? Or maybe I misunderstood. Though how can you misunderstand Brooklyn . . . ?"

In a firm matter-of-fact tone Inez replied, "I threw him the hell out."

Morroe dropped his eyes as if to spare her.

"Yeah, yeah, yeah, I took all his things, I put them in the hall."

"In the hall?" Morroe's voice rang. "Oh, you're kidding!"

"He was going out on a date. I didn't say anything, not a word. I figure, baby, you're going to play around? You want dates? Fine, fine, fine! You fat little slob, I'll give you dates. I ran downstairs, I went to all the stores, I got a bunch of cartons. Whatever he owned I put in. I locked the door from the inside. And I hold my horses. Finally, finally, I hear him shnuffling around. He rings and he bangs and he bangs and he rings. He starts howling and calling me names. 'It's all right,' he tells me, 'tonight we broke up.' You hear? 'We broke up!' Then he starts bringing his stuff downstairs. A dozen trips at least. That I feel guilty about. For all you know he got strained, he damaged his heart."

"Very doubtful," said Morroe. "I would guess it was the least of all the contributing factors." And he began to muse. Leslie should have called me. I would have certainly come down and given a hand. No matter what time, I would have overlooked it. Then a crazy night, like in the old days. Where he would talk and talk, and for all you know we'd make contact again. And I would have brought him home with me and put him up on the couch, or fixed up a couple of chairs with cushions. No matter how Etta carried on. I mean it.

Suddenly Inez ran to the door, saying, "Good, good, good! Here's Pilar, she's got coffee, we'll have coffee, it'll be nice." She hunted up the sugar bowl; the sugar was hard, encrusted and stained brown. As Morroe hacked and hacked with the handle of a spoon, Inez told him, "You know he started in to write smut?"

"Hey, now you're being silly." An astonished grin spread over Morroe's face. "I remember what Wilner wrote about his stories. Sure . . . 'The cerebral is carnal and the carnal is cerebral.' "

"I know what I'm talking about. He said so in a letter. You want to see, you'll see." She launched herself against one of the bookcases and started to drag it from the wall, meanwhile babbling, "It's behind here. . . . How do I know? Because I put it in my winter bag . . . and the lock is no damn good . . . Leslie's presents . . ." Books began to slide and spill from the top shelves, and though breakfast lay heavy on his stomach, Morroe sprang to assist. "Hold the bottom," she instructed, fishing with her hand along the molding. "Push a little more. More. Now give it, like, a lift." My destiny, my fate, Morroe thought, while blood pounded his temples. To *shlepp* for her. Okay, okay, okay." She drew out a wad of paper folded down to matchbook size. "Now you'll read, you'll see."

The letter was typed on blank loose-leaf paper; there were no margins and the ribbon had given out near the end. Morroe drained the sweetened sediment at the bottom of his coffee and sank into the couch. His lips unwittingly moving, he read:

> DEAR INEZ:
>
> So where were you last night? I called and I called, to no avail. She's watching TV, I told myself. She's spread out on the day-bed, shaving her legs or doing her nails, fressing away on ice cream and pistachio nuts, sprinting, during commercials, to the potty. In our Drawer of Love her pessary lies sealed and dry and talcumed between plastic covers. O, sancta simplicimus!
>
> And what's doing with me? Well,
>
> 1) In four weeks I have copped only one quick feel. Even in my wet dreams I'm being rejected.
>
> 2) I have become, in a small way of business, a pornographer.
>
> 3) I have taken a room in Brighton Beach.
>
> Number one I shall charge off to Zeitgeist. Number two— number two is the fate of the artist in mass society, the atomization of the individual, the quality of contemporary experience, the triumph of kitsch, the blight spreading over our moral imagination. All right, all right! One Saturday I'm passing by Marty

Menashim's bookstore. I wave. He runs to the door and pulls me in. He's all around me like a warm bath. One of his biggest customers, a textile king who spends almost four hundred dollars a month with him, has a yen to help the young and promising talents. This poor guy, it hurts him, his disc is slipping because I have to teach and write reviews for two and a half cents a word. And he wants to do something about it, he would definitely like to help. All right, but how? After all, there are the foundations—God forbid he should start competing with the foundations!

He has conceived, therefore, the following proposition: He shall be my patron; I am to write for his eyes alone. So what am I going to write? Well, it should be realistic and, if it's convenient, here and there my characters should administer a little discipline. Stern, mind you, but nothing complicated—no Chinese boots or iron virgins. And, above all, no Jews.

Thus, once a week I deposit my manuscript with Marty, who solemnly delivers over the check. Ten cents a word—was there ever such a fee? The stuff flows, it pours out of me like curses from a Roumanian mouth. And do you know who serves as model, who it is that fevers my fictions? Give a guess! Tsatskeleh meineh, you have been housemaid and nun, overseer of a concentration camp, librarian, Hollywood starlet, lady editor, Eskimo woman. You have been ill used by Lascars, private eyes, prep-school boys, embassy officials, London bobbies and French flics, you have made whoopee with Great Danes and been dildoed by Eurasian midgets.

Which brings us, by commodius vicarius, to Brighton Beach. On that night of nights—and why didn't you close the top on my talcum powder? It spilled over everything—I checked my stuff at Grand Central and wandered, in a state of holy madness, all up and down Times Square. From movie to movie I went, amid the living dead, the sleepwalkers, the Desdemonas and Othellos, the Pucks and Oberons, sustained by pina coladas and coconut drinks and the thinnest of Grant's hamburgers.

At Bickford's in the morning to search the ads. (Let none say a word against those oatmeal cookies!) One, one alone holds my eye. "A very clean room for a nice person." Here are no complex structures, no big deals, no mishmash. "A nice person." The phrase holds open a universe of fixed and eternal values, of certainties unfolding upon certainties. I shlubb down my coffee, I make a wee-wee and, forty-two minutes later—door to door—I present myself to Mrs. Holzberg.

But first let me tell you what a country I have entered. It lies between the heel and instep of the great boardwalk that carries you through the promise of Coney Island and beyond, to Sea Gate, watering place of the once rich. Here is a bazaar, a sun kingdom, here there is no humiliation, no indignity, here all things are endowed with grandeur and significance. (All right, the el can kill you with noise, the fancy-shmancy apartment houses are going under, the bungalows could cave in from a dirty look, the beach is a Castle Garden—never mind!)

Anyway, with Mrs. Holzberg I knew I had fallen into good hands. A few jokes, a Yiddish phrase, and identity was established; I had stepped off on the right foot. Before she even put out the honey cake she let me know she'd been on the Yiddish stage, a singer who had played second fiddle only to Jennie Goldstein. Her late husband, did I know of him? De Hirsch Holzberg. The last of the Yiddish Lears. Even Hollywood had grabbed him, and once in a while he still shows up on an old TV movie. A witch doctor, a mad scientist, a good-natured Indian who begs and begs Sitting Bull not to start up with Custer.

The room is in a back-yard bungalow; the shingles smell a little of flanken, the walls are covered with green oilcloth and the toilet doesn't let up for a minute. But linens like snow, towels upon towels, and over every door a mezuzah. There was a time, Mrs. H. assures me, when she could pick and choose, when people were happy to pay three and four hundred dollars over the summer. Now there's only myself and, two doors down, her son Chester and his wife, Evelyn. Chester is a big fellow who once did all right for himself in the Golden Gloves and still keeps fit with long hours on the handball courts. Every day he's nuhdging me to do some push-ups or to pace him while he runs around the block a few times. An intense Zionist; when he finishes up his dental mechanic's course he will settle in Israel. He talks of long sentry duty in the Negev, scaling walls, leaping ditches, hand-to-hand combat with Arabs. For which he'll be more than ready. And he pinches the roll of fat over my gut.

Evelyn is a kind of gelaymteh: whatever she touches falls from her hands. At Brooklyn College, where she will soon enter her senior year, the authorities are insisting it's time she picks a major. Between education and sociology she is going crazy, she is getting cramps. What do I think? Because if she takes education it's more practical; she can walk into a job; they're begging for teachers. Though she relates better to sociology, and would have received an A for the course if she had not been late with a term paper. She falls back into the beach chair, spent, inert. She can barely get up to go to the bathroom. But at night—ah, that's another story. Then it's pound and thump and huff and puff and zing-a-zing-zing. I lie and I listen. Please, I beg, have a heart, take pity. Then I can't stand it any more. I rush out of bed and I start scribbling my little stories. Which I shall do in a moment, when I have finished this letter. (There's a beauty in the works, about a Tibetan monk with an enormous dong.) And then off, off to the boardwalk, to hang around and watch the kids. Honest, you never saw such kids. Brown and round and mother-loved, fed on dove's milk and Good Humors. At night they pair off under the pavilions—Milton and Sharon, Seymour and Sandra, Heshie and Deborah. They sing stupid songs, an original word doesn't leave their lips and, clearly, not one will ever stand up for beauty or truth or goodness. Yet—do me something! I could stay and watch them for hours. I feel such love, I chuckle and I beam, and if it was in my power I'd walk in their midst, pat their heads and bless them, each and every one. So they don't join YPSL and they never heard of Hound and Horn and they'll end up in garden apartments, with wall-to-wall carpeting. What does it matter? Let them be happy, only be happy. And such is my state that I will remit all sins, even these:

That you have not read my work in three years.

That you do not utter little cries in sex.

That in company you will not laugh at the second hearing of my jokes.

That you have let the Chinese laundry ruin my shirts.

Of course, you know how long this burst of love will last! It'll start to diminish by tomorrow morning, when I get the first jostle on the subway. By the time I hit the city, by the time I search the kiosks for the new quarterlies, it'll disappear altogether. Rankin will have a review, Pankin will have an article, Rifkin will have an excerpt from a novel in progress—and right away I'll eat myself up alive. What can I do, nebbach? Am I the primus

mobilus, am I more than a nachshlepper *in the order of things?*
I'm not the owner, lady, I only work here! To love costs, and
costs dear. Like my grandmother used to say, sometimes you kill
three chickens for one jar of schmaltz.
      Stay well. . . .

LESLIE

P.S. Do me a favor. Send some undershirts. You threw in only
a couple and they're turning green already.

Morroe put aside the letter and sat stiff-backed, in a state of arrest.
In his thoughts he begged, Leave me alone. I feel disgusted, I want
to vomit, I'm sick and tired of everything. Where do I come to this?
I have my own problems. First thing tomorrow morning I have to
start on a new brochure, get a gimmick for the campaign theme. The
fund-raisers are pressing and pressing. And there would probably be
a showdown with Rugoff, the tale bearer, the troublemaker, the
Uriah Heep. So what kind of "love," what kind of bullshit? Yes, and
blessing other kids. His own, though—his own he doesn't even
mention.

After some time Morroe got to his feet and said, "I think we should
start. Till you get a cab, and everything. Plus the fact that you should
arrive a little before everybody else."

But Inez took hold of his arm and drew him back. She said, brooding, "What am I going to do with his clothes? He used to buy and
buy. Sell and you get nothing. You want them? Yeah, yeah, yeah!
You'll come later, I'll put them in valises, you'll take everything."

"They'd never, never fit me," Morroe protested. "Remember, he
was on the broad side. And shorter in the legs. It wouldn't pay with
alterations and everything."

"It's only right," Inez continued, unheeding. "Because he was so
crazy about you. Because he'd always say, this is a real person, a
human being, a *mensch*." She tightened her grip on his arm, then
lunged up and kissed him violently on the lips. The drag of her
weight took him off balance; he toppled to the couch, one knee
folded clumsily under him. "I wished him harm," Inez said, tears
running down her face, her mouth fallen, black and twisted. "I'm
scared. Do I have to kiss him when he's in the box? That's how it is
in my religion. My mother made me do it once to an aunt when
I was a kid—the old bitch! You beg the dead: forgive, take my sins
under with you."

"Foolish, foolish," Morroe cried, stretching out beside her. "I've been to Jewish funerals—too many in my lifetime. And they don't go through any of that stuff. You'll see how foolish you are." He squeezed closer and stroked her hair. "One-two-three. In and out, no big deals." As if by accident he lowered his hand down and down, till it fell near the ridge of her panty-girdle. Whoosh! It dawned on him that on this day anything was possible. But suppose Pilar walked in on them? Never mind. It could be a quickie, sneaked in the name of compassion. Coolly, without caution, Morroe began to gather up the folds of her dress.

And the bell rang. Two short bursts, then a prolonged, tearing peal.

"Wait, wait, wait," Inez cried, deftly stiff-arming him and making for the window. "It's Falvey." She flung up the blinds and bent out. "One second," she howled. "I'll go to the john, I'll wash up and I'm ready." And to Morroe: "My earrings. Are they too loud? Eh, as if they'll even notice."

"Whoa," said Morroe, muddled and fatigued; he had broken into a heavy sweat. "What's the arrangements? I thought you and I would go together."

"I can't talk," Inez snapped. "He's double-parked and it's the beginning of the month. They're giving tickets right and left." She turned away and called for Pilar. Whose face, as she came forward from the kitchen, bore the same wise little smile.

"Then I'll ride down with you," Morroe insisted. "Just let me wash my face, that's all."

Inez gave a nervous shiver and wagged her head. "No room. Where's there room? We have to pick up Falvey's sister. And her kids, she can't leave the kids. We were so close. Could I say no to her, could I say don't come?"

"No room?" Morroe croaked. "That's nice, very nice. You couldn't make better arrangements, hah?" He was ready to say more, much more. But for Pilar's sake he dissembled his anger.

Once again Inez kissed him flush on the mouth, though he shrank from the contact. She said, "You'll call up the boys. You'll let them know. You'll all come together. A big crowd. It'll be nice."

On shaky legs Morroe followed her into the hall. "You didn't tell me where the funeral is. Tell me!" he demanded.

"You know where Ocean Parkway comes into Prospect Park?"

"I think so. Yes."

"Near there. *Parkway Memorial,* or *Parkway Chapel.* You'll see, you'll find it."

"I'm not so sure. Hold it! There must be at least—" But he heard only the knocking of her footsteps on the landing and Pilar's quick-running chatter.

He went back into the apartment and began an aimless wandering of the rooms. Without knowing precisely why, he decided to clear away, straighten up. There was a small carton under the kitchen sink; into this he emptied some of the ash trays and discarded the coffee containers. He adjusted the blinds, climbing on a chair to do what he could for the fraying cords; he shut off the lights, he moved the bookcase back against the wall and, if he had been able to find the vacuum, he would have gone over the rugs. Though he was soon winded and overheated, the effort nevertheless had a settling effect upon him. He rested, smoked a cigarette and rose to make the calls.

His voice was pitched low, somewhat strained and unctuous. With each of the boys he dropped into the same phrases: "A little bad news . . . coronary thrombosis . . . not a bit of warning . . . lousy, rotten deal. . . ." In a few minutes everything was arranged; they were to meet at Sheridan Square, and Holly Levine would pick them up in his Volkswagen.

When Morroe hung up he remained at the telephone table. "Cry," he muttered. "Now cry a little." He bent his head and thought of his Uncle Lazar, of the slights he had suffered over the past month, make it six weeks, of Auschwitz and Buchenwald and the six million. But it was useless.

> *Popular-culture critic Holly Levine has appeared in his Volkswagen, meeting Reiff and Weiner; Ottensteen has yet to arrive.*

"There is a possibility . . ." Levine pressed his right side and blew a tormented breath, ". . . well, a strong likelihood, that I shall be giving a popular culture course this fall. From 'Little Nemo' to 'Li'l Abner.' "

A stir of unbelief went through Weiner.

"Something wrong, Barn?" said Levine, with a sudden tightening of his lips. "You are, ah, perhaps, displeased, old sport?"

"I? I?" Weiner said softly. "*Nahrisher kint!* Except . . ." He scratched behind one of Levine's ears. "Gaah, I don't know. Is that for you? Is it, like they say in the quarterlies, your métier?"

His color deepening, Levine answered, "My piece on John Ford has been twice anthologized. Twice!"

"Granted, granted. Your grasp of the gap between low-middle and high-middle culture—perfect. Your cinematic depth analysis—I don't think I would want better. But when it comes to comic strips and such—unh, unh, man, you doan know shit!" And Weiner shook his head in the slow mournful rhythm of an old darkie.

Levine pursed his lips, as though sucking through a straw.

"Maybe I'm wrong," Weiner placated. "Maybe I am being less than fair. In which case, answer me this: Who used to say, in moments of *Angst*, 'Golly Moses, I got the whim whams all over'?"

"Rooney, Rooney, Little Annie Rooney!" Levine looked around as if for applause.

"Don Winslow of the Navy—his rank!"

"Commander!"

"Now the nemesis of Bim Gump!"

"Wait, wait! She wore a veil . . . she would always drug him . . . MADAM ZENDA!"

"And the protectors of Daddy Warbucks?"

"Punjab," Levine said, delightedly. "Punjab and the Asp."

"The Rinkeydinks," Weiner came back, relentless. "Who and from where?"

"From 'Winnie Winkle.' The club. And there was Perry, the little brother. And there was Spud. . . . There was Chink. . . ."

"And who else?"

"That's all."

"That's all?"

"I give up."

"Come on," Weiner exhorted. "One, one more. The most important one. With the hat. With the moron face. Who would always say, 'Perry, youse is a good boy'?"

"Ah, ah, I remember," said Levine, a sorrowful sweetness passing over his face. "I recall and recollect. Denny Dimwit. Bear in mind, however, that he was the last arrival, that his position with the Rinkeydinks was essentially a fringe position."

"If you get this one . . ." Weiner mumbled, squashed and submissive.

Beaming, Levine braced himself.

"I . . . want . . . the . . . name . . . the name of . . . THE GREEN HORNET'S DRIVER!"

Quietly, without fanfare, Levine answered, "Kato."

Then, drawing Levine's head down and dragging it from side to side, Weiner murmured, "*Ah leben uff der kepele!* Everything he knows, everything he remembers!"

"What is more," said Levine, far gone in triumph, "furthermore, I believe I am one of the few who is able yet to remember the 'Jack Armstrong' theme. In its entirety!"

"Gaah!"

"Rah, rah . . ." Levine began, a little flustered.

Whereupon Morroe offered up a "Boola boola boola boola."

Which Weiner matched with a grudging "Rah rah rah."

And drumming on the seats and slapping their thighs they joined voices:

> "*Wave the flag for Hudson High, boys,*
> *Show them how we stand.*
> *Ever shall our team be champions,*
> *Known throughout the land!*
> *Rah rah boola boola boola boola!*
> *Boola boola boola boo rah rah rah!*
> *Have you tried Wheaties?*
> *They're the whole wheat with all of the bran.*
> *Won't you try Wheaties?*
> *For wheat is the best friend of man.*
> *They're crispy and crunchy the whole year through,*
> *Jack Armstrong never tires of them*
> *And neither will you.*
> *So just buy Wheaties,*
> *The best breakfast food in the land!*"

As they uttered a last "Boola!" and a burst of "Rahs!" there was thumping and thumping on the sun roof, and then the face of Ottensteen darkened a window.

He said, "Such sweet voices, such marvelous mourners. *Yoi,* Leslie, Labeleh, I envy you your friends."

A stillness descended over the car.

At last Weiner broke the silence with a "Harya, Reb Felix!"

"Look who's here, look who is here!" Levine chanted foolishly.

"Felix-*el,* Felix-*el,* what's doing and what's new? cried Morroe in a rush of good feeling.

"You really want to know?" Ottensteen said, telling him with a frown that he would not be happy with the reply.

Morroe gave a submissive shrug.

"Because what's doing is that you're a big *yolt*. What's new—what's new is you sent *der alte* Ottensteen on a fool's errand to Washington Square Park, where, on his sick feet, he had to stand for thirty-three minutes by the clock until he realized he's dealing with a party that has very few brains and no common sense. That's all. Period."

"*I* misdirected? *I* told you Washington Square Park?" Morroe trumpeted.

"A mistake," Weiner said. "It happens."

"What then?" demanded Morroe, consumed with the injustice.

"Naturally, naturally . . . the tension of the moment . . . the bearing of bad news . . ." Levine was all moderation and easy affability. "And now let's give Felix room. Let's make him comfy-cozy and let us get started."

In a broken voice Ottensteen said, "Don't put yourself out, please. For *der alte* Ottensteen you're not going to have to bother."

"Gaah, Felix! Felix, gaah!" Weiner grabbed Ottensteen's arm and drew him half in through the window. "Honestly, I am surprised and ashamed."

"You're surprised?" With both fists Ottensteen knocked away Weiner's hand. "You don't need to be surprised. And when it comes to shame—*der alte* Ottensteen isn't ashamed. *Der alte* Ottensteen is a simple, simple person and individual. He knows how to love, he knows how to hate. Thusly, when a Sholem Asch turns *M'shimid* and no-good bastard, he don't talk to Sholem Asch. And if the Germans kill six million of his people—*his* people—he don't ride in German automobiles."

"On the face of it," interposed Levine, "flawless logic. And yet . . ." He pretended to puzzle over the point.

Ottensteen peered at him as though through frosted glass. He said, at length, "There is an old, a very old saying: 'Who is a hero? He who keeps down a wisecrack.'" He wheeled and strode away, his pants bellying at the knees, his feet, in the high orthopedic shoes, turning out.

"*Shema Yisroel*," said Weiner.

"Let him go," said Levine.

"Whoosh, please, call him back," Morroe exhorted them. "Aw, look, he's older, he's been sick. Call him back, let us be the good ones."

"Gaah, sick, sick!" Weiner answered him coldly. "He'll outlast all things, all systems. He'll—"

But Levine had already started the car, working wheel and gear stick in abrupt jerky movements, racing for the corner and jumping the light to scrape the curb alongside of Ottensteen. Who played dumb at the insistent croaking of the horn.

"Felix! Yay . . . y . . . y! Ottensteen . . . n . . . n!" With the last air in his lungs Morroe cried into the confusion of the street.

Cupping his ear, Ottensteen went through an elaborate pantomime of looking and listening for the voice.

"For Leslie. Is it nice for Leslie? It's not nice!"

Slow, stooped, as though hindered by underbrush, Ottensteen trod to the car.

He said, "Only for Leslie."

> *After attending a memorial service, only to discover it is over a different corpse in the wrong chapel, and after other adventures, the boys arrive at the right cemetery.*

HE COULD OFFER no proof and there was little point mentioning the fact, but Morroe was convinced that the Inez he had last laid eyes on wore taffeta, not silk, open toes, not pumps. The next minute, though, as he began to tally and take stock of the other mourners who milled around the cemetery gate in muted meeting and greeting, he was confounded by greater peculiarities. So that he cried to himself "Ye Gods!" and "Whoosh!"

There was dark Milton Ragner, Milton the unworldly, who had slashed his wrists in a tub of warm water because he could think of no way to get rid of an old mattress.

There was Ozzie Waldman, Ozzie the *kvetch*. For his favor you could die. He gave away nothing, not even a piece of information. Meet him after a visit to his mother, ask him, "Ozzie, where were you?" and he would say, "I saw a woman."

There was Ethel Landsberger, big and shapely and elegant, from the Landsberger Parking System people. She hunted with falcons, she was hot for writers and spent thousands to print her terrible verse. Always in upper case. REMEMBER NO SUCH THING AS IT IS/FORGET WHAT IS ONLY AT ALL.

There was Gideon Pfeffer, the big Latin America specialist. He knew five or six languages, he made special trips for the State Department. he could hold his own against Sidney Hook. But he was with-out charm. He blew matches out under your unlighted cigarette and never bothered introducing you to people.

There was Edgar Segal, Edgar the *macher*. Where there was a mag-azine, he was on the free list. Where there was a forum, he was on the platform, filling the water glasses. Where there were two, he made the third.

There was Maurice Salomon, the editor of *Second Thoughts*, with his Robespierre profile. He had the air of the oldest of men, as if he had been through the Hundred Years' War, taken down Sacco and Vanzetti's last words and seen all movements turn into failure and fiasco. He would be twenty-nine, make it thirty, on his next birthday.

There was Arabelle Talbot Harrington, looking as if she should be fingering a rosary or stamping library cards. Oh, Leslie had a great story about her: how late, late one night at the Devereaux Colony, she paraded nude around the grounds and screamed up into the main guest house, "Will one of you please come down and fuck me!"

There was Cordell Nash. His family had streets named after them and got private audiences with the Pope. Yet all his friends were Jewish. He loved to make jokes like, "Pour me a *goyische kopp* of coffee."

There was Irving Sklare thumping along in his space shoes. They called him "Irving Development" because he was a city planner. Every third word out of his mouth was "environment."

There was Leslie's sister Amelia, fatter than ever, and Lemkuhl the druggist, and there were Colin Bewley the translator and Selma Raab the juvenile editor and Portnoy the veterinarian and Mordecai Roth of *The Naysayer* and Horace Spiro of *Portent* and Inez' old maid Margo and Danny Sherman the gagwriter and Harvey Korn the so-ciologist and many others Morroe knew barely or not at all. Momma, what a crew, what a collection! Who had summoned such numbers so late? Where do you reach them? And by what means? Were there six Inezes working the switchboard of the world? I am in the presence of mystery, Morroe thought, and his gums began to torment him. For a wild moment he had a flash of Inez, a lightly leaping bird shrilling, "Come, come, come!" from window to window, or dancing up the city and down the city, tooting Leslie's old recorder.

Ottensteen, on his right, was lecturing Selma Raab, the juvenile editor. "*Chaval Al De'ovidim.*" Three times he repeated the phrase. "You'll see it on a lot of Jewish stones. To translate—to translate I would say, 'Alas, maybe woe or sorrow for the lost who are never forgotten.' "

Weiner, behind him, had hold of Cordell Nash. Whose choked laugh was already beginning to burst quietly. "And the pool is emptied out, completely empty. And he's soaking and splashing, splashing and soaking. And the manager tippy-toes over and he says, 'How are you, Mr. Shmollowitz, and is everything to your liking?' And he answers him, '*Vun*-derful, *vun*-derful. Now if I only had some money!' "

And Levine, in front, had linked arms with Maurice Salomon and was saying, "I see, then, not a piece which would definitely pigeonhole Leslie—though the, ah, cultural configurations have a critical bearing—but a kind of retrospective reappraisal. In the way that all reappraisals are retrospective. 'Leslie Braverman: the Comic Vision,' or 'The Comic Vision of Leslie Braverman.' "

Kronk!

Creaking and swaying, crunching gravel, with pale radiance of low-beam the hearse, from a devious path, intercepted their path and lumbered ahead at walking pace. Showing the blunt end of the fine wood coffin. Laminated like a scroll. Silver handles and silver screws. Where my friend is laid. Who could polish off, at one sitting, six bialystocken and a half-pound of Novia Scotia lox.

Whoosh!

A fat raindrop spattered one lens. Another exploded in his hair. Storm or sun shower; the day had lacked only this. He saw three clouds move upon each other, collide and merge. To become a bust of Goethe. A dogfight between angry little Spads. An Etruscan warrior. Officer Pupp getting set with his club. Then only the club. Then the sun renewed its thrust.

Morroe wanders toward the grave.

. . . And he concentrated his gaze on headstones, vaults, crypts, monuments, markets, mausoleums, his thoughts on the dead. To them, them, he made silent address.

He said, What can I tell you and what do I know? Your certainty, my problems. We got over the Depression, we got over Hitler. Skeezix is married and has hands full with the kids. My life isn't really connected to anything. Discount houses are very big lately. Likewise mutual funds. Likewise paperback books. Likewise tolerance, brotherhood, human relations, intergroup harmony. Your names and mine at the foot of one page. Now whole families can charter special planes for Israel. We're beginning to see Jewish faces in banks, though not so many. I get very little personal mail. Either people are more nervous lately or there is more to get on their nerves. We are losing India. Black princes from Africa eat at the Automat. I can imagine the day of my death, but not the day after. Everybody seems to have good taste. Bus drivers are becoming more vicious. Macy's has gone downhill. Likewise the big movie houses, the Modern Library series, wrapping paper, pencil sharpeners, kitchen matches, Nedick's orange drink. I have as much in common with the men who rule me as I have with the Gracchi. Big names appear for Jewish causes. Somewhere I read that it costs $3,500 a year to be poor. Comedians are very sad and keep breaking in with, "Seriously, though, folks, seriously . . ." Smilin' Jack is married. Warner Baxter, Richard Dix and Warren William died. Jack Benny is still big. No one talks anymore about Winchell. I don't think you missed too much. Honestly . . .

A dark silent relief enclosed him.

A bird worrying a worm delighted him.

A shimmer of green poplars, make it evergreens, filled him with reverence.

To a fat fly he gave the freedom of his temple.

To a ragged line of ants he yielded right of way.

To Leslie he promised, I'll cry for you. How I'll cry! I'll turn your insults into anecdotes, your *mishugass* into myth. I'll write off the hundred and thirty-seven dollars. Likewise that badger shaving brush and the Miriam Beard *History of the Business Man*, out of print and very scarce.

He altered his gait to a sturdy martial rhythm.

He opened the bottom button of his jacket.

He tuned in to the boys.

To Ottensteen, who was saying to Selma Raab, "More than you realize he took to heart. Once, once on a Sunday he looked pale and green and very strange to me. It was hurting him, he was personally suffering because that minute and that second one-third of the country was watching Ed Sullivan."

To Levine, who was saying to Maurice Salomon, "We must first determine whether we want memoir or critique. If memoir, it behooves us to go easy on the bold and baroque, on his cafeteria-and-dexedrine period. If critique, it behooves us then, or it then behooves

us, to find in his work what I like to think of as, ah, the double image
—that which is, at once, symbolic expression of our time and tragic
protest against it. *Moi-même*, I favor the memoir-critique. The former lending tension to the latter, the latter lending irony to the
former."

To Weiner, who was saying to Cordell Nash, "He loved my mother's split pea soup. True, he didn't mind her sweet and sour cabbage
and he was partial to her honey cake. But he *loved* her split pea soup.
Every Thursday my mother sent along the jar, the big jar for him, and
every Thursday he would walk in. First he would look. Then he would
handle it, like it was the Holy Grail. Then he would turn the cap,
soft, slow, easy, thread by thread, and he would sing a little. *Boi-boi-
bimboi-biddle-bamboi*. Gaah, soft, slow, sweet, easy he'd pour it in the
pot, he'd make sure it didn't overheat, it didn't boil away. And he
would sing a little. *Boi-boi-boi-tzickle-dickle-bimbam*. And he would
eat and while he ate he would explain to me. That food, good food
was the warp and woof, the blood and bone, the spirit and substance,
the very essence of Judaism. Then if there was time we'd go out and
look for pussy."

And Morroe continued his reflections, and his mind gave birth to
warm feelings, good impulses, worthwhile projects. He would keep in
touch with Inez and take her to the best, make it good restaurants for
lunch. He would fix her up with somebody from the office, a decent,
modest, genuine person like Morty Shulman who would dote on her,
take pleasure in her strange ways and go gently with her into a pleasant menopause. He would show an interest in the little girls, treat
them to Radio City, the Statue of Liberty, the Hayden Planetarium
and F.A.O. Schwarz toys on birthdays and special occasions.

If it please God he would try to be . . . a true *mensch*.

.   .   .   .   .   .

Morroe's spirit expanded.

In his shy and goofy way, under his lashes, he gazed at the boys.

He was that minute ready to die for them. Or at least to do them
big favors.

He thought, They may not respect me, but they like me.

He also thought, They wish me no great good, but they wouldn't
want harm to come to me.

And then they went up a little rise.

And then they went down a little incline.

And they bore right.

And they bore half-left.

And the fine warm spray of an alabaster fountain was blown upon them.

And there was a children's plot with little sun dials and a soft blue ark and stone beasts and birds and fishes in the grass, and they passed beyond this.

And there were family plots for Blaustein, Engel, Danzig, Applebome, Barchoff, Schneierson, Nass, Lowey, Diamond, Kratter, and they passed beyond these.

And one was for Braverman, and this one they entered.

And Morroe moistened his lips and braced his shoulders and took down some deep stiff breaths.

And it came to him that so he had often entered Leslie's living room.

And then Levine ran a finger over the flap of Morroe's left pocket and over his left sleeve.

And Levine said to him, "What is this stuff, this substance?"

And Levine further said, "It, ah, feels like, it has the consistency of . . ."

And Levine touched finger to mouth and softly spoke this word: "Salt."

First called up to the graveside was Maurice Salomon, who had this to say: that Leslie's mind and temperament were sternly moral; that it had been his role, his unique function in both fiction and criticism to deal with matters and circumstances which the American character—pluralistic, fragmented and debauched by commercialism— would not readily admit to consciousness; that he had confronted life not with the armor of bias or the cant of dogma, but with a simple openness to the multiplicity of experience; that he undertook to tell us what it was for the individual to be alive at this moment in history; that he had conceded nothing to the times, but had over and again borne personal testimony that IT IS and I AM; that because of the vigor, the purity and passion of this testimony—the moral thrust—he claimed our attention.

Next spoke Arabelle Talbot Harrington, and she lauded Leslie as teacher, as one who delighted in instructing and who instructed by action and example. It gave her great pleasure to remember now that some years back she had been entering a cafeteria with Leslie; and suddenly there had stepped forward a derelict, an outcast, a human discard, a representative of the urban underbelly: a bum. He had begun to exhort them with his whiskey-ruined voice. No, not for a handout, but a loan to be paid back in proper course and due time. You see, Mac, Lady . . . a dishwashing job . . . a week's work . . . put him on his feet again . . . served in the last one, Mac, Lady. Thereupon Leslie had handed over a quarter. And with gravity and gentle ceremony he had proffered an old bill stub bearing his name and address and advised that he would look for payment in an early mail. Arabelle had later chided him. Why the pretense? The farce? Was he so new to the City, to such small swindles? Having been fool for the quarter, must he make himself more fool with the bill stub?

And Leslie had said this, and this is what Leslie had said: "With the quarter I found my own humanness; with the bill stub I restored his."

Next called was Ottensteen. His arms folded, his head low, his gaze turned inward, he said that though he was just now too filled up he would anyway do his best for his dear and very good friend. And he reminded all present, in case they didn't know, that in the Passover Hagadah, when it told in one section about how much God gave the Children of Israel in forty years on the desert, there was after every single item the word *Dayenu:* It would have been sufficient. If, for example, God had just sent manna but didn't bother handing out the Ten Commandments—*Dayenu.* If He handed out the Ten Commandments but didn't see to their drinking water—*Dayenu.* And similar, and such. This word, this *Dayenu* now stood written on his mind. So . . . if Leslie had been only a highly intelligent person and not a writer—*Dayenu.* If he had been only a writer of stories and didn't bother with his articles—again, *Dayenu.* If he had written his articles and didn't have his outstanding personality—once again, *Dayenu.* If he had this personality and didn't like people—again and again, *Dayenu.* If he had just liked people and didn't have on them an influence —*Dayenu* and sufficient. If he had just had an influence and not been sincere with people—sufficient and *Dayenu.* If he had been sincere, sincere but not sweet—

And many minutes later, though he was choking on a *Dayenu,* Ottensteen was eased, gently eased away from the graveside, and there came forward the folksinger, Leroy Gillman. Who said that though he was non-Jewish, though he was a Negro and not too familiar with the observances, he felt it properly right to sing; because that was the way of his people and he knew no better way to let a heart speak. What he would sing had been meant as a farewell, a goodbye for a certain prince hundreds of years back; it was now fittingly natural for this prince of a guy. He accordingly sang:

> "Bonnie Charlie's now awa'
> Safely owre the friendly main;
> Mony a heart will break in twa,
> Should he no come back again.
> Will ye no come back again?
> Will ye no come back again?
> Better lo'ed ye cannot be,
> Will ye no come back again?"

Even after Leroy's last note went pining upward; even after the coffin was rough-handled by the four diggers; even after they had set it on that evil-looking contraption and jacked it up, and it hung and then slid into the pit; even after he flung his handful of dirt; even after the shovels flashed and chipped and smoothed; even after Leslie's little father shouted out, "No man should live to bury a son!"; and even after Ottensteen, Weiner and Levine bawled openly, Morroe held back. Shithead, he labeled himself, horse's ass, peculiar creature. You could cry when the planes shot King Kong off the Empire State Building. You could cry when Wallace Beery slapped Jackie Cooper and then punished his hand. You could cry when Lew Ayres reached for that butterfly.

But even so, nothing wet came from his eyes.

.   .   .   .   .

"I'm home. Honey, I'm home," he told Etta, moving down beside her on the bed.

"Are you sorry?"

"You didn't make me juice and I should be sorry!"

"I made you Jell-O."

"I feel for Jell-O."

"If you'd called—why didn't you call? I could have told you get bananas."

"I'll do without bananas. I can live without bananas in my Jell-O.

And believe me, take my word for it, I couldn't call." He got out of his jacket, his tie and shirt and belt. He began to unzip his pants, stretching them out of shape because he had not first removed his shoes. And because he saw, or thought he saw, a mosquito, he took from the night table a stick of insect repellent and rubbed it all over himself and began to rub it all over Etta; and he said to her, while he worked the sticky stuff over her naked legs and her flanks and over the hem and ribbing of her nightgown and near her nose and cheeks and neck, and into the light pinkness where her hair was parted, he said to her, "Listen, listen, you don't know what a day I had, you don't know. I'll tell you something . . ."

And a long breaking breath.

And whoosh, a tear.

And another, and another, from the mother and father of all sorrows.

And he began to cry freely and quietly.

Herzog

by SAUL BELLOW

Saul Bellow enjoys the distinction of being critically respected and publicly accepted. His novels, from The Dangling Man to Herzog, have placed him on a high plateau of literary eminence. Some have praised his universality, others claim that he falls short of an emotional understanding of his world, though his intellectual comprehension is noteworthy. But none can deny his importance in contemporary American literary history, both Jewish and non-Jewish. Few other writers are so often discussed in academic circles and in the general press.

Bellow has made free and tender use of Jewish family material, but his characters are among the alienated as a rule. One of these is Herzog. The novel is essentially the self-revelation of a man who writes unmailed letters to world personalities and others who enter his thoughts—this is only a stream-of-consciousness device —while he is working through a breakdown. His second wife has gone off to Chicago, taking their little daughter. He makes a stab at action in Chicago, gets ridiculously and pathetically tangled up, and goes back to the country, where, it appears, he is recovering his balance. A Jewish lady who owns a florist shop has her eye on him, and she is good in bed.

Our excerpts touch on the opening, the action episode and its aftermath. There are also examples of Herzog's opinionated letter-writing, filled with erudition and a profundity that sometimes seem to vanish into thin air. These very qualities impart a typicality to Herzog, especially in university communities, and Bellow has shown much insight in the portrayal of the troubled intellectual.

Born in 1915 in Quebec, Bellow attended the University of Chicago, wrote for Partisan Review and other magazines, published The Dangling Man *in 1944*, The Victim *in 1947, and his first big novel*, The Adventures of Augie March, *in 1953. He received the National Book Award in 1965 for Herzog.*

C.A.

I F I AM out of my mind, it's all right with me, thought Moses Herzog.

Some people thought he was cracked and for a time he himself had doubted that he was all there. But now, though he still behaved oddly, he felt confident, cheerful, clairvoyant, and strong. He had fallen under a spell and was writing letters to everyone under the sun. He was so stirred by these letters that from the end of June he moved from place to place with a valise full of papers. He had carried this valise from New York to Martha's Vineyard, but returned from the Vineyard immediately; two days later he flew to Chicago, and from Chicago he went to a village in western Massachusetts. Hidden in the country, he wrote endlessly, fanatically, to the newspapers, to people in public life, to friends and relatives and at last to the dead, his own obscure dead, and finally the famous dead.

It was the peak of summer in the Berkshires. Herzog was alone in the big old house. Normally particular about food, he now ate Silvercup bread from the paper package, beans from the can, and American cheese. Now and then he picked raspberries in the overgrown garden, lifting up the thorny canes with absent-minded caution. As for sleep, he slept on a mattress without sheets—it was his abandoned marriage bed—or in the hammock, covered by his coat. Tall bearded grass and locust and maple seedlings surrounded him in the yard. When he opened his eyes in the night, the stars were near like spiritual bodies. Fires, of course; gases—minerals, heat, atoms, but eloquent at five in the morning to a man lying in a hammock, wrapped in his overcoat.

When some new thought gripped his heart he went to the kitchen, his headquarters, to write it down. The white paint was scaling from the brick walls and Herzog sometimes wiped mouse droppings from the table with his sleeve, calmly wondering why field mice should have such a passion for wax and paraffin. They made holes in paraffin-sealed preserves; they gnawed birthday candles down to the wicks. A rat chewed into a package of bread, leaving the shape of its body in the layers of slices. Herzog ate the other half of the loaf spread with jam. He could share with rats too.

All the while, one corner of his mind remained open to the external world. He heard the crows in the morning. Their harsh call was delicious. He heard the thrushes at dusk. At night there was a barn owl. When he walked in the garden, excited by a mental letter, he saw roses winding about the rain spout; or mulberries—birds gorging in the mulberry tree. The days were hot, the evenings flushed and dusty. He looked keenly at everything but he felt half blind.

His friend, his former friend, Valentine, and his wife, his ex-wife Madeleine, had spread the rumor that his sanity had collapsed. Was it true?

He was taking a turn around the empty house and saw the shadow of his face in a gray, webby window. He looked weirdly tranquil. A radiant line went from mid-forehead over his straight nose and full, silent lips.

Late in spring Herzog had been overcome by the need to explain, to have it out, to justify, to put in perspective, to clarify, to make amends.

At that time he had been giving adult-education lectures in a New York night school. He was clear enough in April but by the end of May he began to ramble. It became apparent to his students that they would never learn much about The Roots of Romanticism but that they would see and hear odd things. One after another, the academic formalities dropped away. Professor Herzog had the unconscious frankness of a man deeply preoccupied. And toward the end of the term there were long pauses in his lectures. He would stop, muttering "Excuse me," reaching inside his coat for his pen. The table creaking, he wrote on scraps of paper with a great pressure of eagerness in his hands; he was absorbed, his eyes darkly circled. His white face showed everything—everything. He was reasoning, arguing, he was suffering, he had thought of a brilliant alternative— he was wide-open, he was narrow; his eyes, his mouth made everything silently clear—longing, bigotry, bitter anger. One could see it all. The class waited three minutes, five minutes, utterly silent.

At first there was no pattern to the notes he made. They were fragments—nonsense syllables, exclamations, twisted proverbs and quotations or, in the Yiddish of his long-dead mother, *Trepverter*

—retorts that came too late, when you were already on your way down the stairs.

He wrote, for instance, *Death—die—live again—die again—live. No person, no death.*

And, *On the knees of your soul? Might as well be useful. Scrub the floor.*

Next, *Answer a fool according to his folly lest he be wise in his own conceit.*

Answer not a fool according to his folly, lest thou be like unto him. Choose one.

He noted also, *I see by Walter Winchell that J. S. Bach put on black gloves to compose a requiem mass.*

Herzog scarcely knew what to think of this scrawling. He yielded to the excitement that inspired it and suspected at times that it might be a symptom of disintegration. That did not frighten him. Lying on the sofa of the kitchenette apartment he had rented on 17th Street, he sometimes imagined he was an industry that manufactured personal history, and saw himself from birth to death. He conceded on a piece of paper,

I cannot justify.

Considering his entire life, he realized that he had mismanaged everything—everything. His life was, as the phrase goes, ruined. But since it had not been much to begin with, there was not much to grieve about. Thinking, on the malodorous sofa, of the centuries, the nineteenth, the sixteenth, the eighteenth, he turned up, from the last, a saying that he liked:

Grief, Sir, is a species of idleness.

He went on taking stock, lying face down on the sofa. Was he a clever man or an idiot? Well, he could not at this time claim to be clever. He might once have had the makings of a clever character, but he had chosen to be dreamy instead, and the sharpies cleaned him out. What more? He was losing his hair. He read the ads of the Thomas Scalp Specialists, with the exaggerated skepticism of a man whose craving to believe was deep, desperate. Scalp experts! So . . . he was a formerly handsome man. His face revealed what a beating he had taken. But he had asked to be beaten too, and had lent his attackers strength. That brought him to consider his character. What sort of character was it? Well, in the modern vocabulary, it was narcissistic; it was masochistic; it was anachronistic. His clinical picture was depressive—not the severest type; not a manic depressive.

There were worse cripples around. If you believed, as everyone now-adays apparently did, that man was the sick animal, then was he even spectacularly sick, exceptionally blind, extraordinarily degraded? No. Was he intelligent? His intellect would have been more effective if he had had an aggressive paranoid character, eager for power. He was jealous but not exceptionally competitive, not a true paranoiac. And what about his learning?—He was obliged to admit, now, that he was not much of a professor, either. Oh, he was earnest, he had a certain large, immature sincerity, but he might never succeed in becoming systematic. He had made a brilliant start in his Ph.D. thesis—*The State of Nature in 17th and 18th Century English and French Political Philosophy*. He had to his credit also several articles and a book, *Romanticism and Christianity*. But the rest of his ambitious projects had dried up, one after another. On the strength of his early successes he had never had difficulty in finding jobs and obtaining research grants. The Narragansett Corporation had paid him fifteen thousand dollars over a number of years to continue his studies in Romanticism. The results lay in the closet, in an old valise—eight hundred pages of chaotic arguments which had never found its focus. It was painful to think of it.

On the floor beside him were pieces of paper, and he occasionally leaned down to write.

He now set down, *Not that long disease, my life, but that long convalescence, my life. The liberal-bourgeois revision, the illusion of improvement, the poison of hope.*

He thought awhile of Mithridates, whose system learned to thrive on poison. He cheated his assassins, who made the mistake of using small doses, and was pickled, not destroyed.

Tutto fa brodo.

Resuming his self-examination, he admitted that he had been a bad husband—twice. Daisy, his first wife, he had treated miserably. Madeleine, his second, had tried to do *him* in. To his son and his daughter he was a loving but bad father. To his own parents he had been an ungrateful child. To his country, an indifferent citizen. To his brothers and his sister, affectionate but remote. With his friends, an egotist. With love, lazy. With brightness, dull. With power, passive. With his own soul, evasive.

Satisfied with his own severity, positively enjoying the hardness and factual rigor of his judgment, he lay on his sofa, his arms rising behind him, his legs extended without aim.

But how charming we remain, notwithstanding.

Papa, poor man, could charm birds from the trees, crocodiles from mud. Madeleine, too, had great charm, and beauty of person also, and a brilliant mind. Valentine Gersbach, her lover, was a charming man, too, though in a heavier, brutal style. He had a thick chin, flaming copper hair that literally gushed from his head (no Thomas Scalp Specialists for him), and he walked on a wooden leg, gracefully bending and straightening like a gondolier. Herzog himself had no small amount of charm. But his sexual powers had been damaged by Madeleine. And without the ability to attract women, how was he to recover? It was in this respect that he felt most like a convalescent.

The paltriness of these sexual struggles.

With Madeleine, several years ago, Herzog had made a fresh start in life. He had won her away from the Church—when they met, she had just been converted. With twenty thousand dollars inherited from his charming father, to please his new wife, he quit an academic position which was perfectly respectable and bought a big old house in Ludeyville, Massachusetts. In the peaceful Berkshires where he had friends (the Valentine Gersbachs) it should be easy to write his second volume on the social ideas of the Romantics.

Herzog did not leave academic life because he was doing badly. On the contrary, his reputation was good. His thesis had been influential and was translated into French and German. His early book, not much noticed when it was published, was now on many reading lists, and the younger generation of historians accepted it as a model of the new sort of history, "history that interests *us*"— personal, *engagée*—and looks at the past with an intense need for contemporary relevance. As long as Moses was married to Daisy, he had led the perfectly ordinary life of an assistant professor, respected and stable. His first work showed by objective research what Christianity was to Romanticism. In the second he was becoming tougher, more assertive, more ambitious. There was a great deal of ruggedness, actually, in his character. He had a strong will and a talent for polemics, a taste for the philosophy of history. In marrying Madeleine and resigning from the university (because she thought he should), digging in at Ludeyville, he showed a taste and talent also for danger and extremism, for heterodoxy, for ordeals, a fatal attraction to the "City of Destruction." What he planned was a history which really took into account the revolutions and mass convulsions of the twentieth century, accepting, with de Tocqueville, the universal and durable development of the equality of conditions, the progress of democracy.

But he couldn't deceive himself about this work. He was beginning seriously to distrust it. His ambitions received a sharp check. Hegel was giving him a great deal of trouble. Ten years earlier he had been certain he understood his ideas on consensus and civility, but something had gone wrong. He was distressed, impatient, angry. At the same time, he and his wife were behaving very peculiarly. She was dissatisfied. At first, she hadn't wanted him to be an ordinary professor, but she changed her mind after a year in the country. Madeleine considered herself too young, too intelligent, too vital, too sociable to be buried in the remote Berkshires. She decided to finish her graduate studies in Slavonic languages. Herzog wrote to Chicago about jobs. He had to find a position for Valentine Gersbach, too. Valentine was a radio announcer, a disk-jockey in Pittsfield. You couldn't leave people like Valentine and Phoebe stuck in this mournful countryside, alone, Madeleine said. Chicago was chosen because Herzog had grown up there, and was well-connected. So he taught courses in the Downtown College and Gersbach became educational director of an FM station in the Loop. The house near Ludeyville was closed up—twenty thousand dollars' worth of house, with books and English bone china and new appliances abandoned to the spiders, the moles, and the field mice—Papa's hard-earned money!

The Herzogs moved to the Midwest. But after about a year of this new Chicago life, Madeleine decided that she and Moses couldn't make it after all—she wanted a divorce. He had to give it, what could he do? And the divorce was painful. He was in love with Madeleine; he couldn't bear to leave his little daughter. But Madeleine refused to be married to him, and people's wishes have to be respected. Slavery is dead.

The strain of the second divorce was too much for Herzog. He felt he was going to pieces—breaking up—and Dr. Edvig, the Chicago psychiatrist who treated both Herzogs, agreed that perhaps it was best for Moses to leave town. He came to an understanding with the dean of the Downtown College that he might come back when he was feeling better, and on money borrowed from his brother Shura he went to Europe. Not everyone threatened with a crackup can manage to go to Europe for relief. Most people have to keep on working; they report daily, they still ride the subway. Or else they drink, they go to the movies and sit there suffering. Herzog ought to have been grateful. Unless you are utterly exploded, there is always something to be grateful for. In fact, he was grateful.

He was not exactly idle in Europe, either. He made a cultural tour for the Narragansett Corporation, lecturing in Copenhagen, Warsaw, Cracow, Berlin, Belgrade, Istanbul, and Jerusalem. But in March when he came to Chicago again his condition was worse than it had been in November. He told his dean that it would probably be better for him to stay in New York. He did not see Madeleine during his visit. His behavior was so strange and to her mind so menacing, that she warned him through Gersbach not to come near the house on Harper Avenue. The police had a picture of him and would arrest him if he was seen in the block.

It was now becoming clear to Herzog, himself incapable of making plans, how well Madeleine had prepared to get rid of him. Six weeks before sending him away, she had had him lease a house near the Midway at two hundred dollars a month. When they moved in, he built shelves, cleared the garden, and repaired the garage door; he put up the storm windows. Only a week before she demanded a divorce, she had his things cleaned and pressed, but on the day he left the house, she flung them all into a carton which she then dumped down the cellar stairs. She needed more closet space. And other things happened, sad, comical, or cruel, depending on one's point of view. Until the very last day, the tone of Herzog's relations with Madeleine was quite serious—that is, ideas, personalities, issues were respected and discussed. When she broke the news to him, for instance, she expressed herself with dignity, in that lovely, masterful style of hers. She had thought it over from every angle, she said, and she had to accept defeat. They could not make the grade together. She was prepared to shoulder some of the blame. Of course, Herzog was not entirely unprepared for this. But he had really thought matters were improving.

All this happened on a bright, keen fall day. He had been in the back yard putting in the storm windows. The first frost had already caught the tomatoes. The grass was dense and soft, with the peculiar beauty it gains when the cold days come and the gossamers lie on it in the morning; the dew is thick and lasting. The tomato vines had blackened and the red globes had burst.

He had seen Madeleine at the back window upstairs, putting June down for her nap, and later he heard the bath being run. Now she was calling from the kitchen door. A gust from the lake made the framed glass tremble in Herzog's arms. He propped it carefully against the porch and took off his canvas gloves but not his beret, as though he sensed that he would immediately go on a trip.

Madeleine hated her father violently, but it was not irrelevant that the old man was a famous impresario—sometimes called the American Stanislavsky. She had prepared the event with a certain theatrical genius of her own. She wore black stockings, high heels, a lavender dress with Indian brocade from Central America. She had on her opal earrings, her bracelets, and she was perfumed; her hair was combed with a new, clean part and her large eyelids shone with a bluish cosmetic. Her eyes were blue but the depth of the color was curiously affected by the variable tinge of the whites. Her nose, which descended in a straight elegant line from her brows, worked slightly when she was peculiarly stirred. To Herzog even this tic was precious. There was a flavor of subjugation in his love for Madeleine. Since she was domineering, and since he loved her, he had to accept the flavor that was given. In this confrontation in the untidy parlor, two kinds of egotism were present, and Herzog from his sofa in New York now contemplated them—hers in triumph (she had prepared a great moment, she was about to do what she longed most to do, strike a blow) and his egotism in abeyance, all converted into passivity. What he was about to suffer, he deserved; he had sinned long and hard; he had earned it. This was it.

In the window on glass shelves there stood an ornamental collection of small glass bottles, Venetian and Swedish. They came with the house. The sun now caught them. They were pierced with the light. Herzog saw the waves, the threads of color, the spectral intersecting bars, and especially a great blot of flaming white on the center of the wall above Madeleine. She was saying, "We can't live together any more."

Her speech continued for several minutes. Her sentences were well formed. This speech had been rehearsed and it seemed also that he had been waiting for the performance to begin.

Theirs was not a marriage that could last. Madeleine had never loved him. She was telling him that. "It's painful to have to say I never loved you. I never will love you, either," she said. "So there's no point in going on."

Herzog said, "I do love you, Madeleine."

Step by step, Madeleine rose in distinction, in brilliance, in insight.

small mirror, the graying hair, the wrinkles of amusement and bitterness. Through the slats of the blind he looked instead at the brown rocks of the park, speckled with mica, and at the optimistic leaping green of June. It would tire soon, as leaves broadened and New York deposited its soot on the summer. It was, however, especially beautiful now, vivid in all particulars—the twigs, the small darts and subtly swelling shapes of green. Beauty is not a human invention. Dr. Emmerich, stooped but energetic, examined him, sounded his chest and back, flashed the light in his eyes, took his blood, felt his prostate gland, wired him for the electrocardiograph.

"Well, you are a healthy man—not twenty-one, but strong."

Herzog heard this with satisfaction, of course, but still he was faintly unhappy about it. He had been hoping for some definite sickness which would send him to a hospital for a while. He would not have to look after himself. His brothers, who had given up on him, more or less, would rally to him then and his sister Helen might come to take care of him. The family would meet his expenses and pay for Marco and June. That was out, now. Apart from the little infection he had caught in Poland, his health was sound, and even that infection, now cured, had been nonspecific. It might have been due to his mental state, to depression and fatigue, not to Wanda. For one horrible day he had thought it was gonorrhea. He must write to Wanda, he thought as he pulled his shirttails forward, buttoned his sleeves. *Chère Wanda*, he began, *Bonnes nouvelles. T'en seras contente*. It was another of his shady love affairs in French. For what other reason had he ground away at his Frazer and Squair in high school, and read Rousseau and de Maistre in college? His achievements were not only scholarly but sexual. And were those achievements? It was his pride that must be satisfied. His flesh got what was left over.

"Then what is the matter with you?" said Dr. Emmerich. An old man, hair grizzled like his own, face narrow and witty, looked up into his eyes. Herzog believed he understood his message. The doctor was telling him that in this decaying office he examined the truly weak, the desperately sick, stricken women, dying men. Then what did Herzog want with him? "You seem very excited," Emmerich said.

"Yes, that's it. I am excited."

"Do you want Miltown? Snakeroot? Do you have insomnia?"

Her color grew very rich, and her brows, and that Byzantine nose of hers, rose, moved; her blue eyes gained by the flush that kept deepening, rising from her chest and her throat. She was in an ecstasy of consciousness. It occurred to Herzog that she had beaten him so badly, her pride was so fully satisfied, that there was an overflow of strength into her intelligence. He realized that he was witnessing one of the very greatest moments of her life.

"You should hold on to that feeling," she said. "I believe it's true. You do love me. But I think you also understand what a humiliation it is to me to admit defeat in this marriage. I've put all I had into it. I'm crushed by this."

Crushed? She had never looked more glorious. There was an element of theater in those looks, but much more of passion.

And Herzog, a solid figure of a man, if pale and suffering, lying on his sofa in the lengthening evening of a New York spring, in the background the trembling energy of the city, a sense and flavor of river water, a stripe of beautifying and dramatic filth contributed by New Jersey to the sunset, Herzog in the coop of his privacy and still strong in the body (his health was really a sort of miracle; he had done his best to be sick) pictured what might have happened if instead of listening so intensely and thoughtfully he had hit Madeleine in the face. What if he had knocked her down, clutched her hair, dragged her screaming and fighting around the room, flogged her until her buttocks bled. What if he had! He should have torn her clothes, ripped off her necklace, brought his fists down on her head. He rejected this mental violence, sighing. He was afraid he was really given in secret to this sort of brutality. But suppose even that he had told *her* to leave the house. After all, it was *his* house. If she couldn't live with him, why didn't she leave? The scandal? There was no need to be driven away by a little scandal. It would have been painful, grotesque, but a scandal was after all a sort of service to the community. Only it had never entered Herzog's mind, in that parlor of flashing bottles, to stand his ground. He still thought perhaps that he could win by the appeal of passivity, of personality, win on the ground of being, after all, Moses—Moses Elkanah Herzog—a good man, and Madeleine's particular benefactor. He had done everything for her—everything!

"Have you discussed this decision with Doctor Edvig?" he said. "What does he think?"

"What difference could his opinion make to me? He can't tell me what to do. He can only help me understand. . . . I went to a lawyer," she said.

"Which lawyer?"

"Well, Sandor Himmelstein. Because he is a buddy of yours. He says you can stay with him until you make your new arrangements."

The conversation was over, and Herzog returned to the storm windows in the shadow and green damp of the back yard—to his obscure system of idiosyncrasies. A person of irregular tendencies, he practiced the art of circling among random facts to swoop down on the essentials. He often expected to take the essentials by surprise, by an amusing stratagem. But nothing of the sort happened as he maneuvered the rattling glass, standing among the frost-scorched drooping tomato vines tied to their stakes with strips of rags. The plant scent was strong. He continued with the windows because he couldn't allow himself to feel crippled. He dreaded the depths of feeling he would eventually have to face, when he could no longer call upon his eccentricities for relief.

In his posture of collapse on the sofa, arms abandoned over his head and legs stretched away, lying with no more style than a chimpanzee, his eyes with greater than normal radiance watched his own work in the garden with detachment, as if he were looking through the front end of a telescope at a tiny clear image.

That suffering joker.

Two points therefore: He knew his scribbling, his letter-writing, was ridiculous. It was involuntary. His eccentricities had him in their power.

There is someone inside me. I am in his grip. When I speak of him I feel him in my head, pounding for order. He will ruin me.

It has been reported, he wrote, *that several teams of Russian Cosmonauts have been lost; disintegrated, we must assume. One was heard calling "SOS—world SOS." Soviet confirmation has been withheld.*

Dear Mama, As to why I haven't visited your grave in so long . . .

Dear Wanda, Dear Zinka, Dear Libbie, Dear Ramona, Dear Sono, I need help in the worst way. I am afraid of falling apart. Dear Edvig, the fact is that madness also has been denied me. I don't know why I should write to you at all. Dear Mr. President, Internal Revenue regulations will turn us into a nation of bookkeepers. The life of every citizen is becoming a business. This, it seems to me, is one of

the worst interpretations of the meaning of human life history has ever seen. Man's life is not a business.

And how shall I sign this? thought Moses. Indignant citizen? Indignation is so wearing that one should reserve it for the main injustice.

Dear Daisy, he wrote to his first wife, *I know it's my turn to visit Marco in camp on Parents' Day but this year I'm afraid my presence might disturb him. I have been writing to him, and keeping up with his activities. It is unfortunately true, however, that he blames me for the breakup with Madeleine and feels I have deserted also his little half-sister. He is too young to understand the difference between the two divorces.* Here Herzog asked himself whether it would be appropriate to discuss the matter further with Daisy and, picturing to himself her handsome and angry face as she read his as yet unwritten letter, he decided against this. He continued, *I think it would be best for Marco not to see me. I have been sick—under the doctor's care.* He noted with distaste his own trick of appealing for sympathy. A personality had its own ways. A mind might observe them without approval. Herzog did not care for his own personality, and at the moment there was apparently nothing he could do about its impulses. *Rebuilding my health and strength gradually*—as a person of sound positive principles, modern and liberal, news of his progress (if true) should please her. As the victim of those impulses she must be looking in the paper for his obituary.

The strength of Herzog's constitution worked obstinately against his hypochondria. Early in June, when the general revival of life troubles many people, the new roses, even in shop windows, reminding them of their own failures, of sterility and death, Herzog went to have a medical checkup. He paid a visit to an elderly refugee, Dr. Emmerich, on the West Side, facing Central Park. A frowzy doorman with an odor of old age about him, wearing a cap from a Balkan campaign half a century gone, let him into the crumbling vault of the lobby. Herzog undressed in the examining room—a troubled, dire green; the dark walls seemed swollen with the disease of old buildings in New York. He was not a big man but he was sturdily built, his muscles developed by the hard work he had done in the country. He was vain of his muscles, the breadth and strength of his hands, the smoothness of his skin, but he saw through this too, and he feared being caught in the part of the aging, conceited handsome man. Old fool, he called himself, glancing away from the

"Not seriously," said Herzog. "My thoughts are shooting out all over the place."

"Do you want me to recommend a psychiatrist?"

"No, I've had all the psychiatry I can use."

"Then what about a holiday? Take a young lady to the country, the seashore. Do you still have the place in Massachusetts?"

"If I want to reopen it."

"Does your friend still live up there? The radio announcer. What is the name of the big fellow with red hair, with the wooden leg?"

"Valentine Gersbach is his name. No, he moved to Chicago when I—when we did."

"He's a very amusing man."

"Yes. Very."

"I heard of your divorce—who told me? I am sorry about it."

Looking for happiness—ought to be prepared for bad results.

Emmerich put on his Ben Franklin eyeglasses and wrote a few words on the file card. "The child is with Madeleine in Chicago, I suppose," said the doctor.

"Yes—"

Herzog tried to get Emmerich to reveal his opinion of Madeleine. She had been his patient, too. But Emmerich would say nothing. Of course not; a doctor must not discuss his patients. Still, an opinion might be construed out of the glances he gave Moses.

"She's a violent, hysterical woman," he told Emmerich. He saw from the old man's lips that he was about to answer; but then Emmerich decided to say nothing, and Moses, who had an odd habit of completing people's sentences for them, made a mental note about his own perplexing personality.

A strange heart. I myself can't account for it.

He now saw that he had come to Emmerich to accuse Madeleine, or simply to talk about her with someone who knew her and could take a realistic view of her.

"But you must have other women," said Emmerich. "Isn't there somebody? Do you have to eat dinner alone tonight?"

Herzog had Ramona. She was a lovely woman, but with her too there were problems, of course—there were bound to be problems. Ramona was a businesswoman, she owned a flower shop on Lexington Avenue. She was not young—probably in her thirties; she wouldn't tell Moses her exact age—but she was extremely attractive, slightly foreign, well-educated. When she inherited the business she was getting her M.A. at Columbia in art history. In fact, she was enrolled in Herzog's evening course. In principle, he opposed affairs with students, even with students like Ramona Donsell, who were obviously made for them.

Doing all the things a wild man does, he noted, *while remaining all the while an earnest person. In frightful earnest.*

Of course it was just this earnestness that attracted Ramona. Ideas excited her. She loved to talk. She was an excellent cook, too, and knew how to prepare shrimp Arnaud, which she served with Pouilly Fuissé. Herzog had supper with her several nights a week. In the cab passing from the drab lecture hall to Ramona's large West Side apartment, she had said she wanted him to feel how her heart was beating. He reached for her wrist, to take her pulse, but she said, "We are not young children, Professor," and put his hand elsewhere.

Within a few days Ramona was saying that this was no ordinary affair. She recognized, she said, that Moses was in a peculiar state, but there was something about him so dear, so loving, so healthy, and basically so steady—as if, having survived so many horrors, he had been purged of neurotic nonsense—that perhaps it had been simply a question of the right woman, all along. Her interest in him quickly became serious, and he consequently began to worry about her, to brood. He said to her a few days after his visit to Emmerich that the doctor had advised him to take a holiday. Ramona then said, "Of course you need a holiday. Why don't you go to Montauk? I have a house there, and I could come out weekends. Perhaps we could stay together all of July."

"I didn't know you owned a house," said Herzog.

"It was up for sale a few years ago, and it was really too big for me, alone, but I had just divorced Harold, and I needed a diversion."

She showed him colored slides of the cottage. With his eye to the viewer, he said, "It's very pretty. All those flowers." But he felt heavy-hearted—dreadful.

"One can have a marvelous time there. And you really ought to get some cheerful summer clothes. Why do you wear such drab things? You still have a youthful figure."

"I lost weight last winter, in Poland and Italy."

"Nonsense—why talk like that! You know you're a good-looking man. And you even take pride in being one. In Argentina they'd call you *macho*—masculine. You like to come on meek and tame, and cover up the devil that's in you. Why put that little devil down? Why not make friends with him—well, why not?"

Instead of answering, he wrote mentally, *Dear Ramona—Very dear Ramona. I like you very much—dear to me, a true friend. It might even go farther. But why is it that I, a lecturer, can't bear to be lectured? I think your wisdom gets me. Because you have the complete wisdom. Perhaps to excess. I do not like to refuse correction. I have a lot to be corrected about. Almost everything. And I know good luck when I see it. . . .* This was the literal truth, every word of it. He did like Ramona.

She came from Buenos Aires. Her background was international—Spanish, French, Russian, Polish, and Jewish. She had gone to school in Switzerland and still spoke with a slight accent, full of charm. She was short, but had a full, substantial figure, a good round seat, firm breasts (all these things mattered to Herzog; he might think himself a moralist but the shape of a woman's breasts mattered greatly). Ramona was unsure of her chin but had confidence in her lovely throat, and so she held her head fairly high. She walked with quick efficiency, rapping her heels in energetic Castilian style. Herzog was intoxicated by this clatter. She entered a room provocatively, swaggering slightly, one hand touching her thigh, as though she carried a knife in her garter belt. It seemed to be the fashion in Madrid, and it delighted Ramona to come on playfully in the role of a tough Spanish broad—*una navaja en la liga;* she taught him the expression. He thought often of that imaginary knife when he watched her in her underthings, which were extravagant and black, a strapless contrivance called the Merry Widow that drew in the waist and trailed red ribbons below. Her thighs were short, but deep and white. The skin darkened where it was compressed by the elastic garment. And silky tags hung down, and garter buckles. Her eyes were brown, sensitive and shrewd, erotic and calculating. She knew what she was up to. The warm odor, the downy arms, the fine bust and excellent white teeth and slightly bowed legs—they all worked. Moses, suffering, suffered in style. His luck never entirely deserted him. Perhaps he was luckier than he knew. Ramona tried to tell him so. "That bitch did you a favor," she said. "You'll be far better off."

Moses! he wrote, *winning as he weeps, weeping as he wins. Evidently can't believe in victories.*

Hitch your agony to a star.

But at the silent moment at which he faced Ramona he wrote, incapable of replying except by mental letter, *You are a great comfort to me. We are dealing with elements more or less stable, more or less controllable, more or less mad. It's true. I have a wild spirit in me though I look meek and mild. You think that sexual pleasure is all this spirit wants, and since we are giving him that sexual pleasure, then why shouldn't everything be well?*

Then he realized suddenly that Ramona had made herself into a sort of sexual professional (or priestess). He was used to dealing with vile amateurs lately. *I didn't know that I could make out with a true sack artist.*

But is that the secret goal of my vague pilgrimage? Do I see myself to be after long blundering an unrecognized son of Sodom and Dionysus—an Orphic type? (Ramona enjoyed speaking of Orphic types.) A petit-bourgeois Dionysian?

He noted: *Foo to all those categories!*

"Perhaps I will buy some summer clothes," he answered Ramona.

I do like fine apparel, he went on. *I used to rub my patent-leather shoes with butter, in early childhood. I overheard my Russian mother calling me "Krasavitz." And when I became a gloomy young student, with a soft handsome face, wasting my time in arrogant looks, I thought a great deal about trousers and shirts. It was only later, as an academic, that I became dowdy. I bought a gaudy vest in the Burlington Arcade last winter, and a pair of Swiss boots of the type I see now the Village fairies have adopted. Heartsore? Yes,* he further wrote, *and dressed-up, too. But my vanity will no longer give me much mileage and to tell you the truth I'm not even greatly impressed with my own tortured heart. It begins to seem another waste of time.*

Soberly deliberating, Herzog decided it would be better not to accept Ramona's offer. She was thirty-seven or thirty-eight years of age, he shrewdly reckoned, and this meant that she was looking for a husband. This, in itself, was not wicked, or even funny. Simple and general human conditions prevailed among the most seemingly sophisticated. Ramona had not learned those erotic monkeyshines in a manual, but in adventure, in confusion, and at times probably with a sinking heart, in brutal and often alien embraces. So now she must yearn for stability. She wanted to give her heart once and for all, and level with a good man, become Herzog's wife and quit being an easy lay. She often had a sober look. Her eyes touched him deeply.

Never idle, his mind's eye saw Montauk—white beaches, flashing light, glossy breakers, horseshoe crabs perishing in their armor, sea robins and blowfish. Herzog longed to lie down in his bathing trunks, and warm his troubled belly on the sand. But how could he? To accept too many favors from Ramona was dangerous. He might have to pay with his freedom. Of course he didn't need that freedom now; he needed a rest. Still, after resting, he might want his freedom again. He wasn't sure of that, either. But it was a possibility.

A holiday will give me more strength to bring to my neurotic life.

Still, Herzog considered, he did look terrible, caved-in; he was losing more hair, and this rapid deterioration he considered to be a surrender to Madeleine and Gersbach, her lover, and to all his enemies. He had more enemies and hatreds than anyone could easily guess from his thoughtful expression.

The night-school term was coming to an end, and Herzog convinced himself that his wisest move was to get away from Ramona too. . . .

> *Herzog goes to Chicago to visit his little daughter, but first stops to see his widowed stepmother and pick up a few remembrances of his father.*

He sat near the very spot where Father Herzog, the year before his death, had threatened to shoot him. The cause of his rage was money. Herzog was broke, and asked his father to underwrite a loan. The old man questioned him narrowly, about his job, his expenses, his child. He had no patience with Moses. At that time I was living in Philadelphia, alone, making my choice (it was no choice!) between Sono and Madeleine. Perhaps he had even heard I was about to be converted to Catholicism. Someone started such a rumor; it may have been Daisy. I was in Chicago then because Papa had sent for me. He wanted to tell me about the changes in his will. Day and night, he thought how he would divide his estate, and thought accordingly of each of us, what we deserved, how we would use it. At odd times, he'd telephone and tell me I had to come right away. I'd sit up all night on the train. And he'd take me into a corner and say, "I want you to hear, once and for all. Your brother Willie is an honest man. When I die, he'll do as we agreed." "I believe it, Papa."

But he lost his temper every time, and when he wanted to shoot me it was because he could no longer bear the sight of me, that look of mine, the look of conceit or proud trouble. The elite look. I don't blame him, thought Moses as Taube slowly and lengthily described her ailments. Papa couldn't bear such an expression on the face of his youngest son. I aged. I wasted myself in stupid schemes, *liberating* my spirit. His heart ached angrily because of me. And Papa was not like some old men who become blunted toward their own death. No, his despair was keen and continual. And Herzog again was pierced with pain for his father.

He listened awhile to Taube's account of her cortisone treatments. Her large, luminous, tame eyes, the eyes that had domesticated Father Herzog, were not watching Moses now. They gazed at a point beyond him and left him free to recall those last days of Father Herzog. We walked to Montrose together to buy cigarettes. It was June, warm like this, the weather bright. Papa wasn't exactly making sense. He said he should have divorced the Widow Kaplitzky ten years ago, that he had hoped to enjoy the last years of his life—his Yiddish became more crabbed and quaint in these conversations—but he had brought his iron to a cold forge. *A kalte kuzhnya, Moshe. Kein fire.* Divorce was impossible because he owed her too much money. "But you have money now, don't you?" said Herzog, blunt with him. His father stopped, staring into his face. Herzog was stunned to see in full summer light how much disintegration had already taken place. But the remaining elements, incredibly vivid, had all their old power over Moses—the straight nose, the furrow between the eyes, the brown and green colors in those eyes. "I need my money. Who'll provide for me—you? I may bribe the Angel of Death a long time yet." Then he bent his knees a little—Moses read that old signal; he had a lifetime of skill in interpreting his father's gestures: those bent knees meant that something of great subtlety was about to be revealed. "I don't know when I'll be delivered," Father Herzog whispered. He used the old Yiddish term for a woman's confinement—*kimpet.* Moses did not know what to say, and his answering voice was not much above a whisper. "Don't torment yourself, Papa." The horror of this second birth, into the hands of death, made his eyes shine, and his lips silently pressed together. Then Father Herzog said, "I have to sit down, Moshe. The sun is too hot for me." He did, suddenly, appear very flushed, and Moses supported him, eased him down on the cement embankment of a lawn. The old man's look was now one of injured male pride. "Even I feel the heat today," said Moses. He placed himself between his father and the sun.

"I may go next month to St. Joe for the baths," Taube was saying. "To the Whitcomb. It's a nice place."

"Not alone?"

"Ethel and Mordecai want to go."

"Oh . . . ?" He nodded, to keep her going. "How is Mordecai?"

"How can he be in his age?" Moses was attentive until she was well started and then he returned to his father. They had had lunch on the back porch that day, and that was where the quarrel began. It had seemed to Moses, perhaps, that he was here as a prodigal son, admitting the worst and asking the old man's mercy, and so Father Herzog saw nothing except a stupid appeal in his son's face—incomprehensible. "Idiot!" was what the old man had shouted. "Calf!" Then he saw the angry demand underlying Moses' look of patience. "Get out! I leave you nothing! Everything to Willie and Helen! You . . . ? Croak in a flophouse." Moses rising, Father Herzog shouted, "Go. And don't come to my funeral."

"All right, maybe I won't."

Too late, Tante Taube had warned him to keep silent, raising her brows—she had still had brows then. Father Herzog rose, stumbling from the table, his face distorted, and ran to get his pistol.

"Go, go! Come back later. I'll call you," Taube had whispered to Moses, and he, confused, reluctant, burning, stung because his misery was not recognized in his father's house (this monstrous egotism making its peculiar demands)—he reluctantly got up from the table. "Quick, quick!" Taube tried to get him to the front door, but old Herzog overtook them with the pistol.

He cried out, "I'll kill you!" And Herzog was startled not so much by this threat, which he did not believe, as by the return of his father's strength. In his rage he recovered it briefly, though it might cost him his life. The strained neck, the grinding of his teeth, his frightening color, even the military Russian strut with which he lifted the gun—these were better, thought Herzog, than his sinking down during a walk to the store. Father Herzog was not made to be pitiful.

"Go, go," said Tante Taube. Moses was weeping then.

"Maybe you'll die first," Father Herzog shouted.

"Papa!"

Half hearing Tante Taube's slow description of Cousin Mordecai's approaching retirement, Herzog grimly recovered the note of that cry. *Papa—Papa.* You lout! The old man in his near-demented way was trying to act out the manhood you should have had. Coming to his house with that Christianized smirk of the long-suffering son. Might as well have been an outright convert, like Mady. He should have pulled the trigger. Those looks were agony to him. He deserved to be spared, in his old age.

And then there was Moses with puffy weeping eyes, in the street, waiting for his cab, while Father Herzog hastily walked up and back before these windows, staring at him in agony of spirit—yes, you got that out of him. Walking quickly there, back and forth in his hasty style, dropping his weight on the one heel. The pistol thrown down. Who knows whether Moses shortened his life by the grief he gave him. Perhaps the stimulus of anger lengthened it. He could not die and leave this half-made Moses yet.

They were reconciled the following year. And then more of the same. And then . . . death.

"Should I make a cup of tea?" said Tante Taube.

"Yes, please, I'd like that if you feel up to it. And I also want to look in Papa's desk."

"Pa's desk? It's locked. You want to look in the desk? Everything belongs to you children. You could take the desk when I die."

"No, no!" he said, "I don't need the desk itself, but I was passing from the airport and thought I'd see how you were. And now that I'm here, I'd like to have a look in the desk. I know you don't mind."

"You want something, Moshe? You took your Mama's silver coin case the last time."

He had given it to Madeleine.

"Is Papa's watch chain still in there?"

"I think Willie took it."

He frowned with concentration. "Then what about the rubles?" he asked. "I'd like them for Marco."

"Rubles?"

"My grandfather Isaac bought Czarist rubles during the Revolution, and they've always been in the desk."

"In the desk? I surely never seen them."

"I'd like to look, while you make a cup of tea, Tante Taube. Give me the key."

"The key . . . ?" Questioning him before, she had spoken more quickly, but now she receded again into slowness, raising a mountain of dilatory will in his way.

"Where do you keep it?"

"Where? Where did I put it? Is it in Pa's dresser? Or somewheres else? Let me remember. That's how I am now, it's hard to remember. . . ."

"I know where it is," he said, suddenly rising.

"You know where it is? So where is it?"

"In the music box, where you always used to keep it."

"In the music . . . ? Pa took it from there. He locked up my social-security checks when they came. He said all the money *he* should have. . . ."

Moses knew he had guessed right. "Don't bother, I'll get it," he said. "If you'll put the kettle on. I'm very thirsty. It's been a hot, long day."

He helped her to rise, holding her flaccid arm. He was having his way—a poor sort of victory and filled with dangerous consequences. Going forward without her, he entered the bedroom. His father's bed had been removed. Hers stood alone with its ugly bedspread—some material that reminded him of a coated tongue. He breathed the old spice, the dark, heavy air, and lifted the lid of the music box. In this house he had only to consult his memory to find what he wanted. The mechanism released its little notes as the cylinder turned within, the small spines picking out the notes from *Figaro*. Moses was able to supply the words:

> *Nel momento*
> *Della mia cerimonia*
> *Io rideva di me*
> *Senza saperlo.*

His fingers recognized the key.

Old Taube in the dark outside the bedroom said, "Did you found it?"

He answered, "It's here," and spoke in a low, mild voice, not to make matters worse. The house was hers, after all. It was rude to invade it. He was not ashamed of this, he only recognized with full objectivity that it was not right. But it had to be done.

"Do you want me to put the kettle on?"

"No, a cup of tea I can still make."

He heard her slow steps in the passage. She was going to the kitchen. Herzog quickly made for the small sitting room. The drapes were drawn. He turned on the lamp beside the desk. In seeking the switch he tore the ancient silk of the shade releasing a fine dust. The name of this color was old rose—he felt certain of it. He opened the cherry-wood secretary, braced the wide leaf on its runners, drawing them out from either side. Then he went back and shut the door, first making sure Taube had reached the kitchen. In the drawers he recognized each article—leather, paper, gold. Swift and tense, veins standing out on his head, and tendons on his hands, he groped, and found what he was looking for—Father Herzog's pistol. An old pistol, the barrel nickel-plated. Papa had bought it to keep on Cherry Street, in the railroad yards. Moses flipped the gun open. There were two bullets. This was it, then. He rapidly clicked it shut and put it in his pocket. There it made too large a bulge. He took out his wallet and replaced it with the gun. The wallet he buttoned in his hip pocket.

Now he began to search for those rubles. Those he found in a small compartment with old passports, ribbons sealed in wax, like gobs of dried blood. *La bourgeoise Sarah Herzog avec ses enfants, Alexandre huit ans, Hélène neuf ans et Guillaume trois ans,* signed by Count Adlerberg *Gouverneur de St. Petersbourg.* The rubles were in a large billfold—his playthings of forty years ago. Peter the Great in a rich coat of armor, and a splendid imperial Catherine. Lamplight revealed the watermarks. Recalling how he and Willie used to play casino for these stakes, Herzog uttered one of his short laughs, then made a nest of these large bills in his pocket for the pistol. He thought it must be less conspicuous now.

"You got what you want?" Taube asked him in the kitchen.

"Yes." He put the key on the enameled metal table.

He knew it was not proper that he should think her expression sheeplike. This figurative habit of his mind crippled his judgment, and was likely to ruin him some day. Perhaps the day was near; perhaps this night his soul would be required of him. The gun weighed on his chest. But the protuberant lips, great eyes, and pleated mouth *were* sheeplike, and they warned him he was taking too many chances with destruction. Taube, a veteran survivor, to be heeded, had fought the grave to a standstill, balking death itself by her slowness. All had decayed but her shrewdness and her incredible patience; and in Moses she saw Father Herzog again, nervy and hasty, impulsive, suffering. His eye twitched as he bent toward her in the kitchen. She muttered, "You got a lot of trouble? Don't make it worser, Moshe."

"There's no trouble, Tante. I have business to take care of. . . . I don't think I can wait for tea, after all."

"I put out Pa's cup for you."

Moses drank tap water from his father's teacup.

"Good-by, Tante Taube, keep well." He kissed her forehead.

"Remember I helped you?" she said. "You shouldn't forget. Take care, Moshe."

He left by the back door; it made departure simpler. Honeysuckle grew along the rainspout, as in his father's time, and fragrant in the evening—almost too rich. Could any heart become quite petrified?

.   .   .   .   .

. . . The familiar odor of the fresh water, bland but also raw, reached him as he sped south. It did not seem illogical that he should claim the privilege of insanity, violence, having been made to carry the rest of it—name-calling and gossip, railroading, pain, even exile in Ludeyville. That property was to have been his madhouse. Finally, his mausoleum. But they had done something else to Herzog—unpredictable. It's not everyone who gets the opportunity to kill with a clear conscience. They had opened the way to justifiable murder. They deserved to die. He had a right to kill them. They would even know why they were dying; no explanation necessary. When he stood before them they would have to submit. Gersbach would only hang his head, with tears for himself. Like Nero—*Qualis artifex pereo.* Madeleine would shriek and curse. Out of hatred, the most powerful element in her life, stronger by far than any other power or motive. In spirit she was his murderess, and therefore he was turned loose, could shoot or choke without remorse. He felt in his arms and in his fingers, and to the core of his heart, the sweet exertion of strangling— horrible and sweet, an orgiastic rapture of inflicting death. He was sweating violently, his shirt wet and cold under his arms. Into his mouth came a taste of copper, a metabolic poison, a flat but deadly flavor.

When he reached Harper Avenue he parked around the corner, and entered the alley that passed behind the house. Grit spilled on the concrete; broken glass and gravelly ashes made his steps loud. He went carefully. The back fences were old here. Garden soil spilled under the slats, and shrubs and vines came over their tops. Once more he saw open honeysuckle. Even rambler roses, dark red in the dusk. He had to cover his face when he passed the garage because of the loops of briar that swung over the path from the sloping roof. When he stole into the yard he stood still until he could see his way. He must not stumble over a toy, or a tool. A fluid had come into his eyes—very clear, only somewhat distorting. He wiped it away with fingertips, and blotted, too, with the lapel of his coat. Stars had come out, violet points framed in roof shapes, leaves, strut wires. The yard was visible to him now. He saw the clothesline—Madeleine's underpants and his daughter's little shirts and dresses, tiny stockings. By the light of the kitchen window he made out a sandbox in the grass, a new red sandbox with broad ledges to sit on. Stepping nearer, he looked into the kitchen. Madeleine was there! He stopped breathing as he watched her. She was wearing slacks and a blouse fastened with a broad red leather and brass belt he had given her. Her smooth hair hung loose as she moved between the table and the sink, cleaning up after dinner, scraping dishes in her own style of abrupt efficiency. He studied her straight profile as she stood at the sink, the flesh under her chin as she concentrated on the foam in the sink, tempering the water. He could see the color in her cheeks, and almost the blue of her eyes. Watching, he fed his rage, to keep it steady, up to full strength. She was not likely to hear him in the yard because the storm windows had not been taken down—not, at least, those he had put up last fall at the back of the house.

He moved into the passageway. Luckily the neighbors were not at home, and he did not have to worry about their lights. He had had his look at Madeleine. It was his daughter he wanted to see now. The dining room was unoccupied—after-dinner emptiness, Coke bottles, paper napkins. Next was the bathroom window, set higher than the rest. He remembered, however, that he had used a cement block to stand on, trying to take out the bathroom screen until he had discovered there was no storm window to replace it. The screen was still in, therefore. And the block? It was exactly where he had left it, among the lilies of the valley on the left side of the path. He moved it into place, the scraping covered by the sound of water in the tub, and stood on it, his side pressed to the building. He tried to muffle the sound of his breathing, opening his mouth. In the rushing water with floating toys his daughter's little body shone. His child! Madeleine had let her black hair grow longer, and now it was tied up for the bath with a rubber band. He melted with tenderness for her, putting his hand over his mouth to cover any sound emotion might cause him to make. She raised her face to speak to someone he could not see. Above the flow of water he heard her say something but could not understand the words. Her face was the Herzog face, the large dark eyes *his* eyes, the nose his father's, Tante Zipporah's, his brother Willie's nose, and the mouth his own. Even the bit of melancholy in her beauty—that was his mother. It was Sarah Herzog, pensive, slightly averting her face as she considered the life about her. Moved, he watched her, breathing with open mouth, his face half covered by his hand. Flying beetles passed him. Their heavy bodies struck the screen but did not attract her notice.

Then a hand reached forward and shut off the water—a man's hand. It was Gersbach. He was going to bathe Herzog's daughter! Gersbach! His waist was now in sight. He came into view stalking beside the old-fashioned round tub, bowing, straightening, bowing—his Venetian hobble, and then, with great trouble, he began to kneel, and Herzog saw his chest, his head, as he arranged himself. Flattened to the wall, his chin on his shoulder, Herzog saw Gersbach roll up the sleeves of his paisley sports shirt, put back his thick glowing hair, take the soap, heard him say, not unkindly, "Okay, cut out the monkey-shines," for Junie was giggling, twisting, splashing, dimpling, showing her tiny white teeth, wrinkling her nose, teasing. "Now hold still," said Gersbach. He got into her ears with the washrag as she screamed, cleaned off her face, the nostrils, wiped her mouth. He spoke with authority, but affectionately and with grumbling smiles and occasionally with laughter he bathed her—soaped, rinsed, dipping water in her toy boats to rinse her back as she squealed and twisted. The man washed her tenderly. His look, perhaps, was false. But he had no *true* expressions, Herzog thought. His face was all heaviness, sexual meat. Looking down his open shirt front, Herzog saw the hair-covered heavy soft flesh of Gersbach's breast. His chin was thick, and like a stone ax, a brutal weapon. And then there were his sentimental eyes, the thick crest of hair, and that hearty voice with its peculiar fraudulence and grossness. The hated traits were all there. But see how he was with June, scooping the water on her playfully, kindly. He let her wear her mother's flowered shower cap, the rubber petals spreading on the child's head. Then Gersbach ordered her to stand, and she stooped slightly to allow him to wash her little cleft. Her father stared at this. A pang went through him, but it was quickly done. She sat again. Gersbach ran fresh water on her, cumbersomely rose and opened the bath towel. Steady and thorough, he dried her, and then with a large puff he powdered her. The child jumped up and down with delight. "Enough of this wild stuff," said Gersbach. "Put on those p-j's now."

She ran out. Herzog still saw faint wisps of powder that floated

over Gersbach's stooping head. His red hair worked up and down
He was scouring the tub. Moses might have killed him now. His left
hand touched the gun, enclosed in the roll of rubles. He might have
shot Gersbach as he methodically salted the yellow sponge rectangle
with cleansing powder. There were two bullets in the chamber. . . .
But they would stay there. Herzog clearly recognized that. Very softly
he stepped down from his perch, and passed without sound through
the yard again. He saw his child in the kitchen, looking up at Mady,
asking for something, and he edged through the gate into the alley.
Firing this pistol was nothing but a thought.

> After a visit to a museum with his daughter, Herzog gets into a
> car accident and is taken, with the child, to a police station. A
> Negro sergeant questions him.

"Okay, you," he then said to Moses. He put on his Ben Franklin
spectacles, two colonial tablets in thin gold frames. He took up his
pen.
"Name?"
"Herzog—Moses."
"Middle initial?"
"E. Elkanah."
"Address?"
"Not living in Chicago."
The sergeant, fairly patient, said again, "Address?"
"Ludeyville, Mass., and New York City. Well, all right, Ludeyville,
Massachusetts. No street number."
"This your child?"
"Yes, sir. My little daughter June."
"Where does she live?"
"Here in the city, with her mother, on Harper Avenue."
"You divorced?"
"Yes, sir. I came to see the child."
"I see. You want to put her down?"
"No, officer—sergeant," he corrected himself, smiling agreeably.
"You're bein' booked, Moses. You weren't drunk were you? Did
you have a drink today?"
"I had one last night, before I went to sleep. Nothing today. Do
you want me to take an alcohol test?"
"It won't be necessary. There's no traffic charge against you. We're
booking you on account of this gun."

Herzog pulled down his daughter's dress.

"It's just a souvenir. Like the money."

"What kind of dough is this?"

"It's Russian, from World War I."

"Just empty your pockets, Moses. Put your stuff down so's I can check it over."

Without protest, he laid down his money, his notebooks, pens, the scrap of handkerchief, his pocket comb, and his keys.

"Seems to me you've got a mess of keys, Moses."

"Yes, sir, but I can identify them all."

"That's okay. There's no law against keys, exceptin' if you're a burglar."

"The only Chicago key is this one with the red mark on it. It's the key to my friend Asphalter's apartment. He's supposed to meet me at four o'clock, by the Rosenwald Museum. I've got to get her to him."

"Well, it ain't four, and you ain't goin' anywhere yet."

"I'd like to phone and head him off. Otherwise, he'll stand waiting."

"Well, now, Moses, why ain't you bringin' the kid straight back to her mother?"

"You see . . . we're not on speaking terms. We've had too many scraps."

"Appears to me you might be scared of her."

Herzog was briefly resentful. The remark was calculated to provoke him. But he couldn't afford to be angry now. "No, sir, not exactly."

"Then maybe she's scared of you."

"This is how we arranged it, with a friend to go between. I haven't seen the woman since last autumn."

"Okay, we'll call your buddy and the kid's mama, too."

Herzog exclaimed, "Oh, don't call her!"

"No?" The sergeant gave him an odd smile, and rested for a moment in his chair as if he had gotten from him what he wanted. "Sure, we'll bring her down here and see what she's got to say. If she's got a complaint in against you, why, it's worse than just illegal possession of firearms. We'll have you on a bad charge, then."

"There isn't any complaint, sergeant. You can check that in the files without making her come all this way. I'm the support of this child, and never miss a check. That's all Mrs. Herzog can tell you."

"Who'd you buy this revolver from?"

There it was again, the natural insolence of the cops. He was being goaded. But he kept himself steady.

"I didn't buy it. It belonged to my father. That and the Russian rubles."

"You're just sentimental?"

"That's right. I'm a sentimental s.o.b. Call it that."

"You sentimental about these here, too?" He tapped each of the bullets, one, two. "All right, we'll make those phone calls. Here, Jim, write the names and numbers."

He spoke to the copper who had brought Herzog in. He had been standing by, fat-cheeked, teasing the bristles of his mustache with his nail, pursing his lips.

"You may as well take my address book, the red one there. Bring it back, please. My friend's name is Asphalter."

"And the other name's Herzog," said the sergeant. "On Harper Avenue, ain't it?"

Moses nodded. He watched the heavy fingers turning the pages of his Parisian leather address book with its scribbles and blots. "It'll put me in bad if you notify the child's mother," he said, making a last attempt to persuade the sergeant. "Why wouldn't it be the same to you if my friend Asphalter came here?"

"Go on, Jim."

The Negro marked the places with red pencil, and went. Moses made a special effort to keep a neutral look—no defiance, no special pleading, nothing of the slightest personal color. He remembered that he once believed in the appeal of a direct glance, driving aside differences of position, accident, one human being silently opening his heart to another. The recognition of essence by essence. He smiled inwardly at this. Sweet dreams, those! If he tried looking into his eyes, the sergeant would throw the book at him. So Madeleine was coming. Well, let her come. Perhaps that was what he wanted after all, a chance to confront her. Straight-nosed and pale, he looked intently at the floor. June changed her position in his arms, stirring the pain in his ribs. "Papa's sorry, sweetheart," he said. "Next time we'll go see the dolphins. Maybe the sharks were bad luck."

"You can sit down if you want," said the sergeant. "You look a little weak in the legs, Moses."

"I'd like to phone my brother to send his lawyer. Unless I don't need a lawyer. If I have to post a bond . . ."

"You'll have to post one, but I can't say how big, yet. Plenty of bondsmen settin' here." He motioned with the back of his hand, or with a wag of his wrist, and Moses turned and saw all sorts of people ranged behind him, along the walls. In fact, there were two men, he now noticed, loitering near, bondsmen by their natty appearance. He neutrally recognized that they were sizing him up as a risk. They had already seen his plane ticket, his keys, pens, rubles, and his wallet. His own car, wrecked on the Drive, would have secured a small bond. But a rented car? A man from out of state, in a dirty seersucker, no necktie? He didn't look good for a few hundred bucks. If it's no more than that, he reflected, I can probably swing it without bothering Will, or Shura. Some fellows always make a nice impression. I never had that ability. Due to my feelings. A passionate heart, a bad credit risk. Asked to make this practical judgment on myself, I wouldn't make it any differently.

It came back to him how he used to be banished to left field when sides were chosen in the sand lot, and when the ball came and he missed it because he was musing about something everyone would cry out, *"Hey! Ikey-Moe. Butterfingers! Fucky-knuckles! You lookin' at the butterflies? Ikey-Fishbones. Fishbones!"* Although silent, he participated in the derision.

His hands were clasped about his daughter's heart, which was beating quickly and lightly.

"Now, Moses, why you been carryin' a loaded gun. To shoot somebody?"

"Of course not. And, please, sergeant, I don't like the kid to hear such things."

"You the one that brought it along, not me. Maybe you just wanted to scare somebody. You sore at somebody?"

"No, sergeant, I was only going to make a paperweight of it I forgot to take out the bullets, but that's because I don't know much about guns so it didn't occur to me. Will you let me make a phone call?"

"By and by. I ain't ready to. Sit down while I take care of other business. You sit and wait for the kid's mama to come."

"Could I get a container of milk for her?"

"Give Jim, here, two bits. He'll fetch it."

"With a straw, eh, June? You'd like to drink it with a straw." She nodded and Herzog said, "Please, a straw with it, if you don't mind."

"Papa?"

"Yes, June."

"You didn't tell me about the most-most."

For an instant he did not remember. "Ah," he said, "you mean that club in New York where people are the most of everything."

"That's the story."

She sat between his knees on the chair. He tried to make more room for her. "There's this association that people belong to. They're the most of every type. There's the hairiest bald man, and the baldest hairy man."

"The fattest thin lady."

"And the thinnest fat woman. The tallest dwarf and the smallest giant. They're all in it. The weakest strong man, and the strongest weak man. The stupidest wise man and the smartest blockhead. Then they have things like crippled acrobats, and ugly beauties."

"And what do they do, Papa?"

"On Saturday night they have a dinner-dance. They have a contest."

"To tell each other apart."

"Yes, sweetheart. And if you can tell the hairiest bald man from the baldest hairy man, you get a prize."

Bless her, she enjoyed her father's nonsense, and he must amuse her. She leaned her head on his shoulder and smiled, drowsy, with small teeth.

.   .   .   .   .

. . . Madeleine arrived. She came in, saying, "Where is my child . . .!" Then she saw June on Herzog's lap and crossed the room quickly. "Come here to me, baby!" She lifted the milk container and put it aside, and took up the girl in her arms. Herzog felt the blood beating in his eardrums, and a great pressure at the back of the head. It was necessary that Madeleine should see him, but her look was devoid of intimate recognition. Coldly she turned from him, her brow twitching. "Is the child all right?" she said.

The sergeant motioned to the Vice Squad to make way. "She's fine. If she had even a scratch on her we'd have taken her to Michael Reese." Madeleine examined June's arms, her legs, felt her with nervous hands. The sergeant beckoned to Moses. He came forward, and he and Mady faced each other across the desk.

She wore a light blue linen suit and her hair fell loose behind her. The word to describe her conduct was *masterful*. Her heels had made a commanding noise clearly audible in this buzzing room. Herzog

took a long look at her blue-eyed, straight, Byzantine profile, the
small lips, the chin that pressed on the flesh beneath. Her color was
deep, a sign with her that consciousness was running high. He
thought he could make out a certain thickening in her face—incipient
coarseness. He hoped so. It was only right that some of Gersbach's
grossness should rub off on her. Why shouldn't it? He observed that
she was definitely broader behind. He imagined what clutching and
rubbing was the cause of that. Uxorious business—but that was not
the right word. . . . Amorous.

"Is this the girl's daddy, lady?"

Madeleine still refused to grant him a look of recognition. "Yes,"
she said, "I divorced him. Not long ago."

"Does he live in Massachusetts?"

"I don't know where he lives. It's none of my business."

Herzog marveled at her. He could not help admiring the perfection
of her self-control. She never hesitated. When she took the milk from
Junie she knew precisely where to drop the container, though she
had been only an instant in the room. By now she had certainly
made an inventory of all the objects on the desk, including the
rubles, and the gun, of course. She had never seen it, but she could
identify the Ludeyville keys by the round magnetic clasp of the ring,
and she would realize the pistol belonged to him. He knew her ways
so well, all her airs, the patrician style, the tic of her nose, the crazy
clear hauteur of the eyes. As the sergeant questioned her, Moses, in
his slightly dazed but intense way, unable to restrain associations,
wondered whether she still gave off those odors of feminine secre-
tions—the dirty way she had with her. That personal sweet and sour
fragrance of hers, and her fire-blue eyes, her spiky glances and her
small mouth ready with any wickedness would never again have the
same power over him. Still, it gave him a headache merely to look at
her. The pulses in his skull were quick and regular, like the tappets
of an engine beating in their film of dark oil. He saw her with great
vividness—the smoothness of her breast, bared by the square-cut
dress, the smoothness of her legs, Indian brown. Her face, especially
the forehead, was altogether too smooth, too glabrous for his taste.
The whole burden of her severity was carried there. She had what the
French called *le front bombé*; in other terms, a pedomorphic forehead. Ultimately unknowable, the processes behind it. See, Moses?
We don't know one another. Even that Gersbach, call him any name
you like, charlatan, psychopath, with his hot phony eyes and his

clumsy cheeks, with the folds. He was unknowable. And I myself, the same. But hard ruthless action taken against a man is the assertion by evildoers that he is fully knowable. They put me down, ergo they claimed final knowledge of Herzog. They *knew* me! And I hold with Spinoza (I hope he won't mind) that to demand what is impossible for any human being, to exercise power where it can't be exercised, is tyranny. Excuse me, therefore, sir and madam, but I reject your definitions of me. Ah, this Madeleine is a strange person, to be so proud but not well wiped—so beautiful but distorted by rage—such a mixed mind of pure diamond and Woolworth glass. And Gersbach who sucked up to me. For the symbiosis of it. Symbiosis and trash. And she, as sweet as cheap candy, and just as reminiscent of poison as chemical sweet acids. But I make no last judgment. That's for them, not me. I came to do harm, I admit. But the first bloodshed was mine, and so I'm out of this now. Count me out. Except in what concerns June. But for the rest, I withdraw from the whole scene as soon as I can. Good-by to all.

"Well, he give you a hard time?" Herzog who had been listening subliminally heard the sergeant put this question.

He said tersely to Madeleine, "Watch it, if you please. Let's not have unnecessary trouble."

She ignored this. "He bothered me, yes."

"He make any threats?"

Herzog waited, tense, for her reply. She would consider the support money—the rent. She was canny, a superbly cunning, very canny woman. But there was also the violence of her hatred, and that hatred had a fringe of insanity.

"No, not directly to me. I haven't seen him since last October."

"To who, then?" The sergeant pressed her.

Madeleine evidently would do what she could to weaken his position. She was aware that her relations with Gersbach offered grounds for a custody suit and she would therefore make the most of his present weakness—his idiocy. "His psychiatrist," she said, "saw fit to warn me."

"Saw fit! Of what!" said Herzog.

Still she spoke only to the sergeant. "He said he was concerned. Doctor Edvig is his name if you want to talk to him. He felt it necessary to advise me . . ."

"Edvig is a sucker—he's a fool," said Herzog.

Madeleine's color was very high, her throat flushed, like pink—like rose quartz, and the curious tinge had come into her eyes. He knew what this moment was to her—happiness! Ah, yes, he said to himself, Ikey-Fishbones has dropped another pop fly in left field. The other team is scoring—clearing all bases. She was making brilliant use of error.

"Do you recognize this gun?" The sergeant held it in his yellow palm, turning it over with delicate fingers like a fish—a perch.

The radiance of her look as it rested on the gun was deeper than any sexual expression he had ever seen on her face. "It's his, isn't it?" she said. "The bullets, too?" He recognized the hard clear look of joy in her eyes. Her lips were pressed shut.

"He had it on him. Do you know it?"

"No, but I'm not surprised."

Moses was watching June now. Her face was clouded again; she seemed to frown.

"Did you ever file a complaint against Moses, here?"

"No," said Mady. "I didn't actually do that." She took a sharp breath. She was about to plunge into something.

"Sergeant," said Herzog. "I told you there was no complaint. Ask her if I've ever missed a single support check."

Madeleine said, "I did give his photograph to the Hyde Park police."

He warned her that she was going too far. "Madeleine!" he said.

"Shut it up, Moses," said the sergeant. "What was that for, lady?"

"In case he prowled around the house. To alert them."

Herzog shook his head, partly at himself. He had made the kind of mistake today that belonged to an earlier period. As of today it was no longer characteristic. But he had to pay an earlier reckoning. When will you catch up with yourself! he asked himself. When will that day come!

"Did he ever prowl?"

"He was never seen, but I know damn well he did. He's jealous and a troublemaker. He has a terrible temper."

"You never signed a complaint, though?"

"No. But I expect to be protected from any sort of violence."

Her voice went up sharply, and as she spoke, Herzog saw the sergeant take a new look at her, as if he was beginning to make out her haughty peculiarities at last. He picked up the Ben Franklin glasses with the tablet-shaped lenses. "There ain't going to be any violence, lady."

Yes, Moses thought, he's beginning to see how it is. "I never intended to use that gun except to hold papers down," he said.

Madeleine now spoke to Herzog for the first time, pointing with a rigid finger to the two bullets and looking him in the eyes. "One of those was for me, wasn't it!"

"You think so? I wonder where you get such ideas? And who was the other one for?" He was quite cool as he said this, his tone was level. He was doing all he could to bring out the hidden Madeleine, the Madeleine he knew. As she stared at him her color receded and her nose began to move very slightly. She seemed to realize that she must control her tic and the violence of her stare. But by noticeable degrees her face became very white, her eyes smaller, stony. He believed he could interpret them. They expressed a total will that he should die. This was infinitely more than ordinary hatred. It was a vote for his nonexistence, he thought. He wondered whether the sergeant was able to see this. "Well, who do you think that second imaginary shot was for?"

She said no more to him, only continued to stare in the same way.

"That'll be all now, lady. You can take your child and go."

"Good-by, June," said Moses. "You go home now. Papa'll see you soon. Give us a kiss, now, on the cheek." He felt the child's lips. Over her mother's shoulder, June reached out and touched him. "God bless you." He added, as Madeleine strode away, "I'll be back."

"I'll finish bookin' you now, Moses."

"I've got to post bond? How much?"

"Three hundred. American, not this stuff."

"I wish you'd let me make a call."

As the sergeant silently directed him to take one of his own dimes, Moses still had the time to note what a powerful police-face he had. He must have Indian blood—Cherokee, perhaps, or Osage; an Irish ancestor or two. His sallow gold skin with heavy seams descending, the austere nose and prominent lips for impassivity, and the many separate, infinitesimal gray curls on his scalp for dignity. His rugged fingers pointed to the phone booth.

Herzog was tired, dragged out, as he dialed his brother, but far from downcast. For some reason he believed he had done well. He was running true to form, yes; more mischief; and Will would have to bail him out. Still, he was not at all heavy-hearted but, on the contrary, felt rather free. Perhaps he was too tired to be glum. That may have been it, after all—the metabolic wastes of fatigue (he was fond of these physiological explanations; this one came from Freud's essay on Mourning and Melancholia) made him temporarily light-hearted, even gay.

"Yes."

"Will Herzog in?"

Each recognized the other's voice.

"Mose!" said Will.

Herzog could do nothing about the feelings stirred by hearing Will. They came to life suddenly at hearing the old tone, the old name. He loved Will, Helen, even Shura, though his millions had made him remote. In the confinement of the metal booth the sweat burst out instantly on his neck.

"Where've you been, Mose? The old woman called last night. I couldn't sleep afterwards. Where are you?"

"Elya," said Herzog, using his brother's family name, "don't worry. I haven't done anything serious, but I'm down at Eleventh and State."

"At Police Headquarters?"

"Just a minor traffic accident. No one hurt. But they're holding me for three hundred bucks bond, and I haven't got the money on me."

"For heaven's sake, Mose. Nobody's seen you since last summer. We've been worried sick. I'll be right down."

He waited in the cell with two other men. One was drunk and sleeping in his soiled skivvies. The other was a Negro boy, not old enough to shave. He wore a fawn-colored expensive suit and brown alligator shoes. Herzog said hello, but the boy chose not to answer. He stuck to his own misery, and looked away. Moses was sorry for him. He leaned against the bars, waiting. The wrong side of the bars—he felt it with his cheek. And here were the toilet bowl, the bare metal bunk, and the flies on the ceiling. This, Herzog realized, was not the sphere of *his* sins. He was merely passing through. Out in the streets, in American society, that was where he did his time. He sat down calmly on the bunk. Of course, he thought, he'd leave Chicago immediately, and he'd come back only when he was ready to do June good, genuine good. No more of this hectic, heart-rent, theatrical window-peering; no more collision, fainting, you-fight-'im-'e-cry encounters, confrontations. The drone of trouble coming from the cells and corridors, the bad smell of headquarters, the wretchedness of faces, the hand that turned the key of no better hope than

the hand of this stuporous sleeper in his urine-stained underpants—
the man who has eyes, nostrils, ears, let him hear, smell, see. The man
who has intellect, heart, let him consider.

Sitting as comfortably as the pain in his ribs would permit, Herzog
even jotted a few memoranda to himself. They were not very coherent or even logical, but they came quite naturally to him. This
was how Moses E. Herzog worked, and wrote on his knee with cheerful eagerness, *Clumsy, inexact machinery of civil peace. Paleotechnic,
as the man would say. If a common primal crime is the origin of
social order, as Freud, Róheim et cetera believe, the band of brothers
attacking and murdering the primal father, eating his body, gaining
their freedom by a murder and united by a blood wrong, then there
is some reason why jail should have these dark, archaic tones. Ah,
yes, the wild energy of the band of brothers, soldiers, rapists, etc.
But all that is nothing but metaphor. I can't truly feel I can attribute
my blundering to this thick unconscious cloud. This primitive blood-
daze.*

*The dream of man's heart, however much we may distrust and
resent it, is that life may complete itself in significant pattern. Some
incomprehensible way. Before death. Not irrationally but incompre-
hensibly fulfilled. Spared by these clumsy police guardians, you get
one last chance to know justice. Truth.*

Dear Edvig, he noted quickly. *You gave me good value for my
money when you explained that neuroses might be graded by the
inability to tolerate ambiguous situations. I have just read a certain
verdict in Madeleine's eyes, "For cowards, Not-being!" Her disorder
is super-clarity. Allow me modestly to claim that I am much better
now at ambiguities. I think I can say, however, that I have been
spared the chief ambiguity that afflicts intellectuals, and this is that
civilized individuals hate and resent the civilization that makes their
lives possible. What they love is an imaginary human situation invented by their own genius and which they believe is the only true
and the only human reality. How odd! But the best-tréated, most
favored and intelligent part of any society is often the most ungrateful. Ingratitude, however, is its social function. Now there's an ambiguity for you! . . . Dear Ramona, I owe you a lot. I am fully aware
of it. Though I may not be coming back to New York right away, I intend to keep in touch. Dear God! Mercy! My God! Rachaim olenu
. . . melekh maimis. . . . Thou King of Death and Life . . . !*

His brother observed, as they were leaving police headquarters,
"You don't seem too upset."

"No, Will."

Above the sidewalk and the warm evening gloom the sky carried the long gilt trails of jets, and the jumbled lights of honky-tonks, just north of 12th Street, were already heaving up and down, a pale mass in which the street seemed to end.

"How do you feel?"

"I feel fine," said Herzog. "How do I look?"

His brother said discreetly, "You could do with a little rest. Why don't we stop and have you looked at by my doctor."

"I don't think that's necessary. This small cut on my head stopped bleeding almost immediately."

"But you've been holding your side. Don't be a fool, Mose."

Will was an undemonstrative man, substantial, shrewd, quiet, shorter than his brother but with thicker, darker hair. In a family of passionately expressive people like Father Herzog and Aunt Zipporah Will had developed a quieter, observant, reticent style.

"How's the family, Will—the kids?"

"Finc . . . What have you been doing, Moses?"

"Don't go by appearances. There's less to worry about than meets the eye. I'm really in very good shape. Do you remember when we got lost at Lake Wandawega? Floundering in the slime, cutting our feet on those reeds? That was really dangerous. But this is nothing."

"What were you doing with that gun?"

"You know I'm no more capable of firing it at someone than Papa was. You took his watch chain, didn't you? I remembered those old rubles in his drawer and then I took the revolver too. I shouldn't have. At least I ought to have emptied it. It was just one of those dumb impulses. Let's forget it."

"All right," said Will. "I don't mean to embarrass you. That's not the point."

"I know what it is," Herzog said. "You're worried." He had to lower his voice to control it. "I love you too, Will."

"Yes, I know that."

"But I haven't behaved very sensibly. From your standpoint . . . Well, from any reasonable standpoint. I brought Madeleine to your office so you could see her before I married her. I could tell you didn't approve. I didn't approve of her myself. And she didn't approve of me."

"Why did you marry her?"

"God ties all kinds of loose ends together. Who knows why! He couldn't care less about my welfare, or my ego, that thing of value.

All you can say is, 'There's a red thread spliced with a green, or blue, and I wonder why.' And then I put all that money into the house in Ludeyville. That was simply crazy."

"Perhaps not," said Will. "It is real estate, after all. Have you tried to sell it?" Will had great faith in real estate.

"To whom? How?"

"List it with an agent. Maybe I'll come and look it over."

"I'd be grateful," said Herzog. "I don't think any buyer in his right mind would touch it."

"But let me call Doctor Ramsberg, Mose, and have him examine you. Then come home and have some dinner with us. It would be a treat for the family."

"When could you come to Ludeyville?"

"I've got to go to Boston next week. Then Muriel and I were going out to the Cape."

"Come by way Ludeyville. It's close to the Turnpike. I'd consider it a tremendous favor. I have to sell that house."

"Have dinner with us, and we can talk about it."

"Will—no. I'm not up to it. Just look at me. I'm stinking dirty, and I'd upset everyone. Like a lousy lost sheep." He laughed. "No, some other time when I'm feeling a little more normal. I look as if I'd just arrived in this country. A D.P. Just as we arrived from Canada at the old Baltimore and Ohio Station. On the Michigan Central. God, we were filthy with the soot."

William did not share his brother's passion for reminiscence. He was an engineer and technologist, a contractor and builder; a balanced, reasonable person, he was pained to see Moses in such a state. His lined face was hot, uneasy; he took a handkerchief from the inner pocket of his well-tailored suit and pressed it to his forehead, his cheeks, under the large Herzog eyes.

"I'm sorry, Elya," said Moses, more quietly.

"Well—"

"Let me straighten myself up a bit. I know you're concerned about me. But that's just it. I'm sorry to worry you. I really am all right."

"Are you?" Will sadly looked at him.

"Yes, I'm at an awful disadvantage here—dirty, foolish, just bailed out. It's just ridiculous. Everything will look a lot different in the East, next week. I'll meet you in Boston, if you like. When I've got myself in better order. There's nothing you can do now but treat me like a jerk—a child. And that's not right."

"I'm not making any judgments on you. You don't have to come home with me, if that embarrasses you. Although we're your own family . . . But there's my car, across the street." He gestured toward his dark-blue Cadillac. "Just come along to the doctor so I can be sure you weren't hurt in the accident. Then you can do what you think best."

"All right. Fair enough. There's nothing wrong. I'm sure of it."

He was not entirely surprised, however, to learn that he had a broken rib. "No lung puncture," the doctor said. "Six weeks or so in tape. And you'll need two or three stitches in your head. That's the whole story. No heavy lifting, straining, chopping, or other violent exercise. Will tells me you're a country gentleman. You've got a farm in the Berkshires? An estate?"

The doctor with grizzled backswept hair and small keen eyes looked at him with thin-lipped amusement.

"It's in bad repair. Miles from a synagogue," said Herzog.

"Ha, your brother likes to kid," Dr. Ramsberg said. Will faintly smiled. . . .

Herzog goes back to the house in Ludeyville.

Herzog's present loneliness did not seem to count because it was so consciously cheerful. He peered through the chink in the lavatory where he used to hide away with his ten-cent volume of Dryden and Pope, reading "I am His Highness' dog at Kew" or "Great wits to madness sure are near allied." There, in the same position as in former years, was the rose that used to give him comfort—as shapely, as red (as nearly "genital" to his imagination) as ever. Some good things do recur. He was a long time peering at it through the meeting of masonry and lumber. The same damp-loving grasshoppers (giant orthoptera) still lived in this closet of masonry and plywood. A struck match revealed them. Among the pipes.

It was odd, the tour he made through his property. In his own room he found the ruins of his scholarly enterprise strewn over the desk and the shelves. The windows were so discolored as to seem stained with iodine, and the honeysuckles outside had almost pulled the screens down. On the sofa he found proof that the place was indeed visited by lovers. Too blind with passion to hunt in darkness for the bedrooms. But they'll get curvature of the spine using Madeleine's horsehair antiques. For some reason it particularly pleased Herzog that his room should be the one chosen by the youth of the

village—here among bales of learned notes. He found girls' hairs on
the curving armrests, and tried to imagine bodies, faces, odors.
Thanks to Ramona he had no need to be greatly envious, but a
little envy of the young was quite natural too. On the floor was one
of his large cards with a note in which he had written *To do justice
to Condorcet* . . . He hadn't the heart to read further and turned it
face down on the table. For the present, anyway, Condorcet would
have to find another defender. In the dining room were the precious
dishes that Tennie wanted, crimson-rimmed bone china, very handsome. He wouldn't need that. The books, muslin-covered, were un-
disturbed. He lifted the cloth and glanced at them with no special
interest. Visiting the little bathroom, he was entertained to see the
lavish fittings Madeleine had bought at Sloane's, scalloped silver
soap dishes and flashing towel racks too heavy for the plaster, even
after they were fastened with toggle bolts. They were drooping now.
The shower stall, for Gersbach's convenience—the Gersbachs had
had no shower in Barrington—was thoughtfully equipped with a
handrail. "If we're going to put it in, let's make it so Valentine can
use it," Mady had said. Ah, well—Moses shrugged. A strange odor
in the toilet bowl attracted his notice next, and raising the wooden
lid he found the small beaked skulls and other remains of birds who
had nested there after the water was drained, and then had been entombed by the falling lid. He looked grimly in, his heart aching somewhat at this accident. There must be a broken window in the attic,
he inferred from this, and other birds nesting in the house. Indeed,
he found owls in his bedroom, perched on the red valances, which
they had streaked with droppings. He gave them every opportunity
to escape, and, when they were gone, looked for a nest. He found the
young owls in the large light fixture over the bed where he and Madeleine had known so much misery and hatred. (Some delight as well.)
On the mattress much nest litter had fallen—straws, wool threads,
down, bits of flesh (mouse ends) and streaks of excrement. Unwilling
to disturb these flat-faced little creatures, Herzog pulled the mattress
of his marriage bed into June's room. He opened more windows, and
the sun and country air at once entered. He was surprised to feel such
contentment . . . contentment? Whom was he kidding, this was joy!
For perhaps the first time he felt what it was to be free from Madeleine. Joy! His servitude was ended, and his heart released from its
grisly heaviness and encrustation. Her absence, no more than her
absence itself, was simply sweetness and lightness of spirit. To her,

at 11th and State, it had been happiness to see him in trouble, and to him in Ludeyville it was a delicious joy to have her removed from his flesh, like something that had stabbed his shoulders, his groin, made his arms and his neck lame and cumbersome. *My dear sage and imbecilic Edvig. It may be that the remission of pain is no small part of human happiness. In its primordial and stupider levels, where now and then a closed valve opens again. . . .* Those strange lights, Herzog's brown eyes, so often overlaid with the film or protective chitin of melancholy, the by-product of his laboring brain, shone again.

It cost him some effort to turn over the mattress on the floor of June's old room. He had to move aside some of her cast-off toys and kiddie furniture, a great stuffed blue-eyed tiger, the potty chair, a red snowsuit, perfectly good. He recognized also the grandmother's bikini, shorts, and halters, and, among other oddities, a washrag which Phoebe had stitched with his initials, a birthday present, a possible hint that his ears were not clean. Beaming, he pushed it aside with his foot. A beetle escaped from beneath. Herzog, lying under the open window with the sun in his face, rested on the mattress. Over him the great trees, the spruces in the front yard, showed their beautiful jaggedness and sent down the odor of heated needles and gum.

It was here, until the sun passed from the room, that he began in earnest, from tranquil fullness of heart, to consider another series of letters.

Dear Ramona. Only "Dear"? Come, Moses, open up a little. *Darling Ramona. What an excellent woman you are.* Here he paused to consider whether he should say he was in Ludeyville. In her Mercedes she could drive from New York in three hours, and it was probable that she would. God's blessing on her short but perfect legs, her solid, well-tinted breasts, and her dashing curved teeth and gypsy brows and curls. *La devoradora de hombres.* He decided, however, to date his letter Chicago and ask Lucas to remail it. What he wanted now was peace—peace and clarity. *I hope I didn't upset you by copping out. But I know you're not one of those conventional women it takes a month to appease because of a broken date. I had to see my daughter, and my son. He's at Camp Ayumah, near Cats-kill. It's turning into a busy summer. Several interesting develop-ments. I hesitate to make too many assertions yet, but at least I can admit what I never stopped asserting anyway, or feeling. The light of truth is never far away, and no human being is too negligible or corrupt to come into it.* I don't see why I shouldn't say that. *But to accept ineffectuality, banishment to personal life, confusion . . .* Why don't you try this out, Herzog, on the owls next door, those naked owlets pimpled with blue. *Since the last question, also the first one, the question of death, offers us the interesting alternatives of disintegrating ourselves by our own wills in proof of our "freedom," or the acknowledging that we owe a human life to this waking spell of existence, regardless of the void. (After all, we have no positive knowledge of that void.)*

Should I say all this to Ramona? Some women think that earnestness is wooing. She'll want a child. She'll want to breed with a man who talks to her like this. *Work. Work. Real, relevant work. . . .* He paused. But Ramona was a willing worker. According to her lights. And she loved her work. He smiled affectionately on his sunlit mattress.

Dear Marco. I've come up to the old homestead to look things over and relax a bit. The place is in pretty good shape, considering. Perhaps you'd like to spend some time here with me, only the two of us—roughing it—after camp. We'll talk about it Parents' Day. I'm looking forward to that, eagerly. Your little sister whom I saw in Chicago yesterday is very lively and as pretty as ever. She received your postcard.

Do you remember the talks we had about Scott's Antarctic Expedition, and how poor Scott was beaten to the Pole by Amundsen? You seemed interested. This is a thing that always gets me. There was a man in Scott's party who went out and lost himself to give the others a chance to survive. He was ailing, footsore, couldn't keep up any longer. And do you remember how by chance they found a mound of frozen blood, the blood of one of their slaughtered ponies, and how thankful they were to thaw and drink it? The success of Amundsen was due to his use of dogs instead of ponies. The weaker were butchered and fed to the stronger. Otherwise the expedition would have failed. I have often wondered at one thing. Hungry as they were, the dogs would sniff at the flesh of their own and back away. The skin had to be removed before they would eat it.

Maybe you and I can take a trip at Xmas to Canada just to get the feel of genuine cold. I am a Canadian, too, you know. We could visit Ste. Agathe, in the Laurentians. Expect me on the 16th, bright and early.

Dear Luke—Be so kind as to post these enclosures. I hope to hear your depression is over. I think your visions of the aunt being rescued by the fireman and of the broads playing piggy-move-up are signs of psychological resiliency. I predict your recovery. As for me. . . . As for you, thought Herzog, you will not tell him how you feel now, all this overflow! It wouldn't make him happier. Keep it to yourself if you feel exalted. Anyway, he may think you've simply gone off your nut.

But if I am out of my mind, it's all right with me.

My dear Professor Mermelstein. I want to congratulate you on a splendid book. In some matters you scooped me, you know, and I felt like hell about it—hated you one whole day for making a good deal of my work superfluous (Wallace and Darwin?). However, I well know what labor and patience went into such a work—so much digging, learning, synthesizing, and I'm all admiration. When you are ready to print a revised edition—or perhaps another book—it would be a great pleasure to talk over some of these questions. There are parts of my projected book I'll never return to. You may do what you like with those materials. In my earlier book (to which you were kind enough to refer) I devoted one section to Heaven and Hell in apocalyptic Romanticism. I may not have done it to your taste, but you ought not to have a look at the monograph by that fat natty brute Egbert Shapiro, "From Luther to Lenin, A History of Revolutionary Psychology." His fat cheeks give him a great resemblance to Gibbon. *It is a valuable piece of work. I was greatly impressed by the section called Millennarianism and Paranoia. It should not be ignored that modern power-systems do offer a resemblance to this psychosis. A gruesome and crazy book on this has been written by a man named Banowitch. Fairly inhuman, and filled with vile paranoid hypotheses such as that crowds are fundamentally cannibalistic, that people standing secretly terrify the sitting, that smiling teeth are the weapons of hunger, that the tyrant is mad for the sight of (possibly edible?) corpses about him. It seems quite true that the making of corpses has been the most dramatic achievement of modern dictators and their followers (Hitler, Stalin, etc.).* Just to see—Herzog tried this on, experimenting—whether Mermelstein didn't have a vestige of old Stalinism about him. *But this fellow Shapiro is something of an eccentric, and I mention him as an extreme case. How we all love extreme cases and apocalypses, fires, drownings, stranglings, and the rest of it. The bigger our mild, basically ethical, safe middle classes* grow the more radical excitement is in demand. Mild or moderate truthfulness or accuracy seems to have no pull at all. Just what we need now! ("When a dog is drowning, you offer him a cup of water," Papa used to say bitterly.) In any case, if you had read that chapter of mine on apocalypse and Romanticism you might have looked a little straighter at that Russian you admire so much—Isvolsky? The man who sees the souls of monads as the legions of the damned, simply atomized and pulverized, a dust storm in Hell; and warns that Lucifer must take charge of collectivized mankind, devoid of spiritual character and true personality. I don't deny this makes some sense, here and there, though I do worry that such ideas, because of the bit of suggestive truth in them, may land us in the same old suffocating churches and synagogues. I was somewhat bothered by borrowings and references which I considered "hit and run," or the use of other writers' serious beliefs as mere metaphors. For instance, I liked the section called "Interpretations of Suffering" and also the one called "Toward a Theory of Boredom." This was an excellent piece of research. But then I thought the treatment you gave Kierkegaard was fairly frivolous. I venture to say Kierkegaard meant that truth has lost its force with us and horrible pain and evil must teach it to us again, the eternal punishments of Hell will have to regain their reality before mankind turns serious once more. I do not see this. Let us set aside the fact that such convictions in the mouths of safe, comfortable people playing at crisis, alienation, apocalypse and desperation, make me sick. We must get it out of our heads that this is a doomed time, that we are waiting for the end, and the rest of it, mere junk from fashionable magazines. Things are grim enough without these shivery games. People frightening one another—a poor sort of moral exercise. But, to get to the main point, the advocacy and praise of suffering take us in the wrong direction and those of us who remain loyal to civilization must not go for it. You have to have the power to employ pain, to repent, to be illuminated, you must have the opportunity and even the time. With the religious, the love of suffering is a form of gratitude to experience or an opportunity to experience evil and change it into good. They believe the spiritual cycle can and will be completed in a man's existence and he will somehow make use of his suffering, if only in the last moments of his life, when the mercy of God will reward him with a vision of the truth, and he will die transfigured. But this is a special exercise. More commonly suffering breaks people, crushes them, and is simply un-

illuminating. You see how gruesomely human beings are destroyed by pain, when they have the added torment of losing their humanity first, so that their death is a total defeat, and then you write about "modern forms of Orphism" and about "people who are not afraid of suffering" and throw in other such cocktail-party expressions. Why not say rather that people of powerful imagination, given to dreaming deeply and to raising up marvelous and self-sufficient fictions, turn to suffering sometimes to cut into their bliss, as people pinch themselves to feel awake. I know that my suffering, if I may speak of it, has often been like that, a more extended form of life, a striving for true wakefulness and an antidote to illusion, and therefore I can take no moral credit for it. I am willing without further exercise in pain to open my heart. And this needs no doctrine or theology of suffering. We love apocalypses too much, and crisis ethics and florid extremism with its thrilling language. Excuse me, no. I've had all the monstrosity I want. We've reached an age in the history of mankind when we can ask about certain persons, "What is this Thing?" No more of that for me—no, no! I am simply a human being, more or less. I am even willing to leave the more or less in your hands. You may decide about me. You have a taste for metaphors. Your otherwise admirable work is marred by them. I'm sure you can come up with a grand metaphor for me. But don't forget to say that I will never expound suffering for anyone or call for Hell to make us serious and truthful. I even think man's perception of pain may have grown too refined. But that is another subject for lengthy treatment.

Very good, Mermelstein. Go, and sin no more. And Herzog, perhaps somewhat sheepish over this strange diatribe, rose from the mattress (the sun was moving away) and went downstairs again. He ate several slices of bread, and baked beans—a cold bean sandwich, and afterward carried outside his hammock and two lawn chairs.

Thus began his final week of letters. He wandered over his twenty acres of hillside and woodlot, composing his messages, none of which he mailed. He was not ready to pedal to the post office and answer questions in the village about Mrs. Herzog and little June. As he knew well, the grotesque facts of the entire Herzog scandal had been overheard on the party line and become the meat and drink of Ludeyville's fantasy life. He had never restrained himself on the telephone; he was too agitated. And Madeleine was far too patrician to care what the hicks were overhearing. Anyway, she had been throwing him out. It reflected no discredit on her.

Dear Madeleine—*You are a terrific one, you are! Bless you! What a creature!* To put on lipstick, after dinner in a restaurant, she would look at her reflection in a knife blade. He recalled this with delight. *And you, Gersbach, you're welcome to Madeleine. Enjoy her*—*rejoice in her. You will not reach me through her, however. I know you sought me in her flesh. But I am no longer there.*

Dear Sirs, The size and number of the rats in Panama City, when I passed through, truly astonished me. I saw one of them sunning himself beside a swimming pool. And another was looking at me from the wainscoting of a restaurant as I was eating fruit salad. Also, on an electric wire which slanted upward into a banana tree, I saw a whole rat-troupe go back and forth, harvesting. They ran the wire twenty times or more without a single collision. My suggestion is that you put birth-control chemicals in the baits. Poisons will never work (for Malthusian reasons; reduce the population somewhat and it only increases more vigorously). But several years of contraception may eliminate your rat problem.

Dear Herr Nietzsche—*My dear sir, May I ask a question from the floor?* You speak of the power of the Dionysian spirit to endure the sight of the Terrible, the Questionable, to allow itself the luxury of Destruction, to witness Decomposition. Hideousness, Evil. All this the Dionysian spirit can do because it has the same power of recovery as Nature itself. Some of these expressions, I must tell you, have a very Germanic ring. A phrase like the "luxury of Destruction" is positively Wagnerian, and I know how you came to despise all that sickly Wagnerian idiocy and bombast. Now we've seen enough destruction to test the power of the Dionysian spirit amply, and where are the heroes who have recovered from it? Nature (itself) and I are alone together, in the Berkshires, and this is my chance to understand. I am lying in a hammock, chin on breast, hands clasped, mind jammed with thoughts, agitated, yes, but also cheerful, and I know you value cheerfulness—true cheerfulness, not the seeming sanguinity of Epicureans, nor the strategic buoyancy of the heartbroken. I also know you think that deep pain is ennobling, pain which burns slow, like green wood, and there you have me with you, somewhat. But for this higher education survival is necessary. You must outlive the pain. Herzog! you must stop this quarrelsomeness and baiting of great men. No, really, Herr Nietzsche, I have great admiration for you. Sympathy. You want to make us able to live with the void. Not lie ourselves into good-naturedness, trust, ordinary middling *human considerations, but to question as has never been questioned before, relentlessly, with iron determination, into evil, through evil, past evil, accepting no abject comfort. The most absolute, the most piercing questions. Rejecting mankind as it is, that ordinary, practical, thieving, stinking, unilluminated, sodden rabble, not only the laboring rabble, but even worse the "educated" rabble with its books and concerts and lectures, its liberalism and its romantic theatrical "loves" and "passions"—it all deserves to die, it will die. Okay. Still, your extremists must survive. No survival, no Amor Fati. Your immoralists also eat meat. They ride the bus. They are only the most bus-sick travelers. Humankind lives mainly upon perverted ideas. Perverted, your ideas are no better than those of the Christianity you condemn. Any philosopher who wants to keep his contact with mankind should pervert his own system in advance to see how it will really look a few decades after adoption. I send you greetings from this mere border of grassy temporal light, and wish you happiness, wherever you are. Yours, under the veil of Maya, M.E.H.*

> Ramona turns up, visiting friends only a few miles away; Herzog invites her to dinner.

To have Ramona coming troubled him slightly, it was true. But they would eat. She would help him with the dishes, and then he'd see her to her car.

I will do no more to enact the peculiarities of life. This is done well enough without my special assistance.

Now on one side the hills lost the sun and began to put on a more intense blue color; on the other they were still white and green. The birds were very loud.

Anyway, can I pretend I have much choice? I look at myself and see chest, thighs, feet—a head. This strange organization, I know it will die. And inside—something, something, happiness . . . "Thou movest me." That leaves me no choice. Something produces intensity, a holy feeling, as oranges produce orange, as grass green, as birds heat. Some hearts put out more love and some less of it, presumably. Does it signify anything? There are those who say this product of hearts is knowledge. "Je sens mon cœur et je connais les hommes." But his mind now detached itself also from its French. *I couldn't say that, for sure. My face too blind, my mind too limited, my instincts too narrow. But this intensity, doesn't it mean anything? Is it an idiot joy that makes this animal, the most peculiar animal of all, exclaim something? And he thinks this reaction a sign, a proof, of eternity? And he has it in his breast? But I have no arguments to make about it. "Thou movest me." "But what do you want, Herzog?" "But that's just it—not a solitary thing. I am pretty well satisfied to be, to be just as it is willed, and for as long as I may remain in occupancy."*

Then he thought he'd light candles at dinner, because Ramona was fond of them. There might be a candle or two in the fuse box. But now it was time to get those bottles from the spring. The labels had washed off, but the glass was well chilled. He took pleasure in the vivid cold of the water.

Coming back from the woods, he picked some flowers for the table. He wondered whether there was a corkscrew in the drawer. Had Madeleine taken it to Chicago? Well, maybe Ramona had a corkscrew in her Mercedes. An unreasonable thought. A nail could be used, if it came to that. Or you could break the neck of the bottle as they did in old movies. Meanwhile, he filled his hat from the rambler vine, the one that clutched the rainpipe. The spines were still too green to hurt much. By the cistern there were yellow day lilies. He took some of these, too, but they wilted instantly. And, back in the darker garden, he looked for peonies; perhaps some had survived. But then it struck him that he might be making a mistake, and he stopped, listening to Mrs. Tuttle's sweeping, the rhythm of bristles. Picking flowers? He was being thoughtful, being lovable. How would it be interpreted? (He smiled slightly.) Still, he need only know his own mind, and the flowers couldn't be used; no, they couldn't be turned against him. So he did not throw them away. He turned his dark face toward the house again. He went around and entered from the front, wondering what further evidence of his sanity, besides refusing to go to the hospital, he could show. Perhaps he'd stop writing letters. Yes, that was what was coming, in fact. The knowledge that he was done with these letters. Whatever had come over him during these last months, the spell, really seemed to be passing, really going. He set down his hat, with the roses and day lilies, on the half-painted piano, and went into his study, carrying the wine bottles in one hand like a pair of Indian clubs. Walking over notes and papers, he lay down on his Récamier couch. As he stretched out, he took a long breath, and then he lay, looking at the mesh of the screen, pulled loose by vines, and listening to the steady scratching of Mrs. Tuttle's broom. He wanted to tell her to sprinkle the floor. She was raising too much dust. In a few minutes he would call down to her, "Damp it down, Mrs. Tuttle. There's water in the sink." But not just yet. At this time he had no messages for anyone. Nothing. Not a single word.

The Chosen

by CHAIM POTOK

The Chosen is one of the phenomenal best sellers of our time. The rabbi-author's first, somewhat halting, novel has had a remarkable appeal to both Jews and non-Jews; oddly enough, its Jewish content is just about as educational for one as for the other.

Unlike so many other Jewish best sellers, The Chosen is "positive" in its approach; it is filled with sound information about life in the religious ghetto, about Hasidism and its denigrators, about synagogue politics, about the problems that arise between young religion-observing Jewish boys during playtime, about the content of religious education, about rabbis and rebbes (Hebrew-school teachers), and, of course, about Jewish fathers and mothers who get their views of life not from reading mass-circulation women's magazines but from their mothers and grandmothers and, above all, from the ancient Jewish traditions.

The sections reprinted here deal with Jewish religious life on various levels, including the American level as seen in the celebrated baseball game between two teams made up of boys from opposing synagogue backgrounds. Rabbi Potok fills this amazing scene with warmth and understanding. Boys are boys, he seems to say, but he quickly shows that boys from orthodox homes have other things to think about even while they are being good pitchers and good hitters.

Part of the attraction of this novel is certainly in the seriousness of the two young men who are its proponents. Quite normal and modern, they are not obsessed with sex, sensation, or far-out experience, but rather with the profound task of discovering their vocations in the world, how best they can fulfill their places in society. Each has a sense of continuation, connected with Judaism, but must find his own route. It is heartening to recognize

*that they are more typical than not—that most young people are
still decent and serious.*

*Chaim Potok was born in New York. After graduating from
Yeshiva University, he attended the Jewish Theological Semi-
nary, and was ordained as a rabbi in 1954. Since 1965 he has
been editor of the Jewish Publication Society in Philadelphia.*

C.A.

FOR THE FIRST FIFTEEN YEARS of our lives, Danny
and I lived within five blocks of each other and neither of us knew
of the other's existence.

Danny's block was heavily populated by the followers of his father,
Russian Hasidic Jews in somber garb, whose habits and frames of
reference were born on the soil of the land they had abandoned.
They drank tea from samovars, sipping it slowly through cubes of
sugar held between their teeth; they ate the foods of their homeland,
talked loudly, occasionally in Russian, most often in a Russian Yiddish, and were fierce in their loyalty to Danny's father.

A block away lived another Hasidic sect, Jews from southern
Poland, who walked the Brooklyn streets like specters, with their
black hats, long black coats, black beards, and earlocks. These Jews
had their own rabbi, their own dynastic ruler, who could trace his
family's position of rabbinic leadership back to the time of the Ba'al
Shem Tov, the eighteenth-century founder of Hasidism, whom they
all regarded as a God-invested personality.

About three or four such Hasidic sects populated the area in which
Danny and I grew up, each with its own rabbi, its own little synagogue, its own customs, its own fierce loyalties. On a Shabbat or
festival morning, the members of each sect could be seen walking
to their respective synagogues, dressed in their particular garb, eager
to pray with their particular rabbi and forget the tumult of the week
and the hungry grabbing for money which they needed to feed their
large families during the seemingly endless Depression.

The sidewalks of Williamsburg were cracked squares of cement,
the streets paved with asphalt that softened in the stifling summers
and broke apart into potholes in the bitter winters. Many of the
houses were brownstones, set tightly together, none taller than three

or four stories. In these houses lived Jews, Irish, Germans, and some Spanish Civil War refugee families that had fled the new Franco regime before the onset of the Second World War. Most of the stores were run by gentiles, but some were owned by Orthodox Jews, members of the Hasidic sects in the area. They could be seen behind their counters, wearing black skullcaps, full beards, and long earlocks, eking out their meager livelihoods and dreaming of Shabbat and festivals when they could close their stores and turn their attention to their prayers, their rabbi, their God.

Every Orthodox Jew sent his male children to a yeshiva, a Jewish parochial school, where they studied from eight or nine in the morning to four or five in the evening. On Fridays the students were let out at about one o'clock to prepare for the Shabbat. Jewish education was compulsory for the Orthodox, and because this was America and not Europe, English education was compulsory as well—so each student carried a double burden: Hebrew studies in the mornings and English studies in the afternoons. The test of intellectual excellence, however, had been reduced by tradition and unvoiced unanimity to a single area of study: Talmud. Virtuosity in Talmud was the achievement most sought after by every student of a yeshiva, for it was the automatic guarantee of a reputation for brilliance.

Danny attended the small yeshiva established by his father. Outside of the Williamsburg area, in Crown Heights, I attended the yeshiva in which my father taught. This latter yeshiva was somewhat looked down upon by the students of other Jewish parochial schools of Brooklyn: it offered more English subjects than the required minimum, and it taught its Jewish subjects in Hebrew rather than Yiddish. Most of the students were children of immigrant Jews who preferred to regard themselves as having been emancipated from the fenced-off ghetto mentality typical of the other Jewish parochial schools in Brooklyn.

Danny and I probably would never have met—or we would have met under altogether different circumstances—had it not been for America's entry into the Second World War and the desire this bred on the part of some English teachers in the Jewish parochial schools to show the gentile world that yeshiva students were as physically fit, despite their long hours of study, as any other American student. They went about proving this by organizing the Jewish parochial schools in and around our area into competitive leagues, and once every two weeks the schools would compete against one another in a variety of sports. I became a member of my school's varsity softball team.

On a Sunday afternoon in early June, the fifteen members of my team met with our gym instructor in the play yard of our school. It was a warm day, and the sun was bright on the asphalt floor of the yard. The gym instructor was a short, chunky man in his early thirties who taught in the mornings in a nearby public high school and supplemented his income by teaching in our yeshiva during the afternoons. He wore a white polo shirt, white pants, and white sweater, and from the awkward way the little black skullcap sat perched on his round, balding head, it was clearly apparent that he was not accustomed to wearing it with any sort of regularity. When he talked he frequently thumped his right fist into his left palm to emphasize a point. He walked on the balls of his feet, almost in imitation of a boxer's ring stance, and he was fanatically addicted to professional baseball. He had nursed our softball team along for two years, and by a mixture of patience, luck, shrewd manipulations during some tight ball games, and hard fist-thumping harangues calculated to shove us into a patriotic awareness of the importance of athletics and physical fitness for the war effort, he was able to mold our original team of fifteen awkward fumblers into the top team of our league. His name was Mr. Galanter, and all of us wondered why he was not off somewhere fighting in the war.

During my two years with the team, I had become quite adept at second base and had also developed a swift underhand pitch that would tempt a batter into a swing but would drop into a curve at the last moment and slide just below the flaying bat for a strike. Mr. Galanter always began a ball game by putting me at second base and would use me as a pitcher only in very tight moments, because, as he put it once, "My baseball philosophy is grounded on the defensive solidarity of the infield."

That afternoon we were scheduled to play the winning team of another neighborhood league, a team with a reputation for wild, offensive slugging and poor fielding. Mr. Galanter said he was counting upon our infield to act as a solid defensive front. Throughout the warm-up period, with only our team in the yard, he kept thumping his right fist into his left palm and shouting at us to be a solid defensive front.

"No holes," he shouted from near home plate. "No holes, you hear? Goldberg, what kind of solid defensive front is that? Close in.

A battleship could get between you and Malter. That's it. Schwartz, what are you doing, looking for paratroops? This is a ball game. The enemy's on the ground. That throw was wide, Goldberg. Throw it like a sharpshooter. Give him the ball again. Throw it. Good. Like a sharpshooter. Very good. Keep the infield solid. No defensive holes in this war."

We batted and threw the ball around, and it was warm and sunny, and there was the smooth, happy feeling of the summer soon to come, and the tight excitement of the ball game. We wanted very much to win, both for ourselves and, more especially, for Mr. Galanter, for we had all come to like his fist-thumping sincerity. To the rabbis who taught in the Jewish parochial schools, baseball was an evil waste of time, a spawn of the potentially assimilationist English portion of the yeshiva day. But to the students of most of the parochial schools, an inter-league baseball victory had come to take on only a shade less significance than a top grade in Talmud, for it was an unquestioned mark of one's Americanism, and to be counted a loyal American had become increasingly important to us during these last years of the war.

So Mr. Galanter stood near home plate, shouting instructions and words of encouragement, and we batted and tossed the ball around. I walked off the field for a moment to set up my eyeglasses for the game. I wore shell-rimmed glasses, and before every game I would bend the earpieces in so the glasses would stay tight on my head and not slip down the bridge of my nose when I began to sweat. I always waited until just before a game to bend down the earpieces, because, bent, they would cut into the skin over my ears, and I did not want to feel the pain a moment longer than I had to. The tops of my ears would be sore for days after every game, but better that, I thought, than the need to keep pushing my glasses up the bridge of my nose or the possibility of having them fall off suddenly during an important play.

Davey Cantor, one of the boys who acted as a replacement if a first-stringer had to leave the game, was standing near the wire screen behind home plate. He was a short boy, with a round face, dark hair, owlish glasses, and a very Semitic nose. He watched me fix my glasses.

"You're looking good out there, Reuven," he told me.

"Thanks," I said.

"Everyone is looking real good."

"It'll be a good game."

He stared at me through his glasses. "You think so?" he asked.

"Sure, why not?"

"You ever see them play, Reuven?"

"No."

"They're murderers."

"Sure," I said.

"No, really. They're wild."

"You saw them play?"

"Twice. They're murderers."

"Everyone plays to win, Davey."

"They don't only play to win. They play like it's the first of the Ten Commandments."

I laughed. "That yeshiva?" I said. "Oh, come on, Davey."

"It's the truth."

"Sure," I said.

"Reb Saunders ordered them never to lose because it would shame their yeshiva or something. I don't know. You'll see."

"Hey, Malter!" Mr. Galanter shouted. "What are you doing, sitting this one out?"

"You'll see," Davey Cantor said.

"Sure." I grinned at him. "A holy war."

He looked at me.

"Are you playing?" I asked him.

"Mr. Galanter said I might take second base if you have to pitch."

"Well, good luck."

"Hey, Malter!" Mr. Galanter shouted. "There's a war on, remember?"

"Yes, sir!" I said, and ran back out to my position at second base.

We threw the ball around a few more minutes, and then I went up to home plate for some batting practice. I hit a long one out to left field, and then a fast one to the shortstop, who fielded it neatly and whipped it to first. I had the bat ready for another swing when someone said, "Here they are," and I rested the bat on my shoulder and saw the team we were going to play turn up our block and come into the yard. I saw Davey Cantor kick nervously at the wire screen behind home plate, then put his hands into the pockets of his dungarees. His eyes were wide and gloomy behind his owlish glasses.

I watched them come into the yard.

There were fifteen of them, and they were dressed alike in white shirts, dark pants, white sweaters, and small black skullcaps. In the fashion of the very Orthodox, their hair was closely cropped, except for the area near their ears from which mushroomed the untouched hair that tumbled down into the long side curls. Some of them had the beginnings of beards, straggly tufts of hair that stood in isolated clumps on their chins, jawbones, and upper lips. They all wore the traditional undergarment beneath their shirts, and the tzitzit, the long fringes appended to the four corners of the garment, came out above their belts and swung against their pants as they walked. These were the very Orthodox, and they obeyed literally the Biblical commandment *And ye shall look upon it*, which pertains to the fringes.

In contrast, our team had no particular uniform, and each of us wore whatever he wished: dungarees, shorts, pants, polo shirts, sweat shirts, even undershirts. Some of us wore the garment, others did not. None of us wore the fringes outside his trousers. The only element of uniform that we had in common was the small, black skullcap which we, too, wore.

They came up to the first-base side of the wire screen behind home plate and stood there in a silent black-and-white mass, holding bats and balls and gloves in their hands. I looked at them. They did not seem to me to present any picture of ferocity. I saw Davey Cantor kick again at the wire screen, then walk away from them to the third-base line, his hands moving nervously against his dungarees.

Mr. Galanter smiled and started toward them, moving quickly on the balls of his feet, his skullcap perched precariously on the top of his balding head.

A man disentangled himself from the black-and-white mass of players and took a step forward. He looked to be in his late twenties and wore a black suit, black shoes, and a black hat. He had a black beard, and he carried a book under one arm. He was obviously a rabbi, and I marveled that the yeshiva had placed a rabbi instead of an athletic coach over its team.

Mr. Galanter came up to him and offered his hand.

"We are ready to play," the rabbi said in Yiddish, shaking Mr. Galanter's hand with obvious uninterest.

"Fine," Mr. Galanter said in English, smiling.

The rabbi looked out at the field. "You played already?" he asked.

"How's that?" Mr. Galanter said.

"You had practice?"

"Well, sure—"

"We want to practice."

"How's that?" Mr. Galanter said again, looking surprised.

"You practiced, now we practice."

"You didn't practice in your own yard?"

"We practiced."

"Well, then—"

"But we have never played in your yard before. We want a few minutes."

"Well, now," Mr. Galanter said, "there isn't much time. The rules are each team practices in its own yard."

"We want five minutes," the rabbi insisted.

"Well—" Mr. Galanter said. He was no longer smiling. He always liked to go right into a game when we played in our own yard. It kept us from cooling off, he said.

"Five minutes," the rabbi said. "Tell your people to leave the field."

"How's that?" Mr. Galanter said.

"We cannot practice with your people on the field. Tell them to leave the field."

"Well, now," Mr. Galanter said, then stopped. He thought for a long moment. The black-and-white mass of players behind the rabbi stood very still, waiting. I saw Davey Cantor kick at the asphalt floor of the yard. "Well, all right. Five minutes. Just five minutes, now."

"Tell your people to leave the field," the rabbi said.

Mr. Galanter stared gloomily out at the field, looking a little deflated. "Everybody off!" he shouted, not very loudly. "They want a five-minute warm-up. Hustle, hustle. Keep those arms going. Keep it hot. Toss some balls around behind home. Let's go!"

The players scrambled off the field.

The black-and-white mass near the wire screen remained intact. The young rabbi turned and faced his team.

He talked in Yiddish. "We have the field for five minutes," he said. "Remember why and for whom we play."

Then he stepped aside, and the black-and-white mass dissolved into fifteen individual players who came quickly onto the field. One of them, a tall boy with sand-colored hair and long arms and legs that seemed all bones and angles, stood at home plate and commenced hitting balls out to the players. He hit a few easy grounders and pop-ups, and the fielders shouted encouragement to one another in Yiddish. They handled themselves awkwardly, dropping easy grounders, throwing wild, fumbling fly balls. I looked over at the young rabbi. He had sat down on the bench near the wire screen and was reading his book.

Behind the wire screen was a wide area, and Mr. Galanter kept us busy there throwing balls around.

"Keep those balls going!" he fist-thumped at us. "No one sits out this fire fight! Never underestimate the enemy!"

But there was a broad smile on his face. Now that he was actually seeing the other team, he seemed not at all concerned about the outcome of the game. In the interim between throwing a ball and having it thrown back to me, I told myself that I liked Mr. Galanter, and I wondered about his constant use of war expressions and why he wasn't in the army.

Davey Cantor came past me, chasing a ball that had gone between his legs.

"Some murderers," I grinned at him.

"You'll see," he said as he bent to retrieve the ball.

"Sure," I said.

"Especially the one batting. You'll see."

The ball was coming back to me, and I caught it neatly and flipped it back.

"Who's the one batting?" I asked.

"Danny Saunders."

"Pardon my ignorance, but who is Danny Saunders?"

"Reb Saunders' son," Davey Cantor said, blinking his eyes.

"I'm impressed."

"You'll see," Davey Cantor said, and ran off with his ball.

My father, who had no love at all for Hasidic communities and their rabbinic overloads, had told me about Rabbi Isaac Saunders and the zealousness with which he ruled his people and settled questions of Jewish law.

I saw Mr. Galanter look at his wristwatch, then stare out at the team on the field. The five minutes were apparently over, but the players were making no move to abandon the field. Danny Saunders was now at first base, and I noticed that his long arms and legs were being used to good advantage, for by stretching and jumping he was able to catch most of the wild throws that came his way.

Mr. Galanter went over to the young rabbi who was still sitting on the bench and reading.

"It's five minutes," he said.

The rabbi looked up from his book. "Ah?" he said.

"The five minutes are up," Mr. Galanter said.

The rabbi stared out at the field. "Enough!" he shouted in Yiddish. "It's time to play!" Then he looked down at the book and resumed his reading.

The players threw the ball around for another minute or two, and then slowly came off the field. Danny Saunders walked past me, still wearing his first baseman's glove. He was a good deal taller than I, and in contrast to my somewhat ordinary but decently proportioned features and dark hair, his face seemed to have been cut from stone. His chin, jaw and cheekbones were made up of jutting hard lines, his nose was straight and pointed, his lips full, rising to a steep angle from the center point beneath his nose and then slanting off to form a too-wide mouth. His eyes were deep blue, and the sparse tufts of hair on his chin, jawbones, and upper lip, the close-cropped hair on his head, and the flow of side curls along his ears were the color of sand. He moved in a loose-jointed, disheveled sort of way, all arms and legs, talking in Yiddish to one of his teammates and ignoring me completely as he passed by. I told myself that I did not like his Hasidic-bred sense of superiority and that it would be a great pleasure to defeat him and his team in this afternoon's game.

The umpire, a gym instructor from a parochial school two blocks away, called the teams together to determine who would bat first. I saw him throw a bat into the air. It was caught and almost dropped by a member of the other team.

During the brief hand-over-hand choosing, Davey Cantor came over and stood next to me.

"What do you think?" he asked.

"They're a snooty bunch," I told him.

"What do you think about their playing?"

"They're lousy."

"They're murderers."

"Oh, come on, Davey."

"You'll see," Davey Cantor said, looking at me gloomily.

"I just did see."

"You didn't see anything."

"Sure," I said. "Elijah the prophet comes in to pitch for them in tight spots."

"I'm not being funny," he said, looking hurt.

"Some murderers," I told him, and laughed.

The teams began to disperse. We had lost the choosing, and they had decided to bat first. We scampered onto the field. I took up my position at second base. I saw the young rabbi sitting on the bench near the wire fence and reading. We threw a ball around for a minute. Mr. Galanter stood alongside third base, shouting his words of encouragement at us. It was warm, and I was sweating a little and feeling very good. Then the umpire, who had taken up his position behind the pitcher, called for the ball and someone tossed it to him. He handed it to the pitcher and shouted, "Here we go! Play ball!" We settled into our positions.

Mr. Galanter shouted, "Goldberg, move in!" and Sidney Goldberg, our shortstop, took two steps forward and moved a little closer to third base. "Okay fine," Mr. Galanter said. "Keep that infield solid!"

A short, thin boy came up to the plate and stood there with his feet together, holding the bat awkwardly over his head. He wore steel-rimmed glasses that gave his face a pinched, old man's look. He swung wildly at the first pitch, and the force of the swing spun him completely around. His earlocks lifted off the sides of his head and followed him around in an almost horizontal circle. Then he steadied himself and resumed his position near the plate, short, thin, his feet together, holding his bat over his head in an awkward grip.

The umpire called the strike in a loud, clear voice, and I saw Sidney Goldberg look over at me and grin broadly.

"If he studies Talmud like that, he's dead," Sidney Goldberg said.

I grinned back at him.

"Keep that infield solid!" Mr. Galanter shouted from third base. "Malter, a little to your left! Good!"

The next pitch was too high, and the boy chopped at it, lost his bat and fell forward on his hands. Sidney Goldberg and I looked at each other again. Sidney was in my class. We were similar in build, thin and lithe, with somewhat spindly arms and legs. He was not a very good student, but he was an excellent shortstop. We lived on the same block and were good but not close friends. He was dressed in an undershirt and dungarees and was not wearing the four-cornered garment. I had on a light-blue shirt and dark-blue work pants, and I wore the four-cornered garment under the shirt.

The short, thin boy was back at the plate, standing with his feet together and holding the bat in his awkward grip. He let the next pitch go by, and the umpire called it a strike. I saw the young rabbi look up a moment from his book, then resume reading.

"Two more just like that!" I shouted encouragingly to the pitcher. "Two more, Schwartzie!" And I thought to myself, Some murderers.

I saw Danny Saunders go over to the boy who had just struck out and talk to him. The boy looked down and seemed to shrivel with hurt. He hung his head and walked away behind the wire screen. Another short, thin boy took his place at the plate. I looked around for Davey Cantor but could not see him.

The boy at bat swung wildly at the first two pitches and missed them both. He swung again at the third pitch, and I heard the loud *thwack* of the bat as it connected with the ball, and saw the ball move in a swift, straight line toward Sidney Goldberg, who caught it, bobbled it for a moment, and finally got it into his glove. He tossed the ball to me, and we threw it around. I saw him take off his glove and shake his left hand.

"That hurt," he said, grinning at me.

"Good catch," I told him.

"That hurt like hell," he said, and put his glove back on his hand.

The batter who stood now at the plate was broad-shouldered and built like a bear. He swung at the first pitch, missed, then swung again at the second pitch and sent the ball in a straight line over the head of the third baseman into left field. I scrambled to second, stood on the base and shouted for the ball. I saw the left fielder pick it up on the second bounce and relay it to me. I was coming in a little high, and I had my glove raised for it. I felt more than saw the batter charging toward second, and as I was getting my glove on the ball he smashed into me like a truck. The ball went over my head, and I fell forward heavily onto the asphalt floor of the yard, and he passed me, going toward third, his fringes flying out behind him, holding his skullcap to his head with his right hand so it would not fall off. Abe Goodstein, our first baseman, retrieved the ball and whipped it home, and the batter stood at third, a wide grin on his face.

The yeshiva team exploded into wild cheers and shouted loud words of congratulations in Yiddish to the batter.

Sidney Goldberg helped me get to my feet.

"That momzer!" he said. "You weren't in his way!"

"Wow!" I said, taking a few deep breaths. I had scraped the palm of my right hand.

"What a momzer!" Sidney Goldberg said.

I saw Mr. Galanter come storming onto the field to talk to the umpire. "What kind of play was that? he asked heatedly. "How are you going to rule that?"

"Safe at third," the umpire said. "Your boy was in the way."

Mr. Galanter's mouth fell open. "How's that again?"

"Safe at third," the umpire repeated.

Mr. Galanter looked ready to argue, thought better of it, then stared over at me. "Are you all right, Malter?"

"I'm okay," I said, taking another deep breath.

Mr. Galanter walked angrily off the field.

"Play ball!" the umpire shouted.

The yeshiva team quieted down. I saw that the young rabbi was now looking up from his book and smiling faintly.

A tall, thin player came up to the plate, set his feet in correct position, swung his bat a few times, then crouched into a waiting stance. I saw it was Danny Saunders. I opened and closed my right hand, which was still sore from the fall.

"Move back! Move back!" Mr. Galanter was shouting from alongside third base, and I took two steps back.

I crouched, waiting.

The first pitch was wild, and the yeshiva team burst into loud laughter. The young rabbi was sitting on the bench, watching Danny Saunders intently.

"Take it easy, Schwartzie!" I shouted encouragingly to the pitcher. "There's only one more to go!"

The next pitch was about a foot over Danny Saunders' head, and the yeshiva team howled with laughter. Sidney Goldberg and I looked at each other. I saw Mr. Galanter standing very still alongside third, staring at the pitcher. The rabbi was still watching Danny Saunders.

The next pitch left Schwartzie's hand in a long, slow line, and before it was halfway to the plate I knew Danny Saunders would try for it. I knew it from the way his left foot came forward and the bat snapped back and his long, thin body began its swift pivot. I tensed, waiting for the sound of the bat against the ball, and when it came it sounded like a gunshot. For a wild fraction of a second I lost sight of the ball. Then I saw Schwartzie dive to the ground, and there was the ball coming through the air where his head had been and I tried for it but it was moving too fast, and I barely had my glove raised before it was in center field. It was caught on a bounce and thrown to Sidney Goldberg, but by that time Danny Saunders was standing solidly on my base and the yeshiva team was screaming with joy.

Mr. Galanter called for time and walked over to talk to Schwartzie. Sidney Goldberg nodded to me, and the two of us went over to them.

"That ball could've killed me!" Schwartzie was saying. He was of medium size, with a long face and a bad case of acne. He wiped sweat from his face. "My God, did you see that ball?"

"I saw it," Mr. Galanter said grimly.

"That was too fast to stop, Mr. Galanter," I said in Schwartzie's defense.

"I heard about that Danny Saunders," Sidney Goldberg said. "He always hits to the pitcher."

"You could've told me," Schwartzie lamented. "I could've been ready."

"I only *heard* about it," Sidney Goldberg said. "You always believe everything you hear?"

"God, that ball could've killed me!" Schwartzie said again.

"You want to go on pitching?" Mr. Galanter said. A thin sheen of sweat covered his forehead, and he looked very grim.

"Sure, Mr. Galanter," Schwartzie said. "I'm okay."

"You're sure?"

"Sure I'm sure."

"No heroes in this war, now," Mr. Galanter said. "I want live soldiers, not dead heroes."

"I'm no hero," Schwartzie muttered lamely. "I can still get it over, Mr. Galanter. God, it's only the first inning."

"Okay, soldier," Mr. Galanter said, not very enthusiastically. "Just keep our side of this war fighting."

"I'm trying my best, Mr. Galanter," Schwartzie said.

Mr. Galanter nodded, still looking grim, and started off the field. I saw him take a handkerchief out of his pocket and wipe his forehead.

"Jesus Christ!" Schwartzie said, now that Mr. Galanter was gone. "That bastard aimed right for my head!"

"Oh, come on, Schwartzie," I said. "What is he, Babe Ruth?"

"You heard what Sidney said."

"Stop giving it to them on a silver platter and they won't hit it like that."

"Who's giving it to them on a silver platter?" Schwartzie lamented. "That was a great pitch."

"Sure," I said.

The umpire came over to us. "You boys planning to chat here all afternoon?" he asked. He was a squat man in his late forties, and he looked impatient.

"No, sir," I said very politely, and Sidney and I ran back to our places.

Danny Saunders was standing on my base. His white shirt was pasted to his arms and back with sweat.

"That was a nice shot," I offered.

He looked at me curiously and said nothing.

"You always hit it like that to the pitcher?" I asked.

He smiled faintly. "You're Reuven Malter," he said in perfect English. He had a low, nasal voice.

"That's right," I said, wondering where he had heard my name.

"Your father is David Malter, the one who writes articles on the Talmud?"

"Yes."

"I told my team we're going to kill you apikorsim this afternoon." He said it flatly, without a trace of expression in his voice.

I stared at him and hoped the sudden tight coldness I felt wasn't showing on my face. "Sure," I said. "Rub your tzitzit for good luck."

I walked away from him and took up my position near the base. I looked toward the wire screen and saw Davey Cantor standing there, staring out at the field, his hands in his pockets. I crouched down quickly, because Schwartzie was going into his pitch.

The batter swung wildly at the first two pitches and missed each time. The next one was low, and he let it go by, then hit a grounder to the first baseman, who dropped it, flailed about for it wildly, and recovered it in time to see Danny Saunders cross the plate. The first baseman stood there for a moment, drenched in shame, then tossed the ball to Schwartzie. I saw Mr. Galanter standing near third base, wiping his forehead. The yeshiva team had gone wild again, and they were all trying to get to Danny Saunders and shake his hand. I saw the rabbi smile broadly, then look down at his book and resume reading.

Sidney Goldberg came over to me. "What did Saunders tell you?" he asked.

"He said they were going to kill us apikorsim this afternoon."

He stared at me. "Those are nice people, those yeshiva people," he said, and walked slowly back to his position.

The next batter hit a long fly ball to right field. It was caught on the run.

"Hooray for us," Sidney Goldberg said grimly as we headed off the field. "Any longer and they'd be asking us to join them for the Mincha Service."

"Not us," I said. "We're not holy enough."

"Where did they learn to hit like that?"

"Who knows?" I said.

We were standing near the wire screen, forming a tight circle around Mr. Galanter.

"Only two runs," Mr. Galanter said, smashing his right fist into his left hand. "And they hit us with all they had. Now we give them *our* heavy artillery. Now *we* barrage *them!*" I saw that he looked relieved but that he was still sweating. His skullcap seemed pasted to his head with sweat. "Okay!" he said. "Fire away!"

The circle broke up, and Sidney Goldberg walked to the plate, carrying a bat. I saw the rabbi was still sitting on the bench, reading. I started to walk around behind him to see what book it was, when Davey Cantor came over, his hands in his pockets, his eyes still gloomy.

"Well?" he asked.

"Well what?" I said.

"I told you they could hit."

"So you told me. So what?" I was in no mood for his feelings of doom, and I let my voice show it.

He sensed my annoyance. "I wasn't bragging or anything," he said, looking hurt. "I just wanted to know what you thought."

"They can hit," I said.

"They're murderers," he said.

I watched Sidney Goldberg let a strike go by and said nothing.

"How's your hand?" Davey Cantor asked.

"I scraped it."

"He ran into you real hard.'

"Who is he?"

"Dov Shlomowitz," Davey Cantor said. "Like his name, that's what he is," he added in Hebrew. "Dov" is the Hebrew word for bear.

"Was I blocking him?"

Davey Cantor shrugged. "You were and you weren't. The ump could've called it either way."

"He felt like a truck," I said, watching Sidney Goldberg step back from a close pitch.

"You should see his father. He's one of Reb Saunders' shamashim. Some bodyguard he makes."

"Reb Saunders has bodyguards?"

"Sure he has bodyguards," Davey Cantor said. "They protect him from his own popularity. Where've you been living all these years?"

"I don't have anything to do with them."

"You're not missing a thing, Reuven."

"How do you know so much about Reb Saunders?"

"My father gives him contributions."

"Well, good for your father," I said.

"He doesn't pray there or anything. He just gives him contributions."

"You're on the wrong team."

"No, I'm not, Reuven. Don't be like that." He was looking very hurt. "My father isn't a Hasid or anything. He just gives them some money a couple times a year."

"I was only kidding, Davey." I grinned at him. "Don't be so serious about everything."

I saw his face break into a happy smile, and just then Sidney Goldberg hit a fast, low grounder and raced off to first. The ball went right through the legs of the shortstop and into center field.

"Hold it at first!" Mr. Galanter screamed at him, and Sidney stopped at first and stood on the base.

The ball had been tossed quickly to second base. The second baseman looked over toward first, then threw the ball to the pitcher. The rabbi glanced up from the book for a moment, then went back to his reading.

"Malter, coach him at first!" Mr. Galanter shouted, and I ran up the base line.

"They can hit, but they can't field," Sidney Goldberg said, grinning at me as I came to a stop alongside the base.

"Davey Cantor says they're murderers," I said.

"Old gloom-and-doom Davey," Sidney Goldberg said, grinning.

Danny Saunders was standing away from the base, making a point of ignoring us both.

The next batter hit a high fly to the second baseman, who caught it, dropped it, retrieved it, and made a wild attempt at tagging Sidney Goldberg as he raced past him to second.

"Safe all around!" the umpire called, and our team burst out with shouts of joy. Mr. Galanter was smiling. The rabbi continued reading, and I saw that he was now slowly moving the upper part of his body back and forth.

"Keep your eyes open, Sidney!" I shouted from alongside first base. I saw Danny Saunders look at me, then look away. Some murderers, I thought. Shleppers is more like it.

"If it's on the ground run like hell," I said to the batter who had just come onto first base, and he nodded at me. He was our third baseman, and he was about my size.

"If they keep fielding like that we'll be here till tomorrow," he said, and I grinned at him.

I saw Mr. Galanter talking to the next batter, who was nodding his head vigorously. He stepped to the plate, hit a hard grounder to the pitcher, who fumbled it for a moment then threw it to first. I saw Danny Saunders stretch for it and stop it.

"Out!" the umpire called. "Safe on second and third!"

As I ran up to the plate to bat, I almost laughed aloud at the pitcher's stupidity. He had thrown it to first rather than third, and now we had Sidney Goldberg on third, and a man on second. I hit a grounder to the shortstop and instead of throwing it to second he threw it to first, wildly, and again Danny Saunders stretched and stopped the ball. But I beat the throw and heard the umpire call out, "Safe all around! One in!" And everyone on our team was patting Sidney Goldberg on the back. Mr. Galanter smiled broadly.

"Hello again," I said to Danny Saunders, who was standing near me, guarding his base. "Been rubbing your tzitzit lately?"

He looked at me, then looked slowly away, his face expressionless.

Schwartzie was at the plate, swinging his bat.

"Keep your eyes open!" I shouted to the runner on third. He looked too eager to head for home. "It's only one out!"

He waved a hand at me.

Schwartzie took two balls and a strike, then I saw him begin to pivot on the fourth pitch. The runner on third started for home. He was almost halfway down the base line when the bat sent the ball in a hard line drive straight to the third baseman, the short, thin boy with the spectacles and the old man's face, who had stood hug-

ging the base and who now caught the ball more with his stomach
than with his glove, managed somehow to hold on to it, and stood
there, looking bewildered and astonished.

I returned to first and saw our player who had been on third and
who was now halfway to home plate turn sharply and start a panicky
race back.

"Step on the base!" Danny Saunders screamed in Yiddish across
the field, and more out of obedience than awareness the third baseman put a foot on the base.

The yeshiva team howled its happiness and raced off the field.
Danny Saunders looked at me, started to say something stopped,
then walked quickly away.

I saw Mr. Galanter going back up the third-base line, his face
grim. The rabbi was looking up from his book and smiling.

I took up my position near second base, and Sidney Goldberg
came over to me.

"Why'd he have to take off like that?" he asked.

I glared over at our third baseman, who was standing near Mr.
Galanter and looking very dejected.

"He was in a hurry to win the war," I said bitterly.

"What a jerk," Sidney Goldberg said.

"Goldberg, get over to your place!" Mr. Galanter called out. There
was an angry edge to his voice. "Let's keep that infield solid!"

Sidney Goldberg went quickly to his position. I stood still and
waited.

It was hot, and I was sweating beneath my clothes. I felt the earpieces of my glasses cutting into the skin over my ears, and I took
the glasses off for a moment and ran a finger over the pinched ridges
of skin, then put them back on quickly because Schwartzie was
going into a windup. I crouched down, waiting, remembering Danny
Saunders' promise to his team that they would kill us apikorsim. The
word had meant, originally, a Jew educated in Judaism who denied
basic tenets of his faith, like the existence of God, the revelation,
the resurrection of the dead. To people like Reb Saunders, it also
meant any educated Jew who might be reading, say, Darwin, and
who was not wearing side curls and fringes outside his trousers. I was
an apikoros to Danny Saunders, despite my belief in God and Torah,
because I did not have side curls and was attending a parochial school
where too many English subjects were offered and where Jewish
subjects were taught in Hebrew instead of Yiddish, both unheard-of

sins, the former because it took time away from the study of Torah, the latter because Hebrew was the Holy Tongue and to use it in ordinary classroom discourse was a desecration of God's Name. I had never really had any personal contact with this kind of Jew before. My father had told me he didn't mind their beliefs. What annoyed him was their fanatic sense of righteousness, their absolute certainty that they and they alone had God's ear, and every other Jew was wrong, totally wrong, a sinner, a hypocrite, an apikoros, and doomed, therefore, to burn in hell. I found myself wondering again how they had learned to hit a ball like that if time for the study of Torah was so precious to them and why they had sent a rabbi along to waste his time sitting on a bench during a ball game.

Standing on the field and watching the boy at the plate swing at a high ball and miss, I felt myself suddenly very angry, and it was at that point that for me the game stopped being merely a game and became a war. The fun and excitement was out of it now. Somehow the yeshiva team had translated this afternoon's baseball game into a conflict between what they regarded as their righteousness and our sinfulness. I found myself growing more and more angry, and I felt the anger begin to focus itself upon Danny Saunders, and suddenly it was not at all difficult for me to hate him.

Schwartzie let five of their men come up to the plate that half inning and let one of those five score. Sometime during that half inning, one of the members of the yeshiva team had shouted at us in Yiddish, "Burn in hell, you apikorsim!" and by the time that half inning was over and we were standing around Mr. Galanter near the wire screen, all of us knew that this was not just another ball game.

Mr. Galanter was sweating heavily, and his face was grim. All he said was, "We light it careful from now on. No more mistakes." He said it very quietly, and we were all quiet, too, as the batter stepped up to the plate.

We proceeded to play a slow, careful game, bunting whenever we had to, sacrificing to move runners forward, obeying Mr. Galanter's instructions. I noticed that no matter where the runners were on the bases, the yeshiva team always threw to Danny Saunders, and I realized that they did this because he was the only infielder who could be relied upon to stop their wild throws. Sometime during the inning, I walked over behind the rabbi and looked over his shoulder at the book he was reading. I saw the words were Yiddish. I walked back to the wire screen. Davey Cantor came over and stood next to me, but he remained silent.

We scored only one run that inning, and we walked onto the field for the first half of the third inning with a sense of doom.

Dov Shlomowitz came up to the plate. He stood there like a bear, the bat looking like a matchstick in his beefy hands. Schwartzie pitched, and he sliced one neatly over the head of the third baseman for a single. The yeshiva team howled, and again one of them called out to us in Yiddish, "Burn, you apikorsim!" and Sidney Goldberg and I looked at each other without saying a word.

Mr. Galanter was standing alongside third base, wiping his forehead. The rabbi was sitting quietly, reading his book.

I took off my glasses and rubbed the tops of my ears. I felt a sudden momentary sense of unreality, as if the play yard, with its black asphalt floor and its white base lines, were my entire world now, as if all the previous years of my life had led me somehow to this one ball game, and all the future years of my life would depend upon its outcome. I stood there for a moment, holding the glasses in my hand and feeling frightened. Then I took a deep breath, and the feeling passed. It's only a ball game, I told myself. What's a ball game?

Mr. Galanter was shouting at us to move back. I was standing a few feet to the left of second, and I took two steps back. I saw Danny Saunders walk up to the plate, swinging a bat. The yeshiva team was shouting at him in Yiddish to kill us apikorsim.

Schwartzie turned around to check the field. He looked nervous and was taking his time. Sidney Goldberg was standing up straight, waiting. We looked at each other, then looked away. Mr. Galanter stood very still alongside third base, looking at Schwartzie.

The first pitch was low, and Danny Saunders ignored it. The second one started to come in shoulder-high, and before it was two thirds of the way to the plate, I was already standing on second base. My glove was going up as the bat cracked against the ball, and I saw the ball move in a straight line directly over Schwartzie's head, high over his head, moving so fast he hadn't even had time to regain his balance from the pitch before it went past him. I saw Dov Shlomowitz heading toward me and Danny Saunders racing to first and I heard the yeshiva team shouting and Sidney Goldberg screaming, and I jumped, pushing myself upward off the ground with all the strength I had in my legs and stretching my glove hand till I thought it would pull out my shoulder. The ball hit the pocket of my glove with an impact that numbed my hand and went through me like an electric shock, and I felt the force pull me backward and throw me off balance, and I came down hard on my left hip and elbow. I saw Dov Shlomowitz whirl and start back to first, and I pushed myself up into a sitting position and threw the ball awkwardly to Sidney Goldberg, who caught it and whipped it to first. I heard the umpire scream "Out!" and Sidney Goldberg ran over to help me to my feet, a look of disbelief and ecstatic joy on his face. Mr. Galanter shouted "Time!" and came racing onto the field. Schwartzie was standing in his pitcher's position with his mouth open. Danny Saunders stood on the base line a few feet from first, where he had stopped after I had caught the ball, staring out at me, his face frozen to stone. The rabbi was staring at me, too, and the yeshiva team was deathly silent.

"That was a great catch, Reuven!" Sidney Goldberg said, thumping my back. "That was sensational!"

I saw the rest of our team had suddenly come back to life and was throwing the ball around and talking up the game.

Mr. Galanter came over. "You all right, Malter?" he asked. "Let me see that elbow."

I showed him the elbow. I had scraped it, but the skin had not been broken.

"That was a good play," Mr. Galanter said, beaming at me. I saw his face was still covered with sweat, but he was smiling broadly now.

"Thanks, Mr. Galanter."

"How's the hand?"

"It hurts a little."

"Let me see it."

I took off the glove, and Mr. Galanter poked and bent the wrist and fingers of the hand.

"Does that hurt?" he asked.

"No," I lied.

"You want to go on playing?"

"Sure, Mr. Galanter."

"Okay," he said, smiling at me and patting my back. "We'll put you in for a Purple Heart on that one, Malter."

I grinned at him.

"Okay," Mr. Galanter said. "Let's keep this infield solid!"

He walked away, smiling.

"I can't get over that catch," Sidney Goldberg said.

"You threw it real good to first," I told him.

"Yeah," he said. "While you were sitting on your tail."

We grinned at each other, and went to our positions.

Two more of the yeshiva team got to bat that inning. The first one hit a single, and the second one sent a high fly to short, which Sidney Goldberg caught without having to move a step. We scored two runs that inning and one run the next, and by the top half of the fifth inning we were leading five to three. Four of their men had stood up to bat during the top half of the fourth inning, and they had got only a single on an error to first. When we took to the field in the top half of the fifth inning, Mr. Galanter was walking back and forth alongside third on the balls of his feet, sweating, smiling, grinning, wiping his head nervously; the rabbi was no longer reading; the yeshiva team was silent as death. Davey Cantor was playing second, and I stood in the pitcher's position. Schwartzie had pleaded exhaustion, and since this was the final inning—our parochial school schedules only permitted us time for five-inning games—and the yeshiva team's last chance at bat, Mr. Galanter was taking no chances and told me to pitch. Davey Cantor was a poor fielder, but Mr. Galanter was counting on my pitching to finish off the game. My left hand was still sore from the catch, and the wrist hurt whenever I caught a ball, but the right hand was fine, and the pitches went in fast and dropped into the curve just when I wanted them to. Dov Shlomowitz stood at the plate, swung three times at what looked to him to be perfect pitches, and hit nothing but air. He stood there looking bewildered after the third swing, then slowly walked away. We threw the ball around the infield, and Danny Saunders came up to the plate.

The members of the yeshiva team stood near the wire fence, watching Danny Saunders. They were very quiet. The rabbi was sitting on the bench, his book closed. Mr. Galanter was shouting at everyone to move back. Danny Saunders swung his bat a few times, then fixed himself into position and looked out at me.

Here's a present from an apikoros, I thought, and let go the ball. It went in fast and straight, and I saw Danny Saunders' left foot move out and his bat go up and his body begin to pivot. He swung just as the ball slid into its curve, and the bat cut savagely through empty air, twisting him around and sending him off balance. His black skullcap fell off his head, and he regained his balance and bent quickly to retrieve it. He stood there for a moment, very still, staring out at me. Then he resumed his position at the plate. The ball came back to me from the catcher, and my wrist hurt as I caught it.

The yeshiva team was very quiet, and the rabbi had begun to chew his lip.

I lost control of the next pitch, and it was wide. On the third pitch, I went into a long, elaborate windup and sent him a slow curving blooper, the kind a batter always wants to hit and always misses. He ignored it completely and the umpire called it a ball.

I felt my left wrist begin to throb as I caught the throw from the catcher. I was hot and sweaty, and the earpieces of my glasses were cutting deeply into the flesh above my ears as a result of the head movements that went with my pitching.

Danny Saunders stood very still at the plate, waiting.

Okay, I thought, hating him bitterly. Here's another present.

The ball went to the plate fast and straight, and dropped just below his swing. He checked himself with difficulty so as not to spin around, but he went off his balance again and took two or three staggering steps forward before he was able to stand up straight.

The catcher threw the ball back, and I winced at the pain in my wrist. I took the ball out of the glove, held it in my right hand, and turned around for a moment to look out at the field and let the pain in my wrist subside. When I turned back I saw Danny Saunders hadn't moved. He was holding his bat in his left hand, standing very still and staring at me. His eyes were dark, and his lips were parted in a crazy, idiot grin. I heard the umpire yell "Play ball!" but Danny Saunders stood there, staring at me and grinning. I turned and looked out at the field again, and when I turned back he was still standing there, staring at me and grinning. I could see his teeth between his parted lips. I took a deep breath and felt myself wet with sweat. I wiped my right hand on my pants and saw Danny Saunders step slowly to the plate and set his legs in position. He was no longer grinning. He stood looking at me over his left shoulder, waiting.

I wanted to finish it quickly because of the pain in my wrist, and I sent in another fast ball. I watched it head straight for the plate. I saw him go into a sudden crouch, and in the fraction of a second before he hit the ball I realized that he had anticipated the curve and was deliberately swinging low. I was still a little off balance from the pitch, but I managed to bring my glove hand up in front of my face just as he hit the ball. I saw it coming at me, and there was nothing

I could do. It hit the finger section of my glove, deflected off, smashed into the upper rim of the left lens of my glasses, glanced off my forehead, and knocked me down. I scrambled around for it wildly, but by the time I got my hand on it Danny Saunders was standing safely on first.

I heard Mr. Galanter call time, everyone on the field came racing over to me. My glasses lay shattered on the asphalt floor, and I felt a sharp pain in my left eye when I blinked. My wrist throbbed, and I could feel the bump coming up on my forehead. I looked over at first, but without my glasses Danny Saunders was only a blur. I imagined I could still see him grinning.

I saw Mr. Galanter put his face next to mine. It was sweaty and full of concern. I wondered what all the fuss was about. I had only lost a pair of glasses, and we had at least two more good pitchers on the team.

"Are you all right, boy?" Mr. Galanter was saying. He looked at my face and forehead. "Somebody wet a handkerchief with cold water!" he shouted. I wondered why he was shouting. His voice hurt my head and rang in my ears. I saw Davey Cantor run off, looking frightened. I heard Sidney Goldberg say something, but I couldn't make out his words. Mr. Galanter put his arms around my shoulders and walked me off the field. He sat me down on the bench next to the rabbi. Without my glasses everything more than about ten feet away from me was blurred. I blinked and wondered about the pain in my left eye. I heard voices and shouts, and then Mr. Galanter was putting a wet handkerchief on my head.

"You feel dizzy, boy?" he said.

I shook my head.

"You're sure now?"

"I'm all right," I said, and wondered why my voice sounded husky and why talking hurt my head.

"You sit quiet now," Mr. Galanter said. "You begin to feel dizzy, you let me know right away."

"Yes, sir," I said.

He went away. I sat on the bench next to the rabbi, who looked at me once, then looked away. I heard shouts in Yiddish. The pain in my left eye was so intense I could feel it in the base of my spine. I sat on the bench a long time, long enough to see us lose the game by a score of eight to seven, long enough to hear the yeshiva team shout with joy, long enough to begin to cry at the pain in my left eye, long enough for Mr. Galanter to come over to me at the end of the game, take one look at my face and go running out of the yard to call a cab.

Malter has been operated on by the most skillful of specialists.

"Hello," Danny Saunders said softly. "I'm sorry if I woke you. The nurse told me it was all right to wait here."

I looked at him in amazement. He was the last person in the world I had expected to visit me in the hospital.

"Before you tell me how much you hate me," he said quietly, "let me tell you that I'm sorry about what happened."

I stared at him and didn't know what to say. He was wearing a dark suit, a white shirt open at the collar, and a dark skullcap. I could see the earlocks hanging down alongside his sculptured face and the fringes outside the trousers below the jacket.

"I don't hate you," I managed to say, because I thought it was time for me to say something even if what I said was a lie.

He smiled sadly. "Can I sit down? I've been standing here about fifteen minutes waiting for you to wake up."

I sort of nodded or did something with my head, and he took it as a sign of approval and sat down on the edge of the bed to my right. The sun streamed in from the windows behind him, and shadows lay over his face and accentuated the lines of his cheeks and jaw. I thought he looked a little like the pictures I had seen of Abraham Lincoln before he grew the beard—except for the small tufts of sand-colored hair on his chin and cheeks, the close-cropped hair on his head, and the side curls. He seemed ill at ease, and his eyes blinked nervously.

"What do they say about the scar tissue?" he asked.

I was astonished all over again. "How did you find out about that?"

"I called your father last night. He told me."

"They don't know anything about it yet. I might be blind in that eye."

He nodded slowly and was silent.

"How does it feel to know you've made someone blind in one eye?" I asked him. I had recovered from any surprise at his presence and was feeling the anger beginning to come back.

He looked at me, his sculptured face expressionless. "What do you want me to say?" His voice wasn't angry, it was sad. "You want me to say I'm miserable? Okay, I'm miserable."

"That's all? Only miserable? How do you sleep nights?"

He looked down at his hands. "I didn't come here to fight with you," he said softly. "If you want to do nothing but fight, I'm going to go home."

"For my part," I told him, "you can go to hell, and take your whole snooty bunch of Hasidim along with you!"

He looked at me and sat still. He didn't seem angry, just sad. His silence made me all the angrier, and finally I said, "What the hell are you sitting there for? I thought you said you were going home!"

"I came to talk to you," he said quietly.

"Well, I don't want to listen," I told him. "Why don't you go home? Go home and be sorry over my eye!"

He stood up slowly. I could barely see his face because of the sunlight behind him. His shoulders seemed bowed.

"I *am* sorry," he said quietly.

"I'll just bet you are," I told him.

He started to say something, stopped, then turned and walked slowly away up the aisle. I lay back on the pillow, trembling a little and frightened over my own anger and hate.

"He a friend of yours?" I heard Mr. Savo ask me.

I turned to him. He was lying with his head on his pillow.

"No," I said.

"He give you a rough time or something? You don't sound so good, Bobby boy."

"He's the one who hit me in the eye with the ball."

Mr. Savo's face brightened. "No kidding? The clopper himself. Well, well!"

"I think I'll get some more sleep," I said. I was feeling depressed.

"He one of these real religious Jews?" Mr. Savo asked.

"Yes."

"I've seen them around. My manager had an uncle like that. Real religious guy. Fanatic. Never had anything to do with my manager, though. Small loss. Some lousy manager."

I didn't feel like having a conversation just then, so I remained silent. I was feeling a little regretful that I had been so angry with Danny Saunders.

I saw Mr. Savo sit up and take the deck of cards from his night table. He began to set up his rows on the blanket. I noticed Billy was asleep. I lay back in my bed and closed my eyes. But I couldn't sleep.

My father came in a few minutes after supper, looking pale and worn. When I told him about my conversation with Danny Saunders, his eyes became angry behind the glasses.

"You did a foolish thing, Reuven," he told me sternly. "You remember what the Talmud says. If a person comes to apologize for having hurt you, you must listen and forgive him."

"I couldn't help it, abba."

"You hate him so much you could say those things to him?"

"I'm sorry," I said, feeling miserable.

He looked at me and I saw his eyes were suddenly sad. "I did not intend to scold you," he said.

"You weren't scolding," I defended him.

"What I tried to tell you, Reuven, is that when a person comes to talk to you, you should be patient and listen. Especially if he has hurt you in any way. Now, we will not talk anymore tonight about Reb Saunders' son. This is an important day in the history of the world. It is the beginning of the end for Hitler and his madmen. Did you hear the announcer on the boat describing the invasion?"

We talked for a while about the invasion. Finally, my father left, and I lay back in my bed, feeling depressed and angry with myself over what I had said to Danny Saunders.

Billy's father had come to see him again, and they were talking quietly. He glanced at me and smiled warmly. He was a fine-looking person, and I noticed he had a long white scar on his forehead running parallel to the line of his light blond hair.

"Billy tells me you've been very nice to him," he said to me.

I sort of nodded my head on the pillow and tried to smile back.

"I appreciate that very much," he said. "Billy wonders if you would call us when he gets out of the hospital."

"Sure," I said.

"We're in the phone book. Roger Merrit. Billy says that after his operation, when he can see again, he would like to see what you look like."

"Sure, I'll give you a call," I said.

"Did you hear that, Billy?"

"Yes," Billy said happily. "Didn't I tell you he was nice, Daddy?"

The man smiled at me, then turned back to Billy. They went on talking quietly.

I lay in the bed and thought about all the things that had happened during the day, and felt sad and depressed.

The next morning, Mrs. Carpenter told me I could get out of bed and walk around a bit. After breakfast, I went out into the hall for a while. I looked out a window and saw people outside on the street. I stood there, staring out the window a long time. Then I went back to my bed and lay down.

I saw Mr. Savo sitting up in his bed, playing cards and grinning.

"How's it feel to be on your feet, Bobby boy?" he asked me.

"It feels wonderful. I'm a little tired, though."

"Take it real slow, kid. Takes a while to get the old strength back."

One of the patients near the radio at the other end of the ward let out a shout. I leaned over and turned on my radio. The announcer was talking about a breakthrough on one of the beaches.

"That's clopping them!" Mr. Savo said, grinning broadly.

I wondered what that beach must look like now, and I could see it filled with broken vehicles and dead soldiers.

I spent the morning listening to the radio. When Mrs. Carpenter came over, I asked her how long I would be in the hospital, and she smiled and said Dr. Snydman would have to decide that. "Dr. Snydman will see you Friday morning," she added.

I was beginning to feel a lot less excited over the war news and a lot more annoyed that I couldn't read. In the afternoon, I listened to some of the soap operas—*Life Can be Beautiful, Stella Dallas, Mary Noble, Ma Perkins*—and what I heard depressed me even more. I decided to turn off the radio and get some sleep.

"Do you want to hear any more of this?" I asked Billy.

He didn't answer, and I saw he was sleeping.

"Turn it off, kid," Mr. Savo said. "How much of that junk can a guy take?"

I turned off the radio and lay back on my pillow.

"Never knew people could get clopped so hard the way they clop them on those soap operas," Mr. Savo said. "Well, well, look who's here."

"Who?" I sat up.

"Your real religious clopper."

I saw it was Danny Saunders. He came up the side aisle and stood alongside my bed, wearing the same clothes he had the day before.

"Are you going to get angry at me again?" he asked hesitantly.

"No," I said.

"Can I sit down?"

"Yes."

"Thanks," he said, and sat down on the edge of the bed to my right. I saw Mr. Savo stare at him for a moment, then go back to his cards.

"You were pretty rotten yesterday, you know," Danny Saunders said.

"I'm sorry about that." I was surprised at how happy I was to see him.

"I didn't so much mind you being angry," he said. "What I thought was rotten was the way you wouldn't let me talk."

"That was rotten, all right. I'm really sorry."

"I came up to talk to you now. Do you want to listen?"

"Sure," I said.

"I've been thinking about that ball game. I haven't stopped thinking about it since you got hit."

"I've been thinking about it, too," I said.

"Whenever I do or see something I don't understand, I like to think about it until I understand it." He talked very rapidly, and I could see he was tense. "I've thought about it a lot, but I still don't understand it. I want to talk to you about it. Okay?"

"Sure," I said.

"Do you know what I don't understand about that ball game? I don't understand why I wanted to kill you."

I stared at him.

"It's really bothering me."

"Well, I should hope so," I said.

"Don't be so cute, Malter. I'm not being melodramatic. I really wanted to kill you."

"Well, it was a pretty hot ball game," I said. "I didn't exactly love you myself there for a while."

"I don't think you even know what I'm talking about," he said.

"Now, wait a minute—"

"No, listen. Just listen to what I'm saying, will you? Do you remember that second curve you threw me?"

"Sure."

"Do you remember I stood in front of the plate afterwards and looked at you?"

"Sure." I remember the idiot grin vividly.

"Well, that's when I wanted to walk over to you and open your head with my bat."

I didn't know what to say.

"I don't know why I didn't. I wanted to."

"That was some ball game," I said, a little awed by what he was telling me.

"It had nothing to do with the ball game," he said. "At least I don't think it did. You weren't the first tough team we played. And we've lost before, too. But you really had me going, Malter. I can't figure it out. Anyway, I feel better telling you about it."

"Please stop calling me Malter," I said.

He looked at me. Then he smiled faintly. "What do you want me to call you?"

"If you're going to call me anything, call me Reuven," I said. "Malter sounds as if you're a schoolteacher or something."

"Okay," he said, smiling again. "Then you call me Danny."

"Fine," I said.

"It was the wildest feeling," he said. "I've never felt that way before."

I looked at him, and suddenly I had the feeling that everything around me was out of focus. There was Danny Saunders, sitting on my bed in the hospital dressed in his Hasidic-style clothes and talking about wanting to kill me because I had pitched him some curve balls. He was dressed like a Hasid, but he didn't sound like one. Also, yesterday I had hated him; now we were calling each other by our first names. I sat and listened to him talk. I was fascinated just listening to the way perfect English came out of a person in the clothes of a Hasid. I had always thought their English was tinged with a Yiddish accent. As a matter of fact, the few times I had ever talked with a Hasid, he had spoken only Yiddish. And here was Danny Saunders talking English, and what he was saying and the way he was saying it just didn't seem to fit in with the way he was dressed, with the side curls on his face and the fringes hanging down below his dark jacket.

"You're a pretty rough fielder and pitcher," he said, smiling at me a little.

"You're pretty rough yourself," I told him. "Where did you learn to hit a ball like that?"

"I practiced," he said. "You don't know how many hours I spent learning how to field and hit a baseball."

"Where do you get the time? I thought you people always studied Talmud."

He grinned at me. "I have an agreement with my father. I study my quota of Talmud every day, and he doesn't care what I do the rest of the time."

"What's your quota of Talmud?"

"Two blatt."

"Two blatt?" I stared at him. That was four pages of Talmud a day. If I did one page a day, I was delighted. "Don't you have any English work at all?"

"Of course I do. But not too much. We don't have too much English work at our yeshiva."

"Everybody has to do two blatt of Talmud a day *and* his English?"

"Not everybody. Only me. My father wants it that way."

"How do you do it? That's a fantastic amount of work."

"I'm lucky." He grinned at me. "I'll show you how. What Talmud are you studying now?"

"*Kiddushin*," I said.

"What page are you on?"

I told him.

"I studied that two years ago. Is this what it reads like?"

He recited about a third of the page word for word, including the commentaries and the Maimonidean legal decisions of the Talmudic disputations. He did it coldly, mechanically, and, listening to him, I had the feeling I was watching some sort of human machine at work.

I sat there and gaped at him. "Say, that's pretty good," I managed to say, finally.

"I have a photographic mind. My father says it's a gift from God. I look at a page of Talmud, and I remember it by heart. I understand it, too. After a while, it gets a little boring, though. They repeat themselves a lot. I can do it with *Ivanhoe*, too. Have you read *Ivanhoe?*"

"Sure."

"Do you want to hear it with *Ivanhoe?*"

"You're showing off now," I said.

He grinned. "I'm trying to make a good impression."

"I'm impressed," I said. "I have to sweat to memorize a page of Talmud. Are you going to be a rabbi?"

"Sure. I'm going to take my father's place."

"I may become a rabbi. Not a Hasidic-type, though."

He looked at me, an expression of surprise on his face. "What do you want to become a rabbi for?"

"Why not?"

"There are so many other things you could be."

"That's a funny way for you to talk. *You're* going to become a rabbi."

"I have no choice. It's an inherited position."

"You mean you wouldn't become a rabbi if you had a choice?"

"I don't think so."

"What would you be?"

"I don't know. Probably a psychologist."

"A psychologist?"

He nodded.

"I'm not even sure I know what it's about."

"It helps you understand what a person is really like inside. I've read some books on it."

"Is that like Freud and psychoanalysis and things like that?"

"Yes," he said.

I didn't know much at all about psychoanalysis, but Danny Saunders, in his Hasidic clothes, seemed to me to be about the last person in the world who would qualify as an analyst. I always pictured analysts as sophisticated people with short pointed beards, monocles, and German accents.

"What would you be if you didn't become a rabbi?" Danny Saunders asked.

"A mathematician," I said. "That's what my father wants me to be."

"And teach in a university somewhere?"

"Yes."

"That's a very nice thing to be," he said. His blue eyes looked dreamy for a moment. "I'd like that."

"I'm not sure I want to do that, though."

"Why not?"

"I sort of feel I could be more useful to people as a rabbi. To our own people, I mean. You know, not everyone is religious, like you or me. I could teach them, and help them when they're in trouble. I think I would get a lot of pleasure out of that."

"I don't think I would. Anyway, I'm going to be a rabbi. Say, where did *you* learn to pitch like that?"

"I practiced, too." I grinned at him.

"But you don't have to do two blatt of Talmud a day."

"Thank God!"

"You certainly have a mean way of pitching."

"How about your hitting? Do you always hit like that, straight to the pitcher?"

"Yes."

"How'd you ever learn to do *that*?"

"I can't hit any other way. It's got something to do with my eyesight, and with the way I hold the bat. I don't know."

"That's a pretty murderous way to hit a ball. You almost killed me."

"You were supposed to duck," he said.

"I had no chance to duck."

"Yes you did."

"There wasn't enough time. You hit it so fast."

"There was time for you to bring up your glove."

I considered that for a moment.

"You didn't want to duck."

"That's right," I said, after a while.

"You didn't want to have to duck any ball that I hit. You had to try and stop it."

"That's right." I remembered that fraction of a second when I had brought my glove up in front of my face. I could have jumped aside and avoided the ball completely. I hadn't thought to do that, though. I hadn't wanted Danny Saunders to make me look like Schwartzie.

"Well, you stopped it," Danny Saunders said.

I grinned at him.

"No hard feelings anymore?" he asked me.

"No hard feelings," I said. "I just hope the eye heals all right."

"I hope so, too," he said fervently. "Believe me."

"Say, who was that rabbi on the bench? Is he a coach or something?"

Danny Saunders laughed. "He's one of the teachers in the yeshiva. My father sends him along to make sure we don't mix too much with the apikorsim."

"That apikorsim thing got me angry at you. What did you have to tell your team a thing like that for?"

"I'm sorry about that. It's the only way we could have a team. I sort of convinced my father you were the best team around and that we had a duty to beat you apikorsim at what you were best at. Something like that."

"You really had to tell your father that?"

"Yes."

"What would have happened if you'd lost?"

"I don't like to think about that. You don't know my father."

"So you practically *had* to beat us."

He looked at me for a moment, and I saw he was thinking of something. His eyes had a kind of cold, glassy look. "That's right," he said, finally. He seemed to be seeing something he had been searching for a long time. "That's right," he said again.

"What was he reading all the time?"

"Who?"

"The rabbi."

"I don't know. Probably a book on Jewish law or something."

"I thought it might have been something your father wrote."

"My father doesn't write," Danny said. "He reads a lot, but he never writes. He says that words distort what a person really feels in his heart. He doesn't like to talk too much, either. Oh, he talks plenty when we're studying Talmud together. But otherwise he doesn't say much. He told me once he wishes everyone could talk in silence."

"Talk in silence?"

"I don't understand it, either," Danny said, shrugging. "But that's what he said."

"Your father must be quite a man."

He looked at me. "Yes," he said, with the same cold, glassy stare in his eyes. I saw him begin to play absent-mindedly with one of his earlocks. We were quiet for a long time. He seemed absorbed in something. Finally, he stood up. "It's late. I had better go."

"Thanks for coming to see me."

"I'll see you tomorrow again."

"Sure."

He still seemed to be absorbed in something. I watched him walk slowly up the aisle and out of the ward.

> *Malter's eye is saved. The two boys have become serious friends. Danny takes Malter to his father's synagogue.*

We were approaching a group of about thirty black-caftaned men who were standing in front of the three-story brownstone at the end of the street. They formed a solid wall, and I did not want to push through them so I slowed my steps, but Danny took my arm with one hand and tapped his other hand upon the shoulder of a man on the outer rim of the crowd. The man turned, pivoting the upper portion of his body—a middle-aged man, his dark beard streaked with gray, his thick brows edging into a frown of annoyance—and I saw his eyes go wide. He bowed slightly and pushed back, and a whisper went through the crowd like a wind, and it parted, and Danny and I walked through, Danny holding me by the arm and nodding his head at the greetings in Yiddish that came in quiet murmurs from the people he passed. It was as if a black-waved, frozen sea had been sliced by a scythe, forming black, solid walls along a jelled path. I saw black- and gray-bearded heads bow toward Danny and dark brows arch sharply over eyes that stared questions at me and at the way Danny was holding me by the arm. We were almost halfway through the crowd now, walking slowly together, Danny's fingers on the part of my arm just over the elbow. I felt myself naked and fragile, an intruder, and my eyes, searching for anything but the bearded faces to look at, settled, finally, upon the sidewalk at my feet. Then, because I wanted something other than the murmured greetings in Yiddish to listen to, I began to hear, distinctly, the tapping sounds of Danny's metal-capped shoes against the cement pavement. It seemed a sharp, unnaturally loud sound, and my ears fixed on it, and I could hear it clearly as we went along. I listened to it intently —the soft scrape of the shoe and the sharp tap-tap of the metal caps— as we went up the stone steps of the stairway that led into the brownstone in front of which the crowd stood. The caps tapped against the stone of the steps, then against the stone of the top landing in front of the double door—and I remembered the old man I often saw walking along Lee Avenue, moving carefully through the busy street and tapping, tapping, his metal-capped cane, which served him for the eyes he had lost in a First World War trench during a German gas attack.

The hallway of the brownstone was crowded with black-caftaned men, and there was suddenly a path there, too, and more murmured greetings and questioning eyes, and then Danny and I went through a door that stood open to our right, and we were in the synagogue.

It was a large room and looked to be the exact size of the apartment in which my father and I lived. What was my father's bedroom was here the section of the synagogue that contained the Ark, the Eternal Light, an eight-branched candelabrum, a small podium to the right of the Ark, and a large podium about ten feet in front of the Ark. The two podiums and the Ark were covered with red velvet. What was our kitchen, hallway, bathroom, my bedroom, my father's study and our front room, was here the portion of the synagogue where the worshipers sat. Each seat consisted of a chair set before a stand with a sloping top, the bottom edge of which was braced with a jutting strip of wood to prevent what was on the stand from sliding to the floor. The seats extended back to about twenty feet from the rear wall of the synagogue, the wall opposite the Ark. A small portion of the synagogue near the upper door of the hallway had been curtained off with white cheesecloth. This was the women's section. It contained a few rows of wooden chairs. The remaining section of the synagogue, the section without chairs, was crowded with long tables and benches. Through the middle of the synagogue ran a narrow aisle that ended at the large podium. The walls were painted white. The wooden floor was a dark brown. The three rear windows were curtained in black velvet. The ceiling was white, and naked bulbs hung from it on dark wires, flooding the room with harsh light.

We stood for a moment just inside the door near one of the tables. Men passed constantly in and out of the room. Some remained in the hallway to chat, others took seats. Some of the seats were occupied by men studying Talmud, reading the Book of Psalms, or talking among themselves in Yiddish. The benches at the tables stood empty, and on the white cloths that covered the tables were paper cups, wooden forks and spoons, and paper plates filled with pickled herring and onion, lettuce, tomatoes, gefülte fish, Shabbat loaves—the braided bread called chalah—tuna fish, salmon, and hard-boiled eggs. At the edge of the table near the window was a brown leather chair. On the table in front of the chair was a pitcher, a towel, a saucer, and a large place covered with a Shabbat cloth—a white satin cloth, with the Hebrew word for the Shabbat embroidered upon it in gold. A long serrated silver knife lay alongside the plate.

A tall, heavyset boy came in the door, nodded at Danny, then noticed me, and stared. I recognized him immediately as Dov Shlomowitz, the player on Danny's team who had run into me at second base and knocked me down. He seemed about to say something to Danny, then changed his mind, turned stiffly, went up the narrow aisle, and found a seat. Sitting in the seat, he glanced at us once over his shoulder, then opened a book on his stand, and began to sway back and forth. I looked at Danny and managed what must have been a sick smile. "I feel like a cowboy surrounded by Indians," I told him in a whisper.

Danny grinned at me reassuringly and let go of my arm. "You're in the holy halls," he said. "It takes getting used to."

"That was like the parting of the Red Sea out there," I said. "How did you do it?"

"I'm my father's son, remember? I'm the inheritor of the dynasty. Number one on our catechism: Treat the son as you would the father, because one day the son will be the father."

"You sound like a Mitnaged," I told him, managing another weak smile.

"No, I don't," he said. "I sound like someone who reads too much. Come on. We sit up front. My father will be down soon."

"You live in this house?"

"We have the upper two floors. It's a fine arrangement. Come on. They're beginning to come in."

The crowd in the hallway and in front of the building had begun coming through the door. Danny and I went up the aisle. He led me to the front row of seats that stood at the right of the large podium and just behind the small podium. Danny sat down in the second seat and I sat in the third. I assumed that the first seat was for his father.

The crowd came in quickly, and the synagogue was soon filled with the sounds of shuffling shoes, scraping chairs, and loud voices talking Yiddish. I heard no English, only Yiddish. Sitting in the chair, I glanced over at Dov Shlomowitz, and found him staring at me, his heavy face wearing an expression of surprise and hostility, and I suddenly realized that Danny was probably going to have as much trouble with his friends over our friendship as I would have with mine. Maybe less, I thought. I'm not the son of a tzaddik. No one steps aside for me in a crowd. Dov Shlomowitz looked away but I saw others in the crowded synagogue staring at me too, and I looked down at the worn prayer book on my stand, feeling exposed and naked again, and very alone.

Two gray-bearded old men came over to Danny, and he got respectfully to his feet. They had had an argument over a passage of Talmud, they told him, each of them interpreting it in a different way, and they wondered who had been correct. They mentioned the passage, and Danny nodded, immediately identified the tractate and the page, then coldly and mechanically repeated the passage word for word, giving his interpretation of it, and quoting at the same time the interpretations of a number of medieval commentators like the Me'iri, the Rashba, and the Maharsha. The passage was a difficult one, he said, gesticulating with his hands as he spoke, the thumb of his right hand describing wide circles as he emphasized certain key points of interpretation, and both men had been correct; one had unknowingly adopted the interpretation of the Me'iri, the other of the Rashba. The men smiled and went away satisfied. Danny sat down.

"That's a tough passage," he said. "I can't make head or tail out of it. Your father would probably say the text was all wrong." He was talking quietly and grinning broadly. "I read some of your father's articles. Sneaked them off my father's desk. The one on that passage in *Kiddushin* about the business with the king is very good. It's full of real apikorsische stuff."

I nodded, and tried another smile. My father had read that article to me before he had sent it off to his publisher. He had begun reading his articles to me during the past year, and spent a lot of time explaining them.

The noise in the synagogue had become very loud, almost a din, and the room seemed to throb and swell with the scraping chairs and the talking men. Some children were running up and down the aisle, laughing and shouting, and a number of younger men lounged near the door, talking loudly and gesticulating with their hands. I had the feeling for a moment I was in the carnival I had seen recently in a movie, with its pushing, shoving, noisy throng, and its shouting, arm-waving vendors and pitchmen.

I sat quietly, staring down at the prayer book on my stand. I opened the book and turned to the Afternoon Service. Its pages were yellow and old, with ragged edges and worn corners. I sat there, staring at the first psalm of the service and thinking of the almost new prayer book I had held in my hands that morning. I felt Danny nudge me with his elbow, and I looked up.

"My father's coming," he said. His voice was quiet and, I thought, a little strained.

The noise inside the synagogue ceased so abruptly that I felt its absence as one would a sudden lack of air. It stopped in swift waves, beginning at the rear of the synagogue and ending at the chairs near the podium. I heard no signal and no call for silence; it simply stopped, cut off, as if a door had slammed shut on a playroom filled with children. The silence that followed had a strange quality to it: expectation, eagerness, love, awe.

A man was coming slowly up the narrow aisle, followed by a child. He was a tall man, and he wore a black satin caftan and a fur-trimmed black hat. As he passed each row of seats, men rose, bowed slightly,

and sat again. Some leaned over to touch him. He nodded his head at
the murmur of greetings directed to him from the seats, and his long
black beard moved back and forth against his chest, and his earlocks
swayed. He walked slowly, his hands clasped behind his back, and as
he came closer to me I could see that the part of his face not hidden
by the beard looked cut from stone, the nose sharp and pointed, the
cheekbones ridged, the lips full, the brow like marble etched with lines,
the sockets deep, the eyebrows thick with black hair and separated by
a single wedge like a furrow plowed into a naked field, the eyes dark,
with pinpoints of white light playing in them as they do in black
stones in the sun. Danny's face mirrored his exactly—except for the
hair and the color of the eyes. The child who followed him, holding
on to the caftan with his right hand, was a delicate miniature of the
man, with the same caftan, the same fur-trimmed hat, the same face,
the same color hair, though beardless, and I realized he was Danny's
brother. I glanced at Danny and saw him staring down at his stand,
his face without expression. I saw the eyes of the congregants follow
the man as he came slowly up the aisle, his hands clasped behind his
back, his head nodding, and then I saw them on Danny and me as he
came up to us. Danny rose quickly to his feet, and I followed, and we
stood there, waiting, as the man's dark eyes moved across my face—
I could feel them moving across my face like a hand—and fixed upon
my left eye. I had a sudden vision of my father's gentle eyes behind
their steel-rimmed spectacles, but it vanished swiftly, because Danny
was introducing me to Reb Saunders.

"This is Reuven Malter," he said quietly in Yiddish.

Reb Saunders continued to stare at my left eye. I felt naked under
his gaze, and he must have sensed my discomfort, because quite suddenly he offered me his hand. I raised my hand to take it, then realized, as my hand was going up, that he was not offering me his hand
but his fingers, and I held them for a moment—they were dry and
limp—then let my hand drop.

"You are the son of David Malter?" Reb Saunders asked me in
Yiddish. His voice was deep and nasal, like Danny's, and the words
came out almost like an accusation.

I nodded my head. I had a moment of panic, trying to decide
whether to answer him in Yiddish or English. I wondered if he knew
English. My Yiddish was very poor. I decided to answer in English.

"Your eye," Reb Saunders said in Yiddish. "It is healed?"

"It's fine," I said in English. My voice came out a little hoarse, and I swallowed. I glanced at the congregants. They were staring at us intently, in complete silence.

Reb Saunders looked at me for a moment, and I saw the dark eyes blink, the lids going up and down like shades. When he spoke again it was still in Yiddish.

"The doctor, the professor who operated, he said your eye is healed?"

"He wants to see me again in a few days. But he said the eye is fine."

I saw his head nod slightly and the beard go up and down against his chest. The lights from the naked bulb on the ceiling gleamed off his satin caftan.

"Tell me, you know mathematics? My son tells me you are very good in mathematics."

I nodded.

"So. We will see. And you know Hebrew. A son of David Malter surely knows Hebrew."

I nodded again.

"We will see," Reb Saunders said.

I glanced out of the sides of my eyes and saw Danny looking down at the floor, his face expressionless. The child stood a little behind Reb Saunders and stared up at us, his mouth open.

"Nu," Reb Saunders said, "later we will talk more. I want to know my son's friend. Especially the son of David Malter." Then he went past us and stood in front of the little podium, his back to the congregation, the little boy still holding on to his caftan.

Danny and I sat down. A whisper moved through the congregation, followed by the rustle of pages as prayer books were opened. An old, gray-bearded man went up to the large podium, put on a prayer shawl, and started the service.

The old man had a weak voice, and I could barely hear him over the prayers of the worshipers. Reb Saunders stood with his back to the congregation, swaying back and forth, occasionally clapping his hands together, and the child stood at his right, swaying too, in obvious imitation of his father. Throughout the entire service, Reb Saunders stood with his back to the congregation, sometimes raising his head toward the ceiling, or raising his hands to cover his eyes. He turned only when the Torah was taken from the Ark and read.

The service ended with the Kaddish, and then Reb Saunders walked slowly back up the aisle, followed by the child, who was still clinging to his father's caftan. As the child passed me, I noticed his dark eyes were very large and his face was deathly pale.

Danny nudged me with his elbow and motioned with his head toward the rear of the synagogue. He rose, and the two of us followed Reb Saunders up the aisle. I could see the eyes of the congregants on my face, and then feel them on my back. I saw Reb Saunders go to the leather chair at the table near the end window and sit down. The child sat on the bench to his left. Danny led me to the table and sat on the bench to his father's right. He motioned me to sit down next to him, and I did.

The congregants rose and came toward the rear of the synagogue. The silence was gone now, burst as abruptly as it had begun, and someone started chanting a tune, and others took it up, clapping their hands in rhythm to the melody. They were filing out the door—probably to wash their hands, I thought—and soon they were coming back in and finding seats at the tables, the benches scraping loudly as they were moved back and forth. The singing had stopped. Our table filled rapidly, mostly with older men.

Reb Saunders stood up, poured water over his hands from the pitcher, the water spilling into the saucer, then wiped his hands, removed the white satin cloth that covered the chalah, said the blessing over bread, cut a section off the end of the chalah, swallowed it, and sat down. Danny got to his feet, washed his hands, cut two slices from the chalah, handed me one, took one for himself, made the blessing, ate, and sat. He passed the pitcher to me, and I repeated the ritual, but I remained seated. Then Danny cut the remainder of the chalah into small pieces, gave a piece to his brother, and handed the plate to the old man sitting next to me. The pieces of chalah disappeared swiftly, grabbed up by the men at the table. Reb Saunders put some salad and fish on his plate and ate a small piece of fish, holding it in his fingers. A man from one of the other tables came over and took the plate. Danny filled another plate for his father. Reb Saunders ate slowly, and in silence.

I was not very hungry, but I made some attempt at eating so as not to insult anyone. Frequently during the meal, I felt rather than saw Reb Saunders' eyes on my face. Danny was quiet. His little brother pecked at the food on his plate, eating little. The skin of his face and hands was almost as white as the tablecloth, drawn tightly over the bones, and the veins showed like blue branches in his face and on the tops of his hands. He sat quietly, and once he began to pick his nose, saw his father look at him, and stopped, his lower lip trembling a little. He bent over his plate and poked at a slice of tomato with a thin, stubby finger.

Danny and I said nothing to each other throughout that entire meal. Once I looked up and saw his father staring at me, his eyes black beneath the thick brows. I looked away, feeling as though my skin had been peeled away and my insides photographed.

Someone began to sing Atah Echad, one of the prayers from the Afternoon Service. The meal was over, and the men began to sway slowly, in unison with the melody. The singing filled the synagogue, and Reb Saunders sat back in his leather seat and sang too, and then Danny was singing. I knew the melody and I joined in, hesitantly at first, then strongly, swaying back and forth. At the end of the song, another melody was begun, a light, fast, wordless tune, sung to the syllables cheeree bim, cheeree bam, and the swaying was a little faster now, and hands were clapped in time to the rhythm. Then tune followed tune, and I felt myself begin to relax as I continued to join the singing. I found that most of the melodies were familiar to me, especially the slow, somber ones that were meant to convey the sadness of the singers over the conclusion of the Shabbat, and the tunes I did not know I was able to follow easily, because the basic melody lines were almost all the same. After a while I was singing loudly, swaying back and forth and clapping my hands, and once I saw Reb Saunders looking at me, and his lips curved into a shadow of a smile. I smiled at Danny and he smiled back at me, and we sat there for about half an hour, singing, swaying, and clapping, and I felt light and happy and completely at ease. So far as I could see, Reb Saunders' little son was the only one in the synagogue not sing-ing; he sat pecking at his food and poking at the slice of tomato on his paper plate with his thin, veined hand. The singing went on and on—and then it stopped. I glanced around to see what had happened, but everyone was sitting very still, looking over at our table. Reb Saunders washed his hands again, and others spilled what was left of the water in their paper cups over their hands. The introductory psalm to the Grace was sung together, and then Reb Saunders began the Grace. He chanted with his eyes closed, swaying slightly in his leather chair. After the opening lines of the Grace, each man prayed quietly, and I saw Danny lean forward, put his elbows on the table, cover his eyes with his right hand, his lips whispering the words. Then the Grace was done, and there was silence—a long, solid silence in which no one moved and everyone waited and eyes stared at Reb Saunders, who was sitting in his chair with his eyes closed, swaying slightly back and forth. I saw Danny take his elbows from the table and sit up straight. He stared down at his paper plate, his face expressionless, and I almost had the feeling that he had gone rigid, tense, as a soldier does before he jumps from shelter into open combat.

Everyone waited, and no one moved, no one coughed, no one even took a deep breath. The silence became unreal and seemed suddenly filled with a noise of its own, the noise of a too long silence. Even the child was staring now at his father, his eyes like black stones against the naked whiteness of his veined face.

And then Reb Saunders began to speak.

He swayed back and forth in the leather chair, his eyes closed, his left hand in the crook of his right elbow, the fingers of his right hand stroking his black beard, and I could see everyone at the tables lean forward, eyes staring, mouths slightly open, some of the older men cupping their hands behind their ears to catch his words. He began in a low voice, the words coming out slowly in a singsong kind of chant.

"The great and holy Rabban Gamaliel," he said, "taught us the following: 'Do His will as if it were thy will, that He may do thy will as if it were His will. Nullify thy will before His will that He may nullify the will of others before thy will.' What does this mean? It means that if we do as the Master of the Universe wishes, then He will do as we wish. A question immediately presents itself. What does it mean to say that the Master of the Universe will do what we wish? He is after all the Master of the Universe, the Creator of heaven and earth, the King of kings. And what are we? Do we not say every day, 'Are not all the mighty as naught before Thee, the men of renown as though they had not been, the wise as if without knowledge, and the men of understanding as if without discernment'? What are we that the Master of the Universe should do our will?"

Reb Saunders paused, and I saw two of the old men who were sitting at our table look at each other and nod. He swayed back and forth in his leather chair, his fingers stroking his beard, and continued to speak in a quiet, singsong voice.

"All men come into the world in the same way. We are born in pain, for it is written, 'In pain shall ye bring forth children.' We are born naked and without strength. Like dust are we born. Like dust can the child be blown about, like dust is his life, like dust is his strength. And like dust do many remain all their lives, until they are put away in dust, in a place of worms and maggots. Will the Master of the Universe obey the will of a man whose life is dust? What is the great and holy Rabban Gamaliel teaching us?" His voice was beginning to rise now. "What is he telling us? What does it mean to say the Master of the Universe will do our will? The will of men who remain dust? Impossible! The will of what men, then? We must say, the will of men who do *not* remain dust. But how can we raise ourselves above dust? Listen, listen to me, for this is a mighty thing the rabbis teach us."

He paused again, and I saw Danny glance at him, then stare down again at his paper plate.

"Rabbi Halafta son of Dosa teaches us, 'When ten people sit together and occupy themselves with the Torah, the Presence of God abides among them, as it is said, "God standeth in the congregation of the godly." And whence can it be shown that the same applies to five? Because it is said, "He had founded his band upon the earth." And whence can it be shown that the same applies to three? Because it is said, "He judgeth among the judges." And whence can it be shown that the same applies to two? Because it is said, "Then they that feared the Lord spake one with the other, and the Lord gave heed and heard." And whence can it be shown that the same applies even to one? Because it is said, "In every place where I cause my name to be remembered I will come into thee and I will bless thee."' Listen, listen to this great teaching. A congregation is ten. It is nothing new that the holy Presence resides among ten. A band is five. It is also nothing new that the holy Presence resides among five. Judges are three. If the holy Presence did not reside among judges there would be no justice in the world. So this, too, is not new. That the Presence can reside even among two is also not impossible to understand. But that the Presence can reside in one! In one! Even in one! That already is a mighty thing. Even in one! If one man studies Torah, the Presence is with him. If one man studies Torah, the Master of the Universe is already in the world. A mighty thing! And to bring the Master of the World *into* the world is also to raise oneself up from the dust. Torah raises us from the dust! Torah gives us strength! Torah clothes us! Torah brings the Presence!"

The singsong chant had died away. He was talking in a straight, loud voice that rang through the terrible silence in the synagogue.

"But to study Torah is not such a simple thing. Torah is a task for all day and all night. It is a task filled with danger. Does not Rabbi Meir teach us, 'He who is walking by the way and studying, and breaks off his study and says, "How fine is that tree, how fine is that field," him the Scripture regards as if he had forfeited his life'?"

I saw Danny glance quickly at his father, then lower his eyes. His body sagged a little, a smile played on his lips, and I thought I even heard him sigh quietly.

"He had forfeited his life! His life! So great is the study of Torah. And now, listen, listen to this word. Whose task is it to study Torah? Of whom does the Master of the Universe demand 'Ye shall meditate over it day and night'? Of the world? No! What does the world know of Torah? The world is Esav! The world is Amalek! The world is Cossacks! The world is Hitler, may his name and memory be erased! Of whom, then? Of the people of Israel! We are commanded to study His Torah! We are commanded to sit in the light of the Presence! It is for this that we were created! Does not the great and holy Rabbi Yochanan son of Zakkai teach us, 'If thou hast learnt much Torah, ascribe not any merit to thyself, for thereunto wast thou created'? Not the world, but the people of Israel! The people of Israel must study His Torah!"

His voice stormed the silence. I found myself holding my breath, my heart thumping in my ears. I could not take my eyes off his face, which was alive now, or his eyes, which were open and filled with dark fire. He struck the table with his hand, and I felt myself go cold with fright. Danny was watching him now, too, and his little brother stared at him as though in a trance, his mouth open, his eyes glazed.

"The world kills us! The world flays our skin from our bodies and throws us to the flames! The world laughs at Torah! And if it does not kill us, it tempts us! It misleads us! It contaminates us! It asks us to join in its ugliness, its impurities, its abominations! The world is Amalek! It is not the world that is commanded to study Torah, but the people of Israel! Listen, listen to this mighty teaching." His voice was suddenly lower, quieter, intimate. "It is written, 'This world is like a vestibule before the world-to-come; prepare thyself in the vestibule, that thou mayest enter into the hall.' The meaning is clear: The vestibule is this world, and the hall is the world-to-come. Listen. In gematriya, the words 'this world' come out one hundred sixty-three, and the words 'the world-to-come' come out one hundred fifty-four. The difference between 'this world' and 'the world-to-come' comes out to nine. Nine is half of eighteen. Eighteen is chai, life. In this world there is only half of chai. We are only half alive in this world! Only half alive!"

A whisper went through the crowd at the tables, and I could see heads nod and lips smile. They had been waiting for this apparently, the gematriya, and they strained forward to listen. One of my teachers in school had told me about gematriya. Each letter of the Hebrew alphabet is also a number, so that every Hebrew word has a numerical value. The word for "this world" in Hebrew is "olam hazeh," and by adding the numerical value of each letter, the total numerical value of the word becomes one hundred and sixty-three. I had heard others do this before, and I enjoyed listening because sometimes they were quite clever and ingenious. I was beginning to feel relaxed again, and I listened carefully.

"Hear me now. Listen. How can we make our lives full? How can we fill our lives so that we are eighteen, chai, and not nine, not half chai? Rabbi Joshua son of Levi teaches us, 'Whoever does not labor in the Torah is said to be under the divine censure.' He is a nozuf, a person whom the Master of the Universe hates! A righteous man, a tzaddik, studies Torah, for it is written, 'For his delight is in the Torah of God, and over His Torah doth he meditate day and night.' In gematriya, 'nozuf' comes out one hundred forty-three, and 'tzaddik' comes out two hundred and four. What is the difference between 'nozuf' and 'tzaddik'? Sixty-one. To whom does a tzaddik dedicate his life? To the Master of the Universe! La-el, to God! The word, 'La-el' in gematriya is sixty-one! It is a life dedicated to God that makes the difference between the nozuf and the tzaddik!"

Another murmur of approval went through the crowd. Reb Saunders was very good at gematriya, I thought. I was really enjoying myself now.

"And now listen to me further. In gematriya, the letters of the word 'traklin,' hall, the hall that refers to the world-to-come, come out three hundred ninety-nine, and 'prozdor,' the vestibule, the vestibule that is this world, comes out five hundred thirteen. Take 'traklin' from 'prozdor,' and have one hundred fourteen. Now listen to me. A righteous man, we said, is two hundred four. A righteous man lives by Torah. Torah is mayim, water; the great and holy rabbis always compare Torah to water. The word 'mayim' in gematriya is ninety. Take 'mayim' from 'tzaddik' and we also have one hundred fourteen. From this we learn that the righteous man who removes himself from Torah also removes himself from the world-to-come!"

The whisper of delight was loud this time, and men nodded their heads and smiled. Some of them were even poking each other with their elbows to indicate their pleasure. That one had really been clever. I started to go over it again in my mind.

"We see that without Torah there is only half a life. We see that without Torah we are dust. We see that without Torah we are abominations." He was saying this quietly, almost as if it were a litany. His eyes were still open, and he was looking directly at Danny now. "When we study Torah, *then* the Master of the Universe listens. *Then* He hears our words. *Then* He will fulfill our wishes. For the Master of the Universe promises strength to those who preoccupy themselves in Torah, as it is written, 'So ye may be strong,' and He promises length of days, as it is written. 'So that your days may be lengthened.' May Torah be a fountain of waters to all who drink from it, and may it bring to us the Messiah speedily and in our day. Amen!"

A chorus of loud and scattered amens answered.

I sat in my seat and saw Reb Saunders looking at Danny, then at me. I felt completely at ease, and I somewhat brazenly smiled and nodded, as if to indicate that I had enjoyed his words, or at least the gematriya part of his words. I didn't agree at all with his notions of the world as being contaminated. Albert Einstein is part of the world, I told myself. President Roosevelt is part of the world. The millions of soldiers fighting Hitler are part of the world.

I thought that the meal was ended now and we would start the Evening Service, and I almost began to get out of my seat when I realized that another silence had settled upon the men at the tables. I sat still and looked around. They seemed all to be staring at Danny. He was sitting quietly, smiling a little, his fingers playing with the edge of his paper plate.

Reb Saunders sat back in his leather chair and folded his arms across his chest. The little boy was poking at the tomato again and glancing at Danny from the tops of his dark eyes. He twirled a side curl around one of his fingers, and I saw his tongue dart out of his mouth, run over his lips, then dart back in. I wondered what was going on.

Reb Saunders sighed loudly and nodded at Danny, "Nu, Daniel, you have something to say?" His voice was quiet, almost gentle.

I saw Danny nod his head.

"Nu, what is it?"

"It is written in the name of Rabbi Yaakov, not Rabbi Meir," Danny said quietly, in Yiddish.

A whisper of approval came from the crowd. I glanced around quickly. Everyone sat staring at Danny.

Reb Saunders almost smiled. He nodded, and the long black beard went back and forth against his chest. Then I saw the thick black eyebrows arch upward and the lids go about halfway down across the eyes. He leaned forward slightly, his arms still folded across his chest.

"And nothing more?" he asked very quietly.

Danny shook his head—a little hesitantly, I thought.

"So," Reb Saunders said, sitting back in the leather chair, "there is nothing more."

I looked at the two of them, wondering what was happening. What was this about Rabbi Yaakov and Rabbi Meir?

"The words were said by Rabbi Yaakov, not by Rabbi Meir," Danny repeated. "Rabbi Yaakov, not Rabbi Meir, said, 'He who is walking by the way and studying, and breaks off his study and—"

"Good," Reb Saunders broke in quietly. "The words were said by Rav Yaakov. Good. You saw it. Very good. And where is it found?"

"In *Pirkei Avos*," Danny said. He was giving the Talmudic source for the quote. Many of the quotes Reb Saunders had used had been from *Pirkei Avos*—or *Avot*, as my father had taught me to pronounce it, with the Sephardic rather than the Ashkenazic rendering of the Hebrew letter "tof." I had recognized the quotes easily. *Pirkei Avot* is a collection of Rabbinic maxims, and a chapter of it is studied by many Jews every Shabbat between Passover and the Jewish New Year.

"Nu," Reb Saunders said, smiling, "how should you not know that? Of course. Good. Very good. Now, tell me—"

As I sat there listening to what then took place between Danny and his father, I slowly realized what I was witnessing. In many Jewish homes, especially homes where there are yeshiva students and where the father is learned, there is a tradition which takes place on Shabbat afternoon: The father quizzes the son on what he has learned in school during the past week. I was witnessing a kind of public quiz, but a strange, almost bizarre quiz, more a contest than a quiz, because Reb Saunders was not confining his questions only to what Danny had learned during the week but was ranging over most of the major tractates of the Talmud and Danny was obviously required to provide the answers. Reb Saunders asked where else there was a statement about one who interrupts his studies, and Danny coolly, quietly answered. He asked what a certain medieval commentator had remarked about that statement, and Danny answered. He chose a minute aspect of the answer and asked who had dealt with it in an altogether different way, and Danny answered. He asked whether Danny agreed with this interpretation, and Danny said he did not, he agreed with another medieval commentator, who had given another interpretation. His father asked how could the commentator have offered such an interpretation when in another passage in the Talmud he had said exactly the opposite, and Danny, very quietly, calmly, his fingers still playing with the rim of the paper plate, found a difference between the contradictory statements by quoting two other sources where one of the statements appeared in a somewhat different context, thereby nullifying the contradiction. One of the two sources Danny had quoted contained a biblical verse, and his father asked him who else had based a law upon this verse. Danny repeated a short passage from the tractate *Sanhedrin*, and then his father quoted another passage from *Yoma* which contradicted the passage in *Sanhedrin*, and Danny answered with a passage from *Gittin* which dissolved the contradiction. His father questioned the validity of his interpretation of the passage in *Gittin* by citing a commentary on the passage that disagreed with his interpretation, and Danny said it was difficult to understand this commentary—he did not say the commentary was wrong, he said it was difficult to understand it— because a parallel passage in *Nedarim* clearly confirmed his own interpretation.

This went on and on, until I lost track of the thread that held it all together and sat and listened in amazement to the feat of memory I was witnessing. Both Danny and his father spoke quietly, his father nodding his approval each time Danny responded. Danny's brother sat staring at them with his mouth open, finally lost interest, and began to eat some of the food that was still on his plate. Once he started picking his nose, but stopped immediately. The men around the tables were watching as if in ecstasy, their faces glowing with pride. This was almost like the pilpul my father had told me about, except that it wasn't really pilpul, they weren't twisting the texts out of shape, they seemed more interested in b'kiut, in straightforward knowledge and simple explanations of the Talmudic passages and commentaries they were discussing. It went on like that for a long time. Then Reb Saunders sat back and was silent.

The contest, or quiz, had apparently ended, and Reb Saunders was smiling at his son. He said, very quietly, "Good. Very good. There is no contradiction. But tell me, you have nothing more to say about what I said earlier?"

Danny was suddenly sitting very straight.

"Nothing more?" Reb Saunders asked again. "You have nothing more to say?"

Danny shook his head, hesitantly.

"Absolutely nothing more to say?" Reb Saunders insisted, his voice flat, cold, distant. He was no longer smiling.

I saw Danny's body go rigid again, as it had done before his father began to speak. The ease and certainty he had worn during the Talmud quiz had disappeared.

"So," Reb Saunders said. "There is nothing more. Nu, what should I say?"

"I did not hear—"

"You did not hear, you did not hear. You heard the first mistake, and you stopped listening. Of course you did not hear. How could you hear when you were not listening?" He said it quietly and without anger.

Danny's face was rigid. The crowd sat silent. I looked at Danny. For a long moment he sat very still—and then I saw his lips part, move, curve slowly upward, and freeze into a grin. I felt the skin on the back of my neck begin to crawl, and I almost cried out. I stared at him, then looked quickly away.

Reb Saunders sat looking at his son. Then he turned his eyes upon me. I felt his eyes looking at me. There was a long, dark silence, during which Danny sat very still, staring fixedly at his plate and grinning. Reb Saunders began to play with the earlock along the right side of his face. He caressed it with the fingers of his right hand, wound it around the index finger, released it, then caressed it again, all the time looking at me. Finally, he sighed loudly, shook his head, and put his hands on the table.

"Nu," he said, "it is possible I am not right. After all, my son is not a mathematician. He has a good head on him, but it is not a head for mathematics. But we have a mathematician with us. The son of David Malter is with us. He is a mathematician." He was looking straight at me, and I felt my heart pound and the blood drain from my face. "Reuven," Reb Saunders was saying, looking straight at me, "you have nothing to say?"

I found I couldn't open my mouth. Say about what? I hadn't the faintest idea what he and Danny had been talking about.

"You heard my little talk?" Reb Saunders asked me quietly.

I felt my head nod.

"And you have nothing to say?"

I felt his eyes on me and found myself staring down at the table. The eyes were like flames on my face.

"Reuven, you liked the gematriya?" Reb Saunders asked softly.

I looked up and nodded. Danny hadn't moved at all. He just sat there grinning. His little brother was playing with the tomato again. And the men at the tables were silent, staring at *me* now.

"I am very happy," Reb Saunders said gently. "You liked the gematriya. Which gematriya did you like?"

I heard myself say, lamely and hoarsely, "They were all very good."

Reb Saunders' eyebrows went up. "All?" he said. "A very nice thing. They were all very good. Reuven, were they *all* very good?"

I felt Danny stir and saw him turn his head, the grin gone now from his lips. He glanced at me quickly, then looked down again at his paper plate.

I looked at Reb Saunders. "No," I heard myself say hoarsely. "They were not all good."

There was a stir from the men at the tables. Reb Saunders sat back in his leather chair.

"Nu, Reuven," he said quietly, "tell me, which one was not good?"

"One of the gematriyot was wrong," I said. I thought the world would fall in on me after I said that. I was a fifteen-year-old boy, and there I was, telling Reb Saunders he had been wrong! But nothing happened. There was another stir from the crowd, but nothing happened. Instead, Reb Saunders broke into a warm, broad smile.

"And which one was it?" he asked me quietly.

"The gematriya for 'prozdor' is five hundred and three, not five hundred and thirteen," I answered.

"Good. Very good," Reb Saunders said, smiling and nodding his head, the black beard going back and forth against his chest, the earlocks swaying. "Very good, Reuven. The gematriya for 'prozdor' comes out five hundred three. Very good." He looked at me, smiling broadly, his teeth showing white through the beard, and I almost thought I saw his eyes mist over. There was a loud murmur from the crowd, and Danny's body sagged as the tension went out of him. He glanced at me, his face a mixture of surprise and relief, and I realized with astonishment that I, too, had just passed some kind of test.

"Nu," Reb Saunders said loudly to the men around the tables, "say Kaddish!"

An old man stood up and recited the Scholar's Kaddish. Then the congregants broke to go back to the front section of the synagogue for the Evening Service.

Danny and I said nothing to each other throughout the service, and though I prayed the words, I did not know what I was saying. I kept going over what had happened at the table. I couldn't believe it. I just couldn't get it through my head that Danny had to go through something like that every week, and that I myself had gone through it tonight.